Canadian Bankruptcy and Insolvency Law

Cases, Text, and Materials
Second Edition

Anthony J. Duggan
Professor
Faculty of Law
University of Toronto

Stephanie Ben-Ishai
Associate Professor
Osgoode Hall Law School
York University

Roderick Wood
Professor
Faculty of Law
University of Alberta

Thomas G.W. Telfer
Associate Professor
Faculty of Law
University of Western Ontario

Jacob S. Ziegel
Professor Emeritus
Faculty of Law
University of Toronto

2009
EMOND MONTGOMERY PUBLICATIONS LIMITED
TORONTO, CANADA

Emond Montgomery Publications Limited
60 Shaftesbury Avenue
Toronto ON M4T 1A3
http://www.emp.ca

Printed in Canada.

We acknowledge the financial support of the Government of Canada through the Book Publishing Industry Development Program (BPIDP) for our publishing activities.

Acquisitions editor: Peggy Buchan
Marketing manager: Christine Davidson
Sales manager: James W. Black
Copy and production editor: Nancy Ennis
Permissions editor: Nick Raymond
Proofreader: Paula Pike

Library and Archives Canada Cataloguing in Publication

Canadian bankruptcy and insolvency law : cases, text and materials / Anthony J. Duggan ... [et al.]. — 2nd ed.

First ed. written by Jacob S. Ziegel, Anthony J. Duggan, Thomas G.W. Telfer.
   Previously published as pt. II of Commercial and consumer transactions. 3rd ed.
ISBN 978-1-55239-322-2

1. Bankruptcy—Canada. I. Duggan, Anthony J. II. Ziegel, Jacob S. Canadian bankruptcy and insolvency law.

KE1485.C353 2009   346.7107'8   C2009-902046-7
KF1536.ZA2C353 2009

Preface

This book had its genesis in Part II of the third edition of Jacob S. Ziegel and Ronald C.C. Cuming, *Secured Transactions in Personal Property, Surety, and Insolvency*, published in 1995. In 2003, Jacob Ziegel joined with Anthony Duggan and Thomas Telfer to publish a separate volume dedicated to bankruptcy and insolvency law, and this book is the second edition of that work. For this edition, Professors Duggan (University of Toronto), Telfer (University of Western Ontario), and Ziegel (University of Toronto) have been joined by Stephanie Ben-Ishai (Osgoode Hall Law School) and Roderick Wood (University of Alberta).

There have been major statutory and case law developments in the six years since the previous edition. Most significant, of course, are the enactment of the *Wage Earner Protection Program Act* and the substantial reforms to the *Bankruptcy and Insolvency Act*, RSC 1985, c. B-3 and the *Companies' Creditors Arrangement Act*, RSC 1985, c. C-36 by Bill C-55, enacted as Statute c. 47 in November 2005, and subsequently amended by Bill C-12, enacted as Statute c. 36 in June 2007. The new laws deal with a wide range of matters, including preferences and transfers at undervalue, the disclaimer of executory contracts, employee protection, the provision of debtor-in-possession financing in restructuring proceedings, and cross-border insolvencies. We discuss all these new provisions in depth, comparing them with the previous law and exploring the underlying policy implications. Among the most important case law developments are the Supreme Court of Canada's decisions in *Peoples Department Stores Inc. (Trustee of) v. Wise*, [2004] 3 SCR 461 (concerning whether directors owe duties to creditors where the company is close to insolvency), *BCE Inc. v. 1976 Debentureholders*, [2008] 3 SCR 560 (concerning the scope of the oppression remedy), and *Saulnier v. Royal Bank of Canada*, [2008] 3 SCR 166 (concerning whether a fishing licence is "property" in the BIA sense) and the Ontario Court of Appeal's decision in *ATB Financial v. Metcalfe & Mansfield Alternative Investments II Corp.* (2008), 296 DLR (4th) 135 (the CCAA asset-backed commercial paper case). These, along with numerous other cases, are extracted and discussed in the following pages.

The book is presented in six parts: Part I (Chapters 1 and 2) deals with the history and policy of the bankruptcy laws, including their constitutional aspects; Part II (Chapters 3 to 11) is devoted to formal (or "straight") bankruptcy proceedings; Part III (Chapters 12 to 15), which is new, provides a comprehensive coverage of CCAA proceedings; Part IV (Chapters 16 and 17) deals with BIA commercial and consumer proposals; Part V (Chapter 18), which is new, covers receiverships; and Part VI (Chapter 19) deals with international insolvencies.

We divided the labour as follows: Professor Duggan was responsible for Chapters 4 (Property of the Estate), 5 (Review of Pre-Bankruptcy Transactions), 6 (Executory Contracts), 12 (CCAA: Introduction), and 13 (Carrying On Business During CCAA Proceedings) (with

Professors Ben-Ishai and Telfer); Professor Ben-Ishai was responsible for Chapters 7 (Claims Against the Estate and Recovery of Claims), 11 (Individual Bankruptcies and Consumer Issues) (with Professor Telfer), 13 (with Professors Duggan and Telfer) and 17 (Consumer Proposals); Professor Telfer was responsible for Chapters 1 (Introduction, Evolution, and Modern Objectives) (with Professor Ziegel), 3 (Initiation of Bankruptcy Proceedings and Consequences of Bankruptcy), 10 (Liability of Corporate Directors and Insolvency), 11 (with Professor Ben-Ishai) and 13 (with Professors Duggan and Ben-Ishai); Professor Wood was responsible for Chapters 8 (Secured Creditors, Crown Claims, and Statutory Deemed Trusts), 9 (Ranking of Creditors and Distribution of Proceeds), 14 (CCAA: Claims), 15 (Approval of CCAA Plans), and 18 (Receiverships); and Professor Ziegel was responsible for Chapters 1 (with Professor Telfer), 2 (Constitutional Aspects and Judicial and Administrative Structure of Bankruptcy System), 16 (BIA Commercial Proposals), and 19 (International Insolvencies). Professor Duggan coordinated the project.

We had anticipated, when we started work on the project, that the 2005-2007 amendments would be in force by the time we went to press. As it happens, most of the new provisions are still unproclaimed. The delay has been due partly to the time it has taken to draft supporting regulations and partly to political events, including the October 2008 general election and the proroguing of the new Parliament in December 2008, which have significantly interrupted government business. We are confident that the amendments will be in force by our publication date, but we have addressed the possibility that they might not be by providing as detailed an account as space allows not only of the amendments themselves but also, as mentioned above, of the laws they (will) replace.

In Chapter 1 of the previous edition of the casebook, we pointed out how Canadian bankruptcy law has evolved from being the preserve of a small number of boutique law firms to its current position, where no large law firm can afford to be without its own team of insolvency specialists. This transformation is no doubt due to the several severe recessions that Canada has suffered over the past 25 years, not to mention the current financial crisis that has gripped much of the industrialized world. It would be nice to think that Canadian law schools have also come to appreciate the intellectual, as well as practical, importance of bankruptcy law as part of a balanced curriculum. An increasing number of law schools have become converted to this view and we hope that this new edition of the casebook will help to attract even more.

We owe many debts: to our conscientious research assistants; to our law schools, for funding assistance; and to the Office of the Superintendent of Bankruptcy, for providing us with statistical information, which we have included in the casebook. We are especially grateful to Nancy Ennis, our production editor, for her meticulous work on the manuscript and to all at Emond Montgomery for encouraging us to persevere and to complete the manuscript by the agreed date.

Canada Day, 2009
A.J.D.
S.B.-I.
T.G.W.T.
R.J.W.
J.S.Z.

Acknowledgments

A book of this nature borrows heavily from other published material. We have attempted to request permission from, and to acknowledge in the text, all sources of such material. We wish to make specific reference here to the authors, publishers, journals, and institutions that have generously given permission to reproduce in this text works already in print. If we have inadvertently overlooked an acknowledgment or failed to secure a permission, we offer our sincere apologies and undertake to rectify the omission in the next edition.

American Bankruptcy Law Journal. Barbara K. Morgan, "Should the Sovereign Be Paid First—A Comparative International Analysis of the Priority for Tax Claims in Bankruptcy" (2000), 74 *Am. Bankr. LJ* 461, at 463-68.

American Review of Insurance Law. Thomas G.W. Telfer, "The Evolution of Bankruptcy Exemption Law in Canada 1867-1919: The Triumph of the Provincial Model," [2008] *Ann. Rev. Insurance L* 578-79 (footnotes omitted).

Annual Review of Insolvency Law. Michael McNaughton and Mary Arzoumanidis, "Substantive Consolidation in the Insolvency of Corporate Groups," [2007] *Ann. Rev. Ins. L*, at 525-29, 540, 543-45 (footnotes omitted).

Stephanie Ben-Ishai. Stephanie Ben-Ishai, "Government Student Loans, Government Debts and Bankruptcy: A Comparative Study" (2007), 44 *CBLJ* 211, at 212-14 and 221-24 (footnotes omitted).

Stephanie Ben-Ishai and Saul Schwartz. Stephanie Ben-Ishai and Saul Schwartz, "Bankruptcy for the Poor" (2007), 45 *Osgoode Hall LJ* 471, at 471-78 and 504-8 (footnotes omitted).

Canadian Bankruptcy Review. Dianne Saxe, "Trustees' and Receivers' Environmental Liability Update" (1997), 49 CBR (3d) 138, at 138-64.

Department of Justice Canada. *Report of the Study Committee on Bankruptcy and Insolvency Legislation* (Canada, 1970) ("Tassé Report"), sections 1.1-1.3 (footnotes omitted).

Government of Canada. Standing Senate Committee on Banking, Trade, and Commerce, *Debtors and Creditors Sharing the Burden: A Review of the Bankruptcy and Insolvency Act and the Companies' Creditors Arrangement Act* (Ottawa: November 2003), at 15 and 190-92.

Hart Publishing. J.S. Ziegel, *Comparative Consumer Insolvency Regimes* (Oxford: Hart Publishing, 2003), at c. 2.14 (footnotes omitted).

Harvard University Press. Thomas H. Jackson, *The Logic and Limits of Bankruptcy Law* (Cambridge, MA: Harvard University Press, 1986), 7-27 (footnotes omitted).

Industry Canada. *Efficiency and Fairness in Business Insolvencies,* Industry Canada, Corporate Law Policy Development, January 2001.

Industry Canada. *Update of Surplus Income Requirements and Payments: Consumer Bankruptcies Filed from 2002–2007,* Report #: BKHQRA-875 Report Date: October 17, 2008.

Andrew J.F. Kent, Wael Rostom, Adam Maerov, and Tushara Weerasooriya. Andrew J.F. Kent, Wael Rostom, Adam Maerov, and Tushara Weerasooriya, "Canadian Business Restructuring Law: When Should a Court Say 'No'?" (2008), 24 *BFLR* 1, at 1 (footnotes omitted).

LexisNexis. Michael B. Rotsztain and Alexandra Dostal, "Debtor-in-Possession Financing," in Stephanie Ben-Ishai and Anthony Duggan, eds., *Canadian Bankruptcy and Insolvency Law: Bill C-55, Statute c. 47 and Beyond* (Toronto: LexisNexis, 2007), at 227-29, 231, 233-34, 236-40.

LexisNexis and Jacob Ziegel. Jacob Ziegel, "Cross-Border Insolvencies," in Stephanie Ben-Ishai and Anthony Duggan, *Canadian Bankruptcy and Insolvency Law: Bill C-55, Statute c. 47 and Beyond* (Toronto: LexisNexis, 2007), chapter 11, at 297-301 (footnotes omitted).

Melbourne University Law Review. Andrew Keay and Mao Zhang, "Incomplete Contracts, Contingent Fiduciaries, and a Director's Duty to Creditors" (2008), 32 *Melbourne ULR* 141-43 and 148 (footnotes omitted).

Ministry of Public Works and Government Services. Kevin Davis and Jacob Ziegel, "Assessing the Economic Impact of a New Priority Scheme for Unpaid Wage Earners and Suppliers of Goods and Services" (prepared for Industry Canada: Corporate Law Policy Directorate, April 30, 1998), 13-15.

New Zealand Law Commission. New Zealand Law Commission, *Priority Debts in the Distribution of Insolvent Estates: An Advisory Report to the Ministry of Commerce* (Wellington, NZ: NZLC, 1999), 6-10.

Office of the Superintendent of Bankruptcy Canada. Personal Insolvency Task Force, *Final Report* (Ottawa: Industry Canada, Office of the Superintendent of Bankruptcy, 2002), at 17-24, 24-26, and 29-33 (footnotes omitted).

Office of the Superintenent of Bankruptcy Canada. Canadian Insolvency Statistics: 1966-2007, Office of the Superintendent of Bankruptcy, Annual Statistical Reports.

Office of the Superintendent of Bankruptcy Canada. Saul Schwartz, "Counselling the Overindebted: A Comparative Perspective" (2005), OSB online, at http://strategis.ic.gc.ca/epic/site/bsf-osb.nsf/en/br01672e.html.

Sweet & Maxwell. R.M. Goode, *Principles of Corporate Insolvency Law*, 3rd ed. (London: Sweet & Maxwell, 2005), 213-15.

Charles J. Tabb. Charles J. Tabb, "Consumer Bankruptcy After the Fall: United States Law Under Section 256" (2006), 43 *CBLJ* 28 (footnotes omitted).

Thomas G.W. Telfer. Thomas G.W. Telfer, "The Canadian Bankruptcy Act of 1919: Public Legislation or Private Interests?" (1995), 24 *CBLJ* 357, at 393 (footnotes omitted).

Thomas G.W. Telfer. Thomas G.W. Telfer, "The Proposed Federal Exemption Regime for the Bankruptcy and Insolvency Act" (2005), 41 *CBLJ* 279, at 283-85 (footnotes omitted).

Thomas G.W. Telfer. Thomas G.W. Telfer, "Transplanting Equitable Subordination: The New Free-Wheeling Equitable Discretion in Canadian Insolvency Law?" (2001), 36 *CBLJ* 36, at 41-43.

Uniform Law Conference of Canada. Tamara M. Buckwold, *Reform of Fraudulent Conveyances and Preferences Law, Part II: Preferential Transfers* (Report prepared for the Uniform Law Conference of Canada, Civil Law Section, August 2008), paras. 4 and 7 to 18 (footnotes omitted).

University of Chicago Law Review. Douglas G. Baird, "Loss Distribution, Forum Shopping, and Bankruptcy: A Reply to Warren" (1987), 54 *University of Chicago Law Review* 815, at 816-22 and 828-31 (footnotes omitted).

University of Chicago Law Review. Elizabeth Warren, "Bankruptcy Policy" (1987), 54 *University of Chicago Law Review* 775-801 (footnotes omitted).

US Government Printing Office. National Bankruptcy Review Commission, *Bankruptcy: The Next Twenty Years* (Washington, DC: US Government Printing Office, 1997), at 315-22 (footnotes omitted).

Virginia Law Review. Alan Schwartz, "A Normative Theory of Business Bankruptcy" (2005), 91 *Virginia Law Review* 1199, at 1224-30 (footnotes omitted).

Jacob Ziegel. Jacob Ziegel, "Consumer Insolvencies, Consumer Credit, and Responsible Lending," 2008 Houlden Fellowship Award Paper (unpublished).

Jacob Ziegel. Jacob S. Ziegel, "Creditors as Corporate Stakeholders: The Quiet Revolution—An Anglo Canadian Perspective" (1993), 43 *UTLJ* 511, at 517-18 (footnotes omitted).

Jacob S. Ziegel. Jacob S. Ziegel, "New and Old Challenges in Approaching Phase Three Amendments to Canada's Commercial Insolvency Laws" (2002), 37 *CBLJ* 75, at 81-83 and 101-3.

Jacob Ziegel. J.S. Ziegel, "Post-Bankruptcy Remedies of Secured Creditors: Some Comments on Professor Buckwold's Article" (1999), 32 *CBLJ* 142 (footnotes omitted).

Jacob S. Ziegel, and R.S. Sahni. J.S. Ziegel and R.S. Sahni, "An Empirical Investigation of Corporate Division 1 Proposals in the Toronto Bankruptcy Region" (2003), 41 *Osgoode Hall LJ* 665, at 673-81 (updated to incorporate references to the 2005-2007 amendments; footnotes omitted).

Short Table of Contents

PART V   RECEIVERSHIPS

PART VI   INTERNATIONAL INSOLVENCIES

Detailed Table of Contents

PART III   The Companies' Creditors Arrangement Act

Table of Cases

A page number in boldface type indicates that the text of the case or a portion thereof is reproduced. A page number in lightface type indicates that the case is quoted briefly or discussed by the authors. An "n" after a page number indicates that the case is to be found in a footnote. Cases mentioned within excerpts are not listed.

Table of Abbreviations

A. REFERENCE TEXTS AND FREQUENTLY CITED TREATISES, REPORTS, AND OTHER MATERIALS

BAIRD AND JACKSON
Adler, Baird, and Jackson's Bankruptcy, Cases, Problems, and Materials, 4th ed. (New York: Foundation Press, 2007)

COLTER REPORT
Report of the Advisory Committee on Bankruptcy and Insolvency (Ottawa: Advisory Committee on Bankruptcy and Insolvency, 1986) (Chair: Gary F. Colter)

FLETCHER
Ian F. Fletcher, *Law of Insolvency*, 4th ed. (London: Sweet & Maxwell, 2009)

HOULDEN AND MORAWETZ
Lloyd W. Houlden, Geoffrey B. Morawetz, and Janis P. Sarra, *The Annotated Bankrupty and Insolvency Act* (Toronto: Carswell, 2009) (annual)

JACKSON
Thomas H. Jackson, *The Logic and Limits of Bankruptcy Law* (Cambridge, MA: Harvard University Press, 1986)

REPORT OF (FEDERAL) ADVISORY COMMITTEE
See COLTER REPORT

TASSÉ REPORT
Report of the Study Committee on Bankruptcy and Insolvency Legislation (Ottawa: Study Committee on Bankruptcy and Insolvency Legislation, 1970)

ZIEGEL
J.S. Ziegel, ed., *Current Developments in International and Comparative Corporate Insolvency Law* (Oxford: Clarendon Press, 1994)

B. FREQUENTLY CITED STATUTES

APA   *Assignment and Preferences Act*, RSO 1990, c. A.33

BIA   *Bankruptcy and Insolvency Act*, RSC 1985, c. B-3,
                            as am. 1992, c. 27; 1997, c. 12

CCAA   *Companies' Creditors Arrangement Act*, RSC 1985,
                            c. C-36

FCA   *Fraudulent Conveyances Act*, RSO 1990, c. F.29

US *Bankruptcy Code*   11 USC (United States Code, Title 11)

WURA   *Winding-Up and Restructuring Act*, RS 1985, c. W-11

Further Readings on Bankruptcy and Insolvency Law

A. Canada

S. Ben-Ishai, *Bankruptcy Reforms* (Toronto: Carswell, 2008).

S. Ben-Ishai and A. Duggan, eds., *Canadian Bankruptcy and Insolvency Law: Bill C-55, Statute c. 47 and Beyond* (Toronto: LexisNexis, 2007).

F. Bennett, *Bennett on Bankruptcy*, 11th ed. (Toronto: CCH, 2009).

F. Bennett, *Bennett on Receiverships*, 2nd ed. (Toronto: Carswell, 1998).

L.W. Houlden, G.B. Morawetz, and J. Sarra, *The 2009 Annotated Bankruptcy and Insolvency Act* (Toronto: Carswell, 2009).

L.W. Houlden, G.B. Morawetz, and J. Sarra, *Bankruptcy and Insolvency Law of Canada*, 3rd ed. (Toronto: Carswell) (looseleaf, 4 vols.) (available on WestlaweCarswell at http://ecarswell.westlaw.com).

J. Sarra, *Creditor Rights and the Public Interest: Restructuring Insolvent Corporations* (Toronto: University of Toronto Press, 2003).

J. Sarra, *Rescue! The Companies' Creditors Arrangement Act* (Thomson Carswell, 2007).

T. Telfer, *Reconstructing Bankruptcy Law in Canada: 1867 to 1919* (Toronto: University of Toronto, Faculty of Law, 1999) (unpublished SJD thesis).

R. Wood, *Bankruptcy and Insolvency Law* (Toronto: Irwin Law, 2009).

B. United States

Adler, Baird and Jackson's Bankruptcy Cases, Problems and Materials, 4th ed. (New York: Foundation Press, 2007).

T. Jackson, *The Logic and Limits of Bankruptcy Law* (Cambridge, MA: Harvard University Press, 1986).

C. Tabb, *The Law of Bankruptcy* (Westbury, New York: Foundation Press, 1997).

C. Tabb and R. Brubaker, *Bankruptcy Law: Principles, Policies, and Practice*, 2nd ed. (New York: LexisNexis Matthew Bender, 2006).

E. Warren and J. Westbrook, *The Law of Debtors and Creditors: Text, Cases, and Problems*, 6th ed. (New York: Aspen Law and Business, 2008).

C. England

V. Finch, *Corporate Insolvency Law Perspectives and Principles*, 2nd ed. (Cambridge: Cambridge University Press, 2009).

I. Fletcher, *Law of Insolvency*, 4th ed. (London: Thomson Sweet & Maxwell, 2009).

R. Goode and R. Stevens, *Goode on Principles of Corporate Insolvency Law*, 4th ed. (London: Thomson Sweet & Maxwell, 2009).

R. Mokal, *Corporate Insolvency Law: Theory and Application* (Oxford: Oxford University Press, 2005).

D. Australia

M. Murray, *Keay's Insolvency: Personal and Corporate Law and Practice*, 6th ed. (Sydney: Thomson Lawbook Co., 2008).

E. Comparative Studies

J. Kilborn, *Comparative Consumer Bankruptcy* (Durham, NC: Carolina Academic Press, 2007).

J. Niemi-Kiesilainen, W. Whitford, and I. Ramsay, *Consumer Bankruptcy in a Global Perspective* (Oxford: Hart Publishing, 2003).

J. Ziegel, *Comparative Consumer Insolvency Regimes: A Canadian Perspective* (Oxford: Hart Publishing, 2003).

J. Ziegel, ed., *Current Developments in International and Comparative Corporate Insolvency Law* (Oxford: Clarendon Press, 1994).

PART I

Introduction

CHAPTER ONE

Introduction, Evolution, and Modern Objectives

Any man's death diminishes me, because I am involved in mankind, and therefore never send to know for whom the bell tolls; it tolls for thee.

    —John Donne, *Meditations from Devotions Upon Emergent Occasions* (1624)

I. INTRODUCTION

A. Why Study Bankruptcy Law?

Casebook editors don't normally feel it necessary to justify their subject. It is assumed that students will either have some prior familiarity with the area or that the title of the casebook will convey sufficient information about its character.

However, these assumptions don't generally hold true for bankruptcy law. For many law students, "bankruptcy" conveys a disagreeable flavour and is associated with financial failure and irresponsible or incompetent debtors. Other students perceive bankruptcy as an intensely practical nuts-and-bolts topic, but one that lacks principles and intellectual rigour. Students are not alone in holding these sentiments. For many years, large downtown law firms avoided bankruptcy work and were content to leave it to small, boutique firms specializing in the area.[1] Law schools also shared this prejudice and, often, when it was offered at all, the teaching of bankruptcy law was entrusted to busy practitioners. Bankruptcy books were largely case annotations on the bankruptcy legislation. There were few law review articles examining the foundations of Canadian bankruptcy law and even fewer dealing with the economic and social aspects of insolvency.

Much of this has changed over the past 25 years. The collapse of dozens of megasized Canadian corporations in the two recessions at the beginning and end of the 1980s brought home to large law firms the importance of having in-house expertise to serve their clients' needs. The risk of a corporate debtor's insolvency, always an important consideration in the

---

[1] In Toronto, one of the best-known bankruptcy firms was that headed by Lloyd Houlden, QC, later a trial judge and then member of the Ontario Court of Appeal. Lloyd Houlden is the eponymous author of the Hon. Mr. Justice Lloyd W. Houlden, the Hon. Mr. Justice Geoffrey B. Morawetz, and Janis Sarra, *Bankruptcy and Insolvency Law of Canada*, 3rd ed. (Toronto: Carswell, looseleaf, 4 vols.). They are also co-authors of *The 2009 Annotated Bankruptcy and Insolvency Act* (Toronto: Carswell, 2009). These are both classic practitioners' texts. Mr. Houlden had a most illustrious career as bankruptcy specialist and judge and continues to edit these texts.

drafting of debt indentures and the provision of security for loans, now loomed more important than ever, as did the exposure of directors of insolvent companies for unpaid wages taxes and for environmental claims.

Developments at the consumer level were no less significant. The rapid growth in the use of consumer credit from the 1970s onward, fuelled by the mass distribution of credit cards and by merchandisers' appreciation of the importance of easy credit facilities as selling tools, led to a commensurate increase in the number of consumer insolvencies: from 2,732 in 1970 to 115,789 at the end of 2008.[2]

Common-law scholars, on both sides of the Atlantic, also began to appreciate the intellectual importance of bankruptcy law. In England, the interest was sparked by the recasting of English insolvency law in the *Insolvency Act 1986*[3] and, as in North America, by the collapse of many large enterprises. In North America, the academic interest was invigorated by the law and economics movement and by debate over alleged abuses involving Chapter 11 of the US *Bankruptcy Code*, and in part by the credit industry's efforts to stem the tide of consumer bankruptcies.[4] The chosen (and highly controversial) vehicle was to have Congress adopt legislation imposing a means test on consumers seeking a fresh start under Chapter 7 of the Code.[5] A third dimension to the bankruptcy picture emerged in the 1980s with the rapid increase in the number of transborder insolvencies resulting from the growth of multinational corporations and global trade. The need here was to harmonize and liberalize the rules for the recognition of foreign insolvencies and to enable foreign administrators to take possession of locally situated assets.

In short, bankruptcy law is no longer, if it ever was,[6] the preoccupation of a few specialists. It permeates many branches of modern corporate, commercial, and consumer law and provides rich intellectual fare even for students not contemplating practising in this field.

---

[2] Office of the Superintendent of Bankruptcy (OSB), *Annual Statistical Report-2007*; OSB, *Overview of Canadian Insolvency Statistics to 2006*. The terminological distinction between bankruptcy and insolvency, and between business, personal, and consumer insolvencies for statistical and legal purposes is explained hereafter.

[3] Now further amended by the *Enterprise Amendment Act 2002*.

[4] Non-business bankruptcy filings in the United States peaked at the astonishing number of 2,039,214 in 2005. This figure covers Chapter 7 and Chapter 13 bankruptcies. Since then numbers have dropped dramatically. In 2007, there were 822,590 non-business filings. The decline coincides with the enactment of the *Bankruptcy Abuse Prevention and Consumer Protection Act of 2005*. This statute is discussed in Chapter 11. See www.abiworld.org. The bankruptcy numbers have climbed again in the light of the subprime mortgage melt down and looming recession in the United States. In 2008 there were 1,074,225 non-business filings.

[5] See further, *infra*, Chapter 11 of this text.

[6] As readers of Charles Dickens and other English novelists will know, 19th century Victorian society was very much absorbed in the bankruptcy phenomenon and the hapless lot of debtors languishing in jail because they could not pay their bills. Between 1831 and 1914, almost 100 bankruptcy bills were introduced in the British Parliament. There were also three royal commissions, at least 10 parliamentary select committees, and one special Lord Chancellor's committee set up to study bankruptcy problems and recommend solutions. See V. Markham Lester, *Victorian Insolvency* (Oxford: Clarendon Press, 1995), 2. In Canada there was a similar fascination with bankruptcy reform. After the federal government repealed the *Insolvent Act of 1875*, Parliament debated 22 reform bills over a near 40-year period before finally enacting the *Bankruptcy Act* of 1919. See T. Telfer, "A Canadian 'World Without Bankruptcy': The Failure of Bankruptcy Reform at the End of the Nineteenth Century" (2004), 8 *Aust. J Legal Hist.* 83.

B. Scope of Casebook

This casebook is designed to give students an overview of the key issues in contemporary Canadian bankruptcy law and some appreciation of the actual operation of the Canadian bankruptcy system. This chapter and the next chapter are introductory in character, but nonetheless important. The balance of the casebook, with the exception of the last chapter, deals with major types of bankruptcy proceedings and their impact on debtors and creditors. Chapters 3 to 10 are concerned with straight bankruptcy proceedings (often referred to as liquidation proceedings to distinguish them from reorganizational proceedings) and provide a sequential account of the chief components of these proceedings. The account begins with the gathering-in of the debtor's estate and ends with the ranking of unsecured creditor claims in the distribution of the net assets, the treatment of secured claims and Crown lien claims, and the liabilities of directors of insolvent companies.[7] Because of their distinctive character and the problems to which they give rise, Chapter 11 is earmarked for a discussion of consumer bankruptcies. Chapters 12 to 15 deal with commercial reorganizations under the *Companies' Creditors Arrangement Act* (CCAA). Chapters 16 and 17 deal with *Bankruptcy and Insolvency Act* (BIA) proposals. Chapter 16 focuses on commercial proposals under Division 1 of Part III of the BIA (hereafter BIA III.1), while Chapter 17 deals with consumer proposals under Division 2 of Part III of the BIA (hereafter BIA III.2). Chapter 18 examines the law of receiverships. Chapter 19, the concluding chapter, addresses cross-border insolvency issues.

C. Bankruptcy Terminology

Unfortunately, bankruptcy terminology is confusing and is not consistent among common-law jurisdictions. Under the BIA, the terms "bankruptcy" and "bankrupt"[8] are confined to straight liquidation proceedings under Part III of the Act and a "bankrupt" is the subject of a "bankruptcy order." All other proceedings under the BIA are known as insolvency proceedings (hence the title of the Act, *Bankruptcy and Insolvency Act*) or are identified by the part and division of the BIA under which the proceedings are brought.[9] The subject of these proceedings is referred to as a "debtor." Importantly, however, unlike the British *Insolvency Act 1986*, the BIA draws no distinction between corporate and personal or individual bankruptcies. All liquidation bankruptcies are basically governed by the same rules. The term reorganization is not actually used in the BIA or the CCAA to describe non-liquidation proceedings designed to enable an insolvent business to stay alive or to enable an insolvent individual to avoid the stigma of bankruptcy by reaching agreement with the debtor's creditors to pay off

---

[7]   Much of the material in these introductory chapters is also relevant in considering the treatment of commercial and consumer reorganizations, infra, Chapters 12 to 17 of this text. The same is true of the liability of corporate directors for company debts, infra, Chapter 10.

[8]   "Bankrupt" is defined in BIA s. 2(1). The expression is of Italian origin, *banke rota* or *bancarupta*, and was used in the Italian city states in the Middle Ages to describe the breaking of the bench of a merchant who had defaulted on his debts: see Tassé Report, extracted above.

[9]   To avoid needless repetition and unless otherwise indicated, references in notes in the casebook to bankruptcy proceedings cover all types of bankruptcy and insolvency proceedings under the BIA and the CCAA.

all or part of the indebtedness over a period of years. Instead, BIA III.1 and III.2 speak respectively of commercial and consumer proposals; the object of proceedings under the CCAA is referred to as an "arrangement." However, "reorganization" (or, increasingly commonly, "restructuring") are the non-technical terms frequently used to describe proceedings under BIA III.1 and the CCAA, and they are used in the same sense in this casebook.

The US *Bankruptcy Code* draws no terminological distinction between straight bankruptcy and reorganizational proceedings. All are referred to as "bankruptcy" or "case" proceedings,[10] and particular bankruptcy proceedings are usually identified by the Code chapter under which they are brought—e.g., Chapter 7 for straight liquidations, Chapter 11 for commercial reorganizations, and Chapter 13 for wage earner debt adjustments. Moreover, Chapters 1, 3, and 5 apply to all case proceedings under the Code unless otherwise provided. The Code also eschews use of the word "bankrupt"; instead persons who are the subject of case proceedings under any chapter of the Code are referred to as "debtors."[11]

In England and Wales (Scotland has its own insolvency legislation) the term "bankruptcy" is restricted to liquidation proceedings involving the assets of *individual* debtors; "winding up" or "winding up order" is the expression used to describe the liquidation of insolvent companies, although under the *Insolvency Act 1986* many of the substantive rules are the same for both individual and company insolvencies.[12]

Unhappily, common law jurisdictions also differ in their terminology in reporting statistical results. The Canadian statistics published by Industry Canada distinguish between personal insolvencies and business insolvencies. "Insolvencies" cover bankruptcy and reorganizational proceedings under the BIA (but not proceedings under the CCAA, for which official statistics are not available). Business insolvencies cover the insolvencies of corporations, partnerships, and individuals where, in the case of individuals, 50 percent or more of the indebtedness is of business origin.[13] Personal insolvencies cover business and consumer insolvencies, whereas consumer insolvencies are restricted to personal, non-business insolvencies. Consumer insolvencies are subdivided into consumer bankruptcy proceedings and consumer proposals under BIA III.2.[14] The other common law jurisdictions—e.g., England

---

[10] US terminology has also been picked up by Canadian media and it is common for news reports to refer to a Canadian company seeking "bankruptcy protection" under the CCAA even though the CCAA is quite independent of the BIA. What is meant is that a stay of proceedings is in effect precluding creditors from suing or invoking remedies against the debtor company while the company is preparing a plan of reorganization to put before its creditors.

[11] Query: should Canada follow suit and also avoid the use of the pejorative term "bankrupt"?

[12] The reason for the distinction is historical but the distinction continues to enjoy popular support in England. The Canadian *Winding-Up and Restructuring Act* (WURA), first adopted in 1882, was copied from British legislation after the federal Parliament repealed the *Insolvent Act of 1875* in 1880. See Section II of this chapter. The WURA is now little used except in cases where its use is mandatory for designated incorporated entities such as banks, insurance companies, and railways. See B. Welling and T. Telfer, "The Winding-Up and Restructuring Act: Realigning Insolvency Law's Orphan to the Modern Law Reform Process" (2008), 24 *BFLR* 235.

[13] This is the definition of business used by the Office of the Superintendent of Bankruptcy. See *Insolvency Statistics in Canada* (OSB, August 2008), at ii.

[14] There are also a small number of orderly payment of debts (OPD) proceedings under Part X of the BIA, but these are statistically insignificant and are often overlooked. In 2007, there were only 596 OPD orders for all of Canada compared to 99,282 consumer insolvencies.

and Australia—use different terminology in reporting personal insolvencies; hence considerable care must be used in comparing their statistics with Canada's.

II. EVOLUTION OF BANKRUPTCY LAW

Report of the Study Committee on Bankruptcy and Insolvency Legislation
(Canada, 1970) ("Tassé Report"), sections 1.1-1.3 (footnotes omitted)

An Expanding Concept: The long history of bankruptcy has been one of an expanding concept. From the harsh and merciless treatment of debtors, the law, through many stages, has come to recognize that, while there may be fraudulent debtors from whom society must be protected, an honest bankrupt is not a contradiction of terms. Upon this cornerstone has been built the modern law of bankruptcy.

In primitive societies, the debtor's lot was hard. There was no exception to the rule that he must pay his debts in full. If he could not pay with his property, he paid with his person.

The Code of Hammurabi: Written more than 4000 years ago, the Code of Hammurabi, King of Babylon, contained several actions concerning the relations between debtors and creditors. According to this Code, the creditor was entitled to levy a "distress" or "pledge," called a *nipûtum*, if the debt was not paid when it became due. It was not necessary for the creditor to first obtain judgment, but he was penalized if he wrongfully levied a distress. While oxen of the plough and grain were exempted from seizure, the debtor's wife, a child or a slave could be brought as *nipûtum* to the creditor's house. There they were put to work until the debt was satisfied. In addition to the *nipûtum*, the Code considered the case where the debtor voluntarily surrendered a dependant into bondage by selling him, with or without right of redemption, to a merchant or to the creditor himself. The position of the dependant in the house of his new master seems to be similar to that of the *nipûtum*, but, in the case of a wife or child, the servitude came to an end after three years service. Finally, if the debt of the creditor was not satisfied one way or another, there seems little doubt that the debtor could be adjudicated to him as a bond-servant.

The Law of Ancient Greece: By the end of the 7th Century, BC, in Athens, the new class of mercantile capitalists virtually owned the entire peasant class with mortgages on nearly every small holding in Attica. The peasants could not resist foreclosures on their lands and on their persons, which often were included in their pledges. The poor were in a state of bondage to the rich, both themselves, their wives, and their children. The political situation was critical. In order to avert a revolution, Solon cancelled all existing mortgages and debts, released debtors from bondage and made illegal those contracts in which a person's liberty was pledged.

The Roman Law: When, in the middle of the 5th Century, BC, Rome decided to codify its laws, it sent three commissioners to Greece to study the laws of Solon. The code that resulted is known as the *Law of the Twelve Tables*. Contrary to the spirit of the reform of Solon, the Roman jurists maintained the execution against the person. After the fulfillment of certain formalities, the unpaid creditor had the power to seize the debtor himself. This seizure, called *manus injectio*, gave the creditor authority to bring the debtor to his home and keep him in chains for sixty days. During this period, the debtor, still the owner of his property and a Roman citizen, could try to settle his debts with his creditor. To allow for the possibility of a ransom being paid, the creditor was required to take him three times to the market place giving notice of the amount of the debt each time. Finally, if at the end of sixty days, the creditor was not fully paid, he could, it would seem, put the debtor to death or sell him into foreign slavery. According to certain modern writers, the creditors could even divide between them the body of the debtor. If this was so, there is no proof that such an inhuman treatment was ever applied. It must also be noted that the *paterfamilias* could, as was the case under the *Hammurabi Code*, in order to avoid his slavery, raise money by leasing out the services of the members of his family. In Roman law, this is known as *mancipium*. During the centuries that followed the promulgation of the *Law of the Twelve Tables*, the severity of the *manus injectio* was progressively reduced. By the end of the Republic, the unpaid creditor could still imprison the debtor or make the debtor work for him in satisfaction of the debt but he could no longer put him to death or sell him into slavery.

· · ·

This was the rule under Roman law until the end of the Republic, when the *Edict of the Praetor* alleviated the harshness of the old quiritarian law. About that time, one praetor developed a method of execution against property known as *venditio bonorum*. This fundamental reform, for the first time, established a link between the assets and the liabilities of a person. Moreover, this was in the nature of a procedure for the collective execution against the property of an insolvent or recalcitrant debtor. To quote W.W. Buckland, "It is in effect the Roman equivalent of bankruptcy proceedings."

Thus, by the end of the Republic, Roman law recognized two methods of execution, one against the person and the other against property. The debtor could, however, by the time of Augustus, avoid execution against his person by making a *cessio bonorum*, that is to say, by surrendering to his creditors everything he owned. About three centuries later, the *cessio bonorum* was not available to debtors who had squandered their property or concealed it from their creditors. According to an imperial ordinance of the year 379, this procedure was only allowed when the insolvency of the debtor was due to an act of God. Under Justinian, the use of the *cessio bonorum* had become so widespread that the *Corpus Juris* scarcely mentions imprisonment for debt.

The Italian Cities: As trade and the use of credit developed, the ordinary law of debtor and creditor became inadequate to cope with the problem of the insolvent trader. Towards the end of the Mediaeval [*sic*] Ages, the Italian cities attempted to deal with this problem and new concepts, such as the "act of bankruptcy" were developed by legal writers of the time. It is from the Italian *bancarupta* that the word "bankrupt" is derived. It may be literally translated as "bank broken" or "bench broken." The allusion is said to be the custom of breaking the table of a defaulting tradesman.

· · ·

The English Law: In England, one of the first insolvency statutes was enacted in 1351. In an attempt to promote commercial integrity, it provided that, if any merchant of the Company of Lombard Merchants acknowledged himself bound in a debt, the Company should answer for it. Apparently, this was by reason of the fact that some of these merchants had, in the past, left the country without paying their debts.

At Common Law, a creditor has to resort to a very expensive, lengthy and cumbersome procedure to obtain an attachment of his debtor's property. Execution cannot (sic) be obtained against a debtor's entire estate but only against the property described in the writ. If there was a plurality of creditors, they took the property of the debtor in the order of their attachments. The race was to the swift. The rule was "first come, first served."

The first Bankruptcy Statutes provided a summary method for the collective execution of all of the debtor's property, both movable and immovable. They stressed the rights of creditors. The only concern shown in respect of the debtor was that he should surrender all of his property and that no fraud on his part should go undetected and unpunished. Under the first of these statutes [Act of 1542 (eds.)], the property was liquidated and distributed "to every of the said creditors a portion, rate and rate alike, according to the quantity of their debts." The preamble of this statute stated: "where divers and sundry persons craftily obtaining into their own hands great substance of other Mens [*sic*] Goods, do suddenly flee to Parts unknown, or keep their Houses not minding to pay or restore to any [*sic*] their Creditors, their Debts and Duties, but at their own Wills and Pleasures Consume the Substance obtained by credit of other Men for their own Pleasure and delicate Living against all Reason, Equity and good Conscience."

Although the English *Bankruptcy Act* of 1542 was directed against any debtor who attempted to defeat his creditors by fraudulent means, the Act of 1571 restricted bankruptcy to those who were engaged in trade. This distinction was to be maintained for almost 300 years. A debtor who was not in trade and who could not pay his debts was imprisoned until some person paid them for him.

The first English Act showing concern for the rehabilitation of the debtor was enacted in 1705 in the reign of Anne. A debtor who was a merchant could get a discharge of all his debts owing at the time of his bankruptcy provided he surrendered all of this property and conformed to the other provisions of the statute. However, the legislator remained very much aware of the continuing problem of the fraudulent debtor. So, while being given new privileges, the debtor had to be free from fraud and submit himself to the control of the Court. Evidence of the concern of the legislator that debtors might abuse the privileges given to them was the severity of the penalty for a debtor who did not strictly comply with the law. The penalty, in the past, had been to stand in the pillory or have an ear cut off. The new penalty was hanging. This penalty applied, for example, if the bankrupt failed to surrender himself to the court, committed perjury on his examination or fraudulently concealed his assets.

In the middle of the 18th Century, Sir William Blackstone, commenting on the Law of England, had this to say about bankruptcy:

The Laws of England, more wisely, have steered in the middle between both extremes: providing at once against the inhumanity of the creditor, who is not suffered to confine an honest bankrupt after his effects are delivered up; and at the same time taking care that all his just debts shall be paid; so far as the effects will extend. But still they are cautious of encouraging prodigality and extravagance by this indulgence to debtors; and therefore they allow the benefit of the laws of bankruptcy to none but actual traders; since that set of men are, generally speaking, the only persons liable to accidental losses, and to an inability of paying their debts, without any fault of their own. If persons in other situations of life run in debt without the power of payment, they must take the consequences of their own indiscretion, even though they may meet with sudden accidents that may reduce their fortunes: for the law holds it to be an unjustifiable practice, for any person but a tradesman to encumber himself with debts of any considerable value. If a gentleman, or one in a liberal profession, at a time of contracting his debts, has a sufficient fund to pay them, the delay of payment is a species of dishonesty, and a temporary injustice to his creditor: and if, at such time, he has no sufficient fund, the dishonesty and the injustice is the greater. He cannot therefore, murmur, if he suffers the punishment which he has voluntarily drawn upon himself. But in mercantile transactions, the case is far otherwise. Trade cannot be carried on without mutual credit on both sides: the contracting of debts is therefore here not only justifiable, but necessary. And if by accidental calamities, as by the loss of a ship in a tempest, the failure of brother traders, or by the non-payment of persons out of trade, a merchant or tradesman becomes incapable of discharging his own debts, it is his misfortune and not his fault. To the misfortunes, therefore, of debtors, the law had given a compassionate remedy, but denied it to their faults: since at the same time that it provides for the security of commerce, by enacting that every considerable trader may be declared a bankrupt, for the benefit of his creditors as well as himself, it has also to discourage extravagance, declared that no one shall be capable of being made a bankrupt, but only a trader, nor capable of receiving the full benefit of the statutes, but only an industrious trader.

. . .

In the early part of the 19th Century, a number of statutes were passed for the relief of insolvent debtors who were not engaged in trade and therefore could not be made bankrupt. Originally, the insolvency acts provided only for the release from imprisonment of the debtor. He was not released of his debts and remained liable for their repayment. Later legislation provided for the discharge of persons who were imprisoned for their debts if they surrendered all of their goods for the benefit of their creditors. In 1812, the laws relating to insolvency were administered by a court of record known as the Court for the Relief of Insolvent Debtors. By the *Bankruptcy Act* of 1861, which made persons other than traders subject to bankruptcy law, this Court was abolished and its jurisdiction transferred to the Court of Bankruptcy. In 1869, by the *Bankruptcy Repeal and Insolvent Court Act*, all insolvency statutes theretofore existing were extinguished. Imprisonment for debt was abolished altogether, except in the case of a dishonest person who could pay his debts but refused to do so. The legal distinction between bankruptcy and insolvency was thus all but eliminated.

In the history of bankruptcy, there is much experimentation concerning who should liquidate and supervise an estate. In 1831, for example, the English legislation provided for the joint administration by official assignees and assignees chosen by the creditors. In 1869, the system of administration, at the insistence of the trading community, reverted to a system of creditor liquidation. The creditors chose the trustee who was supervised by a committee of inspectors also chosen by the creditors. Abuses soon arose, however, particularly in regard to the solicitation of proxies, which often permitted a minority of creditors to control and manipulate the administration of an estate in their interests to the prejudice of the majority of creditors.

It was recognized in England that the system of creditor control over the administration of a bankruptcy estate, as provided by the 1869 Act, had failed. The English *Bank-*

ruptcy Act of 1883 devised a new system of joint official and creditor control. Although minor amendments have been made to this Act, the system of administration, that it created, has not changed in any material respect. When Joseph Chamberlain, the then President of the Board of Trade, spoke on the second reading of the Bill for the 1883 Act, he explained the philosophy of his new legislation as follows:

> He, (Joseph Chamberlain), asked the House to keep in mind two main, and, at the same time, distinct objects of any good Bankruptcy Law. Those were, firstly, in the honest administration of bankrupt estates, with a view to the fair and speedy distribution of the assets among the creditors, whose property they were; and, in the second place their object should be, following the idea that prevention was better than cure, to do something to improve the general tone of commercial morality, to promote honest trading, and to lessen the number of failures. In other words, Parliament had to endeavour, as far as possible, to protect the salvage, and also to diminish the number of wrecks.
>
> His next point was that, with regard to those two most important objects, there was only one way by which they could be secured and that was by securing an independent and impartial examination into the circumstances of each case; and that was the cardinal principle of this Bill. … What happened when a bankruptcy took place which might easily cause misery to thousands of people and bring ruin on many homes? It was treated as if it were entirely a matter of private concern, and allowed to become a scramble between the debtor and his advisers—who were often his confederates—on the one hand, and the creditors on the other. Meanwhile, the great public interests at stake in all these questions were entirely and absolutely ignored, as there was nobody to represent them, and the practice which was followed in the case of other calamities was, in this case, entirely absent. In the case of accidents by sea and by land—railway accidents, for instance—it was incumbent upon a Government Department to institute an inquiry. There were inquiries in the case of accidents in mines, and of boiler explosions, and sad as those disasters were, they did not, in the majority of cases, cause so much misery as a bad bankruptcy, which brought ruin to many families by carrying off the fruits of their labour and industry. …
>
> Now, it would be seen that the provision which he had described (a description of duties and responsibilities of the official receiver, the office of which was first created by this Bill) constituted a system which he thought they might fairly call a system of official inquiry, and which went on all fours with a similar system in the matters of accident to which he had referred. He did not think that without some such limited officialism as this any satisfactory inquiry was even possible. No investigation could be worth anything unless it was conducted by an independent and impartial officer. …

Chapter 2

The Canadian Legislation Since Confederation

Principal Milestones: In the hundred years since Confederation, the following Statutes constitute the important milestones of bankruptcy and insolvency legislation:

1869:	*The Insolvent Act of 1869*	32-33 Vic., Can. S. 1869, c. 16
1875:	*The Insolvent Act of 1875*	38 Vic., Can. S. 1875, c. 16

1880:	*An Act to repeal the Acts Respecting Insolvency*	43 Vic., Can. S. 1880, c. 1
	(now in force in Canada)	
1882:	*An Act respecting Insolvent Banks, Insurance Companies,*	45 Vic., Can. S. 1882, c. 23
	Loan Companies, Building Societies and Trading	
	Corporations, later named the Winding-Up Act	
	(for insolvent companies)	
1889:	*The Winding Up Amendment Act, 1889*	52 Vic., Can. S. 1889, c. 32
	(extended to solvent companies)	
1919:	*The Bankruptcy Act*	9-10 Geo. V, Can. S. 1919, c. 36
1923:	*The Bankruptcy Act Amendment Act, 1923*	13-14 Geo. V., Can. S. 1923, c. 31
	(companies prohibited from making proposals without	
	previously being adjudged bankrupt; office of custodian	
	created; office of official receivers created)	
1932:	*The Bankruptcy Act Amendment Act, 1932*	22-23 Geo., V, Can. S. 1932, c. 39
	(office of Superintendent created)	
1933:	*The Companies' Creditors Arrangement Act, 1933*	23-24 Geo. V, Can. S. 1932-33, c. 36
1934:	*The Farmers' Creditors Arrangement Act, 1934*	24-25 Geo. V, Can. S. 1934, c. 53
1943:	*The Farmers' Creditors Arrangement Act, 1943*	7 Geo. VI, Can. S. 1943, c. 26
1949:	*Bankruptcy Act, 1949*	13 Geo. VI, Can. S. 1949
		(2nd Session), c. 7
1953:	*An Act to Amend the Companies' Creditors Arrangement*	1-2 El. II, Can. S. 1952-53, c. 3
	Act, 1933 (act restricted to arrangement including an	
	arrangement between a company and its bondholders)	
1966:	*An Act to Amend the Bankruptcy Act*	14-15 El. II, Can. S. 1966-67, c. 32

The First Insolvency Legislation After Confederation: The Acts of 1869 and 1875 applied only to insolvent traders. From 1874 to 1878 there was a serious depression in Canada resulting in many commercial failures. This caused much public resentment particularly in the rural areas of the country which led to the enactment of *The Insolvency Acts Repeal Act* in 1880. The following quotations from the debates in the House of Commons indicate something of the public opinion of the time and the reasons for the repeal. The anger directed at those who appeared to be acting fraudulently still has a timeliness:

> *Mr. Colby*: Whatever may have been the necessity of the law when it was passed, I think that now it is unquestionably a fact that it has outlived its usefulness and that public opinion is definitely settled and has declared itself in a way that is unmistakeable, in favour of an immediate and summary repeal of the Act ... (the law) became rather a means of escape for the dishonest and designing debtor than a mere means of relief for the honest and unfortunate debtor ... experience has also shown in this country, and in other countries I believe, that the rapacity of assignees, the dishonesty of debtors, the greed of some creditors, the inattention of others, have thwarted the beneficient intentions of the law; and instead of there being an economical and honest administration of assets, the practical operation of the law has been characterized by a wasteful extravagance, and too often by a dishonest administration. I think it is unmistakeably the case in this country where the law has been a long time on the Statute-Book, that it has tended to the demoralisation of trade, and to lower the standard of com-

mercial morality. It has tended to recklessness in trading and in living to extravagance. It has tempted many persons, wholly unsuited for business, to risk their fortune in business enterprises that were little understood by them. The whole effect of the law in recent years has been unfortunate and disastrous. I think, sir, that it is the sentiment of the people of this country, generally, that it has tended, in some considerable degree, if not to create, at all events to aggravate, the commercial distress which has unhappily prevailed in this country.

· · ·

By a coincidence that appears not to be accidental, the *Bill to Repeal the Insolvency Acts* was read for the third time on March 4, 1880, while on March 5, 1880, assent was given, in Ontario, to "An *Act to Abolish Priorities of and Amongst Execution Creditors*." In the discussion in the House of Commons, it was said that the Ontario Bill, which was similar to the law prevailing in Quebec, would provide for the just and equitable distribution of estates and the hope was expressed that other provinces would enact similar legislation.

The Winding-Up Act: It was soon found that, without an *Insolvency Act*, there was no convenient way to wind up insolvent companies. Boards of Trade, in most of the large cities, passed resolutions requesting new legislation. In 1882, the *Insolvent Banks, Insurance Companies and Trading Corporations Act*, later to be known as the *Winding-Up Act*, was enacted.

In some countries, such as England and Australia, the *Bankruptcy Act* applies only to individuals and there is other legislation for the liquidation of insolvent companies. With the existence of the *Winding-Up Act*, this dichotomy could have developed in Canada. However, when the *Bankruptcy Act* of 1919 was enacted, it applied to both individuals and corporations. From 1919 until 1966, there were, in effect, two separate Acts in competition with each other relating to the insolvency of limited liability companies. These two Acts differ in substance and technique. In bankruptcy, for example, the property of the bankrupt vests in the trustee; under the *Winding-Up Act*, title to the property of the company remains in the company, but its control and management are taken from the directors and placed in the liquidator. The *Bankruptcy Act* binds the Crown, while the *Winding-up Act* does not. Under the *Bankruptcy Act*, an act of bankruptcy must be proved to obtain a receiving order, while, under the *Winding-Up Act*, a winding-up order may be obtained if the debtor is insolvent or deemed to be insolvent. Neither banks, insurance companies nor railway companies may be liquidated under the *Bankruptcy Act*, but they may be wound up under the *Winding-Up Act*. The *Bankruptcy Act* is characterized by an administration, for the most part, controlled by creditors, while, under the *Winding-Up Act*, the administration is controlled by the court. This duality is restricted by the amendments to the *Bankruptcy Act* in 1966 [see now BIA s. 213 (eds.)], which provide in effect that the *Bankruptcy Act* should take precedence over the *Winding-Up Act*. Thus, now, where a petition for a receiving order or an assignment is filed under the *Bankruptcy Act*, in respect of a corporation, the *Winding-Up Act* does not extend or apply to that corporation.

The Period from 1880 to 1919: During the thirty-nine years when there was no federal bankruptcy or insolvency legislation relating to individuals, the only relief available to insolvent individuals was through provincial legislation. There were, in Quebec, articles 763-780 of *The Code of Civil Procedure* and, in the other provinces, the Assignment and

Preferences Acts. The first of these Acts was an *Act Respecting Assignments for the Benefit of Creditors* passed by the Ontario Legislature in 1885, some five years after enacting what is now *The Creditors' Relief Act*.

Under provincial legislation, an insolvent debtor makes an assignment of his property to an authorized trustee licensed by the province. The authorized trustee is then required to liquidate the estate under the supervision of inspectors. For this, he is paid a fee from the debtor's estate. What characterizes provincial legislation, and since 1919, distinguishes it from the *Bankruptcy Act* is that a creditor cannot force a debtor to make an assignment; once an assignment is made, there is no provision in the legislation permitting a debtor to make a composition with his creditors and a debtor does not receive a release of his debts or a discharge.[15]

The 1919 Bankruptcy Act: By 1917, there was considerable agitation across the country in support of the enactment of a national *Bankruptcy Act*. A committee of the Canadian Bar Association was created to draft such an act. This, in turn, disturbed some businessmen and authorized trustees licensed by the provinces. They felt that an act drafted by lawyers would provide for some form of court controlled administration instead of the provincial system of creditor control whereby estates were liquidated by the authorized trustees under the supervision of inspectors. One of the largest firms of authorized trustees, the Canadian Credit Men's Trust Association, retained Mr. H.P. Grundy, KC of Winnipeg, and instructed him to draft a Bill based upon creditor control and retaining the essential features of the provincial Assignments and Preferences Acts.

The Bill, based upon Mr. Grundy's draft, was first introduced in the House of Commons on March 27, 1918 as a war measure. On the motion for first reading, it was said:

> *Mr. Jacobs*: … I think that I can claim for this Bill that it is essentially a war measure at this particular time. We must be prepared when the war comes to a close, to be able to handle the situation which is bound to arise in this country as a result of the long continued struggle and of the readjustments which must be made. … By this measure it is proposed that the courts shall carefully scrutinize the business dealings and the business relations of traders, and shall make a distinction—shall separate the sheep from the goats. When the court is of the opinion that a debtor has been obliged to assign through misfortune, he shall be given the necessary relief. If, on the other hand, it should be found in scrutinizing his affairs, that he wrecked his own business wilfully, then, of course, he should receive no relief whatever.

The Bill, later referred to a special committee and then reintroduced in the House of Commons during the following session, was enacted in 1919.

The Office of the Custodian Created in 1923: It had been hoped that the system of administration established by the 1919 Act and based upon the practice prevailing under the provincial Assignments Acts would prevent the occurring of the abuses that had helped to discredit the old Insolvency Acts. It was soon found, however, that most of the business under the new Act was not going to the experienced organizations of trustees that had efficiently handled most of the business under the provincial Assignments Acts.

---

15 For the history of the 1919 Act, see Thomas G.W. Telfer, "The Canadian Bankruptcy Act of 1919: Public Legislation or Private Interest?" (1995), 24 *CBLJ* 357. [eds.]

The work of a trustee attracted many unqualified and inexperienced persons, and, as there was then not enough business, this resulted in many trustees openly soliciting business and often lead [*sic*] to collusive and inefficient administration of estates.

In an attempt to rectify the abuses surrounding the appointment of trustees, particularly in voluntary assignments where the debtor was nominating his own trustee, the office of custodian was created in 1923. In many respects, the custodian fulfilled several of the functions of the official receiver in England until the first meeting of the creditors. The custodian was in effect the first trustee in every estate. He had to take possession of the property of the debtor and was responsible for its safekeeping until the appointment of the trustee at the first meeting of creditors. In practice, it soon developed that the custodian was invariably appointed trustee. As a result, the office of the custodian served no useful purpose and was ultimately abolished in 1949.

The Office of Superintendent of Bankruptcy created in 1932: The lack of safeguards surrounding the appointment of trustees encouraged the activities of dishonest trustees. There were scandals involving inefficient and collusive liquidations by incompetent and untrustworthy trustees. The supervision of trustees by creditors was ineffectual and the demand grew for some form of government supervision.

At the Annual Meeting of the Canadian Credit Men's Trust Association Ltd., in 1927, attention was called to the office of "Accountant of Court" created under the *Bankruptcy Act* of Scotland. The Accountant, who was appointed by the court on the recommendation of the Crown, had the responsibility to examine the charges and conduct of trustees and inspectors in every proceeding.

In 1929, the late Lewis Duncan, QC, an acknowledged bankruptcy specialist, after comparing the English, French and United States systems, suggested that there was a need in Canada for an adequately staffed bankruptcy department with offices at strategic centres.

In 1932, the office of the Superintendent was created. It was contemplated that the Superintendent would provide an independent, impartial and official supervision of trustees administering estates under the *Bankruptcy Act*. Except for the increased investigatory powers given to it in 1966, the office of the Superintendent has remained unaltered and compares with that of the Inspector General in Bankruptcy established in England in 1883.

The 1949 Bankruptcy Act: The present Canadian *Bankruptcy Act* was enacted in 1949. The intention of the new Act was said to be "to clarify and simplify the legislation." The following extract from Hansard, when the Bill was first introduced in the Senate, explains the history of the Bill and the principal changes:

> *Hon. J. Gordon Fogo*: Honourable senators, it has sometimes been said that legislation in Canada is passed hastily and that those interested and the public in general are not given an opportunity to study its provisions. I do not think that can be said of this Bill F, which appears to have had a rather checkered career. This, I believe, is the fourth time that the bill has been introduced in this honourable House. It was first brought down in the year 1946, in a somewhat different form from the present measure, and was laid over for study for a period during which representations concerning it were made. Subsequently, in 1948, it came up again in a revised form. And, as most honourable senators will remember, it was

introduced for a third time at the first session of this year, but unfortunately, owing to early dissolution, consideration of it was not completed. The present bill, I am informed, with very few exceptions, is practically identical with the bill that was before the Senate last session. … The bill provides a more orderly arrangement of subjects and the language in many sections of the Act has been simplified. One or two of the more notable changes should be mentioned. The bill reinstates a provision which was in the *Bankruptcy Act* of 1919. During the period from 1919 to 1923 the Act contained a provision whereby an insolvent person could make a proposal to his creditors without making an assignment or having a receiving order made against him, and thereby suffering the stigma of bankruptcy. The bill now provides that an insolvent person may make such a proposal without going through the procedure of bankruptcy.

A further change which has been generally accepted as an improvement is a code for the administration of small estates in an economical and inexpensive manner. This section of the bill covers estates with assets of $500 or less, and provides a simplified procedure for their administration.

One other notable innovation of this bill is found in sections 127 to 129, which deal with the discharge of bankrupts. Under the existing legislation it has been necessary for a bankrupt, after the administration was completed, to apply to get his discharge. For various reasons, whether because the debtor did not know he was entitled to do this, or for other reasons, it was not customary for bankrupts to apply to their discharge. Following legislation in other countries—I think in the United States, and perhaps in Australia—this bill incorporates what might be regarded as an automatic application for discharge, because the occurring of the bankruptcy through assignment or receiving order in the first instance is also treated as an application for discharge. The debtor of course has to satisfy the court that he qualifies before he gets his discharge, and the conditions are laid down.

To move on quickly and in a very summary way: there are other miscellaneous provisions which might be mentioned. The new bill vests a greater measure of control in the creditors and inspectors. The powers of the superintendent have been made more explicit. … The remuneration of trustees has been increased; that is, the maximum remuneration has been enlarged from 5 to 7½ per cent. … The office of the custodian is eliminated. …

The 1966 Amendment: During the fifties and early sixties, there was an increasing number of complaints about fraudulent bankruptcies. The complaint was also made that the investigatory machinery was not adequate to cope with the problem. As a result, the *Bankruptcy Act* was amended in 1966 so as to give the Superintendent wider powers of investigation. He may now investigate offences under any Act of Parliament, whether they have occurred before or after bankruptcy.

Many other significant amendments were made in 1966. One relates to non-arms' length transactions, and enables trustees better to deal with the transactions entered into by a debtor to the prejudice of his creditors. Part X of the *Bankruptcy Act* was also enacted. It provides for a system of orderly payment of debts under the supervision of the courts, but it is effective only in provinces where the Lieutenant Governor in Council has requested the Governor in Council to proclaim it in force.

The Companies' Creditors Arrangement Act: Prior to 1914, when most of Canada's financing was done in England, the practice, in issuing securities, was to follow English precedents. As a consequence, almost all trust deeds during this period contained clauses permitting a majority of debenture holders to vary the terms of a trust deed. Sometime later, in the twenties, when financing in the United States became more common, such provisions were no longer included in a great many trust deeds as they were not at that time usual in the United States. When the depression came, many companies needed to be reorganized. Often, to the embarrassment of the directors, it was found that the trust deeds did not contain provisions permitting reorganization by agreement. As a result, without the existence of enabling legislation, there was no way by which such companies could be reorganized.

. . .

The Companies' Creditors Arrangement Act worked well and gave general satisfaction to investors and to companies with secured indebtedness who wished to make arrangements with their creditors. There were, however, abuses of the Act by insolvent companies that used it, instead of the *Bankruptcy Act*, to make arrangements with their unsecured creditors. The *Companies' Creditors Arrangement Act* was never intended for this purpose, as it did not provide an appropriate procedure to give sufficient protection to unsecured creditors against false or misleading statements by the company concerning its affairs, thereby inducing them to accept proposals not in their best interests.

"Debenture holders" did not, however, have to rely solely on this Act for protection. The investing public had other facilities available. Most debentures gave the indenture trustee wide powers to intervene in the affairs of the debtor upon certain conditions. Institutional investors and underwriters that have large blocks of debentures on their hands or in their portfolios would, as a rule, also intervene in order to prevent any serious abuse.

. . .

In 1953, the *Companies' Creditors Arrangement Act* was amended, as originally suggested by the Dominion Mortgage and Investments Association, so as to restrict its application to a debtor company that had an outstanding debenture issue and wished to make a proposal with the debenture holders. [The report continues to point out that the CCAA was seldom used after 1953 because of its restricted application and the fact that trust indentures usually contained their own machinery for the contractual reorganization of financially troubled companies. (eds.)]

. . .

Conclusion: At the end of this brief description of how the bankruptcy and insolvency system developed in Canada, there are a number of comments that come to mind.

Although, at the outset, the legislation was almost entirely borrowed from England, in the course of time, amendments were made to the original legislation to better adapt it to Canadian conditions and special statutes were passed to meet particular problems. Little attempt was made, however, to integrate new legislation with the existing legislation or to make a single comprehensive Act. The result has been a multiplicity of statutes and systems which often lead to inequity and inefficiency.

With the multiplicity of systems, the debtor and the creditor sometimes have the choice of the system under which to proceed and, under certain circumstances, they can fare better under one system than another. A creditor, for example, may be better protected or may have a higher priority for a dividend under one system than another. Similarly, the penalty provisions applicable to debtors may vary.

Many corporations may be liquidated under either the *Winding-Up Act* or the *Bankruptcy Act*. There are transactions that may be set aside as fraudulent preferences under one of these Acts, which could not be set aside, as such, under the other. However, since the 1966 amendments to the *Bankruptcy Act*, the *Winding-Up Act* does not apply to a corporation, where a petition is filed under the *Bankruptcy Act*. While the opportunity of a debtor or creditor to elect to take proceedings under the *Winding-Up Act*, and thus forestall proceedings under the *Bankruptcy Act*, has been reduced, inequities are still possible. The majority of creditors, for example, may wish to take proceedings under the *Winding-Up Act* to reach a creditor who has received a preference that may be set aside as fraudulent under the *Winding-Up Act*, but not under the *Bankruptcy Act*. The creditor who is alleged to have obtained a fraudulent preference, or a creditor friendly to him, may effectively block the proceedings under the *Winding-Up Act* by making a petition under the *Bankruptcy Act*.

There are situations, however, where no choice is given to the debtor or the creditors as to which statute may be used. A number of statutes apply in whole or in part, for example, to particular debtors, such as banks, insurance companies and railways. This situation may also lead to inequity as both debtors and creditors, under the particular statutes, may, without good reason, fare differently than those who come within the provisions of other statutes.

Moreover, in spite of the multiplicity of systems and statutes, there are a number of debtors whose affairs cannot be liquidated under existing federal legislation. The non-trading corporations, for example, would be in that category. It is not clear, either, whether any of this legislation applies to the winding-up, by reason of their insolvency, of some corporations, such as provincial trust companies and certain building societies.

Finally, the existing legislation may also be criticized for being, to a considerable degree, either rudimentary or out-dated. Much of it was designed when social and commercial conditions were very much different than what they are today. In other cases, legislation designed to meet a particular emergency survived long after the emergency had passed and the conditions changed. The procedure for the liquidation of insolvent railways is a good example of rudimentary legislation. Under present conditions, as a practical matter, special legislation would probably be required to effectively liquidate a railway company by reason of its insolvency, as existing legislation is silent in respect to many matters of importance. The *Farmers' Creditors Arrangement Act* is an example of special legislation inspired by a national emergency that has been long out of date, but which has never been repealed, brought up to date or incorporated into the principal statute.[16]

NOTES

1. *Historical update.* Following the publication of the Tassé Report the federal government introduced Bill C-60 in 1975. This was a complete revision of the *Bankruptcy Act* (BA) and adopted most of the Task Force's recommendations. The bill was strongly criticized on

---

16   The Act has now been repealed. [eds.]

technical and policy grounds by various bankruptcy constituencies in hearings before the Senate Banking and Commerce Committee and was withdrawn by the government for further review. A revised bill, Bill C-12, was introduced in 1980 but it, and three other bills introduced over the next four years, never emerged from the committee stage in the House of Commons. See further Comment (1982-83), 8 *CBLJ* 374.

In 1984, the newly elected Mulroney government abandoned further attempts to enact a revised Act and opted instead for incremental changes to the BA. To this end the federal government established an advisory committee (the "Colter Committee") composed of insolvency practitioners and trustees to recommend those changes that were deemed to be most urgent. The committee reported in 1986.

The committee's recommendations were largely adopted in Bill C-22, first introduced in the summer of 1991. The bill nearly came to grief over part I of the bill, which would have enacted a separate *Wage Claim Payment Act*. The bill was given parliamentary approval in 1992 (SC 1992, c. 27), but only after the government had dropped part I entirely. The most important changes contained in the 1992 amendments were the following:

a. A totally revised Part III, Division I, dealing with the reorganization of insolvent business debtors (although, technically speaking, not restricted to business debtors), and a new Division II aimed at the composition of consumer debts.

b. A new Part XI requiring secured creditors to give 10 days' notice to the debtor before seeking to repossess the collateral where the collateral comprises all or substantially all of the debtor's assets or all or substantially all of the debtor's inventory or accounts receivable, and subjecting privately appointed or court appointed receivers and receiver-managers to judicial supervision.

c. The substantial recasting of s. 136 (which deals with the ranking of creditors for the purpose of distributing the net assets of the estate) and the elimination of preferred creditor status for Crown claims.

d. The recognition of deemed trusts, established pursuant to federal and provincial tax legislation, of monies collected and deductions made by a taxpayer on behalf of the Crown (BIA s. 67(3)).

e. Introduction of registration requirements for Crown lien claims as a condition of their recognition in bankruptcy (BIA ss. 86-87).

f. Creation of an unpaid seller's right to recover the goods on the buyer's bankruptcy and, in the case of unpaid farmers, fishermen, and aquaculturists, to claim a charge on the debtor's inventory for the unpaid amounts.

g. Automatic discharge of first-time individual bankrupts nine months after the bankruptcy order unless the discharge is opposed (BIA ss. 168.1-172).

h. Mandatory system of credit counselling of bankrupts as precondition to discharge from bankruptcy (BIA s. 157).

The 1992 Act (s. 92) required Parliament to review the BIA three years after the amendments came into effect. To prepare for this event, Industry Canada established a Bankruptcy and Insolvency Act Advisory Committee (BIAC) in 1993 to consider what further amendments should be recommended. The BIAC in turn established a series of working groups to study the various parts of the Act. The most important groups were those dealing with arrangements and proposals, preferences and priorities, consumer bankruptcies, and international insolvencies. The working group recommendations were then reviewed by the BIAC and, if approved, were incorporated in the BIAC's report to the federal government. The federal government accepted most of the BIAC's recommendations and they were enshrined in Bill C-109 and, later, Bill C-5, amending the BIA and CCAA, and were enacted in 1997 as SC 1997, c. 12. See further R.G. Marantz and R.H. Chartrand, "Bankruptcy and Insolvency Law Reform Continues: The 1996-1997 Amendments" (1997-98), 13 *BFLR* 107 and J.S. Ziegel, "Canadian Bankruptcy Reform, Bill C-109, and Troubling Asymmetries" (1996), 27 *CBLJ* 108.

Some of the important changes made to the BIA and the CCAA were the following:

- Protection against environmental liability was extended to receivers, interim receivers, and trustees under proposals.

- The 1992 provisions involving landlords' claims for leases repudiated by a debtor making a commercial proposal were relaxed to make them more flexible and to afford landlords better protection against unreasonable disclaimers.

- The commercial proposal and CCAA provisions were enlarged to permit corporate debtors to include in the proposal the compromising of claims against directors in their capacities as directors that arose before the proposal was made.

- New provisions were added to the BIA and CCAA governing the recognition of foreign insolvencies and authorizing Canadian courts to provide assistance to foreign insolvency administrators.

- A new Part XII was added dealing with the insolvency of securities firms and the handling of claims against such firms.

- Various amendments, favourable and unfavourable to debtors, were added to the consumer bankruptcy provisions. The single most important amendment was the recasting of s. 68 to make it mandatory for individual bankrupts to remit the bankrupt's surplus income to the trustee until the date of the bankrupt's discharge, the surplus income being determined by directives issued by the Superintendent of Bankruptcy. For further discussion of the surplus income payment requirements see Chapter 13 of this text.

- Important amendments to the CCAA included the following features: the Act was restricted to corporate debtors and their affiliates having a minimum indebtedness of $5 million; the requirements for an outstanding issue of debentures or bonds and a trust deed as preconditions of the Act's applicability were dropped; the court's initial *ex parte* order is only effective for 30 days and a new hearing must be held thereafter; and the court is required to appoint a monitor to protect creditor interests and report to the court at required intervals pending the debtor's preparation of a plan and its being voted on.

The 1997 amendments envisaged a third phase of amendments to the BIA and further possible amendments to the CCAA. They also required the federal government to submit a report to Parliament on the operation of the BIA and the CCAA within five years of the proclamation of the 1997 amendments. In preparation for this event, Industry Canada commissioned a large number of research reports on specific issues.[17]

---

17 Many of the research papers are available in electronic form on Industry Canada's website.

The Superintendent of Bankruptcy also established a Personal Insolvency Task Force (PITF) in 2000 to advise him on desirable amendments to the personal insolvency provisions in the BIA. The PITF's report was published in late 2002[18] and contains a large number of recommendations of varying importance. Some of the more radical recommendations provoked strong dissents within the Task Force.[19] The Insolvency Institute of Canada, an influential body of senior insolvency practitioners across Canada, also conducted its own series of studies on many aspects of the operation of the CCAA and presented its recommendations to the Minister of Industry in March 2002.[20]

Industry Canada published its own statutorily required report in late 2002.[21] The report discussed many of the issues relevant to further amendments to Canada's insolvency legislation. Disappointingly, the report avoided putting forward the Department's own solutions but somehow seemed to expect the Senate Banking, Trade and Commerce Committee (Senate Committee) to do this job for the government. The Senate Committee conducted public hearings in the spring of 2003 and published its substantial report in November of that year.[22] The Report was largely based on the recommendations in the IIC/CAIRP submissions and the recommendations in the PITF Report. The federal government issued no report indicating its own position in the light of these developments. Instead, and rather earlier than expected, the federal government introduced Bill C-55 in the House of Commons in June 2005. This massive 140-page bill involved the most extensive amendments to Canada's insolvency legislation since 1949. The most important changes involved the following areas:

- introduction of a *Wage Earner Protection Program Act* (WEPPA) guaranteeing payment of unpaid wages of employees of a bankrupt employer out of the federal Consolidated Revenue Fund up to a maximum of $3,000 per worker;

- new and revised treatment of executory contracts in straight bankruptcies and commercial proposals;

- revision of provisions involving fraudulent and below-value pre-bankruptcy transactions;

- protection of collective bargaining agreements from interference by the courts;

- conferment of superpriority security status against debtor's assets for unpaid wages up to prescribed amounts and for shortfalls in contributory employer–employee pension plans;

---

[18] See *Final Report* (Ottawa: Personal Insolvency Task Force, 2002).

[19] See, *inter alia*, annex 3 and Chapter 2(V) of the Report.

[20] See Insolvency Institute of Canada (IIC)/Canadian Association of Insolvency and Restructuring Professionals (CAIRP) Joint Task Force on Business Insolvency Law Reform, *Report* (2002) (unpublished), available at www.insolvency.ca.

[21] Industry Canada, Market Framework Policy Branch, Policy Sector, *Report on the Operation and Administration of the Bankruptcy and Insolvency Act and the Companies' Creditors Arrangement Act* (Ottawa: 2002).

[22] Report of the Standing Senate Committee on Banking, Trade and Commerce, *Debtors and Creditors Sharing the Burden: A Review of the Bankruptcy and Insolvency Act and the Companies' Creditors Arrangement Act* (Ottawa: November 2003).

- extension of automatic discharge entitlement for first-time insolvent individuals from 9 months to 21 months;

- substitution of UNCITRAL Model Law Crossborder Insolvency provisions for Part XIII of the BIA;

- major expansion of the skeletal CCAA provisions to cover most of the gaps in the statutory framework previously bridged by court orders made under the judicially crafted "inherent jurisdiction" doctrine;

- replication in CCAA (but often not verbatim) of BIA provisions, as amended, dealing with executory contracts and assignment of contracts and with the treatment of cross-border insolvencies.

- Bill C-55 attracted much criticism from professional groups, not so much on grounds of principle, but because of defects in craftsmanship. One of the most comprehensive critiques of Bill C-55—covering policy as well as drafting issues—was presented to the Industry Committee of the House of Commons in November 2005 by a group of academics.[23] Among the concerns expressed by the academics were the following:

  – the unnecessary duplication of provisions in the revised BIA and the CCAA and inconsistencies between the BIA and the CCAA covering identical topics;

  – the failure to integrate the CCAA as part of the BIA;

  – the need for a complete overhaul and modernization of the BIA, including the BIA regulations, forms and policy statements adopted under the BIA;

  – objections to the extension of the automatic discharge period for first time bankrupts with surplus income from 9 months to 21 months;

  – the need for more studies of the impact of the rapid expansion of consumer credit on the number of consumer insolvencies and the adequacy and fairness of the existing provisions and proposed amendments to the BIA.

The Industry Committee of the House of Commons began hearings on Bill C-55 in October 2005, but was obliged to discontinue (after hearing from only a few witnesses) because Parliament was dissolved on November 25, 2005, in anticipation of forthcoming elections. Before the dissolution of Parliament, the government prevailed on the Senate to approve Bill C-55, without the bill receiving the scrutiny of the Senate's Banking, Trade and Commerce Committee. To secure the Senate's consent, the Martin government gave an undertaking that it would not proclaim Bill C-55, after its enactment, without giving the Senate Committee an opportunity to study the bill in detail. Despite the government's assurance to the Senate, the net result of these events was that the 140-page Bill C-55 (now SC 2005, c. 47) was approved by both Houses of Parliament without scrutiny or serious debate in either House.

The Senate Committee did not in fact study Statute c. 47 in 2007 after Parliament was reconvened following the defeat of the Martin government and the installation of the Harper

---

23 *Academics' Submissions on Bill C-55, 2005: The Wage Earner Protection Program Act and Amendments to the Bankruptcy and Insolvency Act and the Companies' Creditors Arrangement Act* (November 2005).

administration. Rather, the Harper government announced its intention to introduce changes to Statute c. 47 and did so in the form of a Motion to Amend Statute c. 47, which was introduced in the House of Commons in December 2006. The motion was opposed by members of Parliament from Quebec and Saskatchewan representing vested interests in those provinces and the amendments were not adopted.[24] Department of Industry officials spent the next few months negotiating with the opponents of the RRSP amendments in Statute c. 47 and ended up by essentially capitulating to their demands.

In June 2007, the Harper government introduced Bill C-62, a 90-page bill amending Statute c. 47. Bill C-62 died on the Order Paper and was reintroduced in the next Session as Bill C-12. The bill was approved by the House without debate and without being referred to Committee for study. In a remarkable replay of the November 2005 events, government ministers appeared before the Senate Banking, Trade and Commerce Committee in December 2007 and persuaded the Committee to approve the bill without prior study. The ministers justified the request on the ground that the government was anxious to proclaim Statute c. 47 and Bill C-12 (once it was enacted) so that the government could proceed with adoption of the regulations necessary to implement WEPPA. The Senate Committee reluctantly agreed to the government's request, so that, for the second time, a major bankruptcy amendment bill was approved by Parliament without serious debate or scrutiny in either House.

There was one modest glimmer of hope. The Senate reserved the right to hold hearings on Statute c. 47 and on what had now become SC 2007, c. 36. The Senate Banking, Trade and Commerce Committee actually began hearings in February 2008. Because of other commitments, the Committee was not able to complete its hearings in the spring of 2008 and before Parliament adjourned for the summer. As of April 2009, the Committee had still not issued its report. Even if the report had been published, in the opinion of the editors of this casebook, the prospect of the federal government taking the recommendations seriously was negligible.

2. *Further readings:* For further readings on the above topics see S. Ben-Ishai and A.J. Duggan, eds., *Canadian Bankruptcy and Insolvency Law: Bill C-55, Statute c. 47 and Beyond* (Lexis Nexis, 2007), ch. 1.I; J. Ziegel, "Bill C-55 and Canada's Insolvency Law Process" (2006), 43 *CBLJ* 76; J. Ziegel, "The Travails of Bill C-55" (2006), 42 *CBLJ* 440; and Editorial (2007) 45 *CBLJ* 165.

3. *Non-Canadian developments.* Canada is not alone in recognizing the need to modernize its bankruptcy and insolvency legislation. Over the past 25 years, many other industrialized countries have felt the same pressures. The United States adopted a revised *Bankruptcy Code* in 1978, and many amendments were made to the Code between then and 2005. From 1997 onward, there was a powerful, credit-industry-driven and -financed push in the US Congress to amend the *Bankruptcy Code* to curb the growth in the number of consumer bankruptcies, which had tripled since the early 1980s, reaching 1.5 million by 2004. The

---

[24] The opposition was to the amendments in s. 67 of Statute c. 47, involving the exempt status of Registered Retirement Savings Plans (RRSPs). The amendments imposed a ceiling on the size of a plan that could be exempted from the trustee's reach after the RRSP holder became bankrupt. The critics were concerned that these restrictions would make RRSPs less attractive as an investment vehicle and affect their sales by insurance companies and other financial intermediaries. For further discussion of the issues, see PITF Report, pp. 17-23 and Chapter 11 of this text.

efforts bore fruit in President Bush's second term in office with the enactment of the *Bankruptcy Abuse Prevention and Consumer Protection Act 2005* (BAPCPA). The Act requires all consumers filing for bankruptcy relief under Chapter 7 of the *Bankruptcy Code* to satisfy a burdensome means test and show that they had consulted a credit counselling agency about their debt problems before filing. If a debtor fails to satisfy the means test, he is excluded from Chapter 7, but is still free to file a plan under Chapter 13, the US counterpart to consumer proposals under Part III.2 of the BIA.[25]

England completely revamped its corporate and personal bankruptcy law in the *Insolvency Act 1986* and important amendments were approved by the British Parliament in the *Enterprise Act 2002*. The amendments included (1) reducing the period of eligibility for discharge from two years to one year; (2) restructuring the existing disqualifications imposed on a bankrupt and were combining them with a new bankruptcy restriction order regime; and (3) introducing a "fast track" procedure, allowing a bankrupt to enter into an insolvency voluntary arrangement (IVA) (England's counterpart to Canada's consumer proposals under the BIA) and authorizing the official receiver to act as nominee and supervisor of the IVA. Australia completely restructured its corporate insolvency regime in 1992, and adopted important amendments to its bankruptcy law in 1996 and again in 2002. New Zealand enacted significant amendments in relation to personal and corporate insolvency law in 2006. Germany adopted a new insolvency regime in 1993 with special (though complex) provisions for insolvent consumers. Similarly, important new legislation was enacted in France and other EU countries and in Japan and other southeast Asian countries.[26]

There were common reasons for this hectic legislative activity. Much of the legislation being replaced was very old (in the case of the civil law countries some of the legislation was over a hundred years old) and no longer served contemporary needs. A second reason was that post-war recessions of increasing severity and the collapse of large enterprises made it urgent to seek viable alternatives to straight bankruptcies. Third, with the rapid increase in the number of consumer bankruptcies, there was a significant shift in bankruptcy philosophy from one stigmatizing individual bankrupts to a regime more hospitable to enabling the consumer debtor to make a fresh start under prescribed conditions. However, the prescribed conditions vary significantly even among common law countries and even more between common law and civil law jurisdictions.

Philosophically, in a spectrum of bankruptcy regimes, Canada's laws fall in the middle between the American and British approaches. The American *Bankruptcy Code* is more complex and, at least before 2005, was generally more debtor oriented than the BIA and companion Canadian legislation. The British *Insolvency Act 1986*, on the other hand, and true to its 19th century legacy, was until recently more pro-creditor in character, and particularly more deferential to secured creditor claims, than either the Canadian or American regimes. However, the gap has been substantially narrowed as a result of the important amendments in the *Enterprise Act 2002*.

---

[25] For further details and in-depth analysis of the BAPCPA provisions, see "Symposium: Consumer Bankruptcy and Credit in the Wake of the 2005 Act" (2007), *U Ill. L Rev.* 1.

[26] For a fascinating account of the social and economic factors leading to a rapid increase in the number of Japanese consumer bankruptcies, despite the traditional shaming of Japanese debtors who couldn't meet their obligations, see Kent Anderson, "Japanese Insolvency Law After a Decade of Reform" (2006), 43 *CBLJ* 76.

Canadian Insolvency Statistics: 1966-2007

	Bankruptcy		Volume	Proposals			Growth Rate Bankruptcy	
	Consumers	Business	Pre 1993	Div I	Div II	Total	Consumers	Business
1966	1903	2774	425			5102		
1967	1549	2474	253			4276	−18.6%	−10.8%
1968	1308	2481	310			4099	−15.6%	0.3%
1969	1725	2354	266			4345	31.9%	−5.1%
1970	2732	2927	315			5974	58.4%	24.3%
1971	3107	3045	275			6427	13.7%	4.0%
1972	3647	3081	228			6956	17.4%	1.2%
1973	6271	2934	253			9458	71.9%	−4.8%
1974	6992	2790	220			10002	11.5%	−4.9%
1975	8335	2958	202			11495	19.2%	6.0%
1976	10049	3136	211			13396	20.6%	6.0%
1977	12772	3905	254			16931	27.1%	24.5%
1978	15938	5546	234			21718	24.8%	42.0%
1979	17876	5694	312			23882	12.2%	2.7%
1980	21025	6595	403			28023	17.6%	15.8%
1981	23036	8055	392			31483	9.6%	22.1%
1982	30643	10765	435			41843	33.0%	33.6%
1983	26822	10260	470			37552	−12.5%	−4.7%
1984	22022	9578	389			31989	−17.9%	−6.6%
1985	19752	8663	402			28817	−10.3%	−9.6%
1986	21765	8502	543			30810	10.2%	−1.9%
1987	24384	7659	633			32676	12.0%	−9.9%
1988	25817	8031	585			34433	5.9%	4.9%
1989	29202	8664	570			38436	13.1%	7.9%
1990	42782	11642	855			55279	46.5%	34.4%
1991	62277	13496	1239			77012	45.6%	15.9%
1992	61822	14317	1133			77272	−0.7%	6.1%
1993	54456	12527		669	1818	69470	−11.9%	−12.5%
1994	53802	11810		743	1851	68206	−1.2%	−5.7%
1995	65432	13258		838	2419	81947	21.6%	12.3%
1996	79631	14229		1136	3113	98109	21.7%	7.3%
1997	85297	12200		1649	4737	103883	7.1%	−14.3%
1998	75465	10791		1715	7155	95126	−11.5%	−11.5%
1999	72997	10026		1950	9985	94958	−3.3%	−7.1%
2000	75137	10055		2211	12392	99795	2.9%	0.3%
2001	79453	10405		2612	13383	105853	5.7%	3.5%
2002	78232	9472		2826	14268	104798	−1.5%	−9.0%
2003	84251	8844		2920	15400	111415	7.7%	−7.1%
2004	84426	8128		2835	15551	110940	0.2%	−8.8%
2005	84638	7519		3096	16554	111807	0.2%	−8.1%
2006	79218	6756		3036	17619	106629	−6.8%	−11.2%
2007	79796	6307		3241	19486	108830	0.7%	−7.1%

Source: Office of the Superintendent of Bankruptcy, *Annual Statistical Reports*. (The numbers are not final and are subject to verification.)

Beginning in 2008 the OSB changed the way they reported proposals. The OSB website explains the changes:

> [A] significant change has been made to how data on proposals is reported. In previous years, proposals were reported based on the type of procedure: commercial proposals (also called Division I proposals) and consumer proposals (also called Division II proposals). Proposals are now reported based on the type of debt, consumer or business.[27]

Thus, prior to 2008, annual proposal statistics included the total number of Division I and Division II proposals without differentiating the type of debt. For example, the number of Division I proposals in 2007 (3,241) would have included some individuals with consumer debts filing a Division I proposal. In 2008 the number of business proposals did not include individuals with consumer debts. Here are the figures reported in 2008.

			Business	Consumer	Total		
			Proposals (2008)				
2008	90610	6164	1281	25179	123234	13.5%	−2.0%

QUESTIONS

What inferences do you draw from the above table? What accounts for the rapid growth in consumer bankruptcies over the past 40 years? How much is due to population growth and how much to increases in the use of consumer credit? How much of the fluctuations in bankruptcy statistics can be ascribed to the recessions in 1982, 1990, and 2008-9? What is the reason for the much smaller number of business bankruptcies and their smaller rate of growth? Do bankruptcies themselves harm the economy or are they merely *ex post* confirmations of losses ("sunk costs") that have occurred already?

III. MODERN BANKRUPTCY OBJECTIVES

In common law jurisdictions, it is now well established that bankruptcy law serves three principal functions: (1) to solve the "collective action problem" discouraging creditors from collaborating outside bankruptcy and to provide a mechanism in bankruptcy legislation for the orderly liquidation of a bankrupt's estate and distribution of the proceeds among the creditors; (2) to enable basically viable enterprises to reorganize themselves to enable them to stay in business; and (3) to enable overextended debtors to make a "fresh start" by surrendering their non-exempt assets and obtaining a discharge for the balance of their debts.

---

[27] The 2008 Annual Report defines business and consumer as follows:

> **Business:** Any commercial entity or organization, other than an individual, or an individual that has incurred 50 percent or more of total liabilities as a result of operating a business.

> **Consumer:** An individual with more than 50 percent of total liabilities related to consumer goods and services.

[eds.]

The following extracts from the book by Prof. Jackson and the articles by Prof. Elizabeth Warren and Prof. Douglas Baird address the first two questions. The fresh-start policy for individual bankrupts is examined below in Chapter 11. The interaction of reorganization policies and actual reorganization rules is explored in some detail in Chapters 12 to 16.

Thomas H. Jackson, *The Logic and Limits of Bankruptcy Law*
(Cambridge, MA: Harvard University Press, 1986), 7-27 (footnotes omitted)

1. The Role of Bankruptcy Law and Collective Action in Debt Collection

Bankruptcy law and policy have been subject to long-standing debate. This debate is not so much about whether bankruptcy law should exist at all but about how much it should do. All agree that it serves as a collective debt-collection device. Whether, when firms are involved, it should do more is the crux of the dispute. I plan to start by establishing in this chapter what accepted wisdom has already acknowledged—that bankruptcy's system of collectivized debt collection is, in principle, beneficial. Most of this book will then be concerned with exploring how that benefit can be realized and, as importantly, how viewing bankruptcy as a collectivized debt-collection device imposes limits on what else bankruptcy can do well. It is in the latter area that the most conflict arises. It exists because bankruptcy analysts have failed to follow through on the first principles of establishing a collectivized debt-collection system. To show why bankruptcy's principal role limits what other functions it can usefully perform is the objective of this book. Toward that end we shall first examine why bankruptcy law *should* be doing what everyone takes as a given.

Bankruptcy law is a response to credit. The essence of credit economies is people and firms—that can be called *debtors*—borrowing money. The reasons for this are varied. In the case of individuals credit may serve as a device to smooth out consumption patterns by means of borrowing against future income. In the case of corporations and other firms it may be a part of a specialization of financing and investment decisions. And just as the reasons for borrowing are varied, so, too, are the methods. The prototype creditor may be a bank or other financial institution that lends money, but that is only one of many ways in which credit is extended. An installment seller extends credit. So does a worker who receives a paycheck on the first of December for work performed in November. The government, in its role as tax collector, also extends credit to the extent that taxes accrue over a year and are due at the end. Similarly, a tort victim who is injured today and must await payment until the end of a lawsuit extends credit of sorts, although involuntarily and (probably) unhappily. Finally, credit is not extended just by "creditors." First-round purchasers of common and preferred stock of a corporation are also lending money to the debtor. Their repayment rights are distinct (they are the residual claimants), but it is proper to view them, too, as having defined rights to call on the assets of the debtor for payment.

Whatever the reasons for lending and whatever its form, the terms on which consensual credit is extended depend to a substantial extent on the likelihood of voluntary repayment and on the means for coercing repayment. We are not concerned here with the means for getting paid when the debtor is solvent—when it has enough assets to satisfy all its obligations in full—but is simply mean-spirited or is genuinely disputing whether it has a duty of payment (as the debtor might be with our putative tort victim or with a supplier who the debtor believes sold it defective goods). The legal remedies for coercing payment when the debtor is solvent concern the rights of a creditor to use the power of the state in pursuit of its claim. This is a question of debtor-creditor law and one to which bankruptcy law historically has had nothing to add, directly at least.

Bankruptcy law can be thought of as growing out of a distinct aspect of debtor-creditor relations: the effect of the debtor's obligation to repay Creditor A on its remaining creditors. This question takes on particular bite only when the debtor does not have enough to repay everyone in full. Even then, however, a developed system exists for paying creditors without bankruptcy. The relevant question is whether that existing system of creditor remedies has any shortcomings that might be ameliorated by an ancillary system known as bankruptcy law.

To explore that question, it is useful to start with the familiar. Creditor remedies outside of bankruptcy (as well as outside other formal, non-bankruptcy collective systems) can be accurately described as a species of "grab law," represented by the key characteristic of first-come, first-served. The creditor first staking a claim to particular assets of the debtor generally is entitled to be paid first out of those assets. It is like buying tickets for a popular rock event or opera: the people first in line get the best seats; those at the end of the line may get nothing at all.

When the issue is credit, the ways that one can stake a place in line are varied. Some involve "voluntary" actions of the debtor: the debtor can simply pay a creditor off or give the creditor a security interest in certain assets that the creditor "perfects" in the prescribed manner (usually by giving the requisite public notice of its claim). In other cases a creditor's place in line is established notwithstanding the lack of the debtor's consent: the creditor can, following involvement of a court, get an "execution lien" or "garnishment" on the assets of the debtor. Or, sometimes, a place in line may simply be given to a particular claimant by governmental fiat, in the form of a "statutory lien" or similar device.

Although the *methods* for establishing a place in line are varied, the fundamental ordering principle is the same. Creditors are paid according to their place in line for particular assets. With a few exceptions, moreover, one's place in line is fixed by the time when one acquires an interest in the assets and takes the appropriate steps to publicize it. A solvent debtor is like a show for which sufficient tickets are available to accommodate all prospective patrons and all seats are considered equally good. In that event one's place in line is largely a matter of indifference. But when there is not enough to go around to satisfy all claimants in full, this method of ordering will define winners and losers based principally on the time when one gets in line.

The question at the core of bankruptcy law is whether a *better* ordering system can be devised that would be worth the inevitable costs associated with implementing a new system. In the case of tickets to a popular rock event or opera, where there must be winners and losers, and putting aside price adjustments, there may be no better way to allocate available seats than on a first-come, first-served basis. In the world of credit, however, there are powerful reasons to think that there *is* a superior way to allocate the assets of an insolvent debtor than first-come, first-served.

The basic problem that bankruptcy law is designed to handle, both as a normative matter and as a positive matter, is that the system of individual creditor remedies may be bad for the creditors *as a group* when there are not enough assets to go around. Because creditors have conflicting rights, there is a tendency in their debt-collection efforts to make a bad situation worse. Bankruptcy law responds to this problem. Debt-collection by means of individual creditor remedies produces a variant of a widespread problem. One way to characterize the problem is as a multiparty game—a type of "prisoner's dilemma." As such, it has elements of what game theorists would describe as an *end period* game, where basic problems of cooperation are generally expected to lead to undesirable outcomes for the group of players as a whole. Another way of considering it is as a species of what is called a *common pool* problem, which is well known to lawyers in other fields, such as oil and gas.

This role of bankruptcy law is largely unquestioned. But because this role carries limits on what *else* bankruptcy law can do, it is worth considering the basics of the problem so that we understand its essential features before examining whether and why credit may present that problem. The vehicle will be a typical, albeit simple, common pool example. Imagine that you own a lake. There are fish in the lake. You are the only one who has the right to fish in that lake, and no one constrains your decision as to how much fishing to do. You have it in your power to catch all the fish this year and sell them for, say, $100,000. If you did that, however, there would be no fish in the lake next year. It might be better for you—you might maximize your total return from fishing—if you caught and sold some fish this year but left other fish in the lake so that they could multiply and you would have fish in subsequent years. Assume that, by taking this approach, you could earn (adjusting for inflation) $50,000 each year. Having this outcome is like having a perpetual annuity paying $50,000 a year. It has a present value of perhaps $500,000. Since (obviously, I hope) when all other things are equal, $500,000 is better than $100,000, you, as sole owner, would limit your fishing this year unless some other factor influenced you.

But what if you are not the only one who can fish in this lake? What if a hundred people can do so? The optimal solution has not changed: it would be preferable to leave some fish in the lake to multiply because doing so has a present value of $500,000. But in this case, unlike that where you have to control only yourself, an obstacle exists in achieving that result. If there are a hundred fishermen, you cannot be sure, by limiting *your* fishing, that there will be any more fish next year, unless you can also control the others. You may, then, have an incentive to catch as many fish as you can today because maximizing your take this year (catching, on average, $1,000 worth of fish) is better for you than holding off (catching, say, only $500 worth of fish this year) while others scramble and deplete the stock entirely. If you hold off, your aggregate return is only $500, since nothing will be left for next year or the year after. But that sort of reasoning by each of the hundred fishermen will mean that the stock of fish will be gone by the end of the first season. The fishermen will split $100,000 this year, but there will be no fish—and no money—in future years. Self-interest results in their splitting $100,000, not $500,000.

What is required is some rule that will make all hundred fishermen act as a sole owner would. That is where bankruptcy law enters the picture in a world not of fish but of credit. The grab rules of nonbankruptcy law and their allocation of assets on the basis of first-come, first-served create an incentive on the part of the individual creditors, when they sense that a debtor may have more liabilities than assets, to get in line today (by, for example, getting a sheriff to execute on the debtor's equipment), because if they do not, they run the risk of getting nothing. This decision by numerous individual creditors, however, may be the wrong decision for the creditors as a group. Even though the debtor is insolvent, they might be better off if they held the assets together. Bankruptcy provides a way to make these diverse individuals act as one, by imposing a *collective* and *compulsory* proceeding on them. Unlike a typical common pool solution, however, the compulsory solution of bankruptcy law does not apply in all places at all times. Instead, it runs parallel with a system of individual debt-collection rules and is available to supplant them when and if needed.

This is the historically recognized purpose of bankruptcy law and perhaps is none too controversial in itself. Because more controversial limits on bankruptcy policy derive from it, however, less allegorical and more precise analysis is necessary. Exactly *how* does bankruptcy law make creditors as a group better off? To find the answer to that question, consider a simple hypothetical example involving credit, not fish. Debtor has a small printing business. Potential creditors estimate that there is a 20 percent chance that Debtor (who is virtuous and will not misbehave) will become insolvent through bad luck, general economic downturn, or whatever. (By insolvency, I mean a condition whereby Debtor will not have enough assets to satisfy his creditors.) At the point of insolvency—I shall make this very simple—the business is expected to be worth $50,000 if sold piecemeal. Creditors also know that each of them will have to spend $1,000 in pursuit of their individual collection efforts should Debtor become insolvent and fail to repay them. Under these circumstances Debtor borrows $25,000 from each of four creditors, Creditors 1 through 4. Because these creditors know that there is this 20 percent chance, they can account for it—and the associated collection costs—in the interest rate they charge Debtor. Assume that each party can watch out for its own interest, and let us see whether, as in the example of fishing, there are reasons to think that these people would favor a set of restrictions on their own behaviour (apart from paternalism or other similar considerations).

Given that these creditors can watch out for their own interests, the question to be addressed is *how* these creditors should go about protecting themselves. If the creditors have to protect themselves by means of a costly and inefficient system, Debtor is going to have to pay more to obtain credit. Thus, when we consider them all together—Creditors 1 through 4 *and* Debtor—the relevant question is: would the availability of a bankruptcy system reduce the costs of credit?

This requires us to try to identify what bankruptcy's advantages might plausibly be. Identification of abstract advantages is not, however, the end of the issue. One must also compare those possible advantages with the costs of having a bankruptcy system. Determining whether a bankruptcy system would reduce the cost of credit requires a net assessment of charges.

But first the case for bankruptcy's advantages. The common pool example of fish in a lake suggests that one of the advantages to a collective system is a larger aggregate pie. Does that advantage exist in the case of credit? When dealing with businesses, the answer, at least some of the time, would seem to be "yes." The use of individual creditor remedies may lead to a piecemeal dismantling of a debtor's business by the untimely removal of necessary operating assets. To the extent that a non-piecemeal collective process (whether in the form of a liquidation or reorganization) is likely to increase the aggregate value of the pool of assets, its substitution for individual remedies would be advantageous to the creditors as a group. This is derived from a commonplace notion: that a collection of assets is sometimes more valuable together than the same assets would be if spread to the winds. It is often referred to as the surplus of a going-concern value over a liquidation value.

Thus, the most obvious reason for a collective system of creditor collection is to make sure that creditors, in pursuing their individual remedies, do not actually decrease the aggregate value of the assets that will be used to repay them. In our example this situation would occur when a printing press, for example, could be sold to a third party for $20,000, leaving $30,000 of other assets, but the business as a unit could generate sufficient cash so as to have a value of more than $50,000. As such it is directly analogous to the case of the fish in the lake. Even in cases in which the assets should be sold and the business dismembered, the aggregate value of the assets may be increased by keeping groups of those assets together (the printing press with its custom dies, for example) to be sold as discrete units.

This advantage, however, is not the only one to be derived from a collective system for creditors. Consider what the creditors would get if there were no bankruptcy system (putting aside the ultimate collection costs). Without a collective system all of the creditors in our example know that in the case of Debtor's insolvency the first two creditors to get to (and through) the courthouse (or to Debtor, to persuade Debtor to pay voluntarily), will get $25,000, leaving nothing for the third and fourth. And unless the creditors think that one of them is systematically faster (or friendlier with Debtor), this leaves them with a 50 percent chance of gaining $25,000, and a 50 percent chance of getting nothing. A collective system, however, would ensure that they would each get $12,500.

Would the creditors agree in advance to a system that, in the event of Debtor's insolvency, guaranteed them $12,500, in lieu of a system that gave them a 50 percent chance of $25,000—payment in full—and a 50 percent chance of nothing? Resolution of this question really turns on whether the creditors are better off with the one than the other. There are two reasons to think that they are, even without looking to the question of a going-concern surplus and without considering the costs of an individual collection system. First of all, if these creditors are risk averse, assurance of receiving $12,500 is better than a 50 percent chance of $25,000 and a 50 percent chance of nothing. Even if they can diversify the risk—by lending money to many people—it is probably preferable to eliminate it in the first place. This, then, represents a net advantage to having a collective proceeding.

One other possible advantage of a collective proceeding should also be noted: there may be costs to the individualized approach to collecting (in addition to the $1,000 collection costs). For example, since each creditor knows that it must "beat out" the others if it wants to be paid in full, it will spend time monitoring Debtor and the other creditors—perhaps frequently checking the courthouse records—to make sure that it will be no worse than second in the race (and therefore still be paid in full). Although some of these activities may be beneficial, many may not be; they will simply be costs of racing against other creditors, and they will cancel each other out. It is like running on a tread-mill: you expend a lot of energy but get nowhere. If every creditor is doing this, each one *still* does not know if there is more than a fifty-fifty chance that it will get paid in full. But in one sense, unless the creditors can negotiate a deal with each other, the creditors have no choice. Each creditor has to spend this money just to stay in the race because if it does not, it is a virtual certainty that the others will beat it to the payment punch. Of course, a creditor could decide that it did not want to stay in the race, and just charge Debtor at the time of lending the money for coming in last should Debtor become insolvent. Debt-or is not likely, however, to agree to pay a creditor that extra charge for having a lower priority provision, because, once paid that extra amount, the creditor may have an incen-tive to take steps to remain in the race and make money that way. For that reason it may be hard for a creditor to opt out of the race and get compensated for doing so.

These various costs to using an individual system of creditor remedies suggest that there are, indeed, occasions when a collective system of debt-collection law might be preferable. Bankruptcy provides that system. The single most fruitful way to think about bankruptcy is to see it as ameliorating a common pool problem created by a system of individual creditor remedies. Bankruptcy provides a way to override the creditors' pur-suit of their own remedies and to make them work together.

This approach immediately suggests several features of bankruptcy law. First, such a law must usurp individual creditor remedies in order to make the claimants act in an altruistic and cooperative way. Thus, the proceeding is inherently *collective*. Moreover, this system works only if all the creditors are bound to it. To allow a debtor to contract with a credit-or to avoid participating in the bankruptcy proceeding would destroy the advantages of a collective system. So the proceeding must be *compulsory* as well. But unlike common pool solutions in oil and gas or fishing, it is not the exclusive system for dividing up as-sets. It, instead, supplants an existing system of individual creditor remedies, and as we shall see, it is this feature that makes crucial an awareness of its limitations.

Note that the presence of a bankruptcy system does not mandate its use whenever there is a common pool problem. Bankruptcy law stipulates a minimum set of entitle-ments for claimants. That, in turn, permits them to "bargain in the shadow of the law" and to implement a consensual collective proceeding outside of the bankruptcy process. Because use of the bankruptcy process has costs of its own … , if creditors can consensu-ally gain the sorts of advantages of acting collectively that bankruptcy brings, they could avoid those costs. Accordingly, one would expect that consensual deals among creditors outside the bankruptcy process would often be attempted first. The formal bankruptcy process would presumably be used only when individual advantage-taking in the setting of multiparty negotiations made a consensual deal too costly to strike—which may, how-ever, occur frequently as the number of creditors increases. ·

… It is possible that the rules specifying when a bankruptcy petition may be filed prevent the commencement of a collective proceeding until it is too late to save the debt-or's assets from the self-interested actions of various creditors. Another possibility, how-ever, is that the collective proceeding will begin too soon. Forcing all the creditors to re-frain from individual actions (many of which have the effect of monitoring the debtor and preventing it from misbehaving) brings its own costs. Thus, to say that bankruptcy is designed to solve a common pool problem is not to tell us how to design the rules that do that well. These concerns do not, however, undermine the basic insight of what bankruptcy law is all about.

Like all justifications, moreover, this one is subject to a number of qualifications. To say that a common pool problem exists is not to say that individual behavior is entirely self-interested or that legal rules can solve all collective action problems. We often observe people behaving in a cooperative fashion over time even if it appears contrary to their short-run interest. In the credit world, for example, creditors do not always rush to seize a debtor's assets whenever it seems to be in financial trouble. Yet despite this qualification the underlying point remains: sometimes people behave in a self-interested way and would be better off as a group if required to work together. The tragedy of the Texas oil fields in the first half of this century is a notable example of how self-interest led to the depletion of oil that otherwise could have been enjoyed by the group of oil field owners. Creditor relations almost certainly are another area where this essential truth has validity, especially given the fact that creditors may have fewer incentives to cooperate when a debtor is failing than they do when there are greater prospects of repeat dealings with a debtor.

Nor can we be confident that the bankruptcy rules themselves do not create problems. They do, and we will examine later how they should be dealt with. Because these complications play out against a backdrop of basic bankruptcy principles, however, it is preferable for now to make two simplifying assumptions. The first assumption is that insolvency occurs without warning. By this assumption, we eliminate consideration of strategic behavior that is likely to exist when some creditors sense the imminent likelihood of bankruptcy's collective proceeding and attempt to avoid it. ... The second assumption is that bankruptcy proceedings take no time. By this assumption, we can set aside problems that occur through the passage of time and the fact that this passage of time affects various claimants in different ways. We can also set aside the complications that result from a debtor's need to encourage people to deal with it while in bankruptcy and the fact that some of these people may wear both prepetition and postpetition hats. ...

Although imposing these two assumptions is, of course, somewhat unrealistic, doing so clarifies several key features of bankruptcy law. We can later extend our examination by making the inquiry somewhat more realistic. For now, however, it is sufficient to ask whether there is in fact a common pool problem that cannot be solved by creditors contracting among themselves. If the number of creditors is sufficiently small and sufficiently determinate, it may be possible for them to negotiate a solution at the time of insolvency that would avoid many, if not most, of the costs of an individual remedies system, even if they were not bargaining in the shadow of the law. But in cases in which there are large numbers of creditors or the creditors are not immediately known at a particular time (perhaps because they hold contingent or nonmanifested claims), the ability of the creditors to solve the problem of an individual remedies system by an actual agreement may be lost. Bankruptcy provides the desired result by making available a collective system after insolvency has occurred. It is the implications of that view of bankruptcy law that we can now begin to explore.

2. Determining Liabilities and the Basic Role of Nonbankruptcy Law

Bankruptcy provides a collective forum for sorting out the rights of "owners" (creditors and others with rights against a debtor's assets) and can be justified because it provides protection against the destructive effects of an individual remedies system when there are not enough assets to go around. This makes the basic process one of determining *who* gets *what*, in *what order*. *Who* is fundamentally a question of claims, or what shall often be referred to as *liabilities*. *What* is fundamentally a question of property of the estate, or what shall often be referred to as *assets*. At one level there is nothing magical about these basic building blocks. A liability is something that makes you less valuable—that you would pay to get rid of. An asset is something that makes you more valuable—that someone would pay you for.

In looking at all of this, it is helpful to think of bankruptcy as follows. What bankruptcy should be doing, in the abstract, is asking how much someone would pay for the assets of a debtor, assuming they could be sold free of liabilities. The resulting money is then taken and distributed to the holders of the liabilities according to their nonbankruptcy entitlements. Essentially, [the following discussion] simply [fleshes] out this idea against the basic role of bankruptcy law. ... The question [to be] addressed ... is exactly what this means in considering how claimants should be treated in bankruptcy. The basic answer involves seeing the bankruptcy process as protecting, at a minimum, the relative *value* of particular nonbankruptcy entitlements instead of the rights themselves. This is the subject of determining liabilities in bankruptcy and involves the question of how to divide the assets. The question of ... assets is integrally related to the question of liabilities.

The Destructive Effect of Changes of Relative Entitlements in Bankruptcy

Bankruptcy's basic procedures are designed to ameliorate a common pool problem. The key to effective implementation of this goal is to trigger bankruptcy when, and only when, it is in the interests of the creditors as a group. Consider what this means. Insolvency may be an occasion to collectivize what hitherto had been an individual remedies system. It does not, however, justify the implementation of a different set of relative entitlements, unless doing so is necessary as a part of the move from the individual remedies system. It is not just that the need for a collective proceeding does not go hand in hand with new entitlements. It is that the establishment of new entitlements in bankruptcy conflicts with the collectivization goal. Such changes create incentives for particular holders of rights in assets to resort to bankruptcy in order to gain for themselves the advantages of those changes, even when a bankruptcy proceeding would not be in the collective interest of the investor group. These incentives are predictable and counterproductive because they reintroduce the fundamental problem that bankruptcy law is designed to solve: individual self-interest undermining the interests of the group. These changes are better made *generally* instead of in bankruptcy only.

The problem of changing relative entitlements in bankruptcy not only underlies this book's normative view of bankruptcy law but also forms the basis of the bankruptcy system that has been enacted. The Supreme Court made this point in a case that is as important for recognizing it as the actual issue decided is unimportant. The case, *Butner v. United States* [440 US 48], decided in 1979, involved a secured creditor's claim to rents that accrued on the property serving as collateral after the filing of the bankruptcy petition relative to the claims of the unsecured creditors generally. Under relevant state law, as the Supreme Court described it, the debtor was entitled to the rents as long as it remained in possession or until a state court, on request, ordered the rents to be paid over to the secured creditor. In bankruptcy the unsecured creditors of an insolvent debtor can be viewed as the new equity owners of the debtor and hence entitled to what the debtor was entitled to outside of bankruptcy. This gave rise to the conflict between the secured creditor and the trustee, as representative of the unsecured creditors. The issue that the Supreme Court considered in *Butner* was: What should the source of law be (state or federal) in deciding how the secured creditor may realize on the post-bankruptcy rents? The Court saw the source of law as nonbankruptcy and observed that "the federal bankruptcy court should take whatever steps are necessary to ensure that the [secured creditor] is afforded in federal bankruptcy court the same protections he would have under state law if no bankruptcy had ensued." It justified this result as follows:

> Property interests are created and defined by state law. Unless some federal interest requires a different result, there is no reason why such interests should be analyzed differently simply because an interested party is involved in a bankruptcy proceeding. Uniform treatment of property interests by both state and federal courts within a State serves to reduce uncertainty, to discourage forum shopping, and to prevent a party from receiving "a windfall merely by reason of the happenstance of bankruptcy."

In the notion of forum shopping the Supreme Court expressed the fundamental point.

Yet to say that *Butner* denounced changing relative entitlements only in bankruptcy does not end the matter. It is important to understand *why* such rule changes cut against bankruptcy's recognized goal. This requires the separation of two issues that arise when a debtor is in bankruptcy: first, it is necessary to decide what to do with the debtor's assets, and, second, it is necessary to decide who gets them. The principal proposition I wish to establish here is that only by treating the answer to the second question as a nonbankruptcy issue can it be kept from unfavorably altering the answer to the first. To put this another way, in its role as a collective debt-collection device, bankruptcy law should not create rights. Instead, it should act to ensure that the rights that exist are vindicated to the extent possible. Only in this way can bankruptcy law minimize the conversion costs of transferring an insolvent debtor's assets to its creditors.

This point is easiest to demonstrate by examining a case where there is no occasion to use bankruptcy as a response to a common pool problem—where only one person has rights to the debtor's assets. Such a person, the sole owner of the assets, would have no creditors. Irrespective of any thought of bankruptcy, this sole owner would continually re-evaluate his use of the assets. If he were manufacturing buggy whips, at every moment (in theory at least) he would reassess whether this was the best use for those assets. If it was, he would continue; but if it was not, he would stop and either use the assets for some other purpose or sell them, piecemeal or as a unit, to others. This decision would be his alone. And he presumably would make it after determining which action would bring him the most from the assets.

This is, of course, an oversimplification. No person has *full* ownership of assets in the sense that he has absolutely unfettered control over their use. I do not have the right to sell cocaine even if I could make a great deal of money doing so. Similarly, a person making buggy whips may be subject to regulations governing the types of materials he can use, the minimum wages he must pay, or the environmental controls he must observe. These regulations will constrain his decisions and may lead him to choose a different use than he would choose in their absence.

This qualification, however, does not fundamentally undercut the basic point that given an existing array of legal rules, a sole owner would presumably decide to use the assets in the way that would bring him the most. He has, by definition, no need to use bankruptcy to ameliorate a common pool problem because a common pool exists only when there is more than one person with rights. He, accordingly, would be utterly indifferent to bankruptcy policy, unless the debtor's use of it benefited him (by permitting the debtor, for example, to escape an undesirable nonbankruptcy charge). If a charge were placed on assets only in bankruptcy law (such as that a debtor could not go out of business without first protecting employees), this owner would remain free to ignore it by going out of business without using bankruptcy. He would only be obligated to take account of such a charge if it were imposed by nonbankruptcy law.

When rights to assets are spread among a number of people, however, as they almost always are, things change. It then becomes necessary to decide not only how best to deploy the assets but also how to split up the returns from those assets. Because of the diversity of the owners, the deployment question creates a common pool problem. Bankruptcy law exists to solve that problem. But the lessons from the common pool show that the answer to the distributional question should not affect the determination of how to deploy the assets. As a group these diverse owners—bondholders, tort victims, trade creditors, shareholders, and others—would want to follow the same course as a sole owner. It is in the interest of the owners as a *group*, in other words, to keep the distributional question from spilling over into the deployment question.

Bankruptcy law is best approached by separating these two questions—the question of how the process can maximize the value of a given pool of assets and the question of how the law should allocate entitlements to whatever pool exists—and limiting bankruptcy law to the first. This distinction makes clear the relationship between bankruptcy rules and nonbankruptcy rules and provides a principle of bankruptcy policy capable of identifying which nonbankruptcy rules may need to be supplanted.

Because there is perhaps no point in bankruptcy policy that is more easily misunderstood, it is worth proceeding carefully. Let us consider one of the most common views of what bankruptcy law should do. This view is that bankruptcy law exists, in part, to help firms stay in business because of an increased social value and/or the jobs that are saved. In one guise this simply restates the common pool problem—that diverse owners, if unconstrained, will pull apart assets that would be worth more to the group of owners if kept together. Usually, however, the notion of keeping firms in business seems to be meant as an independent policy. For that policy to have independent force, it must mean that, irrespective of the wishes of the owners, a firm's assets should be kept in their current form because somebody—society or workers—is better off.

Incorporating such a policy in a bankruptcy statute, however, would be to mix apples and oranges, if one accepts the view (as everyone seems to) that bankruptcy law also exists as a response to a common pool problem. The question is really one of defining substantive rights. If the group in question—society, or workers, or whatever—deserves such rights, it is counterproductive to locate them only in a bankruptcy statute. Under existing nonbankruptcy law, for example, workers have no substantive entitlements to keep assets in their current form; they are not owners with substantive rights against the assets. For that reason the owners are free to close the business without considering the interests of the workers if doing so brings the owners more money. The fact that those owners have a common pool problem and need to use a collective proceeding to ameliorate it is not a reason to suddenly give a new group—workers—rights that they would not otherwise have and that could be ignored if the bankruptcy process was avoided. The decision whether they should have such rights should not be bankruptcy-specific. It addresses a distributional question as well as a deployment question.

Another way to put this is to note the distinction between saying that something is a problem that Congress should address and saying that something is a problem that Congress should address through bankruptcy law. The first is a federalism question, the second a collective debt-collection question. Whether giving workers substantive rights with regard to how assets are used is desirable, just as whether secured creditors should come ahead of unsecured creditors, is a question of underlying entitlements. Although protecting the victims of economic misfortune who have not been given rights against assets may be an important social and legal question, it is not a question specific to bankruptcy law. However the question is answered, a bankruptcy statute would still be necessary, because answering these substantive questions one way instead of the other does not eliminate the common pool problem. Because the issues of who should have entitlements and how to address a common pool problem are distinct, they should be kept separate in the legal response.

Nor is this simply an academic point. Bankruptcy law cannot both give new groups rights and continue effectively to solve a common pool problem. Treating both as bankruptcy questions interferes with bankruptcy's historic function as a superior debt-collection system against insolvent debtors. Fashioning a distinct bankruptcy rule—such as one that gives workers rights they do not hold under nonbankruptcy law—creates incentives for the group advantaged by the distinct bankruptcy rule to use the bankruptcy process even though it is not in the interest of the owners as a group. The consequences can be seen frequently: many cases are begun where the reason for filing for bankruptcy quite clearly is nothing more than the fact that the entity bringing the case is advantaged because of a bankruptcy rule change. Bankruptcy proceedings inevitably carry costs of their own. When bankruptcy is activated for a rule change that benefits one particular class, the net effect may be harmful to the owners as a group. It is this problem that makes such rule changes undesirable as a matter of bankruptcy law.

Even though a nonbankruptcy rule may suffer from infirmities such as unfairness or inefficiency, if the nonbankruptcy rule does not undermine the advantages of a collective proceeding relative to the individual remedies that exist given those entitlements, imposing a different bankruptcy rule is a second-best and perhaps a counterproductive solution. At bottom, bankruptcy is justified in overriding nonbankruptcy rights *because* those rights interfere with the group advantages associated with creditors acting in concert. If the nonbankruptcy rule—for example, a rule permitting owners to close down a business without considering the plight of workers—is thought undesirable for reasons other than its interference with a collective proceeding, the proper approach for Congress would be to face that issue squarely and to overturn the rule in general, not just to undermine or reverse it in bankruptcy. The latter course is undesirable because, as *Butner* recognized, it creates incentives for strategic "shopping" between the nonbankruptcy and bankruptcy forums.

Elizabeth Warren, "Bankruptcy Policy"
(1987), 54 *University of Chicago Law Review* 775-801 (footnotes omitted)

Bankruptcy is a booming business—in practice and in theory. From headlines about LTV's 10,000-page filing to feature stories about bankrupt consumers (usually Joe-and-Ethel-whose-names-have-been-changed-to-protect-their-privacy), bankruptcy has become an increasingly popular news item in the past few years. Both organized labor and the consumer credit industry made concerted efforts to put bankruptcy issues before the public in their recent pushes to amend the new Bankruptcy Code. Lawyers have been drawn to the bright lights. Firms that did not have a single bankruptcy practitioner five years ago now field large bankruptcy sections. Bankruptcy seminars have been sellouts. And—perhaps the most reliable indicator of increased attention and activity—bankruptcy jokes have begun to make the rounds.

As bankruptcy has flourished in the popular press and in law practice, it enjoys what may be looked back on as a golden age in academe. Law review articles on bankruptcy abound, and enrollments in bankruptcy and related commercial law classes are reported to be on the rise across the country. Uncertainty about how the new Bankruptcy Code will be interpreted and dramatic shifts in the strategic use of bankruptcy have prompted reporters to call law professors for in-depth interviews or quotable statements for the evening news. Rumor has it that requests for expert help are on the increase and consultation fees are up for more than a few academics specializing in bankruptcy. All in all, it's not a bad time to know something about bankruptcy.

In the midst of this attention and noise and clamor, however, there is a quiet but persistent question: what function does bankruptcy serve? After the statutory arguments have been exhausted and the cases have been explored, most academic discussions of bankruptcy can be distilled to this question. Currently, the policies endorsed to support bankruptcy pronouncements are wide-ranging and, at the extremes, very much in opposition. Despite the critical importance of different policy presumptions, the policy elements underlying most discourses are asserted only obliquely, and they are rarely challenged directly.

Professor Douglas Baird and I have undertaken to debate in writing the basis of bankruptcy policy. We offer this paired set of essays in the spirit of the old "Point-Counterpoint" segment of television's "Sixty Minutes." While we cannot promise the dripping invective and snarling satire that made that old feature so delightful, we can try to push forward the debate by making direct challenges and responses. In the belief that a good fight is far more interesting than a host of polite compliments and careful hedgings, Professor Baird and I undertake an aggressive and irreverent debate. In order to join issue more clearly and to narrow the focus of the debate somewhat, Professor Baird and I have agreed to debate the basis of bankruptcy policy in the context of business bankruptcies. While we both believe that the principles we discuss have significance in a consumer setting as well, we recognize that additional issues should be a part of a discussion about consumer bankruptcy policy and that those issues would make the discussion even more complex.

Professor Baird and I hold very different views of the purpose bankruptcy law serves. I see bankruptcy as an attempt to reckon with a debtor's multiple defaults and to distribute the consequences among a number of different actors. Bankruptcy encompasses a number of competing—and sometimes conflicting—values in this distribution. As I see it, no one value dominates, so that bankruptcy policy becomes a composite of factors that bear on a better answer to the question, "How shall the losses be distributed?"

By contrast, Baird has developed a coherent, unified view of bankruptcy that revolves around a single economic construct. According to Baird, the only goal of bankruptcy is to enhance the collection efforts of creditors with state-defined property rights. He explains that all bankruptcy laws are to be tested by a single measure: whether they enhance or diminish the creditors' collective benefits. With that construct, Baird purports to answer a host of wide-ranging questions and translate his policy into specific statutory recommendations.

As Baird and I begin this debate, I am acutely aware that we disagree not only about what bankruptcy policy should be, but also about how that policy should be derived. Baird begins with hypothetical behavior and ends with firmly fixed answers. I begin with a historical observation about legal structures, I surmise the concerns of the drafters, and I end only with tentative conclusions and more complex questions. Baird presumes that there can be a simple answer to explain all of bankruptcy, and that the relationship between statutory law and modification of the behavior of debtors and creditors is known and can be predicted in new circumstances. I see bankruptcy as a more complex and ultimately less confined process than does Baird.

In this paper I discuss our differing views, explaining first the central policy justification of bankruptcy as I see it. In the second section, I contrast my conception of bankruptcy with Baird's view, and I take up his application of theory to the difficult problem of undersecured creditors. In the spirit of forthright debate, I try to expose my ideas enough to provide a target for Baird, and I take direct and specific aim at his work.

I. The Central Policy Justification of Bankruptcy: Coping with Default in an Integrated System

Discussing the debtor-creditor system is much like focusing a camera. Different elements of the system are always in view, but depending on where the focus is directed, different features of the system take on greater importance. I want to begin the discussion of bankruptcy by looking briefly at the role the debtor-creditor system plays in a much broader pattern of promise enforcement.

A. Default and Contract Enforcement

The debtor-creditor system is itself part of a larger, integrated order of public enforcement of promises between individuals. An analysis of promise enforcement should begin with contract law—the laws enforcing private promises—and come full circle with bank-ruptcy law—the laws sanctioning default on private promises. Each element of this sys-tem balances against the other.

The enforcement scheme in debtor-creditor law acknowledges values different from those central to contract law. Idiosyncratic factors involved in the changed circumstances of debtors in extreme financial distress become important. Debtors may not be able to meet their obligations for a host of different reasons. Their stupidity, greed, misfortune, bad judgment, or inadequate foresight may leave them unable to pay. They may not be able to pay over the short term or the long term. They may be victims of their own mis-takes or of unforeseeable circumstances. Contract law need not take account of the val-ues relevant to sanctioning debtor default, because these values are accounted for in the debtor-creditor collection scheme. Without the refined and balanced system of debtor-creditor law—which includes a well-developed concept of bankruptcy—contract law it-self would look very different, and its enforcement would be considerably more constrained.

The definition of an enforceable contract allows some leeway to consider social con-cerns. Contract principles such as impossibility, mutual mistake, and more recently, du-ress and unconscionability undercut any naive view of "strict" enforcement. But for the point of this paper, it is sufficient to note that once an agreement has been struck, the subsequent inability of a party to pay or the high cost of payment is rarely an overt fea-ture of contract doctrine. Relatively strict enforceability of contract can prevail precisely because the debtor-creditor system instills a measure of temperance, an ability to re-spond to changed circumstances, a notion that enforcement should not offend deeply held social norms.

Default—or nonpayment—of debt has long been an essential feature of a system of promise enforcement. Centuries before bankruptcy law became an integrated part of the collection scheme, default existed. Biblical jubilees, medieval English debtor sanctuaries, and poorhouses are evidence of society's past attempts to balance rightful demands for payment with some possibility of escape. When organized forgiveness has been unavail-ing, debtors have devised their own nonpayment plans. Debtors have been known to flee the jurisdiction, to threaten their creditors, or—as an extreme measure—to die. Even to-day, with corporate debtors and risk-spreading creditors, a significant feature of the debt collection system is the possibility of escape from payment through a variety of maneu-vers, both legal and extralegal. Anyone who ever extends credit faces the possibility that repayment will not be forthcoming. Interest is structured, among other things, to pay the creditor for assuming the risk of nonpayment.

B. Default and the Collection System

The current debt collection system has two primary responses to a debtor's default: state collection law and federal bankruptcy law. When discussing the two collection schemes, it is important to bear in mind that property and contract rights are not synonymous with collection rights. Bankruptcy is only a collection scheme; it necessarily depends on other legal rules for the determination of substantive rights underlying bankruptcy claims. Whether a contract is enforceable, a tort has been committed, or an owner has clear title to a piece of land are issues of substantive state or federal law. Similarly, state collection law is different from the underlying substantive law. State collection law presupposes the enforceability of an underlying claim (as does bankruptcy) and focuses on the rights of a creditor to extract the payment owed (as does bankruptcy). State collection law is about judgments, statutory liens, voluntary security interests, exemptions, garnishment, prejudgment remedies, and so on. The state system and the bankruptcy system are both only collection systems.

Although this distinction between substantive rights and collection rules might seem obvious, it is important to the policy debate, which often centers on the degree to which bankruptcy law should "rely" on underlying state law. The answer depends on which underlying state law is under discussion. The real issue is not whether bankruptcy law—or state collection law, for that matter—relies on state law for the definition of substantive rights. The issue is whether the state collection and distribution scheme presumptively should be the federal scheme. That bankruptcy builds on state substantive law does not require it to build on state collection law.

It would, of course, be possible to create a single, fully integrated debt collection scheme rather than the separate state and federal schemes now in effect. But even a unified scheme would have to consider two prototypes of default: first, the single default where only one creditor complains about repayment and the remaining creditors are evidently (even if only temporarily) content with their repayment prospects; and second, the debtor's widespread default and collapse in which every creditor's prospects for repayment are sharply diminished. These two kinds of default involve some overlapping issues about appropriate collection rights, and a factual continuum from a single default to complete collapse better describes the world that includes the two extremes. Nonetheless, the policy issues involved in the two exemplary circumstances differ importantly, and they must be addressed separately whether they are part of one collection system or two.

The current debt collection system treats these issues in different fora: state collection laws cope with a wide spectrum of limited defaults, while the bankruptcy scheme concentrates on default in the context of the debtor's imminent collapse. The state collection scheme occasionally deals with complete collapse, but overall it is rationalized in order to serve a wide variety of collection needs. The federal bankruptcy scheme, by contrast, reckons with a much more limited factual context, and with very different legal devices such as discharge of debt and distribution of unavoidable losses. The different factual contexts change the focus of the policymaking decisions of state collection law and bankruptcy.

. . .

D. Default and Bankruptcy

By contrast with state law, which sees only one default, bankruptcy begins with a presumption of default on every obligation the debtor owes. Although some debtors are able to repay all their debts in bankruptcy, the statutory scheme presumes that some creditors will not enjoy repayment in full. Bankruptcy law aims first to conserve and divide an estate that cannot meet all its obligations, and second to terminate the rights of unpaid creditors. Unlike state law, which considers innumerable circumstances of default, bankruptcy law is sharply focused on the consequences of a debtor's imminent collapse. The difference from state collection law is fundamental. Bankruptcy disputes do not share the debtor-versus-creditor orientation of state collection law. In bankruptcy, with an inadequate pie to divide and the looming discharge of unpaid debts, the disputes center on who is entitled to shares of the debtor's assets and how these shares are to be divided. Distribution among creditors is not incidental to other concerns; it is the center of the bankruptcy scheme. Accordingly, bankruptcy disputes are better characterized as creditor-versus-creditor, with competing creditors struggling to push the losses of default onto others. The Bankruptcy Code reflects this orientation: a significant part of its distributional scheme is oriented toward establishing priorities among creditors.

The battle between secured and unsecured creditors has commanded much interest, but the Bankruptcy Code tackles a wide variety of other distributional issues as well. Some rights are destroyed in bankruptcy, and some are preserved. Priority distributions reorder the competing interests of employees, taxing authorities, fishermen, and farmers. Landlords and business partners receive special treatment. Parties to executory contracts hold an identified place in the bankruptcy pecking order. The beneficiaries of state statutory liens find their rights reordered in bankruptcy. Ordinary course creditors and creditors making contemporaneous exchanges discover that their positions differ from other unsecured creditors. Creditors lending to consumers are distinguished from creditors lending to businesses. Banks with setoff rights are treated differently from banks not in a setoff position. This list is suggestive rather than definitive, but it serves to show that the Bankruptcy Code is concerned with making hard choices about which creditors belong where in a financial hierarchy. These are choices about distribution and redistribution, and they are not controlled by state law.

The distributional design of the Code is even more thorough than the straightforward state law's rank-ordering of easily identified creditors such as fishermen and farmers. The bankruptcy system goes so far as to anticipate the consequences of default on a host of potential creditors, including, for example, future tort claimants who have not yet discovered their injuries or their legal rights and a government agency that might uncover toxic wastes and demand that a debtor clean them up. Bankruptcy law recognizes these rights even though they may not be mature under state law at the time of the bankruptcy filing. In the state law system, these creditors would simply wait until they discovered the injuries and then would sue one at a time for the appropriate remedy. They would take their debtors—tortfeasors or toxic polluters—as they found them when their claims matured, whether the debtors were fat with profits or stripped to a hollow shell after earlier creditors had concluded other disputes.

But because bankruptcy recognizes that the pre-bankrupt debtor will not survive to be sued another day, its distributional scheme necessarily focuses on how to deal with future claimants. Several alternatives are possible. Bankruptcy's distributional scheme could leave future claimants to bear their losses in full, refusing to compensate them at all and effectively barring their future claims. If, instead, their rights to compensation continue notwithstanding the bankruptcy, the distributional consequences of bankruptcy will depend on whether the debtor succeeds or fails in any reorganization attempt.

Still a third distributional scheme is created if the future claimants are participants in a distribution plan and provisions are made for their eventual—if limited—recovery.

The Bankruptcy Code clearly rejects the alternative of leaving future claimants uncompensated. It defines "claim" broadly to pull future creditors into the debtor's distribution plan and to require participation by anticipated claimants. The Code does not specifically address how to establish funds to pay future claimants and determine appropriate payout priorities, and as a result, the courts must take on the difficult task of devising workable plans. Nonetheless, it is clear that dealing with the effects of default on future claimants was intended to be a significant feature of bankruptcy's distributional scheme.

The Bankruptcy Code accomplishes other distributional ends less directly. By providing for impairment of state law collection rights in a court-supervised reorganization, Chapter 11 of the Bankruptcy Code gives bankrupt businesses another opportunity to succeed. The opportunity may not often result in genuine success, but the reports of Toys-R-Us, Wickes, Continental Airlines, Evans Home Products, and a host of other bankruptcy success stories serve as a reminder that at least some Chapter 11 reorganizations conserve and maximize the wealth of the debtor's estate for the benefit of all claimants—an important objective of bankruptcy.

But the revival of an otherwise failing business also serves the distributional interests of many who are not technically "creditors" but who have an interest in a business's continued existence. Older employees who could not have retrained for other jobs, customers who would have to resort to less attractive, alternative suppliers of goods and services, suppliers who would have lost current customers, nearby property owners who would have suffered declining property values, and states or municipalities that would have faced shrinking tax bases benefit from the reorganization's success. By giving the debtor business an opportunity to reorganize, the bankruptcy scheme acknowledges the losses of those who have depended on the business and redistributes some of the risk of loss from the default. Even if dissolution is inevitable, the bankruptcy process allows for delay, which in turn gives time for all those relying on a business to accommodate the coming change.

. . .

E. Distributive Rationales in Bankruptcy

By definition, the distributional issues arising in bankruptcy involve costs to some and benefits to others. Enforcing the state law collection rights of secured creditors often comes at the cost of defeating the state law collection rights of unsecured creditors whose claims are discharged without payment. A priority payment to one unsecured creditor necessarily leaves less for the remaining creditors. The debtor's estate—and thus its creditors—profits from assigning a favorable lease, but this costs the landlord whose lease specifically provided for no assignments. The benefits reaped by the employees or suppliers relying on the continuation of a business are purchased at the expense of every creditor who gives up valuable state collection rights as part of the plan to allow the debtor business a second chance at success.

It might be reasonable to ask about the legitimacy of forcing losses on those with lawful expectations of repayment. The difficulty with this question, however, is that it posits that bankruptcy is the "cause" of the cost. Bankruptcy is not the cause of the cost—it is merely the distributor of the cost. The cost of default is occasioned by the debtor's inability to repay.

Without a bankruptcy system, someone would still bear the costs of default. Perhaps, under the state law collection system, those costs would be borne entirely by unsecured creditors or employees or suppliers or landlords or creditors with loans secured by inventory that is difficult to monitor. But speculation on what would happen at state law is nothing more than the substitution of a different distributional scheme—one created indirectly by focus on the collection of a single debt rather than one created deliberately with an overriding attention to widespread default.

Even if there were no legal scheme to distribute the costs of default, the losses would be distributed by some method. The distribution of losses might be determined by creditor speed (who first backs up to the warehouse with big trucks) or strength (who can carry away the most while others look on) or by debtor favoritism (who gets the first call when the debtor decides to give up). Indeed, outside bankruptcy, it is not clear as an empirical matter whether losses are distributed according to the state law scheme or according to creditor strength, debtor favoritism, or some other factor. But the point is that the costs must be distributed in some manner. Bankruptcy is simply a federal scheme designed to distribute the costs among those at risk.

. . .

II. Baird's Approach: Collectivism Alone

Professor Baird's view of the bankruptcy world is much neater than mine. He explains that there is a single justification for bankruptcy: enhancing the collective return to the creditors. He also explains that there is only one interest to be protected: the interest of those "who, outside of bankruptcy, have property rights in the assets of the firm filing a petition." Baird has rejected the notion that any values other than collectivism may be important in fashioning bankruptcy policy. As the following passage indicates, he at times recognizes the questions that lead eventually to a complex, multifactored analysis:

> Consider the "rehabilitation" goal of a Chapter 11 proceeding. No one, to our knowledge, argues that keeping a firm intact is always a good thing. Yet as soon as one concedes that a reorganization may not always be desirable, one is faced with the problem of understanding and articulating why reorganizations are favored in the first place and how much should be given up to facilitate them.

Yet Baird evidently sees the questions he poses as either unanswerable or too silly to answer, for, having identified them, he says no more. He simply observes:

> The economy of an entire town can be disrupted when a large factory closes. Many employees may be put out of work. The failure of one firm may lead to the failure of those who supplied it with raw materials and those who acquired its finished products. Some believe that preventing such consequences is worth the costs of trying to keep the firm running and jus-

tifies placing burdens on a firm's secured creditors. We think that this view is, as a matter of bankruptcy policy, fundamentally wrong.

Without further discussion, Baird concludes that such attempts are "beyond the competence of a bankruptcy court."

Baird makes a point he can defeat by making it too big. Because bankruptcy will not always save a company, and because sometimes the cost of saving the company is too high, this must never be a goal of any bankruptcy policy. Baird refuses to acknowledge the possibility that bankruptcy might give a corporation a limited opportunity to succeed—an opportunity that balances the cost of trying to the creditors against the likelihood of eventual success. He acknowledges neither the potential benefit of a second chance nor the possibility that bankruptcy policy might aim toward a broad balance between the competing interests of the debtor, the creditors, and the many others who may be injured by the debtor's collapse.

Baird also considers the role of other distributional issues in bankruptcy and concludes that they should play none. He explains, for example, that the question of whether secured creditors should be paid ahead of anyone else "is not one peculiar to bankruptcy law" and then does little more than assert that the arguments for or against favoring the payment rights of secured creditors

> would apply with equal force to any group given favored treatment under nonbankruptcy law. The desirability of secured credit—or other nonbankruptcy property rights—is ultimately not a bankruptcy question and attempting to transform it into one creates incentives that are perverse and counterproductive.

Thus, the distributional issues involved in determining the creditors' legal pecking order are, according to Baird, the same whether the debtor is in default on a single obligation or in a state of complete collapse.

Having dispensed with any other policy considerations, Baird is ready to turn to his single justification for bankruptcy: enhancing the collective return for creditors who have identified property rights. Here Baird purports to use only careful logic to answer some of the most intractable bankruptcy problems, all the while avoiding any discussion of the distributional consequences of his work. The difficulty with Baird's approach is that collectivism alone won't get him where he is going. He necessarily uses—even if he does not discuss—distributional principles. Moreover, Baird endorses the wholesale use of the state law distributional scheme, but he does not defend the distributional rationale of that scheme, nor does he address the possibility that the state scheme was designed to resolve questions significantly different from those to which he applies it.

Baird is engaged in a game of pulling rabbits from other hats. He may actually have a distributional principle to defend; he could argue that state law better distributes risks between secured and unsecured creditors than does current bankruptcy law. We could debate that conclusion, but even that debate would accept the premise that bankruptcy is designed to resolve difficult distributional choices. Instead, Baird purports to avoid distributional concerns—and the attendant normative and empirical issues—by discussing only the "neutral" principle of collectivism. I believe Baird only diverts the debate from the central issues.

A. Collectivism: The Test That Isn't

Collectivism provides a useful way to examine some bankruptcy problems. Baird shows how the need for collectivism can explain why the bankruptcy system substitutes a single, lower-cost action for expensive, multiple individual actions. His analogy between state collection law and the wild car races of "It's a Mad, Mad, Mad, Mad World" makes a delightful story that helps explain a very important function of bankruptcy: bankruptcy calls a halt to the superaggressive, wasteful, and potentially damaging creditor activity permitted by state law.

My dispute with Baird centers instead upon his attempts to use collectivism not only to explain significant features of the bankruptcy system, but also to justify the entire system and to provide answers to specific, complex questions. Baird sees collectivism as something of an intellectual yardstick, a tool that he can use to determine whether a particular bankruptcy proposal is good or bad—solely by measuring whether it promotes or impairs collectivism. Yet Baird ultimately uses collectivism, once a useful theme in a more complex bankruptcy system, to obscure a very different analysis.

Baird chooses to test his collectivist principle in an *American Mariner* situation where he wrestles with the very difficult question of how to determine appropriate rights for the undersecured creditor during a pending bankruptcy proceeding. Baird observes that creditors often have interests hostile to each other in the resolution of a bankruptcy case. The secured creditor is often interested in immediate liquidation, repossession, and repayment from the sale of the repossessed collateral. By contrast, the unsecured creditors— who are likely to receive little or nothing in a liquidation—are interested in allowing the company to retain the collateral and to make one more try at reorganization. Secured creditors claim that unsecured creditors are trying to deny them access to their collateral and to risk its eventual loss, while unsecured creditors claim that secured creditors are destroying the reorganization before it can begin. Baird resolves this impasse with the measuring stick of collectivism: collectivist goals will be met only if the bankruptcy estate (effectively, in Baird's example, the debtor and the unsecured creditors) bears the interest costs of using the secured creditor's collateral during the period of the reorganization and repayment plan. According to Baird, only if all secured creditors—including the undersecured—receive post-petition interest will collectivism be served.

Douglas G. Baird, "Loss Distribution, Forum Shopping, and Bankruptcy: A Reply to Warren"
(1987), 54 *University of Chicago Law Review* 815, at 816-22 and 828-31
(footnotes omitted)

Warren's attack on the theory of bankruptcy that I have developed with Thomas Jackson goes to methodology. Jackson and I claim that we can isolate bankruptcy issues (such as whether the trustee should be able to void preferences) from the question of how losses should be borne in the event that a firm fails (such as whether secured creditors should be paid before tort victims). Warren insists that we cannot do this. The issue, it must be noted, is not *how* losses from a firm failure should be distributed, but whether this question (however hard it may be to answer) is a question of the law generally (as Jackson and I would argue) or one peculiar to bankruptcy law (as Warren would argue).

Even though Warren and I usually end up in the same place, our debate is important. The way in which Jackson and I think about bankruptcy law is so different from the approach of traditional scholars like Warren that we may reach different conclusions about new issues that confront both Congress and the courts. In the first part of my response to Warren, I briefly review the major features of her view of bankruptcy policy and explain why I find it wanting. In the subsequent parts, I try to show what drives my own view of bankruptcy policy.

I. The Traditional View of Bankruptcy Policy

Warren admits that her own view of bankruptcy policy is "dirty, complex, elastic, [and] interconnected" (p. 811). But like most traditional views of bankruptcy policy, it rests on a number of fairly simple propositions: (1) bankruptcy law has a special role to play in determining how losses from a business failure should be borne; (2) creditors as well as others may sometimes be required to give up some of their ultimate rights to the assets of the firm so that the firm will have a better chance of surviving; (3) entrusting a bankruptcy judge with equitable discretion is a useful and unobjectionable way to balance the conflicting and competing interests of the parties; and (4) creditors in bankruptcy have no cause to complain when they lose some rights they had outside of bankruptcy, because bankruptcy is an entirely new game that deals with different kinds of problems. These propositions sound innocuous enough, but none of them can withstand close scrutiny, and adhering to them invites analysis that is unfocused and misguided.

Warren asserts that the law must distribute losses that flow from a business failure and that distributing such losses should be the central concern of bankruptcy law. The second observation, however, does not follow from the first. As long as many firms close or fail outside of bankruptcy, treating the question of how to distribute the losses that flow from a business failure as a bankruptcy question ignores much of the problem and creates perverse incentives. Warren argues, for example, that bankruptcy law should favor those who are least able to bear the costs of a business failure. For this reason, she argues, employees rightly enjoy their limited priority under existing bankruptcy law. Warren, however, needs to explain why those who are least able to bear these costs should nevertheless bear them when the firm closes or fails outside of bankruptcy. (Warren cannot be arguing that the costs should be distributed the same way regardless of whether a bankruptcy petition is filed, because when losses are distributed the same way inside of bankruptcy as outside, distribution of losses is not a *bankruptcy* problem.)

Warren's argument for protecting workers only when the firm is in bankruptcy (and not when a firm closes without defaulting to its creditors or when the creditors work out their differences with the firm without filing a bankruptcy petition) is hard to understand:

> Bankruptcy does not, of course, offer complete protection to all those who might be affected by the outcome of a bankruptcy dispute. ... [T]he *debtor* is always free to redeploy the firm's assets. ... Chapter 11 offers only limited protection against the *creditors'* making the decision to dissolve the business [pp. 788-89, emphasis in original].

Warren seems to derive what bankruptcy law ought to be from what it is, but one cannot derive the normative from the positive. Moreover, it seems odd to argue, as a matter of policy, that existing management should be able to close a plant and throw workers out, but that those who lent money to the management and who come into control of the firm only because the firm failed to meet its obligations to them should not. From the perspective of the workers who are tossed out, the loss is the same in both cases.

Even if one argues that creditors should bear greater legal obligations to workers than should shareholders, it will not do to advocate giving workers a special priority in bankruptcy but not elsewhere. In a world in which workers enjoy a special priority only in bankruptcy, creditors will strive to resolve their differences outside of bankruptcy. To argue that there should be differences between the obligations of the debtor and those of the creditors is not the same as arguing that there should be differences between obligations in and out of bankruptcy.

Warren thinks that the benefits of bankruptcy justify additional burdens on creditors. But the issue is not whether the burdens on creditors in bankruptcy are just, but whether the burdens should exist only in bankruptcy. Creditors enjoy the benefits of the non-bankruptcy debt collection system as well. Why should they not have to take the rights of workers into account when they use that system? More to the point, taxing creditors differently depending on which enforcement mechanism they use invites troublesome forum shopping. But Warren does not take the problem of forum shopping seriously. In Warren's world, workers are protected from the costs of a business failure only when their employer and its creditors choose to enter bankruptcy. Why the rights of workers should turn on the decision of those who have every incentive to ignore them is baffling.

Warren seems to inhabit the middle ground between the position that Jackson and I have developed (that *bankruptcy* policy is limited only to the problems associated with multiple default) and the opposite position (that bankruptcy policy and the problem of distributing losses from firm failures and closings are one and the same). Warren must believe that there is a special set of concerns when a firm fails and at the same time defaults to multiple creditors, for Warren's conception of bankruptcy, like mine, does not extend to cases in which a firm fails or closes without defaulting to multiple creditors. (Indeed, such a conception of bankruptcy would be so foreign that it would be hard to call it bankruptcy.) Warren, however, never explains the link that she and many others see between multiple default and firm failure; she never explains why the presence of a dispute among creditors requires a special set of rules governing the distribution of losses from the closing or failure of a firm.

Warren and others seem to think that a glance at history and situation sense make the link self-evident. Jackson and I, however, have made two points that should give pause to those who find it hard to put aside the lay intuition that a firm that fails is a firm that "goes bankrupt." First, we raise the problem of forum shopping, which I have already mentioned and to which I shall return. Even if bankruptcy's gatekeeping rules were much better than they are, those who want a special legal regime governing loss distribution when a firm fails or closes at the same time it defaults to creditors must expect to see in bankruptcy many cases that do not belong there, and many cases outside bankruptcy that belong in bankruptcy.

The second point is deeper. To argue that a special set of distributional concerns arises when a debtor defaults to many creditors at the same time it fails or closes is to assume a link exists between who has rights to the assets of a firm and how those assets are used. Such links are hard to show and harder to justify, as a large body of literature has shown. Traditional bankruptcy scholars are alone in the academy in their belief that the financing decisions of a firm and its investment decisions are inseparable. Whether a firm continues to manufacture a particular product or even stays in business is an issue utterly distinct from the question of who owns the firm's assets. Thus, in a world in which all assertions of ownership rights are stayed (as they are in bankruptcy), how much a particular owner gets should have *nothing* to do with how a firm's assets are used or whether it stays in business. To assert, as Warren does, that a creditor may need to sacrifice some of its ownership interest so that the firm might survive takes issue with most of what has been written about corporate finance over the last three decades. Warren argues that the legislative history of the Bankruptcy Code shows that some legislators embraced the idea that limiting the rights of creditors may increase a firm's chances of reorganizing successfully. I could dispute whether that is a fair reading of the legislative history, but this is quite beside the point. Limiting the rights of creditors either affects a firm's chance of surviving or it does not. The truth of the proposition is completely independent of what Congress may or may not have thought; the proposition must stand or fall on its own. If Warren wants to rely on it, she should at least acknowledge the body of authority that goes the other way.

Warren relies throughout on the bankruptcy judge to ensure that everything comes out right in the end. But judicial discretion is no panacea, even in a court of equity. Warren puts too much faith in the ability of bankruptcy judges to control the conflicting incentives of the various parties. Controlling a party who has an incentive to misbehave is inherently difficult, and alternatives such as eliminating the incentive entirely are sometimes available. As between eliminating a bad incentive and asking a bankruptcy judge to police misbehavior, Jackson and I favor the former. Allowing someone to gamble with someone else's money is always a bad idea, even when a conscientious judge is looking over the gambler's shoulder. Jackson and I have no objection to judicial discretion per se. The art of judging inevitably requires an intelligent weighing of competing interests. But we live in an imperfect world. Judges, like the rest of us, are prone to error. The advantages and disadvantages of judicial discretion under any set of conditions must be weighed against the alternatives. Our argument is simply that Warren and other traditional scholars are too willing to accept the steady hand of a fair judge when other ways of keeping the parties in line may be preferable.

The last theme that Warren dwells upon arises from her observation that the rights of secured creditors change for better as well as worse when a bankruptcy petition is filed. Tracking down assets may be easier when a bankruptcy petition is filed and a trustee is appointed. From this, Warren draws the conclusion that the secured creditor has nothing to complain about. A creditor who claims both the benefits of bankruptcy procedures and the benefits of substantive rights under nonbankruptcy law is trying to have it both ways.

This strand to Warren's argument, however, is defective in two respects. First, it assumes that Jackson and I would neglect the procedural difficulties that creditors would have under state law in calculating the value of their rights. But we have consistently taken the opposite view. We would insist, for example, that for purposes of adequate protection, the value of the secured creditor's rights should be measured as of the time it would have been able to repossess and sell the collateral under state law. Second, Warren confuses the question of whether an inquiry is difficult and inexact with whether it should be undertaken at all. Jackson and I have argued that powerful reasons exist for ensuring that rights in and outside of bankruptcy remain constant. To assert that maintaining parity is difficult may be an argument for settling on an approximation and being content with rough justice, but it is not an argument against parity. The difficulty of keeping rights constant inside and outside of bankruptcy should not mean that anything goes. ...

All that Jackson and I require is that the differences in the two avenues follow from the reasons for having the two avenues in the first place. We have no objection to differences in multiple avenues of enforcement. We object only to *unnecessary* differences.

Warren agrees that a tension will exist in bankruptcy between senior and junior creditors; but she argues that there are many ways of overcoming these tensions, including, for example, denying recognition to secured creditors in bankruptcy altogether. There are, of course, many ways of ensuring that fights between creditors in bankruptcy do not destroy the value of the firm as a whole, including relying (as Warren would) on the steady hand of a fair bankruptcy judge. But each way is different, and one must have a method for choosing among them. Jackson and I have argued that we should adopt the alternative that minimizes forum shopping. Warren misses that point when she claims that giving all creditors equal status in bankruptcy is the logical extension of our position (p. 804). Allowing priorities outside of bankruptcy but not inside is an open invitation to forum shopping and would exacerbate all the problems Jackson and I want to minimize. Treating secured and unsecured creditors alike in bankruptcy while recognizing priority rights elsewhere makes no more sense than making the rights of workers turn on the city in which the litigation is brought.

IV. *"Rehabilitation," Noncognizable Injuries, and Bankruptcy Policy*

Warren suggests that bankruptcy law should be designed to keep businesses from closing even when those with legally cognizable interests in the business want it to close. She does not, however, explain why special rules in bankruptcy are necessary to achieve this goal. One could, for example, have a federal statute that prevented any business from ceasing operations without making a showing in court that the business was unprofitable, destined to fail, or whatever. One cannot say that bankruptcy is necessary to protect those without legally cognizable interests without first answering the question of why these individuals cannot be given such interests. Similarly, one should not assert that bankruptcy law is necessary to prevent the owners of firms from taking actions that injure third parties without explaining why some other kind of legal rule cannot prevent these injuries without encouraging forum shopping.

The law by omission or commission affects who bears the losses from a failed business, but one must explain why placing the solution in bankruptcy law is the preferred course of action. Business "failure" is not necessarily connected with default. Moreover, default itself is not necessarily connected with bankruptcy. Any time resources are shifted from one use to another, or from one place to another, there are likely to be spill-over effects— both positive and negative. If I run a business that makes widgets, I might decide tomorrow to get out of that business and invest my money elsewhere. I can make that decision even if the business is not insolvent. I can make that decision even if the business is not in default. Indeed, I can make that decision even if the business has no creditors at all. The rust belt is littered with firms that have closed or moved elsewhere, not because these businesses did not have enough to pay off creditors, but because they had better opportunities elsewhere. Such a decision has exactly the same effect on workers and customers and nearby property owners as does the decision to close up shop of an insolvent business after default to numerous creditors and a bankruptcy petition is filed. Warren nowhere explains what it is about default in bankruptcy against those with legally cognizable injuries that suddenly makes the injuries of others relevant. If Warren thinks bankruptcy proceedings are appropriate whenever a firm fails or closes and such dislocations happen, she must contemplate court intervention so dramatically different from current bankruptcy proceedings that using the word "bankruptcy" to describe it is inappropriate.

As I noted earlier, one should not link default and bankruptcy. Default is not necessarily connected with a collective action problem. Indeed, it is because default does not *always* raise a collective problem that there are two avenues of enforcement: the existence of bankruptcy's avenue of enforcement springs from the collective action problem. When Warren focuses on *default,* she does not tell us why default policies should exist only in bankruptcy. To discuss bankruptcy policy, one must discuss default in connection with the existence of more than one procedure for vindicating the legal rights that arise from the default. Linking—without explanation—default to only one of several different avenues of enforcement threatens to undermine whatever justifications exist for having multiple avenues of enforcement in the first instance.

In thinking about bankruptcy policy as applied to corporations and other business entities, one must be careful not to confuse them with flesh-and-blood persons. Warren is rhetorically most effective when she alludes to poorhouses, sanctuaries, and escapes to foreign jurisdictions in discussing the problem of insolvent debtors (p. 780 & n.10), but none of this has much to do with the bankruptcy of a corporation. Legal disputes in corporate bankruptcies frequently are between financial institutions and sophisticated investors. The bankruptcy of a corporation does not necessarily mean that anyone will starve. Warren can argue that we should have a special concern for those who are not professionals, but she must show both that this concern is a bankruptcy concern and that it should affect all bankruptcy disputes—even those between professionals. As a positive matter, Warren is wrong to think that existing bankruptcy law cares about the rights of noncreditors. A bankruptcy judge takes these into account only when there is a dispute between those with legally cognizable claims. Contrary to Warren's assertion, creditors are as free to close a firm down as are its managers, inside of bankruptcy and out, as long as the creditors present a united front.

The problem of retiree health benefits provides a good test for Warren's claim that only bankruptcy law is primarily concerned with priorities when there is not enough to go around. A firm promises health benefits to its workers when they retire. If the firm files a Chapter 7 petition, the retirees probably have only unsecured claims against the firm. Section 507 gives them no special priority. Under existing law, the retirees will receive only a few cents on the dollar for their health claims. If a legislator asked Warren about the problem, what would she say? Would Warren advocate bringing retiree health benefits within the scope of section 507? Would she raise the $ 2,000 cap? Would she insist on empirical data? Would she want to leave the rights of retirees to a bankruptcy judge and have the judge balance the worth of these rights against other interests?

NOTES

1. As will be seen from the above extracts, Jackson and Baird believe that bankruptcy's only legitimate function (using bankruptcy in the broader US sense) is to resolve the collective-action problem existing outside bankruptcy, and that other goals must be eschewed. In particular, they say that pre-bankruptcy rights should not be changed in bankruptcy because this distorts bankruptcy's goals. Do you agree with this criticism?

2. Current Canadian bankruptcy law provides many examples of pre-bankruptcy provincial rights being changed in bankruptcy. The basic rule in BIA s. 72 is that the BIA shall not be deemed to abrogate or supersede the substantive provisions of any other law or statute relating to property or civil rights that are not in conflict with the Act. The following are some of the many exceptions to the general rule:

- Section 68.1 avoids any pre-bankruptcy wage assignment or assignment of receivables given by an individual debtor in respect of wages, commission, or professional fees earned by the debtor after bankruptcy.
- Sections 81 to 81.2 confer rights on unpaid sellers of goods to recover their goods within 30 days following the buyer's bankruptcy, and also confer a charge on the buyer's inventory in respect of supplies provided by farmers, fishers, and acquaculturists.
- Section 136(1) contains a different ranking for the claims of unsecured creditors (and in some cases of non-consensual secured claims) than would obtain outside bankruptcy.
- Section 244 precludes a receiver and/or creditor holding a security interest in all or substantially all of the debtor's inventory, accounts receivable or other property from enforcing the security interest against an insolvent debtor without giving the debtor 10 days' notice of their intention.
- Section 67(3) of the Act imposes a deemed trust on property held by the bankrupt at the time of bankruptcy in respect of federal or provincial taxes collected by the debtor prior to bankruptcy or deductions made on behalf of federal and provincial government agencies and not remitted to them. This provision supersedes any pre-bankruptcy entitlements of other creditors, particularly secured creditors.
- In addition to the existing BIA provisions, the PITF report contains a variety of significant recommendations whose implementation would likely change the pre-bankruptcy entitlements of creditors under existing provincial law. Conceptually, the most important of these recommendations is to establish a list of optional federal personal exemptions and to entitle individual debtors on bankruptcy to avail themselves of the federal list in place of the otherwise applicable provincial exemptions.[28]

---

[28] The purpose of this recommendation is to ensure that all bankrupts, wherever situated in Canada, will have a reasonable level of exemptions and will not have to rely on the vagaries of provincial law which, in many cases, has failed to keep personal exemptions up to date. See Chapter 11.

3. In other respects the BIA provisions, as judicially interpreted, are not consistent in following through a common pool model of bankruptcy legislation. The case law presented below in Chapter 3, in the context of s. 43 of the BIA, shows that Canadian courts are quite willing to entertain an application for a bankruptcy order to assist the petitioner to enforce a claim even where there is no evidence that the debtor's bankruptcy will make the debtor's other creditors better off. Applications for bankruptcy orders are also frequently brought by secured creditors to protect their security interests, again with scant concern about how it will affect the unsecured creditors' welfare. Often, after satisfying secured and preferred creditors' claims, little if anything is left for distribution among general creditors. As a result, there is little incentive for unsecured creditors to present a petition or to take an active interest in the administration of bankruptcy estates. Do these facts mean that Canadian bankruptcy law is not playing its proper role or do we deduce that pre-bankruptcy law is undermining bankruptcy by failing to treat all creditor claims equally?

Constitutional Aspects and Judicial and Administrative Structure of Bankruptcy System

I. CONSTITUTIONAL ASPECTS

A. Introduction

Section 91(21) of the *Constitution Act, 1867* vests "exclusive" power in the federal government to enact laws in relation to "bankruptcy and insolvency." There is much case law testing the scope of the federal power and the validity of provincial laws addressing insolvency issues. Part I of this chapter reproduces extracts from some of the leading cases that illustrate various aspects of these problems. The key issues are: (1) the meaning of "bankruptcy and insolvency" in s. 91(21) of the constitution; (2) restrictions on federal legislation adopted under the bankruptcy and insolvency power and on administrative powers delegated under bankruptcy legislation on courts, trustees, and other officials; and (3) circumstances under which the courts will uphold insolvency-type legislation adopted by the provinces.

As will be seen, the case law is not consistent and Canadian courts have alternated between a narrow view of provincial powers and one that gives the provinces concurrent powers as long as the provincial legislation does not actually conflict with competent federal legislation. The rapid growth in the number of consumer insolvencies since the early 1980s and the much enhanced importance of the judicial role under the CCAA in the reorganization of insolvent businesses have made these questions of growing importance.

Ontario (Attorney General) v. Canada (Attorney General)
[1894] AC 189 (PC)

THE LORD CHANCELLOR: This appeal is presented by the Attorney-General of Ontario against a decision of the Court of Appeal of that province.

The decision complained of was an answer given to a question referred to that Court by the Lieutenant-Governor of the province in pursuance of an Order in Council.

The question was as follows:

> Had the Legislature of Ontario jurisdiction to enact the 9th section of the Revised Statutes of Ontario, c. 124, and entitled "An Act respecting Assignments and Preferences by Insolvent Persons"?

The majority of the Court answered this question in the negative; but one of the judges who formed the majority only concurred with his brethren because he thought the case was governed by a previous decision of the same Court; had he considered the matter *res integra* he would have decided the other way. The Court was thus equally divided in opinion.

It is not contested that the enactment, the validity of which is in question, is within the legislative powers conferred on the provincial legislature by sect. 92 of the *British North America Act, 1867*, which enables that legislature to make laws in relation to property and civil rights in the province unless it is withdrawn from their legislative competency by the provisions of the 91st section of that Act which confers upon the Dominion Parliament the exclusive power of legislation with reference to bankruptcy and insolvency.

The point to be determined, therefore, is the meaning of those words in sect. 91 of the *British North America Act, 1867*, and whether they render the enactment impeached *ultra vires* of the provincial legislature. That enactment is sect. 9 of the Revised Statutes of Ontario of 1887, c. 124, entitled "An Act respecting Assignment and Preferences by Insolvent Persons." The section is as follows:

> An assignment for the general benefit of creditors under this Act shall take precedence of all judgments and of all executions not completely executed by payment, subject to the lien, if any, of an execution creditor for his costs, where there is but one execution in the sheriff's hands, or to the lien, if any, of the creditor for his costs, who has the first execution in the sheriff's hands.

In order to understand the effect of this enactment it is necessary to have recourse to other sections of the Act to see what is meant by the words "an assignment for the general benefit of creditors under this Act."

The first section enacts that if any person in insolvent circumstances, or knowing himself to be on the eve of insolvency, voluntarily confesses judgment, or gives a warrant of attorney to confess judgment, with intent to defeat or delay his creditors, or to give any creditor a preference over his other creditors, every such confession or warrant of attorney shall be void as against the creditors of the party giving it.

The 2nd section avoids as against the other creditors any gift or assignment of goods or other property made by a person at a time when he is in insolvent circumstances, or knows that he is on the eve of insolvency, with intent to defeat, delay, or prejudice his creditors or give any of them a preference.

Then follows sect. 3, which is important:

Its 1st sub-section provides that nothing in the preceding section shall apply to an assignment made to the sheriff of a county in which the debtor resides or carries on business, or to any assignee resident within the province with the consent of his creditors as thereinafter provided for the purpose of paying, rateably and proportionately, and without preference or priority all the creditors of the debtor their just debts.

The 2nd sub-section enacts that every assignment for the general benefit of creditors which is not void under sect. 2 but is not made to the sheriff nor to any other person with the prescribed consent of the creditors shall be void as against a subsequent assignment which is in conformity with the Act, and shall be subject in other respects to the provisions of the Act, until and unless a subsequent assignment is executed in accordance therewith.

The 5th sub-section states the nature of the consent of the creditors which is requisite for assignment in the first instance to some person other than the sheriff.

These are the only sections to which it is necessary to refer in order to explain the meaning of sect. 9.

Before discussing the effect of the enactments to which attention has been called, it will be convenient to glance at the course of legislation in relation to this and cognate matters both in the province and in the Dominion. The enactment's of the 1st and 2nd sections of the Act of 1887 are to be found in substance in sects. 18 and 19 of the Act of the Province of Canada passed in 1858 for the better prevention of fraud. There is a proviso to the latter section which excepts from its operation any assignment made for the purpose of paying all the creditors of the debtor rateably without preference. These provisions were repeated in the Revised Statutes of Ontario, 1877, c. 118. A slight amendment was made by the Act of 1884, and it was as thus amended that they were re-enacted in 1887. At the time when the statute of 1858 was passed there was no bankruptcy law in force in the Province of Canada. In the year 1864 an Act respecting insolvency was enacted. It applied in Lower Canada to traders only; in Upper Canada to all persons whether traders or non-traders. It provided that a debtor should be deemed insolvent and his estate should become subject to compulsory liquidation if he committed certain acts similar to those which had for a long period been made acts of bankruptcy in this country. Among these acts were the assignment or the procuring of his property to be seized in execution with intent to defeat or delay his creditors, and also a general assignment of his property for the benefit of his creditors otherwise than in manner provided by the statute. A person who was unable to meet his engagements might avoid compulsory liquidation by making an assignment of his estate in the manner provided by that Act; but unless he made such an assignment within the time limited the liquidation became compulsory.

This Act was in operation at the time when the *British North America Act* came into force.

In 1869 the Dominion Parliament passed an *Insolvency Act* which proceeded on much the same lines as the Provincial Act of 1864, but applied to traders only. This Act was repealed by a new *Insolvency Act of 1875*, which, after being twice amended, was, together with the Amending Acts, repealed in 1880.

In 1887, the same year in which the Act under consideration was passed, the provincial legislature abolished priority amongst creditors by an execution in the High Court and county courts, and provided for the distribution of any moneys levied on an execution rateably amongst all execution creditors, and all other creditors who within a month delivered to the sheriff writs and certificates obtained in the manner provided for by that Act.

Their Lordships proceed now to consider the nature of the enactment said to be *ultra vires*. It postpones judgments and executions not completely executed by payment to an assignment for the benefit of creditors under the Act. Now there can be no doubt that the effect to be given to judgments and executions and the manner and extent to which they may be made available for the recovery of debts are *prima facie* within the legislative powers of the provincial parliament. Executions are a part of the machinery by which debts are recovered, and are subject to regulation by that parliament. A creditor has no inherent right to have his debt satisfied by means of a levy by the sheriff, or to any priority in respect of such levy. The execution is a mere creature of the law which may determine and regulate the rights to which it gives rise. The Act of 1887 which abolished priority as amongst execution creditors provided a simple means by which every creditor might obtain a share in the distribution of moneys levied under an execution by any particular creditor. The other Act of the same year, containing the section which is impeached, goes a step further, and gives to all creditors under an assignment for their general benefit a right to a rateable share of the assets of the debtor, including those which have been seized in execution.

But it is argued that inasmuch as this assignment contemplates the insolvency of the debtor, and would only be made if he were insolvent, such a provision purports to deal with insolvency, and therefore is a matter exclusively within the jurisdiction of the Dominion Parliament. Now it is to be observed that an assignment for the general benefit of creditors has long been known to the jurisprudence of this country and also of Canada, and has its force and effect at common law quite independently of any system of bankruptcy or insolvency, or any legislation relating thereto. So far from being regarded as an essential part of the bankruptcy law, such an assignment was made an act of bankruptcy on which an adjudication might be founded, and by the law of the Province of Canada which prevailed at the time when the *Dominion Act* was passed, it was one of the grounds for an adjudication of insolvency.

It is to be observed that the word "bankruptcy" was apparently not used in Canadian legislation, but the insolvency law of the Province of Canada was precisely analogous to what was known in England as the bankruptcy law.

Moreover, the operation of an assignment for the benefit of creditors was precisely the same, whether the assignor was or was not in fact insolvent. It was open to any debtor who might deem his solvency doubtful, and who desired in that case that his creditors should be equitably dealt with, to make an assignment for their benefit. The validity of the assignment and its effect would in no way depend on the insolvency of the assignor, and their Lordships think it clear that the 9th section would equally apply whether the assignor was or was not insolvent. Stress was laid on the fact that the enactment relates only to an assignment under the Act containing the section, and that the Act prescribes that the sheriff of the county is to be the assignee unless a majority of the creditors consent to some other assignee being named. This does not appear to their Lordships to be material. If the enactment would have been *intra vires*, supposing sect. 9 had applied to all assignments without these restrictions, it seems difficult to contend that it became *ultra vires* by reason of them. Moreover, it is to be observed that by sub-sect. 2 of sect. 3, assignments for the benefit of creditors not made to the sheriff or to other persons with the prescribed consent, although they are rendered void as against assignments so made, are nevertheless, unless and until so avoided, to be "subject in other respects to the provisions" of the Act.

At the time when the *British North America Act* was passed bankruptcy and insolvency legislation existed, and was based on very similar provisions both in Great Britain and the Province of Canada. Attention has already been drawn to the Canadian Act.

The English Act then in force was that of 1861. That Act applied to traders and non-traders alike. Prior to that date the operation of the Bankruptcy Acts had been confined to traders. The statutes relating to insolvent debtors, other than traders, had been designed to provide for their release from custody on their making an assignment of the whole of their estate for the benefit of their creditors.

It is not necessary to refer in detail to the provisions of the Act of 1861. It is enough to say that it provided for a legal adjudication in bankruptcy with the consequence that the bankrupt was divested of all his property and its distribution amongst his creditors was provided for.

It is not necessary in their Lordships' opinion, nor would it be expedient to attempt to define, what is covered by the words "bankruptcy" and "insolvency" in sect. 91 of the *British North America Act*. But it will be seen that it is a feature common to all the systems of bankruptcy and insolvency to which reference has been made, that the enactments are designed to secure that in the case of an insolvent person his assets shall be rateably distributed amongst his creditors whether he is willing that they shall be so distributed or not. Although provision may be made for a voluntary assignment as an alternative, it is only as an alternative. In reply to a question put by their Lordships the learned counsel for the respondent were unable to point to any scheme of bankruptcy or insolvency legislation which did not involve some power of compulsion by process of law to secure to the creditors the distribution amongst them of the insolvent debtor's estate.

In their Lordships' opinion these considerations must be borne in mind when interpreting the words "bankruptcy" and "insolvency" in the *British North America Act*. It appears to their Lordships that such provisions as are found in the enactment in question, relating as they do to assignments purely voluntary, do not infringe on the exclusive legislative power conferred upon the Dominion Parliament. They would observe that a system of bankruptcy legislation may frequently require various ancillary provisions for the purpose of preventing the scheme of the Act from being defeated. It may be necessary for this purpose to deal with the effect of executions and other matters which would otherwise be within the legislative competence of the provincial legislature. Their Lordships do not doubt that it would be open to the Dominion Parliament to deal with such matters as part of a bankruptcy law, and the provincial legislature would doubtless be then precluded from interfering with this legislation inasmuch as such interference would affect the bankruptcy law of the Dominion Parliament. But it does not follow that such subjects, as might properly be treated as ancillary to such a law and therefore within the powers of the Dominion Parliament, are excluded from the legislative authority of the provincial legislature when there is no bankruptcy or insolvency legislation of the Dominion Parliament in existence.

Their Lordships will therefore humbly advise Her Majesty that the decision of the Court of Appeal ought to be reversed, and that the question ought to be answered in the affirmative.

Decision of Ontario Court of Appeal reversed.

NOTES AND QUESTIONS

1. What was the ratio of the Lord Chancellor's judgment in the *Voluntary Assignment* case? Was it that legislation cannot be characterized as insolvency or bankruptcy legislation unless the insolvency or acts of bankruptcy by the debtor are a precondition of the statute's

applicability, or was it that the legislation does not meet the s. 91(21) threshold requirements unless it covers involuntary bankruptcies as well as voluntary assignments? If the latter answer is the correct interpretation, it clearly conflicts with later Supreme Court of Canada and Privy Council decisions upholding the federal authority to introduce new forms of
insolvency legislation. See, for example, *Reference re Companies' Creditors Arrangement Act*,
[1934] SCR 659. Recall that there was no federal bankruptcy legislation between 1880 and
1919 and therefore no relief available for individual insolvent debtors (insolvent corporate
debtors were covered by the federal *Winding-Up Act* of 1883) before the introduction of the
Bankruptcy Act in 1919. Did this influence the Privy Council's judgment in arguing that
Ontario's *Voluntary Assignment Act* did not trench on the federal government's exclusive
bankruptcy and insolvency power? (See Thomas G.W. Telfer, "A Canadian 'World Without
Bankruptcy Law': The Failure of Bankruptcy Reform at the End of the Nineteenth Century"
(2004), 8 *Aust. J Legal Hist.* 83, esp. at 100-5.) Was the Lord Chancellor hinting that there is
a double aspect to insolvency legislation, thus carving out room for provincial initiatives
where there is no conflicting federal legislation?

2. Meaning of "bankruptcy and insolvency." There is no definitive judicial interpretation of the meaning of these words in s. 91(21). There is a frequently cited dictum of Justice
Rand to the effect that "insolvency" refers to voluntary assignments or liquidation of an insolvent estate and that "bankruptcy" refers to involuntary insolvency proceedings. Even if
the description were accurate (which is doubtful),[1] it is only a description and it doesn't tell
us the meaning of "bankruptcy" or "insolvency." Considerable help in ascertaining what the
1867 drafters may have had in mind can be obtained from the definition of "acts of bankruptcy" in BIA s. 42 and the definition of "insolvent person" in s. 2, because they reflect the
meaning commonly ascribed to these terms in the 19th century and would therefore have
been familiar to the drafters of the *Constitution Act*. Note that a debtor can commit an act
of bankruptcy under s. 42 without being or becoming insolvent (for example, by concealing
his assets or fraudulently conveying them to third parties). The definition of insolvent person in s. 2, on the other hand, reflects a twofold alternative test designed to determine a
debtor's ability to meet his financial obligations, viz., a "liquidity" test and a "balance-sheet"
test, both tests being derived from well-established accounting practices.

3. The insolvency test is also adopted as an alternative prerequisite to the court's jurisdiction to entertain a restructuring application under the CCAA by a "debtor company"
(s. 2(1)), debtor company being defined as any company "that is a bankrupt or insolvent." In
Re Stelco (2004), 48 CBR (4th) 299 (Ont. SCJ). Farley J gave an expansive meaning to "insolvency" and in so doing departed from previous decisions giving "insolvency" the same
meaning as it has received under the BIA. Farley J held that a contextual and purposive approach should be adopted to interpret the term "insolvent person" so that its meaning fits
within the overall context of the rehabilitative process under the CCAA (at para. 23). He
also held that the insolvency requirements should be viewed as "constantly evolving" with the
bankruptcy and restructuring regime in Canada and, in applying these principles, a distinction should be drawn between insolvency in bankruptcy and insolvency in reorganization

---

[1] Beginning in 1864, "insolvent" was featured in the title of pre-Confederation legislation. The *Insolvent Act of
1864* covered both voluntary and involuntary insolvency proceedings. The usage of "insolvent" remained
consistent with early post Confederation legislation: *Insolvent Act of 1869* and *Insolvent Act of 1875*.

(at para. 19). In the first case, insolvency is a precondition to the "end" situation of bankruptcy, and, in the second, it is a precondition to entry to a rehabilitative process. Farley J did not consider the constitutional aspects of his contextual and functional approach and whether s. 91(21) admits of this degree of flexibility. *Re Stelco* is extracted in Chapter 12.

4. In "Should Proof of the Debtor's Insolvency be Dispensed with in Voluntary Insolvency Proceedings?" (2007), *Ann. Rev. Ins. L* 21, an article commenting on Farley J's decision, Ziegel raises the question whether proof of insolvency should be dispensed with altogether as a mandatory requirement in voluntary insolvency proceedings; he favours this approach for two reasons—first, because proof of the debtor's insolvency is not required in voluntary proceedings under the US Bankruptcy Code; and, second, because dispensing with proof of the debtor's insolvency in Canadian proceedings would put Canadian debtors on a level playing field with their US counterparts. This goal is especially important in crossborder insolvency proceedings involving Canadian and US debtors. Ziegel also notes that the insolvency requirement has been abolished for some purposes in the *British Insolvency Act 1986*, as amended in 2002, and that proof of a debtor's insolvency is not required under the UNICITRAL Model Cross-border Insolvency Law (now substantially adopted in the 2005-7 amendments to the BIA and the CCAA) for recognition of foreign insolvency proceedings so long as the proceedings were conducted under a general law dealing with insolvent debtors. However, Ziegel recognizes the substantial difficulties likely to arise in persuading Canadian courts to read out the insolvency requirement, as traditionally understood, as a condition of the federal government's constitutional jurisdiction to regulate and provide relief for debtors in distress.

5. As far as US law is concerned, under the US Code, a debtor can file a petition for relief under a chapter of the Code—for example, Chapter 7 or Chapter 11—without having to prove that the debtor is insolvent. This is because US courts have given a very elastic meaning to "bankruptcy" and to Congressional power under art. 1, s. 8 of the Constitution to adopt bankruptcy legislation. US courts do not treat the word "bankruptcy" as a term of art and the US Supreme Court has consistently refused to restrict Congressional powers to the type of bankruptcy legislation extant in England in 1776. In an oft cited passage, the US Supreme Court, while noting that "[t]he subject of bankruptcies is incapable of final definition," also defined "bankruptcy" as the "subject of the relations between an insolvent or nonpaying or fraudulent debtor and his creditors, extending to his and their relief": *Continental Illinois National Bank & Trust Co. v. Chicago, Rock Island & Pacific Ry. Co.*, 294 US 648, at 668-69 (1935). Tabb states the position still more broadly and claims that "[t]oday virtually any law that addresses the relationship between creditors and a financially distressed debtor, and readjusts the respective rights of those parties, falls within the 'subject of bankruptcies'" (*The Law of Bankruptcy* (1997), at 46).

Reference Re Orderly Payment of Debts Act 1959 (Alberta)
[1960] SCR 571

KERWIN CJC (for himself and Taschereau, Fauteux, Abbott, Judson and Ritchie JJ): Under the provisions of *The Constitutional Questions Act*, RSA 1955, c. 55, the Lieutenant-Governor in Council of the Province of Alberta referred to the Appellate Division of the

Supreme Court of the Province [(1959), 29 WWR 435, 20 DLR (2d) 503] the following question for hearing and consideration:

> Is The *Orderly Payment of Debts Act*, being Chapter 61 of the Statutes of Alberta, 1959, *intra vires* the Legislature of Alberta, either in whole or in part, and if so, in what part or parts, and to what extent?

. . .

George H. Steer, Esq., QC, was appointed as counsel to argue the case on behalf of creditors or other persons who might be opposed to the provisions of the Act. At the hearing counsel for the Attorney General for the Province and one counsel for three credit associations appeared to uphold the Act while Mr. Steer represented argument against its validity. No one else appeared, although the others mentioned above were duly notified. Judgment was reserved and the Court consisting of the Chief Justice, H.J. Macdonald, M.M. Porter and H.G. Johnson, JJA, unanimously decided that the Act was wholly *ultra vires* the Legislature of the Province.

The Attorney General for Alberta appealed to this Court. In accordance with the Rules notice was duly served upon the Attorney-General of Canada and by direction notice was also served upon the Attorney General for each of the other provinces. Before us counsel for the Attorney General for Ontario and for the Attorney General for Saskatchewan supported the appeal. No one else appeared except Mr. Steer. On behalf of the three provinces it was submitted, as apparently it was argued in the Appellate Division, that the Act was within the legislative competence of the Province of Alberta under Heads 13, 14 and 16 of s. 92 of the *British North America Act, 1867*:

Mr. Steer contended that the subject matter of the Act dealt with bankruptcy and insolvency and was therefore within the sole competence of the legislative authority of the Parliament of Canada under Head 21 of s. 91 of the *British North America Act*. He also contended it was *ultra vires* because it encroached upon the following heads of s. 91 of that Act: [the court cited ss. 91(15), 91(18), and 91(19), and continued]:

> 15. Banking, incorporation of Banks and the issue of Paper Money.

> 18. Bills of Exchange and Promissory Notes.

> 19. Interest.

and because it gives to the clerk of a District Court the powers of a judge contrary to the provisions of s. 96 of the *British North America Act*.

I agree with the Appellate Division that the Act is *ultra vires* on the ground that in pith and substance it is bankruptcy and insolvency legislation and that it is therefore unnecessary to consider the other grounds of attack.

Section 3 of *The Orderly Payment of Debts Act* provides:

> 3.(1) This Act applies only
>   (a) to a judgment for the payment of money where the amount of the judgment does not exceed one thousand dollars,
>   (b) to a judgment for the payment of money in excess of one thousand dollars if the creditor consents to come under this Act, and

(c) to a claim for money, demand for debt, account, covenant or otherwise, not in excess of one thousand dollars.

(2) This Act does not apply to a debt due, owing or payable to the Crown or a municipality or relating to the public revenue or one that may be levied and collected in the form of taxes or, unless the creditor consents to come under this Act,

(a) to a claim for wages that may be heard before, or a judgment therefor by, a magistrate under *The Masters and Servants Act*,

(b) to a claim for lien or a judgment thereon under *The Mechanics Lien Act*, or

(c) to a claim for a lien under *The Garagemen's Lien Act*.

(3) This Act does not apply to debts incurred by a trader or merchant in the usual course of his business.

Provision is then made whereby a debtor may apply to the clerk of the District Court of the judicial district in which he resides for a consolidation order, showing by affidavit all his creditors together with the amount he owes to each one, his income from all sources and, if he is married, the amount of the income of his wife, the number of persons dependent upon him, the amount payable for board or lodging or rent or as payment on home property and whether any of his creditors' claims are secured, and if so, the nature and particulars of the security held by each. The clerk is to settle an amount proposed to be paid by the debtor into court periodically or otherwise on account of the claims of his creditors and provide for hearing objections by the latter. After such a hearing, if necessary, a consolidation order is to be made, which order is a judgment of the Court in favour of each creditor, and provision is made for a review by the Court of any such order.

Sections 12, 13 and 14 are important and read as follows:

12. The court may, in deciding any matter brought before it, impose such terms on a debtor with respect to the custody of his property or any disposition thereof or of the proceeds thereof as it deems proper to protect the registered creditors and may give such directions for the purpose as the circumstances require.

13. Upon the making of a consolidation order no process shall be issued in any court against the debtor at the instance of a registered creditor or a creditor to whom this Act applies

(a) except as permitted by this Act or the regulations, or

(b) except by leave of the court.

14.(1) The clerk may at any time require of, and take from, the debtor an assignment to himself as clerk of the court of any moneys due, owing or payable or to become due, owing or payable to the debtor or earned or to be earned by the debtor.

(2) Unless otherwise agreed upon the clerk shall forthwith notify the person owing or about to owe the moneys of the assignment and all moneys collected thereon shall be applied to the credit of the claims against the debtor under the consolidation order.

(3) The clerk may issue a writ of execution in respect of a consolidation order and cause it to be filed with the sheriff of a judicial district and at any land titles office.

While the Act applies only to claims or judgments which do not exceed one thousand dollars, unless in the case of a judgment for the payment of money in excess of one thousand dollars the creditor consents to come under the Act, I can read these provisions in no other way than showing that they refer to a debtor who is unable to pay his debts as they mature. Why else is authority given the Court to impose terms with respect to the custody of his property or any disposition thereof or of the proceeds thereof as it deems proper to protect the registered creditors (s. 12)? And why else may no process be issued in any court against the debtor at the instance of a registered creditor or a creditor to whom the Act applies, except as stated (s. 13)? Section 14 authorizing the clerk to require an assignment to him by the debtor of any monies due, owing or payable or to become due, owing or payable to the debtor, or earned or to be earned by the debtor is surely consonant only with the position of an insolvent debtor. In fact a debtor under the Act is ceasing to meet his liabilities generally as they become due and therefore falls within s. 20(1)(j) of the *Bankruptcy Act*, RSC 1952, c. 14.

In *Attorney-General for British Columbia v. Attorney General for Canada et al.* [[1937] AC 391], Lord Thankerton speaking for the Judicial Committee states at p. 402:

> In a general sense, insolvency means inability to meet one's debts or obligations; in a technical sense, it means the condition or standard of inability to meet debts or obligations, upon the occurrence of which the statutory law enables a creditor to intervene, with the assistance of a Court, to stop individual action by creditors and to secure administration of the debtor's assets in the general interest of creditors; the law also generally allows the debtor to apply for the same administration. The justification for such proceeding by a creditor generally consists in an act of bankruptcy by the debtor, the conditions of which are defined and prescribed by the statute law.

This was said in an appeal affirming the decision of the majority of this Court in the *Reference as to the Validity of The Farmers' Creditors Arrangement Act of the Dominion*, as amended [[1936] SCR 384].

In *Canadian Bankers' Association v. Attorney General of Saskatchewan* [[1956] SCR 31], this Court held that *The Moratorium Act of Saskatchewan* was *ultra vires* as being in relation to insolvency. There the decision of the Judicial Committee in *Abitibi Power and Paper Company v. The Montreal Trust Company* [[1943] AC 536, 4 DLR 1] was relied upon, but, for the reasons given by Mr. Justice Locke, it was held that it had no application. As was pointed out, the Judicial Committee in the 1943 case held that the purpose of the impugned legislation was to stay proceedings in the action brought under the mortgage granted by the Abitibi Company until the interested parties should have an opportunity of considering such plan for the re-organization of the company as might be submitted by a Royal Commission appointed for that purpose. For the same reason that decision is inapplicable here. The older decision of the Privy Council in *Attorney General for Ontario v. The Attorney General of Canada* [[1894] AC 189], dealing with *The Ontario Assignments and Preference Act*, is quite distinguishable, although in my view it is doubtful whether in view of later pronouncements of the Judicial Committee it would at this date be decided in the same sense, even in the absence of Dominion legislation upon the subject of bankruptcy and insolvency.

The Act in question is not legislation for the recovery of debts. It has no analogy to provincial bulk sales legislation because there the object is to make sure that when a person sells his stock of goods, wares, merchandise and chattels, ordinarily the subject of trade and commerce, the creditors will not be placed in any difficulty because of the disappearance of the proceeds of the sale. It is unnecessary to express any opinion as to the validity of s. 156 of *The Division Courts Act of Ontario*, RSO 1950, apparently introduced for the first time in 1950 by c. 16 of the statutes of that year, which provides for a consolidation order.

The debtor under *The Orderly Payment of Debts Act* is not in the same position as the appellant in *L'Union St. Jacques de Montréal v. Bélisle* [(1874) LR 6 PC 31], and the appellant can gain no comfort from *Ladore v. Bennett* [[1939] AC 468, 3 DLR 1], because there it was held that the *City of Windsor (Amalgamation) Act, 1935* and Amendment were in pith and substance Acts passed in relation to "municipal institutions in the Province" and did not encroach upon the exclusive legislative power of the Dominion Parliament in relation to bankruptcy and insolvency, interest, or private rights outside the Province. This was a decision of the Judicial Committee affirming that of the Court of Appeal for Ontario [(1938), 3 DLR 212], which latter, in the meantime, had been applied by the Court of Appeal for British Columbia in *Day v. Corporation of the City of Vancouver*, McGavin and McMullen [(1938), 4 DLR 345]. The legislation in question in each of these cases was quite different from the effort by Alberta in *Board of Trustees of the Lethbridge Northern Irrigation District v. I.O.F.* [[1940] AC 513, 2 DLR 273].

The appeal should be dismissed.

LOCKE J [for himself and Martland J]: ... While the [Alberta] Act does not require that the debtor who applies must be insolvent in the sense that he is unable to pay his debts as they become due, it must, in my opinion, be so construed since it is quite impossible to believe that it was intended that the provisions of the Act might be resorted to by persons who were able to pay their way but do not feel inclined to do so. In my opinion, this is a clear invasion of the legislative field of insolvency and is, accordingly, beyond the powers of the legislature.

There have been bankruptcy laws in England since 1542 dealing with the estates of insolvent persons, and the terms of statutes in force in England prior to 1867 may be looked at as an aid in deciding what subject matters were generally regarded as included in these terms.

The *Bankruptcy Consolidation Act of 1849*, 12-13 Vict., c. 106, which consolidated the law relating to bankrupts, contained in ss. 201 to 223 provisions by which a trader unable to meet his engagements with his creditors might petition the court to approve a composition or scheme of arrangement for the payment of his debts and declared the manner in which such a proposal might be submitted to the creditors and, if approved, to the court for its approval.

The manner in which disputes between the official assignee and the creditors as to the carrying out of a deed of composition or arrangement were to be settled was further dealt with in 1861 in s. 136 of an *Act to amend the law relating to bankruptcy and insolvency in England*, 24-25 Vict., c. 134.

Compositions and schemes of arrangement have thus for more than 100 years past been treated as subject matters falling within the scope of the statutes relating to bankruptcy and insolvency. The provisions dealing with this subject at the present day in England are to be found in the *Bankruptcy Act* of 1914 as amended (see *Williams on*

Bankruptcy, 17th ed., p. 92). When the *Bankruptcy Act* was enacted in Canada in 1919 it contained in s. 13 provisions whereby an insolvent debtor who wished to make a proposal to his creditors for a composition in satisfaction of his debts or an extension of time for payment thereof or a scheme of arrangement of his affairs might, either before or after the making of a receiving order against him or the making of an authorized assignment by him, require in writing an authorized trustee to convene a meeting of his creditors for the consideration of such proposal and provisions whereby the scheme, if approved, might become binding upon the parties concerned. Similar provisions for dealing with such a proposal, a term which is defined to include a proposal for a composition, an extension of time, or for a scheme of arrangement, are contained in the *Bankruptcy Act* as it is today.

These provisions are made applicable to proposals by farmers in Alberta, Manitoba and Saskatchewan by the *Farmers' Creditors Arrangement Act* above mentioned. The Act under consideration appears to be an attempt to substitute for the provisions of the *Bankruptcy Act* and the *Farmers' Creditors Arrangement Act* relating to proposals for an extension of time or a scheme of arrangement which are submitted to the interested creditors for their approval and, if approved, thereafter to the judge in bankruptcy, a scheme whereby the propriety of accepting such a proposal is to be determined by the clerk of the district court and with regard, apparently, only to the claims of those creditors the debts owing to whom are less than one thousand dollars in amount and those to whom greater amounts are owing who consent to come under the Act, leaving other creditors whose claims are greater to resort to such remedies as they may be advised to take for the enforcement of their claims. The provisions of the provincial Act thus conflict with those in the legislation passed by Parliament dealing with the same matters.

In *Attorney General of British Columbia v. Attorney General of Canada* [[1937] AC 391, 1 DLR 695], where the *Farmers' Creditors Arrangement Act 1934* of the Parliament of Canada, as amended by the *Farmers' Creditors Arrangement Act Amendment Act 1935* was considered, Lord Thankerton said in part:

> it cannot be maintained that legislative provision as to compositions, by which bankruptcy is avoided, but which assumes insolvency, is not properly within the sphere of bankruptcy legislation.

and referred to the judgment of this Court in the matter of the *Companies Creditors Arrangement Act* [[1934] SCR 659, 4 DLR 75], where Sir Lyman Duff, delivering the judgment of the majority, said that the history of the law seems to show clearly that legislation in respect of compositions and arrangements is a natural and ordinary component of a system of bankruptcy and insolvency law.

Some support for the validity of this legislation is sought in the judgment of the Judicial Committee in *Attorney General of Ontario v. Attorney General of Canada* [[1894] AC 189]. The question in that appeal was as to whether s. 9 of c. 124, RSO 1887, was within the powers of the legislature. The Act was entitled "An Act respecting assignments and preferences by insolvent persons." A majority of the members of the Court of Appeal who considered the question had found the section to be *ultra vires*. In an earlier case, *Clarkson v. Ontario Bank* [(1890), 15 OAR 166], Haggarty CJO and Osler JA had held the Act as a whole to be *ultra vires* as legislation relating to bankruptcy and insolvency, while

Burton and Patterson JJA considered it to be *intra vires* as being in relation to property and civil rights in the province.

Prior to the passing of that statute the *Insolvency Act of 1875* (c. 16) had been repealed by Parliament by c. 1 of the Statutes of 1880 and there was no *Bankruptcy or Insolvency Act* of the Dominion.

The judgment allowing the appeal was delivered by Herschell LC. The Act, the first two sections of which dealt with fraudulent preferences by insolvents or those knowing themselves to be on the eve of insolvency, permitted a debtor-solvent or otherwise—to make an assignment of his exigible assets to a sheriff for the purpose of realization and distribution pro rata among his creditors. Section 9 provided that such an assignment should take precedence of all judgments and all executions not completely executed by payment. There were no provisions permitting proposals for a composition or extension of time for payment of debts. It was said that the effect to be given to judgments and executions and the manner and the extent to which they might be enforced was *prima facie* within the legislative powers of the legislature and that the validity of the assignment and the application of s. 9 did not depend on whether the assignor was or was not insolvent. Such an assignment, their Lordships said, did not infringe on the exclusive legislative power of Parliament under head 21. The concluding portion of the judgment reads (pp. 200-201):

> Their Lordships do not doubt that it would be open to the Dominion Parliament to deal with such matters as part of a bankruptcy law, and the provincial legislature would doubtless be then precluded from interfering with this legislation inasmuch as such interference would affect the bankruptcy law of the Dominion Parliament. But it does not follow that such subjects, as might properly be treated as ancillary to such a law and therefore within the powers of the Dominion Parliament, are excluded from the legislative authority of the provincial legislature when there is no bankruptcy or insolvency legislation of the Dominion Parliament in existence.

As Parliament has dealt with the matter, the concluding portion of this judgment would be fatal to the appellant's contention, even if the subject of bankruptcy and insolvency were one in relation to which the province might legislate in the absence of legislation by the Dominion. But the language of s. 91 is that the exclusive legislative power of the Parliament of Canada extends to all matters in relation to, *inter alia*, bankruptcy and insolvency, and the provinces are excluded from that field. As Lord Watson said in *Union Colliery v. Bryden* [[1899] AC 580, at 588]:

> The abstinence of the Dominion Parliament from Legislating to the full limit of its power could not have the effect of transferring to any provincial legislature the legislative power which had been assigned to the Dominion by s. 91 of the Act of 1867.

Neither *Ladore v. Bennett* [[1939] AC 468] nor *Abitibi Power and Paper Co. v. Montreal Trust Co.* [[1943] AC 536], affect the question, in my opinion. In the former case the legislation, while it affected the rights of persons who had claims against insolvent municipalities, was found to be in pith and substance in relation to municipal institutions in the province and, as such, was intra vires the legislature under s. 92(8). In the latter case the purpose of the impugned legislation was to stay proceedings in an action brought under a mortgage until the interested parties should have an opportunity of considering a plan for the reorganization of the company, and the true nature of the legislation was held to be to regulate property and civil rights within the province.

[Cartwright J delivered a concurring judgment for himself and Maitland J.]

Appeal dismissed.

NOTE

Following the Supreme Court's decision in the *Orderly Payment of Debts Act Reference*, the federal government amended the *Bankruptcy Act* in 1965 and added a new Part X reproducing the essential features in the Alberta *Orderly Payment of Debts Act*. Part X applies only to those provinces that have elected to adopt it; only six provinces elected to do so. Quebec has its own consolidation provisions, popularly known as the *Lacombe Law*, which were adopted even earlier than the Alberta provisions and have never been challenged constitutionally. See now Quebec Code of Civil Procedure, *Quebec Civil Code*, book IV, arts. 652-659. The number of consolidation orders under Part X dropped off sharply following adoption of the 1992 amendments of the BIA and introduction of the consumer proposal provisions in BIA Part III.2. In 1998, for example, the total number of consolidation orders amounted to 1,539 or about 2 percent of the number of personal bankruptcies declared that year compared with 7,155 consumer proposals or 9.5 percent of the number of consumer bankruptcies. In 2007, there were only 596 consolidations orders. As will be explained in Chapter 17, consumer proposals are much more attractive to insolvent debtors than Part X, because consumer proposals are designed to provide relief from at least part of the consumer's indebtedness, whereas an Orderly Payment Order only gives the debtor more time to discharge the indebtedness.

Donald A. Robinson v. Countrywide Factors Ltd.
[1978] 1 SCR 753

LASKIN CJC (for himself, Martland, Dickson, and de Grandpré JJ) (dissenting): There are two issues in this appeal which is here by leave of this Court. The first is whether a certain transaction and, in particular, a certain debenture, granted on a debtor's stock-in-trade in pursuance of the transaction between the debtor and the respondent creditor, was a fraudulent preference that was impeachable under ss. 3 and 4 of *The Fraudulent Preferences Act*, RSS 1965, c. 397; and the second is whether, if it was so impeachable, those provisions of the provincial Act were *ultra vires* as an invasion of exclusive federal power in relation to bankruptcy and insolvency or, alternatively, were inoperative in the face of the preference provisions of the *Bankruptcy Act*, RSC 1970, c. B-3.

The appellant is trustee in bankruptcy of Kozan Furniture (Yorkton) Ltd. pursuant to a receiving order of November 19, 1968. On November 19, 1966, Kozan entered into a transaction with a pressing creditor, the respondent, whereby it sold certain stock-in-trade to a third person (payment being made to the respondent which reduced Kozan's indebtedness accordingly) and also agreed to give the respondent a debenture on its stock-in-trade for its remaining indebtedness. The debenture was executed on or about March 20, 1967, and duly registered. After the receiving order against Kozan was made, proceedings were taken by the appellant trustee in bankruptcy to set aside the transaction of November 19, 1966, as constituting a fraudulent preference under the provincial *Fraudulent Preferences Act* and to recover the money paid to the respondent and to annul the debenture.

MacPherson J found that Kozan was insolvent at the time of the transaction of November 19, 1966, that there was a concurrent intention of Kozan and the respondent to give and receive a preference, and that, consequently, both the payment made to the respondent and the debenture constituted fraudulent preferences under the provincial statute and were hence impeachable. On appeal, this judgment was set aside on the view of the majority of the Saskatchewan Court of Appeal that the appellant had failed to prove that Kozan was insolvent on November 19, 1966. The trial judge was not called upon to deal with any constitutional issue, and the majority of the Court of Appeal did not have to do so in view of its finding on insolvency. Hall JA who dissented supported the trial judge's finding of insolvency, and in a one sentence assertion, in reliance upon *Re Panfab Corp. Ltd.*, he rejected the contention that *The Fraudulent Preferences Act* was *ultra vires*.

I would not interfere with the findings of the judge of first instance that Kozan was insolvent at the material time and that Kozan intended to give and the respondent intended to receive a preference. This is the view of my brother Spence who, in exhaustive reasons, also concluded that *The Fraudulent Preferences Act* as a whole was not *ultra vires* nor was either s. 3 or s. 4 inoperative in the face of the *Bankruptcy Act*. I have a different opinion on the constitutional issue in this case, as appears from what now follows. That issue does not invite this Court to pronounce on the validity of provincial legislation dealing with fraudulent conveyances or with fraudulent transactions in general. Thus, to take as an example the *Fraudulent Conveyances Act*, RSO 1970, c. 182, nothing said in these reasons is to be taken as impugning the validity of that or similar enactments. They do not, *ex facie*, depend on proof of insolvency or on bankruptcy. In so far as any of the case law, some of it canvassed by my brother Spence, relates to such legislation and carries it into a consideration of the validity of provincial preference legislation which depends, as do ss. 3 and 4 of the Saskatchewan *Fraudulent Preferences Act*, on a condition of insolvency, I find it inapt for the determination of the constitutional question in this appeal.

Sections 3 and 4 aforesaid are in the following terms: …

Sections 8, 9, 10 and 11, to which each of the foregoing provisions is subject, do not affect the constitutional issue, being concerned with *bona fide* sales or payments to innocent purchasers, to valid sales for consideration and to protection of security given up by a creditor. The present cases does not involve ss. 8 to 11.

I approach the question of validity on principle and on authority. So far as principle is concerned, the starting point is in relevant words of the *British North America Act*, namely s. 91(21), "bankruptcy and insolvency," as they relate to s. 92(13), "property and civil rights in the Province." The elucidation of the meaning and scope of s. 91(21), as of the meaning and scope of any other heads of legislative power, can hardly ever be a purely abstract exercise, even where an attempt is made at neutral definition; but I see no reason why judicial pronouncements, especially at the appellate level where they are those of the Court, should not be considered as throwing light upon the integrity of the head of power in the scheme of the *British North America Act* as a whole.

Four things stand out. First, s. 91(21) is an exclusive federal power; second, it is a power confided to the Parliament of Canada notwithstanding anything else in the Act; third, it is a power, like the criminal law power, whose ambit, did not and does not lie frozen under conceptions held of bankruptcy and insolvency in 1867: see the *Farmers' Creditors Arrangement Act* reference, *Attorney-General for British Columbia v. Attorney General for Canada*, at pp. 402-403; and, fourth, the term "insolvency" in s. 91(21) has as much an independent operation in the reservation of an exclusive area of legislative competence to the Parliament of Canada as the term "bankruptcy"; see *Canadian Bankers Association v. Attorney-General of Saskatchewan*, per Rand J, at p. 46.

The view taken by the Privy Council and by this Court as to the meaning of "insolvency," as well after as before the abolition of Privy Council appeals, has been a uniform one. Lord Thankerton, speaking for the Privy Council in the *Farmers' Creditors Arrangement Act* reference, *supra*, at p. 402, expressed it as follows:

> In a general sense, insolvency means inability to meet one's debts or obligations; in a technical sense, it means the condition or standard of inability to meet debts or obligations, upon the occurrence of which the statutory law enables a creditor to intervene with the assistance of a Court, to stop individual action by creditors and to secure administration of the debtor's assets in the general interest of creditors; the law also generally allows the debtor to apply for the same administration.

This definition was referred to with approval in the majority judgment of the Supreme Court of Canada delivered by Kerwin CJC in *Reference re Validity of the Orderly Payment of Debts Act, 1959 (Alta.)*, at p. 576. Earlier in *Reference re Alberta Debt Adjustment Act*, at p. 40, Duff CJC speaking for all but one of the members of the Court took as an additional ground for invalidating the challenged provincial legislation in that case that the powers of the provincial statutory tribunal set up under that legislation would normally "come into operation when a state of insolvency exists"; and he continued: "It is not too much to say that it is for the purpose of dealing with the affairs of debtors who are pressed and unable to pay their debts as they fall due that these powers and duties are created." If it is for Parliament alone to deal with insolvency, indeed to define it where it chooses to do so and to leave it otherwise to judicial definition, there can be no argument about unlawful invasion of provincial power in relation to property and civil rights. A limitation upon such power necessarily inheres in the federal catalogue of powers in s. 91, and it was recognized as early as 1880 in *Cushing v. Dupuy*, at p. 415, in respect of the federal bankruptcy and insolvency power.

I refer to two other propositions before turning to what I consider to be the relevant cases. First, there is the well-recognized proposition that federal abstinence from legislation in relation to an exclusive head of legislative power does not leave that legislative area open to provincial action: see *Union Colliery Co. v. Bryden*, at p. 588. The principle of our Constitution as it relates to legislative power is not one of simple concurrency of authority subject only to a variable doctrine of paramountcy. Exclusiveness is central to the scheme of distribution, save as to a specified number of concurrent powers, such as those in s. 95. It is only under the umbrella of the doctrine of exclusiveness that the relative scope of federal and provincial authority is assessed, the assessment being carried forward to determine whether there is preclusion or supercession where both federal and provincial legislation are in competition. This brings me to the second point. I take the same view here that was taken by Duff CJC in the *Alberta Debt Adjustment Act* reference and I adopt his words at p. 40, namely that although the motives of a provincial Legislature may be laudable ones, it is precluded from seeking to realize its object by entering into a field not open to it.

Attorney-General of Ontario v. Attorney-General for Canada, generally known as the *Voluntary Assignments* case, stands as the general support for provincial legislation that is challenged in the present case. It concerned only one section, s. 9, of the *Ontario Assignments and Preferences Act*, RSO 1887, c. 124, first enacted in 1885 by 1885 (Can.), c. 26. That section was as follows:

> An assignment for the general benefit of creditors under this Act shall take precedence of all judgments and of all executions not completely executed by payment, subject to the lien, if any, of an execution creditor for his costs, where there is but one execution in the sheriff's hands, or to the lien, if any, of the creditor for his costs, who has the first execution in the sherriff's hands.

This Act replaced the earlier pre-Confederation legislation found in CSUC 1859, c. 6, under the title *The Indigent Debtors Act*, which was continued in the post-Confederation legislation of Ontario as *An Act respecting The Fraudulent Preference of Creditors by persons in insolvent circumstances*, and included in RSO 1877, c. 118. What is significant in this earlier legislation is that (as set out in s. 2 of RSO 1877, c. 118) it dealt with "any person being at the time in insolvent circumstances or unable to pay his debts in full, or knowing himself to be on the eve of insolvency." The substituted Act of 1885 continued the reference to insolvency in respect of preferences, but it also introduced new provisions respecting assignments for the benefit of creditors and these provisions, as was noted in the *Voluntary Assignments* case, were not predicated on insolvency and, indeed, were to a large degree separated from the preference provisions of the Act, as is reflected in s. 3 of RSO 1887, c. 124.

Certainly, as the Privy Council noted, the challenged provision, s. 9, had to be taken in the context of the entire Act. There is no doubt, as well, that the issue of validity was recognized as arising at a time when there was no federal bankruptcy or insolvency legislation in force, the only such legislation, the *Insolvency Act* of 1875 having been repealed in 1880 by 1880 (Can.), c. 1. The majority of the Ontario Court of Appeal, to which the question of the validity of s. 9 had been referred, found that it was *ultra vires* as invading exclusive federal power in relation to bankruptcy and insolvency; see *Re Assignments and Preferences Act, Section 9*. The reversal of this judgment by the Privy Council was accompanied by an acknowledgement of the broad scope of federal power under s. 91(21) when affirmatively exercised but it was held that this power was not invaded by an enactment relating to an assignment that was purely voluntary.

The explanation for this result is found in two passages of the Privy Council's reasons. First, "it is to be observed that an assignment for the general benefit of creditors has long been known to the jurisprudence of this country and also of Canada, and has its force and effect at common law quite independently of any system of bankruptcy or insolvency, or any legislation relating thereto" (at p. 198). Second, "the operation of an assignment for the benefit of creditors was precisely the same, whether the assignor was or was not insolvent. ... The validity of the assignment and its effect would in no way depend on the insolvency of the assignor, and their Lordships think it clear that the 9th section would equally apply whether the assignor was or was not insolvent" (at p. 199). What is evident, therefore, from that case is that, unlike the situation here, the operation of the provincial enactment did not depend on insolvency and the Privy Council was willing to treat s. 9 as having an object that was independent of it. This may even be a supportable view today, albeit there is a range of existing federal legislation dealing with bankruptcy and insolvency. I should note, however, that the majority judgment of this Court in *Reference re the Validity of the Orderly Payment of Debts Act, 1959 (Alta.)*, at pp. 576-577, Kerwin CJC referring to the *Voluntary Assignments* reference, said "it is doubtful whether in view of later pronouncements of the Judicial Committee it would at this date be decided in the same sense, even in the absence of Dominion legislation upon the subject of bankruptcy and insolvency."

The later pronouncements of the Privy Council include its judgment in the *Alberta Debt Adjustment Act* reference, as well as in the *Farmers' Creditors Arrangement Act* reference, *supra*. Equally important is the judgment of this Court in *Canadian Bankers Association v. Attorney-General of Saskatchewan*, dealing with the validity of provincial moratorium legislation. It was in line with the decision in the *Alberta Debt Adjustment Act* reference in finding an invasion of federal power in relation to bankruptcy and insolvency. I think it enough, for present purposes, to refer to what Locke J, speaking for the majority of the Court, said, at p. 42:

> Power to declare a moratorium for the relief of the residents of a Province generally in some great emergency, such as existed in 1914 and in the days of the lengthy depression in the thirties is one thing, but power to intervene between insolvent debtors and their creditors irrespective of the reasons which have rendered the debtor unable to meet his liabilities is something entirely different.

Although judgments of the Privy Council and of this Court (and I add to those already cited *Royal Bank of Canada v. Larue*) have recognized the broad power of Parliament to embrace in its legislation in relation to bankruptcy or insolvency provisions which might otherwise fall within provincial competence, I know of no case in those Courts, other than *Ladore v. Bennett*, where provincial legislation has been sustained, either in the absence of or in the face of federal legislation, when such provincial legislation depends for its operation only upon insolvency. *Ladore v. Bennett* can best be explained as involving municipal reorganization and hence as being concerned with the amalgamation and financial restructuring of units of local government for which the provincial Legislature has a direct responsibility, albeit some of the municipalities involved in the legislatively-directed reorganization were insolvent. It is, indeed, a special case of a piece of special legislation enacted in pursuance of the power conferred by s. 92(8) of the *British North America Act*, and I do not regard it as offering any lead to continuing legislation relating to private debtors and their creditors.

It is plain to me that if provincial legislation avowedly directed to insolvency, and to transactions between debtor and creditor consummated in a situation of insolvency, can be sustained as validly enacted, unless overborne by competent federal legislation, there is a serious breach of the principle of exclusiveness which embraces insolvency under s. 91(21). This Court so held in a series of cases where the encroachment on the federal bankruptcy and insolvency power was less obvious than that exhibited here. I refer, of course, to the *Alberta Debt Adjustment Act* reference, *supra*, to the *Canadian Bankers' Association* case, *supra*, and to the *Orderly Payment of Debts Act 1959 (Alta.)* reference, *supra*. It would be a curious reversal of the proposition, enunciated in *Madden v. Nelson and Fort Sheppard Railway Co.*, namely, that you cannot do indirectly what you cannot do directly, to hold that the Province can do directly what it cannot do indirectly.

The case put forward by the appellant and by the intervening Provinces which supported him goes even farther. It is contended that notwithstanding the existence of federal bankruptcy legislation dealing with preferences, the challenged provincial legislation can still operate in respect of a particular preference which is given outside of the time limits within which the federal control operates, so long at least as the provincial provision is not more stringent.

I do not follow this line of reasoning, especially on the submission of greater or lesser stringency. The relevant federal provision is s. 73 of the *Bankruptcy Act* [see now s. 95] which reads as follows: ...

This provision cannot be taken in isolation. The *Bankruptcy Act* is a code on the subject of bankruptcy and insolvency, defining what is an act of bankruptcy, who is an insolvent person, prescribing what are vulnerable settlements as well as what are vulnerable preferences, declaring what is comprised in a bankrupt's estate, providing for priorities in distribution and for rateable distribution. It provides also, as in the present s. 31(1), for the making of an assignment by an insolvent person for the benefit of creditors as well as providing by s. 24(1)(a) that it is an act of bankruptcy to make an assignment for the benefit of creditors whether the assignment is or is not authorized by the *Bankruptcy Act*. In short, apart from the question whether provincial legislation predicated on insolvency is *ipso facto* invalid, I see no room for any assertion that such provincial legislation can continue to have operative effect in the face of the scope of the *Bankruptcy Act* embracing both bankruptcy and insolvency in its provisions.

It is worth a reminder that there is no common law of bankruptcy and insolvency, and hence it cannot be said that there was an existing common law course of decision which was being embraced by provincial legislation. The common law did not distinguish the fraudulent from the insolvent debtor; it was through legislation that such a distinction was made. If a provincial Legislature wishes to proscribe fraudulent transactions, it is compelled by the *British North America Act* to ensure that its legislation dealing with such transactions does not focus on insolvency.

. . .

I wish now to address myself to an issue which, I think, has influenced the approach by single judges to the constitutional question in this case, and wrongly so. That issue is the undesirability of interfering with what appeared to be a practical way of reaching as many alleged preferences in fraud of creditors as possible, to use provincial legislation where federal legislation did not reach far enough, and to use provincial insolvency legislation if nothing else was available. Hence, the approach by way of construction, albeit a dip into a constitutional area was inevitable, avoiding a direct constitutional confrontation.

There are cases even in this Court and on this very subject which have proceeded on a straight construction basis to examine whether operative effect can be given to provincial legislation in the face of a federal enactment. Two examples are *Traders Finance Corp. Ltd. v. Levesque*, and *Produits de Caoutchouc Marquis Inc. v. Trottier*. I do not regard either of these cases as requiring a decision on constitutional grounds. The *Traders Finance* case concerned a largely procedural matter, namely, whether the failure of a trustee in bankruptcy to impeach a preference illegal under the *Bankruptcy Act*, precluded a suit by a creditor to that end. The *Trottier* case dealt with the effect of the *Bankruptcy Act* on the extent of a landlord's claim to rank as a preferred creditor.

· · ·

I conclude, therefore, as follows. Provincial legislation which purports to provide for impeachment of preferences to creditors given by a person who is then insolvent, where insolvency is the *sine qua non* of impeachability, is invalid as a direct invasion of exclusive federal power in relation to bankruptcy and insolvency. Hence, ss. 3 and 4 of Saskatchewan *Fraudulent Preferences Act* are *ultra vires*. Moreover, in so far as these sections prescribe an impeachment period which enables a creditor to set aside a preference made beyond the period fixed by the *Bankruptcy Act*, and hence not impeachable under that Act, it interferes with the operation of the *Bankruptcy Act* and is, indeed, repugnant to it. It must be remembered that where, as in the present case, there has been a receiving order, the intrusion of provincial legislation relating to transactions entered into by an insolvent, must interfere with the rateable distribution of the bankrupt's property according to the scheme of distribution prescribed by the *Bankruptcy Act*. Whether that scheme is faulty in the view of a Court is immaterial; the correction must come from the responsible Legislature. No more under bankruptcy and insolvency law than under the criminal law can a Province make unlawful what is lawful under valid federal legislation, nor make lawful what is unlawful under valid federal legislation.

· · ·

SPENCE J (for the majority): ... I have dealt with what, in my view, are the main cases upon the subject in Canada. Upon considering them *all*, as well as the decision of the Judicial Committee in *A.G. of Ontario v. A.G. for Canada, supra*, I have come to the conclusion that the better view is to confine the effect of what is now s. 73 of the *Bankruptcy Act* to providing for the invalidity of transactions within its exact scope. To that extent, the Parliament of Canada, by valid legislation upon "bankruptcy" and "insolvency," has covered the field but has refrained from completely covering the whole field of transactions avoided by provincial legislation. I am of the opinion that the enactment in 1949 of the provisions now found in s. 50(6) of the *Bankruptcy Act* is a plain indication that Parliament recognized that provisions in provincial statutes dealing with preferential transactions were still valid provincial enactments in reference to "property" and "civil rights" and were valuable aids to trustees in bankruptcy in attacking the validity of such transactions and should be available to the said trustees in bankruptcy.

I am assisted in coming to this conclusion by the view which I believe was behind the Lord Chancellor's reasons in *A.G. of Ontario v. A.G. for Canada, supra*, that the words "bankruptcy" and "insolvency" in s. 91, para. 21, of the *British North America Act* were aimed at legislative schemes which had the purpose of governing the distribution of a debtor's property amongst his creditors. There may well be, and there are, provisions in such legislative schemes, i.e., the *Bankruptcy Act*, dealing with "property" and "civil rights." Such provisions are properly ancillary to the bankruptcy and insolvency legislation, and to the extent to which they do overcome existing valid provincial legislation and bar future provincial legislation *contra* thereto but do not purport to extend beyond that point to invalidate other valid provincial legislation upon "property" and "civil rights."

. . .

BEETZ J: I have had the advantage of reading the opinions of the Chief Justice and of Mr. Justice Spence. I agree with Mr. Justice Spence. To his reasons for judgment I would however like to add some of my own.

The power to repress fraud by avoiding fraudulent conveyances and preferences is an indisputable part of provincial jurisdiction over property and civil rights. The risk of fraud is increased when a debtor finds himself in a situation of impending or actual insolvency and, in my view, provincial laws can, without undergoing a change in nature, focus upon that situation as upon a proper occasion to attain their object. Given their purpose, they do not cease to be laws in relation to property and civil rights simply because they are timely and effective or because Parliament could enact similar laws in relation to bankruptcy and insolvency.

Insolvency has been defined by Lord Thankerton in the *Farmers' Creditors Arrangement Act* reference, *Attorney-General for British Columbia v. Attorney-General for Canada*, at p. 402:

> In a general sense, insolvency means inability to meet one's debts or obligations; in a technical sense, it means the condition or standard of inability to meet debts or obligations, upon the occurrence of which the statutory law enables a creditor to intervene, with the assistance of a Court, to stop individual action by creditors and to secure administration of the debtor's assets in the general interest of creditors; the law also generally allows the debtor to apply for the same administration.

The primary meaning of "insolvency" in s. 91.21 of the Constitution is insolvency in the technical sense, not in the general sense. This Lord Thankerton made just a few lines after the passage quoted above: with respect to the jurisdiction of Parliament under s. 91.21, he referred to "… the statutory conditions of insolvency which enabled a creditor or the debtor to invoke the aid of the bankruptcy laws. …"

There is no common law of bankruptcy and insolvency in the technical sense, but the disruptions resulting from insolvency in the general sense had of necessity to be taken into account by general legal systems such as the common law and the civil law. Insolvency lies at the core of those parts of the common law and of the civil law which relate to such matters as mortgage, pledge, pawning, suretyship and the securing of debts generally which are implicitly or explicitly predicated on the risk of insolvency and which produce their full effect when the risk has been converted into reality; so it is with the rules which determine the rank of privileges and hypothecs or which ordain that an insolvent or bankrupt debtor shall lose the benefit of the term (art. 1092 of the Quebec *Civil Code*). Some of the most fundamental principles of the civil law are expressed in arts. 1980, 1981 and 1982 of the Quebec *Civil Code*:

>   Art. 1980. Whoever incurs a personal obligation, renders liable for its fulfilment all his
> property, moveable and immoveable, present and future, except such property as is specially
> declared to be exempt from seizure.
>   Art. 1981. The property of a debtor is the common pledge of his creditors, and where
> they claim together they share its price rateably, unless there are amongst them legal causes
> of preference.
>   Art. 1982. The legal causes of preference are privileges and hypothecs.

Although not expressly referred to, insolvency forms the web of these articles; there would be little need for them, particularly the last two, were it not for insolvency. But I cannot be persuaded that they are not laws relating to property and civil rights.

When the exclusive power to make laws in relation to bankruptcy and insolvency was bestowed upon Parliament, it was not intended to remove from the general legal systems which regulated property and civil rights a cardinal concept essential to the coherence of those systems. The main purpose was to give to Parliament exclusive jurisdiction over the establishment by statute of a particular system regulating the distribution of a debtor's assets. However, given the nature of general legal systems, the primary jurisdiction of Parliament cannot easily be exercised together with its incidental powers without some degree of overlap in which case federal law prevails. On the other hand, provincial jurisdiction over property and civil rights should not be measured by the ultimate reach of federal power over bankruptcy and insolvency any more than provincial competence in relation to the administration of justice can be determined by every conceivable and potential use of the criminal law power. This, I believe, is the general import of the *Voluntary Assignments* case, *Attorney-General of Ontario v. Attorney-General for Canada*. The Judicial Committee declared that the validity of the provision it had to consider and of the assignments made under the authority of that provision did not depend on the insolvency of the assignor: an assignment was also open "to any debtor who might deem his insolvency doubtful. ..." All that one can say is that legislation of the type considered in the *Voluntary Assignments* case presents little interest for prosperous persons; it is of concern chiefly to debtors in strained circumstances whose solvency is, at best, uncertain. It should be noted that the impugned voluntary assignments enactment did not only deal with assignments: it also provided that an assignment for the general benefit of creditors should take *precedence* of all judgments and of all executions not completely executed by payment.

I am reinforced in those views by a consideration of the *Civil Code of Lower Canada, 1866*, in light of *An Act Respecting Insolvency, 1864* (Can.), c. 17. Both were enacted at a time when Confederation was being discussed. The French title of *The Insolvent Act of 1864*, was "*l'Acte concernant la faillite, 1864*," the word "faillite" being the one now currently used to translate the word "bankruptcy." In spite of its English title, the Act was in fact a bankruptcy act. It applied to all persons in Upper Canada and to traders only in Lower Canada and it contained detailed provisions relating to fraudulent conveyances and preferences. Nevertheless, the *Civil Code* comprised a section of nine articles (arts. 1032 to 1040 incl.), entitled "Of the Avoidance of Contracts and Payments made in Fraud of Creditors," applicable to traders and to non-traders alike except where *The Insolvent Act* was to prevail. The legislative history of those articles was set forth by Mr. Justice

Pigeon in *Gingras v. General Motors Products of Canada Ltd.* Some have been amended. It will suffice to quote a few of them as they then read:

> 1034. A gratuitous contract is deemed to be made with intent to defraud, if the debtor be insolvent at the time of making it.
>
> 1035. An onerous contract made by an insolvent debtor with a person who knows him to be insolvent is deemed to be made with intent to defraud.
>
> 1036. Every payment by an insolvent debtor to a creditor knowing his insolvency, is deemed to be made with intent to defraud, and the creditor may be compelled to restore the amount or thing received or the value thereof, for the benefit of the creditors according to their respective rights.
>
> 1037. Further provisions concerning the presumption of fraud and the nullity of acts done in contemplation of insolvency are contained in *The Insolvent Act of 1864.*

Article 17.23 of the Code defines "bankruptcy" ("faillite") as meaning "the condition of a trader who has discontinued his payments"; insolvency was left undefined, the word being clearly used by the Code in the general sense. Even though articles 1034, 1035 and 1036 are predicated on insolvency, the Commissioners appointed for codifying the laws of Lower Canada in civil matters would have been astonished had they been told that those articles formed no part of the civil law: except perhaps for art. 1036 which appears to be an improvement of relatively modern origin (although it was not considered new law), such provisions were derived from a division of Roman law called Paulian law and, from time immemorial, had constituted a pivot of the civil law system. Other provisions of the Code are of the same nature and also depend on insolvency, such as art. 803 (revocation of a gift made by an insolvent debtor), and art. 2023 (hypothec consented to by an insolvent debtor). Other provisions still, although not expressly predicated on insolvency are related to insolvency and to the protection of creditors, for instance, art. 655 (the creditors of an heir who renounces a succession to their prejudice can have the renunciation rescinded and accept the succession in his stead).

The constitutional validity of such provisions is not in issue: they antedate Confederation and were continued by s. 129 of the Constitution. The only issue which could arise with respect to them is whether they are in conflict with federal law. But the content and integrity of the *Civil Code* are indicative of the extent of provincial jurisdiction over property and civil rights: *Citizens Insurance Company of Canada v. Parsons*, at pp. 110 and 111. The fact that there existed a statutory scheme of bankruptcy and insolvency to which the Code explicitly referred as to a distinct and specific body of law, without curtailing for that reason its own normal ambit, illustrates how the respective domains of property and civil rights and of bankruptcy and insolvency were viewed during the very period when the federal union was being discussed; it also reveals how it was intended that the distribution of powers should operate with respect to those domains.

In the *Alberta Debt Adjustment Act* reference, in *Canadian Bankers Association v. Attorney-General of Saskatchewan*, and in *Reference re Validity of the Orderly Payment of Debts Act, 1959* (Alta.), the various provincial laws found ultra vires were predicated upon insolvency. But they went further and set up elaborate statutory schemes involving one or more of the following features: the denial of creditors' access to courts or the restriction of their right to enforce their claims, the establishment of administrative boards, mediation, composition, arrangements, moratoriums, consolidation orders, staying of proceedings and the relief of debtors from liability to pay their debts. No such features are to be found in the presently impugned Saskatchewan statute where all that is at stake is the avoidance of fraudulent acts for the better enforcement of civil obligations. Some doubt was expressed in the *Orderly Payment of Debts Act*, (1959) (Alta.) reference at pp. 576 and 577 as to whether the Voluntary Assignments case would have been decided in the same way at a later date even in the absence of federal legislation on the subject of bankruptcy and insolvency. But even if this doubt was not expressed in an obiter dictum, I would regard it as questioning not the general principles enunciated in the Voluntary Assignments case, but their application in that particular instance. Accordingly, I do not think that those previous decisions of the Judicial Committee and of this Court preclude my abiding by my conclusions: laws provincial in their purpose, object and nature as those under attack cannot be rendered ultra vires because of virtual federal paramountcy: they can only become inoperative in case of actual repugnancy with valid federal laws.

On this latter point, I believe the test of repugnancy to be applied in this case should not differ from the one which was admitted in *Provincial Secretary of Prince Edward Island v. Egan; O'Grady v. Sparling*, and *Ross v. The Registrar of Motor Vehicles et al.*: provincial law gives way to federal law in case of operational conflict. Even if the test be one of conflict of legislative policies entailing no operational inconsistency and depending solely "upon the intention of the paramount Legislature" as was said by Dixon J, in a passage of *Ex p. McLean*, at p. 483, quoted by Mr. Justice Pigeon in the *Ross* case (at p. 15), I am of the view that s. 50, subs. (6) of the *Bankruptcy Act* provides a clear indication that Parliament, far from intending to depart from the rule of operational conflict, did in fact aim at the highest possible degree of legal integration of federal and provincial laws: attacks upon transactions within the three-month period provided by s. 73 of the *Bankruptcy Act* constitute a minimum but the trustee in bankruptcy is entitled to avail himself of all other rights and remedies provided by provincial law "as supplementary to and in addition to the rights and remedies provided by" the *Bankruptcy Act*.

NOTES AND QUESTIONS

1. Can the Privy Council's decision in the *Voluntary Assignments* case be reconciled with the Supreme Court's decision in the *Orderly Payment of Debts Act Reference*, above? Was Kerwin CJC correct in suggesting in the latter case that *Voluntary Assignments* would be decided differently today? Where does the majority judgment in *Robinson v. Countrywide Factors*, above, fit into this spectrum of judicial views? In other s. 91 areas of the Canadian constitution (for example, trade and commerce and criminal law), the courts have generally allowed considerable play for the exercise of provincial powers under s. 92(13) where there is no direct conflict between the federal and provincial legislation. In the insolvency area, however, the Supreme Court and the Privy Council (before the abolition of appeals to the Privy Council) have generally, though not uniformly, been hostile to upholding the exercise of provincial powers under s. 92(13). Why is this?

2. Generally speaking, the provinces have retained the fraudulent transfer and preferential payment provisions discussed by the Supreme Court in *Robinson*. With a view to reducing the overlap between the federal and provincial provisions and the complexity of litiga-

tion arising from the duplication, a group of law teachers making submissions in 2003 on bankruptcy law reform to the Senate Banking, Trade and Commerce Committee recommended adoption of a provision in the BIA staying any provincial action where proceedings to set aside pre-bankruptcy transactions were initiated after the debtor's bankruptcy. The recommendation was not accepted and no such provision appears in the 2005-7 BIA amendments. However, these amendments did substantially revise the earlier provisions. For the details, see Chapter 5.

Sam Lévy & Associés Inc. v. Azco Mining Inc.
[2001] 3 SCR 978[2]

BINNIE J (for the Court): [1] The long arm of the Quebec Superior Court sitting in Bankruptcy reached out to the appellant in Vancouver, British Columbia, in respect of a claim for shares and warrants and other debts allegedly due to the bankrupt which the trustee in bankruptcy values in excess of $4.5 million. The appellant protested that the dispute, which involves the financing of an African gold mine, has nothing to do with Quebec. It argues that the claim of the respondent trustee in bankruptcy is an ordinary civil claim that rests entirely on agreements that are to be interpreted according to the laws of British Columbia. For this and other reasons of convenience and efficiency, the appellant says, the claim ought to proceed in British Columbia. The bankruptcy court and the Quebec Court of Appeal rejected these submissions and, in my view, the further appeal to this Court ought also to be dismissed.

· · ·

III. Relevant Statutory Provisions

[16]

Bankruptcy and Insolvency Act, RSC 1985, c. B-3
2.(1) In this Act
"locality of a debtor" means the principal place
    (a) where the debtor has carried on business during the year immediately preceding his bankruptcy,
    (b) where the debtor has resided during the year immediately preceding his bankruptcy, or
    (c) in cases not coming within paragraph (a) or (b), where the greater portion of the property of the debtor is situated;
    30.(1) The trustee may, with the permission of the inspectors, do all or any of the following things:

· · ·

    (d) bring, institute or defend any action or other legal proceeding relating to the property of the bankrupt;

---

[2] Also reported *sub nom. Re Eagle International Ltd.* (2001), 30 CBR (4th) 105.

43.(5) The petition shall be filed in the court having jurisdiction in the judicial district of the locality of the debtor.

72.(1) The provisions of this Act shall not be deemed to abrogate or supersede the substantive provisions of any other law or statute relating to property and civil rights that are not in conflict with this Act, and the trustee is entitled to avail himself of all rights and remedies provided by that law or statute as supplementary to and in addition to the rights and remedies provided by this Act.

183.(1) The following courts are invested with such jurisdiction at law and in equity as will enable them to exercise original, auxiliary and ancillary jurisdiction in bankruptcy and in other proceedings authorized by this Act during their respective terms, as they are now, or may be hereafter, held, and in vacation and in chambers:

· · ·

(b) in the Province of Quebec, the Superior Court;

(c) in the Provinces of Nova Scotia and British Columbia, the Supreme Court;

187.(7) The court, on satisfactory proof that the affairs of the bankrupt can be more economically administered within another bankruptcy district or division, or for other sufficient cause, may by order transfer any proceedings under this Act that are pending before it to another bankruptcy district or division.

188.(1) An order made by the court under this Act shall be enforced in the courts having jurisdiction in bankruptcy elsewhere in Canada in the same manner in all respects as if the order had been made by the court hereby required to enforce it.

(2) All courts and the officers of all courts shall severally act in aid of and be auxiliary to each other in all matters of bankruptcy, and an order of one court seeking aid, with a request to another court, shall be deemed sufficient to enable the latter court to exercise, in regard to the matters directed by the order, such jurisdiction as either the court that made the request or the court to which the request is made could exercise in regard to similar matters within its jurisdiction.

Bankruptcy and Insolvency General Rules, CRC, c. 368 (am. SOR/98-240)

3. In cases not provided for in the Act or these Rules, the courts shall apply, within their respective jurisdictions, their ordinary procedure to the extent that that procedure is not inconsistent with the Act or these Rules.

Civil Code of Québec, SQ 1991, c. 64

3135. Even though a Quebec authority has jurisdiction to hear a dispute, it may exceptionally and on an application by a party, decline jurisdiction if it considers that the authorities of another country are in a better position to decide.

· · ·

3148. In personal actions of a patrimonial nature, a Québec authority has jurisdiction where

· · ·

(5) the defendant submits to its jurisdiction.

However, a Québec authority has no jurisdiction where the parties, by agreement, have chosen to submit all existing or future disputes between themselves relating to a specified legal relationship to a foreign authority or to an arbitrator, unless the defendant submits to the jurisdiction of the Quebec authority.

IV. Analysis

[17] Parliament has conferred on the bankruptcy court the capacity and authority to exercise "original, auxiliary and ancillary jurisdiction in bankruptcy and in other proceedings authorized by this Act" (s. 183(1)). On the face of it, the intent of this provision is to confer on the bankruptcy court powers and duties co-extensive with Parliament's jurisdiction over "Bankruptcy" under s. 91(21) of the *Constitution Act, 1867* except insofar as that jurisdiction has been limited or specifically assigned elsewhere by Parliament itself.

[18] While the appellant's motion simply asked that the dispute be transferred to the Vancouver Division of the Supreme Court of British Columbia sitting in Bankruptcy (thereby appearing to concede that the dispute is properly dealt with as a bankruptcy matter), its motion also contended that the trustee's claims are "exclusively contractual" (para. 6) and that the "Superior Court of the Bankruptcy Division of Hull does not have jurisdiction to hear this contractual claim against Azco" (para. 20). Moreover, much of its oral argument suggested that the dispute ought to be tried in the ordinary civil courts. In addition the appellant takes the position that Quebec is not the convenient forum to deal with this dispute, and that the Quebec Superior Court sitting in Bankruptcy lacks a sufficiently long arm to require Azco to take its witnesses east to litigate. The proper forum, it says, is British Columbia because there is no substantial connection at all between this case and the Province of Quebec.

. . .

2. Did the Bankruptcy Court Thereby Acquire Jurisdiction to Deal with Matters Affecting the Bankrupt Estate Arising in British Columbia?

[25] The Act establishes a nationwide scheme for the adjudication of bankruptcy claims. As Rinfret J pointed out in *Boily v. McNulty*, [1928] SCR 182, at p. 186: "This is a federal statute that concerns the whole country, and it considers territory from that point of view." The national implementation of bankruptcy decisions rendered by a court within a particular province is achieved through the cooperative network of superior courts of the provinces and territories under s. 188: *In re Mount Royal Lumber & Flooring Co.* (1926), 8 CBR 240 (Que. CA), per Rivard JA, at p. 246, "The *Bankruptcy Act* is federal and the orders of the Quebec Superior Court sitting as a bankruptcy court under that Act are enforceable in Ontario … ." See also: *Associated Freezers of Canada Inc. (Trustee of) v. Retail, Wholesale Canada, Local 1015* (1996), 39 CBR (3d) 311 (NSCA), at p. 314, and *Kansa General International Insurance Co. (Liquidation de)*, [1998] RJQ 1380 (CA), at p. 1389.

[26] The trustees will often (and perhaps increasingly) have to deal with debtors and creditors residing in different parts of the country. They cannot do that efficiently, to borrow the phrase of Idington J in *Stewart v. LePage* (1916), 53 SCR 337, at p. 345, "if everyone is to be at liberty to interfere and pursue his own notions of his rights of litigation." *Stewart* dealt with the winding up of a federally incorporated trust company in British Columbia. As a result of the winding up, a client in Prince Edward Island instituted a proceeding in the superior court of that province for a declaration that certain moneys held by the bankrupt trust company were held in trust and that the bankrupt trust com-

pany should be removed as trustee. This Court held that the dispute, despite its strong connection to Prince Edward Island, could not be brought before the court of that province without leave of the Supreme Court of British Columbia. Anglin J commented at p. 349:

> No doubt some inconvenience will be involved in such exceptional cases as this where the winding-up of the company is conducted in a province of the Dominion far distant from that in which persons interested as creditors or claimants may reside. But Parliament probably thought it necessary in the interest of prudent and economical winding-up that the court charged with that duty should have control not only of the assets and property found in the hands or possession of the company in liquidation, but also of all litigation in which it might be involved. The great balance of convenience is probably in favour of such single control though it may work hardship in some few cases.

[27] *Stewart* was, as stated, a winding-up case, but the legislative policy in favour of "single control" applies as well to bankruptcy. There is the same public interest in the expeditious, efficient and economical clean-up of the aftermath of a financial collapse. Section 188(1) ensures that orders made by a bankruptcy court sitting in one province can and will be enforced across the country.

[28] I have concluded that the jurisdiction of the Quebec Superior Court sitting in Bankruptcy was properly invoked by the petitioning creditors in this case but counsel for the appellant company says that his client, with its office in British Columbia, is not within its reach. The argument, in part, is that whatever the power of Parliament to confer national jurisdiction on a provincial superior court, that court is nevertheless provincially constituted, and for service of process its long arm statute must be complied with. The factual record does not show precisely how service of the trustee's petition was effected on the appellant, but if the appellant had any concerns regarding the proprieties of service of the petition to initiate proceedings against it, such concerns were waived when Azco did not raise them in its motion brought in Hull. A good deal of time was occupied on the appeal with arguments about how a Quebec court could acquire in personam jurisdiction over a corporation resident in British Columbia, and whether the Quebec rules for service *ex juris* applied. The argument that the Quebec Superior Court sitting in Bankruptcy cannot exercise in personam jurisdiction over creditors in another province under the Act is rejected for the reasons of national jurisdiction already mentioned. Any objections regarding service of process are answered by the fact that Azco not only appeared in Quebec but invoked the jurisdiction of the Quebec Superior Court sitting in Bankruptcy to transfer the proceedings pursuant to s. 187(7) of the Act to the bankruptcy court sitting in Vancouver. Any remaining issue with respect to in personam jurisdiction was thereby waived.

[29] Azco did not, of course, waive its objection to jurisdiction over the subject matter of this particular dispute. That was a major point in its motion. I turn now to that issue.

3. Are Contract Claims Nevertheless Excluded from Federal Bankruptcy Jurisdiction?

[30] The appellant's motion, as stated, argued that the trustee's claims against it are "exclusively contractual in nature" (para. 6) and that "[t]he Superior Court of the Bankruptcy Division of Hull does not have jurisdiction to hear this contractual claim against Azco" (para. 20). The theory underlying these contentions seems to be that contract claims relate to "Property and Civil Rights" within the meaning of s. 92(13) of the *Constitution Act, 1867* and on that account lie outside the jurisdiction of the bankruptcy court. At para. 42 of its factum, for example, the appellant argues:

> Contrary to what the Court of Appeal affirms, the trustee's claim is therefore purely contractual in nature, under the civil law. It is not a remedy specifically provided for under the BIA such as the application to have preferential payments declared void (see sections 91 to 100 BIA). The mere fact that the plaintiff is a trustee does not alter the nature of the claim and does not turn it into a bankruptcy dispute.

[31] Most bankruptcy issues, of course, present a property and civil rights aspect. It is true, however, that some of the decided cases which deny jurisdiction to the bankruptcy court do so on grounds that have a constitutional flavour, e.g., *In re Morris Lofsky* (1947), 28 CBR 164 (Ont. CA), per Roach JA, at p. 167; *Sigurdson v. Fidelity Ins. Co.* (1980), 35 CBR (NS) 75 (BCCA), at p. 102; *Re Holley* (1986), 54 OR (2d) 225 (Ont. CA); *In re Ireland* (1962), 5 CBR (NS) 91 (Que. Sup. Ct.), per Bernier J, at p. 94, and *Falvo Enterprises Ltd. v. Price Waterhouse Ltd.* (1981), 34 OR (2d) 336 (Ont. HCJ).

[32] It is therefore necessary to come to an understanding of what is included in the subject matter of "bankruptcy" within the meaning of s. 91(21) of the *Constitution Act, 1867*.

[33] In *In re The Moratorium Act* (Sask.), [1956] SCR 31, it was stated by Rand J, at p. 46, that:

> Bankruptcy is a well understood procedure by which an insolvent debtor's property is coercively brought under a judicial administration in the interests primarily of the creditors.

[34] The core concept of coercive administration appeared early in our bankruptcy jurisprudence. In *Union St. Jacques de Montréal v. Bélisle* (1874), LR 6 PC 31, Lord Selborne LC, speaking at p. 36 of general laws governing bankruptcy and insolvency, said: "The words describe in their known legal sense provisions made by law for the administration of the estates of persons who may become bankrupt or insolvent, according to rules and definitions prescribed by law, including of course the conditions in which that law is to be brought into operation, the manner in which it is to be brought into operation, and the effect of its operation."

[35] More helpful still was Lord Selborne's description of bankruptcy in the context of the English Act in *Ellis v. Silber* (1872), LR 8 Ch. App. 83, at p. 86:

> That which is to be done in bankruptcy is the administration in bankruptcy. The debtor and the creditors, as the parties to the administration in bankruptcy, are subject to that jurisdiction. The trustees or assignees, as the persons intrusted with that administration, are subject to that jurisdiction. The assets which come to their hands and the mode of administering

them are subject to that jurisdiction; and there may be, and I believe are, some special classes of transactions which, under special clauses of the Acts of Parliament, may be specially
dealt with as regards third parties. But the general proposition, that whenever the assignees
or trustees in bankruptcy or the trustees under such deeds as these have a demand at law or
in equity as against a stranger to the bankruptcy, then that demand is to be prosecuted in
the Court of Bankruptcy, appears to me to be a proposition entirely without the warrant of
anything in the Acts of Parliament, and wholly unsupported by any trace or vestige whatever of authority.

[36] Despite the fact that England is a unitary state without the constitutional limitations imposed by our division of powers, the courts in Canada have generally hewn ever
since 1874 to the basic dividing line between disputes related to the administration of the
bankrupt estate and disputes with "strangers to the bankruptcy." The principle is that if
the dispute relates to a matter that is outside even a generous interpretation of the administration of the bankruptcy, or the remedy is not one contemplated by the Act, the trustee
must seek relief in the ordinary civil courts. Thus in the Quebec case of *Re Ireland*, supra,
the trustee brought proceedings to determine who had the right to proceeds of insurance
policies taken out by the trustee on properties of the bankrupt estate. Bernier J concluded
that the Quebec Superior Court sitting in Bankruptcy lacked jurisdiction over the subject matter of the dispute. The controversy raised purely civil law questions and nothing
in the Act conferred on the bankruptcy court a special jurisdiction to entertain these
matters. Similar arguments prevailed in *Cry-O-Beef Ltd./Cri-O-Boeuf Ltée (Trustee of) v.
Caisse Populaire de Black-Lake* (1987), 66 CBR (NS) 19 (Que. CA); *In re Martin* (1953),
33 CBR 163 (Ont. SC), at p. 169; *In re Reynolds* (1928), 10 CBR 127 (Ont. SC), at p. 131;
Re Galaxy Interiors Ltd. (1971), 15 CBR (NS) 143 (Ont. SC); *Mancini (Trustee of) v. Fal-
coni* (1987), 65 CBR (NS) 246 (Ont. SC), and *In re Morris Lofsky*, supra, at p. 169.

[37] The Quebec Court of Appeal has perhaps led the argument for a more expansive
interpretation of what disputes properly come under the bankruptcy umbrella and can
therefore properly be litigated in the bankruptcy court: *Geoffrion v. Barnett*, [1970] CA
273; *Arctic Gardens inc. (Syndic de)*, [1990] RJQ 6 (CA); *Excavations Sanoduc inc. c.
Morency*, [1991] RDJ 423 (CA). See also the dissenting judgment of LeBel JA, as he then
was, in *Cry-O-Beef Ltd./Cri-O-Boeuf Ltée*, supra, and *In re Atlas Lumber Co. v. Grier and
Sons Ltd.* (1922), 3 CBR 226 (Que. Sup. Ct.); but the push is not confined to Quebec: *In
re Maple Leaf Fruit Co.* (1949), 30 CBR 23 (NSCA); *Re Westam Development Ltd.* (1967),
10 CBR (NS) 61 (BCCA), at p. 65; *Re M.B. Greer & Co.* (1953), 33 CBR 69 (Ont. SC), at
p. 70; *Re M.P. Industrial Mills Ltd.* (1972), 17 CBR 226 (Man. QB).

[38] It seems to me that the decided cases recognize that the word "Bankruptcy" in
s. 91(21) of the *Constitution Act, 1867* must be given a broad scope if it is to accomplish
its purpose. Anything less would unnecessarily complicate and undermine the economical and expeditious winding up of the bankrupt's affairs. Creation of a national jurisdiction in bankruptcy would be of little utility if its exercise were continually frustrated by
a pinched and narrow construction of the constitutional head of power. The broad scope
of authority conferred on Parliament has been passed along to the bankruptcy court in
s. 183(1) of the Act, which confers a correspondingly broad jurisdiction.

[39] There are limits, of course. If the trustee's claim is in relation to a stranger to the bankruptcy, i.e. "persons or matters outside of [the] Act" (*Re Reynolds*, supra, at p. 129) or lacks the "complexion of a matter in bankruptcy" (*Re Morris Lofsky*, supra, at p. 169) it should be brought in the ordinary civil courts and not the bankruptcy court. However, claims for specific property may clearly be advanced in the bankruptcy courts (*Re Galaxy Interiors*, supra, and *Sigurdson*, supra), as can claims for relief specifically granted by the Act (*Re Ireland*, supra, and *Re Atlas Lumber Co.*, supra). That said, it is sometimes difficult to discern the particular "golden thread" running through the cases. L.W. Houlden and L.B. Morawetz observe:

> There has been a great deal of litigation on this issue, and the cases are not always easy to reconcile. The difficulty flows from the division of constitutional powers in Canada, bankruptcy and insolvency being a federal power, and property and civil rights and the administration of justice being provincial powers.

> *Bankruptcy and Insolvency Law of Canada* (3rd ed. (looseleaf)), at I4.

[40] The short answer to the "property and civil rights" argument, however, is that the appellant poses the wrong question. The issue is whether the contractual dispute between it and the respondent trustee properly relates to the bankruptcy. If so, the fact it also has a property and civil rights aspect does not in any way impair the bankruptcy court's jurisdiction.

[Binnie J went on to hold that the contract claim in dispute before the court fell within the Bankruptcy Court's jurisdiction. He also dismissed the appellant's argument that the Quebec bankruptcy court had misdirected itself in refusing the appellant's request under BIA s. 187(7) to transfer the action to a bankruptcy court in British Columbia. Section 187(7) provides that the court, "on satisfactory proof that the affairs of the bankrupt can be more economically administered within another bankruptcy district or division, or for other sufficient cause, may by order transfer any proceedings under this Act that are pending before it to another bankruptcy district or division." The appellant argued that the action should be tried in British Columbia because (1) Azco Mining Co. was incorporated under BC law; (2) the contract between the parties provided that it was to be governed by BC law; and (3) the contract also contained a choice of forum clause in favour of the BC courts. Binnie J held that great deference should be shown to the decision of the bankruptcy court in dealing with s. 187(7) applications and that, in any event, the Quebec bankruptcy court had ample grounds for concluding that no particular hardship would be inflicted on the appellant in allowing the litigation to proceed in Quebec. Binnie J also indicated that bankruptcy courts should pay great deference to a choice of forum clause, but were not absolutely bound by the parties' choice. In any event, in his opinion, there was no choice of forum clause in the contract between the parties.]

Appeal dismissed.

NOTES AND QUESTIONS

1. In *Sam Lévy & Associés Inc.*, above, Justice Binnie clearly accepts the proposition that there are limits to the jurisdiction that Parliament can confer on the federal bankruptcy courts (or, more accurately, on federal powers conferred on provincial Superior Court judges under BIA Part VII). Does he provide clear criteria for determining those limits? What does he mean when he says he approves of earlier case law drawing a distinction between those persons who are subject to the bankruptcy court's jurisdiction and those persons who are "strangers" to the bankruptcy and must be sued in other courts?

Does he provide a clear test for determining who is a stranger to the bankruptcy other than to say that, in interpreting the bankruptcy courts' jurisdiction under s. 91(21), the courts should not give "a pinched and narrow construction" to this head of power under the *Constitution Act, 1867*?

2. Consider also the following questions: (1) Could the BIA provide that class actions against a bankrupt or a reorganizing debtor can only be continued under the supervision of the bankruptcy court; and (2) can the bankruptcy court approve the establishment of a trust fund for the settlement of class action claims and that the debtor is not obliged to make any other payments? Cf. US *Bankruptcy Code*, s. 524(g).

3. Binnie J accepts the proposition that there are clear advantages to all actions by the trustee being brought in the same court as the one in which the bankruptcy is being administered, but he does not spell out what the advantages are. Most bankruptcies, commercial or consumer, generate little litigation for a number of reasons. The trustee usually has no funds with which to initiate expensive litigation (though in some cases the trustee may be able to persuade a lawyer to accept a retainer on a contingency fee basis). If the trustee is in doubt about a claim or needs other guidance from the court, he can make a summary application under BIA s. 35. So far as parties with a claim against the estate are concerned, unless they are trying to recover specific assets in the trustee's hands (for example, because the other party claims to hold a security interest in them) or to obtain a declaration about the status of particular funds, it may not be worth their while to bring the action if a favourable judgment will only result in their being treated as unsecured creditors of the estate for the amount awarded. (Unsecured creditors typically only recover five cents on the dollar on the liquidation of the estate and often not even that.) Recall, too, that in many actions before the bankruptcy courts the courts will be applying non-bankruptcy law (pursuant to BIA s. 72(1)) to resolve the dispute because there are no applicable bankruptcy provisions that provide an answer. In these cases, entitling the trustee to sue in the bankruptcy court where the insolvency was filed gives him a clear logistical advantage if (as Azco Mining argued in the present case) the applicable law and most of the relevant evidence is linked to another province.

4. BIA s. 187(7) was obviously designed to address this type of situation. It is also a familiar one in non-bankruptcy situations where the litigating parties are in different jurisdictions and the defendant argues that, although the court in which the action was brought has jurisdiction under the applicable jurisdictional rules, the court should yield its jurisdiction to another court on *forum non conveniens* grounds. The *forum non conveniens* doctrine is of relatively recent origin in Canadian law; it was first officially embraced by the Supreme Court of Canada in *Amchen Products Inc. v. British Columbia Workers' Compensation Board*, [1993] 1 SCR 897. (A corresponding decision based on the Quebec Civil Code is *Spar Aero-*

space v. American Mobile Satellite, [2002] 4 SCR 205.) A leading Ontario Court of Appeal decision spelling out in great detail the many factors a court should consider in determining a *forum non conveniens* application is *Muscutt v. Courcelles* (2002), 60 OR (3d) 20 (CA). Binnie J, in *Azco Mining*, does not refer to this line of cases. Does this mean that the bankruptcy courts will develop a different (or a more forum-biased) *forum non conveniens* doctrine from the one embraced in non-bankruptcy cases? Would this be desirable?

II. OUTLINE OF CANADA'S BANKRUPTCY SYSTEM

The following notes provide a brief outline of some of the principal features of the BIA and the role played by the principal actors in the BIA's judicial and administrative structure. A more detailed account is provided in subsequent chapters. The account here is essentially descriptive, but readers should not be misled. Many of the features involve important normative and policy decisions and what may appear on the surface to be a simple and straightforward proposition, on closer examination, hides a myriad of ambiguities and unresolved conflicts.

A. Proceedings Under the BIA

Report of the Study Committee on Bankruptcy and Insolvency Legislation
(Canada, 1970) ("Tassé Report"), section 1.3 (adaptation) (footnotes omitted)[3]

Voluntary and Involuntary Bankruptcies: There are two methods by which liquidation of a debtor's property may be initiated under the BIA. First, a debtor may voluntarily enter bankruptcy by making an assignment of his property. Second, a debtor may be forced into bankruptcy by the petition of a creditor.[4] A debtor who has filed a commercial or consumer proposal under BIA III.1 or III.2 may also be forced into bankruptcy if the creditors do not give their approval or if the court either does not ratify or annuls the proposal.

Petition by Creditor: If the debtor has committed an "act of bankruptcy," a creditor may petition for a receiving order.[5] An "act of bankruptcy" may be regarded as an act

---

3 The following description is an updated and amended version of the account in the Tassé Report, below, together with material from other sources. The account is limited to the structure of the BIA and incidental references to the CCAA and does not include the structure of the *Winding-Up and Restructuring Act*, R.S. 1985, c. W-11 (WURA). Proceedings under the CCAA are discussed in Chapters 12 to 15.

4 Most bankruptcies are voluntary bankruptcies, especially in the case of individuals. Can you suggest why? For individuals the great attraction is the prospect of obtaining a discharge from most of the debtor's debts, usually as soon as nine months following the bankruptcy order. See, further, Chapter 11. [eds.]

5 Since 2004, the expression "bankruptcy order" has replaced "receiving order." The change was made because there was no adequate French translation of "receiving order" and because the expression had no counterpart in the *Quebec Civil Code*. The change was also justified on its own merits. Under the English bankruptcy system, a public official, known as the official receiver, actually takes possession of the bankrupt's assets following the receiving order until the official is replaced by a private trustee in bankruptcy appointed at the first meeting of creditors. This system was not adopted in the *Canadian Bankruptcy Act* of 1919 and, although the BIA still recognizes the office of Official Receiver, who is seized of various functions, the official never takes possession of the bankrupt's property and is not responsible for its custody. [eds.]

that raises a presumption that the debtor is either unable to pay his debts or is attempting to avoid their payment. The "act of bankruptcy" most frequently used is that the debtor ceased "to meet his liabilities generally as they become due." The petition is filed with the registrar in bankruptcy. If the debtor consents or if he does not oppose the petition, the registrar may make a receiving order that has the effect of adjudicating the debtor bankrupt. If the petition is opposed, it is heard by a judge.

Interim Receiver: At any time after the filing of a petition, but before a receiving order is made, the court may appoint a licensed trustee to be interim receiver of the property of the debtor, if it is "necessary for the protection of the estate." The interim receiver usually owes her appointment to the recommendation of the petitioning creditor. If a receiving order is subsequently made, the interim receiver, in most cases, is appointed the trustee of the estate.

Assignment by Debtor: A voluntary bankruptcy is commenced by the debtor filing, with the official receiver, a formal assignment of his property. [The document] must be accompanied by a sworn statement showing the property of the debtor, a list of his creditors with their addresses, and the amount owed to each. The official receiver [then completes] the assignment by inserting therein, as grantee, the name of the trustee. In practice, the trustee is chosen by the debtor who, in the majority of cases, has approached the trustee, before the assignment is filed, to ascertain whether or not the trustee is willing to accept the appointment.[6] The trustee, before accepting the appointment, satisfies himself that the proceeds from the realization of the estate will be at least sufficient to secure the payment of his fee. In "no asset cases," cash deposits or third-party guarantees are usually required by the trustee.[7]

Official Receivers: The principal duties of the official receivers are to accept and file assignments; to appoint trustees on assignments; to examine all debtors as to their conduct, the causes of their bankruptcy and the disposition of their property; to fix the amount of the bond to be filed by trustees in both voluntary and involuntary bankruptcies; and to preside over, or nominate someone else to preside over, the first meeting of creditors.

Each Province of Canada is a bankruptcy district, some of which are divided into bankruptcy divisions. For each division, one or more official receivers may be appointed by the governor in council. In Vancouver, Calgary, Edmonton, Toronto, Ottawa, Hull, Montreal, and Quebec City, where the volume of bankruptcies is greater than in other parts of the country, full-time federal civil servants have been appointed as official receivers. Elsewhere, the official receivers are usually provincial civil servants, often court officials.

---

6   Trustees advertise widely in the various media and debtors rarely have difficulties finding a trustee who is willing to accept the appointment. Since the official receiver no longer plays an active role in the selection of trustee, the Personal Insolvency Task Force recommended that the person nominated as trustee in the debtor's assignment be automatically appointed to the position: *Final Report* (2002), at 48. The recommendations were adopted in the 2005-2007 BIA amendments. [eds.]

7   About 90 percent of personal bankruptcies involve no-asset cases—that is, cases where the debtor's assets are exempt from seizure under applicable provincial law. As a result, the current practice is for trustees to enter into a fee and disbursements agreement with the debtor under which the debtor agrees to pay these sums by installments to the extent that the bankrupt's surplus income payable to the trustee under s. 67 of the BIA is not sufficient to cover the trustee's fee and disbursements. The enforceability of the agreements after the debtor's discharge has generated much controversy. See Chapter 11. [eds.]

In Canada, the official receiver is not a receiver in the generally accepted meaning of the word. In England, the official receiver is a true receiver. There, in the interval between the making of a receiving order, which is in the nature of an interim order, and the order adjudging the debtor bankrupt, which is the final order, the official receiver is given control of the debtor's property. The debtor, during this interval, is not deprived of the ownership of her property, but is not entitled to deal with it.[8]

First Meeting: At the first meeting of creditors, the appointment of the trustee is affirmed or another is substituted in his place. One or more, but not exceeding five, inspectors are appointed. Such directions are given to the trustee as the creditors may see fit with reference to the administration of the estate. There are seldom subsequent meetings of creditors as the inspectors are considered to represent them.

Inspectors: The first meeting of inspectors takes place, as a rule, at the conclusion of the first meeting of creditors. The inspectors discuss with the trustee how the estate is to be administered. All major decisions of the trustee relating to the liquidation of the property of the debtor must be authorized by them. Each inspector is entitled to be repaid his actual and necessary travelling expenses incurred in and about the performance of his duties and may be paid a nominal fee per meeting, depending upon the size of the estate.

The Trustee: Only a trustee who has been licensed by the Superintendent of Bankruptcy, may be appointed the trustee of an estate. Most trustees are accountants by training and must pass a qualifying examination before they are eligible to be appointed trustees. Many trustees have also worked for a number of years in one of the regional offices of the Office of the Superintendent of Bankruptcy (OSB). There are about 800 trustees at the present time and many of them are members of the Canadian Association of Insolvency and Restructuring Practitioners (CAIRP), which is a powerful lobbying group.[9] The trustee is an officer of the court and subject to its direction. [The trustee's] main responsibility is to collect the estate of the debtor, to liquidate it, and to distribute the proceeds to the creditors. The trustee does this under the direction and supervision of the creditors, who usually act through the board of inspectors.

Summary Administrations: Many of the administrative provisions applicable to regular estates do not apply to estates where the net value of the estate is less than the prescribed amount—currently, $10,000. See BIA ss. 49(6) and 155. Most consumer bankruptcies [about 90 percent of all individual filings] are administered summarily, thereby greatly simplifying the trustee's work.

The Role of the Creditors: The underlying principle of the BIA is that the creditors should control the administration of an estate in bankruptcy. The theory of creditor control is that, since the assets of the bankrupt are liquidated for the benefit of the creditors, they are in the best position to look after their own interest. As much power as is reasonably possible to give is given to the creditors. They appoint the trustee and may substitute one trustee for another, within the limits of the system requiring trustees to be licensed. In the administration of the estate, the trustee must consider the directions of the creditors, so

---

8   The position has changed as a result of amendments to the *Enterprise Amendment Act 2002* and the official receiver is now automatically appointed trustee in no-asset cases. [eds.]

9   There is no offsetting Association of Insolvents. Why not? [eds.]

long as they are not contrary to the Act. Not only is the trustee bound by these instructions in order for his actions to be valid, but, to avoid being subject to personal liability, he generally requires specific authorization for all that he does. In addition, the trustee is required to report to the creditors, at their request, concerning his administration.

Property Available for Creditors: All the property of a debtor at the date of her bankruptcy, or that may be acquired by, or devolve on, the debtor before his discharge is available for the payment of the debtor's debts. The only exception (and it is a very important exception) is property that, as against a personal bankrupt, is exempt from execution or seizure under the laws of the province within which the property is situated and within whose jurisdiction the bankrupt resides. [See Chapter 4.]

[Since the 1997 BIA amendments, bankrupt individuals have also been obliged to pay over to the trustee their surplus income up to the time of their discharge from bankruptcy. The size of the surplus income depends on the bankrupt's family status and is determined by directives issued by the Superintendent of Bankruptcy. For the details, see Chapter 11.]

The trustee is required to go beyond mere appearances in identifying and taking possession of the property of the bankrupt. Certain transactions entered into within varying suspect periods may be examined and avoided or reviewed under the BIA or the applicable provincial legislation.[10] Examples of such transactions include: (1) certain types of gifts made by a debtor within one year prior to becoming bankrupt; the suspect period is extended to five years where the debtor, at the time of the gift, was unable to pay his debts in full without the aid of the property given away; (2) certain transfers of property, where the intention of the debtor was to defraud his creditors; (3) transfers of property by a debtor to creditors with a view to giving those creditors a preference, where the debtor becomes bankrupt within three months thereafter; the period is extended to 12 months if the debtor and the creditors are related persons; (4) transactions entered into within 12 months prior to bankruptcy by a debtor with persons dealing with him otherwise than at arm's length may be reviewed and, where it is found that the consideration given or received by the bankrupt was conspicuously greater or less than the fair market value of the property or services concerned in the transaction, judgment may be given to the trustee for the difference.

Claims Against the Estate: All persons to whom the bankrupt is indebted, as of the date of bankruptcy, may prove a claim against the estate of the bankrupt. The trustee may disallow the claim or allow it, in whole or in part, subject to an appeal to the court. A secured creditor may prove a claim if he surrenders his security to the trustee for the general benefit of the creditors. Where the creditor realizes his security, he may prove for the balance due to him, after deducting the net amount realized. Instead of realizing his security, the secured creditor may assess the value of his security and claim for the difference. The trustee may redeem the security at the value assessed by the creditor or, if the

---

10   The relevant BIA provisions were extensively amended in 2005-2007. See now BIA ss. 95-98 and the discussion in Chapter 5. [eds.]

secured creditor takes no action, the trustee may redeem the security by paying the debt. [See, further, Chapter 7.]

Distribution of Property: The trustee is required to pay dividends in the course of realizing the property as funds become available, subject to the retention of such sums as may be necessary for the costs of administration. Certain claims are paid in priority to others. After payment of the costs of administration, these claims must be paid in full before a dividend may be paid to the ordinary creditors. The creditors who have a priority include those to whom are owed: (1) wages and salaries for services rendered within six months prior to bankruptcy, to the extent [the claims are not satisfied by the ss. 81.3 and 81.4 liens for unpaid wages and salaries;[11] (2) municipal taxes for a two-year period, if they are not secured by a preferential lien on real property, provided they do not exceed the value of the property against which the taxes are imposed; (3) arrears of rent for a period of three months prior to bankruptcy and accelerated rent for three months, if permitted by the lease, provided the total amount does not exceed the realization from the property on the premises under the lease ... .

[Before the 2005-7 amendments, s. 137 of the BIA contained detailed provisions involving the postponement of claims of relatives and other parties not dealing at arm's length with the bankrupt. These provisions have now been replaced by s. 137(1), providing that a creditor who, at any time before the debtor's bankruptcy, entered into a transaction with the bankrupt and who was not at arm's length with the debtor at that time is not entitled to claim a dividend arising out of the transaction until all claims of the other creditors have been satisfied, unless the transaction was, in the opinion of the trustee, a proper transaction: see Chapter 5.]

Disabilities of Bankrupts: The bankruptcy has the effect of imposing a number of legal disabilities upon the bankrupt until [the bankrupt's] discharge. Some of the most important of these are that: (1) she may not engage in trade or business without disclosing, to all persons with whom she enters into a business transaction, that she is an undischarged bankrupt; (2) she may not obtain credit, for a purpose other than the supply of necessaries for herself and family, to the extent of five hundred dollars or more, without disclosing that she is an undischarged bankrupt; (3) she may not be a director of a limited liability corporation; and (4) she may not be a senator.

Discharge of Bankrupt: For a long time the discharge of individual bankrupts from bankruptcy was a strong bone of contention and could generally not be obtained without the concurrence of the creditors. In Canada, the debtor's eligiblity for a discharge and the opportunity to make a fresh start was not recognized until the adoption of the *Bankruptcy Act* of 1919. Even then, the bankruptcy court was given (and continues to enjoy) a broad discretion to grant or refuse a discharge, suspend it for any period, or require the

---

[11] The 2005-2007 amendments to the bankruptcy legislation also introduced a new feature, the *Wage Earner Protection Program Act* (WEPPA). WEPPA entitles qualifying wage earners to make a claim on the Consolidated Revenue Fund for unpaid wages up to the prescribed amounts. The CRF in turn is subrogated to the wage earners' claims against the bankrupt estate and is also given a super-priority lien over the bankrupt's liquid assets. [eds.]

bankrupt, as a condition of his discharge, to pay such monies, or comply with such other terms, as the court may direct. However, no corporation may obtain a discharge unless it satisfies the claims of its creditors in full.

An important change in this regime adopted in the 1992 amendments to the BIA entitles first-time bankrupts to an automatic discharge nine months after the bankruptcy order unless the discharge is opposed by the trustee, superintendent of bankruptcy, or a creditor.[12] In practice, [well over] 90 percent of first-time bankruptcies are unopposed.[13]

The discharge releases the bankrupt of all the claims of his creditors in the bankruptcy, except: (1) a fine or penalty imposed by a court; (2) a debt arising out of a bail bond; (3) a debt or liability for alimony, maintenance, or support of a spouse or child, living apart from the bankrupt; (4) certain debts incurred by fraud; and (5) a dividend that a creditor would have been entitled to receive on a provable claim not disclosed to the trustee, except where the creditor had notice of the bankruptcy.

Discharge of Trustee: When a trustee has completed the administration of the estate, she is required to apply for her discharge. The court may grant her a discharge if she has accounted, to the satisfaction of the inspectors and the court, for all property that came to her hands. The discharge has the effect of releasing the trustee from all liability in respect of any act done or default made by her in the administration of the property of the bankrupt, and from all liability in relation to her conduct as trustee. For her services, the trustee, unless the court otherwise orders, or the creditors otherwise agree, is entitled to a remuneration not exceeding 7.5 percent of the amount realized. In calculating the trustee's remuneration, however, payments made to secured creditors are not taken into account.

Bankruptcy Offences: In order to ensure their full cooperation in the administration of estates, the BIA imposes upon bankrupts many duties with penalties for their non-performance. Bankrupts are obliged, for example, to make discovery of and deliver their property to the trustee, to prepare a statement of their affairs, to attend the first meeting of creditors, and to examine the correctness of all proofs of claims. The Act also provides that the doing of certain things by the bankrupt, such as a fraudulent disposition of property and the making of a false entry in a statement, constitute an offence. Penalties are also imposed upon inspectors for accepting anything in addition to their fees. There are also a number of offences directed at trustees who abuse their position.

The Superintendent of Bankruptcy: Official control of the bankruptcy process is exercised by the Superintendent of Bankruptcy. The Superintendent heads the OSB, which is an executive agency of the federal government and has its head office in Ottawa. The Superintendent's many responsibilities include the following. He must investigate allegations that offences have been committed under the BIA, where it appears that they would not otherwise be investigated. He also has the responsibility to supervise the administration of all estates to which the Act applies. To do this, he may intervene, as a party, in any matter or

---

[12] Common grounds of opposition to the discharge are that the debtor has not made the required surplus income payments or attended the mandatory two counselling sessions. The 9-months automatic discharge period was changed to 21 months in the 2005-2007 amendments in the case of first-time bankrupts with surplus income. See further, Chapter 11, below. [eds.]

[13] Since the 1998 amendments to the BIA, student loans are now not eligible for discharge until 6 years following the conclusion of student's studies. See, further, Chapter 11. [eds.]

proceeding in court. Every petition for a [bankruptcy] order is served upon the Superintendent. He may thereby get early notice of a matter that might require investigation. In the same way, every bill of costs of a solicitor is served upon him and, if he considers it advisable, he may intervene on the taxation. The Superintendent also examines every statement of receipts and disbursements and the final dividend sheet prepared by the trustee when the administration of an estate is completed. The Superintendent's comments upon these documents are considered by the court when the trustee's accounts are passed. The Superintendent is also responsible for the granting of licences to trustees in bankruptcy.

In short, following the British precedent, the Superintendent and his officials are ultimately responsible for the integrity of Canada's bankruptcy system. An important power that is also vested in the Superintendent is the power to issue directives to facilitate the carrying out of the purposes and provisions of the BIA and the general rules adopted under the Act. See BIA s. 5(4). Directives are not statutory instruments (BIA s. 5(6)) and, therefore, are not subject to parliamentary scrutiny. Nevertheless, directives are widely used by the Superintendent and play a very important role in the administration of the BIA.

Bankruptcy Court Structure: Unlike the United States, Canada has no separate bankruptcy courts and no separate appellate courts in bankruptcy matters. Instead, Part VII, s. 183(1) of the BIA vests in the superior courts of each province "such jurisdiction at law and in equity" as will enable them to exercise original, auxiliary or ancillary jurisdiction in bankruptcy and other proceedings authorized by the BIA.[14] Section 183(2) applies the normal appellate rules for appeals from bankruptcy court decisions unless otherwise provided in the BIA, with a further right of appeal to the Supreme Court of Canada in accordance with its rules.[15] [For further analysis of the bankruptcy court structure, see Binnie J's judgment in *Sam Lévy & Associés Inc. v. Azco Mining Inc.*, above.]

An important feature of the bankruptcy court structure is that while the judges are members of the provincial superior courts, when sitting as bankruptcy judges they are exercising federal powers. Consequently, a bankruptcy court order is effective across Canada and this is made clear in BIA s. 188 requiring bankruptcy courts to enforce each other's orders and requiring "all courts and the officers of all courts" to act in aid of and be auxiliary to each other in all matters of bankruptcy: BIA s. 188(2). This constitutional feature gives bankruptcy proceedings a great advantage over provincially grounded jurisdiction and is another reason why creditors and debtors often resort to the BIA to seek appropriate relief.

Another consequence of the BIA court structure also deserves to be noted. This is that, except in the larger provinces, there is very little bankruptcy specialization among provincial trial judges.[16] In Ontario, the Chief Justice has established a commercial list, which encourages some specialization in bankruptcy matters among trial judges, but

---

14 The minister may also authorize any other court or judge to exercise any of the judicial powers conferred under the BIA, but this power has not so far been exercised. [eds.]

15 BIA s. 183(3). [eds.]

16 Note, however, that s. 185(1) empowers the chief justice of a province to nominate one or more judges in the chief justice's court to handle the bankruptcy work in that jurisdiction. [eds.]

only to a limited extent. This is because the judges are appointed on a rotational basis and because the work of the commercial list is not limited to bankruptcy cases.

B. Role of Registrars in Bankruptcy

Under the BIA,[17] the registrars of the provincial Superior Courts have considerable judicial powers, mainly in relation to procedural matters and unopposed proceedings, but in other important areas as well. This is a feature of the Canadian judicial bankruptcy system that has no counterpart in the US system. The Canadian registrars are the largely unnoticed heroes of the day-to-day judicial administration of the BIA. They carry much of the regular work-load of the bankruptcy courts in their jurisdictions and often develop much expertise on many aspects of the Act.[18]

---

[17] BIA s. 192 reads as follows:

The registrars of the courts have power and jurisdiction, without limiting the powers otherwise conferred by this Act or the General Rules,

(a) to hear bankruptcy applications and to make bankruptcy orders where they are not opposed;

(b) to hold examinations of bankrupts or other persons;

(c) to grant orders of discharge;

(d) to approve proposals where they are not opposed;

(e) to make interim orders in cases of urgency;

(f) to hear and determine any unopposed or *ex parte* application;

(g) to summon and examine the bankrupt or any person known or suspected to have in his possession property of the bankrupt, or to be indebted to him, or capable of giving information respecting the bankrupt, his dealings or property;

(h) to hear and determine matters relating to proofs of claims whether or not opposed;

(i) to tax or fix costs and to pass accounts;

(j) to hear and determine any matter with the consent of all parties;

(k) to hear and determine any matter relating to practice and procedure in the courts;

(l) to settle and sign all orders and judgments of the courts not settled or signed by a judge and to issue all orders, judgments, warrants or other processes of the courts;

(m) to perform all necessary administrative duties relating to the practice and procedure in the courts; and

(n) to hear and determine appeals from the decision of a trustee allowing or disallowing a claim.

[18] A striking feature about bankruptcy registrars is that their number differs widely among the provinces. Ontario has only 3 registrars compared with 59 in Quebec and 26 in British Columbia. Alberta and Manitoba have 7 and 5 registrars, respectively. The Atlantic provinces have 1 each. (*OSB Newsletter 2004-5* (Ottawa: Industry Canada, 2005), 2). Even if one allows for the fact that many of the British Columbia and Quebec bankruptcy registrars have only part-time appointments (in the sense that the rest of their time is spent on other types of registry work), it does not explain Ontario's long-standing reluctance to appoint an adequate number of registrars to serve the needs of the Ontario bankruptcy community, the largest in Canada. Even the Northwest Territories has 4 registrars.

PART II

Bankruptcy

CHAPTER THREE

Initiation of Bankruptcy Proceedings and Consequences of Bankruptcy

I. INTRODUCTION

This chapter deals with two related topics: (1) initiation of bankruptcy proceedings,[1] and (2) the consequences of a bankruptcy order or assignment.[2] There are basic differences in structure under the BIA between an involuntary application for a bankruptcy order brought by creditors under s. 43 and the voluntary assignment by an insolvent person under s. 49. The first is an adversarial proceeding and, predictably, the rules are much stricter. The second proceeding is non-adversarial and the requirements are modest. There is no judicial scrutiny of the assignment at this juncture, only a quick review of the documents by the Official Receiver to ensure formal compliance with the bankruptcy rules. If creditors feel the assignment should not have been made, they must move to have the court annul the bankruptcy pursuant to s. 181. See *Re Wale*, below.

Once the debtor has become a bankrupt, a common set of consequences follow for both voluntary and involuntary bankruptcy proceedings. Section III of this chapter focuses on only one of these consequences, the imposition of an automatic stay of proceedings against the bankrupt. The other consequences are listed in the notes following *R v. Fitzgibbon* and, to the extent they are dealt with at all, are discussed in later chapters.

II. INITIATION OF BANKRUPTCY PROCEEDINGS

In applying for a bankruptcy order under s. 43, in addition to alleging that the debt owing to the applicant creditor or creditors amounts to $1,000, the creditor or creditors must allege

---

[1] The BIA terminology in some of the older cases is somewhat confusing. Until 2004, the BIA used the following terminology for involuntary proceedings: a creditor filed a petition with the court under s. 43. If the petition was successful, a court would issue a receiving order. In 2004, the BIA was amended; now one or more creditors "file an application" and, if the application is successful, the court "makes a bankruptcy order." See *Federal Law—Civil Harmonization Act, No. 2*, SC 2004, c. 25, s. 28. Notwithstanding these legislative changes, some courts continue to use the traditional terminology. A voluntary assignment under s. 49 is "filed" with the Official Receiver in the locality of the debtor but there is no formal order. Once the filing is made, the assignment is deemed complete and the debtor becomes a "bankrupt." See s. 2(1), definition of "bankrupt." To avoid needless repetition, the term "bankruptcy order" will be used hereafter to describe the effects of an assignment and successful application for a bankruptcy order.

[2] Initiation of reorganizational proceedings under BIA III.1 and III.2 and the CCAA are treated separately. See Chapters 12-17 of this text.

that the debtor has committed an act of bankruptcy (listed in s. 42). Creditors frequently rely on the act of bankruptcy found in s. 42(1)(j), alleging that the debtor has ceased to meet liabilities generally as they become due. Whether or not the failure to pay a single creditor can be an act of bankruptcy under s. 42(1)(j) has given rise to a significant number of cases as discussed below. Thomas Jackson has characterized bankruptcy as a way to make multiple creditors act as one by imposing on creditors a *collective and compulsory* proceeding (Chapter 1). As you review the single-creditor line of cases below, consider whether they are consistent with Jackson's view of bankruptcy.

Re Dixie Market (Nurseries) Limited
(1971), 14 CBR (NS) 281 (Ont. SC)

HOULDEN J (orally): This is a petition for a receiving order. The petitioning creditor is the trustee in bankruptcy of The Dixie Fruit Market Ltd. and Co., a limited partnership. The trustee was instructed by an unanimous resolution of a meeting of the creditors of the bankrupt company to file this petition.

The petitioning creditor's debt is in the amount of $26,335; this represents moneys advanced by the bankrupt company to the debtor. According to Ex. 1, the advances by affiliates as at 30th September 1970 total $27,835.03. None of the witnesses, who have given evidence for the debtor, have been able to explain the discrepancy between the two figures. It may be that some payment was made after 30th September 1970 to the petitioning creditor prior to its bankruptcy.

As at 30th September 1970 it appears that there were certain other accounts payable; however, the evidence given for the defence would indicate that all accounts payable have now been paid apart from the debt owing to the petitioning creditor. There is no dispute about the amount owing to the petitioning creditor. Apparently there was no arrangement for payment of the debt and, in the absence of any arrangement for payment, the law of course is that it must be paid within a reasonable time, depending upon the circumstances: *McGregor v. Curry* (1914), 31 OLR 261 at 269, 20 DLR 706, affirmed 25 DLR 771 (PC); *Owchar v. Owchar*, [1949] 2 WWR 97, [1949] 2 DLR 432 (Sask. CA). The debt was owing as at 30th September 1970 and, in my opinion, a reasonable time for payment has elapsed and as at 11th February 1971, the date of the filing of the petition, it was past due.

Counsel for the debtor submits that the reason for the filing of the petition is to use the Bankruptcy Court as a collection agency. I do not think that this is so. I believe the trustee in bankruptcy is well justified in filing the petition. The assets of the debtor consist of two pieces of property in the Oakville area. These properties were purchased for $60,000 about three years ago, and there are presently outstanding mortgages of $42,000. On the basis of the original purchase price, it will be obvious that there is not sufficient equity to pay the debt owing to the petitioning creditor. Furthermore, there is considerable risk that, if the trustee in bankruptcy does not take some positive steps to protect the amount owing to the petitioning creditor, the assets of the debtor may in some way be encumbered to the prejudice of the petitioner. At the present moment, the mortgage payments are up to date although, as appears from Ex. 2, the payment due on the mortgage of Mor Investments Limited was not paid on 1st February 1971. This resulted in a telephone call from the mortgagee, and a letter of 9th February 1971 (Ex. 2) threatening to take legal proceedings.

The rental income from the property is not sufficient to meet the mortgage payments. The taxes on the property, which must be substantial, will soon be falling due and the money will have to be found to pay them.

Turning to the petition, there is no denial of para. 1. As I have pointed out, the debt of the petitioner is admitted so there is no dispute in respect of para. 2. With reference to para. 3, the petitioning creditor has certainly no security. The only paragraph in the petition which is contested, is whether or not the debtor has ceased to meet its liabilities generally as they become due. If there were liabilities to other creditors, there would be a question in this case, as to whether or not the act of bankruptcy has been committed, but this is one of those peculiar situations in which there is only one debt owing and that debt is the amount owing to the petitioning creditor.

Whether or not the failure to pay a single creditor can constitute ceasing to meet liabilities generally as they become due is not an easy question. There have been a number of decisions on this point. However, in this province, the case of *Re Raitblat*, 5 CBR 714, 28 OWN 237, [1925] 2 DLR 1219, affirmed by the Court of Appeal 5 CBR 765, 28 OWN 292, [1925] 3 DLR 446, has decided that a failure to pay a single creditor may constitute ceasing to meet liabilities generally as they become due: see also *Re Freedman*, 4 CBR 499, [1924] 1 DLR 682, reversed on other grounds 5 CBR 47, 55 OLR 206, [1924] 3 DLR 517 (CA) and *Re Glenn* (1941), 23 CBR 81 (Ont.).

I can see no reason why, if there is only a single creditor and there has been a failure to pay that creditor, this cannot constitute ceasing to meet liabilities generally. To hold otherwise would be to deprive the petitioning creditor of the benefits of the *Bankruptcy Act*, RSC 1952, c. 14. If the creditor in the present case is prevented from using the *Bankruptcy Act*, he will be required to use the remedies of a judgment creditor—this means that the assets cannot be disposed of for a year and the sheriff will have control of their disposal.

As I have said, the debt is overdue; the debtor has not been able to suggest any way in which it can be paid and in my opinion, it is a proper case for a receiving order to be made. There will, therefore, be a receiving order and Mr. Sprackman will be the trustee. ...

Petition granted.

Re Holmes and Sinclair
(1975), 20 CBR (NS) 111 (Ont. SC)

HENRY J: ... It is clear that the Courts, in Ontario at least, have granted a receiving order on the basis of a default to one creditor in special circumstances. These circumstances are:

(a) The creditor is the only creditor of the debtor; and the debtor has failed to meet repeated demands of the creditor; in these circumstances he should not be denied the benefits of the *Bankruptcy Act* by reason only of his unique character; or

(b) The creditor is a significant creditor and there are special circumstances such as fraud on the part of the debtor which make it imperative that the processes of the

Bankruptcy Act be set in motion immediately for the protection of the whole class of creditors; or

(c) The debtor admits that he is unable to pay his creditors generally, although they and the obligations are not identified.

I find on the evidence that these circumstances do not exist here.

Because this Court has in some of the recent decisions … made a receiving order on proof of failure to meet a liability to a single creditor, it is not to be taken to have established a new principle that a petitioning creditor need only prove default with respect to the debt owing to him. Those decisions in my judgment do not lay down such a principle; they are, as I see it, merely the application to particular facts of the general rule … that when relying on an act of bankruptcy described in s. 24(1)(j) the petitioning creditor must strictly establish that, in the words of the statute, the debtor "ceases to meet his liabilities generally as they become due;" in all of them the Court was influenced either by the existence of other creditors, or of one of the special circumstances I have set out above. In the non-exceptional case, as in the case at bar, that situation cannot be ordinarily proved by having regard to the experience of one creditor only, even though he may be a major creditor. Resort to the statutory machinery of the *Bankruptcy Act*, rather than to the remedies to enforce a debt or claim in the ordinary Courts, is intended by Parliament to be for the benefit of the creditors of a debtor as a class, and the act of bankruptcy described in s. 24(1)(j) is, in my judgment, an act that singles out the conduct of the debtor in relation to the class, rather than to the individual (as is the case under s. 24(1)(e)). It is for this reason that the Court must be satisfied that there is sufficient evidence from which an inference of fact can fairly be drawn that creditors generally are not being paid. This requires as a minimum some evidence that liabilities other than those incurred towards the petitioning creditor have ceased to be met. The court ought not to be asked to draw inferences with respect to the class on the basis of one creditor's experience where evidence of the debtor's conduct towards other members of the class could, with reasonable diligence, be discovered and produced. The court's intuition is no substitute for the diligence of the petitioning creditor.

In the case before me, the petitioning creditor has not established conduct of the debtors towards other creditors. I am, in effect, asked to infer that there is a group of creditors who have not been paid. It is not possible to say, on the evidence, whether they exist at all, or are few or numerous, or whether their claims individually or in total are significant or, most important, to say whether the debtors have *ceased* to meet their liabilities *generally*. …

Petition refused.

Re Mastronardi
(2000), 195 DLR (4th) 631 (Ont. CA)

MacPHERSON JA (for the Court):

Overview

[1] Three Ohio plaintiffs obtained a huge civil judgment in the Ohio courts because of the negligence in Ohio of an Ontario resident. The Ohio plaintiffs sought unsuccessfully for several months to collect on the judgment. There was evidence that the judgment debtor may have conveyed assets for nominal consideration. Eventually, one of the Ohio creditors turned to the Ontario courts and brought a petition for a receiving order under the *Bankruptcy and Insolvency Act*, RSC 1985, c. B-3 ("BIA"). This appeal invites a consideration of the statutory prerequisites of the BIA in the context of a foreign petitioner whose principal motivation for bringing the petition is a desire to collect money owed to him pursuant to an order of a foreign court.

A. Facts

[2] On a summer day in 1995 two pleasure boats were on Lake Erie, on the American side. The Brabander family of Broadview Heights, Ohio was in one boat. The other boat, a very fast cigarette type boat, was operated by Ollie Mastronardi, a resident of Leamington, Ontario. As the cigarette boat bore down on the Brabander boat, John and Susan Brabander jumped into the water. They survived. Unfortunately, their 24 year old son Scott was killed in the collision of the two boats.

[3] The tragedy on the water gave rise to both criminal and civil proceedings in the Ohio courts. Mr. Mastronardi ("Mastronardi") was convicted in May 1996 of a serious criminal offence in relation to the death of Scott Brabander. He spent several years in an Ohio prison, but is now free.

[4] The Brabander family initiated a civil action against Mastronardi in Ohio. The plaintiffs were successful. On February 12, 1998, following a trial with judge and jury, the three named plaintiffs were awarded damages against Mastronardi as follows:

(1) for John Brabander, administrator of the estate of Scott Brabander, on his survivorship claim on behalf of the estate—$581,705.84 US;

(2) for John Brabander, administrator of the estate of Scott Brabander, on his wrongful death claim on behalf of the next of kin and survivors of Scott Brabander—$1,829,287.56 US;

(3) for John Brabander, personally, for negligent infliction of serious emotional distress—$581,705.83 US; and

(4) for Susan Brabander, personally, for negligent infliction of serious emotional distress—$581,705.83 US.

. . .

[7] On February 24, 1998, Barat [counsel for the Brabander family] wrote to Schrader questioning whether the Brabanders would be able to enforce such a large judgment in Ontario. He invited Schrader "to discuss this with us on review."

[8] Schrader telephoned Barat in March 1998 to discuss the payment of the judgment. Barat informed Schrader he would discuss the matter with Mastronardi's wife Ann and get back to him.

[9] On June 17, 1998, Schrader wrote to Barat as follows:

> Last March I made a demand upon you as the attorney for Ollie Mastronardi regarding payment of the outstanding judgment against your client. No payment of any kind has been made, and you have not returned my calls. The judgment was due and payable at the time of the jury verdict on February 12, 1998.

[10] Schrader followed up this correspondence with another call to Barat. Barat did not return the call or respond to the letter.

[11] On June 22, 1998, John Brabander, acting as administrator of the estate of Scott Brabander, filed a Petition for a Receiving Order in the Ontario Court (General Division) in Bankruptcy in London, Ontario. The petition stated that "Ollie Mastronardi is justly and truly indebted to Brabander in the sum of at least $2,842,738.40 (US)."

[12] The stated ground for the bankruptcy petition was that, contrary to s. 43(1)(b) of the BIA, "Ollie Mastronardi, within the six months next preceding the date of the filing of the petition, has committed the following act of bankruptcy, namely, he has ceased to meet his liabilities generally as they become due."

[13] The petition was heard by Hockin J sitting in London on September 21, 1998. The petitioner called three witnesses, John Brabander, Thomas Schrader and Susan Brabander. The respondent placed in evidence the cross-examination of John Brabander on his Affidavit of Verification, which had been conducted on September 20, 1998, the day before the bankruptcy hearing.

[14] Hockin J dismissed the petition in a written judgment released February 15, 1999. He found that the petitioning creditor had proved that the debt exceeded the threshold figure of $1,000. However, he held that "there is no evidence that the debtor has ceased to meet his liabilities generally as they become due." In reaching this conclusion, he regarded all the Brabanders as a single creditor and said that there were no "special circumstances," within the meaning of the case authorities, to permit this single creditor to invoke the BIA as a means of collecting on its debt. The essence of his reasoning is contained in this passage in the final paragraph of his judgment:

> The evidence is that a demand was made of the debtor but there has really been no attempt to collect on this debt beyond the issuance of the petition. Without more, I am concerned that the Bankruptcy Court would become in this case a collection agency for a single creditor. I do not find that the petitioner has made a serious effort to collect on the debt. The circumstances of the case are otherwise compelling, but I may not for that reason only depart from the cases and the language of the Act.

[15] The petitioner appeals from Hockin J's judgment. He seeks an order setting aside Hockin J's order, adjudging Mastronardi a bankrupt, and appointing Shiner and Associates Inc. as trustee of Mastronardi's property.

B. Issue

[16] The issue on this appeal is: did the bankruptcy judge err in holding that Mastronardi did not commit an act of bankruptcy by ceasing to meet his liabilities as they generally became due?

C. Analysis

[17] The appellant initiated his petition for a receiving order pursuant to sections 43(1) and 42(1)(j) of the BIA, which provide: ...

[18] The bankruptcy judge seemed to rely heavily on two factors in dismissing the petition. First, he treated the Brabanders as a single creditor and held that there were no special circumstances justifying resort to the BIA by a single creditor. Second, he held that the creditor had not made a serious effort to collect on the debt beyond the issuance of the petition. Each of these, in the eyes of the bankruptcy judge, worked against a conclusion that Mastronardi had ceased to meet his liabilities generally as they became due. Presumably, the single creditor conclusion undercut the "liabilities generally" component of s. 42(1)(j) of the BIA and the lack of serious effort to collect the debt counted against a conclusion that the debtor had breached the "ceases to meet his liabilities" component of the same provision. I will consider these two rationales in turn.

(1) Single Creditor/Special Circumstances

[19] There is a line of cases, anchored in *Re Holmes and Sinclair* (1975), 20 CBR (NS) 111 (Ont. Bktcy.), holding that a receiving order should not be made based on a default to only one creditor unless there are "special circumstances." The bankruptcy judge applied *Re Holmes and Sinclair*. He held that the receiving order was being sought by the only creditor of Mastronardi and that none of the special circumstances enumerated by Henry J in *Re Holmes and Sinclair* applied.

[20] In my view, the bankruptcy judge erred in determining that Mastronardi had only one creditor, in effect the Brabander family lumped together. The civil action in Ohio proceeded from start to finish as an action brought by three separate plaintiffs—the estate of Scott Brabander, John Brabander personally and Susan Brabander personally. The final judgment of the Ohio Court of Common Pleas identified each of these three as a separate plaintiff and awarded specific damages to each plaintiff.

[21] The respondent does not quarrel with the fact that only one creditor, John Brabander, acting as administrator of his son's estate, brought the petition for a receiving order. Such a contention would fail because s. 43(1) of the BIA provides that a bankruptcy petition may be filed by "one or more creditors."

[22] However, the respondent does contend that the separate identity of the three Brabander creditors is belied by the fact that the petition, brought on behalf of the single creditor "the estate of Scott Brabander," states that "Mastronardi is justly and truly indebted to Brabander in the sum of at least $2,842,738.40 (US)." This amount, contends the respondent, "constitutes the entire foreign judgment against the Respondent." (factum, paragraph 35).

[23] This is simply not the case. The total judgment in Ohio against Mastronardi was $3,574,405.06 (US). The judgment in favour of the single creditor, the estate of Scott Brabander, was $2,410,993.40 (US). The figure of $2,842,738.40 (US) in the petition represents, as John Brabander testified at the bankruptcy hearing, "the amount awarded the Estate of my son, plus the recovered expenses which was $3,500 or something like that, plus interest since that date at ten percent." In short, the petition was brought by a single creditor and asserts only the debt owed to that creditor.

[24] My conclusion is that the bankruptcy judge erred in determining that Mastronardi had only one creditor. In fact, there are at least three separate creditors. Accordingly, the bankruptcy judge did not need to consider whether there were "special circumstances," within the meaning of *Re Holmes and Sinclair* and its progeny, justifying a receiving order. It was within his discretion to issue a receiving order on the basis that "the existence of two other unpaid debts is ... sufficient to establish the act of bankruptcy": see *Re Joyce* (1984), 51 CBR (NS) 152 (Ont. SC), and *Re Giusto* (1994), 25 CBR (3d) 227 (Ont. Gen. Div.).

(2) Lack of Serious Effort to Collect the Debt

[25] The bankruptcy judge acknowledged that there was evidence that a demand had been made of the debtor. In my view, this observation was correct. During a four month period shortly after the Final Judgment of the Ohio trial court in the civil action the Ohio attorney for the Brabanders attempted to collect on the debt owing to them. He pursued this in precisely the way Mastronardi had instructed him through counsel—by contacting Arthur Barat, Mastronardi's personal and corporate counsel in Windsor. No results were achieved.

[26] The bankruptcy judge recognized the legitimacy of the steps taken by the Brabanders to collect on the debt and he also knew that their efforts had been unsuccessful. Nevertheless, he decided not to grant the receiving order. He said:

> It is the case that there has been no action commenced in Ontario by the Brabander family for the recovery of the amount in the judgment nor any attempt by the family through the Court of Common Pleas of Cuyahoga County to register the judgment in Ontario. In other words, there has been no attempt to execute in Ontario.
>
> • • •
>
> The evidence is that a demand was made of the debtor but there has really been no attempt to collect on this debt beyond the issuance of the petition. Without more, I am concerned that the Bankruptcy Court would become in this case a collection agency for a single creditor.

[27] In my view, the bankruptcy judge erred in dismissing the petition for a receiving order on the basis that the appellant should have pursued other routes to collect on the debt owed by Mastronardi. I reach this conclusion for several reasons.

[28] First, if a petitioner can satisfy the requirements of the BIA, I see no reason for denying him access to the process and remedies of the Act because there may be other civil routes open to him. The BIA is not a second-rate or fallback statute that can only be invoked if other avenues fail. I agree with Ground J who said in *Re Cappe* (1993), 18 CBR (3d) 229 at 235 (Ont. Gen. Div.):

I know of no statutory or common law which requires that a petitioning creditor have exhausted all other remedies available to that creditor to collect the debt owing to him or her before proceeding with a petition for a receiving order. In fact, the jurisprudence would seem to be to the contrary. See also: *Re Chu* (1995), 30 CBR (3d) 78 at 82 (Ont. Gen. Div.).

[29] Second, Mastronardi appears from the record to have made suspect transfers of property at suspect times. Mastronardi was examined in April 1997 in the Ohio civil action. John Brabander and Thomas Schrader testified at the bankruptcy hearing. From these sources the following picture emerges. Mastronardi's principal corporate enterprise, MOS Enterprises, was a multi-million dollar corporation. In Leamington, Ontario, Mastronardi owned or operated a large greenhouse complex with outbuildings and houses, a trucking terminal and employees' quarters. He had a large private residence in Leamington and an oceanfront condominium in Florida. He owned the 38 foot cigarette boat that was involved in the accident. In addition, one of his numbered companies owned a 63 foot Searay valued at approximately $1,000,000.

[30] I do not say that all of the above facts have been conclusively proven. However, they were all in evidence before the bankruptcy judge and Mastronardi introduced no evidence to contradict them. The *prima facie* conclusion I draw is that Mastronardi is a man with substantial personal and business assets.

[31] Did the accident cause him to do anything with these assets? It appears—I put it no higher—that it did. Thomas Schrader testified that in September or October 1995, Mastronardi transferred his entire 51 per cent interest in MOS Enterprises, his central business, to his wife for no consideration. He also testified that at the same time Mastronardi transferred his half interest in the family residence to his wife, again for no consideration. Both of these transactions took place after the accident in June 1995 and after the Brabanders had commenced their civil action in Ohio, but before the Ohio court had made a decision. In his examination in the Ohio action, Mastronardi said that he made the transfers because he could not obtain insurance in Canada after the boat accident. That may or may not be the case (Mastronardi introduced no supporting evidence on this issue at the bankruptcy hearing). However, on the state of the record before the bankruptcy judge, these are highly suspicious transfers of property: see *Bombardier Credit Ltd. v. Find* (1998), 2 CBR (4th) 1 at 10 (Ont. CA).

[32] Moreover, when he was examined in the Ohio civil action in April 1997 (ten months before the judgment in the civil action), Mastronardi admitted that he intended, within weeks, to transfer his half interest in his oceanfront Florida condominium to his wife for $50,000.

[33] All three of these transactions are precisely the kind of transactions that are particularly well-suited to investigation and review by a trustee in bankruptcy. They look vulnerable—again, I put it no higher—to an attack by a trustee as being settlements and, depending on when the Florida transfer was completed, reviewable transactions. To my mind, they constitute a compelling reason why a receiving order should have been granted. If a receiving order were made, time would start running backward from January 1998, when the petition was issued, and the three transactions might fall within the trustee's net under the BIA.

[34] Third, Mastronardi owes three creditors more than $3.5 million pursuant to a valid Ohio court order. He appealed the trial court's order but did not pursue the appeal.

The Ohio court order is truly a final order. Mastronardi is a man with substantial assets. For four months in 1998, his Ohio creditors made demands for payment of the money they were owed. Mastronardi made no response and, importantly, he did not pay a penny on the judgments. In these circumstances, namely a lawful multi-million dollar debt, a person with substantial assets, and no payment at all, the bankruptcy route strikes me as entirely appropriate. There is no need for the petitioning creditor to spend time and money continuing on the ordinary civil track when Mastronardi has not complied with his responsibilities on that track and when the petitioning creditor has established *prima facie* compliance with the statutory conditions of the BIA.

[35] Fourth, the bankruptcy judge's concern "that the Bankruptcy Court would become in this case a collection agency for a single creditor" is, in my view, misplaced. As discussed previously, this is not a single creditor case; there are at least three substantial creditors. Moreover, there is nothing in the record to suggest that the appellant has invoked the BIA for any ulterior purpose, such as trying to force a creditor to deal with him to the exclusion of, or in priority to, other creditors.

[36] The fact that the petitioning creditor desires, as he candidly admitted when he was cross-examined on his Affidavit of Verification in support of the petition, to collect on the debt owing to him, is not an impermissible or disqualifying feature. Virtually every creditor who initiates a bankruptcy petition would have this as an objective. On this point I agree with Catzman J who said in *Re Four Twenty-Seven Investments Limited; Re 495487 Ontario Limited* (1985), 55 CBR (NS) 183 at 188 (Ont. SC), aff'd (1985), 58 CBR (NS) 266 (Ont. CA):

> I also reject the debtor's submission based upon the alleged improper or ulterior motive of the petitioning creditor. It is not an abuse of process or an improper purpose to commence a petition for the collection of a debt. It is not improper to petition to gain remedies not available outside of bankruptcy, including a thoroughgoing investigation of the bankrupt's affairs. Indeed, on the evidence, I consider this to be a prototypal case where the full arsenal of investigatory mechanisms and remedies available to a trustee in bankruptcy would be useful, appropriate and desirable.

[37] I agree with that passage and regard it as equally applicable to the present appeal. Mastronardi owes substantial debts to several creditors, he has made several suspicious transfers of assets and he has not demonstrated any intention or inclination to pay even a penny of the debts he owes. In these circumstances, the petition for a receiving order brought by John Brabander, as administrator of his son's estate, complies with the requirements of the BIA and a receiving order would be "useful, appropriate and desirable."

· · ·

Appeal allowed.

NOTES AND QUESTIONS

1. *Single creditor and application for a bankruptcy order:* As evident from the case law above, the application under s. 43 will not be restricted to cases where a bankruptcy order is necessary to solve common-pool or collective-action problems (see Thomas Jackson, Chapter 1). Is there any inconsistency in the interpretation of s. 42(1)(j)? In *Re Holmes and*

Sinclair, Henry J accepted the proposition that a single creditor would suffice if there were special circumstances—for example, if there was only one creditor, or if the petitioner was the largest creditor. Later cases have accepted this gloss on 42(1)(j), but have not explained how this interpretation can be reconciled with the plain requirements of s. 42(1)(j) that the debtor ceases to meet the debtor's liabilities "generally" as they become due. Nor have the courts explained how the right of a single creditor to put the debtor into bankruptcy can be reconciled with the collective-action theory generally claimed to underlie the BIA provisions. If bankruptcy is intended to resolve the collective-action problem, it is difficult to see why an unsatisfied execution by a single creditor is accepted as an act of bankruptcy without further evidence about its impact on the general body of creditors.

In addition, the courts have not explained why it is sufficient to show (as in *Re Mastronardi*) that the debtor has failed to satisfy the claims of three creditors even when it is obvious (as it surely was obvious in *Mastronardi*) that the debtor had many creditors. Does proof of failure to pay three out of dozens of creditors satisfy the literal wording of s. 42(1)(j)? Indeed, *Mastronardi* relied on earlier jurisprudence to suggest that the existence of two other unpaid debts is sufficient to establish the act of bankruptcy.

2. *Advantages of bankruptcy order over provincial execution remedies: Re Holmes and Sinclair* and, in particular, *Re Mastronardi* illustrate the superiority of bankruptcy over execution orders and conservatory measures, such as a court-appointed receiver, available outside bankruptcy. Note too MacPherson JA's striking observation in *Re Mastronardi* that bankruptcy proceedings should not be regarded as a second-class proceeding or fallback position to enforcement of judgment debts under provincial law. Can the single-creditor line of cases and a willingness to grant a bankruptcy order be explained by judicial recognition of the advantages that bankruptcy proceedings have over provincial execution remedies? See Houlden J's observation in *Re Dixie Market* on the consequences of denying the creditor the benefits of the BIA. Consider, for example, the powers of a sheriff under the *Execution Act*, RSO 1990, c. E-24. The sheriff is vested with broad powers to seize the debtor's real and personal property (ss. 9-22), but in most other respects the sheriff's powers fall short of a trustee's powers under the BIA. The sheriff has no power to examine the debtor (cf. BIA s. 163(1)), and has no power to carry on the debtor's business for even the shortest period of time (cf. BIA ss. 18, 30). However, there are some restrictions on the ability of the trustee to carry on business or sell assets of the bankrupt to related parties. See BIA new ss. 30(4)-(6). The sheriff has no power to seize assets outside his jurisdiction (cf. BIA s. 2 definition of "property" and ss. 16(3) and 17(2)) or to levy execution after the writ has expired. Likewise, the sheriff has no power to set aside impeachable transactions engaged in by the debtor prior to execution, although the execution creditor may be able to do so (cf. BIA ss. 95-98.1). If bankruptcy offers so many advantages, why should a judgment creditor with a major claim bother at all with provincial remedies? The UK *Insolvency Act, 1986* has followed this line of reasoning to its logical conclusion and permits a creditor to launch a bankruptcy petition on proof that the creditor has made a statutory demand for payment of its debt (which must be above a prescribed minimum amount) and that the debt has not been paid. See *Insolvency Act, 1986* (UK), ss. 123(1)(a), 267(2)(c), and 268(1)(a).

3. In the creditor's application for a bankruptcy order, the creditor must allege that the debtor committed an act of bankruptcy within six months preceding the filing of the application (s. 43). If a creditor obtains a judgment before the six-month period and makes no

serious effort to collect on the debt, is there an act of bankruptcy within the six-month period? Consider the following two cases and the notes that follow:

Platt v. Malmstrom
(2001), 198 DLR (4th) 285 (Ont. CA)

FINLAYSON JA (for the Court):

Background

[1] This is an appeal by the debtor Robert Platt from the February 7, 2000 decision of the Honourable Mr. Justice J.M. Farley of the Superior Court of Justice (In Bankruptcy), wherein a judgment for a receiving order was rendered against Platt.

[2] Pursuant to s. 43(6) of the *Bankruptcy and Insolvency Act*, RSC 1985, c. B-3, as amended (the "BIA"), the bankruptcy judge found that the petitioning creditors had established that Mr. Platt:

(a) had ceased to meet his liabilities generally as they became due (s. 42(1) of the BIA);

(b) was indebted to his creditors in a sum in excess of $1,000 (s. 43(1)(a) of the BIA); and

(c) had committed an act of bankruptcy within the six months next preceding the filing of the petition, which was dated June 24, 1999 (s. 43(1)(b) of the BIA).

[3] The debts relied upon by the bankruptcy judge consisted of (a) for 798839 Ontario Limited, a judgment in the amount of $9,895.44 for a cost order taken out by final judgment of the Court of Appeal dated September 15, 1998; (b) for Kaarina Malmstrom, a judgment in the amount of $623.08 issued out of Small Claims Court on March 12, 1991; (c) for Eric Kraushaar, a judgment in the amount of $2,196.56 issued by the Ontario Court (General Division) and confirmed by the Court of Appeal on September 15, 1998; and (d) for Ersen Cogulu, a judgment in the amount of $45,693.54 and costs of $235.00 with interest at a rate of 15 per cent per annum from the date of judgment, being September 12, 1990.

[4] There were two other claims (not taken to judgment) which were accepted by the bankruptcy judge: a claim from the City of Timmins with respect to property taxes in the approximate amount of $7,000, and a 1979 judgment of Barbara Hughes for $600 plus interest.

[5] The bankruptcy judge found that the judgments and orders entered against Platt more than six months before the issuance of the petition were sufficient evidence in themselves of an act of bankruptcy having been committed within six months of the filing date of the petition. He ruled that a demand for payment of the judgments within the six-month period preceding the date of the petition was not necessary in order to establish the act of bankruptcy.

Issue

[6] The two issues in appeal are whether there was any demand for payment made with respect to the debts within six months of the petition and, if there was not, whether such a demand was in fact necessary to establish an act of bankruptcy on the part of the debtor. I will address these issues in reverse order.

· · ·

[7] Section 43(6) of the BIA, read in conjunction with s. 43(1)(b), provides that before a court can grant a receiving order, it must be satisfied that the petitioner has presented proof that an act of bankruptcy was committed within six months preceding the filing of the petition.

[8] The theory behind the six-month period appears to be that a petitioning creditor should not be permitted to rely upon stale-dated debts which have not been pursued in order to establish current acts of bankruptcy. However, it has been accepted that even in situations where a debt has become due more than six months before the date of the petition, a demand for payment made within the six-month period revives the original debt. Such a demand makes the debts current and failure to act on such a demand can serve as a current act of bankruptcy. As noted by Henry J in *Re Harrop of Milton Inc.* (1979), 22 OR (2d) 239, p. 243 OR:

> As I understand those judgments, they interpret the [*Bankruptcy Act*, RSC 1970, c. B-3] as meaning that, where the act of bankruptcy occurred prior to the six-month period and thereafter nothing was done by creditors with respect to the debts in default for a period of six months or more, the act of bankruptcy ceases to be current and cannot found a receiving order. But in my opinion that does not apply where the debtor has received continued demands for payment since the initial defaults and has not paid. This is the case here. ...

[9] In this case, there is some evidence of a demand for payment being made within the six-month period, but leaving that aside for the moment, it is still important to consider the bald question of whether it is necessary to make a demand where the debt is reduced to a judgment of the court pronounced outside the six-month period. In my opinion, this question has not been dealt with satisfactorily in Canada.

[10] It was the view of the bankruptcy judge that court judgments did not require a demand from the judgment creditor within six months of the petition in bankruptcy. As he put it in his reasons of February 7, 2000:

> ... As I discussed before, court judgments and orders are sufficient in themselves. They're the ultimate demand. There is no necessity to keep on demanding on a periodic basis as to the payment under those directions of the Court.

[11] I agree with the position taken by the bankruptcy judge.

[12] As noted by the respondent Malmstrom, the majority of cases cited by the appellant in which it has been found necessary to prove a fresh demand for payment within the six months immediately preceding the issue of the petition appear to be in regard to debts which have not been liquidated to the form of a judgment or an order. In addition, the appellant concedes that there are cases that have held that it is not necessary to make

a demand within the six-month period, as long as there is evidence of a continuing default. See *Re Rayner* (1934), 16 CBR 411 (PEISC); *Re The Pas Foundation & Excavation Ltd.* (1975), 21 CBR (NS) 154 (Man. QB); *Re Aarvi Construction Co.* (1978), 29 CBR (NS) 265 (Ont. SC); *Bayerische Hypotheken-und Wechselbunk Aktiengesellschaft v. Kaussen Estate* (1986), 64 CBR (NS) 97, (Que. Sup. Ct.), affirmed *sub nom. Re Kaussen Estate* (1988), 47 DLR (4th) 626 (Que. CA).

> The object of that limitation clearly is to prevent the filing of a petition for a stale default or isolated act of bankruptcy. It cannot, without disregarding the fundamental purpose of the Act, be held to apply to such a case as the present where a state of bankruptcy is shown to have continued without interruption from a time long prior to and down to the time of presentation of the petition and to be still subsisting; in other words a chronic state of bankruptcy existing for a period more than six months anterior to and down to the time of the presentation of the petition herein.
>
> • • •
>
> … In my opinion the evidence shows the equivalent of a continuous demand for payment by the petitioner and a continuous refusal on the part of the debtor to pay the judgment debt and costs of suit owed by the debtor to the petitioner.

[14] In *Re The Pas Foundation, supra,* Morse J specifically relied upon *Re Rayner,* and stated at p. 157: "To refuse a petition merely because formal demands for payment had not been made in the six months prior to the issuance of the petition would, in my view, be unrealistic."

[15] *Re Aarvi, supra,* was a decision of Saunders J of the Ontario Supreme Court [In Bankruptcy]. Saunders J decided that in circumstances where the debtor had ceased to meet his liabilities generally as they became due for several years, where such situation continued up to a period of time which was within the six months preceding the date of the filing of the petition, and where there was also evidence that the debtor continued to fail to meet its interest obligations on its outstanding loans from the bank, it was unnecessary for the petitioning creditor to have to provide evidence that the demand was made within the six-month period.

[16] In *Re Kaussen, supra,* the bankruptcy judge, Gomery J, who was affirmed by the Quebec Court of Appeal, put it even more broadly at p. 119:

> The reason for the six-month rule was to prevent a petitioning creditor from invoking a stale default as an act of bankruptcy. Where there is no purpose to be achieved in making fresh demands because it is apparent that the debtor cannot or will not pay, the creditor is entitled to consider that default, once clearly established, continues in effect. His recourse should not be excluded because he fails to perform the empty gesture of demanding payment from someone who has already demonstrated his inability to respond.

[17] Of all the cases referred to this court by the parties, I find the case of *Bombardier Credit Ltd. v. Find* (1998), 37 OR (3d) 641 (CA) particularly insightful. While not addressing the specific issue before this court, Charron JA did consider the question of whether an act of bankruptcy had been committed within the requisite limitation period. Charron JA first found that demands for payment made during the six-month period could revive debts that had accrued prior to the notice period. This conclusion was based on a recog-

nition that adopting the contrary view would result in the unnecessary filing of many petitions within six months of a debt accruing due by creditors who, out of an abundance of caution, may seek a remedy under the BIA simply for fear of forever being foreclosed from taking such action at a later time. Charron JA then went on to comment [at p. 9 CBR]:

> Although it is not necessary to consider the matter in this case, I would hasten to add that this decision [*Re Raitblat* (1925), 28 OWN 237 (Ont. SC), aff'd. (1925), 5 CBC 765 (Ont. CA)] should not be interpreted to mean that a fresh demand must be made within the six months preceding the filing of a petition in every case where a s. 42(1)(j) act of bankruptcy is alleged in order to satisfy the requirements of the [BIA]. The issue is not whether a fresh demand has or has not been made but whether the evidence is sufficient to prove that the act of bankruptcy has been committed within the requisite time period. Of course, the making of a fresh demand followed by a repeated default provides cogent evidence on this issue and may be a prudent practice to follow. However, even absent a fresh demand, the circumstances of the case may suffice to support a finding that the ceasing to meet liabilities generally as they become due extends to the relevant period of time.

[18] I agree with the sentiments expressed by Charron JA. Taking a practical approach to the question at bar, once a judgment or order has been entered against a debtor, no purpose would be served by forcing the creditor of that debtor to either file a petition immediately (and possibly prematurely), or to make repeated demands for payment once the petition is filed. It is inappropriate to require a creditor who has proceeded properly through legal channels and become a judgment creditor to make frequent demands for payment to the judgment debtor, only for the purpose of ensuring that the statutory time limitations are complied with. A judgment is a continuing demand for payment by the judgment creditor just as the failure to satisfy the judgment is a continuing refusal by the judgment debtor.

[19] Once a judgment or an order has been entered against a debtor, that judicial decree, even if entered more than six months before the filing of the petition, constitutes sufficient evidence of an act of bankruptcy having been committed within six months of the filing date. There is nothing improper in allowing a petitioning creditor to rely, as proof of bankruptcy, on formal judgments awarded against the debtor before the six-month period. Further, allowing petitioners to rely upon judicial pronouncements in order to establish current acts of bankruptcy is not contrary to the objectives of the BIA.

[20] Accordingly, I do not accept that the bankruptcy judge erred in holding that once a court judgment or order has been entered against a debtor, a demand for payment during the six months preceding the filing of the petition need not have been made in order to comply with the relevant BIA provisions. Therefore, I see no reason to interfere with the order in appeal.

Appeal dismissed.

Valente v. Fancsy Estate
(2004), 70 OR (3d) 31 (CA)

FELDMAN JA: [1] This appeal concerns a disputed petition for a receiving order. For the following reasons, I would allow the appeal, set aside the receiving order, allow the respondent to amend the petition and send the matter back to the bankruptcy judge.

Facts and Findings

[2] The petitioning creditor is the estate of Stephen Fancsy. Before he died, Mr. Fancsy advanced $900,000 to the debtor, Peter Valente, evidenced by a promissory note dated September 12, 1997. The note provided that interest would be at a rate of ten per cent and that the full amount was payable on September 15, 1998. The parties also entered into a share pledge agreement to secure the debt. The agreement provided that it was the sole recourse of the creditor in the event of default on the promissory note. The debtor held the shares in trust for his son, and represented in the share pledge agreement that he had obtained the authorization of the beneficial owner of the shares to pledge them pursuant to the agreement.

[3] The debtor never paid any monies under the note. The creditor's estate obtained summary judgment on the note on May 10, 2000, in the amount of $1,139,178.07 plus costs. No amount was ever paid on the judgment. The creditor conducted a judgment debtor examination on November 21, 2000, at which the debtor acknowledged that at that date there was another outstanding judgment against him for $800,000.

[4] The petition for a receiving order relied on the one debt, the judgment on the promissory note, and recited that the creditor held no security on the debtor's property for payment on the debt. In his notice disputing the petition, the debtor denied that he had failed to meet his liabilities generally as they became due, acknowledged the petitioner's debt and that it had not been paid, but stated that following the judgment representatives of the creditor estate had agreed to take steps to realize on the pledged shares but had not attempted to do so.

[5] The two issues for the bankruptcy judge were: (1) whether the one judgment debt over $1000 constituted the act of bankruptcy defined in s. 42(1)(j) of the *Bankruptcy and Insolvency Act*, RSC 1985, c. B-3, ceasing to meet liabilities generally as they become due; ...

[6] The bankruptcy judge granted the petition. She held: (1) based on this court's decision in *Platt v. Malmstrom* (2001), 53 OR (3d) 502, the judgment automatically qualified as a special circumstance required for a single debt to constitute the act of bankruptcy under s. 42(1)(j); ...

Issues on Appeal

(1) Did the bankruptcy judge err in holding that the single debt owed to the petitioning creditor qualified under s. 42(1)(j) of the B.I.A. as "ceas[ing] to meet ... liabilities generally as they become due"? ...

Analysis

. . .

[8] It is now well-settled in the case law that the failure to pay a single creditor can constitute an act of bankruptcy under s. 42(1)(j) when there are special circumstances, which have been recognized in three categories: (a) where repeated demands for payment have been made within the six-month period; (b) where the debt is significantly large and there is fraud or suspicious circumstances in the way the debtor has handled its assets which require that the processes of the B.I.A. be set in motion; and (c) prior to the filing of the petition, the debtor has admitted its inability to pay creditors generally without identifying the creditors: *Re Holmes* (1976), 9 OR (2d) 240 (Sup. Ct.); see also Houlden and Morawetz, *The 2004 Annotated Bankruptcy and Insolvency Act* (Toronto: Carswell, 2003) at 147 D s. 10(3).

[9] The bankruptcy judge held that there was no evidence establishing criteria (b) or (c). In this case, the debt has been pursued to judgment. The petitioning creditor does not state that repeated demands were made for payment of the judgment debt. Rather, the petitioning creditor relied on the case of *Platt, supra,* for the proposition that a judgment constitutes a continuing demand for payment and the failure to satisfy the judgment is a continuing refusal by the judgment debtor. The bankruptcy judge applied *Platt* and found that the one judgment satisfied the first test from *Holmes* and constituted an act of bankruptcy under s. 42(1)(j).

[10] In *Platt* the issue before the court was whether the act of bankruptcy had occurred within the six months prior to the petition. The concern in *Platt* was that there was no demand within the six months prior to the petition. The court noted that the theory behind the six-month limit is to ensure that a bankruptcy petitioner does not rely on stale-dated debts; however, it has been accepted that continued demands for payment following the debt and within the six-month period can have the effect of reviving the original debt, thus making the debt once again current: *Re Harrap of Milton Inc.* (1979), 22 OR (2d) 239 (Ont. SC). The court also referred to a line of cases that has recognized that no demand is necessary within the six months if there is evidence of a continuing default. See, e.g. *Re Aarvi Construction Co. Ltd.* (1978), 29 CBR (NS) 265 (Ont. SC). The court held that a judgment debt is a continuing demand for payment and in that context, is able to satisfy the statutory time requirement, that is, it can be considered as one of the debts that forms part of an act of bankruptcy within the six-month period prior to the petition. The court stated at para. 18: "It is inappropriate to require a creditor who has proceeded properly through legal channels and become a judgment creditor to make frequent demands for payment to the judgment debtor, *only for the purpose of ensuring that the statutory time limitations are complied with*" (emphasis added).

[11] The petition in *Platt* relied on six debts, four of which were taken to judgment. Each of the debts predated the petition by more than six months. The court was satisfied based on the number of debts and the continuing failure to pay them, that an act of bankruptcy had been committed within the six-month limit.

[12] However, that may not be the case where, for example, a single creditor obtains a judgment and either shortly thereafter petitions the debtor into bankruptcy based on the judgment and the implicit demands, or does nothing for an extended period, then

petitions on the basis that the judgment constitutes a continuing demand. In neither case would the judgment be evidence of failure to meet obligations generally, as contemplated by the special circumstances doctrine.

. . .

[14] The question for this court is whether the concept that a judgment constitutes a continuing demand will render every debt that has been pursued to judgment a special circumstance making that one debt evidence of an act of bankruptcy.

[15] Based on *Platt*, once a debt has been pursued to judgment, because that judgment constitutes a continuing demand for payment, it can form the basis for a finding that it constitutes an act of bankruptcy based on special circumstances. However, one judgment debt will not necessarily constitute special circumstances in every case. Ultimately the issue for the bankruptcy court on a petition for a receiving order is whether the creditor has proved that the debtor committed the act of bankruptcy alleged in the petition. ...

[16] Before the court can be satisfied that the failure to pay one judgment debt is tantamount to failing to meet liabilities generally as they become due, the court must examine and consider all of the circumstances including:

- the size of the judgment—a small unpaid judgment is less likely to indicate an act of bankruptcy than a very large one;
- how long the judgment has been outstanding—there may be reasons why a recently obtained judgment has not been paid as yet, including a potential appeal, the need to arrange for the marshalling of funds, the intent to make arrangements for payment over time or in the case of a default judgment, knowledge of the judgment;
- if a judgment has been outstanding for a long time, it may be that the debtor believes that the creditor is willing to wait for payment, and is paying his or her other debts as they fall due;
- whether the judgment creditor has conducted a judgment debtor examination and the results of that examination—if the judgment creditor can collect without invoking the mechanism of the bankruptcy process, a petition ought not to be granted;
- what steps the judgment creditor has taken to determine whether the debtor has other creditors and the results of those inquiries.

[17] In this case, the bankruptcy court judge appeared to conclude that the one judgment automatically constituted special circumstances and an act of bankruptcy, without considering whether, in all of the circumstances, the petitioning creditor had proved that the debtor was not meeting his liabilities generally as they fell due.

[18] The creditor had conducted a judgment debtor examination, the main thrust of which appeared to have been directed to the issue of the pledged shares. The record does not disclose whether other assets were pursued or whether the sheriff was sent to attempt to levy execution. (A report that there are no assets upon which to levy, itself constitutes an act of bankruptcy under s. 42(1)(e)).

[19] In this case, the only other potentially relevant evidence is the existence of another large judgment debt of $800,000 in favour of the Canadian Imperial Bank of Commerce which was outstanding at the date of Mr. Valente's judgment debtor examination, November 2000, more than six months before the petition. The petition did not rely on

this debt. Nor did the bankruptcy judge consider this evidence an acknowledgement by the debtor that he was failing to meet his liabilities generally as they became due. The petitioning creditor provided no proof that that judgment remained outstanding at the time of the petition. The debtor filed an unsworn Notice of Cause Against the Petition which states that he is able to meet his obligations as they come due and denies committing an act of bankruptcy. Although the debtor could have provided proof that he had paid the Bank of Commerce debt, the onus is on the petitioning creditor to prove the act of bankruptcy: *Re Roy* (1982), 44 CBR (NS) 86 (Ont. SC). The creditor could have called the bank as a witness on the petition or filed an execution certificate showing the continued existence of the debt.

[20] As the bankruptcy judge treated the judgment as automatically constituting an act of bankruptcy without considering the factors identified at para. 16 of these reasons, I would set aside the receiving order, but remit the matter to the bankruptcy judge for further consideration. ...

Appeal allowed.

NOTES AND QUESTIONS

1. In *S.C.M. Farms Limited v. W-4 Holdings Ltd.*, [2008] 2 WWR 73 (Man. QB), the creditor obtained judgment against the debtor in 1991 for $74,000. In 2001, the creditor renewed the judgment (including interest) for the new amount of $133,000. The debtor made no payments on the judgment and in 2007 the creditor applied for a bankruptcy order. The registrar issued the bankruptcy order and the bankrupt appealed on the basis that a judgment issued in 1991 could not form the basis of act of bankruptcy as it had not occurred within the six months prior to the filing of the bankruptcy application. The court dismissed the appeal and upheld the bankruptcy order, relying on the principle in *Platt* that a judgment was a continuing demand for payment (at para. 35):

> The facts of this particular case stretch this principle to the utmost, yet I am persuaded that a judgment of the Court constitutes a continuing demand for payment. A creditor who ignores an outstanding judgment does so at their peril. The lack of any payment against that judgment for 16 years is clear evidence of an act of bankruptcy.

Is *S.C.M. Farms* consistent with *Valente* and *Platt*?

2. In order to rely on s. 42(1)(j), must a creditor prove that the liability in question has in fact become due as of the date of the application for the bankruptcy order? In *Re Inex Pharmaceuticals Corp.* (2006), 20 CBR (5th) 256, the BC Court of Appeal held that in order for a creditor to rely on s. 42(1)(j) the liability must have come due and remain unpaid as of the date of the application.

3. Is there any justification for s. 48, which prohibits involuntary proceedings against various classes of debtors? Are some classes of debtors more worthy of protection from involuntary proceedings?

Moody v. Ashton
(1997), 47 CBR (3d) 91 (Sask. CA)

JACKSON JA (orally): The background facts are fully set out in the judgment under appeal. Thomas, Patrick and Darrell Moody made an application for a receiving order with respect to the assets of Brent Ashton. When the application was heard, Mr. Ashton asserted two positions. First, he argued that he owed no money to the Moodys. Second, he argued that he was able to pay the amount claimed by the Moodys to be owing to them and therefore a receiving order was inappropriate in the circumstances.

After determining that Mr. Ashton owed the Moodys more than $275,000, the learned bankruptcy judge made two other findings critical to this appeal. He found that Mr. Ashton had committed an act of bankruptcy by ceasing to meet his liabilities generally as they became due. But later in the judgment he also found Mr. Ashton was able to repay this amount. He said:

> ... the evidence establishes that Ashton is a wealthy individual who is quite capable of paying his debts, but has simply chosen not do so. He earned over $1.4 million in his last four years as a professional hockey player in the NHL. He has the means to pay his debts and should be required to do so.

He then directed that a receiving order should issue.

In our opinion, these last two findings cannot stand together. If Mr. Ashton was able to pay his debts, s. 43(7) of the *Bankruptcy and Insolvency Act*, RSC 1985, c. B-3 prevented the bankruptcy judge from issuing the receiving order. ...

We see no reason to give these words any meaning other than the one they would ordinarily bear. They are clear on their face. Once a bankruptcy court finds that a debtor is able to pay his or her debts, it "shall dismiss the petition."

Counsel for the Moodys argued that s. 144 of the *Bankruptcy and Insolvency Act* demonstrates that Parliament intended the Act to apply to solvent debtors who are able but unwilling to pay their debts. Section 144 directs that the bankrupt is entitled to any surplus remaining after the creditors have been paid. We agree that in its result, s. 144 can apply only to solvent debtors. But the section is necessary to deal with any surplus, no matter how small, which may arise from the sale of the debtor's assets. There could be many reasons for a surplus including a miscalculation of the value of the debtor's assets or a change in asset value. Since s. 144 serves these purposes, it cannot be read as counsel for the Moodys has asked us to interpret it. It does not override the clear wording of s. 43(7) which prevents a bankruptcy judge from issuing a petition where a debtor is able but unwilling to pay his or her debts.

Interpreting s. 43(7) in this way is consistent with the Act's purposes which permit the orderly payment of the debts of persons who are unable to do so and reintegrates them into society. (See Houlden and Morawetz, *Bankruptcy and Insolvency Law of Canada* (3d ed.), Vol. 1, pp. 1-3 & 1-4 as to the purposes of the Act.)

In reaching this conclusion, we prefer the approach taken in *Re Redbrooke Estates Limited; Re Meco Electric (1960) Inc.* (1970), 13 CBR (NS) 117 (Que. SC) to that followed in *In re Freeholders Oil Company, Limited* (1953), 33 CBR 149 (Sask. QB).

Given the conflicting findings made by the chambers judge, it is necessary to remit the matter to him for a determination as to whether Mr. Ashton was able to pay his debts in light of our interpretation of s. 43(7). The procedure to be followed by the bankruptcy judge on rehearing this aspect of his judgment is left to him.

Until such time as this issue is resolved, the Court is unable to consider the other grounds of appeal raised by Mr. Ashton. Its resolution may determine whether these other grounds are pursued.

Appeal allowed

NOTES AND QUESTIONS

1. In *Moody*, the court did not follow the approach adopted in *Re Freeholders Oil Company, Limited* (1953), 33 CBR 149 (Sask. QB). In *Freeholders*, the Saskatchewan Queen's Bench interpreted the words in s. 43(7) "is able to pay his debts" as meaning "able and willing to pay his debts." What implication would the *Freeholders* approach have on an application for a bankruptcy order where the debtor has significant assets? Does the *Freeholders* approach offer any advantages where the debtor has engaged in a course of conduct aimed at thwarting the collection efforts of the creditor? Compare the *Moody* and *Freeholders* approaches in the context of a debtor who has concealed assets and engaged in fraudulent transfers of funds to an offshore bank account. What would the result of the bankruptcy application be where the debtor produced his or her foreign bank statements showing substantial assets?

Bank of Montreal v. Scott Road Enterprises Ltd.
(1989), 57 DLR (4th) 623 (BCCA)

ESSON JA: This appeal raises the question whether it is open to the court to dismiss a petition in bankruptcy on the ground that it has been brought by a secured creditor solely for the purpose of bringing into effect the scheme of distribution in the *Bankruptcy Act*, RSC 1970, c. B-3, and thus destroying the priority which other creditors would otherwise have had. There is no decision directly on point which is binding on this Court.

This is such a case. The appellant company carried on a substantial car dealership business under a bank line of credit secured by a floating charge debenture. In October, 1987 the bank appointed a receiver who immediately took possession and closed the business. The amount owing to the bank was then about $800,000, about $200,000 more than the maximum amount likely to be realized on liquidation. As the bank's debenture secures it to a limit of $3,000,000 it was obvious from the beginning that it would suffer a shortfall and that no one else could recover anything except someone holding a charge prior to that of the bank.

As with every going concern, there were a number of creditors entitled to such charges. There was unremitted sales tax of about $20,000, WCB assessments of about $4,000 and, most significantly, there was about $39,000 in unpaid wages and vacation pay and some $15,000 in unremitted employee deductions for income tax, Canada Pension Plan and unemployment insurance. The receiver recognized that all of those claims would be secured by statutory liens. I will not refer in detail to the source of those liens and charges except the one securing the wage claims. It arises under s. 15 of the *Employment Standards Act*, SBC 1980, c. 10, which reads:

Lien and charge on property

15(1) Notwithstanding any other Act, unpaid wages constitute a lien, charge and secured debt in favour of the director, dating from the time that the wages were earned, against all the real and personal property of the obligor, including money due or accruing due to the obligor from any source.

(1.1) Unpaid wages set out in an order or decision filed by the Industrial Relations Council pursuant to section 30 of the *Industrial Relations Act* constitute a lien, charge and secured debt in favour named in the order or decision against all the real and personal property of the employer or other person named in the order.

(2) Notwithstanding any other Act, the amount of a lien and charge and secured debt referred to in subsections (1) and (1.1) is payable and enforceable in priority over all liens, judgments, charges or any other claims or rights including those of the Crown in right of the Province and, without limiting the generality of the foregoing, the amount has priority over

(a) and assignment, including an assignment of book debts, whether absolute or otherwise and whether crystallized or not,

(b) a mortgage of personal property,

(c) a debenture charging personal property, whether crystallized or not, and

(d) a contract, account receivable, insurance claim or proceeds of a sale of goods,

whether made or created before or after the date the wages were earned or the date a payment for the benefit of an employee became due.

. . .

It is to be noted that the lien and charge is specifically given priority over assignments of book debts and debentures charging personal property, the broad forms of security most often relied on by banks. I have not reproduced subs. (3) which excludes priority over a registered mortgage or debenture charging land except for advances made after the certificate of judgment was registered.

At one time, it was considered to be settled law in this province that such statutory charges were enforceable according to their tenor in a bankruptcy. A leading case was the judgment of Wilson JA (later CJSC) for this Court in *In Re Clemenshaw* (1962), 4 CBR 238 which concerned the lien of the WCB. But the law laid down in that, and other cases has been overruled by later decisions of the Supreme Court of Canada holding that, on the happening of bankruptcy, such charges securing Crown claims are effectively destroyed and that the order of distribution which must prevail is that set out in s. 136(1), formerly s. 107(1): *Deputy Minister of Revenue v. Rainville in re Bourgault*, [1980] 1 SCR 35, and *Deloitte Haskins and Sells Limited v. The Workers' Compensation Board*, [1985] 1 SCR 785.

Upon learning of the substantial magnitude of the claims secured by statutory liens, the bank and its lawyers pressed the directors of the company to assign it into bankruptcy and, when the directors did not do so, filed the petition in bankruptcy which led to the receiving order now under appeal. We are told that, in light of the law laid down in Rainville, those steps have become routine in such situations.

In the petition, which was launched about six weeks after the appointment of the receiver, the bank asserted that the company had failed to meet its obligations generally as they became due. The company opposed the petition, submitting that it should be dismissed under what is now s. 43(7) (then s. 25(7)), which reads:

> (7) Where the court is not satisfied with the proof of the facts alleged in the petition or of the service of the petition, or is satisfied by the debtor that he is able to pay his debts, or that for other sufficient cause no order ought to be made, it shall dismiss the petition.

The first ground of opposition was that there had been no act of bankruptcy. At the date of the appointment of the receiver, that may have been so but, at the date of filing the petition the company had ceased to meet its obligations. The chambers judge, Mr. Justice McKenzie, held that the relevant date was that of firming the petition. On this appeal, the company did not seriously attack the correctness of that conclusion. The second point raised by the company was rejected by McKenzie J in these words:

> In respect of the device used to satisfy subsection 25(2), I find it to be an effective device to satisfy the provisions of that section and the employment of that or any other device on the part of this or any other creditor to avail itself of the provisions of this Act to enhance its position comes within the decision of Madam Justice McLachlin in [Re Black Bros. (1978) Ltd.] (1982) 41 CBR (NS) 163.
>
> To do what I am invited to do, that is to decline the petition on the grounds that it has been brought for an improper purpose, would be to elevate me without authority to an appellate position that I do not occupy. I am obliged under the Hansard Spruce Mills Limited case to follow a considered decision and I find that Re Black Bros. was one that was considered and applies to the case at bar.
>
> I find no other ground upon which I can consider refusing this petition and according[ly] a Receiv[ing] Order will be granted against the Respondent company.

What was then s. 25(2) is now s. 43(2). It reads:

> (2) Where the petitioning creditor referred to in subsection (1) is a secured creditor, he shall in his petition either state that he is willing to give up his security for the benefit of the creditors in the event of a receiving order being made against the debtor, or give an estimate of the value of his security, and in the latter case he may be admitted as a petitioning creditor to the extent of the balance of the debt due to him after deducting the value so estimated, in the same manner as if he were an unsecured creditor.

The device referred to by the chambers judge is in these paragraphs of the petition:

> 2. THAT SCOTT ROAD ENTERPRISES LTD. is justly and truly indebted to the Petitioner in the sum of $494,003.54 as at December 7, 1987, together with the Receiver's fees and expenses, which indebtedness is in consideration of the Petitioner extending credit to SCOTT ROAD ENTERPRISES LTD. and is evidenced by: a Demand Debenture in the principal amount of $3,000,000, dated for reference June 1, 1987.
>
> 3. THAT the Petitioner holds security for part of the said sum but that the Petitioner will give up such security to the extent of $1,000 for the benefit of the creditors of SCOTT ROAD ENTERPRISES LTD. in the event of a receiving order being made against it.

I question whether that language complies with s. 43(2) which appears to give to the secured creditor the option to take one of two positions. He can give up his security entirely or can give an estimate of its value. The language of para. 3 does neither. That paragraph also seems to be inaccurate in stating that the bank holds security for "part of the said sum." All of the other evidence is to the effect that its security covers all indebtedness.

However, as that question was not made a ground of appeal, we need not reach a decision on it. Were it to be resolved against the bank, the appropriate course might well be to allow it to amend to give a proper estimate of the value of the security. The question of substance is that in respect of which McKenzie J felt bound to follow the decision in *Re Black Bros. (1978) Ltd.* In that case McLachlin J (now CJSC) said at p. 165:

> One purpose—usually the main purpose—of an order in bankruptcy is to secure an equitable distribution of the debtor's property amongst creditors. However, another purpose may be to permit creditors to avail themselves of provisions in the Act which may enhance their positions, for example, by giving them certain priorities which they would not otherwise enjoy. The latter purpose, on the authorities, is a proper and sufficient basis for granting an order. Thus, in *Re Harrop of Milton Inc.* (1979) 22 OR (2d) 239, 29 CBR (NS) 289, 92 DLR (3d) 535 (HC) Henry J found that since the assets were fully encumbered by the petitioner's debenture, there could be no assets available for distribution to the unsecured creditors. However, he went on to hold that a receiving order should go on the ground that it is not improper for a secured creditor to file a petition or procure an assignment in bankruptcy for the purpose of defeating other creditors' priorities, citing in support *Re Develox Indust. Ltd.*, [1970] 3 OR 199, 14 CBR (NS) 132, 12 DLR (3d) 579 (HC), and *Re Gasthof Schnitzel House Ltd.*, 27 CBR (NS) 75, [1978] 2 WWR 756 (BCSC); see *Re Koprel Enterprises Ltd.* (1978), 27 CBR (NS) 22 (BCSC).

The use of bankruptcy proceedings in that way has often been directed against distraining landlords. One such case came before this Court in *Triona Investments Ltd. v. Smythe, McMahon Inc.* (1988), 23 BCLR (2d) 222. In giving judgment for the court, I commented at p. 224:

> The propriety of a secured creditor employing the *Bankruptcy Act* in that way has been established by a line of cases, the correctness of which is not in issue on this appeal. The leading British Columbia cases in that line are the decision of Ruttan J in *Re Gasthof Schnitzel House Ltd. and Sanderson*, [1978] 2 WWR 756, 27 CBR (NS) 75 (BCSC), and that of Legg J in *Re Koprel Ent. Ltd.* (1978), 27 CBR (NS) 22 (BCSC). In each case, it was accepted that there was no possibility of the bankruptcy conferring any benefit on the general creditors. It was nevertheless held to be proper for the secured creditor, in "jockeying for position" against the landlord, to "promote" a bankruptcy in order to defeat the priority which would otherwise be afforded to the landlord.

In the passage quoted from the judgment of McLachlin J in *Re Black Bros.*, that learned judge relied on the judgment of Henry J in *Re Harrop of Milton Inc.* which is the most fully reasoned of the line of cases. It is of some interest that Henry J felt bound to follow the earlier authorities, as he put it at p. 295: "… notwithstanding that I have some misgivings." I detect an implication of similar misgivings in the language of McKenzie J in this case; as there was in my observations in Triona Investments Ltd. (*supra*).

We were also referred to expressions of misgiving by learned commentators. In an article entitled, "Bankruptcy in a Receivership" in (1984), 1 *National Insolvency Review* 23, Alan Kemp-Gee said at p. 27 under the heading, "Is it equitable for a secured creditor to invoke a bankruptcy?":

> Having discussed the technicalities surrounding the secured creditors' use of the *Bankruptcy Act*, a larger issue should be considered: is it appropriate for the secured creditor to invoke a bankruptcy? The Act was intended, after all, to protect unsecured creditors.
>
> It may well be in the best interest of a secured creditor to use the mechanism of a bankruptcy to deal with claims of landlords or the Crown. However, bankruptcy is supposed to be the vehicle available to distribute the assets of a debtor equitably amongst the unsecured creditors. The *Bankruptcy Act* specifically states that, with few exceptions, secured creditors are free to deal with their security in a commercially reasonable fashion outside the Act. Therefore, use of bankruptcy by a secured creditor seems to contravene the spirit of the legislation.

In an article entitled "The Use of the Bankruptcy Act by Secured Creditors" in Bankruptcy—Present Problems and Future Perspectives, Meredith Memorial Lectures, McGill University, 1985, Andre Giroux said at p. 240 under the heading, "Priority Claims":

> One issue that is still debated by creditors who may be entitled to privileges is whether the order of distribution of section 107 applies when the secured creditor proceeds to realize on the basis of his security instrument or when there is no equity for the trustee in the realization of the assets. Although the courts seem to continue to maintain that the ranking order of the privileged creditors is affected by the bankruptcy of a debtor and that therefore the secured creditors are entitled to the proceeds of realization without regard to the claims of these creditors, recent judgments tend to question more and more the use of the *Bankruptcy Act* strictly for the purpose of reversing the priorities. However, there is no doubt that section 107 does apply when the realization of the assets and the distribution of the proceeds are made by the trustee in bankruptcy.

The circumstances of this case illustrate starkly the inequitable consequences which can flow from permitting the debentureholder to employ the *Bankruptcy Act* to destroy the priority which would otherwise have been enjoyed by the Crown and the wage-earners. The affidavit of Mr. Day, a director, states that until October 19, on which day the receiver was appointed, the company had met all its obligations as they became due or within the terms of arrangements with creditors. More specifically, he says, and there is no suggestion that this is not the fact, that until that day the company had been current in all payments for wages and vacation pay, to Revenue Canada for employee deductions, to the Minister of Finance for provincial sales tax, and to the Workers' Compensation Board. The receiver was appointed on a pay day. The bank closed out the payroll account before the cheques could be presented, and thus the default to the employees arose.

The submission of the appellant is, in essence, that what has taken place here is contrary to the spirit, the purpose, and the object of the *Bankruptcy Act*, and is so clearly inequitable in its consequences as to provide "sufficient cause" for refusing to make the order. The bank's first response to that is that there is no real unfairness because, although it is the agents of the Crown and the employees of the bankrupt who may lose their priority, it is not they who are prosecuting this appeal. It is, rather, the company on the instructions of its directors who admittedly are pursuing the matter in an attempt to avoid the liability which may be imposed upon them by statute for the tax deductions, unpaid wages and like liabilities. The bank emphasizes that, if the company was meeting its obligations up to the date of the receivership, it was doing so in reliance on the bank's line of credit and in a way which created a deficit position, and that there is nothing wrong with the bank doing all it can to reduce its ultimate loss as much as possible. While all that may be true, it is no answer to the real question which is whether valid legislative schemes for protecting Crown revenues and wages should be set at nought by the happening of a bankruptcy which serves no useful purpose. Nor is it an answer to throw the liability on the directors, even if they are in a position to meet it.

Were it not for one matter to which I have not yet referred, I would conclude that the facts and circumstances to which I have referred constitute "sufficient cause" why no order ought to be made, and that the petition ought to have been dismissed on that ground. That matter is a decision of the Supreme Court of Canada released since the granting of the petition in this case. On May 26, 1988 the court gave judgment in *Federal Business Development Bank v. Quebec (Commission de la sante et de al securite du travail)*, [1988] 1 SCR 1061. In that case, the contest was between a trustee for bondholders and the Workers' Compensation Commission. The Court of Appeal of Quebec had distinguished *Rainville (supra)* and *Deloitte Haskins, (supra)*, and had granted priority to the Commission. The Supreme Court held that it erred in doing so. The specific facts and issues of the case need not concern us—the decision does not directly touch the issue which has arisen here. But, in giving judgment for the court, Lamer J made an obiter statement which is clearly in point. At p. 1072, he said:

Conclusion

I therefore consider that the claims of the parties to the case must be ranked in the order determined by the *Bankruptcy Act*. As the federal Parliament has exclusive jurisdiction to set priorities in a bankruptcy matter, the scheme of distribution in s. 107 of the *Bankruptcy Act* must be applied here. As respondent's claim was covered by s. 107(1)(h) of the Act, respondent is a preferred creditor whose claim must be ranked after that of appellant, whether or not the trustee realized on his security outside the bankruptcy proceeding. Once the bankruptcy has occurred, the federal statute applies to all creditors of the debtor.

It is true that such a solution may encourage secured creditors to bring about the bankruptcy of their debtor in order to improve their title. On the other hand, this solution has obvious advantages. As soon as the bankruptcy occurs the *Bankruptcy Act* will be applied: the mere fact that a creditor is mentioned in s. 107 of the Act suffices for such creditor to be ranked as a preferred creditor and in the position indicated in that provision. As provincial statutes cannot affect the priorities created by the federal statute, consistency in the order of priority in bankruptcy situations is ensured from one province to another.

It is the last paragraph which is relevant to the issue raised here. This is a case in which the secured creditor brought about the bankruptcy of its debtor solely in order to improve its title. The paragraph represents a considered dictum of the court in relation to a question, essentially one of policy, as to the effect to be given to a federal statute. It is a dictum which, in my view, we are bound to follow and to apply by holding that such a circumstance is not sufficient cause to refuse to grant the receiving order. If the present state of the law is unsatisfactory, it is for Parliament to remedy it.

If the position with respect to the wage-earners is as the bank asserts it to be, the present state of the law may be most unsatisfactory. Wages are not a debt like any other—it has always been recognized that because of their nature they should be accorded a high degree of protection. The *Bankruptcy Act* recognizes that principle by putting wage-earners just after the trustee in the order of distribution in s. 136(1). But, in present-day circumstances, that is an illusory benefit. The section has not been amended since, I believe 1949 and the upper limit of the benefit remains at the archaically modest level of $500. Even that modest protection is illusory because, in the ensuing 40 years, there has developed the virtually universal practice of banks taking floating security on everything, a practice which in combination with the law laid down in Rainville has greatly altered what was earlier thought to be the ordinary balance between the rights of creditors. The illusory nature of the benefit conferred by the *Bankruptcy Act* on wage-earners may have been a factor in the enactment of provisions such as s. 15 of the *Employment Standards Act* and, before Rainville, was probably as effective a kind of protection as could be devised. But, if the rule in Rainville applies to this charge, that protection has itself become illusory in practical terms.

The difficulty thus created for wage-earners may be very serious because the extent to which the legislative scheme can be set at nought by the device employed here may be almost complete. The essence of the legislative scheme is to provide a first charge. Most businesses large enough to have employees carry on at the sufferance of their bankers in the sense that their loans may be called on demand, thus crystallizing the bank's security on every asset of every kind. It follows that, in most cases, the bank will be in a position to do what was done here, i.e. to employ its security to make the debtor effectively bankrupt, and then to petition it into bankruptcy. Because of the inherent flexibility of its security, the bank in all such cases will be in a position to time the appointment of the receiver, as was done here, to arrange matters so that the undertaking will have the benefit of the employees' efforts for a maximum period. In those businesses which are labour intensive, that may be an important consideration. An incidental undesirable consequence of this device is that in addition to the always substantial layer of costs created by a receivership, the happening of bankruptcy will create a further layer of costs to be met before any payment can be made to wage-earners under s. 136(1)(d).

I should not be understood as holding that the charge created by s. 15 of the *Employment Standards Act* is destroyed by the happening of bankruptcy. That issue is not before us and could well be raised at a later stage in this proceeding. To this point I have discussed the matter on the assumption that it will be destroyed because both parties made their arguments on that assumption. We were not, however, referred to any case holding that to be so. The s. 15 charge is different from those in the decisions of the Supreme Court of Canada, which I have called the *Rainville* line of cases, all of which I think have been concerned with charges securing a claim of the Crown. The charge created by s. 15 does not secure a claim of the Crown but may be caught by the reasoning in the *Rainville* line of cases because of the preferred status conferred by s. 136(1)(d). I observe that, if that is the case, the result would seem to be the anomalous one that this small and largely futile preference leaves wage-earners in a worse position than if they were not mentioned in the *Bankruptcy Act*. The question whether that result could have been intended by Parliament cannot be decided on this appeal.

· · ·

Appeal dismissed.

NOTES AND QUESTIONS

1. *Secured creditors invoking involuntary bankruptcy proceedings: Bank of Montreal v. Scott* is authority for the well-settled proposition that an application may be brought by a secured creditor to advance its own interests regardless of how it affects the debtor's other creditors. The *Scott* principle was applied most recently by the Ontario Court of Appeal in *Re Ivaco Inc.* (2006), 83 OR (3d) 108. In *Ivaco*, the Ontario Court of Appeal considered a priority dispute between two classes of creditors. On one side employees and retirees held claims in Ivaco's underfunded pension plans. These claims were covered by the deemed trust and lien provisions of the Ontario *Pension Benefits Act*. (For a more detailed discussion of deemed trusts, see Chapter 9.) The competing claimants were Ivaco's financial and trade creditors who sought to put Ivaco into bankruptcy so as to "take advantage of the scheme of distribution" under the BIA. As the court pointed out, deemed provincial trusts do not "enjoy priority under the federal bankruptcy statute." The superintendent of financial services argued that a bankruptcy order would be unfair, because provincial law had shown a "special solicitude" for pensioners by ensuring that retirees have income security. The Court of Appeal rejected this argument and concluded (at paras. 75-76) that the bankruptcy procedure was proper even if it meant altering non-bankruptcy priorities:

> But federal insolvency law has not shown the same solicitude. It does not accord the claims of "sympathetic" creditors more weight than the claims of "unsympathetic" ones. Subject to specified exceptions, the BIA aims to distribute a bankrupt debtor's estate equitably among all of the estate's creditors. There are undoubtedly compelling policy reasons to protect pension rights in an insolvency. But, as I have said, it is for Parliament, not the courts, to do so. ...
>
> The petitioning creditors have met the technical requirements for bankruptcy. And their desire to use the BIA to alter priorities is a legitimate reason to seek a bankruptcy order. See for example *Bank of Montreal v. Scott Road Enterprises Ltd.* (1989), 57 DLR (4th) 623 (BCCA).

Is this line of cases objectionable on the ground that it distorts bankruptcy law's goals and encourages opportunistic conduct? Why is it all right for a secured creditor to put the debtor into bankruptcy to eliminate a creditor with a superior claim and not acceptable for a debtor to put himself into bankruptcy to frustrate his wife's matrimonial property claims? See *Wale*, below.

2. *Secured creditors and the trustee in bankruptcy:* A secured creditor with a general security interest in the debtor's property often files a s. 43 application even though the secured creditor has installed a privately appointed receiver-manager to enforce its security interest. This does not mean that the receiver-manager is displaced on the appointment of the trustee in bankruptcy, because there is no such requirement in the BIA. On the contrary, s. 71 makes it clear that the vesting of the debtor's property in the trustee is qualified by the (antecedent) rights of the secured creditor. In practice, to reduce costs, the secured creditor's

application under s. 43 will frequently designate the receiver-manager as trustee. This practice is expressly sanctioned in s. 13.4 of the BIA, but could it give rise to a conflict of interests given the fact that the trustee will be wearing two hats? Does s. 13.4 adequately maintain the independence of the trustee?

Re Dahl
(1986), 57 CBR (NS) 296 (Alta. QB)

MacDONALD J: [1] On 29th November 1984 Oscar Martin Dahl (hereinafter referred to as "Dahl") made an assignment of his property to Thorne Riddell Inc. as trustee, for the benefit of his creditors generally, thereby committing an act of bankruptcy pursuant to s. 24(1)(a) of the *Bankruptcy Act*. On 30th November 1984 the official receiver appointed Thorne Riddell Inc. as trustee in the matter of the bankruptcy of Oscar Martin Dahl.

[2] On 19th December 1984 Adolph William Kalau (hereinafter referred to as "Kalau"), as plaintiff, without leave of the court, caused a statement of claim to be issued naming Dahl, Thorne Riddell Inc., Josephine Dahl, James B. McCashin, the North West Life Assurance Company of Canada and Spade Construction Ltd. as defendants. The plaintiff sought a declaration that the bankruptcy of Dahl was a nullity and interim and permanent injunctions.

. . .

[9] It was held in *Eastern Trust Co. v. Lloyd Mfg. Co.; Re Jarvis*, 56 NSR 246, that the bankruptcy rules are a full and complete code and formed for the purpose of providing a summary and expeditious method for determining questions arising in bankruptcy matters with a minimum of cost. The jurisdiction of the court in bankruptcy is given by the *Bankruptcy Act*. In *Re Rousseau; Ont. Equitable Life & Accident Ins. Co. v. Lamarre* (1932), 14 CBR 182, it was held:

> Considering that *The Bankruptcy Act*, is a special statute of the Dominion of Canada dealing with a special subject and its application is, therefore, strictly limited to the rights, remedies, and other matters therein expressly stated, and any matter which is not so expressly declared to be governed by the Act must be deemed to have been intentionally omitted from its application. Similarly, the Bankruptcy Court being a statutory Court, its jurisdiction is limited to that conferred upon it by the Act, and its powers and authority cannot be extended by implication or inference beyond the express terms of the Act;

. . .

[11] In my respectful opinion the Act does not give the court authority either on an interim or permanent basis to stay a receiving order or an assignment. Under s. 25(10) and (11) of the Act the court is given authority to stay petitions but not to stay a receiving order. (See *Re 389179 Ont. Ltd. (No. 2)* (1979), 30 CBR 181). The Act does give the court authority to annul the bankruptcy. It would follow that any legal actions seeking that remedy should be fashioned accordingly. This might be done by notice of motion in accordance with R. 12.

[12] The notice of motion filed in this case does not expressly seek annulment of the bankruptcy on the ground that the assignment ought not to have been filed.

[13] The crux of the dispute between Kalau and Dahl revolves over a shareholder agreement between them dated 1st December 1982. In brief, that agreement provided that upon the death of one of the parties the survivor would purchase the shares of the deceased in Spade Construction Ltd., a company whose shares were held in equal number by Kalau and Dahl. Under the agreement insurance in the sum of $1,000,000 was placed on each party and the policies assigned to James B. McCashin as a party to the agreement as trustee. The agreement provided that the proceeds of the life insurance on a deceased be used for the purchase of the shares of the deceased by the survivor with any surplus of insurance moneys going to the survivor. The agreement provided a method for fixing the price to be paid for the shares. Clause 9 of the agreement gave the right to each shareholder on termination of the agreement to purchase from the trustee the policy of insurance on his own life. Clause 10 of the agreement in subcl. (b) provided:

> Except for the rights and duties provided for in clause 9 hereof, this agreement shall cease and determine on the occurrence of any of the following events namely …
>
> > (b) Bankruptcy or receivership of either or both of the Shareholders.

. . .

[15] It therefore appears that Dahl is in bankruptcy unless or until his bankruptcy is set aside pursuant to s. 151 of the Act. His bankruptcy terminates the agreement between the shareholders except for the provisions of cl. 9 of the agreement. If the shareholder agreement is terminated, Dahl is given the right to purchase the insurance on his life from the trustee holding the insurance. The trustee in bankruptcy has notified the trustee holding the insurance policies that purchase of the insurance is elected.

[16] The background to all this is a deadlock between the two shareholders which they have been unable to resolve. In addition, Dahl is suffering from terminal cancer and is desirous of putting his personal affairs in order. Failing agreement between the shareholders, his going into bankruptcy may offer the means of enabling him to break the deadlock. Each shareholder could become the owner of the insurance on his own life, and death would then cause the proceeds of the insurance to pass to his beneficiary rather than to the trustee of the policy. It seems possible that, on the death of Dahl, Kalau would benefit if the shareholder agreement is in effect.

[17] The issue, then, is whether or not the assignment of Dahl, in the words of s. 151, "ought not to have been filed."

. . .

[21] Even if an assignment is filed to defeat the claim of a judgment creditor, there is nothing unlawful about such assignment and the court will not set it aside: *Irving Oil Co. v. Murphy* (1962), 5 CBR 203.

[22] Under the Australian and English *Bankruptcy Acts*, it is understood that a debtor may petition himself into bankruptcy, thus achieving the same result as an assignment under the Canadian Act. In the case of *Re Mottee; ex parte Mottee v. Official Receiver* (1977), 16 ALR 129 (Fed. Ct. of Bankruptcy), Mrs. M. presented a petition under the *Matrimonial Causes Act* claiming the interest of Mr. M. in the matrimonial home. The court granted an order that the home be sold and permitting Mrs. M. to use the proceeds to purchase another home for herself and the children. The house so purchased was to be treated as the former matrimonial home for the purposes of the petition. Prior to sale

of the matrimonial home Mr. M. petitioned himself into bankruptcy. Mrs. M. made application to the Federal Court of Bankruptcy seeking that the bankruptcy of Mr. M. be annulled. It was held that, where a man who is insolvent or reasonably believes he is insolvent presents a petition against himself and does not thereby commit a fraud on his creditors, his bankruptcy will not be annulled merely because his motive in presenting his petition was "to protect himself from evils which he might otherwise suffer." Even if M. had the ulterior purpose in presenting his petition of causing his interest in the former matrimonial home to vest in the official receiver and so prevent the matrimonial causes court from settling that interest on his former wife, that was not sufficient ground for the court to annul the bankruptcy. Riley J at pp. 137-38 stated:

> The principle which I think may be extracted from the cases to which I have referred is that, where a man who is insolvent, or reasonably believes he is insolvent, presents a petition against himself, and does not thereby commit (as in *Re Betts, supra*) a fraud on his creditors, his bankruptcy will not be annulled merely because his motive in presenting his petition was, in the words of Evershed MR "to protect himself from evils which he might otherwise suffer."

[23] In *Re Dunn; ex parte Official Receiver v. Dunn*, [1949] Ch. 640, the English *Bankruptcy Act* was quoted:

> Where in the opinion of the court a debtor ought not to have been adjudged bankrupt, or where it is proved to the satisfaction of the court that the debts of the bankrupt are paid in full, the court may, on the application of any person interested, by order annul the adjudication.

[24] Evershed MR at p. 392 stated:

> ... I think it clearly emerges from that case that the circumstances that the debtor has filed his petition in order to protect himself from evils which he might otherwise suffer and not with any benevolent intention of benefiting his creditors by securing a fair distribution of assets among his creditors is no reason why an order should not be made. ... There is nothing, I think, in the policy of the Act of 1914 which disentitles the debtor to say: "I will go bankrupt and protect myself from these possibilities and get rid, whether or not they be provable debts, of any claims which are made against me." In my view, there is no ground for saying that the attitude amounts to an abuse of the process of the court and no ground for saying that, without amounting to an abuse of the process of the court, it can be treated as sufficient reason for the court exercising its power under s. 29 and annulling the order.

[25] McLachlin J, in the matter of the bankruptcy of *Re Black Bros. (1978) Ltd.* [(1982), 41 CBR (NS) 163, at 165 (BCSC)], stated:

> One purpose—usually the main purpose—of an order in bankruptcy is to secure an equitable distribution of the debtor's property amongst creditors. However, another purpose may be to permit creditors to avail themselves of provisions in the Act which may enhance their positions, for example, by giving them certain priorities which they would not otherwise enjoy. The latter purpose, on the authorities, is a proper and sufficient basis for granting an order. Thus, in *Re Harrop of Milton Inc.* (1979), 22 OR (2d) 239, Henry J found that, since

the assets were fully encumbered by the petitioner's debenture, there could be no assets available for distribution to the unsecured creditors. However, he went on to hold that a receiving order should go on the ground that it is not improper for a secured creditor to file a petition or procure an assignment in bankruptcy for the purpose of defeating other creditors' priorities, citing in support *Re Develox Indust. Ltd.*, [1970] 3 OR 199, and *Re Gasthof Schnitzel House Ltd.*, 27 CBR 75; see also *Koprel Enterprises Ltd.* (1978), 27 CBR 22.

[26] From these and other cases it would seem that the bankruptcy of the debtor will not be annulled simply because by his assignment he gains benefits for himself, provided that his assignment meets the requirements of the Act. In the case at bar the fact that the assignment may have the effect of terminating the shareholders' agreement, thus giving one or other of the shareholders an economic advantage, and even though the debtor sought that advantage, would not appear to be of sufficient ground for annulling the bankruptcy.

[27] The validity of the assignment, therefore, would depend entirely on the debtor satisfying the requirements of the *Bankruptcy Act* as long as there is no abuse of the process of the court. If I am correct in this, an interested person wishing to have the bankruptcy annulled would adduce evidence to show that the debtor was not an insolvent person when he made his assignment, or alternatively, there is some other ground recognized by the court that satisfies the court that the assignment ought not to have been filed.

[28] Such an application should be made by notice of motion as I have indicated and, if need be, the directions of the court should be sought as to the procedure to be followed. In my opinion this matter is to be resolved in the bankruptcy court where *viva voce* evidence can be heard if need be.

. . .

Motion dismissed.

Re Wale
(1996), 45 CBR (3d) 15 (Ont. Gen. Div.)

O'CONNOR J: [1] Henry John Wale's assignment in bankruptcy was date-stamped by the Official Receiver an hour and a half before the commencement of his family law trial. His former wife brings this motion, under s. 181 of the *Bankruptcy and Insolvency Act*, to annul the bankruptcy and to vest his property in her pending the outcome of the family law trial, or to exempt her claims from the usual stay of creditor proceedings under s. 69.3, and other relief. She argues his filing was motivated solely by his desire to defeat her family law claims and was an abuse of the process of the court. He says he had no such intention, he is an "insolvent person," as defined by the act and is entitled to its protection.

History of the Proceedings

[2] Ms. Wale commenced family law proceedings by application on August 11, 1994. The parties were divorced in October 1995 and he has remarried. On December 15, 1995, McKay J made an interim order, *inter alia*, restraining Mr. Wale from dissipating

assets except in the ordinary course of business. At the outset of the trial on October 16, 1996, Ms. Wale sought an order declaring Mr. Wale in contempt for breach of the interim order, alleging he had sold his inventory and tools, removed all the furnishings from the matrimonial home and attempted to place other assets out of her reach. The court was also advised Mr. Wale had attended on a trustee in bankruptcy the previous week and filed an assignment late Friday afternoon, October 13, 1996. It was received and date-stamped by the Official Receiver at 8:30 am, October 16, 1996, the first day of trial. After one day's evidence and argument the matter was adjourned to October 28, 1996 to permit Ms. Wale to bring this motion to annul the bankruptcy assignment. Pending return of the matter, I ordered Mr. Wale's interest in the matrimonial home and all his assets be held in trust, the contents of the home be returned to it, that he make the mortgage and other payments, that Ms. Wale may occupy the home and the parties cooperate in selling it.

[3] The annulment motion was served on the parties, the trustee and all the creditors. Upon return of the motion the parties and the trustee were represented by counsel. None of the creditors attended or was represented. Pending this ruling I ordered several measures intended to preserve the status quo, including postponing the creditors meeting and requiring Mr. Wale deliver to the trustee $4500 (part of what he received on the sale of his inventory), out of which the trustee is required to pay the mortgage and other household expenses.

Evidence Summary

[4] The Wales lived together and were married for a total of eighteen years. He is a skilled cabinet-maker, specializing in custom-built kitchens. They developed a successful business, first designing and constructing pine furniture and then building and installing kitchens. They built a workshop and showroom behind their home in Chatsworth. She did the books and some of the sales and customer relations work and he built and installed the kitchens. During the several years before their separation in May, 1994 the business prospered and the Wales lived comfortably. At separation she moved out and he stayed in the matrimonial home and continued to run the business. She has one daughter living with her and he has a son and daughter living with him. In October 1995 they were divorced and he has remarried. Ms. Wale's claims in the matrimonial action include child and spousal support and an unequal division of the matrimonial property.

[5] Although it is difficult to determine exact figures for the business because some of it was done for cash, its reported net incomes for the several years before separation were:

Year ended	Net income
February 1990	$73,072
February 1991	$44,182
February 1992	$8,540
February 1993	$27,682
February 1994	$30,575

[6] He says that his business declined severely during 1995 and 1996. He was forced to declare bankruptcy, the close timing to the family law trial being merely coincidental. His reported net incomes for the years after separation were:

Year ended	Net income
February 1995	$ 22,908
December 1995	$(15,334)

[7] However during a part of the year prior to his declaration Mr. Wale continued paying in excess of $1,500 per month against the mortgage, an accelerated rate of about three times that required by the bank. About a week prior to the commencement of the family law trial Mr. Wale met with Richard Burnside, a trustee in bankruptcy. Mr. Burnside advised him an assignment would stay all creditors claims, including those of Ms. Wale, except for support. In the week prior to his declaration Mr. Wale removed all his tools and equipment from his workshop. They were appraised at $18,915 and are security for a line of credit with Scotiabank of about the same amount. He sold his inventory for $8,500 and used this money to pay some creditors and his trustees' fee, $750 to board his dog and cat and he kept $4,500 for "Room and board for 3 children @ $1500 each." He took from the home all the furnishings and contents, appraised at $8896, and stored them at an unknown location. He left a mobile 4′ x 6′ sign at the bottom of the driveway, on Hwy. 10, which read, "Joyce Wale Your Kids Lost Their Home God Bless You. Closed Sorry."

[8] Although he says he lost money over 1996 and is unable to obtain credit to carry on his business, it appears he has been doing a considerable cash business. His trade creditors are owed less than $5700. When confronted with business records Ms. Wale found in the garbage after he moved out, he admitted receiving $17,885.27 in September and October of 1996. When he filed his assignment he had orders for at least five kitchen projects and had received deposits from four of these customers, totalling $3800. Ms. Wale says his usual practice was to take deposits of about 20% of the value of a project before starting it. Projecting the 20% figure, the deposits are evidence of orders for work worth about $19,000. His 1956 MGA sportscar was appraised at $9000 and a lawn tractor at $1200. He claims both are held by a repairman who is owed much of their values.

[9] In his Statement of Affairs, Mr. Wale declares assets of $157,000 and debts of $105,800. However, the values he placed on some of the assets are less than the appraised values mentioned above. Using the appraised values and including the cash he received for the inventory, his assets would total about $19,000 more than declared. Mr. Wale argues this figure may be decreased by an overstatement of the value of some assets, e.g. the home by $7000 and his tools by $1000.

[10] He declared income for himself and new wife of $1593 per month and expenses of $4428.82. However, the declared income does not take into account the $17,855.27 received in September and October, and the expenses appear to be inflated in that they include house taxes, mortgage and other expenses which he has not paid and has no intention of paying, as he had abandoned the house before the assignment.

[11] In summary, Mr. Wale moved out of the house, stored his furniture and tools, discontinued producing kitchens despite a backlog of orders which had been partly paid for, sold his inventory to obtain cash and stopped paying the mortgage and other expenses, apparently prepared to let the house be sold under a power of sale.

[12] Particularly telling of Mr. Wale's scheming are his plans to accelerate his loan payments to the Scotiabank once he finalized the divorce proceedings, as confirmed in

the bank's letter to him, and a handwritten note on a bill to him from a real estate appraiser, "Okay to pay after court case."

The Parties' Positions

[13] Ms. Wale argues the purpose of the bankruptcy filing was obvious. Mr. Wale intended to stop the family law trial from proceeding in any meaningful way by removing the couples' assets from the reach of the court and Ms. Wale's claim for an unequal division of them. She points out that even he now admits his assumption he could no longer carry on the business may have been incorrect. He was determined to move anything movable out of her reach and devalue or destroy anything immovable, i.e. the house and shop, by allowing it to be sold under power of sale.

[14] Mr. Wale and his trustee argue there was nothing improper in his assignment immediately before the trial. He met the definition of an insolvent person. He had debts over $1000, he was "… unable to meet his obligations as they generally become due. …" and he had "… ceased paying his current obligations in the ordinary course of business … ." He had a right to avail himself of the act's protection against all his creditors, including Ms. Wale, who has no special status as his former wife. To grant the annulment would give Ms. Wale a preference over other creditors, which the Court ought not do. The filing in advance of the trial would actually assist the court by apprising it of his true financial circumstances. Annulment is a rarely granted remedy reserved only for cases of clear fraud or abuse of the process of the court. These circumstances do not exist here, he and his trustee argue.

Analysis

[15] Section 181 of the *Bankruptcy and Insolvency Act* reads: …

[16] The jurisdiction of this court, sitting as a bankruptcy court, is limited by the special rules and procedures set out in the Act. The court has no authority, either on an interim or permanent basis to stay an assignment. However, the Act does give the court authority to annul a bankruptcy. *Re Dahl; Kalau v. Dahl et al.* (1985), 57 CBR (NS) 296.

[17] An annulment will be granted only where it is shown either the debtor was not an insolvent person when he made the assignment or where it is shown that the debtor abused the process of the court or committed a fraud on his creditors.

Was Mr. Wale an Insolvent Person When He Made the Assignment?

. . .

[19] Here, Mr. Wale's liabilities exceeded $1000 when he made the assignment. They totalled at least $105,000, and more, if the repair accounts for the sportscar and the lawn tractor are valid. He satisfies the preamble requirement.

[20] Subsections (a), (b) and (c) of the definition are disjunctive. If he has debts exceeding $1000 a person claiming insolvency must show either (a) he is unable to meet his obligations as they generally become due or (b) he has ceased paying his current obligations in the ordinary course of business or (c) establish his assets, if sold, would not yield sufficient money to pay his debts. Mr. Wale does not rely on ss. (c), as his assets,

even allowing for devaluation caused by a quick or forced sale of them, would appear to exceed his liabilities.

[21] He argues he complies with both ss. (a) and (b). However, in considering ss. (a) it appears he had sufficient cash flow in the September and October of this year to meet his obligations as they became due. He received over $17,800, part of which arose from the sale of his inventory, a finished kitchen and part from the receipt of deposits from new orders. His trade debts were about $5700. He had orders for four or five kitchens or smaller jobs which would have produced further income. He declared personal living expenses of $4427 per month, and his loan payment to the Scotiabank was $500 per month. He clearly had an ability to meet his obligations as they generally became due. He simply chose not to do so. He does not meet the criteria under ss. (a).

[22] Mr. Wale had ceased paying his current obligations in the ordinary course of business as they generally became due. The cheques he wrote in payment of some of his trade creditors were returned NSF and he has not replaced them. Perhaps better organiz- ation of his affairs or the use of money he held as cash and put to personal use would have permitted payment of some or all of the trade creditors. However, unlike ss. (a) which re- quires the debtor to show an inability to meet obligations, ss. (b) requires only that the debtor "has ceased paying his current obligations in the ordinary course of business … ." Unlike ss. (a) there is no requirement in ss. (b) for the debtor to show and thus no need to investigate his inability to make payments. If he has ceased paying current obligations, which he had, he meets the criteria of this sub-section. I must assume the reference by parliament to a debtor's "inability" in ss. (a) and not in ss. (b) is intentional and the easier test in the business oriented subsection, i.e. ss. (b), was imposed for a specific reason.

[23] Mr. Wale qualifies as an insolvent person, if only marginally so, and was there- fore entitled to make an assignment in bankruptcy, unless in doing so he abused the process of the court or committed a fraud on his creditors.

Was There an Abuse of the Court's Process?

[24] Numerous cases conclude that the debtor's motive in making an assignment is not generally relevant. There is nothing unlawful in declaring bankruptcy for the sole purpose of defeating the claims of one's creditors. *Irving Oil Co. v. Murphy* (1962), 5 CBR (NS) 203. One of the objectives of bankruptcy legislation is to permit the debtor, in the words of Evershed MR "to protect himself from the evils which he might otherwise suffer." *Re Dunn; Ex Parte Official Receiver v. Dunn*, [1949] 2 All ER 388 (CA). However, this gen- eral principle must always be tempered by the caveat that fraud or abuse of the process will permit a court to annul the assignment. In *Bankruptcy and Insolvency Law of Canada*, by Holden and Morawetz, Third Edition, Vol 2, at page 6-107, the learned authors say:

> The court must consider the rights not only of the debtor and of the creditors but also the rights of the public. A bankrupt should not be permitted to benefit from his own turpitude.

[25] In *Re Fuller; Blaxland et al. v. Fuller* (1990), 2 CBR (3d) 125, Donald J of the BCSC [In Bankruptcy], said at page 127: "If, however, the conduct is tainted by bad motives, then the Court remains able to annul a bankruptcy under s. 181 of the *Bankruptcy Act*."

[26] Under s. 181 the Court has a wide discretion when considering an annulment application. An exhaustive review of the circumstances surrounding the assignment should be made by the Court. There is no single test or principle to be applied. The test is flexible and fact specific. The debtor's motive is the primary consideration is determining abuse of process or fraud. After considering whether the debtor is an insolvent person some of the questions the court might pose to ascertain the debtor's motive are:

(1) Is the debtor's financial situation genuinely overwhelming or could it have been managed?

(2) Was the timing of the assignment related to another agenda or was bankruptcy inevitable in the near or relatively near future?

(3) Was the debtor forthcoming in revealing his situation to his creditors or did he hide assets or prefer some creditors over others?

(4) Did the debtor convert money or assets to himself which would otherwise have been assets in the bankruptcy?

(5) What had been the debtor's relationship with his creditors, particularly his major ones? Was it such that they might have assisted him, if he had approached them, by granting time or terms of repayment or had any goodwill been destroyed by past unfulfilled promises?

(6) Are there other relationships—business partnerships, shareholder arrangements, spousal, competitors for an asset, or simply personal associations which could cast light on a possible bad faith motive for making an assignment?

[27] In *Re Good* (1991), 4 CBR (3d) 12, Rosenberg J of the Ontario Court (General Division) annulled a bankruptcy where he found the husband in a bitter family law dispute filed an assignment because he was "… determined to destroy himself and all of his assets rather than allow his wife the benefit of any of those assets. … In my view, a clear case of abuse of process has been established."

Conclusion

[28] Here, Mr. Wale's motives and conduct compel the Court to exercise its discretion under s. 181 to annul the assignment. He barely meets the definition of an insolvent person. With a modicum of effort and good intentions on his part he could easily have worked his way through his less than formidable financial problems. He was on good terms with Scotiabank, a major creditor which had agreed to reduced payments on its fully secured loan until after his matrimonial difficulties were settled. His mortgage to National Trust, upon which he had been paying three times the required amount within the year prior to the assignment, was current. His trade debts were only $5700 among five creditors with whom he had worked for years. He made no approaches to his mortgagee or his trade creditors to reduce or postpone parts or all of their accounts. The timing of the assignment, the day of his family law trial, is not coincidental, nor motivated by a desire to assist the Court. The visceral antipathy toward his former wife, as evidenced by the mobile sign he left at the property, the holy war that has raged between

them since separation, his egregious conduct in selling assets and pocketing the cash shortly prior to the assignment, contrary to an order of the Court, and his removing and hiding the contents of the matrimonial home all overwhelmingly demonstrate *male fides* by him. I have little difficulty concluding he made his assignment with the intention of removing assets from the reach of the Court and his former wife so as to frustrate her claim for an unequal division of them. The assignment was an abuse of the process of the bankruptcy court and a fraud on at least one of his creditors, his former wife.

Order annulling bankruptcy.

NOTE

Differences between application for bankruptcy order and voluntary assignment: As previously noted, there are important differences between an application for a bankruptcy order brought by a creditor or creditors under s. 43 and a voluntary assignment of property for the benefit of creditors made by an insolvent person (who or which may be a natural person or legal entity) pursuant to s. 49. It seems that an assignment can be made as of right so long as the debtor-assignor satisfies the requirement of "insolvent person" under s. 2(1).[3] No hearing is involved and apparently the Official Receiver has no discretion to refuse an assignment if the paperwork is in order. However, an assignment can be annulled under s. 181 (just as a bankruptcy order can be annulled under the same section), but the basis on which the court can or should exercise its discretion remains unclear. In *Re St. Louis & Peter Co.* (1988), 67 CBR (NS) 176 (Ont. SC) an assignment was set aside on the ground that it would not benefit the bankrupt and would be detrimental to the only creditor (who would have to pay the costs of the bankruptcy). In *Re Kergan* (1966), 9 CBR (NS) 15 (Ont. SC), on the other hand, the court refused to set aside the assignment even though the debtor was making monthly payments that were satisfactory to his creditors. Courts have also repeatedly refused to set aside an assignment on the ground that the debtor had no assets available for distribution among the creditors. See, for example, *Re Linteau* (1944), 26 CBR 244 (Que.). Where does *Re Wale*, above, fit into this decisional pattern?

Contrast the simplicity of an assignment to the much more complex proceedings involved where a creditor (defined in s. 2) brings an application for a bankruptcy order. Here, even if the creditor proves the debtor's "act of bankruptcy" (defined in s. 42(1)), the court may refuse the bankruptcy order if it concludes that the debtor is able to pay his or her debts or that "for other sufficient cause" no order ought to be made (s. 43(7)). How do we explain this basic difference in procedure? Does it have something to do with the "fresh-start" policy for debtors favoured by the BIA?

---

[3] It is important to note that under the US *Bankruptcy Code* there is no requirement that the debtor be insolvent for the purpose of making an assignment or initiating reorganization proceedings under Chapter 11. This dispensation has proven to be a key element in enabling US companies facing mass tort or contract claims to make a Chapter 11 filing and impose an automatic stay on further proceedings. See, for example, *In re Johns-Manville Corp.*, 36 BR 727 (Bkrtcy. SD NY 1984). Canadian women with breast implants manufactured by Dow Corning Corp. have recently felt the impact of these provisions as the result of Dow Corning's decision to file under Chapter 11. The scope of the insolvency requirement under the CCAA is discussed in Chapter 12 of this text.

III. CONSEQUENCES OF BANKRUPTCY ORDER: STAY OF PROCEEDINGS

Vachon v. Canada (Employment & Immigration Commission)
[1985] 2 SCR 417

BEETZ J:

I. Facts and Proceedings

[1] The parties were agreed on the facts summarized by the unanimous judgment of the Federal Court of Appeal:

1. Appellant owed respondent Commission the sum of $922.00 when he made an assignment of his property under the *Bankruptcy Act*;

2. This sum of $922.00 was owed by appellant under ss. 47 and 49 of the *Unemployment Insurance Act, 1971*; however, the debt had been incurred without fraud on the part of appellant, with the result that it was a debt from which he should normally be released by the order of discharge (see s. 148 of the *Bankruptcy Act*);

3. The claim of the Commission was [a] claim provable in bankruptcy and the Commission filed its proof of claim with the trustee;

4. During the bankruptcy, when the Commission had not yet received anything from the trustee and appellant had not yet been discharged, unemployment insurance benefits became payable to appellant;

5. Rather than paying appellant all the benefits owing to him, the Commission withheld the sum of $922.00 owed to it by appellant from these benefits.

[2] On July 3, 1979 an order of discharge was made concerning appellant, and on July 27, 1979 he brought against respondent a declaratory action in which he asked the Federal Court to

[TRANSLATION] DECLARE that defendant acted unlawfully in retaining unemployment insurance benefits amounting to $951, benefits which plaintiff was entitled to during his bankruptcy.

[3] (Counsel for the appellant admitted at the hearing that the amount at issue is in fact $922, as stated by the Federal Court of Appeal, and not $951.)

[4] The Federal Court dismissed the action and the Federal Court of Appeal, which considered the action as one for recovery of the monies retained, affirmed the trial judgment: hence the appeal.

[5] In addition to the facts, the two parties admitted that:

(a) the Crown and respondent are bound by the *Bankruptcy Act*, RSC 1970, c. B-3, in view of s. 187 of that Act;

(b) respondent's claim was a preferred debt under s. 107(1)(h) of the *Bankruptcy Act*, a debt which, if it had not been for the retention of benefits, would have been paid before the claims of ordinary creditors, had there been a distribution;

(c) unemployment insurance benefits which had become payable to appellant could not be assigned, charged, attached, anticipated or given as security, as a consequence of s. 48 of the *Unemployment Insurance Act, 1971*, 1970-71-72 (Can.), c. 48, s. 47 of the *Bankruptcy Act* and art. 553.12 of the *Code of Civil Procedure*.

II. Legislation and Point at Issue

[6] Section 49 of the *Unemployment Insurance Act, 1971* is what imposes on a claimant a duty to repay any overpayment and which provides the procedure for recovery, including in subs. (3) retention from subsequent payments, which respondent applied in the case at bar:

> 49.(1) Where a person has received benefit under this Act or the former Act for a period in respect of which he is disqualified or any benefit to which he is not entitled, he is liable to repay an amount equal to the amount paid by the Commission in respect thereof.
>
> (2) All amounts payable under this section or section 47, 51 or 52 are debts due to Her Majesty and are recoverable as such in the Federal Court of Canada or any other court of competent jurisdiction or in any other manner provided by this Act.
>
> (3) Where a benefit becomes payable to any claimant, the amount of any indebtedness described in subsection (1) or (2) may, in the manner prescribed, be deducted and retained out of the benefit payable to him.

[7] This method of recovering an overpayment, by retention from subsequent benefits, is a technique which is found in many statutes having a social purpose, federal as well as provincial. See, for example, Canada Pension Plan, RSC 1970, c. C-5, s. 65; *Old Age Security Act*, RSC 1970, c. O-6, s. 22; *Pension Act*, RSC 1970, c. P-7, s. 23(8); *Social Aid Act*, RSQ 1977, c. A-16, s. 25; *Act respecting the Quebec Pension Plan*, RSQ 1977, c. R-9, s. 148.

[8] The provision on which respondent's principal argument is based is s. 47 of the *Bankruptcy Act*:

> 47. The property of a bankrupt divisible among his creditors shall not comprise
>
> · · ·
>
> (b) any property that as against the bankrupt is exempt from execution or seizure under the laws of the province within which the property is situated and within which the bankrupt resides,

[9] Finally, the provision which is at the heart of the dispute is s. 49(1) of the *Bankruptcy Act*, which must be cited in both versions:

> 49.(1) Upon the filing of a proposal made by an insolvent person or upon the bankruptcy of any debtor, no creditor with a claim provable in bankruptcy shall have any remedy against the debtor or his property or shall commence or continue any action, execution or other proceedings for the recovery of a claim provable in bankruptcy until the trustee has been discharged or until the proposal has been refused, unless with the leave of the court and on such terms as the court may impose.
>
> 49.(1) Lors de la déposition d'une proposition faite par une personne insolvable ou lors de la faillite de tout débiteur, aucun créancier ayant une réclamation prouvable en matière

de faillite n'a de recours contre le débiteur ou contre ses biens, ni ne doit intenter ou continuer une action, exécution ou autres procédures pour le recouvrement d'une réclamation prouvable en matière de faillite, tant que le syndic n'a pas été libéré ou que la proposition n'a pas été refusée, sauf avec l'autorisation du tribunal et aux conditions que ce dernier peut imposer.

[10] This provision is preceded by the subheading "Suspension des procédures," "Stay of Proceedings."

[11] The question that must be decided is the following: does the recovery of an over-payment by retention from subsequent benefits, applied by respondent, constitute within the meaning of s. 49(1) of the *Bankruptcy Act* a remedy against the debtor or his property, an action, execution or other proceeding which had been stayed except, as provided by this section, with leave of the Court or on such terms as the Court might impose?

III. *Trial Judgment and Judgment a Quo*

[12] The trial judgment simply cited and approved the submissions made by counsel for the defendant Commission. Among the arguments so approved by the trial judge, the following are the two principal ones:

> [TRANSLATION] (1) ... the setoff allowed by ... the *Unemployment Insurance Act*, is neither a remedy nor a proceeding within the meaning of s. 49 of the *Bankruptcy Act*. It is in fact an administrative act of recovery which is allowed by a specific statute and which, in my opinion, is not in the nature of a proceeding.
>
> (2) ... by thus reimbursing itself by recovery, the Unemployment Insurance Commission [sic] is not making payments to itself which are preferential over all other creditors, for its benefits cannot be attached and are not part of the fund available for creditors.

[13] It would appear that the Federal Court of Appeal only adopted the first argument approved by the trial judge. Its entire reasoning is contained, be it said with respect, in one sibylline sentence:

> In my view the right granted to the Commission under subsection 49(3) of the *Unemployment Insurance Act, 1971* is not a remedy, action, execution or proceeding. Subsection 49(1) of the *Bankruptcy Act* does not therefore prevent it from being exercised.

[14] The Federal Court of Appeal did not say why the right granted to the Commission by s. 49(3) of the *Unemployment Insurance Act, 1971* is not a remedy or a proceeding. It may be that this is because the right is not a remedy or proceeding of a judicial nature. It is also possible that this is for other reasons which the Federal Court of Appeal did not disclose.

[15] In this Court, counsel for the appellant sought to show, first, that the remedies and proceedings covered by s. 49(1) of the *Bankruptcy Act* are not confined to remedies and proceedings of a judicial nature and may include recovery by retention from subsequent benefits, such as that applied by respondent. Counsel for the appellant also sought, on the other hand, to answer the second argument approved by the trial judge, and adopted by counsel for the respondent, with further clarification, in support of the findings of the Federal Court of Appeal.

[16] These two points must now be discussed.

IV. General Nature of Stay of Proceedings Imposed by s. 49(1) of the Bankruptcy Act

[17] Appellant in my view properly relied upon the English version of s. 49(1) of the *Bankruptcy Act*, where the word recours is rendered by the word "remedy," giving to it and to the words "autres procédures" ("other proceedings") a very broad meaning which covers any kind of attempt at recovery, judicial or extrajudicial. *Black's Law Dictionary* (5th ed. 1979) defines "remedy":

> The means by which a right is enforced or the violation of a right is prevented, redressed, or compensated.

and below:

> Remedy means any remedial right to which an aggrieved party is entitled with or without resort to a tribunal.

[18] *Jowitt's Dictionary of English Law* (2nd ed. 1977), vol. 2, gives an almost identical definition:

> the means by which the violation of a right is prevented, redressed, or compensated. Remedies are of four kinds: (1) by act of the party injured … ; (2) by operation of law … ; (3) by agreement between the parties … ; (4) by judicial remedy, e.g. action or suit. The last are called judicial remedies, as opposed to the first three classes which are extrajudicial.

[19] The courts have also interpreted the stay of proceedings imposed by s. 49(1) of the *Bankruptcy Act* very broadly.

[20] Thus, in *In re Standard Pharmacy Ltd.* (1926), 7 CBR 424, the City of Edmonton wished to use a proceeding mentioned in its Charter to collect unpaid taxes, consisting alternatively of a distress of personal property or a simple notice to the trustee that there were taxes which had not been paid by the bankrupt. Tweedie J of the Supreme Court of Alberta, sitting in bankruptcy, cited s. 8B of the *Bankruptcy Act*—now s. 49(1)—and wrote, at pp. 430-31:

> This section applies to both judicial and extra-judicial proceedings; and distress being a remedy within the meaning of that section the section is, in my opinion, an absolute bar to any proceedings judicial or otherwise to enforce payment of taxes without the leave of the Court, which was not granted to, nor applied for on behalf of, the city.
>
>   . . .
>
>   In regard to the notice to be given by "the collector or other person authorized to collect the taxes" to the trustee in bankruptcy as provided in sec. 376a of the Charter it is evident from the reading of that section that the notice is a substitute for the distress, and that it was intended that such simple method, instead of the actual physical seizure of the property, should be the remedy to be pursued. Notice is a remedy or proceeding within the meaning of sec. 8B of *The Bankruptcy Act* and what has been said in regard to distress applies with equal force in regard to the notice and the city is deprived of its right to enforce payment in priority by the provisions of sec. 8B of *The Bankruptcy Act*.

[21] At page 430, he gave the reason underlying this decision:

The city by reason of the authorized assignment was deprived of any opportunity of gaining priority in the distribution of the assets which it might have acquired in the enforcement of its remedies.

[22] In *Hudson v. Brisebois Bros. Construction Ltd.* (1982), 42 CBR (NS) 97, the Alberta Court of Appeal ordered that the trustee be repaid money distributed by the sheriff to certain creditors, in ignorance that the debtor was bankrupt at the time of the distribution. At page 103, Lieberman J wrote in the unanimous reasons of the Court:

Section 49(1) has the effect of staying the proceedings taken by the appellant prior to the payment out by the sheriff. Thus the payment out by the sheriff, although completely innocent, contravenes s. 49(1) and is without authority.

[23] In Quebec, public utilities have used s. 73 of the *Gas, Water and Electricity Companies Act*, RSQ 1977, c. C-44, as authority for interrupting the service of a bankrupt subscriber. In a judgment, *Re Plastiques Valsen Inc.; Gaz Metropolitain Inc. v. St-Georges* (1981), 41 CBR (NS) 7 (Que. SC), Jacques Dugas J reviewed the decided cases, which as he recognized are far from being unanimous: but he nevertheless dismissed an application by Gaz Metropolitain Inc. for an order directing the trustee to give him access to the bankrupt's premises in order to cut off the natural gas service. He wrote (at pp. 10-11):

[TRANSLATION] Applicant enjoys no guarantee under the *Bankruptcy Act*. The rule for distributing property of a bankrupt is that the ordinary creditors receive equal shares of the common fund, once the trustee's expenses and secured debts have been paid. It would be contrary to the scheme of the *Bankruptcy Act* if it could by threatening to interrupt the service obtain more than the other ordinary creditors would get.

In *Re Colonial Indust. Equipment Ltd.; Mercure v. Compagnie Bell Téléphone du Can.*, [1971] CA 564, the Court of Appeal vacated the payment which the telephone company had succeeded in prising from its debtor, six days before its bankruptcy, by threatening to interrupt service: this was a cancellable preferential payment. It would be unusual, to say the least, if the applicant could obtain from the trustee preference which the debtor could not give it: surely this is what the applicant is seeking here by making its threat of interrupting service.

. . .

The Court considers that the threat to interrupt service made by applicant is designed to obtain from the trustee preferential treatment for its debt, and this is contrary to the *Bankruptcy Act*. The Court has a duty to protect creditors against abusive use of s. 73 of the *Gas, Water and Electricity Companies Act* so as to obtain advantageous treatment at variance with the scheme of the *Bankruptcy Act*.

[24] This Court of course does not have to decide whether the conclusions of these judgments are correct, but in my opinion the courts were right to give, expressly or by implication, a broad meaning to the stay of proceedings imposed by s. 49(1) of the *Bankruptcy Act*. This broad meaning is confirmed by the fact that the legislator took the trouble to exclude actions against either the creditor or his property.

[25] As Houlden and Morawetz wrote in *Bankruptcy Law of Canada*, vol. 1, p. F-70.1, under s. 49 of the *Bankruptcy Act*:

An ordinary unsecured creditor with a claim provable in bankruptcy can only obtain payment of that claim subject to and in accordance with the terms of the *Bankruptcy Act*. The procedure laid down by that Act completely excludes any other remedy or procedure.

[26] The *Bankruptcy Act* governs bankruptcy in all its aspects. It is therefore understandable that the legislator wished to suspend all proceedings, administrative or judicial, so that all the objectives of the Act could be attained.

[27] Accordingly, I consider that s. 49(1) of the *Bankruptcy Act* is sufficiently broad to include recovery by retention from subsequent benefits, such as the recovery at issue here.

V. Section 49(1) of the Bankruptcy Act and the Immunity from Seizure of Unemployment Insurance Benefits

[28] Respondent replied, however, through its counsel, that even if s. 49(1) of the *Bankruptcy Act* is so broadly worded as to include an extra-judicial remedy or proceeding, such a remedy or proceeding is not a remedy or proceeding within the meaning of s. 49(1) when its purpose is to recover property of the bankrupt which, in view of its immunity from seizure, does not fall within the fund available for his creditors, as provided by s. 47 of the *Bankruptcy Act*.

[29] Respondent submitted that s. 49(1) of the *Bankruptcy Act* must be interpreted in accordance with the principles underlying the Act, and what is in its submission the purpose or reason for the stay of proceedings imposed by s. 49(1).

[30] In the factum submitted by its counsel, respondent explained the purpose of s. 49(1) of the *Bankruptcy Act* as follows:

The true meaning of this section is determined by certain general principles underlying the *Bankruptcy Act*, both as regards the bankrupt's property and with respect to unsecured creditors.

So far as property owned by the bankrupt is concerned, it is worth recalling the rule in s. 50(5) of the *Bankruptcy Act*, that on a receiving order being made or an assignment being filed with an official receiver, "a bankrupt ceases to have any capacity to dispose of or otherwise deal with his property, which shall, subject to this Act and subject to the rights of secured creditors, forthwith pass to and vest in the trustee named in the receiving order or assignment. ..."

As we know, bankruptcy does not have the effect of depriving a bankrupt of all his assets, without exception. The property which passes to the trustee is limited to that which, under s. 47 of the *Bankruptcy Act*, constitutes what the Act calls the property of the bankrupt "divisible among his creditors," that is, property the proceeds from which are to be distributed pari passu among the unsecured creditors.

The property in question includes anything belonging to the bankrupt on the date of the bankruptcy or which may devolve upon him before his discharge. On the other hand, it does not include property which, as against the bankrupt, is immune from seizure. It accordingly follows that in a bankruptcy proceeding the property of a bankrupt actually falls into two categories: what falls within the assets of his bankruptcy and what remains external to it.

If the situation is considered from the standpoint of unsecured creditors, the fundamental principle of the Act is that the latter are to be regarded as on an equal footing in relation to each other: their rights are limited to being collocated pari passu in the proceeds of sale of property held by the bankruptcy, in accordance with the order of priority specified in s. 107 of the *Bankruptcy Act*.

So as to give full effect to the fundamental principles discussed above, it was necessary for the legislator to put property that would be part of the bankruptcy fund beyond the reach of individual actions that might be brought by any of the bankrupt's creditors, seeking payment of their own debts from the property in question and so obtaining an advantage over other creditors. The solution decided on by the legislator was to provide that, from the date of the bankruptcy, no creditor with a claim provable in bankruptcy shall have any remedy, including an execution proceeding, against the debtor or his property, unless with leave of the Court and on such terms as the Court may impose. As can be seen from the wording of s. 49(1), such a prohibition applies to any type of remedy the aim of which is to recover a claim provable in bankruptcy, regardless of whether it is a remedy that can be exercised by an action, or is a remedy in the nature of an execution proceeding.

[31] Respondent concluded with this argument, which constitutes the crux of its second submission:

It follows, therefore, that the only remedies to which s. 49(1) applies are those the effect of which is to take out of the property included in the bankruptcy anything which under the Act devolves on the trustee for the common benefit of creditors of the bankrupt. This section thus clearly cannot be interpreted, in our opinion, as prohibiting the exercise of a right which has no adverse effect on the common fund available to creditors of the bankruptcy.

[32] Respondent submitted that, as unemployment insurance benefits are property which is immune from seizure, they are not part of the common fund available to creditors, and the retentions made by respondent did not have the effect of depriving the ordinary creditors of anything which belonged to the bankruptcy creditors' common fund. Such retentions cannot then be regarded as contravening s. 49(1) of the *Bankruptcy Act*.

[33] To this apparently plausible argument, the gist of which is contained in respondent's factum, counsel for the latter added another in their oral pleading, which also at first sight seems to carry considerable weight. It is the following: in reimbursing itself by retentions from subsequent benefits due to appellant, respondent did something which conferred a benefit on the mass of ordinary creditors—not only did it pay itself from property to which they had no right, but, at the same time, it released those ordinary creditors from the lien which it is given by s. 107(1)(h) of the *Bankruptcy Act* and in accordance with which it would have been paid before them in the event of a distribution.

[34] However, the interpretation suggested by respondent comes up against a major obstacle: without adequate justification, it rejects the method of grammatical or literal interpretation of a very clear provision. This interpretation suggests that words be added to s. 49(1) of the *Bankruptcy Act*, by interpreting the word "property" as referring to "property divisible among his creditors." These words, which are contained in s. 47, are

not found in s. 49(1) of the Act. That subsection uses only the word "property," of which s. 2 of the Act gives a broad definition not including the limitation in s. 47.

. . .

[36] Respondent is thus asking the Court to make a distinction where the legislator makes none, and this *prima facie* is an error of interpretation.

[37] Respondent sought to justify this distinction in reliance on a fundamental objective of the *Bankruptcy Act*, namely, an equitable distribution of property to the creditors.

[38] First, it should be said that this is not the sole objective of the *Bankruptcy Act*. As Estey J wrote, in giving the unanimous judgment of this Court in *Industrial Acceptance Corp. v. Lalonde*, [1952] 2 SCR 109, at p. 120:

> The purpose and object of the *Bankruptcy Act* is to equitably distribute the assets of the debtor and to permit his rehabilitation as a citizen, unfettered by past debts.

[39] The rehabilitation of the bankrupt is not the result only of his discharge. It begins when he is put into bankruptcy with measures designed to give him the minimum needed for subsistence. These measures are contained in s. 47 of the *Bankruptcy Act* concerning, inter alia, the exemption from execution of certain property, and in s. 48, regarding the wages of the bankrupt, which applies notwithstanding s. 47 and which empowers the Court to make

> an order directing the payment to the trustee of such part of the salary, wages or other remuneration as the court may determine having regard to the family responsibilities and personal situation of the bankrupt.

[40] The part of the wages paid to creditors does not necessarily correspond to the part which may be attached. It may be more or less "having regard to the family responsibilities and personal situation of the bankrupt." Houlden and Morawetz, op. cit., vol. 1, write at pp. F-66 and F-69:

> Since the enactment of s. 48, wages have been removed from the operation of s. 47 so that no part thereof vests in the trustee to be divided among creditors unless he makes an application under s. 48 and then only to the extent allowed by the court: *Re Giroux* (1983), 45 CBR (NS) 245, 41 OR (2d) 351, 146 DLR (3d) 103 (SC).
>
> . . .
>
> Applications under s. 48 of the *Bankruptcy Act* come down not to a question of law, but of fact; that is, whether the bankrupt after being given credit for his reasonable living expenses has excess funds which might be used to pay creditors. The Senate Committee poverty lines, while not binding on the court, are persuasive evidence: *Re Michael; Re Superior Films Shops* (1980), 34 CBR (NS) 1 (Ont. SC).

[41] In my view, appellant was right to see an analogy between the wages of a bankrupt and unemployment insurance benefits, and to argue that the partial or complete elimination of the latter may deprive the bankrupt of his means of subsistence, contrary to an other objective of the *Bankruptcy Act*. If retentions from unemployment insurance benefits cannot be made without the Court's authority, as specified in s. 49(1), the Court will ensure that this other objective is not lost sight of.

[42] Moreover, the sole objective of the *Bankruptcy Act* mentioned by respondent, namely an equitable distribution of the bankrupt's property to his creditors, and the interests of the latter, will also be taken into account by the Court, to which the respondent will apply pursuant to s. 49(1) for authority to recover the overpayment by retention from subsequent benefits. The Court may grant such authorization, refuse it or grant it only in part or on certain conditions, taking all the circumstances into account.

[43] In other words, the grammatical or literal interpretation of s. 49(1) of the *Bankruptcy Act*, which makes retentions from unemployment insurance benefits subject to authorization by the Court, is not an obstacle to pursuing any of the objectives of the *Bankruptcy Act*. On the contrary, it makes possible the coherent pursuit of those various objectives, under the supervision of the Court. It may be added that it will also have the effect of facilitating the administration of the bankruptcy by the trustee, who will thus automatically be informed of retentions made by creditors who have also filed claims in the bankruptcy.

[44] I accordingly consider that not only has respondent not shown any justification for an interpretation of s. 49(1) of the *Bankruptcy Act* other than the grammatical or literal one, but the latter is the only possible one in view of the general scheme of the Act.

Appeal allowed.

R v. Fitzgibbon
[1990] 1 SCR 1005

CORY J (for the Court): [1] On the sentencing of an individual who is an undischarged bankrupt, can an order be made by a judge of the criminal court for the restitution of amounts acknowledged to have been defrauded or stolen from victims without giving notice to the trustee in bankruptcy and obtaining the consent of the bankruptcy court? The answer given to the question will resolve this appeal.

Factual Background

[2] The appellant, a lawyer, misappropriated funds entrusted to him. He defrauded and stole money from his clients. In most instances, the appellant assured his clients that he would be placing their money in secure mortgages when in fact he invested their funds in property which had little or no equity. On other occasions, the appellant used his clients' funds, such as the $70,000 entrusted to him by Rudolph Gatien, to make fake "mortgage" payments to other clients.

[3] Disciplinary proceedings were taken against Fitzgibbon, who was permitted to resign his membership in the Law Society of Upper Canada. Claims for compensation were made by his clients to the Law Society. The Law Society authorized payments totalling $359,204.28 out of its Compensation Fund. The sum was paid to 26 claimants, 19 of whom were the victims of the crimes of breach of trust and fraud which Fitzgibbon was convicted of committing. Included in the award of compensation was $25,000 for Rudolph Gatien. Although Gatien had entrusted $70,000 to Fitzgibbon, the Law Society

had fixed a limit of $25,000 for each claimant seeking to recover funds advanced to dishonest solicitors prior to the June 1, 1979. Gatien fell within this category. He therefore personally brought a claim against the appellant for the remaining sum of $45,000.

[4] The appellant was charged with three counts of fraud and one count of breach of trust. Fitzgibbon acknowledged the amounts owing to his clients, pleaded guilty to the charges and was sentenced to three and one-half years imprisonment. As an integral part of his sentence he was ordered to pay by way of compensation the sum of $359,204.28 to the Law Society and $45,000 to Rudolph Gatien. The order for compensation was made pursuant to the provisions of s. 653 of the Criminal Code, RSC 1970, c. C-34, as amended (now RSC, 1985, c. C-46, s. 725). At the time of his sentencing the appellant was an undischarged bankrupt. The statement of affairs in his bankruptcy showed the debts due to Gatien and his other clients. No proceedings seeking leave of the bankruptcy court pursuant to the provisions of s. 49 of the *Bankruptcy Act*, RSC 1970, c. B-3 (now RSC, 1985, c. B-3, s. 69), were taken before the sentence was pronounced.

. . .

Issues

[9]

(1) Must consent be obtained from the bankruptcy court pursuant to s. 49(1) of the *Bankruptcy Act* before a valid compensation order can be made pursuant to s. 653 of the Criminal Code as part of the sentence pronounced against an undischarged bankrupt?

. . .

[10] At the outset, something should be said of the nature of the compensation order and its place in sentencing as an integral and vitally important part of the criminal trial proceedings. A trial judge may, in the exercise of his or her discretion, order that compensation be paid to a victim of the convicted person. Section 653 of the Criminal Code provides:

653.(1) A court that convicts an accused of an indictable offence may, upon the application of a person aggrieved, at the time sentence is imposed, order the accused to pay to that person an amount by way of satisfaction or compensation for loss of or damage to property suffered by the applicant as a result of the commission of the offence of which the accused is convicted.

(2) Where an amount that is ordered to be paid under subsection (1) is not paid forthwith the applicant may, by filing the order, enter as a judgment, in the superior court of the province in which the trial was held, the amount ordered to be paid, and that judgment is enforceable against the accused in the same manner as if it were a judgment rendered against the accused in that court in civil proceedings.

. . .

[18] In summary, it can be seen that compensation orders are an extremely useful part of the sentencing procedure. They are often used in sentencing young persons or first-time offenders who have not committed crimes of violence. Their value cannot be over-emphasized. Much of the efficacy of these orders is the immediacy of their effect. If it is possible, they deserve to be available for consideration in the sentencing of all of-

fenders. It remains only to be determined whether the order could be validly made when the appellant was an undischarged bankrupt at the time of sentencing.

[19] The fact that the appellant is an undischarged bankrupt raises two issues. First, it was recognized in Zelensky that the means of the accused person should be taken into account when a court is considering making a compensation order. However, in the case at bar, the sentencing judge was aware that the appellant was an undischarged bankrupt at the time of the sentencing and nevertheless properly exercised his discretion to make the order. In the Court of Appeal, Martin JA carefully considered the words of Laskin CJ in Zelensky. He concluded that the means of the offender should not in every case be the controlling factor. I agree with that conclusion of Martin JA.

[20] The appellant was a lawyer who defrauded his clients. He used his position to defraud the very persons who had every reason to trust and rely upon him. The fraudulent acts of a lawyer directed against his own clients warranted the imposition of a compensation order even though the lawyer's means at the time of sentencing were minimal. The claims of the victims of fraudulent acts should be paramount. This seems to be recognized by s. 148 (now s. 178) of the *Bankruptcy Act*. That section provides that the discharge of a bankrupt does not release him from any debt or liability arising out of a fraudulent act committed by him while acting in a fiduciary capacity. The *Bankruptcy Act* itself, therefore, permits claims of fraud to survive the discharge of a bankrupt, and the fact that Fitzgibbon is an undischarged bankrupt should not allow him to avoid the imposition of this compensation order as part of his sentence.

[21] Secondly, and more importantly, it must be considered whether the compensation order could be validly made in light of the provisions of s. 49(1) of the *Bankruptcy Act*. That section provides: ...

[22] It is to be observed that the section prohibits the granting of any "remedy against" or "recovery of" any claim against the debtor or his property without leave of the court in bankruptcy. The aim of the section is to provide a means of maintaining control over the distribution of the assets and property of the bankrupt. In doing so, it reflects one of the primary purposes of the *Bankruptcy Act*, namely to provide for the orderly and fair distribution of the bankrupt's property among his or her creditors on a pari passu basis. See Duncan and Honsberger, *Bankruptcy in Canada* (3rd ed. 1961), at p. 4. The object of the section is to avoid a multiplicity of proceedings and to prevent any single unsecured creditor from obtaining a priority over any other unsecured creditors by bringing an action and executing a judgment against the debtor. This is accomplished by providing that no remedy or action may be taken against a bankrupt without leave of the court in bankruptcy, and then only upon such terms as that court may impose.

[23] In contrast, a compensation order is an order made against the person of the offender, imposing upon him or her an obligation to pay the amount ordered. It is only when the compensation order is filed with the Superior Court of the province that it becomes an order enforceable against the person and property of the offender. There is a fundamentally important distinction between the original compensation order, which is an order against the person by which the court recognizes an acknowledged indebtedness, and the subsequent filing in the Superior Court which can convert that personal order into an order against the property of the accused.

[24] Section 49(1) of the *Bankruptcy Act* would preclude the enforcement of the latter. This is because such an enforcement would result in the granting of the very priorities which the *Bankruptcy Act* seeks to avoid. However, the original compensation order made at the time of sentencing is an order against the offender personally recognizing an acknowledged indebtedness and is not immediately enforceable. Until the order is filed with the Superior Court, it simply imposes a future obligation upon the offender to pay. It is neither a remedy nor an order for recovery against the property of the bankrupt offender within the meaning of s. 49(1). Thus s. 49(1) does not prohibit the making of a compensation order.

. . .

[29] I would conclude that the compensation order can be made pursuant to s. 653(1) without obtaining the consent of the bankruptcy court. It is not until such time as the beneficiaries of the compensation order seek to proceed pursuant to s. 653(2) and register the order with the Superior Court of a province that they must first obtain the consent of the bankruptcy court.

Appeal dismissed.

NOTES

1. *Vachon v. Canada and rights of set-off:* The Supreme Court's judgment in *Vachon* is the leading authority on the meaning of the stipulation in what is now s. 69.3(1) of the BIA that no creditor with a provable claim under s. 121 has "any remedy against the debtor or his property" or "shall commence or continue any action, execution or other proceedings for the recovery of a claim provable in bankruptcy." However, for some unexplained reason, the court's judgment does not address the government's right to claim a set-off under BIA s. 97(3). The right of set-off is a basic right, which has been in the BIA from the beginning. Similar rights of set-off are found in most other modern insolvency systems, though the details often differ. Case law illustrating the scope and operation of the s. 97(3) right is reproduced in Chapter 4.

2. *Anatomy of BIA s. 69.4:* Note the following features of s. 69.4. First, a s. 69.4 stay applies only to a "creditor" of a debtor. "Creditor" is defined in s. 2(1) of the BIA as a person having a claim provable as a claim under the Act. This distinguishes the BIA from the US *Bankruptcy Code*, s. 362, which is much broader in its scope and imposes the stay against all "entities," not just the debtor's creditors.

Second, under the BIA, secured creditors are not affected by the stay in straight bankruptcies unless the trustee secures a court order otherwise: see s. 69.3(2). Even then the stay is effective only for a maximum of six months. It seems that, in practice, trustees rarely make such an application—presumably because in most cases the debtor has no equity in the collateral worth worrying about.[4]

---

[4] Note too that if the creditor has, broadly speaking, a general security interest in the debtor's assets, s. 244(2) of the BIA requires the creditor to give the debtor 10 days' notice of the creditor's intention to enforce its security. This amendment was added in 1992 and is designed *inter alia* to give the debtor an opportunity to initiate reorganizational proceedings under BIA III.1 or the CCAA if the debtor's directors feel the business is

A third feature of s. 69.3 is that the stay of proceedings does not affect persons who may have a claim—for example, an employee claim for unpaid wages or a CRA claim for unremitted taxes—against directors or officers of the debtor corporation or a related company of the debtor. This issue often arises in reorganization proceedings and is dealt with below in Chapters 12 to 16. The BIA contains no provision comparable to s. 105(a) of the US Code conferring a residual jurisdiction on the bankruptcy court to issue "any order, process or judgment that is necessary or appropriate to carry out the provisions" of the Code. However, in Canada, the courts have found a similar but implied power in the CCAA for reorganizational purposes as part of the inherent jurisdiction of the court to promote the purposes of the Act.

3. *Sanctions for violation of the stay:* US courts treat violations of the automatic stay under s. 362 of the Code very seriously—as Canadian creditors of US debtors in bankruptcy have found to their cost from time to time. The position is more relaxed in Canada. Section 69 of the BIA does not spell out the consequences of a creditor ignoring the stay of proceedings. However, it has been held that an action begun by the creditor against the debtor after the stay has come into force is a nullity.[5] Presumably a creditor who seizes property in breach of the stay may also be guilty of trespass. A violator may also be guilty of an offence under s. 202(4) of the BIA. However, this is unlikely to be a serious deterrent because provincial prosecutors are notoriously reluctant to prosecute white collar offences of this character. Trustees in bankruptcy and debtors under a proposal are also not likely to be able to afford the costs of a private prosecution or to find a private prosecution worthwhile even if they can afford it. It seems further that violations of a stay of proceedings under s. 69 cannot be treated as a contempt of court because no court order has been breached.[6]

4. *Relief from the stay of proceedings:* BIA s. 69.4 gives the court a seemingly unfettered discretion to lift a stay of proceedings, though it has been held that the discretion must be exercised judicially. Relief applications are often made to allow, for example, a pre-bankruptcy case to proceed to trial, an existing trial to be completed, or a case to be initiated to meet limitation-period requirements. Given the purposes of the stay articulated in *Vachon* and *Fitzgibbon*, above, what tests should a court apply to determine when relief from the stay is appropriate?

5. *Consequences of an assignment or a bankruptcy order:* The following is a list of the most important consequences of an assignment or a bankruptcy order:

s. 69.3   Automatic stay of proceedings against bankrupt unless court grants exemption from stay.

s. 70(1)   Bankruptcy order takes precedence over all outstanding judgments, execution, etc.

---

worth saving or is experiencing only a temporary setback. Note also that a stay of proceedings under s. 69.1(1) of the BIA (in respect of Division 1 proposals) applies to secured as well as unsecured creditors. Under s. 11 of the CCAA, the court has very broad powers to issue an order staying any action by third parties (not just creditors). In practice, s. 11 orders are made almost as a matter of course as soon as the debtor corporation initiates proceedings under the Act. Stays of proceedings under the CCAA are discussed in Chapter 12.

[5] See, for example, *Textiles Tri-Star Ltée v. Dominion Novelty Inc.* (1993), 22 CBR (3d) 213 (Que. SC) and *Amanda Designs Boutique Ltd. v. Charisma Fashions Ltd.* (1972), 17 CBR (NS) 16 (Ont. CA).

[6] The position is different under the CCAA because all s. 11 orders are made by the court.

s. 71   Subject to (mainly) provincially governed exemptions in the case of individuals, all of the bankrupt's present and future property vests in the trustee, and the bankrupt ceases to have capacity to deal with her property. The bankrupt must also pay over any surplus income to the trustee pursuant to s. 68 and the Superintendent's directive. [Exemptions and surplus income payment requirements are discussed in Chapter 11.]

s. 73(2)   Sheriff must deliver to trustee any property of the bankrupt in his hands.

s. 73(4)   Similar effect of bankruptcy order on outstanding distraint for rent or taxes.

s. 199(a)   Offence for undischarged bankrupt to engage in trade or business without disclosing his bankruptcy to the other party; or s. 199(b) to obtain credit to a total of $1000 or more from any person or persons without disclosing his status.

Do these provisions serve a common purpose?

CHAPTER FOUR

Property of the Estate

I. INTRODUCTION

The trustee's main functions are (1) to gather in and determine what assets belong to the estate; (2) where the assets are not already in liquid form, to collect any moneys owing to the estate and to realize the other assets by selling them piecemeal or as an entirety; and (3) to distribute the net residue of the estate in accordance with the creditors' ranking under s. 136(1).

Section 71 provides that on the making of a receiving order or the filing of an assignment, the bankrupt ceases to have the capacity to deal with or dispose of his property and the property forthwith passes to and vests in the trustee. "Property" is comprehensively but non-exhaustively ("'property' includes") defined in s. 2 and covers all forms of property—real and personal, tangible and intangible, present and future, vested or contingent—whether located in Canada or elsewhere.

However, subject to a variety of exceptions and qualifications, the BIA does not specify what property rights the bankrupt in fact has at the time of bankruptcy that vest in the trustee. The question is determined by provincial and other federal laws pursuant to s. 72(1). Section 67(1) provides in part as follows:

> 67(1) The property of a bankrupt divisible among his creditors shall not comprise
>
> (a) property held by the bankrupt in trust for any other person,
>
> (b) any property that as against the bankrupt is exempt from execution or seizure under any laws applicable in the province within which the property is situated and within which the bankrupt resides;
>
> . . .
>
> but it shall comprise
>
> (c) all property wherever situated of the bankrupt at the date of the bankruptcy or that may be acquired by or devolve on the bankrupt before his or her discharge, ... and
>
> (d) such powers in or over or in respect of the property as might have been exercised by the bankrupt for his own benefit.

For a discussion of the relationship between this provision and s. 71, see *Royal Bank of Canada v. North American Life Assurance Co.*, [1996] 1 SCR 325, noted in Chapter 5 (Review of Pre-Bankruptcy Transactions).

This chapter deals with the following topics: (1) the meaning of "property" in the context of ss. 67(1) and 71; (2) the secured creditor exception in s. 71; (3) the claims of bona fide purchasers and the like to trust property (ss. 74, 75, and 99); (4) the trust property exception in s. 67(1)(a); (5) the intersection between bankruptcy and family law; (6) sales (the prepaying buyer); and (7) set-off (s. 97(3)).

149

Other provisions affecting property claims include: ss. 67(2) and (3) (deemed trusts); ss. 81.1 and 81.2 (unpaid suppliers); and ss. 86 and 87 (Crown claims). These provisions are dealt with in Chapter 9. Sections 95, 96, and 101 allow the trustee in a variety of circumstances to claw back funds and other assets transferred by the debtor under impeachable transactions prior to the bankruptcy. These provisions are dealt with in Chapter 5. Sections 70 et seq. govern the precedence of bankruptcy orders and assignments over execution creditors and the like.

II. WHAT IS "PROPERTY"?

Saulnier v. Royal Bank of Canada
[2008] 3 SCR 166

BINNIE J:

. . .

I. Facts

[5] The appellant Saulnier holds four fishing licences (lobster, herring, swordfish and mackerel). Like most fishers, he required loans to finance his business. Accordingly, in April 1999, he signed a General Security Agreement ("GSA") with the Royal Bank. In January 2003, he signed a guarantee (limited to $215,000) to the Royal Bank for the debts of the appellant Bingo Queen, a company of which he was the sole owner. At that time, Bingo Queen also entered into a GSA. The standard form GSA gave the Bank a security interest in: "all ... present and after acquired personal property including ... [i]ntangibles ... and in all proceeds and renewals thereof." The GSA also specified that the term "intangible" would be interpreted according to its definition in the *PPSA*. The GSA contemplated a listing of specific property in Schedule C but in the case of both GSAs in question Schedule C was left blank.

[6] In 2004, the appellants' fishing business faltered. As of July 6, Mr. Saulnier owed the Bank $120,449, and Bingo Queen owed $177,282. On July 8, Saulnier made an assignment in bankruptcy. His Statement of Affairs under the *BIA* showed liabilities of $400,330, of which about $250,000 was owed to the Royal Bank. The trial judge found that according to the evidence, Saulnier's four fishing licences had a market value in excess of $600,000. This amount, if available to creditors, would be sufficient to discharge all debts and provide a surplus.

[7] On November 18, 2004, four months after the bankruptcy, Saulnier purported to lease his lobster licence to Horizon Fisheries Limited, whose principal owner was his common law spouse. In March 2005, the receiver and the trustee in bankruptcy signed an agreement to sell Saulnier's fishing licences and other assets to a third party for $630,000 (the sale was conditional on the trustee being able to effect a transfer of the licences). Saulnier refused to sign the necessary documents. The trustee in bankruptcy and the Royal Bank brought the present application for declaratory relief.

. . .

III. Judicial History

A. Supreme Court of Nova Scotia (2006), 241 NSR (2d) 96, 2006 NSSC 34

[9] Kennedy CJSC found that "the fair and correct approach is to characterize the federal fishing licences based on the reality of the commercial arena" (para. 49). He added that "[t]o accept the argument ... that there can be no property in these licences in the hands of the holder, because of ministerial control would ... foster an unrealistic legal condition based on an historic definition of property that ignores what is actually happening in the commercial world that the law must serve" (para. 53). In his view, the bundle of rights conferred by the licences "constitute marketable property capable of providing security" (para. 54) and also "property for purposes of the *BIA*" (para. 57).

B. Nova Scotia Court of Appeal (Bateman, Hamilton and Fichaud JJA) (2006), 246 NSR (2d) 239, 2006 NSCA 91

[10] Fichaud JA, writing for the court, found that while commercial reality and the market value attached to licences "may be a determinant in the accounting or appraisal contexts" (para. 17), the legal issue should be determined with reference to the definitions of "property" and "personal property" in the *BIA* and the *PPSA*.

[11] Based on his consideration of ss. 2 and 16(1) of the *Regulations*, he concluded that the licence itself is the property of the Crown, and not of the holder. However, "during the term of a license a licensee has a beneficial interest in the earnings from use of the license. That interest, and the right to those earnings, pass to the trustee in bankruptcy of the license holder" (para. 38). An important issue, in his view, was whether Mr. Saulnier had any rights relating to the renewal or reissuance of his licences, and whether these rights pass to the trustee. He considered it important that the holder of a fishing licence not only had the right to request a renewal but a right not to be arbitrarily denied it. In these circumstances [t]he license holder has a legally recognized right—limited though it may be—that constitutes intangible personal property. ... The security holder or trustee in bankruptcy takes the license holder's limited legal right or beneficial interest. The security holder or trustee takes [it] subject to all the risks of non-renewal that applied to the license holder—i.e. nonrenewal on grounds that are not arbitrary. This ensures that the interest of the security holder or trustee in bankruptcy does not degrade the regulatory scheme of the [fisheries] legislation. ... [para. 49].

[12] Fichaud JA cited cases in which bad-faith ministerial decisions had given rise to damages or had been judicially reviewed by the courts including *St. Anthony Seafoods Limited Partnership v. Newfoundland and Labrador (Minister of Fisheries and Aquaculture)* (2004), 245 DLR (4th) 597, 2004 NLCA 59. On the strength of these decisions, he found that "[a] legal right to damages or to set aside a ministerial decision is, in my view, intangible personal property under the broad definition in s. 2 of the *BIA*" (para. 52). Moreover, while "[t]he PPSA's framework to define 'intangible' is less substantial than in the *BIA*," the result concerning the fishing licences is the same (para. 61). The holder's rights in the fishing licences are also personal property ("intangibles") for the purposes of the *PPSA*, in his view.

IV. Analysis

[13] A commercial fisher with a ramshackle boat and a licence to fish is much better off financially than a fisher with a great boat tied up at the wharf with no licence. Financial institutions looking for readily marketable loan collateral want to snap up licences issued under the federal *Regulations*, which in the case of the lobster fishery can have a dockside value that fluctuates up to a half a million dollars or more. Fishers want to offer as much collateral as they can to obtain the loans needed to acquire the equipment to enable them to put to sea.

[14] The Minister's claim to more or less unfettered discretion to renew or not to renew fishing licences each year is based on the legislation as interpreted in *Comeau's Sea Foods Ltd. v. Canada (Minister of Fisheries and Oceans)*, [1997] 1 SCR 12. In that case Major J wrote for the Court:

> Canada's fisheries are a "common property resource," belonging to all the people of Canada. Under the *Fisheries Act*, it is the Minister's duty to manage, conserve and develop the fishery on behalf of Canadians in the public interest (s. 43). Licensing is a tool in the arsenal of powers available to the Minister under the *Fisheries Act* to manage fisheries. [para. 37]

Nevertheless, the fact is that the stability of the fishing industry depends on the Minister's predictable renewal of such licences year after year. Few fishers expect to see their loans paid off with the proceeds of a single year's catch. In an industry where holding one of a very restricted number of licences is a condition precedent to participation, the licence unlocks the value in the fishers' other marine assets.

[15] Yet the appellants are correct to say that just because a "right" or "power" to fish has commercial value, it does not follow that licences also constitute property within the scope of the *BIA* or *PPSA*. Earlier trial level decisions in Nova Scotia had held that fishing licences were not property and were not claimable by the trustee in bankruptcy. See e.g. *Re Jenkins* (1997), 32 CBR (4th) 262 (NSSC), and *Re Townsend* (2002), 32 CBR (4th) 318 (NSSC). We cannot wish away the statutory language however much practical sense is reflected in the result reached by the courts below.

A. A Question of Statutory Interpretation

[16] The questions before the Court essentially raise a dispute about statutory interpretation. We are not concerned with the concept of "property" in the abstract. The notion of "property" is, in any event, a term of some elasticity that takes its meaning from the context. The task is to interpret the definitions in the *BIA* and *PPSA* in a purposeful way having regard to "their entire context, in their grammatical and ordinary sense harmoniously with the scheme of the Act, the object of the Act, and the intention of Parliament" (R. Sullivan, *Sullivan and Driedger on the Construction of Statutes* (4th ed. 2002), at p. 1). Because a fishing licence may not qualify as "property" for the general purposes of the common law does not mean that it is also excluded from the reach of the statutes. For particular purposes Parliament can and does create its own lexicon.

[17] In determining the scope of the definition of "property" in a statutory context, it is necessary to have regard to the overall purpose of the *BIA*, which is to regulate the orderly administration of the bankrupt's affairs, keeping a balance between the rights of

creditors and the desirability of giving the bankrupt a clean break: *Husky Oil Operations Ltd. v. Minister of National Revenue*, [1995] 3 SCR 453, at para. 7. The exemption of designated property from distribution among creditors under s. 67(1) is to allow the bankrupt to continue a living pending discharge and, when discharged, to make a fresh start. Those exemptions do not, it seems to me, bear much similarity to the proposed "exempting" of a valuable asset such as a commercial fishing licence. If Saulnier had "sold" his licences prior to discharge the cash proceeds would, it seems, be after-acquired property that would be divided amongst his creditors under s. 67(1)(c) of the *BIA*.

[18] Within this overall purpose an appropriate interpretation must be given to the following definition of "property" in s. 2 of the *BIA*:

> "property" means any type of property, whether situated in Canada or elsewhere, and includes money, goods, things in action, land and every description of property, whether real or personal, legal or equitable, as well as obligations, easements *and every description of estate, interest and profit, present or future, vested or contingent, in, arising out of or incident to property*. [Emphasis in original.]

[19] The *PPSA*, on the other hand, is designed to facilitate the creation of a security interest to enable holders of personal property to use it as collateral, and to enable lenders to predict accurately the priority of their claims against the assets in question ...

[20] Within that overall purpose, an interpretation must be given to the somewhat circular definitions given in s. 2 of the *PPSA*:

> (w) "intangible" means personal property that is not goods, a document of title, chattel paper, a security, an instrument or money;
>
> ...
>
> (ad) "personal property" means goods, a document of title, chattel paper, a security, an instrument, money or an intangible.

[21] Of course a creditor/lender who enters into a security agreement that is not registerable under the *PPSA* may still have contractual rights against the borrower. However, the objective of lenders is to achieve priority (or to know in advance what priority they *can* achieve) over other claimants. Otherwise a miscreant could enter into a series of unregistered financing agreements purporting to use and re-use the same boat and licence as collateral.

B. The Interest Conferred by a Fishing Licence

[22] The fishery is a public resource. The fishing licence permits the holder to participate for a limited time in its exploitation. The fish, once caught, become the property of the holder. Accordingly, the fishing licence is more than a "mere licence" to do that which is otherwise illegal. It is a licence coupled with a proprietary interest in the harvest from the fishing effort contingent, of course, on first catching it.

[23] It is extremely doubtful that a simple licence could itself be considered property at common law. See generally A.M. Honoré, "Ownership," in A.G. Guest, ed., *Oxford Essays in Jurisprudence* (1961). On the other hand, if not property in the common law sense, a fishing licence is unquestionably a major commercial asset.

[24] Successive Ministers of Fisheries have issued policies underscoring their support for stability in the fishing industry, which necessitates continuity in the ranks of licence holders. Despite a policy favouring stability and continuity, the Minister's *Commercial Fisheries Licensing Policy for Eastern Canada, 1996* seeks to guard against any notion that such licences should be read as conferring a property interest on licence holders, which could possibly impose a fetter on the exercise of the Minister's "absolute discretion" in their issuance. Thus s. 5(a) of the *Licencing Policy* states:

> [a] "licence" grants permission to do something which, without such permission, would be prohibited. As such, a licence confers no property or other rights which can be legally sold, bartered or bequeathed. Essentially, it is a privilege to do something, subject to the terms and conditions of the licence.

The Minister's statement of policy expresses a departmental position that has no regulatory status and which, in the eye of the law, does not add to or subtract from his "absolute discretion" under s. 7(1) of the *Fisheries Act* to issue licences. Nor does this informal policy determine whether the licence can be construed as "property" for the purposes of the *BIA* and *PPSA*. The reality, as found by the courts below, is that the commercial market operates justifiably on the assumption that licences can be transferred on application to the Minister with the consent of the existing licence holder, that licences will be renewed from year to year, and that the Minister's policy will not be changed to the detriment of the existing licence holders. Thus, despite the Minister's protestations, the market attributes a high market value to what might otherwise be seen, as some of the cases put it, as a "transitory and ephemeral" right.

[25] The jurisprudence indicates a number of different approaches.

(i) The Traditional "Property" Approach

[26] The appellants rely on the decision of the Ontario Court of Appeal in *National Trust Co. v. Bouckhuyt* (1987), 61 OR (2d) 640. In that case, the court dismissed the trust company's claim that a valuable tobacco quota listed in a chattel mortgage could properly be made the subject of Ontario *PPSA* registration. Cory JA, as he then was, referred to some traditional *indicia* of rights of property and concluded that renewal of the tobacco quota year to year was subject to the "unfettered discretion of the [Tobacco B]oard" and that the quota itself was "transitory and ephemeral" (pp. 647-48). Accordingly, the quota did "not constitute intangible personal property as that term is utilized" in the Ontario *PPSA* (p. 649). The Quebec Court of Appeal reached a similar conclusion under the *BIA* in relation to a fishing licence in *Re Noel (Syndic)*, [1994] QJ No. 978 (QL) (CA).

[27] The *Bouckhuyt* approach has been followed in some of the Ontario *PPSA* cases; see e.g. *Canadian Imperial Bank of Commerce v. Hallahan* (1990), 69 DLR (4th) 449 (Ont. CA), and *Bank of Montreal v. Bale* (1992), 4 PPSAC (2d) 114 (Ont. CA), but it has been criticized as insufficiently sensitive to the particular context of personal property security legislation, which (so the critics say) commands a broader concept of intangible property if the purposes of that legislation are to be achieved. See, e.g. J.S. Ziegel and D.L. Denomme, *The Ontario Personal Property Security Act: Commentary and Analysis* (1994), at pp. 40-42. As discussed below, more recent cases have tended to restrict *Bouckhuyt* to its

facts. Even in the "regulatory cases" the courts now adopt a more purposeful approach to the definitions in the *BIA* and in personal property security legislation, and consider traditional common law notions of property as less of a stumbling block to recognition of licences and quotas as "property" for statutory purposes. I agree with this evolution.

[28] In any event, there is a significant difference between a quota (as in *Bouckhuyt*) and a fishing licence, which bears some analogy to a common law *profit à prendre* which is undeniably a property right. A *profit à prendre* enables the holder to enter onto the land of another to extract some part of the natural produce, such as crops or game birds (B. Ziff, *Principles of Property Law* (2nd ed. 1996), at pp. 333-34; *The Queen in Right of British Columbia v. Tener*, [1985] 1 SCR 533, M.J. Mossman and W.F. Flanagan, *Property Law: Cases and Commentary* (2nd ed. 2004), at p. 545). Equally, a "profit of piscary" (being a type of *profit à prendre*) is recognized as a property right to fish in the privately owned waters of another.

[29] Fichaud JA in the court below noted numerous cases where it was held that "during the term of a license the license holder has a beneficial interest to the earnings from his license" (para. 37). See also: *Waryk v. Bank of Montreal* (1991), 85 DLR (4th) 514 (BCCA), at pp. 521-24; *British Columbia Packers Ltd. v. Sparrow*, [1989] 4 CNLR 63 (BCCA), at p. 68, and *Buston v. Canada*, [1993] 2 CTC 2720 (TCC), at pp. 2733-34. This is another way of expressing substantially the same idea. The earnings flow from the catch which is lawfully reduced to possession at the time of the catch, as is the case with a *profit à prendre*.

[30] Some analytical comfort may be drawn in this connection from the observations of R. Megarry and H.W.R. Wade on *The Law of Real Property* (4th ed. 2008), at p. 779:

> A licence may be coupled with some proprietary interest in other property. Thus the right to enter another man's land to hunt and take away the deer killed, or to enter and cut down a tree and take it away, involves two things, namely, a licence to enter the land and the grant of an interest (a *profit à prendre*) in the deer or tree.

And at p. 822:

> A right to "hawk, hunt, fish and fowl" may thus exist as a profit, for this gives the right to take creatures living on the soil which, when killed, are capable of being owned.

• • •

[33] … A fishing licence is, no doubt, a creature of the *Fisheries Act* and its *Regulations*. Our Court has already emphasized the broad scope and discretion of the Minister in relation to such licences in *Comeau's Sea Foods*. Nevertheless, there are important points of analogy between the fishing licences issued to the appellant Saulnier and the form of common law property called a *profit à prendre*, which may include a profit of piscary. If the question were whether a fishing licence *is* a *profit à prendre*, the answer would almost certainly be no. But that is not the question. The question before us is whether the fishing licences thus conceived can satisfy the statutory definition of the *BIA* and *PPSA*, purposefully interpreted.

[34] My point is simply that the subject matter of the licence (i.e. the right to participate in a fishery that is exclusive to licence holders) coupled with a proprietary interest in the fish caught pursuant to its terms, bears a reasonable analogy to rights traditionally

considered at common law to be proprietary in nature. It is thus reasonably within the contemplation of the definition of "property" in s. 2 of the *BIA*, where reference is made to a "profit, present or future, vested or contingent, in, arising out of or incident to property." In this connection the property in question is the fish harvest.

[35] Of course, the holder's rights under a fishing licence are limited in time, place and the manner of their exercise by the *Fisheries Act* and *Regulations*. To say that the fishing licence is *coupled* with a proprietary interest does not encumber the Minister's discretion with proprietary fetters. The analogy used for present purposes does not prevail over the legislation. The licence is no more and no less than is described in the relevant legislation. Nevertheless, during its lifetime, however fragile, the fishing licence clearly confers something more than a "mere" permission to do something which is otherwise illegal.

(ii) The Regulatory Approach

[36] *Bouckhuyt* resulted in a line of cases in which licences and quotas were held to be intangible property (or not) according to the degree of renewal discretion vested in the issuing authority. In *Sugarman (in trust) v. Duca Community Credit Union Ltd.* (1999), 44 OR (3d) 257 (CA), the court distinguished *Bouckhuyt* on the basis that the authority issuing nursing home licences was bound to grant licences to operators that qualified, with little discretion to refuse, and an administrative appeal procedure in the event issuance or renewal *was* refused. See also *Re Foster* (1992), 89 DLR (4th) 555 (Ont. Ct. (Gen. Div.)), at pp. 564-65. The Nova Scotia Court of Appeal in the present case adopted a variant of the "regulatory" approach in holding that a licence holder's ability to request a renewal or reissuance of a licence to its designate, and to resist an arbitrary denial by the Minister, forms part of a "bundle of rights" which collectively constitute a type of property in which a security interest can be taken. ...

[37] In my view, the debate about the extent to which licences are "transitory and ephemeral" is of limited value. A lease of land for one day or one hour is undeniably a property interest, as is a lease terminable at pleasure. A third party may be willing to pay "key money" to take over a shop lease that is soon to expire in the expectation (reasonable or not) that a renewal will be forthcoming. Uncertainties of renewal do not detract from the interest presently possessed by the holder, but nor does an expectation of renewal based on a Minister's policy which could change tomorrow, transform a licence into a property interest.

[38] A difficulty with the "regulatory approach" is that there are no clear criteria to determine how much "fetter" on the issuing authority's discretion is enough to transform a "mere licence" into some sort of interest sufficient to satisfy the statutory definitions in the *BIA* and the *PPSA*. In *Bouckhuyt*, the fetters on the authority issuing tobacco quota were considered too weak, the discretion too great, to qualify the tobacco quota as Ontario *PPSA* "property." In *Sugarman* and *Foster* the "fetters" placed on the issuing authorities of nursing home licences and taxi licences, respectively, were thought to be enough to confer a proprietary interest within the terms of the Ontario *PPSA*. The regulatory frameworks in all three cases were different to be sure, but at what point does a licence that does not qualify under personal property security legislation become transformed

into a qualifying licence? ... The cases do not suggest an answer. No doubt criteria will emerge more clearly as cases that rely on a "regulatory approach" evolve. In this respect, however, I do not believe the "judicial review" paradigm offered by the Nova Scotia Court of Appeal in this case is helpful. The *Regulations* permit *anyone* to apply for a fisheries licence and *everyone* is entitled to a ministerial decision that complies with procedural fairness. I cannot agree that these elements are capable, as such, of constituting a licence "property" in the hands of a holder.

[39] In any event, I agree with the observation adopted by Major J in *Comeau's Sea Foods* that he could not find in the fisheries legislation any legal underpinning for the "vesting" of an interest in a licence "beyond the rights which it gives for the year in which it was issued" (p. 25) ... To the extent the regulatory cases are considered relevant here they do not assist the appellants, in my opinion. Section 7(1) of the *Fisheries Act* says that the Minister's discretion is "absolute."

[40] However, I do not believe the prospect of renewal, whether or not subject to an "unfettered" discretion, is determinative. For present purposes the appellants do not have to prove a renewal or even the reasonable prospect of it. The question under the *PPSA* is whether the holder (in this case the appellant Saulnier) had a qualifying interest in the licence either *at the time he entered into a General Security Agreement* with the Royal Bank in April 1999, or at the time the Bank sought to realize on Saulnier's after-acquired property, and the question under the *BIA* is whether he had a qualifying interest within the meaning of that Act *when he made an assignment in bankruptcy* on July 8, 2004.

(iii) The "Commercial Realities" Approach

[41] This approach is well illustrated by the trial decision of Kennedy CJSC in this case, who put the argument succinctly:

> That evidence confirms my understanding, that on the east coast of Canada fishing licenses, particularly for lobster, are commonly exchanged between fishermen for a great deal of money.
>
> Fishing vessels of questionable value are traded for small fortunes because of the licences that are anticipated to come with them.
>
> • • •
>
> To ignore commercial reality would be to deny creditors access to something of significant value in the hands of the bankrupt. That would be both artificial and potentially inequitable. [paras. 51-52 and 58]

• • •

[42] The criticism of this approach is that many things that have commercial value do not constitute property, while the value of some property may be minimal. There is no necessary connection between proprietary status and commercial value ... I agree with the Court of Appeal that "commercial realities" cannot legitimate wishful thinking about the notion of "property" in the *BIA* and the *PPSA*, although commercial realities provide an appropriate context in which to interpret the statutory provisions. The *BIA* and the *PPSA* are, after all, largely commercial statutes which should be interpreted in a way best suited to enable them to accomplish their respective commercial purposes.

(iv) The Preferred Approach

[43] As described above, the holder of a s. 7(1) licence acquires a good deal more than merely permission to do that which would otherwise be unlawful. The holder requires the right to engage in an exclusive fishery under the conditions imposed by the licence and, what is of prime importance, a proprietary right in the wild fish harvested thereunder, and the earnings from their sale. While these elements do not wholly correspond to the full range of rights necessary to characterize something as "property" at common law, the question is whether (even leaving aside the debate about the prospects of renewal) they are sufficient to qualify the "bundle of rights" the appellant Saulnier *did* possess as property for purposes of the statutes.

(a) Fishing Licences Qualify as Property Within the Scope of Section 2 of the BIA

[43]

· · ·

The terms of the [BIA definition of "property"] are very wide. Parliament unambiguously signalled an intention to sweep up a variety of assets of the bankrupt not normally considered "property" at common law. This intention should be respected if the purposes of the *BIA* are to be achieved.

[45] Reliance was placed on s. 16 of the *Regulations* which provides that a fishing licence is a "document" which is "the property of the Crown and is not transferable." From this it was inferred that the licence, in its commercial dimension, is declared by the *Regulations* to be a property right in the hands of the Crown. I think s. 16 merely says that the *Regulations* contemplate that the *documentation* of the licence (as opposed to the licence itself) is the property of the Crown, in the same way that a Canadian Passport is declared to be the property of the Crown, not the holder: *Veffer v. Canada (Minister of Foreign Affairs)*, [2008] 1 FCR 641, 2007 FCA 247, at para. 6. A fisher whose licence is suspended or revoked cannot refuse the Minister's demand for a return of the documentation on the basis the Minister gave it to him and it is now his property.

[46] I prefer to look at the substance of what was conferred, namely a licence to participate in the fishery coupled with a proprietary interest in the fish caught according to its terms and subject to the Minister's regulation. As noted earlier, the *BIA* is intended to fulfill certain objectives in the event of a bankruptcy which require, in general, that non-exempt assets be made available to creditors. The s. 2 definition of property should be construed accordingly to include a s. 7(1) fishing licence.

[47] It is true that the proprietary interest in the fish is contingent on the fish first being caught, but the existence of that contingency is contemplated in the *BIA* definition and is no more fatal to the proprietary status for *BIA* purposes than is the case with the equivalent contingency arising under a *profit à prendre*, which is undeniably a property interest.

[48] Counsel for the Attorney General of Canada was greatly concerned that a holding that the fishing licence is property in the hands of the holder even for limited statutory purposes might be raised in future litigation to fetter the Minister's discretion, but I do not think this concern is well founded. The licence is a creature of the regulatory system. Section 7(1) of the *Fisheries Act* speaks of the Minister's "absolute discretion." The

Minister gives and the Minister (when acting properly within his jurisdiction under s. 9 of the Act) can take away, according to the exigencies of his or her management of the fisheries. The statute defines the nature of the holder's interest, and this interest is not expanded by our decision that a fishing licence qualifies for inclusion as "property" for certain statutory purposes.

[49] It follows that in my view the trustee was entitled to require the appellant Saulnier to execute the appropriate documentation to obtain a transfer of the fishing licences to the third party purchaser.

[50] It may well be that in the course of a bankruptcy the fishing licence will expire, or has already expired. If so, the trustee will have the same right as the original holder of an expired licence to go to the Minister to seek its replacement, and has the same recourse (or the lack of it) if the request is rejected. The bankrupt can transfer no greater rights than he possesses. The trustee simply steps into the shoes of the appellant Saulnier and takes the licence "warts and all."

(b) The Fishing Licence Is Also "Personal Property" Within the Meaning of
     Section 2 of the PPSA

[51] … The [PPSA] definition of "intangible" simply describes something that otherwise constitutes "personal property" but is not one of the listed types of *tangible* personal property. "Intangible" would include an interest created by statute having the characteristics of a licence coupled with an interest at common law as in the case of a *profit à prendre*. Again, to repeat, I do not suggest that a fishing licence constitutes a *profit à prendre* at common law, for clearly there would be numerous conceptual objections to such a characterization. Our concern is exclusively with the extended definitions of "personal property" in the context of a statute that seeks to facilitate financing by borrowers and the protection of creditors. In my view the grant by the Fisheries Minister of a licence coupled with a proprietary interest as described above is sufficient to satisfy the *PPSA* definition.

[52] In this respect, the registration is therefore valid to include the s. 7(1) fishing licence and, in the absence of any other *PPSA* defence, the respondent bank is entitled to proceed with its *PPSA* remedies.

· · ·

Appeal dismissed

NOTES AND QUESTIONS

1. Does the Supreme Court's decision in *Saulnier* resolve the debate about whether a statutory licence is property for the purposes of the BIA? Would a taxi licence qualify as "property" on Binnie J's approach? What about a milk quota, or a nursing home licence? What would the answers to these questions have been if the court had adopted the reasoning of: (1) the trial judge; or (2) the Court of Appeal? Do you agree with Binnie J's reasons for rejecting both these approaches? For a critical analysis of the Supreme Court's decision, see Anthony Duggan, "In the Wake of the Bingo Queen" (2009), 47 *CBLJ* 225. For an

account of the lower court decisions in *Saulnier* and the earlier case law, see Thomas G. W. Telfer, "Statutory Licences and the Search for Property: The End of the Imbroglio" (2007), 45 *CBLJ* 224.

2. *Saulnier* deals with statutory licences. Licences can also be granted by contract. A contractual licence is a form of agreement under which licensor A gives licensee B permission to use A's property. Licensing is a common method for the sharing of intellectual property rights (patents, copyrights, trademarks, and the like). In form, a contractual licence is a promise by A to B that B may use A's property for the duration of the agreement. Assume A grants B a patent licence that incorporates an anti-assignment provision or an *ipso facto* clause and B becomes bankrupt while the licence is still current. (An anti-assignment provision prohibits the licensee from transferring the licence, while an *ipso facto* clause provides for automatic termination of the licence if the licensee becomes bankrupt). Is the licence "property" that passes to B's trustee pursuant to BIA s. 71? The question may arise if the trustee wants to either take over the licence for the benefit of the estate or sell it to a willing buyer. The answer is governed by BIA s. 84.1, which provides that, subject to court approval, the trustee may assign a contract regardless of any restrictions in it, and s. 84.2, which effectively prohibits *ipso facto* clauses. Both these provisions imply that the licence vests in the trustee pursuant to s. 71 and, therefore, that the licence is "property" in the BIA sense. Now assume A, the licensor, becomes bankrupt and A's trustee wants to terminate the licence. The cases establish that the trustee may not do this: "the trustee cannot use her power of disclaimer to disturb accrued rights and interests": see Anthony Duggan, "Partly Performed Contracts," in Stephanie Ben-Ishai and Anthony Duggan, *Canadian Bankruptcy and Insolvency Law: Bill C-55, Statute c. 47 and Beyond* (Toronto: LexisNexis, 2007) 15, at 26 and cases cited there. In other words, B's entitlement is "property" in the sense that it runs with the patent and is enforceable against A's trustee. See Duggan, "In the Wake of the Bingo Queen," above. For a fuller treatment of contract disclaimers and assignments, see Chapter 6, "Executory Contracts," and Chapter 13, Section IV.

3. In *Sittuk Investments Ltd. v. A. Farber & Partners Inc.* (2003), 61 OR (3d) 546 (SCJ), Spence J held that a time-share contract in a vacation resort was not a lease and did not give the holder a proprietary interest in the unit to which the contract relates but only a personal entitlement. The upshot was that the time-share company's trustee-in-bankruptcy was entitled to sell the property free of the holders' interests. However, he went on to grant the time-share contract-holders relief on the grounds of unconscionability and estoppel. (The contracts had described the arrangements as "leases" and the time share company had assured the holders that the contracts would not be adversely affected by any mortgage that might subsequently be placed on the property.)

4. The spate of dot-com company collapses a few years ago raised a new set of questions about the meaning of "property" in the BIA context. For example, is a domain name property? Is a website property? Are customer lists property? In relation to customer lists, does it make a difference whether there are privacy laws in place that restrict transfers or the uses to which the data may be put? These questions take on particular significance in cases where the debtor company has few other assets for the creditors to look to. See Michael Geist, "When Dot.Coms Die: The E-Commerce Challenge to Canada's Bankruptcy Law" (2002), 37 *CBLJ* 34.

5. Section 30(1)(a) of the BIA provides that the trustee may, with the permission of the inspectors, "sell or otherwise dispose of for such price or other consideration as the inspectors may approve all or any part of the property of the company." Can the trustee assign a legal cause of action? The question arises because of the rules against maintenance and champerty. Maintenance is the giving of assistance to a litigant by a person who has no interest in the litigation and no legally valid motive for interference. Champerty is a particular kind of maintenance—namely, maintenance of an action in consideration of a promise to give the maintainer a share of the proceeds. In *Rizzo & Rizzo Shoes Limited* (1998), 38 OR (3d) 280 (CA), the debtor company had retained an accounting firm as a consultant to review its financial situation. Nicholas Rizzo, who was an officer and shareholder of the company, alleged that the accounting firm had taken certain wrongful steps that led to the company's bankruptcy. After the company had gone into bankruptcy, he offered to purchase any claim the bankrupt estate had against the accounting firm for $25,000 and 25 percent of the net proceeds. The inspectors of the estate rejected the offer. Nicholas Rizzo sought an order pursuant to s. 119 of the BIA reversing the inspectors' decision and an order pursuant to s. 37 requiring the trustee to make the assignment. The court refused the order on the ground that it had no jurisdiction in the circumstances to interfere with the inspectors' decision. It went on to consider whether the rules against maintenance and champerty provided an additional ground for refusing the order. It held as follows: (1) a cause of action is a thing in action and so it is "property" within the meaning of BIA s. 2(1); (2) BIA s. 30(1)(a) authorized the trustee, with the concurrence of the inspectors, to assign the cause of action; and (3) the laws against maintenance and champerty do not apply to assignments that are authorized by law. The leading English cases are *Guy v. Churchill* (1889), 40 Ch. D 481 and *Ramsey v. Hartley*, [1977] 2 All ER 673. The court in *Rizzo* doubted whether these authorities applied in a case like the present one, where the court was being asked to make an order *compelling* the assignment: cf. *Re Oasis Merchandising Services Ltd.*, [1997] 2 WLR 764.

Re Holley
(1986), 26 DLR (4th) 230 (Ont. CA)

GOODMAN JA: This is an appeal by the plaintiff from the order of Anderson J sitting in bankruptcy, dated May 17, 1984, whereby he declared that the cause of action referred to in the plaintiff's action is property vested in the trustee in bankruptcy of the plaintiff and is an asset of her estate. He further declared that she had no status to bring or prosecute the action.

The relevant facts are as follows. On March 17, 1980, the appellant made an assignment in bankruptcy. On February 15, 1983, the appellant commenced an action against the respondent (defendant) Gifford-Smith Ltd. claiming damages for wrongful dismissal, including damages for mental distress and punitive damages in relation to the termination on April 3, 1979, of her employment with that respondent. On May 18, 1983, the appellant caused Marshall Children's Foundation to be added as a defendant.

The trustee in bankruptcy by notice dated July 6, 1983, duly advised the respondent Gifford-Smith Ltd. as a creditor who had proved a claim in the bankruptcy proceedings that an application for discharge of the appellant as a bankrupt was returnable on August

9, 1983. On August 2, 1983, Gifford-Smith Ltd. filed a notice of opposition to the discharge of the appellant. On August 3, 1983, the respondent Gifford-Smith Ltd. advised the trustee by a letter from its solicitor that:

> Andrea Holley is suing our client for damages for wrongful dismissal. This action, if successful, would result in funds being made available to Mrs. Holley attributable to the same time period in which Mrs. Holley accumulated sufficient debts to go into bankruptcy. Any recovery, it is our submission, should be for the benefit of all creditors. Although we feel the action is frivolous and vexatious, we thought that this matter should be brought to the attention of the Trustee in bankruptcy.

A copy of that respondent's notice of opposition was enclosed with the letter.

The discharge hearing was adjourned until December 12, 1983. The trustee did not respond to the letter of August 3, 1983, other than to indicate that it would not attend the hearing. On December 12, 1983, the discharge hearing was heard. Counsel for Gifford-Smith Ltd. appeared. No one appeared for the trustee or for the appellant nor did she appear personally. An order was made "that no order of discharge be made at this time."

On or about December 12, 1983, the respondents delivered a statement of defence in the appellant's action alleging inter alia as a ground for denying liability that the cause of action of the plaintiff had vested in the trustee and is an asset of the appellant's estate and, as a result, the appellant had no status to bring the action.

On or about April 12, 1984, the respondents delivered an application by way of notice of motion in bankruptcy court returnable May 17, 1984, seeking a declaration:

> ... that the causes of action referred to in the Supreme Court of Ontario, Judicial District of Waterloo, action no. 8886/84, or part thereof, are properly vested in the Trustee in bankruptcy, Clarke, Henning, Habu and are an asset of the estate of the plaintiff;

and

> ... that the plaintiff has no status to bring this action or part thereof.

No one appeared for the trustee on the motion and Anderson J made the order from which this appeal is taken.

· · ·

[The appellant's] action was not taken until February 15, 1983. In her statement of claim she alleged that she had been employed by one or both of the respondents for two years prior to April 3, 1979, on which date either one or both of the respondents terminated her employment. She alleged that, at the date of her dismissal, she was earning a salary of approximately $20,000 per year together with certain other benefits, including payment of Ontario Hospital Insurance premiums, of which she did not have precise knowledge of the value. She alleged that the respondents failed to give her reasonable notice of termination of her employment and that as a result of the arbitrary and ruthless manner in which her employment was terminated she suffered severe mental and emotional distress, anguish and anxiety.

In her prayer for relief she claimed:

(a) A declaration that either defendant, or both of them, dismissed the plaintiff from her employment with either defendant, or both of them, without lawful justification or excuse;

(b) General damages in the amount of $50,000 including damages for mental distress and loss of the various employment benefits to which she had been entitled previously;

(c) Special damages in the amount of $10,000, including payment of her wages, including overtime pay, cost of living payments, and vacations or holiday pay to the date of her dismissal wrongfully withheld by either defendant, or both of them;

(d) Punitive damages in the amount of $10,000;

(e) Prejudgment interest.

I am of the view that the reasonable interpretation of the claim for special damages is that it relates to a claim for six months' salary and benefits in lieu of notice. This accords with her allegation in the pleading that she earned approximately $20,000 per year and with her statement made to the official receiver. It appears from the pleading that the major portion of her claim is for the sum of $50,000 for mental distress together with the claim of $10,000 for punitive damages.

. . .

The appellant submitted that the bankruptcy court judge erred in finding that the cause of action referred to in the appellant's action was property which vested in the trustee. *Re Hollister* (1926), 30 OWN 328, [1926] 3 DLR 707, 7 CBR 629, was concerned with an action in which the trustee in bankruptcy applied for payment to it of moneys awarded to the debtor, an undischarged bankrupt for personal injuries sustained in an automobile accident. Fisher J said at pp. 708-9 DLR, pp. 630-1 CBR:

> The law is well settled that the *Bankruptcy Act* never intended to increase the assets of an insolvent for division amongst his creditors, by monies recovered in an action for personal injuries, as these monies are awarded as damages to the debtor for his pain, suffering and loss of comfort of life …

and further:

> Causes of action arising from bodily or mental suffering, such as actions for assault, seduction, criminal conversation, and damages for personal injuries, remain in the bankrupt.

In *Wilson et al. v. United Counties Bank, Ltd. et al.*, [1920] AC 102, the House of Lords had occasion to consider an award made by a jury at trial for two amounts:

(1) for the loss occasioned to the bankrupt's estate by the negligence of the defendant bank and in fact resulting in his bankruptcy, and

(2) to the bankrupt personally for injury and loss to his credit and reputation.

In considering whether the bankrupt was entitled to retain for his own use the sum awarded for damages for injury to his credit and reputation, Lord Atkinson pointed out that the same negligence of the defendant bank which caused the bankruptcy also caused the bankrupt pain, humiliation and loss of credit and repute. He indicated that credit and repute of the bankrupt, although of great value to him, were not part of his assets and that injury to them did not lessen or depreciate his property. ...

In *Egan v. Grayson* (1956), 8 DLR (2d) 125, 36 CBR 72, 20 WWR 632, Boyd McBride J, applying these two decisions held that a bankrupt was entitled to sue for damages to his person and reputation in an action for malicious prosecution in his own name and for his personal benefit. He said at p. 128 DLR, pp. 75-6 CBR:

> From the authorities the principle appears clear that the right of action for damages for in-jury to a bankrupt's property which lessened the value of his assets vests in and passes to his trustees and any damages awarded go for the benefit of his creditors, but on the other hand, any right of action for injury to his character and reputation remains vested in the bankrupt and does not pass to the trustee, the bankrupt may sue for damages for such injury in his own name, and if an award is made, it is purely personal to him and he keeps the amount awarded and the trustee cannot intercept it.

In *Cherry v. Ivey et al.* (1982), 37 OR (2d) 361, 136 DLR (3d) 381, 43 CBR (NS) 174, the defendants moved for an order staying the action until the plaintiff, a bankrupt, was discharged from bankruptcy. The plaintiff's action was for damages for malicious pros-ecution and for slander. He alleged that the acts of the defendants had irreparably im-paired his business activities and had caused him embarrassment, anxiety, emotional trauma, mental distress and physical upset. The defendants took the position that the causes of action were essentially claims of action interfering with the plaintiff's business and were therefore property within the definition thereof in the *Bankruptcy Act* and ac-cordingly, only the trustee in bankruptcy could prosecute the actions. Southey J said at pp. 363-4 OR, p. 384 DLR:

> In the case at bar, the causes of action are malicious prosecution and slander, both of which are essentially claims for outrage at the wrongs done to an individual. In my view, such causes of action do not vest in the trustee, simply because the outrage involved the plaintiff in his business. No case was cited to me in which a court has held that an action should be stayed because some of the damages claimed relate to the business of the plaintiff where the cause of action is otherwise clearly a personal one.

He then dismissed the application of the defendants. ...

It is clear that where the damages for which the bankrupt asserts a claim are personal in nature whether it be for physical suffering resulting from physical injuries sustained as a result of the negligence of another person or mental suffering resulting from a libel or slander perpetrated upon him, such cause of action does not become the property of his trustee in bankruptcy because it is not the policy of the law to convert into money for the creditors the mental or physical anguish of the debtor.

In 1976, an English court, for the first time it seems, awarded damages for mental dis-tress resulting from the breach of an employment contract: see *Cox v. Phillips Industries Ltd.* (1976), 1 WLR 638 (QB). ...

In *Brown v. Waterloo Regional Board of Com'rs of Police* (1983), 43 OR (2d) 113 at p. 120, 150 DLR (3d) 729 at pp. 735-6, 23 BLR 41, Weatherston JA, speaking for this Court, expressed the opinion:

The cases that I have referred to show that there may be circumstances where a breach of contract will give rise to a claim for damages for mental distress. In my opinion, the correct rule is stated in Corbin, supra, vol. 5, p. 429, citing the Restatement of the Law of Contracts, para. 341, as follows:

> There is sufficient authority to justify the statement that damages will be awarded for mental suffering caused by the wanton or reckless breach of a contract to render a performance of such a character that the promisor had reason to know when the contract was made that a breach would cause such suffering, for reasons other than pecuniary loss.

In *Pilon v. Peugeot Canada Ltd.* (1980), 29 OR (2d) 711, 114 DLR (3d) 378, 12 BLR 227, a long-term employee had been wrongfully dismissed. The employee had served the company loyally for many years, and that company had led him to expect permanent security of employment. Because the plaintiff had mitigated his loss quite successfully, he was held to be entitled only to damages of about $1,000 in respect of the period of which he ought to have been given notice. Nevertheless the court awarded damages of $7,500 for mental distress.

. . .

Although the only cause of action asserted is that of wrongful dismissal, the appellant has asserted several heads of damages. The respondents in their statement of defence denied that the appellant suffered any damages. The nature of the damages, if any, suffered by the appellant, can only be determined after a trial, with all the attendant pre-trial proceedings available to the parties under the rules of court. The appellant's statement of claim clearly claims damages for mental distress and punitive damages, both of which are personal in nature. The amount claimed under these headings is in excess of the amount which appears to be claimed for damages for salary in lieu of reasonable notice. As may be seen from authorities previously cited, it is possible that the appellant will recover damages solely or principally for mental distress and anxiety. In my view it is only after the nature of the damages, if any, to which the appellant claims to be entitled, has been ascertained, that the court can properly determine whether the cause of action is vested wholly or in part in the appellant or the trustee in bankruptcy. I agree with the opinion expressed by Southey J in *Cherry v. Ivey, supra*, that such question should be determined at trial, although Southey J did not have to consider in that case any proceedings launched in bankruptcy court.

NOTES AND QUESTIONS

1. What is the rationale for excluding certain causes of action from the property of the bankrupt? In *Beckham v. Drake* (1849), 2 HL Cas. 579, Erle J (at 608-9) said the reason was that

> the creditors cannot legitimately have looked to the pain of the bankrupt from a broken limb, or wounded affection, or blasted character, as a source of profit, they being in their nature casual and unforeseen, and unconnected immediately with property. There is a manifest distinction between damages from such sources as these last mentioned and damages in respect of contracts for labour.

The opposing objective is to maximize the debtor's estate for the creditors' benefit: see *Cork (Trustee in Bankruptcy of Rawlins) v. Rawlins*, [2001] EWJ No. 577 (CA). Do you think the cases give sufficient weight to this consideration?

2. In *Re Holley*, the court concluded that "it is only after the nature of the damages, if any, to which the appellant claims to be entitled, has been ascertained, that the court can properly determine whether the cause of action is vested wholly or in part in the appellant or the trustee in bankruptcy. ... The question is to be determined at trial." Who, then, is the proper plaintiff to bring the action—the debtor or the trustee? The answer seems to be either. If the debtor brings the action, she will have to account to the trustee for any damages, other than those for personal loss, recovered. Conversely, if the trustee brings the action, he will have to account to the debtor for the personal loss component of the damages award: see *Cork v. Rawlins*, above, at para. 22 discussing *Ord v. Upton*, [2000] Ch. 352.

3. BIA s. 68 deals with the debtor's obligation to make contributions to the estate from surplus income earned during bankruptcy. Are damages for personal loss to be taken into account in calculating the debtor's surplus income? In *Re Landry* (2000), 192 DLR (4th) 728, the Ontario Court of Appeal held that damages for wrongful dismissal are essentially compensation for unpaid wages and so they are equivalent to income. Section 68 is an exhaustive statement of the debtor's obligation to make income contributions: *Marzetti v. Marzetti*, [1994] 2 SCR 765. The consequence of the court's ruling in *Re Landry* was, therefore, that the trustee could not claim the damages award under the after-acquired property provision in s. 67(1)(c). The 2007 amendments in effect codify the decision by making it clear that, for the purposes of s. 68, "total income" includes "any amounts received as damages for wrongful dismissal."

4. A similar issue arises where the bankrupt is awarded damages for personal injury which include a component for lost wages and loss of future earning capacity. In *Re Anderson* (2004), 2 CBR (5th) 27 (Alta. QB), the court relied on *Marzetti* and *Wallace v. United Grain Growers Ltd.* (1997), 3 SCR 701 in support of the conclusion that s. 68 applied, to the exclusion of s. 67(1)(c). The court noted (at para. 23) that "the bankruptcy laws are not meant or intended to require payments by the bankrupt to the estate after the bankrupt's discharge. To require payment of any of the amount of future loss of wages to the estate would bring about this result." Cf. *Re Mostajo* (2006), 26 CBR (5th) 45 (Ont. SCJ) where the court, without reference to *Re Anderson*, reached the opposite conclusion. For further discussion of the surplus income requirements, see Chapter 11.

5. *Marzetti*, above, establishes that s. 68 takes precedence over s. 67(1)(c). What is the relationship between s. 67(1)(c) and the exempt property provisions in s. 67(1)(b)? In other words, if, after becoming bankrupt, the debtor acquires property that is "exempt from execution or seizure" under provincial law, does the trustee nevertheless have a claim on the basis that the property is after-acquired property to which s. 67(1)(c) applies? See *Monteith (Trustee of) v. Monteith*, [2004] SCJ (Sask. CA), extracted in Chapter 11. For further treatment of the exempt property provisions, see *Re Fields*, below, and Chapter 11.

III. SECURED CREDITORS

BIA s. 71 provides that when a debtor becomes bankrupt his property vests in the trustee, but subject to the "rights of secured creditors." BIA ss. 69.3(1) and (2) provide that when the debtor becomes bankrupt no creditor has any remedy against the debtor or the debtor's property, but, as a general rule, the debtor's bankruptcy does not prevent a secured creditor from enforcing its security interest. Section 127 provides that if a secured creditor enforces its security interest it may file a proof of claim as an unsecured creditor for any shortfall between the value of the collateral and the debt. Alternatively, a secured creditor may surrender its security to the trustee and claim as an unsecured creditor for the whole debt. Sections 136 and following set out the rules for distribution of the estate among creditors who have filed a proof of claim. Section 136(1) provides that these rules are "subject to the rights of secured creditors." Read together, these provisions mean that, generally speaking, a secured creditor has priority over unsecured creditors in a debtor's bankruptcy. See, further, Chapter 8. The PPSAs create an exception by providing that an unperfected security interest is ineffective against the debtor's trustee in bankruptcy. In other words, the secured creditor must take steps to publicize its security interest, typically by taking possession of the collateral or registering a finance statement, if it wants the priority the BIA gives it.

Re Giffen
[1998] 1 SCR 91

IACOBUCCI J: The principal question raised by this appeal is whether s. 20(b)(i) of the *Personal Property Security Act*, SBC 1989, c. 36 ("PPSA"), can render a lessor's unperfected security interest in personal property ineffective against the rights acquired in the property by the trustee in bankruptcy, which finds its authority under the *Bankruptcy and Insolvency Act*, RSC, 1985, c. B-3 ("BIA"). I conclude that s. 20(b)(i) operates, on the present facts, to defeat the unperfected security interest of the respondent Telecom Leasing Canada (TLC) Limited (the "lessor"), in favour of the interest acquired by the appellant R. West & Associates Inc. (the "trustee").

Constitutional questions were raised in this appeal; however, in my view of the case, it is not necessary to address these issues. A reading of the provisions of the BIA and the PPSA in question reveals that no conflict arises in the operation of the legislation.

. . .

On October 27, 1992, the lessor leased a 1993 Saturn car to the BC Telephone Company, which in turn leased the car to one of its employees, Carol Anne Giffen (the "bankrupt"). The bankrupt and her employer were parties to the agreement of lease entitled "Employee Agreement Personal Vehicle Lease Program/Flex Lease Program." The term of the lease was for more than one year. The lease gave the bankrupt the option of purchasing the vehicle from the lessor.

Although the lessor was not a party to the agreement, it played an important role in the arrangement contemplated by the agreement. More specifically, the lessor received a deposit from the bankrupt, it fixed the lease rates, and it was entitled to receive payments directly from the lessee/bankrupt if her employer stopped paying her. Further, the lessor and the bankrupt were named as the owners of the vehicle in the registration and insurance documents relating to the vehicle; the lessor was described as the "lessor" and the bankrupt was described as the "lessee."

The bankrupt made an assignment in bankruptcy on October 12, 1993. Neither the lessor nor the BC Telephone Company had registered financing statements under the PPSA in respect of their leases. The failure to register meant that the lessor's security interest in the car was not perfected, as defined in the PPSA, at the time of the assignment in bankruptcy.

The appellant was appointed as the trustee in bankruptcy. The lessor seized the vehicle and sold it with the trustee's consent; proceeds of $10,154.54 were held in trust by the lessor's counsel. The trustee subsequently brought a motion for an order that it was entitled to the proceeds of sale relying on s. 20(b)(i) of the PPSA. The lessor opposed the claim on the grounds that the bankrupt never owned the car and that the trustee could not have a better claim to the car than the bankrupt had.

Hood J of the Supreme Court of British Columbia held that, by virtue of s. 20(b)(i) of the PPSA, the unperfected security interest of the lessor was of no effect as against the trustee. Hood J ordered that the proceeds from the sale of the vehicle be paid over to the trustee. The lessor appealed to the Court of Appeal for British Columbia; the Attorney General of British Columbia was granted leave to intervene as a party respondent in the appeal. The Court of Appeal allowed the appeal and held that the proceeds properly belonged to the lessor.

. . .

Personal Property Security Act, SBC 1989, c. 36

2.(1) Subject to section 4, this Act applies

(a) to every transaction that in substance creates a security interest, without regard to its form and without regard to the person who has title to the collateral, and

(b) without limiting the generality of paragraph (a), to a chattel mortgage, a conditional sale, a floating charge, a pledge, a trust indenture, a trust receipt, an assignment, a consignment, a lease, a trust, and a transfer of chattel paper where they secure payment or performance of an obligation.

3. Subject to sections 4 and 55, this Act applies to

(a) a transfer of an account or chattel paper,

(b) a commercial consignment, and

(c) a lease for a term of more than one year

that do not secure payment or performance of an obligation.

20. A security interest ...

(b) in collateral is not effective against

(i) a trustee in bankruptcy if the security interest is unperfected at the date of the bankruptcy, ...

21. Where the interest of a lessor under a lease for a term of more than one year or of a consignor under a commercial consignment is not effective against a judgment creditor under section 20 (a) or a trustee or liquidator under section 20 (b), the lessor or consignor is deemed, as against the lessee or consignee, as the case may be, to have suffered, immediately before the seizure of the leased or consigned goods or the date of the bankruptcy or winding-up order, damages in an amount equal to

(a) the value of the leased or consigned goods at the date of the seizure, bankruptcy or winding-up order, and

(b) the amount of loss other than that referred to in paragraph (a) that results from the termination of the lease or consignment.

paid to the lessor.

There is one principal issue in the present appeal: can s. 20(b)(i) of the PPSA extinguish the lessor's right to the car in favour of the trustee's interest, or is the operation of s. 20(b)(i) limited by certain provisions of the BIA?

In my view, this issue can be resolved through a normal reading of the relevant provisions of both the PPSA and the BIA, buttressed by the policy considerations supporting these provisions.

. . .

At the outset, it is important to note that the Court of Appeal's holding in the present appeal rests on the principle that the "property of the bankrupt" shall vest in the trustee (s. 71(2) BIA) and that only the property of the bankrupt shall be distributed among the bankrupt's creditors (s. 67(1) BIA). In the opinion of the Court of Appeal, the bankrupt, as lessee, did not have a proprietary interest in the car, and since the trustee obtains its entitlements to the contents of the bankrupt's estate through the bankrupt, the trustee cannot assert a proprietary interest in the car. In my view, the Court of Appeal, with respect, erred fundamentally in focussing on the locus of title and in holding that the lessor's common law ownership interest prevailed despite the clear meaning of s. 20(b)(i).

The Court of Appeal did not recognize that the provincial legislature, in enacting the PPSA, has set aside the traditional concepts of title and ownership to a certain extent. T.M. Buckwold and R.C.C. Cuming, in their article "The Personal Property Security Act and the Bankruptcy and Insolvency Act: Two Solitudes or Complementary Systems?" (1997), 12 *Banking & Finance L. Rev.* 467, at pp. 469-70, underline the fact that provincial legislatures, in enacting personal property security regimes, have redefined traditional concepts of rights in property:

> Simply put, the property rights of persons subject to provincial legislation are what the legislature determines them to be. While a statutory definition of rights may incorporate common law concepts in whole or in part, it is open to the legislature to redefine or revise those concepts as may be required to meet the objectives of its legislation. This was done in the provincial PPSAs, which implement a new conceptual approach to the definition and assertion of rights in and to personal property falling within their scope. The priority and realization provisions of the Acts revolve around the central statutory concept of "security interest." The rights of parties to a transaction that creates a security interest are explicitly not dependent upon either the form of the transaction or upon traditional questions of title. Rather, they are defined by the Act itself.

In *International Harvester, supra*, the Saskatchewan Court of Appeal recognized that the regime put in place to regulate competing interests in personal property does not turn on title to the collateral (at p. 204):

> There is nothing in the language of the section [s. 20 of the Saskatchewan PPSA which is the equivalent of s. 20 of the British Columbia PPSA], or its relationship with other sections, or

indeed in the overall scheme of the Act to suggest, for example, that an unperfected security interest, because it is rooted in and attached to the title of particular goods in the possession of a debtor, should be treated as superior to the more generally derived and broadly attached interest which an execution creditor comes to have in a debtor's goods. Indeed, the very opposite is suggested not only by the language of the section, but by the overall thrust of the Act.

The Court of Appeal in the present appeal did not look past the traditional concepts of title and ownership. But this dispute cannot be resolved through the determination of who has title to the car because the dispute is one of priority to the car and not ownership in it. It is in this context that the PPSA must be given its intended effect and it is to this question that I now wish to turn.

· · ·

The PPSA applies to "every transaction that in substance creates a security interest, without regard to its form and without regard to the person who has title to the collateral" (s. 2(1)(a)).

Section 1 of the PPSA defines "security interest," in part, as "an interest in goods, chattel paper, a security, a document of title, an instrument, money or an intangible that secures payment or performance of an obligation." This definition is elaborated upon by paragraph 1(a)(iii) of the PPSA, which provides that "security interest" means the interest of "a lessor under a lease for a term of more than one year, whether or not the interest secures payment or performance of an obligation" (emphasis added). Further, s. 3 of the PPSA deems certain agreements, which do not secure payment or performance of an obligation, to be security agreements for the purposes of the PPSA. Section 3 includes leases "for a term of more than one year that do not secure payment or performance of an obligation."

The elements of the definition of "security interest" explicitly include within the definition of "security interest" leases for a term of more than one year. The lessor's interest in the car is the reservation of title in the car; this interest, created by the lease agreement, falls within the ambit of the PPSA.

· · ·

A security interest is valid and enforceable when it attaches to personal property. Section 12(1)(b) of the PPSA provides that a security interest "attaches" when the debtor acquires "rights in the collateral." Section 12(2) states explicitly that "a debtor has rights in goods leased to the debtor ... when he obtains possession of them in accordance with the lease." Thus, upon delivery of the car to the bankrupt, the lessor had a valid security interest in the car that could be asserted against the lessee and against a third party claiming a right in the car. However, the lessor's security interest remained vulnerable to the claims of third parties who obtain an interest in the car through the lessee including, trustees in bankruptcy. In order to protect its security interest from such claims, the lessor must therefore perfect its interest through registration of its interest (s. 25), or repossession of the collateral (s. 24). The lessor did not have possession of the car, and it did not register its security interest. Thus, prior to the bankruptcy, the lessor held an unperfected security interest in the car. This brings us to the BIA.

· · ·

Section 71(2) of the BIA provides that, upon an assignment into bankruptcy, the bankrupt's "property ... shall, subject to this Act and to the rights of secured creditors, forthwith pass to and vest in the trustee." Section 2 of the BIA defines "property" very broadly to include "every description of estate, interest and profit, present or future, vested or contingent, in, arising out of or incident to property."

In my opinion, the bankrupt's right to use and possession of the car constitutes "property" for the purposes of the BIA and the trustee, by virtue of s. 71(2) of the BIA, succeeds to this proprietary right. ...

The trustee assumes the bankrupt's possessory interest in the car through the operation of s. 71(2); it is upon this basis that the trustee can assert a claim to the car.

· · ·

The Saskatchewan Court of Appeal explained the theory behind s. 20 of the Saskatchewan PPSA in *International Harvester* (at pp. 204-5). A person with an interest rooted in title to property in the possession of another, once perfected, can, in the event of default by the debtor, look to the property ahead of all others to satisfy his claim. However, if that interest is not perfected, it is vulnerable, even though it is rooted in title to the goods (at p. 205):

> A third party may derive an interest in the same goods by virtue of some dealing with the person in possession of them, and ... he may become entitled to priority. That is, he may become entitled, ahead of the person holding the unperfected security interest, to look to the goods to satisfy his claim.

Public disclosure of the security interest is required to prevent innocent third parties from granting credit to the debtor or otherwise acquiring an interest in the collateral. However, public disclosure of the security interest does not seem to be required to protect a trustee who is not in the position of an innocent third party; rather, the trustee succeeds to the interests of the bankrupt. In one authority's opinion, trustees are given the capacity to defeat unperfected security interests because of the "representative capacity of the trustee and the effect of bankruptcy on the enforcement rights of unsecured creditors" (R.C.C. Cuming, "Canadian Bankruptcy Law: A Secured Creditor's Heaven" (1994), 24 *Can. Bus. LJ* 17, at pp. 27-28).

Prior to a bankruptcy, unsecured creditors can make claims against the debtor through provincial judgment enforcement measures. Successful claims will rank prior to unperfected security interests pursuant to s. 20. Once a bankruptcy occurs, however, all claims are frozen and the unsecured creditors must look to the trustee in bankruptcy to assert their claims. Cuming describes the purpose of s. 20(b)(i) (at p. 29):

> In effect, the judgment enforcement rights of unsecured creditors are merged in the bankruptcy proceedings and the trustee is now the representative of creditors who can no longer bring their claims to a "perfected" status under provincial law. As the repository of enforcement rights, the trustee has status under s. 20(b)(i) of the BCPPSA to attack the unperfected security interest.

The purpose behind granting a trustee in bankruptcy the power to defeat unperfected security interests was recognized by the Saskatchewan Court of Appeal in *International Harvester* (at p. 206):

Indeed, the fact that a trustee in bankruptcy is a representative of creditors serves to shed light on more than one aspect of the issue. It explains—or at least assists in the explanation of—why a trustee in bankruptcy is included in s. 20, as well as why a trustee is not necessarily confined to the interest of the bankrupt.

The Saskatchewan Court of Appeal again acknowledged the representative role of the trustee in bankruptcy in *Paccar Financial Services*, which also involved a priority contest between a trustee and the unperfected security interest of a lessor. The court stated that the trustee, after bankruptcy, acts as the representative of the unsecured creditors of the bankrupt and asserts "the claim of the unsecured creditors to the goods and possessions of the bankrupt pursuant to the priorities established for competing perfected and unperfected security interests. It is simply a contest as between an unsecured creditor and the holder of an unperfected security interest" (p. 490).

The Court of Appeal erred, in my view, in not recognizing that the purpose of s. 20(b)(i) is, at least in part, to permit the unsecured creditors to maintain, through the person of the trustee, the same status vis-à-vis secured creditors who have not perfected their security interests which they enjoyed prior to the bankruptcy of the debtor.

· · ·

In the present appeal, the trustee's possessory interest in the car, acquired through the bankrupt under the authority of the BIA, comes into competition with the unperfected security interest of the lessor. Section 20(b)(i) of the PPSA states explicitly that a security interest in collateral "is not effective against a trustee in bankruptcy if the security interest is unperfected at the date of the bankruptcy." On a plain reading of s. 20(b)(i), the lessor's interest in the car is ineffective against the trustee.

Section 20(b)(i) does not grant title or any other proprietary interest to the trustee, but it prevents the lessor from exercising rights against the trustee. Admittedly, the effect of s. 20(b)(i), on the present facts, is that the trustee ends up with full rights to the car when the bankrupt had only a right of use and possession. The Court of Appeal refused to accept this result because, in its view, it violated fundamental concepts of bankruptcy law. In this respect, the Court of Appeal cites *Fleeming* [*v. Howden* (1868), LR 1 Sc. & Div. 372 (HL)] and *Flintoft* [*v. Royal Bank of Canada*, [1964] SCR 631] in support of the proposition that a trustee in bankruptcy cannot receive a greater interest in the property than the bankrupt had at the time of the bankruptcy.

With respect, I disagree with the Court of Appeal for two reasons: first, *Fleeming* and *Flintoft* can be distinguished; and second, s. 20(b)(i) modifies the principle that a trustee is limited to the rights in the property enjoyed by the bankrupt.

Both *Fleeming* and *Flintoft* involved circumstances where the contested property was held on trust by the bankrupt and therefore did not form part of the bankrupt's estate. ...

The trustee in bankruptcy cannot succeed to property held on trust by the bankrupt. This principle appears to be the source of comments made in *Fleeming* and *Flintoft* to the effect that a trustee in bankruptcy cannot take a greater interest than the bankrupt had. In my view, the proposition stated in these cases (that a trustee in bankruptcy cannot take a greater interest in property than the bankrupt had) should be restricted to the context in which they were made, namely, where the disputed property is held on trust by the bankrupt debtor. However, the bankrupt in the case on appeal did not hold the car on trust for the lessor.

I accept that there is a principle which provides that a trustee in bankruptcy cannot obtain a greater interest to the goods than the bankrupt (beyond the context of a trust where the goods are not property of the bankrupt). However, s. 20(b)(i) itself modifies that principle. Cases decided prior to the Court of Appeal decision in the case on appeal have consistently accepted that s. 20(b)(i), or its equivalent, can give the trustee a greater interest in the disputed property than that enjoyed by the bankrupt.

. . .

Title could not defeat the trustee's claim under s. 20(b)(i) of the PPSA, but does the lessor's retention of title and the principle of *nemo dat quod non habet* prevent the trustee from selling the car, conferring clear title, and distributing its proceeds under the BIA?

Section 81 of the BIA provides a procedure through which third parties can file claims with the trustee against "property ... in the possession of a bankrupt at the time of the bankruptcy." Subsection 81(2) provides that where the trustee disputes a claim, and the claimant does not appeal within the prescribed time period, then the claimant is "deemed to have abandoned or relinquished all his right to or interest in the property to the trustee who thereupon may sell or dispose of the property free of any lien, right, title or interest of the claimant." Section 81 does not specifically deal with the circumstances where a claimant's claim is defeated, but presumably the trustee would be able to sell the good free of the claim.

The lessor could have made a claim under s. 81 of the BIA. This claim would have been defeated by the trustee in reliance on s. 20(b)(i) of the PPSA. In my view, both the defeat of a claim and the failure to make a claim under s. 81 result in the effective abandonment or relinquishment of any claim to the car; the trustee can therefore sell the car and confer good title.

. . .

Section 136 of the BIA sets out a priority scheme for the division of the property of the bankrupt; the interests of the various creditors are all "[s]ubject to the rights of secured creditors." Section 67 describes that which constitutes the property of the bankrupt.

This Court has held on a number of occasions that provincial legislatures cannot enact legislation which operates to interfere with the priority of distribution set out in the BIA, nor can they confer secured creditor status on a class of creditors not entitled to such status under the BIA.

The Court of Appeal applied this Court's decision in *Husky Oil* to conclude that a provincial law cannot add to the estate of a bankrupt property which the bankrupt never had. In my view, the Court of Appeal erred in its characterization of s. 20(b)(i). Section 20(b)(i) of the PPSA does not offend the priorities set out in the BIA ... ; rather, s. 20(b)(i) is but one element of the provincial legislation which serves to define the rights of the parties involved in a bankruptcy. More particularly, s. 20(b)(i) serves, on the present facts, to define the rights of the lessor and indicates that for the purpose of the bankruptcy, the lessor does not have the status of a secured creditor.

Even though bankruptcy is clearly a federal matter, and even though it has been established that the federal Parliament alone can determine distribution priorities, the BIA is dependent on provincial property and civil rights legislation in order to inform the terms of the BIA and the rights of the parties involved in the bankruptcy. Section 72(1) of the BIA contemplates interaction with provincial legislation.

. . .

Section 20(b)(i) does not reorder federal priorities. Compliance with the perfection requirements of the PPSA is a precondition to maintaining secured creditor status under the BIA. In the event of bankruptcy, the consequences of a failure to perfect are spelled out in s. 20(b)(i). In effect, the secured party with an unperfected security interest becomes an unsecured creditor of the bankrupt.

NOTES AND QUESTIONS

1. *Re Giffen* concerns the interaction between the BIA and the provincial personal property security laws (PPSAs). The PPSAs govern secured transactions, or "security agreements." A security agreement is an agreement that gives the creditor ("secured party") a security interest in personal property belonging to the debtor. The PPSAs apply to all transactions that in substance create a security interest, regardless of form. This means they cover not just transactions that create security interests in the strict sense (the mortgage, the pledge, and the charge), but also transactions that are functionally equivalent to mortgage, charge, and pledge agreements. Examples include conditional sale agreements and a goods lease for a term of more than one year.

There are different kinds of lease. One kind is the simple contract of hire. A familiar example is the car rental agreement. In cases like this the customer has the use of the goods for the period of the agreement and returns them to the lessor when the time is up. Another kind of lease is the finance lease (or "residual-value" lease). This is an in-substance security agreement. It is functionally equivalent to a conditional sale. The customer pays rent for an agreed period but, unlike the simple contract of hire, the parties do not anticipate that the customer will ever return the goods to the lessor. Rather, the agreement either expressly or tacitly gives the customer a right to purchase the goods for a predetermined price (the "residual value") at the end of the term. The finance lease is commonly used in commercial dealings to facilitate the acquisition of vehicles and other equipment. It has income-tax advantages if the goods are for use in a business enterprise, because the rentals can be claimed as deductions, provided the customer uses the leased equipment for income-producing purposes.

In principle, the PPSAs should apply to a lease if it in substance secures payment or performance of an obligation, but not otherwise. However, this distinction is sometimes a hard one to draw and, to avoid litigation, the statutes are expressed to apply to all leases that are for a term of more than one year, the length of the term being a proxy for inquiry into the substance of the transaction.

2. According to Iacobucci J, "the purpose of s. 20(1)(b)(i) [of the BCPPSA] is, at least in part, to permit the unsecured creditors to maintain, through the person of the trustee, the same status vis-à-vis secured creditors who have not perfected their security interests which they enjoyed prior to the bankruptcy of the debtor." Recall Jackson's argument that creditors' relative entitlements should be the same inside bankruptcy as they are outside bankruptcy to prevent creditors from improving their positions relative to one another by using the bankruptcy laws opportunistically: see Chapter 1. There is an obvious tension between this

consideration and the *pari passu* (rateable distribution) principle that supposedly underlies the bankruptcy laws. Given the secured creditor's privileged position in the debtor's bankruptcy, why don't all creditors take security? A security interest is not cost-free. The secured creditor must pay a price, usually in the form of a lower interest rate than it could demand without security. The lower interest rate reflects the secured creditor's reduced risk. These cost considerations imply that the question might just as sensibly be put the other way round—that is, why do creditors *ever* take security? The question in this form has been the subject of intensive discussion in the law and economics literature: see Lucien Arye Bebchuk and Jesse M. Fried, "The Uneasy Case for the Priority of Secured Claims in Bankruptcy: Further Thoughts and a Reply to the Critics" (1997), 82 *Cornell Law Review* 1279 and the literature cited there.

3. At the conceptual level, there is an apparent inconsistency between saying that a perfected security interest is effective against the debtor's trustee in bankruptcy, whereas an unperfected security interest is not. What is the nature of this apparent inconsistency? How did the court in *Re Giffen* resolve it?

4. In *Re Giffen*, the court held that on a plain reading of the BCPPSA, s. 20(1)(b), an unperfected security interest is ineffective against a trustee in bankruptcy. BIA s. 67(1)(b) says that the property of a bankrupt divisible among his creditors shall not comprise any property that "as against the bankrupt is exempt from execution or seizure under the laws of the province within which the property is situated and within which the bankrupt resides." Assume the debtor gives the secured creditor a security interest in goods that are exempt from execution or seizure under the laws of the province concerned. The secured creditor fails to register its security interest in the province. The debtor becomes bankrupt. Is the secured creditor entitled to claim the goods on the ground that, by virtue of BIA s. 67(1)(b), the trustee has no claim to them? See *Re Fields*, below.

Re Fields
(2002), 59 OR (3d) 611 (SC Bktcy.)

POLOWIN J: This is an appeal being brought by the secured creditor, DaimlerChrysler Financial Services (debis) Canada Inc. ("DCFS"). DCFS seeks, in the main, an order reversing the decision of Master Schreider dated October 19, 2001 and a declaration that the Trustee has no interest in, or claim to, the value of the vehicle in question up to the amount of $5,000 and that DCFS maintains its priority to the vehicle to that extent. It is DCFS's position that the Master erred, in fact and law, in dismissing DCFS's Appeal from the Notice of Disallowance of the Trustee.

The facts can be easily stated. James Allen Fields ("Fields") filed an assignment in bankruptcy on June 12, 2001. At the date of the bankruptcy, DCFS was a creditor of Fields pursuant to a conditional sale contract made between Fields and DCFS dated November 19, 1999 in respect of a 1998 Chrysler Intrepid. It is conceded that DCFS had not perfected its security interest in Ontario. It is also agreed that the vehicle has a present worth of at least $11,000.

DCFS filed a Proof of Claim with the Trustee on July 16, 2001, claiming a balance owing in the amount of $22,257.41 pursuant to the conditional sale contract. By Notice of Disallowance dated July 20, 2001, the Trustee disallowed the Proof of Claim of DCFS.

Mr. Fields did not claim any exemption for the subject 1998 Chrysler Intrepid under the Ontario *Execution Act*, RSO 1990, c. E.24 as amended (the "*Execution Act*"). In the Statement of Affairs, the vehicle was shown as non-exempt property. Further, Mr. Fields specifically waived his claim for such exemption in a waiver dated September 12, 2001. In brief reasons, Master Schreider denied DCFS's appeal from the Disallowance.

· · ·

The issue in this case is whether the Trustee has any interest or claim to the bankrupt's motor vehicle up to the amount of $5,000, in light of the applicable sections in the *Execution Act* and the BIA. Stated in another way, does the exempt status of the bankrupt's property (if such property is found to be exempt) prevent the trustee from enjoying priority over DCFS's unperfected security interest.

· · ·

… In [*Perron-Malenfant v. Malenfant (Trustee of)*, [1999] 3 SCR 375, 177 DLR (4th) 257], *supra*, the Supreme Court of Canada considered the interplay of the BIA and a provincial *Execution Act*. The court stated that where a province enacts rules governing seizability, those express rules govern. The *Malenfant* case thus stands for the proposition that this court must look to the specific wording of the Ontario *Execution Act* to determine whether the exemption applies because under s. 67(1)(b), it is the particular province's statutes concerning exemptions that dictate the rights of debtor, creator, and trustee. The BIA sets out the rules of the game. The Ontario *Execution Act* "informs" the BIA. It is the "code" to be applied.

Sections 2 and 3 of the Ontario *Execution Act* provide as follows:

2. The following chattels are exempt from seizure under any writ issued out of any court:

1. Necessary and ordinary wearing apparel of the debtor and his or her family not exceeding the prescribed amount or, if no amount is prescribed, $5,000 in value.

2. The household furniture, utensils, equipment, food and fuel that are contained in and form part of the permanent home of the debtor not exceeding the prescribed amount or, if no amount is prescribed, $10,000 in value.

3. In the case of a debtor other than a person engaged solely in the tillage of the soil or farming, tools and instruments and other chattels ordinarily used by the debtor in the debtor's business, profession or calling not exceeding the prescribed amount or, if no amount is prescribed, $10,000 in value.

4. In the case of a person engaged solely in the tillage of the soil or farming, the livestock, fowl, bees, books, tools and implements and other chattels ordinarily used by the debtor in the debtor's business or calling not exceeding the prescribed amount or, if no amount is prescribed, $25,000 in value.

5. In the case of a person engaged solely in the tillage of the soil or farming, sufficient seed to seed all the person's land under cultivation, not exceeding 100 acres, as

selected by the debtor, and fourteen bushels of potatoes, and, where seizure is made between the 1st day of October and the 30th day of April, such food and bedding as are necessary to feed and bed the livestock and fowl that are exempt under this section until the 30th day of April next following.

6. A motor vehicle not exceeding the prescribed amount or, if no amount is prescribed, $5,000 in value.

3(1) Where exemption is claimed for a chattel referred to in paragraph 3 of section 2 that has a sale value in excess of the amount referred to in subsection (1.1) plus the costs of the sale and other chattels are not available for seizure and sale, the chattel is subject to seizure and sale under a writ of execution and the amount referred to in subsection (1.1) shall be paid to the debtor out of the proceeds of the sale.

3(1.1) The amount for the purposes of subsection (1) is the prescribed amount or, if no amount is prescribed, $10,000.

3(2) The debtor may, in lieu of the chattels referred to in paragraph 4 of section 2, elect to receive the proceeds of the sale thereof up to the amount referred to in subsection (4.1), in which case the officer executing the writ shall pay the net proceeds of the sale if they do not exceed the amount referred to in subsection (4.1) or, if they exceed the amount referred to in subsection (4.1), shall pay that sum to the debtor in satisfaction of the debtor's right to exemption under that paragraph.

. . .

3(4.1) The amount for the purposes of subsection (4) is the prescribed amount or, if no amount is prescribed, $25,000.

It is to be noted that para. 6 of s. 2 was only added to the *Execution Act* in April 2001. Prior to that there was no specific exemption in the legislation dealing with motor vehicles, and the debtor seeking an exemption for a motor vehicle would have to try and fit within one of the other paragraphs in s. 2.

In my view, s. 2(b) is clear in its language. In order for a motor vehicle to be exempt, it must have a value not exceeding $5,000. No other meaning can be given to these words. Thus, the vehicle in question does not qualify for an exemption as it has an admitted value of at least $11,000.

. . .

Thus, for the reasons given, I find that there is no exemption for the vehicle in question. This finding effectively disposes of this appeal. However, I will deal with the alternate positions advanced in this case, in the event that I am found to be incorrect with respect to my interpretation of para. 6 of s. 2.

The bankrupt waived the exemption in this case. Counsel for the Trustee argued that the property of a bankrupt is not considered to be exempt from seizure unless the bankrupt makes the claim for the exemption. He submitted that a creditor couldn't assert the exemption in bankruptcy. Counsel for DCFS argued that a creditor can assert the exemption and relied on the decision of the Alberta Court of Appeal indirect *Rental Centre (West) v. A.C. Waring & Associates Inc. Ltd.* (2001), 205 DLR (4th) 651, 97 Alta. LR (3d) 213 (CA) Thus, squarely in issue before this court is whether a creditor can claim the exemption.

. . .

In this regard, I prefer the reasoning of Mr. Justice Berger in his dissent in the *Direct Rental* case. Justice Berger ... looked to whether the exemptions are privileges which must be claimed by [debtors], or whether they are rights which exist whether asserted or not. Justice Berger referred to the decision in *E.T. Marshall* [*v. Flemming* (1965), 55 WWR 11 (Alta. Dist. Ct.)], which was approved, in obiter by McDonald DCJ in *Winnicky v. Grande Prairie & District Savings & Credit Union Ltd.*, [1976] 1 WWR 80, 61 DLR (3d) 559 (Alta. TD). He also referred to the case of *Spence (Trustee of) v. Yellowhead Feeders Co-operative Ltd.* (1994), 119 Sask. R 24, 25 CBR (3d) 180 (QB), where Baynton J confirmed that under Saskatchewan law, property is not considered exempt unless the bankrupt makes a claim for exemption. Justice Baynton stated at ... p. 192 CBR:

> It makes good sense that a secured creditor who fails to perfect its security is not permitted to defeat other interests by relying on a protection granted by legislation to debtors, not to creditors.

. . .

Justice Berger ... went on to state as follows [at paras. 96-100]:

> The rationale for the requirement that the exemption must be asserted accords with the fact that it is the debtor who has the information needed to establish the exemption. After all, it is the debtor who, in most cases, is the person claiming the exemption, and upon whom the onus to establish that property is exempt should lie. ...
>
> In addition to the foregoing, there are practical impediments that would render it difficult to apply an absolute exemption standard. Suppose, for example, that a number of chattels were held to be absolutely exempt without the assertion of the debtor. If the total market value of the chattels exceeded the prescribed limit, which chattels would be exempt? Which creditors would benefit? If it had been the legislative intention to impose such a regime, a scheme for distribution in those circumstances would, surely, have been enacted.
>
> This accords with the policy reasons underlying the legislative choice to allow for exemptions and is consistent with the justification for exemptions as articulated by C.R.B. Dunlop in *Creditor-Debtor Law in Canada*, 2nd ed., (Carswell: Scarborough, 1995) at 454:
>
>> The obvious justification of exemptions statutes today is that they prevent judgment debtors from being stripped of all the means to support themselves and their families. It is not acceptable that creditors, no matter how just the debt, should have the power to take from debtors the basic necessities of life. Another aim often advanced to support exemptions laws is that they preserve to debtors the means to survive and to earn a living, thus contributing to their rehabilitation as citizens and to their capacity to repay their debts. ... The philosophy of the exemptions laws is to encourage debtors to survive and to carry on their lives as economic and social elements in society.
>
> For all of these reasons, I conclude that an exemption under the [*Civil Enforcement Act*, SA 1994, c. C-10.5] must be claimed and it is only the debtor or bankrupt who is entitled to claim it.

. . .

I wholeheartedly concur with the statement of Mr. Justice Berger that "there is no policy or principled reason to confer upon a creditor who has failed to meet the requirements of the PPSA for perfecting its security interest, an advantage over other unsecured creditors." I accept the assertion that the purpose of the exemptions is to assist a bankrupt in an attempt to re-establish him- or herself. There is no rationale, that I can discern, for the creditor to be able to claim an exemption.

I also note that the Ontario *Execution Act* makes provision for the debtor to make choices about the exemption. Section 3(2) provides that the debtor may, in lieu of the chattels referred to in s. 2(4), elect to receive the proceeds of the sale thereof up to the prescribed amount. Section 6 gives the debtor (and family members) the right to select out of the number of chattels exempt from seizure (a similar provision being noted by Justice Berger in the *Direct Rental* case, in support of his finding that only the debtor can claim the exemption). I agree with the assertion of counsel for the Trustee that, if the legislature had intended that creditors be able to claim the exemption if the debtor chose not to, or to include the right to select among exempt property, it could have enacted provisions to this affect.

I have carefully reviewed the "western" (Alberta/British Columbia) jurisprudence cited by counsel for DCFS, but do not feel constrained to follow same. Counsel for the Trustee cited significant differences between the Ontario *Execution Act* and the pertinent British Columbia and Alberta Statutes. For example, both the British Columbia COEA [*Court Order Enforcement Act*, RSBC 1996, c. 78] and Alberta's CEA (cited above) provide for a distribution scheme recognizing secured creditors, if the value of the exempted property (including motor vehicles) exceeds the prescribed maximum for the exemption (s. 71.2 of the British Columbia COEA and s. 89 of the Alberta CEA). Alberta's CEA specifically allows a bailiff to make selections of property if the debtor does not do so (s. 90). The Ontario *Execution Act* has no such provisions.

Additionally, I find support for my conclusion that the creditor DCFS cannot claim the $5,000 exemption for the motor vehicle in question in the review of the conflicting lines of authority as set out in the majority decision in the *VW Credit* case [*VW Credit Canada Inc. v. Roberts* (2001), 197 DLR (4th) 274 (NSCA)] at pp. 6-10. Justice Roscoe noted that most of the cases were authority prior to the decision of the Supreme Court of Canada in *Re Giffen*, [1998] 1 SCR 91, 155 DLR (4th) 332 which, while not specifically dealing with a claim for exemption, is relevant to the issue of priority between a trustee and a creditor with an unperfected security interest. Justice Roscoe found, given the direction of the Supreme Court of Canada in *Re Giffen*, that the statement in the lower court (Queen's Bench) decision in the *Direct Rental* case, that "the provincial legislature cannot make "non exempt" that which the federal government has made "exempt," questionable. Of the conflicting lines of authority considered, he did not find the reasoning of the *Direct Rental* case to be the most cogent.

Thus, for the reasons given, I find that DCFS cannot claim the $5,000 exemption for the motor vehicle in question. ...

I turn finally to the third prong of the Trustee's argument, that is, that there is no exemption for a purchase money security interest. This argument is premised on the interplay of s. 7(1) of the *Execution Act* and s. 67(1)(b) of the BIA (quoted above). Section 7(1) provides:

> 7(1) The exemptions prescribed in this Act do not apply to exempt any chattel from seizure to satisfy a debt contracted for the purchase of such chattel, except beds, bedding and

bedsteads, including cradles in ordinary use by the debtor and his or her family and the necessary and ordinary wearing apparel of the debtor and his or her family.

RSO 1990, c. E.24, s. 7(1).

The effect of s. 7(1) of the *Execution Act* is that an exemption would not apply to prevent the holder of a purchase money security interest from seizing its collateral. Thus, outside of the bankruptcy, there would be no exemption for the vehicle as against DCFS. However, s. 67(1)(b) of the BIA refers to "any property that as against the bankrupt is exempt from execution or seizure." By virtue of s. 7(1) of the *Execution Act*, there was no exemption with respect to the car as of the date of the assignment in bankruptcy. The BIA does not create exemptions.

The Trustee's position is supported by the Nova Scotia Court of Appeal decision in *VW Credit*. I adopt the reasoning of the court as set out in the paragraphs, which were quoted above [at p. 290 DLR]. In my view, the Court of Appeal quite rightly asked:

> So, if there was no exemption in existence before the bankruptcy, and no exemption if there had been a perfected interest, how can the bankruptcy bring one into existence? How can the fact that the lessor did not perfect its interest, create an exemption?

Thus, I find for the Trustee on the third prong of his argument as well, that is, that there is no exemption for a purchase money security interest.

[The Ontario Court of Appeal affirmed Polowin J's ruling that the motor vehicle was not exempt: (2004), 71 OR (3d) 11. Having ruled on that point, the court did not consider the effect of the secured creditor's unperfected status].

NOTE

Assume that in *Re Fields* the facts were different so that the car *was* exempt property. Now would DCFS be entitled to enforce its unperfected security interest? The cases discussed in *VW Credit Canada Inc. v. Roberts* (2001), 197 DLR (4th) 274 are divided on this question. The debate turns on the meaning of the PPSA rule that an unperfected security interest is ineffective against the debtor's trustee in bankruptcy. One line of cases reads this to mean that the debtor's bankruptcy extinguishes an unperfected security interest. When the debtor claims the exemption, the trustee has to give the property back and the debtor takes it free of the unperfected security interest. The other line of cases reads the rule to mean that an unperfected security interest is ineffective against the trustee himself but not the debtor. When the debtor claims the exemption, the trustee has to give the property back but the debtor takes it subject to the unperfected security interest.

The first line of cases rests on two policy arguments: (1) the purpose of the exemptions is debtor rehabilitation and it would be inconsistent with this purpose if the secured creditor could claim the car; and (2) a secured creditor should not be allowed to use the exemption provisions to escape the consequences of non-perfection. The contrary argument goes like this. If the secured creditor had repossessed the car the day before the debtor's bankruptcy, the debtor could not have stopped it. The PPSA does not say that a security interest must be perfected before the secured creditor can enforce it against the debtor. There is nothing in the BIA to suggest that a different rule applies just because the debtor is bankrupt. If that were the case, the debtor would get a windfall, which would encourage debtors to use the bankruptcy laws opportunistically. In other words, the debtor might put himself or herself into bankruptcy solely for the purpose of avoiding the security interest. *VW Credit v. Roberts*, cited with approval in *Re Fields*, supports this second line of reasoning.

IV. BONA FIDE PURCHASERS AND THE LIKE

Under s. 71 of the BIA, the property of the bankrupt vests in the trustee on the occurrence of bankruptcy, and the bankrupt ceases to have any capacity to dispose of or otherwise deal with the property. Therefore, as a general rule, the bankrupt cannot transfer the property to a third-party purchaser after the occurrence of the bankruptcy. Although the purchaser will not obtain title to the property, the third party will usually have an action against the bankrupt for breach of contract. This claim is not provable in the bankruptcy, because it arises after its commencement. The purchaser therefore cannot participate in the distribution of assets on bankruptcy. As it is not a provable claim, it survives the discharge of the bankrupt. See Chapter 7.

There are two major exceptions to the principle that the bankrupt lacks the capacity to transfer good title to a subsequent purchaser. Section 75 of the BIA provides that a deed, transfer, agreement for sale, mortgage, or charge covering real property in favour of a bona fide purchaser or mortgagee for adequate valuable consideration is valid and effectual unless a bankruptcy order is registered in the land registry system in accordance with the laws of the province in which the property is situated. This protects the integrity of the land registration system, and permits third parties to rely on the register when acquiring interests in the land. Section 74 gives the trustee the right to register a bankruptcy order against the real property. If this is done, a subsequent purchaser will be unable to defeat the claim of the trustee.

The BIA creates a further exception in respect of property that is acquired by the bankrupt after the bankruptcy and before intervention by the trustee. By virtue of s. 67(1)(c) of the BIA, property that is acquired by the bankrupt after the commencement of bankruptcy but before discharge of the bankrupt immediately vests in the trustee and is divisible among the creditors who prove their claims in the bankruptcy. Section 99 of the BIA provides that a dealing between a bankrupt and a person acting in good faith and for value and before the intervention of the trustee is valid as against the trustee in respect of after-acquired property. This gives the bankrupt the power to transfer a good title to a bona fide purchaser if the transaction occurs before the trustee takes possession of or control over the asset. In *Re Van Pelt* (1984), 53 CBR (NS) 28 (Ont. SC), the court held that s. 99 protects a purchaser even if the purchaser had knowledge of the bankruptcy as long as the purchaser was acting in good faith.

V. TRUSTS

BIA s. 67(1)(a) provides that the property of a bankrupt divisible among creditors shall not comprise property of the bankrupt held on trust for any person. The trust is a mechanism for separating legal ownership of an asset from beneficial ownership. Trusts can be created in various ways:

- *By will.* For example, where the testator leaves Blackacre to T on trust for B.

- *By agreement.* For example, where a settlor transfers Blackacre to T on trust for B.

- *By declaration.* For example, where T, the owner of Blackacre, declares that henceforth he holds the property on trust for B.

In all these cases, T is the legal owner of the asset but B is the real or beneficial owner. This is the conceptual basis of s. 67(1)(a).

In some cases, there may be room for argument about whether there is a trust. *Re Ontario Worldair Limited* (1983), 45 CBR (NS) 116 (Ont. SC); aff'd. (1984), 48 CBR (NS) 1121 (OCA) (SC, 1983) is a good example. Ontario Worldair (OWL) subleased aircraft from Air Belgium. There was a "termination adjustment provision" in clause 7 of the sublease agreement stating that in the event of termination, OWL would be liable to Air Belgium for certain payments having to do with engine maintenance. Pursuant to clause 7(b), OWL agreed to open a bank account on trust for maintaining the engines. OWL instructed its bank to open a new account which was to be called the "OWL–Air Belgium Reserve Account," but the instructions said nothing about a trust. OWL became bankrupt. The trustee and Air Belgium both claimed the money in the bank account and the dispute turned on whether a trust had been created. Saunders J concluded that there was no trust: "the overriding circumstance seems to me to be that there is nothing in the letter to the bank which indicates an intention to create a trust and that the provisions in the sub-lease do not indicate that the funds in the account are to be beneficially owned by or available to Air Belgium."

The case demonstrates a basic rule of trusts law—namely, that except for trusts arising by operation of law, there can be no valid trust unless the moving party intended to create one. The sublease agreement provided expressly that OWL would open a bank account on trust. Normally, the express use of trusts language would be sufficient evidence of an intention to create a trust, but, in this case, the court held that the express trust references were undercut by other provisions of the agreement. In particular, the other provisions of the agreement implied that OWL could draw on the account to perform its obligations under the agreement. OWL's right to draw on the account was inconsistent with saying that the account belonged beneficially to Air Belgium. If the sublease agreement had said unequivocally that OWL was to open a trust account, then OWL would have been in breach of trust for failing to keep the Air Belgium money separate and Air Belgium would have had the various remedies a breach of trust gives rise to.

Re Ontario Worldair Limited concerned the existence of an express trust. The express trust is not the only type of trust. Other types include resulting trusts and constructive trusts. A resulting trust is a form of implied trust. Following a transfer, the court may in certain circumstances imply a resulting trust of the property in the transferor's favour. The resulting trust means that the transferee holds the property on trust back for the transferor. For example, in *Barclays Bank Ltd. v. Quistclose Investments Ltd.*, [1970] AC 567, Q loaned money to a related company, R, to finance the payment of a dividend. R paid the money into a separate bank account, but, before it could pay the dividend, the bank purported to set off this account against R's other accounts, which were overdrawn. It was held that the bank had no right of set-off because the money in the account belonged beneficially to Q: the court treated Q as having paid the money to R on trust for the shareholders and, failing the payment, on resulting trust back for Q. Compare *Twinsectra Limited v. Yardley*, [2002] 2 AC 164

(HLE). Resulting trusts have the same status in bankruptcy as express trusts. Accordingly, the *Quistclose* case suggests a means by which an apparently unsecured creditor might in certain circumstances obtain priority: see, for example, *Re Westar Mining Ltd.* (2003), 39 CBR (4th) 313 (BCCA). The better view is that a *Quistclose* trust is not a security interest for PPSA purposes and so it is not registrable: Jacob S. Ziegel and David L. Denomme, *The Ontario Personal Property Security Act: Commentary and Analysis*, 2nd ed. (Toronto: Butterworths, 2000), at 70-71 and Michael G. Bridge et al., "Formalism, Functionalism and Understanding the Law of Secured Transactions" (1999), 44 *McGill LJ* 567, at 610-14. Is it commercially justifiable to give unpublicized claims priority over third-party interests?

A constructive trust is a trust imposed by law, without regard to the parties' intentions, to prevent unjust enrichment or deter wrongful conduct: see, for example, *Baltman v. Melnitzer*, below. Trusts may also be created (or "deemed") by statute. These are dealt with in Chapter 9.

Baltman v. Melnitzer
(1996), 43 CBR (3d) 33 (Ont. Gen. Div.—Bktcy.)

KILLEEN J: This case, brought within the four corners of the bankruptcy of Julius Melnitzer, embraces a fight over the ownership of artwork purchased by Mr. Melnitzer in the five years or so before he was put into bankruptcy on September 26, 1991.

Miss Baltman, the wife of Mr. Melnitzer at the relevant time, claims that she is an owner of some of the artwork by way of gift or special personal arrangement with him. The Royal Bank, which was in a banker-customer and creditor-debtor relationship with Mr. Melnitzer, claims ownership under the combined legal weight of the unjust enrichment principle coupled with the remedial constructive trust doctrine. Coopers & Lybrand and the National Bank assert that the artwork falls into the unsecured assets of the bankruptcy pot and must be available for general creditors of Mr. Melnitzer, subject to a special charging order in favour of Coopers & Lybrand arising from its work as the court-appointed Receiver before the bankruptcy.

Because of the separate and conflicting nature of the claims against the artwork, I propose to deal, first, with the claim of the Royal Bank. ...

By letter dated August 9, 1989, the Bank offered a $3 million line of credit to Mr. Melnitzer in return for collateral security consisting of:

(a) the hypothecation of $1.5 million cash in an interest-bearing account paying market rates;

(b) a guarantee and postponement of claim in the amount of $3 million by Melfan Investments Ltd.;

(c) the hypothecation of the issued shares of Melfan;

(d) a letter of undertaking from the president of Melfan confirming various matters;

(e) A letter of undertaking from Mr. Melnitzer confirming that the advances would be liquidated within three years of the draw-down;

Mr. Melnitzer accepted the offer on September 21, 1989, and the collateral security was later received by the Royal Bank. Funds were, from time to time thereafter, advanced under the line of credit up to July 31, 1991.

It is admitted that Mr. Melnitzer requested the Bank to offer and obtained the $3 million line of credit:

(a) by fraudulently misrepresenting certain of his assets and liabilities to the Bank's London Private Banking Manager, Colin Liptrot; and

(b) by fraudulently (i) preparing (ii) forging and (iii) signing a number of documents to support this application for the line of credit, including financial statements, undertakings, resolutions, a guarantee and even an opinion letter form his own law firm bearing the signature of his partner, Harris W. Cohen.

But for Mr. Melnitzer's fraudulent misrepresentations, forgeries and other related fraudulent conduct, the Bank would clearly not have granted the large line of credit. On July 29, 1991, the Bank offered to increase Melnitzer's line of credit to a starting $8 million, with interest payable at prime plus ½%. The Bank offered to do so following a request by Mr. Melnitzer for an increased line of credit to be secured by the hypothecation of approximately $12 million in "blue-chip" securities. Melnitzer accepted this offer in writing on July 31, 1991. The purported blue-chip securities were delivered to the Bank but later proved to be forged and valueless.

· · ·

At the beginning of August, 1991, Mr. Melnitzer's network of frauds was discovered and an order was issued out of the Ontario Court (General Division) on August 3 freezing his assets and appointing Coopers & Lybrand as Receiver and Manager of his assets. Further, as a result of a bankruptcy petition filed on September 3, 1991, Mr. Melnitzer was adjudged a bankrupt and a receiving order was issued against him on September 26. Additional supplementary orders were also issued on August 9, August 30 and September 26 of that year.

Mr. Melnitzer was indicted later in the fall of 1991 with defrauding the Bank under the $3 million and $8 million lines of credit, was convicted, after pleas of guilty and was given nine year concurrent sentences on the two counts relating to these frauds.

Mr. Melnitzer's indebtedness to the Bank was approximately $2,484,160.51 as of the date of his bankruptcy and is approximately the same today, less certain recoveries effected by the Bank in the interim.

Subsequent investigations after the bankruptcy disclosed that Mr. Melnitzer had used monies drawn on the Bank line of credit to purchase several paintings.

· · ·

It is admitted by all parties that the Bank has not recovered the $477,892.10 drawn on tile line of credit for these paintings. ...

Mr. Neirinck, for the Bank, asks for a declaratory order that it is the beneficial owner of the ten paintings in issue under the principle of unjust enrichment and its remedial tool, the constructive trust.

He started his argument by pointing to the elements of the unjust enrichment cause of action, namely, (1) a benefit to or enrichment of one party (2) a corresponding detriment or deprivation suffered by the other party and (3) an absence of any juristic reason for the benefit or enrichment: *Rathwell v. Rathwell*, [1978] 2 SCR 436 at p. 455. The later cases in the Supreme Court showed that the principle of unjust enrichment could be applied in commercial settings: *International Corona Resources Ltd. v. Lac Minerals Ltd.*, [1989] 2 SCR 574 at pp. 677-78.

With respect to the enrichment/corresponding deprivation elements of the required findings, the conclusion that a plaintiff has suffered a corresponding deprivation is virtually automatic once an enrichment has been found: *Peter v. Beblow*, [1993] 1 SCR 980 at p. 1012 and *Canada (Attorney General) v. Confederation Life Insurance Co.* (1995), 24 OR (3d) 717 (Ont. Gen. Div.) at p. 770. As to these components, Mr. Neirinck submits that it is "self-evident" that Mr. Melnitzer had (1) illegally enriched himself by acquiring these paintings with line-of-credit monies, (2) while, at the same time, illegally depriving the Bank of $477,892.10: see Bank factum at para. 21.

Mr. Neirinck acknowledged, as he had to, that the third component of the required findings—the absence of a juristic reason—involves an examination of the "unjustness" of the situation at hand: *Peter v. Beblow, supra*, at pp. 984, 996, 997 and 1018. Here, Mr. Neirinck relied on several factors or circumstances showing, or tending to show, unjustness: (1) from the outset, there never was a consensual banker-customer or creditor-debtor relationship between the Bank and Mr. Melnitzer because of his "underlying fraudulent conduct"; (2) the Bank would not have lent funds to him but for the fraud surrounding the issuance of the line of credit; (3) Mr. Melnitzer essentially "orchestrated" three thefts from the Bank to acquire the paintings; (4) there is a direct link between the paintings and the $477,892.10 which the Bank advanced for them as a consequence of his fraud and (5) it would be inequitable and unjust to allow either Mr. Melnitzer or someone standing in his shoes, such as the general creditors of the bankrupt estate, to obtain a "windfall" benefit from the paintings.

Mr. Neirinck's final point was that it would be strongly "appropriate" to grant a remedy by way of constructive trust over the paintings in favour of the Bank because (1) given Mr. Melnitzer's bankruptcy, a monetary award would be of little or no assistance to the Bank and (2) there is a "fundamental connecting link" between the paintings, their acquisition and the $477,892.10 loss which the Bank suffered: *Lac Minerals, supra*, at pp. 677-78; *Pettkus v. Becker*, [1980] 2 SCR 834 at p. 852; *Sorochan v. Sorochan*, [1986] 2 SCR 38 at p. 50.

. . .

I conclude, on the facts, that the Bank has made out the enrichment/deprivation elements of the unjust enrichment formula: Mr. Melnitzer received a benefit through the Bank advances and purchase of the paintings and it seems to me that the Bank has made out a showing that it suffered a consequential deprivation. ...

However, I conclude ... that the Bank's claim must founder and fail on the shoals created by the third element of the unjust enrichment cause of action—the absence of a juristic reason—as well as at the remedial stage where the Bank seeks the imposition of constructive trust.

In his now-famous dictum in *Rathwell, supra*, at p. 459, Dickson J described the third element of the formula somewhat delphically:

... for the principle to succeed, the facts must display an enrichment, a corresponding de-privation, and the absence of any juristic reason—such as a contract or disposition of law—for the enrichment.

Later cases have suggested that the formula must be applied flexibly and not ritualisti-cally, depending upon the facts of the given case. In other words, rather inevitably, a case-by-case approach must be taken to the application of the formula. ...

The central core of Mr. Neirinck's argument on the third element is that "there never was a consensual banker/customer or creditor/debtor relationship between Royal and Melnitzer due to Melnitzer's fundamental creditor/debtor relationship ... ." In effect, he is attempting to eviscerate ab initio the contract Mr. Melnitzer entered with the Bank through the letter commitment of August 9, 1989, for a $3 million line of credit because of Mr. Melnitzer's undoubted fraudulent misrepresentations about his net worth, his shareholdings and his interest in Melfan Investments and so on.

In my view, however, Mr. Neirinck cannot so neatly and conveniently turn aside and treat as a non-event the contract for credit between the parties—even though it was un-doubtedly induced by Melnitzer's ingenious and fraudulent conduct.

The plain fact of the matter is that the contract went into effect and stayed in effect for almost two years down to early August, 1991, when Mr. Melnitzer's fraudulent schemes were opened to the light of day.

One should note the following facts about the course of the contract dealings. The Bank entered the contract with its eyes open even though, as I found in the Harowitz case, supra, the Bank was negligent in doing its due diligence leading up to the grant of the credit line to Mr. Melnitzer. The loan commitment was made subject to apparently stringent terms demanded by the Bank, including the hypothecation of $1.5 million in cash by Mr. Melnitzer in an interest-bearing account along with a full-loan guarantee by Melfan Investments, the hypothecation of Melfan Investments shares and other collateral undertakings and guarantees by Mr. Melnitzer personally.

There were no defaults under the credit line down through 1990 and well into 1991. In the interim, Mr. Melnitzer made several draws on the line and the Bank was earning up to $38,000 per month in interest at good rates.

Then, in July, 1991, Mr. Melnitzer succeeded in persuading the Bank to revise the credit line upward to $8 million on the strength of new collateral security in the form of so-called blue chip securities worth $12 million.

· · ·

[All the] documents and transactions in late July and on August 1 clearly show a con-tract relationship is alive between the parties, regardless of whether Mr. Melnitzer has duped the Bank into granting him the credit it did. His conduct cannot make the con-tract of August 9, 1989, void ab initio and the contract provides a sound juristic reason and basis for the credit line and the advances which financed the three purchases of pic-tures in 1990 and 1991.

· · ·

The final coup de grace for his position is, I think, found in ... McLachlin J's powerful judgment in Peter, supra at p. 990. There she concludes that the "fundamental" question to ask under the third component of the unjust enrichment principle is this: What were the legitimate or reasonable expectations of the parties when the deal or occurrences took place? Surely, at the time of the advances in question, the Bank had no expectation whatsoever that it would or could acquire a proprietary interest in the paintings which Mr. Melnitzer was purchasing. It was content with its credit-line arrangements and the collateral it had received, including $1.5 million in cash which was deposited to an interest-bearing account.

I think it is patently absurd to attempt to twist the unjust enrichment principle like a warm pretzel and employ it on these facts.

For the sake of completeness, I now deal with the question of whether, assuming I am wrong in my approach to the application of the unjust enrichment principle, this is a proper case for the imposition of a constructive trust. As I have said, Mr. Neirinck argues that a constructive trust should be imposed because (1) a monetary award would be ineffective and (2) there is a fundamental connecting link between the paintings, their acquisition and the Bank's advances and loss.

It is quite clear that, even where a cause of action for unjust enrichment has been made out, the remedy of constructive trust does not automatically issue. The court must go on to consider the competing equitable interests to decide whether, on balance, a proprietary remedy will be imposed or whether only monetary damages will be ordered.

. . .

On the facts of this case, I do not believe it would be appropriate to award a constructive trust. The factors which I identify telling against its application are these:

(1) the relationship between Mr. Melnitzer and the Bank was a purely commercial and contractual relationship;

(2) while the Bank took certain security interests as it saw fit, such as the $1.5 million deposit account, none of the property at issue—the artwork—was secured by the Bank;

(3) the availability to the Bank of its normal contractual remedies;

(4) the availability to the Bank of its claims as a creditor in the bankruptcy;

(5) the fact that the Bank is asserting a constructive trust only as a result of its own negligence, lack of investigation and breach of its own internal credit-granting rules incidental to the issuance of a credit line to Mr. Melnitzer;

(6) the fact that an otherwise unsecured creditor is seeking, in effect, to "jump the queue" over other unsecured creditors in the bankruptcy;

This is not a case, like *Lac Minerals*, *supra*, where one party effectively stole a property from another party by taking advantage of confidential information. Also, it is not a case where one party has obtained all the fruits of a property on the back of another as in *Rathwell*, *supra*, or *Sorochan*, *supra*. Rather, this is a case where a large and sophisticated commercial enterprise entered a loan contract with a person it was anxiously and almost desperately courting and chose to dictate the terms and conditions of the arrangement. Now, having been burned by the contract, the Bank is attempting to re-write that contract and, after the fact, obtain new security at the expense of other creditors who were also victims of the same fraudster. Equity, in my view, should not come to the aid of that single creditor at the expense of the other equally victimized creditors.

In the result, the claim of the Royal Bank is dismissed.

NOTES AND QUESTIONS

1. What was the bank's argument in *Baltman v. Melnitzer* for saying that the loan contract was not a sufficient juristic reason for the debtor's enrichment? How did the court respond? The bank could have put its argument differently. It might have said that, as a result of the debtor's misrepresentation, it (the bank) did not voluntarily enter into the loan contract or accept the risk of the debtor's insolvency. How do you think the court would have responded?

2. For further discussion of constructive trusts in bankruptcy, see Emily L. Sherwin, "Constructive Trusts in Bankruptcy" (1989), *U Ill. L Rev.* 297; David M. Paccioco, "The Remedial Constructive Trust: A Principled Basis for Priority Over Creditors" (1989), 68 *Can. Bar Rev.* 315, for a similar analysis in the Canadian context; and Anthony Duggan, "Constructive Trusts from a Law and Economics Perspective" (2005), 55 *UTLJ* 217.

VI. THE INTERSECTION OF BANKRUPTCY AND FAMILY LAW

When there is a breakup of an adult family relationship, one of the spouses or partners may assert a claim against the assets owned by the other. Bankruptcy issues come into play if one of the parties goes into bankruptcy. The resolution of the issue will depend on whether it is the party asserting the claim (the non-owning party) or the party who holds legal title to the assets (the owning party) who has gone bankrupt. In the first case, the issue is whether the right to bring an action for a share of the assets is property that vests in the trustee. If it is, the trustee in bankruptcy will be entitled to commence or continue an action against the owning party. In the second case, the issue is whether the non-owning party has any kind of proprietary right in the family assets that can be asserted against the trustee. If the non-owning party does not have any proprietary right to the assets, the non-owning party will at best have a personal claim that must be proven in the bankruptcy. This permits the party to share pro rata with the other unsecured creditors.

A. Bankruptcy of non-owning party. If the parties were married to one another, the non-owning spouse can bring an application under provincial matrimonial property legislation for a share of the assets. This avenue is not available if the parties were not married. Both married and unmarried parties can assert a claim to the assets on the basis of a constructive trust imposed by the court as a remedy for unjust enrichment. See *Peter v. Beblow*, [1993] 1 SCR 980.

Some courts were initially reluctant to permit a trustee in bankruptcy to pursue a non-owning party's claim for a share of family assets. In *Deloitte, Haskins & Sells Ltd. v. Graham* (1983), 47 CBR (NS) 172 (Alta. QB), the court held that a spouse's right to bring a matrimonial property application was not an asset that vested in the trustee, because it did not constitute a present right or entitlement but was "merely a hope that the court will exercise its discretion in favour of the applicant spouse." The Alberta Court of Appeal declined to follow this reasoning in *Tinant v. Tinant* (2003), 46 CBR (4th) 150 (Alta. CA). The court stated (at para. 18):

> The entire purpose of the *MPA* is to achieve an equitable distribution of married people's property after a marriage breakdown has occurred. It is true that the court enjoys a discretion as to

how it distributes the property, but courts often enjoy discretions relating to remedy, especially where equitable principles are factors to be applied. That does not mean, however, that wherever equitable principles come into play that which is being sought or granted no longer relates to property but to an equitable order. Also the *MPA* makes it clear that while judges may take equitable principles into account, once they have done so, they are required to make an order distributing the total property belonging to the married parties.

The trustee's right to bring a matrimonial property application is subject to the same limitations as the applicant spouse's right of action. A spouse is not permitted to bring a matrimonial property application unless there has been a triggering event, such as a divorce or separation. See *Blowes v. Blowes* (1993), 21 CBR (3d) 276 (Ont. CA). If there has not been a triggering event, the spouse has merely an inchoate right that does not vest in the trustee. If the triggering event occurs after bankruptcy but before discharge of the bankrupt, the right of action vests in the trustee as after-acquired property pursuant to s. 67(1)(c) of the BIA. Some commentators have argued that the occurrence of a triggering event is not enough and that the spouse must also have commenced a matrimonial property application. See R. Klotz, *Insolvency and Family Law*, 2nd ed. (Toronto: Carswell, 2001), at 6.1(f). Cases in Alberta have rejected this added requirement. See *Lecerf v. Lecerf* (2004), 2 CBR (5th) 260 (Alta. QB). Courts have similarly permitted the trustee to pursue a bankrupt's claim to a constructive trust. See *Kopr v. Kopr* (2006), 24 CBR (5th) 205 (Alta. QB). In such cases, in contrast to matrimonial property applications, there is no requirement for a triggering event, and therefore the trustee could conceivably bring the action even though the partners are still cohabiting.

B. *Bankruptcy of owning party.* If the owning party goes bankrupt, the issue centres on the nature of the non-owning party's claim. Under matrimonial property legislation, a court has the power to make an order for the payment of money. In that case, the non-owning party's claim is merely a personal one that must be proved in the bankruptcy and entitles the claimant to share *pro rata* with the other unsecured creditors.

In addition to making an order for the payment of money, the court may impose a charge on the owning party's assets to secure the payment. In that case, the non-owning party falls within the BIA definition of "secured creditor" and obtains priority on that basis: see above, *Saulnier*, "III. Judicial History."

As an alternative to making an order for the payment of money, with or without a charge, the court may make an order for the transfer of property to the non-owning spouse. See, for example, the *Family Law Act*, RSO 1990, c. F.3, s. 9. Courts have held that the legislation does not give the non-owning spouse any proprietary right in the family assets prior to the court making an order for the transfer of property. See *Maroukis v. Maroukis*, [1984] 2 SCR 137. If the owning party goes into bankruptcy before such an order is made, the property vests in the trustee and the other spouse merely has a personal claim that can be proven in the bankruptcy. See *Menzies v. Menzies* (2002), 37 CBR (4th) 98 (Sask. QB). On the other hand, if the owning party goes into bankruptcy after the making of the order, the assets in question are no longer the property of the owning party and so they do not vest in the trustee.

The situation is different in respect of a claim for a declaration of constructive trust as a remedy for unjust enrichment. A majority of the Supreme Court of Canada in *Rawluk v.*

Rawluk, [1990] 1 SCR 70 held that the constructive trust arises when the duty to make restitution arises. The assets will therefore be subject to the trust at the time of the bankruptcy, and will not be divisible among the creditors: see above, *Saulnier*, "IV. Analysis." There are, however, some serious difficulties facing a non-owning party in making this claim. The applicant must convince the court that a declaration of constructive trust is appropriate, given that its effect will be to prefer the applicant's claim over the claims of other creditors. See D.M. Paciocco: "The Remedial Constructive Trust: A Principled Basis for Priorities Over Creditors" (1989), 68 *Can. Bar Rev.* 315.

VII. SALES

Consider the following case:

> Seller, a farmer, agrees to sell Buyer a ton of potatoes out of Seller's next crop. The price is $500 and Seller agrees to deliver the potatoes when the crop is harvested in a month's time. Buyer pays the price in advance. Seller becomes bankrupt. Seller's trustee harvests the potatoes. What are Buyer's rights in Seller's bankruptcy?

Section 17 of the *Sale of Goods Act* (SGA), RSO 1990, c. S.1 provides that, in a contract for the sale of unascertained goods, no property in the goods is transferred to the buyer until the goods are ascertained. As cases like *In Re Wait*, [1927] 1 Ch. 606 and *In Re Goldcorp Exchange Ltd.*, [1995] AC 74 demonstrate, this means that a person who buys goods forming part of a larger bulk cannot acquire title to the goods unless and until the goods become ascertained. In the example above, the goods are unascertained for as long as they remain unseparated from the bulk of the harvest, because, until they are separated out, there is no way of telling which potatoes "belong" to Buyer.

These considerations go to the question of legal title. Can Buyer claim an equitable interest in the undivided harvest? The answer is tied up with the question whether Buyer can claim specific performance of her contract with Seller. SGA s. 50 limits specific performance to the case of specific or ascertained goods. Because the potatoes remain unascertained, Buyer cannot claim specific performance. In the absence of a claim to specific performance, Buyer has no equitable interest in the potatoes.

Because Buyer has no legal or equitable interest in the potatoes, she cannot force Seller's trustee to complete the contract. If the trustee fails to deliver the potatoes, Buyer's only remedy is a money claim for recovery of the price and loss of bargain damages (if any). Given Seller's bankruptcy, Buyer's money claim is likely to be worthless, or near enough to worthless: see, further, Chapter 6, on the trustee's power to disclaim unprofitable contracts. The outcome might be different if Buyer held a security interest in Seller's potato crop: see above, Section III. However, the facts do not indicate any security agreement between Seller and Buyer.

The English and Scottish law commissions, in their *Report on Sale of Goods Forming Part of a Bulk* (Law Comm. no. 215, Scots Law Comm. no. 145, 1993), were critical of the rule that a person who buys goods forming part of a larger bulk can have no interest in the goods unless and until they are separated out of the bulk. The commissions thought it was unjust that a prepaying buyer should stand to lose both the price and the goods on the seller's insolvency. (Do you agree?) The commissions recommended that where there is a contract for the sale of a specified quantity of goods forming part of an identified bulk, a buyer who has paid for some or all of the contract goods should obtain an undivided share in the bulk and become a tenant in common of the whole. When the buyer's share of the bulk is separated out and ascertained, property in the goods would pass to the buyer in accordance with the normal rules on the passing of property. The *Sale of Goods Act 1979* (UK) was amended in 1995 to give effect to these recommendations: see ss. 20A and 20B. There have been no corresponding reforms in Canada.

The UK amendments provide a measure of protection to the prepaying buyer, but only in the case where goods are bought from a contractually designated bulk. They do not apply where, for example, the buyer prepays for goods to be manufactured by the seller or to be obtained by the seller from an unspecified source. In cases like these, the buyer will be at risk if the seller becomes insolvent before the goods are appropriated to the contract. This kind of case has attracted a fair amount of attention in recent years, particularly in the context of consumer transactions. The following are some of the solutions that have been proposed.

1. Have the agreement provide that title will pass to the buyer as soon as the seller begins work on the chattel and the buyer has made the first payment. This approach is often adopted in contracts for the construction of vessels, aircraft, and other high-cost, purpose-built goods. It is not a practicable solution in the case of mass-produced items because of problems of identification and the difficulties it would create for manufacturers.

2. Require the seller to hold the buyer's advances in trust until the goods are ready for delivery: see the *Quistclose* case, above. The difficulty about a trust clause is that most sellers would find it an unacceptable restriction because the whole purpose of asking for advance payment is to finance the production of future goods (where the seller is a manufacturer) or to enable the seller to acquire the goods from a third party (where the seller is not the manufacturer).

3. Ask the court to declare a remedial constructive trust in favour of the prepaying buyer on the grounds that (1) not having performed its part of the bargain, it would be unjust to allow the seller to retain the purchase price, and (2) the seller's assets should not be augmented for the benefit of the seller's secured and unsecured creditors. Do you think that these are sufficient grounds for a finding of unjust enrichment in the buyer's favour?

4. Adopt a provision similar to UCC 2-502 entitling the buyer to recover goods identified by the contract where the seller becomes insolvent within 10 days of receiving the first installment of the price. The OLRC Sales Report, at 265, thought the section was of negligible value and also queried whether a province could constitutionally adopt such a provision.

5. Allow the buyer to acquire a buyer's purchase-money security interest (BPMSI) in respect of his prepayments similar to the purchase-money security interest available to the unpaid seller under the PPS acts. See A. Dadson, "A Fresh Plea for the Financing Buyer" (1985-86), 11 *CBLJ* 171. There would be considerable difficulties in adapting the provincial Acts to provide a BPMSI; none of the acts has so far made the effort.

6. In the case of consumer buyers, confer a statutory non-possessory lien in favour of the buyer along the lines proposed in the BC Law Reform Commission's *Report on the Buyer's Lien: A New Consumer Remedy* (LRC 93, 1987) and discussed in Wood (1988), 14 *CBLJ* 118. The recommendations were implemented in the *Consumer Protection Statutes Amendment Act, 1993*, SBC 1993, c. 39, which added a new part 9 to the BC *Sale of Goods Act*. See Arthur Close, "The British Columbia Buyer's Lien—A New Consumer Remedy" (1995), 25 *CBLJ* 127.

7. Establish a compensation fund for the reimbursement of buyers comparable to the compensation funds established in several provinces for the protection of travellers and buyers of motor vehicles. Is it practicable to establish such a scheme for every type of retail merchant or even a majority of merchants?

8. Require the seller under the contract to provide a "standby" letter of credit (SLOC) in the buyer's favour, which the buyer can invoke if she does not receive the goods for which she has paid. SLOCs are becoming increasingly common, in domestic as well as international transactions, but only a buyer in a strong bargaining position can hope to secure one. Even then it will not be worth the trouble unless there is a substantial sum of money at risk.

VIII. SET-OFF

R.M. Goode, *Principles of Corporate Insolvency Law*
3rd ed. (London: Sweet & Maxwell, 2005), 213-15

Set-off is the right of a debtor who is owed money by his creditor on another account or dealing to secure payment for what is owed to him by setting this off in reduction of his own liability. For example, A sells raw materials to B to be made up into finished products which B then sells to A. If A owes B £1,000 for products sold and delivered to him but is owed £400 by B for raw materials then in any claim against him A is not obliged to pay B the £1,000 he owes and then sue separately (or if B is in liquidation, prove in the liquidation in competition with other creditors) for recovery of the £400 he is owed but may set off the latter sum against his indebtedness and discharge the debt by paying B (or B's liquidator) the balance of £600. ...

   Set-off is available both outside and within bankruptcy and liquidation. In both cases it provides a speedy remedy to secure payment but the policy reason for providing the remedy depends on the type of set-off involved. Contractual set-off is recognized as an incident of party autonomy in the conclusion of contracts. The banker's right of combination is similar except that it derives from implied rather than express agreement. In the case of independent (or statutory) set-off the remedy is give primarily to avoid circuity of action. By contrast, the policy underlying transaction (or equitable) set-off is that it would be unjust to allow a party to enforce his money claim without giving credit for the cross-claim if so required. Similarly the provision of insolvency set-off reflects the view that where parties have been giving credit to each other in reliance on their ability to secure payment by withholding what is due from them it would be unjust, on the advent of liquidation, to deprive the solvent party of his security by compelling him to pay what he owes in full and be left to prove for his own claim. This is the policy justification for what is a clear exception to the *pari passu* principle, in that it allows the solvent party to collect payment ahead of other creditors to the extent of the set-off and thus puts him in a position analogous to that of a secured creditor.

Thus set-off is an essential tool in the hands of a debtor who has a cross-claim against his creditor and is particularly used in banking transactions and in mutual dealings in the financial markets.

NOTES

1. Set-off is available both outside and inside bankruptcy. In Canada, the governing provision is BIA s. 97(3), which provides that "the law of set-off applies to all claims made against the estate of the bankrupt and also to all actions instituted by the trustee for the recovery of debts due to the bankrupt in the same manner and to the same extent as if the bankrupt were plaintiff or defendant, as the case may be, except in so far as any claim for set-off is affected by the provisions of this Act respecting frauds or fraudulent preferences."

2. Goode says that the policy behind allowing set-off in bankruptcy is to prevent injustice. Another way of making this point might be to say that provisions like BIA s. 97(3) are necessary to preserve creditors' relative entitlements when the debtor becomes bankrupt: see the Jackson extract in Chapter 1. If bankruptcy were to put an end to rights of set-off, other creditors might use the bankruptcy laws opportunistically to take advantage of the change in relative entitlements.

3. Strictly speaking, set-off is different from the banker's right to combine accounts because set-off presupposes the existence of two distinct claims. However, the two entitlements are functionally similar and the term "set-off" is frequently used to describe them both. The *Quistclose* case involved the banker's right of combination.

Coopers & Lybrand v. Lumberland Building Materials
(1983), 50 CBR (NS) 150 (BCSC)

CAMPBELL LJSC: This is the hearing of a special case pursuant to British Columbia Supreme Court R. 33. The agreed facts are as follows:

1. The Plaintiff is a licensed Trustee in Bankruptcy and is Trustee in Bankruptcy of the Estate of Trans-Lite Distributors Ltd. ("Trans-Lite") which made an assignment for the benefit of its creditors on July 19, 1982.

2. Lumberland Building Materials Ltd. ("Lumberland") is a corporation duly incorporated under the laws of the Province of British Columbia, with its registered office at 5650 Lougheed Highway, Burnaby, Province of British Columbia.

3. Pursuant to an agreement made between Trans-Lite Distributors Ltd. before it became bankrupt, the Plaintiff, Trans-Lite agreed to sell and the Defendant, Lumberland agreed to buy certain goods, namely building supplies and the Defendant agreed to pay Trans-Lite for the goods.

4. Pursuant to the agreement, Plaintiff sold and delivered building supplies to the Defendant, particulars of which have been given to the Defendant, and, as of July 19, 1982, the sum of $11,613.40 was due and owing from the Defendant to Plaintiff on account thereof before allowing for any claim for set-off by the Defendant.

5. In order to induce purchases from, *inter alia*, the Defendant, the Plaintiff had offered its customers a volume sales rebate program for 1982. Attached as Schedule "A" is a true copy of that offer, which was made to the Defendant.

6. The Defendant purchased goods which qualified under the rebate offer, in the amount of $267,256.00 on or before July 19, 1982.

7. The Plaintiff offered the Defendant, *inter alia*, to share the costs of advertising products regularly sold by the Plaintiff. Attached as Schedule "B" is a true copy of the co-operative advertising offer made by the Plaintiff.

8. The Defendant set off the sum of $6,681.40 from the amount owed by it to the Plaintiff as at July 19, 1982 on account of a claimed volume rebate.

9. The Plaintiff claims that the Defendant was not entitled to set-off the sum of $6,681.40.

Schedule "A" to the special case contains, *inter alia*, the following provision:

> Volume earned rebates are based and paid on the plateau achieved by year end. The amount of earned rebate will be paid to you by cheque within sixty (60) days following year end.

The issue is the right of the defendant to set-off against the $11,613.40 owing the plaintiff on the date of bankruptcy the sum of $6,681.40 it says it was entitled to on that date as earned rebate.

Section 75(3) of the *Bankruptcy Act*, RSC 1970, c. B-3 [now s. 97(3)] provides:

> (3) The law of set-off applies to all claims made against the estate and also to all actions instituted by the trustee for the recovery of debts due to the bankrupt in the same manner and to the same extent as if the bankrupt were plaintiff or defendant, as the case may be, except in so far as any claim for set-off is affected by the provisions of this Act respecting frauds or fraudulent preferences.

Section 95(2) and (3) [ss. 121(2) and (3)] provides ... .

The plaintiff says the defendant is not entitled to do so because: (1) there was no rebate due at the date of bankruptcy, i.e. "The amount of earned rebate will be paid ... within sixty (60) days following year end"; and (2) the intervention of the bankruptcy and the lack of crystallization of the amount due destroyed the element of mutuality which is required to permit a set-off.

The defendant says that there is one related agreement as set out in paras. 3 and 5 of the agreed facts which allows the defendant to set off its claim, the amount which can be ascertained, against the plaintiff's liquidated claim and even if there is a loss of mutuality, equity will assist to permit a set-off in the circumstances here.

Section 75 of the *Bankruptcy Act* clearly allows a set-off and I must here determine whether at law one is permitted on the facts here.

There are two kinds of set-off: legal/statutory and equitable set-off. Legal set-off originated in England by statute, s. 13 of Insolvent Debtors Relief (1728), 2 Geo. 2, c. 22, amended and made effective "for ever" by s. 4 of Set-off (1734-35), 8 Geo. 2, c. 24, and carried forward into the law of British Columbia in 1858 by the predecessor of the present s. 2 of the *Law and Equity Act*, RSBC 1979, c. 224. Equitable set-off has its origins in equity and does not rest on the statute of 1729. It followed and even extended the law, the courts of equity holding that certain cases were within the equity of the statute, although not within their actual words.

In *CIBC v. Tuckerr Indust. Inc.*, 48 CBR (NS) 1, [1983] 5 WWR 602, 46 BCLR 8, 149 DLR (3d) 172 (CA), Lambert JA, speaking for the court, held that statutory set-off is available only if two conditions are fulfilled, i.e. (1) both obligations must be debts; and (2) both debts must be mutual cross-obligations, and both conditions must be fulfilled at the same time.

The first requirement is that both the plaintiff's and the defendant's claims be for a debt which can be ascertained with certainty at the time of pleading. (See *Royal Trust Co. v. Holden* (1915), 21 BCLR 185, 8 WWR 500, 22 DLR 660 (CA).) Here, the defendant owes the plaintiff the sum of $11,613.40 for goods purchased. This is a liquidated amount and can be ascertained at the time of pleading. On the other hand the defendant claims entitlement from the plaintiff its share of the advertisement costs and the amount of rebate available to the defendant. These are also ascertainable with certainty at the time of pleading and then amounted to $6,681.40. The rebate programme (previously quoted) provides that value earned rebates are based and paid on the plateau achieved by year-end in accordance with the schedule. After the date of bankruptcy, 19th July 1982, the plaintiff could no longer sell any goods to the defendant. Prior to that, between 1st January 1982 and 19th July 1982, the defendant had purchased goods in an amount entitling it to a rebate in the amount it seeks to set off. Clearly then, on 19th July 1982 the debt owed by the plaintiff to the defendant was a liquidated sum which is ascertainable.

The second condition as stated in the *Tuckerr Indust.* case is that there must be cross-obligations.

A set-off is available only between the same parties and in the same right as the claim. A right of set-off cannot be maintained against a plaintiff suing to enforce his demand or against an assignee when the demand which it is sought to set off arises upon an independent contract and is not due at the date of the suit, for in that case it has not become a "debt" so as to be subject to the statute. The right of set-off depends on the existence of the debt due to the defendant and thus the fact of its debtor being a bankrupt does not prevent the set-off arising. The time that both obligations must exist in a bankruptcy situation is at the time of the bankruptcy, i.e., the assignment in bankruptcy or the pronouncement of a receiving order.

Here, on 19th July 1982 there were mutual and cross-obligations between the parties. On that date the defendant owed the plaintiff the amount of goods purchased and the plaintiff owed the defendant the costs of advertisements and the rebate. Even though the latter amounts were not "due" at that time, that does not defeat the defendant's right of set-off. In *Re Agra & Masterman's Bank, Anderson's Case* (1866), LR 3 Eq. 337 (Ch. D.), the court held that if a company goes into liquidation, debts which accrued before the winding-up may be set off against one another.

The plaintiff relies on *Re Debtor (No. 66 of 1955), Ex parte Debtor v. Trustee of Property of Waite*, [1956] 3 All ER 225 (CA), for the proposition that debts have to be due and cannot be merely accruing due at the time of the bankruptcy. A careful reading of that case discloses the court did not say that the debts have to be due at the date of bankruptcy and could not be accruing due. The court only said that there was no debt at all at that time. Thus, I reject the plaintiff's submission on that point.

So long as there is a debt owed to the defendant by the plaintiff before the date of bankruptcy and a corresponding debt from the defendant to the plaintiff, that satisfies the mutual and cross-obligation condition notwithstanding one of the debts was not actually payable at that time. At the time of bankruptcy there were mutual and cross-obligations between the parties. The trustee in bankruptcy is in the same position as the bankrupt. Thus I find that the defendant is entitled to a legal or statutory set-off in the amount claimed.

Even if I am wrong in that conclusion, I find that the defendant is entitled to the right of equitable set-off. In the *Tuckerr Indust.* case the Court of Appeal said that equitable set-off can apply where the cross-obligations are not debts, or where mutuality is lost or never existed. It may also arise where the cross-obligations arise from the same contract, though mutuality has been lost, or where the cross-obligations are closely related, or where the parties have agreed that a right to set-off may be asserted between them, or where a court of equity could otherwise have permitted a set-off.

In *Abacus Cities Ltd. v. Aboussafy*, 39 CBR (NS) 1, [1981] 4 WWR 660, 124 DLR (3d) 150, 29 AR 607 (CA), the court held that with equitable set-off, even though unliquidated amounts could be set off against liquidated amounts and there is no need of mutuality, nonetheless the claim by the defendant has to be related to the claim by the plaintiff against the defendant.

In addition, in equitable set-off cases the party seeking the benefit of it has to show some equitable ground for being protected against his adversary's demand. In *Rawson v. Samuel* (1841), Cr. & Ph. 161, 41 ER 451 (Ch.), cited in the *Abacus* case at p. 7, the court said that the mere existence of cross-demands is not sufficient. In *Equitable Remedies* by Spry, 2nd ed. (1980), the learned author stated at pp. 170-71:

> What generally must be established is such a relationship between the respective claims of the parties that the claim of the defendant has been brought about by, or has been contributed to by, or is otherwise so bound up with, the rights which are relied upon by the plaintiff that it would be unconscionable that he should proceed without allowing a set-off. Thus if conduct of the plaintiff is such as to induce the defendant to incur an obligation in favour of the plaintiff, and that conduct itself is fraudulent, negligent or otherwise wrongful so as to give a cause of action to the defendant, the plaintiff will not ordinarily be permitted to proceed until he has made good the material claims of the defendant.

In the circumstances here I conclude that the relationship between the parties is one in which it would be inequitable not to allow the defendant to set off its claims. The rebate programme was offered to induce the defendant to purchase more goods. The defendant had fulfilled all the stipulations and qualified for the rebate programme, thus it is equitable that it be allowed to set off the rebate and the advertisement costs against the debt it owes to the plaintiff.

Even if it could be maintained that the obligation owed to the defendant by the plaintiff was not a liquidated debt or there was lack of mutuality, in my view the defendant is still entitled to equitable set-off because the defendant's claim is closely related to the plaintiff's claim and there exist factors that warrant the defendant's protection against the plaintiff's demand.

Therefore, the defendant is entitled at law and in equity to set off its claim against the plaintiff's claim.

NOTES

1. The following are some further examples of cases involving legal set-off:

- *LSUC v. Merker* (1985), 49 OR (2d) 345 (HCJ). The Law Society of Upper Canada operated two plans: a Legal Aid plan and a Compensation Fund plan. A solicitor prior to bankruptcy had money owing to him by the Legal Aid plan but he owed the Compensation Fund plan for money paid out on his behalf to reimburse clients. The court held that the Law Society could set off the amount owing by the Legal Aid plan against the amount the solicitor owed to the Compensation Fund plan.

- *Re Halpern*, [1995] 5 WWR 368 (Alta QB). A real estate salesman had an agreement with his employer to pay certain expenses of the employer. At the date of his bankruptcy, the salesman was owed commission by the employer. The court held that the employer was entitled to set off the expenses against the commission.

- *Re Randell* (1956), 36 CBR 5 (BCSC). A solicitor received money (not in trust) from a client prior to the client's bankruptcy. The court held that the solicitor could set off against the amount received the amount he was owed in fees.

2. Consider the following variation on the facts of the *Lumberland* case:

Lumberland buys building materials from Translite. The price is $12,000. Lumberland was induced to enter into the contract by a misrepresentation that Translite made during the course of negotiations. Lumberland refuses to pay Translite for the building supplies. Translite notifies Lumberland that it plans to sue Lumberland for the price. Lumberland notifies Translite that it plans to sue Translite in tort for damages arising out of Translite's misrepresentation.

Can Lumberland claim set-off?

3. Consider the following variation on the facts of the *Lumberland* case:

Lumberland owes Translite $12,000 for goods sold and delivered. Translite becomes bankrupt. Lumberland discovers that Translite owes another customer (Loser) $5,000 as compensation for a defective shipment. Loser expects to recover only 10 cents on the dollar in Translite's bankruptcy—that is, $500. Lumberland buys Loser's claim for $2,000. Lumberland then sets off the $5,000 claim against the $12,000 it owes the estate. Loser is better off by $1,500 and Lumberland is better off by $3,000. Translite's estate is worse off by $4,500.

Is this sort of transaction allowable? In *Food Group Inc. v. Peat Marwick* (1988), 67 CBR (NS) 159 (NSSC), the court, while denying set-off on the particular facts of the case, left open the larger question of principle. Contrast s. 553(a)(2) of the US *Bankruptcy Code*, which precludes set-off if the creditor acquires its claim after 90 days before the date of the filing and while the debtor was insolvent.

<h2 style="text-align:center">Canada Trustco Mortgage Co. v. Sugarman</h2>

(1999), 179 DLR (4th) 548 (Ont. CA)

CHARRON JA: This appeal turns on whether an accounting firm can claim an equitable set-off against monies held in its capital account to the credit of two of its bankrupt partners, for payment made by the firm, after the bankruptcy of the two partners, to an unsecured creditor of the two bankrupts.

The dispute over the monies is between the appellant, Canada Trustco Mortgage Company ("Trustco"), and the respondent, the Canadian Imperial Bank of Commerce ("CIBC"). Trustco is a creditor of the bankrupts who obtained an order under s. 38 of the *Bankruptcy and Insolvency Act* RSC 1985, c. B-3 ("BIA") authorizing it to bring an action against the accounting firm, Schwartz, Levitsky and Feldman ("SLF") for recovery of monies held in its capital account to the credit of the two bankrupt partners at the time of the bankruptcy. The CIBC is an unsecured creditor of the bankrupts who obtained the monies from SLF after the bankruptcy. SLF paid the CIBC in fulfillment of its undertaking to pay the bankrupts' loan upon the happening of certain events. In return for the payment, the CIBC agreed to indemnify SLF against any resulting liability to Trustco.

Trustco brought a motion for summary judgment in this action against SLF and, in turn, SLF brought a motion for summary judgment against the third party, the CIBC. At the hearing, it was common ground between the parties that Trustco stood in the shoes of the trustee in bankruptcy and the contest was therefore essentially between the trustee in bankruptcy and one unsecured creditor, the CIBC. Somers J resolved the contest in favour of the CIBC on the ground that SLF was entitled to set off the payments made to the CIBC against the monies held in its capital account to the credit of the bankrupts. Consequently, he dismissed Trustco's motion and its action against SLF and, in light of this conclusion, found it unnecessary to deal with SLF's motion for judgment against the CIBC. Trustco appeals from this decision.

It is my view that the trustee in bankruptcy, represented by Trustco in this proceeding, has priority over the monies. The monies held in SLF's capital account to the credit of the two bankrupt partners vested in the trustee in bankruptcy at the time of bankruptcy. At that time, there was no debt owed by the bankrupts to SLF that could give rise to a claim by SLF to a right of set-off against those monies in priority to the rights of the trustee in bankruptcy. Further, SLF's obligation to repay the bankrupts' loan to the CIBC pursuant to its undertaking to do so does not, in the circumstances of this case, give rise to a claim for equitable set-off. Finally, whatever agreement SLF entered into with the CIBC after the bankruptcy cannot affect Trustco's priority over the monies.

. . .

The two bankrupts, David Donald Sugarman and Stacy Brad Mitchell, were chartered accountants. They practised together in partnership until February 1994 when they merged their practice with that of SLF. Upon joining SLF, they were required by SLF to inject capital into the firm. They each borrowed $100,000 from the CIBC for that purpose.

At the time Sugarman and Mitchell joined SLF, they signed a partnership entry agreement and the existing SLF partnership agreement. The partnership entry agreement provided for SLF to assist Sugarman and Mitchell with respect to the capital loans in these terms:

2.3 Provisions Relating to Capital Loans.

The Partnership shall assist Sugarman and Mitchell in arranging bank financing, if required, for the purposes of subsection 2.2(b) in the amount of One Hundred Thousand ($100,000) Dollars each, with a Canadian chartered bank or other lender. So long as such loan is outstanding, the Partnership shall make all payments of interest attributable to it, directly to the financial institution making such loan advance to Sugarman or Mitchell. In the event that either Sugarman or Mitchell ceases to be a Partner, the Partnership shall repay from the capital account of Sugarman or Mitchell as applicable, all principal and interest attributable to such loan, to the extent of such capital account. The parties acknowledge that at no time will the principal amount of any loan advanced by a financial institution to Sugarman or Mitchell pursuant to the provisions of this section exceed the capital account of Sugarman or Mitchell, as applicable.

SLF did accounting work for the CIBC and had a good relationship with the bank. At the request of the CIBC, SLF signed two letters of undertaking, one on behalf of Sugarman and one on behalf of Mitchell. The text in both letters is identical. The letter concerning Sugarman's loan reads as follows:

UNDERTAKING

Manager
Canadian Imperial Bank of Commerce
Private Banking CentreOne Eglinton Avenue East
Toronto, Ontario, M4P 3A1

Dear Sir:

Re: Capital Loan for David Sugarman

In consideration of the bank advancing the sum of $100,000 for the purpose of a Capital contribution to the firm of Schwartz Levitsky Feldman, we hereby agree to the following:

1. The Firm will maintain in their Capital Account at all times an amount equal to the amount outstanding of the Capital Loan maintained by the Bank on behalf of the subject.

2. In the event of the subject's death, withdrawal from the Firm or the dissolution of the Firm or withdrawal of Capital from the Firm for any other reason the Bank will be paid an amount equal to the amount of the Capital Loan outstanding in the name of the subject including accrued interest and other charges.

Dated at Toronto this 22nd day of February, 1994.
Schwartz Levitsky Feldman
Chartered Accountants

Paragraph 12.01 of the SLF partnership agreement also has some bearing on this appeal in that it gives SLF a right of set-off against the value of any withdrawing partner's interest for sums owing by the partner to the partnership:

> In the event of the withdrawal ... of a partner, that such partner shall cease to be a member of the partnership, his partnership interest will terminate and the partnership will pay to such partner the value of his partnership interest as determined in accordance with Article 11.00 of this agreement and as hereinafter provided, minus the amount of any sums owing by the partner in question to the partnership and not already accounted for in the valuation of his partnership interest.

Sugarman and Mitchell suffered a serious financial reversal as a result of a real estate transaction and, in the fall of 1995, each of them filed a proposal under the BIA. The proposals were rejected by their creditors and they were deemed to have made an assignment in bankruptcy as of October 27, 1995. Upon their personal bankruptcy, both Sugarman and Mitchell lost their CA designation. Consequently, they were also deemed to have withdrawn from their partnership in SLF as of the same date.

Upon the bankrupts making their proposal, the CIBC filed proofs of claim with the trustee in bankruptcy for the amounts of the loans as an unsecured creditor and demanded payment from SLF pursuant to the letters of undertaking. The trustee in bankruptcy also demanded that SLF pay the assets of each capital account of Sugarman and Mitchell to the estate. On September 19, 1996, SLF, faced with these competing claims, entered into a settlement agreement with the CIBC. Under the terms of this agreement, repayment of the loans was made to the CIBC by SLF, in return for which the CIBC agreed to indemnify SLF in the event any judgment or order was made against SLF with respect to this repayment. It was also agreed that SLF would take the position that it was entitled to set off the amount of the payments to the CIBC as against the bankrupts' capital accounts.

. . .

Upon the rejection of a proposal pursuant to the BIA, the insolvent person is deemed to have made an assignment in bankruptcy and all property belonging to the bankrupt passes to and vests in the trustee in bankruptcy: s. 57(a) and s. 71(2) of the BIA. Hence, any monies held by SLF in its capital account to the credit of Sugarman and Mitchell vested in the trustee in bankruptcy as of October 27, 1995. It is common ground between the parties that there was the total sum of $200,000 in the capital account at the time of bankruptcy. In this proceeding, Trustco stands in the shoes of the trustee in bankruptcy. Consequently, it is prima facie entitled to judgment for that amount.

However, in certain circumstances, the trustee in bankruptcy will take the property of the bankrupts subject to certain equities. In this case, the respondent takes the position that the monies in the capital account were subject to SLF's right of set-off. The law of set-off is expressly preserved by s. 97(3) of the BIA. ...

In this case, Trustco, standing in the shoes of the trustee, is seeking recovery of monies due to the bankrupts by SLF, namely the monies in the capital account to the credit of each bankrupt, and this claim may be subject to a set-off by SLF against these monies. The question becomes whether SLF has any valid claim for set-off.

A right of set-off may arise by agreement, at law, or in equity: *Telford v. Holt* (1987), 41 DLR (4th) 385 (SCC).

(a) Set-off by Agreement

In this case, the agreement between SLF and Sugarman and Mitchell expressly provided for a right of set-off. As noted earlier, paragraph 12.01 of the partnership agreement provided that, in the event of the withdrawal of a partner, SLF was obliged to pay to the partner the value of his partnership interest (which, by definition in the agreement, included the amount credited to the partner's capital account) minus the amount of any sums owing by the partner to the partnership. However, there were no moneys owed to the firm by either Sugarman or Mitchell at the time of their bankruptcy and, therefore, it is not alleged that any right of set-off arose by agreement.

(b) Legal Set-off

A legal right of set-off exists if both obligations are debts (as opposed to unliquidated claims for damages) and are mutual cross-obligations, although not necessarily connected. The requirement of mutuality can sometimes be difficult to understand from the cases, particularly in situations where an issue arises as to whether the assignment of a debt has destroyed mutuality. However, in this case, it is clear that there is no mutuality. The cross-claims are not owed between the original parties, SLF and Sugarman and Mitchell. Rather, SLF is asserting a right to set off a debt that it owes to a third party, the CIBC, against the debt owed by the firm to the bankrupt estate. The respondent concedes that there is no right of legal set-off at law in this case. Rather, the respondent relies on equitable principles.

(c) Equitable Set-off

Equitable set-off may be available in circumstances where the strict requirements of legal set-off cannot be met. Kelly R. Palmer, in The Law of Set-Off in Canada (1993), reviews the different rationales for allowing equitable set-off as it has evolved over the years, from the need to prevent the harshness of imprisonment for non-payment of debts, to more modern exigencies such as reducing the number of actions and avoiding circuitous claims. Whatever the rationale, it would appear from the cases that the remedy is firmly rooted in the need to achieve fairness between the parties.

One of the main differences between legal set-off and equitable set-off is that, in the latter case, the claims between the parties do not need to be liquidated. Hence, claims for damages are available for equitable set-off. This difference does not matter in this case. Another important difference, and one that is of relevance here, lies in the fact that the requirement for mutuality is relaxed. Hence, equitable set-off may be available even though the situation is not strictly one where A seeks to set off his debt to B against the debt B owes to A. However, for equitable set-off to be available, the cross-claims must be closely connected. It is logical to conclude that this latter requirement arises because mutuality is not strictly insisted upon. After all, it is difficult to imagine why, in the interests of fairness, the courts would allow A to reduce his debt to B by the amount A owes to C, unless it was because of the close connection between the claims. Finally, it is important to note that, just because cross-claims are closely connected to one another, it does not mean that set-off will necessarily follow. Not only must the connection be sufficiently close to warrant an exercise of the equitable jurisdiction of the court, the remedy must not result in any form of inequity.

In order to determine whether equitable set-off should be allowed in this case, it is therefore necessary to look at the connection between the claims and also to consider the effect the remedy would have on the equities between the parties.

It is the respondent's position, as set out in its factum, that the right of set-off claimed by SLF "arises out of the contractual obligation to repay the personal loans to CIBC out of the capital accounts, in accordance with Article 2.3 of the Partnership Entry Agreement between the bankrupts and SLF, as well as the written Undertakings given by SLF to CIBC for the benefit of the bankrupts." The respondent submits that the claims are so connected that it would be unfair to require SLF to pay the monies in the capital account to the trustee in bankruptcy without allowing SLF to offset its obligation to repay the very loan that provided the capital sum in the first place.

In my view, although superficially attractive, this argument cannot hold. I find the argument unconvincing because it ignores the important fact that there has been an intervening bankruptcy in this case. This is not simply a case, for example, where Sugarman and Mitchell would decide to go back to practising on their own and would seek payment of the monies held to their credit in the firm's capital account, leaving SLF behind to pay the loan to the CIBC pursuant to its undertaking. If this were the case, I have no doubt that equity would intervene to allow SLF a right to set off its obligation to the CIBC against the debt to Sugarman and Mitchell, even in the absence of an indemnity agreement between SLF and the two withdrawing partners.

In this case, because of the intervening bankruptcy, the equities are no longer just between SLF and Sugarman and Mitchell or even between SLF and the CIBC. The rights of others have come into play. These rights cannot simply be ignored on the basis that the CIBC lent the money that created the capital account in question. If the respondent's argument was accepted, the unsecured creditor who lent the bankrupt money to buy a car would be able to claim priority over the car based on that fact alone and in the absence of any secured interest in the car. Such a result would be contrary to the scheme of distribution under the BIA. It would result in an unfair preference of one unsecured creditor over other unsecured creditors. Similarly, in this case, the resulting unfairness to SLF, if any, must be assessed in the context of the bankruptcy where other unsecured creditors may stand to lose.

In my view, at the time of bankruptcy, SLF stood in no different position than any other unsecured creditor in the bankrupt's estate. ... At the time SLF gave its undertaking to the bank to repay the loan, it could have obtained some form of security from Sugarman and Mitchell. SLF chose not to do so. SLF is an accounting firm, not an unsophisticated creditor. Obviously, it suited its own purposes to give the undertaking to the CIBC. Indeed, the evidence shows that SLF was receiving two new partners, an injection of $200,000 in the firm's capital account and ongoing accounting business from the CIBC. There is really no reason why SLF should be treated any differently than others who stand to lose as a result of the two partners' bankruptcy.

Further, the ultimate result of granting the remedy of equitable set-off cannot simply be ignored. Given the indemnity it received from the CIBC, SLF does not lose any money. The claim of equitable set-off is made for the CIBC's benefit. Granting relief in this case would be akin to elevating the CIBC's status in the bankruptcy from unsecured to secured creditor to the detriment of other unsecured creditors. There is no justification in this case to so interfere with the scheme of distribution under the BIA.

For these reasons, I would allow the appeal, set aside the order of Somers J and grant judgment to the appellant against Schwartz, Levitsky & Feldman for $200,000 plus interests and costs of the motion, the action and the appeal.

NOTE

Section 533 of the US *Bankruptcy Code* provides that "except as otherwise provided in this section … this title does not affect any right of a creditor to offset a mutual debt owing by such creditor to the debtor." Would set-off be allowable under this provision on facts like those in the *Sugarman* case?

CHAPTER FIVE

Review of Pre-Bankruptcy Transactions

I. INTRODUCTION

This chapter deals with the trustee's powers to claw back assets the bankrupt may have disposed of in pre-bankruptcy transactions. There are three main headings: (1) undervalue the provincial fraudulent conveyance laws; (2) the BIA transfers at undervalue provision; and (3) preferences. The BIA provisions relevant to gifts and transfers at undervalue are s. 96 (transfers at undervalue) and s. 101 (dividends and redemptions of shares). These provisions are supplemented by the provincial fraudulent conveyance laws. The BIA provisions relevant to preferences are in s. 95. These provisions are supplemented by the provincial assignments and preferences laws. In some cases, the provincial laws are the exclusive or predominant basis for challenging a pre-bankruptcy transaction; in other cases, there is substantial overlap between the BIA and the provincial provisions. Where there is no overlap, s. 72 of the BIA appears to envisage continued application of provincial law. This is supported constitutionally by the provincial jurisdiction over property and civil rights (*Constitution Act, 1867*, s. 92(13)).

In *Robinson v. Countrywide Factors Ltd.*, [1978] 1 SCR 753, the Supreme Court, over a strong dissent by Laskin CJ, upheld the constitutional validity of the provincial fraudulent preference laws. The key passage from the judgment of Spence J (for the majority) reads as follows:

> I have dealt with what, in my view, are the main cases upon the subject in Canada. Upon considering them *all*, as well as the decision of the Judicial Committee in *AG of Ontario v. AG for Canada*, [[1893] AC 189], I have come to the conclusion that the better view is to confine the effect of what is now s. 73 of the *Bankruptcy Act* [now s. 95] to providing for the invalidity of transactions within its exact scope. To that extent, the Parliament of Canada, by valid legislation upon "bankruptcy" and "insolvency," has covered the field but has refrained from completely covering the whole field of transactions avoided by provincial legislation. I am of the opinion that the enactment in 1949 of the provisions now found in s. 50(6) [now s. 72(1)] of the *Bankruptcy Act* is a plain indication that Parliament recognized that provisions in provincial statutes dealing with preferential transactions were still valid provincial enactments in reference to "property" and "civil rights" and were valuable aids to trustees in bankruptcy in attacking the validity of such transactions and should be available to the said trustees in bankruptcy.

The practical implication of the decision is that a trustee may rely on either the BIA antipreference provisions or the provincial laws, or both, depending on which system of law is more favourable to the trustee in the particular case.

II. THE PROVINCIAL FRAUDULENT CONVEYANCE LAWS

A. Introduction

The origins of the fraudulent conveyance laws lie in the *Statute of Elizabeth* (the *Statute of Fraudulent Conveyances 1571*). The *Statute of Elizabeth* was received into Canadian provincial law at the time of settlement and it still applies in most parts of Canada on that basis. Four provinces (British Columbia, Manitoba, Newfoundland, and Ontario) have enacted fraudulent conveyances laws codifying the *Statute of Elizabeth*. It is not settled whether the *Statute of Elizabeth* still applies in these provinces (*Royal Bank of Canada v. North American Life Assurance Co.*, [1996] 1 SCR 325), but the question may not matter much because the provincial fraudulent conveyance statutes are, in substance, the same as the *Statute of Elizabeth* (see, further, below). The provincial assignments and fraudulent preferences laws (in all provinces except Manitoba, Newfoundland, and Northwest Territories) also contain fraudulent conveyance provisions, but these apply only if the debtor is insolvent or near insolvency at the date of the transaction. Neither the *Statute of Elizabeth* nor the fraudulent conveyances laws are limited in this way.

The *Statute of Elizabeth* prohibits a conveyance of property by A to B if it is made for the purpose of defeating A's creditors. A creditor can sue to have the conveyance set aside. There are two main kinds of cases:

1. where A transfers an asset to B by way of gift; and

2. where A transfers an asset to B at an undervalue.

The so-called rule in *Freeman v. Pope* (1870), LR 5 Ch. 538 says that, in case (1), the courts will presume A's intention to defeat creditors if A was insolvent at the date of the transaction or the transaction caused A to become insolvent. The rule in *Freeman v. Pope* is a substantial evidentiary concession in favour of a creditor who is attempting to have the transaction set aside. There is no corresponding concession for case (2). In case (2), the courts require actual proof of A's intention to defeat creditors. They also read the statute as requiring proof of B's collusion in A's illegal purpose; if the transaction displays one or more of the badges of fraud (for example, if it is carried out in secret, if A and B are related to one another, or if there is litigation pending against A), this will be enough to establish A's illegal purpose unless A provides an innocent explanation: see *FL Receivables Trust 2002-A (Administrator of) v. Cobrand Foods Ltd.* (2007), 85 OR (3d) 561 (CA).

The policy behind the provincial fraudulent conveyance laws is the prevention of debtor dishonesty. It is the equivalent of theft for A, having made a promise of payment to C, to deprive herself of the capacity for performance by transferring her assets to B. This is the evil that the fraudulent conveyance laws were meant to address. The laws are not specifically bankruptcy laws. Neither the *Statute of Elizabeth* nor the provincial fraudulent conveyance statutes are limited to eve-of-bankruptcy transactions. Theft is theft whether it occurs inside or outside bankruptcy. Outside bankruptcy, the provincial fraudulent conveyance laws give judgment creditors a weapon to attack fraudulent transfers. Inside bankruptcy, the weapon passes to A's trustee to exercise on behalf of all unsecured creditors. The corresponding provision in BIA s. 96 applies only inside bankruptcy, but this is not because the policy is different. It is simply because the BIA is a bankruptcy statute. If A makes a gift to B when A is insolvent or near insolvency, the transfer is voidable under the *Statute of Elizabeth* and the provincial fraudulent conveyance laws. It is important to be clear about the reason why. The reason is not that bankruptcy policy dictates this outcome. It is that, in the circumstances, the courts presume A's intention to defeat creditors. In other words, the rule is an evidentiary one, not a substantive one. The policy is still to prevent dishonesty.

Profile United Industries Ltd. v. Coopers & Lybrand
(1987), 38 DLR (4th) 600 (NBCA)

STRATTON CJNB: This appeal raises two questions: whether a payment made by one related company to another was a "settlement" within the meaning of s. 69 of the *Bankruptcy Act* [now BIA s. 91], RSC 1970, c. B-3; and whether the payment was made in contravention of the *Statute of Elizabeth* (*Fraudulent Conveyances Act*), 1570, 13 Eliz. I, c. 5.

In 1980 the appellant, Profile United Industries Limited ("Profile"), Associated Freezers of Canada Limited ("Freezers") and Associated Fisheries of Canada Limited ("Fisheries"), were associated companies, all controlled by one Joseph Yvon Robichaud.

Fisheries operated a fish processing plant at Shippegan, New Brunswick. On February 29, 1980, Fisheries sold its fish-processing business to Connors Bros. Ltd. for $3,650,000.00. After the payment of several encumbrances Fisheries' solicitors paid the balance of the sale price in the amount of $578,308.06 to Profile. Profile then proceeded to liquidate Fisheries' remaining assets, collect its receivables and pay its outstanding accounts. Among Fisheries' outstanding accounts was one due Profile of $150,570.04, one due Metrocan Leasing Ltd. of $220,149.79 and one due Excel Packaging Ltd. of $220,071.23. Profile off-set against the sums it received its own account with Fisheries while Freezers assumed payment of the Metrocan account.

When the sale by Fisheries to Connors Bros. took place, Excel Packaging Ltd. had commenced legal action in the courts of Quebec to collect its account with Fisheries. In that litigation Fisheries had counterclaimed against Excel for substantially the same amount as was claimed against it. But the counterclaim was unsuccessful and Excel was awarded judgment against Fisheries for the full amount of its account. On July 23, 1981, Excel registered its judgments against Fisheries in New Brunswick. The registered judgment was for $238,638.92. On December 11, 1981, Excel petitioned for a receiving order against Fisheries. On January 8, 1982, a receiving order was made and Coopers & Lybrand Limited was appointed trustee of the estate of Fisheries.

The trustee commenced the present action against Profile claiming that the sum of $578,308.06 that was paid to it by Fisheries' solicitors was paid at a time when Fisheries was unable to pay its debts without these funds, that it was paid with intent to defraud the creditors of Fisheries, and in particular Excel, and that such payment contravened the *Statute of Elizabeth* and was therefore void and should be set aside. At the trial of the action a judge of the Court of Queen's Bench made the following findings:

(1) When the payment of $578,308.06 was made to Profile, Fisheries was insolvent;

(2) The payment made to Profile was not an ordinary business transaction but one which prevented Fisheries from paying its debts in a fair and equitable manner;

(3) The sum of $578,308.06 was paid to Profile so that it could control the payment of Fisheries' accounts and thus exclude Excel;

(4) The assumption by Freezers of Fisheries' account with Metrocan Leasing Limited in the amount of $220,149.79 reduced the Trustee's claim by this amount;

(5) As the Trustee did not contest the set-off by Profile of its own account with Fisheries in the sum of $150,570.04 the Trustee's claim was reduced by this amount;

(6) The payment made to Profile was a "settlement" within the meaning of s. 69(1) of the *Bankruptcy Act* and therefore void as against the Trustee;

(7) Additionally the Trustee was entitled to succeed on the basis of the *Statute of Elizabeth*; and

(8) The Trustee was entitled to judgment against Profile for $263,945.20 together with interest at the rate of 10% per annum from October 31, 1983 and to costs of $11,875.00.

Profile has appealed the decision at trial contending that the learned trial judge erred in law in two respects: (1) in finding that the payment to Profile was a "settlement" within the meaning of s. 69 of the *Bankruptcy Act*, and (2) in finding that the payment to Profile was in contravention of the *Statute of Elizabeth*. The trustee has cross-appealed submitting that the trial judge erred in giving credits to Profile in respect of Profile's own account of $150,507.04 and the account of Metrocan Leasing Ltd. in the amount of $220,149.79.

. . .

Profile contends that the payment of $578,308.06 to it by Fisheries' solicitors did not contravene the *Statute of Elizabeth* because, it argues, the statute does not prohibit a debtor from preferring one creditor to another. Indeed, Profile further submits that even though a debtor may know that a judgment is pending against him or that what is at issue is a substantial portion of the proceeds of sale of the debtor's principal asset yet the statute is not necessarily offended when all creditors save one are paid. There is support for this submission in 17 Hal., 3rd ed., pp. 656-7, para. 1267, where it stated:

> Unlike the bankruptcy laws, the statute does not prohibit a debtor preferring one creditor to another, and therefore a conveyance executed in favour of one or some only of the creditors of the grantor may be bona fide and valid, notwithstanding that the grantor knows at the time that execution is about to be issued against him, or that he is insolvent, and even though the conveyance comprises the whole of the grantor's property. Such an alienation will, however, be avoided if it is a mere cloak to secure a benefit to the grantor, and the fact that one creditor obtains an advantage will not of itself prevent a transaction from being avoided.

It has been said that the *Statute of Elizabeth* was merely declaratory of what was previously the common law of the land. The purpose of its enactment is described in *Kerr on Fraud and Mistake*, 7th ed. (1952), at p. 298, as follows:

> The statute 13 Eliz. c. 5, was made for the protection of creditors. It provided, in effect, that all conveyances and dispositions of property real or personal, made with the intention of delaying, hindering, or defrauding creditors, should be null and void as against them, their

heirs, etc., and assigns. It also provided that nothing therein contained should extend to any estate or interest made on good consideration and bona fide to any person not having, at the time, any notice of such fraud.

The question whether the *Statute of Elizabeth* was in effect in Nova Scotia and the relationship between that enactment and the *Assignments and Preferences Act*, RSNS 1967, c. 16, was widely canvassed by Mr. Justice Hallett of the Nova Scotia Supreme Court in *Bank of Montreal v. Crowell et al.* (1980), 109 DLR (3d) 442, 37 NSR (2d) 292, 34 CBR (NS) 15. In that decision Hallett J concluded that it had been decided many years ago that the law set forth in the *Statute of Elizabeth* was applicable and necessary in that province and therefore in force. In this respect I would observe that there are as well decisions by New Brunswick courts that have adopted the statute as the law of this province: see, for example, *Bank of Montreal v. Vandine et al.*, [1953] 1 DLR 456, 33 MPR 368 (CA). Hallett J also states the following conclusion to which I too would respectfully subscribe (p. 449):

> In my opinion, the *Assignments and Preferences Act*, although it deals with the same subject-matter as the Statute of Elizabeth (fraudulent conveyances), does not repeal the Statute of Elizabeth by implication. The Statute of Elizabeth enables an attack on conveyances made by solvent persons while the *Assignments and Preferences Act* deals with insolvent persons and the matter of preferences which are not subject to attack under the Statute of Elizabeth. The two Acts are not inconsistent or repugnant. I am satisfied that effect can be given to both statutes at the same time and there is therefore no repeal by implication: *Craies on Statute Law*, 7th ed. (1971), p. 366; *Bank of Montreal v. Reis et al.*, [1925] 3 DLR 125, [1925] 2 WWR 169.

I would observe that the *Assignments and Preferences Act*, RSNB 1973, c. A-16, was not raised as an issue either at the trial of this action or on the hearing of the appeal.

It is to be noted that the *Statute of Elizabeth* makes a distinction between voluntary conveyances and *bona fide* transfers for consideration. Section 6 of the statute provides that the statute does not extend to any conveyance made upon good consideration and "bona fide lawfully conveyed" to any person not having notice or knowledge of the fraud or collusion against the creditors. The applicable rule is stated in 17 Hals., 3rd ed., p. 654, at para. 1261, as follows:

> For creditors to be in a position to impeach an alienation of property by their debtor they must prove, in addition to fraudulent intent on the part of the grantor, either that the alienation was not made for valuable consideration or upon good consideration, or that the grantee was privy to the fraud. Otherwise the grantee will be entitled to the protection given by the provision, even where a creditor is in fact defeated by the grant.

The decision in *Bank of Montreal v. Vandine et al.* cited previously involved a conveyance that was made for valuable consideration. In the judgment of Harrison J in that case it was stated at p. 460 DLR, p. 373 MPR:

> Two questions have to be determined under the *Statute of Elizabeth*—(1) Whether the conveyance in question was made by the debtor with the intent "to delay, hinder or defraud" his creditors; and (2) If there was such intent, whether the party buying such property participated in such fraudulent intent.

When a transaction is entered into for good and valuable consideration the burden of proving that it was made in fraud of creditors is upon those who seek to set the transaction aside. Although it is recognized that there can be no hard and fast rule as to what constitutes a fraudulent transaction, since the decision in *Twyne's Case* (1601), 3 Co. Rep. 80b, 76 ER 809, the existence of certain unexplained circumstances have sometimes been looked upon as "badges of fraud" so as to take the case out of the protection afforded to a *bona fide* purchaser. Two of the categories mentioned that have some relevance to the present case are the generality of the transfer, i.e., the inclusion therein of substantially all of the debtors' property, and the transfer of assets *pendente lite*. But overall what must be determined in each case as a question of fact is whether a concurrent intent on the part of the parties to defraud a creditor has been established by a preponderance of evidence.

In the instant case it was established that Fisheries sold its only substantial revenue producing asset, i.e., its fish-processing plant, and diverted the net sale proceeds to Profile in an effort to avoid payment to Excel which had sued it. While it is true that Profile undertook to collect Fisheries' receivables and to pay its outstanding accounts it is also true that Profile, Fisheries and Freezers were associated companies, all controlled by Mr. Robichaud. And as the trial judge took pains to point out, although he was present at the trial, Mr. Robichaud did not testify. In all of the circumstances, the trial judge categorized the diversion of Fisheries' funds to Profile as an unusual business transaction and one which prevented Fisheries from paying its debts in a fair and equitable manner at a time when it was insolvent. More importantly, he also found that Profile shared Fisheries' desire to exclude Excel from the payment of debts. As he put it:

> The balance of the purchase price was paid to a related company, Profile, so that it could choose which of [Fisheries] debts to liquidate. It might be natural that the management of Profile would not want to pay the Excel account which was thought to have caused [Fisheries] downfall.

The learned trial judge therefore concluded that the trustee was entitled to succeed on the basis of the *Statute of Elizabeth* because, he said, as a result of the impugned transaction there were no funds left for Excel "as Profile chose to pay other creditors instead." In my opinion, the trial judge's conclusion is substantiated by the evidence. I would respectfully agree with him that there was present here a shared intention on the part of Fisheries and Profile to delay, hinder or defraud Excel, a potential judgment creditor. Adopting the language of Halsbury, the diversion of Fisheries' funds to Profile "was a mere cloak to secure a benefit" to Fisheries and under the *Statute of Elizabeth* it was void.

Appeal allowed in part.

Optical Recording Laboratories v. Digital Recording Corp.
(1990), 1 OR (3d) 131 (CA)

GRIFFITHS JA (for the Court): On the petition of the respondent creditor, Granger J, by judgment dated August 27, 1989 [now reported 69 OR (2d) 628, 75 CBR (NS) 216 (SC

Bkcy.)], adjudged the appellant debtor bankrupt and issued a receiving order against it finding that the appellant had committed acts of bankruptcy contrary to ss. 42(1)(b) and 42(1)(g) of the *Bankruptcy Act*, RSC 1985, c. B-3 (as amended). The appellant appeals from the receiving order, contending that the trial judge erred in finding the particular acts of bankruptcy. The respondent cross-appeals, contending that the trial judge erred in failing to go further and find that the appellant had committed, in addition, an act of bankruptcy under s. 42(1)(c) of the Act by creating a fraudulent preference.

The Facts

The facts are set out at length in the reasons of the learned trial judge. The following is a summary of those facts pertinent to this appeal.

The appellant, Optical Recording Laboratories Inc. (Laboratories), had a sister company, Optical Recording Corporation (ORC). Mr. G. John Adamson owned all of the common shares of John Adamson Associates Limited which controlled Laboratories and ORC. Adamson was the directing mind of both Laboratories and ORC.

On March 28, 1985 the respondent, Digital Recording Corporation Inc. (Digital), sold a complete experimental facility known as a document storage development system (DSDS) to Laboratories for $21,500,000 of which $2,730,000 was paid in cash and the balance of $18,770,000 was secured by a promissory note made by Laboratories in favour of Digital. The promissory note provided that instalment payments on account of principal and interest would not commence until March 28, 1990 unless there was a default on the part of Laboratories in which case the whole of the principal amount outstanding together with accrued interest thereon would be due and payable immediately. Default under the note would include the following:

1. If Laboratories failed to pay any instalment payment within five days of the due date; or

2. If Laboratories became bankrupt or involved in an insolvency proceeding; or

3. If Laboratories defaulted on any obligation of $100,000 or more which gave the holder of such obligation the right to accelerate payment thereof.

Pursuant to the agreement of March 28, 1985, Laboratories received from Digital the "hard assets," that is, the technology and hardware necessary to undertake research and to develop new products with the DSDS. At the same time as the sale to Laboratories, there was a separate transaction wherein Digital assigned to ORC the patent rights to the technology involved in the DSDS. Under this separate arrangement, ORC was to pay to Digital a certain percentage of royalties received.

On August 31, 1987, Mr. Eli Jacobs (principal shareholder of Digital), Laboratories and ORC entered into a credit arrangement whereby Jacobs was to provide Laboratories and ORC with a line of credit up to $500,000 (US). Laboratories and ORC were jointly and severally liable under this agreement and were, pursuant to the agreement, required to pay monthly interest payments on the principal amount owing.

By January 1988, Laboratories and ORC were indebted to Jacobs under the credit arrangement in the amount of $650,000 (US). On February 12, 1988, Jacobs served Laboratories and ORC with a notice of default under the credit agreement and instituted an action in New York State to recover the amount owing. Jacobs, on behalf of Digital, also took the position that this default under the credit agreement constituted an event of default under the promissory note in that Laboratories had defaulted on an obligation of $100,000 or more. On March 8, 1988, Digital instituted proceedings in the Supreme Court of Ontario against Laboratories for $18,770,000 plus accrued interest owing on the note.

On April 12, 1988, the action brought by Jacobs in New York State was settled and the amount owing under the credit agreement was satisfied when ORC paid approximately $761,000 (US) or $960,000 (Cdn.) directly to Jacobs. Laboratories purported to treat this payment by ORC as a loan to it by ORC. On May 13, 1988, Laboratories executed a general security agreement in favour of ORC purporting to secure the $761,000 US.

On June 30, 1988, Laboratories entered into an asset sale agreement with ORC pursuant to which Laboratories purported to sell all its assets to ORC except the DSDS and a term deposit held in trust for Revenue Canada, for $1,922,000. The terms of the sale were $200,000 cash, assumption of $360,000 of Laboratories' debt and satisfaction of the $1,362,000 of debt owing by Laboratories to ORC.

On July 1, 1988, Laboratories terminated all its employees, who were immediately re-hired by ORC. Laboratories' research business was then carried on by ORC on premises formerly occupied by Laboratories, using the same employees and facilities to carry on the business previously pursued by Laboratories.

On August 8, 1988, Digital petitioned Laboratories for a receiving order. The trial judge granted the order, holding that Laboratories had committed acts of bankruptcy contrary to what are now ss. 42(1)(b) and 42(1)(g) of the *Bankruptcy Act*. Those subsections read:

> 42(1) A debtor commits an act of bankruptcy in each of the following cases:
>
> · · ·
>
> (b) if in Canada or elsewhere he makes a fraudulent conveyance, gift, delivery or transfer of his property or of any part thereof;
>
> · · ·
>
> (g) if he assigns, removes, secretes or disposes of or attempts or is about to assign, remove, secrete or dispose of any of his property with intent to defraud, defeat or delay his creditors or any of them. ...

The learned trial judge declined to make a finding that Laboratories had committed an act of bankruptcy pursuant to s. 42(1)(c) which reads:

> (c) if in Canada or elsewhere he makes any conveyance or transfer of his property or any part thereof, or creates any charge thereon, that would under this Act be void as a fraudulent preference.

The Findings of the Trial Judge

The findings of the trial judge may be summarized as follows:

1. That Digital was a creditor of Laboratories within the meaning of s. 2 of the *Bankruptcy Act*, that is, Digital was a person having a claim "preferred, secured or unsecured, provable as a claim" under the Act.

2. That the issue of whether the entire sum owing under the promissory note was due must await the trial of the Supreme Court action in Ontario brought by Digital against Laboratories and in which Laboratories denied liability under the promissory note and counterclaimed for damages. The trial judge ruled that, until the issue of what was due under the promissory note was settled in the Supreme Court action, he was not prepared to find that Laboratories had committed a fraudulent preference within the meaning of s. 42(1)(c) of the *Bankruptcy Act* since proof of the insolvency of Laboratories at the time of the transfer is an essential requisite under s. 95 of the Act. For the same reasons, the trial judge was not prepared to find that Laboratories had committed an act of bankruptcy within the meaning of s. 42(1)(j) of the *Bankruptcy Act*, that is, had ceased to meet its liabilities generally as they became due.

The general security agreement dated May 13, 1988 and the asset sale agreement dated June 30, 1988 were both fraudulent and constituted acts of bankruptcy within ss. 42(1)(b) and (g) of the *Bankruptcy Act*.

The trial judge found on the evidence that Adamson clearly intended in both instances to protect the assets of Laboratories from "attack by Digital" [p. 635 OR]. He concluded [p. 637 OR] that the "timing of the actions" by Laboratories corroborated the expressed intent of Adamson to protect the assets of Laboratories and defeat Digital, the major creditor.

With respect to the asset sale agreement of June 30, 1988, the trial judge found that the alleged consideration for this transaction, wherein Laboratories purported to sell not only its hard assets but also its potential ability to generate income from the DSDS, was totally inadequate and that this alleged consideration did not "in any manner (breathe) legitimacy into the agreement" [p. 639 OR].

The trial judge found that, by hiring the former employees and taking over Laboratories' former premises, ORC would continue to use the DSDS and research developed by Laboratories. The trial judge said [p. 637 OR] that he was "convinced beyond any doubt that the transfer was fraudulent and an act of bankruptcy within s. 42(1)(b)" of the *Bankruptcy Act*.

Attack on the Findings of the Trial Judge

On this appeal, counsel for Laboratories submitted that the trial judge erred in concluding on the evidence that the two transactions constituted fraudulent conveyances. It is submitted that the general security agreement of May 13, 1988 and the asset sale agreement of June 30, 1988 were each entered into for *bona fide* business purposes and for good consideration.

In arriving at his conclusions, the trial judge made findings of fact that, in my view, were open to him to make on the evidence and an appellate court should not interfere with those findings. The trial judge expressly rejected the position of Laboratories that all of its actions were legitimate business actions and were not fraudulent within the meaning of the *Bankruptcy Act*. The trial judge found, on the testimony of John Adamson, the directing mind of both Laboratories and ORC, that his object in both transactions under attack was to ensure that if the principal sum on the promissory note was due, the income-producing assets developed by Laboratories would be protected from attack by Digital. He found, in effect, that the timing of the transactions and the lack of "good and valuable consideration" raised general suspicion as to the *bona fides* of the transactions. The question of whether both transactions were entered into with an intent to defraud creditors is one of fact, to be decided in the particular circumstances of the case. Here, the trial judge concluded in effect that the actions of Laboratories were intended to de-nude it of all its revenue-producing assets, so that the principal creditor, Digital, could not be repaid. This conclusion was justified on the evidence. The first ground of appeal must fail.

Whether the "Conveyances" Constitute Fraudulent Conveyances in Law

Counsel for Laboratories submitted as a central ground of appeal that the trial judge erred in law in making a finding under the *Bankruptcy Act* that the two transactions in question constituted fraudulent conveyances. Counsel submitted that a fraudulent con-veyance within the meaning of s. 42(1)(b) of the *Bankruptcy Act* and a fraudulent prefer-ence within the meaning of s. 42(1)(c) are mutually exclusive categories. Counsel argued that a fraudulent conveyance is a conveyance to a person who is not a creditor of the transferor. A fraudulent preference, it was submitted, by contrast is a conveyance to a person who is a creditor. ORC was a creditor to some extent at the material time and therefore, it was argued, the conveyance to that company would not qualify as a fraudu-lent conveyance but should only be considered as a possible "fraudulent preference" within the meaning of s. 42(1)(c).

Counsel for Laboratories submits that in order for a conveyance to be considered a fraudulent preference under s. 95 of the *Bankruptcy Act*, the party challenging the con-veyance must prove at the outset that the transferor, Laboratories, was insolvent at the time the conveyance was made. It is submitted that Digital failed to satisfy the trial judge that Laboratories was insolvent at the date of the conveyances and, therefore, the trans-actions would not constitute fraudulent preferences under the Act.

The only authority that counsel for Laboratories cited in support of the proposition that ss. 42(1)(b) and (g) of the *Bankruptcy Act* apply only where the transfer or convey-ances are made to a third party that is not a creditor, was the following statement con-tained in the report of the Ontario Law Reform Commission on the *Enforcement of Judgement Debts and Related Matters* (Toronto, 1983), Part IV:

> Conceptually, and for the purposes of this chapter, a distinction may be drawn between a fraudulent conveyance and a fraudulent or unjust preference. A fraudulent conveyance is a transfer by the debtor of his property to a third party other than a creditor, whereas a fraud-ulent preference is a payment by the debtor to one or more, but not all, of his creditors, the transferee or transferees being preferred thereby. While the language of the *Fraudulent Conveyances Act* would seem to comprehend both fraudulent conveyances and fraudulent preferences, the orthodox view is that the Act is restricted to the voiding of fraudulent conveyances.

No case authority was cited for the above proposition. In my view, the distinction drawn by the authors of the Law Reform Commission report between fraudulent conveyances and fraudulent preferences was drawn solely for the purpose of the discussion that followed in the ensuing chapter.

Although the *Bankruptcy Act* is the governing federal legislation, it has long been recognized that creditors are entitled to make use of the rights and remedies provided under provincial legislation to the extent that such legislation is not in conflict with the *Bankruptcy Act*: see *Re Panfab Corp.*, [1971] 2 OR 202, 15 CBR (NS) 20, 17 DLR (3d) 382 (HCJ), at p. 207 OR *per* Houlden J.

The two provincial statutes that operate concurrently in the area of fraudulent transfers are the *Fraudulent Conveyances Act*, RSO 1980, c. 176 and the *Assignments and Preferences Act*, RSO 1980, c. 33.

There is no definition of "fraudulent conveyance" in the *Bankruptcy Act*. Under the *Fraudulent Conveyances Act*, a debtor makes a "fraudulent conveyance" if he makes a "conveyance" of property "with intent to *defeat, hinder, delay or defraud* creditors or others of their just and lawful actions" (s. 2) (emphasis added). By s. 1(a), the term "conveyance" includes a "charge" on the debtor's property and, accordingly, the general security agreement of May 13, 1988 executed by Laboratories in favour of ORC would qualify as a "conveyance."

The provisions of the *Fraudulent Conveyances Act* defining a fraudulent conveyance in no way limit such transaction to conveyances to third parties other than creditors. In my view, there is no rational reason to read into the legislative definition such a restrictive interpretation. The legislation, being remedial, should be given a liberal construction.

The author C.R.B. Dunlop, in his textbook *Creditor-Debtor Law in Canada* (Toronto: Carswell, 1981), at p. 513, states the purpose of fraudulent conveyance legislation as follows:

> The purpose of the *Statute of Elizabeth* and of the Canadian Acts based on it, as interpreted by the courts, is to strike down all conveyances of property made with the intention of delaying, hindering or defrauding creditors and others except for conveyances made for good consideration and bona fide to persons not having notice of such fraud. *The legislation is couched in very general terms and should be interpreted liberally.* Lord Mansfield concluded that the common law had always been strongly against fraud in every shape and that the Statute of Elizabeth "*cannot receive too liberal a construction, or be too much extended in suppression of fraud.*" *Relying on this policy, the courts have interpreted the statute to include any kind of alienation of property made with the requisite intent, the form of the transaction being immaterial.* Similarly the legislation has been held to invalidate a conveyance of any kind of exigible or attachable property of the debtor, so long as it is of some real value.

(Emphasis added.)

In my view, in determining whether a conveyance is fraudulent under s. 42(1)(b) or (c) of the *Bankruptcy Act*, it is irrelevant whether the transfer was made to a creditor. Instead, what is germane to such an inquiry is the genuineness of the conveyance. To this end, s. 3 of the *Fraudulent Conveyances Act* precludes the impeachment of a conveyance "upon good consideration and *bona fide* to a person not having at the time of the conveyance to him notice or knowledge of the intent set forth" in s. 2 (i.e., to defeat, hinder, delay or defraud creditors). If the argument of Laboratories were correct, debtors could avoid a finding of fraudulent conveyance under the *Fraudulent Conveyances Act*, even though they conveyed assets intending to defeat, hinder or delay their creditors, so long as the recipient of the conveyance was a creditor for any amount, no matter how nominal. In my view, if such a limitation were intended, then it would surely have been expressly stipulated in the legislation.

This second ground fails and, accordingly, the appeal must be dismissed.

The Cross-Appeal

In the cross-appeal, counsel for Digital submits that the learned trial judge erred in failing to find that the sale under the asset sale agreement of June 30, 1988 from Laboratories to ORC was a transfer of property between a debtor and a creditor made within three months of the date of the petition for the receiving order. Counsel argues it was therefore void as a fraudulent preference under s. 95 of the *Bankruptcy Act* because (a) Laboratories was insolvent at the time of the transfer; (b) the transferee, ORC, was a creditor; and (c) the transfer had the effect of giving that creditor a preference over other creditors such as Digital.

There is no question that conditions (b) and (c) are satisfied in the light of the findings of the trial judge. As the trial judge said [pp. 634-35 OR]:

> If the sum of $18,770,000 plus accrued interest was due when ORL (Laboratories) entered into the asset sale agreement, such agreement would have been a transfer by an insolvent company providing a creditor with a preference and therefore deemed fraudulent and void, as made within three months of the bankruptcy.

However, the trial judge declined to make a finding that the sum of $18,770,000 was owing on the promissory note at the material time and that Laboratories was therefore insolvent. He directed his mind to s. 42(1)(j) of the *Bankruptcy Act* which provides:

> 42(1) A debtor commits an act of bankruptcy in each of the following cases:
>
> · · ·
>
> (j) if he ceases to meet his liabilities generally as they become due.

The trial judge held that the issue of whether or not the sum of $18,770,000 was a liability that had become due must await the outcome of the Supreme Court action brought by Digital against Laboratories for recovery of that sum under the note. In that respect, he said [p. 632 OR]:

> That action, however, is for a determination as to whether or not the actions of ORL (Laboratories) constituted a default under the promissory note and thereby rendered the total amount owing, not whether Digital has a claim against ORL. The unliquidated amount of damages ORL alleges are due to it under the counterclaim cannot be set off against Digital's claim and do not affect Digital's status as creditor. Accordingly Digital has status to bring this petition.

Counsel for Digital submits that the trial judge erred in limiting his consideration to the issue of whether Laboratories was insolvent in the sense that it had ceased to meet its liabilities generally as they became due as at May 13, 1988 under s. 42(1)(j) of the *Bank-*

ruptcy Act. Counsel submits that the 1987 and 1988 financial statements filed at trial demonstrate that Laboratories had approximately $400,000 of assets at the time and liabilities in excess of several million dollars made up substantially of the debt owing to Digital. It was submitted that the trial judge should have directed his attention to the definition of "insolvent person" as defined by s. 2 "insolvent person" (c) of the Act as follows:

> "insolvent person" means a person who is not bankrupt and who resides or carries on business in Canada, whose liabilities to creditors provable as claims under this Act amount to one thousand dollars, and
>
> • • •
>
> (c) the aggregate of whose property is not, at a fair valuation, sufficient, or, if disposed of at a fairly conducted sale under legal process, would not be sufficient to enable payment of all his obligations, due and accruing due.

In my respectful view, the learned trial judge erred in failing to make a finding of insolvency within the meaning of the definition in s. 2 "insolvent person" (c). At the material time of the petition, the financial statements filed in the proceedings clearly established that the liabilities of Laboratories far exceeded its assets. In its evidence at trial, Adamson admitted that the obligation of $18,770,000 plus interest *was owing* but disputed whether it was due. In the Supreme Court action brought in Ontario, the counterclaim of Laboratories was for a sum of approximately $200,000 damages. Whatever success Laboratories might enjoy in the pending Supreme Court action, it seems to me improbable that its liabilities on the promissory note, which are now in excess of $23,000,000, would be reduced to a point where its assets at any fair valuation would be sufficient to meet those liabilities. It must not be overlooked, as well, that the trial judge earlier found that Laboratories was a "creditor" of Digital and this finding could only be supported on the basis that money was owing to Digital under the promissory note.

Accordingly, I would allow the cross-appeal and vary the judgment below to include a finding that the appellant committed an act of bankruptcy as well, contrary to s. 42(1)(c) of the *Bankruptcy Act* by making a conveyance of its property and creating a charge thereon that would, under the *Bankruptcy Act*, be void as a fraudulent preference.

• • •

Appeal dismissed with costs;
cross-appeal allowed without costs.

NOTE

In *Perry, Farley & Onyschuk v. Outerbridge Management Ltd.* (2001), 54 OR (3d) 131; (2001), 26 CBR (4th) 64, the Ontario Court of Appeal had to decide what limitation period, if any, applies to an action brought by a creditor under the *Fraudulent Conveyances Act*, RSO 1990 c. F.29. The respondent argued that the FCA claim was barred by the six-year limitation period prescribed by s. 45(1)(g) of the *Limitation Act*, RSO 1990, c. L.15, either as an action on a "simple contract" or as an "action on the case." The court held that the claim did not fit into either category and because the *Limitation Act* does not have a residual or catch-all provision as some other provincial limitations statutes do, the claim was not subject to any limitation period. It was also held that an FCA claim is subject to the equitable defence of laches. However, a party relying on the defence of laches must show a combination of delay and prejudice and, in the present case, the respondent had failed to do this.

III. THE BIA TRANSFERS AT UNDERVALUE PROVISION

A. Prior law

Until the 2007 amendments, the relevant BIA provisions were s. 91 (settlements), s. 100 (reviewable transactions), and s. 101 (dividends and redemptions of shares). The 2007 amendments have repealed ss. 91 and 100 and replaced them with a new s. 96, dealing with gifts and transfers at undervalue. Section 101 is unaffected. The following is a short account of the prior law.

BIA s. 91 dealt with settlements. It said that a settlement of property made within one year, or in some cases five years, before the settlor became bankrupt was void against the trustee. A settlement is a kind of gift. Courts had held that the term "settlement" implies an intention on the part of the debtor that the transferred property be retained for the benefit of the recipient in a form that it can be identified. A definition of "settlement" was added to BIA s. 2(1) in 1992. This provided that "settlement" includes "a contract, covenant, transfer, *gift* and designation of beneficiary in an insurance contract, to the extent that the contract, covenant, transfer, gift or designation is gratuitous or made for merely nominal consideration" (emphasis added). Did this provision expand the meaning of the word beyond its common law sense to cover gifts at large? In *Royal Bank of Canada v. Whalley* (2002), 59 OR (3d) 529, the Ontario Court of Appeal held that it did not. In any event, the BIA settlement provisions overlapped substantially with the provincial fraudulent conveyance laws. Why were the settlement provisions enacted at all? According to Professor Cuming, they were designed to supplement the provincial laws by addressing three situations:

> (i) settlements made by insolvent debtors where, under the *Statute [of Elizabeth]*, the intention to defraud might not be presumed as a result of the insolvency [that is, to confirm the rule in *Freeman v. Pope*]; (ii) settlements by a solvent debtor just prior to bankruptcy where fraudulent intent could not be established; and (iii) certain types of settlements made as part of marriage settlements that could not be attacked under the Statute because they were transactions for value and the double fraudulent intention required by the Statute could not be established.

(Ronald C.C. Cuming, *Gifts and Transfers at Undervalue: Reformulation of Section 91 of the Bankruptcy and Insolvency Act* (Report prepared for the Corporate Review Policy Directorate, Industry Canada, December 1997), text following note 17.)

BIA s. 100 dealt with reviewable transactions. A reviewable transaction was a transfer at undervalue by A to B where A and B are not at arm's length (for example, where A and B are related to one another): BIA s. 3 ("reviewable transaction") and s. 4(2) ("related persons"). Section 100 said that where the debtor enters into a reviewable transaction within one year before bankruptcy, the trustee may apply to the court for an order requiring the other party to the contract to pay the value shortfall. BIA s. 100 overlapped substantially with the provincial fraudulent conveyance laws. The main differences were as follows:

1. the provincial laws are not limited to non-arm's-length transactions;

2. BIA s. 100 did not require proof of A's intention to defeat creditors or B's collusion in A's illegal purpose; and

3. the provincial laws allow A's creditors to set aside the transaction, whereas BIA s. 100 gave the trustee, at the court's discretion, a money claim against B for recovery of the value shortfall.

BIA s. 101 deals with the purchase or redemption by a corporation of its own shares in a bankruptcy context. These transactions are the functional equivalent of a gift, because they do not return value to the corporation; therefore, they have the potential to defeat creditors. BIA s. 101 supplements federal and provincial corporations laws that, generally speaking, prevent a corporation from purchasing or redeeming its shares if it is insolvent. BIA s. 101 also catches the declaration of a dividend at a time when the corporation is insolvent on the theory that this, too, is the functional equivalent of a gift by the corporation to its shareholders.

B. Shortcomings of Prior Law

The main shortcoming of BIA s. 91 was that it only applied to settlements of property and did not catch other gratuitous transactions that diminish the value of the debtor's estate. The main shortcomings of s. 100 were as follows:

1. It was unclear whether the provision was limited to non-arm's-length transactions or whether all transactions that fell within the one-year review period were potentially reviewable.

2. In any event, there was no good policy reason for limiting the provision to non-arm's-length transactions. It should be sufficient for the trustee to show that the transfer took place within the prescribed review period and that the debtor either intended to defeat creditors or was insolvent at the time.

3. The remedy structure lacked a rational basis. The trustee had a choice of remedies if he could make a case under both s. 100 and the provincial fraudulent conveyance laws. However, if he could make a case under one but not the other, he would be limited to either damages or avoidance of the transaction.

4. The discretionary nature of the s. 100 remedy increased the uncertainty of litigation outcomes.

Sections 91 and 100 together were open to the following criticisms:

1. Gifts and transfers at undervalue both have a gift element and there is no reason for separate provisions to govern them. In other countries—for example, the United States, the United Kingdom, and Australia—bankruptcy law deals with both types of transaction under the umbrella of a single provision.

2. The provisions were both incomplete and inconsistent. For example, a gift of property fell outside s. 91 unless it was a settlement. Section 100 may have applied, but

only if the transaction took place within the one-year review period. By contrast, the review period under s. 91 was five years if the debtor was insolvent at the time or in consequence of the transaction. Moreover, if s. 100 applied, the trustee's remedy was damages representing the fair market value of the property. On the other hand, if s. 91 applied, the remedy was avoidance and the trustee got the property back.

3. The concurrent application of the provincial fraudulent conveyance laws is open to question. There is a case for leaving fraudulent conveyances law entirely to the provinces. The only possible justification for including fraudulent conveyance provisions in the BIA rests on the ground of administrative convenience. However, this objective is significantly compromised by the trustee's capacity to fall back on provincial laws where the BIA provisions do not apply or are less advantageous.

C. The 2007 BIA Amendments

The 2007 amendments address the first two of these criticisms, but not the third. The amendments repeal ss. 91 and 100 and replace them with a new s. 96, governing transfers at undervalue. "Transfer at undervalue" is defined to mean "a disposition of property or provision of services for which no consideration is received by the debtor or for which the consideration received by the debtor is conspicuously less than the fair market value of the consideration given by the debtor." In summary, the main features of new s. 96 are:

1. The provision applies to both arm's-length and non-arm's-length transactions (as to the meaning of an arm's-length transaction, see s. 4).

2. In the case of an arm's-length transaction, the review period is one year before the date of the initial bankruptcy event; in the case of a non-arm's length transaction, the review period is five years.

3. In the case of an arm's-length transaction, the trustee must prove (a) that the debtor was insolvent at the time of the transaction or the transaction rendered the debtor insolvent; *and* (b) that the debtor intended to defeat the interests of creditors.

4. In the case of a non-arm's-length transaction occurring within one year before the date of the initial bankruptcy event, the trustee must prove *neither* that (a) the debtor was insolvent at the time of the transaction or the transaction rendered the debtor insolvent; *nor* (b) that the debtor intended to defeat the interests of creditors.

5. In the case of a non-arm's length transaction occurring between two and five years before the date of the initial bankruptcy event, the trustee must prove that (a) the debtor was insolvent at the time of the transaction or was rendered insolvent by the transaction; *or* (b) the debtor intended to defeat the interests of creditors.

6. The trustee has a choice of remedies, either to avoid the transfer or sue the counterparty for the value shortfall.

For a critical analysis of s. 96, see Anthony Duggan and Thomas G.W. Telfer, "Gifts and Transfers at Undervalue," in Stephanie Ben-Ishai and Anthony Duggan, eds., *Canadian*

Bankruptcy and Insolvency Law: Bill C-55, Statute c. 47 and Beyond (Toronto: LexisNexis, 2007) 175, at 190-98.

The following two cases deal with BIA s. 100. The s. 100 case law remains relevant because new s. 96 is similar in many respects to the former provision. In particular, both provisions refer to a "conspicuous disparity" between the fair market value of the property or services and the amount given or received for it; both provisions use permissive language, suggesting that the court has the discretion to grant relief that extends beyond the factors specifically enumerated in the provision itself; and both provisions make remedies available against a party who is privy to the transfer, in addition to the immediate parties.

Standard Trustco Ltd. (Trustee of) v. Standard Trust Co.
(1995), 26 OR (3d) 1 (CA)

WEILER JA (Abella JA concurring): Trustco made a capital injection worth $25 million into STC, a related company, and received subordinated debt and common shares of STC in exchange. Within one year of this transaction Trustco went bankrupt. Non-arm's length dealings between related companies are deemed to be reviewable under ss. 3 and 4 of the *Bankruptcy Act*, RSC 1985, c. B-3 (now the *Bankruptcy and Insolvency Act*, as renamed by SC 1992, c. 27, s. 2). Pursuant to s. 100(1) of the Act, the court "may" inquire into the transaction at the request of the trustee. If the inquiry proceeds and a "conspicuous" difference is revealed between the amount STC received and the fair market value of the property STC gave, then, under s. 100(2), the court "may" order STC to make up the difference. According to s. 100(3), the values on which the court makes a decision as to whether the transaction took place at fair market value "shall" be the values stated by the trustee in bankruptcy unless other values are proven.

The issue in this appeal is whether Farley J, the motions judge, correctly interpreted s. 100, and more particularly, s. 100(2) of the Act, when he declared that if there was a conspicuous difference in the fair market value received by Trustco, the trustee was entitled to judgment for the difference against STC and that there was no discretion to refuse to make the order.

· · ·

Should an inquiry be conducted under s. 100(1)?

I have had the benefit of reading the reasons of Doherty JA. He is of the opinion that the word "may" in s. 100(1) does give the court a discretion whether to conduct an inquiry or not, and that Farley J, the motions judge, recognized that he had such a discretion. In deciding whether the discretion should be exercised, Doherty JA agrees with Farley J that the intention with which the transaction was done and the legality of the transaction were irrelevant considerations. Rather, Doherty JA would recognize a discretion not to allow the action to proceed under s. 100(1) only if (a) the creditors of Trustco had given their informed consent to the transaction before it occurred, (b) if the trustee had been guilty of laches in pursuing a remedy against STC, or (c) if to allow the inquiry to proceed would be an abuse of the court's process.

I agree with Doherty JA's conclusion that the exercise of discretion under s. 100(1) would include equitable considerations. While I see no need to say that only some equitable considerations may be considered and not others, I am of the opinion that s. 100(1) is not the main focus of this appeal. STC's motion for dismissal of the proceeding commenced against it by PW was denied. STC was also denied leave to appeal to the Divisional Court from that interlocutory decision. This court's interpretation of s. 100(1) cannot, therefore, result in the inquiry being stopped. If I am wrong in this conclusion I would nevertheless conclude that the court's discretion to allow the inquiry to go ahead under s. 100(1) was properly exercised in this case. STC and the intervenor CDIC take the position that because a regulatory government body was involved in the transaction it should be exempt from review; I do not agree.

· · ·

Where the conditions of s. 100(2) have been satisfied, does the court have a discretion as to whether to grant judgment?

· · ·

By virtue of s. 3(1) of the *Interpretation Act*, RSC 1985, c. I-21, the expression "may" is to be construed as permissive unless a contrary intention appears. I do not disagree with the proposition that in certain circumstances the word "may" in a statute must be taken to mean "shall." But where, as here, the word "may" as well as the word "shall" are used within s. 100 the presumption that "may" is intended to be discretionary is strengthened: *Smith & Rhuland Ltd. v. R.*, [1953] 2 SCR 95 at p. 97, [1953] 3 DLR 690 at p. 692. In addition, consistency of expression requires that the same words used within a section be given the same meaning: R. Sullivan, *Driedger on the Construction of Statutes*, 3rd ed. (Markham: Butterworths, 1994) at p. 163. Once equitable considerations are found to be relevant with respect to s. 100(1), as Doherty JA has found, consistency of interpretation requires, in my opinion, that equitable considerations be taken into account under s. 100(2).

· · ·

When a contextual approach is adopted it is apparent that although the conditions of the section have been satisfied the court is not obliged to grant judgment. The court has a residual discretion to exercise. The contextual approach indicates that the good faith of the parties, the intention with which the transaction took place, and whether fair value was given and received in the transaction are important considerations as to whether that discretion should be exercised.

· · ·

I agree that generally the purpose underlying s. 100 is a recognition that when normal market forces do not operate, there is a loss to the bankrupt company and, as a result, the interests of creditors suffer. Here, however, Trustco's lenders knew in advance that Trustco's original $74 million investment in STC was an investment in an industry which is regulated in the public interest for the protection of depositors and that normal market forces are not allowed to operate without regard to that interest. They were also aware that Trustco's $25 million injection of capital into STC at the behest of the Regulator could result in their interests being enhanced if Trustco's already substantial investment in STC was to be saved. ...

DOHERTY JA (dissenting): ... The appellants have not argued that STC was not a beneficiary of the transaction. The appellants rely on the bona fides of the transaction and the regulatory context in which it took place in submitting that PW should be denied relief under s. 100(2), even if it was determined that Trustco received conspicuously less than fair market value in return for the $25 million advanced to STC. With respect to the bona fides of the transaction, the appellants submit that had Trustco not complied with the regulators' demand for an additional $25 million in regulatory capital, the regulators would have immediately terminated the operation of STC. Had that occurred, Trustco's very substantial investment in STC ($73,800,000) would have been lost. By injecting the additional $25 million, Trustco protected its existing investment and thereby served the interests of its shareholders and creditors. The appellants point out that the injection did not contravene any agreements with existing creditors and was accurately disclosed to the creditors immediately after it was made.

The appellants' submissions seem well-founded on the facts. However, in my view, they are relevant only to the valuation of the consideration received by Trustco. The submissions amount to an assertion that when the entirety of the circumstances are considered, Trustco in fact received fair market value for the $25 million it advanced to STC. At the trial of the issue directed by Farley J, STC can adduce evidence of the value received by Trustco. It may attempt to show that the value included not only the value of the property received from STC, but also the value inherent in the opportunity to salvage Trustco's existing large investment in STC. If STC advances this claim, the trial judge will decide, based on the evidence, what value, if any, should be given to this opportunity to salvage Trustco's investment. If, however, the trial judge concludes, after considering all aspects of the valuation question, that Trustco in fact received conspicuously less than fair market value, I cannot read s. 100(2) as allowing the court to refuse the remedy because Trustco entered into the transaction believing that it got good value and was acting in the best interests of its shareholders and creditors. To so read s. 100(2) would be to replace fair market evaluation with one based on the bankrupt's perception of the commercial efficacy of the transaction.

With respect to the regulatory context in which the transaction occurred, the appellants contend that the transaction was part of a solution devised by Trustco and the regulators in an attempt to preserve STC and protect the members of the public who had placed deposits with STC. The appellants argued that broader policy concerns than those which usually dictate commercial transactions were at play in this case, and must be acknowledged when deciding whether to "undo" the transaction by means of a s. 100(2) order. I agree with Farley J at pp. 39-40 that absent statutory protection, transactions otherwise captured by s. 100(2) are not placed beyond the reach of that section because they were initiated by regulatory agencies with a view to fulfilling their obligation to protect the investing public. As with the argument based on the bona fides of the transaction, I regard this submission as relevant to the valuation exercise required by s. 100(2). It may be that the regulatory context will impact on the assessment of the value received by Trustco. This, too, is a matter to be decided by the trial judge on the basis of the evidence adduced by the parties.

In summary, while I agree with the appellants' submission that s. 100(1) and (2) contain a discretionary component and that the word "may" should be read as permissive, I cannot agree that the discretion found in either section could assist STC.

Appeal allowed.

Peoples Department Stores Inc. (Trustee of) v. Wise
[2004] 3 SCR 461, 2004 SCC 68

[The facts are set out in a second extract from the case that appears in Chapter 10, Section III. Peoples' trustee sued the Wise brothers, alleging breach of their duties as directors to Peoples' creditors under s. 122(1) of the *Canada Business Corporation Act*. This is the aspect of the case dealt with in Chapter 10. In the alternative, the trustee claimed that the Wise brothers were privy to transactions in which Peoples' assets had been transferred to Wise for conspicuously less than fair market value within the meaning of BIA s. 100. The following extract deals with this aspect of the case.]

MAJOR and DESCHAMPS JJ:

. . .

[79] The trustee also claimed against the Wise brothers under s. 100 of the BIA. ...

[80] The provision has two principal elements. First, subs. (1) requires the transaction to have been conducted within the year preceding the date of bankruptcy. Second, subs. (2) requires that the consideration given or received by the bankrupt be "conspicuously greater or less" than the fair market value of the property concerned.

[81] The word "may" is found in both ss. 100(1) and 100(2) of the BIA with respect to the jurisdiction of the court. In *Standard Trustco Ltd. (Trustee of) v. Standard Trust Co.* (1995), 26 OR (3d) 1, a majority of the Ontario Court of Appeal held that, even if the necessary preconditions are present, the exercise of jurisdiction under s. 100(1) to inquire into the transaction, and under s. 100(2) to grant judgment, is discretionary. Equitable principles guide the exercise of discretion. We agree.

[82] Referring to s. 100(2) of the BIA, in *Standard Trustco, supra*, at p. 23, Weiler JA explained that:

> When a contextual approach is adopted it is apparent that although the conditions of the section have been satisfied the court is not obliged to grant judgment. The court has a residual discretion to exercise. The contextual approach indicates that the good faith of the parties, the intention with which the transaction took place, and whether fair value was given and received in the transaction are important considerations as to whether that discretion should be exercised.

We agree with Weiler JA and adopt her position; however, this appeal does not turn on the discretion to ultimately impose liability. In our view, the Court of Appeal did not interfere with the trial judge's exercise of discretion in reviewing the facts and finding a palpable and overriding error.

[83] Within the year preceding the date of bankruptcy, Peoples had transferred inventory to Wise for which the trustee claimed Peoples had not received fair market value in consideration. The relevant transactions involved, for the most part, transfers completed in anticipation of the busy holiday season. Given the non-arm's length relationship between Wise and its wholly-owned subsidiary Peoples, there is no question that these inventory transfers could have constituted reviewable transactions.

[84] We share the view of the Court of Appeal that it is not only the final transfers that should be considered. In fairness, the inventory transactions should be considered

over the entire period from February to December 1994, which was the period when the new policy was in effect.

[85] In *Skalbania (Trustee of) v. Wedgewood Village Estates Ltd.* (1989), 37 BCLR (2d) 88 (CA), the test for determining whether the difference in consideration is "conspicuously greater or less" was held to be not whether it is conspicuous to the parties at the time of the transaction, but whether it is conspicuous to the court having regard to all the relevant factors. This is a sound approach. In that case, a difference of $1.18 million between fair market value and the consideration received by the bankrupt was seen as conspicuous, where the fair market value was $6.6 million, leaving a discrepancy of more than 17 percent. While there is no particular percentage that definitively sets the threshold for a conspicuous difference, the percentage difference is a factor.

[86] As for the factors that would be relevant to this determination, the court might consider, *inter alia*: evidence of the margin of error in valuing the types of assets in question; any appraisals made of the assets in question and evidence of the parties' honestly held beliefs regarding the value of the assets in question; and other circumstances adduced in evidence by the parties to explain the difference between the consideration received and fair market value: see L.W. Houlden and G.B. Morawetz, *Bankruptcy and Insolvency Law of Canada* (3rd ed. (loose-leaf)), vol. 2, at p. 4-114.1.

[87] Over the lifespan of the new policy, Peoples transferred to Wise inventory valued at $71.54 million. As of the date of bankruptcy, it had received $59.50 million in property or money from Wise. As explained earlier, the trial judge adjusted the outstanding difference down to a balance of $4.44 million after taking into account, *inter alia*, the reallocation of general and administrative expenses, and adjustments necessitated by imported inventory transferred from Wise to Peoples. Neither party disputed these figures before this Court. We agree with the Court of Appeal's observation that these findings directly conflict with the trial judge's assertion that Peoples had received no consideration for the inventory transfers on the basis that the outstanding accounts were "neither collected nor collectible" from Wise. Like Pelletier JA, we conclude that the trial judge's finding in this regard was a palpable and overriding error, and we adopt the view of the Court of Appeal.

[88] We are not satisfied that, with regard to all the circumstances of this case, a disparity of slightly more than 6 percent between fair market value and the consideration received constitutes a "conspicuous" difference within the meaning of s. 100(2) of the BIA. Accordingly, we hold that the trustee's claim under the BIA also fails.

[89] In addition to permitting the court to give judgment against the other party to the transaction, s. 100(2) of the BIA also permits it to give judgment against someone who was not a party but was "privy" to the transaction. Given our finding that the consideration for the impugned transactions was not "conspicuously less" than fair market value, there is no need to consider whether the Wise brothers would have been "privy" to the transaction for the purpose of holding them liable under s. 100(2). Nonetheless, the disagreement between the trial judge and the Court of Appeal on the interpretation of "privy" in s. 100(2) of the BIA warrants the following observations.

[90] The trial judge in this appeal had little difficulty finding that the Wise brothers were privy to the transaction within the meaning of s. 100(2). Pelletier JA, however, preferred a narrow construction in finding that the Wise brothers were not privy to the transactions. He held, at para. 135 QL, that:

[TRANSLATION]... [T]he legislator wanted to provide for the case in which a person other than the co-contracting party of the bankrupt actually received all or part of the benefit resulting from the lack of equality between the respective considerations.

To support this direct benefit requirement, Pelletier JA also referred to the French version which uses the term *ayant intérêt*. While he conceded that the respondent brothers received an indirect benefit from the inventory transfers as shareholders of Wise, Pelletier JA found this too remote to be considered "privy" to the transactions (paras. 139-40 QL).

[91] The primary purpose of s. 100 of the BIA is to reverse the effects of a transaction that stripped value from the estate of a bankrupt person. It makes sense to adopt a more inclusive understanding of the word "privy" to prevent someone who might receive indirect benefits to the detriment of a bankrupt's unsatisfied creditors from frustrating the provision's remedial purpose. The word "privy" should be given a broad reading to include those who benefit directly or indirectly from and have knowledge of a transaction occurring for less than fair market value. In our opinion, this rationale is particularly apt when those who benefit are the controlling minds behind the transaction.

[92] A finding that a person was "privy" to a reviewable transaction does not of course necessarily mean that the court will exercise its discretion to make a remedial order against that person. For liability to be imposed, it must be established that the transaction occurred: (a) within the past year; (b) for consideration conspicuously greater or less than fair market value; (c) with the person's knowledge; and (d) in a way that directly or indirectly benefited the person. In addition, after having considered the context and all the above factors, the judge must conclude that the case is a proper one for holding the person liable. In light of these conditions and of the discretion exercised by the judge, we find that a broad reading of "privy" is appropriate.

NOTES

1. *Royal Bank of Canada v. North American Life Assurance Co.*, [1996] 1 SCR 325 concerned the interaction between the settlements provision in BIA s. 91 and the exempt property provision in s. 67(1)(b). Dr. Ramgotra had savings in two Registered Retirement Savings Plans (RRSPs). In June 1990, he transferred his savings from the RRSPs into a Registered Retirement Income Fund (RRIF). The RRIF was in the form of a life insurance annuity and Dr. Ramgotra named his wife as the beneficiary. Dr. Ramgotra was solvent at the time and his purpose was not to defeat creditors. He took out the RRIF at the suggestion of his investment adviser. A few months later, Dr. Ramgotra's financial position took a turn for the worse and in February 1992 he went into bankruptcy. His trustee in bankruptcy brought an action claiming the RRIF for the estate.

Section 158(2) of the *Saskatchewan Insurance Act*, RSS 1978, c. S-26 provides that a life insurance policy is exempt from seizure if the insured designates his spouse as the beneficiary. BIA s. 67(1)(b) provides that property of the debtor divisible among creditors does not include property that is exempt from seizure under provincial law. The debtor argued on this basis that the RRIF was not property divisible among creditors. The trustee argued that Ramgotra's beneficiary designation in his wife's favour was a settlement; s. 91(2) avoided the beneficiary designation; and without the beneficiary designation, the RRIF was not exempt from seizure. Section 91(2) provided that any settlement of property made within the period beginning on the day that is five years before the date of the initial bankruptcy event in respect of the settlor and ending on the date that the settlor became bankrupt, both dates included, "is void against the trustee if the trustee can prove that the settlor was, at the time of making the settlement, unable to pay all [the settlor's] debts without the aid of the property comprised in the settlement *or that the interest of the settlor in the property did not pass on the execution thereof*" (emphasis added).

The leading judgment in the Supreme Court was delivered by Gonthier J. He held that the beneficiary designation was a settlement and that it was caught by the closing words of s. 91(2). Consequently, the beneficiary designation was void under BIA s. 91(2) and so the RRIF policy passed to Dr. Ramgotra's trustee in bankruptcy under s. 71(2) (now s. 71). However, by virtue of BIA s. 67(1)(b) read in conjunction with the *Saskatchewan Insurance Act*, the policy was exempt property and thus not property divisible among creditors. Therefore, the trustee held the policy on trust for Dr. Ramgotra and had to give it back.

2. According to Gonthier J, the BIA divides the trustee's functions into two stages: (a) the "property-passing" stage; and (b) the "estate administration" stage. This distinction was central to his judgment because it allowed him to avoid the apparent conflict between ss. 67(1)(b) and 91. Gonthier J said there was no conflict because the two provisions belonged to different stages of the process: s. 91 went to the property-passing stage, whereas s. 67(1)(b) went to the estate-administration stage. This reasoning is open to question on a number of grounds. In the first place, if the beneficiary designation was void, how could the RRIF still qualify as exempt property? The court's answer was that if s. 91(2) applies, the settlement is "void against the trustee," but only against the trustee. It is not void against "the claims of creditors under the provincial legislation which s. 67(1)(b) incorporates." This is a strained construction of s. 91(2), which overlooks the fact that the trustee is the creditors' representative. Second, on Gonthier J's reasoning, property may vest in the trustee under s. 71, but still not be property divisible among creditors. This involves reading s. 71 in isolation from s. 67. There is no textual or historical basis for this. The better view is that if property is not divisible among creditors under s. 67, then it does not vest in the trustee under s. 71. Correspondingly, if property vests in the trustee pursuant to s. 71, it is property divisible among creditors. For a critical analysis of the *Royal Bank* case ("*Ramgotra*"), see: Lisa H. Kerbel Caplan, "Prebankruptcy Settlements: Royal Bank of Canada v. North American Life Assurance Company and Balvir Singh Ramgotra" (1996), 27 *CBLJ* 458. The 2007 amendments have repealed s. 91 and replaced it with a new s. 96. Consequently, the parts of the case that deal specifically with s. 91 are no longer relevant. On the other hand, Gonthier J's observations about the relationship between the "property-passing" provisions of the BIA and the "estate administration provisions" apply, *mutatis mutandis*, to the new s. 96.

3. The provincial courts have taken up Gonthier J's invitation in *Ramgotra* to give the fraudulent conveyance laws a "broad and liberal interpretation": see, for example, *Re Sykes* (1998), 156 DLR (4th) 105 (BCCA), where the court held that an RRSP beneficiary designation was a "disposition of property" within the meaning of the BC *Fraudulent Conveyance Act*, s. 1. Would new BIA s. 96 catch a beneficiary designation in an insurance policy? The courts may take the view that if a beneficiary designation is a "disposition of property" for the purposes of the provincial fraudulent conveyance laws then, likewise, it is a "transfer" for the purposes of BIA s. 96. Note, though, that new s. 96 would not have applied in

Ramgotra's case. Ramgotra and his wife were not at arm's length and so the five-year review period would apply. However, the trustee would have to show either that Ramgotra was insolvent at the time of the transfer (which he was not) or that he intended to defeat creditors (which he did not).

4. The reason for Gonthier J's strained construction in *Ramgotra* is that he was trying to get to what was arguably the right policy result. If he had applied s. 91(2) literally, Dr. Ramgotra would have lost his RRIF. This might have been a justifiable outcome if Dr. Ramgotra had been trying to defeat his creditors, but he wasn't: he was solvent at the time he bought the RRIF and his purpose was simply to improve his retirement prospects. In these circumstances, taking away his RRIF would have been contrary to the policy of debtor rehabilitation that lies behind the exempt-property provisions. In summary, the case exposes the tension between the debtor-rehabilitation goal of the bankruptcy laws, on the one hand, and the goals of maximizing the returns to creditors and preventing debtor fraud, on the other. The 2007 amendments introduce a new s. 67(1)(b.3), which provides that property in an RRSP or RRIF is exempt from seizure, with the exception of contributions made in the 12 months preceding the bankruptcy. Does this provision, read in conjunction with the new s. 96, satisfactorily balance the competing goals? See Chapter 11 for further discussion.

5. Consider the following case:

Debtor lives in Alberta. He is on the verge of bankruptcy. His main asset is a share portfolio valued at $40,000. Debtor and his family live in a rented apartment. Debtor sells the shares and uses the sale proceeds to buy a mobile home. Debtor and his family move out of their rented apartment and into the mobile home. Three months later, Debtor makes an assignment into bankruptcy. Can the trustee claim the mobile home? (Note that the *Civil Enforcement Act*, RSA 1994, s. 171 exempts from execution or seizure a debtor's principal place of residence to the value of $40,000, which includes a mobile home if actually lived in.)

The case involves the exchange of non-exempt property (the shares) for exempt property (the mobile home). Prior to the 2007 amendments, this kind of transaction was often described as a "self-settlement." In *Ramgotra*, Gonthier J, overruling provincial decisions to the contrary, held that a self-settlement is not a "settlement" for the purposes of BIA s. 91 because for a settlement there must be a transfer of property from one person to another. For similar reasons, a self-settlement would not be open to attack under the provincial fraudulent conveyance laws or the new transfers at undervalue provision in BIA s. 96. What is there to stop a debtor from defeating creditors by taking advantage of this loophole? New BIA s. 69(1)(b.3) addresses this concern in the specific context of RRSPs and RRIFs, but the 2007 amendments make no attempt to tackle the issue more generally.

IV. THE BIA PREFERENCE PROVISIONS

Broadly speaking, a preference is a payment of money or transfer of property made by a debtor to a creditor on the eve of the debtor's bankruptcy that is for a larger amount than the creditor would recover in a bankruptcy distribution. Here are three simple examples:

a. Fred has five unsecured creditors, A, B, C, D, and Wilma. A, B, C, and D are all trade creditors. Wilma is Fred's wife. Each of the five debts is for $100. Fred's total assets are $200. He pays Wilma her $100 and a week later goes into bankruptcy. If Fred had not paid Wilma, there would have been $200 for distribution among A, B, C, D, and Wilma. The basic bankruptcy distribution rule is pro rata, so that each would have recovered $40. Fred's payment to Wilma means there is now only $100 for distribution among A, B, C, and D. They each get $25 on a pro rata basis, but Wilma has $100.

b. Fred is the director and controlling shareholder of Flintstone Enterprises Limited (FEL). FEL has five unsecured creditors, A, B, C, D, and Rubble Bank. A, B, C, and D are all trade creditors; Rubble Bank is FEL's general lender. FEL owes all five creditors $100 each. Fred has given a personal guarantee in support of FEL's debt to Rubble Bank. FEL's total assets are $200. Fred causes FEL to pay Rubble Bank its $100. A week later, FEL goes into bankruptcy. The effect on A, B, C, and D of the payment to Rubble is the same as in example a.

c. Fred runs a retail store specializing in the sale of dinosaur parts. He has five unsecured creditors, A, B, C, D, and Barney. He owes them each $100. His total assets are $200. Barney is Fred's main inventory supplier. Barney threatens to cancel further deliveries until Fred pays him. Fred pays Barney because he needs the inventory to stay in business. Unfortunately, the business fails anyway, and, two weeks later, Fred goes into bankruptcy.

BIA s. 95 addresses cases like these. Prior to the 2007 amendments, s. 95 provided that the trustee in bankruptcy could avoid the transaction if it was made within 3 months of the debtor's bankruptcy (or 12 months if the parties were related to one another), but the trustee had to prove the debtor intended to prefer the creditor. However, if the transaction had the effect of giving a preference, the section presumed the debtor's intention to prefer, in the absence of proof to the contrary, and it went on to specify that evidence of pressure was not admissible to support the transaction. The thinking behind the extended review period for related-party transactions was that, if the parties are related to one another, the preferred creditor is more likely to have inside knowledge of the debtor's financial problems and this means the parties might time the payment to avoid the standard review period: see, for example, the *Benallack* case, extracted below.

The purpose of the presumption was to reduce the burden on the trustee and make it easier for her to win cases. Why was evidence of pressure not admissible? The purpose was to shore up the presumption. Before the pressure exception was enacted, all the preferred creditor had to do was show that it had given the debtor some sort of ultimatum. Then there was a fair chance the court would say that the debtor's motive was not to prefer the creditor, but simply to get the creditor off his back. The pressure exception was meant to foreclose this line of argument. However, the courts have reintroduced the doctrine of pressure by the back door. They have done this by inventing a so-called diligent-creditor defence. The thinking is that a creditor should not be penalized just because its collection methods are more efficient than its competitors. Unfortunately, there is no easy way of telling on which side of the line a creditor's conduct will fall. For instance, in example c, above, some courts might say that Barney's threat to cancel further deliveries is just Barney being diligent and so he can rely on the threat to rebut the presumption.

Other courts might say it is pressure and so the evidence is inadmissible. Another tack Barney might take is to argue that Fred's motivation was not to prefer Barney, but simply to make sure Barney would keep supplying him so that he could stay in business: see *Hapco Farms* and *St. Anne Nackawic*, both extracted below. This line of cases reveals two competing policy considerations: (1) the importance of facilitating transactions that may improve the return to creditors in the debtor's bankruptcy (as in *St. Anne Nackawic*) or, better still, help the debtor trade out of its difficulties and avoid bankruptcy altogether; and (2) the importance of preventing one creditor from obtaining an advantage over the others.

The 2007 amendments have made some changes to s. 95. The new provision distinguishes between arm's-length and non-arm's-length transactions. In the case of an arm's-length transaction, the law is the same as before (see above). In particular, the trustee must prove the debtor's intention to prefer, subject to the presumption. However, in the case of a non-arm's-length transaction, the trustee only needs to prove that the transaction has the effect of giving the creditor a preference. In other words, in the case of a non-arm's-length transaction, if the transaction has the effect of giving the creditor a preference, there is, so to speak, an irrebuttable presumption that the debtor intended to prefer the creditor. Example c, above, illustrates the practical implications of this reform. The transaction between Fred and Barney clearly has the effect of giving Barney a preference. Therefore, if Fred and Barney are at arm's length, there is a presumption that Fred intended to prefer Barney, but Barney can rebut the presumption by leading evidence of the kind described above. However, if Fred and Barney are not at arm's length, Barney does not have a leg to stand on. What is the justification for discriminating in this way between arm's-length and non-arm's-length transactions? A possible explanation is that, if the parties are not at arm's length, the debtor is more likely to have intended a preference. However, this consideration supports at most a rebuttable presumption. Why should the creditor not be free to prove that, despite the parties' relationship, the transaction was an innocent one? In the United States, the debtor's intention to prefer is irrelevant; if the trustee can show that the transaction has the effect of giving the creditor a preference, then, subject to various "safe-harbour provisions," she can recover the payment: *Bankruptcy Code*, s. 547. The 2007 amendments could be seen as a step toward the US position, but, if that is the case, why retain the requirement for proof of intention at all?

The explanation for the resistance to an across-the-board effects-based test is concern among stakeholders, most notably the Insolvency Institute of Canada, that an effects-based test would make it too easy for the trustee to set payments aside. In other words, the concern is with finality of transactions: if creditors cannot be sure of keeping the debtor's repayments, this increases the risks of lending and may affect the cost and availability of credit. On the other hand, if the overriding concern is really with the finality of transactions, then it needs to be asked whether the preference provisions should be repealed altogether: see Schwartz, "A Normative Theory of Business Bankruptcy," below.

There are three competing versions of the need for anti-preference laws: debtor deterrence, creditor deterrence, and equal sharing. The debtor deterrence rationale can be traced back to Lord Coke's statement in *The Case of Bankrupts* (1584), 76 ER 441, at 473: "there ought to be an equal distribution … ; [for] if, after the debtor becomes bankrupt, he may prefer a [creditor] and defeat and defraud many other poor men of their true debts, it would be unequal and unconscionable, and a defect in the law." In other words, the debtor should not play favourites among creditors in defiance of the bankruptcy laws: paying out friends, relatives, and business connections ahead of other creditors is wrong because, given the debtor's looming bankruptcy, it deprives "other poor men of their true debts." Another way of making the same point is to say that the debtor may not set herself up as the lawgiver in a bankruptcy distribution. This is how Lord Mansfield expressed the idea in *Alderson v. Temple* (1768), 96 ER 384, two hundred or so years later.

The creditor-deterrence rationale derives from Thomas Jackson, *The Logic and Limits of Bankruptcy Law* (Cambridge, MA: Harvard University Press, 1986), Chapter 6. The basic idea is that we do not want creditors jumping the queue on the eve of the debtor's bankruptcy because this might cause a scramble for payment, leaving only the "tag ends and remnants" of the debtor's assets for distribution in the bankruptcy proceedings. In other words, preferential payments are inconsistent with the basic purpose of the bankruptcy laws. A related consideration is that if preferences were allowed, every creditor would want to monitor every other creditor as well as the debtor herself to make sure they were not left behind in any eve-of-bankruptcy collection race. The preference laws avoid these monitoring costs.

According to the equal-sharing rationale, the purpose of the preference provisions is to make sure that all creditors are treated equally in bankruptcy. Statements like this should not be taken literally, however, given the large number of exceptions to the *pari passu* principle. In real life, creditors are not treated equally in bankruptcy. For example, secured creditors get paid ahead of unsecured creditors, and some classes of unsecured creditor are entitled to priority payment ahead of others—for example, employees and landlords.

A better statement of the equal-sharing rationale might be to say that creditors should share in accordance with the overall scheme of distribution the bankruptcy laws provide for. The key feature of the equal-sharing rationale is that it focuses on the outcome of the bankruptcy distribution, not on the debtor's supposed fraud in giving the preference or on the creditor's supposed fraud in receiving it. For a fuller discussion of the policies underlying the preference laws, see Anthony Duggan and Thomas G.W. Telfer, "Voidable Preferences," in Stephanie Ben-Ishai and Anthony Duggan, eds., *Canadian Bankruptcy and Insolvency Law: Bill C-55, Statute c. 47 and Beyond* (Toronto: LexisNexis, 2007), Chapter 6.

The choice between these competing explanations is important, because it affects the shape of the legislation and, therefore, case outcomes. For example, if we conceive of preferential transactions as fraudulent conduct on the debtor's part, it makes sense to limit the preference provisions by requiring proof of the debtor's intention to prefer. On the other hand, if we view preferences as strategic behaviour on the creditor's part, the more appropriate response is to limit the provisions by requiring proof of the creditor's state of mind (as pre-1978 US bankruptcy law did). Yet again, if our primary objective is to achieve some sort of equality between creditors in the bankruptcy distribution, the debtor's state of mind and the creditor's state of mind are both irrelevant and a strict liability rule should apply. Which of these three objectives did the drafting of the pre-2007 version of BIA s. 95 most closely reflect? What is the policy underlying the new s. 95? The preference provision in s. 547 of the US *Bankruptcy Code* imposes a strict liability rule. Does this reflect a commitment to the equal-sharing rationale? The preference provisions in the provincial assignments and preferences statutes, which apply in tandem with BIA s. 95 (see Section V), require proof of *concurrent* intention: see *Benallack*, below. Can this limitation be justified in terms of any of the theories discussed above? In example a, above, it seems Fred intended to give Wilma a preference and, similarly, Wilma was likely conscious of receiving one. On this footing, Fred's payment to Wilma would be a preferential one under any of the preference-law models identified above. In example b, it seems that Fred intended to prefer Rubble Bank, but it is at least possible that Rubble Bank was unaware of the payment's preferential effect. On this footing, the payment is a potentially preferential one under the pre- and post-2007 versions of BIA s. 95, as well as post-1978 US bankruptcy law, but not under the provincial laws or pre-1978 United States bankruptcy law. In example c, Fred's immediate reason for paying Barney may have been to guarantee future supplies rather than to prefer Barney (but see *Hapco*, below). On this footing, the payment is not a preference under the pre-2007 version of BIA s. 95 or under the provincial preference laws, it may be a preference under the post-2007 version if Fred and Barney are not at arm's length, and it may or may not be a preference under s. 547 of the US *Bankruptcy Code*, depending on whether it falls within the "ordinary-course-of-business" safe harbour in s. 547(c)(2). Which of these sets of outcomes do you prefer?

Alan Schwartz, "A Normative Theory of Business Bankruptcy"
(2005), 91 *Virginia Law Review* 1199, at 1224-30 (footnotes omitted)

The preference sections of the Code ... create incentives for the trustee to redistribute wealth from some creditors—those that received preferences—to other creditors—those that did not. These redistributions ... come at positive cost, and thus reduce the net value of the bankrupt estate. The Code permits the trustee to recover payments to a creditor made in the ninety days before bankruptcy unless (a) the creditor made a contemporaneous transfer to the debtor; or (b) the payment was made in the ordinary course of the debtor's business. Payments in the former category do not reduce the value of the firm because cash out is replaced with cash or goods in. The exception for payments in category (b) has a similar justification. Shipments in the ordinary course, over time, will offset payments in the ordinary course; the typical transaction sequence thus will not deplete the firm's value. The trustee's power otherwise to avoid preferences can be partly restricted by private agreement. A firm may contract out of the law by issuing security. An eve-of-bankruptcy payment to a secured creditor is not a preference: The creditor has a property right in the firm's assets, and it is entitled to realize that right in whatever way the security agreement permits.

There are two traditional justifications for preventing distressed firms from preferring some general creditors over others: the prohibition is *ex post* efficient, and the prohibition treats all general creditors equally. This part shows the following: (a) the preference law is *ex post* inefficient; (b) a mandatory rule prohibiting the payment of preferences is *ex ante* inefficient; rather, the preference law should be a default; and (c) the pursuit of *ex post* equality among general creditors is without justification.

The *ex post* efficiency case for prohibiting preferences is thought to follow from the justification for bankruptcy law itself. A firm's survival prospects may be fatally worsened by last minute depletions of its capital. Some such firms may be only financially distressed, however, and so should be continued. Prohibiting preferences thus advances the goal of saving viable firms.

A distressed firm would pay preferences, in the traditional theory, either because it may yield to creditor pressure or because the firm's principals may be in league with powerful creditors. The former reason is unpersuasive because creditors cannot force a distressed firm to pay preferences. To be sure, in the absence of a bankruptcy filing, creditors will attach property pursuant to judicial orders. The debtor, however, need not make voluntary payments. Creditors can threaten attachment in order to force the debtor to pay, but the debtor can respond by credibly threatening to file, which would stay all attachments. Thus, if the preference law were repealed, distressed firms would pay preferences because they wanted to, not because they had to.

The question when a distressed firm would want to prefer some creditors has never been seriously explored. If no preference law existed, a distressed firm would pay preferences only if it expected to be liquidated. To see why, recall that the pro rata bankruptcy distribution rule requires each general creditor to receive a sum that equals the firm's ratio of total value to total debt times the creditor's unpaid debt. A distressed firm that pays one creditor more than this must pay at least one other creditor less. When would a distressed firm default in this asymmetric way? Consider first a firm that believes its continuation value to exceed its liquidation value (that is, that it is liquidity-constrained but only financially distressed). The firm could either file for bankruptcy or attempt to settle privately with its creditors. Suppose that the firm preferred to settle. To prefer a creditor is to pay it more than its pro rata bankruptcy share. Nonpreferred creditors, however, would reject a work-out offer that offered them less than their pro rata bankruptcy payoffs. Instead, these creditors would bring suit and attempt to attach the distressed firm's assets. These efforts would cause the firm to file. From the firm's point of view, then, the goals of settling privately and paying preferences are inconsistent. Rather, a firm that wants to settle privately would offer each creditor its pro rata share plus a portion of the cost savings from avoiding bankruptcy. In other words, the pro rata rule precludes a firm interested in survival from paying today what are de-fined as preferences. Consequently, a separate prohibition against preferences does not materially increase a financially distressed firm's commitment to the pro rata rule.

Now consider a firm that believes its liquidation value to exceed its continuation value. This debtor, in its capacity as a firm, is indifferent as to how its assets are divided because the firm will disappear with certainty. It has no incentive to adhere to any rule of distribution. The firm's principals, in their individual capacities, however, may not be indifferent as to whom the firm pays. Rather, the principals may cause the firm to pay particular creditors either to ensure good will for the principals, in consequence of a personal relationship, or to avoid liability exposure if a principal has guaranteed the firm's debt. The trustee's power to recover preferences thus is exercised *only on behalf of the general creditors of economically failing firms*. Redistributing the assets of a failed firm among its general creditors amounts to redecorating the Titanic's salon. Because redecoration is costly, enforcing the preference prohibition diminishes the value of the bankrupt estate. The preference law is actually *ex post* inefficient.

Turning to *ex ante* efficiency, … legal rules which reduce the value of distressed firms raise interest rates. Thus, parties would wish to avoid the rules if possible. This reasoning implies that the parties' current ability to contract out of the preference law by giving security should be expanded. It is a more difficult question whether the default rule should permit distressed firms to pay whomever they choose, so that firms would have to contract into the preference law, or whether current law should be the default, so that firms would have to contract out. It is worth stressing, however, that the question regarding what the default should be is the ground on which preference law should be discussed. Bankruptcy reasons cannot justify the Code's current mandatory rule.

A preliminary consideration of the default question should begin with a possible strategy of creditors who are unsure, *ex ante*, whether the debtor, if economically distressed, would later prefer anyone. The equilibrium strategy is to charge interest rates that assume preferences will be paid. The interest rate increases from this "assume the worst" strategy could exceed the interest rate reductions that repeal of the preference law would produce. Hence, if repealing the preference law altogether would materially increase uncertainty, current law should be the default because parties would commonly prefer it.

Any increase in uncertainty, however, is unlikely to be of this magnitude. A creditor with the power to exact a preference often will be the firm's main bank. Primary bank lenders commonly require borrowers to keep their accounts with the bank, and the bank will set off the borrower's debt to it against the bank account. Because set-offs are not considered preferences under the Code, current creditors must price the bank's ability to get them. Creditors today thus face the uncertainty of material asymmetric defaults. In addition, which creditors will likely receive preferences seems predictable. This reasoning suggests that the better default would permit the firm to pay whomever it chooses.

Turning from efficiency to equity, the pro rata rule gives each creditor the same proportional payoff. Making the preference law a default sometimes would subvert this *ex post* equality result. That bankruptcy law should pursue equality of any type, however, is a position whose correctness is incorrectly assumed. Principles of equality are principles of entitlement. Thus, in conditions of scarcity, each actor who has an equal entitlement is entitled to an equal share. An actor can have such an entitlement either instrumentally (respecting the entitlement would advance an independent goal) or intrinsically (equality in the context at issue is a good in and of itself). Making the pro rata rule mandatory, it has been shown here, is inefficient, and no other non-equality goal has been identified that a mandatory preference law would advance. Business bankruptcy also is an inappropriate arena in which to pursue intrinsic equality claims. For example, the equal welfare doctrine holds that the disadvantaged are entitled to more pleasure because they have the capacity to experience more pleasure. Such reasoning would be misplaced if applied to business firms. There is, therefore, no good reason, in the business bankruptcy context, to temper the pursuit of efficiency with equality considerations. And to summarize the argument of this section, although the current preference law is mandatory as regards monetary payments, it should be a default that would permit insolvent firms to make irreversible payments to creditors at any time preceding the filing of a bankruptcy petition.

Blaine L. Hudson, Trustee v. Benallack
[1976] 2 SCR 168

DICKSON J:

I

This appeal raises a question of statutory construction which, one should think, would not cause difficulty, but which has indeed given rise to an abundance of conflicting legal opinion and a thoroughly obfuscated state of the law. The question is whether the words "with a view to giving such creditor a preference" contained in s. 73(1) of the *Bankruptcy Act*, RSC 1970, c. B-3, require only an intention on the part of the insolvent debtor to prefer or a concurrent intent on the part of both debtor and creditor. Sections 73 and 74 of the Act [BIA s. 95] read as follows:

. . .

Any conveyance or transfer of property or payment made by an insolvent person in favour of any creditor with a view to giving such creditor a preference over other creditors is deemed fraudulent and void as against the trustee in bankruptcy if the insolvent person becomes bankrupt within three months thereafter or within twelve months where the insolvent person and the preferred creditor are related persons.

II

In the present case the transaction impugned is the assignment on March 1, 1972, by G.S. & D. Construction Ltd. to the respondents, John Alexander Benallack and Lillian M. Benallack, of the assignor's interest, as purchaser, in an agreement for sale of certain lands in the City of Calgary. The consideration for the assignment was stated to be $15,250. At the time the assignor company was indebted to the assignees in the amount of $15,000 with interest and this indebtedness was used to offset the purchase price of the assignor's interest in the agreement of sale. All of the issued shares of G.S. & D. Construction Ltd. were owned by George Bayard Benallack and Shirley Edna May Benallack, the son and daughter-in-law respectively of the respondents. G.S. & D. Construction Ltd. made an assignment in bankruptcy on June 27, 1972, within the 12-month period mentioned in s. 74 of the Act, and the appellant Hudson was named as trustee. The learned Chambers Judge, Cullen J, made a number of findings, of which the following are of moment:

1. On March 1, 1972, the date of the assignment, the bankrupt company was an insolvent person within the meaning of the *Bankruptcy Act*;

2. The bankrupt and the respondents were related persons within the meaning of the Act and s. 74 applied;

3. The respondents received a preference over other creditors as a result of the assignment;

4. The bankrupt intended to give the respondents a preference over its other creditors.

Cullen J held against the need for concurrent intent and declared the assignment to be void as against the trustee in bankruptcy. The Appellate Division of the Supreme Court of Alberta reversed.

III

On the question whether proof of concurrent intent on the part of the debtor and creditor must be shown before the transaction can be set aside, there is, as I have indicated, a wide divergence of opinion. There are many decisions in which it has been held that concurrent intent must be proved; others in which it has been held that the Court is concerned only with the intent of the debtor; and still others in which the point has been left unresolved.

IV

Although the Courts of the country appear divided, more or less evenly, on the need for a concurrent intent before invalidating a transaction, the textbook writers and commentators do not evidence such divergence of opinion. The editors of Duncan & Honsberger, *Bankruptcy in Canada*, 3rd ed., p. 485, point out that s. 64 (now s. 73) makes no reference to the view of the creditor and that the cases in England and in the other Dominions on corresponding sections in *Bankruptcy Acts* contain no references to the view of the creditor, the view of the debtor alone being considered. The editors of Houlden & Morawetz, *Bankruptcy Law of Canada*, Cumulative Supplement, 1974, at p. 83, say:

> In view of the plain meaning of Sec. 73, the concurrent intent of both debtor and creditor is not necessary to show a fraudulent preference. The intention of the debtor alone is to be considered.

[A]nd in Bradford & Greenberg's *Canadian Bankruptcy Act*, 3rd ed., p. 163, the authors cite "an intention on the part of the debtor to prefer" as one of the two circumstances constituting a fraudulent preference. See also 2 CED (Ont. 3rd) 15-334: "The intention of the debtor alone is to be considered" and *Comment* in (1958-59), 37 CBR 153, and *Notes on Section 64 of the Bankruptcy Act* by Professor Réginald Savoie in (1967), 9 CBR (NS) 1.

V

If this Court is free to decide the issue of concurrent intent untrammelled by earlier decisions, there would seem to be at least three reasons why we should not engraft upon s. 73 of the *Bankruptcy Act* an additional concept, that of concurrent intent: first, the policy of the *Bankruptcy Act*; second, the history of the Act; third, the language of s. 73.

The object of the bankruptcy law is to ensure the division of the property of the debtor rateably among all his creditors in the event of his bankruptcy. Section 112 of the Act provides that, subject to the Act, all claims proved in the bankruptcy shall be paid *pari passu*. The Act is intended to put all creditors upon an equal footing. Generally, until a debtor is insolvent or has an act of bankruptcy in contemplation, he is quite free to deal with his property as he wills and he may prefer one creditor over another but, upon becoming insolvent, he can no longer do any act out of the ordinary course of business which has the effect of preferring a particular creditor over other creditors. If one creditor receives a preference over other creditors as a result of the debtor acting intentionally and in fraud of the law, this defeats the equality of the bankruptcy laws.

The cognizance of the creditor or its absence should be irrelevant. One can sympathize with the rationale of concurrent intent, which is the desire to protect an innocent creditor who accepts payment of a debt in good faith, but it is hard to reconcile this point of view with the language of the statute, with the history of bankruptcy legislation, and with the right of other innocent creditors to equal protection.

VII

I come now to consider the decision of this Court in *Benallack v. Bank of British North America*. The case has stood on the books for seventy years. Many judges have considered it controlling on the question of concurrent purpose as applied to s. 73(1) of the *Bankruptcy Act*. I approach the case, therefore, with the respect to which those considerations entitle it, but I must at once observe that the case was decided in 1905, some fourteen years before the enactment of the Canadian *Bankruptcy Act* in 1919. It concerned a Yukon Ordinance having to do with preferential assignments, c. 38 of the Consolidated Ordinances of the Yukon Territory 1902. To permit comparison with s. 73(1) of the *Bankruptcy Act*, I will give the Ordinance in its entirety:

> **An Ordinance Respecting Preferential Assignments.**
>
> 1. Every gift, conveyance, assignment or transfer, delivery over or payment of goods, chattels or effects or of bonds, bills, notes, securities or of shares, dividends, premiums or bonus in any bank, company or corporation made by any person at any time when he is in insolvent circumstances or is unable to pay his debts in full or knows that he is on the eve of insolvency with intent to defeat or delay or prejudice his creditors or to give to any one or more of them a preference over his other creditors or over any one or more of them or which has such effect shall as against them be utterly void.
>
> 2. Every such gift, conveyance, assignment, transfer, delivery over or payment whether made owing to pressure or partly owing to pressure or not, which has the effect of defeating, delaying or prejudicing creditors or giving one or more of them a preference shall as against the other creditors of such debtor be utterly void.
>
> 3. Nothing in this Ordinance shall apply to any deed of assignment made and executed by a debtor for the purpose of paying and satisfying rateably and proportionately and without preference or priority all the creditors of such debtor their just debts or any *bona fide* sale of goods or payment made in the ordinary course of trade or calling, to innocent purchasers or parties.

The wording of the Ordinance differs from that of s. 73(1) of the *Bankruptcy Act*; in particular s. 3 introduces concepts of *bona fides* and "innocent purchasers or parties" not found in s. 73(1).

The action in the 1905 *Benallack* case was brought to set aside several instruments, consisting of a chattel mortgage, land transfer and book debt assignments, in favour of a bank, as being void against creditors under the Ordinance. The bank was ignorant of the true financial condition of the debtor. Idington J, who delivered the unanimous judgment of a five-man Court, after referring to the cases of *Stephens v. McArthur*, and *Gibbons v. McDonald*, said:

> And if a fraudulent preference to whom is the having such a purpose to be attributed?
>
> Is it enough to shew that the assignor may have had such an intent?
>
> Must not the assignee as well as the assignor be a party to the fraudulent intent?

Such would seem to be the result of a long line of decisions upon which the commercial world has had a right to act for a long time past. And though there may not have been any express decision on the point upon this legislation in this Court the late Chief Justice, Sir William Ritchie, in *Gibbons v. McDonald*, at page 589 indicates that in his view there must be

a concurrence of intent on the one side to give and on the other to accept a preference over other creditors.

Counsel for the appellants properly conceded that the evidence here did not show knowledge on the part of the bank such as would enable us to find this concurrence of purpose.

Until the legislature obliterates the element of intent in such legislation and clearly declares that, quite independently of intent, the preferential result or effect of the transaction impeached is to govern, it will be exceedingly difficult to arrive at any other conclusion in cases of this kind. The results that might flow from such legislation ought not to be brought about without such purpose being most clearly expressed by the legislature.

The case is unsatisfactory, if I may, with respect, say so, in that none of the "long line of decisions" upon which Idington J relies is identified and no reasons are given for concluding that the intent to which the Ordinance refers must be entertained by the creditor as well as the debtor. In the later case of *Salter & Arnold, Ltd. v. Dominion Bank, supra*, as I have already mentioned, Duff J observed that whatever else may be said about the intention to give a preference envisaged by s. 31 (now s. 73) "it must be an intention entertained by the debtor." These words have been interpreted by some judges to mean that the intention with which one is concerned is only that of the debtor. I think, however, that we must give effect to the words of Duff J "whatever else may be said about it." What Duff J intended, in my opinion, was merely to leave the matter open, just as Cartwright J, as he then was, did in the penultimate paragraph of his judgment in *Velensky v. Canadian Credit Men's Trust Association Limited* (reported in 38 CBR 162 as *In re Bernard Motors Ltd.*). The paragraph in question, for some reason, was not printed in the report of the case in the Supreme Court Reports but is contained in the 38 Canadian Bankruptcy Reports, p. 167 and reads:

Before parting with the matter, I wish to observe that Bridges J suggests a doubt as to whether if he were untrammelled by authority he would hold that, on the true construction of s. 64, to render void a preference in fact it is necessary that there be an intention on the part of the creditor to be preferred as well as an intention on the part of the debtor to prefer. In *In re Blenkarn Planer Ltd.* (1958), 37 CBR 147, 26 WWR 168, 14 DLR (2d) 719, 1958 Can. Abr. 55, Ruttan J examines a number of decisions and expresses the opinion that the view of the debtor alone has to be considered. I mention this for the purpose of making it clear that in the case before us this point does not require decision and I express no opinion upon it.

I have concluded that a finding of concurrent intent is not necessary in order to set aside a payment as a fraudulent preference under s. 73 of the *Bankruptcy Act*. I do not believe that the decision of this Court in *Benallack v. Bank of British North America* is authoritative in interpreting s. 73 of the *Bankruptcy Act*. However similar may be the wording, I do not think that a phrase in a provincial or territorial Ordinance of three paragraphs dealing with preferential assignments and having a particular legislative history and jurisprudence should govern the language of a federal Act of some 213 sections dealing with bankruptcy and having an entirely different legislative history and jurisprudence.

One must recall that fraudulent preference statutes and fraudulent conveyance statutes outside of the bankruptcy laws have generally contained a section exempting from the application of the statute any assignment or payment or *bona fide* sale of goods made in the ordinary course of trade to innocent purchasers. Such saving provisions are contained in our provincial fraudulent preference statutes and in each of the cases relied on in the 1905 *Benallack* judgment a similar statute was under consideration. These statutes required consideration of the knowledge or *bona fides* of the creditor. Under the law relating to bankruptcy the rule has been different, as the English authorities cited earlier in these reasons will confirm.

I am further of the view that s. 3 of the Yukon Ordinance plays the same role in the interpretation of the Ordinance as the proviso to s. 92 of the English Act of 1869 played in *Butcher v. Stead*, requiring consideration of the knowledge and intent and privity of the creditor; but there is no counterpart of s. 3 of the Ordinance to be found in s. 73(1) of the *Bankruptcy Act*. Section 75(1) of the Act, which protects certain transactions, is the only section in which the *bona fides* of the creditor emerges. Section 75(1) is very limited in scope. It is expressly made "Subject to the foregoing provisions of this Act … with respect to the avoidance of certain settlements and preferences …" and only comes into operation when s. 73(1) does not apply. Section 75(1) in express terms calls for double intent whereas s. 73(1) does not.

Our duty is to construe the language of s. 73 of the *Bankruptcy Act* within the ambit and policy of that Act; if we go to the words of the statute we find that what is to be considered as fraudulent and void is:

> "Every conveyance … of property" (i.e., the assignment in favour of respondents) "… made by any insolvent person" (i.e., G.S. & D. Construction Ltd.) "in favour of any creditor" (i.e. the respondents) "… with a view to giving such creditor a preference …"

It seems to me plain from the quoted words that the view, the only view, with which s. 73(1) of the Act is concerned is that of the insolvent person making the conveyance and we should not be diverted to any other conclusion by reliance upon a case in which a different statute in different language was construed. Whether or not a conveyance or payment is a fraudulent preference depends entirely on the intention of the debtor. The trial judge has found against the respondents on this point.

. . .

Appeal allowed.

Canadawide Fruit Wholesalers Inc. (Trustee of) v. Hapco Farms Inc.
[1998] QJ no. 1527 (QL) (CA)

MAILHOT JA: This is an appeal from a judgment of the Honourable Daniel H. Tingley (Superior Court, Bankruptcy & Insolvency Division, District of Montreal, November 9, 1994), dismissing the trustee's petition to annul as preferential two payments made by the debtor company (Canadawide) to respondent (Hapco).

. . .

Applicable law

Section 95(1) of the *Bankruptcy and Insolvency Act* ... concerning fraudulent preferences provides that every payment made by any insolvent person in favour of any creditor with a view to giving that creditor a preference over the other creditors shall, if the person making it becomes bankrupt within three months after the date of making it, be deemed fraudulent and void as against the trustee in the bankruptcy.

Subsection (2) provides that where any payment mentioned in subsection (1) has the effect of giving any creditor a preference over other creditors, or over any one or more of them, it shall be presumed, in the absence of evidence to the contrary, to have been made with a view to giving the creditor a preference over other creditors.

In other words, if, in the three-month period prior to the bankruptcy of his debtor, one creditor is paid over other creditors, that payment is presumed to be preferential. The onus is on the creditor to prove he was not paid by preference, but in the ordinary course of his debtor's business. If the creditor fails to satisfy the Court that the payment was made in the ordinary course of his debtor's business, the payment is considered fraudulent (a legal or constructive fraud) and void as against the trustee.

In my opinion, this principle was not correctly applied in the first instance.

Facts

Canadawide is a wholesaler of fruits and vegetables. As a result of financial problems, its bank appointed a consultant to supervise its affairs in November of 1992. All accounts payable, including the disputed payments to Hapco, were approved by the consultant.

Hapco is an American wholesaler and exporter of fruits and vegetables. Canadawide began buying from Hapco in early 1993. It placed only three orders with Hapco in February and March 1993. The last two orders are at issue in these proceedings.

Hapco delivered a first shipment of fruit to Canadawide on February 19, 1993, for a price of slightly over US$14,000.00. Canadawide made out a cheque on April 6, 1993. A second shipment of fruit was made to Canadawide on March 15, 1993, for over US$20,000.00.

The cheque for the first shipment was not honoured by Canadawide's bank, due to insufficient funds. Hapco discovered this fact only after Canadawide had received the second shipment. One of Hapco's representatives called Canadawide to ask for a replacement cheque. Canadawide's representative, Mr. Katsabanis, explained to the Hapco representative that his company was in financial difficulty. Canadawide was however willing to issue a replacement cheque, but on the condition that Hapco would undertake to supply Canadawide with additional products in the future. According to Katsabanis' uncontradicted testimony, Hapco made such an undertaking. Katsabanis authorized the issuance of the replacement cheque, which was subsequently approved by the bank consultant. The cheque for the second shipment dated May 19, 1993 was cleared by Canadawide's bank on May 31, 1993. The replacement cheque for the first shipment dated June 1, 1993 was cleared by the bank on June 9, 1993.

Thereafter Canadawide called Hapco several times to request quotes on produce. Mr. Katsabanis testified that the quotes he received were above market prices or he was told that the requested product was not available. No orders were received from Hapco after the second shipment.

Canadawide's financial situation did not improve over time. The company filed a Notice of Intention to make a Proposal on August 30, 1993. At that time, the company carried a debt load of some 13 million dollars and was running a deficit of approximately 11 million dollars.

Since the payments to Hapco were made in the three months prior to the filing of the notice of intention, the trustee asked the Court to declare them void and to order Hapco to remit the sum of CDN$42,792.74, with interest and costs, under s. 95 of the *Bankruptcy Act*.

The trial judge concluded that Canadawide was insolvent when it made the two payments. The effect of these payments was to give Hapco a preference in fact over other ordinary creditors, i.e. those who had not undertaken to continue doing business with Canadawide. But the judge found that these payments did not constitute fraudulent preferences, because they were not made with a view of giving Hapco a preference over other creditors.

The payments to Hapco were made pursuant to a policy intended to keep Canadawide in business, wrote the judge. Canadawide had decided in April 1993, undoubtedly in concert with its bank, to pay only the claims of those of its creditors who were prepared to continue trading with it, so as to permit it to continue its operations.

His specific words are as follows:

> The most probable effect of this payment policy was that a creditor could expect to be paid on a cash basis for all future deliveries or services. Hapco was paid in the pursuit of this policy which was intended, not to prefer, but to encourage all creditors to continue to trade with the debtor company.
>
> The Court concludes that the trustee has not established an intention on the part of the debtor company to give Hapco a preference over its other creditors. It dealt with Hapco in the same way it intended to deal with all its other creditors who undertook to continue trading with it. By doing so, it hoped to stay in business.

The judge then stated that had the trustee succeeded in proving an intention to prefer, he would have considered Hapco had rebutted the presumption established by subsection 95(2), because the payments were made in the normal course of Canadawide's business, given the context at the time.

Discussion

[Houlden and Morawetz] comment [on] s. 95 of the *Bankruptcy Act* as follows:

> Under s. 95 the trustee is required to prove: (1) that the conveyance, transfer, payment, etc.,
> took place within three months or one year of bankruptcy; (2) that the debtor was an insol-
> vent person at the date of the alleged preference; and (3) that at the date when the convey-
> ance, transfer, payment, etc., was made, it gave the creditor a preference in fact over other
> creditors [...] . When the trustee has proved these three essentials, s. 95(2) provides that the
> conveyance, transfer, payment, etc., is presumed to have been made with a view to giving
> the creditor a preference over other creditors [...] .

In the instant case, the three conditions mentioned above are met. It is undisputed
that the payments occurred in the three months prior to the notice of proposal and that
Canadawide was insolvent when it made these payments. The payments gave also Hapco
a preference in fact over other creditors, simply because Hapco was paid, while other
creditors, who also had debts outstanding, were not.

In my respectful opinion, the trial judge erred at law when he required the trustee to
first establish the debtor's intention to prefer for subsection 95(2) to apply. I also find, as
a matter of law, that the trustee had no more to do than simply prove a preference in fact.
In this case the evidence quite obviously demonstrates that Hapco was paid, while other
creditors were not.

Since the trustee has established the necessary conditions for the prima facie presumption of subsection 95(2) to apply, the onus should properly have rested on Hapco to
prove, by balance of probabilities, that the payments were not fraudulent, because they
were not made with a view to prefer.

There are a number of ways to achieve this. The authors Houlden and Morawetz list
thirteen examples ... . The trial judge seems to have considered two, i.e. that the payments were intended to keep the company in business and that they were made in the
ordinary course of business.

The trial judge held that Canadawide had adopted a policy of paying only the claims
of its creditors who were prepared to continue trading with it, so as to continue its operations. These payments were made in the pursuit of this policy and were intended to keep
Canadawide in business.

The trustee argues before us that Hapco knew of Canadawide's insolvency at the time
the payments were made because of the NSF cheque and because Mr. Katsabanis had explained the financial difficulties to Hapco. The trustee submits Hapco then deceptively
offered to supply further goods if the invoices were paid, but had actually no intention of
doing so, adding that such trade practices should not be sanctioned by the Court, because it allows a creditor to make a promise it does not intend to fulfil in order to escape
the principle of equal distribution among creditors.

Mr. Katsabanis testified that Canadawide payed Hapco to obtain more goods, so as to
stay in business. ... That was no doubt his reason for paying. But to do so, Canadawide
had no choice but to prefer Hapco over its other suppliers with debts outstanding. The
first judge ruled that the probable effect of the payment policy was that creditors could
expect to be paid on a cash basis for future deliveries. I agree. If Hapco had indeed been

paid cash on delivery, the presumption would have been rebutted. It could have been easily argued that the deliveries were necessary to carry on business. However, there were no orders pending with Hapco at the time of payment. Mr. Katsabanis' expectations were founded on the hope that Hapco would fulfil future orders. I find his hope unreasonable, given that he had just told Hapco of Canadawide's financial difficulties and that it was too tempting for Hapco, which was not a major supplier of Canadawide and which did not depend on its business, far from it, to say whatever it had to in order to secure immediate payment. In short, Mr. Katsabanis' expectation that this payment would help Canadawide stay in business was unreasonable.

The judge also held that the payments were not made outside the normal course of Canadawide's business, given the circumstances. The trustee answers that Canadawide's "ordinary course of business" must be judged objectively, not subjectively. A company experiencing financial difficulty, running under the supervision of a consultant appointed by its bank, systematically preferring certain creditors over others and delaying payment is not operating in the ordinary course of its business. It would be a bad precedent, claims the trustee, for the Court to conclude that an extraordinary course of business carried out by an insolvent debtor, making desperate moves to avoid bankruptcy, is an ordinary course of business for the purposes of the *Bankruptcy Act*. Creditors who were preferred, due to this extraordinary means of carrying on business, should not be able to justify the payments in question by the argument that they were made in the ordinary course of business.

I agree with the trustee. I see nothing "ordinary" about Canadawide's operations at the time the payments were made. The trial judge focuses on the fact that the payment terms of 45 days for the first invoice and of 65 days for the second were not abnormal under the circumstances. I find these considerations irrelevant given the more general context, namely that Canadawide had implemented a policy of paying only certain creditors under certain conditions.

Appeal allowed.

St. Anne Nackawic Pulp Co. (Trustee of) v. Logistec Stevedoring (Atlantic) Inc.
2005 NBCA 55

J.T. ROBERTSON JA: [1] We are asked to decide whether the application judge erred in holding that a $500,000 payment made by an insolvent debtor to one of its creditors qualifies as a fraudulent preference within the meaning of s. 95 of the *Bankruptcy and Insolvency Act*, RSC 1985, c. B-3 (BIA). In my respectful view, the application judge erred. Specifically, he failed to ask whether the impugned payment was made with the "dominant intent" of preferring one creditor over the others. When that test is applied to the facts of the present case, it is evident that the debtor harboured no such intent. Admittedly, the creditor in receipt of the payment received a "preference in fact," but that is not a sufficient basis for declaring the payment a fraudulent preference. As will be explained, s. 95 has no application in circumstances where the insolvent debtor is effecting a payment with a view to generating income to be applied against the debts of both secured and unsecured creditors. This remains true even if it were unrealistic to expect that the unsecured creditors would share in the income generated.

[2] The essential facts are as follows. Until September 15, 2004, St. Anne Nackawic Pulp Company Ltd. had been operating a pulp mill in Nackawic, New Brunswick. That corporation is a wholly owned subsidiary of St. Anne Industries Ltd. St. Anne Industries is also the primary secured creditor of St. Anne Pulp under a registered general security agreement, the validity of which is being challenged in other proceedings. Finally, St. Anne Industries is a wholly owned subsidiary of Parsons & Whittemore Inc. of New York. On September 15, 2004, St. Anne Pulp made a voluntary assignment in bankruptcy. A trustee was appointed on that date, but later replaced by the respondent, A.C. Poirier & Associates Inc. Prior to the bankruptcy, it was customary for St. Anne Pulp to transport its pulp to Saint John where it was stored in a dockside warehouse belonging to the appellant, Logistec Stevedoring (Atlantic) Inc. Logistec was also responsible for loading of pulp onto ships and trucks. On September 14, 2004, one day prior to the filing for bankruptcy, Logistec was informed by St. Anne Pulp that it would be ceasing operations but that it wanted to ensure that the 10,800 tonnes of pulp, being presently stored in Logistec's warehouse, would be released and loaded onto two ships that were to arrive in Saint John on or about September 18, 2004. As well, one shipment was to be effected by truck. In response, Logistec asserted that it possessed a warehouseman's lien on the goods and refused to release and load any pulp unless it received prior payment, in full, with respect to past due accounts. Logistec informed St. Anne Pulp that it was owed $562,574.72 plus amounts not yet posted to the account. Initially, Logistec demanded payment from anyone other than St. Anne Pulp in order to avoid the possibility of someone alleging the payment was a fraudulent preference. Eventually, Parsons & Whittemore agreed to indemnify Logistec in the event the payment from St. Anne Pulp to Logistec was successfully challenged. The impugned payment was made on September 14, 2004. The next day St. Anne Pulp made a voluntary assignment in bankruptcy. On the same date, St. Anne Industries appointed a receiver under the terms of its security agreement. On September 16, 2004, Logistec determined that a further $232,945.91 would be needed to settle the account. The receiver paid this amount with funds drawn on St. Anne Pulp's bank account, over which St. Anne Industries had taken security. As of September 27, 2004, all the pulp in the warehouse had been shipped.

[3] On December 10, 2004, the respondent trustee filed an application for a declaration that the $562,574.72 payment was fraudulent and void under s. 95 of the BIA. Correlatively, the trustee sought judgment for that amount. On December 21, 2004, the application was heard. On the same date the application judge granted the relief requested. His decision is now reported at [2004] NBJ No. 477 (QB) (QL). The reasons for judgment address two issues. The first was whether the application proceedings should be converted into an action. On this issue, the application judge ruled in favour of the trustee. Although Logistec pursued this issue on appeal, there is no need to convert this matter into an action. The only factual matter which the parties failed to resolve concerns the extent to which the $500,000 payment related to work already performed, as opposed to work to be performed. However, that factual determination is only relevant if the payment in question were declared a fraudulent preference, in which case part of the payment may have been valid. As I find that the payment in question does not constitute a fraudulent

preference, there is no need to dwell on the first issue. As to the second issue, I turn to s. 95. ...

[4] The law is settled with respect to the interpretation and application of s. 95 of the BIA. In order for a payment to a creditor to qualify as a fraudulent preference three conditions precedent must be met: (1) the payment must have been made within three months of bankruptcy; (2) the debtor must have been insolvent at the date of the payment; and (3) as a result of the payment the creditor must have in fact received a preference over other creditors (see *Re Van der Liek* (1970), 14 CBR (NS) 229 (Ont. HCJ).

[5] Once the three conditions precedent have been met, a presumption arises that the payment was made "with a view to giving that creditor a preference over the other creditors." However, it is a rebuttable presumption. In that regard, the courts have interpreted the above-quoted phrase as placing an onus on the creditor to establish that the debtor's dominant intent was not to prefer that creditor. The genesis of the dominant intent test is invariably traced to the following passage in *Re Van der Liek*, at pages 231-32:

> When the trustee has proved these three essentials, he need proceed no further and the onus is then on the creditor to satisfy the court, if he can, that there was no intent on the part of the debtor to give a preference. If the creditor can show on the balance of probabilities that the dominant intent of the debtor was not to prefer the creditor but was some other purpose, then the application will be dismissed, but if the creditor fails to meet the onus, then the trustee succeeds.

[6] Certain factors may or may not be relevant to the task of ascertaining the debtor's dominant intent. Based on the Supreme Court's decision in *Hudson v. Benallack*, [1976] 2 SCR 168, it is settled law that the creditor's knowledge of the debtor's insolvency at the time of the payment is an irrelevant consideration. On the other hand, it is relevant that the corporate debtor knew of its insolvency at the date of the payment. If the debtor is related to the creditor the payment will be scrutinized with greater care and suspicion. However, it is no defence to an allegation of fraudulent preference that the creditor exerted pressure on the insolvent debtor to secure the payment. According to s. 95(2), pressure is no longer a ground for upholding a transaction which is otherwise preferential within the meaning of s. 95(1). Finally, as the dominant intent test is an objective one, we need not be concerned with the subjective intent of the insolvent debtor at the time of the payment. The requisite intent will be drawn from all of the relevant circumstances, as opposed to the debtor's personal ruminations. See generally Lloyd W. Houlden & Geoffrey B. Morawetz, *Bankruptcy & Insolvency Law of Canada*, looseleaf (Toronto: Carswell, 1992) at 4-66 to 4-67, 4-79.

[7] Returning to the facts of the present case, the parties agree that conditions precedent (1) and (2) have been met. However, Logistec argues that it was not the beneficiary of a preference in fact and, therefore, s. 95 has no application. A concise and accurate statement of the law as to the relationship between the concept of preference in fact and dominant intent is found in *Re Norris* (1996), 193 AR 15 at para. 16 (CA):

> In considering this section, it is well to keep in mind the distinction between preference in fact and fraudulent preference as that latter is defined in the Act. There can be no doubt in this case that Revenue Canada received a preference in fact from the payment of tax made

by this debtor on November 25, 1992. Its debt was paid where the debts owing to other ordinary creditors were not. What would render that preference in fact a fraudulent one under
s. 95 is the accompanying intent of the insolvent debtor who in the face of imminent bankruptcy is moved to prefer or favour, before losing control over his assets, a particular credit-
or over others who will have to wait for and accept as full payment their rateable share on
distribution by the Trustee in the ensuing bankruptcy. It is called fraudulent because it prejudices other creditors who will receive proportionately less, or nothing at all, and upsets the
fundamental scheme of the Act for equal sharing among creditors. That accompanying intent to favour one creditor over another is what makes a preference in fact a fraudulent
preference and is referred to in the cases as the "dominant intent." ...

[8] In my view, Logistec's argument would have been persuasive had the impugned
payment related solely to work or services to be performed in regard to the pulp that was
being stored in Logistec's warehouse at the time of the payment. In other words, had the
entire $500,000 payment related to the storage and shipping of the 10,800 tonnes of pulp
in Logistec's warehouse, Logistec's argument would have been well founded. The situation would be no different had Logistec sold St. Anne Pulp a piece of machinery within
the three months preceding the bankruptcy and St. Anne Pulp paid in cash. Such a payment would not qualify as a preference, but rather as a purchase and sale made in the ordinary course of business. However, counsel for Logistec conceded that part of the
$500,000 was to be applied against amounts already owing for work undertaken in the
past. In these circumstances, Logistec did receive a preference in fact when contrasted
with St. Anne Pulp's other creditors who were also awaiting payment of their outstanding
accounts. That said, the mere establishment of a preference in fact does not lead to the
conclusion that the payment qualifies as a fraudulent preference within the meaning of
s. 95 of the BIA. What we are left with is a rebuttable presumption that the payment in
question so qualifies.

[9] Logistec bore the onus of establishing that St. Anne Pulp's dominant intent was
not to prefer Logistec over the other creditors. Alternatively stated, the onus was on Logistec to establish that St. Anne Pulp's dominant intent was to achieve a purpose other
than to prefer Logistec. Regrettably, the application judge did not address that issue. For
this reason, this court must draw the necessary inference from the primary findings of
fact, as found by the application judge. Those facts are not in dispute.

[10] St. Anne Pulp's dominant intent may be formulated in at least one of four ways.
First, it can be argued that it intended to bestow a preference on Logistec over the other
creditors. This is the position of the trustee in bankruptcy. Second, it can be argued that
St. Anne Pulp made the payment in order to honour its contractual obligations to its
customers who had purchased the pulp and, hence, to ensure that the goods were duly
shipped. This is the position of Logistec. The third and fourth characterizations flow
from the second. Third, it can be argued that St. Anne Pulp's dominant intent was to
generate income in the form of accounts receivable. Moneys collected would be applied
against amounts owing to creditors and in the order of priority established at law. Fourth,
it can be argued that St. Anne Pulp's dominant intent was to maximize St. Anne Industries' recovery on its secured debt. This characterization is a logical extension of the reality that, as the primary secured creditor, St. Anne Industries is entitled to the proceeds

arising from the sale of inventory in priority to the unsecured creditors. If it can be fairly said that St. Anne Pulp's dominant intent falls within either the second, third or fourth formulations, it is my view that the payment in question does not qualify as a fraudulent preference under s. 95 of the BIA. I so find. My formal reasoning is as follows.

[11] At common law and even after passage of the *Statute of Elizabeth* in 1570 (fraudulent conveyances) there was no impediment against an insolvent debtor preferring one creditor over another. The question of why a debtor would prefer one creditor over another goes to the question of the debtor's underlying motive, which text writers point out is irrelevant to the issue of dominant intent. Admittedly, it is easy to blur the legal distinctions often drawn between motive, intent, purpose or object. Be that as it may, one cannot help but ask why a debtor would prefer one creditor over another. In some cases the answer is self-evident. The common law allowed an insolvent debtor to engage in selective generosity by paying first those he liked most. Thus, payment to a creditor who is a family member or friend is more apt than not to qualify as a fraudulent preference within the meaning of s. 95 of the BIA: see *Craig (Trustee of) v. Devlin Estate* (1989), 63 Man. R (2d) 122 (CA). Ironically, there is also a reported case in which the debtor allegedly made the payment to a non-related creditor (Revenue Canada) in order to prefer a creditor who was a close but distant relative [sic]: see *Norris (Re)*. But even if there is no close relationship between the debtor and the preferred creditor, the payment may be caught by s. 95. For example, where the payment is made to a creditor with respect to an indebtedness that had been guaranteed by the debtor's spouse, the payment has been held to be a fraudulent preference: see *Royal Bank of Canada v. Roofmart Ontario Ltd.* (1990), 74 OR (2d) 633 (CA) and also *Re Royal City Chrysler Plymouth Limited* (1998), 38 OR (3d) 380 (CA).

[12] As a general observation, it is evident that the cases in which the creditor has been unable to rebut the presumption arising under s. 95 of the BIA generally involve two factual patterns. First, the insolvent debtor and the creditor in receipt of the payment are somehow related (e.g., family members). Second, the payment to an arm's length creditor has the subsidiary effect of conferring an unjustified benefit or advantage on the insolvent debtor or a family member. While these factual patterns are not exhaustive, it is clear that the facts of the present case do not support a finding that St. Anne Pulp's dominant intent was to prefer Logistec over the other creditors. But that is not the end of the matter. It is still necessary to isolate, by inference, St. Anne Pulp's dominant intent. In my view, its ultimate goal was to generate income from its accounts receivable, the proceeds of which would be applied first against the debt owing to St. Anne Industries, the primary secured creditor. In brief, St. Anne Pulp's dominant intent was to maximize the amount that the receiver would recover on behalf of St. Anne Industries from the sale of the existing inventory. Does this inference support the allegation of fraudulent preference under s. 95 of the BIA? In my view, it does not for two reasons. First, s. 95 speaks of fraudulent preference in terms of the creditor who received the payment. In this case, it was Logistec who received the payment, not St. Anne Industries. Second, and more importantly, St. Anne Industries cannot be accused of obtaining a fraudulent preference when as a matter of law it is entitled to a preference as a secured creditor of St. Anne Pulp. It is St. Anne Industries that has priority over the unsecured creditors by virtue of its security agreement. St. Anne Industries is to be paid first. If the income generated resulted in a

surplus that surplus would be shared pro-rata amongst the unsecured creditors. The fact that St. Anne Pulp made the impugned payment to Logistec with a view to generating income which would be applied first against the debt owing to the secured creditor, St. Anne Industries, and then against amounts owing to the unsecured creditors, cannot be regarded as a valid basis on which to declare the payment to Logistec a fraudulent preference.

[13] My understanding of the law is that in circumstances where an insolvent debtor pays one creditor at the expense of another for purposes of carrying on business, the payment will more likely than not be deemed not to constitute a fraudulent preference within the meaning of s. 95 of the BIA. I need only refer to two cases in support of this proposition. In *Davis v. Ducan Industries Ltd.* (1983), 45 CBR (NS) 290 (Alta. QB) the bankrupt was a manufacturer of recreational vehicles. The creditor who received the questionable payment was a supplier of parts that the debtor used in its business. The supplier refused to continue to do business with the debtor unless payments were made towards its large outstanding account. Less than three months before the bankruptcy, the debtor made payments to the supplier. Once the debtor became bankrupt, another creditor challenged this transaction as a fraudulent preference. The court found that the dominant intent of the bankrupt in making the payments to the supplier was to secure supplies to continue to run its business and not to give the creditor a preference. Similarly, in *Econ Consulting Ltd. (Trustee of) v. Deloitte, Haskins & Sells* (1985), 31 Man. R (2d) 313 (CA) the bankrupt made a payment of $10,000 to accountants in respect of an outstanding account sixteen days prior to making an assignment in bankruptcy. The debtor's income tax returns were due and the accountants required the payment before they would prepare income tax returns for the debtor. The Court of Appeal cited this finding of the application judge with approval:

> I am satisfied that Econ made this payment not to give a preference to Deloitte but to get what it needed and required, i.e. its income tax returns prepared. I think that Deloitte would not have received payment if it had not been necessary for Econ to do so in order to persuade Deloitte to do the work that had to be done.

[14] Under Canadian law, if a creditor refuses to perform an act for an insolvent debtor, such as delivering goods or preparing income tax returns, unless its existing account is paid in full or in part, and the account is so paid in order to have the act performed, the transaction will not be deemed a fraudulent preference. This is because the debtor made the payment, not for purposes of preferring the creditor, but rather to obtain the performance of an act which is consistent with what is expected of someone who is acting in the ordinary course of business: see Houlden & Morawetz at 4-79 to 4-80.

[15] I admit that in the present case St. Anne Pulp did not make the payment for purposes of carrying on its pulp business in the long term. The impugned payment was made one day prior to St. Anne Pulp's voluntary assignment in bankruptcy. In the interim, however, it was entitled to carry on business albeit for a day. The truth of the matter is that St. Anne Pulp was acting in the best interests of all concerned when it made the payment to Logistec. Let me explain.

[16] It would have been irresponsible for either St. Anne Pulp, the trustee or the privately appointed receiver to allow the inventory of pulp to sit in Logistec's warehouse. St. Anne Pulp had entered into binding contracts for the sale of this product. The goods had

to be shipped, otherwise St. Anne Pulp would have been in breach of its contractual obligations and liable for any consequential damages. When completed, those contracts generated income for St. Anne Pulp. The net amount invoiced on the three contracts in question was $1.3 million (US), $2.3 million (US) and $300,000 (Cdn.). Together, the shipment of the pulp generated more than $4.6 million (Cdn.) in accounts receivable. That amount is net of the $800,000 paid to Logistec to ensure the shipment of the pulp ($562,574.72 + $232,945.91 = $795,520.63). In effect, for every $1 paid to Logistec, St. Anne Pulp generated at least $5 in accounts receivable. In addition, by fulfilling the pulp contracts, future pulp sales might not otherwise be jeopardized if the trustee or the receiver decided to operate St. Anne Pulp pending a disposition of the mill.

[17] What the trustee fails to appreciate is that although a debtor is insolvent, it is entitled to carry on in the ordinary course of business even if only for a day, so long as it is acting in a commercially reasonable manner and, therefore, in the best interests of all concerned. As well, the trustee appears to be proceeding on the mistaken assumption that prior to the voluntary assignment in bankruptcy any moneys held in St. Anne Pulp's bank account could be used only for purposes of effecting a settlement of all debts on a pro-rata basis. The reality is that if anyone possessed a priority with respect to moneys in St. Anne Pulp's bank account, it was St. Anne Industries under its general security agreement. That security extended not only to St. Anne Pulp's accounts receivable and inventory, but also to all moneys held on St. Anne Pulp's account. It is out of that bank account that the receiver paid Logistec $232,000 in order to secure shipment of the pulp. Had St. Anne Pulp not made the payment to Logistec on September 14, 2004, here is what would have happened. On the following day, the newly appointed receiver would have seized the moneys held in St. Anne Pulp's bank account. From that account the receiver would have paid the full amount owing to Logistec, for both past and present work. As it happens, the fact that a substantial payment was made one day prior to the bankruptcy is of no moment. Finally, I should point out that the payment to Logistec will work to the benefit of the unsecured creditors in the event St. Anne Industries' security agreement is successfully challenged and declared invalid. The income generated by that payment ($5 for every $1 paid to Logistec) would become available to all unsecured creditors.

[18] At first blush the "optics" of this case cast a long shadow over the actions of St. Anne Pulp, St. Anne Industries and, ultimately, Parsons & Whittemore. It is understandable that Logistec was adamant that it receive an indemnity from Parsons & Whittemore with respect to the possibility the payment in question would be successfully challenged as a fraudulent preference under s. 95 of the BIA. The fact that the payment was made one day prior to the voluntary assignment in bankruptcy, and that both Logistec and St. Anne Pulp were aware of the latter's insolvency, threw suspicion over the transaction. However, when properly viewed, the transaction made good commercial sense. There is no doubt that St. Anne Industries was the true beneficiary of St. Anne Pulp's payment to Logistec. But no one can complain of the preferential treatment being accorded that secured creditor. The preference arises as a matter of the security contract and is sanctioned by both the common law and the BIA.

V. THE PROVINCIAL PREFERENCE PROVISIONS

Tamara M. Buckwold, *Reform of Fraudulent Conveyances and Fraudulent*
Preferences Law, Part II: Preferential Transfers
(Report prepared for the Uniform Law Conference of Canada, Civil Law Section,
August 2008), paras. 4 and 7 to 18 (footnotes omitted)

Provincial preferential transfer legislation is a product of the introduction of creditors'
relief legislation during the late 19th century as part of a package of legislation designed
to fill the void created by the absence of federal bankruptcy law. Although elements of
the provincial package were repealed when the federal government reentered the field
with the *Bankruptcy Act* of 1919, the creditors' relief and companion preferences legislation generally continued in effect.

. . .

[P]ayments and the provision of security resulting in satisfaction of a debt owed to
one creditor in circumstances in which others of equal rank will be unsatisfied or receive
a proportionately smaller amount are regulated in most provinces by provincial legislation and, where bankruptcy or restructuring proceedings have been commenced under
federal legislation, by provisions of the *Bankruptcy and Insolvency Act*. Because secured
creditors are able to recover through resort to their collateral the concern in both contexts is the equal satisfaction of unsecured debts through enforcement against the debt-
or's unencumbered assets.

Provincial preferences legislation differs in name and in various points of detail as
among jurisdictions and the interpretational overlay added by the judiciary is far from
uniform. What follows below is therefore of necessity only an outline of regularly appearing provisions and principles.

Transactions Regulated by the Statute

The language defining the scope of the Alberta *Fraudulent Preferences Act* is representative
of the provincial statutes generally. It provides that "every gift, conveyance, assignment,
transfer, delivery over or payment of ... any property, real or personal" made in the circumstances prescribed is "void as against the creditor or creditors injured, delayed, prejudiced or postponed." However, qualifying provisions substantially limit the scope of the
legislation by exempting the various transactions described further below from challenge,
most notably payments of money to a creditor. Therefore the word "payment" used in relation to the operation of the provincial statutes should be understood to refer to a payment through the transfer of property other than money and to include the transfer of
an interest in property by way of security for antecedent debt. A transfer of value through
the provision of services or the assumption of an obligation is not subject to challenge.

Only transfers to a "creditor" can be challenged. The statutes provide an expanded
definition under which "creditor" includes a surety and the endorser of a promissory
note or bill of exchange who may become a creditor on fulfillment of their legal obligations, as well as a *cestui que trust* "or other person to whom liability is equitable only."

Requirement of Insolvency

A transfer to a creditor may only be avoided if made by a person who is insolvent or who knows him or herself to be on the eve of insolvency. As indicated above, the assumption is that a payment made by a solvent debtor cannot be a preference because he or she is by definition financially able to satisfy all creditors in full. Whether or not this is in fact so may depend upon the definition of insolvency applied and whether the value of exempt property is taken into account in the determination. The state of insolvency is not defined in the statute and courts have taken various approaches. However to quote a leading author, "[w]hat must be established is incapacity to pay one's debts."

Debtor's Intention

A preferential transfer may be avoided only if it is established that the debtor *intended* to give the recipient creditor a preference. The requirement of intention to prefer has been part of Canadian preferences law since its inception and, as the discussion below indicates, its suitability as the factor determining the legal vulnerability of a preferential payment is the most significant issue in reform of this area of law.

What is required to establish the requisite intention to prefer varies depending the period of time that has elapsed between the date of the challenged transaction and the commencement of proceedings to set it aside. If the challenge is mounted within a prescribed period the debtor is presumed to have intended to prefer the creditor to whom the payment was made if it had the effect of giving that creditor a preference over others, provided the debtor was insolvent or knowingly on the eve of insolvency at the date of the transaction. If action is commenced outside the prescribed time period the plaintiff must bring evidence establishing an actual intention to prefer.

Proof of Intention Outside the Prescribed Time Period. Proof that the debtor knows he or she is insolvent when a creditor is paid may be accepted as proof of an intention to prefer, since the necessary consequence of the payment is that the recipient creditor is advantaged relative to those who cannot be satisfied. However there is little doubt that any such inference is rebuttable, since the courts will not find an intention to prefer when it is established that the debtor acted pursuant to another dominant motive. Thus a debtor who responds to a creditor's pressure to pay will likely not be regarded as having acted with the requisite intention to prefer, on the view that the payment is not truly voluntary. Similarly a preferential payment made by a debtor in the genuine hope of staying in business may not be subject to avoidance. The difficulty of proving the debtor's intention to prefer along with uncertainty over what will be accepted by the courts as an exculpatory motive and the evidence required to establish it has severely limited the ability of creditors to successfully use the provincial statutes to set aside a payment that has preferential effect.

Proof of Intention within the Presumptive Time Period. In most provinces the presumption of intention to prefer arising from the preferential effect of a payment operates when it is challenged through the commencement of litigation within 60 days of the date the payment was made, though in Alberta the period is a full year. In Ontario the presumption is *"prima facie"* so it may be rebutted by evidence proving a contrary motive, though not on the basis of pressure exerted by the benefiting creditor. In the western provinces the presumption is explicitly irrebuttable. In jurisdictions in which the statutory language is ambiguous the presumption will likely be regarded as rebuttable.

Intention of Preferred Creditor

Under the terms of the statute, the state of mind of a creditor receiving a preferential payment is irrelevant. Nevertheless the courts have protected creditors by refusing to set aside a transfer if the recipient did not in some fashion participate in or at least know of the debtor's intention to confer a preference. Judicial proclivity to impose a dual intention requirement varies as among jurisdictions, and one province has explicitly abolished it as a relevant consideration. This inconsistency in judicial approach is exacerbated by uncertainty over the degree of creditor participation required to warrant avoidance of a transfer.

Standing to Challenge a Transfer or Payment

Since a preferential transfer is void as against "the creditor or creditors injured, delayed, prejudiced or postponed," only a person who is a creditor at the time it occurs has standing to challenge a transfer under the statute. The expanded definition noted under heading "a." above applies in this context, but the weight of authority indicates that the holder of an unliquidated or contingent claim is not otherwise a creditor. Although a secured creditor is a "creditor" in the strict sense such a creditor is ordinarily not adversely affected by a preferential payment and will not have standing under the statute, except to the extent the debt is unsecured.

Protected Transactions

The law of all jurisdictions in some way shelters preferential transfers that are regarded as legitimate or that for reasons of commercial stability should not be disrupted, regardless of the intention of the debtor in making them. The statutes differ slightly in their definition of transactions that are above challenge, and the terms by which the exceptions are defined are generally far from clear. However the range of such transactions includes, along with payments of money noted earlier, those listed below, cast in language sprinkled liberally throughout with references to "bona fides" and good faith:

Transactions involving an exchange in which the money paid or property transferred bears a "fair and reasonable relative value to the consideration for it," in the form of:

- A sale or payment made in the ordinary course of business to an "innocent" party."
- A conveyance or delivery of property in exchange for a reciprocal sale or delivery of goods or other property or a money payment.
- A transfer by way of security for a present advance of money.
- A payment given to a creditor who has in good faith given up a security, unless the value of the security is restored.
- The provision of one form of security in substitution for another.
- A security given for pre-existing debt that induces a further advance intended to enable the debtor to carry on business and satisfy creditors in full.
- An assignment made for the purpose of paying creditors rateably.

NOTE

The provincial preference provisions are different in a number of material respects from BIA s. 95. Does it make sense to have preference provisions at both the federal and the provincial level, particularly given the differences between them? (Recall that there is no constitutional issue involved: see Chapter 2.) Here is what the Standing Senate Committee on Banking, Trade and Commerce has said:

> [T]here should be a uniform system nationwide for the examination of fraudulent and review-able transactions in situations of insolvency. At present, there is a lack of fairness, uniformity and predictability by virtue of both federal and provincial/territorial legislation addressing fraudu-lent and reviewable transactions. We feel that a national standard is needed for reviewable transactions that diminish the value of the insolvent debtor's estate and thereby reduce the value of creditors' realizable claims. Provincial/territorial legislation would continue to exist for trans-actions not occurring in the context of insolvency. A national system for review of such trans-actions would provide the fairness and predictability that we want in our insolvency system.

(Standing Senate Committee on Banking, *Trade and Commerce, Debtors and Creditors Shar-ing the Burden: A Review of the Bankruptcy and Insolvency Act and the Companies' Creditors Arrangement Act* (Ottawa: November, 2003), at 122.)

One cost of retaining the provincial preference provisions is the threat to national uni-form laws inside bankruptcy. This point should not be understated. Canadian bankruptcy and insolvency law is by and large a federal responsibility and this reflects a commitment to the value of national uniformity. As the above-quoted passage implies, the continued con-current operation of provincial laws is inconsistent with having federal bankruptcy laws in the first place. Uniformity is not the only issue. Another potential cost of retaining the prov-incial laws is that the concurrent operation of federal and provincial laws creates the poten-tial for confusion at the policy level—for example, where provincial laws allow a trustee in bankruptcy to circumvent limitations on the scope of the federal preference provisions. It also adds to the complexity of the law because it requires parties, their legal advisers, and the courts to negotiate two layers of provisions instead of just one.

CHAPTER SIX

Executory Contracts

I. INTRODUCTION

Consider the following cases:

1. Landlord owns a shopping centre development. Debtor leases a shop space from Landlord for a five-year term and opens a clothing store. Three years into the lease, Debtor becomes bankrupt. Trustee wants to sell Debtor's business on a going-concern basis. She estimates that she will get a better price if she can close down Debtor's unprofitable stores first. The store in Landlord's mall is unprofitable and Trustee wants to close it down, but this involves terminating the lease. Can Trustee terminate the lease and, if so, subject to what conditions?

2. Debtor agrees to sell Buyer 2,000 tonnes of wheat for $150 per tonne to be delivered by installments over a three-year period. Some months later, and before any deliveries have been made, Debtor goes into bankruptcy. The price of wheat has fallen in the meantime and so Buyer wants to get out of the contract. On the other hand, Trustee is keen to perform the contract with a view to maximizing the returns to the estate. Does Trustee have the right to take over performance of the contract?

3. Debtor supplies gymnasium equipment to fitness centres on long-term lease along with service and repair facilities. Debtor goes into bankruptcy and Trustee proposes to sell the business as a going concern to Successor. The deal envisages that Successor will take over the lease and service agreements. The agreements all prohibit assignment without the lessee-fitness centre's written consent. Some of the fitness centres refuse to give consent. Can Trustee proceed with the assignments to Successor?

This chapter addresses the trustee's right to disclaim a contract (case 1), affirm a contract with a view to performance (case 2), and assign contracts (case 3). Similar questions concerning the status of partly performed contracts also arise in the context of CCAA and BIA proposal proceedings: see Chapters 13 and 16. This chapter's focus is on straight bankruptcy proceedings.

Provincial landlord and tenant legislation, apart from Quebec and Newfoundland and Labrador, provides for the disclaimer, affirmation, and assignment of commercial tenancy agreements in the tenant's bankruptcy, and BIA s. 146 incorporates these provisions by reference. However, until the 2007 amendments, there was no corresponding legislation for other contracts and thus the trustee's rights depended on common-law principles. The 2007 amendments enact statutory rules relevant to the disclaimer, affirmation, and assignment of contracts: new BIA ss. 65.11, 84.2, and 84.1, respectively. However, the disclaimer provision in s. 65.11 does not apply in bankruptcy (it is limited to proposals). The upshot is that, in bankruptcy, the trustee's right of disclaimer remains subject to the provincial landlord and tenant laws (for commercial tenancy agreements) and common-law principles (for other contracts). By contrast, new BIA ss. 84.1 and 84.2 *do* apply in bankruptcy and they extend to contracts at large, including commercial tenancy agreements. For an analysis of the reforms, see Anthony Duggan, "Partly Performed Contracts," in Stephanie Ben-Ishai and Anthony Duggan, eds., *Canadian Bankruptcy and Insolvency Law: Bill C-55, Statute c. 47 and Beyond* (Toronto: LexisNexis, 2007), Chapter 2.

II. DISCLAIMER

A. Introduction

Outside bankruptcy, a party (Debtor) can disclaim a contract if he wants to, but, in the absence of a lawful excuse, he will be liable to the counterparty (Counterparty) for loss of bargain damages. Generally speaking, the same rule applies inside bankruptcy: the trustee (Trustee) can disclaim a contract, but this gives Counterparty a damages claim: see *New Skeena Forest Products*, extracted below. If Trustee makes no election one way or the other, she is deemed to have disclaimed the contract: see *Re Thomson Knitting Co.*, extracted below.

Is Counterparty's damages claim a provable one in Debtor's bankruptcy? If not, it would survive an individual debtor's bankruptcy because the bankruptcy discharge applies only to provable claims. In most cases, this would make disclaimer an unattractive proposition from Debtor's point of view, unless Debtor is a corporation (as a general rule, a bankrupt corporation cannot obtain a discharge: BIA s. 169(4)). On the other hand, if Counterparty's claim is a provable one, Counterparty will have to lodge a proof of claim with Trustee, and the likelihood is that Counterparty [will end up recovering only a few cents on the dollar as part of the bankruptcy distribution. This makes disclaimer a more attractive option inside bankruptcy than outside: outside bankruptcy, if Debtor disclaims a contract, she will have to pay Counterparty's damages in full. But inside bankruptcy, if Trustee disclaims, the estate will only have to pay a fraction of Landlord's claim.

BIA. s. 121(1) defines "provable claim" to mean

> all debts and liabilities, present or future, to which the bankrupt is subject on the day the bankrupt becomes bankrupt or to which the bankrupt may become subject before the bankrupt's discharge by reason of any obligation incurred before the day on which the bankrupt becomes bankrupt.

In other words, only pre-filing claims are provable claims. On that basis, Counterparty's claim would not be a provable one because it does not materialize until Trustee disclaims—that is, it is a post-filing claim. As it happens, though, Counterparty's claim is a provable one, even though it is a post-filing claim and this rule is an exception to the general rule that only pre-filing claims are provable. In the case of commercial tenancy agreements, the exception derives by implication from the provincial landlord and tenant statutes read in conjunction with BIA s. 136(1)(f). In the case of other kinds of contract, the exception has been established by case law: *Re Doman* (2004), 45 BLR (3rd) 78 (BCSC) (extracted in Chapter 13).

B. Landlord and Tenant Agreements

BIA s. 146 incorporates by reference the provisions in provincial landlord and tenant statutes relating to the disclaimer, affirmation, and assignment of commercial tenancy agreements. Sections 38 and 39 of the *Commercial Tenancies Act*, RSO 1990, c. L.7, reproduced below, are reasonably representative. Section 39(1) gives a trustee the right by notice in writing to surrender or disclaim a lease. This more or less restates the common-law position. But assume the trustee makes no election either to disclaim or affirm the lease: at common law, the default rule is that the trustee is deemed to have disclaimed. Does the statute, by requiring notice in writing of disclaimer, displace the common-law default rule? BIA s. 136(1)(f) displaces the common-law rules about how much a landlord can claim: it gives the landlord a claim for three months' arrears of rent and three months' accelerated rent. In *Re Vrablik* (Ont. Sup. Ct., 1993), extracted below, the court held that the claim for three months' accelerated rent was in substitution for loss of bargain damages. In other words, a landlord cannot claim loss of bargain damages on top of the claim that s. 136(1)(f) gives him.

Section 136(1)(f) gives the landlord a preferred claim. This means the trustee has to pay the landlord's claim in full before the ordinary unsecured creditors get anything. On the other hand, s. 136(1) is "subject to the rights of secured creditors." This means the landlord's preferred claim ranks behind the right of a secured creditor to enforce its security interest. The preferred claim is for three months' arrears of rent and three months' accelerated rent. Assume the tenant is more than three months in arrears of rent. Can the landlord file a proof of claim for the balance? The answer is yes: s. 136(3) provides that a creditor whose rights are restricted by s. 136(1) is entitled to rank as an unsecured creditor for any balance of claim due to him. Consequently, the landlord ranks as a preferred creditor for three months' arrears of rent and an ordinary unsecured creditor for any arrears of rent beyond three months.

The preferred claim may not exceed the "realization from the property on the premises under lease." The reference is to the value of the tenant's goods. The *Commercial Tenancies Act* gives a commercial landlord a right of distress for non-payment of rent. This means that, outside bankruptcy, the landlord can seize the tenant's goods and sell them, using the sale proceeds to pay off the rent. BIA s. 70(1) takes away the landlord's right of distress when the tenant becomes bankrupt. The s. 136(1)(f) preferred claim is meant to compensate the landlord for loss of the right of distress, hence the limitation. Assume the value of the tenant's goods is less than the three months' arrears of rent. Can the landlord claim the difference? The answer is yes: again, s. 136(3) applies.

The closing words of s. 136(1)(f) say that any payment on account of accelerated rent shall be credited against the amount payable by the trustee for occupation rent. Section 38(2) of the *Commercial Tenancies Act* gives the trustee three months to elect between affirming or disclaiming the lease. The trustee is liable for occupation rent during that period. The landlord cannot claim both occupation rent and accelerated rent, because that would be double-dipping.

Commercial Tenancies Act
RSO 1990, c. L.7, ss. 38, 39

38(1) In case of an assignment for the general benefit of creditors, or an order being made for the winding up of an incorporated company, or where a receiving order in bankruptcy or authorized assignment has been made by or against a tenant, the preferential lien of the landlord for rent is restricted to the arrears of rent due during the period of three months next preceding, and for three months following the execution of the assignment, and from thence so long as the assignee retains possession of the premises, but any payment to be made to the landlord in respect of accelerated rent shall be credited against the amount payable by the person who is assignee, liquidator or trustee for the period of the person's occupation. RSO 1980, c. 232, s. 38(1).

(2) Despite any provision, stipulation or agreement in any lease or agreement or the legal effect thereof, in case of an assignment for the general benefit of creditors, or an order being made for the winding up of an incorporated company, or where a receiving order in bankruptcy or authorized assignment has been made by or against a tenant, the person who is assignee, liquidator or trustee may at any time within three months thereafter for the purposes of the trust estate and before the person has given notice of intention to surrender possession or disclaim, by notice in writing elect to retain the leased premises for the whole or any portion of the unexpired term and any renewal thereof, upon the terms of the lease and subject to the payment of the rent as provided by the lease or agreement, and the person may, upon payment to the landlord of all arrears of rent, assign the lease with rights of renewal, if any, to any person who will covenant to observe and perform its terms and agree to conduct upon the demised premises a trade or business which is not reasonably of a more objectionable or hazardous nature than that which was thereon conducted by the debtor, and who on application of the assignee, liquidator or trustee, is approved by a judge of the Ontario Court (General Division) as a person fit and proper to be put in possession of the leased premises. RSO 1980, c. 232, s. 38(2), *revised*.

39(1) The person who is assignee, liquidator or trustee has the further right, at any time before so electing, by notice in writing to the landlord, to surrender possession or disclaim any such lease, and the person's entry into possession of the leased premises and their occupation by the person, while required for the purposes of the trust estate, shall not be deemed to be evidence of an intention on the person's part to elect to retain possession under section 38.

(2) Where the assignor, or person or firm against whom a receiving order has been made in bankruptcy, or a winding up order has been made, being a lessee, has, before the making of the assignment or such order demised any premises by way of under-lease, approved or consented to in writing by the landlord, and the assignee, liquidator or trustee surrenders, disclaims or elects to assign the lease, the under-lessee, if the under-lessee so elects in writing within three months of such assignment or order, stands in the same position with the landlord as though the under-lessee were a direct lessee from the landlord but subject, except as to rental payable, to the same liabilities and obligations as the assignor, bankrupt or insolvent company was subject to under the lease at the date of the assignment or order, but the under-lessee shall in such event be required to covenant

to pay to the landlord a rental not less than that payable by the under-lessee to the debtor, and if such last mentioned rental was greater than that payable by the debtor to the said landlord, the under-lessee shall be required to covenant to pay to the landlord the like greater rental. RSO 1980, c. 232, s. 39(1, 2).

(3) In the event of any dispute arising under this section or section 38, the dispute shall be disposed of by a judge of the Ontario Court (General Division) upon an application. RSO 1980, c. 232, s. 39(3), *revised*.

Re Vrablik
(1993), 17 CBR (3d) 154 (Ont. Gen. Div.)

MALONEY J: This is a motion brought by the Trustee in this bankruptcy for:

1. An Order of the Court determining whether the contingent claim of Donald Raymond Stasiuk, Kathryn Marta Stasiuk, Andrew Findlay Coffey, Roberta Joan Coffey and 705514 Ontario Limited is a provable claim;

2. If the contingent claim is a provable claim then, an Order of the Court valuing the claim;

The reason for the bringing of the motion is that the above-named landlords of the bankrupt tenant are claiming damages in lieu of payments which would otherwise be due under the portion of the lease as yet unexpired at the time of the assignment in bankruptcy made by the tenant on November 16th, 1989.

On June 10, 1988 Melanie Vrablik (the "Tenant") entered into a commercial lease with Donald Raymond Stasiuk, Kathryn Marta Stasiuk, Andrew Findlay Coffey, Roberta Joan Coffey and 705514 Ontario Limited (hereinafter referred to as the "Landlord") as the lessor. The tenant had hoped to establish a fitness and exercise salon. The leased premises were known municipally as 104 North Syndicate Avenue in the City of Thunder Bay. The term of the lease was from July 1, 1988 to June 30, 1993. The monthly rental under the lease was $1,606.67. The tenant was responsible for the payment of municipal taxes, hydro, water and maintenance costs as set out in the lease. On November 16, 1989 the Tenant filed an assignment in bankruptcy (Bankruptcy No. 027144), the Trustee in Bankruptcy of the Estate of Melanie Vrablik being Ignit Stetsko (the "Trustee"). The landlord filed Proof of Claim dated December 11, 1989 in the amount of $99,412.59. A portion of this claim was a preferred claim, being the arrears of rent for a period of three months immediately preceding the bankruptcy of the tenant and the accelerated rent for a period of three months following the bankruptcy of the tenant. The Proof of Claim dated December 11, 1989 disclosed a sum of $13,886.09 as the preferred claim. A revised Proof of Claim dated November 22, 1991 filed by the Landlord reduced that sum to $8,167.41. The Proof of Claim dated December 11, 1989 also disclosed that the landlord has advanced a contingent and unliquidated claim in the amount of $85,526.50 based on the damages the landlord alleges it has sustained as a result of the tenant's default under the lease. The revised Proof of Claim dated November 22, 1991 outlines the landlord's unliquidated claim as follows:

(1)	rent from February 16, 1990 to	
	August 1, 1991 at $1,606.67....................	$ 28,116.72
(2)	1989 taxes...................................	$ 2,949.81
(3)	1990 taxes...................................	$ 4,685.94
(4)	1991 taxes to August 1, 1991..................	$ 3,043.64
(5)	maintenance in 1990........................	$ 1,121.95
(6)	maintenance in 1991........................	$ 839.08
(7)	shortfall on re-letting August 1, 1991 to	
	June 30, 1993...............................	$ 5,623.44
		$ 46,380.58

In summary, the Revised Proof of Claim dated November 22, 1991 lists the landlord's preferred claim at $8,167.41 and the unliquidated claim at $46,380.58. Section 38 of the *Landlord and Tenant Act*, RSO 1990, c. L.7 (*"Landlord Tenant Act"*) gives a landlord a preferential lien for the arrears of rent due during the period of three months preceding the assignment in bankruptcy and for three months following the execution of the assignment of bankruptcy:

> 38(1) In case of an assignment for the general benefit of creditors, or an order being made for the winding up of an incorporated company, or where a receiving order in bankruptcy or authorized assignment has been made by or against a tenant, the preferential lien of the landlord for rent is restricted to the arrears of rent due during the period of three months next preceding, and for three months following the execution of the assignment, and from thence so long as the assignee retains possession of the premises, but any payment to be made to the landlord in respect of accelerated rent shall be credited against the amount payable by the person who is assignee, liquidator or trustee for the period of the person's occupation.

Section 136 of the *Bankruptcy Act*, RSC 1985, c. B-3 (*"Bankruptcy Act"*) lays out a scheme of distribution of priorities subject to the rights of secured creditors. It is interesting to note that the preferential lien granted to a landlord in s. 38 of the Ontario *Landlord and Tenant Act*, reflects exactly the lien granted by s. 136(1) of the *Bankruptcy Act* and Parliament in its wisdom has ranked this priority sixth behind various other security interests:

> 136(1) Subject to the rights of secured creditors, the proceeds realized from the property of a bankrupt shall be applied in priority of payment as follows;
>
> • • •
>
> (f) the landlord for arrears of rent for a period of three months immediately preceding the bankruptcy and accelerated rent for a period not exceeding three months following the bankruptcy if entitled thereto under the lease, but the total amount so payable shall not exceed the realization from the property on the premises under lease, and any payment made on account of accelerated rent shall be credited against the amount payable by the trustee for occupation rent;

The preference provided by the *Bankruptcy Act*, *supra*, is only to the extent of the availability of property of the bankrupt on the premises at the time of the bankruptcy and is subject to the rights of other secured creditors having a higher priority under the *Bankruptcy Act*. The law is quite explicit in designating the Landlord as a preferred creditor compensating him for his vacant premises and in substitution of his right to distrain. This motion is brought on the basis of the combined strength of s. 121 of the *Bankruptcy Act* and Rule 94 of the *Bankruptcy Rules* which state that when an unliquidated claim is made, the Trustee in Bankruptcy must apply to the Court to determine whether or not the claim is provable, and if provable to have the claim valued. Counsel have all agreed that the central issue is whether or not the contingent, unliquidated claim is provable.

Upon making an Assignment in Bankruptcy or Receiving Order, all of the obligations and rights of the tenant in the lease vest in the Trustee in Bankruptcy as per s. 71(2) of the *Bankruptcy Act*:

> 71(2) On a receiving order being made or an assignment being filed with an official receiver, a bankrupt ceases to have any capacity to dispose of or otherwise deal with his property, which shall, subject to this Act and to the rights of secured creditors, forthwith pass to and vest in the trustee named in the receiving order or assignment, and in any case of change of trustee the property shall pass from trustee to trustee without any conveyance, assignment or transfer.

The Trustee in Bankruptcy has the right for a period of up to three months from the date of bankruptcy in which to elect whether to retain, assign, surrender or disclaim the lease as per s. 38(2) of the *Landlord Tenant Act* [see *supra*].

The Trustee in this case decided to disclaim and surrendered the lease in question to the landlord on December 11, 1989. Upon this action on the part of the Trustee, all rights and obligations of the Trustee under the lease are terminated as of the effective date of the disclaimer or surrender.

Counsel for the landlord in this matter argues that the landlord possesses a valid claim against the tenant or Trustee for amounts falling due *after* the date of the surrender or disclaimer of the lease. He relies upon the 1971 Supreme Court of Canada decision in *Highway Properties Ltd. v. Kelly, Douglas & Co.*, [1971] SCR 562, 17 DLR (3d) 710 ("*Highway Properties*") for this proposition. In that case, a major tenant in a shopping centre repudiated an unexpired lease. The landlord resumed possession of the premises and gave notice to the defaulting tenant that it would be held liable for damages suffered by the landlord as a result of the admittedly wrongful repudiation. In deciding whether or not to allow the damages, Laskin J, as he then was, considered the various options open to a landlord when faced with a repudiation of a lease:

1. The landlord may refuse to accept the repudiation of the lease by the tenant. Nothing is done to alter the landlord-tenant relationship. The landlord simply insists on the performance of the terms of the lease and sues for rent or damages as they accrue on the basis that the lease remains in force.

2. The landlord may elect to terminate the lease and retake possession of the premises. In this case, the landlord may sue for rent accrued due, or for damages to the date of termination for previous breaches of the covenant. The landlord may not sue for prospective damages because it is a principle of common law that once the lease is terminated, all obligations under the lease cease to exist.

3. The landlord may advise the tenant that he refuses to accept the repudiation of the lease but that he proposes to re-enter the premises and, unless otherwise directed by tenant, relet the property *on the tenant's behalf* and hold the original tenant liable for any deficiency in rental for the balance of the lease term.

Noting the increasing intermingling of property law with contract law in the area of leasehold estates in land, Laskin J recognized the common law principle that a lease of land for a term of years, under which possession is taken, creates an estate in land. In many situations legislation or a strict literal reading of contractual terms have superseded the common law, for example, the provision of payment of rent in advance, and the provision of re-entry for non-payment of rent or for breaches of other covenants by the tenant. For some reason the courts had stopped short in refusing to apply to leasehold estates in land the contractual doctrine of anticipatory breach and its accompanying principle governing relief upon repudiation of contract. On p. 716 [DLR] he continues after noting that this doctrine has been applied without question to contracts for the sale of land:

> I think it is equally open to consider its application to a contractual lease, although the lease is partly executed. Its anticipatory feature lies, of course, in the fact that instalments of rent are payable for future periods, and repudiation of the lease raises the question whether an immediate remedy covering the loss of such rent and of other advantages extending over the unexpired term of the lease may be pursued notwithstanding that the estate in the land may have been terminated.

In allowing a new, fourth alternative—the right of the landlord to sue for prospective damages—Laskin J overruled *Goldhar v. Universal Sections & Mouldings Ltd.* (1963), 36 DLR (2d) 450 (Ont. CA) ("*Goldhar*"). *Goldhar* formulated the doctrine of surrender such that once a lease is terminated, there can be no claim for prospective damages because that claim may only be founded on rights accruing to the tenant under the lease when still alive. Laskin J did not think it fair that, once an election to terminate the lease had been communicated through repudiation, all covenants and potential claims for relief in damages are terminated. At p. 721 [DLR] he made this observation:

> It is no longer sensible to pretend that a commercial lease, such as the one before this Court, is simply a conveyance and not also a contract. It is equally untenable to persist in denying resort to the full armoury of remedies ordinarily available to redress repudiation of covenants, merely because the covenants may be associated with an estate in land.

Counsel for the Landlord has urged that the analysis and decision in *Highway Properties* be adopted in the present case. This would be a grave error in that the present case involves a bankruptcy, which is quite different from an outright repudiation of contract. A bankruptcy is a final and irreversible situation. In fact the Legislature has foreseen the present situation in that it has very distinctly created a comprehensive scheme for administering the leasehold interests of bankrupt tenants. It is not a coincidence that s. 38 of the *Landlord Tenant Act* reflects almost verbatim s. 136(1)(f) of the federal *Bankruptcy Act*. Section 136(1)(f) outlines the priority of a landlord for arrears and accelerated rent as against other secured and unsecured creditors. When it comes to the rights of the landlord and tenant with regards to the repudiation of the lease contract because of the bankruptcy, s. 146 of the *Bankruptcy Act* refers the parties back to the wording of the appropriate sections of the *Landlord Tenant Act* and not to the common law as counsel for the Trustee has stated:

> 146. Subject to priority of ranking as provided by section 136 and subject to subsection 73(4) [*right to distrain for arrears of rent*], the rights of landlords shall be determined according to the laws of the province in which the leased premises are situated. [insert added]

It has been argued that the "laws of the province" referred to in s. 146 are the common law as well as the statute law and that in this situation the common law right to sue for prospective damages as outlined in *Highway Properties* should be adopted in this case. Despite this argument, the "laws of the province in which the leased premises are situated" are, of course, ss. 38 and 39 of the *Landlord Tenant Act*. As stated above, the combined effect of the *Bankruptcy Act* and the *Landlord Tenant Act* provides a comprehensive scheme for the administration of the leasehold interest of bankrupt tenants, *Re Limestone Electrical & Supply Co.*, [1955] OR 291 (Ont. CA).

Quite often Trustees in Bankruptcy elect under s. 38(2) to assign the lease with the approval of the Ontario Court (General Division). This is the kinder option for the landlord but it is only possible if an assignor can be found and approved by the Court. In an effort to promote fairness in commercial dealings, Trustees in Bankruptcy have been held personally liable for occupation rent during the time of disposal of the bankrupt's assets where there has been no clear agreement waiving such rights between the landlord and the Trustee, *Sasso v. D & A MacLeod Co.* (1991), 3 OR (3d) 472 (Gen. Div.); *Re Auto Experts Ltd.* (1921), 3 CBR 591 (Ont. CA). Nonetheless, where the Trustee legally disclaims the lease as per s. 39(1) of the *Landlord Tenant Act*, the effect of such a surrender is the same as if the lease had been surrendered with the consent of the lessor: *Re Mussens Ltd.* (1933), 14 CBR 479 (Ont. SC) at p. 482; *Cummer-Yonge Investments Ltd. v. Fagot*, [1965] 2 OR 152 (HC), affirmed [1965] 2 OR 157 (note) (CA); *Titan Warehouse Club Inc. (Trustee of) v. Glenview Corp.* (1988), 67 CBR (NS) 204 (Ont. HC). Any cause of action under the lease that arises against a tenant prior to bankruptcy remains a liability of the tenant and is accordingly, a responsibility of the Trustee as per s. 38(1) of the *Landlord Tenant Act*. However, a claim for rent after bankruptcy is restricted to the statutory three months next following the execution of assignment in bankruptcy or for so long as the Trustee elects to retain possession of the property. This is the law of this province. The landlord's claim for damages is therefore not provable in this bankruptcy and the Trustee's motion is hereby determined accordingly, and I am relieved of the necessity of assessing quantum.

Motion determined
no assessment of quantum.

NOTES AND QUESTIONS

1. *Re Vrablik* should be compared with the Supreme Court's decision in *In re Gingras Automobile Ltée* (1962), 4 CBR (NS) 123 (SCC). In the latter case, the landlord claimed

three months' arrears of rent and $1,398.22 for the cost of repairs the landlord was entitled to recover under the terms of the lease. The trustee allowed the first claim but disallowed the second. The landlord relied on the provisions of the (old) Quebec *Civil Code* (CC) giving him a privilege for both claims and on CC 1994 ranking a landlord's claim seventh among the claims of competing creditors. The Supreme Court held (1) that *Bankruptcy Act* (BA) s. 95(1)(f) (now BIA s. 136(1)(f)) exclusively determines the landlord's priority; (2) that s. 105 of the BA (now BIA s. 146) relates only to the validity of the landlord's claim and not to its priority; (3) that a landlord is not a secured creditor for the purposes of s. 2 of the Act; and (4) (*semble*), even if the landlord's *privilège* could be so construed, s. 107(1)(f) inferentially denies it that status.

2. Faced with limited rights of recovery under the BIA and provincial law, landlords have sought to work their way around the problem, but their success has been divided. In *885676 Ont. Ltd. v. Frasmet Holdings Ltd.* (1993), 12 OR (3d) 62 (Gen. Div.), R.A. Blair J held that while disclaimer of a lease deprived the landlord of the right to sue the trustee for damages, the trustee was not entitled to an order restraining the landlord from demanding payment from the issuer of an irrevocable letter of credit (LOC) to cover the landlord's damages. The trustee was concerned because the bankrupt had given security to the issuer of the LOC and release of the security would obviously be jeopardized if the issuer honoured the LOC. On the other hand, in *Peat Marwick Thorne Inc. v. Natco Trading Corp.* (1995), 22 OR (3d) 727 (Gen. Div.), Feldman J held that a landlord could not enforce security given by a tenant to collect future rent or damages under the lease upon the tenant's bankruptcy. Her reasoning was that the security was only as good as the underlying claim and, because the combined effect of the BIA and the Ontario *Landlord and Tenant Act* was to relieve the estate from further liability if the trustee elected to disclaim, there were no remaining obligations to support the security. She did not question the soundness of the decision in *Frasmet Holdings* and acknowledged that a letter of credit or other security could be so drafted as to survive termination of the lease by the landlord and the landlord's claim for damages. Is this reasoning sound where enforcement of the LOC or security interest will oblige the trustee to make good the third-party's loss, as apparently was true in *Frasmet*? Would this not undermine the statutory intent?

3. Why should realty leases be singled out for special treatment in the BIA and why does the BIA defer to provincial legislation in straight bankruptcies and not in the case of Part III proposals (see s. 65.2)? Assuming the appropriateness of allowing the trustee to disclaim a lease, why should the landlord's damages be limited to a preferential claim for three months' accelerated rent following the bankruptcy (and then only if the realized amount from the property on the premises is sufficient to cover the claim and subject to a deduction for any amount payable by the trustee for occupation rent)?

These questions received much attention in 1994, in the context of Part III of the BIA, by the Working Group of BIAC studying the desirability of amending s. 65.2. Landlords complained loudly that owners of chain stores were often invoking Part III so that they could disclaim leases and that the results were grossly unfair to them. Do you agree?

C. Other Contracts

New Skeena Forest Products Inc. v. Don Hull & Sons Contracting
(2005), 251 DLR (4th) 328 (BCCA)

BRAIDWOOD JA: ... [21] Although it is not necessary for me to decide for the purposes of this case, in light of the Intervenor's submissions on the confusion in the law regarding the power of trustees to disclaim contracts, and with a view to clarifying the matter, I make these observations.

[22] There is no provision in the *Bankruptcy & Insolvency Act*, RSC 1985, c. B-3 that gives a trustee power to disclaim contracts. The Act only addresses those powers that may be exercised with permission of inspectors. Thus, under s. 30(1)(k) of the *Bankruptcy & Insolvency Act* the trustee may disclaim a "lease of, or other temporary interest in, any property of the bankrupt."

[23] The power to disclaim contracts has been included in statutes in other common-law jurisdictions. Notably, s. 23 of the English *Bankruptcy Act, 1869* (32 & 33 Vict.), c. 71 first gave trustees the power to disclaim contracts of the bankrupt. The modern English statute, *Insolvency Act 1986* (UK), 1986, c. 45, s. 315 confers the same right upon a trustee. Similarly, in both Australia *(Bankruptcy Act 1966*, (Cth.), s. 133) and the United States (11 USC § 365) there is a statutory power for trustees to disclaim contracts.

[24] However, the power of trustees to disclaim contracts has its roots in the English law where there was a common-law power in assignees (who took control of debtor property prior to use of trusteeships in bankruptcy) to disclaim contracts. There is a weight of authority supporting the existence of such a power prior to the enactment of the 1869 Act.

[25] In his 1922 text, Lewis Duncan, in *The Law and Practice of Bankruptcy in Canada* (Toronto: Carswell, 1922) at 304-5, cites several venerable English cases for the proposition that:

> There is no section in the Canadian *Act* corresponding with section 54 of the English *Act* [earlier s. 23] which gives the trustee the right to disclaim onerous contracts or property. The law under *The* [Canadian] *Bankruptcy Act* will be the same as the law in England before the Act of 1869 was passed, with the exception that section 44 of the *Bankruptcy Act* gives a right of proof against the estate of the debtor with respect to contracts entered into before the date of the receiving order or authorized assignment. The law under the *Bankruptcy Act* would seem to be that a trustee may at his option perform the contract into which the bankrupt has entered or he may abandon it.

[26] In *In re Sneezum ex parte Davis* (1876), 3 Ch. D 463 (CA) at 472, James LJ said that at common law, prior to the passing of the *1869 Act*, assignees in bankruptcy had the option of deciding whether or not to carry on with performance of an executory contract.

[27] To similar effect, in *Gibson v. Carruthers* (1841), 8 M & W 321 at 326-27, a case in which the assignees wished to assume a contract under which the defendant, who had contracted with the bankrupt, had agreed to deliver 2000 quarters of linseed to a charter ship, Gurney B said:

... it is clear that assignees of a bankrupt are entitled to the benefit of all contracts entered into by the bankrupt and which are in fieri at the time of the bankruptcy. They may elect to adopt or reject such contracts, according as they are likely to be beneficial or onerous to the estate.

[28] In Canada, the Ontario Supreme Court Appellate Division in *Re Thomson Knitting Company*, [1925] 2 DLR 1007 (Ont. SC (AD)) recognized such a power; see also *Denison v. Smith* (1878), 43 UCR 503 (QB); *Stead Lumber Co. v. Lewis* (1958), 37 CBR 24, 13 DLR (2d) 34 at 43 (Nfld. SC); *Re Salok Hotel Co.* (1967), 11 CBR (NS) 95, 66 DLR (2d) 5 at 8 (Man. QB).

[29] In more recent times, L.W. Houlden & G.B. Morowetz in their text *Bankruptcy and Insolvency Law of Canada*, 3d ed, looseleaf (Toronto: Thomson Carswell, 2004) at F§ 45.2 state quite unequivocally that a trustee may disclaim a contract entered into by the bankrupt. Similarly, in a case comment on *Potato Distributors Inc. v. Eastern Trust Co.* (1955), 35 CBR 161 at 166 (PEICA), L.W. Houlden writes:

> It is well established law that a trustee may elect to carry on with a contract entered into prior to bankruptcy, provided he pays up arrears and is ready to perform the contract. The trustee could also, if he saw fit, elect not to go on with the contract in which event the vendor would have the right to prove a claim for damages.

[30] I observe that several Canadian commentators have recently opined that in the absence of an express statutory power, trustees in Canada may not disclaim executory contracts, specifically licences: see Piero Ianuzzi, "Bankruptcy and the Trustee's Power to Disclaim Intellectual Property and Technology Licencing Agreements: Preventing the Chilling Effect of Licensor Bankruptcy in Canada" (2001) 18 CIPR 367; Gabor F.S. Takach and Ellen Hayes, "Case Comment," *Re Erin Features #1 Ltd.* (1993) 15 CBR (3d) 66 (BCSC).; Mario J. Forte and Amanda C. Chester, "Licences and the Effects of Bankruptcy and Insolvency Law on the Licensee" (2001) 13 Comm. Insol. R 25. However, the position taken by the authors of these articles departs from the traditional understanding of the law in this area.

[31] In view of the position in the English authorities pre-dating the English Act of 1869, there is a common-law power in trustees to disclaim executory contracts. This power has been relied on for many years by trustees, and in the absence of a clear statutory provision overriding the common law, in my view trustees should have this power to assist them fulfill the duties of their office.

[32] I observe that recently, in its 2002 *Report on the Operation of the Administration of the Bankruptcy and Insolvency Act and the Companies' Creditors Arrangements Act*, Industry Canada's Marketplace Framework Policy Branch considered the extent to which insolvency law should intervene in private contracts to ensure fair distribution or maximize value during an insolvency. The Report notes there is not universal support for the enactment of a detailed statutory provision like the American one. In a 2001 report on business insolvency law reform, the Insolvency Institute of Canada and the Canadian Association of Insolvency & Restructuring Professionals proposed the enactment of more detailed rules for both powers of trustees to disclaim executory contracts ... . Ultimately, it may therefore be preferable for the legislature to move to include a power in

the statute, but until that time, in my view, trustees enjoy the power protected by the common law.

In re Thomson Knitting Co.
(1924-25), 5 CBR 189 (Ont. SC); aff'd. (1925), 5 CBR 489 (Ont. CA)

FISHER J: The debtor company was incorporated under *The Ontario Companies Act*, RSO, 1914, ch. 178, and carried on business at Bowmanville as wholesale and retail manufacturers of hosiery and designers and dealers in textile products.

Bever & Wolf carried on business in Bradford, England.

In October, 1922, the debtor company ordered from the creditors 5,000 pounds of artificial silk wool, of which 3,240 pounds were delivered. On December 29, 1922, the debtor company ordered 10,000 pounds and only 307 pounds were delivered. On January 5, 1923, the debtor company ordered 10,000 pounds; no delivery was made under this order. On January 13, 1923, the debtor company ordered 2,500 pounds and only 379 pounds were delivered. The wool was to be delivered in instalments.

Exhibits (1) (2) (3) (4) (5) and (6) show the contracts entered into and the correspondence in connection therewith.

Slater & Company were the Toronto agents of the creditors, and it was through these agents that all the orders were obtained.

On September 23, 1923, the debtor company made an authorized assignment and the creditors filed with the trustee the usual declaration proving their claim. The trustee admitted the claim, excepting as to any amount the creditors were claiming damages for, because of the insolvent company's failure to take delivery of the goods as ordered.

The facts and terms of the contracts are not in dispute. The goods were to be paid for, net 60 days from date of invoice.

One of the conditions in all the contracts reads:

If any payment is in arrear, either under this or any other contract, deliveries may be suspended or contract cancelled at our option.

The purchasers confirmed all the contracts in these words:

To Bever & Wolf: We have received your contract dated ... and we hereby accept and confirm.

Yours Truly,
(Sgd.) Thomson Knitting Co. Ltd.

The creditors now claim £675-16-5, as damages by reason of the insolvent company's failure to take delivery.

Counsel for both parties agreed that if it was found the creditors were entitled to any damages for breach of contract, they would agree on the *quantum* of damages.

Slater was the only witness called on behalf of the creditors, and he swore that the only reason deliveries were not made was because the insolvent company was unable to make payments for the goods already sold and delivered and for the goods they subsequently requisitioned under their contracts. All the correspondence, excepting that referred to in Exs. (1) (2) (3) (4) (5) and (6), was put in as Ex. (7).

From the correspondence it appears the purchasers were endeavouring, through Slater & Company, to obtain deliveries, and Slater communicated with the vendors. The correspondence indicates the purchasers were always hard-pressed for money. Slater & Company at one time were satisfied the company was in a position to pay and so communicated to the vendors. Slater & Company went even so far as to become personally responsible for a portion of some of the deliveries. They also obtained the personal guarantee of the directors of the debtor company and forwarded it to the vendors; Slater & Company agreeing to be personally responsible, and the guarantee, relieved the situation somewhat, but the vendors were not satisfied with the guarantee and so stated in the correspondence, because there was too much money owing.

It is only necessary to refer to a few of the letters to show the readiness on the part of the vendors to deliver and the desire on the part of the purchasers to obtain delivery and the inability on their part to pay.

. . .

The learned counsel for the trustee does not attack the contracts but contends that as the contracts called for delivery at certain stated periods, if there is any liability, it is at the time a delivery was to be made; that failure by the purchasers to pay does not relieve the vendors from the necessity of delivering, and that, whilst the vendors, on failure to pay, could have cancelled the contracts, not having done so there can now be no claim for damages; that the vendors cannot say "we will refuse delivery" and then claim damages for failure to pay; that the vendors having elected to retain the goods cannot now come into competition, on a claim for damages, with those creditors who had sold and delivered goods to the purchaser and were unpaid when they became insolvent, and that in any event, even if there was a failure to pay, it was the duty of the vendors, if they wished to hold the purchasers liable in damages for breach of contract, to have tendered the goods.

The learned counsel for the vendors contends that as they had not cancelled the contracts, and as they had kept in stock goods for the purpose of fulfilling the contracts when the purchasers called for deliveries, they are entitled to damages for breach of the contracts as of the date of its cancellation.

The questions for determination are: Are these creditors entitled to any damages; and if so, at what time is the damage to be ascertained?

The trustee's contention that the vendors' refusal to make deliveries operated as a rescission of the contracts is not borne out by the facts, as the correspondence clearly indicates there never was any intimation by the purchasers they would and could not pay, but on the contrary the purchasers were repeatedly calling for deliveries, making occasional payments and promising to pay, and as I have stated there was always readiness on the part of the vendors to deliver if payments were made. All the circumstances point to an intention on the part of both vendors and purchasers to have the contract continued. There was only a suspension of deliveries, and I hold the contract was not cancelled, and on these findings *Morgan v. Bain* (1874), LR 10 CP 15, 44 LJCP 47, 31 LT 616, 23 WR 239, relied on by counsel for the trustee, has no application.

A vendor is entitled to consider his contract cancelled on the insolvency of the purchaser if the trustee within a reasonable time after his appointment fails to notify the vendor he intends to adopt the contract, and a reasonable time, in my opinion, would be after the first meeting of creditors, as there is no one, until that meeting is called, authorized to act for the debtor. If a trustee remains silent a vendor is entitled to assume the contract is at an end.

The trustee in this case did not notify the vendors he intended to carry out the contract, and I therefore hold, if the vendors can prove any damages, they will be measured as of the date of the first meeting of creditors.

The law is well settled that a contract for the purchase of goods is not cancelled merely on account of the purchaser becoming bankrupt; see *Boorman v. Nash* (1829), B & C 145, 7 LJKB 150; *Griffiths v. Perry* (1859) 1 E & E 680, 28 LFQB 214, 5 Jur. (NS) 1076. It seems to me the terms of the contracts must govern. The vendors expressly provided, if payments were in arrear for two separate and distinct contingencies, namely, at their option (1) suspension of deliveries and (2) cancellation of their contracts. They could adopt either. The purchasers made their first default under the contracts on or about January 14, 1924, and according to the correspondence, at the solicitation of the purchasers, several deliveries were subsequently made and payments on account received from time to time. The vendors did not know the purchasers were going into insolvency, and they had a right to believe they might be able to pay for the goods purchased, and in order that they could make deliveries instead of cancelling the contracts kept them alive. The purchasers at any time up to the insolvency, if they could have provided for payment of the money, the contracts not having been cancelled, could have compelled the vendors to deliver all the goods covered by the contracts. But the evidence in this case is that the purchasers did not want the contracts cancelled, on the contrary they wanted them continued.

This is not a case where there was only one default by the purchasers (they were always in default) but rather that of a case where the sellers were ready and willing to deliver and were anxious for the buyers to take delivery. There was no object in the vendors tendering the goods, as default had already been made, and the correspondence shows the purchasers could not pay. In such circumstances the vendors were not bound to tender deliveries. See *Ex parte Chalmers; In re Edwards* (1873), LR 8 Ch. 289, 42 LJ Bk. 37, 28 LT 325, 21 WR 349, and at p. 291, Mellish LJ, said:

> The first question that arises is, what are the rights of the seller of goods when the purchaser becomes insolvent before the contract for sale has been completely performed. I am of opinion that the result of the authorities is this—that in such a case the seller, notwithstanding he may have agreed to allow credit for the goods, is not bound to deliver any more goods under the contract until the price of the goods not yet delivered is tendered to him; and that, if a debt is due to him for goods already delivered, he is entitled to refuse to deliver any more till he is paid the debt due for those already delivered as well as the price of those still to be delivered.

And at p. 293:

> I am, therefore, of opinion that, in the present case, when the insolvency of the purchaser had been declared the vendor was not bound to deliver any more goods until the price of

the goods delivered in November, as well as those which were to be delivered in December, had been tendered to him.

· · ·

There must be a finding that these contracts were outstanding and uncancelled at the date of the debtor company's bankruptcy; and, as the trustee refused to take them over and accept delivery of the goods, there will be judgment in favor of the creditors, and the damages, if any, will be measured as of the date of the first meeting of creditors.

· · ·

Judgment for creditors.

Creditel of Canada Ltd. v. Terrace Corp.
(1983), 4 DLR (4th) 49 (Alta. CA)

BELZIL JA: The appellants appeal a judgment against them for $11,991 and costs.

The plaintiff's action in its final form as amended at trial alleged a debt owing by the appellant to Formex Ltd. The debt is alleged to have been assigned by Formex Ltd. to Formex Location Rental Inc., and by the latter to the present respondent, Creditel of Canada Ltd., on October 1, 1980. The assignment from Formex Location to Creditel filed as an exhibit at trial was an assignment of an account or debt receivable. Notwithstanding that the action was pleaded in debt, the judgment awarded was for damages for breach of contract, without amendment of the pleading to fit the evidence. This discrepancy between the award of damages and the pleading in debt was raised before us but apparently not before the trial judge. ...

The assignment from Formex Ltd. to Location Formex Rental Inc. was not filed as an exhibit. It appears from the evidence of Norbert Dubois, an officer of both corporations, that Location Formex Rental Inc. was entirely owned by Formex Ltd., that Formex Ltd. went into bankruptcy on February 23, 1978, and that Formex Location Rental Inc. bought all the assets of Formex Ltd. on September 19, 1979, presumably from a trustee in bankruptcy, although that is not indicated in evidence.

The debt sued for is alleged to be due under an agreement for the fabrication and sale by Formex Ltd. to the appellants of three metal forms for the moulding of pre-cast concrete construction panels for a building being undertaken by the appellants in Edmonton. The trial judge found, correctly on the evidence, that there was one contract for the three forms. That contract is evidenced by quotation from Formex Ltd. submitted to and accepted by the appellants for fabrication of the units as per the appellants' design.

The first two units required modification of the design at extra cost. Responsibility for the additional cost was settled amicably by the parties and the two first units so modified were delivered and likewise specified by the appellants, over and above the modifications made to the first two units. Formex Ltd. sent a quotation to the appellants covering those extra modifications and requested approval of the extra costs by issuance of a supplementary purchase order. The appellants did not formally respond to this request, although it is indicated in evidence that there were telephone consultations between the parties. On February 13, 1978, Formex Ltd. sent a telegram to the appellants reaffirming its quotation for the modified third unit and again requesting a purchase order to cover. On February 27, 1978, Formex Ltd. sent a follow-up telegram to the appellants advising that work on the unit was being delayed pending advice from the appellants. The appellants did not respond because in the meantime they had received information from an employee of Formex Ltd. that Formex Ltd. was in bankruptcy. The trial judge found that the action of Formex Ltd. in delaying completion of the work on the third unit did not amount to a breach disentitling it to payment for work already done on the unit. He attributed fault to the appellants for having failed to supply a purchase order as requested. He awarded judgment to the value of the work done by Formex Ltd. on the third unit.

While the learned trial judge did not specifically qualify the award as one in damages, it obviously must have been so intended. It could not be for the contract debt since the contract remained uncompleted. It could only succeed in damages or *quantum meruit* and then only if the appellants had repudiated the contract by failing to furnish a new purchase order in acceptance of the quotation of Formex Ltd.

The learned trial judge did not take into account the effect on the contract of the bankruptcy of Formex Ltd. That effect is stated concisely as follows in *Re Thomson Knitting Co. Ltd., Ex p. Bever & Wolf*, [1925] 2 DLR 1007 at p. 1008, 56 OLR 625 at p. 631, 5 CBR 489:

> While the bankruptcy did not of itself constitute a breach of the contract, it did not on the other hand cast any further burden upon the vendors. But it had this effect: it entitled the vendors to treat the contract as broken if the trustee did not, within a reasonable time, approbate the contract and call for its completion.

In *Emden and Watson's Building Contracts and Practice*, 6th ed. (1962), the proposition is stated as follows at p. 220:

> *Rights which Pass to Trustee*—Ordinarily the benefits and rights under contracts which would pass as part of the bankrupt's personal estate to his personal representatives if he had died, pass to the trustee as part of the bankrupt's property, subject to the trustee's right to disclaim unprofitable contracts …
>
> *Election to Perform or Disclaim*—As regards those contracts which the trustee can perform, he has an election and may disclaim them, in which cases the persons who have contracted with the bankrupt may prove in the bankruptcy for damages to the value of any injury sustained by them, or the trustee may insist on the contract being performed, and in such case must perform the bankrupt's part of the contract, as and when the bankrupt should have done so himself.

There is no evidence to show that an election to perform was ever made by the trustee in bankruptcy, and certainly no evidence that such an election was ever communicated to the appellants. The issue was never addressed at trial. In these circumstances, the appellants could not be found in breach of the contract for their failure to issue a purchase order to the bankrupt vendor after learning of the bankruptcy. No case was made out by the plaintiff to support an award either in damages or in debt.

Appeal allowed.

A NOTE ON TECHNOLOGY LICENCES

The most common approach to the distribution of software technology is for the owner of the technology to copyright the software and license its use to others. A licence agreement is a form of permission by the licensor (A) for the licensee (B) to use some property belonging to A for a specified purpose: *Re T. Eaton Co.*, [1999] OJ no. 4216 (QL), at para. 12, per Farley J. The licence may be exclusive or non-exclusive. A software licence agreement is a promise by A to B that A will not enforce its copyright in the software for the duration of the licence. The consideration is usually in the form of royalties payable by B to A while the agreement continues. The agreement may be a software-distribution licence agreement or a software end-use licence agreement. In the case of a software-distribution licence agreement, B will need the rights to: (1) copy the software, and (2) distribute copies to the public by way of sale, lease, and so on. The agreement gives B these rights. In the case of an end-use licence agreement, B will need the right to use the software free of legal restrictions that might otherwise apply. The agreement gives B this right: see J. Dianne Brinson, "Software Distribution Agreements and Bankruptcy: The Licensor's Perspective" (1989), 64 *Washington Law Review* 497, at 501-10.

The business uses of software have increased dramatically in recent times. Dot-com enterprises depend almost entirely on software, but software is important for brick and mortar enterprises as well. Many business organizations rely on software to carry out key operations, such as the processing of customer orders, payrolls, and warehouse movements: see Michael Geist, "When Dot-coms Die: The E-commerce Challenge to Canada's Bankruptcy Law" (2002), 37 *CBLJ* 34. In these cases, A (the software producer or distributor) contracts with B (the end user) to develop and supply the software. A will often also contract to supply B with support services such as training, maintenance, update facilities, and the like. The contract is likely to be in the form of a licence giving B end-user rights to the software together with associated benefits. If A becomes bankrupt, A's trustee may want to terminate the agreement because: (1) he does not want to have to provide the support services; or (2) he wants to resell the licence rights to a third party. Loss of the right to use the software may devastate B's business. The risk of this outcome may discourage B from contracting with A in the first place. In other words, it may inhibit the development and supply of software systems and limit the commercial uses to which software systems are put.

In *Lubrizol Enterprises v. Richmond Metal Finishers Inc.*, 756 F 2d 1943 (4th Cir. 1985), the court held that a technology licence was an executory contract to which s. 365 of the US Bankruptcy Code applied, in substance because there were outstanding obligations still to be performed on both sides. This meant that A's trustee was entitled to reject the contract subject to the court's approval. The court approved the trustee's election. The effect of the rejection was to cancel the licence. A software licence is probably also an executory contact to which Code s. 365 applies. The decision had a potentially chilling effect on the development and exploitation of intellectual property. In 1988, Congress enacted s. 365(n) to reverse the outcome. Section 365(n) gives B two options: (1) to treat the contract as terminated if A's rejection would constitute a breach outside bankruptcy; or (2) to retain its rights under the agreement, including the right to enforce any exclusivity provision, subject to a continued obligation to make the royalty payments. If B chooses option (1), he has a claim against A's estate for any loss caused by the rejection. If B chooses option (2), he can continue to use the technology for the duration of the term, but he has no right to compel specific performance of other aspects of the agreement (for example, A's obligation to provide training, maintenance, or update facilities). In other words, s. 365(n) allows B to enforce A's negative obligations under the agreement, but not the positive obligations. In this respect, the provision attempts to strike a balance between B's individual interest in having the agreement enforced and the collective interests of A's creditors in having it set aside.

In Canada, new BIA s. 65.11, which was enacted as part of the 2007 amendments, provides for the disclaimer of contracts in BIA commercial proposal proceedings and new CCAA s. 32 is a parallel provision applicable in CCAA proceedings. Both provisions make a specific exception for intellectual property licences as follows:

> [I]f the debtor has granted a right to use intellectual property to a party to an agreement, the disclaimer or resiliation does not affect the party's right to use the intellectual property—including the party's right to enforce an exclusive use—during the term of the agreement, including any period for which the party extends the agreement as of right, as long as the party continues to perform its obligations under the agreement in relation to the use of the intellectual property.

This provision loosely corresponds with s. 365(n) of the Bankruptcy Code in the United States. What is the status of technology licence agreements in straight bankruptcy proceedings? There is no statutory right to disclaim contracts in bankruptcy (with the exception of commercial tenancy agreements), but there is a corresponding common law right: see the *New Skeena* case, extracted above. Outside bankruptcy, courts will typically grant an injunction to restrain breach by the licensor of a negative covenant in a licensing agreement. (The negative covenant is A's express or implied promise not to assert its ownership rights against B for the duration of the agreement). There is no case law directly in point, but the better view is that the same rule applies in the licensor's bankruptcy: see Wendy A. Adams and Gabor G.S. Takach, "Insecure Transactions: Deficiencies in the Treatment of Technology Licences in Commercial Transactions Involving Secured Debt or Bankruptcy" (2000), 33 *CBLJ* 321, at 356-61; Duggan, "Partly Performed Contracts," above, at 26-27. If the better view is right (as better views tend to be), then the licensor's trustee cannot refuse to honour the licence. If the trustee tries to revoke the licence without cause, the licensee can sue for an order to restrain her.

On the other hand, the trustee remains free to assign the technology to which the licence relates and, in the absence of agreement, the assignee may not be bound by the licence: *Royal Bank of Canada v. Body Blue Inc.*, 2008 CanLII 19227 (Ont. Sup. Ct). In *Body Blue*, the debtor, Body Blue, held the intellectual property rights to certain technology. The debtor granted Herbal Care an exclusive licence to use the technology in the manufacture and sale of products. The debtor later went into receivership and the receiver sold certain assets, including the technology, to a third-party purchaser. The sale was effected by court order ("the Approval and Vesting Order"), dated May 17, 2006. Herbal Care claimed that the licence was unaffected by the Approval and Vesting Order. Morawetz J disagreed, holding that, under the terms of the Approval and Vesting Order, the purchaser acquired the technology free and clear of any claim by Herbal Care. The main ground of the decision was that, although Herbal Care was aware of the vesting order, it took no steps to appeal during the time allowed. However, the case could be read as suggesting that a licence is not property in the sense of an entitlement that runs with the underlying asset and thus, even if Herbal Care had appealed the vesting order in time, it still might not have been successful. The Supreme Court's decision in *Saulnier* lends some support to this suggestion (note Binnie J's repeated statements that a licence is not property at common law). The reasoning in *Body Blue* would presumably have been the same if the debtor had gone into bankruptcy and the trustee had sold the assets in question. What explains the courts' reluctance to treat licences as property? The answer may be tied up with verification costs: in the absence of a workable registration scheme, the assignee of the underlying technology may have no easy way of discovering the licensee's interest and, if the licence were enforceable against the assignee, this might have a chilling effect on dealings in the technology: see Anthony Duggan, "In the Wake of the Bingo Queen: Are Licences Property?" (2009), 47 *Can. Bus. LJ* 225.

In the CCAA context, new CCAA s. 36 (not yet in force) may offer a solution. Section 36 precludes a debtor in CCAA proceedings from selling assets outside the ordinary course of business without court approval. In reaching its decision, the court must consider various factors, including "the effects of the proposed sale or disposition on the creditors and *other interested parties.*" Section 36 would apply to the proposed sale of an intellectual property right and, if the intellectual property right is subject to a current licence, the licensee would qualify as an interested party. It follows that, in making a s. 36 application, the debtor would have to disclose the existence of the licence to the court and the court would have a discretion either to disallow the sale altogether or to allow the sale subject to the continuance of the licence. New BIA s. 65.13 is a corresponding provision applicable in BIA commercial proposal proceedings. There is no equivalent for straight bankruptcy proceedings.

To recapitulate, in straight bankruptcy proceedings, the trustee's right of disclaimer depends on the common law and, probably, at common law, the trustee cannot disclaim a licence given by the debtor. Why should the law permit a debtor-licensee to disclaim, but not a debtor-licensor (or landlord)?

Can the trustee refuse to honour ancillary covenants, such as a covenant to provide support services (training, maintenance, update facilities, and the like)? The basic covenant is a negative promise—in other words, a promise to refrain from taking action to enforce the licensor's intellectual property rights. Ancillary covenants to provide support services are affirmative provisions. They require positive action on the licensor's part. Outside bankruptcy, the usual remedy for breach of such undertakings is damages. Equitable relief is not normally available. Presumably the same rule applies inside bankruptcy. The licensor's trustee may want to refuse the provision of support services because to honour the obligations would be burdensome to the estate. The court will not order the trustee to perform, but it will award the licensee damages against the estate for breach of contract. The licensee will have to prove in the bankruptcy for the claim and will rank for payment with the other unsecured creditors. In this limited sense, the licensor's trustee does have a right of disclaimer. She can refuse to perform the positive covenants. This is a breach of contract sounding in damages but the licensee will be denied full recovery due to the licensor's bankruptcy. Note that the specific provision for intellectual property licences in new BIA s. 65.11 (commercial proposals) and CCAA s. 32 (CCAA proceedings) only applies to the licensee's "right to use the intellectual property"; consequently, the debtor remains free to disclaim ancillary covenants, subject to the rules governing disclaimer the section lays down.

The foregoing discussion addresses the status of the licence in the licensor's bankruptcy. Assume A grants B a patent licence that incorporates an anti-assignment provision or an *ipso facto* clause and B becomes bankrupt while the licence is still current. Can B's trustee disclaim the licence? In straight bankruptcy proceedings, the answer is subject to the same common principles as apply to contracts at large: see above. In BIA commercial proposal proceedings and CCAA restructuring proceedings, the answer is governed by BIA s. 65.11 and CCAA s. 32: see Chapter 13, Section IV, "Executory Contracts." (Why should the law allow disclaimer of a licence in a debtor-licensee's bankruptcy, but not in the bankruptcy of the debtor-licensor? See Duggan, "Partly Performed Contracts," above, at 26-27.) Can B's trustee take over the licence? See below, Section III, "Affirmation." Can B's trustee assign the licence to a willing buyer? See Section IV, "Assignment."

Armadale Properties Ltd. v. 700 King St. (1997) Ltd.
(2001), 25 CBR (4th) 198 (Ont. SC—Bktcy.)

LAX J: This motion is brought by Deloitte & Touche Inc. in its capacity as Construction Lien Trustee and in its capacity as Trustee in Bankruptcy. It raises the issue whether the Trustee should perform an agreement for the purchase and sale of land where the estate will receive no benefit from the transaction. The facts are unique.

700 King Street (1997) Ltd. was incorporated to convert 700 King Street West to mixed residential and commercial condominium use. Richard Crenian was its sole officer and director. He was also president and a 50% owner of Peregrine Hunter, a real estate developer and the project manager for 700 King. Armadale Properties Limited was a principal investor and 50% owner of the King Street project.

On February 9, 2001, Armadale obtained an order appointing Deloitte & Touche Inc. as Trustee and Receiver and Manager of 700 King and of 140085 Ontario Limited, a company which held title to the remaining real property assets of 700 King. On February 19, 2001, 700 King was assigned into bankruptcy and Deloitte & Touche Inc. was also appointed Trustee in Bankruptcy.

Yotam Goldschlager was directly or indirectly a purchaser of three residential units and one commercial unit at 700 King. The residential units were purchased for members of his family. The commercial unit, Unit 8, was purchased for his business. With respect to each of these purchases, Goldschlager dealt exclusively with Crenian, who had apparent and actual authority to enter into the agreements of purchase and sale on behalf of 700 King. This motion concerns the purchase of Unit 8.

On March 20, 1999, Goldschlager, through a numbered company as purchaser, entered into an Agreement of Purchase and Sale with Peregrine Homes Ltd. and 700 King as vendors. The purchase price provided in the Agreement of Purchase and Sale was $185,000 and by Amending Agreement dated January 5, 2000 was increased to $206,082. The uncontradicted evidence of Goldschlager is that initially, he was only prepared to pay $185,000 for Unit 8 and Crenian was only willing to sell it to him at that price if he paid a deposit of $100,000. Goldschlager agreed to this. Goldschlager's company provided cheques for $100,000 in May 1999, $22,557.74 in June 2000 (in accordance with the Amending Agreement) and $85,000 (the balance of the purchase price) in December 2000, with the result that the entire purchase price was paid by way of deposit. At the request of Crenian, the cheques were made payable to Peregrine Homes Ltd. In July 2000,

Goldschlager moved his business from its former premises to Unit 8 and spent about $80,000 in improvements and moving costs.

The residential units closed on January 5, 2001. The transfer date for Unit 8 was scheduled for January 15, 2001 and postponed to February 7, 2001, but did not take place. The Receivership and Bankruptcy followed shortly after.

After its appointment, the Trustee proceeded to close sales of the residential and commercial units that had been sold. When it reviewed the files for Unit 8, it became apparent that all of the purchase monies for this unit had been paid by way of deposit to Peregrine Homes Limited, which was a personal company of Crenian, and had never been received by 700 King. There are no further funds to be delivered to the Construction Lien Trustee or to the Trustee in Bankruptcy upon the closing of the transaction. There is therefore no benefit to the creditors of the bankrupt in completing the transaction. The Trustee now applies for the advice and direction of the court.

The Trustee advances two arguments. First, it submits that the manner of payment is an essential term of a contract and that payment to one of two joint vendors in the absence of a written direction relieves the other contracting party from performing. Second, it submits that as the Trustee and the court must protect the assets of the estate for the benefit of the creditors, where the estate will receive no benefit, the court should direct the Trustee to disclaim the contract. In any event, as Trustee in Bankruptcy, it can only convey the bankrupt's interest, which is subject to mortgage and lien claims. Goldschlager would not accept this title. Although its powers as Construction Lien Trustee permit it to convey clear title, it questions whether it would be appropriate for the Trustee to use its lien powers in this way.

In my opinion, these arguments are both answered in the circumstances of this case and the Trustee should be directed to use its lien powers to convey clear title to Goldschlager in accordance with the Agreement of Purchase and Sale and consistent with the Statement of Adjustments that was prepared in anticipation of the scheduled closing.

As to the Trustee's first argument, I was provided with no case that stands for this proposition, but assuming this is sound law, it cannot apply in this case. The Trustee concedes that Crenian had actual authority to enter into the Agreement of Purchase and Sale and to direct the manner in which the funds were to be paid. This is precisely what occurred. Crenian determined that the funds should be paid to Peregrine Homes Ltd. and Goldschlager complied with this direction. It makes no difference that there is no written direction for payment. Crenian did not pay the funds to 700 King, but this cannot affect the performance obligations of 700 King under the contract.

As to the second argument, the circumstances under which a trustee can disclaim a contract entered into by a bankrupt prior to its bankruptcy have long been the subject of uncertainty: *Re Triangle Lumber and Supply Co. Ltd.* (1978), 21 OR (2d) 221; *Re Erin Features 91 Ltd.* (1991), 8 CBR (3d) 205 (BCSC). Assuming a trustee has this right, section 75 of the *Bankruptcy and Insolvency Act*, RSC 1985, c. B-3 prevents the Trustee from disclaiming this contract. As was noted by Saunders J in *Re Triangle*, *supra*:

> A reading of s. 53 [now, s. 75] would appear to dispose of the problem. An agreement for sale in favour of a bona fide purchaser or mortgagee for valuable consideration is valid and effectual as if no receiving order had been made. It would therefore appear that the Trustee is bound by the agreement and may not disclaim it.

In the event that I am wrong and section 75 does not apply, I would not allow the Trustee to disclaim this contract. It is clear that a trustee can only succeed to the rights of a bankrupt and has no higher or greater interest. A trustee cannot terminate property rights that have passed under the contract prior to the bankruptcy: *Re Triangle, supra*; *Re Erin Features 91, supra*. The equitable interest under this contract passed prior to the bankruptcy and Goldschlager could have enforced the transfer of title by way of specific performance. In my opinion, the property was validly conveyed and all that remained was the delivery of a deed.

I was referred to the decision in *Re Bakermaster Foods Limited* (1985), 56 CBR (NS) 314 as contrary authority. In that case, if the Trustee had closed the transaction, there would have been a substantial deficit, which could only be made up from the funds in the estate to the prejudice of the unsecured creditors. The Trustee was directed not to close the transaction. In my view, these were exceptional circumstances, which have no application here.

The Trustee submitted that Goldschlager was the author of his own misfortune in providing the entire purchase monies as deposit and it is therefore he and not the creditors of 700 King who should bear this loss. In my view, if there is culpability, it does not rest with Goldschlager. He had no relationship with Crenian except as a purchaser of real estate. He has offered an explanation for providing the deposit he did. Although Peregrine Homes Ltd. had no beneficial interest in Unit 8, it was the bankrupt that gave Crenian apparent authority to act as he did. Prior to the bankruptcy, 700 King could not assert as against Goldschlager that Crenian lacked the authority to direct payment of the funds to Peregrine Homes Ltd. As the Trustee stands in the shoes of the bankrupt, it cannot now complain of the very loss to the estate that the bankrupt brought about.

Finally, the Trustee is an officer of the court and must act fairly to all parties with an interest in the estate. It would be dishonourable for the Trustee to disclaim this contract. I therefore find that the Trustee is bound by the contract in the same manner and to the same extent as the bankrupt was at the time of the bankruptcy and has no power to disclaim the contract. The Trustee is directed to complete the transaction in its capacity as Construction Lien Trustee. It may discharge the caution registered on title by 1333203 Ontario Limited. The Trustee and the numbered company should have their costs out of the estate. I fix the costs of the numbered company at $2500.

NOTES AND QUESTIONS

1. Why did the trustee want to disclaim the contract? The reason is that Goldschlager had already paid the whole of the purchase price. Therefore there was no benefit to the creditors in completing the contract. By disclaiming the contract, the trustee was attempting to keep both the unit and Goldschlager's money, leaving Goldschlager in return with only a right to prove in the bankruptcy for the amount of his payment.

2. Do you agree with Lax J's decision? There are two competing principles involved. The first is that the trustee in bankruptcy gets no larger property rights than the debtor himself had. The second is that unsecured creditors are entitled to share pro rata in the bankruptcy distribution. The first principle suggests that, in a case like *Armadale*, the purchaser should still be allowed to sue for specific performance even though the vendor is bankrupt. The

second principle suggests that the purchaser should not have a right of specific performance in bankruptcy, because that gives him an advantage over the other unsecured creditors: in effect, his claim is satisfied in full, leaving less in the kitty for everyone else. Lax J's decision in *Armadale* is consistent with the first principle, but inconsistent with the second one. Section 365(i) of the US *Bankruptcy Code* allows a purchaser of real estate to sue for specific performance, but only if he has gone into possession of the land. If he has not gone into possession, the Code reduces his claim to damages and he ranks for payment equally with the other unsecured creditors. One reason for the different rules is that a purchaser in possession is likely to have spent money on the property (for improvements, and so on), and the specific performance remedy protects her reliance interest.

3. Assume Debtor is Tenant's landlord. Debtor becomes bankrupt and Trustee wants to disclaim the lease, perhaps because he can get more rent by letting the property to someone else, or perhaps because he can sell the property for a higher price if it is untenanted. Can Trustee disclaim the lease? *Armadale Properties* suggests that the answer is "no": Trustee's right of disclaimer cannot override established property rights. The US *Bankruptcy Code* also disallows rejection in a case like this. On the other hand, it does allow rejection of a landlord and tenant agreement if Debtor is the tenant. Likewise, in Canada, new BIA s. 65.11 (disclaimer in commercial proposals) and CCAA s. 32 (disclaimer in CCAA proceedings) specifically exclude "a lease of real property ... if the debtor is the lessor." Why allow rejection (disclaimer) if Debtor is the tenant, but not if she is the landlord? There are at least two reasons. First, outside bankruptcy, Debtor could not dispossess Tenant so long as Tenant paid the rent and observed the other terms of the lease. Trustee's rights against Tenant should be no larger than Debtor's rights outside bankruptcy because, otherwise, Debtor's creditors will have an incentive to use the bankruptcy laws opportunistically as a means of avoiding the lease. The second reason is that Tenant is likely to have spent money either on the property itself or otherwise in reliance on the lease and disallowing disclaimer protects Tenant's reliance interest. Failure to protect Tenant's reliance interest would increase the upfront risk to prospective tenants and presumably lower both the demand for rental properties and the rent tenants are willing to pay. Furthermore, dispossession might trigger Tenant's own financial crisis, putting in train a whole new set of bankruptcy proceedings, and this would be too high a price to pay for facilitating Debtor's own proceedings.

III. AFFIRMATION

A. Introduction

Affirmation is the other side of the coin from disclaimer. Disclaimer is Trustee's decision not to proceed with performance of a contract Debtor negotiated before becoming bankrupt. Affirmation is Trustee's decision to adopt the contract. As the *Thomson Knitting* case indicates, disclaimer does not require a positive election on Trustee's part; the default rule, subject to any statutory provision to the contrary, is that if Trustee fails to make an election she will be deemed to have disclaimed the contract. On the other hand, affirmation does require a positive choice. The reason is that Debtor and Trustee are separate persons and Trustee does not automatically become party to Debtor's pre-bankruptcy contracts. Assume Trustee affirms a contract, but subsequently fails to perform, so that Counterparty has a claim for damages. Counterparty's claim lies against the estate and is payable, as an administrative expense, in priority to the unsecured creditors: BIA ss. 31(4) and 32 and *Re North American Steamships Ltd.*, extracted below. This priority can be rationalized as a form of *quid pro quo* to Counterparty for forcing it to accept performance from Trustee.

B. Landlord and Tenant Agreements

Provincial landlord and tenant statutes give the trustee of a bankrupt tenant the right to affirm a commercial tenancy agreement. In Ontario, the governing provision is *Commercial Tenancies Act*, s. 38(2), extracted above, which provides that, despite any provision in the lease agreement to the contrary, the trustee may, within three months after the debtor goes into bankruptcy and by notice in writing to the landlord, elect to retain the leased premises. The trustee must pay rent as provided for in the lease and these payments come out of the estate.

Section 38(2) deals with the trustee's right to affirm the lease and also with the right of assignment. The 2007 BIA amendments override the assignment part of the provision (see below, Section IV), but they do not affect the affirmation part.

In *Re Limestone Electrical & Supply Co. Ltd.*, [1955] OR 291 (Ont. CA), Laidlaw JA described the operation of the affirmation part of the provision as follows:

> The procedure and requisites for the acquisition and exercise of the rights created by the subsection, and as prescribed therein, are these:
>
> 1. The right to retain the leased premises for the period of three months described above does not depend upon any condition or stipulation, but is unqualified and unconditional.
>
> 2. In order to acquire the right to retain the leased premises for any period after the expiration of the three months described above, it is essential to comply with the following statutory requirements:
>
>   (a) that the assignee, liquidator or trustee elect by notice in writing to retain the leased premises for the whole or any portion of the unexpired term and any renewal thereof, upon the terms of the lease and subject to the payment of the rent as provided therein;
>
>   (b) that such notice be given by the assignee, liquidator or trustee within the period of three months;
>
>   (c) that the notice be given before the assignee, liquidator or trustee has given notice of intention to surrender possession or disclaim."

C. Other Contracts

Professionally drafted agreements commonly provide that a party's bankruptcy or insolvency entitles the other party to cancel or amend the agreement, demand the return of goods (in the case of chattel leases or bailments), and claim damages that may be in a liquidated amount. Such provisions are known as *ipso facto* clauses. Prior to the 2007 amendments, the status of *ipso facto* clauses in bankruptcy was uncertain. The question turned on whether the counterparty's right of cancellation fell within the terms of the stay in BIA s. 69.3. BIA s. 84.2, which was enacted as part of the 2007 amendments, resolves the uncertainty by providing that no person may terminate or amend a contract with the debtor by reason only of the debtor's bankruptcy. The 2007 amendments do not expressly give the trustee power to affirm contracts, but s. 84.2 assumes such a power because there would be no point in prohibiting *ipso facto* clauses unless the trustee, but for such a clause, had the option of keeping the contract on foot. BIA s. 30(1)(c) gives the trustee power to carry on the business of the bankrupt, so far as may be necessary for the beneficial administration of the estate and this provision, also by implication, gives the trustee power to continue existing contracts, in addition to entering new ones.

Potato Distributors Inc. v. Eastern Trust Company
(1955), 35 CBR 161 (PEICA)

TWEEDY J: This is an appeal from a judgment of my Lord the Chief Justice, upon an application by Potato Distributors Incorporated for an order declaring a certain contract to be frustrated and void by reason of bankruptcy of the debtor, or in the alternative, for an order that the trustee in bankruptcy disclaim the said contract as onerous.

The learned Chief Justice refused the application and as to the alternative order sought he held it clearly could not be considered upon the application before him as the above appellant was only a contractor and not a creditor at that time.

Since then, however, Russell Hammill and Russell Ching, two creditors of the debtor, have been added as intervenants. Some objection was made to this procedure, but for the purpose of this appeal it was agreed that the appeal be considered as properly before the Court and that the appeal should be heard and determined upon its merits.

The contract in question is dated April 9, 1955, and is between the debtor of the one part and the appellant of the other part and is for sale and delivery by the debtor to the appellant in each of the years, 1955, 1956, and 1957, of 25,000 bags of certified Number One Canada A Grade Sebago Seed Potatoes and also 1,750 bags of certified Number One Canada A Grade Small Sebago Seed Potatoes, ship's tackle at Summerside, Charlottetown or Souris in Prince Edward Island.

The date of delivery of said potatoes in each of the said three years was to be during the months of November and December, and the price agreed to be paid by the purchaser appellant to the debtor was $1.75 United States funds per 100 pound bag.

On August 25, 1955, a receiving order was made against the debtor and the respondent was appointed trustee in bankruptcy. No potatoes have been delivered under the contract.

The grounds of appeal are as follows:

1. From the very nature of bankruptcy, performance of a three year contract by the trustee is inapt.

2. More especially is this so where, as in the present case, performance of the contract involves gambling on the potato market.

3. *The Bankruptcy Act* does not contemplate carrying on the business of the bankrupt by the trustees where that business is of a highly speculative nature.

4. Carrying on business by the trustee must be confined to such business as will promote a reasonably speedy winding up of the estate.

5. The undertaking given by the trustee in the present case would be worthless in certain circumstances, and His Lordship therefore erred in refusing the appellant's application upon such an undertaking.

The argument was devoted mainly to s. 10(1)(c) of *The Bankruptcy Act*, 1949, 2nd Sess. (Can.), c. 7 [now BIA s. 30(1)], which reads as follows:

The trustee may, with the permission of the inspectors, do all or any of the following things: ...

(c) carry on the business of the bankrupt, so far as may be necessary for the beneficial administration of the estate.

It was contended by the appellant that the completion of the contract by the trustee is the carrying on of the business of the debtor; business that is not necessary for the beneficial administration of the estate.

Our *Bankruptcy Act* was no doubt modelled after and largely copied from the English Act, 1914, c. 59. An examination of the English cases therefore will be of some assistance in the consideration of this case.

The original *Bankruptcy Act* was enacted by the Dominion Parliament in the Session of 1919 (9-10 Geo. V, c. 36) and was to become operative by Royal Proclamation. A proclamation was issued on December 31, 1919, bringing the Act into force on July 1, 1920.

Various amendments were passed and these were consolidated and revised and the new *Bankruptcy Act* was contained in RSC 1927, c. 11.

What is now s. 10(1)(c) already quoted, was s. 43(1)(b) in RSC 1927, c. 11, and was s. 20(1)(b) of *The Bankruptcy Act*, 1919 and amendments thereto with this variation:

Section 43(1)(b) of RSC 1927, c. 11 reads as follows:

43. The trustee may, with the permission in writing of the inspectors, do all or any of the following things: ...

(b) carry on the business of the debtor, so far as may be necessary for the beneficial winding-up of the same.

From a perusal of the English cases, it would appear that this section of the English *Bankruptcy Act* reads exactly the same way.

However, our *Bankruptcy Act*, 1949, in s. 10 does not require the permission of the inspectors to be in writing; refers to the "debtor" as a "bankrupt" in s. 10(1)(c) and states that the business should be carried on "so far as may be necessary for the beneficial administration of the estate," not "so far as may be necessary for the beneficial winding-up of the business of the debtor."

It is contended by the appellant that "administration" and "winding-up" are the same thing. I realize that the words are used interchangeably in the English cases. Also that Morawetz's 3rd edition of *Bradford & Greenberg's Canadian Bankruptcy Act* at p. 43 states that "Para. (c) corresponds to former para. (b)." I cannot help feeling, however, that there is a difference in meaning in the words of the two sections. One of the dictionary meanings of "administration" is "The management and disposal of the estate of a deceased person."

The dictionary meaning of "wind-up" is to close, conclude, finish.

A very common use of the word administration is in connection with the administration of estates of deceased persons. In that use it does not mean that contracts of the deceased be frustrated or voided or that the administrator should disclaim contracts of the deceased as being onerous.

Neither do I think that Parliament intended this to be the case when it deliberately changed the wording of the section as used in the English Act, *The Bankruptcy Act*, 1919 and *The Bankruptcy Act*, 1927.

However, it is not necessary for the disposition of this appeal that I should determine this point although I must confess it is fascinating and very interesting.

[To deal] now with the main question whether or not by carrying out this contract the trustee is carrying on business not necessary for the beneficial administration of the estate.

I was much impressed with the argument and the cases cited. I am quite prepared to admit too that the pith and substance of this section is whether or not the carrying on of the bankrupt business is necessary for the beneficial administration of the estate. See *In re Wreck Recovery and Salvage Company* (1880), 15 Ch. D 353, per Jessel MR at p. 360: "Now the word 'necessary' means that it must not be merely beneficial but something more. ... Then it must be for the 'beneficial winding-up' of the business of the company, therefore it must be with a view to the winding-up of the company, not with a view to its continuance."

I am also in agreement with the quotation from the judgment of Macdonald J in *In re Sechart Fisheries Limited* (1929), 10 CBR 565 at 569, [1929] 2 WWR 413, 41 BCR 323, [1929] 4 DLR 536, 3 Can. Abr. 442, where he states: "... in my opinion it is the duty of a trustee to speedily realize the assets, and divide the proceeds among the creditors."

In re Delisle (Colonial Construction Co.), Bonnier and Fels, 23 CBR 333, [1942] Que. SC 72, Abr. Con. 285, and *In re Grobstein and Capra* (1929), 11 CBR 250, 3 Can. Abr. 443, were cited by the appellant as cases showing where it was proper that the business of the bankrupt debtor should be carried on for a time.

The leading English case of *Clark v. Smith*, [1940] 1 KB 126, [1939] 4 All ER 59, while it is very interesting and illuminating, yet is not of much assistance in the present case.

After carefully considering all the above cases and the other cases cited, I cannot reach the conclusion that the trustee in this case is carrying on business of the bankrupt that is not necessary for the beneficial administration of the estate.

The potato business of the bankrupt was only one branch of many other lines of business carried on by it. Among others mentioned were plumbing, feed business, hardware business and many others.

All the trustee is trying to do by carrying out this contract is to endeavour to mitigate the liabilities as much as possible and not try to make a profit.

As so often pointed out, *The Bankruptcy Act* was passed for two main objects: 1. To secure the creditors the best result, i.e., an economical administration, and 2. To enable an honest bankrupt to obtain a discharge and to make a fresh start.

The Bankruptcy Act was passed primarily for the purpose of securing to creditors the wreckage of bankrupt estates, and extricating from an intolerable situation the unfortunate trader who, through no fault of his own, finds himself weighed down with financial burdens which he cannot discharge: *Per* Barry, CJKBD, in *In re Holdengraber; Ex parte Royal Brand Clothing Co.* (1927), 8 CBR 411 at 413, 3 Can. Abr. 662.

> "In the performance of his duties a trustee … should have regard to the fact that his principal duty is to realize the assets of the debtor … and distribute such assets *pari passu* amongst the unsecured creditors after having satisfied all preferred creditors. … The trustee cannot carry on the business for the purpose of making a profit for the debtor or with a view of saving the business for him, but only for the purpose of beneficially winding-up the business in the interest of the general body of creditors:" *Per* Maclennan J, in *In re Gareau; Ex parte Joseph Bros.* (1922), 3 CBR 76, 3 Can. Abr. 486.

Here the inspectors instructed the trustee to carry out the contract under consideration.

The whole scope of *The Bankruptcy Act* indicates that in the administration of the estate of a debtor the governing authority shall be the inspectors and not the Court. If, however, they act fraudulently or in bad faith and not for the benefit of the estate, the Court may interfere, but otherwise the policy of the Act is to leave the matter entirely in their hands: *In re J.L. Jacobs & Co.* (1941), 22 CBR 208, Abr. Con. 323.

It is not as though the trustee were entering upon some new project. Here he is trying to do the best possible, guided by the views of his inspectors for the creditors as a body and not for any one group.

I am of the opinion, therefore, that the learned Chief Justice was right in refusing to grant an order declaring the contract to be frustrated and void subject to the express undertaking given by the trustee that no distribution of assets would be made among the creditors until after the date of the completion of the three-year contract with the appellant, and that the assets of the bankrupt in the hands of the trustee would be answerable to the appellant for any damages arising from a breach of the contract.

Appeal dismissed.

[MacGuigan J delivered a short concurring judgment.]

NOTE

Why does the BIA impose the condition that the trustee can only carry on the debtor's business "so far as may be necessary for the beneficial administration" of the estate of the bankrupt (s. 30(1)(c))? Whose interests are being protected? Is it likely that the inspectors would encourage the trustee to gamble on the success of continuing in business? Why is the inspectors' business judgment of the merits of the trustee being allowed to carry on the business not sufficient? For a discussion of the role and purpose of inspectors under the BIA, see *Impact Tool & Mould Inc. (Trustee of) v. Impact Tool & Mould (Windsor) Inc. (Receiver of)* (2006), 79 OR (3d) 241 (CA).

In re Gareau (1922), 3 CBR 76 (Que. SC) shows the advisability of not fettering the inspectors' discretion. The bankrupt was a manufacturer and retailer of woolen clothing (men's suits) and apparently had a large number of orders and cloth in hand at the time of its assignment. With the inspectors' consent, the trustee continued the business. Fifteen stores had been closed and seven more were shortly to be closed. Suits to the value of $390,000 had been manufactured and had realized 67.5 percent of their inventory value. This was much more than the goods were supposed to be worth at the time of the assignment.

The trustee had also sold suits for a total amount of $1,152,000; had paid all related expenses; paid the secured creditors $88,000 and a dividend of 12.5 percent to ordinary creditors; and had on hand a further $96,000 for distribution to ordinary creditors, whose remaining claims amounted to $1,112,000. The trustee expected to be able to pay a further dividend of 12.5 percent to ordinary creditors at the end of the spring season in 1922.

So it is clear that an orderly liquidation of a bankrupt business is much to be preferred over a fire sale.

In the Matter of the Bankruptcy of North American Steamships Ltd.
2007 BCSC 267

TYSOE J:

Introduction

[1] The Trustee in Bankruptcy (the "Trustee") of North America Steamships Ltd. (the "Bankrupt") applies for two declarations in connection with the necessity and effect of the Trustee affirming two freight forward swap agreements between the Bankrupt and AWB Geneva S.A. ("Geneva") and one freight forward swap agreement between the Bankrupt and Pioneer Metal Logistics, B.V.I. ("Pioneer").

[2] On January 10, 2007, I granted an *ex parte* Order declaring that the reasonable time for affirmation by the Trustee of these freight forward swap agreements (the "Geneva/Pioneer Swap Agreements" or the "Swap Agreements") would not expire until five business days after a decision by the court of an application set for hearing with respect to the liability of the Trustee in the event it affirmed the Geneva/Pioneer Swap Agreements. The Trustee subsequently made a separate application for a declaration that it is not required to affirm the Swap Agreements. I heard these two applications concurrently.

Background

[3] The Bankrupt began carrying on a ship brokering business in 1993 or 1994. Its focus shifted after a few years to the ship chartering business. In 2004, the Bankrupt acted as agent for another company in dealing with a swap agreement in the shipping industry. It became involved in swap agreements on its own account in 2005.

[4] In simple terms, a swap agreement in the shipping industry is considered to be a derivative product that does not actually involve shipping physical products. It can be used as a hedge by parties involved in shipping products to protect themselves against fluctuation in shipping rates or, as was the case with the Bankrupt, it can be a form of trading in futures. It was referred to in the submissions before me as a form of gambling.

[5] A representative of the Trustee described the main elements of the swap agreements entered into by the Bankrupt as follows in his affidavit:

(a) the [swap agreement] is entered into between two parties—a Buyer and a Seller;

(b) the parties agree on a route;

(c) the parties agree on a day, month and year of settlement;

(d) the parties agree on the contract quantity (ie. number of days, although I believe that it must be a minimum of 3 months);

(e) the parties agree on a Contract Rate and Settlement Rate. The Settlement Rate is established by an independent Index or Baltic Exchange (the "Exchange");

(f) essentially, the Buyer is wagering that the Settlement Rate on the Exchange will be higher than the Contract Rate at a future time. Conversely, the Seller is wagering that the Settlement Rate on the Exchange will be lower than the Contract Rate at a future time;

(g) settlement is made by the parties in cash within five days following the end of each calendar month; and

(h) the transactions under the [swap agreements] are derivative products only—i.e. there are no physical shipping transactions involved.

[6] The Bankrupt became insolvent as a result of losses of approximately $13 million under swap agreements covering all or parts of 2006. During the course of 2006, the Bankrupt entered into approximately 20 swap agreements for the 2007 year. Most of the 2007 agreements are anticipated to result in losses. The Trustee estimates that the total losses under the 2006 and 2007 swap agreements will be approximately $55 million. As at the time of the hearing of the *ex parte* application, the Trustee had collected approximately $3.5 million and had additional receivables.

[7] While the Bankrupt was largely unsuccessful with respect to the swap agreements it entered into during the past two years, the likely outcome of the Geneva/Pioneer Swap Agreements is positive. The Bankrupt is the buyer under each of the Swap Agreements, and the contract period for each of them expires on December 31, 2007 (two of them had contract periods of one year and the third had a contract period of one-half year). The contract rates under the Swap Agreements range from US $13,700 a day to US $17,500 a day, while the current settlement rate is approximately US $36,000 a day. If the settlement rate were to stay at US $36,000 for the entire year, the Trustee estimates that the payments due to the Bankrupt under the Swap Agreements would amount to US $18.3 million. The concern of the Trustee is that there is a possibility that the settlement rate could fall below the contract rates and that monies could be owing to Geneva and Pioneer under the Swap Agreements.

[8] Each of the Geneva/Pioneer Swap Agreements incorporated by reference the 1992 ISDA Master Agreement (Multicurrency—Cross Border) (without Schedule) (the "Master Agreement"). This is a detailed agreement developed by the International Swap Dealers Association. One of the provisions of the Master Agreement is that if one of the

parties goes bankrupt, the other party may terminate the swap agreement, in which case the payments due under the agreement are determined by a market quotation of the average settlement rate for the year. The quoted rate for 2007 is US $31,625, which would mean that Geneva and Pioneer would have to pay the Bankrupt an amount somewhat less than the US $18.3 million figure mentioned above if they were to elect to terminate the Swap Agreements at the present time.

Issues

[9] The issues raised by the Trustee's applications are as follows:

(a) is it necessary for the Trustee to affirm the Geneva/Pioneer Swap Agreements in order to take the benefit of them?

(b) if the Trustee does affirm the Geneva/Pioneer Swap Agreements, will the Trustee be personally liable in respect of the obligations of the buyer under the Swap Agreements or will the liability of the Trustee be limited to the assets in the bankruptcy estate?

Discussion

(a) Necessity to Affirm

[10] The requirement for a trustee in bankruptcy to affirm a contract entered into by the bankrupt stems from the decision in *Re Thomson Knitting Co. Ltd.* (1925), 5 CBR 489 (Ont. SC (AD)). In that case, the bankrupt had entered into a contract for the purchase of goods from the vendor. At issue was whether the vendor qualified as a creditor of the bankrupt in respect of damages for breach of contract. In holding that the vendor was a creditor, the Court said the following at p. 490:

> While the bankruptcy did not of itself constitute a breach of the contract, it did not on the other hand cast any further burden upon the vendors. But it had this effect: it entitled the vendors to treat the contract as broken if the trustee did not, within a reasonable time, approbate the contract and call for its completion. Nor was it necessary for the vendors first to tender the goods to the trustee: *Ex parte Stapleton; In re Nathan* (1879), 10 Ch. D 586, 40 LT 14, 27 WR 327. And the trustee could not insist upon delivery of the balance of the goods except upon full payment, not only of the prices of the goods so delivered, but also of all the arrears. In other words, the trustee cannot call for completion of the contract by the vendors without full performance on his part of all the purchasers' obligations thereunder: *William Hamilton Mfg. Co. v. Hamilton Steel and Iron Co.* (1911), 23 OLR 270.

[11] The Appellate Division of the Ontario Supreme Court did not explain why the trustee should be required to approbate the contract and call for its completion. In my view, such a requirement is reasonable and makes commercial sense. If a party to a contract becomes bankrupt, a question arises as to whether the obligations of that party under the contract will be performed. The bankrupt itself is no longer in a position to perform the obligations and one could consider the contract to be frustrated unless someone else standing in the place of the bankrupt (i.e., the trustee in bankruptcy) is prepared to

perform the obligations. It is not reasonable for the other party to be bound to perform its obligations under the contract after the date of bankruptcy without knowing how the obligations of the bankrupt will be treated if they are not performed. If the other party performs its obligations, it is entitled to know that it will not simply become an unsecured creditor of the bankrupt if the obligations of the bankrupt under the contract are not performed. Thus, if the trustee in bankruptcy wants to benefit from the contract, it is incumbent on it to affirm the contract and thereby assure the other party that it will not be treated as an unsecured creditor of the bankrupt in respect of the obligations it performs after the date of bankruptcy.

[12] A similar point arose in *Potato Distributors Inc. v. Eastern Trust Company* (1955), 35 CBR 161 (PEICA), where a party to a contract with the bankrupt applied for an order declaring the contract to be frustrated and void by reason of the bankruptcy. The Prince Edward Island Court of Appeal said the following at p. 166 in holding that the contract was not frustrated:

> I am of the opinion, therefore, that the learned Chief Justice was right in refusing to grant an order declaring the contract to be frustrated and void subject to the express undertaking given by the trustee that no distribution of assets would be made among the creditors until after the date of the completion of the three-year contract with the appellant, and that the assets of the bankrupt in the hands of the trustee would be answerable to the appellant for any damages arising from a breach of the contract.

In that case, the trustee had not explicitly approbated or affirmed the contract but the undertaking given by the trustee had the same effect. The trustee was undertaking that the bankruptcy estate would stand behind the obligations of the bankrupt under the agreement in priority to the claims of the bankrupt's unsecured creditors.

[13] In the present case, counsel for the Trustee submits that these authorities do not apply in the present circumstances because the Geneva/Pioneer Swap Agreements contain provisions allowing Geneva and Pioneer to terminate the Swap Agreements as a result of the bankruptcy of the Bankrupt. In other words, the contracting parties turned their minds to the possibility of one of them becoming bankrupt and provided a remedy for the protection of the non-bankrupt party. With respect, I do not accept this submission.

[14] While Geneva and Pioneer have the option of terminating the Swap Agreements as a result of the bankruptcy, they are entitled to know whether the Trustee is prepared to commit the assets in the bankruptcy estate towards the obligations of the Bankrupt under the Swap Agreements if they do not choose the termination option. In my view, nothing turns on whether the bankruptcy of one of the contracting parties does constitute a breach of the contract or otherwise entitles the other party to terminate the contract.

[15] There is potentially an important difference between the termination of the contract in accordance with its provisions and the contract coming to an end due to frustration of the contract. In the present case, there is a significant difference between the two alternatives. If Geneva and Pioneer were to terminate the Swap Agreements in accordance with their provisions at the present time, they would have to make a significant payment to the Trustee. On the other hand, if the Swap Agreements are frustrated, they are entitled to treat them at an end without making any further payment.

[16] Another way of looking at the point is to consider the right of the trustee in bankruptcy to disclaim a contract entered into by the bankrupt, in which case the other party to the contract may claim as an unsecured creditor of the bankrupt in respect of the damages suffered by it. The BC Court of Appeal recently had occasion to consider the right of trustees in bankruptcy to disclaim contracts in the decision of *New Skeena Forest Products Inc. v. Don Hull & Sons Contracting Ltd.*, 2005 BCCA 154. The Court said the following at ¶ 29:

> In more recent times, L.W. Houlden & G.B. Morawetz in their text *Bankruptcy and Insolvency Law of Canada*, 3d ed, looseleaf (Toronto: Thomson Carswell, 2004) at F§ 45.2 state quite unequivocally that a trustee may disclaim a contract entered into by the bankrupt. Similarly, in a case comment on *Potato Distributors Inc. v. Eastern Trust Co.* (1955), 35 CBR 161 at 166 (PEICA), L.W. Houlden writes:
>
>> It is well established law that a trustee may elect to carry on with a contract entered into prior to bankruptcy, provided he pays up arrears and is ready to perform the contract. The trustee could also, if he saw fit, elect not to go on with the contract in which event the vendor would have the right to prove a claim for damages.

In his case comment, L.W. Houlden cited the *Thomson Knitting* decision immediately following the passage quoted above.

[17] A trustee in bankruptcy has two alternatives with respect to contracts entered into by the bankrupt. The trustee can either affirm or disclaim the contract. Support for this proposition is found in *Saan Stores Ltd. v. United Steelworkers of America, Local 596 (Retail Wholesale Canada, Canadian Service Section Division)* (1999), 172 DLR (4th) 134 (NSCA) at p. 151:

> As a general rule, with respect to contracts that a trustee can perform, the trustee may, within a reasonable time, elect to either adopt the contracts or to disclaim them (*Re Thomson Knitting Company* (1925), 2 DLR 1007 (Ont. SC); Houlden, L.W. and C.H. Morawetz, *Bankruptcy and Insolvency Law of Canada*, 3rd ed. (Toronto: Carswell, 1993) paragraph F45.2).

[18] The trustee cannot choose to do nothing. It must elect between the two alternatives because the other contracting party is entitled to know whether it will be a creditor of the bankrupt or a creditor of the bankruptcy estate (or the trustee personally) with respect to any unfulfilled obligations on the part of the bankrupt. The other contracting party is entitled to know which alternative the trustee is choosing irrespective of whether it is entitled to terminate the contract as a result of the bankruptcy.

[19] Counsel for the Trustee made submissions to the effect that the obligation to affirm a contract of a bankrupt only applies when the contract is executory in nature and that a contract is not executory in nature when the only obligation remaining is payment. In my view, the requirement of affirmation should apply if there is a prospect that obligations on the part of the bankrupt under the contract may have to be performed prior to the end of the contract. Such a prospect exists in this case and, indeed, it is the existence of this prospect that has caused the Trustee to make these applications.

(b) Personal Liability of the Trustee

[20] The history of personal liability of trustees in bankruptcies was reviewed in the decision of *Transalta Utilities Corporation v. Hudson* (1982), 44 CBR (NS) 97 (Alta. QB). Registrar Funduk concluded after his review that until 1949 a trustee was *prima facie* personally liable for debts incurred in operating the business of the bankrupt and that the trustee was required to rebut this presumption if he wished to establish that the debt was incurred on behalf of the bankruptcy estate. This was changed in 1949 with the enactment of what is now s. 31(4) of the *Bankruptcy and Insolvency Act*, RSC 1985, c. B-3, as amended, which reads as follows:

> All debts incurred and credit received in carrying on the business of a bankrupt are deemed to be debts incurred and credit received by the estate of the bankrupt.

Registrar Funduk concluded, correctly in my view, that liability in respect of post-bankruptcy liabilities now lies *prima facie* with the bankruptcy estate and that the onus is on the creditor to show that the liability rests with the trustee personally.

[21] This is consistent with the following passage from the decision of the Ontario Court of Appeal in *Re St. Marys Paper Inc.* (1994), 26 CBR (3d) 273 at p. 288:

> Nor do we see any impediment to that conclusion in the BIA. Section 31(4) of the BIA deems all debts incurred in carrying on the business of a bankrupt to be incurred by the estate of the bankrupt. This presumption is not irrefutable, nor is it incompatible with the personal liability of the trustee, in appropriate circumstances. In a section entitled "Trustee Protecting Himself Against Liability for Debts and Liabilities Incurred in Carrying on the Business of the Bankrupt," Houlden and Morawetz state, in *Bankruptcy and Insolvency Law of Canada*, 3rd ed., Vol. 1 (Toronto: Carswell, 1992) at pp. 103-04:
>
>> Notwithstanding s. 31(4), there are still situations where a trustee may be personally liable for obligations incurred in carrying on the debtor's business. Thus, if a trustee enters into a contract to act as agent for a secured creditor in realizing its security and in doing so carries on the business of the bankrupt, s. 31(4) is no protection to the trustee. In these circumstances, the trustee is personally liable to account to the secured creditor for the proceeds of the realization and if he fails to do so, judgment will be given against him personally for the amount owing: *Re P.E. Lapierre Inc.; Bank of Nova Scotia v. Gagnon* (1970), 16 CBR (NS) 43 (Que. SC). Again, if a supplier will not supply goods unless the trustee pledges his personal credit and the trustee accepts the goods on that basis, the trustee will, notwithstanding s. 31(4), be personally liable to the supplier: *Transalta Utilities Corp. v. Hudson* (1982), 44 CBR (NS) 97, 22 Alta. LR (2d) 139, 40 AR 134 (MC).

[22] This result is also consistent with the reasoning in the decision of *Potato Distributors Inc.* which I quoted above. The decision was made after 1949, and the court held that there was sufficient affirmation if the trustee in bankruptcy undertook that the assets in the bankruptcy estate would be answerable for any damages arising from a breach of the contract. It was not necessary for the affirmation to have been done by the trustee in his personal capacity.

[23] It has been suggested that, as s. 31(4) refers to "debts" and not "liabilities," the provision may not reverse the presumption against personal liability of trustees in bankruptcy in respect of liabilities which are not debts (see *Glick v. Jordan* (1967), 11 CBR (NS) 70 (Ont. SC (HCJ)), where a plaintiff was suing a trustee in bankruptcy in his personal capacity for the tort of negligence). As I am satisfied that any amounts which the buyer may have to pay under the Geneva/Pioneer Swap Agreements to Geneva and Pioneer would constitute "debts" in the ordinary sense of the word, I need not consider whether "debts" should be given a broader meaning.

[24] Counsel for Geneva and Pioneer submits that I do not have the jurisdiction to immunize the Trustee against personal liability. I agree with this proposition but I am able to make a declaration with respect to the circumstances in which the Trustee will not be personally liable according to law. While the court is usually reluctant to make prospective declarations, s. 34(1) of the *Bankruptcy and Insolvency Act* specifically contemplates that trustees in bankruptcy may apply to the court for directions in relation to any matter affecting the administration of the bankruptcy estate.

[25] As there is only a rebuttable presumption against personal liability on the part of trustees in bankruptcy, I cannot make the unequivocal declaration which the Trustee seeks. However, I am able to make a declaration of a general nature.

Conclusion

[26] I declare as follows:

(a) it is necessary for the Trustee to affirm the Geneva/Pioneer Swap Agreements in order to take the benefit of them; and

(b) the affirmation of the Geneva/Pioneer Swap Agreements by the Trustee will not itself make the Trustee personally liable in respect of the obligations of the buyer under the Swap Agreements as long as the Trustee affirms the Swap Agreements on behalf of the bankruptcy estate and not in its personal capacity.

IV. ASSIGNMENT

Does a trustee in bankruptcy have the right to assign a pre-bankruptcy contract between Counterparty and Debtor regardless of Counterparty's wishes? Does it make any difference if there is a provision in the contract prohibiting assignments? Prior to the 2007 amendments, provincial landlord and tenant laws provided for the assignment of commercial tenancy agreements in bankruptcy. The governing provision in Ontario was *Commercial Tenancies Act*, s. 38(2), extracted above. Section 38(2) overrode any anti-assignment clause in the lease and it relieved the trustee from post-assignment liability for non-payment of rent and other breaches. However, it also enacted safeguards for the landlord's protection. The requirements for a valid assignment were that: (1) the trustee must pay all arrears of rent; (2) the assignee must covenant to observe and perform all the terms of the lease and agree to conduct on the premises "a trade or business which is not reasonably of a more objectionable or hazardous nature than that which was thereon conducted by the debtor"; and (3) the court must approve the assignee as a fit and proper person. Prior to the 2007 amendments, there was no statutory right of assignment for contracts other than commercial tenancy agreements.

A new BIA s. 84.1 was enacted as part of the 2007 amendments and this provision creates a statutory right of assignment for all contracts, including commercial tenancy agreements. In so far as it applies to commercial tenancy agreements, it displaces the provincial provisions described above. The section provides that the court must approve a proposed assignment and the factors it has to consider include: (1) whether the assignee is able to perform the obligations; and (2) whether it is "appropriate" to assign the contract to the assignee. The case law on whether the assignee is a "fit and proper person" within the meaning of s. 38(2) of the Ontario *Commercial Tenancies Act* and the corresponding provision in other provinces will provide some guidance as to the exercise of the court's discretion under new BIA s. 84.1: see *Re Darrigo Holdings*, below.

Re Darrigo Consolidated Holdings
(1987), 63 CBR 216 (Ont. SC)

EBERLE J: ... I turn now to the second objection, which is a substantive one. It is based upon the unsuitability and, particularly, the financial unsuitability of the proposed assignees. Specifically the landlords ask for security, such as by way of a bank letter of credit for the balance of the rental payments which will fall due to them under the two leases in question. Counsel relies for this request upon the decision in *Re FigurMagic Int. Ltd.* (1974), 19 CBR (NS) 310 (Ont. Div. Ct.), where it appears that some security or prepayment of at least part of the balance of the rent was provided for.

I think that the present case should be regarded on the basis of what was said in *Re Griff and Sommerset Mgmt. Services Ltd.* (1978), 19 OR (2d) 209, 26 CBR (NS) 205, 4 BLR 72, 3 RPR 225 (sub nom. *Re Sommerset Mgmt. Services and Yolles Furniture Co.; Re Yolles Furniture Co. (Ont.) and Modernage Furniture Ltd.*), 84 DLR (3d) 386 (CA), concerning the factors which should be considered by a judge asked to approve an assignment of a lease under s. 38(2).

At pp. 219-20 [OR], and continuing on to 221, certain factors are prescribed for the court's consideration. I regard what the court there said about those factors as meaning that they are to be considered in sum, and that, weighing all of them together, approval should or should not be granted, according to the case. I do not read what is said by the court on this subject to have established each of the elements or factors as a precondition to the granting of approval. The operation, as I see it, is a weighing of the various elements.

When one looks at the facts of this case, it is quite clear that the financial position of the proposed assignees is not as sound as many would like it to be. The proposed assignees are incorporated companies which were only recently incorporated and have no business history. The principal behind all of them is Hilda Darrigo, the wife of one of the former partners, and I use that term not in any legal sense, in the Darrigo business. The two brothers have, I am told, had a substantial falling out, and must be very much at loggerheads, for it is said that that produced the bankruptcy. It appears that relations within the family are no better now than they were at the time of the bankruptcy. Mrs. Darrigo, it is said, had some connection with the business before the bankruptcy, although I gather it was not an extensive connection. Her husband has been retained as a consultant on behalf of the assignees if they should obtain the businesses.

The material discloses that the tender made by Hilda Darrigo is the best tender, well above any other, and that among those others was a tender by the other Darrigo brother. The material also discloses that the prices tendered by Mrs. Darrigo are for a going business, and that they are prices and amounts which total well above the break-up value of the assets, if they were to be sold on that basis.

It must be to the benefit of the creditors of the bankrupt company, and particularly the unsecured creditors, that the businesses be disposed of on a going concern basis, and, in any event, that the maximum return be obtained on disposition. It is to be observed that the sale of the businesses on a going concern basis has already received an approval by the court by order made 18th December 1986, which approved the acceptance by the receiver and manager of the property of an offer or offers made by Mrs. Darrigo in trust for company or companies to be incorporated. Such an order does not, of course, render unnecessary the application presently made. However, a refusal of approval of the present application would nullify that part of the order of 18th December 1986.

The landlords' concern at the present time is with respect to the rental payments that would accrue to them during the balance of the two leases. It appears to be clear, however, that if there is default in payment of any of those rental payments the landlords will have their usual remedies, including retaking possession of the property. It is suggested that that may not be as easy in this case, as it might be in some other case, because of the family dispute, and because of the fact that, with respect to each of the properties in this case, the landlord is owned by the wives of the two feuding brothers. In view of the time limit imposed by s. 38(2) upon the trustee electing to retain the leases, it seems to me there is a reasonable probability that, if the present application is not granted, there will be no assignment of the leases, and no recovery of money with respect to these two properties on a going concern basis, and on 4th February the landlords will be entitled to take over these two properties. Whatever difficulty may exist in the future about retaking possession of the properties will certainly exist on 4th February.

In other words, I can see little difference in the landlords' position whether the present application is granted or not. And particularly, I am unable to see any real prejudice to the landlords by the granting of the application. It appears to me that to give the landlords full security, such as by a bank letter of credit, for future rent payments, is to give them a security and an advantage which they do not presently possess. I have been referred to no authority with the possible exception of the *FigurMagic* case, where such an improvement in the landlord's position is mandated, and I am unaware of any ground in principle why the landlord's position should be better upon an assignment subject to a bankruptcy than it was prior to the bankruptcy.

In this case, the interests of the creditors are important, and particularly those of the unsecured creditors. In view of the shortness of time remaining out of the three months, it is most unlikely that any other assignee can be found and the necessary approvals obtained; and that, accordingly, if the present application is refused, there will be a substantial deterioration in the position of the unsecured creditors as compared to their position, if the application is granted.

Accordingly, the best conclusion that I can come to, in endeavouring to consider the interests of the landlords, and of the unsecured creditors, is that the application should be granted.

I referred earlier to the weaknesses in the assignees' financial position, and I keep them in mind. Nevertheless, that is but one of the factors to be considered. I consider as well the other factors mentioned in *Re Griff and Sommerset Mgmt. Services Ltd.* The business reputation of the assignees in the present circumstances is practically non-existent in a technical sense. However, on the other hand, there is the connection of Mrs. Darrigo herself, and of her husband, who has, it need hardly be said, had considerable experience in operating this kind of business. There is no change in the use of the premises. I am satisfied that the facts in evidence establish a reasonable motivation and a reasonable ability on the part of the assignees to honour their covenants, and I see a considerable advantage to the unsecured creditors, without any significant disadvantage, if indeed there is any disadvantage, to the landlords at all.

. . .

Application granted.

NOTE

In *Micro Cooking Centres (Can.) Inc. (Trustee of) v. Cambridge Leaseholds Ltd.* (1988), 68 CBR (NS) 60 (Ont. HC), the debtor leased retail premises in two shopping centre developments where it sold microwave ovens and cooking appliances. The trustee wanted to assign the leases to a company that planned to sell frozen yoghurt and fruit juices. Both leases contained a "user covenant," which stated that the premises were only to be used as a retail store for the sale of microwave ovens and kitchenware. The landlord objected on the ground that the shopping centre depended on a pre-arranged business mix and the assignee's proposed business was inconsistent with the mix. The trustee argued that the assignee had agreed "to conduct upon the demised premises a trade or business which is not reasonably of a more objectionable or hazardous nature than that which was thereon conducted by the debtor," as required by s. 38(2), and therefore the court should approve the application. The court rejected the application on the ground that the assignee was not a fit and proper person to be put in possession of the leased premises: "to confer a right on the assignee to ignore the user clause in the lease would be to emasculate the terms of the lease by sweeping aside, what in the context of a shopping mall, is a fundamental term." Note that the court could have found for the landlords on the alternative ground that s. 38(2) states that the proposed assignee must agree to observe the terms of the lease and these would include the user covenant. Under new BIA s. 84.1, the case would presumably turn on whether it was "appropriate" to assign the premises to the assignee.

CHAPTER SEVEN

Claims Against the Estate and Recovery of Claims

I. INTRODUCTION

To be entitled to participate in the debtor's bankruptcy, a creditor must have a "provable" claim: BIA s. 2(1), "creditor." The amount of the creditor's claim matters because it determines the size of its dividends. For example, assume there are enough assets in the estate to pay unsecured creditors 5 cents on the dollar. If the creditor's claim is for $200, it will receive $10. If its claim is for $500, it will receive $25. The amount of a creditor's claim also matters because it determines the number of votes it can cast in a creditor's meeting: BIA s. 115. In the context of commercial proposals under BIA, Part 3, Div. 1, the amount of a creditor's claim determines its voting power in a class meeting to approve a proposal: BIA s. 54(1) provides that a proposal is accepted if all classes of unsecured creditors vote in favour by a majority in number and two thirds in value: see further, Chapter 16. CCAA s. 6 enacts a similar rule for CCAA plans: see Chapter 14.

This chapter addresses two issues:

1. What is a provable claim?

2. What are the rules for valuing claims?

Provable claims. BIA s. 121(1) provides:

> All debts and liabilities, present or future, to which the bankrupt is subject on the day on which the bankrupt becomes bankrupt or to which the bankrupt may become subject before the bankrupt's discharge by reason of any obligation incurred before the day on which the bankrupt becomes bankrupt shall be deemed to be claims provable in proceedings under this Act.

The definition covers present debts (debts that are owing to the creditor on the date the debtor goes into bankruptcy); future debts (debts that are owing, but not payable on the date of the bankruptcy); contingent debts (debts subject to a condition that has not been fulfilled); and unliquidated claims (claims for an amount that is undetermined at the date of the bankruptcy). However, the definition is limited to pre-bankruptcy claims and, as a general rule, debts and liabilities incurred after the date of bankruptcy are not provable claims: *Re Sanderson* (1978), 29 CBR (NS) 92 (Ont. CA). One exception is post-filing claims for environmental clean-up costs: BIA s. 14.06(8). Another exception arises in the context of executory contracts: disclaimer of a contract in bankruptcy gives the counterparty a claim for damages, which is a provable claim even though it arises post-filing (see Chapter 6, Section II).

Section 124(1) provides that every creditor must prove his claim and a creditor who does not prove his claim is not entitled to share in any distribution. Section 178(2) provides that, as a general rule, an order of discharge releases the debtor from all claims provable in the bankruptcy. The upshot is that if a creditor has a provable claim and does not file a proof of claim pursuant to s. 124(1), it cannot enforce its claim once the debtor has been discharged. This gives a creditor who has a provable claim a strong incentive to file a proof of claim under s. 124(1). The corollary is that if a creditor's claim is not a provable claim, it may not file a proof of claim under s. 124(1) and its claim is not released when the debtor is discharged. The consequences of failing to lodge a proof of claim in restructuring proceedings are roughly comparable: see Chapters 14 and 16.

Valuation of claims. A contingent claim or an unliquidated claim will be an unprovable claim if it turns out to be too difficult to value. This follows from ss. 121(2) and 135 read in combination. Section 121(2) provides that the determination whether a contingent or unliquidated claim is a provable claim and the valuation of such a claim shall be made in accordance with s. 135. Section 135(1.1) provides that the trustee shall determine whether any contingent or unliquidated claim is a provable claim and, if it is a provable claim, the trustee shall value it. If the trustee makes a determination under this provision, the creditor has 30 days to appeal to the court: s. 135(4).

The scheme is driven by 2 competing policy considerations: (1) debtor rehabilitation; and (2) the need for finality of bankruptcy proceedings. In the case of an individual debtor, one of the objects of the bankruptcy laws is to wipe the slate clean so the debtor can make a fresh start. This means that "provable claim" should be defined as widely as possible so the debtor is not left with outstanding liabilities after the discharge. The discharge provisions only apply to individuals, but where the debtor is a company, the fresh start policy is to be found in the restructuring laws (BIA, Part III, Div. 1 and the CCAA). A BIA proposal, if accepted by creditors, releases the debtor from provable claims except for payments the debtor agrees to make under the proposal, and the same is true for CCAA plans. Again, in the restructuring context, it makes sense in terms of the fresh start policy to define "provable claim" as widely as possible.

The countervailing factor is the need for finality of bankruptcy proceedings. Unliquidated and contingent claims are by definition uncertain. The only sure way to resolve the uncertainty in the case of an unliquidated claim is to wait and see what the court hearing the claim decides. Similarly, the only sure way to resolve the uncertainty in the case of a contingent claim is to wait and see whether the contingency materializes. The difficulty is that the wait and see option may take years and it would be undesirable to hold up bankruptcy or restructuring proceedings indefinitely. The main solutions are to estimate the present value of the claim and admit it to proof on that basis or, alternatively, if the estimation is too difficult, determine that the claim is not a provable claim. The first option is consistent with the rehabilitation goal of the bankruptcy laws, but it means doing rough and ready justice so far as the value of the creditor's claim is concerned. The second option is consistent with the need for finality in bankruptcy proceedings, but it is inconsistent with the fresh start policy.

In many estates these issues create no problems, particularly because there is often not enough left in the estate to make it worthwhile for unsecured creditors to press their claims. As noted, problems arise where the claim is unliquidated or contingent in character. Even more difficult issues arise in the case of mass tort claims (such as those involving asbestosis claims, or claims involving medical devices and implants), where many of the victims may not even be aware of the fact that they have, or may have a claim, and may not be able to bring a claim under applicable provincial law until they can establish an injury and quantify their damages. The cases that follow illustrate some of these problems in the context of BIA proceedings as well as the innovative approach taken by US courts in resolving deadlocks.

II. ILLUSTRATIVE CASES

Ontario New Home Warranty Program v. Jiordan Homes Ltd.
(1999), 45 OR (3d) 756, [1999] OJ no. 944 (QL) (Gen. Div.)

FERGUSON J:

The Facts

The defendant is a former shareholder in Jiordan which was in the business of building houses.

The sequence of events is this:

July 14, 1989—the defendant signed a guarantee in which he agreed to indemnify the plaintiff if it had to make good any obligations of Jiordan

July 17, 1989—Jiordan agreed to indemnify the plaintiff if it had to make good any obligations of Jiordan under an agreement of purchase and sale

August 14, 1991—Jiordan agreed to sell a house to Ramos with a closing date of March 30, 1992

November 14, 1991—the defendant filed an assignment in bankruptcy

March 30, 1992—the sale of the house did not close

October 29, 1992—the defendant was discharged from bankruptcy

October 30, 1992—Ramos made a claim against the plaintiff for the return of the deposit it had paid Jiordan under the sale agreement

January 22, 1993—the plaintiff paid Ramos compensation of $8,000 pursuant to s. 14 of the *Ontario New Home Warranties Plan Act*, RSO 1990, c. O.31.

The plaintiff is claiming the $8,000 from the defendant under his personal guarantee.

There are two issues: first, did the bankruptcy terminate the guarantee? Second, if not, is the claim barred because of the defendant's bankruptcy?

Counsel advise me there are no cases on point.

I shall consider the two issues in reverse order.

Is the Claim Barred by Section 69 [now s. 69.3] of the Bankruptcy Act?

Section [69.3(1)] of the *Bankruptcy and Insolvency Act*, RSC 1985, c. B-3, as amended, states that a creditor has no remedy against an insolvent for a claim provable in bankruptcy.

Section 121(1) states:

> 121(1) All debts and liabilities, present or future, to which the bankrupt is subject at the date of the bankruptcy or to which he may become subject before his discharge by reason of any obligation incurred before the date of the bankruptcy shall be deemed to be claims provable in proceedings under this Act.

Subsection (2) provides that the court shall on application by the trustee determine whether any contingent claim is a provable claim. No such application was made.

It appears to me that when the defendant went bankrupt, the claim by the plaintiff against the defendant was a future liability to which the defendant might theoretically become subject before his discharge by reason of an obligation incurred before the date of the bankruptcy. The obligation was the indemnity agreement.

The theoretical risk was this: before the defendant's discharge, Jiordan had failed to close the sale, and if it did not repay the deposits, Ramos might claim the amount from the plaintiff, and the plaintiff might pay and claim the amount from the defendant. However, s. 121(1) makes the claim a provable claim only if the defendant "is subject" to a liability before his discharge; that is, it is a provable claim only if the defendant actually becomes liable before his discharge. While the section includes liabilities which may become due at a future time after discharge, it appears to me that it does not include liabilities which do not arise until after discharge.

Here, the defendant did not become subject to a liability until the plaintiff made the payment for which it claims indemnity and that payment was made after discharge.

Consequently, I conclude that the claim in this action was not a provable claim in the defendant's bankruptcy and this action is not barred by s. [69.3(1)] of the *Bankruptcy and Insolvency Act*, as amended.

Did the Bankruptcy Terminate the Guarantee?

There appears to be no provision in the Act which governs this issue.

It may seem anomalous that where a person's wealth is erased by bankruptcy, and that wealth is the reason why he was asked for and gave a guarantee, that he should continue to be liable on the guarantee after bankruptcy for claims which were not provable in bankruptcy and therefore not erased by it. However, I can see no indication in the Act that the guarantee should somehow evaporate in the bankruptcy. If the bankrupt were a party to other kinds of contracts which imposed obligations on him then these would not evaporate because of the bankruptcy.

I conclude that the guarantee here survives the bankruptcy and that the Act does not bar this action.

NOTE

For a critical analysis of this decision, see Scott A. Bomhof, "Case Comment on Ontario New Home Warranty Program v. Jiordan Homes Ltd." (1999), 10 CBR-ART 5, 10 CBR (4th) 5. Bomhof makes the following point:

It appears that the Honourable Judge attempted to draw a distinction between claims arising from pre-bankruptcy obligations which may be asserted by a creditor of the bankrupt at a future time and liabilities which do not arise at all until after the bankrupt's discharge. However, it is respectfully submitted that such an interpretation misconstrues the meaning of a "provable claim." If such an interpretation is followed by the Courts, it would open the door for parties with claims against a bankrupt, which are contingent on a triggering event which is within the control of the creditor, to simply wait out the period of the bankruptcy and proceed with their claim, for its full amount, against the bankrupt following his or her discharge.

Do you agree?

Re Dunham
(2005), 9 CBR (5th) 205, 2005 NSSC 57

REG. CREGAN:

Introduction

[1] This is an application of National Bank Financial Ltd. ("NBFL") to appeal under subsection 135(4) of the *Bankruptcy and Insolvency Act*, RSC 1985, c. B-3, as amended (the "Act") the determination by the Trustee, McCuaig & Company Inc., dated December 30, 2004, that the claim of NBFL in the Proposal of Craig Anthony Dunham is a contingent or unliquidated claim and that the valuation of the claim is $0.00 dollars.

Preliminary Facts

[2] Craig Anthony Dunham ("Mr. Dunham") is a self-employed individual who resides in New Minas, Nova Scotia. In August 2004, he filed a Division I Proposal (the "Proposal") pursuant to section 50 of the Act. McCuaig & Company Inc. was named the Trustee (the "Trustee"). Robert L. McCuaig ("Mr. McCuaig") is the personal trustee involved in the matter. NBFL is the largest creditor subject to the Proposal. Mr. Dunham had been the owner of a business which was sold to Knowledge House Inc. ("KHI"). As part of the transaction he acquired shares in KHI. In this context he also formed a broker–client relationship with Bruce E. Clarke ("Mr. Clarke"), an investment advisor associated with NBFL.

[3] Mr. Dunham maintained a brokerage account with NBFL ("the Account"). On or about March 15, 2000, he entered into a Margin Account Agreement with NBFL (" the Margin Account"). This permitted him to borrow money to purchase securities for the Account. The money borrowed was collateralized by the securities. The Margin Account provided that any outstanding debit balance would incur interest at a rate set by NBFL.

[4] On or about September 6, 2001, NBFL demanded immediate payment from Mr. Dunham of $362,350.00, the approximate negative balance of the Account at that time. Mr. Dunham did not respond to this demand.

[5] Later in the month, NBFL commenced an action against Mr. Dunham in the Supreme Court of Nova Scotia for that amount together with interest as provided in the

Margin Account. Mr. Dunham filed a defence and counterclaim to this action. NBFL filed a defence to the counterclaim. The entire action has been dormant and now with the current Proposal is stayed.

[6] There was a meeting of creditors on September 17, 2004, at which the Proposal was approved. NBFL had not received notice of it. Thus it did not file a proof of claim and did not attend the creditors' meeting. On learning of the meeting, it filed a Proof of Claim dated October 5, 2004, claiming the sum of $397,149.71, being the $353,021.96 owing as of December 31, 2001, and interest of $44,127.75 calculated according to the Margin Account to the date of the filing of the Proposal, Also it brought an application before this court on November 25, 2004, and was granted an order declaring the creditors' meeting a nullity and directing that a new meeting be called.

[7] On December 30, 2004, NBFL received a notice from the Trustee advising that he had determined that NBFL's proven claim was a contingent or unliquidated claim which was valued at $0.00, and also notice of the new creditors' meeting to be held on January 11, 2005. At this meeting NBFL voted its claim of $0.00 against the Proposal. The Proposal was passed with 83% of the creditors in number voting in favour and 100% of the creditors in dollars voting in favour.

What Is a "Provable Claim"?

[8] I shall first set out the authorities relating to the presentation of claims provable in bankruptcy. A "provable claim" is defined in subsection 2(1) of the Act to include "any claim or liability provable in proceedings under this Act by a creditor."

[9] I quote subsections 121(1) and (2): ...

[10] By subsection 66(1) the provisions of the Act apply with such modification as circumstances required to proposals made under Division I.

[11] The actual procedure for filing the proof of claim is laid out in section 124 of the Act ...

[12] The procedure by which the Trustee examines the proof is laid out in section 135 ...

[13] The proof of claim filed by NFBL was for the amount of $397,149.71, being the balance owing as of the date of the Proposal including interest. It was supported by a statement of account confirming that figure. On its face it appears to be framed in accordance with the foregoing statutory requirements. Mr. McCuaig in cross-examination on his affidavit acknowledged that it was in normal form.

. . .

Liquidated, Unliquidated, Contingent Claims

[24] I should make clear what is meant by liquidated, unliquidated and contingent claim. The definition in *The 2005 Annotated Bankruptcy and Insolvency Act*, Houlden & Morawetz at G § 29, paragraphs (2) and (5) are as follows:

> A contingent claim is a claim which may or may not ever ripen into a debt, according as some future event does or does not happen: *Gardner v. Newton* (1916), 29 DLR 276, 10 WWR 51, 26 Man. R 251 (KB).

A liquidated claim is in the nature of a debt, i.e., a specific sum of money due and payable under or by virtue of a contract. Its amount must either be already ascertained or capable of being ascertained as a mere matter of arithmetic. If the ascertainment of a sum of money, even though it be specified or named as a definite figure, requires investigation beyond mere arithmetical calculation, then the claim is an unliquidated claim: *Re A Debtor* (No. 64 of 1992), [1994] 1 WLR 264 (HC) ...

Position of the Trustee

[25] Although the evidence before the court shows the claim as liquidated having been calculated to the last cent, the Trustee says it is not. It is either unliquidated or contingent. It views the debt not as a separate legal transaction, but as a component of a larger complicated legal relationship between NBFL and Mr. Dunham. All components in the Trustee's view need to be resolved before a liquidated amount, positive or negative, can be placed on the claim. Until then the claim is contingent or unliquidated.

[26] An alternative view though not strongly urged by the Trustee would be that there is a proper liquidated claim, but it is subject to a set-off for what damages might be awarded in the counterclaim. The difficulty with this is that the claim appears to be framed in tort or in breach of contract for which general damages would be awarded. The thrust of authority is that one cannot set such damages off against a claim for a liquidated debt.

[27] In support of the Trustee's position that the creditor's claim can only be liquidated by first considering the debtor's counterclaim and all the surrounding circumstances, it relies on the following cases.

[28] *Re Scotland Woollen Mills Co.* (1923), 3 CBR 636 (Ont. Bktcy.) (Fisher J) concerns the claim of a woolen mill in England against the estate in bankruptcy of a Canadian company to whom it had sold woolen cloth to be made into men's business suits. The cloth was defective. The company incurred loses with respect to the cloth. The mill filed a proof of claim for the amount owing for the cloth and the company counterclaimed for damages arising from breach of contract for delivering defective goods. The court allowed that the company was able to present evidence of a counterclaim for the damages sustained. This does not help the Trustee, because it has not presented any evidence to support its counterclaim,

[29] *Re Thomas Electric Co.* (1981), 39 CBR (NS) 20 (Ont. Bktcy.) (Ont. Registrar Ferron). A contractor claimed a set-off against money it owed to the bankrupt, a subcontractor. The point of this case is clearly put in the head note:

The amounts claimed for damages were speculative and conjectural, or based on estimates, and could therefore not be allowed. The contractor had the right to set off only the amount of the claim which was actually proved.

[30] In effect damages for poor workmanship, not quantified could not be set off, but the cost of replacing defective parts which had been quantified (liquidated) could be set off.

[31] Houlden & Morawetz speaking of set off at F § 109(1) says:

The object of set-off is to avoid the perceived injustice to a man who has had mutual dealings with a bankrupt of having to pay in full what he owes to the bankrupt while having to rest content with a dividend on what the bankrupt owes him. At the time the effect of the set-off is to prefer one creditor over the general body of creditors, and accordingly, it is confined within narrow limits. The principal limiting requirement is that of mutuality. If there is no mutuality there is no set-off. The requirement of mutuality is central to bankruptcy set-off and is rigorously enforced: *Re Bank of Credit and Commerce International S.A. (No. 8),* [1996] 2 WLR 631.

This is directly on point as indicated elsewhere herein.

[32] These cases and commentary do not help the Trustee in the contention that, notwithstanding the claim of NBFL is essentially for a liquidated amount, in valuing the claim defences and counterclaims should be considered. They only allow such where in fact the counterclaim or defence is proved with evidence.

[33] A further difficulty with what is urged by the Trustee is not just that there is no evidence to support it, but that no legal theory has been put to me whereby a proven liquidated debt can be vitiated. There is no suggestion of fraudulent misrepresentation, negligent misrepresentation, legal incompetence, illegality or the like.

Finding

[34] I am satisfied that NBFL has provided evidence in the manner required by the Act to substantiate its claim for $397,149.71. This is a liquidated amount. No further calculation is required. The claim is in proper form signed by the proper officer with the appropriate statement attached and all confirmed by the sworn affidavit of Mr. Anderson, NBFL's officer. The Trustee has not questioned this calculation nor the facts on which it is based and has offered no competent evidence to substantiate its allegation that there are other factors to be taken into account in proving the amount of the claim, nor has the Trustee submitted any firm analysis as to how its allegations may be legally categorized. I therefore find that NBFL has a valid proved claim in the liquidated amount of $397,149.71.

[35] The Trustee made certain submissions that, if accepted, would result in a different finding. Let me explain why I reject them.

Improper Purpose

[36] The Trustee submits that I should be concerned with the intentions of NBFL in pressing this appeal.

[37] The Trustee relies on *Laserworks Computer Services Inc., Re,* [1998] NSJ No. 60, 6 CBR (4th) 69, 165 NSR (2d) 297 (NSCA). In this case a competitor of the debtor had bought debts owing to creditors for the purpose of being able to vote to defeat the debtor's proposal and thereby put the debtor out of business. The Court of Appeal confirmed the Registrar's determination that the votes of the competitor should not be considered. Thus the proposal was approved. The purpose of the Act is to provide for the orderly distribution of the debtor's assets to its creditors. The competitor was not a creditor, but one who went about buying up debts one by one from several creditors, not in the interest of collecting the proportionate share of the assets provided for under the Act, but with the intention of destroying the debtor, something the original creditors would not have wanted to do.

[38] What is before me is the concern of NBFL, that with the $0.00 valuation, it could not vote its true dollar claim at the creditors' meeting. As a result the proposal was

approved at the creditors' meeting. It wants to have its claim accepted for its face value so that, when the proposal comes before the court for approval, it will have a basis for submitting that it not be approved.

[39] The Trustee suggests that the NBFL is using the situation to bankrupt Mr. Dunham and thereby rid itself of the counterclaim. This the Trustee says should be balanced against the inconvenience to NBFL of having to wait until its claim is settled and then share in the proceeds of the proposal.

[40] I do not think the principles behind the *Laserworks Computer Services Inc.* case apply. The competitor was not originally a creditor. It bought status as creditor as a way to destroy the debtor. The Act exists to provide for a fair distribution of the debtor's assets among its creditors. The competitor attempted to use it not to receive its share on the debts purchased, but to use the votes related to the debts to bankrupt and in effect put the debtor, a competitor, out of business. This is not a purpose contemplated by the Act. Our Court of Appeal has affirmed that one cannot take advantage of the mechanics of the Act to effect a perverse result, quite unrelated to the distribution of assets among creditors. NBFL has no such perverse motive. It simply wants to have the value of its Margin Account claim to be recognized. The evidence for it is clear. If there is a valid counterclaim or set off against it, it does not relate to the value of the claim and must be resolved in other proceedings.

[41] The issues in the counterclaim may be constituents of a larger contest of which the Margin Account is also a constituent, but they are not necessarily legally connected, or at least there is no evidence before me that they are. NBFL is simply making the proper use of the Act to have its proof of claim accepted. It will have to deal with the counterclaim, if it is pursued.

[42] It is suggested that the putting of Mr. Dunham into bankruptcy will result in the abandonment of the counterclaim. This does not necessarily follow. It will be open to the Trustee, other creditors, or Mr. Dunham himself to pursue it, if they wish.

[43] I cannot see that NBFL is making any improper use of the Act. It merely wants its claim to be properly characterized and valued and to be properly considered in the application to have the proposal approved.

[44] The Trustee further suggests that NBFL having missed out on voting on the proposal has nothing to lose by letting its claim be valued in due course after a trial and then sharing in the assets in proportion to what ever claim it may be determined to have. It is said this will not result in any prejudice. That is not necessarily so. The status of its claim as determined in this decision may have some bearing on the approval procedure before a judge. Whether the counterclaim can be set off against the claim on the Margin Account will also affect how the assets are distributed. It may make significant difference in the final distribution of assets whether there are two distinct claims, one by NBFL for the claim under the Margin Account, and the other by Mr. Dunham by way of general damages or simply one claim, as the Trustee seems to assume. NBFL should not be prevented from seeking the remedies to which the Act entitles it.

· · ·

Application granted.

Claude Resources Inc. (Trustee of) v. Dutton
(1993), 22 CBR (3d) 56 (Sask. QB)

NOBLE J: [1] When the issues arising out of the bankruptcy of Claude Resources Inc., (Claude) came before me there were three matters up for discussion: …

> 3. A motion by the Trustee pursuant to s. 121(2) of the Act to determine whether contingent claims against the bankrupt's estate by Dutton and J.M.D. are provable claims and if so the value of the claims. As part of this motion the Court by agreement of counsel is also to consider a proof of claim by Dutton for $50,385.79 dated June 18, 1993 which was filed with the Trustee but denied. Technically this claim is under appeal to the Court but counsel for Dutton concedes that it is a contingent claim and can be treated the same as the other two above referred to.

[2] The application to approve the Trustee's proposal was adjourned at the request of counsel for Claude to August 30 next to allow for a valuation of certain assets of Claude to be filed and perhaps other information counsel felt the Court should have before it. At this stage counsel for Dutton and J.M.D. was not in a position to indicate whether or not they would consent to the order sought.

[3] This leaves the other two matters to be considered and the Court heard argument in relation to them. The first issue to be decided is whether or not the contingent claims of Dutton and J.M.D. can be designated as "provable claims" under s. 121(2) and if so what value should be attached to each. If the contingent claims are established then Dutton and J.M.D. will have status to appear before the Court on the Trustee's application to approve the proposal. If not, then not being a creditor with a "provable claim," Dutton and J.M.D. will have no standing on that motion and coincidentally will not be entitled to examine the Trustee on the proposal (No. 2 above).

[4] The proposal of Claude includes some timely deadlines that in my view must be reckoned with. Accordingly, a full and complete statement of the very long and complicated relationship between these parties is not practical at this stage. However, in order to explain the conclusions I have reached on the issue of whether or not the contingent claims of Dutton and J.M.D. are "provable claims," I must trace briefly some of the facts before me.

The Facts

(a) Pre-bankruptcy

1. In November 1988 Dutton incorporated Western Canada Shopping Centres Inc. (W.C.S.C.) for the purpose of operating the business of an immigration investment fund pursuant to the Business Immigration Program of the Governments of Canada and Saskatchewan.

2. Dutton, as sole shareholder, director and president of W.C.S.C. promoted investment by immigrants up to $34 million through a debenture offering which was designed to use the proceeds to acquire and develop commercial, non-residential, income producing properties in Saskatchewan.

3. By early 1990 W.C.S.C. had raised approximately $22 million. At this point Claude and W.C.S.C. entered into a series of transactions whereby W.C.S.C. loaned Claude this money by way of the purchase and development by W.C.S.C. of certain surface facilities and a gold mill which was thereafter leased to Claude.

4. As part of this transaction Dutton sold his shares in W.C.S.C. to Claude for $3,200,000.00 and at the same time Claude entered into an employment agreement with Dutton dated May 15, 1990 and a management agreement with J.M.D. (Dutton's company) which paid them a total of $250,000.00 a year. At the same time Claude became the beneficial owner of W.C.S.C. through a shell corporation called Mantle Investments Ltd. (Mantle) in which Claude held 49% of the stock and Dutton 51%. Dutton continued under these arrangements to be in control of W.C.S.C. as its president and continued to pursue the raising of immigrant investment monies on its behalf.

5. From May 15, 1990 until April 1991, W.C.S.C., under Dutton's guidance, had accumulated additional funds from immigrant investors. Claude sought further loans of $9,450,000.00 and $2,565,000.00. These sums were made available by W.C.S.C. to Claude. who needed further capital but not until (indeed not unless) Claude bought out the contracts of Dutton and J.M.D. Claude paid $649,000.00 to buy out the employment and management on about May 9, 1991. At the same time Claude entered into a release and indemnity agreement with Dutton and J.M.D. which purported in fairly broad terms to indemnify both, *inter alia*, from any or all claims arising out of the various transactions between them from "any actions or inactions of Dutton or J.M.D. in their capacities as an officer and director and manager respectively of W.C.S.C. in relation to the investment and placement of W.C.S.C. debenture holders' funds from and after May 15, 1990." However, the indemnity agreement also did not extend to any claim, demand or liability occasioned by:

(a) the gross negligence, wilful misconduct or wilful default of Dutton or J.M.D.; and

(b) an action of J.M.D. or Dutton outside the scope of the management agreement or employment agreement, as the case may be, without the knowledge and approval of an officer or director, other than Dutton, of W.C.S.C.

6. On December 31, 1991 Claude defaulted on payment of interest to W.C.S.C.'s loan advances. At this point in time it appears that Claude was in breach of its obligation to repay total loan advances of $34,065,000.00 plus interest.

7. On February 7, 1992 Dutton launched a lawsuit seeking to have a receiver appointed to manage the affairs of W.C.S.C. and restrain Claude (and Mantle) from interfering in the affairs of W.C.S.C. Nothing came of this action although Dutton includes the legal fees he expended under his claim of $50,385.79 which the Trustee rejected.

8. On May 14, 1992 in Alberta, W.C.S.C. and representative holders of the debentures issued by W.C.S.C. sued Dutton, J.M.D. and a number of their advisers on the formation and activities of the money raising scheme W.C.S.C. had been engaged in under Dutton's direction claiming $34,065,000.00 and interest. Sometime later, on April 26, 1993 the plaintiffs amended their claim to include Claude, some of its officers and advisors for a return of the outstanding loans made to it by W.C.S.C. and other claims for damages of one sort or another.

9. It appears that very little occurred as between the parties until March 4, 1993 when Claude filed a notice of intention to make a proposal to its creditors under Division 1 of Part III of the Act. It is apparent that in the meantime Claude had divested itself of ownership in W.C.S.C.—apparently handing it over to the immigrant investor plaintiffs in the Alberta Court action. In addition one can draw the inference from reading the proposal to its creditors filed by Claude that it was engaged in negotiations to settle the claim by the plaintiffs in the Alberta action and various other creditors of Claude.

(b) After bankruptcy

10. On June 17, 1993 Claude lodged its proposal pursuant to Division 1, Part III of the Act with the Trustee. A meeting of the creditors was held on July 8, 1993 but neither Dutton nor J.M.D. were represented.

11. On receiving notice of Claude's proposal Dutton and J.M.D. filed the three proof of claims above referred to with the Trustee on July 5. These included a liquidated claim by Dutton for $50,385.75 respecting legal fees. This is as indicated earlier now being treated as a contingent claim. In addition Dutton filed a contingent claim based on his alleged exposure under the Alberta lawsuit totalling $53,323,125.00. J.M.D. also filed a contingent claim based on its exposure under the Alberta action which totalled $11,675,000.00.

12. On July 7, 1993 the Trustee advised Dutton that the so-called liquidated claim for $50,385.79 was being disallowed. At the same time the Trustee advised both Dutton and J.M.D. that it would be applying to the Court under s. 121(2) of the Act and Rule 94 to determine whether or not their respective contingent claims are claims provable in bankruptcy and if so, the value of such claims.

13. The Trustee then held the meeting of creditors out of which the proposal which he seeks approval for was agreed to by those attending. The motion respecting the contingent claims was filed returnable July 22, but for one reason or another did not come on for argument until August 18 leaving little time to decide the issue since the Trustee's proposal by its very words must be dealt with by the Court on or before September 1 next.

The Position of Dutton and J.M.D.

[5] I turn now to discuss the basis upon which Dutton and J.M.D. contend that their contingent claims are "provable" under s. 121(1) of the Act. I note first that a "provable claim" does not entitle the creditor who establishes it a right to vote on the proposal of the bankrupt. It would entitle such a creditor the standing to support or oppose the approval of that proposal before the Court. (See s. 59(1).)

[6] I also note that the alleged contingent claims of Dutton and J.M.D. are unsecured so that they are only entitled if their claims are "provable" to share in the distribution of $390,000.00 which is earmarked in the proposal for the unsecured creditors.

[7] As a matter of law it has been held in a number of cases that unliquidated claims for damages arising out of contract or tort are claims provable in bankruptcy pursuant to s. 121(1). See: In Re *Angelstad* (1991), 4 CBR (3d) 235 as an example. As I understand the position of Dutton and J.M.D. they contend that the action taken against them by W.C.S.C. and the immigrant investors in Alberta constitutes a contingent liability which, by virtue of the said indemnity agreement they have with Claude, will become a "provable claim" against Claude if the plaintiffs obtain a judgment. This is so according to their

submission whether or not the nature and amount of the plaintiffs' claim is uncertain and yet to be determined. In other words the mere fact that the plaintiffs' action against Dutton and J.M.D. is in existence is sufficient to deem it "provable" under s. 121(1) of the Act. As to the value of the contingent claims of Dutton and J.M.D. it is submitted that the only appropriate way to determine that is to await the outcome of the Alberta action. Once the Court concludes their contingent claims are "provable," then under s. 148(2) of the Act "... where the validity of any claim has not been determined the Trustee shall retain sufficient funds to provide payment thereof ... ." Thus Dutton and J.M.D. seek an order that all three contingent claims are "provable"; that they be valued by allowing the Alberta action to run its course and that the Trustee reserve funds to take care of the claims in due course.

Claude's Position

[8] Claude raises a number of questions about the validity of the position being advanced by Dutton and J.M.D. that the existence of the Alberta action when combined with the indemnity agreement on its face adds up to a "provable" claim under s. 121(1).

[9] Firstly, Claude submits that simply relying on the fact that they are exposed to a court action in Alberta which may or may not result in a judgment against them is not sufficient. They must in Claude's view satisfy the Court that there is a real likelihood or probability that will be the result. Claude contends there is no evidence before the Court which goes beyond a possibility of liability arising from the action. But even if the plaintiffs succeed in obtaining a judgment against Dutton and J.M.D. would they still be entitled to claim over against Claude under the terms of the indemnity agreement? So Claude argues that the position of Dutton and J.M.D. is not just a straightforward matter that they have been sued by W.C.S.C. and therefore a contingent claim by way of a judgment might arise and that becomes a "provable" claim in bankruptcy. They must then meet the second contingency of bringing the potential judgment under the indemnity agreement before they are entitled to collect from Claude. This, so the argument goes, is a double contingency with the first contingency being subject to the wording of the indemnity.

[10] Claude goes further and invites the Court to examine the nature of the claim against Dutton and J.M.D. in the statement of claim issued in Alberta. Time and space will not permit setting out here all of the allegations in the statement of claim of the Alberta action, but the following will suffice to illustrate the point that Claude attempts to make: ...

[11] Next Claude points to the terms of the indemnity agreement that are set out in para. no. 5 of the statement of facts (*supra*). These seem to say that Claude indemnifies Dutton and J.M.D. from any actions arising out of their actions while directing the affairs of W.C.S.C. in relation to the sale of debentures from and after May 15, 1990. It also limits Claude's liability where Dutton and J.M.D. are accused of gross negligence, wilful misconduct or wilful default or any action against them outside the scope of the management or the employment agreements without the knowledge and approval of Claude (the only other interested party after May 15, 1990).

[12] Based on this scenario Claude argues that the Alberta action does not give rise to a contingent liability for Dutton and J.M.D. as against Claude because 1) the action is

based on actions taken prior to May 15, 1990; 2) the action is based on allegations of negligence, recklessness, *mala fides*, breach of fiduciary duty and other allegations that suggest wrongful and wilful attempt to mislead the plaintiffs, particularly the immigrant investors; 3) the indemnity agreement does not cover such activity in any event so even if Dutton and J.M.D. are found liable they cannot pass their liability along to Claude under the terms of the indemnity agreement.

[13] So, as I understand Claude's submission it argues that the Alberta action against Dutton and J.M.D. does not fall into the category of a "provable" claim under s. 121 because:

(a) it relies on two contingencies, not one; first that Dutton and J.M.D. will be found liable and secondly that the judgment against them will be one that they are entitled to be indemnified against by Claude.

(b) therefore, because of the improbability of the claims meeting both contingencies the Court should reject the argument that this is a realistic claim provable in bankruptcy.

Conclusion

[14] In attempting to assess the validity of a "provable" claim under s. 121(1) of the Act, it is clear that the Court cannot get into the merits of the alleged contingent liability beyond noting the nature of the claim as set out, in this case, in the Alberta statement of claim. Similarly the Court is not in a position to assess whether any judgment that might be awarded the plaintiffs against Dutton and J.M.D. would qualify as a viable claim under the terms of the indemnity agreement they have with Claude for the obvious reason that the nature of the Alberta claim is founded on all sorts of allegations of wrongdoing and it is speculative in the extreme to conclude which, if any, of the allegations made against Dutton or J.M.D. might succeed in the eyes of the Court that tries it. There is simply no way of predicting what the outcome might be. This it seems to me is a weakness in the submission of Dutton and J.M.D. that this lawsuit falls into the category of a probable liability which qualifies as a "provable" claim in bankruptcy.

[15] There are other problems with the nature of the Alberta lawsuit that can be gleaned from the statement of claim without in any way attempting to assess the merits of it. It appears, given the number of defendants named and the extent of the allegations against each that all sorts of claim-overs, cross-claims and attempts to blame the other defendants are likely to arise before the action gets to trial. The action was started in May 1992 and aside from the amendments in April 1993 to extend the claim to Claude no further steps have been taken by the plaintiffs. The claim of the plaintiffs' involves large sums of money and can fairly be described as extensive, complex and speculative in nature.

[16] In addition if the only way the Court can arrive at a value of the alleged "provable" claim under s. 121(2) is to let the Alberta action take its course, it is apparent it will at the very least be a very long time in coming if indeed it is ever determined. Claude has settled its claim with the plaintiffs W.C.S.C. and the investors. It has no control over the progress of the action nor do Dutton or J.M.D. There is no evidence to suggest the action will ever get to trial. It is fair to conclude the establishment of this alleged "provable" claim and the value of it cannot be made known for a very long time.

[17] In my opinion the rights of a potential creditor of a bankrupt to establish a "provable" claim under s. 121 goes beyond evidence that the creditor has been sued and therefore the Court should recognize the potential and contingent liability that might flow from that claim. Surely there has to be some element of probability about the contingent liability arising from the Court action. In this instance the claimants Dutton and J.M.D. cannot rely just on the Alberta action resulting in a judgment—they must be able to claim indemnity against Claude before the claim becomes "provable." As I see it there are just too many "ifs" about the action itself and the applicability of the indemnity agreement to bring their claims into the "provable" category and in any event the valuation of it at this stage is speculative in the extreme.

[18] As a result I have concluded that the contingent claims of Dutton and J.M.D. are so remote and speculative they do not meet the definition of a "provable" claim under s. 121(2); therefore they cannot be recognized as valid claims against the assets of Claude on the evidence before me. I include in the contingent claims of Dutton both his alleged liability under the Alberta action and his other claim for mostly legal fees in the amount of $50,385.79.

[19] Also the Court cannot ignore the potential disruption to the proposal made by Claude to its creditors which the Court must rule on next August 30. The proposal indicates that Claude by negotiating a settlement with W.C.S.C. and the other plaintiffs in the Alberta action as well as its unsecured creditors will be able to carry on business and perhaps work its way out of the financial difficulties it currently has. Surely this is an objective the Court should attempt to foster not only for Claude's sake but for its creditors as well. The alleged contingent claims of Dutton and J.M.D. will disrupt this possibility for Claude because the proposal and the agreement it reached with its unsecured creditors would become subject to the intervening claims totalling over $60 million dollars. It seems to me that this is just another reason for insisting that if a potential creditor of the bankrupt comes forward with a contingent claim that he argues is "provable" and capable of "valuation" by the Court that the claim on its face must be a lot clearer than the ones being put forward by Dutton and J.M.D. in this case.

[20] For all of the foregoing reasons I conclude in answer to the motion by the Trustee to determine whether the alleged contingent claims of Dutton ($53,323,125.00) and J.M.D. ($11,675,000.00) arising out of the Alberta action are "provable" claims under s. 121(2) that they are not. I also find that the contingent claim of Dutton for $50,385.79 brought to me by way of appeal from the Trustee's disallowance does not fall into the category of a "provable" claim within the meaning of s. 121(2).

· · ·

Contingent claims disallowed.

Re Wiebe
(1995), 30 CBR (3d) 109 (Ont. Gen. Div.)

KOZAK J: [1] This is an application pursuant to Rule 94 of the *Bankruptcy Act* for a determination as to whether the contingent claim of the Thunder Bay District Health Unit is a provable claim and, if so, the value of the said claim.

Factual Background

[2] The bankrupt, Peter Victor Wiebe, is a dentist who is licensed and duly qualified to carry on a private practice in the Province of Ontario. An assignment in bankruptcy was filed on his behalf on November 5, 1993. On November 25, 1993, a proof of claim was filed by the Thunder Bay District Health Unit in which the sum of $94,458.58 was shown as an unsecured debt owing by the bankrupt to the said creditor. The amount shown as being owing arises out of an agreement, in writing, dated January 2, 1992 under which the Thunder Bay District Health Unit advanced to Doctor Wiebe the sum of $94,458.58 for the purpose of becoming qualified as a Dental Director in Public Health so that the Health Unit could hire him as its Dental Director. In this regard I take it that Doctor Wiebe successfully completed the necessary courses to qualify himself to practice as a Dental Director in Dental Public Health in the Province of Ontario, and that he commenced employment with the Health Unit in that capacity on September 1, 1993. The affidavit material filed indicates that he continues to be so employed.

[3] Paragraph 5 of the agreement between Doctor Wiebe and the Health Unit states:

> Provided the Dentist successfully obtains the necessary qualifications and is employed by the Health Unit for the period September 1, 1993 to February 28, 1998 as its Dental Director then all monies loaned to him or paid on his behalf by the Health Unit shall be forgiven.

On the other hand, paragraph 3(d) states:

> Except in the occurrence of death or permanent disability in the event that the Dentist enters employment with the Health Unit but his employment is terminated before completing the required period of service of 54 months commencing September 1, 1993 to February 28, 1998 of such service, then all monies advanced to the Dentist or on his behalf pursuant to paragraph 2 shall forthwith be due and payable on demand by him to the Health Unit together with interest at the rate of 11 percent per annum calculated from the dates of the respective advances or payments on his behalf.

[4] On August 5, 1994 a discharge hearing took place at which time the bankrupt's discharge was ordered suspended for a period of four months and he was discharged on December 5, 1994. Subsequent to the discharge the trustee came into possession of an unexpected sum in the amount of $2,500.00 and now wishes to have this amount paid out to the unsecured creditors. Hence the need to have the contingent claim of the Thunder Bay Health Unit determined as a provable claim and valued.

Legal Considerations

[5] Section 121(1) makes it clear that only debts to which the debtor is liable before the date of the bankruptcy or those to which he may become subject before his discharge, by reason of an obligation incurred before the bankruptcy, share in the assets vested in the trustee.

[6] Rule 94(1) provides that when a contingent or unliquidated claim is filed with the trustee, he shall, unless he compromises the claim, apply to the Court to determine whether the claim is a provable claim and, if so, to value the claim.

[7] A provable claim must be one recoverable by legal process (*Farm Credit Corp. v. Holowach* (1988), 68 CBR (NS) 255 (Alta. CA)). To be a provable claim under Section 121(2), a claim must not be too remote and speculative. To establish that a contingent claim or unliquidated claim is a provable claim, a creditor must prove more than he has been sued, and that he has an indemnity agreement from the bankrupt. There has to be an element of probability of liability arising from the Court proceedings. If there are too many ifs about the action and the applicability of the indemnity agreement before a provable claim comes into being, the claim is not a provable claim under Section 121(2). See *Claude Resources Inc. v. Dutton* (1993), 22 CBR (3d) 56.

Decision

[8] This is a case where the bankrupt has now been employed as the Dental Director of the Health Unit since September 1, 1993 and it would appear that he is performing his job function in a satisfactory manner. According to the Trustee, there is no present intention, on the part of the bankrupt, to leave his current employment, nor is there any indication at the present time, on behalf of the Health Unit, to terminate the employment of the bankrupt. The parties are content with the present arrangement which has existed for the past 18 months, and it is anticipated that the status will prevail until February 28, 1998 at which time the loan to the bankrupt will be forgiven. And yet, the contingency that the bankrupt might leave his employment or be terminated by his employer prior to February 28, 1998 and thereby incur liability for the loan is not so speculative or remote a probability as to render the creditor's claim unprovable. There are any number of reasons as to why a person might leave a position such as this or be terminated for cause. The bankrupt might receive a better job offer, wish to return to private practice, or move to another area. On the other hand, there might be misconduct or misbehaviour on the part of the bankrupt in the performance of his duties that could result in his dismissal prior to the expiration of the 54 month period. There is a case to be made for the Court to consider some factor for the happening of the contingency in this case. Accordingly, it is the finding of this Court that the creditor, Thunder Bay District Health Unit has proven its claim.

[9] As to the value of the said claim, the Court must look to what is reasonable in the circumstances. Given the current state of satisfaction of the parties, the tenure of the bankrupt on the job and the period remaining in the agreement, this Court values the claim at approximately ten percent of its face value which would be $9,500.00.

Contingent claim allowed.

Bukvic v. Bukvic
(2007), 86 OR (3d) 297 (Sup. Ct.)

D.J. GORDON J:

. . .

[79] The *Divorce Act* and *Family Law Act* have long been considered to create a debtor–creditor relationship when one spouse is obliged to make payment, either as to property or for support, to the other spouse.

[80] Prior to the amendments to the *BIA*, support recipients were not considered creditors in insolvency matters. In *Burrows, Re*, [1996] OJ No. 2825 (Ont. Gen. Div. [Commercial List]), the bankrupt support payor sought to have his support arrears declared provable such that enforcement would be stayed. Feldman J, as she then was, in finding the arrears were not provable, set out the common law position on support in the bankruptcy context, saying, at para. 7:

> In my view the Director's position is correct. Although the genesis of the rule is correctly articulated by the debtor, that is, because support payments can always be varied they cannot be quantified for proof in bankruptcy, it has become accepted law that maintenance and support payments including all arrears, whether court-ordered or made by agreement between the parties do not amount to a claim provable in bankruptcy.

[81] The rationale for the common law, as I understand it, was:

a) support claims were too uncertain; and,
b) the support debt would continue to exist post-bankruptcy and the support recipient was free to enforce the obligation on non-excluded property during bankruptcy.

The common law was seen as a hindrance to support recipients and, thus, legislative amendment was deemed necessary.

[82] The 1997 amendments to the *BIA* included what is now section 121(4). Support obligations were recognized as a provable claim where:

a) there is a debt or liability of the bankrupt to pay support;
b) such support is payable pursuant to an order or agreement made before the bankruptcy date;
c) the spouses are separated; and,
d) periodic support or lump sum amounts are provided in the order or agreement.

[83] In the case at bar, the wife meets this threshold test. The support order granted 23 February 2006 obligated the husband to pay periodic support, thus creating a liability.

[84] There were no support arrears on the bankruptcy date. Section 121(1), however, speaks of "all debts and *liabilities*, present or *future* … ." Future support obligations are an obvious liability. Section 121(2) refers to "contingent and unliquidated claims" and section 121(3) addresses "debts payable at a future time," all of which are provable claims if such are capable of calculation.

[85] There appears to be some disagreement as to the interpretation of section 121 with respect to support.

[86] As noted previously, Mr. Klotz is of the view section 121(4) only applies to support arrears arising before the bankruptcy date. Other commentators offer a similar interpretation. For example, Ronald E. Pizzo, in his paper *"Support Claims in Bankruptcy and Related Enforcement Issues"* 1999, 16 *National Insolvency Review* at p. 21 said:

> The new amendments affect only pre-bankruptcy arrears which arose while the spouses were living separate and apart. All other support obligations, including ongoing periodic support obligations and arrears arising after the date of bankruptcy, have not been affected by the new amendments. These claims are not provable in bankruptcy.

[87] Section 121(4) makes no mention of "support arrears" and, in my view, the above interpretation is incorrect. It would appear these commentators may be relying on the initial draft amendments as contained in Bill C-109. Bill C-109, which expired on the order paper, would have restricted provable support amounts to those assigned priority under section 136(1)(d.1). Bill C-5, as passed by Parliament, deleted such a restriction from section 121(4). It is logical to conclude Parliament thus intended to allow all support, "present or future," to be a provable claim. Support arrears accruing in the year prior and any lump sum payments in arrears are then left as priority claims under section 136(1)(d.1).

[88] Tamara M. Buckwold, in her book review *"Bankruptcy, Insolvency and Family Law,* 2nd ed., by Robert A. Klotz (Toronto, Carswell, 2001)," (2002) 37 *Can. Bus. LJ* 469, at pp. 471-2, provides this comment:

> In the same chapter, Klotz expresses in unqualified terms, and without supporting authority, the proposition that the provability of support arrears (and the special priority attaching to them under BIA s. 136) is limited to arrears accrued up to, but not after, the date of bankruptcy. This appears to represent a misreading of BIA s. 121. Subsection (4), specifically addressing the provability of support claims, might have been worded more clearly. However, it must be read in conjunction with subsection (1), which stipulates that provable claims include "liabilities, present or future … to which the bankrupt may become subject before the bankrupt's discharge by reason of any obligation incurred before the date on which the bankrupt becomes bankrupt." This must mean that support obligations payable after the date of bankruptcy but before the bankrupt payor's discharge are to be included in the provable claim, provided that they arise under a pre-bankruptcy agreement or order. This point, which may be significant in some circumstances, reappears at several other junctures in the book.

[89] Prof. Buckwold, in my view, provides the correct interpretation of section 121 as found in the present legislation.

[90] Accordingly, I conclude the wife has a provable claim although it does not have priority. Clearly, the bankrupt's obligation for future support arose by virtue of the court order prior to the bankruptcy date. The wife is, therefore, an unsecured creditor of the bankrupt estate.

[91] Mr. Snider relied on Misener J's decision in *Burson v. Burson* (1990), 29 RFL (3d) 454 (Ont. Gen. Div.) where, at para. 24, he said:

> Whatever might have been the effect of any of the provisions of the *Family Law Reform Act,* none of the provisions of the *Family Law Act, 1986* grant to one spouse a legal or beneficial

interest in any property of the other spouse at any stage. At the highest, the *Family Law Act,
1986* statutorily created a creditor–debtor relationship between the spouses upon permanent separation, with the calculation of the amount of the debt to be made by a formula that
requires the valuation of their respective properties. There are, of course, provisions that
empower the court to order the transfer of the property of one spouse to the other, either
for the satisfaction of the debt or as security for the debt, but these provisions are remedial
only, and discretionary at that. Absent the actual making of such an order pursuant to them,
those sections cannot possibly be construed so as to grant, on their face, property rights.

[92] This passage has been cited with approval on several occasions. For example, in
Gaudet (Litigation Guardian of) v. Young Estate (1995), 11 RFL (4th) 284 (Ont. Gen. Div.),
LaForme J, at para. 16, concluded:

> I am of the view that the more recent cases of *Burson* and *Nevare Holdings Ltd.* more prop-
> erly reflect the law than does *Beck*. These recent cases are consistent with the view, which I
> share, that a spouse should not have priority over business creditors. Spouses should only
> share in the profits of a marriage generated during the relationship. As a result, Patricia
> Young's interest arising out of the continuing preservation order and her right to equaliza-
> tion, does not grant her priority over third party creditors of the estate.

[93] *Burson* and *Gaudet*, although decided prior to the 1997 amendments to the *BIA*,
dealt with property issues, specifically equalization of net family property. Accordingly,
these decisions are distinguishable and ought not be relied upon in connection with support issues.

[94] Sections 178(1)(b) and (c), *BIA*, provide that a discharge order does not release
the bankrupt from support obligations. As well, pursuant to section 69.41, support enforcement proceedings are not stayed by an assignment in bankruptcy. Accordingly, in
the vast majority of cases, support recipients will pursue their claim personally against
the support payor, particularly by garnishment of wages.

[95] When the bankrupt has left the jurisdiction and abandoned his family, as here,
there is no reasonable likelihood of the support recipient receiving future support. In
those circumstances, she may wish, and must be allowed, to prove her claim as against
the bankrupt estate.

[96] The practical difficulty, in most cases, will be in quantifying the future support
obligation. As noted by Professor Buckwold above, section 121(1) includes provable support claims "... payable after the date of bankruptcy but before the bankrupt payor's discharge." The discharge date for most first-time bankrupts, pursuant to section 168.1,
automatically occurs nine months after the bankruptcy date.

[97] In this case, however, the husband will not be seeking a discharge and, in my
view, he is also ineligible for such relief. The husband has not participated in mandatory
counselling pursuant to section 157.1(3), a prerequisite for discharge. He has fled the
jurisdiction in circumstances which make it unlikely he will return. It appears, as I have
found, the husband left with the money accumulated from financial institutions which
may be a bankruptcy offence under section 198.

[98] Accordingly, the wife's claim is not restricted to nine months but, rather, includes the whole of the husband's future support obligation. This claim is capable of vali-

dation as such has already been calculated and converted into a lump sum amount as provided in my order granted 20 December 2006. The amount required from the bankrupt support payor is $389,666. This amount, therefore, is the provable claim of the wife against the bankrupt estate of the husband pursuant to section 121(1).

[99] From a policy perspective, it would be an obvious injustice if support creditors were not treated as creditors under the *BIA*. This proposition is amply supported by the comments in *Marzetti* and *Backman* previously mentioned. At the very least, all unsecured creditors, including support recipients, must be treated equally. Just as unconscionable as was the conduct of the husband in abandoning his family obligations, so too would be the action of a commercial creditor in attempting to assert absolute priority over a support recipient and thus subjecting her to a state of poverty.

[100] There is, in my view, a strong argument, from a policy perspective, for absolute priority in favour of provable spousal and child support claims, liability for such which occurs prior to the bankruptcy date. Priority, however, is restricted to the circumstances described in section 136(1)(d.1). Accordingly, it would not be proper for the court to declare a higher priority. Such is a function of Parliament. …

[101] For the above reasons, an order shall issue on the following terms:

...

b)   declaring Visnja Bukvic to be an unsecured creditor of the bankrupt estate with a provable claim in the amount of $389,666; …

Order accordingly.

Bittner v. Borne Chemical Company, Inc.
691 F 2d 134 (3rd Cir. 1982)

GIBBONS Cir. J: Stockholders of The Rolfite Company appeal from the judgment of the district court, affirming the decision of the bankruptcy court to assign a zero value to their claims in the reorganization proceedings of Borne Chemical Company, Inc. (Borne) under Chapter 11 of the Bankruptcy Code (Code), 11 USC §§1-151326 (Supp. IV 1981). Since the bankruptcy court neither abused its discretionary authority to estimate the value of the claims pursuant to 11 USC §502(c)(1) nor relied on clearly erroneous findings of fact, we affirm.

I.

Prior to filing its voluntary petition under Chapter 11 of the Code, Borne commenced a state court action against Rolfite for the alleged pirating of trade secrets and proprietary information from Borne. The Rolfite Company filed a counterclaim, alleging, *inter alia*, that Borne had tortiously interfered with a proposed merger between Rolfite and the Quaker Chemical Corporation (Quaker) by unilaterally terminating a contract to manufacture Rolfite products and by bringing its suit. Sometime after Borne filed its Chapter 11 petition, the Rolfite stockholders sought relief from the automatic stay so that the state court proceedings might be continued. Borne then filed a motion to disallow temporarily the Rolfite claims until they were finally liquidated in the state court. The bankruptcy court lifted the automatic stay but also granted Borne's motion to disallow temporarily the claims, extending the time within which such claims could be filed and allowed if they should be eventually liquidated.

Upon denial of their motion to stay the hearing on confirmation of Borne's reorganization plan, the Rolfite stockholders appealed to the district court, which vacated the temporary disallowance order and directed the bankruptcy court to hold an estimation hearing. The parties agreed to establish guidelines for the submission of evidence at the hearing, and, in accordance with this agreement, the bankruptcy court relied on the parties' choice of relevant pleadings and other documents related to the state court litigation, and on briefs and oral argument. After weighing the evidence, the court assigned a zero value to the Rolfite claims and reinstated its earlier order to disallow temporarily the claims until such time as they might be liquidated in the state court, in effect requiring a waiver of discharge of the Rolfite claims from Borne. Upon appeal, the district court affirmed.

II.

Section 502(c) of the Code provides:

> There shall be estimated for purposes of allowance under this section—
>
> (1) any contingent or unliquidated claim, fixing or liquidation of which, as the case may be, would unduly delay the closing of the case. ...

The Code, the Rules of Bankruptcy Procedure, 11 USC App. (1977), and the Suggested Interim Bankruptcy Rules, 11 US CA (1982), are silent as to the manner in which contingent or unliquidated claims are to be estimated. Despite the lack of express direction on the matter, we are persuaded that Congress intended the procedure to be undertaken initially by the bankruptcy judges, using whatever method is best suited to the particular contingencies at issue. The principal consideration must be an accommodation to the underlying purposes of the Code. It is conceivable that in rare and unusual cases arbitration or even a jury trial on all or some of the issues may be necessary to obtain a reasonably accurate evaluation of the claims. See 3 *Collier on Bankruptcy* ¶ 502.03 (15th ed. 1981). Such methods, however, usually will run counter to the efficient administration of the bankrupt's estate and where there is sufficient evidence on which to base a reasonable estimate of the claim, the bankruptcy judge should determine the value. In so doing, the court is bound by the legal rules which may govern the ultimate value of the claim. For example, when the claim is based on an alleged breach of contract, the court must estimate its worth in accordance with accepted contract law. See, e.g., 3 *Collier on Bankruptcy* ¶ 57.15[3.2] (14th ed. 1977). However, there are no other limitations on the court's authority to evaluate the claim save those general principles which should inform all decisions made pursuant to the Code.

In reviewing the method by which a bankruptcy court has ascertained the value of a claim under section 502(c)(1), an appellate court may only reverse if the bankruptcy court has abused its discretion. ...

According to the Rolfite stockholders, the estimate which section 502(c)(1) requires is the present value of the probability that appellants will be successful in their state court action. Thus, if the bankruptcy court should determine as of this date that the Rolfite stockholders' case is not supported by a preponderance or 51% of the evidence but merely by 40%, they apparently would be entitled to have 40% of their claims allowed during the reorganization proceedings, subject to modification if and when the claims are liquidated in state court. The Rolfite stockholders contend that instead of estimating their claims in this manner, the bankruptcy court assessed the ultimate merits and, believing that they could not establish their case by a preponderance of the evidence, valued the claims at zero.

We note first that the bankruptcy court did not explicitly draw the distinction that the Rolfite stockholders make. Assuming however that the bankruptcy court did estimate their claims according to their ultimate merits rather than the present value of the probability that they would succeed in their state court action, we cannot find that such a valuation method is an abuse of the discretion conferred by section 502(c)(1).

The validity of this estimation must be determined in light of the policy underlying reorganization proceedings. In Chapter 11 of the Code, Congress addressed the complex issues which are raised when a corporation faces mounting financial problems.

> The modern corporation is a complex and multi-faceted entity. Most corporations do not have a significant market share of the lines of business in which they compete. The success, and even the survival, of a corporation in contemporary markets depends on three elements: First, the ability to attract and hold skilled management; second, the ability to obtain credit; and third, the corporation's ability to project to the public an image of vitality. …
>
> One cannot overemphasize the advantages of speed and simplicity to both creditors and debtors. Chapter XI allows a debtor to negotiate a plan outside of court and, having reached a settlement with a majority in number and amount of each class of creditors, permits the debtor to bind all unsecured creditors to the terms of the arrangement. From the perspective of creditors, early confirmation of a plan of arrangement: first, generally reduces administrative expenses which have priority over the claims of unsecured creditors; second, permits creditors to receive prompt distributions on their claims with respect to which interest does not accrue after the filing date; and third, increases the ultimate recovery on creditor claims by minimizing the adverse effect on the business which often accompanies efforts to operate an enterprise under the protection of the *Bankruptcy Act*.

124 Cong. Rec. H 11101-H 11102 (daily ed. Sept. 28, 1978) (statement of Rep. D. Edwards of California, floor manager for bankruptcy legislation in the House of Representatives). Thus, in order to realize the goals of Chapter 11, a reorganization must be accomplished quickly and efficiently.

If the bankruptcy court estimated the value of the Rolfite stockholders' claims according to the ultimate merits of their state court action, such a valuation method is not inconsistent with the principles which imbue Chapter 11. Those claims are contingent and unliquidated. According to the bankruptcy court's findings of fact, the Rolfite stockholders' chances of ultimately succeeding in the state court action are uncertain at best. Yet, if the court had valued the Rolfite stockholders' claims according to the present probability of success, the Rolfite stockholders might well have acquired a significant, if not controlling, voice in the reorganization proceedings. The interests of those creditors with liquidated claims would have been subject to the Rolfite interests, despite the fact that the state court might ultimately decide against those interests after the reorganization. The bankruptcy court may well have decided that such a situation would at best unduly complicate the reorganization proceedings and at worst undermine Borne's attempts to rehabilitate its business and preserve its assets for the benefit of its creditors and employees. By valuing the ultimate merits of the Rolfite stockholders' claims at zero, and temporarily disallowing them until the final resolution of the state action, the bankruptcy court avoided the possibility of a protracted and inequitable reorganization proceeding while ensuring that Borne will be responsible to pay a dividend on the claims in the event that the state court decides in the Rolfite stockholders' favor. Such a solution is consistent with the Chapter 11 concerns of speed and simplicity but does not deprive the Rolfite stockholders of the right to recover on their contingent claims against Borne.

III.

The Rolfite stockholders further contend that, regardless of the method which the bankruptcy court used to value their claims, the court based its estimation on incorrect findings of fact. Rule 810 of the Rules of Bankruptcy Procedure permits an appellate court to overturn a bankruptcy referee's findings of fact only when they are clearly erroneous. ... A bankruptcy court may not, however, mask its interpretation of the law as findings of fact. In determining the legal merits of a case on which claims such as those of the Rolfite stockholders are based, the bankruptcy court should be guided by the applicable state law. The determination of such law is of course subject to plenary review. ...

The Rolfite stockholders argue that in assessing the merits of its state court action for the purpose of evaluating their claims against Borne, the bankruptcy court erred both in finding the facts and in applying the law. In reviewing the record according to the standards we have just described, we cannot agree. ...

The court's ultimate finding of fact—that the Rolfite stockholders' claims in the reorganization proceeding were worth zero—must also be upheld since it too is not clearly erroneous. The subsidiary findings of the court plainly indicated that the Rolfite counterclaim in the state action lacked legal merit. Faced with only the remote possibility that the state court would find otherwise, the bankruptcy court correctly valued the claims at zero. On the basis of the court's subsidiary findings, such an estimation was consistent both with the claims' present value and with the court's assessment of the ultimate merits.

District court judgment affirmed.

QUESTIONS

1. The court in *Bittner* effectively adopted a wait-and-see approach. This was exactly what the court in *Claude Resources v. Dutton* declined to do. Are these cases distinguishable?

2. The court in *Bittner* could have valued Rolfite's claim by assigning a present probability to its likelihood of success in the state court. Why did the court reject this approach?

3. The court's ruling in *Bittner* meant that the trustee had to keep funds in reserve to meet the claim if it materialized. The court's ruling in *Claude Resources* avoided this requirement. Presumably the amount of Rolfite's claim in *Bittner* was not so large that the creation

of a reserve fund would have derailed the reorganization. The court's ruling in *Bittner* meant that the Rolfite claim was released once the creditors voted to accept the debtor's plan and the court approved it. By contrast, the court's ruling in *Claude Resources* meant that the Alberta plaintiffs' claims were not released. Both decisions can be understood in terms of the fresh-start objective: in *Claude Resources*, the chances of the claims ever materializing were remote and so the debtor's continued exposure to them did not pose a significant risk; in *Bittner*, the chance of the Rolfite claim maturing was presumably higher and so it made sense in terms of the fresh start policy to include it in the plan.

In re Chavez
381 BR 582 (Bktcy. EDNY 2008)

CARLA E. CRAIG Chief US Bktcy. J: This matter comes before the Court on the motion ("Motion") of the debtor, Marco Antonio Chavez (the "debtor" or "Mr. Chavez") to estimate proof of claim No. 6 under 11 USC § 502(c) at one dollar, representing nominal damages to *pro se* claimant Carla Duncan (the "claimant" or "Ms. Duncan"). For the reasons set forth below, Ms. Duncan's claim, which arose from her wrongful eviction by the debtor from her apartment, is estimated at $28,916.04 representing compensatory and punitive damages, including $4,416.04, representing prejudgment interest at the rate of 9% per annum provided by CPLR §§ 5001(b).

. . .

Legal Standard

The debtor's motion to estimate the Claim is governed by § 502(c) of the *Bankruptcy Code*, which provides:

> (c) There shall be estimated for purpose of allowance under this section—
> (1) any contingent or unliquidated claim, the fixing or liquidation of which, as the case may be, would unduly delay the administration of the case;

11 USC §502(c).

Bankruptcy courts are required to estimate claims "[t]o achieve reorganization, and/or distributions on claims, without awaiting the results of legal proceedings." *In re Adelphia Business Solutions, Inc.*, 341 BR 415, 423 (Bankr. SDNY 2003) (citation omitted); "[W]hen the liquidation of a claim is premised on litigation pending in a non-bankruptcy court, and the final outcome of the matter is not forthcoming, the bankruptcy court should estimate the claim." *In re Lionel L.L.C.*, Case No. 04-17324, 2007 WL 2261539, at 2, 2007 Bankr. LEXIS 2652, at *7 (SDNY August 3, 2007) (citation omitted).

Ms. Duncan's action for damages has already continued for several years in the Civil Court, only to be transferred to the Supreme Court for further litigation. It is clearly within this Court's authority to estimate Ms. Duncan's claim to avoid further delay in the administration of the debtor's bankruptcy case.

"Neither the Bankruptcy Code nor the Federal Rules of Bankruptcy Procedure provide any procedures or guidelines for estimation." *DeGeorge Financial Corp. v. Novak (In re DeGeorge Financial Corp.)*, Case No. 3:01CV0009(CFD), 2002 WL 31096716, at 10, 2002 US Dist. LEXIS 17621, at 34 (D.Conn. July 15, 2002). Courts addressing the issue have held that bankruptcy judges may use "whatever method is best suited to the particular contingencies at issue." *Id.* (quoting *Bittner v. Borne Chemical Co.*, 691 F 2d 134, 135 (3d Cir. 1982)). "The methods used by courts have run the gamut from summary trials to full-blown evidentiary hearings to a mere review of pleadings [and] briefs." *Id.* at 10, 2002 US Dist. LEXIS 17621 at 35 (citations omitted). In exercising this broad discretion, the "[c]ourt must apply 'the legal rules which govern the ultimate value of the claim,' which ordinarily requires the application of state law." *In re Enron Corp.*, Case No. 01-16304, 2006 WL 544463, at 4, 2006 Bankr. LEXIS 4294, at 10 (SDNY January 17, 2006) (quoting *In re Brints Cotton Marketing, Inc.*, 737 F.2d 1338, 1341 (5th Cir. 1984)). "In general, the truncated trial process that can be developed under 502(c) has been found to be consistent with the dictates of due process of law." *Lionel*, 2007 WL 2261539, at 5, 2007 Bankr. LEXIS 2652, at 16-17 (citations omitted).

Wrongful Eviction

The debtor testified that he locked Ms. Duncan out of the Apartment because he believed that she had voluntarily moved out. The Court finds that the debtor's account lacks credibility for many reasons.

For one thing, the debtor failed even once to mention, let alone to explain, the flood and resulting water damage in the Apartment, although Ms. Duncan introduced numerous photographs into evidence showing that it had occurred. (Claimant's Exhibits 2-A, 2-K, 2-M, 2-N and 25.) Ms. Duncan also introduced Officer Boyette's testimony that the kitchen was dismantled, and the cabinets removed, and introduced additional photographs showing that closet doors were broken and removed from their hinges. The condition of the Apartment described by Mr. Boyette and shown in the photographs is consistent with the explanation offered by Ms. Duncan for the debtor's actions—that he locked her out because he knew that he had rented her an illegal basement apartment and that the authorities were investigating this as a result of her complaint, and he wanted to get rid of the evidence that the basement was being used as an apartment. (Tr. 2, 14:5-6; 38:1-3; Claimant's Exhibits 3-A, 3-F.)

The debtor's omission of any mention of the flood and damage to the Apartment from his testimony adds credibility to Ms. Duncan's version of events. The debtor's failure to offer any alternative explanation why the Apartment was flooded and the kitchen cabinetry and appliances removed is difficult to understand and undermines the credibility of his testimony. (Tr. 2, 14:5-6; 38:2.) In fact, the debtor's entire story lacked credibility. His testimony was peppered with omissions, obvious falsehoods, and inconsistencies. The debtor's only supporting evidence was provided by his brother, Enrique Chavez, whose testimony was equally lacking in credibility.

For example, the debtor and his brother testified that they resided in the Apartment with Ms. Duncan and her daughter, and that Ms. Duncan and her daughter were guests and were never asked to pay any rent in exchange for living there. (Tr. 2, 29:11-13; 24:12-13; 93:2-8.) This distinction is not relevant to Ms. Duncan's claim for wrongful eviction; even the landlord of a squatter may not resort to self-help "[w]hen a landlord gives permission, whether implicit or express, to occupy his property." *Walls v. Giuliani*, 916 F Supp. 214, 218 (EDNY 1996). Apparently, however, the debtor believes that Ms. Duncan's status as a rent-paying tenant is relevant to whether it was legal for the Apartment to be used by her as a dwelling. Mr. Chavez states in his Declaration dated July 16, 2006, submitted in connection with the Debtor's Objection to Proof of Claim Number Six, that "[t]he basement does not contain a legal apartment or dwelling space, so it could not be rented to her, but it was habitable. I never requested any money from Ms. Duncan because of her relationship with my brother." (Declaration dated 7/10/06, ¶ 2.) The fact that the debtor concocted this patently incredible story of a communal living arrangement in the Apartment adds credibility to Ms. Duncan's explanation of events: there would be no reason for the debtor to fabricate such a story unless he was concerned about liability for renting an illegal basement apartment.

. . .

Officer Boyette's testimony directly contradicted the debtor's, and was unbiased, credible and uncontroverted. Officer Boyette's testimony further undermined the debtor's credibility, and added to the credibility of Ms. Duncan's version of events. Based on Ms. Duncan's and Officer Boyette's testimony, and based on the lack of credibility of the testimony offered by the debtor, this Court finds that the debtor locked Ms. Duncan out of the Apartment and removed and disposed of her property.

Damages

"One who enters upon lands by permission of the owner without any term being prescribed or without reservation of rent is a tenant at will and, as such, is entitled to one month's notice to quit." *Fisher v. Queens Park Realty Corp.*, 41 AD 2d 547, 549, 339 NYS 2d 642, 645 (2d Dept. 1973); see also *Walls v. Giuliani*, 916 F Supp. at 219 (A landlord may terminate a tenancy at will only by delivering written notice of at least 30 days demanding the tenant leave the premises). The debtor did not employ lawful process for evicting Ms. Duncan from the Apartment. The debtor had no right to lock Ms. Duncan out of the Apartment or to remove her possessions, and is therefore liable for any resulting damages.

Compensatory Damages

"The measure of compensatory damages for wrongful eviction is the value of the unexpired term of the lease over and above the rent the lessee must pay under its terms, together with any actual damages flowing directly from the wrongful eviction." *Long Isl. Airports Limousine Serv. Corp. v. Northwest Airlines*, 124 AD 2d 711, 713, 508 NYS 2d 223, 225 (2d Dept. 1986). Damages measured by the value of the unexpired term of the lease would be inapplicable here, as Ms. Duncan was a tenant at will. However, Ms. Duncan may recover the value of her personal property lost, stolen or discarded during the course of the wrongful eviction.

The value of Ms. Duncan's personal property need not be determined to an exact certainty. "Receipts are not required to establish the value of [Ms. Duncan's] property; actual monetary loss, value of the property to the owner, [and] reasonable value ... are all admissible to prove damages." *Foxworth v. Tjutjulis*, 4 Misc. 3d 133A, 791 NYS 2d 869, 2007

NY Misc. LEXIS 1061, 2004 WL 1574703 (NY Misc. 2d Dept. 2004) (some testimonial or other evidence is required to establish the items lost and their estimated value); *N. Main Bagel Corp. v. Duncan*, 37 AD 3d 785, 787, 831 NYS 2d 239, 242 (NY App. Div. 2d Dept. 2007) (holding that the Supreme Court erred in not granting the tenants the value of personal property lost in the unlawful eviction based on a lack of documentation showing exact prices paid, because there was credible testimony that the items were actually purchased and of their estimated values, and no evidence was offered by the landlord to the contrary.)

Ms. Duncan testified that she valued the items lost from the Apartment at $25,000, because that is the upper limit of damages available in Civil Court. (Tr. 2, 186: 11-12.) That is obviously not an appropriate method of valuing the items she lost. Though she testified generally that she lost food, clothes, toys, and household goods (Tr. 2, 166), Ms. Duncan was unable to provide testimony identifying with any specificity the items she lost and their approximate value. (Tr. 2, 183-196.)

Ms. Duncan did, however, specifically identify the value of several items of property she lost as a result of the debtor's actions; she testified that she lost $5,000 in cash which she kept in the Apartment (Tr. 2, 167:15), as well as a blender, for which she paid $200, and a microwave, for which she paid $300 (Tr. 2, 189:3-4.) Ms. Duncan's testimony on these points was credible. Ms. Duncan testified that she did not have a bank account because she was a traveling surgical technician and had recently gone through an acrimonious divorce. (Tr. 2, 173:25; 174:1-3.) She stated that she would cash her pay checks weekly, and keep the money in the only closet in the Apartment that had a lock. (Tr. 2, 167:15-18; 174:6-8.) She further testified that she did not think that the debtor necessarily stole the $5,000 she had in her closet at the time she was locked out, but that he possibly threw it out along with the rest of her belongings. (Tr. 2, 167:23-25; 168:1-4.) In either event, the funds were lost as a result of the wrongful eviction, and the debtor is liable.

It is clear from Ms. Duncan's testimony as well as Officer Boyette's that Ms. Duncan lost other household goods, and although Ms. Duncan was unable to provide testimony concerning the value of those items, this Court assigns a value of $1,000 for estimation purposes to the other items of property lost by Ms. Duncan as a result of the debtor's actions. Ms. Duncan's claim for property damage is therefore estimated at $6,500.

Treble Damages

Section 853 of the *New York Real Property Actions and Proceedings Law* ("RPAPL") provides in pertinent part:

> If a person is disseized, ejected, or put out of real property in a forcible or unlawful manner, or after he has been put out, is held and kept out by force or by putting him in fear of personal violence or by unlawful means, he is entitled to recover treble damages in an action therefor against the wrong-doer.

RPAPL § 853.

"Damages for the removal, destruction or discarding of property in the course of an unlawful eviction are included under § 853." *H & P Research, Inc. v. Liza Realty Corp.*, 943 F Supp. 328, 330 (SDNY 1996). The record supports the conclusion that the debtor put Ms. Duncan out of the Apartment in an unlawful manner. Ms. Duncan is therefore entitled to treble damages, for a compensatory award of $19,500.

Punitive Damages

"An award for treble damages pursuant to RPAPL § 853 does not preclude an additional award of punitive damages." *H & P Research, Inc.*, 943 F Supp. at 330. Punitive damages is a common-law remedy which is "only available in the extreme cases where the [landlord] is shown to have been motivated by actual malice or to have acted in such a reckless, wanton or criminal manner so as to indicate a conscious disregard of the rights of others." *Lyke v. Anderson*, 147 AD 2d 18, 31, 541 NYS 2d 817, 825-826 (2d Dept. 1989). The record supports a finding that the debtor acted with a complete disregard for Ms. Duncan's property, for her safety and that of her daughter, and for her legal rights. *Suffolk Sports Center v. Belli Construction Corp.*, 212 AD 2d 241, 248, 628 NYS 2d 952, 956 (2d Dept. 1995) (Punitive damages are appropriate when denying such damages "[c]ould be interpreted as tacit permission for a landlord to engage in threats and intimidation ... conversely, the sanctioning of punitive damages will serve the public good by acting as [a] deterrent to similar actions in the future.") In this case, the record, including the debtor's patently incredible account of his living arrangements with Ms. Duncan, and his failure to offer any credible explanation of the circumstances under which he locked her out of the Apartment, or any account at all of the flooding of the Apartment and destruction of the kitchen, supports the conclusion that he acted in an attempt to force her out in order to cover up the fact that he had rented her an illegal apartment. As noted by the court in *Pleasant East Associates v. Cabrera*:

> This case cries out for the imposition of punitive damages. Such a remedy should serve to deter the petitioner from repeating such conduct and serve as a warning to others.

125 Misc. 2d 877, 883-884, 480 NYS 2d 693 (NY City Civ. Ct. 1984) (citations omitted).

The measure of punitive damages must be proportionate to the amount of compensatory damages and to the nature of the landlord's conduct. In *Suffolk Sports Center*, 212 AD 2d at 248, 628 NYS 2d 952, the court set aside the amount awarded for punitive damages, stating that although punitive damages were appropriate where a landlord "embarked upon a calculated effort to vitiate the landlord–tenant relationship between it and [its tenant]," the $300,000 awarded should be reduced to $60,000, which the court found to be proportionate to the $99,364.45 compensatory damages awarded. *Id.* This Court finds an award of $4,000 in estimated punitive damages satisfies the purpose and public policy set forth above in light of the debtor's conduct and that such an award is proportionate to the $6,500 awarded in estimated compensatory damages.

Emotional Distress

The emotional distress suffered by Ms. Duncan as a result of the trauma of losing her home and her belongings may be compensable damage. "The principle of awarding damages for emotional distress is not unknown in New York and the application of such principle to a case where a tenant is unceremoniously evicted from [her] home is entirely in accord with analogous decisions and 'civilized public policy.'" *Williams v. Llorente*, 115

Misc. 2d 171, 173, 454 NYS 2d 930, 932 (NY App. Term 1982) (citations omitted) (quoting *Stiles v. Donovan*, 100 Misc. 2d 1048, 1050, 420 NYS 2d 453, 455 (Civ. Ct. NY Cty. 1979)) (awarding $250 for emotional distress finding sufficient testimony given by the tenant regarding the emotional impact of being unlawfully locked out of his apartment and having his belongings removed.); *Lopez v. City of NY*, 78 Misc. 2d 575, 577, 357 NYS 2d 659, 661 (Civ. Ct. NY Cty. 1974) (awarding $500 to the tenant for emotional distress where the landlord unlawfully and forcibly evicted the tenant and, destroyed and discarded his belongings.); *Bianchi v. Hood*, 128 AD 2d 1007, 1008, 513 NYS 2d 541, 542 (3d Dept. 1987) (awarding $1,000 for pain and suffering and mental distress based on the testimony of the tenant and her father, who verified the tenant's emotional distress and the aggravation to an ankle injury as a result of the "flagrant, unlawful interference by [the landlord] with [her] right to enjoy and possess her leased premises.") The record here supports an estimated award of $1,000 in damages for emotional distress. Ms. Duncan testified to the mental anguish she suffered because of the debtor's actions, as well as to her diagnosis of bipolar disorder and depression and the exacerbation of these problems as a result of the debtor's actions. (Tr. 2, 196:10-12; 203:1-3.)

Prejudgment Interest

Ms. Duncan is entitled to recover prejudgment interest because of the debtor's interference with her "possession or enjoyment of property." NYCPLR §§ 5001(a); see *also* *N. Main Bagel*, 37 AD 3d 785 at 787, 831 NYS 2d 239 ("Prejudgment interest should be awarded on the plaintiff's recovery, from … the date of the wrongful eviction"). "Such interest is to be calculated at the simple rate of 9% per annum." *H & P Research, Inc.*, 943 F Supp. at 332. Therefore, Ms. Duncan's estimated award shall be increased by $4,416.04, representing 9% interest or $6.04 per diem, from May 8, 2004 through May 9, 2006, the date this bankruptcy case was commenced.

Conclusion

For the reasons stated in this opinion, this Court holds that proof of claim No. 6, filed by Ms. Duncan, is estimated in the amount of $28,916.04, representing compensatory, treble and punitive damages, including prejudgment interest of 9% per annum from May 8, 2004 through May 9, 2006. A separate order will be issued herewith.

In re FV Steel and Wire Co.
372 BR 446 (Bktcy. ED Wis., 2007) (footnotes omitted)

SUSAN V. KELLEY Bktcy. J:

Background and Facts

In 1989, the United States Environmental Protection Agency ("EPA") named various parties, including the Glidden Company and DeSoto, Inc., now known as Sherman Wire Company (the "Debtor"), as potentially responsible parties ("PRPs") liable for the cleanup of the Chemical Recycling, Inc. hazardous waste site located in Wylie, Texas (the "site" or the "CRI Site"). Without admitting liability, the PRPs entered into the Chemical Recycling, Inc. Site Agreement for Participation (the "Agreement") to jointly manage the cleanup. The Agreement created the CRI Steering Committee (the "CRI Committee") to organize the initiative and apportion the liability among the parties. The EPA issued an Administrative Consent Order on August 4, 1989, and the PRPs contributed funds to the cleanup. Various drums and tanks were removed in the 1989 to 1990 timeframe, and the site was fenced, but very little else occurred at the site until 2004, when a new EPA On Scene Coordinator was appointed. The EPA issued Action Memoranda which purported to modify the Statement of Work in 2005 and 2006, but no work has been done at the site (except for testing and monitoring) since 1990.

The Debtor filed a chapter 11 petition on February 26, 2004. The claims bar date for nongovernmental entities was July 1, 2004, and the claims bar date for governmental units was August 24, 2004. The CRI Committee and Glidden filed timely proofs of claim related to the site, but, although it had filed claims related to the cleanup of other sites in which the Debtor was involved, the EPA did not file a proof of claim related to the CRI Site. After the claims bar date expired, the Debtor withdrew from the Agreement. The CRI Committee and Glidden then sought leave to file a late proof of claim on behalf of the EPA, claiming that excusable neglect operated to excuse its failure to file this claim prior to the bar date. Although this Court ruled that the doctrine of excusable neglect as dictated by the 7th Circuit Court of Appeals did not permit the late filing of the claim, this decision was reversed on appeal by the District Court. On remand, this Court disallowed the claims filed by Glidden and the CRI Committee based on Bankruptcy Code § 502(e)(1)(B), which bars contingent claims for contribution and reimbursement. However, the court permitted the CRI Committee to file the claim on behalf of the EPA and proceeded with an estimation hearing under 11 USC § 502(c)(1). The parties have filed post trial briefs.

. . .

Claim Estimation Analysis

The Debtor objected that the CRI Committee's estimate and classification as a removal action is excessive and questioned why the CRI Committee and the EPA did not analyze less expensive remedial options. The CRI Committee's estimate is $1.9 million, and the Debtor believes the actual cleanup costs will be no more than $75,000. "To value contingent liability it is necessary to discount it by the probability that the contingency will occur and the liability become real." *In re Xonics Photochemical, Inc.*, 841 F 2d 198, 200 (7th Cir. 1988). After considering the evidence, and the relevant authorities, the Court concludes that the Debtor's estimate is closer to the allowable amount of the claim.

CERCLA provides the EPA with a framework of tools to achieve the efficient and effective cleanup of hazardous waste sites. See 42 USC § 9601; *Frey v. EPA*, 403 F 3d 828, 833 (7th Cir. 2005); *United States v. Occidental Chem. Corp.*, 200 F 3d 143 (3d Cir. 1999). CERCLA § 104 authorizes the President (who has delegated most of his authority under CERCLA to the EPA) to use Superfund money to respond to any threatened or actual release of any hazardous substance that may pose an imminent and substantial threat to public health. See 42 USC § 9604. CERCLA § 107 provides for the recovery of response costs from all persons responsible for the release of a hazardous substance. *In re Bell Petroleum Servs.*, 3 F 3d 889, 894 (5th Cir. 1993).

To establish a *prima facie* case under § 107(a) of CERCLA, the EPA must prove five elements: (1) the defendant is among the four categories of responsible parties enumerated in § 107(a); (2) the site is a "facility" as defined in § 101(9); (3) there was a "release" or "threatened release" of "hazardous substances" at the facility; (4) the United States incurred costs responding to the release or threatened release; and (5) the costs and response actions conform to the national contingency plan under CERCLA § 107(a)(4)(A) as administered by the EPA. *United States v. 175 Inwood Assocs. LLP*, 330 F. Supp. 2d 213, 220-221 (EDNY 2004), citing *B.F. Goodrich v. Betkoski*, 99 F 3d 505, 514 (2d Cir. 1996); *United States v. Alcan Aluminum Corp.*, 990 F 2d 711, 719-20 (2d Cir. 1993). In this case, there is little doubt that the Debtor is a person who arranged for the disposal of hazardous substances at the site, and thus is a covered person under the statute. Also, it is not disputable that the site is a facility at which a release or threatened release occurred. However, the Debtor disputes that the United States has incurred unreimbursed costs responding to the release, and contends that if such costs are incurred in the future, the estimate contained in the Claim filed on behalf of the EPA by the CRI Committee does not conform to the requirements of the national contingency plan.

At first blush, there appears to be merit in the Debtor's argument that the "surrogate claim" filed by the CRI Committee on behalf of the EPA must be disallowed because the EPA itself is not spending the response costs. The funds to be expended for the remaining cleanup will in all likelihood come from the CRI Committee and the other PRPs who have not filed bankruptcy and not the government itself. However, in disallowing the CRI Committee's and Glidden's individual claims under § 502(e)(1)(B) of the Bankruptcy Code, this Court necessarily found that those parties are liable with the Debtor to the EPA. See *In re Hemingway Transp.*, 993 F 2d 915 (1st Cir. 1993). If the Debtor is not liable to the EPA because the EPA has not spent any money, then the provisions of § 502(e)(1)(B) do not apply, and Glidden and the CRI Committee can prove their own contingent claims for the cleanup. The Debtor cannot escape liability to all parties, simply because the amount of the claim is contingent and unliquidated. While there cannot be multiple claims for the same contingent, unliquidated liability, there can be one claim, the claim at issue in this case. See *id.*, 993 F 2d at 923 (sole purpose of Bankruptcy Code § 502(e)(1)(B) is to "preclude redundant recoveries on identical claims against insolvent estates" and "double-dipping" resulting from EPA and PRP claim for the same future CERCLA response costs.) Accordingly, the Debtor's objection based on the EPA's failure to have spent any money is denied, and the issue for decision is whether the costs estimated by the CRI Committee would conform to the national contingency plan under CERCLA.

"CERCLA response actions fall into two categories: removal and remedial actions. Removal refers to a short-term action taken to halt risks posed by hazardous wastes immediately. Remedial actions involve permanent solutions, taken instead of or in addition to removal, such as the destruction of hazardous materials." *Frey*, 403 F 3d at 835. *Frey* concerned a remedial action, because it dealt with "actions consistent with permanent remedy" including a long-term excavation and destruction of hazardous materials. 42 USC § 9601(24).

The distinction is important because if the cleanup is a remedial action, regulations require that the site be included on the National Priorities List and that the EPA consider the cost effectiveness of the remediation. *United States v. W.R. Grace & Co.*, 429 F 3d 1224, 1226 (9th Cir. 2005), cert. denied,___US___, 127 S.Ct. 379, 166 L Ed. 2d 268 (2006). "In contrast, the regulatory requirements for removal actions, which provide the EPA with substantial flexibility to tailor prompt and effective responses to immediate threats to human health and the environment, are considerably relaxed." *Id.* Determining whether the cleanup is a remedial or removal action is complicated by the fact that "(e)lements of either response action may overlap and semantics often obscure the actual nature of the cleanup being performed." *Pub. Serv. of Colo. v. Gates Rubber Co.*, 175 F 3d 1177, 1182 (10th Cir. 1999).

The CRI Committee alleges that this cleanup is a removal action, and the Debtor disagrees. The standard for determining allowed costs of a removal action is two-fold. First, the EPA's costs must be upheld unless the party challenging the claim proves the method chosen for the cleanup was arbitrary and capricious. Second, the EPA action must be properly characterized as a removal action. See *W.R. Grace & Co.* at 1233. The arbitrary and capricious standard of review instructs a court to make the narrow determination of whether the EPA's decision is based upon consideration of relevant factors and is not a clear error of judgment. *Motor Vehicle Mfg. Ass'n of US Inc. v. State Farm Mut. Auto.*, 463 US 29, 43, 103 S Ct. 2856, 77 L Ed. 2d 443 (1983). The agency must present a clear explanation of the relevant data, and the reviewing court will not substitute its judgment for the agency. *Id.* However, this Court has not heard from the EPA, and is cognizant that it should not "supply a reasoned basis for the agency's action that the agency itself has not given." *Id.*

National Contingency Plan regulations require the EPA to consider eight factors before deciding whether to conduct a removal action:

   (i)   Actual or potential exposure to nearby human populations, animals, or the food chain from hazardous substances or pollutants or contaminants;

  (ii)   Actual or potential contamination of drinking water supplies or sensitive ecosystems;

 (iii)   Hazardous substances or pollutants or contaminants in drums, barrels, tanks, or other bulk storage containers, that may pose a threat of release;

 (iv)   High levels of hazardous substances or pollutants or contaminants in soils largely at or near the surface, that may migrate;

  (v)   Weather conditions that may cause hazardous substances or pollutants or contaminants to migrate or be released;

 (vi)   Threat of fire or explosion;

 (vii)   The availability of other appropriate federal or state response mechanisms to respond to the release; and

(viii)   Other situations or factors that may pose threats to public health or welfare of the United States or the environment.

40 CFR § 300.415(b)(2).

In *W.R. Grace & Co.*, a removal decision was upheld when the EPA's consideration of these factors was supported by extensive documentation. The EPA's findings "detailed specific threats with carefully documented reasoning." *W.R. Grace & Co.*, 429 F 3d at 1233. By contrast, in *United States v. Wash. State DOT*, 2007 US Dist. LEXIS 8796 (February 7, 2007), the court found the evidence to support the removal decision lacking, for many of the same reasons that exist in this case. For example, in discussing a contaminated plume of groundwater that was allegedly migrating toward uncontaminated wells, the court said "[I]t is unclear how this evidence may be used to support a time-sensitive removal. ... [T]he groundwater path does not evidence the rate of migration. The parties agree that at least some of the contamination is traceable to events that occurred in 1970. The Court therefore concludes that the record of evidence of groundwater flow does not demonstrate how this contamination, of which the City and the EPA had been aware since 1993, became an urgent concern in 1997." *Id.* at *34 (internal citations omitted). In denying the costs of the removal action, the court concluded: "While much of the EPA's analysis references scientific evidence in the record, the evidence cited is often of little or no relevance to the overall question of whether the conditions at the Site were such that cleanup, in the form of a *time-sensitive removal*, was appropriate." *Id.* at *44 (emphasis in original).

In this case, it is similarly impossible to conclude that the evidence justifies a "time-sensitive response to public health threats," when there has been no cleanup for 17 years. In fact, it appears that in the absence of immediate attention the CRI Site has remained stable. For example, there is no evidence that the groundwater has or even could carry hazardous substances off the site, and the CRI Site is fenced in and bordered by railroad tracks and a highway, presumably preventing children from entering. The site is lush and green with vegetation, reducing the risk of the contaminated soils becoming airborne, and natural attenuation seems to have mitigated a great deal of the problem. Given the lack of any evidence that public health or safety has been threatened during the long period of inactivity, it is highly doubtful that the site in fact requires "immediate attention," and extremely speculative that an expensive removal procedure in which 80 trucks full of contaminated soil are driven across several states to a treatment facility is justifiable under the CERCLA standards and national contingency plan regulations·

Further, it is important to reiterate that the CRI Committee did not produce any witnesses from the EPA to discuss how the site poses an imminent public health threat nor to explain how much, if any, soil will need to be excavated. Such testimony could have clarified and supported the CRI Committee's position that a removal action complies with the NCP and will cost $1.7 to $1.9 million. While some documents exist in the form of findings from Golder Associates, the conclusions and methodology were challenged by the Debtor's expert, and the EPA's own report suggests that far less soil may be required to be removed than Golder's report suggests. It is also important to note that after participating in the 1989 removal action, the Debtor withdrew from the CRI Committee and the Participation Agreement after a long period of inactivity. The CRI Committee has presented no evidence to show that the Debtor did anything to the CRI Site in the meantime that contributed to the alleged need to take emergency action in 2007.

The CRI Committee has not presented any clear evidence that the EPA actually views the CRI Site as an imminent threat to human health or the environment warranting a removal action or that the EPA could support such a decision with appropriate documentation. The CRI Site is a commercial site used only for industrial purposes, is fenced and secure, and no migrating groundwater issues exist. The contaminated soil has existed untreated since at least 1989, and natural attenuation appears to be reducing the contamination. Assuming that some cleanup is required, there is insufficient evidence that the most expensive and least desirable process of removing and trucking the soil across two states would be upheld, especially without considering less expensive, but equally protective options. In a remediation, "Costs that are grossly excessive compared to the overall effectiveness of alternatives may be considered as one of several factors used to eliminate alternatives. Alternatives providing effectiveness and implementability similar to that of another alternative by employing a similar method of treatment or engineering control, but at greater cost, may be eliminated."

Conclusion

After careful consideration of the evidence presented in the claim estimation hearing, and the extremely well-presented arguments of the parties, the court estimates the Claim filed by the CRI Committee on behalf of the EPA at the high end of the range given by the Debtor's expert: $75,000. Although it is arguable that the Debtor is not jointly and severally liable for 100% of this amount, the Debtor did not present evidence suggesting apportionment, and no such apportionment will be ordered by this court.

However, the CRI Committee stipulated that the Debtor is entitled to a $53,100 credit for funds previously paid to the CRI Committee under the 1989 Consent Order. This amount should be offset from the Claim, reducing the Claim to $21,900. The Debtor's rights to seek contribution and reimbursement from Glidden and the CRI Committee for the amounts to be paid on this Claim are not properly before this Court.

An Order will be entered allowing the Claim in the amount of $75,000, less credit for the overpayment of $53,100, for a total allowed claim of $21,900.

III. MASS TORT CLAIMS

NOTE ON THE MEANING OF "CLAIM" AND "CREDITOR" IN THE CONTEXT OF MASS TORTS

American courts have on several occasions had to wrestle with the meaning of "creditor" and "claim" under the *Bankruptcy Code* when corporations sought protection under Chapter 11 against current and prospective mass tort claims brought, or liable to be brought, against them by alleged victims of asbestosis (Johns-Manville Corp.) or wearers of the Dalkon Shield (A.H. Robins Co.). According to Baird and Jackson (Douglas G. Baird and Thomas H. Jackson, *Cases, Problems and Materials on Bankruptcy*, 2d ed. 1989, 151), writing in 1989, the case law was "conflicting, contradictory, and, from time to time, confused." In one such case, *In re UNR Industries*, 29 Bankr. 741 (Bankr. ND Ill. 1983), appeal dismissed, 725 F 2d 1111 (7th Cir. 1984), Judge Hart refused to appoint a representative to file claims on behalf of individuals who might develop asbestosis from past exposure to products manufactured and sold by UNR, and reasoned as follows (Baird and Jackson, 151):

The debtors contend that the putative claimants are holders of contingent claims. Three principles determine the question presented here:

1. A claim of which a bankruptcy court may take cognizance must be one that is recognized by state or federal law. ... The asbestos claims and rights all arise under state law.

2. The existence of a claim turns on when it arose. ... In the case of a claim sounding in tort, it is not the wrongful or negligent act which gives rise to the claim. Instead, no claim arises until the plaintiff suffers an injury. ...

3. The claim of an asbestos plaintiff (including a putative claimant) does not arise under state law until the plaintiff knows or should have known about the injury. ...

Therefore, under the definition imposed in the debtors' Application, the putative claimants—who have been exposed to asbestos some time in their lives but do not now have or do not know that they have an asbestos-related disease—have no claims under state law, and therefore do not have claims cognizable under the Code. Further, by the debtors' own definition the claims of the putative claimants will not have arisen either "at the time of or before the order for relief," 11 USC §101(9) [now §101(10)], since a putative claimant is one who does not know that he has an asbestos-related disease.

The Code provision for the possibility of the evaluation and discharge of a *contingent* claim does not change the definition of "claim." It is not true that any conceivable claim is contingent. The contingency must be one that arises out of the prior contractual relationship of the claimant and the debtor. A tort claim does not meet this requirement. Instead, a tort action brought against a debtor is covered by other definitions: it is a "right to payment [not yet] reduced to judgment [that is] unliquidated [and] disputed." 11 USC §101(4)(A) [now §105(A): "right to payment, whether or not such right is reduced to judgment, liquidated, unliquidated, fixed, contingent, matured, unmatured, disputed, undisputed, legal, equitable, secured, or unsecured"].

On appeal, Judge Posner, writing for the Seventh Circuit, did not reach the merits of the case on the ground that Judge Hart's order in which he refused to appoint a representative was not "final" within the meaning of 28 USC §1291 and hence was not appealable, 725 F 2d at 1118. However, he went on to suggest what his own views of the cognizability of asbestosis claims might be if the issue were before him (Baird and Jackson, above, 152-53):

The practical difficulties of identifying, giving constitutionally adequate notice to, and attempting to estimate the damages of the thousands upon thousands of people who have been exposed to asbestos sold by UNR but have not yet developed asbestosis are formidable, and possibly insurmountable. Yet if any of them have already suffered a tort there would be no basis we can think of for not letting them file claims in this bankruptcy proceeding. And some, at least, probably have suffered a tort. The states differ on whether a cause of action in an asbestosis case accrues upon inhalation ... or not until there is palpable disease ... or the disease is discovered. ... Even in a "discovery" state the cause of action may "exist" before it "accrues"—that is, before the statute of limitations on bringing it begins to run. ... These states postpone the date of accrual of the cause of action not in order to prevent the early filing of claims but in order to lift the bar of the statute of limitations to later filings. Since there is "medical evidence that the body incurs microscopic injury as asbestos fibers become lodged in the lungs and as the surrounding tissue reacts to the fibers thereafter," *Keene Corp. v. Insurance Co. of North America*, 667 F 2d 1034, 1042 (DC Cir. 1981), and since no particular amount of injury is necessary to create tort liability, courts in these states might hold that a tort claim arises as soon as asbestos fibers are inhaled, however much time the victim might have for bringing suit. In any event, some at least of the many thousands of workers who have been exposed to asbestos sold by UNR must have been exposed in states such as Indiana and New York where the cause of action accrues upon inhalation, and their claims against the bankrupt estate—accrued tort claims— would appear uncontroversially to be provable in bankruptcy.

Even in states where exposed workers are not injured in a tort sense till the disease manifests itself, and therefore do not have an accrued tort claim in any sense, and even assuming that an unaccrued tort claim cannot be a "claim" within the meaning of 11 USC §101(4)(A) [now §101(5)(A)], ... a bankruptcy court's equitable powers ... just might be broad enough to enable the court to make provision for future asbestosis claims against the bankrupt when it approved the final plan of reorganization. The date on which a person exposed to asbestos happens to develop a diagnosable case of asbestosis is arbitrary. Could it not be argued therefore that a bankruptcy court can and should use its equitable powers, which traditionally "have been invoked to that end that ... substance will not give way to form, that technical considerations will not prevent substantial justice from being done" [*Pepper v. Litton*, 308 US 295, 305 (1939)] (especially, perhaps, in a reorganization case, see *In re Michigan Brewing Co.*, 24 F Supp. 430 (WD Mich. 1938)), to prevent the liquidation or discharge of the bankrupt before provision is made for such persons? And more than arbitrariness is involved. If future claims cannot be discharged before they ripen, UNR may not be able to emerge from bankruptcy with reasonable prospects for continued existence as a going concern. In that event, and assuming that UNR's going-concern value would exceed its liquidation value, both UNR (which is to say the creditors who will own UNR at the conclusion of the reorganization) and future plaintiffs would be made worse off, and UNR's current creditors would not necessarily be made better off, by the court's failure to act along the lines proposed by UNR.

In re Roman Catholic Archbishop of Portland in Oregon
44 Bankr. Ct. Dec. 54 (Bankr. D Or. 2005) (footnotes omitted)

PERRIS Bktcy. J: At the November 19, 2004 hearing, I approved the appointment of a future claims representative ("FCR") to represent the interests of certain unknown individuals holding claims against debtor who will fail to formally assert those claims by the bar date. The pertinent claims result from "Tortious Misconduct by any priest, representative, agent, volunteer, or employee of the Debtor which occurred prior to the Petition Date." Debtor's Amended Motion for an Order (1) Fixing a Bar Date for Filing Proofs of Claim, and (2) Approving a Proof of Claim Form, Bar Date Notices, Actual Notice Procedure, and Mailing and Media Notice Program, 9:12-14. There is no dispute that the FCR should represent the interest of individuals who are currently minors and whose parent or legal guardian does not file a timely claim (hereinafter "minors") and those with repressed memory who have no knowledge of the wrongful conduct resulting in their claim against debtor.

Debtor's position is that the scope of the FCR's authority should be limited to minor and repressed memory claimants. The Tort Claimants Committee ("the TCC") advocated for a broader scope of representation. At the November 19 hearing, I sustained the TCC's objection and ruled that, in addition to minors and those with repressed memory, the FCR would represent the interests of those persons who know they were subjected to sexual contact as children but who have "not discovered the [resulting] injury or the causal connection between the injury and the child abuse, nor in the exercise of reasonable care should have discovered the injury or the causal connection between the injury and the child abuse." This language comes from an Oregon statute, ORS 12.117(1), which would be pertinent to all the possible Tortious Misconduct for which debtor may be liable, because of the geographic location of debtor's operations. ORS 12.117(1) states as follows:

> Notwithstanding ORS 12.110, 12.115 or 12.160, an action based on conduct that constitutes child abuse or conduct knowingly allowing, permitting or encouraging child abuse accruing while the person who is entitled to bring the action is under 18 years of age shall be commenced not more than six years after that person attains 18 years of age, or if the injured person has not discovered the injury or the causal connection between the injury and the child abuse, nor in the exercise of reasonable care should have discovered the injury or the causal connection between the injury and the child abuse, not more than three years from the date the injured person discovers or in the exercise of reasonable care should have discovered the injury or the causal connection between the child abuse and the injury, whichever period is longer.

The purpose of this memorandum is to explain the basis for my decision and to point out that the scope of the FCR's representation is more limited than some of the lawyers' arguments would suggest.

A. All Alleged Victims of Prepetition Sexual Abuse Have Claims Within the Meaning of the Bankruptcy Code

As an initial matter, I acknowledge, and all parties appear to agree, that the alleged victims of prepetition sexual abuse by priests or other representatives of debtor are "creditors" holding "claims" against debtor as those terms are defined under the Bankruptcy Code.

A creditor includes an "entity that has a claim against the debtor that arose at the time of or before the" petition date. § 101(10). "While state law determines the existence of a claim based on a cause of action, federal law determines when the claim arises for bankruptcy purposes." *In re Hassanally*, 208 BR 46, 50 (9th Cir. BAP 1997). The Bankruptcy Code defines a claim to be a

> (A) right to payment, whether or not such right is reduced to judgment, liquidated, unliquidated, fixed, contingent, matured, unmatured, disputed, undisputed, legal, equitable, secured, or unsecured; or
> (B) right to an equitable remedy for breach or performance if such breach gives rise to a right to payment, whether or not such right to an equitable remedy is reduced to judgment, fixed, contingent, matured, unmatured, disputed, undisputed, secured or unsecured.

§ 101(5). Congress adopted the expansive definition of claim set forth above to ensure that "all legal obligations of the debtor, no matter how remote or contingent, will be able to be dealt with in the bankruptcy case." HR Rep. No. 595, 95th Cong., 2d Sess. 1, 309 (1978), *reprinted* in 1978 USCCAN 5963, 6266.

In re Jensen, 995 F 2d 925, 929 (9th Cir. 1993). Indeed, the breadth of the definition of claim is essential to achieve the Bankruptcy Code's goal of providing debtors with a fresh start.

In *Jensen*, the Ninth Circuit applied a "fair contemplation test" to determine when an environmental claim arose. The fair contemplation test has been described as equivalent to the test set forth in *In re Piper Aircraft Corp.*, 58 F 3d 1573 (11th Cir. 1995), see *Hassanally*, 208 BR at 52, which requires some prepetition or preconfirmation relationship, such as "contact, exposure, impact, or privity" between the debtor and the claimant. *Piper*, 58 F 3d at 1577. Under this test, "[t]he debtor's prepetition conduct gives rise to a claim to be administered in a case only if there is a relationship established before confirmation between an identifiable claimant or group of claimants and that prepetition conduct." *Id.* There is no dispute that this requirement is met in this case. Therefore, all the future claimants to be represented by the FCR, including the minors and those with repressed memory, hold claims against debtor within the meaning of § 101(5).

B. Scope of the FCR's Representation

As I stated at the hearing, the fact that the future claimants have claims does not answer the question of whether there should be a FCR or of the appropriate scope of the FCR's authority. The debtor sought the appointment of a FCR, because it had unknown creditors who might be unaware that they had claims. Memorandum in Support of Debtor's Amended Motion for an Order (1) Fixing a Bar Date for Filing Proofs of Claim, and (2) Approving a Proof of Claim Form, Bar Date Notices, Actual Notice Procedure, and Mailing and Media Notice Program, 18:11-13. Debtor recognized that, absent the appointment of a FCR, it was questionable whether it could accomplish through this bankruptcy a global resolution and discharge of the abuse claims. The narrow scope of representation proposed by debtor for the FCR is inconsistent with the approach taken in other bankruptcy cases, and with debtor's stated purpose in invoking the relief afforded under chapter 11.

In October of this year, the United States Bankruptcy Court for the District of Arizona entered an order approving the appointment of an Unknown Claims Representative ("the UCR") in the chapter 11 case of the Catholic Diocese of Tucson ("the Tucson case"). The UCR in the Tucson case has wide-ranging duties, including the authority to file a proof of claim on behalf of the class he represents, which class is comprised of "those persons who are of adult age whose claims currently exist but who do not realize and who will not realize, prior to the April 15, 2005 deadline for filing claims, that they have claims against the estate." Case No. 4-04-bk-04721-JMM, Order Appointing an "Unknown Claims" Representative and a Guardian Ad Litem, 1:12-14. The scope of representation approved by the court in the Tucson case is even broader than that which I approved. In this case, the FCR will represent only those individuals who, "in the exercise of reasonable care," have failed to discover that they have been injured by debtor's conduct or the causal connection between debtor's conduct and their injury. ORS 12.117(1). There is no such limitation imposed in the Tucson case.

The approach taken in the Tucson case, and in this case, is consistent with that taken in the "mass tort" asbestos bankruptcy cases. The seminal asbestos bankruptcy case is that of the Johns-Manville Corporation. In that case, the court, citing § 105(a) and § 1109(b), approved the appointment of a future claims representative to represent all persons who, on or before a certain date, came into contact with asbestos or asbestos-containing products mined, fabricated, manufactured, supplied or sold by Manville and who have not yet filed claims against Manville for personal injuries or property damage. These claimants may be unaware of their entitlement to recourse against Manville due to the latency period of many years characterizing manifestation of all asbestos related diseases.

In re Johns-Manville Corp., 36 BR 743, 745 (Bankr. SDNY 1984), aff'd, 52 BR 940 (SDNY 1985). Other bankruptcy courts followed suit, appointing representatives for those who, whether knowingly or not, had already been exposed to asbestos, but for whom injury had not yet manifested itself. See, e.g., *In re Forty-Eight Insulations*, Inc., 58 BR 476 (Bankr. ND Ill. 1986); *In re UNR Indus.*, Inc., 46 BR 671 (Bankr. ND Ill. 1985). In *In re Amatex Corp.*, 755 F 2d 1034 (3d Cir. 1985), the Third Circuit affirmed the bankruptcy court's appointment of a representative for future claimants who had been exposed to asbestos but who had not yet manifested an injury.

The possibility of a long latency period before which injury becomes manifest is an important factual similarity between this case and the asbestos cases. The Oxford English Dictionary Online (2002) defines "manifest" as follows: "Clearly revealed to the eye, mind, or judgment; open to view or comprehension; obvious." The evidence in this case is that, when childhood sexual abuse causes an injury, the injury may not be manifest for many years.

Debtor cites *In re Dow Corning Corp.*, 211 BR 545 (Bankr. ED Mich. 1997), in support of its position that a future claims representative is not necessary to represent the interests of those potential claimants who know they have been subjected to abuse, but have not yet manifested an injury. The *Dow Corning* chapter 11 case arose out of a flood of lawsuits connected to the debtor's involvement with silicone breast implants. The court in that case explained that it had not appointed a future claims representative, because "[a]ll who have received a breast implant are cognizable of this fact." *Id.* at 598 n. 55. However, the court also explained that a future claims representative was unnecessary, because

> [i]t has been the consistent view of the official committee representing all tort claimants that "any person who has received a silicone-gel breast implant ... has already suffered an injury and is therefore a present, as opposed to a future claimant.
>
> Order Dismissing Motion of Alan B. Morrison for Appointment as the Legal Representative of Future Breast Implant Claimants, Oct. 10, 1995.

This case is distinguishable from the *Dow* case for at least two reasons. First, the very nature of the tortious conduct alleged in this case can result in cognitive and psychological injuries, making the injured person incapable of recognizing that he or she has been injured or of identifying the causal connection between the abuse and the injury. Declaration of Jon R. Conte, Ph.D, 8; 9; 13-14. The potential injuries resulting from exposure to silicone breast implants are not of this type. Second, in this case, unlike the *Dow* case, the TCC does not take the position that all those exposed to childhood sexual abuse have been damaged in a legal sense, or purport to represent the interests of such persons. The *Dow* court did not disapprove of the approach taken in the asbestos cases. In fact, the court in *Dow* acknowledged that "[f]uture tort claims problems come in all shapes and sizes [,]" and cautioned against an oversimplified approach to such problems. *Dow*, 211 BR at 598 n. 55.

In a chapter 11 case involving future claims, a court must "balance the competing interests of the debtor's fresh start with the creditor's right to compensation. Largely, the issue of adequate notice to inform and bind the future claimant and notions of fundamental fairness determine the outcome." *Hassanally*, 208 BR at 53 n. 9. As I discuss above, the appointment of a FCR is appropriate, given that the tortious conduct at issue in this case does not consistently produce injury, and that when injury does result, it can take many years for it to become manifest. In addition, childhood sexual abuse can result in cognitive and psychological injuries making the injured person incapable of currently recognizing that he or she has been injured or of identifying the causal connection between the abuse and the injury.

ORS 12.117(1) recognizes the unique nature of the potential damages caused by childhood sexual abuse by providing an unusually extended period to assert claims based on such conduct. Oregon case law acknowledges that decades may pass between the childhood abuse and the date the victim either manifests the injury or reasonably should have known of the casual connection between the abuse and the injury. See, e.g., *P.H. v. F.C.*, 127 Or. App. 592, 873 P 2d 465 (Or. Ct. App. 1994).

While counsel for ACE is correct that the bankruptcy claims bar dates operate regardless of state statutes of limitation, that does not address the question of whether a FCR is appropriate. When there is a class of claimants that is incapable of asserting a claim, either because of a long latency period between the wrongful conduct and the manifestation of damages, or because the nature of the wrongful conduct is such that it disables the claimant from being reasonably able to recognize the injury, it is appropriate for the court to appoint a FCR to protect the interests of the class.

It is important to point out that the FCR does not represent all alleged childhood abuse victims who do not assert claims. The representation is much more limited. The only claimants represented are (1) minors; (2) those with repressed memory; and (3) those persons who know they were subjected to sexual contact as children but who have "not discovered the [resulting] injury or the causal connection between the injury and the child abuse, nor in the exercise of reasonable care should have discovered the injury or the causal connection between the injury and the child abuse." ORS 12.117(1). Counsel for debtor and the insurance companies argue that, by including the third category, the court effectively excuses from filing individual childhood abuse victim claimants "who know that the conduct took place, people who do have the memory of that conduct, but … are ashamed, embarrassed, reluctant, [or] don't want to come forward. …" Transcript of November 19, 2004 Hearing, 118:5-10. This is incorrect.

I am not authorizing the FCR to represent claimants who decline to assert their own claims because of embarrassment, shame or a desire not to come forward. It is only those child abuse claimants who are minors, have repressed memory, or who have not discovered, "nor in the exercise of reasonable care should have discovered" their injury or that the abuse caused the injury. ORS 12.117(1). The limited scope of the third category, qualified by the objective requirement of the exercise of reasonable care, prevents the wholesale vitiation of the claims bar date that counsel for the insurance companies and debtor assert may happen.

C. Conclusion

Debtor's representatives and counsel have stated on numerous occasions in this court, that debtor's purpose in filing a chapter 11 petition was to resolve, fairly, finally and in a global fashion, the sexual abuse claims asserted against it. For example, debtor's Director of Business Affairs stated as follows in connection with the November 19 hearing:

> One of the principal reasons for seeking relief under chapter 11 was to enable the Debtor to use the chapter 11 process to address in a comprehensive manner all tort claims asserted against it in one forum, determine the extent of the Debtor's liability with respect thereto, and address such claims and all other claims against the Debtor in a fair and equitable manner.

Declaration of Paulette Furness in Support of Debtor's Motion for an Order (1) Fixing a Bar Date for Filing Tort Proofs of Claim, and (2) Approving a Tort Proof of Claim Form, Bar Date Notices, Actual Notice Procedure, and Media Notice Program, 3:5-9. The appointment of a FCR to represent the interests of those persons who know they were subjected to abuse but who have not discovered the resulting injury or the causal connection between the injury and the abuse will effectuate debtor's stated goals and will assure equitable treatment of future as well as present claimants.

QUESTIONS

How would these issues be decided under the BIA? Can it be argued that BIA s. 121(1) is more broadly worded than USC §§101(5) and (10) insofar as s. 121(1) applies to all debts and liabilities, present and future, to which the bankrupt is subject on the day on which the bankrupt become bankrupt "or to which the bankrupt may become subject before the bankrupt's discharge"? Alternatively, should the court interpret the language, as Judge Posner did in the US context, in the light of the underlying purposes of reorganization and bankruptcy proceedings?

National Bankruptcy Review Commission, *Bankruptcy: The Next Twenty Years*
(Washington, DC: US Government Printing Office, 1997),
at 315-22 (footnotes omitted)

Treatment of Mass Future Claims in Bankruptcy

Massive tort or contract liabilities can have an enormous impact on otherwise viable enterprises that are vital to the American economy. Parties have found that traditional individual tort or contract litigation for mass torts or mass contract is unwieldy and too expensive for all parties, and has forced them to seek more efficient alternatives. The bankruptcy system offers a structured system to manage multiple liabilities and has provided a forum for companies with massive liabilities to attempt to do so. At least 15 asbestos manufacturers, including UNR, Amatex, Johns-Manville, National Gypsum, Eagle-Picher, Celotex, and Raytech, have reorganized or liquidated in attempts to address massive numbers of known and unknown asbestos claimants using the Bankruptcy Code. The fact pattern is not unique to asbestos; manufacturers of other products also must find ways to deal with mass claimants alleging injury or damages from products such as silicone implants, polybutylene pipe, airplanes, and intrauterine devices, and some are resorting to bankruptcy to do so.

Treating massive claims is inherently complicated, partly because of the sheer number of the claims. In addition, a more difficult conceptual issue arises with "future claims" that have not manifested but that are relatively certain to manifest in the future and are based on prior acts of the debtor. A collective process that commences well before the damages or injuries develop might be the only opportunity for future claimants to receive any compensation, both because otherwise early claimants may take all the assets of the company or the company's extraordinary potential liability will dry up access to all capital needed for ongoing business operations. A company may not be able to preserve its going concern value and its work force if it is not able to deal collectively and definitively with all actions arising out of a certain activity. Acknowledging these issues, Congress took the first step in recognizing the treatment of future claimants in bankruptcy in amending the Bankruptcy Code in 1994 to authorize the treatment of future asbestos-related demands against a debtor. Now, after several years of experience with future claims in the bankruptcy system under the 1994 amendments, the Commission recommends additional provisions, not limited to asbestos, to guide the structured treatment of mass future claims in the bankruptcy system.

Recommendations

2.1.1 Definition of Mass Future Claim

A definition of "mass future claim" should be added as a subset of the definition of "claim" in 11 USC §101(5). "Mass future claim" should be defined as a claim arising out of a right to payment, or equitable relief that gives rise to a right to payment that has or has not accrued under nonbankruptcy law that is created by one or more acts or omissions of the debtor if:

1) the act(s) or omission(s) occurred before or at the time of the order for relief;

2) the act(s) or omission(s) may be sufficient to establish liability when injuries ultimately are manifested;

3) at the time of the petition, the debtor has been subject to numerous demands for payment for injuries or damages arising from such acts or omissions and is likely to be subject to substantial future demands for payment on similar grounds;

4) the holders of such rights to payments are known or, if unknown, can be identified or described with reasonable certainty; and

5) the amount of such liability is reasonably capable of estimation.

The definition of "claim" in section 101(5) should be amended to add a definition of "holder of a mass future claim," which would be an entity that holds a mass future claim.

2.1.2 Protecting the Interests of Holders of Mass Future Claims

The Bankruptcy Code should provide that a party in interest may petition the court for the appointment of a mass future claims representative. When a plan includes a class or classes of mass future claims, the Bankruptcy Code should authorize a court to order the appointment of a representative for each class of holders of mass future claims. A mass future claims representative shall serve until further order of the bankruptcy court.

The Bankruptcy Code should provide that a mass future claims representative shall have the exclusive power to file a claim or claims on behalf of the class of mass future claims (and to determine whether or not to file a claim), to cast votes on behalf of the holders of mass future claims and to exercise all of the powers of a committee appointed pursuant to section 1102. However, a holder of a mass future claim may elect to represent his, her, or its own interests and may opt out of being represented by the mass future claims representative.

The Bankruptcy Code should provide that prior to confirmation of a plan of reorganization, the fees and expenses of a mass future claims representative and his or her agents shall be administrative expenses under section 503. Following the confirmation of a plan of reorganization, and for so long as holders of mass future claims may exist, any continuing fees and expenses of a mass future claims representative and his or her agents shall be an expense of the fund established for the compensation of mass future claims.

The Bankruptcy Code should provide that a mass future claims representative shall serve until further orders of the bankruptcy court declare otherwise, shall serve as a fiduciary for the holders of future claims in such representative's class, and shall be subject to suit only in the district where the representative was appointed.

2.1.3 Determination of Mass Future Claims

Section 502 should provide that the court may estimate mass future claims and also may determine the amount of mass future claims prior to confirmation of a plan for purposes of distribution as well as allowance and voting. In addition, 28 USC §157(b)(2)(B) should specify that core proceedings include the estimation or determination of the amount of mass future claims.

2.1.4 Channeling Injunctions

Section 524 should authorize courts to issue channeling injunctions.

2.1.5 Plan Confirmation and Discharge; Successor Liability

Sections 363 and 1123 should provide that the trustee may dispose of property free and clear of mass future claims when the trustee or plan proponent has satisfied the requirements for treating mass future claims. Upon approving the sale, the court could issue, and later enforce, an injunction to preclude holders from suing a successor/good faith purchaser.

Discussion

As a consequence of modern technology and a global marketplace, there is an unlimited list of products that might cause massive liabilities. Unlike typical liabilities that are addressed every day in the bankruptcy system and in individualized adjudication, mass tort and mass contract liabilities often have geographically widespread effects and a "long tail;" this means that once a product is distributed, it may take one or several decades for individuals to discover their injuries or property damage caused by that product. As a corollary, widespread damage caused by the product will appear at sporadic times, not all at once.

Asbestos provides a classic example. After asbestos exposure occurs, diseases generally do not manifest for another 15 to 40 years. This means that 100 people might have been exposed to asbestos simultaneously but their injuries are revealed at 100 different times. Fundamental principles of justice require that a person who develops asbestosis 40 years after exposure should have the same entitlement to compensation as a person who got asbestosis 25 years earlier from the same exposure. However, providing reasonable and equitable compensation to victims is not simple, evidenced by the inadequate results of traditional tort litigation:

> Dockets in both federal and state courts continue to grow; long delays are routine; trials are too long; the same issues are litigated over and over; transaction costs exceed the victims' recovery by nearly two to one; exhaustion of assets threatens and distorts the process; and future claimants may lose altogether.

The bankruptcy system is designed to provide equality of distribution to similar creditors in a collective proceeding while ameliorating the devastating effect that a huge liability may have on the worth of a business and, correspondingly, the compensation available to all victims. Bankruptcy therefore provides an appropriate vehicle to resolve massive liabilities. In theory, incorporating all claimants into the collective bankruptcy process should be workable and universally beneficial: mass future claimants would benefit from the segregation of assets on their behalf, which otherwise will be exhausted long before they would be entitled to collect, while present creditors would benefit by the enhancement in the debtor's going concern value and the company's rejuvenated ability to attract new capital that will accompany a global resolution to the company's massive liability problems.

As commentators amply have highlighted, notwithstanding its inherent advantages, the bankruptcy system has to correct several significant ambiguities and shortcomings if it is to deal with mass future claims fairly and with certainty. In the absence of statutory guidance, courts have reached vastly different determinations of the ability to treat and discharge future claims in bankruptcy. Since the early 1980s, a large handful of courts have presided over cases dealing with uncertain future liabilities, and some have confirmed plans using channeling injunctions to protect the reorganized entity against individual collection attempts while providing a pool of resources for the claimants' treatment. Yet, because the Bankruptcy Code did not contain express authorization for these procedures, the resulting uncertainty over the legality of the resolutions restricted access to capital and depressed public stock value.

Recognizing these concerns, Congress enacted amendments in the *Bankruptcy Reform Act* of 1994 to provide explicit legislative guidance to ensure equitable treatment of mass future asbestos claimants in bankruptcy. Marking an important first step, these amendments introduced a series of additional detailed provisions with limited application to section 524 of the Bankruptcy Code.

As their name suggests, the "asbestos amendments" apply exclusively to demands for payment on account of asbestos injuries. Legislative response to other types of massive future liabilities was specifically reserved for another day. In recent years, it has become even clearer that products other than asbestos give rise to massive liability issues. Similar problems already have arisen in the context of intrauterine devices, polybutylene pipe, lead-related injuries, and silicone implants. The 1994 asbestos amendments have not precluded the use of bankruptcy to deal with other types of mass future claims, and cases currently are pending that might result in plans that deal with mass future claims. However, all parties to such cases continue to suffer the consequences of uncertainty that formerly plagued asbestos cases. Moreover, these cases remain subject to disparate treatment in the courts due to the lack of statutory guidance. The Commission's Proposal is not limited to a certain type of liability or industry. Instead, the Proposal focuses on determining the conditions under which it is appropriate to treat mass future claims in the bankruptcy process and the safeguards required in such cases.

The scope of the asbestos provisions enacted in 1994 is limited in other ways too. The provisions are available only to Chapter 11 debtors, and yet mass future claimants of a debtor liquidating in Chapter 7 also should be entitled to equal priority with present claimants. The amendments authorize the establishment only of trusts constructed and funded exactly like the Johns-Manville trust, and therefore do not foster innovation and flexibility that might accommodate other circumstances or yield more successful results. Moreover, the 1994 amendments treat asbestos injuries as "future *demands*," not *claims*, a distinction that calls into question the applicability of other provisions of the Bankruptcy Code to the holders of these future demands. Although the asbestos amendments spell out different procedures for asbestos demand holders, depriving demand holders of "claim" status in the bankruptcy process strips parties with asbestos injuries of the other protections of the Bankruptcy Code, and thus, in a sense, provides them with inferior treatment in the course of the case but discharges their claims as if they were claimholders. At the same time, several attributes of the asbestos amendments afford present claimants with more leverage, potentially undercutting the notion of equality of distribution to similar claimants. The Commission's Recommendations address all three of these issues.

By enacting the 1994 asbestos amendments, Congress made clear that those amendments were a much-needed and important first step in giving legislative approval to the treatment of mass future claims in bankruptcy, but also acknowledged the potential need for a mechanism to deal fairly with *non*asbestos mass future claims. Building on the spirit of the 1994 amendments, these Proposals are intended to be the second step in establishing procedures to assure that future claimholders receive fair and equitable treatment in the bankruptcy process by addressing some of the issues left open in 1994.

In both reorganizations and liquidations, the Proposals should further the equality of distribution among claimholders, preserve the going concern value of viable businesses, and enhance the likelihood of compensation for parties who might otherwise end up with no compensation. These objectives are applicable in all cases, but the Proposals offer a workable solution for future liabilities in the most pressing and most complex cases, where the claims that are contingent and likely to give rise to future liability are so massive that they warrant special procedures and protections of the type suggested here. Consideration of whether it will be necessary to develop a statutory framework expressly articulating the approach to deal with individual future claims has been reserved for another day. In the meantime, the Commission's Proposals would not change in any way the general handling of obligations that fall within the statutory definition of "claim," including contingent, unmatured, and unliquidated claims, which currently are treated under the Bankruptcy Code.

CHAPTER EIGHT

Secured Creditors, Crown Claims, and Statutory Deemed Trusts

I. INTRODUCTION

Anglo-Canadian law has long been respectful of secured creditors' claims on a debtor's bankruptcy and this continues to be the case. So, for example, BIA s. 71 provides that the debtor's property vests in the trustee subject to the rights of secured creditors. There are two reasons for this favourable treatment. The first is political: in England and Canada, banks and other financial intermediaries have historically played an influential role in the shaping of bankruptcy rules. The second reason is conceptual and economic. Anglo-Canadian common law (including, importantly, equity) permits a creditor to secure a business debt with all of the debtor's present and after-acquired property, a phenomenon that gave rise to the famous fixed and floating charge over all of a debtor's assets. This liberal tradition is continued in the *Personal Property Security Acts* now in force in all the common law provinces and territories. (In Quebec, *sûreté mobilières* were also greatly liberalized in the new Civil Code of 1994.) For the details, see Anthony J. Duggan and Jacob S. Ziegel, *Secured Transactions in Personal Property*, 5th ed. (Toronto: Emond Montgomery, 2009), Chapter 1.

Obviously, secured creditors are anxious to ensure that bankruptcy law recognizes their pre-bankruptcy claims, because it is on the debtor's insolvency that secured creditors most often find it necessary to enforce their security. The BIA recognizes the logic of this reasoning and, with some important exceptions in the consumer area (see Chapter 11), allows secured creditors to enforce their claims after the debtor's bankruptcy. What remains to be determined are the mechanisms adopted by the BIA for regulating the exercise of secured creditor's rights.

This solicitous attitude vanishes when the claimant is the Crown and the proprietary right that secures the obligation is created by statute rather than through a consensual agreement between the parties. The Crown often occupies the position of a creditor. This may result from the debtor's failure to remit income tax, Canada Pension Plan, or employment insurance contributions from the pay of employees or sales tax that has been collected from customers. Or it may result from the failure to pay workers compensation assessments or other obligations when due. Federal and provincial governments attempted to use two techniques to confer an elevated priority status on their claims. First, they enacted statutes that gave the Crown a proprietary right in the debtor's property to secure the obligation. The statute would usually create a statutory lien or charge on the debtor's assets. Sometimes the statute would also provide a priority rule that gave the statutory lien or charge priority over a prior secured creditor. Second, the Crown would create a statutory deemed trust in its favour. The legislation provided that a deemed statutory trust is imposed on the debtor's property, even if the property was not kept separate and apart. The legislation sometimes also included a priority rule that gave the statutory deemed trust priority over a prior secured creditor. The Crown's ability to rely on such devices to claim a secured status was originally curtailed by the judiciary, and the 1992 amendments to the BIA have imposed legislative restrictions on the use of these devices.

II. SECURED CREDITORS' CLAIMS

A. Introduction

One of the fundamental principles of Canadian bankruptcy law is that only the property of the bankrupt is made available to satisfy the claims of the creditors of the bankrupt. A trustee in bankruptcy therefore has no right to confiscate the property of a third party, notwithstanding that it may be in the possession or control of the bankrupt. This principle applies even if the third party has only a limited proprietary right in the property, as opposed to full ownership of it. This explains the treatment of secured creditors in bankruptcy. Secured creditors have a limited proprietary right in the debtor's property, which gives them the right to enforce their claims against the collateral in the event of default.

The proprietary right of a secured creditor is largely unaffected by a bankruptcy of the debtor. Upon default, the secured creditor may enforce the security interest through seizure and sale of the property or through foreclosure of the security interest. A secured creditor thereby withdraws the asset from the bankrupt estate. If there is a surplus after the secured creditor and any subordinate interests are satisfied, it must be paid over to the trustee in bankruptcy. If there is a deficiency (the proceeds from the sale of the collateral are insufficient to satisfy the obligation secured), the secured creditor may prove for it as an ordinary unsecured creditor in the bankruptcy of the debtor. The trustee in bankruptcy has only a limited ability to interfere with the right of a secured creditor to enforce its security.

There is an exception to the principle that the rights of a secured creditor are largely unaffected by a bankruptcy. Provincial law may provide that certain registration or perfection requirements must be satisfied in order for a security interest to have priority over a trustee in bankruptcy. Provincial personal property security legislation provides that an unperfected security interest is subordinate to a trustee in bankruptcy. The Supreme Court of Canada in *Re Giffen*, [1998] 1 SCR 91 (excerpted in Chapter 4, Section III) upheld the constitutionality of these provisions. Provincial statutes governing real property do not contain equivalent provisions that subordinate an unregistered interest in land to a trustee in bankruptcy. A secured creditor is therefore able to enforce its security against the trustee in bankruptcy despite its failure to register its interest in a land titles or land registration system. See *Citifinancial Canada East Corp. v. Morrow Estate* (2005), 20 CBR (5th) 74 (NBQB); *Re Canadian Engineering & Contracting Co.* (1994), 28 CBR (3d) 136 (Ont. Gen. Div.).

B. Definition of Secured Creditor

The definition of secured creditor in BIA s. 2 is of pre-PPSA vintage and raises two important questions: (1) does it cover security interests not enumerated in the definition—for example, conditional sales and some types of equipment leases; and (2) does it include non-consensual security interests arising by operation of law and not by agreement? So far as the first question is concerned, in *R v. Ford*, below, Austin J assumed almost as a matter of course that the definition in s. 2 includes conditional sales. We believe he was right, not because the inclusion of conditional sales is implicit in the enumeration of security interests in the definition, but because serious practical difficulties would otherwise arise in applying the BIA provisions governing the enforcement of security interests.

The answer to the second question is clearly "yes," although there is surprisingly little authority that states this explicitly. The reasons for this construction are that the definition of secured creditor is not confined to consensual claims and that the terms "liens," "charge," and, in Quebec, privilege (*privilège*) have long covered non-consensual as well as consensual property claims. A repairer who has a common-law possessory lien therefore qualifies as a secured creditor, as would a person who is entitled to claim a statutory lien on goods pursuant to legislation such as the *Repair and Storage Liens Act*, RSO 1990, c. R.25 or the *Garage-keepers' Lien Act*, RSA 2000, c. G-2.

A landlord's distress for unpaid rent originally qualified as a secured claim, because it gave the landlord an interest akin to a lien on the goods. However, in 1949, the *Bankruptcy Act* was changed. A landlord's right to distrain for unpaid rent was taken away and the landlord was instead afforded the status of a preferred claimant. Any property that had been seized under a distress for rent had to be turned over to the trustee, unless the process had been fully completed by payment to the landlord before the occurrence of the bankruptcy. See BIA ss. 73(4) and 136(1)(f). The courts held that these changes indicated that Parliament intended that landlords were no longer to be treated as secured creditors in bankruptcy proceedings. See *Re Radioland Ltd.* (1957), 36 CBR 158 (Sask. CA); *Re Gingras Automobile Ltée*, [1962] SCR 676.

Although statutory liens and charges in favour of the Crown qualify as secured claims and give the Crown the status of a secured creditor, the Crown's ability to assert such claims in a bankruptcy has been restricted by ss. 87-88 of the BIA. Although statutory deemed trusts have essentially the same function as statutory liens and charges, they are afforded different treatment under the BIA. A person who has the benefit of a statutory deemed trust is not regarded as a secured creditor under Canadian bankruptcy law. The courts have treated the holder of the claim as a beneficiary of a trust. However, ss. 67(2) and (3) of the BIA have greatly restricted the ability of the Crown to assert such claims in a bankruptcy.

C. Enforcement of Security Interests

BIA s. 69.3 establishes the basic principle that the general stay of proceedings consequent on the debtor's bankruptcy does not apply to secured claims unless the court imposes a stay at the trustee's request. Even then the stay can only be of limited duration and is rarely granted in practice. However, there is an unresolved conflict in the case law whether a secured creditor may engage in self-help in repossessing the collateral or whether it must file a proof of claim and comply with the requirements in BIA s. 81. See *R v. Ford Credit Canada Limited*, below.

In addition to these provisions that apply only in bankruptcy proceedings, s. 244 of the BIA limits the ability of a secured creditor to enforce the security. The secured creditor must give the debtor a 10-day notice before enforcing a security on all or substantially all the inventory, accounts receivable, or other property of the debtor. This limitation applies outside the bankruptcy context as well, and frequently arises when a secured creditor appoints a privately appointed receiver. It is discussed in Chapter 18.

Assuming that the secured creditor has seized and/or realized the collateral after the debtor's bankruptcy, BIA ss. 127-130 then come into play to determine the trustee's and secured creditor's rights. Students should examine these provisions themselves and assess their practical importance. (There appears to be little case law on these sections.) Consider also the interaction between ss. 128-130 and the PPSA provisions governing the enforcement of security interests and the duties incumbent on secured creditors after repossessing the collateral. Can the provisions coexist and will the BIA provisions prevail in case of conflict? Can the trustee invoke either set of provisions at his discretion?

If there is a deficiency in the amount owing to the secured creditor after the collateral has been realized, s. 127 allows the secured party to file a proof of claim for the balance. However, in the case of an individual debtor, any unpaid balance will be discharged upon the debtor's discharge from bankruptcy under s. 169 or 172. (For discussion of consumer discharges from bankruptcy, see Chapter 11.)

R v. Ford Credit Canada Limited
(1990), 78 CBR (NS) 266 (Ont. SC)

AUSTIN J: This case considers the respective rights of a secured creditor and a trustee in bankruptcy. Section 49(1) [now s. 69.3(1)] of the *Bankruptcy Act* stays proceedings against a bankrupt. Section 49(2) [now s. 69.3(2)] says, in effect, that s. 49(1) does not apply to secured creditors. Section 174 [now s. 203] makes it an offence, in certain circumstances, to take property from the bankrupt or the trustee. The issue, in a nutshell, is whether s. 174 applies to secured creditors.

Mr. and Mrs. Szucsko bought a Ford Tempo from Delhi Ford Sales Ltd. on 25th April 1987. The vehicle was taken in Mrs. Szucsko's name. It was financed by Ford Credit Canada Limited. The financing statement filed by Ford under the *Personal Property Security Act* was in the name of Mr. Szucsko.

The Szucskos made a voluntary assignment in bankruptcy on 30th October 1987. The trustee left the motor vehicle in the possession of Mrs. Szucsko. Mrs. Szucsko listed Ford as a secured creditor for $10,000. The trustee gave notice of the bankruptcy to Ford. Ford filed a proof of claim on 21st December 1987 for $8,626.14 and claimed the vehicle as security.

On 22nd December 1987 the trustee asked Ford for further documentation. Ford demanded the vehicle. The trustee indicated that he was not yet satisfied with the security. The trustee also advised Ford that any repossession would be contrary to the *Bankruptcy*

Act and that if such action were taken, Ford would be charged with theft. Ford seized the car from Mrs. Szucsko on 11th January 1988.

On 21st January 1988 the trustee demanded the return of the vehicle. On 8th February 1988 Ford asked the trustee to pay Ford out or to waive his rights to the vehicle. The trustee did neither.

At some stage Ford applied to the bankruptcy court for a declaration that it had a security interest in the vehicle valid and subsisting in priority to the interest of the trustee. Such a declaration was made on 21st March 1989.

In November 1988 the trustee had a charge laid against Ford under s. 174 of the *Bankruptcy Act*. That section reads as follows:

> 174. A person, except the trustee, who, within thirty days after delivery to the trustee of the proof of claim mentioned in section 59, or who, in case no such proof has been delivered, removes or attempts to remove the property or any part thereof mentioned in such section out of the charge or possession of the bankrupt, the trustee or other custodian of such property, unless with the written permission of the trustee, is guilty of an offence and is liable on summary conviction to a fine not exceeding five thousand dollars, or to imprisonment for a term not exceeding two years, or to both.

The charge under the *Bankruptcy Act* was heard by His Honour Judge P.R. Mitchell in Hamilton on 2nd August 1989. It was dismissed. This is an appeal by the Crown from that dismissal.

In its argument, the Crown relied on three western cases. Their fact situations are very close, if not identical, to the present case. The first of the three is *R v. Ford Motor Credit Co.*, [1977] 6 WWR 241, 25 CBR (NS) 283 (Man. Prov. Ct.). Klassen Concrete went bankrupt and gave possession of its four motor vehicles to the trustee. The trustee wrote to Ford Credit, which held the conditional sales agreement. The trustee asked Ford to file a proof of claim and the security documents. Ford replied to the effect that its policy was to take possession notwithstanding the bankruptcy. Ford seized the motor vehicles despite the efforts of the trustee. Subsequently, Ford provided a proof of claim and the security documents for the four motor vehicles and the trustee gave releases for two of them to Ford. Ford was charged under s. 174 with respect to the other two and was convicted.

In that case, as in the present case, the Crown relied upon s. 59 [now s. 81] of the *Bankruptcy Act*. It reads as follows:

> . . .

The defendant relied upon s. 49(2) [now s. 69.3(2)]. It reads as follows:

> . . .

Kopstein Prov. J held that there was no conflict between s. 49(2) and s. 59. He found that even secured creditors had to comply with s. 59 and that, in seizing the motor vehicles before such compliance, Ford had violated s. 174.

This decision was followed in *R v. Mathers* (1979), 30 CBR (NS) 133 (Sask. Prov. Ct.). There the creditor held a chattel mortgage and filed a proof of claim which was rejected by the trustee. The creditor then seized the trucks from the possession of the trustee on the premises of the bankrupt. The creditor was charged under s. 174. There, as in the present case, a separate proceeding determined that the creditor did have title to the vehicle.

Wedge Prov. J followed Kopstein Prov. J and at p. 138 held that if the security is in the possession of the trustee, a secured creditor must comply with s. 59.

At the same page he held that s. 57 and ss. 98 to 105 "do not derogate from the right of a trustee in possession to demand proper proof of claim before giving up possession or custody."

He said at p. 139 that: "The purpose of the relevant sections of the *Bankruptcy Act* is to ensure the orderly and speedy settlement of a bankrupt's affairs."

Ford and *Mathers* were followed in *R v. Bank of Montreal*, 53 CBR (NS) 287, [1985] WWR 259 (Man. Prov. Ct.). The bank held a chattel mortgage on some vehicles and equipment. It filed a proof of claim pursuant to s. 59. The trustee did not take physical possession of the mortgaged items but went to the various farms where they were located and made arrangements to leave them in place. The bank agreed with this arrangement. Norton Prov. J found that the trustee had taken possession.

The bank argued that the Act intended to distinguish between creditors with proprietary interests in the property and those who only had security interests in it. The bank contended that s. 59 only applied where a proprietary interest was claimed and since it had only claimed a security interest, s. 59 had no application.

The learned trial judge gave no effect to that argument. At p. 291, he said:

> In my view, s. 174 simply sets forth the time frame in which the removal of the assets from the bankrupt after filing a claim would constitute an offence, or, failing to file a claim, the removal of the property from the possession or charge of the trustee becomes an offence unless done with the prior written permission of the trustee.

He went on to comment that:

> Apart from the above conclusion, if such were not the case it might well become possible to defeat what Wedge Prov. J stated in *R v. Mathers* [p. 13], "The purpose of the relevant sections of the *Bankruptcy Act* is to ensure the orderly and speedy settlement of the bankrupt's affairs," if a secured creditor could arbitrarily seize its security and make no accounting to the trustee. This is precisely what the bank did in this case.

That decision was appealed to the Manitoba Court of Queen's Bench, 58 CBR (NS) 45, [1986] 2 WWR 573. In dismissing the appeal, Lockwood J said at p. 47 that it was irrelevant whether the bank's interest in the property was proprietary or security because s. 174 does not exclude secured creditors.

It is apparent from the reasons of the learned trial judge that those three cases were presented to him. He chose, however, to follow another line of cases which included *Re Leblanc; Cie Eagle Lumber Ltée v. Rochon* (1966), 11 CBR (NS) 13 (Que.), and *Re Bradford; Household Fin. Corp. v. Davis*, 17 CBR (NS) 171, [1972] 4 WWR 484 (Alta.).

In *Leblanc*, Eagle sold lumber to Rochon and registered a privilege against Rochon's real property for the amount owing. Rochon went into bankruptcy and Eagle issued a writ to enforce its privilege. The trustee then sent Eagle a notice disallowing its claim on the ground that the granting of a privilege constituted a preference under the *Bankruptcy Act*. Eagle did not appeal the disallowance. In the action the trustee pleaded that the action should be dismissed upon the ground that the disallowance of the claim was final and conclusive. Batshaw J held that, by virtue of s. 40(2), the plaintiff as a secured creditor was entitled to realize upon its security without seeking the permission of the court.

At p. 15, Batshaw J said:

> 1. It is the policy of the *Bankruptcy Act* not to interfere with secured creditors except insofar as may be necessary to protect the estate as to any surplus on the assets covered by the security.
>
> 2. In the opinion of the court, once the trustee received the plaintiff's writ to enforce the privilege, he should have contested the action on the merits if he wished to challenge its claim as a secured creditor rather than seek to do so through the disallowance of the claim as such.

. . .

In the *Household Fin.* case, the lender took a wage assignment as security for a loan. When the borrower went bankrupt, the lender sent a copy of the assignment to the trustee and at the same time served the employer. The trustee disallowed the claim as contrary to the *Bankruptcy Act* and then applied to the court for directions.

The lender also appealed the disallowance of its claim. At p. 485, Riley J held:

> I am of the opinion that there is no such jurisdiction in the trustee to determine whether a claim is secured or not, and that the proper method is to bring the matter before a bankruptcy court by way of notice of motion for advice and directions.

At pp. 487-488, he went on:

> To my mind the case authorities are conclusive that if there is a dispute as to whether or not a claim is secured, as there is in this case, the proper procedure of the trustee is to bring an application to the Bankruptcy Court for advice and directions on this issue, but he has no jurisdiction pursuant to s. 106, or any other section of the *Bankruptcy Act*, to disallow an alleged secured claim or determine by himself the question of the validity of the security.

At first blush, it is difficult to see why Judge Mitchell in the present case chose to follow *Re Leblanc* and *Household Fin.* rather than the reasoning of Kopstein Prov. J in *R v. Ford* and the cases which followed. Those latter cases are directly on point and their facts are identical, or almost so, to the present case. *Leblanc* and *Household Fin.*, on the other hand, are factually different and are not directly on point. They deal with the extent, if any, to which a trustee has the power to disallow the claim of a secured creditor. If the rationale of *Leblanc* and *Household Fin.* is pursued, however, it can be seen where conflict will arise with the reasoning in *Ford*, *Mathers* and *Bank of Montreal*.

Those latter cases hold that a secured creditor must comply with s. 59. If s. 59 is applicable to secured creditors, then s. 59 gives the trustee power to dispute or disallow the claim. According to s. 59(2), the claimant must then appeal if he wishes to preserve his rights. *Leblanc* and *Household Fin.*, however, say clearly that the trustee has no power to disallow the claim of a secured creditor and that there is no obligation on a secured creditor to appeal and that the proper course for the trustee to follow is to apply to the court for advice and directions. How then to reconcile these decisions?

One of the matters discussed on the argument of this appeal was whether Ford's interest was proprietary or security. This question arises by virtue of a distinction drawn between the two kinds of interests in such cases as *Re Festival Singers of Can.* (1980), 32 CBR (NS) 193 (Ont. SC), *Re Shibou* (1982), 42 CBR (NS) 132, 134 DLR (3d) 568 (Man. QB) and *Bank of Montreal.*

The distinction arises from the different language used in ss. 49(2) and 59(1). Section 49(2) refers to a "secured creditor" dealing "with his security." Section 59(1), on the other hand, deals with the situation "where a person claims any property, or interest therein, in the possession of the bankrupt." It is clear that s. 59 is intended to deal with a bailment situation, e.g., where a person leaves his suit with the drycleaner and the drycleaner goes bankrupt. Whether it applies to more than bailments need not be decided here. Section 59 sets out a code or procedure to be followed in those circumstances. The claimant must file a proof of claim. The trustee may allow it or dispute it. If disputed, the claimant may appeal. If he does not, he is deemed to have abandoned the property. The onus of establishing a claim is on the claimant. Section 59 provides the only method of determining such a claim.

It is clear that the procedure to be followed where a security claim only is made is quite different. In the event of a dispute, the trustee's recourse is not to give notice of disallowance but to apply to the court for directions: *Household Fin. v. Davis.* Section 59 does not provide an exclusive procedure for this situation: *Re Leblanc.*

This difference in procedure raises the question whether Parliament intended s. 59 to have any application at all where a security interest only is claimed. Having regard to the language of s. 49(2) and of s. 59, it would appear that Parliament did not.

On its face, s. 49(2) indicates that s. 59 does *not* apply. Section 49(2) says that with certain exceptions, a secured creditor may deal with his security as if this section had not been passed. "This section" refers to s. 49(1). The "certain exceptions" are set out in ss. 57 [now s. 79] and 98 to 105 [now ss. 127-134]. They are commented on below, but none of those sections has any application in the present circumstances. Section 59 is not even mentioned in s. 49(2). On a plain reading of s. 49(2), therefore, it is not subject to s. 59. Since s. 174 is only applicable to the property or property interest referred to in s. 59, it would appear that s. 174 is not applicable to security.

Section 57 [now s. 79] deals with property of the bankrupt held by another as a pledge, pawn or other security. In such a case, the trustee may inspect the property and redeem it. On receipt of notice from the trustee, the holder is not to realize the security until the trustee has had an opportunity to inspect, and if he so wishes, to redeem. That section has no application here as the property was in the possession of Mrs. Szucsko at the time of the bankruptcy.

Sections 98 to 105 [now ss. 127-134] are under the heading "Proof by Secured Creditors." Section 98(1) says that where a secured creditor realizes his security, he may prove (as an ordinary creditor) for the balance of the debt.

Section 98(2) provides that where the creditor surrenders his security to the trustee, he may file a proof of claim for the whole amount of his claim. Clearly s. 98 has no application to the present circumstances.

Section 99 [now s. 128] provides that where a secured creditor neither realizes nor surrenders his security, he shall, if the trustee so demands, value the security. If he does this, he is entitled to share in the bankruptcy only to the extent that his claim exceeds the stated value of the security. The trustee, for his part, may accept the creditor's valuation and may redeem the security if he so wishes.

Section 100 [now s. 129] deals with the situation where the secured creditor has failed to value his security or the trustee is not satisfied with the creditor's valuation. In either of these events, the trustee may require that the security be put up for sale.

Section 101 [now s. 130] empowers the creditor to require the trustee to elect whether he is going to redeem or require a sale. This was what Ford purported to do on 8th February 1988. No response from the trustee is revealed in the evidence.

Sections 102 and 103 [now ss. 131 and 132] deal with amending the valuation of the security.

Section 104 [now s. 133] provides that if a secured creditor does not comply with ss. 98 to 103, he shall be excluded from any dividend.

Section 105 provides that subject to s. 101, a creditor shall not receive more than 100 cents on the dollar, plus interest.

As noted above, none of ss. 57 or 98 to 105 is directly applicable to the circumstances of the present case. They suggest that a secured creditor may deal with the security as if the *Bankruptcy Act* had not been passed, subject to certain exceptions, and that a secured creditor need not file any proof of claim, except as an unsecured creditor for any amount by which his claim exceeds the value of his security.

The issue in the present appeal is the same as in the three western cases. That is, whether s. 174 applies to property in the possession of the bankrupt which is security for a debt of the bankrupt.

The Crown argues that s. 174 *is* applicable because it applies to anyone who is "a person," with the sole exception of the trustee. Had it been intended to exempt secured creditors, it is argued, they would have been listed along with the trustee. There can be no doubt that the meaning would have been clearer had secured creditors been so listed. As it is, something must be read in, in order to reconcile s. 49(2) and s. 174. Either s. 174 should be added to the exceptions in s. 49(2) or secured creditors should be added to the exception in s. 174. I would resolve that question as the learned trial judge has done, by finding that s. 49(2) is the more specific section in that it deals only with secured creditors and that "a person" in s. 174 is not intended to include secured creditors.

The Crown argues that s. 174 does not interfere with the operation of s. 49(2), it simply sets forth the time frame in which, after filing a claim, removal of the assets from the bankrupt would constitute an offence. This, it is argued, is to ensure the orderly and speedy settlement of the bankrupt's affairs. Finally, if a secured creditor could arbitrarily seize its security and make no accounting to the trustee, the purpose of the Act would be frustrated.

In my view the "time frame" argument ignores the fact that speed may be very important to the realization of security. It also ignores the specific language of s. 49(2) that, subject to some exceptions, a secured creditor may treat s. 49(1) as if it did not exist. Seizure by a secured creditor is not necessarily "arbitrary"; it may only be done in accordance with the terms of the agreement between debtor and creditor. Nor need there be an absence of accounting. Sections 57, 99 and 100 give the trustee certain rights in this regard.

It is argued as well by the Crown that irrespective of his status under s. 49(2), a secured creditor must always file a proof of claim pursuant to s. 59 in order to get possession when the trustee already has possession. While that would certainly fit in with the
"orderly scheme" argument, I do not interpret s. 59 in that manner.

As I read that section, it would apply to goods left with a drycleaner who goes bankrupt, or a car left with a garage for repair where the garage operator goes bankrupt. The
claimant would be the real owner of the goods; he is not claiming just a security interest
in the goods. He claims both title and possession. In such a case, the trustee does have
power to disallow the claim, by virtue of s. 59(2). This is not the situation dealt with in
Household Fin. v. Davis; that case dealt with a secured claim.

Returning to the decision of Kopstein Prov J in *R v. Ford Motor Credit*, at the conclusion of his reasons he said:

> In my opinion, there is no conflict between s. 49(2) and s. 59. What is dealt with under
> s. 49(2) in the context of this case is an exception enabling the secured creditor to take
> action upon his security without awaiting the discharge of the bankrupt. That enabling pro-
> vision, however, does not negate or nullify the requirement that he first comply with s. 59.
> That his rights may be prejudiced by the delay involved in compliance with s. 59 appears to
> be an unavoidable result of s. 59, but such prejudice does not minimize or negate the
> requirement.

In my view, it is an error to find that a secured creditor must comply with s. 59. As indicated above, s. 59 does not apply to secured claims but to situations where the bankrupt has possession, as, for instance, as bailee.

Some cases appear to have been decided upon the basis of whether the creditor had
title to the property in question. In *Re Festival Singers of Can.*, the registrar, Master Ferron, suggested at p. 195 that:

> … in cases involving conditional sales agreements title to the property never passed to the
> bankrupt, and since it remained in the claimant he could properly assert his interest as
> owner under that section.

He was referring to s. 59 and I understand the registrar to mean that in cases where
the creditor claims under a conditional sales agreement, s. 59 applies because the creditor
has title. The registrar went on to say, "It is not the case where other security is involved
such as under a chattel mortgage." I understand this to mean that, in the case of a chattel
mortgage, the creditor does not have title and therefore s. 59 does not apply. But a chattel
mortgagee does have title so that, in that respect, he would be in the same position as a
conditional vendor: Barron and O'Brien, Chattel Mortgages and Bills of Sale, 3rd ed.
(1927), p. 3.

I raise the broader question—was s. 59 intended to apply to situations where the
creditor is a conditional vendor or chattel mortgagee?—that is, where the claimant may
have title for legal purposes, but is not the "real owner" in practical terms and does not
have possession. Clearly, such a claimant is "a person [claiming] any property, or interest
therein"—the language of s. 59(1). In my view, however, s. 59 should be limited to the
cases where the claimant has *only* a proprietary interest; the person who left his suit with
the drycleaner would be an example, as would the man leaving his vehicle with the

garage operator for repairs. Where the claimant has a security interest, either in isolation or together with a proprietary interest, then he can rely on his security interest. In this event, he can exercise his rights under s. 49(2) and need not proceed under s. 59. This approach appears to be consistent with the reasoning of Scollin J in *Re Shibou*.

A reason for drawing a distinction between the assertion of a proprietary right and the assertion of a security right lies in the different requirements of a trustee in those two situations. In the case of the suit left with the drycleaner who went bankrupt, the trustee would be entitled to the cost of the cleaning, if it had been done, nothing more. In the case of the assertion of a security interest, however, the trustee must be concerned about the value of the security, whether it will yield money in excess of the claim of the secured creditor, or whether on the other hand there will be a deficiency and a claim by the creditor for that deficiency. To meet these exigencies, the trustee is given the powers and duties set out in s. 57 and in ss. 98 to 105: *Re Festival Singers of Can.*, at p. 195, para. 3. To meet the circumstances of a purely proprietary claim, the trustee is given the powers and duties set out in s. 59.

It was suggested earlier in these reasons that in order to reconcile ss. 49(2) and 174, something had to be read into one or other of them. I would read into s. 174 that it does not apply to property in the possession of the bankrupt which is security for a debt of the bankrupt. To do otherwise is to make s. 49(2) subject to s. 174. To do that is to import into s. 49(2) the code of procedure set out in s. 59. That, it seems to me, is entirely contrary to the apparent objective of s. 49(2).

Whether Ford in the present case had a proprietary interest is irrelevant. It was a secured creditor. It was bound to observe the requirements of ss. 49(2), 57 and 98 to 105. It was not bound to observe the requirements of s. 59. Because s. 59 did not apply, neither did s. 174. The learned trial judge was correct and the appeal should be dismissed.

Appeal dismissed.

NOTES

1. Do you agree with the decision in *Ford Credit* and with Austin J's rationalization of the distinction between BIA ss. 69.3(2) and 81(1)? Is there a meaningful distinction between a security claim and a proprietary claim? If there is, why would Parliament put a trustee in a stronger position vis-à-vis proprietary claimants (for example, bailors of goods left with the bankrupt for storage or dry cleaning) than toward secured parties? How is the secured party prejudiced by having to comply with s. 81(1)? Given the unsettled state of the case law, should the conflict not have been resolved in the amendments to the BIA?

2. Section 362(a)(4) of the US *Bankruptcy Code* makes it clear that the automatic stay triggered on the filing of a bankruptcy petition (and Chapter 11 filing) also applies to the enforcement of security interests. However, under s. 362(d), the court may grant relief from the stay under the following circumstances: (1) for cause, including the lack of adequate protection of an interest in property of the party in interest; and (2) where the stay applies to an act against property, if (a) the debtor does not have an equity in such property; and (b) such property is not necessary to an effective reorganization.

The meaning of "adequate protection" is explained in s. 361, but the definition has attracted considerable litigation and scholarly discussion because it does not address the issue of the time value of money or its equivalent. See Baird and Jackson, *Cases, Problems and Materials on Bankruptcy*, 2nd ed. (Boston: Little, Brown, 1990), 620-23. The American theory of the automatic stay appears to be that secured creditors, as well as other creditors, will be better off if the trustee is allowed to deal with all the assets of the estate. The Canadian theory, on the other hand (embodied in s. 69.3(2)), adopts the view that the secured creditor's bargain (which includes the right to foreclose and sell the collateral on default or other prescribed events) should be respected in bankruptcy as well as outside bankruptcy. The Canadian position is supported in F.H. Buckley, "A Corporate Governance Theory of Repossessory Rights" (1994), 23 *CBLJ* 96. However, in the light of the American doctrine of adequate protection, is there a practical difference between the Canadian and American positions? As we have noted at the beginning of the chapter, it is common for a privately appointed receiver to also act as trustee of the estate and, where there is no privately appointed receiver, the secured party may agree to allow the trustee to realize the collateral on its behalf. Frequently, the secured party will have repossessed the collateral before the filing of the bankruptcy application.

3. An argument that could be made in favour of applying the automatic stay to straight bankruptcies is that it would assist the trustee in valuing the collateral and in determining whether the debtor still has an equity in it. BIA ss. 127-134 address these issues as well as other questions affecting the collateral. Do these provisions, which are not predicated on the trustee's having possession of the collateral, prove that an automatic stay is not essential for the protection of the estate? Or is the main purpose of the stay to enable the trustee to determine whether the business can be sold as a going concern? Consider also that a trustee in bankruptcy may file a notice of intention to make a proposal under BIA s. 50(1). If filed, the automatic stay of proceedings will stay the proceedings of a secured creditor as long as the secured creditor has not yet taken possession of the secured assets for the purposes of realization and as long as the 10-day notice period under BIA s. 244 has not expired. See BIA s. 69(2).

4. The BIA supports secured creditors' claims at almost every stage. Is this sound policy? See R.C.C. Cuming, "Canadian Bankruptcy Law: A Secured Creditors Heaven" (1994), 24 *CBLJ* 17; compare J.S. Ziegel, "The New Personal Property Security Regimes: Have We Gone Too Far?" (1990), 28 *Alta. L Rev.* 739. The pervasive use of secured credit that encompasses all of the debtor's assets has led some jurisdictions to provide that a portion of the debtor's assets must be turned over to the bankrupt estate for the benefit of the unsecured creditors. In the United Kingdom, the *Insolvency Act, 1986* was amended to provide that a prescribed percentage of a company's assets must be made available for distribution to the ordinary unsecured creditors. In Canada, the trend has been to create a statutory charge in favour of certain types of claimants who are considered to be particularly vulnerable in terms of their reliance on the debt owed to them and their inability to adjust by restricting credit or charging a higher interest rate. See Chapter 9.

D. Secured Creditors' Right to Post-Bankruptcy and Post-Discharge Collateral

An important practical and conceptual issue has arisen in the case law where the secured creditor holds a security interest in the debtor's after-acquired property as well as in present property. Will the after-acquired property clause attach to property interests acquired by the debtor between the time of bankruptcy and the time of discharge? Will it pick up property interests only acquired by the debtor *after* discharge?

Holy Rosary Parish (Thorold) Credit Union Ltd. v. Robitaille (Trustee of)
[1965] SCR 503

SPENCE J (for the Court): This is an appeal by special leave from the judgment of the Court of Appeal for Ontario pronounced on September 12, 1963. The judgment of that Court confirmed that of the Honourable Mr. Justice Smily pronounced May 6, 1963, in which he declared

> that the assignment of wages made by the said bankrupt, Herbert Léger Robitaille, to the Holy Rosary Credit Union dated the 10th of April 1962, and presently filed with the Empire Rug Mills Limited, employer of the said bankrupt, on the 27th day of November 1962, is void and unenforceable as against the said The Premier Trust Company, Trustee of the estate of the said bankrupt, and it is ordered and adjudged accordingly.

On April 10, 1962, the said Herbert Léger Robitaille borrowed certain funds from the Holy Rosary (Thorold) Credit Union Limited and on that date gave to the Credit Union an assignment of 30 per cent of all the wages, salary, commission, or other moneys owing to him or thereafter to become owing to him, or earned by him in the employ of the Empire Rug Mills Limited, or any other person, firm or corporation by whom he might thereafter be employed. Default having occurred in a payment of the instalments of indebtedness due by the said Robitaille to the Credit Union, the Credit Union notified his employer, Empire Rug Mills Limited, on November 27, 1962, of the assignment of wages.

On January 8, 1963, the said Robitaille made an assignment in bankruptcy to the Premier Trust Company Limited and its position as trustee was confirmed by a meeting of creditors held on January 22, 1963. The appellant Credit Union was notified by the trustee of the fact of the assignment and was supplied with a proof of claim form but never filed any proof of claim or appeared in the bankruptcy.

On March 14, 1963, the trustee by letter notified the Empire Rug Mills Limited that it required the said company to pay to it the funds deducted from Robitaille's wages up till that date. The Empire Rug Mills Limited took the position that it would hold the money pending an order of the Court declaring the assignment of wages dated April 10, 1962 to be void and unenforceable. An application for that declaration was made on behalf of the trustee on March 29, 1963, and Smily J so declared on May 6, 1963.

On May 23, 1963, the bankrupt Robitaille applied for and obtained his unconditional discharge from the bankruptcy.

No reasons in writing were delivered by the Court of Appeal but Smily J in giving judgment said:

I am, of course, bound by the judgment in the *Lundy v. Niagara Falls Railway Employees Credit Union* case, [1960] OWN 539, 1 CBR (NS) 201, 26 DLR (2d) 47.

There are two distinctions between that decision and the present case. In the first place, in the *Lundy v. Niagara Falls* case, the only notice of the assignment to the employer was given after the bankruptcy. This was relied upon by the Credit Union in the present case in the argument before Smily J but in this Court counsel for the Credit Union placed no reliance at all on such distinction. Secondly, in the *Lundy v. Niagara Falls* case, the creditor filed a claim in bankruptcy and although it did not value its security its manager was nominated as the sole inspector of the estate and actively engaged in the administration of the bankruptcy. As I shall point hereafter, that circumstance might well have determined the action in favour of the trustee as it would appear that in so doing the Credit Union had released its security.

The only other authority in Canada dealing with the issue as between the assignee of future wages and the trustee in bankruptcy which was cited to us or which I could discover would seem to be *In re Hunt* [(1954), 34 CBR 120, 12 WWR (NS) 552], in which Graham J held in the Court of Queen's Bench of Saskatchewan that such assignment was valid as against the trustee despite the creditor's failure to notify the employer until after the bankruptcy occurred, and despite the fact that the creditor had filed a claim in the bankruptcy. *In re Hunt* does not seem to have been referred to in the consideration in the Court of Appeal of the *Lundy v. Niagara Falls* case, *supra*.

The definition of "property" in s. 2(o) of the *Bankruptcy Act*, RSC 1952, c. 14, reads as follows:

(o) "Property" includes money, goods, things in action, land, and every description of property, whether real or personal, movable or immovable, legal or equitable, and whether situate in Canada or elsewhere and includes obligations, easements and every description of estate, interest and profit, present or future, vested or contingent, in, arising out of, or incident to property.

Disregarding for the moment the assignment of the wages, there is no doubt that in Canada after-acquired wages or salaries of a bankrupt, subject to a fair and reasonable allowance to the debtor for maintenance of himself and his family, go to the trustee as property of the bankrupt: *In re Tod, Clarkson v. Tod* [[1934] SCR 230, 15 CBR 253, 2 DLR 316], and *Industrial Acceptance Corporation and T. Eaton Co. Ltd. of Montreal v. Lalonde* [[1952] 2 SCR 109, 32 CBR 191, 3 DLR 348].

In my opinion, it is equally well established that an assignment for valuable consideration of property to be obtained in the future is a valid equitable assignment and one which is enforceable in equity so soon as the property comes into the possession of the assignor: *Tailby v. Official Receiver* [(1888), 13 App. Cas. 523, 58 LJQB 75].

In re Lind, Industrial Finance Syndicate v. Lind [(1915), 84 LJ Ch. 884], Swinfen Eady LJ said at p. 895:

It is clear from these authorities that an assignment for value of future property actually binds the property itself, directly if it is acquired, automatically on the happening of the event, and without any further act on the part of the assignor, and does not merely rest in and amount to a right in contract giving rise to an action. The assignor, having received the consideration, becomes in equity, on the happening of the event, trustee for the assignee of the property devolving upon or acquired by him, and which he had previously sold and been paid for.

Phillimore LJ said at p. 897:

But, notwithstanding these allusions to the specific performance of contracts, it is, I think, well and long settled that the right of the assignee is a higher right than the right to have specific performance of a contract, that the assignment creates an equitable charge, which arises immediately upon the property coming into existence. Either then no further act of assurance from the assignor is required, or, if there be something necessary to be done by him to pass the legal estate or complete the title, he has to do it, not by reason of a covenant for further assurance, the persistence of which, through bankruptcy, it is unnecessary to discuss, but because it is due from him as trustee for his assignee.

Bankes LJ said at p. 902:

It appears to me to be manifest from these statements of the law that equity regarded an assignment for value of future-acquired property as containing an enforceable security as against the property assigned quite independent of the personal obligation of the assignor arising out of his imported covenant to assign. It is true that the security was not enforceable until the property came into existence, but nevertheless the security was there, and the assignor was the bare trustee of the assignee to receive and hold the property for him when it came into existence.

The Lind case was not one of an assignment of wages to be earned in the future but it was an assignment of property to be acquired in the future, and a bankruptcy did follow the assignment.

Indeed, the valid and enforceable character of the assignment as an equitable assignment was upheld by the Court of Appeal for Ontario in *Niagara Falls Railway Employees Credit Union v. International Nickel Co. Ltd.* [[1960] OWN 42, 23 DLR (2d) 215]. In that Court, the argument that such an assignment was contrary to public policy was also disposed of. Such an argument was suggested in this Court upon the present argument but it was not relied upon. If the assignment of the wages to be acquired thereafter is a valid, equitable assignment and creates a valid, equitable security, there is no reason why the property of the debtor in those after-acquired wages should not pass to the trustee subject to such security. In my view, such result is not affected materially by the decisions in a series of cases exemplified by *Re Jones, Ex. p. Nichols* [(1883), 22 Ch. D 782, 52 LJ Ch. 635].

· · ·

Laidlaw JA, in giving the judgment for the Court of Appeal in *Lundy v. Niagara Falls Railway Employees Credit Union, supra,* quoted *Williams on Bankruptcy,* 17th ed., at p. 75, as follows:

At common law a document purporting to be an assignment of property thereafter to be acquired by the assignor passes no property to the assignee unless and until there be, besides the acquisition of the property by the assignor, some *actus interveniens,* such as seizure

> by the assignee; but in equity, although a contract engaging to transfer property not in existence as the property of the assignor cannot operate as an immediate alienation, yet, if the assignor afterwards becomes possessed of property answering the description in the contract, it will transfer the beneficial interest to the purchaser immediately upon the property being acquired, provided it appear therefrom that such is the intention of the parties; but not if it appear that the intention of the parties is that there shall be merely a power to seize after-acquired property as distinguished from an interest therein on its acquirement.

And continued:

> That statement of law must be read with s. 39 of the *Bankruptcy Act*, quoted *supra*. I can find no ambiguity in the relevant language of that section and no doubt arises therefrom in my mind. The wages earned and falling due to the appellant after he made an assignment in bankruptcy did not form part of his property at the date of the assignment in bankruptcy. He acquired the right to those wages after his bankruptcy and before his discharge. In my opinion, that right became property of the bankrupt appellant and vested in the trustee in bankruptcy by virtue of s. 39 of the *Bankruptcy Act*.

But by the very terms of s. 39(a), the property of the bankrupt shall not comprise property held by the bankrupt in trust for any other person. And the whole import of the cases which I have cited, *supra*, is to the effect that so soon as those after-acquired wages are due to the bankrupt then the assignment operates in equity to transfer the property there in to the assignee.

. . .

Judgment for Credit Union.

Holy Rosary Parish (Thorold) Credit Union Ltd. v. Bye
[1967] SCR 271

JUDSON J (for the court): In *Holy Rosary Parish (Thorold) Credit Union Ltd. v. Premier Trust Company* [[1965] SCR 503, 51 DLR (2d) 591, 7 CBR (NS) 169], the Premier Trust Company, as trustee in bankruptcy of one Robitaille, a wage-earner, sought a declaration that an assignment of wages given by Robitaille to the credit union was void and unenforceable against it. This application was eventually dismissed in this Court but, at the same time, the Court said that the effect of the discharge of the bankrupt upon the credit union's right to obtain a portion of the wages earned by the bankrupt after his discharge was not in issue in the appeal and that the Court expressed no opinion thereon. This problem is now before the Court.

On May 30, 1961, Bye obtained a loan from Holy Rosary Parish (Thorold) Credit Union Limited and at the same time assigned 30 per cent of his wages.

. . .

This is the same form of assignment that was under consideration in the Premier Trust case and appears to be authorized by s. 7(6) of *The Wages Act*, RSO 1960, c. 421, as amended by 9-10 Elizabeth II, c. 103. This subsection reads:

(6) Any contract hereafter made may provide for the assignment by the debtor to the creditor of a portion of the debtor's wages up to but not exceeding the portion thereof that is liable to attachment or seizure under this section, and any provision of any contract hereafter made that provides for the assignment by the debtor to the creditor of a greater portion of the debtor's wages than is permissible under this subsection is invalid.

On October 3, 1961, Bye made an assignment in bankruptcy. On January 11, 1962, an order was made for his unconditional discharge from bankruptcy. On April 26, 1965, the credit union filed the assignment with Overland Express Limited and requested them to act upon it. Bye then brought a motion for an order declaring

(a) that he was released from all debts and liabilities incurred by him on or before the 3rd of October 1961; and

(b) that the assignment of wages was now void and unenforceable.

Bye relies upon the *Bankruptcy Act*, RSC 1952, c. 14, s. 135(2), which reads:

135.(2) An order of discharge releases the bankrupt from all other claims provable in bankruptcy.

There is no doubt that the borrowing by Bye from the credit union did create a debt provable in bankruptcy. The credit union did not prove in bankruptcy. The debt has now gone by operation of law. The assignment was given as a means of collection of the debt. The statutory release of the debtor under the *Bankruptcy Act* renders the assignment ineffective as a means of collection. Both the judge of first instance and the Court of Appeal [(1966), 54 DLR (2d) 590] have so held and in my opinion correctly.

Appeal dismissed.

J.S. Ziegel, "Post-Bankruptcy Remedies of Secured Creditors: Some Comments on Professor Buckwold's Article"
(1999), 32 *CBLJ* 142 (footnotes omitted)

All of us who toil in the insolvency field are deeply indebted to Professor Buckwold for her thoughtful, powerfully reasoned and scholarly investigation in the April 1999 issue of the *Canadian Business Law Journal* of two much neglected aspects of secured obligations in bankruptcy. The first concerns the requirement for reaffirmation by a debtor of the contract where the debtor remains in possession of the collateral after bankruptcy and the secured creditor seeks to hold the debtor liable for a deficiency on the debtor's default. The second issue involves a secured creditor's right to claim any accretion in value of the security interest after the debtor's discharge where the underlying debt has been discharged pursuant to s. 178(2) of the *Bankruptcy and Insolvency Act* (BIA).

I agree with much that appears in Professor Buckwold's article but I also find myself in disagreement with important aspects of her analysis. The purpose of this short comment is to indicate the principal areas of disagreement, to encourage other commentators to contribute their own insights, and not least to highlight the need for better data on the first issue and improved legislation on both issues.

· · ·

2. The Status of Postdischarge Security Interests

I also have the misfortune to differ from Professor Buckwold on two important aspects of her treatment of this topic. Briefly put, (1) I query whether her "pool of assets" or "economic value" characterization of modern security interests is soundly based, and (2) I cannot accept her proposition that the Supreme Court's decision in *Bye*, with or without the gloss added to it by the Ontario Court of Appeal in *Pelyea and Canada Packers Employees Credit Union Ltd: (Re)*, is indisputably correct. I appreciate of course that until the Supreme Court revisits its decision it is a binding precedent. Nevertheless, it is legitimate in the context of a serious law journal to remind the reader of how deeply the court's decision conflicts with previously well established bankruptcy policy and leading precedents in England and the United States, and of the arbitrary results engendered by the court's distinction between security interests "acquired" by the debtor before and after a s. 178(2) discharge although in both cases the collateral was given as security under a prebankruptcy security agreement.

(a) The Proper Characterization of Modern Security Interests

With much skill and eloquence, Professor Buckwold distinguishes between the old-style title-based security interests, such as the common law realty mortgage and modern functionally oriented security interests such as those created under the Torrens Land Title systems, and the provincial *Personal Property Security Acts*. She argues, unless I have misconstrued her meaning, that these types of security interests are only as good as the pool of assets supporting them and that when the economic value ceases to exist so (apparently) does the security interest. She applies this conceptualization to the facts in *Andrew v. FarmStart* and criticizes the Saskatchewan's Court of Appeal's reasoning on the ground that "There were no units of value available in the 'pool' to be applied to payment of [FarmStart's] claim. Though FarmStart had registered a claim against the debtor's title, there was no property to which a third mortgage could attach."

I could live with her conceptualization if it were clear that she means to limit it to postdischarge assets for the purpose of applying the *Bye* and *Pelyea* prescriptions in a bankruptcy context. It seems clear, however, that Professor Buckwold does not intend to confine her conceptualization to this narrow band, and this is what troubles me. Taken to its logical conclusion it would lead to dramatic results. It would mean, for example, that a security interest may never come into existence if the collateral has no economic value at the time of its purported creation or attachment. Similarly, a security interest that was supported by economic value may drop out of sight because of a dramatic decline in value. Logically, it should also lead to the conclusion that a debtor should have the right to redeem the security at its current market value or, if the security interest is no longer supported by economic value, to seek a court declaration that the security interest has ceased to exist.

I see nothing in the *Personal Property Security Acts* that remotely supports either Professor Buckwold's conceptualization or these and many other potential results. To overcome the difficulties I have described[,] Professor Buckwold argues that a distinction must be drawn between the "substantive rights" associated with a security interest and the "procedural rights" ascribed to secured creditors under the legislation. I confess I find this distinction equally unpersuasive. There is no provision I am aware of in the Ontario Act, for example, that entitles a court to expunge an otherwise valid and perfected security interest on the ground that it has lost all economic value, even if there is a proper hearing and all other due process requirements have been met. So far as the right to redeem is concerned, the provincial PPSAs only entitle the debtor to exercise the right by tendering fulfilment of all obligations secured by the collateral together with the secured party's expenses.

It is true bankruptcy law has established a value test for some purposes. The exceptions, however, mainly flow from the need to determine the quantum of debt for which a secured creditor should be treated as secured or unsecured. It is not legitimate to extrapolate from the exceptions to lay the foundations for a radically new theory of security interests.

(b) Discharge of Security Interests: The Bye Heresy

This brings me to the Supreme Court's decision in *Bye*, which, as I have indicated, provides the basis for Professor Buckwold's criticism of *FarmStart* and similar decisions. To appreciate the impact of *Bye* we need to remind ourselves of a little bit of legal history.

Holroyd v. Marshall, decided in 1862, laid the foundation for modern chattel security financing in its holding that a security interest in future goods is binding and enforceable in equity. The decision was carried a step further by the law lords' decision in *Tailby v. Official Receiver*, which made it clear that the security interest fastened on the future property as soon as the debtor acquired an interest in it and that the secured party was not required to take further steps to perfect its security interest.

England adopted a comprehensive *Bankruptcy Act* in 1883, which was substantially re-enacted in the *Bankruptcy Act 1914*. The 1914 Act provided the conceptual framework for the Canadian *Bankruptcy Act* of 1919 and its later progeny, including the current *Bankruptcy and Insolvency Act*. Among others, the 1883 Act enshrined the following basic building blocks. First, it recognized and gave effect to prebankruptcy security interests if they had been validly created before bankruptcy, and gave broad immunity to secured creditors from the bankruptcy process. In particular, secured creditors were generally free to enforce their security interests as if no bankruptcy had intervened and it was left up to them to decide, *inter alia*, whether they wished to value their security and file proof of claim for any unsecured amount or whether they preferred to segregate themselves entirely from unsecured creditors and file no proof of claim at all. The second important feature of the 1883 Act was that for the first time consumer debtors were given a general right to apply for a discharge of their debts.

The interaction of these two great principles was tested before the English Court of Appeal in the leading case of *In re Lind*. The facts are important because the court's decision is in direct conflict with the Supreme Court's later decision in *Bye*. In 1905, L gave

N a mortgage in an expectancy in L's mother's estate. In 1908, he gave a second mortgage in the expectancy to A, subject to the first mortgage. In August 1908, L was adjudged bankrupt and in 1910 he obtained his discharge. Neither N nor A proved in L's bankruptcy.

In 1911 L gave an assignment of the expectancy to the I Syndicate. In 1914, L's mother died and L's share of the estate fell into his possession. Two principal issues were argued before the Court of Appeal. The first was whether N and A had acquired an effective security interest in the expectancy. The second was whether the security interests had survived L's discharge from bankruptcy. A strong court answered both questions affirmatively.

So far as the second question was concerned, Swinfen Eady LJ wrote:

> It was urged by the appellants that having regard to the wide language of s. 37 of the *Bankruptcy Act, 1883*, with regard to debts and liabilities provable in bankruptcy, all liability of the assignor of every kind, under the mortgages of 1905 and 1908, was provable; and that as the debts created by the mortgage deeds were extinguished by the bankruptcy, the contract relating to the future property, which was merely ancillary to and for the purpose of securing the debt, was also discharged. The answer is that the mortgagees under the deeds of 1905 and 1908 elected to rely upon their security, and not to prove, and therefore as mortgagees they stand outside the bankruptcy; and, moreover, that any contract contained in those deeds far vesting the future property in the mortgagees was ancillary not to the debt, but to the mortgage by which the debt was secured, in like manner as the covenant not to revoke a will which had appointed a sum of money to a mortgagee was so held in *Robinson v. Ommanney* 8 both by Kay J and the Court of Appeal.

Bankes LJ responded similarly.

In re Lind is still good law in England and the current English *Insolvency Act 1986* makes it clear that secured parties are not affected by the debtor's discharge if they do not prove in respect of the debts. Though US bankruptcy law is generally much less favourable to secured creditors' rights than Anglo-Canadian law, the postdischarge survival of valid prebankruptcy security interests has been an established axiom since the US Supreme Court's decision in *Long v. Bullard* (1886).

In re Lind appears to have attracted little judicial attention in Canada before the Supreme Court was asked to determine in *Holy Rosary Parish (Thorold) Credit Union Ltd. v. Premier Trust Co.* the validity in bankruptcy of a prebankruptcy wage assignment given as security to the debtor's credit union. Issues of public policy were argued as well as the status of future security interests in bankruptcy. Speaking through Spence J, the Supreme Court found little difficulty in answering both questions in the Credit Union's favour. So far as the general issue was concerned, Spence J cited approvingly from the Court of Appeal's judgments in *In re Lind*. However, he added an important rider to the effect that he was not expressing an opinion on the credit union's right to continue to enforce its security interest after the debtor had obtained a discharge.

It was this reservation that provided the basis for the Supreme Court's subsequent decision in *Bye* and Judson J's remarkably short judgment (only three pages in the *Supreme Court Reports* and the *Canadian Bankruptcy Reports*) for a case of this importance. Once again the court was confronted with a prebankruptcy wage assignment in favour of a credit union but with the difference that this time the debtor had already obtained a discharge. The credit union did not prove for its debt. In the Ontario Court of Appeal, in an equally short judgment, Schroeder JA agreed with the trial judge that since the discharge had extinguished the debt the assignment too was no longer operative. He did not refer to *In re Lind* although it seems unlikely that his attention was not drawn to its relevance.

In the Supreme Court, Judson J also focused exclusively on the discharge provisions in the *Bankruptcy Act* (s. 135(2)), and then continued:

> There is no doubt that the borrowing by Bye from the credit union did create a debt provable in bankruptcy. The credit union did not prove in bankruptcy. The assignment was given as a means of collection of the debt. The statutory release of the debtor under the *Bankruptcy Act* renders the assignment ineffective as a means of collection. Both the Judge of first instance and the Court of Appeal have so held and in my opinion correctly.

He did not examine the other provisions in the *Bankruptcy Act* or the history of the treatment of security interests in the English and Canadian insolvency legislation. Similarly, he did not address his mind to the question of the status of collateral received or earned by the debtor before his discharge but not yet seized and realized by the secured creditor.

That question came before the Ontario Court of Appeal in *Pelyea* [(1969), 13 CBR (NS) 284]. The security given the credit union in this case consisted of the debtor's share in an employee profit-sharing plan. It appears, however, that under the terms of the plan Pelyea was not entitled to receive any money until after his discharge and it was those funds to which the credit union laid claim. Not surprisingly, on the strength of *Bye*, MacKay JA held that the credit union's claim must fail. However, he also distinguished between collateral to which the debtor was entitled and that had been collected or realized by the secured creditor before the debtor's discharge, and collateral that only came into existence after the discharge. It was only the postdischarge collateral, in his opinion, that was affected by the discharge.

MacKay JA rejected counsel's argument that the discharge totally extinguished the assignment in the following passage:

> As to the respondent's first submission, what is extinguished by s. 135(2) of the *Bankruptcy Act* in the case of a secured creditor is the debt owing by the debtor at the time of the bankruptcy, not the security which was validly in existence at the date of the bankruptcy. It remains a valid security that the creditor is entitled to realize on or have valued pursuant to the provisions of ss. 40(2), 86 and 87 of the Act, and the debt owing by the bankrupt, insofar as s. 135(2) is concerned, is the balance remaining of the original debt after the security has been realized and applied on account or valued.

I find the reasoning baffling. If, as *In re Lind* held, the security has an autonomous existence and is not affected by the discharge, then the secured party should be entitled to continue to claim the collateral. This is what *In re Lind* decided, and *Bye* denied. But, conversely, if the debt and the security interest are interdependent, surely the collateral must be released together with the debt. I see no logical halfway house.

3. Where Do We Go from Here?

As Professor Buckwold's examination of the post-*Pelyea* case law shows, MacKay JA's compromise leads to some quite arbitrary results. So far as wage assignments and assignments of other earnings are concerned, their status is now settled in s. 68.1 of the BIA. Significantly, they are simply disallowed on bankruptcy because they jeopardize the debtor's livelihood. It is all the other possible permutations that secured creditors and debtors must worry about. Debtors have an obvious incentive to secure the earliest possible discharge although that goal will now be much more difficult because of the new discharge provisions adopted in the 1997 amendments to the BIA and the emphasis on steering the debtor away from a straight bankruptcy and towards a consumer proposal under Part 111.2 of the Act. Secured creditors, for their part, will find it that much more difficult to assess the risk of loss if the survival of their collateral depends on the accident of whether it falls into possession before or after the discharge and, if before, on whether or not they are able to realize it before the discharge. The same complexities arise in determining whether the accrual to a debtor's equity occurred before or after discharge.

NOTES

1. Section 68.1(1) provides that an after-acquired property clause is ineffective against property acquired after the commencement of bankruptcy proceedings in respect of wage assignment. Note that in some provinces the use of wage assignments has been curtailed with the result that the problem will not arise. See, for example, *Fair Trading Act*, RSA 2000, c. F-2, s. 53. Section 68.1(2) provides that an assignment of amounts payable as a result of services rendered by an individual is also of no effect in respect of amounts earned or generated after the bankruptcy.

2. Suppose that a secured creditor has a security interest in accounts. Following a bankruptcy of the debtor, the trustee in bankruptcy sells some of the bankrupt's assets or operates the business so as to produce an account. Can the secured creditor claim priority over the account as against the trustee? Why or why not? See *Re Anderson & Hiltz Ltd.* (1985), 57 CBR (NS) 222 (Ont. SC); *Wilmot v. Allen* (1897), 1 QB 17 (CA).

3. Professors Cuming, Walsh, and Wood, *Personal Property Security Law* (Toronto: Irwin Law, 2005), at 430-37, question whether the enactment of the modernized personal property security legislation may have altered the analysis in cases such as *Re Lind*. The PPSA adopts the concept of attachment under which a security interest attaches when the debtor has rights in the collateral and value is given. Does after-acquired property vest momentarily in the debtor or do future assets vest directly in the trustee? What difference would this make in respect of the attachment of the security interest? Although BIA s. 67(1)(c) makes it clear that post-bankruptcy/pre-discharge assets are divisible among the creditors, it does not shed any light on this question. BIA s. 71 provides that upon a bankruptcy, the debtor's property immediately vests in the trustee, but it is silent about the vesting of after-acquired assets.

III. CROWN CLAIMS

A. Introduction

Should Crown claims have priority status in a debtor's insolvency? The standard argument in favour runs as follows. "[A] debt owing to the Crown is a debt owing to the public at large and the inability to collect debts owing to the Crown will affect the ability of government to function": Ronald C.C. Cuming, "An Approach to the Rationalization of Enforcement of Federal and Provincial Crown Claims" (October 1999) (unpublished, prepared for Industry Canada: Corporate Law Policy Directorate), at 78. Another way of stating the argument is to say that the Crown is a "non-adjusting creditor" in the debtor's bankruptcy. It is a non-adjusting creditor in the sense that, because the amount of its entitlement is set by statute, it cannot prospectively adjust its claim against any given debtor to account for the risk of the debtor's insolvency: Lucien Arye Bebchuk and Jesse M. Fried, "The Uneasy Case for the Priority of Secured Claims in Bankruptcy: Further Thoughts and a Reply to the Critics" (1997), 82 *Cornell Law Review* 1279, at 1288-99. Like involuntary creditors (tort claimants and the like), non-adjusting creditors are not compensated for assuming the risk of the debtor's insolvency. Therefore, on both efficiency and fairness grounds, their claims should be preferred to the claims of other creditors.

The standard argument against Crown priority is that "the burden of tax left unpaid by the bankrupt should be divided among all the tax-paying public rather than being borne by the creditors, who have already suffered losses": Canada, Advisory Committee on Bankruptcy and Insolvency, *Proposed Bankruptcy Act Amendments: Report of the Advisory Committee on Bankruptcy and Insolvency* (Ottawa: Minister of Supply and Services Canada, 1986), at 79 ("Colter Committee Report"). Federal and provincial legislatures use a wide variety of measures to secure for Crown claims priority over other creditors, both inside and outside bankruptcy:

> A wide range of legal techniques, such as expedited seizure, expedited garnishment and distress and third party liabilities have been developed to facilitate enforcement of Crown claims. Other devices such as liens, charges, security interests, deemed trusts and statutory subordination are used to give these claims the highest possible priority relative to other claims.

See Ronald C.C. Cuming, "An Approach to the Rationalization of Enforcement of Federal and Provincial Crown Claims," above, at 1.

The effectiveness of Crown priority claims outside a debtor's bankruptcy or insolvency varies depending on the terms of the statute that governs the Crown's claim. For example, the statute may give the Crown a lien, charge, or security interest over assets of the debtor to secure payment of the Crown claim. In that case, the statute may set out priority rules to apply where a third party claims a competing interest in the same collateral. Alternatively, the statute may say nothing about priorities. If it says nothing, the courts will have to imply a priority rule to cover the case. If the statute does deal with the priorities question, there are all sorts of possible variables. For example, it may say the Crown's interest has priority over a party who acquires a later competing interest in the collateral, but not a party who has an earlier interest. Or it may say the Crown's claim has priority over both earlier and later interests. With respect to later interests, the statute may say the Crown has priority only if the later interest holder had notice of the Crown's claim. Or it may state or imply that the Crown's claim has priority regardless of notice. Some statutes make the Crown's priority depend on registration by the Crown, the holder of the competing interest, or both. Others make no reference to registration.

Instead of, or as well as, giving the Crown a lien, charge, or security interest, the statute may provide for a deemed trust in the Crown's favour of assets under the debtor's control. The statute may expressly or by implication limit the trust to the case where the subject property remains separate and identifiable in the debtor's hands. Alternatively, it may assert a trust even if the subject property is no longer traceable. The statute may provide expressly for the latter case by saying that the trust extends to other property in the debtor's hands of equivalent value. If it does not, the trust is likely to fail for want of subject matter in cases where the debtor deals with the subject property so that it can no longer be traced. If the statute does create a deemed trust over the debtor's other property, it may set out priority rules to apply where a third party claims a prior competing interest. Alternatively, the statute may say nothing about priorities. If the statute says nothing, a court is likely to say the holder of the competing interest has priority over the Crown's trust claim on the ground that, in the absence of a clear indication of the legislature's intention to the contrary, a statute should not be construed in a manner that could deprive third parties of their pre-existing property rights.

Prior to 1992, the BIA ranked Crown claims as preferred claims under s. 136. Although one of the fundamental principles of bankruptcy law is the equal treatment of creditors, s. 136 sets out a number of different claims that are entitled to be paid before ordinary unsecured creditors. (Preferred claims under s. 136 are covered in more detail in Chapter 9.) Although the pre-1992 position of Crown claims ranked ahead of unsecured claims, Crown claims, like all other preferred claims in s. 136, ranked behind secured claims. Federal and provincial Crowns long felt that they deserved to be treated much better and rather than waiting for Parliament to revise the BIA, the federal and provincial governments addressed the issue in the *Excise Tax Act*, RSC 1985, c. E-15, the *Income Tax Act*, RSC 1985 c. 1 (ITA), the *Employment Insurance Act*, SC 1996, c. 23, the *Canada Pension Plan*, RSC 1985, c. C-8, and the workers' compensation acts by deeming deductions not remitted to the governmental agencies to be held in trust for the Crown and creating a first lien on all the debtor's assets ranking ahead of all other claims. In other cases, where no deductions or collections by the debtor were involved, the legislation created a super-priority lien in favour of the Crown. The deemed trusts or deemed liens "were intended to rank in priority to the claims of secured creditors" (Colter Committee Report, above, at 76).

Predictably, this led to fierce (and ongoing) litigation. Consensual secured creditors took the position that the governmental agencies were trying to circumvent the ranking prescribed in BIA s. 136(1). The Supreme Court of Canada agreed with the secured creditors and, in a quartet of cases decided in the 1980s, decided that provincial legislation could not be used to bypass the s. 136(1) ranking by converting Crown claims into lien claims. In the last of the four cases, *British Columbia v. Henfrey Samson Belair Ltd.* (1989), 59 DLR (4th) 726 (SCC), the court also held that a deemed trust created under the BC *Social Service Tax Act* in respect of sales tax collected by the bankrupt, but not remitted to the province, did not qualify as a trust under s. 67(1) of the pre-1992 BIA. In 1995, the Supreme Court of Canada added a fifth decision, discussed below.

Husky Oil Operations Ltd. v. Canada (Minister of National Revenue—MNR)
(1995), 128 DLR (4th) 1 (SCC)

GONTHIER J: ...

(ii) The Principles and Philosophy Embodied in the Quartet

What principles should be distilled from the quartet? The intervener Attorney General for Saskatchewan suggested that there are two possible interpretations of these decisions: what it called a broader "bottom line" approach which posits that "any time provincial law affects the final result of a bankruptcy, the province is improperly attempting to alter the priorities of distribution"; and a narrower "jump the queue" approach to the effect that "the province cannot attempt to alter the position of a person within the scheme of distribution created by Parliament, vis-à-vis the other creditors who are claiming from the bankrupt's estate."

My colleague Iacobucci J properly rejects the broader "bottom line" approach since, as he indicates, such an approach "risks nullifying the broad array of provincial legislation underpinning the *Bankruptcy Act*" (para. 142). It is trite to observe that the *Bankruptcy Act* is contingent on the provincial law of property for its operation. The Act is superimposed on those provincial schemes when a debtor declares bankruptcy. As a result, provincial law necessarily affects the "bottom line," but this is contemplated by the *Bankruptcy Act* itself. Indeed, it is no exaggeration to say that there is no "bottom line" without provincial law. The "bottom line" approach is therefore not the appropriate characterization of the quartet.

However, even rejecting the simplistic "bottom line" approach, I do not agree that the quartet stands for the sole proposition that the provinces cannot "jump the queue." In my opinion, the quartet embodies a consistent and general philosophy as to the purposes of the federal system of bankruptcy and its relation to provincial property arrangements. That philosophy cannot be captured in the pithy but limited proposition that the provinces cannot "jump the queue."

The quartet is better stated, in my view, as standing for a number of related propositions which are themselves part of a consistent philosophy. In their lucid and thorough study of the quartet, "The Conflict Between Canadian Provincial Personal Property Security Acts and the Federal Bankruptcy Act: The War is Over" (1992), 71 *Can. Bar Rev.* 77, at pp. 78-79, Andrew J. Roman and M. Jasmine Sweatman state that the quartet stands for the following four propositions:

(1) provinces cannot create priorities between creditors or change the scheme of distribution on bankruptcy under s. 136(1) of the *Bankruptcy Act*;

(2) while provincial legislation may validly affect priorities in a non-bankruptcy situation, once bankruptcy has occurred section 136(1) of the *Bankruptcy Act* determines the status and priority of the claims specifically dealt with in that section;

(3) if the provinces could create their own priorities or affect priorities under the *Bankruptcy Act* this would invite a different scheme of distribution on bankruptcy from province to province, an unacceptable situation; and

(4) the definition of terms such as "secured creditor," if defined under the *Bankruptcy Act*, must be interpreted in bankruptcy cases as defined by the federal Parliament, not the provincial legislatures. Provinces cannot affect how such terms are defined for purposes of the *Bankruptcy Act*.

See also for concurrence with Roman and Sweatman's general conclusions drawn from the quartet, Jacob S. Ziegel, "Personal Property Security and Bankruptcy: There is no War!—A Reply to Roman and Sweatman" (1993), 72 *Can. Bar Rev.* 44, at p. 45.

My colleague Iacobucci J states at para. 141 that the quartet "stands for the position that only those provincial laws which *directly* improve the priority of a claim upon the actual property of the bankrupt over that accorded by the *Bankruptcy Act* are inoperative" (emphasis added). This statement falls within Roman and Sweatman's proposition 1. However, as my summary of those cases has hopefully indicated, the quartet is clearly not limited to provincial "laws which directly improve the priority of a claim." To quote Roman and Sweatman, supra, at p. 78:

> ... the reasoning in [the quartet] is not limited to trusts, nor to situations of colourable legislation attempting to give an artificial preference to government. Rather, these rulings are broad enough to encompass any potential area of conflict between provincial power to legislate in the area of property and civil rights, and exclusive federal jurisdiction over bankruptcy and insolvency.

In a similar vein these authors add at p. 81:

> The Supreme Court of Canada's quartet of decisions, although dealing with provincial statutory trusts which affected priorities in bankruptcy, has progressively and finally provided a definite ruling on the relationship between priorities under the *Bankruptcy Act* and *any* other provincial statute which directly or indirectly affects priorities. [Emphasis in original.]

Importantly, they conclude at p. 105:

> The law, in our opinion, is settled by these four judgments of the Supreme Court of Canada. In all four cases the issues were not whether the provinces could directly and blatantly attempt to alter the scheme of interests of secured and other creditors under what is now section 136(1) of the *Bankruptcy Act*. Rather, the issue was whether a province could indirectly influence priorities under the *Bankruptcy Act*. Even in this weaker version of influence, the Supreme Court of Canada has held that the provinces could not.

And in so concluding, they are also quick to caution at p. 106:

> It is also incorrect to state that in all four cases the provinces attempted to redistribute or change priorities by explicitly elevating one of the lower ranked claims to a higher rank. As seen from an examination of the dissenting judgments in *Deloitte Haskins* and *Henfrey*, the provinces were not attempting specifically to target the bankruptcy situation but, rather, to create a general priority.

As a result, the "jump the queue" or "directly improve bankruptcy priorities" approach captures only part of the reasoning of the quartet. As Roman and Sweatman noted, in the

Deloitte Haskins and *Henfrey Samson* cases, for example, the provinces were not directly or intentionally attempting to influence bankruptcy priorities. Rather, the provinces enacted laws of general application which sought to create a general priority not necessarily targeted to bankruptcy, but which had the effect of altering bankruptcy priorities. This Court nevertheless ruled that such provincial laws were inapplicable in the event of bankruptcy.

I underline that the "effect" which Roman and Sweatman speak of is the effect on bankruptcy priorities (Roman and Sweatman, *supra*, at pp. 81-105). Consequently, clear conflict, that is an inconsistent or mutually exclusive result, which in this case entails a reordering of federal priorities, is necessary in order to declare a provincial law to be inapplicable in bankruptcy.

I also think it is important to emphasize the importance of Roman and Sweatman's proposition 3. While I agree with my colleague Iacobucci J that complete standardization of the distribution of property in bankruptcies is not possible across Canada having regard to the diversity of provincial laws relating to property and civil rights, yet the value of a national bankruptcy system is confirmed by the placing of bankruptcy under exclusive federal jurisdiction. As Professor Hogg has explained (supra, at pp. 25-1 and 25-2):

> … debtors may move from one province to another, and may have property and creditors in more than one province. A national body of law is required to ensure that all of a debtor's property is available to satisfy his debts, that all creditors are fairly treated, and that all are bound by any arrangements for the settlement of the debtor's debts. Indeed, without these assurances, lenders would be reluctant to extend credit to persons who could evade their obligations simply by removing themselves or their assets across a provincial boundary.

Furthermore, as my overview of the quartet hopefully indicated, the goal of maintaining a nationally homogeneous system of bankruptcy priorities has properly been a constant concern of this Court. Were the situation otherwise, "Canada [would] have a balkanized bankruptcy regime which [would] diminish the significance of the exclusivity of federal jurisdiction over bankruptcy and insolvency. … Otherwise there could be a different scheme in every jurisdiction; ten different bankruptcy regimes would make ordinary commercial affairs extremely complex, unwieldy and costly, not only for Canadians but also for our international trading partners" (Roman and Sweatman, *supra*, at pp. 80, 104). This is a prospect which this Court has been acutely mindful of in the past, and its vigilance has ensured the continuing vitality of our nation's bankruptcy legislation. In my view, its past vigilance commends itself to the present and, barring an amendment to s. 91(21) of the *Constitution Act, 1867*, also to the future.

In this regard, I agree with Iacobucci J, at para. 147, that a bankruptcy priority is a category, and also that provincial law may result in the content of such categories being different from province to province. However, provincial law does not and cannot define the content of bankruptcy priorities or categories without limitation. Indeed, crucial limitation is imposed by the order of priorities in the *Bankruptcy Act* itself. Thus, while individual provinces can define and rank categories such as "secured creditor" and "trust" as they each have their own purposes, those provincial laws which enter into conflict with the provisions of the *Bankruptcy Act* are simply without application in bankruptcy. Such, indeed, was this Court's unequivocal holding in *Re Bourgault, Deloitte Haskins,* and

FBDB with respect to "secured creditors" and in *Henfrey Samson* with respect to "trusts."

Finally, I would observe that while in agreement with the above four propositions as embodying the reasoning of the quartet, in my view the list would be more complete with the addition of a fifth and sixth, as follows:

(5) in determining the relationship between provincial legislation and the *Bankruptcy Act*, the form of the provincial interest created must not be allowed to triumph over its substance. The provinces are not entitled to do indirectly what they are prohibited from doing directly;

(6) there need not be any provincial intention to intrude into the exclusive federal sphere of bankruptcy and to conflict with the order of priorities of the *Bankruptcy Act* in order to render the provincial law inapplicable. It is sufficient that the effect of provincial legislation is to do so.

NOTES AND QUESTIONS

1. A secured creditor, which is subordinate to a Crown claim under provincial or non-bankruptcy federal law, is able to produce a "priority flip" or "inversion of priorities" by invoking the *Bankruptcy and Insolvency Act*. See T. Buckwold and R. Wood, "Priorities," in *Canadian Bankruptcy and Insolvency Law: Bill C-55, Statute c. 47 and Beyond*, S. Ben-Ishai and A. Duggan, eds. (Markham, ON: LexisNexis Canada, 2007). In other words, the BIA provisions governing Crown claims in bankruptcy improve the position of other creditors relative to the Crown when the debtor becomes bankrupt. Rules that improve creditor A's entitlements relative to creditor B's inside bankruptcy are contrary to good bankruptcy policy. The reason is that they create an incentive for A to put the debtor into bankruptcy in order to obtain a priority advantage over B. The danger is that the debtor may end up in bankruptcy prematurely. While this may be in A's individual interest, it will not be in the interest of the creditors as a group. Bankruptcy is likely to result in the dismantling of the debtor's business. The interest of the creditors as a group lies in maximizing the returns from realization of the debtor's assets. The debtor's business may be worth more if it sold as a going concern rather than piecemeal: Thomas H. Jackson, *The Logic and Limits of Bankruptcy Law* (Cambridge, MA: Harvard University Press, 1986), Chapter 1. Professor Cuming assessed the impact of the quintet and the 1992 reforms:

> Over the past 25 years a revolution in provincial secured financing law has occurred which has resulted in regimes that greatly facilitate the use of security interests in all types of movable property. Accompanying this has been a dramatic increase in the use of secured financing transactions, particularly in business financing. The result is that, in a large number of cases involving business bankruptcies, three types of claims predominate: secured claims, claims of the Crown (generally unpaid or unremitted taxes) and claims of unpaid former employees. In this context, the effect of the Quintet is to place secured creditors in the position of being able to defeat provincial law (that otherwise regulates all aspects of their rights as secured parties unless they hold *Bank Act* security interests) designed to give priority to Crown claims or claims for unpaid wages of former employees. In other words, the Court has developed an approach to a central feature of bankruptcy law that, in its application, has little to do with the historic

raison d'être of bankruptcy law: fair treatment of the claims of unsecured creditors. The *Bankruptcy and Insolvency Act* has become a source of federally superimposed priority rules, which heavily favour secured creditors, applicable to two areas which are socially and commercially very important to provincial legislators: priority for provincial Crown claims and priority for unpaid wages of employees or former employees of bankrupt business organizations. Short of dramatically limiting the circumstances in which security interests can be taken under provincial law, provincial legislators are powerless to introduce balance into the system of secured financing law so as to protect other interests from over-reaching. ... The effect of the Quintet is to put into the hands of Parliament the exclusive power to control matters which, in most other contexts, are properly within the provincial legislative competence. A very respectable argument can be made that this power has not been exercised in a manner that recognizes the important public policy issues that are of crucial importance to the provinces and which, in other contexts, fall within provincial jurisdiction. It is a matter of speculation as to whether the dismal record of Parliament in this area will change in the foreseeable future.

(Ronald C.C. Cuming, "The Supreme Court, Commerce and the Consumer: Making the Most of Limited Opportunities" (2001), 80 *Can. Bar Rev.* 42, at 59-61.)

2. Professor Wood in *Bankruptcy and Insolvency Law* (Toronto: Irwin Law, 2008) identifies four different situations where an inversion of priorities can arise. The first occurs where a creditor is given a preferred creditor status under the BIA. This was the ground that was used to subordinate statutory liens and charges in favour of the Crown. Note that the BIA was amended in 1992, such that the Crown is no longer listed as a preferred claim. The priorities of Crown claims are now covered by ss. 86 and 87. However, this ground is still important where other interests are involved. The subordination of a landlord's right of distress occurs because the landlord is listed as a preferred creditor. The same also held true in respect of claims of employees for unpaid wages, although this has been significantly altered by the 2007 reforms to the BIA and the enactment of the *Wage Earner Protection Program Act*. See Chapter 9. The second situation is in respect of Crown claims that are secured by a lien or charge. These are fully effective outside bankruptcy, and they are often given a super-priority over prior security interests. However, in bankruptcy they are effective only if registered and, even if this is done, they are rendered subordinate to a prior security. See the discussion of Crown claims under the 1992 reforms below. The third situation involves statutory deemed trusts. Section 67(2) provides that a deemed trust in favour of the Crown is ineffective unless it would constitute a valid trust in the absence of the statutory provisions. The fourth situation arises when a secured creditor is subordinate to a writ or judgment held by an ordinary unsecured creditor. For example, a writ creditor may have registered a writ of execution against the debtor's land prior to the granting of a mortgage to a lender. Under non-bankruptcy law, the writ has priority over the mortgage. However, by invoking bankruptcy, the secured creditor will cause the writ to cease to have any effect. See *Westcoast Savings Credit Union v. McElroy* (1981), 39 CBR (NS) 52 (BCSC); *James Hunter & Associates Inc. v. Citifinancial Inc.* (2007), 40 CBR (5th) 149 (Ont. SCJ).

3. Professors Buckwold and Wood, above, argue that the current state of the law produces the possibility of regime shopping under which a creditor has a strong incentive to invoke the insolvency regime—bankruptcy, restructuring, or receivership—that gives it the best priority ranking. Courts have permitted the restructuring regimes to be used to effect

a going-concern sale of the business. Thus, all three insolvency regimes can be used to effect a liquidation, yet the priorities that govern are often markedly different. In particular, Crown claims that are afforded a secured status and statutory deemed trusts are effective outside bankruptcy, but are limited by ss. 86-87 and BIA s. 67(2) when bankruptcy proceedings are commenced.

4. What solutions are available in the light of the these problems? The ability of secured creditors to invoke bankruptcy proceedings was considered in *Re Bank of Montreal v. Scott Road Enterprises Ltd.* (1989), 57 DLR (4th) 623 (BCCA), reproduced in Chapter 3. The position of unpaid employees is considered in more detail in Chapter 9.

B. The 1992 Reformed Approach to Crown Claims

The status of Crown claims in bankruptcy was fundamentally altered in the 1992 amendments to the BIA. Section 136(1)(h) and (j) were modified so that Crown claims and Workers' Compensation Board claims that arose after November 30, 1992 were no longer afforded the status of a preferred claim in a bankruptcy. This means that the quintet of SCC decisions that culminated in *Huskey Oil*, above, were no longer applicable because there was no longer an operational conflict between BIA s. 136 and the provincial legislation. Sections 86 and 87 were added to the BIA, and these provisions now govern the status of Crown claims.

Re Gillford Furniture Mart Ltd.
(1996), 36 CBR (3d) 157 (BCCA)

GOLDIE JA (orally): This is an appeal from the judgment of Mr. Justice Collver pronounced 22 March 1994 [reported at 25 CBR (3d) 4], exercising the jurisdiction of the Supreme Court of British Columbia in Bankruptcy under the provisions of the *Bankruptcy and Insolvency Act*, RSC 1985, c. B-3. I will refer to the *Bankruptcy and Insolvency Act* as the "Act."

The trial judge described the manner in which the issue came before him in his reasons for judgment [at 5]:

> A bailiff, acting on the instructions of the Commissioner administering the *Social Service Tax Act*, RSBC 1979, c. 388, seized the inventory of a struggling retailer in an effort to collect unpaid provincial sales taxes of $26,192.85. When the bailiff submitted a Proof of Claim pertaining to seizure costs of $15,256.26 to the retailer's trustee in bankruptcy, the bailiff claimed entitlement to a first charge for "the costs of distress," pursuant to s. 73(4) of the *Bankruptcy and Insolvency Act*, RSC 1985, c. B-3 [as amended]. The trustee disallowed the claim, ruling that the bailiff's charges are to be dealt with only as a preferred claim. The bailiff has appealed that decision.

He dismissed the bailiff's appeal.

The appeal is taken by Her Majesty the Queen in Right of the Province of British Columbia as the assignee of the bailiff's claim and as the secured creditor on behalf of whom the bailiff acted. No one appeared for the bailiff.

It is necessary to enlarge somewhat upon the facts. Under the *Social Service Tax Act,* RSBC 1979, c. 388, and amendments thereto, the Province has armed itself with a number of ways in which the Commissioner may recover taxes collected on behalf of the Crown which have not been remitted.

A relevant provision here is found in s. 18.1 of the *Social Service Tax Act.* Subsection (2) enables the Commissioner to create a lien against personal property of the delinquent "… by designating the amount owing as a lien and entering the amount together with the date of the entry in an accounts receivable system maintained by the commissioner." This is said by a collection supervisor in the Ministry of Finance and Corporate Affairs as registering the debt as a lien.

In fact, a further step was taken. Prior to the date of the assignment in bankruptcy the lien was registered in the Provincial Personal Property Registry under the provisions of the *Miscellaneous Registrations Act, 1992,* SBC 1992, c. 16.

The Commissioner next utilized the provisions of s. 21 of the *Social Service Tax Act* and filed a Certificate of Indebtedness in a District Registry of the Supreme Court. The effect of this is to give the Certificate the same force and effect as a judgment of that Court and upon which proceedings may be taken for the recovery of the amount owing.

The Certificate in respect of the sum of $26,000 plus is dated 5 February 1993 and was filed the same day. A writ of seizure and sale was issued 11 February 1993 and was placed in the bailiff's hands. It is acknowledged that the bailiff was acting in the manner as a sheriff would act under a writ of execution. Indeed, a writ of seizure and sale is a writ of execution.

The writ directed the bailiff to realize the sum of $26,192.05 and costs. The bailiff went into possession a day or so before the bankrupt executed an assignment for the benefit of creditors which was filed with the Official Receiver on 21 April. Before this occurred a second writ of seizure and sale was issued directing realization of some $4,300. It was not registered in the Personal Property Registry. After some exchanges between the trustee and the bailiff the latter surrendered possession of the seized goods to the trustee who, I understand, has caused them to be sold. We need not decide whether the bailiff's surrender was a mistake, as the Province says it was.

The trustee has recognized the claim of the Province to be treated as a secured creditor in the amount of taxes owing under the first writ of seizure and sale but has declined to recognize the costs sought by the bailiff as a secured claim nor to recognize as a secured claim the Province's claim under the second writ of seizure and sale. All of the foregoing reflects the effect as perceived by the trustee of provisions of the Act to which I will now turn.

· · ·

It is acknowledged the lien in question falls within the description in s. 87(1) as a "security provided for … the sole or principal purpose of securing a claim of Her Majesty in right of … a province." It is also acknowledged that registration of lien in respect of the second amount claimed, that is to say, under the second writ of seizure and sale, was not perfected before the bankruptcy of the debtor: see s. 87(1)(b) of the Act.

I will refer to other sections of the Act when I come to Mr. Butler's principal argument.

He says on behalf of the Province that the chambers judge erred in his analysis of all relevant statutory provisions. He contends, not that the costs of execution are themselves a secured claim, but, rather, that the security created by provincial law extends to the net amount owing. And, he says, as the province is entitled to realize under valid provincial legislation net of costs so must the notional realization here be net of costs.

He contends that realization net of costs is expressly authorized by valid provincial legislation and that the Act recognizes provincial legislation determines this result. As a first step, he referred us to s. 54 of the *Court Order Enforcement Act*, RSBC 1979, c. 75, which provides:

> 54. The sheriff or other officer shall pay over to the execution creditor the money recovered, or a part of it as is sufficient to discharge the amount by the writ of execution directed to be levied; and if, after satisfaction of the amount directed to be levied, together with sheriff's fees, poundage and expenses, any surplus remains in the hands of the sheriff or other officer, it shall be paid to the execution debtor.

There is no doubt this entitles the sheriff to deduct from the amount realized his costs. Mr. Butler says the same result must follow in the case at bar by virtue of s. 127 of the Act. ...

I think it clear s. 127 reflects a basic premise of the Act, namely, the right of a secured creditor to realize on his security. ...

This now brings me to the primary issue here, the construction of s. 86 and s. 87 of the Act in light of Mr. Butler's contentions with respect to the effect of provincial legislation.

I think the plain meaning of subs. (1) of s. 86 is clear: claims on behalf of the Crown in Right of either Canada or a Province rank as unsecured claims subject to subss. (2) and (3). Mr. Butler does not question the right of Parliament to enact s. 86. In my view the exceptions in subss. (2) and (3) are to be construed consistently with the scope of s. 86.

We are not concerned with the exceptions provided in subs. (2)(a) of s. 86; the security in question is not available to persons other than Her Majesty and its sole purpose is to create what I would call "after the fact" security.

Clause (b) of subs. (2) of s. 86 is relevant. The words "to the extent" which are found at the beginning of cl. (b) imply the exception is qualified, something less than a complete reversal of the unsecured ranking provided in s. 86(1).

The extent to which that ranking is to be varied is as follows: the words at the end of cl. (b)—"if the security is registered in accordance with that subsection"—is a condition precedent, the requirements of which are to be found in subs. (1) of s. 87. We go then to s. 87(1) and from that it is clear the registration in question must occur before the act of bankruptcy. That is sufficient, of course, to rule out the second writ of seizure and sale.

Then, going to subs. (2) of s. 87 I refer to cl. (b), which provides that the registration is valid "only" in respect of amounts owing to Her Majesty at the time of that registration. The emphatic "only" is exclusionary of other amounts. This is made clear by the clause that follows which permits the addition of interest accrued subsequent to the time of registration. No other addition to the sum owing at the time of registration is recognized.

Turning to the Act as a whole I am not persuaded s. 127 requires us to read s. 86 or s. 87 in a strained fashion as would be the case if we recognized the bailiff's costs which arise subsequent to registration are to be an exception to the general provision. Sections 86 and 87 deal with a particular problem and I see no reason why the general should govern the particular. I do not think s. 127 opens the door to a construction that flies in the face of the plain wording of s. 86 and s. 87.

We were also referred to s. 72(1) of the Act which provides:

> 72(1) The provisions of this Act shall not be deemed to abrogate or supersede the substantive provisions of any other law or statute relating to property and civil rights that are not in conflict with this Act, and the trustee is entitled to avail himself of all rights and remedies provided by that law or statute as supplementary to and in addition to the rights and remedies provided by this Act.

I do not think this assists Mr. Butler. Indeed, I would be inclined to the view that the construction he wishes to place on the provincial legislation in relation to the relevant federal legislation is in conflict with the Act but the constitutional issue is not before us.

I do not consider the result is either absurd or in conflict with the general scheme of the Act. If Parliament meant to provide for subsequent additions to the principal debt other than interest it could have done so. As it now stands, the effect is that only security to the extent to which public notice has been given is recognized.

The proposition that the bailiff's costs fall under s. 73(4) of the Act as costs of distress was not pressed. In my view it would fail as under any definition the proceeding taken by the Commissioner was not a distress.

Appeal dismissed.

NOTES AND QUESTIONS

1. Unlike some of the other priority rules of the BIA that apply to both bankruptcies and receiverships (see, for example, BIA ss. 14.06(7) and 81.1), ss. 86 to 87 apply only in bankruptcy proceedings. As a consequence, secured creditors will continue to have a strong incentive to put a debtor into bankruptcy if there are Crown claims that are afforded priority by statute over the claim of the secured creditor.

2. The *Bankruptcy and Insolvency General Rules*, CRC 368, s. 111, provide that a "prescribed system of registration," referred to in s. 86(2), "is a system of registration of securities that is available to Her Majesty in right of Canada or a province and to any other creditor holding a security, and is open to the public for inspection or for the making of searches." The provincial personal property security registries are therefore used in respect of security in personal property, while the provincial land registry systems are used in connection with real property.

3. Section 87(3) provides an exception in respect of the statutory garnishment device created by s. 224(1.2) of the *Income Tax Act*. This gives the Canadian Revenue Agency (CRA) the right to intercept debts that are owed by third parties to the debtor. The statute provides that this remedy has priority over a prior secured creditor who has a security interest in the debtor's accounts.

4. The personal property registries provide a notice filing system that permit a secured creditor to register a financing statement before a security agreement is entered into and a single registration may cover more than one security interest. Section 87(2) does not permit pre-registration of a Crown claim, and the registration of a Crown claim only covers obligations that are in existence at the time of the registration. What reasons might explain these restrictions on pre-registration of Crown claims?

C. Statutory Deemed Trusts

Although statutory deemed trusts are also created in an attempt to promote the ranking of certain kinds of claims, they do so through a different means. Instead of creating a lien or charge on the debtor's assets, they seek to create a trust in favour of the claimant. The legislation often contains an additional priority provision that gives the statutory deemed trust priority over the interests of a prior secured creditor.

British Columbia v. Henfrey Samson Belair Ltd.
(1989), 59 DLR (4th) 726 (SCC)

McLACHLIN J: The issue on this appeal is whether the statutory trust created by s. 18 of the British Columbia *Social Service Tax Act*, RSBC 1979, c. 388, gives the province priority over other creditors under the *Bankruptcy Act*, RSC 1970, c. B-3.

Tops Pontiac Buick Ltd. collected sales tax for the provincial government in the course of its business operations, as it was required to do by the *Social Service Tax Act*. Tops mingled the tax collected with its other assets. When the Canadian Imperial Bank of Commerce placed Tops in receivership pursuant to its debenture and Tops made an assignment in bankruptcy, the receiver sold the assets of Tops and applied the full proceeds in reduction of the indebtedness of the bank.

The province contends that the *Social Service Tax Act* creates a statutory trust over the assets of Tops equal to the amount of the sales tax collected but not remitted ($58,763.23), and that it has priority over the bank and all other creditors for this amount.

The chambers judge held that the *Social Service Tax Act* did not create a trust and that the province did not have priority [5 BCLR (2d) 212, 61 CBR (NS) 59]. On appeal the receiver conceded that the legislation created a statutory trust, but contended that the chambers judge was correct in ruling that the province did not have priority because the *Bankruptcy Act* did not confer priority on such a trust. The British Columbia Court of Appeal accepted this submission [40 DLR (4th) 728, 13 BCLR (2d) 346, [1987] 4 WWR 673, 65 CBR (NS) 24, 5 ACWS (3d) 47]. The province now appeals to this court.

The section of the *Social Service Tax Act* which the province contends gives it priority provides:

18(1) Where a person collects an amount of tax under this Act

(a) he shall be deemed to hold it in trust for Her Majesty in right of the Province for the payment over of that amount to Her Majesty in the manner and at the time required under this Act and regulations, and

(b) the tax collected shall be deemed to be held separate from and form no part of the person's money, assets or estate, whether or not the amount of the tax has in fact been kept separate and apart from either the person's own money or the assets of the estate of the person who collected the amount of the tax under this Act.

(2) The amount of taxes that, under this Act,

(a) is collected and held in trust, in accordance with subsection (1); or

(b) is required to be collected and remitted by a vendor or lessor

forms a lien and charge on the entire assets of

(c) the estate of the trustee under paragraph (a);

(d) the person required to collect or remit the tax under paragraph (b); or

(e) the estate of the person required to collect or remit the tax under paragraph (d).

The province argues that s. 18(1) creates a trust within s. 47(a) [now s. 67(1)(a)] of the *Bankruptcy Act*, which provides:

47. The property of a bankrupt divisible among his creditors shall not comprise

(a) property held by the bankrupt in trust for any other person;

The respondents, on the other hand, submit that the deemed statutory trust created by s. 18 of the *Social Service Tax Act* is not a trust within s. 47 the *Bankruptcy Act*, in that it does not possess the attributes of a true trust. They submit that the province's claim to the tax money is in fact a debt falling under s. 107(1)(j) of the *Bankruptcy Act*, the priority to which falls to be determined according to the priorities established by s. 107.[4]

107(1) Subject to the rights of secured creditors, the proceeds realized from the property of a bankrupt shall be applied in priority of payment as follows:

. . .

(j) claims of the Crown not previously mentioned in this section, in right of Canada or of any province, *pari passu* notwithstanding any statutory preference to the contrary.

Discussion

The issue may be characterized as follows. Section 47(a) of the *Bankruptcy Act* exempts trust property in the hands of the bankrupt from distribution to creditors, giving trust claimants absolute priority. Section 107(1) establishes priorities between creditors on distribution: s. 107(1)(j) ranks Crown claims last. Section 18 of the *Social Service Tax Act* creates a statutory trust which lacks the essential characteristics of a trust, namely, that the property impressed with the trust be identifiable or traceable. The question is whether the statutory trust created by the provincial legislation is a trust within s. 47(a) of the *Bankruptcy Act* or a mere Crown claim under s. 107(1)(j).

In my opinion, the answer to this question lies in the construction of the relevant provisions of the *Bankruptcy Act* and the *Social Service Tax Act*.

In approaching this task, I take as my guide the following passage from Driedger, *Construction of Statutes*, 2nd ed. (1983), at p. 105:

The decisions ... indicate that the provisions of an enactment relevant to a particular case are to be read in the following way:

1. The Act as a whole is to be read in its entire context so as to ascertain the intention of Parliament (the law as expressly or impliedly enacted by the words), the object of the Act (the ends sought to be achieved), and the scheme of the Act (the relation between the individual provisions of the Act).

2. The words of the individual provisions to be applied to the particular case under consideration are then to be read in their grammatical and ordinary sense in the light of the intention of Parliament embodied in the Act as a whole, the object of the Act and the scheme of the Act, and if they are clear and unambiguous and in harmony with that intention, object and scheme and with the general body of the law, that is the end.

With these principles in mind, I turn to the construction of ss. 47(a) and 107(1)(j) of the *Bankruptcy Act*. The question which arises under s. 47(a) of the Act concerns the meaning of the phrase "property held by the bankrupt in trust for any other person." Taking the words in their ordinary sense, they connote a situation where there is property which can be identified as being held in trust. That property is to be removed from other assets in the hands of the bankrupt before distribution under the *Bankruptcy Act* because, in equity, it belongs to another person. The intention of Parliament in enacting s. 47(a), then, was to permit removal of property which can be specifically identified as not belonging to the bankrupt under general principles of trust law from the distribution scheme established by the *Bankruptcy Act*.

Section 107(1)(j), on the other hand, has been held to deal not with rights conferred by general law, but with the statutorily created claims of federal and provincial tax collectors. The purpose of s. 107(1)(j) was discussed by this court in *Re Bourgault* (1979), 105 DLR (3d) 270, [1980] 1 SCR 35 *sub nom. Deputy Minister of Revenue v. Rainville*, 33 CBR (NS) 301, Pigeon J, speaking for the majority, stated at p. 278:

> There is no need to consider the scope of the expression "claims of the Crown." It is quite clear that this applies to claims of provincial governments for taxes and I think it is obvious that it does not include claims not secured by Her Majesty's personal preference, but by a privilege which may be obtained by anyone under general rules of law, such as a vendor's or a builder's privilege.

If ss. 47(a) and 107(1)(f) are read in this way, no conflict arises between them. If a trust claim is established under general principles of law, then the property subject to the trust is removed from the general distribution by reason of s. 47(a). Following the reasoning of Pigeon J in *Rainville*, such a claim would not fall under s. 107(1)(j) because it is valid under general principles of law and is not a claim secured by the Crown's personal preference.

This construction of ss. 47(a) and 107(1)(j) of the *Bankruptcy Act* conforms with the principle that provinces cannot create priorities under the *Bankruptcy Act* by their own legislation, a principle affirmed by this court in *Re Deloitte, Haskins & Sells Ltd. and Workers' Compensation Board* (1985), 19 DLR (4th) 577, [1985] 1 SCR 785, [1985] 4 WWR 481 (SCC). As Wilson J stated at p. 592:

> … the issue in *Re Bourgault* and *Re Black Forest* was not whether a proprietary interest has been created under the relevant provincial legislation. It was whether provincial legislation,

even if it did create a proprietary interest, could defeat the scheme of distribution under s. 107(1) of the *Bankruptcy Act*. These cases held that it could not, that while the provincial legislation could validly secure debts on the property of the debtor in a non-bankruptcy situation, once bankruptcy occurred s. 107(1) determined the status and priority of the claims specifically dealt with in the section. It was not open to the claimant in bankruptcy to say: By virtue of the applicable provincial legislation I am a secured creditor within the meaning of the opening words of s. 107(1) of the *Bankruptcy Act* and therefore the priority accorded my claim under the relevant paragraph of s. 107(1) does not apply to me. In effect, this is the position adopted by the Court of Appeal and advanced before us by the respondent. It cannot be supported as a matter of statutory interpretation of s. 107(1) since, if the section were to be read in this way, it would have the effect of permitting the provinces to determine priorities on a bankruptcy, a matter within exclusive federal jurisdiction.

While *Re Deloitte, Haskins & Sells Ltd. and Workers' Compensation Board* was concerned with provincial legislation purporting to give the province the status of a secured creditor for purposes of the *Bankruptcy Act*, the same reasoning applies in the case at bar.

To interpret s. 47(a) as applying not only to trusts as defined by the general law, but to statutory trusts created by the provinces lacking the common law attributes of trusts, would be to permit the provinces to create their own priorities under the *Bankruptcy Act* and to invite a differential scheme of distribution on bankruptcy from province to province.

Practical policy considerations also recommend this interpretation of the *Bankruptcy Act*. The difficulties of extending s. 47(a) to cases where no specific property impressed with a trust can be identified are formidable and defy fairness and common sense. For example, if the claim for taxes equalled or exceeded the funds in the hands of the trustee in bankruptcy, the trustee would not recover the costs incurred to realize the funds. Indeed, the trustee might be in breach of the Act by expending funds to realize the bankrupt's assets. Other difficulties would arise in the case of more than one claimant to the trust property. The spectre is raised of a person who has a valid trust claim under the general principles of trust law to a specific piece of property, finding himself in competition with the Crown claiming a statutory trust in that and all the other property. Could the Crown's general claim pre-empt the property interest of the claimant under trust law? Or would the claimant under trust law prevail? To admit of such a possibility would be to run counter to the clear intention of Parliament in enacting the *Bankruptcy Act* of setting up a clear and orderly scheme for the distribution of the bankrupt's assets.

In summary, I am of the view that s. 47(a) should be confined to trusts arising under general principles of law, while s. 107(1)(j) should be confined to claims such as tax claims not established by general law but secured "by her Majesty's personal preference" through legislation. This conclusion, in my opinion, is supported by the wording of the sections in question, by the jurisprudence of this court, and by the policy considerations to which I have alluded.

I turn next to s. 18 of the *Social Service Tax Act* and the nature of the legal interests created by it. At the moment of collection the trust property is identifiable and the trust meets the requirements for a trust under the principles of trust law. The difficulty in this, as in most cases, is that the trust property soon ceases to be identifiable. The tax money is mingled with other money in the hands of the merchant and converted to other property so that it cannot be traced. At this point it is no longer a trust under general principles of law. In an attempt to meet this problem, s. 18(1)(b) states that tax collected shall be deemed to be held separate from and form no part of the collector's money, assets or estate. But, as the presence of the deeming provision tacitly acknowledges, the reality is that after conversion the statutory trust bears little resemblance to a true trust. There is no property which can be regarded as being impressed with a trust. Because of this, s. 18(2) goes on to provide that the unpaid tax forms a lien and charge on the entire assets of the collector, an interest in the nature of a secured debt.

Applying these observations on s. 18 of the *Social Service Tax Act* to the construction of ss. 47(a) and 107(1)(j) of the *Bankruptcy Act* which I have earlier adopted, the answer to the question of whether the province's interest under s. 18 is a "trust" under s. 47(a) or a "claim of the Crown" under s. 107(1)(j) depends on the facts of the particular case. If the money collected for tax is identifiable or traceable, then the true state of affairs conforms with the ordinary meaning of "trust" and the money is exempt from distribution to creditors by reason of s. 47(a). If, on the other hand, the money has been converted to other property and cannot be traced, there is no "property held ... in trust" under s. 47(a). The province has a claim secured only by a charge or lien, and s. 107(1)(j) applies.

In the case at bar, no specific property impressed with a trust can be identified. It follows that s. 47(a) of the *Bankruptcy Act* should not be construed as extending to the province's claim in this case.

The Province, however, argues that it is open to it to define "trust" however it pleases, property and civil rights being matters within provincial competence. The short answer to this submission is that the definition of trust which is operative for purposes of exemption under the *Bankruptcy Act* must be that of the federal Parliament, not the provincial legislatures. The provinces may define "trust" as they choose for matters within their own legislative competence, but they cannot dictate to Parliament how it should be defined for purposes of the *Bankruptcy Act*: *Re Deloitte, Haskins & Sells Ltd. and Workers' Compensation Board.*

Nor does the argument that the tax money remains the property of the Crown throughout withstand scrutiny. If that were the case, there would be no need for the lien and charge in the Crown's favour created by s. 18(2) of the *Social Service Tax Act.* The province has a trust interest and hence property in the tax funds so long as they can be identified or traced. But once they lose that character, any common law or equitable property interest disappears. The province is left with a statutory deemed trust which does not give it the same property interest a common law trust would, supplemented by a lien and charge over all the bankrupt's property under s. 18(2).

The province relies on *Re Phoenix Paper Products Ltd.* (1983), 3 DLR (4th) 617, 44 OR (2d) 225, 48 CBR (NS) 113, where the Ontario Court of Appeal held that accrued vacation pay mixed with other assets of a bankrupt constituted a trust under s. 47(a) of the *Bankruptcy Act.* As the Court of Appeal in this case pointed out, the Ontario Court of Appeal in *Re Phoenix Paper Products Ltd.*, in considering the two divergent lines of authority presented to it, did not have the advantage of considering what was said in *Re*

Deloitte, Haskins & Sells and Workers' Compensation Board, and the affirmation in that case of the line of authority which the Ontario Court of Appeal rejected.

• • •

Conclusion

For the reasons stated, I conclude that s. 47(a) of the *Bankruptcy Act* does not apply in this case and the priority of the province's claim is governed by s. 107(1)(j) of the Act. I would decline to answer the alternative question posed by the appellants.

Appeal dismissed.

NOTE

BIA s. 67(2) provides that property of a bankrupt shall not be regarded as held in trust for the purposes of s. 67(1)(a) unless it would be so regarded in the absence of statutory provision. This provision governs when a statutory deemed trust is created in favour of the Crown. However, sometimes a statutory deemed trust is conferred on a person other than the Crown—for example, the Ontario *Pension Benefits Act, 1987*, SO 1987, c. 35 contains the following provisions:

> 57(3) An employer who is required to pay contributions to a pension fund shall be deemed to hold in trust for the beneficiaries of the pension plan an amount of money equal to the employer contributions due and not paid into the pension fund.
>
> s. 57(5) The administrator of the pension plan has a lien and charge on the assets of the employer in an amount equal to the amounts deemed to be held in trust under subsections (1), (3) and (4).

There is both a narrow and a broad interpretation of the *Henfrey* decision. The narrow view is that the decision must be restricted to cases where a province is attempting to use a statutory deemed trust to elevate a claim that is designated as a preferred claim under the BIA. On this view, *Henfrey* would not apply in respect of a statutory deemed trust that is created in favour of an ordinary unsecured creditor; the claimant could therefore assert the trust in the bankruptcy. The broad view is that the court in *Henfrey* intended to establish the general proposition that, in order to fall within BIA s. 67(1)(a), every trust must satisfy the requirements of a trust under principles of trust law. The Ontario Court of Appeal in *Re Ivaco* (2006), 275 DLR (4th) 132 (Ont. CA) adopted this broad view and held that a statutory deemed trust in respect of unpaid pension contributions (which is not designated as a preferred claim under s. 136(1) of the BIA) did not qualify as a trust under s. 67(1)(a) of the BIA.

D. Deemed Trusts Under the Income Tax Act

One of the most significant deemed trusts recognized by the BIA is the claim of the CCRA arising under s. 227(4.1) of the *Income Tax Act*. The scope of the deemed trust is wide and it has been described as providing the CRAL with a "superpriority." What is the nature of the so-called superpriority and what is the rationale for protecting this Crown claim in this manner? In *First Vancouver Finance v. Canada (Minister of National Revenue—MNR)* (2002), 212 DLR (4th) 615, at 624 (SCC), Iacobucci J offered the following justification for the deemed trust arising under the *Income Tax Act*:

> The collection of source deductions has been recognized as "at the heart" of income tax collection in Canada: see *Pembina on the Red Development Corp. v. Triman Industries Ltd.* (1991), 85 DLR (4th) 29 (Man. CA), at p. 51, per Lyon JA (dissenting), quoted with approval by Gonthier J (dissenting on another issue) in *Royal Bank of Canada v. Sparrow Electric Corp.*, [1997] 1 SCR 411, at para. 36. Because of the importance of collecting source deductions, the legislation in question gives the Minister the vehicle of the deemed trust to recover employee tax deductions which employers fail to remit to the Minister.
>
> It has also been noted that, in contrast to a tax debtor's bank which is familiar with the tax debtor's business and finances, the Minister does not have the same level of knowledge of the tax debtor or its creditors, and cannot structure its affairs with the tax debtor accordingly. Thus, as an "involuntary creditor," the Minister must rely on its ability to collect source deductions under the ITA: Pembina on the Red Development, *supra*, at pp. 33-34, per Scott CJM, approved by Cory J in Alberta (Treasury Branches), *supra*, at paras. 16-18. For the above reasons, under the terms of the ITA, the Minister has been given special priority over other creditors to collect unremitted taxes.

The justification for priority of government tax claims has been debated widely. As the following extract indicates, the claim that the Crown is an involuntary creditor is a contentious issue.

Barbara K. Morgan, "Should the Sovereign Be Paid First—A Comparative International Analysis of the Priority for Tax Claims in Bankruptcy"
(2000), 74 *Am. Bankr. LJ* 461, at 463-68

Traditionally, there have been several justifications for the priority for tax claims. First, unlike the claims of private commercial creditors, tax claims are for the benefit of the entire community. The priority protects the revenue base for the common good, and avoids shifting the burden of the debtor's unpaid taxes to other taxpayers.

Second, unlike private creditors, taxing authorities are involuntary creditors, unable to choose their debtor or obtain security for debt before extending credit. The priority compensates for this disadvantage, giving the taxing authorities an opportunity to assess the amounts due and mobilize their collection remedies.

Third, with regard to taxes for which the debtor acts as the government's tax collector—such as sales tax, value added tax, or employee withholding tax—the argument is made that, if no priority or trust is imposed, the moneys collected by the debtor will increase the estate for the benefit of unsecured creditors. In these circumstances, the tax priority operates to prevent a windfall to general unsecured creditors who have no fair claim to the collected funds.

Fourth, some argue that if the taxing authorities are not reasonably secure they will be discouraged from negotiating payment terms with debtors, thus forcing premature and possibly unnecessary business failures.

Finally, it can be argued that the priority is needed to effectuate an individual debtor's discharge, where tax liabilities are made nondischargeable in order to discourage tax evasion through bankruptcy. Granting priority to those nondischargeable tax debts supports the individual debtor's rehabilitation, making it more likely that the tax claims will be paid in a personal bankruptcy and that the debtor will be left with fewer nondischargeable debts at the conclusion of the proceeding.

· · ·

As new forms of taxation have been created and tax rates have increased, tax claims have consumed more and more of an insolvent debtor's estate, leading to questions about the tax priority. Critics of the priority reject the community interest argument, contending that the debt owed to the government is unlikely to be significant in terms of total government receipts, whereas the loss to private creditors may cause substantial hardship and precipitate additional insolvencies. Moreover, to the extent private creditors receive a higher return on their claims, part of the loss to the taxing authorities can be recouped through additional taxes paid by those creditors. And, of course, a loss of priority does not prevent the taxing authorities from sharing in an insolvent estate pro rata with general unsecured creditors.

Critics of the priority similarly reject the involuntary creditor argument, on the ground that the government has other enhancements of its ability to collect debts, offsetting its involuntary position, that are not shared by private creditors, including (1) the imposition of penalties and relatively high interest rates, (2) third party liability, and (3) collection procedures such as statutory lien and levy. Furthermore, there is no general rule that involuntary creditors should receive priority—several other categories of involuntary creditors are not entitled to any kind of priority.

Critics also argue that abolishing priority for tax claims will provide a greater incentive to the taxing authorities to collect taxes in a commercially reasonable manner, by removing reliance on an artificial ability to be paid ahead of other creditors. These critics reject the argument that priority can be beneficial to the rehabilitation process and argue instead that any incentive to delay collection is counterproductive. According to this view, delaying collection compromises the uniform enforcement of the tax laws and constitutes a state subsidy, which undermines the disciplinary force of an effective insolvency law. Particularly in situations where the debtor is acting as tax collector, the taxing authorities have better information available about the debtor's financial condition than general business creditors. The debtor is required to submit periodic returns in connection with payroll, value added taxes, sales taxes, and taxes withheld from employee wages, and the authorities receiving these returns are likely to know without delay when there is a delinquency. Allowing tax debts to accumulate under those circumstances can unfairly disadvantage other unsecured creditors who go on trading with the debtor not knowing that there is a tax delinquency.

NOTES AND QUESTIONS

1. Does the existence of the deemed trust have any impact on the Crown's incentive to monitor for arrears? For contrasting views see: Andrew Keay and Peter Walton, "The Preferential Debts Regime in Liquidation Law: In the Public Interest?" (1999), 3 *CFILR* 84; Susan

Cantlie, "Preferred Priority in Bankruptcy," in Jacob S. Ziegel, ed., *Current Developments in International and Comparative Corporate Insolvency Law* (Oxford: Clarendon Press, 1994), 413. The CCRA position on monitoring is contained in its policy document "Deemed Trust—A Responsible Application Policy" (CCRA, Accounts Receivable Division Publications, 2001-01, March 7, 2002):

> Since the Crown's priority results from legislation that is binding on third parties, the CCRA is not obliged to monitor the person's business, to issue forms or claims, or to register or publish notice of its priority rights. However, within the limits imposed by the ITA ... provisions regarding confidentiality of information, every reasonable effort will be made to give third parties timely notice of any claims of deemed trust by the CCRA.

2. The CCRA (now CRA) claims the "payroll withholding ... [mechanism] generate[s] not only most of the funds required for the federal government's own operations, but also the amounts redistributed through various social programs." ("Deemed Trust—A Responsible Application Policy," above. Does this justify the deemed trust priority?

3. Secured creditors have long objected to the Crown's attempt to override consensual security interests. Ziegel notes that secured creditors object to the "unfairness and destabilizing effect of super-priority liens that undermine security agreements made in good faith by a secured creditor before the taxpayer was in default in its statutory obligations or, at any rate, where the secured creditor was not privy to the default and had done nothing to encourage it" (Jacob S. Ziegel, "Conditional Sales and Superpriority Crown Claims Under the ITA s. 227" (2003), 38 CBR (4th) 161). In the face of the existence of the deemed trust, secured creditors have sought to convince the courts to give a narrow interpretation to the provisions. In some instances, secured creditors have been successful. However, as Ziegel notes "[s]uch victories, however, are usually short-lived because the federal government has often reacted quickly to reverse an unfavourable judicial construction by amending the ITA" (Jacob S. Ziegel, "Conditional Sales and Superpriority Crown Claims Under the ITA s. 227" (2003), above).

4. One such victory over the Crown occurred in *Royal Bank of Canada v. Sparrow Electric Corp.* (1997), 143 DLR (4th) 385 (SCC). In *Sparrow*, the court was called on to interpret the scope of the deemed trust as it then existed under ss. 227(4) and 227(5) of the ITA. See Kevin Davis, "Priority of Crown Claims in Insolvency: Royal Bank of Canada v. Sparrow Electric Corp. ((1997) 143 DLR 4th 385) and Its Aftermath?" (1997), 29 *CBLJ* 145. The *Sparrow* decision and the consequent 1998 amendments to the ITA were discussed by the Supreme Court of Canada in *First Vancouver Finance v. Canada (Minister of National Revenue—MNR*, below.

First Vancouver Finance v. Canada (Minister of National Revenue—MNR)
(2002), 212 DLR (4th) 615 (SCC)

IACOBUCCI J (for the Court): This Court had occasion to interpret the deemed trust provisions in *Sparrow Electric, supra*. At that time, the relevant provisions were ss. 227(4) and 227(5) of the ITA which read as follows:

227(4) Every person who deducts or withholds any amount under this Act shall be deemed to hold the amount so deducted or withheld in trust for Her Majesty.

(5) Notwithstanding any provision of the *Bankruptcy Act*, in the event of any liquidation, assignment, receivership or bankruptcy of or by a person, an amount equal to any amount

(a) deemed by subsection (4) to be held in trust for Her Majesty, or

· · ·

shall be deemed to be separate from and form no part of the estate in liquidation, assignment, receivership or bankruptcy, whether or not that amount has in fact been kept separate and apart from the person's own moneys or from the assets of the estate.

In *Sparrow Electric*, both Royal Bank and the Minister claimed an interest in the proceeds of inventory of the tax debtor. In characterizing the nature of the deemed trust provisions, Gonthier J (dissenting, but not on this issue) stated at para. 34 that, even if collateral was subject to a fixed charge at the time of a triggering event such as bankruptcy or liquidation, the deemed trust operated to attach the Minister's interest to such collateral as long as it was not subject to the fixed charge at the time the source deductions were made:

Thus, s. 227(5) [now 227(4.1)] alternatively permits Her Majesty's interest to attach retroactively to the disputed collateral if the competing security interest has attached *after* the deductions giving rise to Her Majesty's claim in fact occurred. Conceptually, the s. 227(5) deemed trust allows Her Majesty's claim to go back in time and attach its outstanding s. 227(4) interest to the collateral before that collateral became subject to a fixed charge. [Emphasis in original.]

Royal Bank's interest was characterized as a fixed and specific charge over the inventory of the tax debtor. This had the effect of making the bank the legal owner of inventory as it came into possession of the tax debtor, subject to the debtor's equitable right of redemption. The majority of the Court concluded that, since the inventory was subject to the bank's security interest before the deductions giving rise to the deemed trust occurred, the bank's interest attached to the inventory in priority to Her Majesty's interest under the deemed trust.

However, in reaching this conclusion, the majority of the Court noted at para. 112 that Parliament was free to grant absolute priority to the deemed trust by adopting the appropriate language:

Finally, I wish to emphasize that it is open to Parliament to step in and assign absolute priority to the deemed trust. A clear illustration of how this might be done is afforded by s. 224(1.2) ITA, which vests certain moneys in the Crown "notwithstanding any security interest in those moneys" and provides that they "shall be paid to the Receiver General in priority to any such security interest." All that is needed to effect the desired result is clear language of that kind.

In response to *Sparrow Electric*, the deemed trust provisions were amended in 1998 (retroactively to 1994) to their current form. Most notably, the words "notwithstanding any security interest … in the amount so deducted, or withheld" were added to s. 227(4).

As well, s. 227(4.1) (formerly s. 227(5)) expanded the scope of the deemed trust to include "property held by any secured creditor ... that but for a security interest ... would be property of the person." Section 227(4.1) was also amended to remove reference to the triggering events of liquidation, bankruptcy, etc., instead deeming property of the tax debtor and of secured creditors to be held in trust "at any time an amount deemed by subsection (4) to be held by a person in trust for Her Majesty is not paid to Her Majesty in the manner and at the time provided under this Act." Finally, s. 227(4.1) now explicitly deems the trust to operate "from the time the amount was deducted or withheld."

It is apparent from these changes that the intent of Parliament when drafting ss. 227(4) and 227(4.1) was to grant priority to the deemed trust in respect of property that is also subject to a security interest regardless of when the security interest arose in relation to the time the source deductions were made or when the deemed trust takes effect. This is clear from the use of the words "notwithstanding any security interest" in both ss. 227(4) and 227(4.1). In other words, Parliament has reacted to the interpretation of the deemed trust provisions in *Sparrow Electric*, and has amended the provisions to grant priority to the deemed trust in situations where the Minister and secured creditors of a tax debtor both claim an interest in the tax debtor's property.

As noted above, Parliament has also amended the deemed trust provisions in regard to the timing of the trust. Reference to events triggering operation of the deemed trust such as liquidation or bankruptcy have been removed. Section 227(4.1) now states that the deemed trust begins to operate "*at any time* [source deductions are] not paid to Her Majesty in the manner and at the time provided under this Act" (emphasis added). Thus, the deemed trust is now triggered at the moment a default in remitting source deductions occurs. Further, pursuant to s. 227(4.1)(a), the trust is deemed to be in effect "from the time the amount was deducted or withheld." Thus, while a default in remitting source deductions triggers the operation of the trust, the trust is deemed to have been in existence retroactively to the time the source deductions were made. It is evident from these changes that Parliament has made a concerted effort to broaden and strengthen the deemed trust in order to facilitate the collection efforts of the Minister.

NOTES AND QUESTIONS

1. In *First Vancouver*, the court considered whether after-acquired property (that is, property that came into the tax debtor's hands after the deemed trust arose) was subject to the trust. In addition, the court also considered whether the sale of trust property releases property from the trust. The court held (at 619) that the "trust arises the moment the tax debtor fails to remit source deductions by the specified due date, but is deemed to have been in existence from the moment the deductions were made. ... [Therefore,] at any given point in time, whatever property then belonging to the tax debtor is subject to the deemed trust." The court also held that property that is sold is released from the trust. However, the proceeds of the sale are "captured by the trust."

2. The deemed trust is subject to the right of an unpaid supplier to repossess goods (s. 81.1) and the special rights of farmers, fishermen, and aquaculturalists (s. 81.2). These provisions are discussed in Chapter 9. In light of the all encompassing nature of the deemed trust, why would Parliament carve out an exception for unpaid suppliers?

3. Section 227(4.2) of the ITA excludes certain limited prescribed security interests and thus provides further limited exceptions to the deemed trust. Section 2201 of the *Income Tax Regulations* says that a mortgage on land or a building that was voluntarily given and "registered pursuant to the appropriate land registration system before the time the amount is deemed to be held in trust by the person" is a prescribed security interest. Such a specified security interest will take priority over the deemed trust. However, where such a secured creditor has security interests over other forms of property, the value of those other interests will be taken into account in assessing the secured creditor's position *vis-à-vis* the Crown: s. 2201(2) of the *Income Tax Regulations*.

4. As noted above, secured creditors have sought to convince the courts to take a narrow interpretation of the deemed trust. A relevant interpretive issue is the definition of "security interest." As the deemed trust takes priority over secured creditors, the scope of such priority will turn on how the court interprets that term as defined in s. 224(1.3) of the ITA.

Canada (Deputy Attorney General) v. Schwab Construction Ltd.
[2002] 4 WWR 628 (Sask. CA)

LANE JA (for the court): The Federal Government ("Crown"), as represented by the Minister of Customs and Revenue, appeals a decision out of Queen's Bench chambers dismissing its application to have a receiver appointed for the purpose of collecting and disposing of the assets of the bankrupt, Schwab Construction Ltd. ("Schwab" or "bankrupt"). The Crown contended that all of the equipment of the bankrupt is property beneficially owned by the Crown in priority to the interests of the respondents by virtue of ss. 227(4) and (4.1) of the *Income Tax Act* [RSC 1985, c. 1, 5th Supp.] ("the Act"), the so-called superpriority provisions.

The application also involved the Saskatoon Credit Union, the Kenaston Credit Union, and Joe Gourley Construction Ltd. as secured creditors of the bankrupt, however on appeal the credit unions did not defend their interests and the Crown abandoned its appeal of that portion of the order pertaining to the construction company.

The respondents' position below and on appeal is they do not have secured interests as defined in s. 224 of the *Income Tax Act* as leases do not come within such definition.

The facts are more completely set out in the judgment below but a brief summary is as follows: the bankrupt did not submit the required payroll source deductions for income tax, Canada pension, and employment insurance totalling over $350,000 including interest and penalties. The Crown claimed the sum of approximately $272,000 as the amount it claimed to be held in trust as property beneficially owned by the Crown pursuant to the provisions of ss. 227(4) and (4.1) of the Act. The Crown claimed each of the respondents was a secured creditor of the bankrupt having supplied to, or financed the acquisition of, equipment held by the bankrupt and that each held a security interest in the equipment.

All agreements in issue were described as "leases," with the title to the equipment being reserved and not passing until the financing institution was fully paid, the exception being a Mack truck financed by the Canadian Western Bank (CWB) which was to be returned to the vendor after 30 months. Save for that piece of equipment the bankrupt had the option to purchase at the end of the lease, the equipment financed by the CWB for $100 per lease agreement. In the cases of Ford and GMAC, there was a buy back option with a residual price of an estimated depreciated value at the end of the lease. The details of the agreements are set out in the decision of the chambers judge.

The following are the relevant provisions of the Act:

[The court set out in full ss. 224(1.3), 227(4), and 227(4.1).]

The Crown took the position the equipment, in all cases, was the property of the bankrupt because of all of the "incidents" of ownership supported only a finding the equipment was owned by Schwab. In the Canadian Western Bank agreement the appellant says the master lease agreement was, in effect, a money purchase plan and not a lease because there was only a nominal sum required to be paid by the bankrupt to obtain title after all obligations were met.

The Crown argued the definition of "security interest" is broad enough to include "leases" of the nature of those in question. The Crown contended it was entitled to a priority over all of the property and did not argue it was entitled to only a priority over any equity or property interest, if any, the bankrupt may have had in any of the equipment. Further, the Crown argued the agreements in issue are agreements "to secure the payment or performance of an obligation."

I am of the view the chambers judge was correct. The equipment covered by the lease was not the property of the bankrupt and the leases were not "a security interest" within the meeting of s. 224(1.3) of the Act. As the chambers judge stated, "[t]o decide otherwise would allow the applicant (the Crown) to claim as part of its deemed trust property not owned by the bankrupt but owned by an innocent third party who had just agreed to allow the bankrupt to use its property for a certain price pursuant to the terms of a lease agreement." She correctly found that finding the Crown had a priority interest would offend the principle as set out in *Royal Bank of Canada v. Sparrow Electric Corporation*, [1997] 1 SCR 411 by Gonthier J:

> This provision does not permit Her Majesty to attach Her beneficial interest to property which, at the time of liquidation, assignment, receivership or bankruptcy, in law belongs to a party other than the tax debtor. Section 227(4) and (5) are manifestly directed towards the property of the tax debtor, and it would be contrary to well-established authority to stretch the interpretation of section 227(5) to permit the expropriation of the property of third parties who are not specifically mentioned in the statute. [At para. 39.]

I might add he went on to refer to the presumption against expropriation of property where he quoted Twaddle JA in *Re Pembina on the Red Development Corp. Ltd. v. Triman Industries Ltd.* [(1991), 85 DLR (4th) 29 (Man. CA)]: "It is a long-established principle of law that, in the absence of clear language contrary, a tax on one person cannot be collected out of property belonging to another." [at p. 46]

The appeal must therefore be dismissed with costs on double Column V.

NOTE

In *DaimlerChrysler Financial Services (debis) Canada Inc. v. Mega Pets Ltd.* (2002), 212 DLR (4th) 41 (BCCA), the court also considered the definition of "security interest" under the ITA. The court held that the interest under a conditional sales agreement does not create a security interest as defined under the ITA. This case is reproduced and discussed in Anthony Duggan and Jacob S. Ziegel, *Secured Transactions in Personal Property and Suretyships: Cases, Text and Materials*, 5th ed. (Toronto: Emond Montgomery Publications, 2009), Chapter 10. Ziegel argues that Newbury JA in *DaimlerChrysler* was too quick to reject the relevance of the BCPPSA as an aid in construing s. 224(1.3). Further, he argues that the wording of s. 224(1.3) illustrates that Parliament intended "security interest" to have the same meaning as under provincial personal property security acts. What language of s. 224(1.3) suggests that Parliament intended the provision to be interpreted in the light of provincial PPS statutes? See Jacob S. Ziegel, "Conditional Sales and Superpriority Crown Claims Under the ITA s. 227" (2003), 38 CBR (4th) 161.

E. Reform Options

The priority of Crown claims continues to be raised as an area in need of reform. Professor Cuming, in a report prepared for Industry Canada, canvassed a number of reform options including comprehensive legislation to cover Crown security interests. See Ronald C.C. Cuming, "An Approach to the Rationalization of Enforcement of Federal and Provincial Crown Claims" (October 1999) (unpublished, prepared for Industry Canada: Corporate Law Policy Directorate). The Cuming Crown claims paper argues the case for a new statutory regime to rationalize and simplify the law. It recommends a new uniform system of rules to govern Crown claim priorities inside and outside bankruptcy. The paper identifies four main policy objectives (at 88):

1. to ensure that effective remedies are available to the Crown to enforce Crown claims;

2. to facilitate legal risk assessment in order to give as much certainty as possible to private financing transactions;

3. to avoid, wherever possible, confiscation of existing third-party interests to pay Crown claims; and

4. to eliminate the initiation of bankruptcy proceedings by secured creditors in order to trigger a priority flip.

The paper argues that the most significant issue needing to be addressed is the effect of Crown claims on secured creditors' rights. The reason is that, in the case of a business insolvency, secured creditors typically have the first legal right to enforce their claims against the debtor's assets. There is unlikely to be much left over for unsecured creditors. This means that unsecured creditors in many cases will be relatively indifferent to whether Crown claims have priority or not. Therefore the main consideration that needs to be taken into account is not "fairness" to unsecured creditors but, rather, the effect that giving priority to Crown claims has on the practices of secured credit providers and their willingness to lend (*supra*, at 80). Other commentators take a different view: see, for example, the Tassé Report, at 123.

The paper acknowledges that the capacity of the federal government to reform the laws governing Crown claim priorities is subject to constitutional constraints. As far as Canada Crown claims are concerned, the government has carte blanche. However, as far as provincial Crown claims are concerned, the government must rely on the bankruptcy and insolvency power. This means that it can legislate with respect to provincial Crown claim priorities only in cases where the debtor is bankrupt or has made a BIA or CCAA reorganization proposal (Tassé Report, at 78-79). Subject to these constitutional constraints, the paper recommends the enactment, in a federal Crown priorities act, of a system for priority of Crown claims based on concepts contained in the provincial personal property security laws. There would be appropriate modifications to reflect the special features of Crown claims and the position of the Crown as a non-adjusting creditor.

The main features of the Cuming proposal are as follows.

1. The new Act would establish two regimes, one to deal with federal Crown claim priorities in non-bankruptcy situations (including receiverships), and the other to deal with both federal and provincial Crown claim priorities in bankruptcy and insolvency proceedings.

2. Outside bankruptcy:

   a. the priority of a provincial Crown claim would be determined by reference to the provincial statute that creates the claim; and

   b. the priority of a Canada Crown claim would be determined by the new Act.

3. Inside bankruptcy, the priority of provincial and Canada Crown claims would be determined by the new Act.

4. A Crown claim ("Crown security interest")

   a. in personal property would be registerable as a security interest in the PPSA registry of the province where the debtor is located; or

   b. in real property would be registerable in the real property registry of the province where the real property is located.

5. A Crown security interest would not be registrable until the debtor has defaulted on its obligation to the Crown. When the debtor moves to another jurisdiction, a Crown security interest relating to personal property would be registrable in the PPS registry of the new jurisdiction within 60 days of the date the relevant government agency acquires notice of the debtor's move. As a general rule, if a Crown security interest is registered within the 60-day period, it would be deemed to have been continuously registered in the new jurisdiction from the date it was first registered in the old jurisdiction.

6. As a general rule, a registered Crown security interest would have priority over a prior interest in the collateral to the same extent as a registered or perfected subsequent consensual security interest other than a purchase money security interest would have priority.

7. A person who acquires an interest in property that is subject to a Crown security interest would take free of the Crown security interest if, at the time of the acquisition, the Crown security interest was not registered. Otherwise the person would, as a general rule, take subject to the Crown security interest.

8. A buyer or lessee of goods for personal or family purposes without knowledge of the Crown security interest would take free of the Crown security interest.

9. The priority that a Crown security interest has by virtue of registration would extend to all amounts owing by the debtor to the Crown that are covered by the claim, including all amounts that become owing prior to the discharge of the registration.

10. The Crown's priority would extend to after-acquired property.

11. As a general rule, a registered Crown security interest would be subordinate to prior registered security interests.

12. A registered Crown security interest would not be subordinate to a prior perfected security interest with respect to advances made by the holder of the prior perfected security interest after being given notice of the Crown security interest.

13. In the case of a competition between: (1) a registered Crown security interest affecting accounts of a debtor who has collected money on behalf of the Crown but has failed to remit the proceeds, and (2) a prior registered consensual security interest in the accounts, the Crown would have priority after notice of the Crown security interest has been given to the accounts security holder.

14. In a case where there were two or more security interests, the amount of the Crown claim would be distributed on a pro rata basis between them.

The concept of a Crown priorities act (CPA) is also discussed in David Baird and Scott Bomhof, "Crown Priorities Forum: Lawyers Perspective" (March 22, 2002) (unpublished). See also Canada, Corporate Law Policy Directorate and Revenue Collections Directorate, "Crown Priorities in Business Insolvencies" (Industry Canada and CCRA, 2001). While the Cuming and Baird and Bomhof proposals differ on some issues, they agree on one central feature. Both proposals would require that Crown claims be registered in the appropriate provincial personal property or land registry. A federal CPA, which would cover both federal and provincial Crown claims, would provide a priority scheme to rank consensual secured creditors and Crown claims. Both the Cuming and Baird and Bomhof proposals contemplate exceptions or special priority rules for certain types of Crown claims.

CHAPTER NINE

Ranking of Creditors and Distribution of Proceeds

I. THE BANKRUPTCY SCHEME OF DISTRIBUTION

From the creditors' perspective, no bankruptcy topic is more controversial than the ranking of creditors' claims in the distribution of the bankrupt's estate—understandably so because the creditors are fighting over their share in what is almost invariably a seriously depleted estate. Under the BIA (ss. 136-141), creditors' claims are ranked in the following order:

1. secured creditors' claims;
2. preferred creditors (s. 136(1));
3. ordinary unsecured creditors (s. 141); and
4. postponed creditors (ss. 137-140.1).

Technically speaking, secured creditors do not share in the proceeds of the estate at all because they are entitled to withdraw the secured assets from the estate pursuant to s. 69.3(2) and to realize the assets themselves. This is why s. 71 provides that the debtor's property passes to the trustee "subject to ... the rights of secured creditors" and why s. 136(1) provides that "*[s]ubject to the rights of secured creditors*, the proceeds realized from the property of the bankrupt shall be applied in priority of payment as follows ... ." (For a discussion of secured creditors, see Chapter 8.)

Further, the distribution scheme must take into account the important concept of property. Section 136 only purports to distribute "the proceeds realized from *the property of the bankrupt*" (see Chapter 4). Thus, property held on trust by the debtor or deemed to be held in trust (where the BIA recognizes such a deemed trust—see Chapter 8) is not available to the trustee for distribution: see s. 67 and Jacob S. Ziegel, "Preferences and Priorities in Insolvency Law: Is There a Solution?" (1995), 39 *St. Louis ULJ* 793.

In addition to these four classes of creditors, the BIA affords special treatment to the following classes of claims:

1. claims of unpaid suppliers of goods (ss. 81.1 and 81.2);
2. claims of unpaid employees (s. 81.3);
3. claims for unpaid pension contributions (s. 81.5); and
4. environmental claims (s. 14.06(7)).

These claimants are given either a charge on the assets of the debtor or a right to repossess certain identifiable property. In either case, the claimant generally obtains priority over other claimants. These claims are different from ordinary secured claims. In the case of ordinary secured claims, the BIA does not create the security interest or charge but simply recognizes the secured status created by some other body of provincial or federal law. The special claims listed above are different in that the BIA creates a special status for such claims that otherwise would not exist. In some instances, the effect is to elevate the claim from that of an ordinary secured creditor. In other cases, the provisions displace provincial provisions that create a proprietary interest in respect of the claims and that might otherwise give the interest a higher priority ranking.

These special claims will be examined first, because they allow the claimant to withdraw the asset or its value from the bankrupt estate thereby leaving less for the other claimants. This will be followed by an examination of the bankruptcy scheme of distribution, which establishes the ranking of the claims in respect of the residue of the bankrupt estate.

II. UNPAID SUPPLIERS

Jacob S. Ziegel, "New and Old Challenges in Approaching Phase Three Amendments to Canada's Commercial Insolvency Laws"
(2002), 37 *CBLJ* 75, at 101-3

(a) Introduction

If we had to compile a list of unsecured creditors whose ranking under the BIA deserves a higher priority, the claims of unpaid suppliers would surely appear near the bottom. We would see them quintessentially as consensual creditors who should be able to assess and diversify their credit risks and be able to protect their own interests. In Canada, these assumptions have turned out to be wrong. On paper at least, unpaid suppliers won a substantial victory in the 1992 amendments and there is every indication that the industry is ready to resume the battle at the next round of Parliamentary hearings.

How do we explain this surprising *dénouement*? I have not made a systematic study of the many factors but I believe they include some of the following. The recessions of the 1980s and early 1990s hit the Canadian retail industry particularly hard. Dozens of retail chains and many large department stores were forced to close or had to be radically restructured. Second, much of the soft and hard goods retail trade is seasonal in character. Suppliers may ship a large quantity of goods in a 30-day period representing a significant proportion of sales for the whole year. Suppliers also complained that frequently when a retailer became bankrupt they suffered serious losses. This was because the old Bankruptcy Act provisions encouraged retailers to "juice up" their inventory for the benefit of secured creditors so as to reduce the directors' liabilities under personal guarantees given to inventory financiers. A third factor is that many suppliers, especially in the garment trade, are privately owned and do not have sophisticated credit systems. Even if they did, it would not do them much good. Small suppliers do not have leverage over large buyers. They cannot force them to hand over balance sheets or disclose their current financials. Similarly, we are told, for the most part retailers categorically refuse to give buyers a purchase money security interest because that would jeopardize the retailers' line of credit with their banks. Given these and other arguments, the suppliers argued in 1991 that they should have a right to reclaim their goods on the buyer's insolvency similar to the right enjoyed by suppliers under the Quebec Civil Code.

(b) 1992 Amendments

Of course, there is another side to the debate. The Colter Committee was completely opposed to giving unpaid suppliers a special status in the ranking of a debtor's creditors, as was the banking community. Apart from issues of fairness among unsecured creditors, they argued that giving unpaid suppliers repossessory rights on bankruptcy would seriously disrupt banking lines of credit and throw a major wrench in the prospects for successful restructuring of struggling retailers.

The House of Commons Standing Committee was more sympathetic to the suppliers' pleas and responded with two additions to the 1992 amendments. Section 81.1 confers rights on unpaid suppliers of goods to reclaim goods supplied to a debtor within 30 days preceding the bankruptcy providing the goods have not been resold and can still be identified, and provided a large number of other conditions are satisfied. Section 81.2 applies only to farmers, fishermen and aquaculturists and treats their claims differently. They are given the benefit of a first lien on all inventory held by the debtor at the time of bankruptcy for goods supplied during the 30-day prebankruptcy period.

NOTES AND QUESTIONS

1. The Alberta Court of Appeal in *Stereo People of Canada Ltd. (Trustee of) v. Royal Bank of Canada*, [1997] 1 WWR 204 considered the purpose of s. 81.1 at paras. 11-12:

> The intention of Parliament in enacting this section is clear. Parliament intended to grant to suppliers who have recently delivered goods, limited relief from the inequities imposed upon them in the earlier legislation. These inequities include the complete loss of all unpaid goods shipped by the supplier to the bankrupt, leaving the suppliers subject to the risk that a debtor will order goods just prior to bankruptcy to improve his position in the bankruptcy. As pointed out by Farley J in *Re Rizzo Shoes (1989) Ltd.* (1995), 29 CBR (3d) 270, at 272:

>> It appears that the repossession section was included in the 1992 amendment of the BIA to protect "recent" unsecured creditors, especially in those situations where the bankrupt has "bulked up" with inventory to liquidate so as to generate funds to pay third parties.

> The protection accorded to suppliers is strictly limited to goods recently supplied which have not been paid for, which have not been resold, and which are in the same state as they were on delivery. Parliament ensured that rights of innocent third parties who obtained an interest in the goods subsequent to delivery would not be affected. We see no inequity to the secured creditor who is not given recourse against inventory, the cost of which has not been paid by the bankrupt.

2. Notwithstanding the special right of repossession granted by s. 81.1, Professor Ziegel concludes that unpaid suppliers "won a largely symbolic victory. The number of successful unpaid suppliers' claims under the new legislation appears to be very small." Jacob S. Ziegel,

"New and Old Challenges in Approaching Phase Three Amendments to Canada's Commercial Insolvency Laws," above, at 103. See also Jacob S. Ziegel, "The Modernization of Canada's Bankruptcy Law in a Comparative Context" (1999), 4 CBR (4th) 151, at note 108 (citing the small number of s. 81.1 claims based on survey evidence). What elements of s. 81.1 appear to provide the most difficulty for unpaid suppliers? The following case extracts and the subsequent notes and questions raise a number of interpretive issues that arise under s. 81.1.

Thomson Consumer Electronics Canada, Inc. v. Consumers Distributing Inc. (Receiver Manager of)
(1996), 43 CBR (3d) 77 (Ont. Gen. Div.)

FARLEY J: Section 81.1 provides an exception to the general policy of the BIA (a *pari passu* sharing amongst unsecured creditors) by giving a right to reclaim property to certain unsecured creditors (suppliers) of a bankrupt which is not available to the general body of unsecured creditors. Thus the court is required to narrowly construe such an exception to the fundamental policy of the BIA; see *Barrette v. Crabtree Estate*, [1993] 1 SCR 1027; *Langille v. Toronto-Dominion Bank* (1981), 37 CBR (NS) 35 (NSCA) aff'd. 131 DLR (3d) 571 (SCC). I also agree that it is an established canon of statutory interpretation that when legislation confers a right or benefit on persons which they would not have had at common law, the conditions which the legislation prescribes for the acquisition of that right or benefit are mandatory: see *Goodison Thresher Co. v. McNab* (1909), 19 OLR 188 at p. 214 (CA) aff'd. (1910), 44 SCR 187; *Czerwonka v. Paskawski* (1989), 8 RPR (2d) 73 (Sask. CA); Bennion, F., *Statutory Interpretation*, 2nd ed. (London: Butterworths, 1992) at p. 32.

. . .

I would also note the other aspect of the applicants not having satisfied that the goods said to be 30 day goods are, in fact, same. In this regard see *Re Stokes Building Supplies Ltd.* (1994), 30 CBR (3d) 36 (Nfld. TD) at p. 37:

> Clearly, the onus is on the applicant, Window Land, to establish on the balance of probabilities that the goods are so identifiable. In considering this matter, I accept that identification under s. 81.1 need not be apparent on the face of the goods. In other words one need not have serial numbers or other distinctive stamps on the face of the goods, although that obviously would be sufficient. Identification can come from records such as invoices, purchase orders and from the evidence of representatives of suppliers and purchasers. To use an example if evidence established that Window Land had supplied Stokes goods only within the preceding thirty days that would be identification although the goods might not be stamped, marked or otherwise distinctive.

Thus I would agree that if the applicants were shown to have supplied goods in the 30 day period and at the start of that period I was shown that there was a zero inventory of those goods, that would be sufficient identification. However once one gets beyond that one is into very boggy ground. Essentially what the applicants are relying on is the testing by the receiver Coopers—but it was acknowledged by Mr. Holmes of Coopers that he was operating from a logical but wrong premise. It was claimed by Mr. Johnston of T&B

that T&B storage methodology in practice did not accord under the assumptions and logic of Coopers. It is unfortunate that neither Mr. Holmes nor Mr. Johnston had any direct involvement with the applicants "goods" in the period June 29-July 29, 1996. Their information is thus second hand. We are therefore left with the unresolved aspect of Johnston claiming that there was significant movement of goods within the warehouse which would not show up on the computer or be obvious from an inspection—eg. whether the boxes on the pallet (which pallet was tagged) had been used up and the pallet strength replenished from the overstock area. However it was apparently the view of personnel speaking to Coopers personnel that such movement was not significant. However, it appears that the computer system was designed to track numbers of goods rather than to track the specific goods—thus gets into a question of identifying what should be there rather than what is there and is a variation of the "book count" problems.

Unfortunately, for the applicants' case, in addition it appears that a number of the invoices of the applicants show delivery to warehouses other than T&B Cambridge. As well many of the delivery slips are dated more than 30 days prior to delivery of demand kicking in. Further it would seem that there is a problem with linking invoices with specific goods said to be delivered to the warehouse. It would seem that this compounds the problem of proof—the onus of which is on the applicants. A difficulty is shown by example in the Evenflo situation where the demand kick in would only catch goods sold and delivered from July 6–July 29, 1996; however, Evenflo was not precise enough and has claimed for goods said to be sold and delivered in the June 29–July 5 period. See also the difficulty of Spencer's unprecise affidavit as to paras. 21-22 and the reference as well to Ex N (ie. p. 122). Spencer says she identified the goods but does not say how.

It would not seem to me that the state of the goods was changed by their being removed from bulk shrink wrap. This would seem to be packing or packaging of the goods—and not a change to the goods themselves. They apparently would be sold in their intended state as sold by the supplier—ie: in their original form (including perhaps individual boxing). Certainly there has been no transformation of the goods (or incorporation into other goods).

Acceptance of the goods as being 30 day goods by the Receiver in these circumstances would not be binding in these circumstances upon T&B. It would also seem to me that the applicants have not sufficiently overcome the hurdle of showing that they meet the requirements of s. 81.1(1)(c) and so they would not meet the onus, except where they have demonstrated that there was a zero inventory where the period began to run.

NOTES

On appeal, the Ontario Court of Appeal in *Thomson Consumer Electronics Canada, Inc. v. Consumers Distributing Inc. (Receiver of)* (1999), 170 DLR (4th) 115 (Ont. CA) dismissed the appeal on the ground that the supplier did not have a right of repossession under s. 81.1 because neither the trustee in bankruptcy nor the receiver appointed by the secured creditors had possession of the goods. The goods were in fact in the possession of a warehouse-keeper. The fact that a third party has actual physical possession of the goods is not in itself sufficient to preclude the operation of s. 81.1. If the third party is holding the goods as agent for the debtor and is bound to hand them over to the debtor on demand, the supplier's right to repossess the goods is not affected because the third party holds possession of the goods on behalf of the debtor. The 2005-2007 amendments have reworded s. 81.1 to provide that the right to repossess may be exercised if the supplier "delivered the goods to the purchaser or to the purchaser's agent." The problem was that the warehousekeeper had two valid bases for retaining the goods, and was therefore entitled in law to refuse to deliver them to the trustee in bankruptcy. The warehousekeeper had a possessory lien on the goods in respect of the storage charges. Additionally, the debtor had given the warehousekeeper a security interest in the debtor's goods stored in the warehouse.

Port Alice Specialty Cellulose Inc. (Bankruptcy) v. ConocoPhillips Co.
(2005), 11 CBR (5th) 279, 2005 BCCA 299

LEVINE JA:

Introduction

[1] A supplier which has delivered goods for which it has not been fully paid may demand repossession of them from a person who has become bankrupt, provided the goods are "identifiable," pursuant to s. 81.1 of the *Bankruptcy and Insolvency Act*, RSC 1985, c. B-3. The question that arises in this case is whether goods that are commingled with other goods are "identifiable" for the purposes of this statutory provision.

[2] A Supreme Court chambers judge determined that the respondent, ConocoPhillips Company, was entitled to recover fuel oil delivered to the pulp mill at Port Alice and not paid for, in spite of the fact that the fuel oil had been pumped into a storage tank in which there was a quantity of fuel oil remaining from previous deliveries.

[3] The Trustee of the bankrupt company claims on appeal that the unpaid fuel oil was not "identifiable" and Conoco's demand for repossession must fail.

[4] Conoco cross-appeals the chambers judge's determination of how much of the remaining oil it was entitled to repossess.

[5] For the reasons that follow, I am of the opinion that the chambers judge adopted the proper approach to the interpretation of the statutory provision and the determination of how much oil Conoco was entitled to repossess. I would dismiss the appeal and the cross-appeal.

Background

[6] Conoco was a supplier of fuel oil to the pulp mill at Port Alice. On October 6, 2004 it delivered 23,598 barrels of fuel oil (the "New Oil") to the mill. At the time, there were 18,801 barrels (the "Old Oil") in the storage tank. On November 17, 2004, there were 24,417 barrels of fuel oil remaining in the storage tank. Port Alice Specialty Cellulose Inc. became bankrupt on November 22, 2004.

[7] It is common ground that Conoco had provided all fuel oil to Port Alice since June 2004; it had been the sole supplier of the last four of five deliveries before the bankruptcy. Conoco was not paid the invoiced amount of $749,102.82 for the last delivery.

[8] Conoco made a demand for repossession of the fuel oil under s. 81.1(1) of the *BIA* ... .

[9] The Trustee in Bankruptcy sought directions from the Supreme Court as to Conoco's entitlement to repossess fuel oil in Port Alice's storage tank. The only issue in dispute was whether Conoco could satisfy the requirement of s. 81.1(1)(c)(ii) that "the goods are identifiable as the goods delivered by the supplier and not fully paid for." The Trustee took the position that the New Oil was commingled with and could not be separated from the Old Oil and therefore the oil remaining in the storage tank when Conoco demanded respossession could not be identified as oil delivered within the 30 days prior to the bankruptcy. (Conoco's demand was made on November 29, 2004, which was more than 30 days after delivery. There was an intervening proposal under the *BIA*, during which the 30 day period in s. 81.1(1) was suspended (by s. 81.1(4)).

[10] Mr. Justice Masuhara determined that s. 81.1 (which had not previously been subject to court review in British Columbia and had not been interpreted in relation to fungible goods in any jurisdiction) should not be interpreted narrowly, as sought by the Trustee, "but in such a way as to allow it to operate fairly and practically to protect the interest of a supplier who has delivered within the 30-day period having regard to the specific circumstances and the goods in question." He noted that "no particular type of good is excluded from the right of possession or repossession granted under Section 81.1 and that includes liquid hydrocarbons which are fungible goods," and that excluding fungible goods "would not be consistent with the intent of this provision." (The chambers judge's oral reasons for judgment are unreported: (25 February 2005), Vancouver Registry, B041848 (BCSC). The quotes are from para. 11.)

[11] In determining the intent of s. 81.1, the chambers judge referred to the 2003 Report of the Senate Standing Committee on Bank, Trade and Commerce, "Debtors and Creditors: Sharing the Burden" (which may be found at http:// www.parl.gc.ca/37/2/parl-bus/commbus/senate/com-e/bank-e/rep-e/bankruptcy-e.pdf), where the intent of s. 81.1 was summarized as follows (at p. 106):

> The "30-day goods rule" was introduced to protect suppliers—who often lack a realistic ability to demand security for the transaction—from harm by insolvent debtors who ordered excessive amounts of inventory prior to bankruptcy as a means of increasing the assets available to satisfy secured creditors, a practice that is sometimes referred to as "juicing the trades." It also, however, can assist businesses in financial difficulty; because suppliers can recover their goods under certain circumstances, they may be willing to continue supplying to these businesses.

[12] The chambers judge concluded that the New Oil was sufficiently identifiable on the basis of the following facts (para. 15):

(a) The new fuel was delivered to a single tank and was stored there.

(b) All of the previous deliveries since the previous June were made by Conoco and no deliveries of any further fuel subsequent to October have been made.

(c) The qualities of the New and Old Oil are the same and the fuel in the Tank remains as such.

(d) The volume of the fuel in the Tank before delivery of the New Oil into the Tank is known and ascertained.

(e) The volume of the New Oil pumped into the Tank is known and ascertained.

(f) The volume of fuel oil drawn down is known and ascertained.

(g) The fuel in the Tank can be inferred to have been evenly drawn down.

[13] He rejected Conoco's argument that its entitlement to fuel oil in the storage tank should be determined by applying the "first in, first out" principle. Instead, he found Conoco to be entitled to the same proportion of the remaining fuel oil that the New Oil was to the New Oil and Old Oil in the storage tank on October 6, 2004, the date of delivery of the New Oil. That proportion was found to be 56 per cent.

The Appeal

. . .

[24] The Trustee's second ground of appeal is that the trial judge misinterpreted s. 81.1.

[25] There is no dispute that the proper approach to the interpretation of s. 81.1 is that described in E.A. Driedger's *Construction of Statutes* (2nd ed. 1983), at p. 87:

> Today there is only one principle or approach, namely, the words of an Act are to be read in their entire context and in their grammatical and ordinary sense harmoniously with the scheme of the Act, the object of the Act, and the intention of Parliament.

[26] This approach has been approved by the Supreme Court of Canada in numerous cases. The Supreme Court has also said that this approach is confirmed by s. 12 of the *Interpretation Act*, RSC 1985, c. I-21, which provides that every enactment "is deemed remedial, and shall be given such fair, large and liberal construction and interpretation as best ensures the attainment of its objects": see *Barrie Public Utilities v. Canadian Cable Television Assn.*, [2003] 1 SCR 476 (SCC) at para. 20; *Bell ExpressVu Ltd. Partnership v. Rex*, [2002] 2 SCR 559 (SCC) at para. 26.

[27] In interpreting the *BIA*, courts have noted that it is a commercial statute used by business people and should not be given an overly narrow or legalistic approach: see *McCoubrey, Re*, [1924] 4 DLR 1227 (Alta. TD), at 1231-32; *A. Marquette & fils Inc. v. Mercure* (1975), [1977] 1 SCR 547 (SCC), at 556; *Maple Homes Canada Ltd., Re*, 2000 BCSC 1443 (BCSC) at para. 21.

[28] In my opinion, the chambers judge properly applied these principles to the interpretation of s. 81.1.

[29] Firstly, he noted that the words of s. 81.1(1) did not exclude fungible goods such as fuel oil. An interpretation of "identifiable" that would have the effect of excluding a class of goods would narrow the application of the section in a manner that would be inconsistent with the "grammatical and ordinary sense" of the words.

[30] In considering the context of the words of s. 81.1, the chambers judge noted (at para. 6) the argument of the Trustee that s. 81.1 should be construed narrowly because, in the context of the *BIA*, it is an exception to the general rule that unsecured creditors

share *pro rata* in the property of the bankrupt. In this Court, the Trustee also argued that the context of s. 81.1 includes the provisions of s. 81.2, which provide additional security for farmers, fishers and agriculturalists who deliver their products to a person who becomes bankrupt within 15 days. The Trustee claims that s. 81.2 indicates that fungible goods are not included in s. 81.1.

[31] As noted by the chambers judge (at para. 16), s. 81.1 provides special protection for unpaid suppliers and its interpretation should be approached by applying the principles applicable to all statutory provisions. Section 81.2 does not assist the Trustee in narrowing the interpretation of s. 81.1. It is not a complete code for the protection of suppliers of fungible goods. It provides additional protection for some suppliers of such goods in the form of security over the inventory of a bankrupt, but the security is expressly subject to a supplier's right to repossess goods under s. 81.1 (s. 81.2(1)) and it preserves the rights of farmers, fishers and agriculturalists under s. 81.1 (ss. 81.2(4) and (5)).

[32] The chambers judge determined that the intent of s. 81.1, to protect unpaid suppliers, would be denied if it were not applicable to goods such as fuel oil in a tank. He considered such a result to be unfair. The Trustee points out that the result of the application of many of the provisions of the *BIA* may be unfair to particular creditors or classes of creditors because of the nature of the problem it addresses: the division of scarce resources among multiple claimants. The Trustee says that if a supplier is denied the special protection provided by s. 81.1 because it is unable to identify its goods, that is not unfair, but simply the result of the application of the statute.

[33] I do not quarrel with the Trustee's submission that the effect of the *BIA* may be unfair in particular cases, but do not find his analysis of assistance in this case where the issue is whether commingled goods are excluded entirely from the protection of s. 81.1. In my opinion, there is nothing in the words of the section, in their context, read harmoniously with the scheme and object of the Act and the intention of Parliament, that leads to the conclusion that goods such as the fuel oil in this case are not capable of being identified, for the purposes of s. 81.1, in the manner determined by the trial judge.

[34] Section 81.1 has been considered in three cases in other jurisdictions, where the courts have adopted a narrower interpretive approach, urged on the chambers judge and this Court by the Trustee.

[35] In *Stokes Building Supplies Ltd., Re* (1994), 30 CBR (3d) 36 (Nfld. TD), the Court found that the supplier of identical windows before and after the 30-day period could not identify which of the windows in the bankrupt's possession had been delivered within 30 days of the bankruptcy. In that case, the windows had no identifiable markings to distinguish old and new stock. There was evidence that the stock was not rotated uniformly and that old stock was not sold first. The Court said (at para. 16):

> In my view section 81.1 does not confer a broad discretion on the Court to make a general equitable adjustment between the parties. I cannot allocate goods between the receiver and the supplier on the assumption that old stock was sold first. The items which are to be taken under repossession must themselves be identifiable.

[36] In *Bruce Agra Foods Inc. v. Everfresh Beverages Inc. (Receiver of)* (1996), 45 CBR (3d) 169 (Ont. Gen. Div.), the issue was whether a claim for repossession (of orange juice) could be made against an interim receiver. Rejecting the claim, Farley J said (at para. 5):

The 30 days rights of section 81.1 are not triggered unless the purchaser (Everfresh here) is a bankrupt or there is a section 243(2)(b) receiver. While section 12 of the *Interpretation Act*, RSC 1985, Chapter I-21 provides that "every enactment is deemed remedial and shall be given such fair, large and liberal construction and interpretation as best ensures the attainment of its objects," this does not provide that proper regard not be paid to the canons of statutory interpretation and where the legislature confers a right or benefit on persons which they would not have had at common law, the conditions which the legislature prescribes for the acquisition of that right or benefit are mandatory: [citations omitted]

[37] In *obiter*, Justice Farley commented (at para. 8):

[I]t was certainly more likely on the probabilities that the new shipment was pumped into a continuing mixture—thus destroying the identifiability of this most fungible good (as opposed to having been pumped into an empty vat).

[38] In *Thomson Consumer Electronics Canada Inc. v. Consumers Distributing Inc. (Receiver of)* (1999), 5 CBR (4th) 141 (Ont. CA), the issue was whether the goods were in the "possession" of the bankrupt, the trustee or the receiver. They were stored in a warehouse where they were subject to a warehouseman's lien claim as well as other security. The Court said, in regard to the application of s. 81.1 (at para. 22):

Section 81.1 of the *BIA*, which was first enacted in 1992, gives unpaid suppliers a right to repossess goods sold and delivered to a purchaser who has been adjudged bankrupt or who has been placed in receivership, provided the suppliers' claims meet the requirements set out in the section. This preferential claim for unpaid suppliers is an exception to the general rule in bankruptcy proceedings that unsecured creditors share equally in the bankrupt estate.

[39] The chambers judge distinguished these cases, and they are not binding on this Court in any event: see *Wolf v. R* (1974), [1975] 2 SCR 107 (SCC). In *Stokes Building Supplies Ltd.*, the windows were not commingled in the way the New Oil was commingled with the Old Oil in this case. It was possible to physically identify them, with serial numbers or other markings, as is the case for electronic goods such as DVD players or computers, referred to by the Trustee as also being "fungible goods." In *Everfresh*, Farley J's comments about whether the orange juice could be identified if it was not delivered to a clean vat were clearly *obiter*. And in *Thompson*, O'Connor JA for the Court observed, in *obiter*, that a narrow interpretation of s. 81.1 may be contrary to the intention of Parliament (at para. 51):

Further, I would observe that a narrow interpretation of the meaning of "possession" in s. 81.1 that excludes all third party possessions ignores the commercial reality that some purchasers and certainly some trustees and receivers will take possession of goods and arrange to have the goods held on their behalf by third party warehouses. While I agree with Farley J that s. 81.1 is an exception to the general rule that unsecured creditors share equally in the bankrupt estate, an interpretation of the meaning of "possession" in s. 81.1 which excludes possession in these types of circumstances may unnecessarily restrict the rights that parliament intended to confer on unpaid suppliers.

[40] In my opinion, the chambers judge properly interpreted s. 81.1 of the BIA.

[41] It follows that I would dismiss the appeal.

The Cross-Appeal

[42] The chambers judge concluded that Conoco should be allowed to repossess a *pro rata* share of the oil in the storage tank: that is, the proportion that the New Oil was to the total oil in the tank before any was drawn down, 56 per cent or 13,674 barrels. He rejected Conoco's argument that the "first in, first out" ("FIFO") principle should be applied to determine Conoco's share, stating that it "does not reflect the operational or process reality of how fuel is drawn from the Tank," which is "uniformly."

[43] Conoco cross-appealed, claiming that the application of the FIFO principle would be consistent with a liberal approach to the interpretation of s. 81.1 to allow an unpaid supplier in its circumstances to recover goods for which it is unpaid.

[44] The FIFO principle was discussed extensively, in the context of a dispute over moneys commingled in a trust account, in *Ontario (Securities Commission) v. Greymac Credit Corp.* (1986), 30 DLR (4th) 1 (Ont. CA) aff'd [1988] 2 SCR 172 (SCC). It was decided that it was not appropriately applied where the dispute was not between a debtor and creditor but among competing equal claimants to a trust fund. Conoco distinguishes *Greymac* on the basis that in this case there are no competing claimants for the fuel oil.

[45] In my view, that is an overly simplistic view of this case. Conoco, as an unsecured creditor, competes with the other unsecured creditors for a *pro rata* share of the property of the bankrupt Port Alice. Conoco has not offered any principled reason why FIFO is more appropriate than the *pro rata* method chosen by the chambers judge to balance the rights of Conoco and the other unsecured creditors, in the circumstances of this case.

[46] I would dismiss the cross-appeal.

Appeal and cross-appeal dismissed.

NOTES AND QUESTIONS

1. Following involves identifying the location of a thing, usually as it passes from one person to another. The inquiry is usually a simple factual inquiry, but it can be complicated if the property is mixed with similar property owned by others. The principles that are used to follow goods into mixtures are similar to the principles of tracing. The difference between following and tracing is that, in the former, the goods have lost their identity by virtue of being mixed with similar goods—for example, your grain is mixed with my grain. Tracing involves a substitution—an assertion that the claimant's property was used to acquire some other asset. This allows the claimant to claim the new asset—for example, you sold my grain and received cash proceeds for it. I can assert a claim to the cash as the traceable proceeds of my property. Tracing principles were developed by courts to cover situations where the traceable proceeds were mixed with property belonging to other persons—for example, you deposit into your bank account the cash proceeds arising out of the sale of my property and thereby mix them with your own funds. See L. Smith, *The Law of Tracing* (Oxford: Clarendon Press, 1997), at 6-8.

2. A's goods may be mixed with B's goods. If some of the goods comprising the mixture are subsequently withdrawn, it must be determined whether they were A's goods, B's goods, or some of each that were withdrawn. Courts have held that if a person mixes his or her property with those of another person and then withdraws some of the mixture, that person

is presumed to withdraw his or her own property first. See *Re Hallet's Estate* (1880), 13 Ch. D 696 (CA). If the goods of two innocent parties are mixed together, this principle cannot be applied. Instead, a pro rata depletion rule is applied. See *Ontario (Securities Commission) v. Greymac Credit Corp.*, [1988] 2 SCR 172. This was the approach taken by the court in *Re Port Alice Specialty*, above. One commentator who has questioned whether the court was correct in applying a pro-rata depletion rule has suggested that the court ought to have applied the principle that subsequent withdrawals are to come from the buyer's portion of the mixture. See A. Duggan, "Tracing Canadian-Style: Re Graphicshoppe and Other Recent Cases" (2006), 43 *CBLJ* 292.

3. The original version of s. 81.1 provided that the right to repossess the goods must be exercised within a period of 30 days after delivery of the goods to the purchaser. This created difficulties for the supplier, because the time would often begin to run before the supplier had any knowledge of the bankruptcy of the purchaser. The 2005-2007 amendments changed this element of the provision. The right must now be exercised within a 15-day period after the purchaser becomes bankrupt and is exercisable against goods sold and delivered during the 30-day period preceding the bankruptcy. Do you think that this change together with the less-strict approach to identifiability of the goods reflected in *Re Port Alice*, above, will result in a greater use of the repossessory right by suppliers?

4. If the terms of the agreement provide that title and property in the goods do not pass until the goods have been fully paid for, is s. 81.1 applicable? See *R.A. Warren Equipment Ltd. v. KPMG Inc.* (1999), 11 CBR (4th) 110; aff'd. on other grounds (1999), 14 CBR (4th) 274 (Man. CA). What would be the outcome if title passes to the purchaser under the agreement, but the supplier reserved a security interest in the goods to secure the unpaid purchase price?

5. A supplier's right to repossess will be defeated if the goods have been resold at arm's length or are subject to any agreement for sale at arm's length: ss. 81.1(1)(c)(iv) and (v). See, for example, *Re ITI Education Corp.* (2002), 38 CBR (4th) 41 (NSCA); *Re Commercial Body Builders Ltd.* (1993), 21 CBR (3d) 218; aff'd. (1994), 29 CBR (3d) 155 (BCCA); and *Re Barrington and Vokey Ltd.* (1995), 34 CBR (3d) 187 (NSSC).

6. What is the effect of a reorganization on the right to repossess? Should the right to repossess be treated differently depending on whether there is a reorganization or a straight bankruptcy? See, for example, *Re Woodward's Ltd.* (1993), 100 DLR (4th) 133 (BCSC), with additional reasons at (1993), 17 CBR (3d) 253 (BCSC); leave to appeal refused (1993), 22 CBR (3d) 25 (BCCA).

7. Compare the operation of s. 81.1 with that of s. 81.2. The latter provision gives farmers, fishermen, and aquaculturalists a security on all of the purchaser's inventory to secure unpaid claims in respect of products sold and delivered for use in the purchaser's business where delivery has occurred in the 15-day period preceding the bankruptcy. How is the issue of identifiability of goods handled under this provision? What happens when several different suppliers supply products to the purchaser during the 15-day period? Will it make any difference if some of the suppliers have reserved security interests in the goods that they supply to the purchaser?

III. WAGE CLAIMS

Kevin Davis and Jacob Ziegel, "Assessing the Economic Impact of a New Priority Scheme for Unpaid Wage Earners and Suppliers of Goods and Services"
(prepared for Industry Canada: Corporate Law Policy Directorate,
April 30, 1998), 13-15

It is sometimes said that wage earners are non-consensual creditors because there is no formal agreement for the extension of credit. The characterization is incorrect because even the wage earner who is paid on an hourly basis gives credit for at least the hour before he or she is entitled to payment. However, it may be true to say that because the employee does not anticipate non-payment the employee's wages are unlikely to include a risk premium to offset the risk of the employer failing to pay wages because of insolvency. Even if the employee appreciated the risk of non-payment it is unlikely that the typical employee, especially at a non-executive level, would bother to bargain for a risk premium or some other form of protection against the risk of the employer becoming insolvent ... .

Employers and secured creditors benefit from any failure on the part of wage earners to bargain for a risk premium. This is because issuing secured debt allows employers to transfer bankruptcy-related risk from creditors who are granted security interests to the wage earners whose preferred claims will be subordinated to those of the secured creditors. This directly benefits the secured creditors and indirectly benefits the employer if the secured creditors provide credit on more favourable terms than they would if their claims did not have priority over those of other creditors. Meanwhile, the wage earners who are not compensated for bearing the additional risk of bankruptcy-related losses are prejudiced. This strikes many people as unfair. Allowing firms to shift bankruptcy-related risk to their employees without compensation is also potentially inefficient because it allows firms to avoid internalizing all of the costs associated with their operations. This is undesirable from a societal perspective as it may result in excessive resources being allocated to firms with a high risk of going bankrupt.

Even if wage earners are able to bargain for compensation for bearing bankruptcy-related risk it may not be efficient for them to bear that risk. This is because it can be argued that, relative to other creditors, wage earners are poor risk bearers, meaning that it is more costly to society for a typical wage earner to bear a given amount of bankruptcy risk than it is for another creditor to bear the same risk. There are two reasons why this might be the case. First of all, other creditors may have the resources, knowledge and experience to monitor the employer's financial condition and either reduce the amount of credit extended or bargain for a risk premium as the probability of bankruptcy increases. By contrast, wage earners often have little information about their employer's financial position and, unless they can readily obtain other employment, may find it impracticable either to cease extending credit to their employer (e.g. by quitting) or to bargain for an increase in wages as the employer's financial position worsens. A second consideration is that creditors other than wage earners may be in a better position either to diversify the risk of non-payment across a large number of debtors or to obtain some form of credit insurance. Granting super-priority to the claims of wage earners is one way of relieving them of the need to bear the risk of losses associated with the bankruptcy of their employer.

NOTES

1. Wage claims of employees were originally afforded the status of a preferred claim. With the growth of secured credit, the preferred status was found to be inadequate to protect the interests of unpaid employees, because the assets were often insufficient to satisfy the higher-ranking claim of the secured creditor. Some provinces attempted to improve the status of employee claims by creating a statutory lien or charge in their favour that had priority over prior secured creditors. Although these statutory devices were fully effective outside bankruptcy, they were rendered inoperative upon the bankruptcy of the employer. The Supreme Court of Canada held that Parliament intended that such claims should be given a preferred status and that it was not open to the provinces to create interests that gave the claims any higher priority. Secured creditors would frequently instigate a bankruptcy for the sole purpose of obtaining priority over such competing interests, and courts held that this did not constitute an abuse of process or provide grounds for the exercise of the court's discretion to refuse a bankruptcy order. See *Bank of Montreal v. Scott Road Enterprises Ltd.* (1989), 57 DLR (4th) 623 (BCCA), discussed in Chapter 3.

2. Between 1975 and 1992 Canada considered a series of proposals to remedy the problem of the unpaid wage earner in a bankruptcy. These proposals included increasing the amount of the wage-earner preferred claim, establishing full superpriority protection for up to $2,000 in wage claims, and the creation of a wage-earner protection fund. As previously explained in Chapter 1, the Mulroney government wanted to adopt a wage-earner protection act as part of the Bill C-22 package of amendments introduced in 1991, but was unable to overcome opposition from within its own caucus. The government therefore contented itself with some marginal improvements on the pre-1992 position by increasing the amount of wages eligible for preferred treatment to $2,000 and the eligible expenses of travelling salesmen to $1,000.

3. The wage-earner issue subsequently became a political issue immediately prior to the 2006 federal election, and legislation was introduced with consent from all the political parties. A bankruptcy reform bill was introduced, the centrepiece of which was the *Wage Earner Protection Program Act* (WEPPA). This legislation created an insurance scheme to protect unpaid employees where their employer has gone into bankruptcy or receivership. Neither the employers nor the employees are required to make contributions into the program—the expenditures are funded out of the general revenue. However, the Crown is subrogated to the claims held by the employees: see WEPPA s. 36. (A right of subrogation permits the substitution of a party for another party who holds a claim. In the present context, the right of subrogation allows the Crown to assert the employee's right in respect of a claim for unpaid wages.) The BIA was amended to give the employees a security to secure their unpaid wages to a maximum of $2,000 for each employee: see BIA s. 81.3. The security covers current assets, which are defined as "cash and cash equivalents, including negotiable instruments and demand deposits—inventory or accounts receivable or the proceeds from the

dealing with those assets." The security ranks above any other security against the bankrupt's assets, except for unpaid supplier's rights provided for in BIA ss. 81.1 and 81.2.

4. There are a number of limitations on employee claims under the WEPPA. They are not covered to the extent that their claims exceed $3,000 or an amount equal to four times the maximum weekly insurable earnings under the *Employment Insurance Act*, SC 1996, c. 23, whichever is greater. Nor are they covered to the extent that their wage claims fall outside the six-month period preceding the bankruptcy. See WEPPA s. 7. Originally, the WEPPA definition of "wages" did not include severance or termination pay. Bill C-10, which implements the January 27, 2009 federal budget, changed the definition so that it now includes both. Although Bill C-10 came into force on March 12, 2009, the amendment is made retroactive to January 27, 2009. An individual is ineligible to receive a payment in respect of wages earned during a period in which the individual was an officer or director or the employer, if he or she had a controlling interest in the employer or occupied a managerial position with the employer, or if he or she was not acting at arm's length with such a person. See WEPPA s. 6.

5. If the current assets are insufficient to satisfy the BIA s. 81.3 security, the claimant can prove as a preferred creditor for the balance of the claim. The superpriority that the s. 81.3 security enjoys over other secured creditors afforded to this claim may mean that there will be insufficient current assets to satisfy the claims of the secured creditors. The secured creditor may prove as a preferred creditor in the bankruptcy of an employer for the amount that it loses by virtue of this superpriority. An employee who is not eligible under the WEPPA may prove the claim as an ordinary unsecured creditor in the bankruptcy of the employer.

QUESTIONS

1. A supplier sells inventory to a business pursuant to a conditional sales agreement under which property in the goods does not pass until the full purchase price is paid. The business goes bankrupt and its employees are left with unpaid wage claims. Does the s. 81.3 security have priority over the interest of the supplier? Consider the approach taken by the court in *Canada (Deputy Attorney General) v. Schwab Construction Ltd.* and *DaimlerChrysler Financial Services (debis) Canada Inc. v. Mega Pets Ltd.*, discussed in Chapter 8.

2. Provincial and federal employment standards legislation and business corporations statutes give unpaid employees a right of recovery against a director of an employer corporation. In many instances, the conditions for making such claims are less restrictive than under the WEPPA. For example, the employment standards legislation in Ontario and Alberta provide that the right to recover against a director extends to all wages that become payable up to a maximum of six months. How do the new wage protection provisions affect this right? See WEPPA s. 36. See Chapter 10 for further treatment of the employment standards legislation.

IV. PENSION FUND CONTRIBUTIONS

Re Graphicshoppe Ltd.
(2005),15 CBR (5th) 207 (Ont. CA)

MOLDAVER JA: ... [119] ... The salient facts are not in dispute. It is accepted that Graphicshoppe held its employees pension contributions in trust when it deducted them from their pay. At that moment, the trust property was identifiable and the trust met the requirements for a trust under established principles of trust law.

[120] Shortly thereafter however, the trust property ceased to be identifiable. The employee contributions were co-mingled with Graphicshoppe's funds and prior to the date of bankruptcy, they were converted into other property and were no longer traceable. On this point, it is clear from the record that as of the date of bankruptcy, none of the employee contributions that had been deposited into Graphicshoppe's bank account remained intact. We know that with certainty because prior to the date of bankruptcy, the account went into a negative balance. We likewise know that the funds in the account on the date of bankruptcy came from Textron, the company that was factoring Graphicshoppe's receivables. Replenishment is a non-issue on the facts before us.

[121] Against that backdrop, the central issue on appeal is whether the trustee in bankruptcy was correct in concluding that the employee contributions did not constitute trust funds at the date of bankruptcy within the meaning of s. 67(1)(a) of the *BIA*. With respect, I believe that he was.

[122] On the facts of this case, I am of the view that McLachlin J's majority decision in *British Columbia v. Henfrey Samson Belair Ltd.*, [1989] 2 SCR 24 (SCC) ("*Henfrey Samson*") vindicates the position taken by the trustee in bankruptcy. My colleague has reviewed the salient facts of that case and they need not be repeated. The passages that I consider to be apposite are found at pp. 741 and 742. They are reproduced below:

> I turn next to s. 18 of the *Social Service Tax Act* and the nature of the legal interests created by it. At the moment of collection of the tax, there is a deemed statutory trust. *At that moment the trust property is identifiable and the trust meets the requirements for a trust under the principles of trust law. The difficulty in this, as in most cases, is that the trust property soon ceases to be identifiable. The tax money is mingled with other money in the hands of the merchant and converted to other property so that it cannot be traced.* At this point it is no longer a trust under general principles of law. In an attempt to meet this problem, s. 18(1)(b) states that tax collected shall be deemed to be held separate from and form no part of the collector's money, assets or estate. *But, as the presence of the deeming provision tacitly acknowledges, the reality is that after conversion the statutory trust bears little resemblance to a true trust. There is no property which can be regarded as being impressed with a trust.* Because of this, s. 18(2) goes on to provide that the unpaid tax forms a lien and charge on the entire assets of the collector, an interest in the nature of a secured debt.
>
> • • •
>
> Nor does the argument that the tax money remains the property of the Crown throughout withstand scrutiny. If that were the case, there would be no need for the lien and charge in the Crown's favour created by s. 18(2) of the *Social Service Tax Act. The province has a*

trust interest and hence property in the tax funds so long as they can be identified or traced. But once they lose that character, any common law or equitable property interest disappears. The province is left with a statutory deemed trust which does not give it the same property interest a common law trust would, supplemented by a lien and charge over all the bankrupt's property under s. 18(2) [emphasis added].

[123] For present purposes, I am prepared to accept that *Henfrey Samson* falls short of holding that co-mingling of trust and other funds is, by itself, fatal to the application of s. 67(1)(a) of the *BIA*. Once however, the trust funds have been converted into property that cannot be traced, that is fatal. And that is what occurred here.

• • •

[126] In the case at bar, the employees had a trust interest and hence a right to seek a proprietary remedy with respect to the pension contributions so long as they could be identified or traced. However, as McLachlin J noted at p. 742 of *Henfrey Samson*, once the contributions lost that character, any common law or equitable property interest disappeared. While this may seem harsh, it must be remembered that in the commercial context and particularly in the realm of bankruptcy, innocent beneficiaries may well be competing with innocent unsecured creditors for the same dollars. This raises policy considerations which the courts in *Greymac* and *LSUC* did not have to face.

• • •

[133] For these reasons, I am satisfied that the trustee in bankruptcy was correct in holding that the pension plan contributions made by the employees did not constitute trust funds within the meaning of s. 67(1)(a) of the *BIA*. Accordingly, I would allow the appeal, set aside the order of Lax J and in its place, substitute an order upholding the trustee's disallowance of the employees' proof of claim.

[134] With respect to costs both here and below, if the parties cannot agree, the appellant may file submissions with the court within fifteen days of the release of these reasons. The respondents shall reply within ten days thereafter. The submissions shall not exceed five pages double-spaced. If so advised, counsel for the appellant may file a reply within five days of the receipt of the respondents' submission, limited to three pages double-spaced.

Appeal allowed.

NOTES AND QUESTIONS

1. The 2007 amendments to the BIA have improved the position of employees in respect of their claims for unpaid pension contributions. BIA s. 81.5 creates a security on all the employer's assets, which secures pension contribution arrears, contributions owed by an employer for the normal costs of the plan, and contributions owed by an employer to a defined contribution plan. These amounts are not covered by the WEPPA. The statutory security is wider than the s. 81.3 security that secures wage claims; it is not subject to a monetary limit and the security is not limited to current assets, but covers all of the employer's assets. Section 81.5(2) establishes the priority ranking of the security. It has priority over every other claim, right, charge, or security against the bankrupt's assets except for the

rights of suppliers under ss. 81.1 and 81.2, statutory deemed trusts covered by s. 67(3) (that is, those that cover source deductions of income tax, employment insurance, and CPP), and the security in favour of wage earners in ss. 81.3 and 81.4.

2. Does the absence of a monetary limit in respect of the pension contribution charge make it more difficult for a secured creditor to predict the potential risk associated with losing priority to the charge? What measures might a secured creditor implement to confirm that pension contributions are being made?

V. ENVIRONMENTAL CLAIMS

Until the 1992 amendments, the BIA did not address the problem of ranking claims for the cost of environmental cleanups under federal and provincial legislation. Under environmental legislation, the occupier of premises or the person in control of a business is typically held responsible for the costs of the cleanup, regardless of when the pollution was first caused and whether the occupant was at fault. In *Re Big Sky Living Inc.* (2002), 37 CBR (4th) 42 (Alta. QB) Slatter J at para. 43 noted that

> [t]he increased societal sensitivity to environmental damage and contamination created new issues for receivers and trustees in bankruptcy. Particularly problematic were provisions in environmental legislation that imposed liability not only on those who contaminated property, but on those who thereafter came to own or control that property.

Not surprisingly, such provisions in environmental legislation have made lenders nervous about enforcing security interests against premises suspected of being contaminated, and have made receivers and trustees equally circumspect about accepting office without iron clad indemnities if they are held liable. In 1992 Parliament sought to address these problems by limiting the liability of trustees for environmental damage and extending that protection to receivers and interim receivers in 1997. Further, in 1997, Parliament established a superpriority charge for the costs of remedying any environmental condition or environmental damage. The following extract explains the background to the 1992 and 1997 amendments and raises some important interpretive issues with respect to the new superpriority claim.

Dianne Saxe, "Trustees' and Receivers' Environmental Liability Update"
(1997), 49 CBR (3d) 138, at 138-64

Bankruptcy law is essentially a private system for the resolution of monetary disputes. There is a limited, identifiable list of affected parties. Each party has a limited and identifiable amount at stake. To a considerable extent, the risk has already materialized, and most of the money has been lost. Bankruptcy is therefore a defined procedure for allocating defined harms which have already occurred among a defined group. This structure does not accommodate, and was not designed to manage, risks of unlimited future harm to unlimited and unidentified parties. Some environmental conditions present exactly this sort of risk. In the late 1980s, Canadian courts ruled that these sorts of environmental risks (urgent requirements to prevent serious future risks) could "trump" the normal bankruptcy system of priorities. This was done by recognizing environmental requirement as both "costs of administration" of a debtor's estate and (at least arguably) the personal responsibility of the trustee. The most immediate practical consequence was that trustees refused appointments. The *Bankruptcy and Insolvency Act* was amended in 1992 to limit a trustee's personal liability. The 1997 amendments have limited that liability even further.

· · ·

III. The First Cases on Lender Liability, 1989-1992

The leading case on environmental protection orders in a non-bankrupt insolvency is still *Canada Trust Co. v. Bulora Corp.* (1981), 39 CBR (NS) 152 (Ont. CA). In that case, the Ontario Court of Appeal held that a receiver-manager was obliged to comply with a provincial administrative order necessary in the public interest, prior to paying the claim of the secured creditor who had appointed him. The assets of the debtor (who was not bankrupt) included a residential subdivision. The fire marshal ordered the debtor to tear down certain of the homes, because they were fire hazards to nearby residents. As the secured creditor's claim exceeded the value of the estate, there were no funds available to pay for the demolition except those owed to the secured creditor. The creditor had a prior, perfected, legitimate claim to the funds. On the other hand, failure to demolish the houses could endanger the lives and property of all other residents of the subdivision. The Court held that the *urgent need to protect public safety* took priority over the rights of the creditor. The receiver-manager was required to comply with the order prior to paying the secured creditor.

· · ·

Until 1990, it was not clear what effect provincial environmental requirements would have in a bankruptcy. There is no doubt that provincial environmental statutes are constitutionally valid within the province, but when they conflict with federal laws such as the *Bankruptcy and Insolvency Act*, the federal laws prevail. What priority does a provincial environmental protection order have in a bankruptcy?

· · ·

This question was addressed by a Canadian court for the first time in *Panamericana de Bienes y Servicios S.A. v. Northern Badger Oil & Gas Ltd.*, [1991] 5 WWR 577 (Alta. CA). Northern Badger Oil and Gas Limited was an oil and gas producer. It operated a number of valuable wells. However, it was also the named operator of seven old, disused wells, which could cause significant contamination unless properly decommissioned, as required by provincial law. Northern Badger Oil and Gas Limited became insolvent without decommissioning the old wells. Creditors began making their claims. A receiver-manager was appointed by the principal secured creditor, followed shortly by a trustee in bankruptcy.

The receiver-manager operated the business while arranging to realize the assets. However, it did not decommission the wells, despite a formal order to do so issued by the provincial Energy Resources Conservation Board (the "ERCB"). Instead, the receiver deliberately arranged a complicated sale of the assets of the estate, designed to ensure that all of the valuable assets were realized for the benefit of the secured creditor, leaving for the trustee in bankruptcy only the burdensome "assets" such as the disused wells. The arrangement worked by "selling" all of the assets, but on the condition that the purchaser could refuse to accept any asset. This arrangement was made without notice to the ERCB, despite its express request and clear interest, and without drawing the fact to the attention of the court which approved the sale. On the day of closing, the purchaser declined to accept the seven old wells, thus leaving them in the estate.

Most of the funds realized (more than $1 million) were promptly paid to the secured creditors, leaving enough to complete the administration of the estate, but not enough to decommission the wells. When all other matters had been completed, the receiver applied to the court for permission to pay the remaining funds to the secured creditor, to turn over the unrealized property, including the seven old wells, to the trustee, and to be discharged. The ERCB moved for an order requiring the receiver to first decommission the wells.

At trial, Mr. Justice MacPherson upheld the validity of the ERCB's order, recognizing that the wells were dangerous in their present condition. However, he held that the receiver was not obliged to comply with the order. He characterized the order to properly decommission the wells as a "claim" within the meaning of the *Bankruptcy and Insolvency Act*, and characterized the ERCB as a creditor seeking to use provincial law to evade the scheme of priorities set out in the Act.

The Court of Appeal ... required the receiver to comply with the order in priority to the claims of the secured creditors. The court held that an obligation to comply with the law, whether a statute or an administrative order, is a "liability," but it is not a "claim" as defined by the *Bankruptcy and Insolvency Act*. Nor was the Energy Resources Conservation Board a "creditor" of the bankrupt estate when it ordered the receiver to properly seal the abandoned wells.

The court held that it did not matter that the debtor, Northern Badger, had only a 10-per-cent ownership interest in the wells. The receiver, as manager of the wells, had operating control of them, and was therefore bound to obey the provincial law which governed those wells and which required the abandonment. The obligation to properly abandon wells is not a liability owed to the particular government agency which enforces the law; it is a duty owed by all citizens to all of their fellow citizens. A public authority which enforces the law does not thereby become a creditor of those persons bound to obey the law. Accordingly, the ERCB's order took priority over the rights of the secured creditor; the receiver was obliged to do whatever was necessary to obey the law before disbursing funds to the bank which had appointed it.

The Court of Appeal also stressed that a court-appointed receiver is a fiduciary on behalf of all parties with an interest in the debtor's property. As such, he is held to the highest standards of propriety and of respect ... for the law. The receiver's conduct in deliberately diverting all valuable assets for the benefit of the secured creditor, thus ensuring that no funds would be left to decommission the wells, while concealing these facts from the ERCB, did not meet these standards. For this reason, the receiver was ordered to perform the abandonment (at an estimated cost of more than $250,000), notwithstanding the fact that there were no longer sufficient assets in the debtor's estate. There was no indication in the decision as to whether the deficiency would have to be made up by the receiver personally, or whether he could look to the secured creditor for indemnity.

IV. The 1992 Amendments to the Bankruptcy and Insolvency Act

The *Panamericana* case put everyone in the lending community on notice that they must be concerned about the environmental status of their debtors. Unfortunately, the risk of uncertain and unlimited liability rapidly caused significant difficulty in persuading trustees and receivers to take appointments. This came to a head in *Re Lamford Forest Products Ltd.* (1991), 10 CBR (3d) 137 (BCSC). No one could be found to act as trustee of this large company, without the assurance that they would be paid. The British Columbia Supreme Court in Bankruptcy therefore ruled that the cost of compliance with an environmental protection order has priority over the claims of all secured and unsecured creditors, *except for the fee of the trustee.*

The court made an exception for the trustee because it would not be possible, otherwise, to appoint trustees in cases involving serious contamination. The court also held that a trustee in bankruptcy is not *personally* liable for [the] cost of complying with an environmental protection order which was issued to the bankrupt before the trustee was appointed. However, the court refused to decide whether, and in what circumstances, the trustee would have personal liability for breaches of environmental laws committed during the administration of the estate.

Soon afterwards, on November 1, 1992, the *Bankruptcy and Insolvency Act* was amended to provide trustees in bankruptcy with this measure of personal protection. [See subsections 14.06(2) and 14.06(3) as enacted by SC 1992, c. 27, s. 9(1).]

. . .

These *Bankruptcy and Insolvency Act* amendments gave trustees (but not receivers) some protection for their personal assets, but still allowed the Crown to put environmental requirements before the claim of the secured creditors.

. . .

VII. The 1997 Amendments to the Bankruptcy and Insolvency Act

On April 25, 1997, the 1992 *Bankruptcy and Insolvency Act* provisions were replaced by new provisions [SC 1996-97, c. 12, s. 15(1)] to come into force in September 1997. The key changes are:

- the personal protection given to trustees in 1992 now also extends to receivers and interim receivers: [14.06(1.1)].
- the standard for personal liability of trustees has been raised from mere negligence (failure to exercise due diligence) to gross negligence or willful misconduct: [14.06(2)(b)].
- the estate can abandon contaminated sites; if so, the trustee is not personally liable to comply with orders relating to that site, and clean-up costs for that site do not rank as costs of administration: [14.06(4); 14.06(6)].

- when an administrative order is issued, the trustee has 10 days' grace, during which it can abandon the property, appeal the order, or seek a stay of order while considering its options: [14.06(4)].
- clean-up costs are provable claims, no matter when they arise: [14.06(8)].
- the Crown has a superlien against the contaminated property, but not against other assets of the estate, e.g., accounts receivable: [14.06(7)].

The most important substantive change is that trustees (including receivers) have acquired the qualified right to abandon contaminated property. When property has been abandoned, the trustee cannot be required to comply with any remedial order relating to that property. Costs of cleaning up property which has been abandoned are still a claim provable in the bankruptcy, but they are not costs of administration. The amount actually expended by the Crown in right of Canada or a province for "remedying any environmental condition or environmental damage affecting real property of the debtor" can be recovered by a special "superlien" which attaches to that property and to any other real property of the debtor that is contiguous to the affected property and is related to the activity that caused the environmental damage. However, these clean-up costs do not have any special priority as against the other assets of the debtor, but will rank as ordinary unsecured claims.

· · ·

A. The Impact of These Changes

Now that the trustees and receivers can abandon properties, and thereby substantially protect the debtors' remaining assets, we may expect trustees to take more aggressive positions in their negotiations with the provincial Ministries of the Environment. These negotiations will continue to be necessary. The *Bankruptcy and Insolvency Act* amendments do not directly aid a trustee who goes into possession of contaminated property and does not abandon it. In such cases, the trustee will still be obliged to negotiate with provincial regulators a cap on the proportion of proceeds to be devoted to environmental matters.

However, the amendments may strengthen the trustee's bargaining position. Provincial regulators must be aware that clean-up costs expended by the trustee while in possession of contaminated property will rank as costs of administration, and therefore will be paid for out of all the assets of the estate in priority to all other claims. If the trustee renounces the property, the Crown is still free to do the work itself and to attempt to recover the funds, but it will have priority only as against the affected property and its neighbours, which is often an asset of dubious value. The Crown is also increasingly unwilling to fund clean-ups out of its own purse, as it would be required to do once the trustee abandons it. Accordingly, provincial regulators should be anxious to convince trustees to retain possession of problem properties, even more than they have been in the past. The staff cuts experienced by provincial regulators may also contribute to increased regulator interest in standardized lender agreements for modest but definite environmental improvements.

B. Questions of Interpretation

Numerous questions of interpretation are likely to arise as the new sections are applied to insolvencies across the country. For example:

- What will constitute "gross negligence or willful misconduct" on behalf of a trustee? Was Price Waterhouse guilty of gross negligence or wilful misconduct in exhausting the estate in its attempt to expand the landfill, rather than, as the Ministry preferred, in controlling the leachate plume? Nothing in the amendments gives either regulators or trustees guidance in making these tradeoffs.
- In s. 14.06(7), the Crown's superlien applies to "an environmental condition affecting real property." There are cases in which contamination has moved from the polluter's property into the property of a neighbour. Administrative orders are not infrequently issued to the polluter requiring the remediation of off-property contamination. If so, does subs. (7) apply? To what property?
- Subsection (7) extends the lien to any other real property of the debtor that is "contiguous to" the affected property. Will it apply where the second parcel is across a municipal street? What are the defining characteristics of property "related to the activity that caused the environmental condition or environmental damage"? Does it matter whether the polluting activity was carried on by a person other than the debtor, or whether the parcels were in separate ownership at the time the contamination occurred? How will it be applied where the cause of the contamination is unknown, or where the responsibility for the contamination could have arisen from similar operations on adjacent parcels?
- How will lenders manage the risk of losing their priority on a secured property because of (past or future) contamination on a "contiguous" site?
- Are the "costs of remediating any environmental condition or environmental damage," for which the Crown may claim priority, limited to those costs which the Crown has already incurred, or do they include the costs of those activities which the Crown has ordered someone to carry out, but which no one has performed?

• • •

VIII. Conclusion

Ten years ago, environmental issues in a bankruptcy were presented to the courts as urgent requirements to take timely action to avoid threatened, substantial, irreversible harm to significant public interests. In these extreme cases, environmental requirements should, and did, "trump" the monetary allocation framework of the *Bankruptcy Act*.

This conclusion, however, required, and received, re-evaluation. Aggressive efforts by environmental regulators to extend liability to those without fault have met strong opposition, particularly from those with bargaining power, such as the lending community. It has become apparent that many environmental claims are directed at correction of past harms, or merely at the collection of money, rather than at urgent, future dangers to the public welfare. Moreover, the urgency and social value of environmental demands are sometimes modest in comparison with the other social values that must be balanced in a bankruptcy. It is therefore no surprise that environmental issues no longer automatically trump other priorities.

How, then, should the balance be struck? In an ideal system, bankruptcy priorities would reflect a functional analysis: urgent needs to prevent future harm to significant public interests would take priority over mere monetary claims; environmental monetary claims would rank with other monetary claims. This is not, however, the approach taken in the current *Bankruptcy and Insolvency Act* provisions. It is difficult to discern any clear principle which underlies them; instead, they suggest arbitrary truce lines drawn out of exhaustion in the midst of a prolonged battle. We should expect continuing struggles as the lending and environmental regulatory communities continue to pursue their separate agendas on the murky battlefield of the *Bankruptcy and Insolvency Act*.

NOTES AND QUESTIONS

1. In *Re Lamford Forest Products Ltd.* (1991), 10 CBR (3d) 137, at 145 (BCSC) (a case decided prior to the 1992 amendments, and discussed above) Harvey J, in the absence of specific provisions in the BIA, concluded, "The balancing of values in this case falls in favour of protecting the health and safety of society over the rights of creditors." Do the amendments strike the appropriate balance between the societal interests of health and safety and the rights of creditors?

2. In *Canadian Imperial Bank of Commerce v. Isobord Enterprises Inc.* (2002), 44 CELR (NS) 281 (Man. QB), Manitoba Conservation claimed a charge in priority to all other claims under s. 14.06(7) of the BIA for the costs incurred in implementing a rodent-control program. The terms of the Manitoba *Environment Act*, CCSM c. E125 provided that costs incurred by the government of Manitoba to remedy an environmental situation are debts owed to the government. In this case, the Crown did not follow the proper steps as required by the provincial legislation. It did not apply for an order authorizing an environmental officer to enter the affected area. The Crown went ahead and contracted with exterminators to develop a rodent-control program without a court order. The court held that where the Crown did not follow the proper steps as required by the provincial legislation, no claim could be asserted by the Crown. As the Crown did not acquire a claim against the debtor under the provincial law it could not assert any priority claim under s. 14.06(7).

VI. PREFERRED CLAIMS

In *Husky Oil Operations Ltd. v. Canada (Minister of National Revenue—MNR)* (1995), 128 DLR (4th) 1, at 8-9 (SCC), Iacobucci J stated:

> It has long been accepted that the first goal of ensuring an equitable distribution of a debtor's assets is to be pursued in accordance with the federal system of bankruptcy priorities. ... Parliament has created an equitable distribution wherein the general rule is that creditors are to rank equally, with claims provable in bankruptcy being paid rateably (*Bankruptcy Act*, s. 141). The rule of creditor equality is subject to 10 classes of debt which are accorded priority in a stated order, the so-called list of "preferred" creditors (s. 136). ... Lastly, the entire scheme of distribution is "[s]ubject to the rights of secured creditors" (s. 136) which, as Professor Hogg has noted, "enables secured creditors to realize their security as if there were no bankruptcy."

What is the rationale for the equitable treatment of creditors? Does bankruptcy law actually achieve an equitable distribution to creditors? Why does the law tolerate exceptions to the equality principle by creating a class of preferred creditors? See, for example, R. Mokal, "Priority as Pathology: The Pari Passu Myth" (2001), *CLJ* 581; A. Keay and P. Walton, "The Preferential Debts Regime in Liquidation Law: In the Public Interest" (1999), *CFILR* 84; and Susan Cantile, "Preferred Priority in Bankruptcy," in Jacob Ziegel, *Current Developments in International and Comparative Corporate Insolvency Law* (Oxford: Clarendon Press, 1994), 438. The following extract considers the rationale for preferred claims.

New Zealand Law Commission, *Priority Debts in the Distribution of Insolvent Estates: An Advisory Report to the Ministry of Commerce* (NZLC SP2, 1999), 6-10

In our view, the purpose of insolvency law is to provide rules based on notions of fairness and justice, which can be applied in any given case to avoid inefficiencies which would result from an individualized resolution of claims within a bankruptcy or liquidation. In an insolvency, it is axiomatic that loss will be suffered. The issue is how the incidence of loss will be borne. The granting of priority status to a creditor affects the incidence of loss as particular creditors may be paid in full while others receive little or nothing.

We agree with Professor Goode that the fundamental principle of insolvency law:

> is that of *pari passu* distribution, for creditors participating in the common pool in proportion to the size of their admitted claims. (Goode, *Principles of Corporate Insolvency Law* (Sweet & Maxwell, London 1990) 59)

. . .

Our starting point is that after payment of secured creditors, the proceeds of realisation of property of an insolvent entity should be distributed *pari passu* to remaining creditors *unless* there are compelling reasons to justify giving preferential status to a particular debt. No submissions made to us seriously challenged that starting proposition.

We have endeavoured to articulate the policy factors which should be taken into account when determining whether compelling reasons exist to grant preferential status to any particular type of debt. We have come to the view that the following are the relevant policy factors:

. . .

- The balancing of private rights should *generally* be given precedence over public interest issues. Because insolvency law draws lines which determine which creditors suffer more loss than others, it is the competing rights of those creditors which should be given paramountcy. While certain types of priority may be considered desirable on public interest grounds (for example, the desirability of protecting the country's revenue base, the social imperative involved in protecting employees, and, in other jurisdictions, the priority afforded to the costs of remedying environmental damage), the issue is whether it is appropriate *in the particular case* for these matters to be taken into account for insolvency law purposes. Care should be taken to ensure that social imperatives that might be taken into account cannot be met more readily through social welfare or other legislation.

- The need to create incentives for creditors to manage credit efficiently. The granting of preferential status to a class of debt may tend to reduce the incentive for a creditor to manage credit efficiently, as that creditor is more likely to receive payment from the realised assets of the insolvent. The cost of any laxity will be borne by other (unsecured) creditors.

· · ·

In our view, having balanced the considerations to which we have just referred, it is necessary to stand back and make an objective judgment as to whether the proposed priority:

- is one which can be justified by reference to principles of fairness and equity likely to command general public acceptance;
- intrudes unnecessarily upon the law as it otherwise affects property rights and securities; and
- provides encouragement for the effective administration of insolvencies or, at least, does not provide any disincentive to administer insolvent estates efficiently.

While we have taken the view that, generally, the balancing of private rights should be given precedence over public interest issues, there will, no doubt, be occasions when community expectations demand that public interest considerations be given primacy. In our view, it is entirely appropriate in a democracy for community expectations to be the value underpinning a priority, *provided* the grounds for the expectation are articulated clearly so that proper debate can take place as to whether priority status is the best way of achieving the policy goal.

NOTES AND QUESTIONS

1. The World Bank in *Principles and Guidelines for Effective Insolvency and Creditor Rights Systems* (April 2001), at 9, adopted a similar view of preferred claims:

Principle 16(C) Following distribution to secured creditors and payment of claims related to costs and expenses of administration, proceeds available for distribution should be distributed *pari passu* to remaining creditors unless there are compelling reasons to justify giving preferential status to a particular debt. Public interests should not be given precedence over private rights. The number of priority classes should be kept to a minimum.

2. Examine the various classes of preferred creditors contained in s. 136. In light of the principles discussed by the New Zealand Law Commission, what justifications can be offered for the specific categories of preferred creditors in s. 136?

3. Note that paragraphs 136(1)(h) and (j) are effectively spent in their effect. The preferred status is afforded to these claims only if the debtor went into bankruptcy before the prescribed date of November 30, 1992. See *Bankruptcy and Insolvency General Rules*, CRC c. 368, s. 137.

4. One author suggests that *pari passu* has suffered a progressive erosion due to the ever-increasing proliferation of preferred debts. It is argued that this is a result of the political nature of priorities:

> As priorities are granted by legislation, every pressure group tries to influence parliaments in order to reach a better treatment for their credits. The development of legislation is the consequence of the political struggle among social groups, leading to a race for the top in the creditors' graduation. The legislative power has sought to satisfy the demands for protection of very different categories of creditors: the legislature feels free to grant a preferential status, because new priorities do not suppress previous ones. Superimposition has become the rule in the field of priorities: legislation superimposes new preferential credits on old ones, so that old preferential credits are not eliminated, but displaced to a lower position in the graduation.
>
> [Jose M. Garrido, "The Distributional Question in Insolvency: Comparative Aspects" (1995), 4 *Int. Insol. Rev.* 25, at 34.]

Does this statement apply to the Canadian context? Can you identify any preferred claim in s. 136 that might be said to be the result of interest-group influence? Was the government's decision to eliminate the Crown's preferred status in 1992 (discussed in Chapter 8) consistent with the author's argument above?

Re Milad
(1984), 50 CBR (NS) 113 (Ont. CA)

ZUBER JA (orally): [1] This is an appeal from an order made by White Prov. J, upon the application of the bankrupt for discharge.

[2] This appeal raises the issue of whether or not in such an order there is power in the judge sitting in bankruptcy to require that the bankrupt consent to judgment in favour of one creditor in preference to other creditors of the same class.

[3] Section 142 of the *Bankruptcy Act*, RSC 1970, c. B-3, provides as follows:

> 142.(1) On the hearing of the application, the court may either grant or refuse an absolute order of discharge or suspend the operation of the order for a specified time, or grant an order of discharge subject to any terms or conditions with respect to any earnings or income that may afterwards become due to the bankrupt or with respect to his after-acquired property.
>
> (2) The court shall on proof of any of the facts mentioned in section 143
>
> (a) refuse the discharge,
>
> (b) suspend the discharge for such period as the court thinks proper, or
>
> (c) require the bankrupt, as a condition of his discharge, to perform such acts, pay such moneys, consent to such judgments, or comply with such other terms, as the court may direct.

[4] Mr. Quirt argues that the language of this section is broad enough to empower the judge to make the order which is the subject of this appeal.

[5] With respect to the learned judge sitting in bankruptcy we do not agree. In our view, the powers conferred by this section are not sufficiently wide to enable the bankruptcy judge to make an order which is inconsistent with a fundamental principle of the *Bankruptcy Act*, namely, the principle of *pari passu* distribution amongst creditors of the same rank: see s. 112 of the *Bankruptcy Act*.

[6] Other courts have also reached this conclusion, although I am obliged to say that the pattern of authorities is not entirely consistent. We rely upon the principles expressed by trial judges in the following cases: *Re Billone* (1980), 33 CBR (NS) 86 (Ont. HC); *Re Harrison* (1983), 47 CBR (NS) 316, 45 BCLR 167 (BCSC); and *Re Lockyer* (1978), 28 CBR (NS) 80, 7 BCLR 361 (SC).

[7] In the result, the appeal is allowed and the order of White Prov. J will be varied to provide that the payments ordered by White Prov. J will be made to the trustee in bankruptcy and not to the creditor and that the consent judgment of the deputy registrar be varied so as to be in favour of the trustee instead of the creditor.

NOTE

The 2005 amendments to the BIA contained a provision that gave a court the discretion to order that money paid by a bankrupt to satisfy the terms of a conditional discharge be paid to a particular creditor rather than to the trustee. However, this provision was subsequently repealed in the 2007 amendments to the BIA. Should the court have the discretion to direct that these funds be paid to a particular creditor? Under what circumstances would it be appropriate for a court to exercise such discretion?

VII. CONTRACTUAL SUBORDINATION

Re Air Canada
(2004), 2 CBR (5th) 4 (Ont. SCJ)

FARLEY J: Canadian Imperial Bank of Commerce, Greater Toronto Airports Authority, Airbus, Cara Operations Limited and IBM Canada Limited (collectively "Trade Creditors") moved:

(A) for a declaration that the holders of Subordinated Perpetual Debt

(a) 5¾% Subordinated Bonds 1986ff (Swiss fr 200,000,000);

(b) 6¼% Subordinated Bonds 1986ff (Swiss fr 300,000,000);

(c) 6⅜% Interest-Adjustable Subordinated Bonds 1987ff (DM 200,000,000);

(d) Subordinated Loan Agreement (Yen 20,000,000,000); and

(e) Subordinated Loan Agreement (Yen 40,000,000,000)

(collectively "SP Debt") are not entitled to vote or receive any dividend or other distribution from Air Canada unless and until the claims of all unsecured creditors, including those whose claims are in respect of borrowed money, have been paid in full;

(B) a declaration that any entitlement of holders of [SP Debt] must be distributed not to such holders but to all unsecured creditors *pro rata* in relation to their proven claim; and

(C) such further and other relief as this Honourable Court deems just.

· · ·

Each of the SP Debt instruments contains subordination provisions. While all the provisions are not identical, they are substantially similar. The following are definitions from the November 14, 1989 Yen Loan Agreement:

> *"Indebtedness"*—the principal, premium, if any, and unpaid interest (including interest accrued after the commencement of any reorganization or bankruptcy proceedings) or any indebtedness of the Borrower for borrowed money, whether by way of loan or evidenced by a bond, debenture, note or other evidence of indebtedness and whether secured or unsecured, including indebtedness for borrowed money of others guaranteed by the Borrower;
>
> *"Senior Indebtedness"*—means all Indebtedness, present or future, which is not expressly subordinated to or ranking *pari passu* with the Loan whether by operation of law or otherwise, in the event of a winding-up, liquidation or dissolution, whether voluntary or involuntary, whether by operation of Law or by reason of insolvency legislation;

The end result is that upon the happening of the relevant triggering event, the holders of the SP Debt have contractually agreed that they will be subordinated to Senior Indebtedness. The Trade Creditors assert that there will be untold difficulty in determining what is "borrowed money" as this is an undefined term. With respect, I disagree as not every term has to be defined in an agreement in order to determine its meaning and it would not appear to me to be all that difficult to draw the line if, as and when that becomes necessary.

The Trade Creditors also submit that as among the unsecured debt, as the unsecured SP Debt is subordinated to Senior Indebtedness (also unsecured), then the doctrine of subordination requires that the SP Debt be subordinated to all unsecured debt (that is, not only the Senior Indebtedness but also all unsecured debt). They rely upon what they say is "a fundamental principle of Canadian insolvency law that, excepting only specifically enumerated preferred creditors, all unsecured creditors are entitled to *pro rata* distribution" and that this principle is reflected in s. 141 of the *Bankruptcy and Insolvency Act* ("BIA"):

> 141 Subject to this Act, all claims proved in a bankruptcy shall be paid rateably.

However, this is a CCAA insolvency proceeding not a BIA one. The jurisprudence in CCAA proceedings is that any plans of arrangement are treated as contracts amongst the parties (including the minority voting against) and that the court in a sanction hearing will review the creditor approved plan to see if it is fair, reasonable and equitable, wherein equitable does not necessarily mean equal. See *Alternative Fuel Systems Inc., Re* (2004), 24 Alta. LR (4th) 1 (Alta. CA); *Sammi Atlas Inc., Re* (1998), 3 CBR (4th) 171 (Ont. Gen. Div. [Commercial List]).

The Trade Creditors rely upon *Re Maxwell Communications Corporation PLC*, [1993] 1 WLR 1402 where at pp. 1411-2 in approving the proposed distribution, Vinelott J concluded that a bilateral subordination between a debtor and a creditor can be effective:

> The question is whether this underlying consideration of public policy should similarly invalidate an agreement between a debtor and a creditor postponing or subordinating the claim of the creditor to the claims of other unsecured creditors and preclude the waiver or subordination of the creditor's claim after the commencement of a bankruptcy or winding up. I do not think that it does. It seems to me plain that after the commencement of a bankruptcy or a winding up a creditor must be entitled to waive his debt just as he is entitled to decline to submit a proof.
>
> *If the creditor can waive his right altogether I can see no reason why he should not waive his right to prove, save to the extent of any assets remaining after the debts of other unsecured creditors have been paid in full;* ...
>
> So also, if the creditor can waive his right to prove or agree the postponement of his debt after the commencement of the bankruptcy or winding up, I can see no reason why he should not agree with the debtor that his debt will not be payable or will be postponed or subordinated in the event of a bankruptcy or winding up.

(emphasis by Trade Creditors)

However, I would caution that this quote must be taken in context; similarly for the second Vinelott J quote. Then in reliance upon Vinelott J's views at p. 1416, the Trade Creditors submitted in their factum:

> 20. Accordingly, the Court gave effect to the bilateral subordination provisions as a waiver of the credit to its entitlement to receive any distribution until *all unsecured* creditor claims have been paid in full.
>
> 21. In giving effect to the subordination, the Court distinguished on the facts previous decisions of the English courts that had addressed arrangements that disturbed rateable distribution among unsecured creditors. The Court, however endorsed the fundamental principle that a debtor cannot validly contract with one unsecured creditor for any advantage denied to other unsecured creditors.

Vinelott J stated at p. 1416:

> [If] the clearance arrangements had had the effect contended for by Air France they would clearly have put a member of the clearance arrangements in a position which would have been better than the position of other unsecured creditors. *The arrangements would therefore unquestionably have infringed a fundamental principle of bankruptcy law, which is reflected in but not derived from section 302 or its predecessor, that a creditor cannot validly contract with his debtor that he will enjoy some advantage in a bankruptcy or winding-up which is denied to other creditors.*
>
> In my judgment I am not compelled by the decisions of the House of Lords in the *Halesowen* and *British Eagle* cases, or by the decisions of the Court of Appeal in those cases or in *Rolls Razor Ltd. v. Cox*, [1967] 1 QB 552, to conclude that a contract between a company and a creditor, providing for the debt due to the creditor to be subordinated in the insolvent

winding up of the company to other unsecured debt, is rendered void by the insolvency legislation.

(emphasis by Trade Creditors)

The Trade Creditors went on at paras. 23-24 of their factum:

> 23. However, also consistent with the decision of the English Court in *Maxwell* and cases enforcing the policy of rateable distribution among unsecured creditors which were accepted in *Maxwell*, such agreement cannot be enforced to provide an unsecured creditor (or any subset of unsecured creditors) an advantage in an insolvency proceeding which is denied to other unsecured creditors. Put simply, the [SP Debt] holders are free to waive claims if they choose, but neither they nor the debtor can direct that the resulting benefit shall be distributed preferentially to some unsecured creditors and not others.
>
> 24. Treating the holders of [SP Debt] as being subordinated to all unsecured creditors is consistent with key principles of Canadian insolvency law and with the terms of the subordination itself. Such holders should not be entitled to receive any dividend until creditors with "borrowed money" claims are paid in full. As claims arising from "borrowed money," in the case, are unsecured claims, they are entitled to receive *pro rata* distributions under Air Canada's plan of arrangement with all other unsecured creditors and will be paid in full only when all other unsecured claims are paid in full.

With respect, I disagree. The Trade Creditors did not bargain or pay for any benefit or advantage in respect of the SP Debt nor are they parties to any agreements in respect thereto and it is important to observe that they have not been designated as third party beneficiaries (nor have they asserted that they were). The cases cited by the Trade Creditors would not appear to me to have much if any relevance to the situation in this case. *Ex parte MacKay* (1873), 8 Ch App 643 dealt with a situation where a creditor had bargained with the debtor for additional rights upon the bankruptcy of that debtor. *British Eagle International Airlines Ltd. v. Compagnie Nationale Air France*, [1975] 1 WLR 780 (HL) involved the applicability of the laws of bankruptcy to the existence of mutual debts existing as of the date of bankruptcy. *Gingras automobile Ltée, Re* (1962), 34 DLR (2d) 751 (SCC) deals with the legal question of paramountcy. *Hamilton and others v. Law Debenture Trustee Ltd. and others*, [2001] 2 BCLC 159 (Ch Div); *Maxwell, supra*; *Re British & Commonwealth Holdings PLC (No. 3)*, [1992] 1 WLR 672 (Ch Div) each dealt with instruments that had rights on their face that were subordinated to the rights of *all other creditors*.

Even within a bankruptcy context there is no impediment to a creditor agreeing to subordinate his claim to that of another creditor. See *Rico Enterprises Ltd., Re* (1994), 24 CBR (3d) 309 (BCSC [In Chambers]) where Tysoe J observed at pp. 322-3:

> ... If one creditor subordinates its claim to the claim of another party without subordinating to other claims ranking in priority to the claim of the other party, it is my view that a distribution of the assets of the bankrupt debtor should be made as if there was no subordination except to the extent that the share of the distribution to which the subordinating creditor would otherwise be entitled should be paid to the party in whose favour the subordination was granted.

It is not appropriate to simply take the subordinating creditor out of the class to which it belongs and put it in the class ranking immediately behind the holder of the subordination right. I say this for two reasons. First, the creditors in the same class as the subordinating creditor should not receive the benefit of a subordination agreement to which they are not a party and on which they are not entitled to rely. They would receive a windfall benefit by the removal of the subordinating creditor from their class in the event that there were insufficient monies to fully pay their class because the total indebtedness of the class would be reduced and the pro rata distribution would be increased. Second, if the parties to the subordination agreement turned their minds to it, they would inevitably agree that the subordinating creditor should receive its normal share of the distribution and give it to the party in whose favour the subordination was granted. The party receiving the subordination would agree because it would be paid a portion of a distribution to a higher class of creditor that it would not otherwise receive and the subordinating creditor would agree because it would not receive the money in either event.

See also *Bank of Montreal v. Dynex Petroleum Ltd.* (1997), 145 DLR (4th) 499 (Alta. QB) at p. 529; (reversed on appeal on other grounds [1999 CarswellAlta 1271 (Alta. CA)]); Roy Goode, *Legal Problems of Credit and Security*, 3rd ed. (Sweet & Maxwell: London, 2003) at p. 55. It would seem to me that a guide-lining principle should be that as discussed in A.R. Keay, *MacPherson's Law of Company Liquidation* (London; Sweet & Maxwell, 2001) at p. 717:

> However, they [the courts] would permit a liquidator to distribute according to an agreement made along the lines of the latter situation providing that to do so would not adversely affect any creditor not a party to the agreement, *i.e.*, creditors not involved in the subordination agreement would not receive less under that agreement than would have been received if distributions had been made on a *pari passu* basis.

See also J.L. Lopes, "Contractual Subordinations and Bankruptcy" (1980), 97 No. 3 *Banking Law Journal*, 204 at p. 206.

> At the conclusion of the bankruptcy proceedings, a dividend is allocated to all unsecured creditors, including the subordinated creditor, on a pro rata basis. The dividend allocated to the subordinated creditor is paid over to the senior creditor, to the extent of its claim, with the subordinated creditor retaining the remainder of the dividend if the senior creditor is paid in full.* This process neither affects the amount of claims against the debtor nor the dividend paid to unsecured creditors. (*See, e.g., *In re Associated Gas & Elec. Co.*, 53 F. Supp. 107, 114 (S.D.N.Y. 1943).)

· · ·

In the end result I do not see that there is any problem with the SP Debt being selectively subordinated to the Senior Indebtedness. This subordination to that "borrowed money" does not result in the SP Debt being subordinated to all the unsecured debt, Senior Indebtedness and non-Senior Indebtedness alike.

Motion dismissed.

NOTE

The court in *Re Maxwell Communications Corporation plc*, [1993] 1 WLR 1402 distinguished between contractual subordination (in which a creditor contractually agreed to the subordination of its claim) and turnover subordination (in which a creditor agreed to turn over any amounts received to the creditors who were given the benefit of the subordination). Turnover subordination is often effected by means of a trust under which the subordinating creditor undertakes to hold the proceeds of any distribution for the benefit of the benefiting creditor up to the amount agreed to be postponed. Are there any significant differences in outcome that depend upon which type of subordination is employed? Consider the case where both the subordinating creditor and the debtor are insolvent. What is the nature and status of the benefiting creditor's claim to the funds that are payable to the subordinating creditor?

VIII. POSTPONED CLAIMS

A. Postponement Under the BIA

In addition to granting creditors enhanced priority or special repossession rights, the BIA also postpones certain types of claims. The postponed claims are listed in ss. 137-140.1. Section 137 provides that a creditor who has entered into a non-arm's-length transaction with a debtor at any time prior to bankruptcy is not entitled to claim a dividend in respect of that transaction until all other claims of the creditors have been satisfied.

Section 139 postpones claims of silent partners. If an advance of money is made to a borrower whereby the lender receives an interest rate varying with the profits and the borrower subsequently becomes bankrupt, the lender of the money is not entitled to recover anything in respect of the loan until the claims of all other creditors of the borrower have been satisfied. However, this provision will not prevent a profit-sharing lender from obtaining a security interest to secure the obligation. In this case, the claim will only be postponed to the extent that the collateral is insufficient to satisfy the obligation secured. See *Sukloff v. A.H. Rushforth & Co. Estate*, [1964] SCR 459.

Claims by shareholders for the return of equity do not rank as claims of creditors in bankruptcy. Therefore, shareholders do not recover anything unless the claims of all creditors are satisfied: this principle has been codified by the 2007 amendments (see new BIA s. 140.1, discussed further in the notes following the *Blue Range* case, below). However, shareholders may sometimes attempt to assert a claim against the corporation and claim as an unsecured creditor. A shareholder might assert a claim for damages for fraudulent misrepresentation against a corporation in respect of the issuance of shares. Alternatively, a shareholder might bring a restitutionary action for the recovery of money upon the rescission of a contract for the purchase of shares. Shareholders may also attempt to claim as unsecured creditors in respect of dividends that were declared or other corporate distributions that became owing to shareholders prior to the bankruptcy.

Re Blue Range Resource Corp.
(2000), 15 CBR (4th) 169 (Alta. QB)

Introduction

ROMAINE J: [1] This is an application for determination of three preliminary issues relating to a claim made by Big Bear Exploration Ltd. against Blue Range Resource Corporation, a company to which the *Companies' Creditors Arrangement Act*, RSC 1985, c. C-36, as amended, applies. Big Bear is the sole shareholder of Blue Range, and submits that its claim should rank equally with claims of unsecured creditors. The preliminary issues relate to the ranking of Big Bear's claim, the scope of its entitlement to pursue its claim and whether Big Bear is the proper party to advance the major portion of the claim.

[2] The Applicants are the Creditors' Committee of Blue Range and Enron Canada Corp., a major creditor. Big Bear is the Respondent, together with the MRF 1998 II Limited Partnership, whose partners are in a similar situation to Big Bear.

Facts

[3] Between October 27, 1998 and February 2, 1999, Big Bear took the following steps:

(a) it purchased shares of Blue Range for cash through The Toronto Stock Exchange on October 27 and 29, 1998;

(b) it undertook a hostile takeover bid on November 13, 1998, by which it sought to acquire all of the issued and outstanding Blue Range shares;

(c) it paid for the Blue Range shares sought through the takeover bid by way of a share exchange: Blue Range shareholders accepting Big Bear's offer received 11 Big Bear shares for each Blue Range share;

(d) it issued Big Bear shares from treasury to provide the shares used in the share exchange.

[4] The takeover bid was accepted by Blue Range shareholders and on December 12, 1998, Big Bear acquired control of Blue Range. It is now the sole shareholder of Blue Range.

[5] Big Bear says that its decision to undertake the takeover was made in reliance upon information publicly disclosed by Blue Range regarding its financial situation. It says that after the takeover, it discovered that the information disclosed by Blue Range was misleading, and in fact the Blue Range shares were essentially worthless.

[6] Big Bear as the sole shareholder of Blue Range entered into a Unanimous Shareholders' Agreement pursuant to which Big Bear replaced and took on all the rights, duties and obligations of the Blue Range directors. Using its authority under the Unanimous Shareholders' Agreement, Big Bear caused Blue Range to apply for protection under the CCAA. An order stipulating that Blue Range is a company to which the CCAA applies was granted on March 2, 1999.

. . .

Issue #1

[12] With respect to the alleged share exchange loss, without considering the principle of equitable subordination, is Big Bear:

(a) an unsecured creditor of Blue Range that ranks equally with the unsecured creditors of Blue Range; or

(b) a shareholder of Blue Range that ranks after the unsecured creditors of Blue Range.

[13] At the hearing, this question was expanded to include reference to the transaction costs and cash share purchase damage claims in addition to the alleged share exchange loss.

Summary of Decision

[14] The nature of the Big Bear claim against Blue Range for an alleged share exchange loss, transaction costs and cash share purchase damages is in substance a claim by a shareholder for a return of what it invested *qua* shareholder. The claim therefore ranks after the claims of unsecured creditors of Blue Range.

Analysis

[15] The position of the Applicants is that the share exchange itself was clearly an investment in capital, and that the claim for the share exchange loss derives solely from and is inextricably intertwined with Big Bear's interest as a shareholder of Blue Range. The Applicants submit that there are therefore good policy reasons why the claim should rank after the claims of unsecured creditors of Blue Range, and that basic corporate principles, fairness and American case law support these policy reasons. Big Bear submits that its claim is a tort claim, allowable under the CCAA, and that there is no good reason to rank the claim other than equally with unsecured creditors. Big Bear submits that the American cases cited are inappropriate to a Canadian CCAA proceeding, as they are inconsistent with Canadian law.

[16] There is no Canadian law that deals directly with the issue of whether a shareholder allegedly induced by fraud to purchase shares of a debtor corporation is able to assert its claim in such a way as to achieve parity with other unsecured creditors in a CCAA proceeding. It is therefore necessary to start with basic principles governing priority disputes.

[17] It is clear that in common law shareholders are not entitled to share in the assets of an insolvent corporation until after all the ordinary creditors have been paid in full: *Re Central Capital Corp.* (1996), 132 DLR (4th) 223 (Ont. CA) at page 245; *Canada Deposit Insurance Corp. v. Canadian Commercial Bank* (1992), 97 DLR (4th) 385 (SCC) at pages 402 and 408. In that sense, Big Bear acquired not only rights but restrictions under corporate law when it acquired the Blue Range shares.

. . .

[19] In *Canada Deposit Insurance* (*supra*), the Supreme Court of Canada considered whether emergency financial assistance provided to the Canadian Commercial Bank by

a group of lending institutions and government was properly categorized as a loan or as an equity investment for the purpose of determining whether the group was entitled to rank *pari passu* with unsecured creditors in an insolvency. The court found that, although the arrangement was hybrid in nature, combining elements of both debt and equity, it was in substance a loan and not a capital investment. It is noteworthy that the equity component of the arrangement was incidental, and in fact had never come into effect, and that the agreements between the parties clearly supported the characterization of the arrangement as a loan.

[20] *Central Capital Corp. (supra)* deals with the issue of whether the holders of retractable preferred shares should be treated as creditors rather than shareholders under the CCAA because of the retraction feature of the shares. Weiler JA commented at page 247 of the decision that it is necessary to characterize the true nature of a transaction in order to decide whether a claim is a claim provable in either bankruptcy or under the CCAA. She stated that a court must look to the surrounding circumstances to determine "whether the true nature of the relationship is that of a shareholder who has equity in the company or whether it is that of a creditor owed a debt or liability."

[21] The court in *Central Capital Corp.* found that the true nature of the relationship between the preferred shareholders and the debtor company was that of shareholders. In doing so, it considered the statutory provision that prevents a corporation from redeeming its shares while insolvent, the articles of the corporation, and policy considerations. In relation to the latter factor, the court commented that in an insolvency where debts will exceed assets, the policy of federal insolvency legislation precludes shareholders from looking to the assets until the creditors have been paid (*supra*, page 257).

[22] In this case, the true nature of Big Bear's claim is more difficult to characterize. There may well be scenarios where the fact that a party with a claim in tort or debt is a shareholder is coincidental and incidental, such as where a shareholder is also a regular trade creditor of a corporation, or slips and falls outside the corporate office and thus has a claim in negligence against the corporation. In the current situation, however, the very core of the claim is the acquisition of Blue Range shares by Big Bear and whether the consideration paid for such shares was based on misrepresentation. Big Bear had no cause of action until it acquired shares of Blue Range, which it did through share purchases for cash prior to becoming a majority shareholder, as it suffered no damage until it acquired such shares. This tort claim derives from Big Bear's status as a shareholder, and not from a tort unrelated to that status. The claim for misrepresentation therefore is hybrid in nature and combines elements of both a claim in tort and a claim as shareholder. It must be determined what character it has in substance.

[23] It is true that Big Bear does not claim rescission. Therefore, this is not a claim for return of capital in the direct sense. What is being claimed, however, is an award of damages measured as the difference between the "true" value of Blue Range shares and their "misrepresented" value—in other words, money back from what Big Bear "paid" by way of consideration. Although the matter is complicated by reason that the consideration paid for Blue Range shares by Big Bear was Big Bear treasury shares, the Notice of Claim filed by Big Bear quantifies the loss by assigning a value to the treasury shares. A tort award to Big Bear could only represent a return of what Big Bear invested in equity of Blue Range. It is that kind of return that is limited by the basic common law principal

that shareholders rank after creditors in respect of any return on their equity investment. Whether payment of the tort liability by Blue Range would affect Blue Range's stated capital account is irrelevant, since the shares were not acquired from Blue Range but from its shareholders.

[24] In considering the question of the characterization of this claim, it is noteworthy that Mr. Tonken in his March 2, 1999 affidavit in support of Blue Range's application to apply the CCAA did not include the Big Bear claim in his list of estimated outstanding debt, accounts payable and other liabilities. The affidavit does, however, set out details of the alleged misrepresentations.

[25] I find that the alleged share exchange loss derives from and is inextricably intertwined with Big Bear's shareholder interest in Blue Range. The nature of the claim is in substance a claim by a shareholder for a return of what it invested *qua* shareholder, rather than an ordinary tort claim.

[26] Given the true nature of the claim, where should it rank relative to the claims of unsecured creditors?

· · ·

[28] Although there are no binding authorities directly on point on the issue of ranking, the Applicants submit that there are a number of policy reasons for finding that the Big Bear claim should rank subordinate to the claims of unsecured creditors.

[29] The first policy reason is based on the fundamental corporate principle that claims of shareholders should rank below those of creditors on an insolvency. Even though this claim is a tort claim on its face, it is in substance a claim by a shareholder for a return of what it paid for shares by way of damages. The Articles of Blue Range state that a holder of Class A Voting Common Shares is entitled to receive the "remaining property of the corporation upon dissolution in equal rank with the holders of all other common shares of the Corporation." As pointed out by Laskin J in *Central Capital* (*supra* at page 274):

Holding that the appellants do not have provable claims accords with sound corporate policy. On the insolvency of a company the claims of creditors have always ranked ahead of the claims of shareholders for the return of their capital. Case law and statute law protect creditors by preventing companies from using their funds to prejudice creditors' chances of repayment. Creditors rely on these protections in making loans to companies.

[30] Although what is envisaged here is not that Blue Range will pay out funds to retract shares, the result is the same: Blue Range would be paying out funds to the benefit of its sole shareholder to the prejudice of third-party creditors.

· · ·

[33] Another policy reason which supports subordinating the Big Bear claim is a recognition that creditors conduct business with corporations on the assumption that they will be given priority over shareholders in the event of an insolvency. This assumption was referred to by Laskin J in *Central Capital* (*supra*), in legal textbooks (Hadden, Forbes and Simmonds, *Canadian Business Organizations Law* Toronto: Butterworths, 1984 at 310, 311), and has been explicitly recognized in American case law. The court in *Matter of Stirling Homex Corp.*, 579 F 2d 206 (US 2nd Cir. NY 1978) at page 211 referred to this assumption as follows:

Defrauded stockholder claimants in the purchase of stock are presumed to have been bargaining for equity type profits and assumed equity type risks. Conventional creditors are
presumed to have dealt with the corporation with the reasonable expectation that they
would have a senior position against its assets, to that of alleged stockholder claims based
on fraud.

[34] The identification of risk-taking assumed by shareholders and creditors is not
only relevant in a general sense, but can be illustrated by the behaviour of Big Bear in this
particular case. In the evidence put before me, Big Bear's president described how, in the
course of Big Bear's hostile takeover of Blue Range, it sought access to Blue Range's books
and records for information, but had its requests denied. Nevertheless, Big Bear decided
to pursue the takeover in the absence of information it knew would have been prudent
to obtain. Should the creditors be required to share the result of that type of risk-taking
with Big Bear? The creditors are already suffering the results of misrepresentation, if it
occurred, in the inability of Blue Range to make full payment on its trade obligations.

[35] The Applicants submit that a decision to allow Big Bear to stand *pari passu* with
ordinary creditors would create a fundamental change in the assumptions upon which
business is carried on between corporations and creditors, requiring creditors to re-
evaluate the need to obtain secured status. It was this concern, in part, that led the court
in *Stirling Homex* to find that it was fair and equitable that conventional creditors should
take precedence over defrauded shareholder claims (*supra* at page 208).

[36] The Applicants also submit that the reasoning underlying the *Central Capital
Corp.* case (where the court found that retraction rights in shares do not create a debt
that can stand equally with the debt of shareholders) and the cases where shareholders
have attempted to rescind their shareholdings after a corporation has been found insolvent is analogous to the Big Bear situation, and the same result should ensue.

[37] It is clear that, both in Canada and in the United Kingdom, once a company is
insolvent, shareholders are not allowed to rescind their shares on the basis of misrepresentation: *Re Northwestern Trust Co.*, [1926] SCR 412 (SCC) at 419; *Milne v. Durham
Hosiery Mills Ltd.*, [1925] 3 DLR 725 (Ont. CA); *Trusts & Guarantee Co. v. Smith* (1923),
54 OLR 144 (Ont. CA); *Re National Stadium Ltd.* (1924), 55 OLR 199 (Ont. CA); *Oakes
v. Turquand* (1867), [1861-73] All ER Rep. 738 (UKHL) at page 743-744.

[38] The court in *Northwestern Trust Co.* (*supra* at page 419) in *obiter dicta* refers to
a claim of recission for fraud, and comments that the right to rescind in such a case may
be lost due to a change of circumstances making it unjust to exercise the right. Duff J
then refers to the long settled principle that a shareholder who has the right to rescind
his shares on the ground of misrepresentation will lose that right if he fails to exercise it
before the commencement of winding-up proceedings, and comments:

> The basis of this is that the winding-up order creates an entirely new situation, by altering
> the relations, not only between the creditors and the shareholders, but also among the
> shareholders *inter se*.

[39] This is an explicit recognition that in an insolvency, a corporation may not be
able to satisfy the claims of all creditors, thus changing the entire complexion of the corporation, and rights that a shareholder may have been entitled to prior to an insolvency
can be lost or limited.

[40] In the Blue Range situation, Big Bear has actively embraced its shareholder status despite the allegations of misrepresentation, putting Blue Range under the CCAA in an attempt to preserve its equity value and, in the result, holding Blue Range's creditors at bay. Through the provision of management services, Big Bear has participated in adjudicating on the validity of creditor claims, and has then used that same CCAA claim approval process to attempt to prove its claim for misrepresentation. It may well be inequitable to allow Big Bear to exercise all of the rights it had arising from its status as shareholder before CCAA proceedings had commenced without recognition of Blue Range's profound change of status once the stay order was granted. Certainly, given the weight of authority, Big Bear would not likely have been entitled to rescind its purchase of shares on the basis of misrepresentation, had the Blue Range shares been issued from treasury.

. . .

[57] Based on my characterization of the claim, the equitable principles and considerations set out in the American cases, the general expectations of creditors and shareholders with respect to priority and assumption of risk, and the basic equitable principle that claims of defrauded shareholders should rank after the claims of ordinary creditors in a situation where there are inadequate assets to satisfy all claims, I find that Big Bear must rank after the unsecured creditors of Blue Range in respect to the alleged share exchange loss, the claim for transaction costs and the claim for cash share purchase damages.

. . .

Order accordingly.

NOTES AND QUESTIONS

1. Section 510(b) of the US *Bankruptcy Code* provides that a claim arising from rescission of a purchase or sale of a security of the debtor or for damages arising from the purchase or sale of the security, shall be subordinated to all claims or interests that are senior to or equal the claim or interest represented by such security.

The *Blue Range* decision imported a similar rule into Canadian bankruptcy law.

2. The 2007 amendments enact a new BIA s. 140.1: "a creditor is not entitled to a dividend in respect of an equity claim until all claims that are not equity claims have been satisfied." "Equity claim" is defined to mean:

a claim that is in respect of an equity interest, including a claim for, among other things,

(a) a dividend or similar payment,

(b) a return of capital,

(c) a redemption or retraction obligation,

(d) a monetary loss resulting from the ownership, purchase or sale of an equity interest or from the rescission, or, in Quebec, the annulment, of a purchase or sale of an equity interest, or

(e) contribution or indemnity in respect of a claim referred to in any of paragraphs (a) to (d).

"Equity interest" means, in effect, a share or like interest in a corporation: new BIA s. 2.

These provisions codify the *Blue Range* decision, but they go further. In common with s. 510(b) of the United States Bankruptcy Code, *Blue Range* only deals with one kind of equity claim—that is, a rescission or damages claim arising from the purchase or sale of a security. The amendments extend the rule to all equity claims, including shareholder claims for return of capital. New BIA s. 60(1.7) enacts a corresponding rule for BIA commercial proposal proceedings and new CCAA s. 6(8) enacts a corresponding rule for CCAA proceedings: see Chapter 15, Section IV.

3. As a matter of policy, is it right to treat shareholder claims for misrepresentation and the like as equity claims? According to *Blue Range*, the answer is "yes," in part because shareholders take the risk of equity-type losses in exchange for equity-type profits and they can't have one without the other. But is it true to say that ordinary investors also assume the risk of being lied to in company prospectuses and the like?

According to the provincial securities laws, the answer to this question is "no" and they give defrauded investors a range of remedies. The aim is to preserve investor confidence in securities markets. But what is the point of provincial laws giving defrauded investors the right to sue for damages and the like if the bankruptcy laws subordinate the investors' claims?

The bankruptcy law reformers justify their position by saying that subordination of equity claims is important to preserve creditor confidence: if creditors do not have priority over shareholder claims, they may be less willing to lend and they will probably charge more. On the other hand, according to the securities law makers, we need remedies for defrauded investors to maintain confidence in securities markets: if there are no effective remedies for fraud, investors may be less willing to invest and the company's securities will be worth less. In summary, there is a tension between the need to preserve creditor confidence in credit markets and the need to preserve investor confidence in securities markets. The new bankruptcy reforms were apparently enacted without consideration of this point and without input from securities laws specialists: see Janis Sarra, "From Subordination to Parity: An International Comparison of Equity Securities Claims in Insolvency Proceedings (2007), 16 *International Insolvency Law Review* 181; Anita Anand, "Should Shareholders Rank with Unsecured Creditors in Bankruptcy?" (2008), 24 *BFLR* 169.

4. In the United States the *Sarbanes-Oxley Act* has special provisions allowing the SEC to collect civil penalties on behalf of defrauded investors ("the fair funds provision"). The fair funds provision, at least to some extent, counteracts s. 510(b) of the *Bankruptcy Code*: it means that defrauded investors will get some compensation, via the SEC, even though they themselves are subordinated creditors in the issuing company's bankruptcy. As matters now stand, there is nothing like the fair funds provision in Canada.

5. Defrauded investors also receive a measure of protection in both the United Kingdom and Australia. In the United Kingdom, s. 74(2)(f) of the *Insolvency Act* provides that claims owing to a person in the person's capacity as a member of the company by way of dividends, profits, or otherwise are postponed until all other debts are satisfied. Section 563A of the Australian *Corporations Act 2001* is a similar provision. The House of Lords in *Soden v. British & Commonwealth Holdings Plc.*, [1998] AC 298 read down the provision by holding that it does not apply in respect of a claim to an independent cause of action that was not connected with the statutory contract that defined the rights of the shareholder. The rule was not that the "rights of members come last." Rather, it was that the "rights of members as

members come last." As the members have an independent cause of action for fraudulent misrepresentation, this claim was not affected by the legislative subordination (although claims for an unpaid dividend or for money owing by the company upon the exercise of a retraction right would be postponed). A similar conclusion was reached by the High Court of Australia in *Sons of Gwalia Ltd. v. Margaretic* (2007), 81 ALJR 525. The difference was that, in *Soden*, the House of Lords drew a distinction between subscriber investors and transferee investors, holding that the exception applied only to the latter, whereas the High Court in *Sons of Gwalia* held that there was no basis for this distinction and that the exception applied equally to both types of investor.

6. *I. Waxman & Sons Ltd (Re)* (2008), 40 CBR (5th) 307 (Ont. SCJ) appears to support the proposition that, once an equity claim is reduced to judgment, it acquires the character of an ordinary debt and thus the reasoning in *Blue Range* does not apply. Does this distinction make sense in terms of the policy considerations discussed above? How does new BIA s. 140.1 affect the question?

B. Equitable Subordination

Beyond the express statutory provisions for postponement contained in the BIA, there is an issue about whether Canadian courts have an equitable power to postpone claims along the lines of the US doctrine of equitable subordination. Starting with *Pepper v. Litton*, 308 US 295 (1939) and *Taylor v. Standard Gas & Electric Co.*, 306 US 307 (1939), US courts have embraced a doctrine of equitable subordination. The doctrine applies where a claimant, not dealing at arm's length with the bankrupt, has exploited its controlling position by taking unfair advantage of the bankrupt or securing a benefit over the bankrupt's other creditors that would not otherwise have accrued to it. The wrongdoer may be a majority shareholder in a single corporation or it may be a parent corporation in a position to dictate decisions to a subsidiary. The advantage may consist in the dominant shareholder causing the corporation to confess to judgment in the shareholder's favour with respect to a long-dormant wage claim (as in *Pepper v. Litton*); or it may involve a parent company causing the subsidiary to declare large dividends in the parent company's favour (as in *Taylor*, above) where the dividends cannot be justified on economic grounds.

Where such inequitable conduct is found, the remedy applied by US courts is to subordinate the wrongdoer's claim, in whole or in part, until the claims of the bankrupt's other creditors have been satisfied.

> **Thomas G.W. Telfer, "Transplanting Equitable Subordination: The New Free-Wheeling Equitable Discretion in Canadian Insolvency Law?"**
> (2001), 36 *CBLJ* 36, at 41-43

The ruling [in *Pepper*] began a long debate over the meaning of these highly abstract concepts, and indeed one author suggests that it is impossible to extract from the decision a basic rule that can be followed consistently. Nine years later, the [US] Supreme Court in *Comstock v. Group of Institutional Investors* [335 US 211 (1948)] divided 5-4 on the scope of the doctrine … . It was not until 1977 that a framework emerged to provide some consistency to the principles of equitable subordination.

In 1977, the Fifth Circuit in *Re Mobile Steel* [563 F2d 692] distilled the principles from the earlier case law and developed a three-part test for equitable subordination … . Before exercising the power of equitable subordination, a court must be satisfied that:

> (i) The claimant must have engaged in some type of inequitable conduct; (ii) The misconduct must have resulted in injury to the creditors of the bankrupt or conferred an unfair advantage on the claimant; (iii) Equitable subordination of the claim must not be inconsistent with the provisions of the Bankruptcy Act.

The *Mobile Steel* three-part test quickly became the new framework by which courts analyzed equitable subordination. The following year, Congress gave statutory recognition to the power of equitable subordination. In enacting the provision, Congress purposely left the wording vague, thus allowing the courts the freedom to continue to develop and define the scope of the doctrine. Section 510(c) of the Bankruptcy Code provides that after notice and a hearing, the court may,

> (1) under the principles of equitable subordination, subordinate for purposes of distribution all or part of an allowed claim to all or part of another claim or all or part of an allowed interest to all or part of another interest; (2) or order that any lien securing such a subordinated claim be transferred to the estate.

The principles developed by the courts, including the *Mobile Steel* test, continue to provide the only guidelines on the meaning of the doctrine. The United States Supreme Court in the 1996 decision of *United States v. Noland* [517 US 535] endorsed the *Mobile Steel* three-part test.

NOTES AND QUESTIONS

1. There is no specific statutory provision in either the CCAA or the BIA that expressly permits the application of the doctrine of equitable subordination. However, under s. 183 of the BIA, courts are "invested with such jurisdiction at law and in equity as will enable them to exercise original, auxiliary and ancillary jurisdiction in bankruptcy." Does s. 183 permit a court to import US concepts of equity into Canadian law? What provisions of the CCAA might permit a court to invoke the doctrine?

2. Prior to 1992, Canadian courts were divided on the issue of whether a comparable doctrine existed in Canadian law. The BC Court of Appeal in *Laronge Realty Ltd. v. Golconda Investments Ltd.* (1986), 7 BCLR (2d) 90 did not rule out the existence of a broad equitable jurisdiction. In contrast, Chadwick J in *AEVO Co. v. D & A Macleod Co.* (1991), 4 OR (3d) 368 (Gen. Div.) rejected the doctrine:

> To incorporate the doctrine of equitable subordination into the Bankruptcy Act would create chaos and lead to challenges of security agreements based on the conduct of the secured creditor. If the Parliament of Canada felt that this doctrine had some application I am confident that in their wisdom they would have incorporated similar provisions into our statute.

3. In *Canada Deposit Insurance Corp. v. Canadian Commercial Bank* (1992), 97 DLR (4th) 385 (SCC), the possibility was left open that equitable subordination is available under Canadian bankruptcy law. While citing the three-part test in *Mobile Steel,* the court expressly refrained from ruling on the question whether the doctrine of equitable subordination should become part of Canadian insolvency law and held that there was no evidence of inequitable conduct on the part of the creditor that would justify the application of the doctrine on the assumption that it did apply. The ruling in *CDIC* equitable subordination continues to remain an open question. The Ontario Court of Appeal similarly left the matter unresolved in *Olympia & York Developments Ltd. v. Royal Trust Co.* (1993), 14 OR (3d) 1, at 17. Canadian case law since 1992 falls into three lines of authority: "(1) explicit rejection of the doctrine, (2) ambivalence about whether equitable subordination applies but willingness to consider the test in relation to the facts of the case, and (3) receptivity to the doctrine or its application." See Telfer, above, at 56.

4. In *Harbert Distressed Investment Fund, L.P. v. General Chemical Canada Ltd.* (2006), 22 CBR (5th) 298 (Ont. SCJ), at para. 92, Justice Mesbur stated:

> It should be remembered, however, that equitable subordination has been used sparingly by Canadian courts. Inequitable conduct requires the court to conduct a broad inquiry into the conduct of the parties to determine what is right and just in all the circumstances. The test is a "sense of simple fairness. Equitable subordination is not used, however, to "adjust the legally valid claim of an innocent party who asserts the claim in good faith merely because the Court perceives the result as inequitable. The court must therefore be careful not to approach the question on the basis of who the competing creditors are (i.e., the "innocent and vulnerable" employees, as opposed to the "sophisticated and wealthy" lender), but rather by the nature of their respective claims.

5. A Joint Report of the Insolvency Institute of Canada and the Canadian Association of Insolvency and Restructuring Professionals made the following recommendation with respect to equitable subordination:

> 69. Provide that there is no doctrine of equitable subordination in Canada.

> The US doctrine of equitable subordination allows superior courts to exercise their equitable jurisdiction to subordinate claims that are valid against the insolvent debtor's estate but arise from, or are connected with, inequitable conduct prejudicial to the interests of creditors. Canadian courts have not yet clarified whether the doctrine applies to the Canadian insolvency context. Proposal #69 specifies that the doctrine of equitable subordination would not be applicable to reviewable transactions in the Canadian context, thus creating some certainty for parties in their financing transactions.

(Joint Report of Insolvency Institute of Canada and the Canadian Association of Insolvency and Restructuring Professionals (Toronto: Joint Task Force on Business Insolvency Law Reform, March 15, 2002).)

6. What specific remedy is appropriate if a court applies the doctrine? See Robert C. Clark, "The Duties of the Corporate Debtor to Its Creditors" (1977), 90 *Harv. L Rev.* 505, at 519-20. Clark suggests that the remedy may involve the subordination of all the claims of the controlling party ("full-subordination" rule); it may be restricted to a deduction of the

unfair benefit received by the insider from the insider's claim ("offset" rule); or the insider's entitlement to share in the proceeds of the estate will be calculated as if no tainted transaction had taken place and the insider is then considered to have received an anticipatory distribution equal to the amount of the unjust benefit previously received by it ("constructive distribution" rule).

7. Is there any need for a Canadian doctrine of equitable subordination in light of the existing statutory powers of postponement that exist in the BIA? Are there other statutes outside the BIA that might provide an adequate remedy to deal with problems that arise in cases such as *Pepper*? Reilly J in *Unisource Canada Inc. (c.o.b. Barber-Ellis Fine Papers) v. Hong Kong Bank of Canada* (1998), 43 BLR (2d) 226 (Ont. Gen. Div.); aff'd. in part (2000), 131 OAC 24 (CA) questioned the need for equitable subordination given existing Canadian statutory provisions at para. 134:

> It might be noted in passing that the Bankruptcy and Insolvency Act, together with provincial legislation such as the Fraudulent Conveyances Act, the Personal Property Security Act and the Assignments and Preferences Act provide for a statutory scheme of distribution of the estate of a bankrupt that enshrines most of the "equitable principles" that form the basis for many "equitable subordination" decisions in American cases (see, for example, secs. 3, 4, 91, 95, 96, 100, 101 and 136-147 of the Bankruptcy and Insolvency Act). Principles such as settlement of property, fraudulent preferences, reviewable transactions and the rules for priority and postponement of claims involving non-arm's length transactions or related parties are all recognized within the legislation. A Court presiding in bankruptcy clearly has an equitable jurisdiction (see s. 183, Bankruptcy and Insolvency Act). ... However, barring evidence of fraud or misrepresentation, in my view the Court should exercise great caution in departing from the statutory scheme for distribution and relief.

8. Beyond equitable subordination, what other means might be available to attack the series of transactions? See Robert C. Clark, "The Duties of the Corporate Debtor to Its Creditors" (1977), 90 *Harv. L Rev.* 505, at 530-32. Are there any advantages to pursuing a case such as *Pepper* under the rubric of equitable subordination?

9. Creditors, and more recently trustees in bankruptcy, have been able to rely on the oppression remedy found in Canadian corporation statutes. Under s. 241(2) of the CBCA, for example, a court may order relief for conduct that is "oppressive or unfairly prejudicial to or that unfairly disregards the interests of any security holder, creditor, director or officer." The scope of the oppression remedy is considered in Chapter 10 in the context of director liability. Does the oppression remedy offer any possibility of achieving the equivalence of equitable subordination? The range of orders available under the oppression remedy is broad, including the general power of the court to grant "any interim or final order it thinks fit": CBCA s. 241(3).

10. Are there alternative mechanisms available in the common law that might allow a court to achieve the functional equivalence of equitable subordination? In *Sittuk Investments Ltd. v. A. Farber & Partners Inc.* (2002), 61 OR (3d) 546 (Ont. SCJ), the court held that a claim may be postponed where the claimant acted unconscionably toward the other claimants. Time-share agreements were marketed as leases when in fact they did not give the holder a proprietary right in the land. The holders of the time-share agreements therefore could only claim as ordinary unsecured creditors in the bankruptcy of the company

that entered into these contracts. An affiliated company (the applicant company) had a sizable claim against the bankrupt company. Normally, the claims would be required to share pro rata. The court concluded:

> As president and sole shareholder and director of the applicant company, he was and is its controlling mind. He knew or had reason to know that a borrowing authorized by him on behalf of the bankrupt company and the applicant company would prospectively give the applicant company a *pari passu* claim against the unit holders. Thus, it was unconscionable for him to authorize the borrowing transaction for each of the parties to it. If the borrowing had instead been made from an unrelated third party such as a bank, without actual or constructive knowledge on its part, the case would be a different one as regards any claim that might have been asserted by the unrelated third party. It would have been a stranger to the unconscionable conduct.

CHAPTER TEN

Liability of Corporate Directors and Insolvency

I. INTRODUCTION

The insolvency of a corporation raises the issue of whether directors should take some responsibility for the debts of the corporation. While traditional company law principles treat the corporation as a separate entity, there are a number of statutes in Canada that will hold directors personally liable for some aspects of the corporation's debts.[1] Section II of this chapter considers a range of statutes that impose director liability for debts of the corporation. For example, director liability arises for unpaid wages under federal and provincial corporations statutes, as well as under employment standards legislation. Similarly, directors face the prospect of personal liability for unpaid remittances by the corporation of income tax.

Section III focuses on sanctions for director conduct that is detrimental to creditors. Traditionally corporate law has taken the position that directors must act in the best interests of the corporation. However, do directors of a corporation owe a duty to the corporation's creditors when the company is insolvent or in the vicinity of insolvency? This question has been considered by courts in England, Australia, New Zealand, and the United States. Section III examines how the Supreme Court of Canada answered that question in *Peoples Department Stores Inc. (Trustee of) v. Wise*. The chapter concludes with a study of the oppression remedy and a comparative examination of wrongful or reckless trading statutes found in other jurisdictions. While the parameters of the topic of director liability are wide, this chapter focuses on specific instances of director liability in the context of bankruptcy and insolvency.

---

[1] See, for example, Janis P. Sarra and Ronald B. Davis, *Director and Officer Liability in Corporate Insolvency* (Markham, ON: Butterworths, 2002), at 12.

II. DIRECTORS' PERSONAL LIABILITY FOR CORPORATE DEBTS

Barrette v. Crabtree Estate
[1993] 1 SCR 1027

L'HEUREUX-DUBÉ J: [1] This appeal concerns the interpretation of s. 114(1) of the *Canada Business Corporations Act*, SC 1974-75-76, c. 33 ("CBCA") (now s. 119(1) of the *Canada Business Corporations Act*, RSC, 1985, c. C-44). Specifically, the question is whether, under that provision, the directors of a corporation against which employees have obtained a judgment, can be held personally liable for sums of money awarded by a court as pay in lieu of notice of dismissal.

. . .

I. Facts

[2] On May 17, 1985 Wabasso Inc. (hereinafter "the corporation") closed its plant at Trois-Rivières after experiencing serious financial difficulties. The appellants, 29 former managerial employees, were laid off. There being no agreement as to the amount to be paid by the corporation to its managerial employees in lieu of notice of dismissal, the appellants brought an action in the Quebec Superior Court. By judgment dated December 14, 1987, JE 88-416, Laroche J ordered the corporation to pay the appellants $300,358.66 as pay in lieu of notice of dismissal, in addition to the indemnity provided for in art. 1078.1 CCLC.

[3] That decision was not appealed.

[4] On January 27, 1988, after the corporation became insolvent, the appellants brought an action in the Court of Quebec pursuant to s. 114(1) CBCA seeking a personal order against the directors of the corporation (the respondents). By judgment dated May 25, 1989 Judge Gagnon allowed the appellants' action and ordered the respondents jointly and severally to pay the appellants the sum of $300,358.66 as well as the additional indemnity provided for in art. 1078.1 CCLC.

[5] On April 15, 1991 the Quebec Court of Appeal allowed the respondents' appeal.

. . .

[11] The Court of Appeal therefore concluded, unlike the Court of Quebec judge, that the sums awarded by the Superior Court did not fall within the scope of s. 114 CBCA.

III. Issue

[12] The only issue in this Court is whether the sums awarded by the Superior Court as pay in lieu of notice of dismissal were "debts ... for services performed for the corporation" within the meaning of that expression in s. 114(1) CBCA.

. . .

IV. Analysis

[14] According to the appellants, the rules of statutory interpretation generally give a broad meaning to the word "debts" in s. 114(1) CBCA. Thus, by reason of the remedial nature of that provision, a broad and liberal interpretation should be adopted so as to include the amounts awarded by the Superior Court as pay in lieu of notice. The respondents, on the other hand, point out that s. 114(1) CBCA imposes a liability on them that goes beyond what the law ordinarily prescribes, being an exception to the general rule that directors are not liable for a company's debts. The respondents accordingly submit that, given the exceptional nature of directors' personal liability, s. 114(1) CBCA requires instead a strict interpretation.

. . .

(B) Origin and Background of Section 114(1) CBCA

(1) New York Legislation

[16] The remedy provided for in s. 114(1) CBCA is based on a New York State law dating from 1848. That statute, *An Act to authorise the formation of corporations for manufacturing, mining, mechanical or chemical purposes, NY Laws 1848*, c. 40, s. 18, provided that shareholders of companies covered by the law "shall be jointly and severally individually liable for all debts that may be due and owing to all their laborers, servants and apprentices, for services performed for such corporation."

. . .

(2) Canadian Legislation

[22] Unlike its American precursor, the federal provision at issue here places the liability for certain debts of the corporation to its employees on the shoulders of the directors, rather than on those of the shareholders. Its original wording goes back to the first general legislation dealing with the incorporation of federal companies. Section 49 of the *Canada Joint Stock Companies Letters Patent Act*, 1869, SC 1869, c. 13, read as follows:

> 49. The Directors of the Company shall be jointly and severally liable to the laborers, servants and apprentices thereof, for all debts, not exceeding one year's wages, due for services performed for the Company whilst they are such Directors respectively; but no Director shall be liable to an action therefor, unless the Company has been sued therefor within one year after the debt became due, nor yet unless such Director is sued therefor within one year from the time when he ceased to be such Director, nor yet before an execution against the Company has been returned unsatisfied in whole or in part; and the amount due on such execution shall be the amount recoverable with costs against the Directors.

[23] By specifying that the sums paid by one director could be recovered from other directors, the federal statute avoided reproducing one of the flaws inherent in the American provision. Similarly, by placing this liability on the shoulders of directors rather than shareholders, the federal provision avoided the problem of the potential liability of shareholders with small holdings who had no part in the administration of the company. On

the other hand, unlike its New York counterpart, the Canadian provision never formulated a specific definition of the amounts covered by the remedy.

. . .

[25] Accordingly, the issue in this case is whether, in the absence of a specific definition of the nature of the debts Parliament had in mind, s. 114(1) CBCA applies to amounts awarded by a court as pay in lieu of notice. Parliament places the liability imposed by s. 114(1) CBCA on the shoulders of directors, on the one hand, for the benefit of a particular category of creditors, on the other. While clarifying the context of the remedy, both the case law and the doctrine indicate that these two facets are inseparable from its purpose.

(C) Purpose and Context of the Remedy

[26] The primary purpose of the remedy provided for in s. 114(1) CBCA is to protect employees in the event of bankruptcy or insolvency of the corporation. This protection is part of a range of legislative measures which go far beyond the bounds of company law:

> [TRANSLATION] According to traditional wisdom, Parliament always was or should have been concerned with protecting employees affected by bankruptcy or insolvency.
>
> This concern to provide protection can take various forms. It can be demonstrated by giving priority to a wage claim against the debtor's assets or against immovable property the value of which was increased by the employee's work, up to the amount of the value added. It can also take the form of providing a preferred claim in the debtor's bankruptcy or in the liquidation of the company.
>
> *In addition to these measures … the protection of employees can take the form of a remedy against third parties, primarily* the bank which has taken possession of the debtor's assets under s. 178(6) of the *Bank Act*, the beneficiary of an assignment of inventory and *the directors of an insolvent company.* [Emphasis added.]
>
> (A. Bohémier and A.-M. Poliquin, "Réflexion sur la protection des salariés dans le cadre de la faillite ou de l'insolvabilité" (1988), 48 R du B 75, at p. 81.)

[27] This overview of the general context indicates that the recourse provided for in s. 114(1) CBCA is distinguishable because it is brought against third parties, the directors. The observations of Hall J in *Fee v. Turner* (1904), 13 Que. KB 435, clearly summarize the rationale underlying the remedy itself (at p. 446):

> For lack of any other reason it occurs to me that what must have been had in view, was to protect to a limited extent those who were employed by such companies in positions which do not enable them to judge with any special intelligence what is the company's real financial position. The directors have personally this knowledge or should have it, and if, aware of the company's embarrassed affairs, and specially of the danger of a speedy collapse and insolvency, they continue to utilize the services of employees who have no means of securing this knowledge and who give their time and labour upon their sole reliance, often, on the good faith and respectability of the company's directors, it is not inequitable that such directors should be personally liable, within reasonable limits, for arrears of wages, thus given to their service.

[28] Scholarly commentary has endorsed these observations concerning the purpose of the protection inherent in such measures. Thus, distinguishing employees from the corporation's other creditors, Professor Marie-Louis Beaulieu dismisses as follows the argument that directors' liability is penal in nature:

> [TRANSLATION] And why would this penalty involve requiring them to pay the employees rather than the company's other creditors?
>
> It will perhaps be said that such creditors deserve special consideration by the law: that is very true; and it is more logical to say that Parliament wished to protect the worker and nothing more, to give him a remedial action, a guarantee of payment, in view of his often difficult situation. As he has nothing to do with administration, he should not suffer the consequences of a disaster; he does not speculate, he will be paid for what his work is worth, whatever the company's profits.

> ("De la responsabilité des directeurs de compagnies pour le salaire des employés" (1930-31), 9 R du D 218 and 483, at p. 220.)

[29] Iacobucci, Pilkington and Prichard similarly justify the protection at issue here by the special vulnerability of employees as compared with other creditors of the corporation:

> This liability is an intrusion on the principle of corporate personality and limited liability, but it can be justified on the grounds that directors who authorize or acquiesce in the continued employment of workers when the corporation is not in a position to pay them should not be able to shift the loss onto the shoulders of the employees. Other creditors who supply goods and services to a failing corporation are not entitled to this kind of preference, but neither are they as dependent on the corporation as employees, nor as vulnerable.

> (Canadian Business Corporations (1977), at p. 327.)

. . .

[31] Section 114(1) CBCA is located within a specific legal framework. In terms of the general principles governing company law, the provision is exceptional in at least three respects. First, the rule departs from the fundamental principle that a corporation's legal personality remains distinct from that of its members. In so doing, s. 114(1) CBCA creates an exception to the more general principle that no one is responsible for the debts of another. Further, unlike other statutory rules which may impose personal liability on directors, s. 114(1) CBCA does not contain an exculpatory clause as such:

> Contrary to the liability resulting from the inappropriate declaration of dividends, inappropriate financial assistance to shareholders and other statutorily created liability of directors, the statutes do not contain any exculpatory availabilities with respect to unpaid wages: the mere fact of having been a director at the time that the services were rendered by the employee renders the directors jointly and severally liable, provided the various statutory procedural requirements are fulfilled by the employee.

> The only possible exculpation, therefore, is proof by the director that he was *not* a director at the time the liability was incurred, that he was not sued within the proper prescriptive or statute of limitations period, or that the employee did not fulfil the relevant statutory pre-conditions which give rise to the director's liability. [Emphasis in original.]

(Yoine Goldstein, "Bankruptcy As it Affects Third Parties: Some Aspects," in Meredith Memorial Lectures 1985, Bankruptcy—Present Problems and Future Perspectives (1986), 198, at p. 212.)

[32] Finally, the provision in question imposes on directors a positive obligation. This distinguishes it from most statutory rules, which prohibit directors from engaging in certain acts or transactions. As Marc Chabot points out:

[TRANSLATION] In general, the statutory liability of directors involves the prohibition of certain actions. Liability is then associated with a decision which they took at some point on their own initiative. The obligation imposed on them is to avoid certain decisions in certain circumstances. The liability of directors for unpaid wages is perhaps the only case where a positive obligation is imposed on them: they must ensure that wages are paid in the event ·of bankruptcy or insolvency.

(La protection des salaires en cas de faillite ou d'insolvabilité (1985), at p. 91.)

[33] It is against this background that the present appeal must be considered. While its purpose is to ensure that certain sums, including wages, are paid to employees in the event the corporation becomes bankrupt or insolvent, s. 114(1) CBCA constitutes a major exception to the fundamental principles of company law applicable to directors' liability. As we have seen, it also overrides the more general principle that no one is liable for the debts of another.

[34] In this regard, there are two important parameters in connection with the employee's remedy. First, the directors' maximum liability is set at six months' wages. This parameter provides a ceiling which, while establishing a quantitative limit to the liability of the directors, does not in so doing determine the nature of the amounts covered by the action. The nature of the sums which Parliament had in mind must be considered instead from a second angle: regardless of quantum, the amounts claimed must be "debts … for services performed for the corporation." I therefore cannot subscribe to the appellants' arguments that the first question to be answered is whether the job loss compensation falls within the broad concept of "wages." In the context of s. 114(1) CBCA, the word "wages" refers solely to the quantum of the directors' liability and cannot in itself guide the Court in disposing of the present case.

[35] The parameter which is at the heart of the appeal is therefore not the concept of "wages," but the expression "debts … for services performed for the corporation." In thus limiting the debts covered by the remedy, Parliament indicated that directors will not be personally liable for all debts assumed by the corporation to its employees. As Beauregard JA pointed out in *Schwartz v. Scott*, [[1985] CA173], at pp. 716-17:

[TRANSLATION] The purpose of this provision is not to make directors liable for all the debts which a corporation may at its option assume more or less retroactively to its employees for past services.

[36] In order to determine whether the amounts awarded as job loss compensation are "debts … for services performed for the corporation," the nature of pay in lieu of notice of dismissal must therefore be examined in light of this criterion.

· · ·

[L'Heureux-Dubé J noted that where there is an employment contract for an indefinite term, either of the parties may terminate the contract at any time by giving the other party reasonable notice.]

[40] In light of the foregoing, it seems necessary to mention two separate errors made by the lower courts. These relate, first, to the characterization of the amounts awarded by the Superior Court, and second, to the requirements of s. 114(1) CBCA.

[41] After stressing that the notice of dismissal was mandatory and necessary, the trial judge concluded (at p. 12):

> [TRANSLATION] *The notice period is therefore not comparable to damages since its purpose is to minimize the impact of the job loss by allowing the employee to make reasonable advance provision for the effects of dismissal. Reasonable notice of dismissal is therefore an integral part of the employment contract* for an indefinite term, as was the case with the plaintiffs. Accordingly, this debt is associated with the performance of services for the corporation. [Emphasis added.]

[42] With respect, the outcome of the appeal cannot depend simply on whether or not the obligation to give reasonable notice is part of the contract for an indefinite term. First, since the employer's failure to give reasonable notice is a contractual fault, the penalty for that failure must necessarily take the form of contractual damages. Second, as I noted earlier, the purpose of s. 114(1) CBCA is not to cover all debts assumed by the corporation to its employees. This point cannot be disregarded. Accordingly, the fact that the employer has an obligation under a contract of employment cannot in itself be conclusive for purposes of an action brought by the employee.

[43] On the other hand, the fact that an obligation imposed on the employer is not expressed in specific monetary terms under the law or in the employment contract cannot be a bar to a remedy under s. 114(1) CBCA. By concluding that this provision applied only to a debt [TRANSLATION] "the amount of which is known because the rates are specified in the employment contract (individual or collective, as the case may be) or by law" (p. 1196), the Court of Appeal added a condition that is not found in the wording of the provision. Section 114(1) CBCA establishes a quantitative limit on the amounts for which directors will be personally liable, and that is a sum equivalent to six months' wages. Directors are therefore in a position to know in advance the maximum amount of their potential liability in the event the company becomes bankrupt or insolvent. For the purposes of the present appeal, it does not seem necessary to dispose of the controversy that may arise as to the interpretation of the word "debts" taken in isolation. I am thus prepared to assume, without deciding, that the amounts payable in lieu of notice of dismissal are "debts" within the meaning of s. 114(1) CBCA. However, the appellants' appeal must fail on another ground.

[44] The term "debts" cannot be dissociated from the context in which it is used. According to the language used by Parliament, the debts must result from "services performed for the corporation." An amount payable in lieu of notice does not flow from services performed for the corporation, but rather from the damage arising from non-performance of a contractual obligation to give sufficient notice. The wrongful breach of the employment relationship by the employer is the cause and basis for the amounts

awarded by the Superior Court as pay in lieu of notice. It is primarily for this reason that the Ontario Court of Appeal has excluded this type of compensation from the scope of s. 114(1) CBCA (see *Mesheau v. Campbell*, [(1982), 141 DLR (3d) 155 (Ont. CA)], at p. 157, and *Mills-Hughes v. Raynor* (1988), 47 DLR (4th) 381, at pp. 386-87). In the absence of additional legislative indicia, the performance of services by the employee remains the cornerstone of the directors' personal liability for debts assumed by the corporation. On the pretext of a broad interpretation, this Court cannot add to the text of the provision words which it does not contain. Taking account of the context in which s. 114(1) CBCA was enacted and the nature of the specific liability which departs from what the law ordinarily prescribes, it seems to me that only one conclusion logically follows.

. . .

(E) Conclusion

[49] As with the examination of context surrounding the remedy provided for in s. 114(1) CBCA, reference to comparative law makes it clear that the ambiguity of the provision in question should not be resolved by a mechanical application of a given rule of construction. Although the purpose of this provision is to ensure that certain sums are paid to employees in the event that the corporation becomes bankrupt or insolvent, the rule it states cannot be separated from either the legal context or the language in which Parliament has chosen to state the rule. In such circumstances, amounts awarded by a court for damages the basis of which is located, as here, in the non-performance of a contractual obligation and the wrongful breach of a contract of employment by the employer are not "debts ... for services performed for the corporation" for which the corporation's directors can thus be personally liable.

[50] However much sympathy one may feel for the appellants, who have here been deprived of certain benefits resulting from the contract of employment with their employer, that does not give a court of law the authority to confer on them rights which Parliament did not intend them to have. In the absence of the provision here at issue, the employees would have suffered the same fate as any creditor dealing with an insolvent debtor, in this case the bankrupt employer. The Act provides a remedy, giving them recourse against the directors of the corporation, but it has limited that remedy both in quantity and in duration. Only Parliament is in a position, if it so wishes, to extend these benefits after weighing the consequences of so doing. This, in the final analysis, remains a political choice and cannot be the function of the courts.

NOTES AND QUESTIONS

1. As noted by Justice L'Heureux-Dubé, the remedy against directors for unpaid wages can be traced back to the 19th century. Eric Tucker describes the history as follows:

The recurring demand for wage protection arises from the near universal practice of paying workers in arrears—that is, after they have provided service. As a result, workers become their employers' creditors and bear some risk that they will not be paid. It is clearly unacceptable, however, for workers not to be remunerated for the service they provided: non-payment of wages is a breach of employers' most fundamental contractual obligation to workers. It is a cause of hardship to workers and their dependent family members who, without the cushion of significant savings or accumulations of property, rely on wages to meet their basic needs.

. . .

[I]n parts of Canada and the United States the demand for wage protection did not arise to confront a preexisting corporate law, but was present in the process of its creation, needing to be accommodated in the first general incorporation statutes. Numerous Canadian and American legislatures responded to this demand by making shareholder and later director liability for unpaid workers' wages a condition of granting widespread access to the privilege of forming limited liability corporations. Yet within a short time, judicial decision making inverted this understanding of the conditionality of limited liability. It reconstructed limited liability as a basic norm of capitalist legality rather than as an exceptional privilege.

In so doing, the courts also transformed the protection of workers' wages from a normative and legal condition of granting corporate investors and managers the privilege of limited liability into an exceptional privilege granted by the state in derogation of the norm of limited liability. Then, on the basis of this inversion, judges narrowly interpreted the scope of director liability for unpaid workers' wages both in relation to who and what was protected.

"Shareholder and Director Liability for Unpaid Workers' Wages in Canada: From Condition of Granting Limited Liability to Exceptional Remedy" (2008), 26 *Law & Hist. Rev.* 57, 58-59, 95 (footnotes omitted).

2. Is the decision in *Crabtree* a further example of what Professor Tucker describes as a narrow interpretation of the director liability provisions? To what extent is *Crabtree* consistent with the rationale in *Fee v. Turner*, quoted above?

3. What is the distinction between debts incurred to employees for services performed during employment and amounts awarded by a court as pay in lieu of notice?

4. The *Canada Business Corporations Act* (CBCA), RSC 1985, c. C-44 now contains a due diligence defence for directors. A director will not be liable under s. 119 "if the director exercised the care, diligence and skill that a reasonably prudent person would have exercised in comparable circumstances": s. 123(4). See SC 2001, c. 14.

5. Directors also face liability for unpaid wages under provincial corporations law and/ or employment standards legislation. In the Maritime provinces there is no provincial statutory liability on directors for unpaid wage claims. See, for example, *Employment Standards Act*, RSBC 1996, c. 113, ss. 87 and 96, as am.; *Employment Standards Code*, RSA 2000, c. E-9, s. 112; *Business Corporations Act*, RSA 2000, c. E-9, as am., s. 119(1); *Employment Standards Act, 2000*, SO 2000, c. 41, as am., s. 81; *Business Corporations Act*, RSO 1990, c. B.16, as am., s. 131(1) (OBCA).

In *Canadian-Automatic Data Processing Services Ltd. v. CEEI Safety & Security Inc.* (2004), 246 DLR (4th) 400, the Ontario Court of Appeal set out the framework of s. 131 of the OBCA:

Broadly speaking, s. 131 of the OBCA is in the nature of employee protection legislation. The primary purpose of legislation of that nature, which is found in the corporate legislation of the federal government and that of most provinces, is to protect employees in the event of bankruptcy or insolvency of their corporate employers.

. . .

Therefore, as with corporate statutes in most other Canadian jurisdictions, s. 131 sets out a legislative framework that enables employees to pursue claims for unpaid wages, not exceeding six months' wages, against the directors of corporate employers. Although s. 131(1) speaks of directors being liable to employees for certain debts payable to a corporation's employees while the directors hold office, the directors are not primarily liable for these debts. The preconditions to a director's liability in s. 131(2) and (3) make it clear that the primary liability for debts to the employees rests with the corporation.

. . .

Two conclusions follow from the foregoing discussion. First, without s. 131 of the OBCA, an employee would have no remedy against the director of a corporation that has failed to pay his or her wages. Second, a director's liability to an employee for unpaid wages is secondary to that of his or her corporate employer.

... [T]he liability of directors under s. 131 of the OBCA to pay unpaid wages arises only when such wages are in fact unpaid. This liability arises only when the corporation has defaulted on its primary contractual obligation as an employer to pay its employees' wages.

6. Among the provinces that do regulate director liability for unpaid wages, there is some variation in terms of the extent of liability. For example, compare the BC *Employment Standards Act*, s. 96 with s. 81(7) of the Ontario *Employment Standards Act, 2000*. Compare s. 131 of the OBCA with s. 119 of the CBCA. Is there any justification for the diverse treatment of director liability of unpaid wages? For a detailed discussion of the provincial statutes, see: J. Sarra and R. Davis, *Director and Officer Liability in Corporate Insolvency* (Markham, ON: Butterworths, 2002), at 83-117.

7. What is the significance of the Maritime provinces not having director liability provisions for unpaid wages? What impact will the absence of director liability provisions in the Maritimes have on the decision of non-Maritime corporations to incorporate or not in the Maritimes? As a matter of national policy, should the BIA and CCAA not contain provisions imposing personal liability on directors of Canadian-based enterprises for unpaid wages regardless of the province of incorporation or whether the bankrupt debtor corporation is federally or provincially incorporated?

8. Business corporation statutes and labour standards acts are not the only legislation protecting employees against the prospect of unpaid wages: *Bank Act*, SC 1991, c. 46. Rather than imposing liability on directors for unpaid wages, the *Bank Act* subordinates a bank's security interest to the claims of unpaid employees. Under s. 427(7) of the *Bank Act*, if the employer becomes bankrupt "claims for wages, salaries or other remuneration owing in respect of the period of three months immediately preceding the making of the order or assignment, to employees ... have priority over the rights of the bank in a security given to the bank under this section."

See also s. 40 of the Ontario *Employment Standards Act, 2000*, which provides that "[e]very employer shall be deemed to hold vacation pay accruing due to an employee in trust for the employee whether or not the employer has kept the amount for it separate and apart."[2] This provision interacts with s. 30(7) of the Ontario *Personal Property Security Act*,

---

[2] Section 40(2) of the *Employment Standards Act, 2000* provides that an amount equal to vacation pay becomes a lien and charge on the assets of the employer.

RSO 1990, c. P.10. Under s. 30(7) of the PPSA, "[a] security interest in an account or inventory and its proceeds is subordinate to the interest of a person who is the beneficiary of a deemed trust arising under the *Employment Standards Act*."[3] Would this deemed trust survive the bankruptcy of the employer?

9. Directors also face personal liability under the *Income Tax Act*, RSC 1985, c. 1 (5th Supp.), as am. Section 153(1) of the *Income Tax Act* imposes a duty on corporations to withhold taxes and other source deductions from an employee's salary. Where the corporation fails to remit such amounts, s. 227.1(1) imposes liability on directors for unremitted source deductions. Directors have a s. 227.1(3) due diligence defence and will not be liable if they can establish that they "exercised the degree of care, diligence and skill to prevent the failure that a reasonably prudent person would have exercised in comparable circumstances." In *Soper v. Canada* (1997), 119 DLR (4th) 297, the Federal Court of Appeal explained the rationale for s. 227.1 of the *Income Tax Act* as follows:

> Prior to the coming into force of section 227.1 of the Act, the Department of National Revenue faced two related but distinct problems. The first was the non-payment of corporate taxes per se and the second was the non-remittance of taxes that were to be withheld at source on behalf of a third party (e.g. employees). The 1981 recession exacerbated both of these problems. As companies experienced difficult financial times, corporations and directors actively and knowingly sought to avoid the payment of taxes in a variety of ways. For example, some companies allowed themselves to be stripped of their assets by a related entity, and left with an uncollectible I.O.U., with the result that the Crown's claim for unpaid corporate taxes could not be satisfied. Yet other corporations that were short of capital "sold" their unused investment tax credits or scientific research deductions with little concern for whether the company would subsequently be able to fulfil its obligations under the Act. Non-remittance of taxes withheld on behalf of a third party was likewise not uncommon during the recession. Faced with a choice between remitting such amounts to the Crown or drawing on such amounts to pay key creditors whose goods or services were necessary to the continued operation of the business, corporate directors often followed the latter course. Such patent abuse and mismanagement on the part of directors constituted the "mischief" at which section 227.1 was directed. ...

> • • •

> The standard of care laid down in subsection 227.1(3) of the Act is inherently flexible. Rather than treating directors as a homogeneous group of professionals whose conduct is governed by a single, unchanging standard, that provision embraces a subjective element which takes into account the personal knowledge and background of the director, as well as his or her corporate circumstances in the form of, *inter alia*, the company's organization, resources, customs and conduct. Thus, for example, more is expected of individuals with superior qualifications (e.g. experienced business-persons).

10. Directors also face personal liability under s. 323 of the *Excise Tax Act*, RSC 1985, c. E-15 for failure to remit GST. Section 323(3) also contains a due diligence defence.

---

[3] Section 30(7) of the PPSA also subordinates the interest of a person who is the beneficiary of a deemed trust arising under s. 57 of the *Pension Benefits Act*, RSO 1990, c. P.8.

11. The BIA creates a number of bankruptcy offences under s. 198. If a corporation commits an offence under s. 204, a director who "directed, authorized, assented to, acquiesced in or participated in the commission of the offence" is a party to the offence and is liable to conviction whether or not the corporation has been prosecuted or convicted.

12. Under CCAA s. 5.1, "[a] compromise or arrangement made in respect of a debtor company may include in its terms a provision for the compromise of claims against directors of the company that arose before the commencement of the proceedings under [the CCAA]." The compromise of claims against the directors must relate to the "obligations of the company where the directors are by law liable in their capacity as directors for the payment of such obligations." Such compromises of claims against directors are not available where the claim (1) relates to contractual rights of one or more creditors; or (2) where the claim is based on allegations of misrepresentations made by directors to creditors or of wrongful or oppressive conduct by directors. The court has the power under s. 5.1(3) to declare that "a claim against directors shall not be compromised if it is satisfied that the compromise would not be fair and reasonable in the circumstances." A similar provision is found in s. 50(13) of the BIA. The provisions were added in 1997. The Ontario Court of Appeal, in *ATB Financial v. Metcalfe & Mansfield Alternative Investments II Corp.* (2008), 45 CBR (5th) 163, at 199 (Ont. CA), leave to appeal refused [2008] SCCA no. 337 concluded:

> The rationale behind these amendments was to encourage directors of an insolvent company to remain in office during a restructuring, rather than resign. The assumption was that by remaining in office the directors would provide some stability while the affairs of the company were being reorganized.

13. Director and officer liability (D&O) insurance may be available to meet some of the claims against directors. Once the company has commenced proceedings under the CCAA, a debtor company may make application for an order that all or part of the company's property is subject to a charge in favour of any director or officer to indemnify the director or officer against obligations and liabilities incurred as a director or officer of the company after the commencement of proceedings. The charge will not be available where the debtor company can obtain adequate indemnification insurance for directors and officers at a reasonable charge. Such a charge will not apply to a liability that was incurred as a result of the director's or officer's gross negligence or wilful misconduct. Because the court may order that the charge take priority over other secured claims, the application for the charge must be on notice to secured creditors likely to be affected by the charge.

14. Note the response of the Standing Senate Committee on Banking, Trade and Commerce to concerns about the potential adverse incentive effects of directors' personal liability:

> Federal and provincial/territorial statutes expose corporate directors to personal liability for a range of corporate debts, including unpaid wages and taxes. While due diligence and/or good faith reliance defences are available in most cases, directors are subject to absolute liability for some debts, and no defence is possible. Even in the former instances, however, there is some risk.
>
> This liability may dissuade highly competent individuals from becoming corporate directors, and from remaining with the organization during periods of financial difficulty. From this

perspective, reduced exposure to personal liability might encourage desirable individuals to accept positions as directors. A high level of personal liability, however, might be supported on the basis that it should lead to highly responsible behaviour by directors in order to reduce their risks. ...

Our 1996 report *Corporate Governance* recommended incorporating provisions covering directors' liability for wages into the BIA, with a due diligence defence. Furthermore, in our 1997 report on Bill C-5, we recommended legislating, in the BIA, a generally applicable due diligence defence against personal liability for directors. We continue to support this change, and believe that it is, in essence, a question of fairness and responsibility. We also hope that such a change might have the desirable effect of increasing the number of competent individuals who wish to serve as directors, since in our June 2003 report *Navigating Through "The Perfect Storm": Safeguards to Restore Investor Confidence* we identified the concern of some about the limited pool of directors in Canada. For this reason, the Committee recommends that: The *Bankruptcy and Insolvency Act* be amended to include a generally applicable due diligence defence against personal liability for directors.

(Standing Senate Committee on Banking, Trade and Commerce, *Debtors and Creditors Sharing the Burden: A Review of the Bankruptcy and Insolvency Act and the Companies' Creditors Arrangement Act* (Ottawa: 2003), at 118-20.)

What are the advantages and disadvantages of this proposal? Might it create an incentive for strategic behaviour on the part of directors? What trade offs would be gained by the creation of a due diligence defence?

15. Another reform possibility, known as the exoneration or safe-harbour model, would release directors from specific liabilities that arise within a specific time prior to the commencement of the BIA or CCAA proceedings. Janis Sarra and Ron Davis suggest that an exoneration model or the creation of a safe-harbour period will remove an important protection for one of the most vulnerable groups in insolvency: employees. How might directors react with respect to wage claims as the corporation approaches insolvency under an exoneration model? Should a safe-harbour regime be automatic, or should the court have some discretion whether to grant directors protection? See Sarra and Davis, above, at 79-81.

III. SANCTIONS FOR DIRECTOR AND OFFICER CONDUCT DETRIMENTAL TO CREDITORS

A. Directors' Duties and the Interests of Creditors: The Evolution of the Duty

Jacob S. Ziegel, "Creditors as Corporate Stakeholders: The Quiet Revolution—An Anglo Canadian Perspective"
(1993), 43 *UTLJ* 511, at 517-18 (footnotes omitted)

The time-honoured formula for describing directors' duties in British and Canadian company law is that directors must act "honestly and in good faith with a view to the best interests of the corporation." [CBCA s. 122(1)(a); OBCA s. 134(1)(a)] For more than a century "best interests of the corporation" has been held to mean the interests of share-holders. Creditors were wholly excluded, even when they were bondholders, unless the legislation gave them a specific status in the corporation's decisional machinery. The re-sult was that the directors had no accountability to the company's creditors even where the creditors' stake in the company's fortunes were much larger than the shareholders' stake, as typically is true in many highly leveraged modern businesses.

The directors owed them no fiduciary duties and no prudential rules of care and skill. The directors were completely free to ignore creditors' welfare, subject only to specific prohibitions in the corporate legislation and subject to such restraining rules as were imposed by general tort and contract rules. Even when corporate rules were clearly designed for the protection of creditors—as with respect to rules governing the mainten-ance of shared capital and the prohibition of financial assistance for the purchase of the company's securities—the creditors had no standing to attack violations; only the share-holders, by bringing a derivative action (an unlikely event), and the company's liquidator on the voluntary or involuntary winding up of the company could do so.

This passive view of creditors' rights changed radically from 1976 onwards, starting with Mason J's judgment in the High Court of Australia in *Walker v. Wimborne* [(1976), 50 ALJR 446, at 449], as Australian, New Zealand, and British trial and appellate courts rendered judgments emphasizing that the best interests of the company were not re-stricted to shareholder interests but included creditors' interests as well. Indeed, we have been told, creditors' interests are pre-eminent if the company is insolvent or close to in-solvency at the time of the impugned action or if the proposed action will jeopardize the company's solvency. In several of the cases judgments were actually rendered against di-rectors for breaching this new-found duty to creditors.

Andrew Keay and Mao Zhang, "Incomplete Contracts, Contingent Fiduciaries, and a Director's Duty to Creditors"
(2008), 32 *Melbourne ULR* 141-43, 148 (footnotes omitted)

It is now almost accepted without question, in the courts of a number of common law jurisdictions including Australia and the United Kingdom, that directors of a firm owe a fiduciary duty to their company to consider the interests of creditors ahead of the inter-ests of shareholders when the firm is actually insolvent. But over the years, there has also been a gradual acknowledgement by courts in various jurisdictions that directors owe a fiduciary duty to the company to consider the interests of the company's creditors as well as its shareholders when the firm is short of actual insolvency but near to, or in danger of, it. In the case of *Credit Lyonnais Bank Nederland NV v. Pathe Communications Cor-poration* [1991 WL 277613 (Del. Ch.)] ("*Credit Lyonnais*"), Chancellor Allen of the Dela-ware Chancery Court ruled that "[a]t least when a corporation is operating in the vicinity of insolvency, a board of directors is not merely the agent of the residue risk bearers [shareholders], but owes its duty to the corporate enterprise [including creditors]."

The Anglo-Australian jurisprudence on this subject can be traced back to the well-known dictum of Mason J of the High Court of Australia in the case of *Walker v. Wim-borne* [(1976), 50 ALJR 446] ("*Walker*") in 1976. His Honour said [at 449]:

In this respect it should be emphasized that the directors of a company in discharging their duty to the company must take account of the interest of its shareholders and its creditors. Any failure by the directors to take into account the interests of creditors will have adverse consequences for the company as well as for them.

Later, in something of a controversial judgment, Lord Templeman in the House of Lords' decision in *Winkworth v. Edward Baron Development Co. Ltd.* [[1987] 1 All ER 114] ("*Winkworth*") said [at 118]:

A duty is owed by the directors to the company and to the creditors of the company to ensure that the affairs of the company are properly administered and that its property is not dissipated or exploited for the benefit of the directors themselves to the prejudice of the creditors.

All three judges recognised that when a company is in financial difficulty, some element of obligation is owed to creditors by directors at some point. ...

The reason given for the shift to consider creditor interests either along with, or in substitution for, shareholder interests is the gradual realisation that if the company is insolvent, in the vicinity of insolvency or embarking on a venture which it cannot sustain without relying totally on creditor funds, "the interests of the company are in reality the interests of existing creditors alone." At this time, the shareholders are no longer the owners of the residual value of the firm as they have been usurped by the creditors, whose rights are transformed into equity-like rights. Thus, the directors are effectively playing with the creditors' money, which means that the creditors may instead be seen as the major stakeholders in the company. ...

Perhaps the most severe damage that has been done in relation to the concept of a direct duty has been in Australia and Canada, where the highest courts in both jurisdictions have rejected a direct duty. For the first time since *Walker*, the Australian High Court had an opportunity to consider the issue in *Spies v. The Queen* [(2000) 201 CLR 603] ("*Spies*"). However, the case did not turn on whether directors owed a responsibility to creditors and what the Court had to say on the topic only constituted dicta at best. The Court denied, clearly, that directors owe an independent duty to creditors. The same result occurred in *Peoples Department Stores Inc. (Trustee of) v. Wise* ("*Peoples Department Stores*") [see extract, below].

Peoples Department Stores Inc. (Trustee of) v. Wise
[2004] 3 SCR 461

MAJOR and DESCHAMPS JJ:

I. Introduction

[1] The principal question raised by this appeal is whether directors of a corporation owe a fiduciary duty to the corporation's creditors comparable to the statutory duty owed to the corporation. For the reasons that follow, we conclude that directors owe a duty of

care to creditors, but that duty does not rise to a fiduciary duty. We agree with the dispo-sition of the Quebec Court of Appeal. The appeal is therefore dismissed.

[2] As a result of the demise in the mid-1990s of two major retail chains in eastern Canada, Wise Stores Inc. ("Wise") and its wholly-owned subsidiary, Peoples Department Stores Inc. ("Peoples"), the indebtedness of a number of Peoples' creditors went unsatis-fied. In the wake of the failure of the two chains, Caron Bélanger Ernst & Young Inc., Peoples' trustee in bankruptcy (the "trustee"), brought an action against the directors of Peoples. To address the trustee's claims, the extent of the duties imposed by s. 122(1) of the *Canada Business Corporations Act*, RSC 1985, c. C-44 ("CBCA"), upon directors with respect to creditors must be determined ... .

[3] In our view, it has not been established that the directors of Peoples violated ei-ther the fiduciary duty or the duty of care imposed by s. 122(1) of the CBCA. ...

II. Background

[Wise Stores Inc. ("Wise") operated clothing stores mainly in urban Quebec. Wise was controlled by the three Wise brothers. Peoples Department Stores Inc. ("Peoples") oper-ated stores in rural areas from Ontario to Newfoundland and Labrador. Peoples experi-enced financial difficulties posting annual losses of $10 million. In 1992, Wise acquired Peoples from Marks & Spencer Canada Inc. for a purchase price of $27 million. The agreement provided that $5 million was payable at the closing of the transaction, while the balance of the transaction was payable in installments over an eight-year period. The initial $5 million payment was financed by TD Bank. The Supreme Court described the sale as a "fully leveraged buyout." The agreement prohibited Wise from merging with Peoples prior to the complete payment of the purchase price. The agreement also pre-cluded Peoples from providing financial assistance to Wise. However, in 1993, as a result of a corporate reorganization, Peoples became a subsidiary directly owned and con-trolled by Wise. The three Wise brothers became Peoples' only directors.

After the amalgamation, Wise sought to consolidate the operations of Wise and Peo-ples to maximize profits. Wise gradually merged operations and head office services with Peoples. By 1993, there was a consolidation of administration, advertising and purchas-ing departments of Peoples and Wise. However, the expected benefits of the consolida-tion of operations did not arise. The merger of shipping, receiving, and storage activities created a number of difficulties, often leading to the misdirection of inventory to the wrong store. This resulted in incorrect inventory records for each company. In October 1993, the Wise brothers, in response to the numerous problems, approved a new domes-tic joint inventory procurement system that had been recommended by the vice presi-dent of Wise. The new system integrated the inventory management for Wise and Peo-ples as if the two entities comprised a single company operating 125 stores. Under the new system, Wise would make all purchases from overseas suppliers. Peoples assumed responsibility for all purchases of North American inventory for the two companies. Peoples in turn charged Wise for any inventory transferred to Wise. The new policy ex-posed Peoples to substantial debt, particularly when Wise did not pay Peoples for the in-ventory. Approximately 82 percent of the total inventory of the two companies was pur-chased from North American suppliers. The directors were aware of the new policy but it was never established in writing or approved by a formal board meeting or resolution. In January 1995, Wise and Peoples were declared bankrupt.]

[25] Following the bankruptcy, Peoples' trustee filed a petition against the Wise brothers. In the petition, the trustee claimed that they had favoured the interests of Wise over Peoples to the detriment of Peoples' creditors, in breach of their duties as directors under s. 122(1) of the CBCA. ...

[27] The trial judge, Greenberg J, relying on decisions from the United Kingdom, Australia and New Zealand, held that the fiduciary duty and the duty of care under s. 122(1) of the CBCA extend to a company's creditors when a company is insolvent or in the vicinity of insolvency. Greenberg J found that the implementation, by the Wise brothers qua directors of Peoples, of a corporate policy that affected both companies, had occurred while the corporation was in the vicinity of insolvency and was detrimental to the interests of the creditors of Peoples. The Wise brothers were therefore found liable and the trustee was awarded $4.44 million in damages. ...

[28] The Quebec Court of Appeal... allowed the appeals by Chubb and the Wise brothers. The Court of Appeal expressed reluctance to follow Greenberg J in equating the interests of creditors with the best interests of the corporation when the corporation was insolvent or in the vicinity of insolvency, stating that an innovation in the law such as this is a policy matter more appropriately dealt with by Parliament than the courts. ...

III. Analysis

...

[30] ... This case came before our Court on the issue of whether directors owe a duty to creditors. The creditors did not bring a derivative action or an oppression remedy application under the CBCA. Instead, the trustee, representing the interests of the creditors, sued the directors for an alleged breach of the duties imposed by s. 122(1) of the CBCA. The standing of the trustee to sue was not questioned. ...

[32] Subsection 122(1) of the CBCA establishes two distinct duties to be discharged by directors and officers in managing, or supervising the management of, the corporation:

> 122(1) Every director and officer of a corporation in exercising their powers and discharging their duties shall
> (a) act honestly and in good faith with a view to the best interests of the corporation; and
> (b) exercise the care, diligence and skill that a reasonably prudent person would exercise in comparable circumstances.

The first duty has been referred to in this case as the "fiduciary duty." It is better described as the "duty of loyalty." We will use the expression "statutory fiduciary duty" for purposes of clarity when referring to the duty under the CBCA. This duty requires directors and officers to act honestly and in good faith with a view to the best interests of the corporation. The second duty is commonly referred to as the "duty of care." Generally speaking, it imposes a legal obligation upon directors and officers to be diligent in supervising and managing the corporation's affairs.

[33] The trial judge did not apply or consider separately the two duties imposed on directors by s. 122(1). As the Court of Appeal observed, the trial judge appears to have confused the two duties. They are, in fact, distinct and are designed to secure different ends. For that reason, they will be addressed separately in these reasons.

A. The Statutory Fiduciary Duty: Section 122(1)(a) of the CBCA

[34] Considerable power over the deployment and management of financial, human, and material resources is vested in the directors and officers of corporations. For the directors of CBCA corporations, this power originates in s. 102 of the Act. For officers, this power comes from the powers delegated to them by the directors. In deciding to invest in, lend to or otherwise deal with a corporation, shareholders and creditors transfer control over their assets to the corporation, and hence to the directors and officers, in the expectation that the directors and officers will use the corporation's resources to make reasonable business decisions that are to the corporation's advantage.

[35] The statutory fiduciary duty requires directors and officers to act honestly and in good faith *vis-à-vis* the corporation. They must respect the trust and confidence that have been reposed in them to manage the assets of the corporation in pursuit of the realization of the objects of the corporation. They must avoid conflicts of interest with the corporation. They must avoid abusing their position to gain personal benefit. They must maintain the confidentiality of information they acquire by virtue of their position. Directors and officers must serve the corporation selflessly, honestly and loyally: see K.P. McGuinness, *The Law and Practice of Canadian Business Corporations* (1999), at p. 715. ...

[37] The issue to be considered here is the "specific substance" of the fiduciary duty based on the relationship of directors to corporations under the CBCA.

[38] It is settled law that the fiduciary duty owed by directors and officers imposes strict obligations: see *Canadian Aero Service Ltd. v. O'Malley* (1973), [1974] SCR 592 (SCC), at pp. 609-10, *per* Laskin J (as he then was), where it was decided that directors and officers may even have to account to the corporation for profits they make that do not come at the corporation's expense. ...

[39] However, it is not required that directors and officers in all cases avoid personal gain as a direct or indirect result of their honest and good faith supervision or management of the corporation. In many cases the interests of directors and officers will innocently and genuinely coincide with those of the corporation. If directors and officers are also shareholders, as is often the case, their lot will automatically improve as the corporation's financial condition improves. Another example is the compensation that directors and officers usually draw from the corporations they serve. This benefit, though paid by the corporation, does not, if reasonable, ordinarily place them in breach of their fiduciary duty. Therefore, all the circumstances may be scrutinized to determine whether the directors and officers have acted honestly and in good faith with a view to the best interests of the corporation.

[40] In our opinion, the trial judge's determination that there was no fraud or dishonesty in the Wise brothers' attempts to solve the mounting inventory problems of Peoples and Wise stands in the way of a finding that they breached their fiduciary duty. ...

[41] As explained above, there is no doubt that both Peoples and Wise were struggling with a serious inventory management problem. The Wise brothers considered the

problem and implemented a policy they hoped would solve it. In the absence of evidence of a personal interest or improper purpose in the new policy, and in light of the evidence of a desire to make both Wise and Peoples "better" corporations, we find that the directors did not breach their fiduciary duty under s. 122(1)(a) of the CBCA. See *820099 Ontario Inc. v. Harold E. Ballard Ltd.* (1991), 3 BLR (2d) 123 (Ont. Gen. Div.) (aff'd. (1991), 3 BLR (2d) 113 (Ont. Div. Ct.)), in which Farley J, at p. 171, correctly observes that in resolving a conflict between majority and minority shareholders, it is safe for directors and officers to act to make the corporation a "better corporation."

[42] This appeal does not relate to the non-statutory duty directors owe to shareholders. It is concerned only with the statutory duties owed under the CBCA. Insofar as the statutory fiduciary duty is concerned, it is clear that the phrase the "best interests of the corporation" should be read not simply as the "best interests of the shareholders." From an economic perspective, the "best interests of the corporation" means the maximization of the value of the corporation: see E.M. Iacobucci, "Directors' Duties in Insolvency: Clarifying What Is at Stake" (2003), 39(3) *Can. Bus. LJ* 398, at pp. 400-1. However, the courts have long recognized that various other factors may be relevant in determining what directors should consider in soundly managing with a view to the best interests of the corporation. For example, in *Teck Corp. v. Millar* (1972), 33 DLR (3d) 288 (BCSC), Berger J stated, at p. 314:

> A classical theory that once was unchallengeable must yield to the facts of modern life. In fact, of course, it has. If today the directors of a company were to consider the interests of its employees no one would argue that in doing so they were not acting *bona fide* in the interests of the company itself. Similarly, if the directors were to consider the consequences to the community of any policy that the company intended to pursue, and were deflected in their commitment to that policy as a result, it could not be said that they had not considered bona fide the interests of the shareholders.
>
> I appreciate that it would be a breach of their duty for directors to disregard entirely the interests of a company's shareholders in order to confer a benefit on its employees: *Parke v. Daily News Ltd.*, [1962] Ch. 927. But if they observe a decent respect for other interests lying beyond those of the company's shareholders in the strict sense, that will not, in my view, leave directors open to the charge that they have failed in their fiduciary duty to the company.

The case of *Olympia & York Enterprises Ltd. v. Hiram Walker Resources Ltd.* (1986), 59 OR (2d) 254 (Ont. Div. Ct.), approved, at p. 271, the decision in *Teck, supra.* We accept as an accurate statement of law that in determining whether they are acting with a view to the best interests of the corporation it may be legitimate, given all the circumstances of a given case, for the board of directors to consider, inter alia, the interests of shareholders, employees, suppliers, creditors, consumers, governments and the environment.

[43] The various shifts in interests that naturally occur as a corporation's fortunes rise and fall do not, however, affect the content of the fiduciary duty under s. 122(1)(a) of the CBCA. At all times, directors and officers owe their fiduciary obligation to the corporation. The interests of the corporation are not to be confused with the interests of the creditors or those of any other stakeholders.

[44] The interests of shareholders, those of the creditors and those of the corporation may and will be consistent with each other if the corporation is profitable and well

capitalized and has strong prospects. However, this can change if the corporation starts to struggle financially. The residual rights of the shareholders will generally become worthless if a corporation is declared bankrupt. Upon bankruptcy, the directors of the corporation transfer control to a trustee, who administers the corporation's assets for the benefit of creditors.

[45] Short of bankruptcy, as the corporation approaches what has been described as the "vicinity of insolvency," the residual claims of shareholders will be nearly exhausted. While shareholders might well prefer that the directors pursue high-risk alternatives with a high potential payoff to maximize the shareholders' expected residual claim, creditors in the same circumstances might prefer that the directors steer a safer course so as to maximize the value of their claims against the assets of the corporation.

[46] The directors' fiduciary duty does not change when a corporation is in the nebulous "vicinity of insolvency." That phrase has not been defined; moreover, it is incapable of definition and has no legal meaning. What it is obviously intended to convey is a deterioration in the corporation's financial stability. In assessing the actions of directors it is evident that any honest and good faith attempt to redress the corporation's financial problems will, if successful, both retain value for shareholders and improve the position of creditors. If unsuccessful, it will not qualify as a breach of the statutory fiduciary duty.

[47] For a discussion of the shifting interests and incentives of shareholders and creditors, see W.D. Gray, "*Peoples v. Wise* and *Dylex*: Identifying Stakeholder Interests upon or near Corporate Insolvency—Stasis or Pragmatism?" (2003), 39 *Can. Bus. LJ* 242, at p. 257; E. M. Iacobucci & K.E. Davis, "Reconciling Derivative Claims and the Oppression Remedy" (2000), 12 *SCLR* (2d) 87, at p. 114. In resolving these competing interests, it is incumbent upon the directors to act honestly and in good faith with a view to the best interests of the corporation. In using their skills for the benefit of the corporation when it is in troubled waters financially, the directors must be careful to attempt to act in its best interests by creating a "better" corporation, and not to favour the interests of any one group of stakeholders. If the stakeholders cannot avail themselves of the statutory fiduciary duty (the duty of loyalty, *supra*) to sue the directors for failing to take care of their interests, they have other means at their disposal.

[48] The Canadian legal landscape with respect to stakeholders is unique. Creditors are only one set of stakeholders, but their interests are protected in a number of ways … . The oppression remedy of s. 241(2)(c) of the CBCA and the similar provisions of provincial legislation regarding corporations grant the broadest rights to creditors of any common law jurisdiction: see D. Thomson, "Directors, Creditors and Insolvency: A Fiduciary Duty or a Duty Not to Oppress?" (2000), 58(1) *UT Fac. L Rev.* 31, at p. 48. One commentator describes the oppression remedy as "the broadest, most comprehensive and most open-ended shareholder remedy in the common law world": S.M. Beck, "Minority Shareholders' Rights in the 1980s" in *Corporate Law in the 80s* (1982), 311, at p. 312. While Beck was concerned with shareholder remedies, his observation applies equally to those of creditors.

[49] The fact that creditors' interests increase in relevancy as a corporation's finances deteriorate is apt to be relevant to, *inter alia*, the exercise of discretion by a court in granting standing to a party as a "complainant" under s. 238(d) of the CBCA as a "proper person" to bring a derivative action in the name of the corporation under ss. 239 and 240 of the CBCA, or to bring an oppression remedy claim under s. 241 of the CBCA.

[50] Section 241(2)(c) authorizes a court to grant a remedy if

> (c) the powers of the directors of the corporation or any of its affiliates are or have been exercised in a manner that is oppressive or unfairly prejudicial to or that unfairly disregards the interests of any security holder, creditor, director or officer … .

A person applying for the oppression remedy must, in the court's opinion, fall within the definition of "complainant" found in s. 238 of the CBCA: …

> (d) any other person who, in the discretion of a court, is a proper person to make an application under this Part.

Creditors, who are not security holders within the meaning of para. (a), may therefore apply for the oppression remedy under para. (d) by asking a court to exercise its discretion and grant them status as a "complainant."

[51] Section 241 of the CBCA provides a possible mechanism for creditors to protect their interests from the prejudicial conduct of directors. In our view, the availability of such a broad oppression remedy undermines any perceived need to extend the fiduciary duty imposed on directors by s. 122(1)(a) of the CBCA to include creditors. …

[53] In light of the availability both of the oppression remedy and of an action based on the duty of care, which will be discussed below, stakeholders have viable remedies at their disposal. There is no need to read the interests of creditors into the duty set out in s. 122(1)(a) of the CBCA. Moreover, in the circumstances of this case, the Wise brothers did not breach the statutory fiduciary duty owed to the corporation.

B. The Statutory Duty of Care: Section 122(1)(b) of the CBCA

. . .

[57] … Indeed, unlike the statement of the fiduciary duty in s. 122(1)(a) of the CBCA, which specifies that directors and officers must act with a view to the best interests of the corporation, the statement of the duty of care in s. 122(1)(b) of the CBCA does not specifically refer to an identifiable party as the beneficiary of the duty. Instead, it provides that "[e]very director and officer of a corporation in exercising his powers and discharging his duties shall … exercise the care, diligence and skill that a reasonably prudent person would exercise in comparable circumstances." Thus, the identity of the beneficiary of the duty of care is much more open-ended, and it appears obvious that it must include creditors. …

[59] That directors must satisfy a duty of care is a long-standing principle of the common law, although the duty of care has been reinforced by statute to become more demanding. Among the earliest English cases establishing the duty of care were *Dovey v. Cory*, [1901] AC 477 (Eng. HL); *Brazilian Rubber Plantation & Estates Ltd., Re*, [1911] 1 Ch. 425 (Eng. Ch. Div.); and *City Equitable Fire Insurance Co., Re* (1924), [1925] 1 Ch. 407 (Eng. CA). In substance, these cases held that the standard of care was a reasonably relaxed, subjective standard. The common law required directors to avoid being grossly negligent with respect to the affairs of the corporation and judged them according to their own personal skills, knowledge, abilities and capacities. See McGuinness, *supra*, at p. 776: "Given the history of case law in this area, and the prevailing standards of competence

displayed in commerce generally, it is quite clear that directors were not expected at common law to have any particular business skill or judgment." ...

[63] The standard of care embodied in s. 122(1)(b) of the CBCA was described by Robertson JA of the Federal Court of Appeal in *Soper v. R* (1997), [1998] 1 FC 124 (Fed. CA), at para. 41, as being "objective subjective." Although that case concerned the interpretation of a provision of the *Income Tax Act*, it is relevant here because the language of the provision establishing the standard of care was identical to that of s. 122(1)(b) of the CBCA. With respect, we feel that Robertson JA's characterization of the standard as an "objective subjective" one could lead to confusion. We prefer to describe it as an objective standard. To say that the standard is objective makes it clear that the factual aspects of the circumstances surrounding the actions of the director or officer are important in the case of the s. 122(1)(b) duty of care, as opposed to the subjective motivation of the director or officer, which is the central focus of the statutory fiduciary duty of s. 122(1)(a) of the CBCA.

[64] The contextual approach dictated by s. 122(1)(b) of the CBCA not only emphasizes the primary facts but also permits prevailing socio-economic conditions to be taken into consideration. The emergence of stricter standards puts pressure on corporations to improve the quality of board decisions. The establishment of good corporate governance rules should be a shield that protects directors from allegations that they have breached their duty of care. However, even with good corporate governance rules, directors' decisions can still be open to criticism from outsiders. Canadian courts, like their counterparts in the United States, the United Kingdom, Australia and New Zealand, have tended to take an approach with respect to the enforcement of the duty of care that respects the fact that directors and officers often have business expertise that courts do not. Many decisions made in the course of business, although ultimately unsuccessful, are reasonable and defensible at the time they are made. Business decisions must sometimes be made, with high stakes and under considerable time pressure, in circumstances in which detailed information is not available. It might be tempting for some to see unsuccessful business decisions as unreasonable or imprudent in light of information that becomes available *ex post facto*. Because of this risk of hindsight bias, Canadian courts have developed a rule of deference to business decisions called the "business judgment rule," adopting the American name for the rule.

[65] In *Maple Leaf Foods Inc. v. Schneider Corp.* (1998), 42 OR (3d) 177, Weiler JA stated, at p. 192:

> The law as it has evolved in Ontario and Delaware has the common requirements that the court must be satisfied that the directors have acted reasonably and fairly. The *court looks to see that the directors made a* <u>reasonable</u> *decision* <u>not a perfect decision</u>. *Provided the decision taken is within a range of reasonableness, the court ought not to substitute its opinion for that of the board even though subsequent events may have cast doubt on the board's determination. As long as the directors have selected one of several reasonable alternatives, deference is accorded to the board's decision.* This formulation of deference to the decision of the Board is known as the "business judgment rule." The fact that alternative transactions were rejected by the directors is irrelevant unless it can be shown that a particular alternative was definitely available and clearly more beneficial to the company than the chosen transaction. [Italics added; emphasis in original; references omitted.]

[66] In order for a plaintiff to succeed in challenging a business decision he or she has to establish that the directors acted (i) in breach of the duty of care and (ii) in a way that caused injury to the plaintiff: W.T. Allen, J.B. Jacobs, and L.E. Strine, Jr., "Function Over Form: A Reassessment of Standards of Review in Delaware Corporation Law" (2001), 26 *Del. J Corp. L* 859, at p. 892.

[67] Directors and officers will not be held to be in breach of the duty of care under s. 122(1)(b) of the CBCA if they act prudently and on a reasonably informed basis. The decisions they make must be reasonable business decisions in light of all the circumstances about which the directors or officers knew or ought to have known. In determining whether directors have acted in a manner that breached the duty of care, it is worth repeating that perfection is not demanded. Courts are ill-suited and should be reluctant to second-guess the application of business expertise to the considerations that are involved in corporate decision making, but they are capable, on the facts of any case, of determining whether an appropriate degree of prudence and diligence was brought to bear in reaching what is claimed to be a reasonable business decision at the time it was made.

[68] The trustee alleges that the Wise brothers breached their duty of care under s. 122(1)(b) of the CBCA by implementing the new procurement policy to the detriment of Peoples' creditors. After considering all the evidence, we agree with the Court of Appeal that the implementation of the new policy was a reasonable business decision that was made with a view to rectifying a serious and urgent business problem in circumstances in which no solution may have been possible. The trial judge's conclusion that the new policy led inexorably to Peoples' failure and bankruptcy was factually incorrect and constituted a palpable and overriding error.

[69] In fact, as noted by Pelletier JA, there were many factors other than the new policy that contributed more directly to Peoples' bankruptcy. Peoples had lost $10 million annually while being operated by M & S. Wise, which was only marginally profitable and solvent with annual sales of $100 million (versus $160 million for Peoples), had hoped to improve the performance of its new acquisition. Given that the transaction was a fully leveraged buyout, for Wise and Peoples to succeed, Peoples' performance needed to improve dramatically. Unfortunately for both Wise and Peoples, the retail market in eastern Canada had become very competitive in the early 1990s, and this trend continued with the arrival of Wal-Mart in 1994. ...

[70] The Wise brothers treated the implementation of the new policy as a decision made in the ordinary course of business and, while no formal agreement evidenced the arrangement, a monthly record was made of the inventory transfers. Although this may appear to be a loose business practice, by the autumn of 1993, Wise had already consolidated several aspects of the operations of the two companies. Legally they were two separate entities. However, the financial fate of the two companies had become intertwined. In these circumstances, there was little or no economic incentive for the Wise brothers to jeopardize the interests of Peoples in favour of the interests of Wise. In fact, given the tax losses that Peoples had carried forward, the companies had every incentive to keep Peoples profitable in order to reduce their combined tax liabilities.

[71] Arguably, the Wise brothers could have been more precise in pursuing a resolution to the intractable inventory management problems, having regard to all the troublesome circumstances involved at the time the new policy was implemented. But we, like

the Court of Appeal, are not satisfied that the adoption of the new policy breached the duty of care under s. 122(1)(b) of the CBCA. The directors cannot be held liable for a breach of their duty of care in respect of the creditors of Peoples. ...

Appeal dismissed.

NOTES AND QUESTIONS

1. Beyond the oppression remedy are there any other legal mechanisms that creditors may utilize to protect their interests from possible prejudicial conduct on the part of directors?

2. The Supreme Court acknowledged that any honest and good faith attempt to redress the corporation's financial problems will, "if *unsuccessful* ... *not* qualify as a breach of the statutory fiduciary duty" (emphasis added). What must a director show to establish an honest and good faith effort? Should an unsuccessful attempt to save the company be a breach of the statutory fiduciary duty?

3. The Supreme Court concluded that "[t]he directors' fiduciary duty does not change when a corporation is in the nebulous 'vicinity of insolvency.'" That phrase has not been defined; moreover, it is incapable of definition and has no legal meaning." Why? Christopher Nicholls explains as follows:

> There are several ways of formulating the rationale upon which a director's or officer's duty to a corporation's creditors might be said to be based, at least when a firm is in the vicinity of insolvency ... [I]t appears sensible to mandate some duty on the part of the directors to consider the interests of creditors when a corporation is on the verge of insolvency. After all, at that point in a corporation's life only the creditors have a non-trivial economic interest in the corporation. Yet this argument does bring to mind a variation of Zeno's paradox. Before a company becomes insolvent, there must be an earlier moment when it is almost insolvent. Before that moment, there must be still an earlier point in time when the firm is *almost* almost insolvent. And so on. Since the obligations of the firm in insolvency will be to preserve the assets of the corporation, surely such an obligation should also exist the instant before insolvency. Yet, if the obligation arises the instant before insolvency, why, then, not the instant before that? And the instant before that? And so on, back, presumably, to the moment of original incorporation. Perhaps directors *should* owe a duty to creditors from the moment of incorporation, but the supporters of the "vicinity of insolvency" approach do not necessarily argue that such a duty would be necessary or desirable.
>
> A weakness of the "vicinity of insolvency" approach revealed by this paradox is that it tends to minimize the significance of the shift of duties that occurs upon an insolvency. Consider the case of an individual debtor who becomes bankrupt or insolvent. Although we properly forbid all types of fraudulent conveyances or preferences occurring within some period of time prior to such an insolvency, we do not typically forbid an individual to continue a high risk career while approaching insolvency, or even from switching careers from one of low financial risk to one of high financial risk. Similarly, in the case of corporate debtors, while fraudulent conveyances and preferences ought rightly to be prevented, it is not as clear that significant constraints

should be placed on (non-fraudulent) business activities undertaken prior to insolvency, notwithstanding that they might involve an assumption of greater risk.

("Liability of Corporate Officers and Directors to Third Parties" (2001), 35 *CBLJ* 1, at 34-35.)

4. Many aspects of the *Peoples* decision have been criticized by legal scholars. See, for example, "Symposium on Supreme Court's Judgment in the Peoples Department Stores Case" (2005), 41 *CBLJ* 167-246. See also Janis Sarra, "Canada's Supreme Court Rules No Fiduciary Obligation Towards Creditors on Insolvency—Peoples Department Stores v. Wise" (2006), 15 *Int'l. Ins. Rev.* 1; Robert Flannigan, "Reshaping the Duties of Directors" (2005), 84 *Can. Bar Rev.* 365. Another issue in *Peoples* was the application of BIA s. 100 (the reviewable transactions provision). This aspect is dealt with in Chapter 5.

5. Compare *Peoples* with the decision of the Delaware Supreme Court in *Gheewalla*, extracted below.

North American Catholic Educ. Programming Found. v. Gheewalla
930 A 2d 92, 99-101, 103 (Del. 2007) (footnotes omitted)

This procedural requirement requires us to address a substantive question of first impression that is raised by the present appeal: as a matter of Delaware law, can the creditor of a corporation that is operating within the zone of insolvency bring a direct action against its directors for an alleged breach of fiduciary duty?

It is well established that the directors owe their fiduciary obligations to the corporation and its shareholders. While shareholders rely on directors acting as fiduciaries to protect their interests, creditors are afforded protection through contractual agreements, fraud and fraudulent conveyance law, implied covenants of good faith and fair dealing, bankruptcy law, general commercial law and other sources of creditor rights. Delaware courts have traditionally been reluctant to expand existing fiduciary duties. Accordingly, "the general rule is that directors do not owe creditors duties beyond the relevant contractual terms."

. . .

In *Production Resources* [*v. NCT Group*, 863 A 2d, at 790], the Court of Chancery remarked that recognition of fiduciary duties to creditors in the "zone of insolvency" context may involve:

> using the law of fiduciary duty to fill gaps that do not exist. Creditors are often protected by strong covenants, liens on assets, and other negotiated contractual protections. The implied covenant of good faith and fair dealing also protects creditors. So does the law of fraudulent conveyance. With these protections, when creditors are unable to prove that a corporation or its directors breached any of the specific legal duties owed to them, one would think that the conceptual room for concluding that the creditors were somehow, nevertheless, injured by inequitable conduct would be extremely small, *if extant*. Having complied with all legal obligations owed to the firm's creditors, the board would, in that scenario, ordinarily be free to take economic risk for the benefit of the firm's equity owners, so long as the directors

comply with their fiduciary duties to the firm by selecting and pursuing with fidelity and prudence a plausible strategy to maximize the firm's value.

In this case, the Court of Chancery noted that creditors' existing protections—among which are the protections afforded by their negotiated agreements, their security instruments, the implied covenant of good faith and fair dealing, fraudulent conveyance law, and bankruptcy law—render the imposition of an additional, unique layer of protection through direct claims for breach of fiduciary duty unnecessary. It also noted that "any benefit to be derived by the recognition of such additional direct claims appears minimal, at best, and significantly outweighed by the costs to economic efficiency." The Court of Chancery reasoned that "an otherwise solvent corporation operating in the zone of insolvency is one in most need of effective and proactive leadership—as well as the ability to negotiate in good faith with its creditors—goals which would likely be significantly undermined by the prospect of individual liability arising from the pursuit of direct claims by creditors." We agree. ...

In this case, the need for providing directors with definitive guidance compels us to hold that no direct claim for breach of fiduciary duties may be asserted by the creditors of a solvent corporation that is operating in the zone of insolvency. When a solvent corporation is navigating in the zone of insolvency, the focus for Delaware directors does not change: directors must continue to discharge their fiduciary duties to the corporation and its shareholders by exercising their business judgment in the best interests of the corporation for the benefit of its shareholder owners. Therefore, we hold the Court of Chancery properly concluded that Count II of the NACEPF Complaint fails to state a claim, as a matter of Delaware law, to the extent that it attempts to assert a direct claim for breach of fiduciary duty to a creditor while Clearwire was operating in the zone of insolvency. ...

[The court considered the separate argument of whether directors of an *insolvent* corporation owed a direct fiduciary duty to creditors.]

Recognizing that directors of an insolvent corporation owe direct fiduciary duties to creditors, would create uncertainty for directors who have a fiduciary duty to exercise their business judgment in the best interest of the insolvent corporation. To recognize a new right for creditors to bring direct fiduciary claims against those directors would create a conflict between those directors' duty to maximize the value of the insolvent corporation for the benefit of all those having an interest in it, and the newly recognized direct fiduciary duty to individual creditors. Directors of insolvent corporations must retain the freedom to engage in vigorous, good faith negotiations with individual creditors for the benefit of the corporation.

Accordingly, we hold that individual creditors of an insolvent corporation have no right to assert direct claims for breach of fiduciary duty against corporate directors. Creditors may nonetheless protect their interest by bringing derivative claims on behalf of the insolvent corporation or any other direct nonfiduciary claim, as discussed earlier in this opinion, that may be available for individual creditors.

Conclusion

The creditors of a Delaware corporation that is either insolvent or in the zone of insolvency have no right, as a matter of law, to assert direct claims for breach of fiduciary duty against its directors. ...

Judgment affirmed.

NOTES

1. Did the court in *Gheewalla* define the zone of insolvency? See *Teleglobe Communs Corp. v. BCE, Inc.* 493 F 3d 345 (3rd Cir., 2007). Do creditors need protection outside the zone of insolvency? According to the Delaware Supreme Court, where are those creditor protections found in US law?

2. The debate over the scope of directors' duties continues in the United States after *Gheewalla*. See, for example, Henry T.C. Hu and Jay Lawrence Westbrook, "Abolition of the Corporate Duty to Creditors" (2007), 107 *Colum. L Rev.* 1321; Frederick Tung, "The New Death of Contract: Creeping Corporate Fiduciary Duties for Creditors" (2008), 57 *Emory LJ* 809; Jonathan C. Lipson, "The Expressive Function of Directors' Duties to Creditors" (2007), 12 *Stan. JL. Bus. & Fin.* 224.

3. The US doctrine of "deepening insolvency" provides an alternative theory for imposing liability on directors. It has not been accepted in Canada and the scope of the doctrine is subject to debate in the United States. Jassmine Girgis summarizes the doctrine as follows:

Deepening insolvency holds directors liable for harms suffered by the corporation when its life is wrongfully prolonged. The doctrine imposes on directors a duty to the corporation, but it also indirectly benefits creditors: first, by bringing money into the debtor's estate to repay creditors if the claim against the directors is successful, and second, by restraining the actions of directors when the corporation is suffering financially, through the threat of liability. ...

In 1983, the term "deepening insolvency" was coined when the United States Court of Appeals for the Seventh Circuit recognized the damage that can be accrued when management continues to operate an insolvent corporation ... . "Deepening insolvency" is a nonstatutory doctrine that does not appear anywhere in the Bankruptcy Code. The absence of a statutory definition renders the doctrine uncertain in scope and, consequently, deepening insolvency has neither been universally defined nor applied, nor has it been universally accepted in the United States.

Directors, officers or other parties who exercise control over the corporation engage in deepening insolvency when they wrongfully incur further corporate debt while the corporation is insolvent and has no reasonable prospect of recovering. Deepening insolvency is premised on the acknowledgment that incurring such debt harms the corporation. Accordingly, the harm brought about by directors' failure to stop trading under the above circumstances can be avoided through the creation of personal liability under the doctrine of deepening insolvency. The objective of the liability imposed by the doctrine is to motivate directors to recognize this harm and cease trading as soon as saving the corporation is no longer a feasible prospect. ...

Without the threat of personal liability, directors may be no worse off even if they continue to incur debt when the corporation is insolvent. Even if it is unlikely that the corporation could trade into a profitable financial state, directors have an incentive to take that chance. If they are successful, they will once again have a profitable corporation; they will keep their jobs and, if they are also shareholders, regain value in their shares. If they are unsuccessful, other than the damage done to their reputations as directors, they will suffer no additional financial loss because the limitation of their liability ensures that they are not responsible for the corporation's debts. ...

Specifically, the injury caused to the corporation can include the decline in value of the remaining corporate assets through the incurrence of additional debt. It can cause a hastening of bankruptcy through the dissipation of corporate assets and an undermining of the relationships between the corporation and its "customers, suppliers, and employees." Due to the broad definition of deepening insolvency, while the claim is usually brought against directors and officers, it may include other defendants such as lenders or auditors.

Nevertheless, to fall within the scope of the deepening insolvency doctrine, the prolongation of the corporation's life must usually have been the result of fraud.

"Deepening Insolvency in Canada?" (2008), 53 *McGill LJ* 167, at 169, 175-77.

Is the adoption of deepening insolvency in Canada necessary? Consider this question in light of the oppression remedy below.

B. The Oppression Remedy

BCE Inc. v. 1976 Debentureholders
2008 SCC 69

THE COURT:

I. Introduction

[1] These appeals arise out of an offer to purchase all shares of BCE Inc. ("BCE"), a large telecommunications corporation, by a group headed by the Ontario Teachers Pension Plan Board ("Teachers"), financed in part by the assumption by Bell Canada, a wholly owned subsidiary of BCE, of a $30 billion debt. The leveraged buyout was opposed by debentureholders of Bell Canada on the ground that the increased debt contemplated by the purchase agreement would reduce the value of their bonds. ... [The debentureholders] ... opposed the arrangement under s. 241 of the CBCA on the ground that it was oppressive to them.

· · ·

II. Facts

· · ·

[4] At issue is a plan of arrangement valued at approximately $52 billion, for the purchase of the shares of BCE by way of a leveraged buyout. The arrangement was opposed by a group [the debentureholders], comprised mainly of financial institutions, that hold debentures issued by Bell Canada. The crux of their complaints is that the arrangement would diminish the trading value of their debentures by an average of 20 percent, while conferring a premium of approximately 40 percent on the market price of BCE shares.

· · ·

[7] Bell Canada's debentures were perceived by investors to be safe investments and, up to the time of the proposed leveraged buyout, had maintained an investment grade rating. The debentureholders are some of Canada's largest and most reputable financial institutions, pension funds and insurance companies. They are major participants in the debt markets and possess an intimate and historic knowledge of the financial markets.

. . .

[14] In a press release dated April 17, 2007, BCE announced that it was reviewing its strategic alternatives with a view to further enhancing shareholder value. On the same day, a Strategic Oversight Committee ("SOC") was created. None of its members had ever been part of management at BCE. Its mandate was, notably, to set up and supervise the auction process.

[15] Following the April 17 press release, several debentureholders sent letters to the Board voicing their concerns about a potential leveraged buyout transaction. They sought assurance that their interests would be considered by the Board. BCE replied in writing that it intended to honour the contractual terms of the trust indentures.

. . .

[17] Offers were submitted by three groups. All three offers contemplated the addition of a substantial amount of new debt for which Bell Canada would be liable. All would have likely resulted in a downgrade of the debentures below investment grade. The initial offer [was] submitted by the appellant 6796508 Canada Inc. (the "Purchaser"), a corporation formed by Teachers and affiliates of Providence Equity Partners Inc. and Madison Dearborn Partners LLC. ...

[18] The Board, after a review of the three offers and based on the recommendation of the SOC, found that the Purchaser's revised offer was in the best interests of BCE and BCE's shareholders ... . The Board did not seek a fairness opinion in respect of the debentureholders, taking the view that their rights were not being arranged.

[19] On June 30, 2007, the Purchaser and BCE entered into a definitive agreement. On September 21, 2007, BCE's shareholders approved the arrangement by a majority of 97.93 percent.

. . .

[21] As a result of the announcement of the arrangement, the credit ratings of the debentures by the time of trial had been downgraded from investment grade to below investment grade. From the perspective of the debentureholders, this downgrade was problematic for two reasons. First, it caused the debentures to decrease in value by an average of approximately 20 percent. Second, the downgrade could oblige debentureholders with credit-rating restrictions on their holdings to sell their debentures at a loss.

. . .

IV. Issues

[30] The issues, briefly stated, are whether the Court of Appeal erred in dismissing the debentureholders' s. 241 oppression claim ... . These questions raise the issue of what is required to establish oppression of debentureholders in a situation where a corporation is facing a change of control ... .

. . .

V. Analysis

A. Overview of Rights, Obligations, and Remedies Under the CBCA

. . .

[36] The directors are responsible for the governance of the corporation. In the performance of this role, the directors are subject to two duties: a fiduciary duty to the corporation under s. 122(1)(a) (the fiduciary duty); and a duty to exercise the care, diligence and skill of a reasonably prudent person in comparable circumstances under s. 122(1)(b) (the duty of care). ... [T]his case does involve the fiduciary duty of the directors to the corporation, and particularly the "fair treatment" component of this duty, which, as will be seen, is fundamental to the reasonable expectations of stakeholders claiming an oppression remedy.

[37] The fiduciary duty of the directors to the corporation originated in the common law. It is a duty to act in the best interests of the corporation. Often the interests of shareholders and stakeholders are co-extensive with the interests of the corporation. But if they conflict, the directors' duty is clear—it is to the corporation: *Peoples Department Stores* [[2004] 3 SCR 461].

[38] The fiduciary duty of the directors to the corporation is a broad, contextual concept. It is not confined to short-term profit or share value. Where the corporation is an ongoing concern, it looks to the long-term interests of the corporation. The content of this duty varies with the situation at hand. At a minimum, it requires the directors to ensure that the corporation meets its statutory obligations. But, depending on the context, there may also be other requirements. In any event, the fiduciary duty owed by directors is mandatory; directors must look to what is in the best interests of the corporation.

[39] In *Peoples Department Stores*, this Court found that although directors *must* consider the best interests of the corporation, it may also be appropriate, although *not mandatory*, to consider the impact of corporate decisions on shareholders or particular groups of stakeholders [see para. 42 in *Peoples*].

. . .

[40] In considering what is in the best interests of the corporation, directors may look to the interests of, *inter alia*, shareholders, employees, creditors, consumers, governments and the environment to inform their decisions. Courts should give appropriate deference to the business judgment of directors who take into account these ancillary interests, as reflected by the business judgment rule. The "business judgment rule" accords deference to a business decision, so long as it lies within a range of reasonable alternatives: see *Maple Leaf Foods Inc. v. Schneider Corp.* (1998), 42 OR (3d) 177 (CA); *Kerr v. Danier Leather Inc.*, [2007] 3 SCR 331 ... . It reflects the reality that directors ... are often better suited to determine what is in the best interests of the corporation. This applies to decisions on stakeholders' interests, as much as other directorial decisions.

[41] Normally only the beneficiary of a fiduciary duty can enforce the duty. In the corporate context, however, this may offer little comfort. The directors who control the corporation are unlikely to bring an action against themselves for breach of their own fiduciary duty. The shareholders cannot act in the stead of the corporation; their only power is the right to oversee the conduct of the directors by way of votes at shareholder assemblies. Other stakeholders may not even have that.

. . .

[45] ... [T]he oppression remedy focuses on harm to the legal and equitable interests of stakeholders affected by oppressive acts of a corporation or its directors. This remedy is available to a wide range of stakeholders—security holders, creditors, directors and officers.

. . .

B. The Section 241 Oppression Remedy

. . .

[56] In our view ... [o]ne should look first to the principles underlying the oppression remedy, and in particular the concept of reasonable expectations. If a breach of a reasonable expectation is established, one must go on to consider whether the conduct complained of amounts to "oppression," "unfair prejudice" or "unfair disregard" as set out in s. 241(2) of the CBCA.

[57] We preface our discussion of the twin prongs of the oppression inquiry by two preliminary observations that run throughout all the jurisprudence.

[58] First, oppression is an equitable remedy. It seeks to ensure fairness—what is "just and equitable." It gives a court broad, equitable jurisdiction to enforce not just what is legal but what is fair ... . It follows that courts considering claims for oppression should look at business realities, not merely narrow legalities ... .

[59] Second, like many equitable remedies, oppression is fact-specific. What is just and equitable is judged by the reasonable expectations of the stakeholders in the context and in regard to the relationships at play. Conduct that may be oppressive in one situation may not be in another.

[60] Against this background, we turn to the first prong of the inquiry, the principles underlying the remedy of oppression. In *Ebrahimi v. Westbourne Galleries Ltd.*, [1973] AC 360 (HL), at p. 379, Lord Wilberforce, interpreting s. 222 of the UK *Companies Act, 1948*, described the remedy of oppression in the following seminal terms:

> The words ["just and equitable"] are a recognition of the fact that a limited company is more than a mere legal entity, with a personality in law of its own: that there is room in company law for recognition of the fact that behind it, or amongst it, there are individuals, with rights, expectations and obligations *inter se* which are not necessarily submerged in the company structure.

[61] Lord Wilberforce spoke of the equitable remedy in terms of the "rights, expectations and obligations" of individuals. ... It is left for the oppression remedy to deal with the "expectations" of affected stakeholders. The reasonable expectations of these stakeholders is the cornerstone of the oppression remedy.

[62] As denoted by "reasonable," the concept of reasonable expectations is objective and contextual. The actual expectation of a particular stakeholder is not conclusive. In the context of whether it would be "just and equitable" to grant a remedy, the question is whether the expectation is reasonable having regard to the facts of the specific case, the relationships at issue, and the entire context, including the fact that there may be conflicting claims and expectations.

[63] Particular circumstances give rise to particular expectations. Stakeholders enter into relationships, with and within corporations, on the basis of understandings and

expectations, upon which they are entitled to rely, provided they are reasonable in the context: see: ... *Main v. Delcan Group Inc.* (1999), 47 BLR (2d) 200 (Ont. SCJ). These expectations are what the remedy of oppression seeks to uphold.

[64] Determining whether a particular expectation is reasonable is complicated by the fact that the interests and expectations of different stakeholders may conflict. The oppression remedy recognizes that a corporation is an entity that encompasses and affects various individuals and groups, some of whose interests may conflict with others. Directors or other corporate actors may make corporate decisions or seek to resolve conflicts in a way that abusively or unfairly maximizes a particular group's interest at the expense of other stakeholders. The corporation and shareholders are entitled to maximize profit and share value, to be sure, but not by treating individual stakeholders unfairly. Fair treatment—the central theme running through the oppression jurisprudence—is most fundamentally what stakeholders are entitled to "reasonably expect."

[65] Section 241(2) speaks of the "act or omission" of the corporation or any of its affiliates, the conduct of "business or affairs" of the corporation and the "powers of the directors of the corporation or any of its affiliates." Often, the conduct complained of is the conduct of the corporation or of its directors, who are responsible for the governance of the corporation. However, the conduct of other actors, such as shareholders, may also support a claim for oppression ... *GATX Corp. v. Hawker Siddeley Canada Inc.* (1996), 27 BLR (2d) 251 (Ont. Ct. (Gen. Div.)). In the appeals before us, the claims for oppression are based on allegations that the directors of BCE and Bell Canada failed to comply with the reasonable expectations of the debentureholders, and it is unnecessary to go beyond this.

[66] The fact that the conduct of the directors is often at the centre of oppression actions might seem to suggest that directors are under a direct duty to individual stakeholders who may be affected by a corporate decision. Directors, acting in the best interests of the corporation, may be obliged to consider the impact of their decisions on corporate stakeholders, such as the debentureholders in these appeals. This is what we mean when we speak of a director being required to act in the best interests of the corporation viewed as a good corporate citizen. However, the directors owe a fiduciary duty to the corporation, and only to the corporation. People sometimes speak in terms of directors owing a duty to both the corporation and to stakeholders. Usually this is harmless, since the reasonable expectations of the stakeholder in a particular outcome often coincides with what is in the best interests of the corporation. However, cases (such as these appeals) may arise where these interests do not coincide. In such cases, it is important to be clear that the directors owe their duty to the corporation, not to stakeholders, and that the reasonable expectation of stakeholders is simply that the directors act in the best interests of the corporation.

[67] Having discussed the concept of reasonable expectations that underlies the oppression remedy, we arrive at the second prong of the s. 241 oppression remedy. Even if reasonable, not every unmet expectation gives rise to claim under s. 241. The section requires that the conduct complained of amount to "oppression," "unfair prejudice" or "unfair disregard" of relevant interests. "Oppression" carries the sense of conduct that is coercive and abusive, and suggests bad faith. "Unfair prejudice" may admit of a less culpable state of mind, that nevertheless has unfair consequences. Finally, "unfair disregard" of interests extends the remedy to ignoring an interest as being of no importance, contrary to the

stakeholders' reasonable expectations ... . The phrases describe, in adjectival terms, ways in which corporate actors may fail to meet the reasonable expectations of stakeholders.

[68] In summary, the foregoing discussion suggests conducting two related inquiries in a claim for oppression: (1) Does the evidence support the reasonable expectation asserted by the claimant? and (2) Does the evidence establish that the reasonable expectation was violated by conduct falling within the terms "oppression," "unfair prejudice" or "unfair disregard" of a relevant interest?

. . .

(a) Proof of a Claimant's Reasonable Expectations

[70] At the outset, the claimant must identify the expectations that he or she claims have been violated by the conduct at issue and establish that the expectations were reasonably held. As stated above, it may be readily inferred that a stakeholder has a reasonable expectation of fair treatment. However, oppression, as discussed, generally turns on particular expectations arising in particular situations. The question becomes whether the claimant stakeholder reasonably held the particular expectation. Evidence of an expectation may take many forms depending on the facts of the case.

[71] It is impossible to catalogue exhaustively situations where a reasonable expectation may arise due to their fact-specific nature. A few generalizations, however, may be ventured. Actual unlawfulness is not required to invoke s. 241; the provision applies "where the impugned conduct is wrongful, even if it is not actually unlawful": Dickerson Committee (R.W.V. Dickerson, J.L. Howard and L. Getz), *Proposals for a New Business Corporations Law for Canada* (1971), vol. 1, at p. 163. The remedy is focused on concepts of fairness and equity rather than on legal rights. In determining whether there is a reasonable expectation or interest to be considered, the court looks beyond legality to what is fair, given all of the interests at play ... . It follows that not all conduct that is harmful to a stakeholder will give rise to a remedy for oppression as against the corporation.

[72] Factors that emerge from the case law that are useful in determining whether a reasonable expectation exists include: ... [see, below, factors (i)-(vii), paras. 73-88].

(i) Commercial Practice

[73] Commercial practice plays a significant role in forming the reasonable expectations of the parties. A departure from normal business practices that has the effect of undermining or frustrating the complainant's exercise of his or her legal rights will generally (although not inevitably) give rise to a remedy. ...

(ii) The Nature of the Corporation

[74] The size, nature and structure of the corporation are relevant factors in assessing reasonable expectations ... .Courts may accord more latitude to the directors of a small, closely held corporation to deviate from strict formalities than to the directors of a larger public company.

(iii) Relationships

[75] Reasonable expectations may emerge from the personal relationships between the claimant and other corporate actors. Relationships between shareholders based on

ties of family or friendship may be governed by different standards than relationships between arm's length shareholders in a widely held corporation. As noted in *Re Ferguson and Imax Systems Corp.*, (1983), 150 DLR (3d) 718 (Ont. CA), "when dealing with a close corporation, the court may consider the relationship between the shareholders and not simply legal rights as such" (p. 727).

(iv) Past Practice

[76] Past practice may create reasonable expectations, especially among shareholders of a closely held corporation on matters relating to participation of shareholders in the corporation's profits and governance: *Gibbons v. Medical Carriers Ltd.* (2001), 17 BLR (3d) 280 [(Man. QB)] … . For instance, in *Gibbons*, the court found that the shareholders had a legitimate expectation that all monies paid out of the corporation would be paid to shareholders in proportion to the percentage of shares they held. The authorization by the new directors to pay fees to themselves, for which the shareholders would not receive any comparable payments, was in breach of those expectations.

[77] It is important to note that practices and expectations can change over time. Where valid commercial reasons exist for the change and the change does not undermine the complainant's rights, there can be no reasonable expectation that directors will resist a departure from past practice: *Alberta Treasury Branches v. SevenWay Capital Corp.* (1999), 50 BLR (2d) 294 (Alta. QB), aff'd (2000), 8 BLR (3d) 1 … .

(v) Preventive Steps

[78] In determining whether a stakeholder expectation is reasonable, the court may consider whether the claimant could have taken steps to protect itself against the prejudice it claims to have suffered. Thus it may be relevant to inquire whether a secured creditor claiming oppressive conduct could have negotiated protections against the prejudice suffered … .

(vi) Representations and Agreements

[79] Shareholder agreements may be viewed as reflecting the reasonable expectations of the parties … *Lyall v. 147250 Canada Ltd.* (1993), 106 DLR (4th) 304 (BCCA).

[80] Reasonable expectations may also be affected by representations made to stakeholders or to the public in promotional material, prospectuses, offering circulars and other communications … .

(vii) Fair Resolution of Conflicting Interests

[81] As discussed, conflicts may arise between the interests of corporate stakeholders *inter se* and between stakeholders and the corporation. Where the conflict involves the interests of the corporation, it falls to the directors of the corporation to resolve them in accordance with their fiduciary duty to act in the best interests of the corporation, viewed as a good corporate citizen.

[82] The cases on oppression, taken as a whole, confirm that the duty of the directors to act in the best interests of the corporation comprehends a duty to treat individual stakeholders affected by corporate actions equitably and fairly. There are no absolute rules. In each case, the question is whether, in all the circumstances, the directors acted

in the best interests of the corporation, having regard to all relevant considerations, including, but not confined to, the need to treat affected stakeholders in a fair manner, commensurate with the corporation's duties as a responsible corporate citizen.

[83] Directors may find themselves in a situation where it is impossible to please all stakeholders. The "fact that alternative transactions were rejected by the directors is irrelevant unless it can be shown that a particular alternative was definitely available and clearly more beneficial to the company than the chosen transaction": *Maple Leaf Foods*, *per* Weiler JA, at p. 192.

[84] There is no principle that one set of interests—for example the interests of shareholders—should prevail over another set of interests. Everything depends on the particular situation faced by the directors and whether, having regard to that situation, they exercised business judgment in a responsible way.

[85] On these appeals, it was suggested on behalf of the corporations that the "*Revlon* line" of cases from Delaware support the principle that where the interests of shareholders conflict with the interests of creditors, the interests of shareholders should prevail.

[86] The "*Revlon* line" refers to a series of Delaware corporate takeover cases, the two most important of which are *Revlon Inc. v. MacAndrews & Forbes Holdings Inc.*, 506 A 2d 173 (Del. 1985), and *Unocal Corp. v. Mesa Petroleum Co.*, 493 A 2d 946 (Del. 1985). In both cases, the issue was how directors should react to a hostile takeover bid. *Revlon* suggests that in such circumstances, shareholder interests should prevail over those of other stakeholders, such as creditors. *Unocal* tied this approach to situations where the corporation will not continue as a going concern, holding that although a board facing a hostile takeover "may have regard for various constituencies in discharging its responsibilities, ... such concern for non-stockholder interests is inappropriate when ... the object no longer is to protect or maintain the corporate enterprise but to sell it to the highest bidder" (p. 182).

[87] What is clear is that the *Revlon* line of cases has not displaced the fundamental rule that the duty of the directors cannot be confined to particular priority rules, but is rather a function of business judgment of what is in the best interests of the corporation, in the particular situation it faces. In a review of trends in Delaware corporate jurisprudence, former Delaware Supreme Court Chief Justice E. Norman Veasey put it this way:

> [It] is important to keep in mind the precise content of this "best interests" concept—that is, to whom this duty is owed and when. Naturally, one often thinks that directors owe this duty to both the corporation and the stockholders. That formulation is harmless in most instances because of the confluence of interests, in that what is good for the corporate entity is usually derivatively good for the stockholders. There are times, of course, when the focus is directly on the interests of the stockholders [i.e., as in *Revlon*]. But, in general, the directors owe fiduciary duties to the *corporation*, not to the stockholders. [Emphasis in original.]

> (E. Norman Veasey with Christine T. Di Guglielmo, "What Happened in Delaware Corporate Law and Governance from 1992–2004? A Retrospective on Some Key Developments" (2005), 153 *U Pa. L Rev.* 1399, at p. 1431)

[88] Nor does this Court's decision in *Peoples Department Stores* suggest a fixed rule that the interests of creditors must prevail. In *Peoples Department Stores*, the Court had to consider whether, in the case of a corporation under threat of bankruptcy, creditors

deserved special consideration (para. 46). The Court held that the fiduciary duty to the corporation did not change in the period preceding the bankruptcy, but that if the directors breach their duty of care to a stakeholder under s. 122(1)(b) of the CBCA, such a stakeholder may act upon it (para. 66).

(b) Conduct Which Is Oppressive, Is Unfairly Prejudicial or Unfairly Disregards the Claimant's Relevant Interests

[89] Thus far we have discussed how a claimant establishes the first element of an action for oppression—a reasonable expectation that he or she would be treated in a certain way. However, to complete a claim for oppression, the claimant must show that the failure to meet this expectation involved unfair conduct and prejudicial consequences within s. 241 of the CBCA. Not every failure to meet a reasonable expectation will give rise to the equitable considerations that ground actions for oppression. The court must be satisfied that the conduct falls within the concepts of "oppression," "unfair prejudice" or "unfair disregard" of the claimant's interest, within the meaning of s. 241 of the CBCA. Viewed in this way, the reasonable expectations analysis that is the theoretical foundation of the oppression remedy, and the particular types of conduct described in s. 241, may be seen as complementary, rather than representing alternative approaches to the oppression remedy, as has sometimes been supposed. Together, they offer a complete picture of conduct that is unjust and inequitable, to return to the language of *Ebrahimi*.

[90] In most cases, proof of a reasonable expectation will be tied up with one or more of the concepts of oppression, unfair prejudice, or unfair disregard of interests set out in s. 241, and the two prongs will in fact merge. Nevertheless, it is worth stating that as in any action in equity, wrongful conduct, causation and compensable injury must be established in a claim for oppression.

[91] The concepts of oppression, unfair prejudice and unfairly disregarding relevant interests are adjectival. They indicate the type of wrong or conduct that the oppression remedy of s. 241 of the CBCA is aimed at. However, they do not represent watertight compartments, and often overlap and intermingle.

[92] The original wrong recognized in the cases was described simply as oppression, and was generally associated with conduct that has variously been described as "burdensome, harsh and wrongful," "a visible departure from standards of fair dealing," and an "abuse of power" going to the probity of how the corporation's affairs are being conducted ... . It is this wrong that gave the remedy its name, which now is generally used to cover all s. 241 claims. However, the term also operates to connote a particular type of injury within the modern rubric of oppression generally—a wrong of the most serious sort.

[93] The CBCA has added "unfair prejudice" and "unfair disregard" of interests to the original common law concept, making it clear that wrongs falling short of the harsh and abusive conduct connoted by "oppression" may fall within s. 241. "[U]nfair prejudice" is generally seen as involving conduct less offensive than "oppression." Examples include squeezing out a minority shareholder, failing to disclose related party transactions, changing corporate structure to drastically alter debt ratios, adopting a "poison pill" to prevent a takeover bid, paying dividends without a formal declaration, preferring some shareholders with management fees and paying directors' fees higher than the industry norm ... .

[94] "[U]nfair disregard" is viewed as the least serious of the three injuries, or wrongs, mentioned in s. 241. Examples include favouring a director by failing to properly prosecute claims, improperly reducing a shareholder's dividend, or failing to deliver property belonging to the claimant ... .

C. Application to These Appeals

[95] As discussed above (at para. 68), in assessing a claim for oppression a court must answer two questions: (1) Does the evidence support the reasonable expectation the claimant asserts? and (2) Does the evidence establish that the reasonable expectation was violated by conduct falling within the terms "oppression," "unfair prejudice" or "unfair disregard" of a relevant interest?

[96] The debentureholders in this case assert two alternative expectations. Their highest position is that they had a reasonable expectation that the directors of BCE would protect their economic interests as debentureholders in Bell Canada by putting forward a plan of arrangement that would maintain the investment grade trading value of their debentures. Before this Court, however, they argued a softer alternative—a reasonable expectation that the directors would consider their economic interests in maintaining the trading value of the debentures.

[97] ... [T]he trial judge proceeded on the debentureholders' alleged expectation that the directors would act in a way that would preserve the investment grade status of their debentures. He concluded that this expectation was not made out on the evidence, since the statements by Bell Canada suggesting a commitment to retaining investment grade ratings were accompanied by warnings that explicitly precluded investors from reasonably forming such expectations, and the warnings were included in the prospectuses pursuant to which the debentures were issued.

[98] The absence of a reasonable expectation that the investment grade of the debentures would be maintained was confirmed, in the trial judge's view, by the overall context of the relationship, the nature of the corporation, its situation as the target of a bidding war, as well as by the fact that the claimants could have protected themselves against reduction in market value by negotiating appropriate contractual terms.

[99] The trial judge situated his consideration of the relevant factors in the appropriate legal context. He recognized that the directors had a fiduciary duty to act in the best interests of the corporation and that the content of this duty was affected by the various interests at stake in the context of the auction process that BCE was undergoing. He emphasized that the directors, faced with conflicting interests, might have no choice but to approve transactions that, while in the best interests of the corporation, would benefit some groups at the expense of others. He held that the fact that the shareholders stood to benefit from the transaction and that the debentureholders were prejudiced did not in itself give rise to a conclusion that the directors had breached their fiduciary duty to the corporation. All three competing bids required Bell Canada to assume additional debt, and there was no evidence that bidders were prepared to accept less leveraged debt. Under the business judgment rule, deference should be accorded to business decisions of directors taken in good faith and in the performance of the functions they were elected to perform by the shareholders.

[100] We see no error in the principles applied by the trial judge nor in his findings of fact, which were amply supported by the evidence. We accordingly agree that the first expectation advanced in this case—that the investment grade status of the debentures would be maintained—was not established.

[101] The alternative, softer, expectation advanced is that the directors would consider the interests of the bondholders in maintaining the trading value of the debentures. ...

[102] The evidence, objectively viewed, supports a reasonable expectation that the directors would consider the position of the debentureholders in making their decisions on the various offers under consideration. As discussed above, reasonable expectations for the purpose of a claim of oppression are not confined to legal interests. Given the potential impact on the debentureholders of the transactions under consideration, one would expect the directors, acting in the best interests of the corporation, to consider their short and long-term interests in the course of making their ultimate decision.

[103] Indeed, the evidence shows that the directors did consider the interests of the debentureholders. A number of debentureholders sent letters to the Board, expressing concern about the proposed leveraged buyout and seeking assurances that their interests would be considered. One of the directors, Mr. Pattison, met with Phillips, Hager & North, representatives of the debentureholders. The directors' response to these overtures was that the contractual terms of the debentures would be met, but no additional assurances were given.

[104] It is apparent that the directors considered the interests of the debentureholders and, having done so, concluded that while the contractual terms of the debentures would be honoured, no further commitments could be made. This fulfilled the duty of the directors to consider the debentureholders' interests. It did not amount to "unfair disregard" of the interests of the debentureholders. As discussed above, it may be impossible to satisfy all stakeholders in a given situation. In this case, the Board considered the interests of the claimant stakeholders. Having done so, and having considered its options in the difficult circumstances it faced, it made its decision, acting in what it perceived to be the best interests of the corporation.

[105] What the claimants contend for on this appeal, in reality, is not merely an expectation that their interests be considered, but an expectation that the Board would take further positive steps to restructure the purchase in a way that would provide a satisfactory purchase price to the shareholders and preserve the high market value of the debentures. At this point, the second, softer expectation asserted approaches the first alleged expectation of maintaining the investment grade rating of the debentures.

[106] The difficulty with this proposition is that there is no evidence that it was reasonable to suppose it could have been achieved. BCE, facing certain takeover, acted reasonably to create a competitive bidding process. The process attracted three bids. All of the bids were leveraged, involving a substantial increase in Bell Canada's debt. It was this factor that posed the risk to the trading value of the debentures. There is no evidence that BCE could have done anything to avoid that risk. Indeed, the evidence is to the contrary.

[107] We earlier discussed the factors to consider in determining whether an expectation is reasonable on a s. 241 oppression claim. These include commercial practice; the size, nature and structure of the corporation; the relationship between the parties; past practice; the failure to negotiate protections; agreements and representations; and the fair

resolution of conflicting interests. In our view, all these factors weigh against finding an expectation beyond honouring the contractual obligations of the debentures in this particular case.

[108] Commercial practice—indeed commercial reality—undermines the claim that a way could have been found to preserve the trading position of the debentures in the context of the leveraged buyout. This reality must have been appreciated by reasonable debentureholders. More broadly, two considerations are germane to the influence of general commercial practice on the reasonableness of the debentureholders' expectations. First, leveraged buyouts of this kind are not unusual or unforeseeable, although the transaction at issue in this case is noteworthy for its magnitude. Second, trust indentures can include change of control and credit rating covenants where those protections have been negotiated. Protections of that type would have assured debentureholders a right to vote, potentially through their trustee, on the leveraged buyout, as the trial judge pointed out. This failure to negotiate protections was significant where the debentureholders, it may be noted, generally represent some of Canada's largest and most reputable financial institutions, pension funds and insurance companies.

[109] The nature and size of the corporation also undermine the reasonableness of any expectation that the directors would reject the offers that had been presented and seek an arrangement that preserved the investment grade rating of the debentures. As discussed above (at para. 74), courts may accord greater latitude to the reasonableness of expectations formed in the context of a small, closely held corporation, rather than those relating to interests in a large, public corporation. Bell Canada had become a wholly owned subsidiary of BCE in 1983, pursuant to a plan of arrangement which saw the shareholders of Bell Canada surrender their shares in exchange for shares of BCE. Based upon the history of the relationship, it should not have been outside the contemplation of debentureholders acquiring debentures of Bell Canada under the 1996 and 1997 trust indentures, that arrangements of this type had occurred and could occur in the future.

[110] The debentureholders rely on past practice, suggesting that investment grade ratings had always been maintained. However, as noted, reasonable practices may reflect changing economic and market realities. The events that precipitated the leveraged buyout transaction were such realities. Nor did the trial judge find in this case that representations had been made to debentureholders upon which they could have reasonably relied.

[111] Finally, the claim must be considered from the perspective of the duty on the directors to resolve conflicts between the interests of corporate stakeholders in a fair manner that reflected the best interests of the corporation.

[112] The best interests of the corporation arguably favoured acceptance of the offer at the time. BCE had been put in play, and the momentum of the market made a buyout inevitable. The evidence, accepted by the trial judge, was that Bell Canada needed to undertake significant changes to continue to be successful, and that privatization would provide greater freedom to achieve its long-term goals by removing the pressure on short-term public financial reporting, and bringing in equity from sophisticated investors motivated to improve the corporation's performance. Provided that, as here, the directors' decision is found to have been within the range of reasonable choices that they could have made in weighing conflicting interests, the court will not go on to determine whether their decision was the perfect one.

[113] Considering all the relevant factors, we conclude that the debentureholders have failed to establish a reasonable expectation that could give rise to a claim for oppression. As found by the trial judge, the alleged expectation that the investment grade of the debentures would be maintained is not supported by the evidence. A reasonable expectation that the debentureholders' interests would be considered is established, but was fulfilled. The evidence does not support a further expectation that a better arrangement could be negotiated that would meet the exigencies that the corporation was facing, while better preserving the trading value of the debentures.

[114] Given that the debentureholders have failed to establish that the expectations they assert were reasonable, or that they were not fulfilled, it is unnecessary to consider in detail whether conduct complained of was oppressive, unfairly prejudicial, or unfairly disregarded the debentureholders' interests within the terms of s. 241 of the CBCA. Suffice it to say that "oppression" in the sense of bad faith and abuse was not alleged, much less proved. At best, the claim was for "unfair disregard" of the interests of the debentureholders. As discussed, the evidence does not support this claim.

. . .

VI. *Conclusion*

[166] We conclude that the debentureholders have failed to establish ... oppression under s. 241 of the CBCA ... .

Appeals allowed. Cross-appeals dismissed.

Sidaplex-Plastic Suppliers Inc. v. Elta Group Inc.
(1995), 131 DLR (4th) 399 (Ont. Ct. Gen. Div.)

R.A. BLAIR J:

Background

[1] The primary question to be addressed on this application is whether its facts give rise to one of those rare situations in which the "oppression remedy" provisions of the Ontario *Business Corporations Act*, RSO 1990, c. B.16 [OBCA], apply in the absence of bad faith or want of probity on the part of the respondents. There is also an issue under the *Bulk Sales Act*, RSO 1990, c. B.14.

[2] The corporate parties are all companies engaged in the production and sale of plastics and film in the graphic arts industry. Sidaplex-Plastic Suppliers, Inc. is a judgment creditor of the defendant, the Elta Group Inc. The judgment, in the amount of $97,076.30, was obtained on consent and as part of an overall arrangement whereby a further claim by Sidaplex involving approximately $10,000 would be tried together with an outstanding action by Elta against Sidaplex claiming substantial damages for breach of fiduciary duty and breach of contract. Although the terms of the judgment itself provided that the moneys were to be paid in cash to the solicitors for Sidaplex, the parties entered into an agreement whereby the judgment would instead be secured by an irre-

vocable letter of credit in favour of Sidaplex, to be automatically renewed pending the disposition of the issues remaining outstanding between the parties.

[3] A letter of credit was arranged by Elta, through its bank, but instead of being renewable automatically, the letter of credit was for a fixed term. It expired on February 21, 1995. As the application for the letter of credit had sought an instrument that would be renewable automatically, the parties apparently assumed that such was the case. The letter of credit itself had been forwarded to Elta's solicitors who, in turn, forwarded it to Sidaplex's solicitors. No one apparently noticed that it was for a fixed term. Through what appears to be sheer inadvertence, the letter of credit was not renewed.

[4] Thus, Sidaplex's security for its judgment lapsed with the expiration of the letter of credit.

[5] In the meantime, Elta entered into an agreement whereby it sold the bulk of its assets to the defendant Kimoto Canada Inc., a competitor and sometimes supplier of both Sidaplex and Elta. The proceeds of sale—something in excess of $533,000—were utilized to eliminate Elta's indebtedness of $320,000 at the bank, and at the same time eliminate the liability of the defendant Frank Lin—Elta's sole shareholder, director and officer—to the bank on his guarantee of that indebtedness. The balance of the sale proceeds was used in one fashion or another to pay off other Elta indebtedness, including two other letters of credit totalling approximately $168,000.

[6] The sale did not comply with the provisions of the *Bulk Sales Act*. Neither Elta nor Kimoto filed particulars of the asset sale with the court, nor did they obtain an order exempting the application of the Act. Kimoto did not demand a statement of creditors pursuant to s. 4.

[7] Elta is no longer carrying on business in the graphic arts field. It has no assets.

[8] In these circumstances Sidaplex applies to the court, in its capacity as creditor, seeking to invoke the oppression remedy provisions of the OBCA against both Elta and Mr. Lin, in order to rescue it from its lost security position. It also relies upon the provisions of the *Bulk Sales Act*, asking that the asset transaction between Elta and Kimoto be set aside, or that Kimoto be required to pay it a sum of money in compensation for the value of the lost security.

Issues

[9] The following issues arise out of this:

1. Was the inadvertent failure of Elta to renew and maintain the letter of credit "oppressive conduct," as that term is employed in s. 248 of the OBCA, in the sense that it was unfairly prejudicial to or that it unfairly disregarded the rights of Sidaplex as creditor?

2. Was the inadvertent failure of Mr. Lin—the sole shareholder, director and officer of Elta—to cause the company to renew and maintain the letter of credit similarly "oppressive conduct," giving rise to personal liability on the part of Mr. Lin?

3. Does the failure to comply with the *Bulk Sales Act* render Kimoto liable to reimburse the applicant for the loss it has sustained as a result of the disappearance of its security?

Law and Analysis

. . .

[10] Section 248 of the OBCA provides as follows:

> 248(1) A complainant ... may apply to the court for an order under this section.
>
> (2) Where, upon an application under subsection (1), the court is satisfied that in respect of a corporation or any of its affiliates,
>
> > (a) any act or omission of the corporation of any of its affiliates effects or threatens to effect a result;
> >
> > (b) the business or affairs of the corporation or any of its affiliates are, have been or are threatened to be carried on or conducted in a manner; or
> >
> > (c) the powers of the directors of the corporation or any of its affiliates are, have been or are threatened to be exercised in a manner,
>
> that is oppressive or unfairly prejudicial to or that unfairly disregards the interests of any security holder, creditor, director or officer of the corporation, the court may make an order to rectify the matters complained of.

[11] A "complainant," in addition to being a current or former shareholder, director or officer of the company, is defined in s. 245 to include:

> (c) any other person who, in the discretion of the court, is a proper person to make an application under this Part.

[12] It is well established now that a creditor has status to bring an application as a complainant, pursuant to s. 245(c) noted above. ...

[13] In terms of "oppression," each of these cases turns upon its own particular facts. As Brooke JA noted, in *Ferguson v. Imax Systems Corp.* (1983), 150 DLR (3d) 718 at p. 727, 43 OR (2d) 128, 21 ACWS (2d) 443 (CA): "[w]hat is oppressive or unfairly prejudicial in one case may not necessarily be so in the slightly different setting of another." Moreover, while some degree of bad faith or lack of probity in the impugned conduct may be the norm in such cases, neither is essential to a finding of "oppression" in the sense of conduct that is unfairly prejudicial to or which unfairly disregards the interests of the complainant, under the OBCA: see *Brant Investments Ltd. v. KeepRite Inc.* (1991), 80 DLR (4th) 161 at pp. 173-81, 1 BLR (2d) 225, 3 OR (3d) 289 (CA) (per McKinlay JA); *First Edmonton Place Ltd. v. 315888 Alberta Ltd.* [(1988), 40 BLR 28 (Alta. QB)], at pp. 55-7.

[14] This is, in my view, one of those rare cases where the oppression remedy is applicable, notwithstanding the facts do not demonstrate any bad faith or lack of probity on the part of Elta or Mr. Lin.

[15] What the OBCA proscribes is "any act or omission" on the part of the corporation which "effects" a result that is "unfairly prejudicial to or that unfairly disregards the interests" of a creditor. The failure to renew the letter of credit is unquestionably an "omission" which has "effected a result" that is "prejudicial" to Sidaplex. Sidaplex has lost the security which assured payment of its judgment at a time when all other creditors, apparently, have been looked after, including unsecured trade creditors, and including Mr. Lin—the sole shareholder, officer and director of the company—who has been released from a substantial personal guarantee.

[16] Do these circumstances amount to an "unfair" prejudice, or to an "unfair" disregard of the creditor's interests, however? In my opinion, they do. In *First Edmonton Place, supra,* Mr. Justice McDonald considered the factors to be assessed in considering whether a remedy under the comparable provisions of the Alberta *Business Corporations Act* should lie. He said at p. 57:

> Assuming the absence of fraud, in what other circumstances would a remedy under s. 234 be available? In deciding what is unfair, the history and nature of the corporation, the essential nature of the relationship between the corporation and the creditor, the type of rights affected, and general commercial practice should all be material. More concretely, the test of unfair prejudice or unfair disregard should encompass the following considerations: the protection of the underlying expectation of a creditor in its arrangement with the corporation, the extent to which the acts complained of were unforeseeable or the creditor could reasonably have protected itself from such acts, and the detriment to the interests of the creditor. The elements of the formula and the list of considerations as I have stated them should not be regarded as exhaustive. Other elements and considerations may be relevant, based upon the facts of a particular case.

[17] Here, Sidaplex and Elta had an ongoing business relationship for some time, Elta being a purchaser and distributor of Sidaplex product. The continuing nature of this relationship would appear to be reflected in the consensual process that was established to settle the outstanding differences between them: that is, the consent to the judgment for $97,076.36 and the referral of the additional $10,000 dispute for trial along with the complaints by Elta against Sidaplex. This was designed to preserve for Sidaplex, and protect, the liquidated amount which was clearly owing, while allowing the remaining, and less clear, issues to be litigated between them. It was the reasonable expectation of Sidaplex that this security would be preserved.

[18] Underlying intentions, understandings and expectations are now accepted as important underpinnings of the "oppression" remedy—using that term in its broad sense. This is as true whether the complainant is a minority shareholder or a creditor, in my opinion.

[19] Balanced against the underlying expectations of the creditor, in the set of criteria put forward in *First Edmonton Place, supra,* is the extent to which the acts complained of were unforeseeable or the creditor could reasonably have protected itself from such acts. This factor must be considered here. Counsel for Elta and Mr. Lin argues that the solicitors for Sidaplex were provided with a copy of the letter of credit and could either have refused to accept it—because it did not conform to the agreement—or, at least, have written reminding Elta that the letter of credit needed to be renewed. There is some merit in this argument, perhaps. In the end, however, it does not carry the day. Moreover, it neatly places the focus on the solicitors for Sidaplex, and sidesteps the fact that Elta's solicitors apparently never provided Elta or Mr. Lin with a copy of the letter of credit as issued either.

[20] It is Elta which had the contractual relationship with the bank vis-à-vis the letter of credit, and only Elta, through Mr. Lin, could have arranged for the letter of credit to be renewed. Sidaplex had no right or power to do so. Moreover, it was Sidaplex which was entitled to be protected, and it was Elta which had the obligation to ensure that such protection continued. In considering where the ultimate risk of the inadvertent failure to

renew the letter of credit should fall, it seems to me that the proper balance is for it to fall upon the obligor, Elta and its sole directing mind, Mr. Lin.

[21] What of the liability of Mr. Lin himself?

[22] Courts have made orders against directors personally, in oppression remedy cases: see, for example, Canadian Opera Co. v. Euro-American Motor Cars [(1989) 69 OR (2d) 532 (HCJ), aff'd. (1990) 75 OR (2d) 720 (Div. Ct.)]; Prime Computer of Canada Ltd. v. Jeffrey, supra; Tropxe Investments Inc. v. Ursus Securities Corp., [(1991)] 6 OR (3d) 733 (Gen. Div.)]. These cases, in particular, have involved small, closely held corporations, where the director whose conduct was attacked has been the sole controlling owner of the corporation and its sole and directing mind; and where the conduct in question has redounded directly to the benefit of that person.

[23] Such is the case here. Mr. Lin is the sole shareholder, director and officer of Elta. He is the one who has benefitted personally from the events that have transpired because he has been relieved of his substantial exposure under his personal guarantee of Elta's indebtedness to the bank. Sidaplex, on the other hand, appears to be the only loser. All other creditors have been paid. Sidaplex has been deprived of the security for which it bargained, and on which it relied, and left with a "paper" judgment when it should not have been. That security—the letter of credit—while not directly guaranteed by Mr. Lin personally, was based upon the company's line of credit at the bank, which was in turn buttressed by Mr. Lin's guarantee. The evidence is that the bank looked primarily to that guarantee for its security, and the bank's testimony, at least, is that it would have been prepared to renew the letter of credit had Mr. Lin made the request and had he been prepared to support the renewal with his guarantee.

[24] Lawyers and judges tend to worry and fuss a great deal about whether or not a given set of circumstances permits the piercing of the "corporate veil." They do so for legitimate reasons pertaining to corporate law. While personal liability of a director in an oppression remedy situation may be founded upon such a base—as it was in the authorities referred to above—the issue, in my view, is not so much one of piercing the corporate veil as it is a question of the overall application of s. 248(2) of the OBCA and the interplay between its various provisions.

[25] When "oppressive" conduct (in the broad sense), has been found to have occurred under s. 248, the court has a very broad discretionary power to "make an order to rectify the matters complained of." That broad discretionary power, under s. 248(3) is to "make any interim or final order it thinks fit," including:

> (j) an order compensating an aggrieved person;

[26] In its targeting of the kinds of conduct encompassed by the oppression remedy provision of the Act, the legislature has focused specifically upon the acts or omissions of the corporation (s. 248(2)(a)), the business or affairs of the corporation (s. 248(2)(b)), and the exercise of the powers of the directors (s. 248(2)(c)). In a small, closely held corporation such as Elta, it is the director who is in the position of a Mr. Lin, who is the source of all such conduct. When the power of the director is exercised in a fashion which causes an act or omission of the corporation which effects an unfairly prejudicial result, or a result which unfairly disregards the interests of the complainant—or which causes the business or affairs of the corporation to be conducted in a manner which has

the same effect—those powers themselves have been "exercised in a manner" which is caught by the section, in my opinion. Liability therefore lies directly with the director, under the section, in appropriate cases.

[27] This, in my view, is one of those cases. The proper way in which to rectify the matters complained of in this case is to make an order directing that Mr. Lin pay to Sidaplex the amount of Elta's judgment debt that should have been continually secured by the letter of credit, but which was not. That amount, as I have indicated, is $97,076.36, together with accrued interest. I so order.

. . .

Conclusion

[34] In the summary, then, I hold that the conduct of Elta, and of Mr. Lin as its sole director, in failing to ensure that the letter of credit was renewed, in the circumstances, constitutes conduct that is unfairly prejudicial to or that unfairly disregards the interests of Sidaplex as a creditor of Elta. Elta has no assets, and there is little point in making an order against it, particularly since Sidaplex already has a judgment in its favour against Elta. Mr. Lin has been relieved from his obligations to the bank under his personal guarantee, however, in circumstances where that guarantee would in all probability have been required to be kept in place either to buttress the line of credit at the bank to support a renewed letter of credit or, more directly, to support the letter of credit itself. The appropriate disposition, in my view, in order to rectify the matter complained of, is to require Mr. Lin to compensate Sidaplex for its loss as a result of the lapsed letter of credit. That amount, as I have previously indicated, is $97,076.36, plus interest.

[35] The application against Kimoto is dismissed.

Danylchuk v. Wolinsky
(2007), 38 CBR (5th) 173 (Man. CA)

M.A. MONNIN JA: [1] This is an appeal from findings of oppression under the provisions of s. 241 of the *Canada Business Corporations Act*, RSC 1985, c. C-44 (the "CBCA"), and an order that the appellants, Costas Ataliotis (Ataliotis) and David Wolinsky (Wolinsky), in their personal capacities, are liable, jointly and severally, to pay to the respondents an amount equal to one-half of their original investments or advancements as the case may be.

[2] The total amount of the judgment, for which the appellants are liable, is in the order of $875,000.

Introduction

[3] The appellants allege that the judge erred, firstly, in deciding the issue before her on the strength of challenged and disputed affidavit evidence instead of referring the matter for the trial of an issue and, secondly, by ordering a money award to be paid by both appellants jointly and severally.

[4] The appellants were shareholders and directors of Protos International Inc. (Protos) and Maple Leaf Distillers Inc. (Maple Leaf). Protos was a holding company which held shares in various businesses of which Maple Leaf was the most important. The respondents are either shareholders who invested in Protos or are creditors who loaned money to Protos.

. . .

[8] [The trial judge] ... proceeded to review the allegations made by the respondents and the countervailing position of the appellants and came to the following findings (at para. 64):

I am satisfied on the affidavit evidence filed that the applicants have demonstrated oppression. The respondents have unfairly disregarded the interests of the applicants, as follows:

1) by using the companies which they controlled as their personal bank accounts;

2) by making unauthorized payments of personal expenses or expenses which had no valid corporate purpose;

3) by preferring the interest of some shareholders over the interest of others;

4) by disregarding the interests of some creditors to the advantage of others;

5) by not having regular shareholders' meetings to update the shareholders;

6) by not providing timely financial statements to the shareholders.

. . .

[11] Dealing with the remedy, the appellants argue that a money judgment should not have been ordered for the simple failures of providing financial statements and calling meetings of shareholders, or for that matter for making payments as against their shareholder loans.

[12] Furthermore, the appellants also argue that there was no basis on which to make them personally and severally liable.

. . .

Conclusions with Respect to Oppression

[40] I concede that the appellants presented evidence that they were entitled to proceed as they did and that there was nothing illegal in the manner in which they proceeded. That, however, does not change the fact that such conduct, as found by the judge, was oppressive as the term has been defined in the jurisprudence, namely, that the conduct of the companies' affairs by the appellants was unfairly prejudicial to, or that it unfairly disregarded the interest of shareholders and creditors. Illegality and oppression are two entirely different concepts and oppressive actions can be, and are probably most times, legal actions.

[41] The conduct of the appellants was unfairly prejudicial to and unfairly disregarded the interest of the respondents as those terms have been defined in the decisions that I have referred to in these reasons. In arriving at her findings, the judge, according to the Act, had wide discretionary powers and she exercised them judicially and fairly.

[42] I would, therefore, dismiss the appeal with respect to the issue of finding oppression.

Remedy

[43] This now leaves the issue of the remedy imposed by the judge. She initiates her analysis of the appropriate remedy to apply in these words (at para. 65):

> What is the appropriate remedy to be given? The applicants have asked for the return of their initial investments in Protos or the amount secured by the promissory notes in the case of the creditors. No authority has been provided by counsel for the applicants to show that this remedy has ever been granted in Canada by any court pursuant to the CBCA. I appreciate that the scope of the remedy section is extremely wide and allows for creative remedies to be fashioned in appropriate circumstances without the expense and time necessary to proceed to trial by statement of claim.

[44] And then she goes on to conclude (at paras. 67-69):

> The applicants invested in Protos expecting a significant return for their investment, but knowing at the same time that this was somewhat speculative. Had personal expenses not been paid and charged against the shareholders' loans by Ataliotis and Wolinsky, Protos and Maple Leaf might still have gone into receivership by virtue of the inability to finalize a lucrative contract in 2005 with Angostura Ltd. Without the oppressive actions of Wolinsky and Ataliotis the applicants may very well have still lost all of their investment. Nonetheless, the access by the respondents to funds in Protos and Maple Leaf without divulging that to the other shareholders and without allowing them to have drawn a proportionate amount of money, in my view, is unfair. And if the money accessed against the shareholders' account had been left in the company, its liquidity may have been better. That being said, it would not be equitable to force Wolinsky and Ataliotis to return the full investment as requested by the applicants.
>
> I believe an equitable remedy to be to order Wolinsky and Ataliotis jointly and severally to be liable to the applicants in the amount of one-half of their original investment or advancement, as the case may be.
>
> At first blush this might seem arbitrary. I believe it to be appropriate for a number of reasons. Section 241 of the CBCA allows for equitable remedies to be granted, including compensation to an aggrieved person. It would be almost impossible to quantify the exact amount that Wolinsky and Ataliotis accessed under circumstances that unfairly disregarded the interests of the shareholders and creditors in this application. Even if the matter was to proceed by way of statement of claim rather than application, oppression would be easily demonstrated by the applicants as it has been in this application but quantification would remain difficult even with a forensic accounting, and would be extremely costly to all parties. In arriving at this percentage I have attempted to balance the potential total loss of investment by the applicants with the substantial accessing of company funds by the respondents. Thus, the remedy has been fashioned as set out above.

• • •

[47] The appellants argue that the remedy imposed by the judge is unprecedented and completely disproportionate to the manner in which they conducted the affairs of the company even if that conduct was found to be oppressive. They argue that the acts of oppression found to exist by the judge have no connection with the losses suffered by the shareholders or creditors and that their actions did not result in the failure of Protos.

They point out that even if the respondents have lost their investments, they themselves have lost more than all of the respondents combined. They also argue that they gained no personal benefits or financial gains as a result of their conduct.

· · ·

[49] Finally, the appellants argue that the purpose of the legislation, and particularly the remedial portion thereof, is to rectify oppressive situations and not to reimburse investors in an enterprise that went wrong.

· · ·

[54] Before dealing specifically with the remedy imposed by the judge, it is useful to consider cases in which similar remedies have been imposed.

[55] *Loveridge Holdings Ltd. v. King-Pin Ltd.* (1991), 5 BLR (2d) 195 (Ont. Gen. Div.), is a decision in which a money judgment was awarded. Chapnik J stated in oral reasons (at paras. 20, 22-25):

> ... The applicant made certain allegations of fraud and illegality against the respondent. I am not prepared to make those findings. On the evidence before me, I do not believe that the respondents acted in bad faith in that they deliberately intended to do harm to the applicant; they may well have thought that they were carrying on business for legitimate business reasons. The evidence indicates that they had carried on business in a similar fashion for several years in the past. However, in this situation, where there is a minority shareholder who has no say in the business and whose rights are being prejudiced, they cannot continue to do so.
>
> In the case of *Palmer v. Carling O'Keefe Breweries of Canada Ltd.* (1989), 67 OR (2d) 161 (Div. Ct.), the directors of the defendant company treated the company as though it was a private enterprise when it still had other shareholders. Thus, the court, although it found no bad faith, ordered the company to make an offer to redeem preference shares owned by some of its shareholders. At p. 172 [OR], Southey J stated:
>
> > Section 247 does not expressly require proof of bad faith. Whatever may be the rule in an oppression case, I do not think the statements in *Re Brant Investments Ltd. and KeepRite Inc.* (1987), 60 OR (2d) 737, 42 DLR (4th) 15, 37 BLR 65 (HCJ); *Re Pizza Pizza Ltd.* (unreported, August 17, 1987), and *Bank of Montreal v. Dome Petroleum Ltd.* (1987), 67 CBR (NS) 296 (QB), are authority for the proposition that bad faith must be shown before an order to rectify a complaint may be made in a case of this nature.

· · ·

[57] Further guidance can be obtained from the Ontario Court of Appeal decision in *Budd v. Gentra Inc.* (1998), 111 OAC 288 (Ont. CA) ... . After a review of the principles of limited liability of directors at common law, Doherty JA goes on to distinguish the remedies available at common law with the remedies provided for under the Ontario oppression statute. He wrote (at para. 29):

> Section 241(3) vests the court with broad remedial powers. It provides that in rectifying the matter complained of "the court may make any interim or final order it thinks fit." Those words are followed by a list of 14 orders which may be made and the express indication that those specific orders do not limit the generality of the remedial power given in the opening language of s. 241(3). The specific orders referred to in s. 241(3) include the power to require

"any other person to pay to a security holder any part of the monies paid by him for securities" (s. 241(3)(g)), and the power to compensate an aggrieved person (s. 241(3)(j)). Both orders can be made against the company and/or individuals, including directors and officers.

[58] And he continues (at paras. 33-35):

If the conduct of the corporation is oppressive, unfairly prejudicial to, or unfairly disregards the interest of corporate stakeholders, the court may impose a "fit order." The nature and scope of that order is circumscribed by the requirements that the order "rectify the matter complained of" and address only the aggrieved parties' interests as corporate stakeholders: *Naneff v. Con-Crete Holdings Limited et al.* ... at pp. 489-490 ... . By providing for remedies against individuals, including directors and officers, s. 241 recognizes that the rectification of harm done to corporate stakeholders by corporate abuse may necessitate an order against individuals through whom the company acts. To the extent that the section contemplates that individuals will bear the remedial burden flowing from the oppressive exercise of corporate powers, s. 241 takes a different approach to assigning responsibility for corporate conduct than does the common law. The section permits the court to address the harm done by the conduct described in s. 241 from a broader perspective than that permitted by a simple inquiry into the true identity of the actor.

This broader perspective is entirely consistent with the purpose of the section which is aptly described by D. Peterson in *Shareholder Remedies in Canada* (loose leaf), at p. 18.1:

The oppression remedy may be considered the *Charter of Rights and Freedoms* of corporate law. It is a relatively new creature of statute, so it is little developed. It is broad and flexible, allowing any type of corporate activity to be the subject of judicial scrutiny. The potential protection it offers corporate stakeholders is awesome. Nevertheless, the legislative intent of the oppression remedy is to balance the interests of those claiming rights from the corporation against the ability of management to conduct business in an efficient manner. The remedy is appropriate only where as a result of corporate activity, there is some discrimination or unfair dealing amongst corporate stakeholders, a breach of a legal or equitable right, or appropriation of corporate property.

Where a plaintiff seeks a remedy against a director or officer personally under s. 241, I do not think it is accurate to suggest that the plaintiff is attempting to "circumvent the principles with respect to personal liability of directors and officers." On the contrary, the plaintiff is making a fundamentally different kind of claim than is contemplated in cases like *Peoples* [*Montreal Trust Co. of Canada et al. v. Scotia McLeod Inc. et al.* (1995), 87 OAC 129]. The plaintiff is not alleging that he was wronged by a director or officers acting in his or her personal capacity, but is asserting that the corporation, through the actions of the directors or officers, has acted oppressively and that in the circumstances it is appropriate (i.e., fit) to rectify that oppression by an order against the directors or officers personally.

[59] And he comes to the following conclusion (at paras. 46-47):

In my view, Farley J erred in holding that a director or officer could only be personally liable for a monetary order under s. 241 of the CBCA where the claim against the director or officer met the *Peoples* criteria. A director or officer may be personally liable for a monetary order under that section if that director or officer is implicated in the conduct said to constitute the oppression and if in all of the circumstances, rectification of the harm done by the oppressive conduct is appropriately made by an order requiring the director or officer to personally compensate the aggrieved parties.

In deciding whether an oppression action claiming a monetary order reveals a reasonable cause of action against directors or officers personally, the court must decide:

- Are there acts pleaded against specific directors or officers which, taken in the context of the entirety of the pleadings, could provide the basis for finding that the corporation acted oppressively within the meaning of s. 241 of the CBCA?
- Is there a reasonable basis in the pleadings on which a court could decide that the oppression alleged could be properly rectified by a monetary order against a director or officer personally?

[60] Finally, although stated in *obiter*, the Supreme Court of Canada in *People's Department Stores Ltd. (1992) Inc., Re*, [2004] 3 SCR 461 (SCC), recognized the extraordinarily wide powers available under oppression remedy legislation [*Peoples*, above, paras. 48 and 51].

. . .

[62] I would conclude from the above that since the Supreme Court of Canada considers that creditors of insolvent companies can avail themselves of the remedies provided under oppression legislation and seek redress from directors of those companies, that at the very least the respondents before us are in the same if not a stronger position.

[63] At the outset, I must state that I reject out of hand the appellants' contention that a monetary remedy should not be imposed unless the finding of oppression comes following a trial of an issue. The law specifically provides that evidence of oppression may be adduced by way of affidavit evidence. Evidence is evidence whether it is presented to a judge in the form of affidavit or *viva voce* evidence and that evidence is not automatically less reliable because it happens to be in written form.

[64] A judge has a wide discretion in imposing a remedy that she or he thinks appropriate and an appellate court can only interfere with that decision if it concludes that there was an error in principle on the part of the judge or if the remedy imposed in all of the circumstances is an unjust order. I cannot come to that conclusion in this case.

[65] The appellants were both clearly implicated in the oppressive conduct of Protos as together they had total control of the company on a day-to-day basis. The respondents had advanced funds or invested in Protos because of their personal relationships and confidence with the appellants. The findings of oppression made by the judge are directly and wholly attributable to the appellants. They easily fit into the *Budd v. Gentra Inc.* criteria of instances where a monetary judgment can be deemed appropriate. In addition, the cases I have cited are of more than sufficient authority to justify and maintain the remedial order made by the judge.

[66] I concede that the remedy imposed is, to say the very least, significant but so are the losses incurred by the respondents. Any investor in a company such as Protos takes some element of risk with his or her investment but that investor is entitled to have that investment dealt with fairly. That was not the case with respect to Protos. There well might be no illegality in the manner the appellants dealt with the company, but their conduct prevented the shareholders and creditors from managing their investments in

an informed and knowledgeable manner. They were entitled to much more than what they received from the appellants.

[67] The judge in her wisdom and discretion framed a remedy which she thought appropriate and equitable. She demonstrated no error in doing so and, therefore, I am not in a position to interfere with it even if I might consider it severe or significant.

Appeal dismissed.

NOTES AND QUESTIONS

1. The Ontario Court of Appeal affirmed Blair J's ruling in *Sidaplex* on the oppression remedy: see *Sidaplex-Plastics Suppliers Inc. v. Elta Group Inc.* (1998), 162 DLR (4th) 367 (Ont. CA). The Court of Appeal, relying on the earlier decision of *Brant Investments Ltd. v. KeepRite Inc.* (1991), 3 OR (3d) 289 (Ont. CA) noted at para. 4 that "it is no longer necessary to prove bad faith or want of probity to show a right to a remedy under s. 248." Would the outcome in *Sidaplex* be altered by the Supreme Court of Canada's decision in *BCE*? Does the *BCE* decision provide a workable framework for analyzing oppression cases?

2. In *BCE* the Supreme Court of Canada (at para. 66) referred to a "director being required to act in the best interests of the corporation viewed as a good corporate citizen." Further on (at para. 82), the court referred to "the corporation's duties as a responsible corporate citizen." Is there a distinction between a good and responsible corporate citizen? Does the court define these terms? What meaning should these terms have in the light of the court's analysis of the oppression remedy?

3. In *Downtown Eatery (1993) Ltd. v. Ontario* (2001), 200 DLR (4th) 289 (Ont. CA), leave to appeal dismissed [2001] SCCA no. 397 (QL), a judgment creditor of the corporation sought an oppression remedy against the directors of the corporation. Prior to the judgment being granted, the directors engineered a reorganization of the corporation and, subsequently, the corporation ceased trading. The judgment creditor sought to invoke the oppression remedy against the directors, alleging that the directors' decision to reorganize the company and cease operations left the corporation without assets capable of responding to a judgment against it. The trial judge dismissed the claim for an oppression remedy on the basis that the reorganization was not undertaken for the purpose of depriving the creditor of recovery of judgment. The Court of Appeal overturned this ruling, concluding (at para. 56):

> In our view, the trial judge failed to appreciate that the "oppressive" conduct that causes harm to a complainant need not be undertaken with the intention of harming the complainant. Provided that it is established that a complainant has a reasonable expectation that a company's affairs will be conducted with a view to protecting his interests, the conduct complained of need not be undertaken with the intention of harming the plaintiff. If the effect of the conduct results in harm to the complainant, recovery under s. 248(2) may follow.

4. As discussed in *Peoples*, a creditor may obtain standing as a complainant to pursue an oppression remedy. Can a trustee in bankruptcy rely on the oppression remedy? In *Olympia & York Developments Ltd (Trustee of) v. Olympia & York Realty Corp.* (2003), 68 OR (3d) 544, the Ontario Court of Appeal (at para. 45) held that "the trustee is neither automatically barred from being a complainant nor automatically entitled to that status. It is for the judge

at first instance to determine in the exercise of his or her discretion whether in the circumstances of the particular case, the trustee is a proper person to be a complainant."

5. Can the creditor seek to rely on the oppression remedy to obtain a judgment against the corporate director as a means of debt collection against the corporation? If so, is it relevant whether the creditor had sought to obtain director guarantees or obtain a security interest in corporate assets before advancing the loan? In *Royal Trust Corp. of Canada v. Hordo* (1992), 10 BLR (2d) 86 (Ont. Gen. Div.), the court said (at 92):

> It does not seem to me that debt actions should be routinely turned into oppression actions ...
> I do not think that the court's discretion should be used to give complainant status to a creditor where the creditor's interest in the affairs of the corporation is too remote or where the complaints of the creditor have nothing to do with the circumstances giving rise to the debt or if the creditor is not proceeding in good faith. Status as a complainant should also be refused where the creditor is not in a position analogous to that of a minority shareholder and has no particular legitimate interest in the manner in which the affairs of the company are managed.

Is this statement consistent with the Supreme Court of Canada's analysis in *BCE*?

6. In the light of the decision in *Wolinsky*, it appears that a court has a great deal of discretion in fashioning an oppression remedy. In *Wonlinsky*, the Manitoba Court of Appeal upheld the trial judge's order that the appellants, in their personal capacities, were liable, jointly and severally, to pay to the respondents an amount equal to one-half of their original investments or loan advances. On what basis did the trial judge arrive at the one-half allocation? In your view was it arbitrary? What factors led to the court's finding of oppression? How would the *Wolinsky* facts be analyzed using the framework from *BCE*?

7. In 2002, the Insolvency Institute of Canada and the Canadian Association of Insolvency and Restructuring Professionals recommended the adoption of a national oppression standard within the BIA. Recommendation 65 states:

> Canadian courts for the most part have recognized the ability of creditors to bring oppression remedy applications under the *Canada Business Corporations Act* and similar provincial corporation legislation. However, the creditor must establish that it is a position analogous to a minority shareholder before the court will generally allow the case to proceed. An oppression provision under the BIA could contain the same standard as corporations statutes. ... The provision would be tempered by a safe harbour provision, creating a balance between the ability of the debtor to make business decisions in the period before and during the firm's financial distress and the ability of creditors to obtain a remedy where the conduct is oppressive, unfairly prejudicial to or unfairly disregards their interests.

> (Canada, Joint Task Force on Business Insolvency Law Reform, "Joint Report of the Insolvency Institute of Canada and the Canadian Association of Insolvency and Restructuring Professionals" (Industry Canada, 2002))

The Joint Task Force recommended that a separate BIA oppression provision would apply once the corporation entered insolvency proceedings. This would mean that provincial oppression provisions would no longer apply through the creation of a new national standard of oppression remedy to govern insolvent corporations.

C. Wrongful and Reckless Trading Statutes

One way to prevent the possibility of abuse of the corporate form is to impose statutory liability on the directors where the company continues to trade while insolvent. New Zealand,[4] England,[5] and Australia[6] have all adopted provisions that impose personal liability on directors for defined notions of wrongful, insolvent, or reckless trading. The idea behind these statutes is to inhibit directors from continuing to operate an insolvent company at the expense of creditors. However, the imposition of statutory liability on directors may also involve costs. The legal regime must balance the need to protect creditors against the risk that a director liability regime will discourage a company's ability to innovate and take appropriate business risks. Risk taking is recognized as one of the fundamental features of company law. Professor Roy Goode concludes that "risk is inherent in business activity, and if entrepreneurial activity is to be encouraged we have to accept the failure of some enterprises as the price to be paid": Goode, "Insolvent Trading Under English and Australian Law" (1998), 16 *CSLJ* 170, at 175. There is, therefore, a tension between the desirability of risk taking and the importance of deterring reckless trading. While there might be agreement on the underlying principle that directors should not continue to trade and gamble with creditors' money, the difficulty is defining precisely the point at which director liability should be imposed. Thus far, Canada has not opted to adopt a specific wrongful or reckless trading statute, but it has been debated in the past.

Efficiency and Fairness in Business Insolvencies
Industry Canada, Corporate Law Policy Development, January 2001

The issue of sanctions for conduct by directors and officers detrimental to creditors was raised as long ago as 1970, in the report of the Study Committee on Bankruptcy and Insolvency Legislation—the Tassé Committee. The report noted problems with individuals hiding under the corporate veil and commented that the inconvenience of bankruptcy to the principals of a bankrupt company often lasts no longer than the time needed to incorporate a new company. The Committee recommended imposing the status of bankrupt on a bankrupt corporation's directors and officers for up to five years, which would have made them ineligible to serve as directors under most corporations laws. It also recommended providing that no contracts with these persons should be enforceable. It further recommended exposing directors and officers to liability for the deficiency in

---

[4]   *Companies Act 1993* (No. 105), ss. 135 and 136. See Thomas G.W. Telfer, "Risk and Insolvent Trading," in C. Rickett and R. Grantham, eds., *Corporate Personality in the 20th Century* (Oxford: Hart Publishing, 1998), at 127.

[5]   Section 214 of the *Insolvency Act 1986* (UK). See A. Keay, *Company Directors' Responsibilities to Creditors* (New York: Cavendish-Routledge, 2007); Andrew Keay, "Wrongful Trading and the Liability of Company Directors: A Theoretical Perspective" (2005), 25 *LS* 431.

[6]   Section 588G of the *Corporations Act 2001* (Cth). Papers on the Australian, New Zealand, and United Kingdom provisions can be found in Ian Ramsay, ed., *Company Directors' Liability for Insolvent Trading* (Sydney: CCH Australia and the Centre for Corporate Law and Securities Regulation, 2000).

corporate assets when transactions made were not in the corporation's interest, when a director used his company's property as his own, or when a director was responsible for defrauding creditors.

Bill C-60 of 1975, the first of a series of six omnibus bankruptcy reform bills introduced between 1975 and 1984, adopted most of the Study Committee's recommendations on directors' and officers' improper conduct. The bill contained provisions imposing liability on "agents," including directors and officers, for deficiency in the estate of a bankrupt company if the agent, in his own interest or that of a related person, caused the company, while insolvent, to carry on business or to enter into transactions contrary to the company's interest, to continue the business by ruinous borrowing or sales below cost, or to conduct the business so as to defraud, impede, obstruct or delay creditors. It also contained provisions enabling agents to be deemed bankrupt and hence ineligible to enter into enforceable credit contracts or to act as officers or directors if they were found primarily responsible for the company's insolvency. In addition, it provided that bankrupts could not act as directors or officers.

The agent liability provisions in Bill C-60 received support at the Parliamentary Committee stage. However, the provisions deeming agents to be bankrupt were criticized and the committee recommended that they be replaced by provisions prohibiting individual bankrupts or agents from carrying on the same business for two years. In fact, the deeming provisions of Bill C-60 were dropped from later bills. Bill C-17 of 1984, contained agent liability and disqualification provisions. It also proposed that liability be imposed on directors and officers of a bankrupt company for creditors' losses. The liability provision was similar to that of Bill C-60, the main difference being that it contained a good faith reliance defence. The bill also provided that, if a "caveat" was filed in respect of an agent, that person could not, while the caveat was in effect, act as a director or officer of a corporation or engage in any trade or business without disclosing the caveat. The bill also made bankrupts ineligible to act as directors or officers.

The Colter Committee reviewed Bill C-17 and recommended that directors be subject to personal liability and disqualification for wrongful conduct. Stakeholders responding to the Colter Committee's report generally supported provisions holding "responsible person(s)" to account, although the need to carefully define the terms used, such as "responsible person" or "wrongful trading," was stressed. Some concern was raised about the need to balance liability with the need to attract qualified people to take on directorships, especially during reorganizations. The Colter Committee's recommendations on "responsible persons" were not included in the 1991 bill. The issue was not discussed in the deliberations of the Bankruptcy and Insolvency Advisory Committee (BIAC), nor was it addressed in the 1997 bill.[7]

---

7 In 1986 the Colter Committee considered the following as a possible solution to the issue of wrongful trading:

> A director of a company could be personally liable for the loss suffered by creditors to the extent determined by the court if a director allowed a company to continue trading with the result that the position of existing creditors worsened or additional liabilities were incurred which were not paid and the directors knew or ought to have known that there was no reasonable prospect of avoiding that

NOTES AND QUESTIONS

1. Assume that acting on the 1986 recommendation of the Colter Committee, Parliament has adopted ss. 135 and 136 of the New Zealand *Companies Act 1993*, set out below. How would you advise a director in the example that follows?

Sections 135 and 136 of the *Companies Act 1993* (1993 No. 105) (NZ) provide as follows:

135. Reckless trading—A director of a company must not—

a) Agree to the business of the company being carried on in a manner likely to create a substantial risk of serious loss to the company's creditors; or

b) Cause or allow the business of the company to be carried on in a manner likely to create a substantial risk of serious loss to the company's creditors.

136. Duty in relation to obligations—A director of a company must not agree to the company incurring an obligation unless the director believes at that time on reasonable grounds that the company will be able to perform the obligation when it is required to do so.

Example

An engineer has an idea for a new laser switch (drug or biotech marvel) and needs funds to build an operational prototype. Whatever equity he had put into his company to fund his research is exhausted. He now seeks first-stage financing in anticipation of creating an operational prototype, generating customers, and beginning manufacturing operations. His firm's balance sheet shows negative equity and best projections show negative earnings for at least another five years. Both he and his lenders understand that only 1 in 5 high-tech companies end up turning a profit, and only 1 in 10 end up a substantial success. But the lenders are willing to fund the company with convertible debt. The lenders calculate that they can diversify their lending over 10 or more companies and ask for a rate of return on each that will leave them a profit when 8 fail, 1 shows a profit, and 1 is a success.[8]

Is the director able to obtain the financing from the venture capital firm without the risk of personal liability under the statute? If the company fails, is the venture capital firm, which makes a calculated risk to invest in the high-tech firm, truly deserving of protection?

2. In the absence of a wrongful or reckless trading provision, can directors continue to let the company trade if they know the company is insolvent? In *USF Red Star Inc. v. 1220103 Ontario Ltd.* (2001), 13 BLR (3d) (295) (Ont. SCJ), Hawkins J stated:

---

situation. This liability would arise where officers or directors of an insolvent company have authorized the company to make additional purchases of inventory in order to enhance the amount available for realization by a secured creditor whose debt they have guaranteed.

(Canada, Advisory Committee on Bankruptcy and Insolvency, *Proposed Bankruptcy Act Amendments: Report of the Advisory Committee on Bankruptcy and Insolvency* (Ottawa: Minister of Supply and Services, 1986), at 113 ("Colter Committee Report").) [eds.]

[8] See Dale A. Oesterle, "Corporate Directors' Personal Liability for 'Insolvent,' 'Reckless,' and 'Wrongful' Trading: A Recipe for Timid Directors, Hamstrung Controlling Shareholders and Skittish Lenders" (2001), 7 *NZBLQ* 20, at 26.

I conclude that directors of a company may, with impunity, cause the company to order goods and services which they have no objective reason to believe the company can pay for in the absence of a preference or fraudulent activities which impair the company's ability to meet its obligations.

Is this an accurate statement of Canadian law? Would your answer differ if the director's motive for the inventory order was to reduce the director's personal guarantee to a secured creditor holding a security interest over existing and after-acquired property of the company?

3. In relation to note 2, the unpaid supplier provisions in BIA ss. 81.1 and 81.2, discussed in Section II of Chapter 9, which protect the inventory supplier by giving it priority, in limited circumstances, over the claims of other unsecured creditors.

CHAPTER ELEVEN

Individual Bankruptcies and Consumer Issues

I. INTRODUCTION

In previous chapters we examined the general structure of the BIA concepts and rules. In this chapter we focus on those aspects of Canada's insolvency system that are specially designed to address the problems of individual and consumer bankruptcies. There are good reasons for the distinction between business and consumer bankruptcies. Functionally, consumer bankruptcies raise very different social, economic, and legal issues than business bankruptcies, and over the past 30 years there has been phenomenal growth in the number of consumer insolvencies. (Consumer insolvencies are subdivided into consumer bankruptcy proceedings and consumer proposals under BIA III.2. See Chapter 1, generally, and Office of the Superintendent of Bankruptcy (OSB), *Annual Statistical Report—2008*; OSB, *Overview of Canadian Insolvency Statistics to 2006*. See also Canadian Insolvency Statistics: 1966-2008, in Chapter 1.) More than any other chapter in the casebook, this chapter reflects the interplay of social, economic, and legal issues and the absence of an effective consumer voice in the drafting of the BIA consumer insolvency provisions.

A. Growth in Consumer Insolvencies

As shown by the table at the end of Section II in Chapter 1, consumer insolvencies grew from 3,647 in 1972 to 21,025 in 1980 and 115,789 in 2008. A variety of reasons explain the phenomenal growth in the number of consumer insolvencies since 1972. Probably the single most important factor is the commensurate growth in all forms of consumer credit during the same period and, since the mid-1970s, the impact of the availability of credit cards to most Canadian consumers. A number of empirical studies have been conducted in Canada over the past 25 years to identify the types of Canadians who go bankrupt and the reasons given by bankrupts (and, in some cases, by the trustees in bankruptcy) for their financial difficulties.

Among the most common reasons cited for bankruptcy were those related to credit card debt, adverse employment changes, and business failure. (See: Iain D.C. Ramsay, "Individual Bankruptcy: Preliminary Findings of a Socio-Legal Analysis" (1999), 37 *Osgoode Hall LJ* 15 and Saul Schwartz, "The Empirical Dimensions of Consumer Bankruptcy: Results from a Survey of Canadian Bankrupts" (1999), 37 *Osgoode Hall LJ* 83.)

The trustees themselves, in their reports to creditors and the court at the time of the debtor's application for discharge, often blame the bankrupts' poor money management skills. Creditors also endorse this explanation, but put much of the blame on Canada's insolvency system. Many of them believe it is too easy for debtors to go bankrupt and obtain a discharge from outstanding debts. The 1997 amendments to the BIA were meant to stanch the flow of bankruptcies by introducing the regime of mandatory payments of surplus income by debtors in s. 68 of the Act (see below, Section IV), but these and other amendments have only slowed the rate of bankruptcies. The basic problems remain substantially the same as before.

Canadian statistics show that consumer bankrupts are overwhelmingly asset poor. A survey conducted for the Personal Insolvency Task Force of the Canadian Office of the Superintendent of Bankruptcy, which involved a study of receipts and disbursements in a random sample of 900 completed "summary administration" estates out of 81,400 summary administration bankruptcies opened in 1998, tells the story graphically. Median receipts from the estates were CDN$1,795.13; average total receipts were $2,460.84. The latter figure was broken down as follows: realization of non-exempt assets, $583.28; voluntary payments from the debtor to the trustee, $1,045.13; tax refunds, $50.10; refund of federal sales tax, $125.51; conditional order payments, $57.47; interest earned on assets realized or moneys collected by the trustee, $49.44; and surplus income payments, $9.90. The typical file derived 6.2 percent of its receipts from the realization of non-exempt vehicles, but only 129 out of 891 files showed this as a source of estate funds.

The OSB in its report on the period leading up to 2006 notes that the average net annual income of consumers having filed for bankruptcy was $19,300, which is 30.8 percent lower than the Canadian average of $27,900. (See Office of the Superintendent of Bankruptcy, *Overview of Canadian Insolvency Statistics up to 2006* (Ottawa: Industry Canada, 2007).) Given these statistics, it is not difficult to see why so many of the debtors in the Canadian studies rank excessive debt as a primary cause of their undoing.

II. ROLE OF TRUSTEES

A. Initiation of Proceedings

As we saw in Chapter 3, it is easy for Canadian consumer debtors to make an assignment in bankruptcy. Similarly, there is no shortage of trustees willing to offer their services and to administer the estate once the assignment has been filed with the official receiver. Trustees advertise widely—in the yellow pages of telephone directories, on radio, television, cable, and the Internet—and encourage debtors to consult them about their debt problems. The difficulty debtors face at this stage is to know how to pay for the trustee's services. Most debtors cannot afford to pay even a substantial part of the trustee's fee and disbursements (now amounting to about $1,600); often, too, the debtor's estate contains only a negligible amount of non-exempt assets that could be realized to satisfy the trustee's fee and expenses. Thus, it is common for the debtor to sign an agreement with the trustee agreeing to pay the trustee's fees and disbursements by installments. If the debtor has a substantial amount of surplus income payable to the trustee under BIA s. 68 before the debtor's discharge, this, coupled with other income sources, may be sufficient to cover the trustee's bill before the debtor's usual discharge nine months after the bankruptcy: see ss. 168 and 170.

In "Bankruptcy for the Poor," below, Stephanie Ben-Ishai and Saul Schwartz challenge the conventional wisdom that the poor are not heavy users of the insolvency system because creditors are unwilling to take risks on them and because many of the poor are judgment-proof. Consider whether you agree with the authors' recommendations.

Stephanie Ben-Ishai and Saul Schwartz, "Bankruptcy for the Poor"
(2007), 45 *Osgoode Hall LJ* 471, at 471-78 and 504-8 (footnotes omitted)

Introduction

Bankruptcy need not be synonymous with poverty. Indeed, in North America, consumer bankruptcy is a middle-class phenomenon with debtors filing for bankruptcy from a wide array of occupations and income levels. Filing for bankruptcy requires a few thousand dollars in out-of-pocket costs in Canada and the US. Most of those considering bankruptcy can afford to pay, drawing either upon their earnings or their friends and family.

Our concern here is with debtors who need bankruptcy but who cannot afford to pay the required costs of filing. We will call them "poor debtors" and the first task is to define what we mean by this term. ... In our view, the defining characteristic of poor debtors is the strong likelihood that they will experience *persistent* poverty, with or without their debts. They are not using the bankruptcy system to discharge their debts and then move on to a comfortable middle-class existence. We will use the term "poor debtors" to refer to debtors seeking bankruptcy who cannot pay the fees associated with filing and who seem unlikely to attain anything but a low income for the foreseeable future. ...

In this article, we address several questions concerning the situation of poor debtors in the Canadian context. First, how common is it for low-income Canadians to have significant debts? If the poor cannot easily borrow, it is unlikely that they will accumulate enough debt to warrant bankruptcy. Second, do poor debtors need bankruptcy? Many will be judgement-proof, facing no real prospect that a court would allow their creditors to take any action against them. And, third, do existing procedures provide sufficient access to bankruptcy for poor debtors? A Canadian government program called the Bankruptcy Assistance Program (BAP) is available to those who cannot afford the required fees and, as we will see, private efforts also aid such debtors. ...

Our conclusions are easily stated. We believe that the poor now have wide access to credit, fueled by the easy availability of credit cards, by the ease with which consumer durables can be bought on credit and, for some, by government-subsidized student loans. When the poor find themselves unable to meet their repayment obligations, they are often subject to intense and invasive collection efforts, even if they are judgement-proof. Despite the efforts of some trustees in some cities to provide bankruptcy at a reduced price, an unknown number of poor debtors remain without access to bankruptcy. Moreover, the Office of the Superintendent of Bankruptcy's (OSB) BAP is poorly designed, poorly understood and in great need of modernization.

Do the Poor Need Bankruptcy?

The poor in the context of consumer bankruptcy are not only insolvent at the time of filing for bankruptcy, but are likely to have been poor for some time and are likely to remain in poverty for the foreseeable future. Their current earnings prospects are dim and their life circumstances are such that any upward economic mobility will be impeded by significant barriers.

However, for one of two reasons, some might question whether the poor need bankruptcy. The first reason has already been discussed. Many of the poor are judgement-proof and, in principle, can simply refuse to respond to collection efforts. Nonetheless, that seemingly simple refusal is far more difficult than one might think and judgement-proof debtors frequently appear in trustees' offices seeking bankruptcy protection.

The second reason for believing that the poor do not need bankruptcy is the idea that the poor do not accumulate very large debts and therefore have little need for bankruptcy protection. In this section, we use the 1999 Survey of Financial Security to illustrate that the so-called "democratization of credit"—the extension of credit throughout the income distribution—has proceeded to the point where even families in the lowest deciles of family income have significant debts.

Tables 1 and 2 show the distribution of various kinds of debt across the deciles of family income. Families in the bottom three deciles almost certainly have incomes that are less than the relevant Statistics Canada Low Income Cut-Off (LICO) and therefore might qualify as poor by our definition.

Table 1 makes clear that significant proportions of the poor have debts in each of the categories listed. To be sure, families in the lowest three deciles are *less* likely to have various types of debts than those in the higher deciles, but one in four has credit card debt (e.g., 0.25 in the lowest decile) and one in six (0.17 in the lowest decile) has other debts. Since bankruptcy is a situation facing only a minority of debtors, these proportions are large enough to suggest that a significant minority of poor families will have significant debts coming due at a time when their income is low. The amounts shown in Table 2 are averages only for those who have positive amounts of debt in each category, but their size once again suggests that poor families may acquire significant debts, especially in relation to their low income. For example, among those in the lowest decile with credit card debt, the average amount owed was $2,064.

Overview of the Canadian System

Since bankruptcies are administered by private-sector trustees, a poor debtor seeking bankruptcy protection must find a trustee willing to take their case. Not surprisingly, trustees consider whether they are likely to be paid for their efforts before they agree to take on a case. Trustees are paid from the money that they collect on behalf of the creditors, money that defines the estate of the debtor. Rule 128(1) of the *Bankruptcy and Insolvency Act* (BIA) sets out the method by which maximum fees are to be calculated. Essentially, the maximum fees are a function of the amount of receipts coming into the estate. At most, a trustee can collect the first $975 of receipts, plus 35 percent of the next $1,025, plus 50 percent of everything above $2,000 to a maximum of $10,000. In practice, it seems that trustees try to realize at least $1,500 to $1,700 on each file. Of course, they are free to take less if they so choose.

Table 1 Proportion of Families with Various Types of Debt

Deciles of Family Income	Mortgage	Vehicle Loans	Credit Cards	Student Loans	Other Debts	Total Debt
Less than						
$12,250	0.07	0.06	0.25	0.13	0.17	0.50
12,250-18,000	0.09	0.09	0.24	0.09	0.15	0.47
18,000-24,700	0.14	0.14	0.32	0.10	0.20	0.57
24,700-31,850	0.22	0.19	0.39	0.10	0.24	0.65
31,850-40,000	0.32	0.24	0.42	0.12	0.27	0.72
40,000-49,000	0.41	0.28	0.46	0.10	0.32	0.78
49,000-60,850	0.45	0.31	0.47	0.11	0.35	0.81
60,850-76,800	0.53	0.34	0.48	0.12	0.40	0.84
76,800-105,300	0.52	0.34	0.45	0.10	0.39	0.83
More than						
105,300	0.47	0.23	0.30	0.05	0.39	0.76

Source: 1999 Survey of Financial Security (unweighted). See S. Schwartz and S. Baum, "How Much Debt Is Too Much? Benchmarks for Manageable Debt in Canada and the United States," in Bruce Doern and Christopher Stoney, eds., *Universities and the Powering of Knowledge: Policy, Regulation and Innovation* (University of Toronto Press, 2008), Chapter 7.

Note: All debts are reported for the family as a whole.

Table 2 Amount of Debt Outstanding for Families with Non-negative Debt

Deciles of Family Income	Mortgage	Vehicle Loans	Credit Cards	Student Loans	Other Debts	Total Debt
Less than						
$12,250	$62,260	$6,968	$2,064	$11,961	$6,562	$19,430
12,250-18,000	52,348	8,338	1,957	12,013	8,601	19,875
18,000-24,700	51,815	8,113	2,233	9,983	6,307	23,651
24,700-31,850	51,783	9,393	2,551	11,593	8,171	29,248
31,850-40,000	58,804	9,835	2,696	10,611	9,021	39,202
40,000-49,000	65,158	10,897	2,998	10,093	9,126	48,871
49,000-60,850	70,281	11,005	3,186	9,619	11,740	58,561
60,850-76,800	75,093	12,054	3,479	9,979	14,589	69,382
76,800-105,300	80,899	14,469	3,786	9,769	17,632	77,080
More than						
105,300	117,558	16,108	4,721	12,354	33,266	109,512
No. of Families.......	5,098	3,506	5,993	1,615	4,592	10,543

Source: 1999 Survey of Financial Security (unweighted). See S. Schwartz and S. Baum, "How Much Debt Is Too Much? Benchmarks for Manageable Debt in Canada and the United States," in Bruce Doern and Christopher Stoney, eds., *Universities and the Powering of Knowledge: Policy, Regulation and Innovation* (University of Toronto Press, 2008), Chapter 7.

Note: All debts are reported for the family as a whole.

Two major sources of receipts for the estate, and thus for trustee fees, are selling the debtor's non-exempt assets and filing the debtor's tax refunds. In many cases, however, debtors have no non-exempt assets and the amounts that can be expected from their tax returns are not enough to bring the receipts of the estate up to an acceptable level. In such cases, trustees are allowed to ask the debtors to make voluntary payments to the estate, over the course of the nine months of the bankruptcy. In a significant minority of bankruptcies, these voluntary payments comprise the bulk of the receipts of the estate.

The problem for the poor debtors is that trustees may decide, rightly or wrongly, that the receipts of the estate, including any voluntary payments that the debtor can afford, are not likely to reach an acceptable level. If so, the trustee need not accept the case.

In talking to the trustees, we realized that a poor debtor who decides to seek bankruptcy in Canada and cannot afford to make the voluntary payments required by most trustees has two options. First, the debtors may try to find a trustee who will handle the file at a lower-than-normal price. Second, the debtors might seek help from the BAP operated by the OSB. ...

Recommendations

... We propose ... recommendations [to] addresses the two principal flaws we believe are present in the current Canadian system:

a. No national and even local uniformity exists in the treatment of poor debtors.

b. Poor debtors face informational and financial barriers that may impede equal access to the fresh start provided by bankruptcy.

[Some of our recommendations] may be implemented quite quickly and with limited cost. Others will take longer to implement and will require additional consultation and funding. In particular, further review will be necessary to determine the exact budgetary implications of our recommendations.

The two flaws highlighted by our research do not lead us to recommend the adoption of a separate bankruptcy scheme for poor debtors or NINA [no-income, no-asset] debtors. Instead, we recommend that Canada adopt a Bankruptcy Assistance Program (BAP) that eliminates the out-of-pocket costs for poor debtors. These costs could be eliminated with a combination of fee waivers (e.g., waiving the OSB's filing fee) and government subsidy (e.g., having the OSB pay for the mandatory counselling sessions). A BAP program that demands no out-of-pocket payments by poor debtors would address the financial barriers they face. To deal with the informational barriers, we recommend the creation of an impartial agency that provides advice and support to poor debtors trying to deal with collection efforts. We recognize that in some instances bankruptcy might not be the appropriate solution for poor debtors and other options should be available to deal with creditor aggression. By making the judgement-proof status of poor debtors clear, such advice and support provided by an impartial agency would limit the number of debtors who use the bankruptcy process. Finally, to increase the uniformity and certainty of bankruptcy across the country, we propose a method for creating parity while encouraging the voluntary agreements among trustees that exist in some cities.

In addition to the trustee interviews, our recommendations are informed by the analysis found in our comparative account in Part 5 of this article. In particular, we believe that the situation in New Zealand and Australia provides low-cost access to the bankruptcy process but we do not agree with corresponding to changes to the system that make the process more burdensome for "poor debtors." At the same time, we are persuaded by the arguments in favor of eliminating fees made as part of the reform process in New Zealand, Australia, the United Kingdom, and the United States.

Reform of BAP Regulation. Our research suggests that a thorough revision of the rules governing the operation of the BAP program is necessary. Our review of the program suggests that the following changes are highly desirable.

Widespread and improved publicity of the BAP is required. One reason for the infrequent use of the BAP is that the OSB has made no systematic efforts to make its existence known to poor debtors. Much more information on the operation of the BAP program should be made easily accessible to debtors and trustees. Detailed information on the BAP should be provided to poverty clinics, credit counsellors and trustees. The information on the OSB website related to the BAP should be updated and improved. The information is difficult to find and does not give a balanced and accurate sense of the program. For example, the website currently gives the impression that the BAP requires pro bono work by trustees.

A clear eligibility standard for the BAP should be put into place. Further consultation should be undertaken to determine the exact nature of a new BAP eligibility standard. Based on our research to date, we recommend a standard involving low current income and a long-term history of receipt of government transfers. Using low current income alone might lead to abuse by debtors who only temporarily have low income. The appropriate requirement might be that eligible debtors must be in receipt of government transfers (such as income assistance, unemployment insurance or disability benefits) for twelve of the previous eighteen months. The critique of the New Zealand model presented by Brown and Telfer warns against moving to a standard for eligibility which allows for any significant degree of subjectivity. In addition, some form of procedural fairness will need to be built into such a bright line eligibility standard. For example, appeals should be allowed by a debtor who is newly poor or disabled and likely to stay that way.

Under this new eligibility standard, the requirement that debtors must visit two trustees to qualify for the BAP should be eliminated. This requirement imposes an additional barrier to bankruptcy that higher income debtors do not face. The current requirement has a detrimental impact on women in particular, as they must often find child care for their children as they move around the city obtaining opinions from two trustees.

Fees for debtors who qualify for the BAP should be waived. Ideally, poor debtors should be able to file for bankruptcy without paying any of the out-of-pocket costs. Receipts from tax refunds would remain in the estate as would any proceeds from the sale of non-exempt assets. The fee waiver could be financed by a combination of OSB waivers, OSB payments to trustees for counselling or pro bono work by trustees. Further consultation needs to be done with trustees, combined with a careful cost analysis by the OSB, in order to determine the ideal solution. In the interim, we recommend that the $75 filing fee be eliminated and that the OSB cover the cost of both counselling sessions. The high mean level of fees in BAP cases means that trustees can recover significant amounts without voluntary payments.

The BAP should provide that the OSB will file the bankruptcy as a last resort. The regulations (and the expanded publicity recommended above) should indicate the OSB's commitment to ensuring that the bankruptcy will be filed in a timely fashion even if no private trustee is forthcoming, and even if an OSB official must administer the bankruptcy.

Working Toward Uniformity. In comparison to the other jurisdictions considered, the issue of uniformity appears to be a uniquely Canadian issue. Poor debtors throughout Canada should have access to the reformed BAP. However, our interviews suggested that trustees are not happy with the existing BAP and, where possible, prefer to rely on voluntary agreements among area trustees or on the good will of individual trustees. At least until the reformed BAP can gain the trust of trustees, we recommend that the voluntary agreements among trustees be encouraged and perhaps expanded in scope. However, these voluntary systems should be at least as cheap as BAP. A first step would be to assess the extent of the geographic coverage of the agreements. CAIRP could become involved by surveying their members to make an inventory of such agreements. Second, the OSB should keep track of files where receipts are low to see if they are spread, in a representative way, across the country.

The OSB should establish, by directive, a system for registering city specific fee agreements reached by trustees. While we believe that the voluntary agreements should be encouraged, we also think the OSB should make sure that it is aware of all such agreements and that the terms of the agreements are consistent with the aim of the reformed BAP—ease of access and low out-of-pocket costs to the debtor. In the end, it is not obvious whether it will be better to have only a reformed BAP, only a set of voluntary agreements or a combination of the two. Informed decision-making about the need for the BAP can only be made if a close watch is kept on the operation of the voluntary agreements.

An impartial agency should be created to give poor debtors advice on how to deal with their debt. Currently, Canadian debtors have no place to turn for impartial debt advice. Debtors can seek advice from credit counseling services but these are either financed by creditors or are for-profit, fee-charging entities; most require 100 percent repayment. Trustees are another possible source of advice but they have a clear incentive to recommend bankruptcy. The creation of a neutral agency that provides advice on debtors' rights vis-à-vis their creditors and suggests the most appropriate remedy is recommended. We recommend the creation of an impartial debt advice agency in 2 to 3 pilot sites in the short term (Toronto, Montreal, and Vancouver).

NOTE

See also Jacob Ziegel, "Indigent Debtors and the Financial Accessibility of Consumer Insolvency Regimes" [2004] *Ann. Ins. Rev.* 499.

B. Trustee Fees

A question litigated before Canadian courts is whether the trustee is entitled to oppose the debtor's discharge on the ground that money is still owing to the trustee under the agreement or under the prescribed tariff in the bankruptcy rules. The following cases illustrate the courts' reactions to this issue.

Re Berthelette
(1999), 174 DLR (4th) 577 (Man. CA) (footnotes omitted)

PHILP JA (for the court):

Introduction

[1] The amount in issue in this summary administration bankruptcy proceeding is $196.00. The Superintendent of Bankruptcy (the superintendent) argues, however, that important questions affecting the summary administration of estates under the *Bankruptcy and Insolvency Act*, RSC 1985, c. B-3 (the Act), are raised which have resulted in disparate judgments in the courts of other provinces.

The Facts

[2] The issues arise out of uncomplicated factual circumstances that, apart from one inference the Court is invited to draw, are not disputed. On January 4, 1994, Nicole Marie Berthelette (the bankrupt), a first-time bankrupt, made an assignment in bankruptcy under the Act. On the same day, she signed a document entitled "Agreement Letter," which provided:

> I, Nicole Marie Bethelette [*sic*], hereby agree to pay David I. Guttman, Trustee in Bankruptcy, any deficiency in fees arising out of my Assignment in Bankruptcy.

[3] The bankrupt's realizable assets were negligible, and the administration of her bankruptcy proceeded summarily. On March 29, 1995, she received an absolute discharge.

[4] The trustee filed its final statement of receipts and disbursements on September 12, 1996. The statement disclosed receipts totalling $1,080.25 and disbursements of $231.90, leaving $848.35 for the trustee's fees. The fees to which a trustee is entitled for the summary administration of an estate are calculated, pursuant to Rule 115(1) [now rule 128] of the Bankruptcy and Insolvency General Rules, CRC 1978, c. 368, on the receipts of the estate. On receipts of $1,080.25, the amount of the fees under the Rule is $1,011.84. (The trustee's statement erroneously shows this calculation to be $1,009.58.)

[5] There was, therefore, a shortfall or deficiency of $163.49 between the trustee's fees calculated pursuant to the Rule and the amount available for distribution.

[6] On October 31, 1996, the trustee received a payment of $196.00 from the bankrupt pursuant to the agreement letter. Four days later, on November 4, 1996, the trustee filed an amended statement of receipts and disbursements, which included the payment of $196.00 as a receipt of the estate. In the amended statement, the receipts total $1,276.25 and the trustee's fees, calculated on those receipts pursuant to Rule 115(1), are shown as $1,080.44.

[7] The amount available for payment of the trustee's fees in the amended statement has increased to $1,044.35 ($848.35, the amount available in the first statement, plus the payment of $196.00). The revised amount available is insufficient to pay his re-calculated fees, but more than sufficient to pay the fees calculated in the first statement on receipts of the estate before the payment of $196.00.

[8] The superintendent raised concerns that the trustee had not obtained an order under s. 68 of the Act with respect to the post-bankruptcy payment of $196.00 and with regard to the trustee's authority to collect or receive that payment after the bankrupt's absolute discharge. The superintendent requested that the trustee's accounts be taxed.

[9] To complete the factual circumstances, the superintendent invites the Court to make the finding not made by the registrar or the motions court judge that the payment of $196.00 came out of the bankrupt's modest monthly take-home pay. That is likely not an unreasonable inference to draw in light of her impecunious circumstances, but because of the conclusion I have reached with respect to the application of s. 68 of the Act, it is an inference I need not draw.

The Issue

[10] The registrar identified the issue before her as ((1997), 120 Man. R (2d) 302, at para. 1):

> [W]hether the payment of $196 received from the bankrupt after her discharge should be included in the receipts on which the trustee's fee is based.

On appeal, Jewers J, the motions court judge, identified the issue in similar words. In this Court, the parties agree that the issue is:

> Did the Learned Motions Court Judge err in law in holding that there is no statutory provision, regulation, directive or policy which prevents the Trustee from accepting, and basing its fee upon, payments made by a bankrupt after the bankrupt's discharge pursuant to an agreement with the Trustee?

[11] As we will see, broader questions than those that have been put before the courts emerge from the factual circumstances.

Pertinent Legislation

[12] Sections 68(1), (2) and (8), 121(1), 178(1) and (2), and 202(1)(h) of the Act, as they were at the times relevant to the facts of this appeal, are set out in the appendix that follows these reasons. Section 68 was amended in 1997. A different regime for the attachment of a bankrupt's post-assignment (or post-receiving order) remuneration now applies to bankruptcies in respect of which proceedings are commenced after April 30, 1998 (the date the new section came into force). The earlier version, which applies to the circumstances of this appeal, is set out in the appendix.

Judgments

[13] The registrar concluded (at para. 9):

> [T]here is no statutory provision, regulation, directive or public policy which prevents the trustee from accepting, and basing its fee upon, payments made by a bankrupt after her discharge pursuant to an agreement with the trustee. Nor is there any judicial authority which binds or persuades me otherwise.

[14] In arriving at that conclusion, the registrar reasoned, and the motions court judge agreed, that court approval under s. 68 of the Act was not required "if the trustee and the bankrupt are in agreement."

[15] The registrar also reasoned (at para. 16) that any claim arising from the agreement letter arose "by reason of an *obligation incurred on the day she became a bankrupt*" and therefore "would not be a claim provable in a bankruptcy and would therefore not be released by s. 178(2)" (my emphasis). She declined to follow *Privé (Re)* (1995), 36 CBR (3d) 152 (Que. SC), in which Guthrie J concluded (at para. 20) that s. 178(1) "must cover 'all debts' and not just 'claims provable in bankruptcy' (s. 178(2))" and that "[t]herefore, the 'debt' of the bankrupt towards the trustee, under the terms of their agreement, would also be released!"

[16] The motions court judge adopted the reasons of the registrar with respect to the application of s. 68 of the Act and the effect of s. 178(2). He, too, declined to follow *Privé (Re)*. He wrote ((1998), 124 Man. R (2d) 261, at para. 28):

> However, I agree with [counsel for the intervener] that the reference to "all debts" must be to debts provable in bankruptcy. The trustee can only certify that the debts provable in bankruptcy are released because the discharge obviously cannot and does not affect debts which are not provable in bankruptcy.

Analysis

Section 68

[17] I agree that s. 68 of the Act has no application to the circumstances of this bankruptcy, but not for the reasons given by the registrar and adopted by the motions court judge. The argument of the superintendent that "a trustee can only access [*sic*] a bankrupt's wages and salary for the purposes of making [*sic*] a deficiency in the minimum fees and disbursements that the trustee has set for its own internal purposes through a s. 68" order has no application to the facts before the Court. While it might be reasonable to infer that the payment of $196.00 came out of the bankrupt's wages or salary, it is not a reasonable inference that the payment, made 19 months after her discharge, was made out of her earnings after her assignment and prior to her discharge. The requirement for an order under s. 68 attaching post-assignment income of the bankrupt never arose in the factual circumstances of this appeal.

[18] Parenthetically, it should be noted that s. 68 of the Act, as re-enacted in 1997, provides a quite different regime for the attachment of the post-assignment income of a bankrupt. The trustee is now required, without an application to the court, to fix the amount the bankrupt must pay to the bankrupt estate.

[19] *Marzetti v. Marzetti*, [1994] 2 SCR 765, 116 DLR (4th) 577, it would appear, was not referred to the registrar or motions court judge, or considered by them. In that decision, Iacobucci J, writing for the Court, concluded (at p. 794) that s. 68 (the 1992 version) is "a substantive provision, one which is intended to operate as a complete code in respect of a bankrupt's salary, wages, or other remuneration."

[20] The registrar and the motions court judge appear to have concluded that, notwithstanding s. 68, nothing in the Act prevented agreements between a bankrupt and

his/her trustee relating to post-assignment remuneration. Courts in Quebec have reached a similar conclusion. ... In *Re Clark* (Alta. QB, April 6, 1998) [reported 8 CBR (4th) 2], Forsyth J was of a different view. He rejected the conclusion of the motions court judge in this appeal and found "that agreements of this nature are not contemplated by the *Bankruptcy Act.*"

[21] *Marzetti*, it seems to me, resolves the dichotomy. I do not see how agreements relating to a bankrupt's post-assignment earnings can survive the Supreme Court's characterization of s. 68 as "a substantive provision ... a complete code in respect of a bankrupt's salary, wages, or other remuneration." However, that is a conclusion that need not be made in the circumstances of this appeal.

Sections 121(1) and 178(2)

[22] As noted above, the registrar concluded that the bankrupt's obligation under the agreement letter "would not be a claim provable in a bankruptcy and would therefore not be released by s. 178(2)." That is so, she reasoned, because the obligation was incurred on the day the bankrupt became a bankrupt. The registrar did not consider the other arm of claims provable under s. 121(1); namely, "[a]ll debts and liabilities, present or future, *to which the bankrupt is subject on the day on which the bankrupt becomes bankrupt*" (my emphasis).

[23] From information provided to the Court at the second hearing of the appeal, it would appear that the assignment, statement of affairs, and agreement letter were signed by the bankrupt at the same time and in that order, and that the assignment and statement of affairs were filed later the same day with the official receiver.

[24] In Houlden and Morawetz, *The 1999 Annotated Bankruptcy and Insolvency Act* (1998), the authors acknowledge (at p. 436) that:

> The expression "the day on which the bankrupt becomes bankrupt" is ambiguous; presumably, it means the date on which the assignment is filed or the receiving order is made. A debt or liability incurred by the bankrupt after the filing of the petition but prior to the making of a receiving order is a provable claim: *Re Tunnell* (1924), 5 CBR 73, ... (Ont. CA).

Other sections of the Act support that interpretation. Section 49(3) provides that an assignment "is inoperative until filed with [the] official receiver," and s. 71(1) provides that "[a] bankruptcy shall be deemed to have relation back to, and to commence at the time ... of the filing of an assignment with the official receiver."

[25] Applying that interpretation to the factual circumstances of this appeal, I conclude that whatever debt or liability arose under the agreement letter was one "to which the bankrupt [was] subject on the day on which the bankrupt becomes bankrupt." Assuming that the bankrupt's obligation under the agreement letter was enforceable at law—a conclusion questioned by counsel for the trustee at the appeal hearing, but not an issue before the Court for determination on the appeal—the obligation was a claim provable in bankruptcy pursuant to s. 121(1) of the Act. On the bankrupt's absolute discharge on March 29, 1995, her obligation under the agreement letter was released—s. 178(2). She was under no legal obligation to pay any sum to the trustee under the agreement letter after her absolute discharge. The sum of $196.00 which the bankrupt paid to the

trustee on October 31, 1996, was not a receipt of the estate for the purpose of calculating the fees of the trustee pursuant to Rule 115(1).

[26] Permit me a few obiter comments that are prompted by the reasons of the registrar and the motions court judge and by the shifting arguments that were put before the Court by counsel as the appeal progressed.

[27] Firstly, s. 202(1)(h) of the Act was cited to the Court by counsel for the superintendent. He argued that the motions court judge erred in concluding (at para. 18):

[I]n this case the remuneration to which the trustee was entitled exceeded that actually charged and Parliament could not have intended to make it an offence for the trustee to agree with the bankrupt that the latter should make up any deficiency in the fees and disbursements properly payable under the Act.

He points out, as the motions court judge recognized, that "there is no minimum fee under Rule 115" and argues, therefore, "there can never be any 'deficiency' in the fees and disbursements 'properly' payable under the Act." However, whether or not the agreement letter constituted an offence under s. 202(1)(h) is a question that is not before the Court for determination on this appeal.

[28] Secondly, the thrust of the argument of the trustee (and the intervener) is that "[t]he payment of $196.00 is a *voluntary payment* made by the bankrupt to the Trustee pursuant to the agreement made on the date of the bankruptcy" (my emphasis). That is a contradiction in terms. The argument that the agreement letter was "collateral to the assignment" and was "inoperative until the assignment was filed" is simply an attempt to put too fine a point on an issue that need not be determined on this appeal.

[29] Finally, the provisions in the Act for the summary administration of estates may invite a relaxed interpretation of the statutory duties and obligations imposed upon the trustee in the administration of a bankruptcy. Policy considerations—the ability of debtors like the bankrupt in this appeal, who possess few, if any, realizable assets, to obtain access to the scheme of the Act and to become rehabilitated unfettered by his/her past debts and liabilities—would seem to support that kind of interpretation. The registrar and the motions court judge concluded that the Act did not prevent payments by a bankrupt to his/her trustee pursuant to an agreement. However, Forsyth J observed in *Re Clark*:

[I]f it is determined that such agreements are of benefit to the creditors as a whole, it is up to parliament and not to this court to make amendments to the Act sufficient to make it clear that arrangements of this nature are in order.

[30] The trustee referred the Court to Directive No. 11, issued by the superintendent on October 23, 1986, entitled Bankruptcy Assistance Program. That directive outlines a program to accommodate overburdened debtors [who] are unable to demonstrate to a trustee that sufficient funds will be available in the estate to cover administration costs" and are therefore "unable to secure services of a trustee to administer their bankruptcy." Paragraph 18 of the directive provides:

In cases where a debtor's income is in excess of the amounts determined by the Superintendent's guidelines (which are based on the Senate Committee Poverty Lines (SCPL) as amended), the debtor is expected *to provide voluntary payments to the estate* in accordance with the SCPL guideline. In those circumstances where the debtor, without valid reasons, refuses to abide by these guidelines, the trustee may refuse to grant the debtor's request for bankruptcy service. [My emphasis.]

[31] However commendable the purposes of the directive and the provision for "voluntary payments" by a bankrupt may be, the authority of a trustee to attach the earnings of a bankrupt, even by the expectation that the bankrupt will provide voluntary payments to the estate, has been put in doubt by the decision of the Supreme Court in *Marzetti*. In any event, the directive has no application to the circumstances in this appeal. There is no evidence that the bankrupt availed herself of the program or that the trustee was a "participating" trustee "designated" to act under the program in providing services to her. And the purpose of the agreement letter was not to have the bankrupt "provide voluntary payments to the estate in accordance with the SCPL guideline"; it was an agreement by the bankrupt to pay the trustee "any deficiency in fees arising out of my Assignment in Bankruptcy."

. . .

Appeal allowed.

NOTES

1. For a discussion of *Re Berthelette*, see J.S. Ziegel, "Financing Consumer Bankruptcies, Re Berthelette, and Public Policy" (2000), 33 *CBLJ* 294. The question of how the unpaid balance of a trustee's fee should be handled in a discharge hearing was one of the most hotly contested issues before the Personal Insolvency Task Force (PITF). A majority of the members ultimately adopted the following recommendation:

The Task Force recommends ... that the BIA allow trustees to enter into voluntary payment agreements with bankrupts who do not have surplus income. There should be a ceiling on the payments made through these voluntary agreements, a ceiling related to the sum of trustees' fees and other administrative costs of the bankruptcy. If the receipts of the estate exceed this province-specific amount, a dividend to creditors is generated. The Task Force recommends that the ceiling on the amount that can be collected through voluntary agreements between bankrupts and trustees be set at the maximum level of estate receipts possible without generating dividends to creditors. In determining the post-discharge payments, any other assets realized must be taken into account in setting the maximum. For example, if the trustee has been able to realize $1,000, during the bankruptcy, from the bankrupts' assets, the maximum amount that could be collected through the voluntary agreement would be the ceiling minus the $1,000. The bankrupt would receive an automatic discharge at the end of nine months unless the discharge is opposed.

A limit as to the maximum length of time for which additional payments would be required would be set out in the BIA. The Task Force recommends that the legislation provide that voluntary payments occur for no more than 12 months after discharge. There would also be a requirement that any such agreement entered into by trustees and bankrupts should not cause undue hardship to the bankrupts.

In the event that bankrupts choose not to sign a voluntary agreement, trustees would have the option of opposing their discharge, and the appropriate order would be made by the court. Task Force members who were trustees stated that the vast majority of bankrupts want to pay trustees for their services, and that most would honour their agreements even if they had already received a discharge. If discharged bankrupts who have made voluntary agreements with a trustee do not make the specified payments, the trustee would decide whether or not to pursue the bankrupt for the payments, based on the same factors that any creditor would consider.

While there was general consensus on the above approach, one Task Force member did not support the recommendations. The member believes that a fresh start will not be afforded to newly discharged bankrupts who have agreed to make post-discharge payments (see PITF, *Final Report* (Ottawa: Industry Canada, Office of the Superintendent of Bankruptcy, 2002), at 44).

2. Following *Re Berthlette*, in *Re Weatherbee* (2001), 25 CBR (4th) 133 (NSSC), Registrar Hill rejected a trustee's attempt to oppose the discharge of a bankrupt on the basis that she could not pay his fees. Registrar Hill held, at paragraph 15, that "the holding up of an individual's discharge because they lack the financial capacity to pay the trustee's fee within a reasonable time is not only not contemplated in the BIA, but is also contrary to the well established principle that a bankrupt is entitled to retain from his or her income a reasonable amount to maintain his or her family." What are the potential consequences for the debtors that Registrar Hill was attempting to protect in rendering this decision?

3. The 2007 amendments introduce a new s. 156.1 to the BIA that permits trustees to enter into binding contracts with debtors for payment of trustee's fees for up to a year following the debtor's discharge even where the debtor has no surplus income. Do you think that this amendment addresses the concerns highlighted in the Ben-Ishai and Schwartz paper? What are the limitations of this provision?

4. Also note that the 2007 amendments modify s. 67(1)(c) so that income tax refunds now vest in the trustee as after-acquired property and are not covered by s. 68 as surplus income. Trustees therefore will be able to look to the refund to recoup their fees.

III. EXEMPT PROPERTY

A. General Considerations and Purposes of Exemption Law

Exempt property is another troublesome area of consumer bankruptcy policy. Section 67(1)(b) of the BIA provides that the trustee is entitled to all of the debtor's property with the exception, *inter alia*, of property exempt from execution or seizure under any laws applicable in the province within which the property is situated and within which the bankrupt resides. From a very early date, the common law exempted a debtor's apparel, tools, and household utensils from execution, but little else. In particular, there was no exemption for the debtor's home (in England and Australia and in several Canadian provinces there still are no such exemptions.)

What general purposes or objectives underlie exemption law? The Saskatchewan Court of Appeal in *Investors Group Trust Co. v. Eckhoff*, [2008] 9 WWR 306 recently stated that "the purpose of exemptions legislation is to ensure a minimum asset base for execution debtors so as to keep them from having to seek social assistance." In *Saulnier v. Royal Bank of Canada*,

[2008] 3 SCR 166, Justice Binnie concluded (at para. 17) that "the exemption of designated property from distribution among creditors under s. 67(1) is to allow the bankrupt to continue a living pending discharge and, when discharged, to make a fresh start." See also *Re Pearson* (1997), 46 CBR (3d) 257. Are there any other justifications for exemption law?

Thomas G.W. Telfer, "The Proposed Federal Exemption Regime for the Bankruptcy and Insolvency Act"
(2005), 41 *CBLJ* 279, at 283-85 (footnotes omitted)

· · ·

Most explanations for provincial exemption statutes begin with the fundamental premise that the statutes preserve a minimum level of subsistence and dignity for the debtor and the debtor's family. Professor Dunlop argues that "It is not acceptable that creditors, no matter how just the debt, should have the power to take from debtors the basic necessities of life." Exemption statutes permit the debtor to retain some essentials or what has been called the "basics of life while making the bulk of his or her assets available to satisfy judgment creditors." However, recent reform proposals suggest that a broader view should be taken of a necessity. In a 2001 report, *Modernization of Saskatchewan Money Judgment Enforcement Law*, Professors Buckwold and Cuming recognized that beyond maintaining "a subsistence standard of living" exemption law should also permit a debtor and a debtor's family "to function as healthy, productive and contributing members of society." This broader rationale might justify a wider scope of necessities that are related to the reasonable educational, health and recreational needs of the debtor and the debtor's dependents.

Existing provincial exemption statutes, however, reflect a traditional concern to protect a minimal level of existence. Under the general category of necessities many provincial exemption statutes include such items as household furniture, wearing apparel, food and fuel. Some jurisdictions recognize a motor vehicle as a basic necessity up to a fixed dollar amount. A debtor's basic necessity may also include shelter and some jurisdictions provide some form of exemption for residential property. However, there is no consensus among the provinces and territories on the scope of the residential property exemption or whether such an exemption should exist at all.

A second major theme of exemption statutes involves preserving the means for debtors to "survive and to earn a living, thus contributing to their rehabilitation as citizens and to their capacity to repay their debts." Debtors should not be "deprived of an immediate means of livelihood." To accomplish this goal, exemption statutes protect items of personal property, such as tools of trade or agricultural implements, which assist a debtor in earning an income. Within this livelihood rationale, some provinces exempt farmland.

Preserving the economic vitality of the debtor has been justified from the broader perspective of the public interest. If creditors were permitted to "destroy debtors' economic viability, their continued maintenance would fall to society." Exemptions are said to shift the burden of support for the debtor from the "public to private credit sources." Debtors should not be "cast upon the community with nothing, penniless with the likelihood of becoming a public charge." Finally, exemption statutes minimize the judgment debtor's loss that may occur through forced execution sales. While the exempt property may be of value to the debtor, many of the debtor's personal possessions may yield little value at a sheriff's sale and in turn may impose considerable hardship on the debtor. Even where the creditor does not intend to follow through with its threat to seize and sell, "the coercive effect of a threatened seizure of necessaries often can be used to enforce direct payment from a defaulting creditor." Some provincial statutes protect items of sentimental value.

B. The Choice of Provincial Law for Federal Bankruptcy Exemptions

In the 19th century, many western US states adopted very generous homestead and farmstead exemptions in order to attract new settlers, and these provisions have survived to this day. One of the key issues in 19th century US debates about the need for national bankruptcy legislation was whether federal bankruptcy law should impose a uniform set of exemptions or whether the exemptions should continue to be governed by the law of the bankrupt's residence. The 1898 *Bankruptcy Act* adopted the latter solution. The report of the 1973 US Bankruptcy Commission recommended the adoption of a uniform federal standard. However, Congress rejected this approach and substituted a federal set of exemptions that the states are free to exclude if they wish. See US *Bankruptcy Code*, s. 522. A majority of the states have made this election.

The drafter of the Canadian *Bankruptcy Act, 1919*, H.P. Grundy, chose to incorporate provincial exemption legislation to determine the types and values of property that would be exempt in a bankruptcy. As a result, bankruptcy exemptions vary widely among the provinces, though not as widely as in the United States. In particular, the western provinces are much more generous in their homestead and farmstead allowances than the other provinces. In deferring to the provinces to set exemptions, was Canada simply following the US *Bankruptcy Act* of 1898?

**Thomas G.W. Telfer, "The Evolution of Bankruptcy Exemption Law in Canada
1867-1919: The Triumph of the Provincial Model"**
[2008] *Ann. Rev. Ins. L* 578-79 (footnotes omitted)

The *Personal Insolvency Task Force (PITF) Final Report*, published in 2002, suggests that the reliance upon provincial exemption law in the BIA can be traced to the influence of the US *Bankruptcy Act* of 1898. The *PITF Final Report* offers a tentative conclusion that the provincial exemption model in the *Bankruptcy Act of 1919* "was apparently copied" from the US *Bankruptcy Act* of 1898. Under the US *Bankruptcy Act*, "a bankrupt's exemptions depended on the law of the state in which the bankrupt resided at the time of bankruptcy."

Although the US *Bankruptcy Act* of 1898 may have been an influence, there are several other explanations that explain the policy choice to incorporate provincial exemptions laws into the *Bankruptcy Act* in 1919. First, the provincial model found in the 1919 Act was consistent with provisions found in the earlier Canadian bankruptcy legislation and bills which pre-dated the US *Bankruptcy Act* of 1898. Second, and perhaps more importantly, the diversity of provincial exemption laws precluded the adoption of a uniform bankruptcy exemption regime in 1919. Personal property exemption lists varied from province to province both in terms of value and types of property exempted. Additionally the existence of generous homestead exemptions in Manitoba, Saskatchewan, and Alberta and the absence of similar regimes in other provinces would have made it difficult for H.P. Grundy to draft some kind of compromise acceptable to each region. Beyond the statutory differences, a review of the case law reveals further regional differences and approaches to the interpretation of exemption statutes. Reconciliation of the provincial lists would have been nearly impossible.

If American law had any influence in Canada it was state homestead exemption statutes that provided a ready model for the Canadian western provinces of Manitoba, Saskatchewan and Alberta. The 160-acre homestead exemption could be found north and south of the border. The extensive homestead exemption, which was adopted in the Canadian west but not in other provinces, provided an important source of diversity among the provinces. However, Canadian provinces did not copy US state homestead law as a matter of convenience. The three western provinces were in a competition for immigrants with states to the south. Without such a homestead exemption north of the border there was a fear that immigrants would avoid the Canadian west in favour of the United States. The homestead exemption became a necessity in the Canadian west.

Thus when H.P. Grundy began to draft the 1919 Act, he was not starting with a clean slate, at least when it came to exemptions. The near forty-year period without a bankruptcy law had placed provincial debtor creditor law, including exemptions, at the forefront. The starting point for Parliament in 1919 was the old and diverse provincial law that had been enacted at various times and in response to various needs.

NOTE

Jacob Ziegel, writing in 2003, noted that Canadian provinces "differ widely in their exemption policies ... . In overall impact, Alberta and Saskatchewan confer the most generous exemptions with British Columbia arguably ranking third. Among the provinces, prior to amendments adopted in 2000, Ontario had the dubious distinction of having the lowest exemptions." Jacob Ziegel, *Comparative Consumer Insolvency Regimes—A Comparative Perspective* (Oxford: Hart Publishing, 2003), at 22.

C. Personal Insolvency Task Force Recommendations

The PITF felt the current disparities among the provincial exemption statutes were too great and that, at a minimum, all Canadian personal bankrupts, wherever situated, should be able to avail themselves at their option of a set of federal exemptions. The extract that follows describes the task force's position.

Personal Insolvency Task Force, *Final Report*
(Ottawa: Industry Canada, Office of the Superintendent of Bankruptcy, 2002),
at 24-26 (footnotes omitted)

Exemptions in the US vary enormously across the states, from the excessively generous to the very parsimonious, and this disparate result has given rise to much criticism because of the abuses to which it leads and the inherent unfairness of such a checkerboard system. Strenuous efforts were made in the US during the passage of the *Bankruptcy Code* of 1978 to substitute a uniform federal set of exemptions for the state-determined exemptions. However, the Congress could only agree on an optional set of federal exemptions that the debtor would be free to elect if state legislation did not preclude the debtor from doing so. These optional provisions appear in Section 522 of the US *Bankruptcy Code*.

The Canadian position is similar to the position that prevailed in the US before 1978. There is a wide disparity among the provinces and territories with respect to the types of property that are exempt from seizure by the debtor's creditors, and therefore also exempt from seizure in bankruptcy, and the value of the property that is exempt. For example, some of the Canadian jurisdictions grant no exemptions in respect of the debtor's residence while others fail to include motor vehicles in the list of exempt assets. The value of the debtor's residence that is exempt from seizure in Saskatchewan, Alberta and British Columbia is substantially higher than the level of exemptions in most of the other provinces. Also, the exemption provisions in many of the provinces are badly dated and have failed to keep pace with increases in the cost of living and changes in the life styles and needs of ordinary Canadians.

These results conflict with the general theory of Canadian bankruptcy law, which proceeds from the premise that bankrupts and their creditors should be treated alike regardless of the residence or place of business of the debtor or the debtor's creditors. For example, Section 68 of the BIA, adopted in 1997, does not leave it up to the provinces to determine how much of the debtor's income shall be treated as surplus to the debtor's essential requirements. Instead, the Superintendent of Bankruptcy is required to determine the appropriate standards by directive, standards which are adjusted at regular intervals to reflect changes in the relevant consumer price index (CPI).

Ideally, therefore, the status of a debtor's property in bankruptcy should be treated the same way as the debtor's surplus income, and the kinds and levels of exemption should be determined by the BIA and not by delegation to provincial or territorial law. However, after full discussion, the Task Force concluded that a more modest approach is called for at the present time and that individual bankrupts should be able to opt for a list of federally prescribed exemptions in place of the otherwise applicable provincial or territorial exemptions. In this way the BIA will ensure that all bankrupts will have access to what is regarded as a reasonable set of exemptions regardless of the bankrupt's place of residence or weaknesses and gaps in the provincial or territorial legislation.

The recommendations of the Task Force are as follows:

    a. There should be a federal exemptions list which the debtor, and only the debtor, can select in preference to the otherwise applicable provincial or territorial exemptions.

b. Debtors will have to make their election promptly following their assignment in bankruptcy or the making of a bankruptcy order. Where there is a joint assignment by related debtors, both parties must elect to be governed in their entirety by the federal or provincial list of exemptions; they cannot "cherry pick" among the different items in each list. If there is a deadlock between the debtors, they will be deemed to have elected the federal exemptions.

c. The specific exemptions and exemption levels recommended by the Task Force are:

1.	Apparel & household furnishings	$7,500
2.	Medically prescribed aids and appliances and medication for use or consumption by the debtor or the debtor's family	No limit
3.	One motor vehicle whether used for personal, trade or business purposes	$3,000
4.	Tools of the trade and professional books but *not* including motor vehicles used in the trade or business	$10,000
5.	Debtor's residence, defined to include a house, apartment, mobile home and house boat	$5,000

d. There should be an exemption for real and personal property used by a debtor whose livelihood is derived from farming, fishing, forestry and other activities related to the natural resource sector of the economy. The amount of the exemption should be governed by applicable provincial/territorial law but is to be not less than $10,000 and not more than $20,000.

e. Registered pension plans and tax exempt life insurance annuities, but not Registered Retirement Savings Plans or RRSPs, shall continue to be governed by applicable federal or provincial law.

f. The above exemptions (other than exemptions governed by item (e)) shall extend to proceeds from the sale of, or the raising of a mortgage on, the exempt property.

g. Exemption levels are to be adjusted to the CPI as determined by regulation under the BIA or, preferably, by exercise of the Superintendent's Directive powers. The value of property for the purpose of the above exemptions shall be the fair market value of the property at the time of the assignment or the making of the bankruptcy order.

h. The exemptions will not apply in respect of a creditor's claim arising out of a maintenance, alimony and other family related support order governed by federal or provincial law.

i. The federal statutory exemptions, if elected by the debtor, cannot be waived by a debtor before the debtor's bankruptcy in favour of the debtor's unsecured creditors, and cannot be waived in favour of a secured creditor holding an unenforceable lien as described below in the Task Force recommendation concerning non-purchase money security interests.

NOTES AND QUESTIONS

1. Note the double test applied under s. 67(1)(b) of the BIA. Which law applies if the debtor resides in province A and owns property in province B? Does it mean that any property located outside Canada is totally non-exempt even if essential for the debtor's well being and even though exempt under the law of the bankrupt's foreign residence?

2. Is there any justification for continued local control over bankruptcy exemptions?

3. It has been suggested that exempt property in a bankruptcy is very much tied to the rehabilitative function of the bankruptcy discharge. Does this suggest that provincial exemption statutes, which are enacted with non-bankruptcy objectives in mind, can never fulfill the larger goal of bankruptcy rehabilitation?

4. The PITF recognized the importance of medically prescribed aids and appliances as exempt property. Not all provinces have included medical aids as a category of exempt property. The case below reveals the outcome where the provincial statute has failed to include a medical aid as exempt property.

Re Guest
(2003), 38 CBR (4th) 209 (Sask. QB)

REGISTRAR HERAUF: There are times, admittedly rare, when as presiding judicial officer in any given matter, you come across a situation where the law and one's concept of justice are at odds. This is one of those cases. Allow me to elaborate.

The trustee applied by motion pursuant to s. 34(1) of the *Bankruptcy and Insolvency Act* ... for direction concerning the bankrupt's claim to exemption on a 1994 Chevrolet van. The trustee disputes the validity of the claim. The personal circumstances of the bankrupt pull this from an ordinary application to that of the extraordinary.

The bankrupt, who is 52 years of age, is a quadriplegic as a result of a motor vehicle accident. The van in question is specially equipped to accommodate his medical condition. The bankrupt is not employed in the ordinary sense that one would associate with the term employment; that is, he does not have an occupation, profession, trade or business that consumes his time or attention for which he receives remuneration. This should not be interpreted to mean that the bankrupt is idle—far from it. The bankrupt, who survives on disability benefits, maintains a volunteer schedule with the Regina Qu'Appelle Health Region that would make Mother Teresa blush. The volunteer activities include such things as peer counselling for individuals recently afflicted with quadriplegia and paraplegia, providing rides to shut-ins with disabilities, and delivering groceries and toiletries to individuals with disabilities.

It is against this factual background that I have the unenviable task of deciding whether the bankrupt can retain his van.

An examination of this issue must start with a look at the statutory provisions that are relevant to an exemption claim on a motor vehicle.

Section 67(1)(b) of the *Bankruptcy and Insolvency Act* implicitly incorporates provincial exemption legislation ... .

Section 2(1) paragraph 5 of *The Exemptions Act*, RSS 1978, c. E-14 exempts from seizure: "One motor vehicle where it is necessary for the proper and efficient conduct of the execution debtor's business, trade, calling or profession."

There is no shortage of jurisprudence in this jurisdiction relating to this particular provision of *The Exemptions Act*. I have carefully reviewed a number of cases but, for the purpose of this application, need only to refer to two cases. The process that one has to go through to determine this question is set out in *Re Kurty* (1998), 6 CBR (4th) 245 (Sask. QB) In *Kurty*, this court adopted the two step analysis identified by Cameron J (as he then was) in *Canadian Acceptance Corp. v. Laviolette* (1981), 11 Sask. R 121 (Sask. QB). The two questions addressed in the course of the judgment were:

1. Is the respondent engaged in a "business, trade, calling or profession"?
2. If so, and assuming the vehicle is necessary for the respondent to get to and from the place where he carries on his "business trade, calling or profession," can it be said that the vehicle is "necessary" for the proper and efficient conduct thereof?

When determining the first question I was urged by counsel for the bankrupt to apply a broad and liberal interpretation to the word "calling" (there was no suggestion that volunteer work could be considered a business, trade or profession) as was endorsed by the Saskatchewan Court of Appeal in *W.W. Gleave Construction Ltd. v. Hampton* (1986), 53 Sask. R 163 (Sask. CA).

. . .

Mr. Dowling, on behalf of the bankrupt, suggests that the liberal interpretation of calling outlined in *Hampton* by the Court of Appeal could be applied in the case at bar to recognize the bankrupt's volunteer work even though there is a non-monetary aspect attached to it. Counsel for the bankrupt also utilized terminology such as compassion, necessity, liberty in his valiant effort to sway the court to his client's viewpoint. While use of these words exemplify the emotional aspect of this case, they do nothing to resolve the legal issue. For that I must look to the legislation. I cannot, in good conscience, interpret the legislation to include volunteer work as a calling. No matter how meritorious the bankrupt's volunteer work, I must do my duty and interpret the legislation as it presently stands. Therefore, I must side with the trustee, who is also doing his duty, and hold that the 1994 Chevrolet van is not exempt property.

Before closing I should mention that the provision of *The Exemptions Act* in question was likely implemented at a time when people with the bankrupt's medical condition, if they survived at all, were certainly not expected to live independently. The medical community has made great strides in doing what it can to ameliorate the symptoms associated with quadriplegia and paraplegia so that individuals, such as the bankrupt, can and do become independent and valued members of society. The legal component necessary to ensure this has not kept up. There is absolutely nothing in the legislation that would recognize and exempt health aids or devices required by the bankrupt due to his physical disability. As a consequence, this decision effectively deprives this bankrupt of the very item that ensures his independence. I take no pride in coming to this conclusion and offer my apologies to Mr. Guest.

NOTES AND QUESTIONS

1. Could Registrar Herauf have "reinterpreted" the Saskatchewan exemption legislation to enable the bankrupt to retain the van?

2. Could the Registrar have resorted to the "inherent jurisdiction of the courts" doctrine to reinterpret the manifestly obsolete/inadequate legislative language?

3. What does *Re Guest* tell us about the effectiveness of consumer interests in the drafting of exemption legislation?

D. Time for Determining the Exempt Status of Property

The time for determining the exempt status of property is at the date of bankruptcy. If the debtor has sold an exempt asset prior to the bankruptcy, the debtor will not be able to claim an exemption in respect of the proceeds unless the proceeds are also given an exempt status by the applicable exemption law. In most provinces, a voluntary sale or other disposition of an exempt asset will result in the loss of the exemption. However, if the transfer was an involuntary one, as in the case of a forced sale by a secured creditor, the proceeds were afforded an exempt status. See *Higgins Co. v. McNabb* (1979), 33 CBR 243 (Sask. CA).

In Alberta and Newfoundland and Labrador, if the proceeds of a sale of exempt property are not intermingled with other funds of the debtor, they themselves are exempt for 60 days from the day of the sale. See *Civil Enforcement Regulation*, Alta. Reg. 276/1995, s. 37(2); *Judgment Enforcement Act*, SNL 1996, c. J-1.1, s. 134. If a bankrupt acquires an asset after the date of the bankruptcy, the determination of its exempt status is made at the time that the bankrupt acquired it. See *Monteith (Trustee of) v. Monteith* (2004), 6 CBR (5th) 47 (Sask. CA).

E. Consequences of Disposition of Exempt Assets

In most provinces, a voluntary disposition of an exempt asset, absent a bankruptcy, will cause the loss of the exempt status in respect of the proceeds of sale in the hands of the debtor. What principle applies when there is a disposition in bankruptcy? Do the proceeds retain their exempt status or are they available to creditors? These issues are discussed in the following case. What policy considerations influenced the court in *Re Gruber*?

Re Gruber
(1993), 22 CBR (3d) 262 (Alta. QB)

FORSYTH J: In this application, the Trustee seeks the advice and direction of this Honourable Court with respect to the following matter:

Do the proceeds from the bankrupt's sale of his joint interest in his home which was claimed exempt at the date of his Assignment in Bankruptcy which was sold by him prior to his discharge form an asset of the bankrupt's estate, or are these proceeds exempt?

The facts in this matter are fairly straightforward. The Bankrupt made an Assignment in Bankruptcy of February 14th, 1992, pursuant to which Deloitte & Touche Inc. was appointed as Trustee. At the time of his Assignment, the Bankrupt claimed as exempt his interest as joint tenant of certain real property which was indicated on his Statement of Affairs as having an estimated value of $138,000 subject to a mortgage in favour of Royal Trust in the amount of $90,000. At the time of the Assignment, the Bankrupt was in actual occupation of this property.

On or about May 22nd, 1992, while still an undischarged bankrupt, the Bankrupt and his wife sold their home generating a net sale of proceeds after payment of realtor's commission, legal fees, etc. of approximately $40,000. The undisputed evidence before me is that these funds have subsequently been used by the Bankrupt and his wife to support himself and his family during his bankruptcy. It should be noted that the sale of the property also was motivated in part from threats of foreclosure proceedings due to the mortgage on the property being substantially in arrears.

Complete disclosure was made by the Bankrupt to the Trustee in Bankruptcy prior to the sale of the property. The Bankrupt proceeded with the sale on the basis and understanding that the net proceeds insofar as his share was concerned would continue to be exempt to be used as he saw fit.

The concern that arises in this case appears to flow from the fact that notwithstanding that the Bankrupt was under considerable pressure to resolve the question of arrears on his mortgage he entered into what might be considered a voluntary sale rather than a forced sale and whether those circumstances change his entitlement to an exemption with respect to the net proceeds of the sale.

· · ·

Section 1(1)(k) of the *Exemptions Act*, RSA 1980, c. E-15, as amended, provides that:

> 1(1) The following real and personal property of an execution debtor is exempt from seizure under a writ of execution: ...
>
>> (k) the house actually occupied by the execution debtor and buildings used in connection with it, and the lot or lots on which the house and buildings are situated according to the registered plan thereof, if the value of the house, building and the lot or lots does not exceed $40 000, but if the value does exceed $40 000, the house, building and lot or lots may be offered for sale and if the amount bid at the sale after deducting all costs and expenses exceeds $40 000 the property shall be sold and the amount received from the sale to the extent of the exemption shall be paid at once to the execution debtor and is until then exempt from seizure under any legal process, but the sale shall not be carried out or possession given to any person until the execution debtor has received $40 000.

· · ·

It is to be noted that s. 1(1)(k) of the *Exemptions Act* requires that in order for the house for which exemption is claimed to be exempt from seizure under a writ of execution, the house must be actually occupied by the execution debtor.

There is clear case authority and it flows from the wording of the *Exemptions Act* that, absent bankruptcy, if the debtor abandons his occupation of the property or sells same, the *Exemptions Act* no longer applies to the proceeds of same and same may be subject to attachment by his execution creditors.

As previously noted, case authority is clear that the effective date for determination of the status of the exemption occurs on the date of bankruptcy. At that date the Bankrupt's property was severed into two estates: one estate that vests with the Trustee and is divisible amongst the Bankrupt's creditors, and one that remains with the Bankrupt because it is exempt under the provincial law. It should be noted that the Trustee may acquire other property of the Bankrupt if it consists of property that may be acquired by or devolve on the Bankrupt before his discharge as set forth in s. 67(c) of the *Bankruptcy Act*.

In *Re Pearson* [(1997), 23 CBR (NS) 44 (Ont. SC], the trustee, as the successor to the bankrupt's estate, sought to change the designated beneficiaries of the bankrupt's RRSP so as to render it exigible under Ontario's *Insurance Act*. Henry J denied the trustee's application, stating at pp. 456-457 that:

> In my opinion, the view expressed by Houlden J is right and I respectfully adopt it. What comes into the hands of the trustee on the occurrence of the bankruptcy is the rights and interests of the insured in the insurance money and in the contract as they stood at the date of bankruptcy. ... *In my opinion, so far as the creditors of the bankrupt are concerned, that situation crystallized at the time the bankruptcy occurred and that property by virtue of s. 47(b) of the Bankruptcy Act [now s. 67(1)(b) of the Act], was impressed with its character as not divisible among the creditors, for all the purposes of the bankruptcy.* ... *[O]nce the bankruptcy occurred the provincial statute had spent its force.* There was no continuing operation of that statute in relation to creditors that could be altered by any act of the bankrupt or the trustee so as to displace the effect that s. 47(b) of the *Bankruptcy Act* had in relation to the property on the occurrence of the bankruptcy (emphasis added).

A similar view is expressed in *Pannell Kerr MacGillivray Inc. v. Beer* [(1988), 69 CBR (NS) 203, 53 Man. R (2d) 200 (QB)], where the facts are somewhat similar to the case at bar in that after bankruptcy, the bankrupt moved off the property and sold the property but before he was discharged from bankruptcy. The Court there held that the debtor was entitled to the proceeds from the sale of that property and Simonsen J stated at p. 206:

> I have no doubt that as of the date of bankruptcy the realty in question was exempt under s. 13(1) of the *Judgments Act*. The trustee, however, contends that the exemption was lost when the bankrupt disposed of the asset during the period when he was an undischarged bankrupt.
>
> *In my view the effective date for determination of the status of the exemption occurs on the date of bankruptcy.* Support for this conclusion is found in the decision of MacDonald J in *Re Hammill* (1984), 52 CBR (NS) 125, 32 Alta. LR (2d) 79 (QB). *If after the date of bankruptcy the bankrupt elects to convert an exempt asset into another form by selling it, the proceeds of sale do not become property which vests in the trustee for division amongst creditors.* [Emphasis added.]
>
> ...

I subscribe to the view espoused in *Re Pearson*, supra, and *Pannell Kerr MacGillivray Inc. v. Beer*, supra, that once an assignment in bankruptcy has been made, the determination of the property of the bankrupt which is assigned to the trustee and the property to which he can claim an exemption is made, as of the date of the assignment. As previously noted, property that may come into the hands of the bankrupt after the date of the assign-ment into bankruptcy may well properly flow through to the trustee in bankruptcy as property of the bankrupt estate. However, I am not satisfied that those decisions dealing with exempt assets losing their exemption have any application whatsoever in the case of a bankruptcy. If the determination of the division of property is made as of the date of bankruptcy, provisions of the *Exemptions Act* are no longer applicable after that date. In general terms, the intent of the *Bankruptcy and Insolvency Act* is, *inter alia*, to allow a bankrupt to reorganize his affairs and in due course be discharged from bankruptcy, and hopefully to maintain a solvent position thereafter. It surely could not have been intended that where a bankrupt is forced by financial constraints to sell an exempt asset in order to support his family or otherwise that he should lose that exemption even if the sale is voluntary, and thus be penalized for attempting to reduce his expenses to the benefit of his creditors. I am satisfied that an asset which is validly exempt at the date of bankruptcy remains exempt, notwithstanding the nature of any subsequent dealings with that asset.

Accordingly, turning to the facts in issue in this case, I find that the Bankrupt was en-titled to the exemption of his interest in his home at the date of the bankruptcy as he was in actual occupation, and the equity was less than $40,000. The fact that he subsequently sold that property prior to his discharge, does not affect his entitlement to one-half of the net proceeds of that sale as exempt property. Therefore, the Bankrupt's interest in the net sale proceeds from his home which was claimed exempt at the date of his Assignment but subsequently sold by him is property exempt and does not comprise an asset of his bankrupt estate.

Order accordingly.

F. Exempt Property and Valuation Issues

Provincial exemption legislation may exempt certain types of property regardless of value or the legislation may specify that some types of property will be exempt up to a maximum dollar value. Generally, property exceeding that capped amount is available to creditors. Where an exemption is subject to a value cap when should a valuation of that exemption take place? Should the valuation take place as of the date of bankruptcy? Alternatively, should the trustee in bankruptcy or a creditor be entitled to ask for a valuation post-discharge where the exempt property has significantly appreciated in value? *Re McKay* exam-ines valuation issues in relation to a value-capped exemption.

Re McKay
(2002), 35 CBR (4th) 275 (Alta. QB)

REGISTRAR FUNDUK: This is an application by Canadian Imperial Bank of Commerce ("CIBC") for an order that the bankrupt pay $21,375 to it, which is what the bankrupt netted above his $20,000 exemption when the co-owned principal residence was volun-tarily sold some time after the date of bankruptcy.

. . .

In 1996 the bankrupt made a proposal, which was approved by the Court in March, 1997. The bankrupt carried on with the proposal for some time but eventually found it impossible to continue. On June 18, 1999 he assigned himself into bankruptcy. On that date he and his wife were the joint owners of the house and it was their principal residence.

The *Bankruptcy and Insolvency Act* ("BIA") requires a bankrupt to provide a sworn statement giving certain information: s. 49(2). It is called a statement of affairs.

In the statement of affairs which accompanied the assignment the bankrupt shows the house to have an "estimated dollar value" of $300,000 and that it is encumbered with a mortgage for $274,000.

The bankrupt is a second time bankrupt so he was not entitled to an automatic discharge. He had to come to Court to get a discharge [and the] bankrupt's application for discharge was heard ... on August 23, 2000.

The bankrupt gave affidavit evidence in support of his discharge. He does testify about the house but the evidence is about the money that he had spent to repair and upgrade it. The house is over 65 years old and is in the Old Glenora area in Edmonton. The bankrupt, who is a lawyer, is not qualified to give opinion evidence about the value of the house. He does not do so.

The bankrupt was cross-examined by CIBC's lawyer in March 2000. The cross-examination does touch on the house, but of course does not deal with its value. All that is in evidence is that the house was bought in July, 1995 for $275,000. ... The exhibits to the cross-examination and the answers to undertakings are not relevant to the value of the house at the date of bankruptcy.

The trustee's s. 170 report, which is required for every application for discharge, says that the house is "exempt" and that its value "as per Statement of Affairs" is $300,000.

On August 23, 2000 Registrar Alberstat gave a conditional order for discharge. The operative part of the order, for today, is that the bankrupt pay 45 monthly payments of $1,500. The formal order says nothing about the house. It does not show that what the bankrupt was ordered to pay includes a "component" for the bankrupt's equity in the house, whatever it might be.

CIBC was present at the application for discharge. It was an objecting creditor.

The underlying facts which bring the parties before me are these. In February 2001 the bankrupt and his wife sold the house. At that date the bankrupt was still in bankruptcy, although there is the conditional order of discharge. The sale netted the bankruptcy $21,375 *above* the $20,000 exemption that s. 88(g) *Civil Enforcement Act* ("CEA") combined with s. 37(1)(e) Alta. Reg. 276/95 gives a debtor who is a joint tenant of the principal residence.

The trustee demanded that the bankrupt pay him the $21,375. The bankrupt refused. Mr. McCabe, for the bankrupt, replied to the trustee on September 6, 2001. That part of his reply relevant to the issue before me is as follows:

> The real cause of the exceptional sale price received by the MacKay's appears to be that houses, generally, and more particularly, houses in Old Glenora have gone up in value, dramatically, since the summer of 1999.

> Our position is that the value of property, and the calculation of any equity, is to be done as of the date of bankruptcy. That was done, here, and as you correctly concluded, the available exemption was less than the reasonable costs to sell the property. As far as we are concerned, that is the end of the matter.

The trustee declined to challenge the bankrupt's position and invited CIBC to get a s. 38 BIA order. CIBC got an order on March 12, 2002. The operative paragraph says:

> 1. [CIBC] may and is hereby authorized to commence proceedings in his own name and at his own risk and expense, for entitlement to $21,355.00, which represents the Bankrupt's equity in the Bankrupt's residence which is over and above the Bankrupt's exemption.

> . . .

In Alberta exemptions are a matter of legislation, either by the Legislature acting within its constitutional jurisdiction or by Parliament acting within its constitutional jurisdiction. The most common Alberta legislation relevant to exemptions is the *Civil Enforcement Act*, although it is not the only Alberta exemptions legislation.

In a bankruptcy the bankrupt's property passing to the trustee falls into three general classes:

(1) property which is not exempt;

(2) property which is wholly exempt regardless of its value;

(3) property which the bankrupt has a limited exemption for.

The first class needs no explanation, and it is not relevant to the issue before me.

The second class of property is where the legislation gives an exemption without a quantitative limit. One example is a life insurance policy which fits within s. 580(2) *Insurance Act*: see *McCallum, Re* (2001), 283 AR 282 (Alta. QB). That insurance contract is exempt regardless of its value. Another example is an insurance policy which fits within s. 688(2) *Insurance Act*. That insurance contract is exempt regardless of its value. An example of that is *Re Pearson* (1977), 23 CBR (NS) 44 (Ont. SC), referred to in *Royal Bank of Canada v. North American Life Assurance Co.*, [1966] 1 SCR 325. In that case the bankrupt was the owner of the insurance contract and the insured and his wife the designated beneficiary. The relevant Ontario legislation is set out in the decision and is identical to Alberta's s. 688(2) *Insurance Act*.

If property is wholly exempt regardless of its value there is no need to debate at which point in time it should be valued for exemption purposes. That which is wholly exempt regardless of value remains wholly exempt. The value of wholly exempt property is simply not relevant for realization purposes because the trustee is prohibited from realizing on it. ...

The third class of property is that for which the bankrupt has a limited exemption. Those most commonly run across in both bankruptcy and non-bankruptcy cases is property identified in s. 88 *Civil Enforcement Act*. Some is limited by a dollar amount set by Alta. Reg. 276/95: clauses (b), (c), (d), (g) and (h). Some has a non-money limit: clauses (a), (e), and (f) and (i). Where any equity in the property exceeds the limited exemption the property is subject to realization by creditors, s. 89(1), subject to the protection given to the debtor by s.-s. (2).

In the application before me the house was the bankrupt's principal residence [s.88(g)] at the date of bankruptcy so he has *as a matter of law* whatever exemption the law gives him at that time. ...

I do not accept that the relevant value of limited exemption property for realization purposes should be its value at the date of bankruptcy to give bankrupts immediate certainty. A bankruptcy is not a one day circus with the finale being at the end of the day. An assignment is a start of a legal process which will continue for some time. Only time will spell the finale. The only certainties for a bankrupt at the date of bankruptcy are:

(1) he has assigned all his property to the trustee;

(2) his unsecured creditors cannot proceed against him without leave of the Court;

(3) when he exits the bankruptcy he can keep that which the law says is exempt.

. . .

At the "estate-administration stage" of the bankruptcy the trustee cannot exercise his distribution powers to use that which is exempt for the benefit of the creditors: *Ramgotra*, para. 48. But that which is exempt is the "maximum exemption" set out in the Regulation. The trustee is not required to transfer back to the bankrupt more than that and the bankrupt is not entitled to get back more than that. I turn now to Mr. McCabe's third position.

Nobody says that there need not be a cut-off date for dealing with the issue posed before me. I agree that the bankrupt should not be left to twist in the wind indefinitely. *Zemlak (Trustee of) v. Zemlak* (1987), 42 DLR (4th) 395 (Sask. CA) recognizes that. It indicates that the issue should be at least dealt with at the bankrupt's application for discharge, pp. 403-04:

> In the factual context of this case we conclude that a non-exempt equity did not exist at the time of the application for discharge. On that ground alone the caveat should be vacated if it were not for the trustee's position that any increase in the equity will accrue to the benefit of the creditors. In argument before this court the appellant's counsel used the following example in his factum to illustrate the ultimate result—a result which was not disputed by the respondent:
>
>> The following is submitted as a specific example of the ultimate result if the Learned Chambers Judge is correct:
>>
>> i.   At the date of discharge of the Trustee a Bankrupt's home is valued at $50,000.00;
>>
>> ii. The $50,000.00 is apportioned by way of an $18,000.00 real property mortgage and $32,000.00 exempt equity.
>>
>> iii. At the time of discharge, the Trustee does not specifically return the home to the Bankrupt pursuant to s. 22(1);
>>
>> iv. Some 30 or 40 years later the discharged bankrupt has paid off the mortgage and the home, through inflation, is then valued at $82,000.00;
>>
>> v.   When the discharge bankrupt moves to a retirement home, he would be entitled to his $32,000.00 exemption and the Trustee would distribute the $50,000.00 non-exempt

> equity to the creditors without any obligation to maintain or administer the home in the intervening years.

> If this result were permitted, property acquired by the debtor after an absolute discharge in bankruptcy would be appropriated to payment of the discharged debtor's debts. The equity built up in the property after issue of an absolute order would form a realizable fund for creditors at some future date, notwithstanding the final discharge. Such a result does not comport with the philosophy of the Act.

> We have no doubt that the Registrar in Bankruptcy would have recognized the importance of this issue if the material had alerted him to it. Since the registrar is familiar with the established practice of title clearing in the Land titles Office upon filing of the certificate of the bankrupt's discharge, he would undoubtedly have suggested that the bankrupt obtain counsel to deal with the matter at that stage. Accordingly, the respondent should not now be heard to say that it is entitled to maintain the caveat.

I agree with that approach.

A trustee can realize for the surplus equity in limited exemptions property before the bankrupt's application for discharge. *ICI Paints* [*v. Gazette* (2001), 24 CBR (4th) 54 (Alta. QB)] does not prohibit that. The trustee can also decide to deal with that on the bankrupt's application for discharge if he considers that to be the best time and best method for realizing on the surplus. Again, this is a practical decision by the trustee: *Rassell, Re* [(1999), 12 CBR (4th) 316 (Alta. CA)].

It is not uncommon for a trustee to wait until the bankrupt's application for discharge to deal with the surplus equity. An example is *Re Swatsky* [(2001), 28 CBR (4th) 116 (Alta. QB)]. Conditional orders of discharge are sometimes a practical and effective means to deal with a surplus equity in property, be it land or chattels. I have given such orders over the years and I am confident others have also done so.

There are advantages to surplus equity being realized that way. First, the trustee must do a s. 170 report and he makes recommendations about what order is appropriate. If he recommends a conditional order of discharge for the surplus equity proved creditors (who are given a copy of the report) might not be as opposed to the bankrupt's discharge. Second, a conditional order is a cost effective method of realizing on the surplus equity. Third, a bankrupt who wants to keep the property and pay a reasonable price for the surplus equity may not presently have the money to do it. Instead of adjourning the application for discharge until the bankrupt is able to pay and has paid the conditional order gives a present finality, which is necessary at some point. In effect, the bankrupt buys now on time. The conditional order can even be ordered to be a charge against the property and be registered as such.

The trustee is not the only person who can ask for a conditional order of discharge as a way to realize on the surplus equity in property. Proved creditors have a status to ask for that. If a trustee declines to realize on surplus equity prior to the application for discharge or declines to ask for a conditional order of discharge creditors have a right to pursue surplus equity in a timely manner. It is not uncommon for creditors to appear on applications for discharge and submit that the bankrupt should not be unconditionally discharged.

If a surplus equity has not been realized on by the trustee, creditors who want realization have two options. First, they can appear at the application for discharge and ask for a conditional order for payment of the surplus equity. If that is given the surplus equity is shared between all proved creditors. Alternatively, a creditor can get a s. 38 order in a timely manner to let it realize for the surplus equity and if it gets the order and does realize on the surplus equity it does not have to share with other creditors. ...

Ramgotra speaks of a two-stage analysis, the second stage being the estate-administration stage. At the estate-administration stage the trustee deals with limited exemption property. He cannot use that which is exempt for the benefit of creditors; para. 48.

If the trustee has not dealt with limited exemption property prior to the bankrupt's discharge the discharge is to be considered as an estate-administration stage for that property. That brings finality for all. Viewing the discharge as part of the estate-administration stage for dealing with wholly exempt or limited exemption property fits within the second stage of the *Ramgotra* analysis.

Regardless whether a bankrupt has gotten an absolute, suspended or conditional discharge nobody can *later* raise an issue about surplus equity in a house. The discharge is the latest time that that issue is to be dealt with, if anyone wants to make that an issue.

If a conditional order is given requiring the bankrupt to pay for the surplus equity nobody can later ride the market, up or down, to revisit that. If the house value later goes up the trustee and creditors cannot ask that the bankrupt now pay more. If the house value later goes down the bankrupt cannot ask that he now pay less.

I have in my recitation of the facts outlined the sequence of events. There is nothing in the Court record showing that the bankrupt's equity in the house was an issue at any time prior to the discharge or at his application for discharge.

CIBC did not raise an issue about the bankrupt's equity in the house until some months after the conditional order of discharge and only after the house was sold some months after the conditional order of discharge.

It is too late. ...

The message to trustees and creditors is—advance claims for surplus equity in limited exemptions property by no later than the bankrupt's application for discharge, or forget it.

Application dismissed

G. Non-Purchase Money Security Interests in Exempt Personal Property

If the debtor has given a creditor a pre-bankruptcy security interest in exempt property, in general, provincial law does not prevent the secured party from enforcing its security interest. This is true where the secured party holds a purchase money security interest in the chattel. For example, provincial exemption law will not prevent a dealer or bank that has financed the purchase of a motor vehicle from repossessing the vehicle after the debtor's bankruptcy. This is generally (though not uniformly) regarded as a fair result. However, the position may be viewed very differently if the secured party holds a non-purchase money security interest in exempt property.

For example, in *Re Vanhove* (1994), 20 OR (3d) 653 (Gen. Div.) the debtor granted a security interest by way of a chattel mortgage over household furniture and the secured party perfected its interest. Under s. 2 of the Ontario *Execution Act* household furniture is an exempt category of personal property. The debtor defaulted under the terms of the security agreement. The court held that the secured party was not precluded from enforcing its security interest against the household furniture because the *Execution Act* only applied to execution proceedings such as the enforcement of a judgment and not to secured creditors enforcing a security interest. The court held that the secured creditor was entitled to an order requiring delivery of the household furniture.

Many of the provinces now make non-purchase money security interests in exempt property unenforceable. See for example s. 62(2) of the Ontario PPSA. The PITF recommended the inclusion of a provision to deal with non-purchase money security agreements in the BIA to ensure uniform treatment of bankrupts across Canada. See PITF, *Final Report* (2002), at 27-28.

H. RRSP Exemptions in Bankruptcy

Personal Insolvency Task Force, *Final Report*
(Ottawa: Industry Canada, Office of the Superintendent of Bankruptcy, 2002),
at 17-19, 23 (footnotes omitted)

The federal government has made a policy choice favouring retirement savings. The rationale for this policy choice is the importance of encouraging Canadians to plan for their retirement, so as to promote individual financial responsibility and to ensure that senior citizens do not become solely reliant on the public purse. The policy choice is evidenced by the exempt status afforded to Registered Pension Plans (RPPs) available to employed Canadians, through significant tax incentives available both for RPPs and RRSPs, and through the prohibition against lenders taking security against RRSP investments.

While pensions are "inexigible," meaning that they are entirely exempt from creditors' claims, RRSPs vary in the extent to which they are exigible.

- Conventional RRSPs held by banks, brokerages or self-directed funds are fully exigible through execution and in bankruptcy.
- Insurance-type RRSPs, held by provincially-regulated insurers in the form of annuities, are exempt under certain circumstances, primarily where the designated beneficiary is the spouse, parent or child of the holder of the RRSP.
- Locked-in RRSPs, created when ex-employees withdraw from pension plans upon termination of employment after the pension rights have vested, are exempt under pension legislation and cannot be accessed until retirement.

Only a very small proportion of bankrupts have RRSPs among their assets at the time of filing. In 1998, about 30% of all Canadians contributed to an RRSP. The percentage of bankrupts holding RRSPs probably understates their importance in insolvency proceedings, however, since any debtors with RRSPs are likely to have cashed them well before filing for bankruptcy.

As a result of the treatment of RRSPs, employees with pension plans can safely accumulate exempt retirement savings but self-employed individuals and non-pensioned employees normally lose their RRSP investments upon bankruptcy, even though their contributions may have been made many years before their insolvency.

The existence of the exempt insurance-type RRSPs has led to several other unsatisfactory aspects of the current bankruptcy treatment of RRSPs. First, only a small proportion of Canadians are aware of the exempt status of insurance-type RRSPs. For that reason, only especially prudent self-employed individuals and non-pensioned employees, or those with good advisors, are able to creditor-proof their retirement funds. Second, those facing the possibility of bankruptcy might be tempted to convert non-exempt RRSPs into exempt insurance-type RRSPs. By virtue of the Supreme Court of Canada's *Ramgotra* [*Ramgotra (Trustee of) v. North American Life Assurance Co.*, [1996] 1 SCR 325—eds.] decision, however, only a cumbersome fraud test is available to the trustee, under provincial fraudulent conveyance legislation, to set aside such pre-bankruptcy transactions.

Even if the RRSP is exempt, the bankruptcy court hearing the debtor's discharge may require that the bankrupt, in effect, draw down the RRSP by way of a conditional discharge order made in specific contemplation of the RRSP. Not doing so, and leaving the bankrupt with substantial exempt assets, has been held to undermine the integrity of the bankruptcy system. Such views are never advanced in respect of pensions, even if their capitalized value is very high, because pensions are inaccessible until after retirement.

In considering reforms to the current treatment of RRSPs under the BIA, the Task Force acknowledged that it would be inappropriate if the bankruptcy system treated RRSPs in exactly the same way as pensions. This is because there are several key differences that call for different treatment.

First, pension contributions are normally mandatory as a condition or benefit of employment, and normally include an employer's contribution. RRSPs are voluntary and normally fully self-funded, perhaps through borrowing. Second, pension contributions are normally regular, periodic and fixed in amount. RRSP contributions are self-determined in amount, often irregular, and are purely a matter of individual planning. Third, pensions cannot normally be accessed until retirement. RRSPs are normally liquid so that they can be cashed or collapsed at any time, subject to a tax penalty. Fourth, RRSPs are often utilized as tax-deferred savings vehicles and are not intended exclusively, or even primarily, for retirement.

Sound public policy ought to support and encourage prudent retirement planning. Existing provincial and federal legislation already exempts pensions and some varieties of RRSPs. It would be consistent with both retirement and bankruptcy policies if bankruptcy legislation afforded exempt status to RRSP savings that have accumulated through prudent retirement savings practices before the period of insolvency. At the same time, the BIA ought not to be available for strategic use by those who intend to shelter their assets from the reach of impending or foreseeable creditors. An overly generous exemption policy would invite abuse.

As well, the integrity of the bankruptcy system would suffer if debtors succeeded in preserving their RRSPs through the bankruptcy process, only to be in a position to access the preserved cash shortly following, or even during, the bankruptcy. This would flout the retirement policy goals for the exemption, and would lead to well-warranted creditor frustration.

The aim of the Task Force has been to devise a mechanism for RRSP exemption that would accommodate these competing concerns in a fair, efficient and principled manner.

Key Recommendations

RRSPs should be eligible for exemption in bankruptcy on the basis of several inter-related elements. The three most important elements of the Task Force recommendation are presented immediately below. A number of other elements are also important and these are set out in the discussion below. All elements of the complete recommendation are then repeated at the end of this section. ...

a. An RRSP exemption will be available to bankrupts only if they convert the RRSP, shortly following the date of bankruptcy, into a locked-in RRSP or annuity that will be accessible only after their retirement. In effect, the RRSP will be converted into a locked-in RRSP similar to that prescribed by pension legislation when an employee's vested pension rights are terminated due to a loss of employment status.

b. All RRSP contributions (including contributions to a spousal RRSP) made by the debtor within three years of the date of the initial bankruptcy event, will accrue to the trustee as property divisible among creditors. This will be an irrebuttable vesting; that is, it will not be dependent upon any fraud test or judicial determination. Contributions outside the three-year mark will continue to be subject to fraudulent conveyance attack under existing provincial legislation.

c. The income or proceeds from the locked-in RRSP, when it is being paid out following retirement, will be treated as income that is subject to the surplus income standards in Section 68 of the BIA. The trustee will be entitled to enforce the surplus income obligation against such income.

d. The exemption will be capped. The maximum amount exempted will be equal to the maximum RRSP contribution limit in the year of bankruptcy multiplied by the number of years that the bankrupt's age exceeds 21, to a limit of age 65.

NOTES AND QUESTIONS

1. New BIA s. 67(1)(b.3) now expressly provides an exemption for RRSPs. The provision confirms that property in an RRSP is not property that is divisible among the bankrupt's creditors. However, the protection extended to bankrupts in s. 67(1)(b.3) does not cover property contributed to such a plan in the 12 months, or any longer period that the court may specify, before the date of the bankruptcy. What is the rationale for this exception?

2. The Senate Committee on Banking, Trade and Commerce, in its report *Debtors and Creditors Sharing the Burden* (2003), recommended (at 29) that the "*Bankruptcy and Insolvency Act* be amended to exempt funds in all Registered Retirement Savings Plans from seizure in bankruptcy, provided that three conditions are met: the Registered Retirement Savings Plan is locked in; contributions made to the Registered Retirement Savings Plan in the one-year period prior to bankruptcy are paid to the trustee for distribution to creditors; and the exempt amount is no greater than a maximum amount to be set by regulation and increased annually in accordance with increases in the cost of living as measured by the Consumer Price Index." Examine s. 67(1)(b.3). How does the provision differ from the recommendations of the PITF or the Senate Committee Report?

3. Should RRSPs be considered in the same context as other categories of exempt property such as household furniture, tools of trade, motor vehicles, or, in the case of some provinces, residential homes or farm land? In other words do the same policy justifications that have been offered for the traditional categories of exempt property apply to RRSPs?

4. There is an interplay between provincial law and s. 67(1)(b.3). The federal exemption specifies that it does not limit the existing provincial exemptions. Several provinces, including Saskatchewan, Manitoba, Quebec, and Newfoundland and Labrador have amended their exemptions law to provide an exemption for an RRSP. In these provinces, the RRSP will be fully exempt, including the contributions made immediately before the bankruptcy. In other provinces, an exempt status is afforded to future income retirement plans only if they take the form of an annuity with an insurance company. In these provinces, the funds will be fully exempt under provincial law only if the bankrupt has contributed into this type of insurance annuity product. If the bankrupt has contributed into an ordinary RRSP it is not exempt under provincial law. Therefore, the only exemption that is available is that created by s. 67(1)(b.3), and the bankrupt therefore cannot claim the exemption in respect of any contribution made in the 12 months prior to the bankruptcy.

5. Revised s. 67(1)(b.3) is a further illustration of interest group influence over the consumer insolvency law reform process. The provision, which departs from the PITF's recommendation on exemptions for RRSP contributions, came about as a result of Quebec and Saskatchewan MPs refusing to approve the Motion to Amend Bill C-55. The Motion to amend the 2005 Bill required unanimous approval to proceed.

IV. DEBTOR'S OBLIGATION TO CONTRIBUTE SURPLUS INCOME TO THE ESTATE

Before 1966, the BIA contained no explicit provisions dealing with the disposition of the debtor's income during bankruptcy. The only relevant provision was s. 67(1)(c) entitling the trustee to claim the debtor's non-exempt property, which the Supreme Court held in *Industrial Acceptance Corp. v. Lalonde*, [1952] 2 SCR 109 included the debtor's income. However, that decision left it unclear what part of the debtor's income remained exempt. To clarify the position, s. 68 was added to the BIA in 1966 (SC 1966-67, c. 32, s. 10) authorizing the trustee, and requiring him to do so if required by the inspectors, to make an application to the court for an income payment order. Initially, the amendment applied only to the debtor's earnings from employment but was subsequently enlarged to include other forms of remuneration. The court was given complete discretion in responding to the application "having regard to the family responsibilities and personal situation of the debtor." In a later decision, the Supreme Court of Canada held that s. 68 constituted a complete code with respect to the trustee's power to attach a debtor's earnings. (*Marzetti v. Marzetti*, [1994] 2 SCR 765.) For background to s. 68, see Jacob Ziegel, *Comparative Consumer Insolvency Regimes—A Canadian Perspective* (Oxford: Hart Publishing, 2003), at 27-28.

Creditors were unhappy with the way trustees applied s. 68 in practice and thought it left too much to the trustee's discretion. As a result, s. 68 was completely revised in 1997, making it *mandatory* for the bankrupt to pay over to the trustee the surplus portion of his income as determined by policy directives issued by the Superintendent of Bankruptcy. Surplus income was again an issue in the most recent round of reforms in 2005 and 2007.

The Standing Senate Committee on Banking, Trade and Commerce, in its 2003 report, *Debtors and Creditors Sharing the Burden*, at 60, estimated that between 15-20 percent of bankrupts have surplus income. "The Committee, in the interests of fairness and responsibility, believes that bankrupts with surplus income should be required to make contributions to their estate that would increase the moneys available for distribution to creditors" (61-62). The 2005 and 2007 amendments clarify what constitutes "total income" as well as setting out a new statutory standard of "surplus income." The following materials address the impact of the surplus income requirements.

In *Kallenberger v. Beck (Trustee of)* (2005), 18 CBR (5th) 113 (Alta. QB), at para. 15, the court concluded that "[s]ection 68 recognizes a reality of life, namely, even a bankrupt needs something to live on while their affairs are being controlled by their Trustee." However, the courts suggest that a balance must be struck between the interests of the bankrupt and creditors. "The Act holds that the bankrupt must be entitled to a fair and reasonable amount for the maintenance of himself or herself and the family. On the other hand, certain sacrifices have to be made for the benefit of the creditors." See *Re Jakola* (2005), 13 CBR (5th) 198 (Ont. SCJ), at para. 30.

At issue is how one determines the appropriate standard of surplus income such that a bankrupt is able to maintain a reasonable standard of living. Under s. 68(1) of the BIA, the "Superintendent shall, by directive, establish ... the standards for determining surplus income." See Directive No. 11R, "Surplus Income." According to BIA s. 68(3) the "trustee *shall*, having regard to the applicable standards and to the personal and family situation of the bankrupt, determine whether the bankrupt has surplus income" (emphasis added). But consumer bankrupts and social welfare agencies have no input into the design of the surplus income tables in Directive No. 11R. Appendix A in Directive No. 11R, which establishes the Superintendent's Standards, relies on low income cut-offs (LICO) compiled by Statistics Canada.

The LICO standards were developed by Statistics Canada for quite different purposes. If the Surplus Income Directive does not accurately reflect the financial position of debtors and their dependants, it will have an impact on whether the bankrupt will be able to make surplus income payments. The implications of not being able to make surplus income payments are significant because those bankrupts will not be able to secure a nine-month discharge. Does Directive No. 11R give the trustee any discretion to take into account the debtor's family situation or the debtor's social, economic, or geographic situation? See Jacob Ziegel, *Comparative Consumer Insolvency Regimes*, above, at 30. For an examination of how s. 68 has been operating in practice, see Jacob Ziegel, "What Can the United States Learn from the Canadian Means Testing System?" [2007] *Ill. L Rev.* 195.

The chart on the facing page compiled by the OSB provides data on the surplus income requirements and payments for consumer bankruptcies filed between 2002 and 2007.

Re Landry
(2000), 192 DLR (4th) 728 (Ont. CA) (footnotes omitted)

CHARRON JA (for the Court): [1] The respondent, Nycole Landry, declared bankruptcy on June 4, 1997 and the appellant, Deloitte & Touche, was appointed trustee of the bankrupt's estate. Landry has been discharged from bankruptcy on October 15, 1998. The

Report #: BKHQRA-875   Report Date: October 17, 2008

Update of Surplus Income Requirements and Payments: Consumer Bankruptcies Filed from 2002–2007

Year filed	Above requirement	At requirement	Below requirement	No requirement to pay	Total
2002	7358	7941	1061	61706	78066
2003	8038	8663	1086	66470	84257
2004	8060	8946	1116	66442	84564
2005	8578	9422	1206	65538	84744
2006	8507	9162	1104	60561	79334
2007	9061	9693	1451	59741	79946
Total	49602	53827	7024	380458	490911

Surplus income payments by band

Year filed	No requirement to pay	<$100	$100–$200	$200–$300	$300–$400	$400–$500	$500–$600	$600–$700	$700–$800	$800–$900	$900–$1000	>$1000	Total
2002 (# of estates)	61706	945	7894	3707	1682	884	532	258	137	97	55	169	78066
(percentage)	79.04	1.21	10.11	4.75	2.15	1.13	0.68	0.33	0.18	0.12	0.07	0.22	
2003 (# of estates)	66470	931	8401	4134	1893	1011	537	305	202	131	75	167	84257
(percentage)	78.89	1.1	9.97	4.91	2.25	1.2	0.64	0.36	0.24	0.16	0.09	0.2	
2004 (# of estates)	66442	940	8217	4380	1983	1099	601	353	182	120	81	166	84564
(percentage)	78.57	1.11	9.72	5.18	2.34	1.3	0.71	0.42	0.22	0.14	0.1	0.2	
2005 (# of estates)	65538	907	8408	4698	2296	1178	622	393	229	162	92	221	84744
(percentage)	77.34	1.07	9.92	5.54	2.71	1.39	0.73	0.46	0.27	0.19	0.11	0.26	
2006 (# of estates)	60561	845	8016	4727	2183	1103	702	428	221	159	110	279	79334
(percentage)	76.34	1.07	10.1	5.96	2.75	1.39	0.88	0.54	0.28	0.2	0.14	0.35	
2007 (# of estates)	59741	859	8157	5021	2421	1380	812	556	322	206	124	347	79946
(percentage)	74.73	1.07	10.2	6.28	3.03	1.73	1.02	0.7	0.4	0.26	0.16	0.43	
Total (# of estates)	380458	5427	49093	26667	12458	6655	3806	2293	1293	875	537	1349	490911

Surplus income payments

Number of Estates	Mean	Median
110278	$263.76	$200.00

trustee has not yet been discharged and is still attempting to realize upon the assets of the bankrupt's estate for the benefit of the creditors. This proceeding concerns one potential asset.

A. The Facts

. . .

[3] In 1993, Landry was dismissed from her employment as a pilot with First Air. That same year, she brought a claim for unjust dismissal against First Air under the Canada Labour Code, RSC 1985, c. L-2. At the end of a first hearing, the arbitrator found that Landry had been unjustly dismissed.

[4] The employer successfully appealed the arbitrator's finding and a new hearing was ordered. Shortly before the second hearing, Landry changed solicitors. In May 1997, the first solicitor's costs were assessed in the amount of $77,500. Landry declared bankruptcy on June 4, 1997. The first solicitor is the main, if not the only, creditor in the bankruptcy.

[5] Landry obtained an absolute discharge from her bankruptcy on October 15, 1998 which effectively discharged her from her debt to the first solicitor. The trustee did not oppose the discharge but made it clear to Landry that the trustee maintained the right to claim any part of an eventual award of damages for unjust dismissal.

[6] In December 1998, at the conclusion of a second hearing under the Canada Labour Code, a different arbitrator also found that Landry was unjustly dismissed. When the trustee became aware of the arbitrator's decision, the trustee unsuccessfully attempted to intervene in the proceedings to claim the first solicitor's costs.

[7] The arbitrator's decision on the award has not yet been delivered and apparently awaits the outcome of this appeal. Although the exact amount is uncertain, the parties agree that Landry can expect to receive, as part of the award, some moneys for lost wages.

B. The Trustee's Motion

[8] In the spring of 1999, the trustee moved before Chadwick J under ss. 67, 68 and 71 of the *Bankruptcy and Insolvency Act*, RSC 1985, c. B-3 (the "BIA") for various forms of relief with respect to the expected arbitrator's award. The trustee sought a declaration that any amount awarded in relation to lost wages constituted property of the bankrupt that vested in the trustee for the benefit of the creditors, either through the automatic operation of ss. 67 and 71(2) or pursuant to an order that the court should make under s. 68. (Simply put, s. 67 defines the property of the bankrupt that is divisible among the creditors, s. 71(2) is a general vesting provision and s. 68 makes specific provisions with respect to either the "total income" of the bankrupt, if the current provision applies, or the bankrupt's "salary, wages, or other remuneration" from employment, if the former version applies.) The trustee also sought a declaration that Landry's claim against First Air vested in the trustee on the date of bankruptcy and that the trustee was therefore entitled to intervene in the proceedings before the arbitrator to seek an order for costs in relation to the first solicitor's account. Finally, the trustee sought an order for a lien under s. 34 of the *Solicitors Act*, RSO 1990, c. S.15.

C. *The Decision Under Appeal*

[9] Chadwick J held that, even if that part of the settlement related to wages in lieu of notice could arguably form part of the bankrupt estate under s. 67, 80 per cent of this amount would be exempt pursuant to the provisions of the *Wages Act*, RSO 1990, c. W.1 incorporated under s. 67(1)(b) of the BIA. In view of the small amount of money that could be apportioned, the motions judge stated that he was not prepared to make any order under s. 67. The motions judge held further that the current s. 68 applied but that the trustee was precluded from resorting to its provisions because the section applied only to undischarged bankrupts and because the trustee had not followed the procedure set out under s. 68. On the question of costs, the motions judge held that neither the trustee nor the former solicitors had any status in seeking an order for costs before the arbitrator as the costs are those of the client Landry and that she had waived her claim for costs as a result of her bankruptcy. Finally the motions judge refused to make an order for a lien under the *Solicitors Act* and dismissed the trustee's motion. The trustee appeals from this decision on all questions except that the trustee does not pursue the request for a lien under the *Solicitors Act*.

D. *The Issues on the Appeal*

[10] This appeal therefore raises the following questions:

1. Does Landry's claim against First Air or any part of the resulting award constitute property of the bankrupt that vests in the trustee under ss. 67 and 71(2) of the BIA?

2. If so, does any exemption apply pursuant to s. 67(1)(b) so as to except any part of the property from the estate of the bankrupt?

3. Is s. 67 superseded by the provisions of s. 68 in relation to a bankrupt's wages?

4. If so, which provision applies, the former s. 68, which was in force at the time Landry declared bankruptcy, or the present s. 68, which was in force at the time the trustee brought its motion?

5. Is the trustee precluded from resorting to s. 68 after the discharge of the bankrupt?

6. Is the trustee precluded from resorting to the current s. 68 because the procedure set out thereunder has not been followed?

7. Does the trustee have standing to intervene in the proceeding under the Canada Labour Code to claim Landry's costs incurred at the first arbitration hearing?

E. Analysis

1. Does Landry's Claim Against First Air or Any Part of the Resulting Award Constitute Property of the Bankrupt That Vests in the Trustee Under Sections 67 and 71(2) of the BIA?

[11] As stated earlier, s. 71(2) is a general vesting provision. It reads as follows: ...

[12] "Property" is defined under s. 2 of the BIA as including: ...

[13] "Things in action" encompass a claim for damages for breach of contract, including an action for wrongful dismissal: *Wallace v. United Grain Growers Ltd.*, [1997] 3 SCR 701. The parties do not dispute that Landry's claim against her former employer under the Canada Labour Code is a "thing in action" and therefore constitutes "property" for the purpose of the BIA. Hence, pursuant to s. 71(2), Landry's claim against her former employer would vest in the trustee on the date she declared bankruptcy and she would cease to have any capacity to deal with it. However, s. 71(2) is subject to the other provisions of the BIA.

[14] Section 67 of the BIA defines what property of a bankrupt is divisible among her creditors and can serve to restrict the ambit of s. 71(2). ...

[15] It is clear that s. 67(1)(c) is wide enough to encompass Landry's claim against her former employer and, consequently, any award of damages (other than those relating to personal claims, see fn. 1, supra) would form part of the property divisible among her creditors under that provision. A question then arises whether any part of the property falls within the exception made for exempt property under s. 67(1)(b).

2. Does any Exemption Apply Pursuant to Section 67(1)(b) so as to Except Any Part of the Property from the Estate of the Bankrupt?

[16] As provided under s. 67(1)(b), the property of the bankrupt divisible among her creditors shall not comprise any property that as against Landry is exempt from execution or seizure under the laws of Ontario. Landry relies on s. 7(2) of the Ontario *Wages Act* which provides that "80 per cent of a person's wages are exempt from seizure or garnishment." Therefore, if any part of the arbitrator's award constitutes "wages" within the meaning of s. 7(2), 80 per cent of that amount would not constitute property divisible among Landry's creditors and, hence, would not vest in the trustee.

[17] At the hearing, counsel did not seriously dispute that the case of *Wallace, supra*, provides support for the contention that the arbitrator's award of damages for unjust dismissal, in so far as it relates to lost wages, can be equated to actual wages.

[18] Wallace made a voluntary assignment into personal bankruptcy and remained an undischarged bankrupt when he commenced an action for wrongful dismissal against his former employer. A question arose whether Wallace could bring this action in his own name given the vesting provisions under s. 71(2) of the [then] *Bankruptcy Act* which, as s. 71(2) of the present BIA, provided that a bankrupt ceases to have any capacity to deal with his property.

[19] Iacobucci J, in the majority judgment (all justices were in agreement on this issue), stated (para. 58) that the wording of the Act is clear and that an undischarged

bankrupt has no capacity to deal with his or her property, including an action for breach of contract, outside the circumstances described in s. 99(1) (which circumstances are of no relevance to this appeal). The court held further that the Act made no distinction whether that property was acquired before or after the assignment in bankruptcy. However, the court went on to consider the provisions of s. 68(1) of the *Bankruptcy Act* as it then read (this is the provision which was in force at the time Landry declared bankruptcy) and concluded that it carved out an additional exception to this general rule. Section 68(1), in this earlier version, provided as follows:

> 68(1) Notwithstanding subsection 67(1), where a bankrupt
>
> (a) is in receipt of, or is entitled to receive, any money as salary, wages or other remuneration from a person employing the bankrupt …
>
> the trustee may, on the trustee's own initiative or, if directed by the inspectors or the creditors, shall, make an application to the court for an order directing the payment to the trustee of such part of the money as the court may determine, having regard to the family responsibilities and personal situation of the bankrupt.

[20] More will be said about the effect of s. 68 later in these reasons. What is of relevance to the question presently under consideration is the finding by the court that Wallace, an undischarged bankrupt, could maintain his action against his former employer for damages for wrongful dismissal not because of the timing of the acquisition of the property "but rather, because of the nature of the property in question" (para. 59) which the court equated to "wages." Iacobucci J wrote as follows (paras. 65-66):

> As I see the matter, the underlying nature of the damages awarded in a wrongful dismissal action is clearly akin to the "wages" referred to in s. 68(1). In the absence of just cause, an employer remains free to dismiss an employee at any time provided that reasonable notice of the termination is given. In providing the employee with reasonable notice, the employer has two options: either to require the employee to continue working for the duration of that period or to give the employee pay in lieu of notice: D. Harris, *Wrongful Dismissal* (1989 (loose-leaf)), at p. 3-10. There can be no doubt that if the employer opted to require the employee to continue working during the notice period, his or her earnings during this time would constitute wages or salary under s. 68(1) of the Act. The only difference between these earnings and pay in lieu of notice is that the employee receives a lump sum payment instead of having that sum spread out over the course of the notice period. The nature of those funds remains the same and thus s. 68(1) will also apply in these circumstances.
>
> In the event that an employee is wrongfully dismissed, the measure of damages for wrongful dismissal is the salary that the employee would have earned had the employee worked during the period of notice to which he or she was entitled: *Sylvester v. British Columbia*, [1997] 2 SCR 315. The fact that this sum is awarded as damages at trial in no way alters the fundamental character of the money. An award of damages in a wrongful dismissal action is in reality the wages that the employer ought to have paid the employee either over the course of the period of reasonable notice or as pay in lieu of notice. Therefore, in accordance with the exception which is carved out in s. 68(1) for "salary, wages or other remuneration," this money is not divisible among a bankrupt's creditors and does not vest in the trustee. The right of action is the means of attaining these damages and is similarly exempt.

[21] On the authority of Wallace, I conclude that, to the extent that the arbitrator's award relates to the pay Landry should have received in lieu of notice, the moneys would constitute "wages" for the purpose of the s. 67(1)(b) exception. However, what is also clear from Wallace is that s. 67 must be considered in conjunction with s. 68. This brings us to the next question.

3. Is Section 67 Superseded by the Provisions of Section 68 in Relation to a Bankrupt's Wages?

[22] Two versions of s. 68 must be taken into account: the former version under the *Bankruptcy Act* that was considered in Wallace and the current version under the BIA which will be discussed shortly. There are two reasons why both versions must be examined. The first is that the former version and its interconnection with s. 67 was considered by the Supreme Court of Canada in Wallace and in *Marzetti v. Marzetti*, [1994] 2 SCR 765 and the question arises whether the reasoning in those cases applies to the new version. The second reason is that the trustee contends that the former version is applicable to this case since it was in force at the time Landry declared bankruptcy rather than the current version which was in force at the time the motion was brought. This latter argument forms the subject-matter of the next question on this appeal and will be dealt with later. I will now deal with the interpretation of s. 68 and its interconnection with s. 67.

(a) The Former Section 68

[23] Section 68 under the *Bankruptcy Act* provided the trustee with the means to obtain part of a bankrupt's salary, wages or other remuneration from employment notwithstanding the provisions contained in s. 67(1). For our purposes, it is only necessary to consider s. 68(1) and I reproduce it again for convenience: …

[24] This provision was considered at length by the Supreme Court of Canada in *Marzetti*. The particular facts and a number of other issues in *Marzetti* are not relevant to our discussion. What is relevant to this case is the Court's consideration of the interconnection between s. 67 and s. 68. Iacobucci J, in writing for the court, set out the issue as follows (at p. 786):

> … I must determine whether s. 68 always controls the disposition of a bankrupt's wages. Is s. 68 a substantive provision, that is, one which always removes wages from the scope of s. 67, or does it simply create a procedural device for trustees?

[25] Following his analysis, he concluded as follows (at p. 794):

> To summarize briefly, it is my opinion that the language of s. 68, the inferred purpose of that provision, and the decision of this Court in *Vachon* [*v. Canada Employment and Immigration Commission*, [1985] 2 SCR 417] all support the conclusion that s. 68 is a substantive provision, one which is intended to operate as a complete code in respect of a bankrupt's salary, wages, or other remuneration. These forms of property cannot fall within s. 67(c) of the *Bankruptcy Act* as a bankrupt's after-acquired "property," and they cannot be considered "property of a bankrupt divisible among his creditors" for the purposes of s. 67. They do not vest in the trustee through the simple operation of law.

[26] Hence, the Supreme Court in *Marzetti*, and later in *Wallace*, has authoritatively determined that s. 68 supersedes the provisions of s. 67 in so far as "salary, wages or other remuneration" from employment are concerned. It follows that, if this provision is applicable to this case, the Ontario *Wages Act* does not apply and neither does any other part of s. 67. There is no automatic vesting of Landry's claim against First Air or of any part of the arbitrator's award. The trustee, and the court, must look exclusively to s. 68 to determine what part, if any, of the award will form part of the bankrupt's estate for distribution to the creditors. The question becomes, does the same interpretation apply to the current s. 68 under the BIA?

(b) Section 68 Under the BIA

[27] The current s. 68 in the BIA differs from the former version in a number of respects. The full text is appended to these reasons for ease of reference. First, the section does not refer to "salary, wages or other remuneration" but to "total income." "[T]otal income" is defined for the purpose of s. 68 as including, "notwithstanding s. 67(1)(b) and (b.1), all revenues of a bankrupt of whatever nature or source." The section still allows the trustee to apply to the court for a determination of the amount that a bankrupt is required to pay to the estate of the bankrupt out of her total income but an elaborate procedure must be followed before such an application is made. For our purposes, this procedure can be summarized as follows.

[28] First, the superintendent is directed to establish standards for determining the portion of the total income of an individual bankrupt that exceeds that which is necessary to enable the bankrupt to maintain a reasonable standard of living. Second, the trustee, having regard to these standards and to the personal and family situation of the bankrupt, must fix the amount that the bankrupt is required to pay, inform the official receiver of his decision and take reasonable measures to ensure that the bankrupt complies with the requirement to pay. Third, where the official receiver determines that the fixed amount is not in accordance with the applicable standards, the official receiver must recommend an appropriate amount. Fourth, where the trustee and the bankrupt disagree on the amount to be paid, the trustee must send to the official receiver a request that the matter be determined by mediation. A creditor can also make a request for mediation. Fifth, the mediation takes place in accordance with prescribed procedures.

[29] In addition to this procedure, an application may be made to the court under s. 68(10): ...

[30] In my view, the reasoning in *Marzetti* and *Wallace* that led to the conclusion that s. 68 was a complete code with respect to wages applies equally to this new section. The current provision applies to the "total income" of the bankrupt and, as such, is even wider than the earlier reference to "salary, wages and other remuneration"; the provision expressly excludes the application of s. 67(1)(b); its purpose is no different than that described in *Marzetti* (except that applications to the court now appear to be limited to those cases where the issue cannot be otherwise resolved); and the jurisprudential principles reviewed by the Supreme Court in *Marzetti* are equally relevant.

[31] I therefore conclude that s. 67 is superseded by the provisions of the current s. 68 in so far as the "total income" of the bankrupt is concerned. It follows that, as in *Wallace*,

Landry's claim against her former employer and any consequent award relating to lost wages do not automatically vest in the trustee under ss. 67 and 71. Resort can only be had to s. 68 for payment of any portion thereof to the estate of the bankrupt.

. . .

5. *Is the Trustee Precluded from Resorting to Section 68 After the Discharge of the Bankrupt?*

[35] The motions judge held that s. 68 was no longer available to a trustee after the discharge of a bankrupt. First, the motions judge noted that s. 68 refers to "a bankrupt" and that s. 2 defined "bankrupt" as "a person who has made an assignment or against whom a receiving order has been made or the legal status of that person." Second, the motions judge held that the section was intended to apply in the period from the assignment in bankruptcy or the receivership order until the discharge of the bankrupt. He therefore concluded that s. 68 applied to a bankrupt and not to a discharged bankrupt.

[36] In my view, this interpretation cannot be supported.

[37] First, it disregards the fact that the definition of "bankrupt" does not only refer to "the legal status of [the] person"—since Landry has been discharged, it is correct to say that she is no longer in the state of bankruptcy, but also to "a person who has made an assignment"—a description that clearly applies to Landry.

[38] Second, the motions judge erred in his interpretation of the scope of the section. Although, from a practical standpoint, s. 68 may apply more commonly to periodic wages received during the period of time between the assignment and the discharge, I see nothing in the language of the provision that restricts its application to this time frame. It is clear from *Wallace* and *Marzetti* that s. 68 applies because of the nature of the property in question, regardless of the timing of the acquisition of the property or of the fact that the payment is made in a lump sum.

[39] Third, I do not see any policy reason why, in situations such as in this case where the income is only to be received after the discharge, resort to s. 68 would nonetheless have to be made before the discharge. Indeed, given the procedure set out under s. 68, it may be impossible to resort to its provisions before payment is made or at least its quantum ascertained. Further, if resort to s. 68 were to be limited to the pre-discharge period, the trustee or the creditors would likely oppose any discharge if any payment of income was still pending at the time the bankrupt applied for a discharge. I am therefore concerned that such an interpretation would have the effect of unnecessarily postponing discharges until the full administration of the estate is completed. In cases where there is pending litigation over the payment of such income, the delay in obtaining a discharge could prove quite substantial. This result, in my view would militate against the prompt rehabilitation of the bankrupt. Finally, such an interpretation runs contrary to the established principle and practice that the trustee's obligation to realize and distribute the estate of the bankrupt continues until the trustee is discharged regardless of the prior discharge of the bankrupt: see *Re Salloum* (1990), 1 CBR (3d) 204 (BCCA).

[40] I therefore conclude that the trustee is not precluded from resorting to s. 68 by the fact that Landry has been discharged.

Appeal allowed.

NOTES AND QUESTIONS

1. Does the new definition of total income in s. 68(2) alter the result in *Landry*? What strategic behaviour on the part of bankrupts is the definition of total income trying to avoid?

2. Why did Parliament exclude from the definition of "total income" amounts received by the bankrupt between the date of the bankruptcy and the date of the discharge as a gift, a legacy, or an inheritance or as any other windfall? See s. 68(2)(b).

3. Is income earned from exempt property included within the definition of "total income"?

4. If a debtor has surplus income it will have an impact on the time period a debtor will have to wait for his or her discharge. This is discussed below under Section V, Discharge.

5. In *Cargill Ltd. v. Meyers Norris Penny Ltd.* (2008), 47 CBR (5th) 214 (Man. CA), the Manitoba Court of Appeal considered the rights of secured creditors and s. 68. In *Cargill*, a farmer executed security agreements in favour of two secured creditors. The security agreements contained after-acquired property clauses. Both secured parties perfected their security interests. The farmer subsequently made an assignment in bankruptcy. After the bankruptcy, the Canadian Agricultural Income Stabilization Program (CAIS), a federal government assistance program designed to help farmers, made a payment of $159,000 to the trustee. The Court of Appeal considered whether the secured creditors were entitled to the whole amount of the fund or whether s. 68 of the BIA applied to allow an amount for the bankrupt to maintain a reasonable standard of living.

Cargill Ltd. v. Meyers Norris Penny Ltd.
2008 MBCA 104

Against this background the judge held that "it is only after the requirements of s. 68 of [the Act] have been met that the equitable assignment of Cargill and CIBC can attach the CAIS proceeds" (at para. 54). This meant that the CAIS Money was only available to creditors of the bankrupt to the extent that the CAIS Money exceeded what was necessary for the bankrupt to maintain a reasonable standard of living.

In making this finding, it is my view, with respect, that the judge erred. It is important to keep in mind that, as argued here by the Creditors, "the rights of secured creditors are dealt with outside the confines" of the Act, except if there is specific statutory language to the contrary. This is effectively explained in The Honourable L.W. Houlden, The Honourable Geoffrey B. Morawetz & Dr. Janis P. Sarra, *The 2008 Annotated Bankruptcy and Insolvency Act* (Toronto: Carswell, 2007) at 630: "Where a debtor has made an assignment ... the policy of the Act is not to interfere with secured creditors except insofar as may be necessary to protect the estate as to any surplus in the assets covered by the security ... ." Once the CAIS Money was in the hands of the Trustee, it was presumptively captured by the security agreements, unless some statutory or other governing provision clearly negated that result.

Section 68 is intended to assist the trustee in accessing the bankrupt's wages for the benefit of the estate's creditors; ... there is no indication in the legislation that s. 68 was intended to alter the position of secured creditors *vis-à-vis* the bankrupt. Section 69.3(2) states that the position of secured creditors is not altered by the bankruptcy of the debtor and ss. 71 and 136(1) confirm the priority granted to secured creditors by the bankruptcy regime. ...

Marzetti did not involve the rights of a secured creditor. None of the other cases cited in relation to this issue involved the rights of secured creditors. Section 68 of the Act does not limit or restrict a secured creditor's interest in a bankrupt's assets which, by that section, are characterized as "total income." The Trustee is, of course, limited and restricted by the provisions of s. 68, and it must apply distributable funds in accordance with that section, but funds in the Trustee's hands to which a secured creditor has a supervening right cannot fall within that category.

In my opinion, the law is clear that, unless otherwise expressly provided in the Act or another governing provision, to quote again from Houlden, Morawetz & Sarra, "secured creditors may ignore the bankruptcy and deal with their security in the usual manner" (at p. 630) (*Federal Business Development Bank v. Quebec (Commission de la santé et de la sécurité du travail)*, [1988] 1 SCR 1061). This is so even though the monies in question have been realized through the efforts of the Trustee.

The general scheme of distribution under the Act (s. 136(1)) is stated to be "[s]ubject to the rights of secured creditors." Moreover, while there are a few sections in the Act which provide that particular provisions apply to secured creditors (see, e.g., s. 69.3(2), among others), none have been identified here that could defeat the present claims of the Creditors.

I will add that, in my opinion, Menzies J went a little too far in *Lintott v. Bank of Montreal*, 2004 MBQB 214, 188 Man. R (2d) 228, when he said that "[s]ection 68 is a complete code for determining what if any portion of a bankrupt's total income will be made available for distribution among creditors whether secured or not" (at para. 25). As indicated, the rights of secured creditors are not impaired by bankruptcy unless expressly so provided in legislation, and s. 68 does not so provide.

To summarize, nothing has been pointed out, in the Act or elsewhere, that could adversely affect and limit the rights of the Creditors to claim the CAIS Money under their admittedly valid and perfected security agreements. Absent explicit legislative provisions ... the interests of secured creditors prevail over those of a bankruptcy trustee, even with respect to the income of the bankrupt. ... [I]t follows that the Creditors prevail over the Trustee, as s. 68 has no application to them. This is not to say that payments from CAIS may not form part of a bankrupt's "total income" for the purposes of s. 68, but that question does not arise in this case, as s. 68 has no application to the Creditors here.

Accordingly, I would hold that the rights and interests of the Creditors by virtue of their security agreements apply to the CAIS Money without reduction as a result of the application of s. 68 of the Act, and in this respect I would allow the cross-appeal.

NOTE

If *Cargill* is rightly decided, bankrupts will be at the mercy of whatever provincial legislation there may be restricting or invalidating assignment of wages and other earnings. Is this consistent with the policy of BIA s. 68? Should BIA s. 67 be amended to impose restrictions on the validity of security interests affecting an individual debtor's income without waiting for provincial initiatives? (Note that the provincial PPSAs have a provision outlawing after-acquired property clauses in consumer contexts. See, for example, Ontario PPSA s. 12(2)(b). Does the PPSA provision go far enough in this context?)

NOTE ON THE US MEANS TEST

**Charles J. Tabb, "Consumer Bankruptcy After the Fall:
United States Law Under Section 256"**
(2006), 43 *CBLJ* 28 (footnotes omitted)

On October 17, 2005, a new era came to pass in the history of the United States consumer bankruptcy laws, as s. 256, the *Bankruptcy Abuse Prevention and Consumer Protection Act* of 2005, took effect. Signed into law by President George W. Bush on April 20, 2005, s. 256 marks a retrenchment from a history of substantial bankruptcy protection for consumer debtors in the United States, and hails a long sought legislative victory for the consumer credit industry. Indeed, the credit industry had vigorously attempted to reverse the pro-debtor thrust of the United States consumer bankruptcy law almost from the time the ink was dry on the *Bankruptcy Reform Act* of 1978.

The heart of the retrenchment is the enactment of a "means test" for consumer debtors. That test serves as a gate-keeping device to bar consumer debtors from immediate discharge of debts in a chapter 7 straight liquidation bankruptcy, if they have the supposed "means" to pay a small amount of their debts to unsecured creditors in a chapter 13 payment plan.

. . .

Section 256 dramatically reshapes the United States consumer bankruptcy laws in favor of financial institutions and to the detriment of needy individual debtors. For many debtors the promise of a financial "fresh start" in life that the United States bankruptcy law has offered for over a century has become, as I once wrote, a "cruel and ephemeral illusion."

. . .

Debtors whose income exceeds allowed expenses by a certain amount are deemed to have the "means" to repay their creditors. The idea is to "requir[e] bankrupts to repay their debts when they have the ability to do so." A debtor who fails the means test will be dismissed from chapter 7, thus leaving a chapter 13 repayment plan as the debtor's only remaining bankruptcy alternative.

. . .

The long battle is over. The well-funded creditor lobby won. Individual consumer debtors lost. The consumer bankruptcy regime in the United States has now become much more like that in much of the rest of the world. That might not be so objectionable, but the United States otherwise has a very limited social welfare system. For good or ill, for over a century the de facto system in the States was to utilize consumer bankruptcy as a back-stop social safety net, in lieu of meaningful social welfare. Now we may have the worst of both worlds—little social welfare, and weakened bankruptcy protection.

NOTE

For a comparative examination of the American means test legislation and the Canadian surplus income regime see Stephanie Ben-Ishai, "Means-Testing" in Stephanie Ben-Ishai and Anthony Duggan, *Canadian Bankruptcy and Insolvency Law: Bill C-55, Statute c. 47 and Beyond* (Markham, ON: LexisNexis, 2007), 344.

V. DISCHARGE

A. The Canadian Discharge Regime

The question whether individual bankrupts should be entitled to a discharge from their debts after they have gone into bankruptcy and surrendered their non-exempt property was a heated topic for debate throughout much of the 19th century in the United States, England, and Canada. In England and Canada, the debate only affected traders and merchants because, for the most part, the legislation only applied to them. In the United States, the critical turning point came with the adoption of the 1898 *Bankruptcy Act*, which provided for an unconditional discharge for all individual debtors with the exception of non-dischargeable debts. The British *Bankruptcy Act 1883* also applied to all types of individuals but creditors were entitled to oppose the discharge and the judge was given a broad discretion to grant or refuse the application or to grant it conditionally and on terms.

It was the British model that was adopted in the Canadian Act of 1919. The US fresh-start model was rejected because of its laxity, which one critic described as a "sort of constant jubilee." The essential features of the 1919 Act were the following. The debtor could apply for a discharge at any time. When he did, the court had complete discretion in dealing with the application unless the debtor had committed an offence or had otherwise misconducted himself, or if the realizable assets were worth less than 50 cents on the dollar. If these restrictions did not apply, the court could grant or refuse the discharge, suspend the discharge, or make a conditional discharge order linked to the debtor's future earnings or the debtor's income or after-acquired property. The court had to refuse the application or suspend it for two years if the debtor had committed a bankruptcy offence.

The 1949 Act introduced an important procedural change in deeming the bankrupt to have made a discharge application no earlier than 3 months after the bankruptcy order and no later than 12 months. In the case of a first-time individual bankrupt, the 1992 amendments simplified the procedure still further in deeming the application to be made 9 months from the date of the bankruptcy order unless the debtor had waived this entitlement.

From the beginning, a discharge application was accompanied by a report from the trustee about the debtor's conduct and the factors leading to the debtor's bankruptcy. The 1997 amendments retained this requirement and tightened it substantially. The trustee is now also required to report on (1) whether the debtor had made the required surplus income payments and (2) whether the debtor could have made a viable proposal, as well as to provide the court with the trustee's own recommendations. In setting up this seemingly complex discharge structure, the federal Parliament was obviously striving to strike a balance between enabling a "poor and unfortunate" Canadian debtor to make a fresh start and sending a strong signal to debtors that debts could not be sloughed off easily regardless of the debtor's financial circumstances, past conduct, and capacity to make future payments.

Nevertheless, on paper at least, the provisions are heavily creditor-oriented and retain a 19th century anti-discharge bias.

The application of these provisions in practice has been very different and tells a markedly different story about the universe of overcommitted debtors seeking relief from the burden of debt. For many years, between 80 and 90 percent of discharge applications involved no-asset cases and an absolute or automatic discharge was granted in the great majority of cases. For example, in 1998, out of a total of 83,431 discharge applications, 79,999 (96 percent) involved summary estates and 3,432 involved regular estates. Of the combined cases, 60,178 (72.1 percent) resulted in an automatic discharge; 17,736 (21 percent) were given an absolute discharge and 5,480 (6.5 percent) a suspended discharge. Only 14 received a conditional discharge (0.0016 percent) and only 4 applications were refused. By way of comparison, Prof. Ramsay reports the following results from 1,118 discharge applications in his sample of 1994 bankrupts. 85.4 percent were unopposed. Of those who opposed the application, 5.7 percent were creditors, 8.6 percent were trustees, and 0.3 percent came from the Office of the Superintendent of Bankruptcy. Apparently, most of the trustees' opposition related to non-payment of the trustee's fee and expenses or the debtor's failure to complete the mandatory counselling sessions. Commercial creditors rarely file an opposition to the application. It is notable that more recent comprehensive statistics on discharge are currently unavailable but would be the subject of a worthwhile future empirical study. The OSB currently keeps data only on the number of estates that are closed each year. In 2007, 95,325 bankruptcy estates were closed (including business and personal). By way of context, there were 86,103 bankruptcy filings (79,796 personal and 6,307 business) in the same year.

Thomas G.W. Telfer, "The Canadian Bankruptcy Act of 1919: Public Legislation or Private Interests?"
(1995), 24 *CBLJ* 357, at 393 (footnotes omitted)

The federal government passed the *Bankruptcy Act, 1919* after an almost 40-year absence from legislating in the field of bankruptcy law. Parliament first debated the legislation in 1918 and, after extensive committee hearings, the government introduced the bill the following year. While the Act of 1919 marked a new beginning for federal government involvement in bankruptcy matters, the law did not originate in the cabinet meeting room or with the civil service. Like its predecessors, the bankruptcy bill of 1919 was the product of private initiative, drafted by a member of the Manitoba Bar, H.P. Grundy, on behalf of his clients, the Canadian Credit Men's Trust Association. However, unlike the numerous private bills of the 1880's, the government adopted Grundy's bill as a framework for the *Bankruptcy Act, 1919*.

Several factors explained the success of this bill. First, provincial laws did not adequately deal with debtors. With the repeal of federal insolvency legislation in 1880, the provinces attempted to regulate the field of bankruptcy and insolvency. However, the defects in the provincial laws, including their lack of uniformity, became more glaring as inter-provincial trade increased. Demands for a national discharge, compulsory assignments, regulated composition agreements and a uniform federal law emerged as a result of the inadequate provincial legislation.

These demands coincided with the downturn in the economy just prior to the First World War and the economic uncertainty caused by the war. The growth of new national lobby groups, such as the Canadian Bar Association (CBA) and the Canadian Credit Men's Trust Association (CCMTA), gave a national voice to some of those advocating new legislation. Additionally, advocates of reform were able to point to bankruptcy legislation in other countries. In 1919, Canada was at last joining other commercial nations, such as England and the United States, in regulating debtor-creditor relations through a national bankruptcy act.

The *Bankruptcy Act, 1919*, contained several important provisions that were a marked improvement on the provincial legislation. In addition to creating uniformity, it granted debtors a right of discharge, and created a formal composition proceeding that allowed debtors to bind minority creditors through a court order. Neither of these features existed under provincial law. The Act also continued a debtor's ability to make a voluntary assignment.

However, the *Bankruptcy Act* was not enacted at the request of debtors and should not be viewed as pro-debtor legislation. The Act was drafted on behalf of and in the interests of a group representing both creditors and organizations which acted in liquidating debtors' assets under provincial legislation. Therefore, the provisions of the Act should not be analyzed in terms of the protection afforded debtors but rather in terms of how it maintained the rights of creditors.

In drafting the legislation, the lawyer representing the CCMTA sought to remedy the defects of the provincial law from a creditor perspective. The Act allowed creditors to petition debtors into bankruptcy, and the discharge provisions followed the conservative English model that focused on debtor conduct. The discharge released individuals from the burden of debt and returned them to the community of borrowers. Further, statutory regulation of discharges served the public interest as well as creditors' interests by protecting the community from dishonest debtors. Creditors acting individually had not been able to monitor debtor conduct effectively under the provincial regimes.

In addition, the drafter of the bill desired to retain certain elements of the provincial assignment Acts that had been of benefit to his clients. Grundy, in drafting the provisions on the administration of debtors' estates, rejected the court-supervised model found in the English and American systems. In some aspects, he followed the model of the provincial assignments Acts on the basis of lower court costs and greater control by trustees in the administration of estates. Therefore, debate over bankruptcy reform not only included a desire for change but also an attempt to maintain some elements of the status quo in favour of creditors.

B. The Theory of the Bankruptcy Discharge

1. Why should there be a right of discharge? The traditional argument in favour of the discharge is that it causes debtors to work more after bankruptcy: if debtors had to pay all or part of their future earnings to creditors, they would have less incentive to work: *Local Loan Co. v. Hunt*, 202 US 234 (1934). An additional compelling argument, supported by Thomas Jackson, is that the discharge encourages debtors to take risks and fuel market activity. (See Thomas Jackson, *The Logic and Limits of Bankruptcy Law* (Washington, DC:

Beard Books, 2001). It does so by offering a form of consumption insurance—if a debtor has a financial reversal, she loses her non-exempt assets and income but the rest of her personal wealth, including her human capital is protected. The discharge shifts the risk of bad spending decisions from the debtor to her creditors. This shift is justified by the fact that creditors are more likely to be repeat players in the market for credit and, accordingly, in a better position to assess the debtor's risk. Further, creditors are better able to limit their risk by diversifying—that is, by lending to numerous debtors.

2. *Why is the discharge non-waivable?* Why can't individual debtors and creditors agree that the discharge will not apply to their agreement and reduce the cost of credit to the debtor accordingly? The primary answer comes from behavioral economics:

- A waiver may make the debtor's family worse off because its members bear most of the cost, but the debtor may not take his family's welfare sufficiently into account when he decides to give a waiver.

- Debtors may underestimate the probability of a financial reversal and thus give a waiver even when it is against their self-interest (incomplete heuristics argument).

In addition, various externalities may be created by allowing individual debtors and creditors to waive the discharge:

- If the debtor cannot discharge her debts, she has less incentive to work; thus, if waivers were allowed, there might be social costs in the form of reduced productivity.

- Prohibiting waivers benefits the government itself. The discharge is a partial substitute for social welfare programs; if waivers were allowed, the government might have to spend more on social welfare.

3. *Why isn't the discharge free?* The discharge is not free. In return for the discharge, the debtor has to give up his non-exempt assets and also a portion of his future earnings (to the extent BIA s. 68 requires). There is also a second-order cost: by using bankruptcy to obtain a discharge, the debtor sends out a negative signal about her creditworthiness and this may affect her access to credit in future. Given the benefits of the discharge, why not make it free—in other words, give the debtor a discharge without requiring her to surrender assets or income? According to Jackson (at 250), the answer is that "the availability of the discharge presents a cost as well as a benefit to the individual debtor: the more readily available the benefit, the higher the cost of credit."

Re McAfee
(1998), 49 DLR (4th) 401 (BCCA)

LOCKE JA (for the Court):

. . .

This appeal concerns the principles to be applied on an application to discharge a bankrupt, and considers some of the factors to be taken into account in setting a condition.

The chambers judge imposed as a condition of discharge that the bankrupt consent to a judgment for $40,000. Westmore, a principal creditor, opposed the discharge, and now appeals, arguing that this is inequitable under the circumstances and is not enough. Broadly, the grounds for appeal are that the chambers judge erred in law and misconstrued relevant facts when he held that the bankrupt was blameless in relation to his financial problems, and conducted himself properly during bankruptcy; and in particular failed to give due weight to the bankrupt's present and future large income.

• • •

The respondent, John A. McAfee, practised law in Kelowna, BC but has always engaged in business. From the mid-1970s up until the spring of 1982, he controlled and operated a company called Old MacDonald's Farms Ltd. ("MacDonalds") in the Okanagan which operated a children's amusement park. In the spring of 1982 the facility was sold to third parties for $1,500,000.

In 1978 he and others promoted a large amusement park development in Calgary known as "Calaway Park." The land was purchased, approvals were obtained and construction started in the spring of 1981 and opened in the summer of 1982. It was a financial disaster and all investors lost their equity. The Bank of America, the Northland Bank and the Royal Bank of Canada were all involved in financing this venture; with the collapse of the real estate market the loans were called and in November of 1982 McAfee was on a guarantee for $17.5 million. He entered into negotiations to attempt to resolve his liability and managed to restructure the liability and settled it by liquidating some major assets but lost something more than half of his net worth, which in 1980 he estimated at near $4 million.

The appellant, Hilton H. Westmore, through his company Enchant Resources Ltd. ("Enchant"), on January 15, 1978, bought 20 shares of the capital stock of MacDonald's and advanced $144,000 to it by way of a shareholder loan. On April 30, 1980, the parties entered into two agreements, which in substance provided for the repurchase by McAfee of Westmore's shares by paying out the shareholders' loan, together with an immediate cash payment. The first payment under these agreements was to be made on September 30, 1983. On April 1, 1982, the company sold its assets for $1.5 million. Because McAfee believed that Westmore, by virtue of the agreements, had ceased to be a shareholder of the company and that Enchant was otherwise adequately secured, he caused his company to engage in certain corporate manoeuvres which had the effect of seeing that large cash payments were made by way of dividend to himself and used by him to pay off guarantees to various banks. In giving judgment in the action, *Westmore v. Old MacDonald's Farms Ltd.* (1986), 70 BCLR 332, in an action brought by Westmore to enforce payment of the money due under the agreements of 1980, Macdonald J concluded two things: first, the transactions involved had been unfairly prejudicial and oppressive to Westmore, but second, that McAfee was under the mistaken but honest belief that Westmore had ceased to be a shareholder of the company. In the result, a claim for breach of fiduciary duties was dismissed but judgment to complete the sale in the sum of $300,000 was given against McAfee, his wife Brenda McAfee and his private company, McAfee Enterprises Inc.

When MacDonald's was sold, McAfee took back as part of the purchase price, a debenture of $550,000 payable to him and the purchasers defaulted. He repurchased the enterprise in 1983 as described, but it continued to lose money and, on November 28, 1985, the Northland Bank who had assisted in the purchase demanded payment in full of the debt of MacDonald's in the sum of $897,132.72, guaranteed personally by McAfee. On January 14, 1986, just prior to the Westmore action hearing, McAfee negotiated a settlement with the bank whereby he was released from this guarantee in return for the grant of a second mortgage in favour of the bank in the sum of $85,000 over his residence in Kelowna.

After the judgment was obtained and up until July, 1986, McAfee negotiated with Westmore with regard to his large liability to Westmore but Westmore was furious and would not entertain any of the comparatively small settlement proposals and demanded payment of the full amount. At the same time, Revenue Canada advanced a claim of nearly a quarter of a million dollars, some of the liability arising from non-payment of tax on the MacDonald's dividends.

In the meantime, McAfee had gone back to practising law in earnest in Kelowna. Westmore had threatened to levy execution and McAfee went to the Law Society and disclosed his financial position, received some assurances that he would be able to continue practice, and ultimately on July 31st, executed an assignment for the general benefit of creditors. On November 5, 1986, a proposal in bankruptcy made by Brenda McAfee was rejected by her creditor (Westmore) and, pursuant to s. 39 of the *Bankruptcy Act*, RSC 1970, c. B-3, she was thereupon deemed to have made an assignment on that same day.

Nine months later, on March 27, 1987, McAfee petitioned the court for an order of discharge.

. . .

McAfee filed his business records which disclosed his violent irregularities in income but he estimated his net income for the year ending October, 1987, at about $100,000. The chambers judge had the advantage of hearing the respondent examined and cross-examined in open court. Westmore's counsel submitted the offer of $12,000 was wholly inadequate and suggested $200,000 as more appropriate. Following this, the chambers judge reserved and when he gave his judgment next day he made two important findings:

1. For the most part McAfee had conducted himself properly and should not be criticized because bad economic times and poor judgment brought about his financial collapse.
2. The fact that no moneys were paid to the trustee since the declaration of bankruptcy in August, 1986, was a proper matter to take into account in settling any terms or conditions for discharge in view of the fact that he was able to earn a substantial income at the present time and into the future.

He then ordered the respondent to enter into a consent judgment for $40,000 as a condition of discharge.

. . .

The trustee is to give his opinion in the statutory report and s. 140(5) states that the report is evidence of the statements therein contained. It is to be noticed that there is a difference in the burden of proof as to s. 143(1)(a) and the remaining 12 subsections. As to this, an important point was settled by the Quebec Court of Appeal in *Samson v. L'Alliance Nationale* (1935), 60 Que. KB 311 at p. 317, 17 CBR 304, under slightly different wording, where Mr. Justice Barclay said:

Under section 141(8), for the purposes of this section 143a, the report of the trustees shall be prima facie evidence of the statements therein contained.

This report of the trustees cannot be disregarded. As was said in *Re Gorman* (1922), 2 CBR 454, the trade creditors who oppose the application must

> show conclusively some misconduct or impropriety on the part of the bankrupt other than what is to be inferred from the small dividend paid, before they are in a position to contend effectively against his discharge.

> There is, therefore, prima facie evidence contained in the trustees' report which shifts the onus of proof to the opposing creditor.

> . . .

Most of the principles of law governing the discharge of a bankrupt are found in *Links v. Robinson* (1971), 16 CBR (NS) 180. These were adopted by this court in *Patterson v. Royal Bank of Canada* (1984), 57 CBR (NS) 6, and in *Re Markel* [(1986), 63 CBR (NS) 7 (BCCA)]. Underlying principles were also put succinctly by Hutcheon JA in *Re Marshall* [(1986), 62 CBR (NS) 118 (BCCA)], where he said: "On that point it would seem to me that the judge in bankruptcy must consider two principles: the first is that of the rehabilitation of the bankrupt, and the second is that of the integrity of the bankruptcy system ..."

I would wish to adopt, without referring to the authorities other than *Re Posner* (1960), 3 CBR (NS) 49, a statement of Anderson J in *Re Raftis* (1984), 53 CBR (NS) 19 at pp. 22-3, where he gave a compendious expression of the sometimes conflicting principles of discharge extracted from the cases:

> 1. In considering the question of discharge, the Court must have regard not only to the interests of the bankrupt and his creditors, but also to the interests of the public ...
>
> 2. The Legislature has always recognized the interest that the State has in a debtor being released from the overwhelming pressure of his debts, and that it is undesirable that a citizen should be so weighed down by his debts as to be incapable of performing the ordinary duties of citizenship ...
>
> 3. One of the objects of the *Bankruptcy Act* was to enable an honest debtor, who had been unfortunate in business, to secure a discharge so he might make a new start ...
>
> 4. The bankruptcy courts should not be converted into a sort of clearing-house for the liquidation of debts irrespective of the circumstances under which they were created ...
>
> 5. The success or failure of any bankruptcy system depends upon the administration of the discharge provisions of the Act ...
>
> 6. The Court is not to be regarded as a sort of charitable institution ...
>
> 7. It is incumbent upon the Court to guard against laxity in granting discharges so as not to offend against commercial morality. It is nevertheless the duty of the Court to administer the *Bankruptcy Act* in such a way as to assist honest debtors who have been unfortunate ...
>
> 8. The discharge is not a matter of right ...

These principles impose upon a judge the obligation of considering and balancing the interests of the bankrupt, of the creditors and of the public.

When Westmore opposed the discharge he took the following grounds as I appreciate them:

1. that the primary reason the bankrupt made an assignment was to avoid the consequences of the Westmore judgment;

2. that the respondent's conduct before and after bankruptcy should have been subject to censure;

3. that the court in making its order failed to consider the respondent's extravagant style of living during bankruptcy, but, of more importance, the fact that he was continuing his practice as a lawyer with some substantial assurance of future income.

The first ground was that the order for discharge should have been refused because the financial situation of the respondent did not arise from circumstances for which he could not justly be held responsible, i.e., he was culpably responsible for his own condition.

The trustee stated that he:

> ... does not believe that the bankrupt can be held responsible for his insolvency, which appears to have arisen from guarantees of corporate debts ... Mr. McAfee executed a settlement agreement with the Northland Bank reducing this debt from $897,000 to $85,000 based on the assumption that this debt was the last of his onerous financial problems. Subsequently the court found him liable as guarantor of loans by Enchant Resources Ltd. to Old Macdonald's Farms of some $335,000. He could not meet this obligation and was forced to consider bankruptcy. For these reasons, the trustee does not believe the bankrupt can be held responsible for his insolvency ...

This is a pretty sketchy and not wholly accurate account of the causes of the bankruptcy, as it was conceded by the respondent that the debts to the appellant and to Revenue Canada—his principal liabilities—did not arise from guarantees at all.

The argument rests upon *Kozack v. Richter*, [1974] SCR 832, where Pigeon J for the court, where the debt had arisen from a judgment for damages arising out of grossly negligent driving, said [at 615]:

> In the present case, the respondent's bankruptcy was precipitated by his condemnation to pay damages to the appellant. This being due to a finding of "wilful and wanton misconduct" on his part, certainly his financial predicament cannot be said to have arisen "from circumstances for which he cannot justly be held responsible"

and in those circumstances the court declined to make an order of discharge.

. . .

I cannot find here anything other than a superficial resemblance between the case at bar and *Kozack*. McAfee swore he arranged to satisfy his outstanding liabilities as far as he could so that he could in the end avoid bankruptcy. The trial judge accepted this, and from my independent review of the facts I see no ground for disturbing his conclusion.

However, this is not to say that the facts are to be forgotten in the exercise of a discretion.

. . .

The authorities above are all examples of the court examining widely varying patterns and endeavouring to balance the three interested parties of bankrupt, creditor and public. In the circumstances displayed in *Markel* the discharge was originally granted on a $40,000 condition. In *Raftis* the balance was struck at $60,000; In *Harley*, BCCA February 11, 1986 (unreported), $100,000 was ordered; and in *Atkin* [*Re* (1987), 65 CBR (NS) 296 (Ont. SC)] $150,000 was deemed to be fair. No one formula will do.

Here the bankrupt discharged the onus he has of establishing that his assets had not diminished through his own culpability. However, McAfee did not, as did Markel, make any substantial effort after the assignment to make any payments to anybody out of his income; all of his efforts were devoted to preserve his own assets and himself. This is not a bankruptcy offence, but is a factor. A monthly income in excess of the Superintendent's guidelines by $50,000 a year must surely be considered, and the style of living which he continues is appropriate to a wealthy man, but the appearance of wealth is not essential to enable one to successfully practise law. I think on principle that appropriate appearances ought to be maintainable. But in view of the past and the future, I think that more than a modest living standard is inappropriate. The fact that children go to university or to private school is desirable and acknowledged by every parent, but life sometimes does not permit it. There are other schools, and there are student loans.

I would not venture to alter the chamber judge's assessment of all the factors did I not deem it a matter of degree. I have had the advantage of considering a long argument and many authorities not quoted to him. When I look at this application for discharge I see a man who has met many misfortunes but at the same time he is now rid of half a million dollars of liability. It appears to me he has a future. In view of the authorities and the facts in this case, I would set as an appropriate condition, a consent to judgment in the sum of $80,000 plus the taxed costs of this appeal. I would further wish to adopt a procedure mentioned in some of the Ontario cases to which I have referred: rather than set a timetable and an amount per month or per year, I would leave it to the discretion of the trustee to set an appropriate schedule of payments, with an acceleration clause on default, and I would direct that as this will lengthen the term of his engagement the trustee should be appropriately remunerated by McAfee, and that there be liberty to apply to this court if the details cannot be satisfactorily arranged. McAfee therefore stands absolutely discharged subject to consenting to an appropriate form of judgment.

. . .

Appeal allowed in part.

C. The 2007 Amendments

The 2007 amendments impact three components of the bankruptcy discharge: (1) automatic discharge; (2) creditors' participation and pay-out; and (3) bankrupts with high income tax debt.

1. Automatic Discharge. Building on the recommendations in the PITF Report and the 2003 Senate Report, the 2007 reforms increase the availability of the automatic discharge while, at the same time, increasing for some debtors the period before eligibility for an automatic discharge. Bankrupts with surplus income will no longer be eligible for the automatic discharge after 9 months. Rather, they will be required to wait for the expiration of a 21-month period while continuing to make surplus income payments to the trustee. In addition, there will be an automatic discharge for second-time bankrupts who do not have surplus income following the expiration of a 24-month period. Where a second-time bankrupt has surplus income, the automatic discharge will be available following the expiration of a 36-month period, during which the bankrupt must make surplus income payments to the trustee: see BIA s. 168.1.

2. Creditors' Participation and Pay-Out. Both the PITF and Senate reports proposed measures to increase the participation of creditors in the bankruptcy process. The 2007 reforms seek to implement these recommendations. They provide for a party opposing the discharge to submit evidence orally under oath, by affidavit or otherwise. See BIA s. 172(2).

3. Bankrupts with High Income Tax Debt. The 2007 reforms provide that bankrupts with more than $200,000 (including principal, interest, and penalties) in personal income tax debt (federal and/or provincial) representing 75 percent or more of their total unsecured debts will not be eligible for an automatic discharge and an application for discharge will be required. For a first- and second-time bankrupt, the timing of the automatic discharge (including the new timing for surplus income payers) dictates the first time that an application for discharge may be made. Where a bankrupt has been bankrupt on more than two other occasions, the hearing may not be held until 36 months have expired.

On an application for discharge, the court cannot grant an absolute discharge for bankrupts that fall under the section: see BIA s. 172.1(1). A court may refuse the discharge, suspend the discharge, or provide a conditional discharge. The onus is on the bankrupt to justify the relief that is requested. The statute directs the court to consider the following factors: (1) the bankrupt's circumstances at the time the personal income tax debt was incurred; (2) the efforts made by the bankrupt to pay the personal income tax; (3) whether the bankrupt paid other debts while failing to make reasonable efforts to pay the personal income tax debt; and (4) the bankrupt's financial prospects for the future. The court may modify the discharge order after one year: see BIA s. 172.1.

For a critical analysis of these reforms and the argument that they have the potential to entrench the "deviant-debtor" construct in Canada's consumer bankruptcy system, thus positioning bankruptcy law as a response to deviant behaviour, see Stephanie Ben-Ishai, "Discharge," in Ben-Ishai and Duggan, above, at 357.

D. Non-Dischargeable Debts and Liabilities

A general principle behind consumer bankruptcy in Canada is that, following discharge from bankruptcy, an individual is free from her debts and, at the same time, she retains her experiences, knowledge, and values, which can contribute to her becoming a productive member of society again and provide her with a fresh start. Recognizing that not all individuals who attempt to make use of the bankruptcy process are honest but unfortunate debtors with the types of debts for which it is intended, a number of exceptions to the fresh start are provided for under existing legislation: see BIA s. 178. These exceptions are in addition to BIA s. 173, which confers broad discretion on courts to attach conditions to discharge and to deny it entirely if objection is raised to the discharge. It is important to note that the exceptions from discharge cover much more than dishonest or criminal conduct by the bankrupt. Canada is not alone in making various types of debts and liabilities non-dischargeable, and the list varies from jurisdiction to jurisdiction. In recent history, a common form of debt found in the list is student loans. A consideration of this exception to the discharge provides a good vehicle for better understanding the theory behind the discharge and is also a significant issue in bankruptcy policy. The following excerpt highlights a number of the key issues.

Stephanie Ben-Ishai, "Government Student Loans, Government Debts and Bankruptcy: A Comparative Study"
(2007), 44 *CBLJ* 211, at 212-14 and 221-24 (footnotes omitted)

Policy makers, post-secondary educational institutions, student groups and the media project an increase in the number and the value of loans for post-secondary education funded by the federal and provincial governments in Canada. Given this projection and calls for reform to the treatment of these loans in bankruptcy, this article provides a comprehensive review of the treatment of government-funded student loans in bankruptcy in Canada. Recognizing that a number of other jurisdictions have recently considered the issue and enacted reforms, this article considers the treatment in bankruptcy of loans funded by the government for a post-secondary education in a comparative context.

· · ·

A review of the current position and historical trajectory of the treatment of government student loans in bankruptcy in Canada, Australia, England, the United States and New Zealand suggests that all five jurisdictions are converging on a model where the bankruptcy system provides limited to no relief for loans transacted under a program funded or guaranteed by a government unit to fund a post-secondary education. This article argues that the two key justifications relied upon to justify this model—student abuse of the bankruptcy process and the need to protect the public interest—should be put to rest as they are unsubstantiated. The evidence from Canada and from all of the other jurisdictions under review demonstrates that students are not abusing the bankruptcy process. The evidence also demonstrates that, with the exception of the United States, government-funded student loans are the only government debts that are excepted from the bankruptcy discharge. This is in opposition to the trend in every jurisdiction under review to remove the special treatment previously accorded to Crown debts. Further, given the growth of securitization markets for student loans, the special treatment for government-funded student loans in bankruptcy that is justified as protecting the public interest is in fact being sold to private investors.

Following from the argument for dispensing with the justifications for the current exception to the bankruptcy discharge for government-funded student loans, this article does not advocate tweaking the waiting period for the exception to discharge for government-funded student loans. Rather, reform efforts should be directed at the substantive and procedural aspects of the exception. The process for making decisions about these features must be informed by empirical data. Adopting this approach, the article suggests that the current exception to discharge for government-funded student loans in Canada should be abolished. The current system, which places the onus on the bankrupt to apply to the court and demonstrate good faith and financial hardship, is ineffective due to procedural obstacles relating to the onus and substantive obstacles relating to the role of bankruptcy registrars. The onus should be placed on the government to oppose a discharge where the bankrupt has not experienced financial hardship in repaying government-funded student loans and/or where there is evidence of bad faith.

· · ·

A central facet of the Canadian consumer bankruptcy system in its current form is an individual's right to a "fresh start" provided by the bankruptcy discharge. Following bankruptcy an individual is free from most of her debts and at the same time retains her experiences, knowledge and values, often referred to as human capital, which can contribute to her becoming a productive member of society again. However, a number of exceptions to the bankruptcy discharge are provided for under existing legislation. These exceptions apply to both bankruptcies and consumer proposals under the *Bankruptcy and Insolvency Act* [BIA]. While a literature has developed around the justifications for a mandatory, or non-waivable, bankruptcy discharge, a comprehensive normative theory of the appropriate scope of the discharge and accompanying exceptions has eluded commentators for some time. A common explanation for this list of exceptions is that they all concern fraud or similar misbehavior against creditors and excluding these categories of bankrupts from discharge is intended to deter this conduct. However, the list excludes a large number of "wrongdoers," such as bankrupts who have committed torts other than the three that are identified by the Act. In particular, bankrupts who owe tax and non-tax debts to the government, such as unemployment insurance overpayments or small business loans, are not included on the list. There is no obvious rationale for this list of debts.

Government Student Loans are found on the existing list of exceptions to discharge. The inclusion of Government Student Loans was justified on the basis that without the exception to discharge, a significant number of students were blatantly manipulating the bankruptcy system by finishing their post-secondary studies, and then going bankrupt to erase their Government Student Loans before profiting from professions such as law or medicine.

· · ·

The status of Government Student Loans in bankruptcy also received significant attention in the two recent Canadian government reports on bankruptcy: the Personal Insolvency Task Force Report published in December 2002 and the Senate Report published in November 2003. Both reports advocated reforms to address the current exception to the bankruptcy discharge for Government Student Loans, which provides for limited relief on financial hardship grounds, on an all-or-nothing basis, following a costly court application that is only possible 10 years after the bankrupt or former bankrupt has ceased to be a full- or part-time student. Both reports referenced empirical data that detailed the dire financial circumstances of bankrupts with student loans relative to those without student loans and demonstrated that such bankrupts were generally not high-income professionals attempting to defraud the system. Further, the reports indicated that the existing legislation was ill-equipped to address intervening life events such as illness, disability and family breakdown which often accounted for unpaid Government Student Loans and warranted a fresh start. To this end, both reports recommended that the exception to discharge for Government Student Loans should be amended to apply only to situations where it had been less than five years since the bankrupt completed full- or part-time studies that the loans had funded. As well, both reports recommended that courts be provided with the discretion to confirm the discharge of all or a portion of a Government Student Loan before the five-year period had lapsed, in cases where the bankrupt could establish that the burden of maintaining the liability for some or all of the debt would result in financial hardship.

The 10-year exception to discharge has also been met with a great deal of criticism by bankruptcy trustees and student groups. Bankruptcy trustees, concerned with the impact the 10-year exception has on their ability to come up with a reasonable solution to debtors' financial distress, have criticized the exception as unduly harsh. Student groups supported what was ultimately an unsuccessful legal action to challenge the exception under the equality provisions of the *Canadian Charter of Rights and Freedoms*.

In the last year, two bills have been introduced that attempt to vary the timing of the exception to discharge for Government Student Loans. On October 20, 2004, Alexa McDonough (Halifax, NDP) introduced Bill C-236, which would have amended the BIA to "reduce, from ten to two years after a bankrupt leaves school, the period of time during which an order of discharge does not release the bankrupt from the reimbursement of his or her student loan." The bill was subsequently defeated in a motion held on April 13, 2005.

Most recently, on June 3, 2005, the federal government, in Bill C-55, unveiled a package of long awaited amendments to Canadian bankruptcy legislation. ... Bill C-55 reduces the period for the exception to discharge for Government Student Loans from 10 years to seven years following the completion of full- or part-time studies. The bill also reduces the period of time before an application for relief from the exception to discharge can be made from 10 years to five years. Similar to Bill C-236 and the government reports that have recommended changes to the timing of the exception, Bill C-55 does not provide a principled amendment to the substance of the exception. For example, the bill leaves intact the requirement that a bankrupt submit a judicial application for relief following the waiting period, in order for any relief from the exception to be granted.

NOTE

The 2007 amendments are the same as the Bill C-55 amendments to the treatment of student loans. Government student loans are non-dischargeable for seven years after the debtor ceases to be a student. Bankrupts who had non-dischargeable student loans at the time of bankruptcy are entitled to make an application for discharge of these student loans. See BIA ss. 178(1) and (1.1). Consider whether these reforms would have produced a different result in *Re Kelly*, below.

Re Kelly
(2000), 20 CBR (4th) 251 (Ont. SC)

DEPUTY REGISTRAR SPROAT: [1] This is one of four applications heard together, for an order under subsection 178(1.1) of the *Bankruptcy and Insolvency Act* (the "BIA") that paragraph 178(1)(g) of the BIA no longer applies to the bankrupt. Such an order would have the effect of releasing the bankrupt from liability for student loans, as defined in paragraph 178(1)(g). For the purpose of these reasons, I will simply refer to such indebtedness as "student loans." The application is opposed by both the Ontario Student Loans Plan and Canada Student Loans Program.

The Facts

[2] The bankrupt obtained Canada student loans and Ontario student loans of about $8,000 and $15,278, respectively, for furthering her post-secondary education. She attended York University from 1992 to 1996 and graduated in 1996 with a Bachelor of Arts degree in Psychology and a Bachelor of Arts degree in Education. She is a qualified teacher. She searched for a teaching position for about 1 to 2 years and did volunteer work in various private and public schools in the hopes of "getting her foot in the door." As a mother of two teenaged children, she received family benefits during this period.

[3] The bankrupt was unable to secure employment as a teacher and, in August, 1997, she obtained work as a receptionist with Security Insurance Company of Hartford ("Hartford"). She earned $24,000 per annum in this position. She has remained employed with Hartford continuously since August, 1997. The bankrupt has proven to be a good employee and was recently promoted. She is now an underwriting assistant with Hartford, which has been described as an administrative position. She earns $37,000 per annum and has enjoyed a bonus in the past years (the latest being $1,350 received March, 2000).

[4] The bankrupt claims that she had difficulty servicing her debts and therefore she made an assignment in bankruptcy on October 6, 1997, two months after securing full-time employment with Hartford. She had limited contact from the administrators of the Ontario Student Loans Plan and said that she contacted a representative of the Royal Bank of Canada and her MPP about her student loan. She admitted, however, that she largely ignored the situation of her student loans and, in fact, she made no payments on account of this indebtedness.

[5] On August 13, 1998, the bankrupt obtained a conditional order of discharge from the court. The condition related to the completion of the mandatory counselling requirement. She fulfilled this condition and obtained her discharge in May, 2000.

Discussion

[6] The bankrupt brings this application under subsection 178(1.1) of the BIA. Before turning to the merits of this application, it may be helpful to provide some history as to

debts or obligations in respect of loans made under the *Canada Student Loans Act* and other similar legislation. Until 1997, such liabilities were released by an order of discharge from bankruptcy, by operation of subsection 178(2) of the BIA, which provides that all claims provable in bankruptcy (with the exception of debts referred to in subsection 178(1)) are released by an order of discharge.

[7] However, in 1997, the BIA was amended. Subsection 178(1) of the BIA was amended to add paragraph 178(1)(g), which thereby excepted student loans from the operation of subsection 178(2) of the BIA. The amendment came into force on September 30, 1997. Thus, if the date of bankruptcy was after September 30, 1997, student loans were not automatically released by an order of discharge. A further amendment (subsection 178(1.1) of the BIA) was enacted to permit the bankrupt to effectively apply for the release of student loans upon the expiry of two years after the bankrupt ceased to be a full or part-time student.

[8] These amendments were motivated by the recognition that a bankrupt had and would continue to have the benefit from the education he or she obtained with the assistance of the student loans and to address a perceived abuse of the bankruptcy process. It was said that:

> The broad purpose of the Act is to permit honest but unfortunate debtors to obtain a discharge of their obligations in order to facilitate a return to stable participation in social and economic life, while balancing this objective against the interests of creditors. Section 178(1)(g) reflects a policy decision which accords with this objective and recognizes that student loans involve a situation where funds are advanced when there is no existing capacity of the debtor to repay the debt, but education obtained will hopefully enable the debtor to begin active and fruitful participation in the economy at some later date.
>
> Realization of earning potential associated with education can take some period of time after leaving school, so Parliament saw fit to disallow the immediate discharge of student loans, in this case for two years after ceasing to be a student. This measure addressed the perceived abuse of students using the Act to obtain a discharge of student loans prior to making reasonable efforts to realize upon their earning potential achieved through education.

(See *Re Minto* (1999), 14 CBR (4th) 235 (Sask. QB) at paragraph 16.)

[9] Thus, the date on which the bankrupt filed for bankruptcy is of importance as to whether student loans are or are not automatically released. If a bankrupt made an assignment on or after September 30, 1997, liabilities for student loans were not released upon an order of discharge. In such a bankruptcy, to be released of liability for student loans, the bankrupt is required to bring an application under subsection 178(1.1) of the BIA, after the expiry of two years from the date the bankrupt ceased being a full or part-time student, for the requisite order.

[10] To complicate matters somewhat further, the BIA was again amended in 1998 to increase the time after which the bankrupt could apply to the court for an order under subsection 178(1.1). Thus, if the date of bankruptcy was on or after June 18, 1998, the bankrupt was not entitled to bring an application for the release of student loans until after the expiry of 10 years (as opposed to the 2 year period resulting from the 1997 amendments) from the date the bankrupt ceased being a full or part-time student.

[11] Thus, there are now three relevant time periods, insofar as student loan obligations are concerned. They are:

1. if the date of bankruptcy was after December, 1992 but before September 30, 1997, debts or obligations in respect of student loans were released by an order of discharge;

2. if the date of bankruptcy was on or after September 30, 1997 but before June 18, 1998, the bankrupt's student loans were not released by an order of discharge and the bankrupt was obligated to wait 2 years from the time the bankrupt ceased being a full or part-time student before applying to the court for an order that the student loans be released; and

3. if the date of bankruptcy was on or after June 18, 1998, the bankrupt's student loans were not released and the bankrupt was obligated to wait 10 years from the time the bankrupt ceased being a full or part-time student before applying to the court for an order that the student loans be released.

[12] In this case, the date of bankruptcy is October 6, 1997. The bankrupt ceased being a full time student in April, 1996 and two years have since lapsed. The bankrupt is therefore entitled to bring this application for a release of her student loan obligations.

[13] The test which the bankrupt must meet on this application is set forth in subsection 178(1.1) of the BIA which provided (in 1997) as follows:

At any time after two years after a bankrupt who has a debt referred to in paragraph (1)(g) ceases to be a full- or part-time student, as the case may be, under the applicable Act or enactment, the court may, on application, order that subsection (1) does not apply to the debt if the court is satisfied that

(a) the bankrupt has acted in good faith in connection with the bankrupt's liabilities under the loan; and

(b) the bankrupt has and will continue to experience financial difficulty to such an extent that the bankrupt will be unable to pay the liabilities under the loan.

[14] The test is conjunctive and the bankrupt therefore has the onus of establishing on a balance of probabilities that she has acted in good faith and has and will continue to experience financial difficulty such that she will be unable to pay her student loan liabilities.

(a) Good Faith

[15] Given the existence of the two year waiting period before an application could be brought for an order releasing student loans, there have been few occasions (until recently) where the court was required to consider the test set forth in subsection 178(1.1) of the BIA and what factors the court should consider on such an application.

[16] In Re Minto, supra, Registrar Herauf referred to the factors which the court had considered on applications for discharge of a bankrupt with student loans and determined that these same factors were relevant to an application under subsection 178(1.1) of the BIA. I agree. In Re Minto, Registrar Herauf summarized the following factors as

relevant to the determination of the issue of "good faith": whether the money was used for the purpose loaned, whether the applicant completed the education, whether the applicant derived economic benefit from the education (i.e. is the applicant employed in an area directly related to the education), whether the applicant has made reasonable efforts to repay the debts and whether the applicant has made use of available options such as interest relief, remission, etc.

[17] However, I do not see these factors as exhaustive. I would add that the timing of the bankruptcy and whether the student loans form a significant part of the bankrupt's overall indebtedness as of the date of bankruptcy are factors that the court could consider in the determination of the good faith aspect of the test. I am of this view given the purpose of and the policy reasons for the 1997 amendments to the BIA.

[18] Having regard to the facts of this case, I am of the view that the bankrupt has not acted in good faith. I am not satisfied that the bankrupt made reasonable efforts to secure employment as a teacher (although I think that she did make some efforts). However, that is not all. I find as fact that the bankrupt failed to make any inquiries or at least meaningful inquiries as to the options which might have been available to her to reduce or avoid, at least in part, the burden relating to her student loans. For example, she may have been entitled to interest relief or loan forgiveness. She did not pursue these avenues of relief and admittedly ignored her student loan obligations.

[19] I think it also significant that she made her assignment in bankruptcy two months after she secured gainful employment. She claimed to have done so because she could not service her debts. In addition, the bankrupt had financial ability to make some provision for her student loans. She has, over the period August, 1997 to the present, managed to contribute about $4,500 into an RRSP plan (presumably on a receptionists' salary of $24,000 given that her promotion was recent). Yet, the bankrupt has made no provision for her student loans. In my view, the bankrupt has not made reasonable efforts to pay the student loans.

[20] I therefore find that the bankrupt fails on the first branch of the test on this application.

(b) Financial Difficulty

[21] As to the second branch of the test, it is necessary for the bankrupt to establish that she has *and* will continue to experience financial difficulty to such an extent that she will be unable to pay the student loans.

[22] The issue as to whether a bankrupt "will continue to experience financial difficulty" will in most cases pose the biggest obstacle for bankrupts bringing a subsection 178(1.1) application. The BIA does not provide any guidance to the court as to the appropriate duration of time into the future wherein the bankrupt must experience this financial difficulty. I agree with Registrar Herauf that the time period cannot be established with certainty and is dependent upon the facts of the particular case.

[23] In this case, I am not satisfied that the bankrupt has, in the past, experienced financial difficulty to such an extent that she was unable to pay her student loans. I come to this view as she has been employed on a full-time basis for about 3 years. During this

period of time, she was capable of making contributions to an RRSP plan at the rate of about $85 every two weeks (which is roughly $184 per month).

[24] In addition, I am of the view that the bankrupt had and will have, in my view, sufficient income with which to make some provision for her student loans. Her monthly budget filed in support of the application revealed net income of $2,153, which figure was arrived at by multiplying her net income (for a two week pay period) of $994.19 by 26 pay periods and dividing by 12. However, the bankrupt neglected to include in her net income the $184 deduction automatically made from her pay on account of her RRSP contribution. If one adds the $184 RRSP contribution and the $170 child tax credit to her income, the total net income is $2,507. Her stated expenses are $2,286. Thus, the excess income of $221 would be available to make some provision on account of her student loans.

[25] Lastly, I note that she has about $4,500 in her RRSP that she could cash out and pay towards her student loans. She has failed to do so. She does not wish to do so. This is a liquid asset now available to her to pay down her student loan. She has also enjoyed income tax refunds of about $1,300 yearly. She has also enjoyed bonuses from her employer of a similar amount. These too could have been paid against the student loans. For these reasons, I do not think that the bankrupt has experienced financial difficulty to such an extent that she was unable to pay her student loans.

Application dismissed.

VI. REAFFIRMATION OF DISCHARGED LIABILITIES

Important but often overlooked questions in Canadian consumer insolvency law are (1) to what extent can a discharged debt be reaffirmed by a bankrupt person, and (2) what will amount to a reaffirmation? The answer to the first question is that the BIA does not outlaw reaffirmation of discharged debts. The answer to the second question is that a reaffirmation will bind the debtor if it meets normal contractual requirements and, in particular, if there is consideration for the debtor's promise to pay the discharged debt—for example, the creditor's agreement to issue a new credit card to the debtor or to revive a line of credit.

Particular difficulties arise when there is no express promise by the debtor to pay the discharged debt and reaffirmation is based on the debtor's conduct, such as post-discharge retention by the debtor of a vehicle leased from the creditor and the debtor continuing to make rental payments. *Seaboard Acceptance Corp. v. Moen*, below, is a good example of the latter type and the constructional difficulties to which it gives rise. A much broader question is whether reaffirmations should be allowed at all and, if they are to be permitted, what safeguards need to be put in place to protect consumer bankrupts against unconscionable practices.

Seaboard Acceptance Corp. v. Moen
(1986), 62 CBR (NS) 143 (BCCA)

LAMBERT JA (for the Court): This is an appeal from the judgment of the Honourable Judge Campbell in which he awarded summary judgment under Rule 18A in favour of the plaintiff against the defendant.

On April 16th, 1982, Seaboard Acceptance Corporation Ltd. (whom I will call Seaboard) entered into a standard form of written contract with the defendant under which the defendant agreed to lease a motor vehicle for three years.

Clause 3(e) of the contract required the defendant to pay Seaboard a rental for the use of the vehicle, a sum called a fixed rental charge to be paid monthly. The contract also required that at the conclusion of the three year rental period a calculation would be made, based on the value of the vehicle at the start of the contract, which was agreed to by all parties, and based also on the value set at the conclusion of the contract, based on the highest wholesale bid for the purchase of the vehicle. There were other factors in the calculation and in the end an amount was to be determined at the conclusion of the contract which might be an amount payable by the defendant to Seaboard, or it might be an amount payable by Seaboard to the defendant.

There was also a clause in the contract which provided that if the defendant became insolvent or if any proceedings were taken in bankruptcy in relation to the defendant, whether voluntary or otherwise, the defendant then agreed that Seaboard should have the right to immediately retake and repossess the vehicle.

The terms of clause 8 were that the defendant would remain liable for all rentals payable, for all payments under the contract, and for costs.

The contract provided that in the event of premature termination the defendant would pay Seaboard all monies due under the agreement.

The defendant took possession of the vehicle in April, 1982 when the contract was signed. On 7 December, 1983, the defendant made a voluntary assignment into bankruptcy. She did not inform the Trustee in Bankruptcy of the lease contract with Seaboard or the terms by which she had possession of the automobile. That bankruptcy went through the procedures under the *Bankruptcy Act* and an absolute order of discharge was made on 22nd, May, 1984.

The defendant made the required payments until 14 September, 1984, that is, from before the bankruptcy, right through the bankruptcy, past the time of her discharge, and several payments after the discharge had been granted. But, in September, 1984, default occurred and in the end the vehicle was returned to Seaboard in November, 1984. At that time Seaboard calculated the amount owing under the contract in accordance with the terms of the contract just as if no bankruptcy had occurred and Seaboard made a demand for the balance owing.

At that time Seaboard had no knowledge of the bankruptcy. Seaboard learned of the bankruptcy in December, 1984.

No funds were realized by the Trustee in Bankruptcy for the benefit of creditors, nor were any dividends paid out to the unsecured creditors from the bankrupt's estate.

In February, 1985, Seaboard began this action against the defendant claiming $2,934.48, which was the balance said to be due on the lease. Both Seaboard and the defendant brought applications for judgment under Rules 18 and 18A.

Judgment was given by the Honourable Judge Campbell dismissing the defendant's application and giving judgment in favour of Seaboard for the amount claimed of $2,934.48. The reasons discussed whether this was a claim provable in bankruptcy and turn on the fact that, in the opinion of Judge Campbell, this was not a claim provable in bankruptcy but a claim for individual monthly payments and that when each payment was made, as it was up to the date of bankruptcy, that payment discharged the debt and there was no further debt until a further payment became due.

A question called "novation" was also mentioned by Judge Campbell, but was specifically not dealt with by him. By the term "novation" I understand Judge Campbell to mean those arguments in relation to the conduct of the parties throughout the bankruptcy, and particularly after the bankruptcy, in relation to whether there was an existing contractual relationship between the parties after the bankruptcy.

We were referred by counsel for the appellant to s. 95, and particularly subsections (1), (2) and (3) of that section in the *Bankruptcy Act*. We were referred also to s. 148, and particularly to subsection (1)(f) and to subsection (2). On the basis of those provisions counsel for the appellant argued that at the time of the bankruptcy there was a claim provable by Seaboard in the bankruptcy for the full amount then calculable as owing under the contract, either because of breach or because of the termination provisions of clause 8. The argument continues with the submission that if there were a claim payable in bankruptcy that claim could not survive the discharge except as a claim to a dividend equal to the dividend in the bankruptcy.

It is not necessary for me to deal with that argument in this case. I do not wish to make any decision as to whether there was or was not a claim provable in bankruptcy. But, on the assumption that there was a claim provable in bankruptcy, I pass on to consider what occurred between these parties.

The contractual payments were made throughout the period of the bankruptcy and the defendant retained possession of the vehicle throughout that period. After she had obtained her discharge from the bankruptcy she continued to retain possession of the vehicle and she continued to make the contractual payments. Under what basis was that possession retained and on what basis were those payments made? In my opinion, the proper view is that the contract continued throughout the bankruptcy and continued after the discharge from bankruptcy; it was never terminated in accordance with its provisions for termination, and the fact that there might have been a claim provable in bankruptcy, or that a claim provable in bankruptcy might have been made, does not affect the fact that the contract itself continued and continued to regulate the relationship of the parties after the discharge from bankruptcy.

In my opinion, what occurred in this case was not, strictly speaking, a novation, as that term is properly understood, but was merely a continuation of the contract, and a continued abiding by the terms of the contract that had been made between the parties. In effect the contract was endorsed by the defendant after the discharge. In those circumstances no other order is possible in relation to damages than that the contractual provisions apply and they must set the quantum of damages in the amount for which judgment was given by the Honourable Judge Campbell.

We were referred in the course of argument in relation to the question of endorsement of the contract to the decision of the Superior Court of Quebec in Bankruptcy in the case of *In Re Napoleon Godin* (1926) 7 CBR 726. That case deals with whether the partial payment to a debtor after the discharge from bankruptcy would restore the full amount of the debtor's claim. That case is distinguishable from this case because in this case there was a continuing contract with continuing benefits flowing both ways through the continued possession of the vehicle and the continuation of making payments. So I do not disagree with that decision, but say it has no application to the facts of this case.

Appeal dismissed.

NOTE

For a lively exchange of views on the *Moen* case and related issues, see Tamara Buckwold (1999), 31 *CBLJ* 335; J.S. Ziegel (1999), 32 *CBLJ* 142; and Tamara Buckwold (2000), 33 *CBLJ* 128. What is the ratio of *Moen*? Is the decision based on the bankrupt's retention of the vehicle after bankruptcy without disclosing the lease to the trustee, or is it based on the bankrupt's failure to make contact with the lessor?

Bank of Nova Scotia v. Jorgensen
(2008), 41 CBR (5th) 236 (Ont. Sup. Ct.)

P.F. LALONDE J:

Introduction

. . .

The question before the Court in the case concerning defendant Peter Jorgensen (Mr. Jorgensen) is whether his December 22, 1999 assignment in bankruptcy extinguished his debt to the plaintiff even though he continued to make payments on the SCL [Scotia Credit Loan] after his bankruptcy.

In the case of defendant Susan Mary Jorgensen, née Boucher (Mrs. Jorgensen), the question is whether she can escape liability for repayment of the loan as the plaintiff failed to give her monthly statements and keep her informed that Mr. Jorgensen was drawing on the Scotia line of credit that ought to have been paid in full.

. . .

The Law

Plaintiff's Position

Counsel for the plaintiff referred to *Royal Bank v. The King*, [1931] 2 DLR 685 (Man. KB) ("*Royal Bank*"), where Mr. Justice Dysart of the King's Bench of Manitoba sets out four principles with respect to the right to recover money paid under mistake of fact as follows:

> [10] First, that the mistake is honest. There must be on the part of the person paying the money the genuine bona-fide belief that certain facts exist which really do not exist. It is not what he ought to believe or what he ought to have learned. His laches or negligence will not

of themselves affect his belief. Knowledge will not be imputed to him; however ample may be the means of knowledge which he has on hand, or however readily accessible those means may be, they do not constitute knowledge; and knowledge will not be imputed to him or inferred against him, unless he wilfully abstains from enquiry.

• • •

[13] The second condition is that the mistake must be as between the person paying and the person receiving the money. In other words, the receiver must in some way be a party to the mistake, either as inducing it, or as responsible for it, or connected with it.

[14] The third condition is that the facts, as they are believed to be impose an obligation to make the payment: *Aiken v. Short* (1856) 1 H & N 210, at 215, 25 LJ Ex. 321. This obligation must be legal or equitable or moral ... .

[15] The fourth condition to recovery is that the receiver of the money has no legal or equitable or moral right to retain the money as against the payer.

The *Royal Bank* case was considered and applied in the recent Ontario Court of Appeal decision of *Pinnacle Bank, N.A. v. 1317414 Ontario Inc.*, [2002] OJ No. 281 (CA) ("*Pinnacle*"). In *Pinnacle* the bank's client had directed it to transfer a sum of money to the corporate defendant. The plaintiff bank then wired an identical amount three days later as the result of a clerical error. The error was discovered two weeks later, and the bank requested the return of those funds. The corporate defendant refused on the basis that the bank's client owed it additional sums of money and that it was entitled to same. Further, the money had already been used to pay suppliers of goods. The trial judge found, and it was upheld on appeal, that the bank was entitled to recover the additional sum of money that had been mistakenly wired to the corporate defendant. The Court of Appeal in *Pinnacle* applied the principles set out in *Royal Bank* in order to reach the conclusion that the corporate defendant was liable to the plaintiff for the return of funds, which had been mistakenly paid out by the plaintiff.

Next, dealing with the impact of Peter Jorgensen's bankruptcy on his indebtedness to the plaintiff, counsel for the plaintiff argued that the *Bankruptcy and Insolvency Act*, RSC 1985, c. B-3, ss. 178(1) and (2) (the "BIA") provide for the release of a bankrupt from all his liabilities incurred pre-bankruptcy. The BIA also makes specific exceptions to this release of liability for certain enumerated claims/debts, including restitutionary orders.

The plaintiff argued that the $90,000.00 advanced to the defendants must be returned for two reasons. Firstly, the law dictates that monies advanced under mistake must be returned. Secondly, there was fresh consideration for keeping the $90,000.00 debt alive after the bankruptcy. The consideration was that the line of credit enabled the defendants to keep their home without selling it for 18 months after the bankruptcy. The defendants' home increased in value during that time to the defendants' benefit. There is also an added benefit to the defendants in that the loan was life insured and if either defendant had died, the loan would have been paid off in full.

Counsel for the plaintiff argued that even if s. 178 of the BIA does not help his client, the common law does. The plaintiff argues that a creditor is protected by the common law where a bankrupt continues paying a pre-bankruptcy debt and does so for fresh consideration. In this case, the fresh consideration was that the bank did not force the Jorgensens out of their home and offered them a renewal of the debt on new terms. The defendants also received life insurance protection on the loan.

The plaintiff filed a signed mortgage renewal form showing different terms and rates, claiming that Peter Jorgensen had agreed to the offer of a renewal loan and had made, through his wife Susan Jorgensen, payments on the line of credit as well. Counsel for the plaintiff relies on the British Columbia Court of Appeal decision in *Seaboard Acceptance Corp. v. Moen* (1986), 62 CBR (NS) 143 for the proposition that when a pre-bankruptcy contract continues to be affirmed by the bankrupt after the occurrence of the bankruptcy the contract's terms remain enforceable against the bankrupt. A contract with continuing benefits flowing both ways is enforceable post bankruptcy. It is distinguishable from a partial payment on a debt made post bankruptcy on the basis that the parties in a continuing contract both enjoy post bankruptcy consideration. The fact that a claim provable in bankruptcy arose from the contract and could have been made in bankruptcy does not affect the fact that the contract itself continued, and continues, to regulate the parties' relationship.

In connection with Susan Jorgensen, the plaintiff believes that while it is true that she was left in the dark by her husband concerning his further use of the credit agreement, she has to take her complaints to her husband and not to the bank. She signed the credit application to cover the $3,089.00 overdraft that showed the $90,000.00 debt on the line of credit and she cannot be excused from liability because she did not read the application.

Peter Jorgensen's Position

Counsel for Mr. Jorgensen criticized the cases cited by counsel for the plaintiff by stating that they address the situation of a secured creditor relationship, where even if the debt is proved in bankruptcy and there is a deficiency, the bankruptcy has no effect because the security is a continuing contract. In such a case, a provision of services on a pre-bankruptcy secured debt is enough to keep the debt alive. This, however, is not the case at hand.

This defendant contends that in his case the offer by the plaintiff to have him make minimum payments on the line of credit in exchange for not foreclosing on his house mortgage is not a new deal to repay a $90,000.00 debt already dead by his assignment in bankruptcy. He claims that, at best, the plaintiff used coercion to have him pay a discharged debt.

Counsel for Mr. Jorgensen relies on Lissaman J's decision in *Engels v. Merit Insurance Brokers Inc.*, [2000] OJ No. 2233 (SCJ), dated June 12, 2000. In that case, Lissaman J had to decide whether the defendants' loan to the plaintiff had been extinguished by his personal bankruptcy and subsequently revived by an alleged promise to repay the loan to the defendant if the defendant did not oppose his discharge from bankruptcy. Lissaman J states at paragraph 17:

> [17] … The plaintiff's bankruptcy was not one where the Trustee was seeking sanctions against the bankrupt. In my view the opposition of the defendant to the discharge because of bankruptcy offences would have been of no effect at all. I find that the alleged consideration to be of no value. It is also my view that the concept of "creditors and debtors" making side deals to avoid the *Bankruptcy Act* is somewhat unsavory and should not be judicially encouraged.

He further states at paragraph 18:

> [18] Judges are entitled to draw inferences. In the case at bar, I am of the opinion that Merit at all material times used its position to coerce the plaintiff in paying a discharged debt. Such conduct should not be in any way condoned by a Court.

It is clear from the cases cited by this defendant that he maintains the position that no new consideration was given and therefore his debt is extinguished by operation of law and the plaintiff cannot recover on it. Counsel for this defendant also points out that the plaintiff is relying on cases where a security was involved as the cases of *Seaboard Acceptance Corp. v. Moen* (1986), 62 CBR (NS) 143 (BCCA) (a chattel lease), *CIBC Mortgage Corp. v. Stenerson* (1998), 4 CBR (4th) 226 (Alta. QB) (a mortgage) and *Superior Credit Corp. v. Andrews*, [1999] MJ No. 350, 1999 CarswellMan 374 (Man. QB) (vehicles and household goods). In the case at bar, the debt is unsecured.

Susan Jorgensen's Position

Counsel claims that the only debt his client knew about and had signed for was discharged when the $140,000.00 mortgage was advanced by the plaintiff. Susan Jorgensen did not consent to anything else even if she did sign an application for credit to cover an overdraft on March 20, 2000, that showed $90,805.00 was owed for a line of credit. Susan Jorgensen did not read the document, the debt was not brought to her attention by Brett Patterson, the bank manager, and although she had consented to borrow the original $90,000.00 she had not consented to this $90,000.00 debt surreptitiously drawn over time by Peter Jorgensen.

The plaintiff considered the second $90,000.00 a Peter Jorgensen debt. The file was opened in his name, he received all statements at a postal box in Kingston that Susan Jorgensen never knew existed. The monthly bank statements were made in the name of Peter Jorgensen only and were mailed to him at a postal box number, preventing Mrs. Jorgensen from finding out about the debt. Counsel for Mrs. Jorgensen claims that his client was not connected with the debt and that the mistake was not between the person paying and the person receiving the money, a requirement made essential in the *Royal Bank* case.

Decision

I find that there was no new consideration for the $90,000.00 indebtedness and that the plaintiff compounded its mistake by not suing for the debt once the mistake was discovered. The *Bankruptcy and Insolvency Act* is clear that a discharge from bankruptcy acts to extinguish a debt provable in bankruptcy. The renewals of the mortgage the plaintiff granted to Peter Jorgensen after the bankruptcy was no consideration at all. As Lissaman J stated in *Engels v. Merit Insurance Brokers Inc.*, I am entitled to draw an inference that at all material times the plaintiff was in a position to coerce Peter Jorgensen into paying a discharged debt. This inference is not displaced by the fact that it was Peter Jorgensen who contacted the plaintiff when the Jorgensen overdraft came to the attention of the bank.

The case of *Chamandy Brothers v. Albert* [1928] 2 DLR 577 does not help the plaintiff's case as the debtor reneged on a proposal he made to his creditors in that case. The debt was never extinguished by operation of law as it was in this case.

The plaintiff's claim against Susan Jorgensen is also dismissed. She never consented to a second advance of $90,000.00 on the original line of credit. By its actions, the plaintiff ensured that Susan Jorgensen never knew that Peter Jorgensen was surreptitiously drawing out monies from a line of credit that she knew was paid off by the registration of the mortgage. The plaintiff considered the loan a Peter Jorgensen loan, as indicated by the loan statements which were addressed to Peter Jorgensen only. To make matters worse the statements were mailed to a postal station box away from the defendants' residence. Even if Susan Jorgensen did not open her husband's mail, if the statements were sent to her home there was a better chance for her to discover that the line of credit was not cancelled.

While it is true that she signed a credit application during the year 2000, she is fully justified in thinking she was attending at a bank where she owed money on a mortgage on which payments were current and for a $3,089.00 overdraft that existed. The $3,089.00 overdraft was her reason to attend at the plaintiff's bank in the first place. As a result, Susan Jorgensen escapes liability to repay a loan she did not contract for with the plaintiff, and her consent in 1992 cannot be used to pay the second $90,000.00 line of credit because of a mistake made by the bank.

Susan Jorgensen's escape from liability in this litigation is also made possible because of another contract she had with the Bank of Nova Scotia. As stated earlier, that contract was made in 1993 to borrow $140,000.00 on a mortgage and as the mortgage application recites "customer paying off collateral first," the $90,000.00 debt was paid off. This was a contract for valuable consideration and that debt could not be revived without Susan Jorgensen's consent no matter how many times the second $90,000.00 appeared on subsequent documents.

Appeal dismissed.

Personal Insolvency Task Force, *Final Report*
(Ottawa: Industry Canada, Office of the Superintendent of Bankruptcy, 2002) at 29-33 (footnotes omitted)

It is a fundamental principle of the Canadian insolvency system, embodied in Section 178(2) of the BIA, that bankrupts should receive a fresh start upon being discharged from bankruptcy. To that end, Section 178(2) releases discharged bankrupts from all liabilities, with the exception of the few described in Section 178(1).

Reaffirmations occur when bankrupts revive, or reaffirm, personal responsibility for liabilities which have been released upon discharge. Hence, reaffirmation is inconsistent with the fresh start principle. There are two kinds of reaffirmation: reaffirmation by conduct and reaffirmation by express agreement.

Reaffirmation by conduct occurs when bankrupts continue to make payments to creditors even though the relevant debts have been discharged. In a line of cases that began with the *Moen* decision in 1986, the courts have interpreted such conduct as reaffirming, or reestablishing, the bankrupts' promise to make the payments.

If the law is to be consistent with the fresh start philosophy, bankrupts should be released from such promises—also called personal covenants or covenants to pay—when they are discharged from bankruptcy. In the *Moen* line of cases, Canadian courts have instead held that discharged bankrupts must uphold their pre-bankruptcy covenant to pay once they have continued to make payments after their discharge. If the bankrupts later stop making the payments, the courts have granted judgments against them. The Task Force believes that bankrupts did not, in general, intend to reaffirm their pre-bankruptcy promises; instead, they probably continued to make the payments in order to retain possession of the leased or mortgaged asset and did not appreciate that they were reaffirming their covenant to pay.

Reaffirmation by express agreement occurs when bankrupts enter into agreements with creditors to repay debts even if the debts were released upon the discharge from bankruptcy. In the United States, reaffirmation agreements are regulated by the US *Bankruptcy Code* and are quite common. There are no statistics available in Canada but there is ample anecdotal evidence to demonstrate that creditors are attempting to get discharged bankrupts to sign reaffirmation agreements.

The Task Force recommends that the BIA should deal with reaffirmations. In general terms, it is recommended that:

a. The *Moen* line of cases should be statutorily overruled so that reaffirmation cannot occur through the continuation of payments or through any other conduct.

b. Reaffirmation agreements in respect of unsecured transactions should be prohibited in all circumstances.

c. Reaffirmation agreements in respect of secured transactions should be prohibited except to the extent described in detail below.

d. Except in the circumstances described below, it should be an offence under the BIA for a creditor who knows about a bankrupt's discharge from bankruptcy to accept payment of any indebtedness released upon the bankrupt's discharge. Any impermissible payments should be recoverable from the creditor.

The rationale for each of these recommendations and the specific details of the last two recommendations will now be presented.

Why shouldn't reaffirmation by conduct be allowed? The view of the Task Force is that the *Moen* line of cases offends against the fresh start principle and against the spirit of Section 178 of the BIA. While reaffirmations should be permitted in certain circumstances, they should not be implied from the possibly uninformed decisions by bankrupts to continue making payments. The Task Force believes that bankrupts should make a conscious and informed decision before becoming again personally liable for indebtedness released when they were discharged from bankruptcy.

Why should reaffirmation of unsecured debt be disallowed? The Task Force recommends that reaffirmation agreements in respect of unsecured transactions be prohibited for three reasons. First, they offend against the fresh start principle. Second, they have the effect of giving one creditor preference over other creditors and such preferences are generally discouraged by the BIA. Third, the discussion between creditors and bankrupts about such reaffirmations will likely occur at a time when the bankrupts are quite vulnerable and subject to pressure. For example, a creditor might offer the continued use of a credit card in exchange for the discharged bankrupt signing a reaffirmation agreement in respect of the pre-bankruptcy credit card indebtedness. The discharged bankrupt may be having difficulty in obtaining credit and may foolishly agree to pay indebtedness which was released upon the discharge of the bankrupt.

Although the Task Force has concluded that reaffirmation agreements in respect of unsecured transactions should not be permitted in any circumstances, it recognizes that there will be situations where discharged bankrupts may legitimately want to repay certain debts. For example, a bankrupt might want to repay a loan from a family member, even if that debt has been legally discharged. Such repayment will be allowed under the conditions, discussed below, of the recommendation dealing with the offence provisions of the BIA.

Should reaffirmation agreements of secured debt be permitted? The Task Force recommends that reaffirmation agreements be permitted in respect of secured transactions subject to a number of conditions. The rationale for this recommendation is that it will allow bankrupts to retain the assets covered by the security agreement and to thus avoid disruption in their lives. The secured creditors will be in the same position as they would have been in if they had to enforce the security and realize upon the asset.

NOTE

The PITF Report's recommendations have received a mixed reaction and have been criticized for their complexity, and because they were not based on any empirical evidence of existing Canadian practices. One member of the Task Force (see the Report, at 32, note 31) also objected strongly to criminalizing a creditor's receipt of payment of a discharged debt that did not meet the Report's conditions. What would *you* recommend?

VII. CREDIT GRANTING PRACTICES AND THEIR IMPACT ON BANKRUPTCY FILINGS

Until the recent period leading up to the 2008 credit crisis, the response to increasing consumer bankruptcy rates from regulators and creditors was to focus on the conduct of debtors. Only recently, with the subprime crisis in the United States and the growth of alternative credit instruments, has the focus broadened to also consider the impact of credit-granting practices on bankruptcy filing. Further research is needed into the relationship between insolvency and modern credit instruments—for example, how have modern instruments of consumer credit, such as unsecured lines of credit, remortgaging/refinancing offers, and aggressive solicitations by credit card issuers affected the number or rate of consumer insolvencies? Are there particular practices in the credit market that merit particular attention? Is a policy regarding responsible borrowing/lending possible for Canada? Are there international examples in this regard that could provide valuable lessons for Canada?

Jacob Ziegel, "Consumer Insolvencies, Consumer Credit, and Responsible Lending"
2008 Houlden Fellowship Award Paper (unpublished)

Canadian professional reaction to these escalating insolvency figures differs. Leaving aside cases of personal and unpredictable misfortunes (such as unemployment, marital problems, and serious illnesses), credit counselors and trustees in bankruptcy have long been of the view that many Canadian consumers do not know how to manage their budgets. This perception led to the establishment of voluntary credit counseling services in metropolitan Toronto and other parts of Canada and, more importantly, to the introduction of mandatory counselling requirements in the 1992 amendments to the federal *Bankruptcy and Insolvency Act* (BIA).

Another reaction came principally from creditors. This was that it was too easy for consumers to initiate personal bankruptcy proceedings and to obtain an early discharge from their debts without being required to make a meaningful (or any) contribution to the reduction of their debts. This perception led to the adoption of the surplus income payment regime as part of the 1997 amendments to the BIA requiring the debtor to make prescribed payments from the debtor's income as determined by the low income cut-off (LICO) standards established by the Superintendent of Bankruptcy. The provisions are still in force.

A striking feature of this reaction to the escalating insolvency figures was the assumption that the creditors themselves were blameless and bore no responsibility for the credit practices that often lead to a debtor's downfall. The thesis of this paper is that the assumption is incorrect and that there is abundant evidence of creditors' contribution toward debtors' difficulties. The writer is not alone in voicing these concerns. They have received much attention in recent studies, reports, and testimony by witnesses in the United States, the European Union, and the United Kingdom, and have led to new laws and regulations designed to promote greater creditor responsibility in the granting of credit. In the United States, the same concerns have often also been expressed by consumer groups, welfare organizations, and academics specializing in consumer insolvency and consumer credit problems.

NOTES AND QUESTIONS

Distinguished Harvard insolvency law scholar Professor Elizabeth Warren argues that it is safer to buy a toaster than to enter into a complex debt agreement. For example, it is impossible to change the price of a toaster once it has been purchased, but it is possible to triple the price of credit even after a credit agreement has been entered into. She explains the difference between the two markets with the "R-word": regulation. On this basis she makes a strong case for a "financial product safety commission" that has gained popularity, even among proponents of free markets, in the current crisis. See Elizabeth Warren, "Unsafe At Any Rate" (2007), *Democracy: A Journal of Ideas* 8. See also Robert Shiller, *The Subprime Solution* (Princeton, NJ: Princeton University Press, 2008), where Yale economist Shiller includes the financial product safety commission in his solution to the current crisis, which is based on fostering more market activity. What do you think about this proposal?

PART III

The Companies' Creditors Arrangement Act

CHAPTER TWELVE

The Companies' Creditors Arrangement Act: Introduction

I. ORIGINS, PHILOSOPHY, EVOLUTION, AND COMPARATIVE ASPECTS

There is little doubt that over the past 30 years or so the dominant theme in business insolvencies has revolved around the need to avert business bankruptcies by facilitating business reorganization or restructuring,[1] and thereby saving jobs and, sometimes, communities, and updating dated laws to provide a modern statutory framework. This is not to suggest that the restructuring of insolvent business debtors as an alternative to liquidation is, economically or legally, a modern concept. England adopted legislation as far back as 1870, although it was heavily circumscribed. In the United States, court sanctioned receiverships were widely used in the 19th century to address the problems of insolvent railroads and these generated a large body of complex case law before the introduction of regulatory legislation in 1933 and 1938. In Canada, the *Bankruptcy Act of 1919* contained a separate part dealing with proposals, which was moderately used in practice prior to the 1992 amendments. The main shortcomings of the provisions were that they did not apply to secured creditors, could only be invoked after the debtor was in bankruptcy, and contained no provisions for a stay of proceedings before the proposal was actually filed.[2] These were some of the reasons why, at the height of the Great Depression, Parliament deemed it necessary to adopt the *Companies' Creditors Arrangement Act*. The sources of the Act were some skeletal provisions

---

1. The terms "reorganization" and "restructuring" are used interchangeably in Canada and the United States to describe the restructuring of the debts of an insolvent business, but neither term is used in the Canadian legislation. The CCAA speaks of an arrangement, but without defining the term. Part III, Division 1 of the BIA uses the term "proposal." "Proposal" is defined in BIA s. 2 as "including" a proposal for a composition, for an extension of time, or for a scheme of arrangement. "Composition" and "arrangement" are not defined, but, given the non-exhaustive definition of "proposal," it probably does not matter. Composition is usually understood to mean an arrangement whereby creditors agree to accept less than full repayment of what is owing to them as contrasted with a proposal for an extension of time, which simply gives the debtor more time to pay the debts. A scheme of arrangement usually implies a more elaborate proposal possibly involving a restructuring of the classes of creditors and equity holders in the debtor corporation coupled with a reduction in the amount that is repayable and the period in which it must be paid: see *ATB Financial v. Metcalfe & Mansfield Alternative Investments II Vorp.* (2008), 296 DLR (4th) 135 (Ont. CA), at paras. 60 and 61. In this casebook, "reorganization" and "restructuring" are used in a non-technical sense to denote any and all of these methods of rescuing an insolvent business.

2. In practice, the last difficulty was overcome by the trustee filing a "holding" proposal.

in the English *Companies Act of 1929*. As drafted, the CCAA was only designed to facilitate the restructuring of large corporations. This feature was emphasized in the 1953 amendments, which restricted the Act to companies that had an outstanding issue of bonds or debentures and a trustee to protect the interests of the bond or debenture holders. See *Re Metcalfe & Mansfield Alternative Investments II Corp.*, 2008 ONCA 587, extracted below. Another equally important feature was the skeletal character of the Act, which, prior to the 1997 amendments, only contained 22 sections.

So far as Canada was concerned, two major recessions in the 1980s made it urgent to revise and augment the earlier legislation. The same need was felt in many other countries. The Tassé Study Committee, reporting in 1970 (see Chapters 1 and 2) recommended the repeal of the CCAA and adoption of a new set of reorganizational provisions as part of the new bankruptcy act recommended by the Committee. As we saw in Chapter 1, efforts between 1975 and 1984 to persuade Parliament to adopt a revised act proved unsuccessful and, in 1984, the new Mulroney administration appointed the Colter Committee to make recommendations with respect to those amendments to the BIA that, in the Committee's view, were most urgent. The Committee's 1986 report paid particular attention to the need to enact modern and efficient alternatives to business and consumer bankruptcies. These recommendations were largely adopted in the 1992 amendments to the BIA. Part III of the Act was greatly expanded and was divided into two divisions. Division 1 deals with business proposals, although, technically speaking, it is not limited to business insolvencies; Division 2 is restricted to consumer proposals. Division 1 business proposals are dealt with in Chapter 16; consumer proposals are examined in Chapter 17.

The Colter Committee did not indicate what should be done with the CCAA. Some practitioners thought it would die from disuse; the House of Commons Committee examining Bill C-22 in 1991 recommended repeal of the CCAA at the end of a three-year period. However, that did not happen for the following reasons. Between 1986 and 1992, Canadian courts had shown themselves remarkably creative in adapting the skeletal provisions of the CCAA to meet the restructuring needs of medium-sized and large corporations; insolvency practitioners found that they preferred the court-driven and, as judicially construed, flexible provisions of the CCAA to the much more rule-driven new BIA Part III.1 provisions. This philosophy was also shared by the members of the BIA Advisory Committee established by the federal government in 1994 to make recommendations for the next round of insolvency amendments. The Committee recommended retention of the CCAA, but with important amendments, which were enacted as part of the 1997 CCAA amendments. One of the amendments (see now CCAA s. 3(1)) restricts access to the CCAA to a debtor company or affiliated debtor companies where the total claims against the company or its affiliates exceeds $5 million. Subject to this exception, corporate debtors in Canada now have a choice of two very differently inspired regimes to reorganize their affairs.

Briefly stated, the difference between the two regimes is that the debtor initiates the BIA reorganization procedure by filing either a proposal or a notice of intention to make a proposal. The procedure is an administrative one and there is no need for a court application. Creditors meet and vote on the proposal subject to rules that are spelled out in the statute itself. The court's main function is to approve the proposal once creditors have voted on it. (The court's other functions include hearing applications for extensions of time to file a proposal and applications by creditors opposing the proposal to terminate the proceedings.)

In contrast, the debtor initiates the CCAA reorganization procedure by making an application to the court. The debtor puts together a plan for submission to creditors subject to time lines the court imposes on a case-by-case basis. Creditors meet and vote on the plan subject to the court's direction, and, at the end of the process, the court decides whether or not to approve the plan. In short, the BIA business proposals regime is a statute-driven one, while the CCAA regime is a court-driven one. Proponents of the bifurcated system argue that the two regimes serve different interests: large firms prefer the greater flexibility that the CCAA offers, while smaller firms prefer the BIA regime because it is cheaper and, given its greater reliance on bright-line statutory rules, more predictable. Largely on the basis of these views, the Standing Senate Committee on Banking, Trade and Commerce in its 2003 Report, *Debtors and Creditors Sharing the Burden: A Review of the Bankruptcy and Insolvency Act and Companies' Creditors Arrangement Act*, recommended (at 170-73) that "the *Bankruptcy and Insolvency Act* and the *Companies' Creditors Arrangement Act* continue to exist as separate statutes." However, the 2007 amendments make a number of changes to the CCAA, most of which are aimed at reducing the court's discretion by substituting statutory rules (examples include the new provisions governing debtor-in-possession financing, executory contracts and asset sales); of course, the more rule-oriented the CCAA becomes, the weaker the argument for maintaining the separate regimes: see, further, Jacob Ziegel, "The BIA and CCAA Interface," in Stephanie Ben-Ishai and Anthony Duggan, eds., *Canadian Bankruptcy and Insolvency Law: Bill C-55, Statute c. 47 and Beyond* (Toronto: LexisNexis, 2007), 307.

In terms of the number of filings, BIA proposals far exceed CCAA proceedings. Keith Pritchard reports that between 1997 and 2002 there were 79 new CCAA proceedings. Of these, 29 were successful, 36 were unsuccessful, and 14 were ongoing: "Analysis of Recent CCAA Cases" (2004), 40 *CBLJ* 116. In contrast, in the 12-month period ending August 31, 2008, there were 1,308 BIA commercial proposals: Office of the Superintendent of Bankruptcy, *Bankruptcy Statistics 2008* (Ottawa, 2008). In other words, in a single year, there were about 15 times the number of CCAA cases reported by Pritchard in the 5-year period 1997-2002. On the other hand, the dollar amounts in CCAA proceedings are much larger (on average, about 10 times the amounts involved in BIA commercial proposals).

A. Comparative Developments

In the United States, Chapter 11 of the *Bankruptcy Code* of 1978 completely replaced the pre-World War II reorganization legislation and greatly encourages enterprises of all sizes facing financial difficulties[3] to seek protection from creditors. Chapter 11 has been amended frequently since 1978, but its basic structure remains the same. Chapter 11 is rule-driven and addresses systematically, in conjunction with the rest of the Code, most of the questions likely to arise in the course of a reorganization. In the United Kingdom, the *Insolvency Act*

---

3. Chapter 11 does not require a petitioning debtor to allege or prove its insolvency, and it is well-established that the US government's insolvency power is not restricted to companies that are technically insolvent. This is one of the reasons why US corporations facing mass tort claims can readily avail themselves of Chapter 11, even though they may be currently solvent and the value of the claims against them not established for years to come, if ever.

1986 introduced new provisions for an "administration order," which may lead to the presentation of a reorganization proposal. Many other industralized countries, including France, Germany, and Australia, also revamped their insolvency legislation in the 1980s and 1990s to facilitate corporate reorganizations.

It needs to be emphasized, however, that while the above initiatives share common goals, the techniques adopted in the legislation and their commitment to a rescue philosophy differ widely. It is generally agreed that US Chapter 11 is the most debtor-oriented of the postwar regimes. Because of this, its underlying philosophy and practical effects have engendered a lively controversy among lawyers, economists, and bankruptcy scholars. In a widely cited 1992 article,[4] Bradley and Rosenzweig argued that corporate creditors were significantly worse off than they were under the pre-1978 insolvency regime and that, generally, Chapter 11 was an inefficient and heavily biased solution to corporate debt problems. They therefore argued for a radical overhaul of Chapter 11 principles. Bradley and Rosenzweig's factual assertions were hotly disputed by other scholars.[5] There is much evidence that the academic controversy will continue at a broader level among law and economcs scholars, but it seems so far to have had little impact on the US Congress.

The British administration order provisions proved to be a great disappointment[6] and were substantially amended in the *Enterprise Amendment Act 2002*, largely to deprive fixed and floating charge holders of the right to veto the appointment of an administrator. Overall, British legislative developments over the past 25 years have exercised little influence in Canada.

II. THE OBJECTIVES OF RESTRUCTURING LAW

Re Lehndorff General Partner Ltd.
(1993), 17 CBR (3d) 24 (Ont. Gen. Div.)

FARLEY J: ... The CCAA is intended to facilitate compromises and arrangements between companies and their creditors as an alternative to bankruptcy and, as such, is remedial legislation entitled to a liberal interpretation. It seems to me that the purpose of the statute is to enable insolvent companies to carry on business in the ordinary course or otherwise deal with their assets so as to enable a plan of compromise or arrangement to be prepared, filed and considered by their creditors and the court. In the interim, a judge has great discretion under the CCAA to make orders so as to effectively maintain the status quo in respect of an insolvent company while it attempts to gain the approval

---

4. "The Untenable Case for Chapter 11" (1992), 101 *Yale LJ* 1043. See also Douglas Baird, "The Uneasy Case for Corporate Reorganization" (1986), 15 *J Legal Stud.* 127.

5. See Lynn LoPucki, "Strange Visions in a Strange World: A Reply to Professors Bradley and Rozenzweig" (1992), 91 *Mich. L Rev.* 79 and Elizabeth Warren, "The Untenable Case for Repeal of Chapter 11" (1992), 102 *Yale LJ* 437.

6. The provisions suffered from two main difficulties. The first was that holders of fixed and floating charges could opt out of them entirely, and often did; the second was that once an order was made, management was displaced and an administrator was put in charge of the debtor company's business. This obviously gave debtor companies little incentive to make use of the administration regime.

of its creditors for the proposed compromise or arrangement which will be to the benefit of both the company and its creditors. ...

The CCAA is intended to provide a structured environment for the negotiation of compromises between a debtor company and its creditors for the benefit of both. Where a debtor company realistically plans to continue operating or to otherwise deal with its assets but it requires the protection of the court in order to do so and it is otherwise too early for the court to determine whether the debtor company will succeed, relief should be granted under the CCAA. ... It has been held that the intention of the CCAA is to prevent any manoeuvres for positioning among the creditors during the period required to develop a plan and obtain approval of creditors. Such manoeuvres could give an aggressive creditor an advantage to the prejudice of others who are less aggressive and would undermine the company's financial position making it even less likely that the plan will succeed. ... The possibility that one or more creditors may be prejudiced should not affect the court's exercise of its authority to grant a stay of proceedings under the CCAA because this effect is offset by the benefit to all creditors and to the company of facilitating a reorganization. The court's primary concerns under the CCAA must be for the debtor and all of the creditors. ...

One of the purposes of the CCAA is to facilitate ongoing operations of a business where its assets have a greater value as part of an integrated system than individually. The CCAA facilitates reorganization of a company where the alternative, sale of the property piecemeal, is likely to yield far less satisfaction to the creditors. Unlike the *Bankruptcy Act*, RSC 1985, c. B-3, before the amendments effective November 30, 1992 to transform it into the *Bankruptcy and Insolvency Act* ("BIA"), it is possible under the CCAA to bind secured creditors. It has been generally speculated that the CCAA will be resorted to by companies that are generally larger and have a more complicated capital structure and that those companies which make an application under the BIA will be generally smaller and have a less complicated structure. Reorganization may include partial liquidation where it is intended as part of the process of a return to long term viability and profitability. ... It appears to me that the purpose of the CCAA is also to protect the interests of creditors and to enable an orderly distribution of the debtor company's affairs. This may involve a winding-up or liquidation of a company or simply a substantial downsizing of its business operations, provided the same is proposed in the best interests of the creditors generally. ...

It strikes me that each of the applicants in this case has a realistic possibility of being able to continue operating, although each is currently unable to meet all of its expenses, albeit on a reduced scale. This is precisely the sort of circumstance in which all of the creditors are likely to benefit from the application of the CCAA and in which it is appropriate to grant an order staying proceedings so as to allow the applicant to finalize preparation of and file a plan of compromise and arrangement.

NOTE

In *Cliffs Over Maple Bay Investments Ltd v. Fisgard Capital Corp.* (2008), 296 DLR (4th) 577 (BCCA), the debtor filed for CCAA protection following the breakdown of a development project. Its restructuring plan was to secure funds to complete the project and, upon completion, to sell the development and use the sale proceeds to pay off its creditors. Tysoe JA, for the court, stated (at para. 26):

> [T]he ability of the court to grant or continue a stay under s. 11 is not a free standing remedy that the court may grant whenever an insolvent company wishes to undertake a "restructuring," a term with a broad meaning including such things as refinancings, capital injections and asset sales and other downsizing. Rather, s. 11 is ancillary to the fundamental purpose of the CCAA [which is to facilitate compromises and arrangements between companies and their creditors], and a stay of proceedings freezing the rights of creditors should only be granted in furtherance of the CCAA's fundamental purpose.

In *Fisgard*, there was no evidence that the debtor intended to propose an arrangement or compromise with its creditors before proceeding with its restructuring plan and so the court concluded that the CCAA proceedings were inappropriate.

At first glance, this decision seems to be inconsistent with *Lehndorff*. However, Tysoe JA suggested that the inconsistency could be avoided by reading Farley J's statement in *Lehndorff* (at para. 32) as applying only if "the sale, winding up or liquidation is part of the arrangement approved by the creditors and sanctioned by the court." Compare *Royal Bank of Canada v. Fracmaster* (1999), 244 AR 93, where the Alberta Court of Appeal went further, holding (at para. 16) that, "although there are infrequent situations in which a liquidation of a company's assets has been concluded under the CCAA, the proposed transaction must be in the best interests of the creditors generally," "there must be an ongoing business entity which will survive the asset sale," and "a sale of all or substantially all the assets of a company to an entirely different entity, with no continued involvement by former creditors and shareholders, does not meet this requirement." For further discussion of asset sales, and the apparent split between the courts from province to province on the question, see Chapter 13, Section VII.

ATB Financial v. Metcalfe & Mansfield Alternative Investments II Corp.
(2008), 296 DLR (4th) 135 (OCA)

BLAIR JA: ... [44] The CCAA is skeletal in nature. It does not contain a comprehensive code that lays out all that is permitted or barred. Judges must therefore play a role in fleshing out the details of the statutory scheme. The scope of the Act and the powers of the court under it are not limitless. It is beyond controversy, however, that the CCAA is remedial legislation to be liberally construed in accordance with the modern purposive approach to statutory interpretation. It is designed to be a flexible instrument and it is that very flexibility which gives the Act its efficacy: *Canadian Red Cross Society (Re)* (1998), 5 CBR (4th) 299 (Ont. Gen. Div.). As Farley J noted in *Re Dylex Ltd.* (1995), 31 CBR (3d) 106 at 111 (Ont. Gen. Div.), "[t]he history of CCAA law has been an evolution of judicial interpretation." ...

[50] The remedial purpose of the CCAA—as its title affirms—is to facilitate compromises or arrangements between an insolvent debtor company and its creditors. In *Chef Ready Foods Ltd. v. Hongkong Bank of Canada* (1990), 4 CBR (3d) 311 at 318 (BCCA), Gibbs JA summarized very concisely the purpose, object and scheme of the Act:

Almost inevitably, liquidation destroyed the shareholders' investment, yielded little by way of recovery to the creditors, and exacerbated the social evil of devastating levels of unemployment. The government of the day sought, through the CCAA, to create a regime whereby the principals of the company and the creditors could be brought together under the supervision of the court to attempt a reorganization or compromise or arrangement under which the company could continue in business.

[51] The CCAA was enacted in 1933 and was necessary—as the then Secretary of State noted in introducing the Bill on First Reading—"because of the prevailing commercial and industrial depression" and the need to alleviate the effects of business bankruptcies in that context: see the statement of the Hon. C.H. Cahan, Secretary of State, *House of Commons Debates (Hansard)* (April 20, 1933) at 4091. One of the greatest effects of that Depression was what Gibbs JA described as "the social evil of devastating levels of unemployment." Since then, courts have recognized that the Act has a broader dimension than simply the direct relations between the debtor company and its creditors and that this broader public dimension must be weighed in the balance together with the interests of those most directly affected: see, for example, *Elan Corp. v. Comiskey (Trustee of)* (1990), 1 OR (3d) 289 (CA), *per* Doherty JA in dissent; *Re Skydome Corp.* (1998), 16 CBR (4th) 125 (Ont. Gen. Div.); *Re Anvil Range Mining Corp.* (1998), 7 CBR (4th) 51 (Ont. Gen. Div.).

[52] In this respect, I agree with the following statement of Doherty JA in *Elan, supra*, at pp. 306-307:

> [T]he Act was designed to serve a "broad constituency of investors, creditors and employees." Because of that "broad constituency" the court must, when considering applications brought under the Act, *have regard not only to the individuals and organizations directly affected by the application, but also to the wider public interest.* [Emphasis added.]

Andrew J.F. Kent, Wael Rostom, Adam Maerov, and Tushara Weerasooriya, "Canadian Business Restructuring Law: When Should a Court Say 'No'?"
(2008), 24 *BFLR* 1, at 1 (footnotes omitted)

Courts have generally held that the purpose of the CCAA is "to preserve an insolvent company as a viable operation and to reorganize its affairs to the benefit not only of the debtor but of the creditors." Implicit in this purpose is the belief that restructurings have such economic and social value as to render them preferable to liquidation or sale. It has been argued that from a macroeconomic perspective, there is little to be gained in liquidating viable enterprises that are experiencing temporary financial hardship.

The flaw in these types of motherhood statements is that they lack a fundamental theoretical basis upon which we can formulate concrete objectives. In the United States there are competing theories of bankruptcy law. For example, one theory, the creditor's bargain theory, focuses on the position and expectations of creditors. Alternatively, we could ascribe to Professor Warren's position that bankruptcy reorganization should preserve the debtor's business for the benefit of many constituencies, such as employees, customers and suppliers and judge the success of a restructuring by how many jobs were saved or customer/supplier relationships maintained.[7] It is unclear what theory informs Canadian insolvency laws. Is the primary value as simple as getting to a deal, whatever that deal may be?

Consider for instance the position of debtor's counsel advising its client on the eve of a CCAA filing. Should counsel tell the debtor's board of directors that post-filing it should look only to protection of shareholder interests and the enterprise as a whole because Canadian corporate law does not recognize a shift in the board's duties to creditors within an insolvency? Should counsel advise the debtor to terminate its employees and make termination and severance payments before the filing on the basis that the employees, particularly unionized employees, are more likely to put up an organized fight, while unsecured creditors have less capacity to advance their interests? Should counsel assure the debtor that in all likelihood any plan put forward by the debtor will be approved by the Court (even where substantive rights of third parties, like landlords, are compromised or unilaterally changed), as long as the result is said to be better than a liquidation? There are no simple answers to these questions and counsel, whose primary duty is to serve the interests of the client, must advise the debtor to act in a manner that is advantageous to the debtor's interests, without regard to the consequences such actions may have on the restructuring system as a whole.

The absence of definitive guidance and rules governing the behaviour of the debtor in an insolvency, has resulted in the transfer of the governance burden (perhaps unfairly) to the judiciary who must maintain the integrity of the system through the exercise of judicial discretion and inherent jurisdiction. However, the nature of the Canadian Court process is such that it requires Courts to adjudicate specific disputes between particular parties. While the Court can and must be relied on implicitly to adjudicate such matters in a manner that is fair and just, the case by case consideration of issues is not always conducive to promoting high level policy objectives. For example, the decision of a court to approve a particular course of conduct while justifiable in the circumstances, may lead to injustices in the future. In the absence of specific legislative rules that speak to when and, in what circumstances, such conduct should be approved, that one decision of the Court is itself elevated to a "rule" which must be followed or at least considered in every subsequent case. The result is that Courts have become bound by a set of decisions made (in large part) to address very specific disputes and facts and which together do not necessarily reflect the principles that would collectively have been agreed upon by parties designing the system.

What is clear is that when it comes to the governance of parties participating in a restructuring process, particularly the debtor, there is a gap in the legislation. While this gap has, to a certain extent, been filled by corporate law and by the common law or the civil code on an ad hoc basis, it does not provide the "necessary degree of predictability and consistency in the application of the law, which is essential to investors, creditors, employees and other interested parties in developing a successful restructuring plan."

---

7. See Elizabeth Warren, "Bankruptcy Policy" (1987), 54 *U. Chicago L Rev.* 775, extracted in Section III of Chapter 1; compare Douglas Baird, "Loss Distribution, Forum Shopping and Bankruptcy: A Reply to Professor Warren" (1984) 54 *U. Chicago L Rev.* 815. [eds.]

III. SCOPE OF THE CCAA

The application of the CCAA is subject to the following limitations (CCAA ss. 2(1), 3(1)):

1. the Act applies only if the debtor is a company or an income trust, but not if the debtor is a bank, a railway or telegraph company, an insurance company, or a company to which the *Trust and Loan Companies Act* applies;

2. total claims against the debtor or its affiliated companies must exceed $5 million; and

3. the debtor must be bankrupt or insolvent, or have committed an act of bankruptcy or be subject to winding-up proceedings under the *Winding-up and Restructuring Act*.

The following cases address the insolvency requirement.

Enterprise Capital Management Inc. v. Semi-Tech Corp.
(1999), 10 CBR (4th) 133 (Ont. SCJ)

GROUND J: [1] This application is brought by Enterprise Capital Management Inc. ("Enterprise"), on its own behalf and on behalf of funds managed by it, and with the support of other holders of Senior Secured Discount Notes (the "Notes") of Semi-Tech Corporation ("Semi-Tech") for, *inter alia*, an order declaring that Semi-Tech is a corporation to which the *Companies' Creditors Arrangement Act*, RSC 1985, Chapter C-36 (the "CCAA") and the *Business Corporations Act*, RSO 1990, Chapter B.16 (the "OBCA") apply, for an order authorizing the applicant to file a plan or plans of compromise or arrangement in respect of Semi-Tech under the CCAA and the OBCA, an order appointing KPMG Inc. ("KPMG") as monitor of Semi-Tech to assist Enterprise in developing the plan and to monitor the property of Semi-Tech and conduct the business and affairs of Semi-Tech until discharged by this Court. The application also seeks orders restricting the management and control of Semi-Tech and its operations by prohibiting Semi-Tech from making any payments to certain senior officers and directors, from voting any of the shares of Semi-Tech (Global) Company Limited ("Global") or the Singer Company NV ("Singer"), altering any material contracts between controlling parties and corporations in which Semi-Tech has a substantial equity interest, prohibiting Semi-Tech and its officers and directors from dealing with its assets or making payments to creditors except in the ordinary course of business and removing the current directors of Semi-Tech and appointing directors to be specified in the plan.

Background

[2] Semi-Tech is a holding company. Its common shares trade on the Toronto Stock Exchange. Its primary direct holdings are control blocks of two public companies, Singer and Global. Singer trades on the New York Stock Exchange and Global trades on the Hong Kong Stock Exchange. Both Singer and Global hold controlling interests in other public companies. For example, Singer holds approximately 80% of the common shares of G.M. Pfaff AG ("Pfaff") which shares are traded on the Frankfurt Stock Exchange.

Global holds direct and indirect controlling interests in Akai Electric Co. Ltd. ("Akai") and Sansui Electric Co. Limited ("Sansui") whose shares are traded on the Tokyo, Osaka and Nagoya Stock Exchanges as well as Tomei International Holding Limited ("Tomei"), whose shares are traded on the Hong Kong Stock Exchange.

[3] As the financial statements of the companies are based on United States dollars, the dollar references herein are to United States dollars.

[4] Semi-Tech acquired its interest in Singer from Global in 1993. The acquisition price of $848 million was funded by a public issue of common shares raising $548 million and the issuance of the Notes, raising $300 million. In the 1993 Prospectus filed in connection with the issuance of its common shares and Notes, Semi-Tech described the purpose of its acquisition of Singer and described Global's plans for continued investment in turnaround opportunities in the developing word, particularly Asia. The terms of the Notes were negotiated with the original holders. The Notes provide that no payments of principal are due until 2003 and no interest is payable until 2001.

[5] The Notes are secured by a pledge of 25,300,000 shares of Singer, representing approximately 50% of the outstanding shares of Singer. The trust indenture dated August 18, 1993 (the "Trust Indenture"), under which the Notes are secured, provides that, if an Event of Default were to occur, the Noteholders, acting through their trustee and in accordance with the terms set out in the Trust Indenture, could accelerate the maturity date of the Notes and enforce their security in the Singer shares.

[6] I am satisfied that the Applicant would be able to establish that Semi-Tech has breached certain of the covenants contained in the Trust Indenture. However, in that the appropriate notices of covenant defaults have not been given and the time periods allowed to remedy defaults following such notices have not elapsed, it is conceded that at this date there is no "Event of Default" as defined in the Trust Indenture.

[7] The most recent audited and unaudited financial statements for Semi-Tech, Singer and Global indicate substantial shareholders' equity in each company although the audited financial statements for the companies as at the end of their January, 1999 fiscal years are not yet issued and are not before this Court. The market prices of the shares of Singer and Global are depressed and the total market value of the shares of Singer and Global held by Semi-Tech as of the date of the application was approximately $120,000,000. The total principal amount of the Notes outstanding as of September 30, 1998 was approximately $531,000,000 and it is alleged by Enterprise that this amount has been increasing by approximately $5,000,000 per month since September, 1998 as the redemption price of the Notes gradually increases toward their ultimate maturity date. There are no other significant liabilities of Semi-Tech.

Submissions

[8] It is conceded that there is no evidence before this Court of Semi-Tech being unable to meet its obligations as they generally became due. It appears to be the position of Enterprise that Semi-Tech is insolvent under the test set out in clause (c) of the definition of "insolvent person" in subsection 2(1) of the *Bankruptcy and Insolvency Act*, RSC 1985, c. B-3 as amended (the "BIA"), which definition is applicable to defining a "debtor company" as being "insolvent" under section 2 of the CCAA. It is the position of Enterprise

that, having regard to the market value of the shares of Singer and Global, which are effectively the only assets of Semi-Tech, they are not, in the aggregate, at a fair valuation or if disposed of at a fairly conducted sale under legal process, sufficient to enable payment of Semi-Tech's obligations due and accruing due.

[9] Enterprise submits that in determining obligations "due and accruing due" for purposes of the insolvency test in clause (c) of the definition of "insolvent person" in subsection 2(1) of the BIA, the Court should not limit its consideration to debts which have matured and that accordingly a debtor is insolvent if its present assets are insufficient to meet its liabilities at maturity. Enterprise relies on certain American authorities to support this proposition.

[10] Enterprise further takes the position that the principal amount of Notes outstanding are obligations due and accruing due because of the occurrence of defaults under certain covenants in the Trust Indenture which defaults have not been waived. Enterprise relies on an Abstract of issues discussed by the Emerging Issues Committee of the Canadian Institute of Chartered Accountants as contained in the CIAC Handbook which recommends that, if there has been a default under certain types of covenants in an instrument under which debt securities are outstanding and such default has not been waived or arrangements in place to cure the default, the principal amount of such debt securities should be included in current liabilities in a financial statement.

[11] Semi-Tech submits that the determination of whether the value of its property is sufficient to enable payment of its obligations due and accruing due is a "present exercise" and that the Court should not speculate as to whether the company will eventually be unable to meet its liabilities as they fall due. Semi-Tech states that its audited financial statements are appropriate evidence of solvency sufficient to rebut any allegations of insolvency, that such financial statements indicate substantial shareholders equity in Semi-Tech, that no reduction has been made by its auditors in the market value of the securities it holds and that the Notes have not been recorded as current liabilities as would be recommended by the CICA Handbook provision referred to above.

[12] It is the further submission of Semi-Tech that the market value of the shares of Singer and Global is not determinative of the value of the assets of Semi-Tech which are controlling interests in Singer and Global and which would attract a control block premium and that, to determine the value of such assets, would require expert evidence from underwriters or others at a trial. In addition, Semi-Tech submits that, to value such assets, one must have regard to the financial statements of Singer and Global. The financial statements of Singer and Global before this Court indicate a substantial shareholders' equity in each of Singer and Global which would indicate the value of the controlling interests in each of those companies. Semi-Tech also submits that the CICA Handbook is not definitive of the question of whether the Notes are obligations "due or accruing due" for purposes of the insolvency test and that the Notes are not now due or accruing due in that no payments of interest or principal are due until the years 2001 and 2003 respectively and no Event of Default has occurred under the Trust Indenture accelerating the maturity date of the Notes.

Reasons

[13] I accept the submission of Semi-Tech that to determine the fair valuation of Semi-Tech's assets, being principally the control blocks of shares of Singer and Global, one cannot simply multiply the number of shares by their current market prices. The Court must recognize that the control blocks, if disposed of by Semi-Tech, would attract control block premiums and that accordingly a determination of fair valuation would require expert evidence from underwriters or others as to the market value of such control blocks. It does seem to me however that, if the Notes represent obligations "due and accruing due" in an amount in excess of $531,000,000, it is highly unlikely that control block premiums would increase the fair valuation of such control blocks from the value of $120,000,000 based on current share prices to anything approaching $531,000,000.

[14] I am not satisfied that one can rely upon the fact that the financial statements of Semi-Tech indicate a shareholders equity to rebut a finding of insolvency based on a comparison of fair valuation of assets to the amount of obligations due and accruing due. Financial statements are based upon historic figures and on a going concern assumption and do not necessarily reflect what would result if the company as of this date sold all its assets at a fair valuation and was required to pay all of its obligations due and accruing due. In *Lin v. Lee* (June 27, 1996), Doc. Vancouver C944487 (BCSC), Coultas J referred to this assumption as stated in the CICA Handbook.

> An assumption underlying the preparation of financial statements in accordance with generally accepted accounting principles is that the enterprise will be able to realize assets and discharge liabilities in the normal course of business for the foreseeable future. This is commonly referred to as the going concern assumption.

[15] It therefore becomes necessary to determine whether the principal amount of the Notes constitutes an obligation "due or accruing due" as of date of this application.

[16] There is a paucity of helpful authority on the meaning of "accruing due" for purposes of a definition of insolvency. Historically in 1933, in *P. Lyall & Sons Construction Co. v. Baker*, [1933] OR 286 (Ont. CA), the Ontario Court of Appeal, in determining a question of set-off under the Dominion *Winding Up Act* had to determine whether the amount claimed as a set-off was a debt due or accruing due to the company in liquidation for purposes of that Act. Marsten JA at pages 292-293 quoted from Moss JA in *Mail Printing Co. v. Clarkson* (1898), 25 OAR 1 (Ont. CA) at page 8:

> A debt is defined to be a sum of money which is certainly, and at all event, payable without regard to the fact whether it be payable now or at a future time. And an accruing debt is a debt not yet actually payable, but a debt which is represented by an existing obligation; *per* Lindley LJ in *Webb v. Stenton* (1883) 11 QBD at p. 529.

[17] Whatever relevance such definition may have had for purposes of dealing with claims by and against companies in liquidation under the old winding up legislation, it is apparent to me that it should not be applied to definitions of insolvency. To include every debt payable at some future date in "accruing due" for the purposes of insolvency tests would render numerous corporations, with long term debt due over a period of years in the future and anticipated to be paid out of future income, "insolvent" for purposes of the BIA and therefore the CCAA. For the same reason, I do not accept the state-

ment quoted in the Enterprise factum from the decision of the Bankruptcy Court for the Southern District of New York in *Centennial Textiles Inc., Re*, 220 BR 165 (USNYDC 1998) that "if the present saleable value of assets are less than the amount required to pay existing debt as they mature, the debtor is insolvent." In my view the obligations, which are to be measured against the fair valuation of a company's property as being obligations due and accruing due, must be limited to obligations currently payable or properly chargeable to the accounting period during which the test is being applied as, for example, a sinking fund payment due within the current year. Black's Law Dictionary defines "accrued liability" as "an obligation or debt which is properly chargeable in a given accounting period but which is not yet paid or payable." The principal amount of the Notes is neither due nor accruing due in this sense.

[18] In addition, even if the reference in the CICA Handbook is applicable to the covenant defaults alleged by Enterprise, this simply means that it is recommended that, in applicable situations for purposes of preparing a financial statement, the accountants should show long term debt as a current liability. As stated above, I do not think reference should be made to financial statements for the purpose of determining whether a company is "insolvent" as that term is defined in the BIA and applicable to the CCAA. In the case at bar, where the Notes do not mature until 2003, there has been no Event of Default and no acceleration of the maturity of the Notes, the fact that accountants may, in certain circumstances of a covenant default, determine to show long term debt as a current liability in the financial statements, presumably with some explanatory note, is not in my view determinative of such debt being an obligation "accruing due" for purposes of the insolvency test.

[19] Accordingly, on the basis of the evidence now before this Court, I am unable to conclude that Semi-Tech is insolvent within the meaning of clause (c) of the definition of "insolvent person" in subsection 2(1) of the BIA which definition is applicable to the CCAA.

[20] Although it is moot in view of my finding that Semi-Tech is not insolvent within the meaning of clause (c) of subsection 2(1) of the BIA, I wish to comment on certain other aspects of this application. Even where the Court has found a company to be insolvent, the Court must in exercising its discretion under the CCAA, determine whether in all the circumstances it is appropriate that an order be made pursuant to the CCAA. In making such determination, the Court must have regard to the interests of all the stakeholders, not only those represented before the Court on the application, and must take into account any public interest involved.

[21] I adopt the statement of Blair J in his November 27, 1998 endorsement in the application of *Skydome Corp., Re* [(November 27, 1998), Blair J (Ont. Gen. Div.)] under the CCAA:

> Thus there is a broader public dimension which must be considered and weighed in the balance on this Application as well as the interests of those most directly affected: see *Anvil Range Mining Corporation*, unreported decision of the Ontario Court of Justice, General Division, August 20, 1998. As was stated in that case:
>
>> The court in its supervisory capacity has a broader mandate. In a receivership such as this one which works well into the social and economic fabric of a territory, that

mandate must encompass having an eye for the social consequences of the receivership too. These interests cannot override the lawful interests of secured creditors ultimately but they can and must be weighed in the balance as the process works its way through.

The *Anvil Range* case concerned a CCAA proceeding which had been turned into a receivership but the same principles apply in my view to a case such as this.

[22] In addition the Court must be conscious of the purpose and intent of the CCAA. The statute was originally enacted in 1933 to provide for an alternative to bankruptcy or liquidation of companies in financial difficulties during the depression years and for court sanction of plans of compromise and arrangement between companies and their creditors which would permit a restructuring and the continued operation of the companies' businesses and continued production and employment by the companies. In the Houlden and Morawetz annotated *Bankruptcy and Insolvency Act* at page 10A-2, the authors describe the purpose and intent of the CCAA as follows:

> The CCAA has a broad remedial purpose giving a debtor an opportunity to find a way out of financial difficulties short of bankruptcy, foreclosure or the seizure of assets through receivership proceedings. It allows the debtor to find a plan that will enable him to meet the demands of his creditors through refinancing with new lending, equity financing or the sale of the business as a going concern. This alternative may well give the creditors of all classes a larger return and protect the jobs of the company's employees: *Diemaster Tool Inc. v. Skvortsoff (Trustee of)* (1991), 3 CBR (3d) 133 (Ont. Gen. Div.).

[23] It is usual on initial applications under the CCAA for the applicant to submit to the Court at least a general outline of the type of plan of compromise and arrangement between the company and its creditors proposed by the applicant. The application now before this Court is somewhat of a rarity in that the application is brought by an applicant representing a group of creditors and not by the company itself as is the usual case. Enterprise has submitted that it is not in a position to submit an outline of a plan to the Court in that it lacks sufficient information and has been unable to obtain such information from Semi-Tech. Enterprise points out that, in the usual case, the application is brought by the company, the company has all the necessary information at hand and has usually had the assistance of a firm which is the proposed monitor and which has worked with the company in preparing an outline of a plan.

[24] I have some difficulty with the submission of Enterprise that it does not have sufficient information available to submit an outline of a plan. Semi-Tech is a public company, as are Singer and Global and a number of the subsidiaries of Singer and Global, and I would have thought that sufficient information is easily accessible by Enterprise to prepare a general outline of what compromises or arrangements are proposed as between Semi-Tech and its creditors and in particular what is proposed as to either a disposition of the shares of Singer and/or Global or a restructuring of either of those companies. There is no such information before the Court and no indication that Semi-Tech will be involved in the preparation of a draft plan to be put before the Court other than as a source of information.

[25] In the absence of any indication that Enterprise proposes a plan which would consist of some compromise or arrangement between Semi-Tech and its creditors and permit the continued operation of Semi-Tech and its subsidiaries in some restructured form, it appears to me that it would be inappropriate to make any order pursuant to the CCAA. If the Noteholders intend simply to liquidate the assets of Semi-Tech and distribute the proceeds, it would appear that they could do so by proceeding under the Trust Indenture on the basis of the alleged covenant defaults, accelerating the maturity date of the Notes, realizing on their security in the shares of Singer and recovering any balance due on the Notes by the appointment of a receiver or otherwise.

[26] If any such steps were taken by the Noteholders, Semi-Tech could at that time bring its own application pursuant to the CCAA outlining a restructuring plan which would permit the continued operation of the company and its subsidiaries and be in conformity with the purpose and intent of the legislation. I am conscious however that, although the evidence before this Court on this point was somewhat inconclusive, the application is alleged to be brought with the consent of an informal committee of Noteholders representing 52.3% in principal amount of the outstanding Notes and that the holder of a further 20% in principal amount of outstanding Notes is alleged to support the application. In view of this, it would appear unlikely that any plan brought forward by Semi-Tech would receive the approval of creditors required by the CCAA. ...

Application dismissed

Re Stelco Inc.
(2004), 48 CBR (4th) 299 (Ont. SCJ)

FARLEY J: As argued this motion by Locals 1005, 5328 and 8782 United Steel Workers of America (collectively "Union") to rescind the initial order and dismiss the application of Stelco Inc. ("Stelco") and various of its subsidiaries (collectively "Sub Applicants") for access to the protection and process of the *Companies' Creditors Arrangement Act* ("CCAA") was that this access should be denied on the basis that Stelco was not a "debtor company" as defined in s. 2 of the CCAA because it was not insolvent. ...

The Union, supported by the International United Steel Workers of America ("International"), indicated that if certain of the obligations of Stelco were taken into account in the determination of insolvency, then a very good number of large Canadian corporations would be able to make an application under the CCAA. I am of the view that this concern can be addressed as follows. The test of insolvency is to be determined on its own merits, not on the basis that an otherwise technically insolvent corporation should not be allowed to apply. However, if a technically insolvent corporation were to apply and there was no material advantage to the corporation and its stakeholders (in other words, a pressing need to restructure), then one would expect that the court's discretion would be judicially exercised against granting CCAA protection and ancillary relief. In the case of Stelco, it is recognized, as discussed above, that it is in crisis and in need of restructuring—which restructuring, if it is insolvent, would be best accomplished within a CCAA proceeding. Further, I am of the view that the track record of CCAA proceedings in this country demonstrates a healthy respect for the fundamental concerns of interested parties and stakeholders. I have consistently observed that much more can be achieved by negotiations outside the courtroom where there is a reasonable exchange of information, views and the exploration of possible solutions and negotiations held on a without prejudice basis than likely can be achieved by resorting to the legal combative atmosphere of the courtroom. A mutual problem requires a mutual solution. The basic interest of the CCAA is to rehabilitate insolvent corporations for the benefit of all stakeholders. To do this, the cause(s) of the insolvency must be fixed on a long term viable basis so that the corporation may be turned around. It is not achieved by positional bargaining in a tug of war between two parties, each trying for a larger slice of a defined size pie; it may be achieved by taking steps involving shorter term equitable sacrifices and implementing sensible approaches to improve productivity to ensure that the pie grows sufficiently for the long term to accommodate the reasonable needs of the parties. ...

On a practical basis, I would note that all too often corporations will wait too long before applying, at least this was a significant problem in the early 1990s. In *Re Inducon Development Corp.* (1991), 8 CBR (3d) 306 (Ont. Gen. Div.), I observed:

> Secondly, CCAA is designed to be remedial; it is not, however, designed to be preventative. CCAA should not be the *last* gasp of a dying company; it should be implemented, if it is to be implemented, at a stage prior to the death throe.

It seems to me that the phrase "death throe" could be reasonably replaced with "death spiral." In *Re Cumberland Trading Inc.* (1994), 23 CBR (3d) 225 (Ont. Gen. Div.), I went on to expand on this at p. 228:

> I would also observe that all too frequently debtors wait until virtually the last moment, the last moment, or in some cases, beyond the last moment before even beginning to think about reorganizational (and the attendant support that any successful reorganization requires from the creditors). I noted the lamentable tendency of debtors to deal with these situations as "last gasp" desperation moves in *Re Inducon Development Corp.* (1992), 8 CBR (3d) 308 (Ont. Gen. Div.). To deal with matters on this basis minimizes the chances of success, even if "success" may have been available with earlier spade work.

I have not been able to find in the CCAA reported cases any instance where there has been an objection to a corporation availing itself of the facilities of the CCAA on the basis of whether the corporation was insolvent. Indeed, as indicated above, the major concern here has been that an applicant leaves it so late that the timetable of necessary steps may get impossibly compressed. That is not to say that there have not been objections by parties opposing the application on various other grounds. Prior to the 1992 amendments, there had to be debentures (plural) issued pursuant to a trust deed; I recall that in *Nova Metal Products Inc. v. Comiskey (Trustee of)*, (1990), 1 CBR (3d) 101; 1 OR (3d) 280 (CA), the initial application was rejected in the morning because there had only been one debenture issued but another one was issued prior to the return to court that afternoon. This case stands for the general proposition that the CCAA should be given a large and liberal interpretation. I should note that there was in *Enterprise Capital Management Inc. v. Semi-Tech Corp.* (1999), 10 CBR (4th) 133 (Ont. SCJ) a determination that in a creditor application, the corporation was found not to be insolvent, but see below as to BIA test (c) my views as to the correctness of this decision. ...

I note in particular that the (b), (c) and (d) aspects of the definition of "debtor company" all refer to other statutes, including the BIA; (a) does not. Section 12 of the CCAA defines "claims" with reference over to the BIA (and otherwise refers to the BIA and the *Winding-Up and Restructuring Act*). It seems to me that there is merit in considering that the test for insolvency under the CCAA may differ somewhat from that under the BIA, so as to meet the special circumstances of the CCAA and those corporations which would apply under it. In that respect, I am mindful of the above discussion regarding the time that is usually and necessarily (in the circumstances) taken in a CCAA reorganization restructuring which is engaged in coming up with a plan of compromise and arrangement. The BIA definition would appear to have been historically focussed on the question of bankruptcy—and not reorganization of a corporation under a proposal since before 1992, secured creditors could not be forced to compromise their claims, so that in practice there were no reorganizations under the former *Bankruptcy Act* unless all secured creditors voluntarily agreed to have their secured claims compromised. The BIA definition then was essentially useful for being a pre-condition to the "end" situation of a bankruptcy petition or voluntary receiving order where the upshot would be a realization on the bankrupt's assets (not likely involving the business carried on—and certainly not by the bankrupt). Insolvency under the BIA is also important as to the Paulian action events (eg., fraudulent preferences, settlements) as to the conduct of the debtor *prior* to the bankruptcy; similarly as to the question of provincial preference legislation. Reorganization under a plan or proposal, on the contrary, is with a general objective of the applicant continuing to exist, albeit that the CCAA may also be used to have an orderly disposition of the assets and undertaking in whole or in part.

It seems to me that given the time and steps involved in a reorganization, and the condition of insolvency perforce requires an expanded meaning under the CCAA. Query whether the definition under the BIA is now sufficient in that light for the allowance of sufficient time to carry through with a realistically viable proposal within the maximum of six months allowed under the BIA? I think it sufficient to note that there would not be much sense in providing for a rehabilitation program of restructuring/reorganization under either statute if the entry test was that the applicant could not apply until a rather late stage of its financial difficulties with the rather automatic result that in situations of complexity of any material degree, the applicant would not have the financial resources sufficient to carry through to hopefully a successful end. This would indeed be contrary to the renewed emphasis of Parliament on "rescues" as exhibited by the 1992 and 1997 amendments to the CCAA and the BIA.

Allow me now to examine whether Stelco has been successful in meeting the onus of demonstrating with credible evidence on a common sense basis that it is insolvent within the meaning required by the CCAA in regard to the interpretation of "debtor company" in the context and within the purpose of that legislation. ... It seems to me that the CCAA test of insolvency advocated by Stelco and which I have determined is a proper interpretation is that the BIA definition of (a), (b) or (c) of insolvent person is acceptable with the caveat that as to (a), a financially troubled corporation is insolvent if it is reasonably expected to run out of liquidity within reasonable proximity of time as compared with the time reasonably required to implement a restructuring. That is, there should be a reasonable cushion, which cushion may be adjusted and indeed become in effect an encroachment depending upon reasonable access to DIP between financing. In the present case, Stelco accepts the view of the Union's affiant, Michael Mackey of Deloitte and Touche that it will otherwise run out of funding by November 2004. ...

In my view, the Union's position that Stelco is not insolvent under BIA (a) because it has not entirely used up its cash and cash facilities (including its credit line), that is, it [has] not yet as of January 29, 2004 run out of liquidity conflates inappropriately the (a) test with the (b) test. The Union's view would render the (a) test necessarily as being redundant. ...

It seems to me that if the BIA (a) test is restrictively dealt with (as per my question to Union counsel as to how far in the future should one look on a prospective basis being answered "24 hours") then Stelco would not be insolvent under that test. However, I am of the view that that would be unduly restrictive and a proper contextual and purposive interpretation to be given when it is being used for a restructuring purpose even under BIA would be to see whether there is a reasonably foreseeable (at the time of filing) expectation that there is a looming liquidity condition or crisis which will result in the applicant running out of "cash" to pay its debts as they generally become due in the future without the benefit of the stay and ancillary protection and procedure by court authorization pursuant to an order. I think this is the more appropriate interpretation of BIA (a) test in the context of a reorganization or "rescue" as opposed to a threshold to bankruptcy consideration or a fraudulent preferences proceeding. On that basis, I would find Stelco insolvent from the date of filing. Even if one were not to give the latter interpretation to the BIA (a) test, clearly for the above reasons and analysis, if one looks at the meaning of "insolvent" within the context of a CCAA reorganization or rescue solely, then of necessity, the time horizon must be such that the liquidity crisis would occur in the sense of running out of "cash" but for the grant of the CCAA order. On that basis Stelco is certainly insolvent given its limited cash resources unused, its need for a cushion, its rate of cash burn recently experienced and anticipated.

What about the BIA (c) test which may be roughly referred to as an assets compared with obligations test. See *New Quebec Reglan Mines Ltd. v. Blok-Andersen*, [1993] OJ No. 727 (Gen. Div.) as to fair value and fair market valuation. The Union observed that there was no intention by Stelco to wind itself up or proceed with a sale of some or all of its assets and undertaking and therefore some of the liabilities which Stelco and Stephen took into account would not crystallize. However, as I discussed at the time of the hearing, the (c) test is what one might reasonably call or describe as an "artificial" or notional/hypothetical test. It presumes certain things which are in fact not necessarily contemplated to take place or to be involved. ...

To my view the preferable interpretation to be given to "sufficient to enable payment of all his obligations, due and accruing due" is to be determined in the context of this test as a whole. What is being put up to satisfy those obligations is the debtor's assets and undertaking *in total*; in other words, the debtor in essence is taken as having sold everything. There would be no residual assets and undertaking to pay off any obligations which would not be encompassed by the phrase "all of his obligations, due and accruing due." Surely, there cannot be "orphan" obligations which are left hanging unsatisfied. It seems to me that the intention of "due and accruing due" was to cover off all obligations of whatever nature or kind and leave nothing in limbo. ...

In the end result, I have concluded on the balance of probabilities that Stelco is insolvent and therefore it is a "debtor company" as at the date of filing and entitled to apply for the CCAA initial order. My conclusion is that (i) BIA test (c) strongly shows Stelco is insolvent; (ii) BIA test (a) demonstrates, to a less certain but sufficient basis, an insolvency; and (iii) the "new" CCAA test again strongly supports the conclusion of insolvency. I am further of the opinion that I properly exercised my discretion in granting Stelco and the Sub Applicants the initial order on January 29, 2004 and I would confirm that as of the present date with effect on the date of filing. The Union's motion is therefore dismissed.

NOTES AND QUESTIONS

1. Leave to appeal in the *Stelco* case was refused both by the Ontario Court of Appeal (*Re Stelco*, [2004] OJ no. 1903 (QL)) and the Supreme Court of Canada (*Re Stelco*, [2004] SCCA no. 336 (QL).)

2. The decisions in *Semi-Tech* and *Stelco* appear to be contradictory. Note, though, that in *Semi-Tech* the CCAA proceedings were initiated by a creditor, whereas in *Stelco* the proceedings were initiated by the debtor itself. Are the cases distinguishable on this basis?

3. In the United States, a petitioning creditor does not have to allege or prove insolvency under Chapter 11. What function does the insolvency requirement perform under the CCAA? Would there be any advantage in abolishing the insolvency requirement under the CCAA for voluntary proceedings? Might there be constitutional implications in doing this? See J. Ziegel, "Should Proof of the Debtor's Insolvency Be Dispensed with in Voluntary Insolvency Proceedings?" [2007] *Ann. Rev. Ins. L* 21.

IV. THE INITIAL FILING

CCAA proceedings are initiated by means of an application to the court by the debtor, a creditor, or the debtor's trustee in bankruptcy or liquidator: CCAA ss. 4 and 5 ("the initial application"). The application may be made to a court in the province within which the company has its head office or chief place of business. If the company has neither, then the application may be made in the province within which any of the assets of the company are situated.

An application for an initial order under the CCAA can be made on an *ex parte* basis. This may be useful if there is a real prospect that creditors will attempt to exercise their enforcement remedies against the debtor's assets before the court hears the matter. Sometimes the initial application is made only with notice to the major creditors if it is impracticable to identify and notify all the creditors. A projected cash-flow statement and copies of financial statements prepared in the prior year must be submitted with an application for an initial order.

The initial application usually requests an order containing the following components:

- abridging service of notice of the application;

- declaring the debtor company to be one to which the CCAA applies;

- authorizing the debtor company to continue its business operations and continue in possession of its property;

- staying proceedings against the debtor company;

- appointing a monitor;

- authorizing the debtor company to obtain interim financing (DIP financing);

- indemnifying the debtor company's directors and officers for liability that they incur following the date of the initial order;

- creating charges against the property that secure the administrative expenses, the interim financing, and the indemnification of directors and officers and that give priority over all other security interests and encumbrances;

- authorizing the debtor company to file a plan of arrangement; and

- permitting interested parties to apply to the court for variation or amendment of the order (a "comeback" clause).

The stay of proceedings provided for in the initial order cannot exceed 30 days. The applicant will therefore need to bring a subsequent application before the court for a stay of proceedings of a longer duration. This permits parties affected by the initial order to have an opportunity to express their views concerning the eligibility of the debtor or the appropriateness of the order. The monitor must notify every known creditor who has a claim of more than $1,000 against the company and advise them of the order.

In a number of provinces, insolvency practitioners, working in conjunction with the courts, have developed an initial-order template. The aim is to both expedite the commencement of proceedings and mimize the risk of prejudice to interested parties who may not have had an opportunity to read the proposed order or make submissions on it. Parties are free to vary the template to suit their circumstances, but all variations must be black-lined for easy identification by other parties and the court. The Ontario initial-order template was developed by the Commercial List User's Committee. The Commercial List is a specialized commercial court within the Ontario Superior Court of Justice in Toronto, which deals exclusively with commercial and insolvency matters. The Commercial List Users' Committee comprises judges, practitioners, and court administrators. There are similar initial-order templates in Quebec, British Columbia, and Alberta. The current version of the Ontario initial-order template can be viewed at www.ontariocourts.on.ca/scj/en/commerciallist/forms/SF.doc. However, the document needs updating to take account of the 2007 amendments.

CCAA s. 11.02(3) provides that, to qualify for a stay order, the applicant must satisfy the court that the order is "appropriate" and, in the case of an application other than an initial application, that "the applicant has acted, and is acting, in good faith and with due diligence." The court may rule against the applicant on the appropriateness ground if there is evidence suggesting that the restructuring has no reasonable chance of success: see *Bargain Harold's Discount*, extracted below. *San Francisco Gifts*, also extracted below, addresses the meaning of "good faith."

Bargain Harold's Discount Ltd v. Paribas Bank of Canada
(1992), 10 CBR (3d) 23 (Ont. Gen. Div.)

AUSTIN J: This is an application by Bargain Harold's Discount Limited for an order under s. 11 of the *Companies' Creditors Arrangement Act*, RSC 1985, c. C-36 (the CCAA or the Act). It is opposed by a number of secured creditors. Paribas is the first secured creditor in terms of priority. It has either commenced an action or intends to do so and in that action has brought a motion for the appointment of a receiver and manager. ...

The jurisprudence is clear that if it is obvious that no plan will be found acceptable to the required percentages of creditors, then the application should be refused. The fact that Paribas, the Royal Bank and K Mart now say there is no plan that they would approve, does not put an end to the inquiry. All affected constituencies must be considered, including secured, preferred and unsecured creditors, employees, landlords, shareholders, and the public generally. ...

As to the degree of persuasion required, Doherty JA in *Elan* [*Corp. v. Comiskey (Trustee of)* (1990), 1 OR (3d) 289 (CA)] said at p. 316 OR, p. 129 CBR:

> I agree that the feasibility of the plan is a relevant and significant factor to be considered in determining whether to order a meeting of creditors: Edwards, "Re-organizations under the *Companies' Creditors Arrangement Act*," *supra*, at pp. 594-95. I would not, however, impose a heavy burden on the debtor company to establish the likelihood of ultimate success from the outset. As the Act will often be the last refuge for failing companies, it is to be expected that many of the proposed plans of re-organization will involve variables and contingencies which will make the plan's ultimate acceptability to the creditors and the court very uncertain at the time the initial application is made.

In *Ultracare Management Inc. v. Gammon* (1990), 1 OR (3d) 321, 3 CBR (3d) 151 (Gen. Div.), Hoilett J, at p. 330f OR, p. 162 CBR, suggests that the test is whether the plan, or in the present case, any plan, "has a probable chance of acceptance."

These two standards are in conflict, *Ultracare* requiring the probability of success, and *Elan* requiring something less. Having regard to the nature of the legislation, I prefer the test enunciated by Doherty JA in *Elan*. In *First Treasury Financial Inc. v. Cango Petroleums Inc.* (1991), 3 CBR (3d) 232, 78 DLR (4th) 585 (Ont. Gen. Div.), at p. 238 CBR, p. 590 DLR I expressed the view that the statute required "a reasonable chance" that a plan would be accepted.

A court must be concerned with the nature of the evidence presented in cases such as this. The applicant's main affidavit was sworn on February 25, Paribas' affidavit on the 26th, and the applicant's in response on the 26th. There has been no opportunity for cross-examination. As a consequence, there is a very heavy responsibility on counsel and the court must be mindful of the frailties of the evidence.

Section 6 of the CCAA requires approval of the plan or arrangement by a majority in number representing three-fourths in value of the creditors. Where there are different classes of creditors, the section requires a majority in number representing three-fourths in value of the creditors in each class. Having regard to the evidence presented and its shortcomings, I am unable to conclude that there is any reasonable prospect of the applicant being able to devise a plan or arrangement which would meet the approval requirements of s. 6 of the Act. Amongst the most important elements in reaching this decision is the fact that the applicant still does not know the precise nature of the problem which brought about its present financial circumstances. According to its own auditors, the cause or causes may never be known. There is also the fact, probably related to this first element, that the applicant has no specific idea how its operation can be salvaged, other than to suggest "downsizing." There is no reason to believe that that downsizing can be done any more efficiently by the applicant than by a receiver.

Next is the need to borrow still more money from the Royal Bank in order to continue in business at all. The fact that the Royal Bank may be paid out on March 6 is irrelevant. In order to carry on during the proposed stay period, the applicant requires funds. No source other than the Royal Bank, or in its shoes, K Mart, has been suggested. More to the point, perhaps, no offer has been made by QECC or by CCFL, both of whom are substantial shareholders and both of whom, it was argued, are in a position to assist in refinancing.

Another factor is the failed or abandoned attempt to raise $15 million in October 1992. Yet another is the complete loss of confidence in the management of the company. To this is added the failure of the applicant to suggest who the new management might be.

The only proposal suggested by way of an alternative to a CCAA order was the appointment of a receiver and manager. As in *Cango*, there is no reason to believe that if a receiver were appointed, any more unemployment would result than if the present applicant were left in charge.

At the conclusion of the hearing of this matter on February 26, I indicated my intention to reserve my decision. Counsel for the applicant indicated that as its financial difficulties were now a matter of public knowledge, some order should be made to protect the company pending my decision. As counsel were unable to agree on anything, I made an interim order under s. 11 of the CCAA and appointed Price Waterhouse monitor for the interim period. That order and monitorship is now terminated.

An order will go dismissing the CCAA application. An order will also go appointing Price Waterhouse as receiver and manager of the applicant, effective immediately. If there is any difficulty in settling the form of order, I may be spoken to. Although the question was not raised during the course of argument, the order should confer upon the receiver the power to make an assignment in bankruptcy should it be so advised. A major asset of Bargain Harold's consists of leases. A trustee in bankruptcy has much wider powers to deal with leases than does a receiver.

Re San Francisco Gifts Ltd.
(2005), 10 CBR (5th) 275 (Alta. QB)

TOPOLINSKI J:

Introduction

The San Francisco group of companies (San Francisco) obtained *Companies' Creditors Arrangement Act* (CCAA) protection on January 7, 2000 (Initial Order). Key to that protection was the requisite stay of proceedings that gives a debtor company breathing room to formulate a plan of arrangement. The stay was extended three times thereafter with the expectation that the entire CCAA process would be completed by February 7th, 2005. That date was not met. Accordingly, San Francisco now applies to have the stay extended to June 30, 2005.

A small group of landlords opposes the motion on the basis of San Francisco's recent guilty plea to *Copyright Act* offenses and the sentencing judge's description of San Francisco's conduct as: "… a despicable fraud on the public. Not only not insignificant but bordering on a massive scale … ." The landlords suggest that this precludes any possibility of the company having acted in "good faith" and therefore having met the statutory prerequisite to an extension. Further, they contend that extending the stay would bring the administration of justice into disrepute.

San Francisco acknowledges that its conduct was stupid, offensive and dangerous. That said, it contends that it already has been sanctioned and that it has "paid its debt to society." It argues that subjecting it to another consequence in this proceeding would be akin to double jeopardy. Apart from the obvious consequential harm to the company itself, San Francisco expresses concern that its creditors might be disadvantaged if it is forced into bankruptcy.

While there has been some delay in moving this matter forward towards the creditor vote, this delay is primarily attributable to the time it took San Francisco to deal with leave to appeal my classification decision of September 28, 2004. Despite the opposing landlords' mild protestations to the contrary, it is evident that the company has acted with due diligence. The real focus of this application is on the meaning and scope of the term "good faith" as that term is used in s. 11(6) of the CCAA, and on whether San Francisco's conduct renders it unworthy of the protective umbrella of the Act in its restructuring efforts. It also raises questions about the role of a supervising court in CCAA proceedings.

Background

San Francisco operates a national chain of novelty goods stores from its head office in Edmonton, Alberta. It currently has 62 locations and approximately 400 employees.

The group of companies is comprised of the operating company, San Francisco Gifts Ltd., and a number of hollow nominee companies. The operating company holds all of the group's assets. It is 100 percent owned by Laurier Investments Corp., which in turn is 100 percent owned by Barry Slawsky (Slawsky), the driving force behind the companies.

Apart from typical priority challenges in insolvency matters, this proceeding has been punctuated by a series of challenges to the process and its continuation, led primarily by a group of landlords that includes the opposing landlords.

On December 30, 2004, San Francisco pleaded guilty to nine charges under s. 42 of the *Copyright Act*, which creates offences for a variety of conduct constituting wilful copyright infringement. The evidence in that proceeding established that:

(a) An investigation by the St. John's, Newfoundland, Fire Marshall, arising from a complaint about a faulty lamp sold by San Francisco, led to the discovery that the lamp bore a counterfeit safety certification label commonly called a "UL" label. The RCMP conducted searches of San Francisco stores across the country, its head office, and a warehouse, which turned up other counterfeit electrical UL labels as well as counterfeit products bearing the symbols of trademark holders of Playboy, Marvel Comics and others.

(b) Counterfeit UL labels were found in the offices of Slawsky and San Francisco's Head of Sales. There was also a fax from "a Chinese location" found in Slawsky's office that threatened that a report to Canadian authorities about the counterfeit safety labels would be made if payment was not forthcoming.

(c) *Copyright Act* charges against Slawsky were withdrawn when San Francisco entered a plea of guilty to the charges.

(d) The sentencing judge accepted counsels' joint submission that a $150,000.00 fine would be appropriate. In passing sentence, he condemned the company's conduct, particularly as it related to the counterfeit labels, expressing grave concern for the safety of unknowing consumers.

(e) San Francisco was co-operative during the RCMP investigation and the Crown's prosecution of the case.

(f) San Francisco had been convicted of similar offences in 1998.

Judge Stevens-Guille's condemnation of San Francisco's conduct was the subject of local and national newspaper coverage.

The company paid the $150,000.00 fine from last year's profits.

Analysis

. . .

The well established remedial purpose of the CCAA is to facilitate the making of a compromise or arrangement by an insolvent company with its creditors to the end that the company is able to stay in business. The premise is that this will result in a benefit to the company, its creditors and employees. The Act is to be given a large and liberal interpretation.

The court's jurisdiction under s. 11(6) [now s. 11.02(3)] to extend a stay of proceedings (beyond the initial 30 days of a CCAA order) is preconditioned on the applicant satisfying it that:

(a) circumstances exist that make such an order appropriate; and
(b) the applicant has acted, and is acting, in good faith and with due diligence.

Whether it is "appropriate" to make the order is not dependant on finding "due diligence" and "good faith." Indeed, refusal on that basis can be the result of an independent or interconnected finding. Stays of proceedings have been refused where the company is hopelessly insolvent; has acted in bad faith; or where the plan of arrangement is unworkable, impractical or essentially doomed to failure. ...

The court's role during the stay period has been described as a supervisory one, meant to: "... preserve the *status quo* and to move the process along to the point where an arrangement or compromise is approved or it is evident that the attempt is doomed to failure." That is not to say that the supervising judge is limited to a myopic view of balance sheets, scheduling of creditors' meetings and the like. On the contrary, this role requires attention to changing circumstances and vigilance in ensuring that a delicate balance of interests is maintained.

Although the supervising judge's main concern centres on actions affecting stakeholders in the proceeding, she is also responsible for protecting the institutional integrity of the CCAA courts, preserving their public esteem, and doing equity. She cannot turn a blind eye to corporate conduct that could affect the public's confidence in the CCAA process but must be alive to concerns of offensive business practices that are of such gravity that the interests of stakeholders in the proceeding must yield to those of the public at large.

Conclusions

While "good faith" in the context of stay applications is generally focused on the debtor's dealings with stakeholders, concern for the broader public interest mandates that a stay not be granted if the result will be to condone wrongdoing.

Although there is a possibility that a debtor company's business practices will be so offensive as to warrant refusal of a stay extension on public policy grounds, this is not such a case. Clearly, San Francisco's sale of knockoff goods was illegal and offensive. Most troubling was its sale to an unwitting public of goods bearing counterfeit safety labels. Allowing the stay to continue in this case is not to minimize the repugnant nature of San Francisco's conduct. However, the company has been condemned for its illegal conduct in the appropriate forum and punishment levied. Denying the stay extension application would be an additional form of punishment. Of greater concern is the effect that it would have on San Francisco's creditors, particularly the unsecured creditors, who would be denied their right to vote on the plan and whatever chance they might have for a small financial recovery, one which they, for the most part, patiently await.

San Francisco has met the prerequisites that it has acted and is acting with due diligence and in good faith in working towards presenting a plan of arrangement to its creditors. Appreciating that the CCAA is to be given a broad and liberal interpretation to give effect to its remedial purpose, I am satisfied that, in the circumstances, extending the stay of proceedings is appropriate. The stay is extended to July 19, 2005. The revised time frame for next steps in the proceedings is set out on the attached Schedule.

Although San Francisco has paid the $150,000.00 fine, the Monitor is satisfied that the company's current cash flow statements indicate that it is financially viable. Whether San Francisco can weather any loss of public confidence arising from its actions and resulting conviction is yet to be seen. Its creditors may look more critically at the plan of arrangement, and its customers and business associates may reconsider the value of their continued relationship with the company. However, that is sheer speculation.

NOTE ON CONSOLIDATION OF CCAA PROCEEDINGS

A question of growing importance, domestically and internationally, is whether a court can make a single bankruptcy order for a group of companies, or permit them to make a consolidated application under the CCAA or a consolidated proposal under Part III of the BIA.

The effect of such an order is to create a single corpus of assets and liabilities; as a result, some creditors will recover more and others less than if there were no consolidation. Such "substantive consolidations" must be distinguished from "procedural consolidations," which are merely mechanisms for the more efficient administration of related insolvent debtors and involve no commingling of assets and liabilities of members of the group.

Substantive consolidation orders are usually sought where the debtor and its creditors have themselves treated the related corporations as a single enterprise (in some cases, the creditors may not even have been aware of the multiple legal personalities) or where assets and liabilities of members of the group have been so completely commingled that it would be expensive to try to disentangle them. (The latter scenario applied to the group affairs of the Bank of Credit and Commerce International (BCCI), which went bankrupt in the early 1990s with unmet liabilities to depositors of about $10 billion. The British courts approved a recommendation from the liquidators that the assets and liabilities of the group be consolidated for greater efficiency.)

US courts have long accepted the doctrine of substantive as well as procedural consolidation, but they have been divided about the tests to be applied in determining when a consolidation order should be made. There are no provisions in Canadian insolvency legislation authorizing consolidation orders. Nevertheless, according to one count, at least 16 plans of arrangement were attempted under the CCAA in the 1980s and early 1990s and several well-known ones were approved by the courts. The best known of these is the consolidation order made in the *Northland Properties Ltd.* CCAA proceedings.

Michael McNaughton and Mary Arzoumanidis, "Substantive Consolidation in the Insolvency of Corporate Groups"
[2007] *Ann. Rev. Ins. L*, at 525-29, 540, 543-45
(footnotes omitted)

Large corporations are increasingly structured as corporate groups to accommodate the complexities of operating in the modern business environment. In fact, the corporate group is the most typical corporate structure of a large enterprise. Although each member of the corporate group retains a separate legal personality, the affairs of the corporate group are often conducted as if it were a single commercial entity. This may be evidenced through the use of extensive inter-company loans, commingling of assets, overlap in personnel, and a failure to keep proper financial records for each individual member of the group.

In the context of insolvency, the complex structure of corporate groups creates unique problems. Corporate groups test the limits of the separate legal personality principle since the insolvency no longer concerns a single debtor, but rather a bundle of related companies. The insolvency of a group of companies also raises the fundamental problem of ascertaining which assets within the corporate group belong to which company, and which creditor claims exist against each related company. Consequently, these difficulties necessitate a closer look into the interrelationship of the component parent, subsidiary and related companies in order to determine the extent of integration between the separate legal entities constituting the group. This considerably increases the complexity of the insolvency proceedings and poses new demands on the legal system to yield novel doctrines that address the inherently difficult problems associated with the insolvency of a corporate group.

In a liquidation or reorganization of a corporate group, the doctrine of substantive consolidation has emerged in order to provide a mechanism whereby the court may treat the separate legal entities belonging to the corporate group as one. In particular, substantive consolidation allows for the combination of the assets and liabilities of two or more members of the group, extinguishes inter-company debt and creates a single fund from which all claims against the consolidated debtors are satisfied. In effect, under substantive consolidation, claims of creditors against separate debtors instantly become claims against a single entity. ...

At the outset, substantive consolidation should be distinguished from procedural consolidation; the latter is a distinct device permitting the joint administration of the estates of related companies. In Canada, as in the United States, an order for procedural consolidation is almost *de rigueur* in insolvency proceedings under the CCAA and the . BIA. Procedural consolidation merely promotes administrative convenience and cost efficiency since a single court has jurisdiction over multiple related debtors. Unlike substantive consolidation however, procedural consolidation does not have substantive consequences. It does not alter the substantive rights and liabilities of creditors and debtors, nor does it affect the allocation of assets or the *pro rata* satisfaction of claims. Further, since procedural consolidation does not eliminate inter-company claims, the possibility to attack inter-company transfers as fraudulent or preferential transactions still exists. Accordingly, procedural consolidation results in each debtor remaining separate and distinct, with the substantive rights of all concerned intact. ...

The primary aim of substantive consolidation is to ensure the equitable treatment of all creditors. Even though substantive consolidation should not effectively benefit one group of creditors to the detriment of another group, its effects can be quite dramatic on creditor recoveries. Substantive consolidation effectively redistributes wealth among creditors of the related entities and individual creditors will invariably realize asymmetric losses or gains. Separate debtors forming part of a corporate group will have differing ratios of assets-to-liabilities, varying levels of solvency or disparities in encumbered assets. In substantive consolidation, creditors of entities with lower ratios of assets-to-liabilities will benefit from the higher asset-to-liability ratio of the consolidated group. Creditors of entities with higher asset-to-liability ratios will receive a proportionately smaller satisfaction of their claims as a result of consolidation.

The effects of substantive consolidation on creditor recoveries may be illustrated by the following example. Assume Company A has $6 million in liabilities and $1 million in assets. Assume further that Company B is a related company and has $4 million in liabilities and $2 million in assets. Outside substantive consolidation, creditors of Company A would receive 17 cents on the dollar for their claims, while creditors of Company B would receive 50 cents on the dollar. In substantive collaboration, all creditors will receive 30 cents on the dollar for their claims. ...

The few reported decisions do provide a set of factors that a Court [in Canada] may consider in determining whether to grant substantive consolidation. These factors include:

- the degree of difficulty in identifying each company's individual assets and liabilities;

- the extent of intermingling of assets and operational functions between each individual company;

- the extent to which costs associated with administering each estate separately would reduce or diminish the potential recoveries of creditors; and

- the degree of prejudice that each creditor might suffer upon consolidation.

What emerges from the few decided cases under the CCAA is that where substantive consolidation has been approved, the courts have emphasized that no injury was being done to any particular creditor or creditors or that no objection was made. ...

The CCAA does not contain any provisions that specifically authorize a court to consolidate the assets and liabilities of two separate entities. As a result, where the courts have authorized consolidation order, they have relied on their equitable jurisdiction and discretionary powers under the CCAA to consolidate the estates of related debtors.

In the context of CCAA proceedings, one of the first and only reported decisions to consider and analyze the issue of substantive consolidation was the decision of the British Columbia Superior Court in *Northland Properties Ltd., Re*. In that case, the debtor companies sought, *inter alia*, a prospective order approving the preparation of a single reorganization plan for all the companies. The Court however determined that consolidation was not appropriate at that stage of the proceedings and refused to make the order. ...

In considering whether substantive consolidation was appropriate in this case, Justice Trainor noted the paucity of Canadian jurisprudence and thus relied upon various US decisions which set out the tests to he considered on an application for substantive consolidation. He began his analysis by adopting the balancing test articulated in *Baker & Getty Financial Services Inc., Re*, which stated as follows:

> The propriety of ordering substantive consolidation is determined by a balancing of interests. The relevant enquiry asks whether the "creditors will suffer greater prejudice in the absence of consolidation than the debtors (and any objecting creditors) will suffer from its imposition.

After adopting this test, Trainor J listed the factors identified in *Vecco*, commonly referred to as the "elements of consolidation," which were developed by the courts to assist in the balancing of interests and then considered the test set out in *Re Snider Brothers Inc.*, where the Court stated in making an application for substantive consolidation, "it must be clearly shown that not only are the 'elements of consolidation' present ... but that the court's action is necessary to prevent harm or prejudice, or to effect a benefit generally." Ultimately it was found inappropriate in this case to make a consolidating order without first obtaining creditor approval since the effect of the order would be to approve an amalgamation of the companies. However, Justice Trainor stated that the debtor companies could return for court sanction of a consolidated plan once they obtained the approval of their creditors. Hence, it was implicit in Justice Trainor's decision that the court had authority to approve a consolidation plan under the appropriate circumstances. ...

On appeal, the British Columbia Court of Appeal affirmed Justice Trainor's decision and thereby confirmed that a CCAA court has the jurisdiction to entertain a consolidated plan. The Court of Appeal accepted that the correct test for substantive consolidation was that set out in *Re Snider Bros.* and interestingly also found statutory authority to make a consolidation order in s. 20 of the CCAA. ...

Although the decisions stemming from the Northland proceedings confirm that substantive consolidation is part of Canadian law, the courts failed to provide significant analysis of the principles to be applied in making a consolidation order. Since those decisions, few cases have addressed the issue of substantive consolidation in any meaningful way, and even fewer have offered any guidance as to how courts should attack the consolidation inquiry. More significantly, none of the subsequent cases have explicitly considered the decision in *Northland Properties* and have instead focused on facts of each particular case.

V. SCOPE OF THE STAY

Re Doman Industries (Trustee of)
(2003), 41 CBR (4th) 29 (BCSC)

TYSOE J: ... The law is clear that the court has the jurisdiction under the CCAA to impose a stay during the restructuring period to prevent a creditor relying on an event of default to accelerate the payment of indebtedness owed by the debtor company or to prevent a non-creditor relying on a breach of a contract with the debtor company to terminate the contract. It is also my view that the court has similar jurisdiction to grant a permanent stay surviving the restructuring of the debtor company in respect of events of default or breaches occurring prior to the restructuring. In this regard, I agree with the following reasoning of Spence J at para. 32 of the supplementary reasons in *Playdium*:

> In interpreting s. 11(4), including the "such terms" clause, the remedial nature of the CCAA must be taken into account. If no permanent order could be made under s. 11(4) it would not be possible to order, for example, that the insolvency defaults which occasioned the CCAA order could not be asserted by the Famous Players after the stay period. If such an order could not be made, the CCAA regime would prospectively be of little or no value because even though a compromise of creditor claims might be worked out in the stay period, Famous Players (or for that matter, any similar third party) could then assert the insolvency default and terminate, so that the stay would not provide any protection for the continuing prospects of the business. In view of the remedial nature of the CCAA, the Court should not take such a restrictive view of the s. 11(4) jurisdiction.

Spence J made the above comments in the context of a third party which had a contract with the debtor company. In my opinion, the reasoning applies equally to a creditor of the debtor company in circumstances where the debtor company has chosen not to compromise the indebtedness owed to it. The decision in *Luscar Ltd. v. Smoky River Coal Ltd.*, is an example of a permanent stay being granted in respect of a creditor of the restructuring company.

Accordingly, it is my view that the court does have the jurisdiction to grant a permanent stay preventing the Senior Secured Noteholders and the Trustee under the Trust Indenture from relying on events of default existing prior to or during the restructuring period to accelerate the repayment of the indebtedness owing under the Notes. It may be that the court would decline to exercise its jurisdiction in respect of monetary defaults but this point is academic in the present case because the Doman Group does intend to pay the overdue interest on the Notes upon implementation of the Reorganization Plan. ...

The third issue is whether the court has the jurisdiction to effectively stay the operation of Section 4.16 of the Trust Indenture. Although I understand that there is an issue as to whether the giving of 85% of the equity in the Doman Group to the Unsecured Noteholders as part of the reorganization would constitute a change of control for the purposes of the current version of the provincial forestry legislation, counsel for the Doman Group conceded that it would constitute a Change of Control within the meaning of Section 4.16.

The language of s. 11(4) of the CCAA, on a literal interpretation, is very broad and the case authorities have held that it should receive a liberal interpretation in view of the remedial nature of the CCAA. However, in my opinion, a liberal interpretation of s. 11(4) does not permit the court to excuse the debtor company from fulfilling its contractual obligations arising after the implementation of a plan of compromise or arrangement.

In my view, there are numerous purposes of stays under s. 11 of the CCAA. One of the purposes is to maintain the status quo among creditors while a debtor company endeavours to reorganize or restructure its financial affairs. Another purpose is to prevent creditors and other parties from acting on the insolvency of the debtor company or other contractual breaches caused by the insolvency to terminate contracts or accelerate the repayment of the indebtedness owing by the debtor company when it would interfere with the ability of the debtor company to reorganize or restructure its financial affairs. An additional purpose is to relieve the debtor company of the burden of dealing with litigation against it so that it may focus on restructuring its financial affairs. As I have observed above, a further purpose is to prevent the frustration of a reorganization or restructuring plan after its implementation on the basis of events of default or breaches which existed prior to or during the restructuring period. All of these purposes are to facilitate a debtor company in restructuring its financial affairs. On the other hand, it is my opinion that Parliament did not intend s. 11(4) to authorize courts to stay proceedings in respect of defaults or breaches which occur after the implementation of the reorganization or restructuring plan, even if they arise as a result of the implementation of the plan.

Re Richtree Inc.
(2005), 74 OR (3d) 174 (SCJ)

LAX J: [1] Richtree Inc. is a reporting issuer in Ontario and in several other Canadian jurisdictions. It brings this motion requesting an exemption by way of extension from the requirement to file its audited financial statements and other continuous disclosure documents with the Ontario Securities Commission (the "OSC") and the equivalent regulatory authorities in British Columbia, Alberta, Saskatchewan, Manitoba, Newfoundland and Labrador and Nova Scotia. Following submissions, I dismissed the motion with reasons to follow. These are the reasons.

Background

[2] At the time of the motion, Richtree had filed an Application with the Superior Court of Justice, Commercial List, and received creditor protection under the *Companies' Creditors Arrangement Act*, RSC 1985, c. C-36 ("CCAA"). This proceeding is ongoing.

[3] On November 24, 2004, it made an Application under the Mutual Reliance Review System for Exemptive Relief Applications (the "MRRS System") for an exemption from the obligation to meet its filing requirements with the OSC. The MRRS System permits reporting issuers to request exemptions from multiple Canadian securities regulators with a single application. As Richtree had appointed the OSC as the principal regulator, its staff had primary carriage of the Application for Exemption. The exemptions sought were exemptions from the filing with the OSC the 2005 Q1 Interim Financial Statements and the 2005 Q1 Management's Discussion and Analysis by December 8, 2004; and, the 2004 Annual Financial Statements, the 2004 Management's Discussion and Analysis and the 2004 Annual Information Form by December 10, 2004.

[4] Shortly before the formal filing of the Application for Exemption, OSC staff informed Richtree that they would not recommend that the OSC grant the exemption. On December 1, 2004, OSC staff confirmed its recommendation and also informed Richtree that staff of the other regulators would also recommend that their securities commissions refuse the request for exemption. The OSC staff offered to convene a joint hearing before a panel of the OSC, with the other jurisdictions participating by conference, or a hearing before the OSC if the other jurisdictions agreed to abide by the decision of the OSC. Richtree refused the hearing and brought this motion on December 7, 2004, which was the day before its first filings were due.

Analysis

[5] Richtree concedes that the OSC has statutory jurisdiction to grant an exemption to a reporting issuer: *Securities Act*, RSO 1990, c. S.5, s. 80. However, it submits that the court has inherent jurisdiction to grant this relief consistent with its discretionary powers under section 11 of the CCAA to accomplish the goal of facilitating the restructuring of a debtor company. It points to examples of stays in the nature of "tolling provisions." These are frequently granted in Initial CCAA Orders and constrain creditors or third parties from exercising rights so as to provide the necessary stability for the debtor company to restructure its affairs. It submits that the court has a variety of discretionary powers arising from its inherent jurisdiction to make orders to do justice between the parties and also to do what practicality demands. For this proposition, it relies on dicta of Farley J in *Re Royal Oak Mines Inc.* (1999), 7 CBR (4th) 293 (Ont. Gen. Div. [Commercial List]) where he said at p. 296:

> … In light of the very general framework of the CCAA, judges must rely upon inherent jurisdiction to deal with CCAA proceedings. However, inherent jurisdiction is not limitless

if the legislative body has not left a functional gap or vacuum, then inherent jurisdiction should not be brought into play. The same limitations are applicable to a Court's use of a discretion granted by statute. I appreciate that there may have been some blurring of distinction among discretion, inherent jurisdiction and general jurisdiction (including the common law facility). This combination is implicitly recognized in *Baxter Student Housing Ltd. v. College Housing Cooperative Ltd.* (1975), 57 DLR (3d) 1 SCC) in Dickson J's analysis of inherent jurisdiction at pp. 4-5. ...

[6] In *Baxter*, Dickson J emphasized that inherent jurisdiction does not empower a judge to negate an unambiguous expression of the legislature. Neither may it be exercised to conflict with a statute or rule. It is a special and extraordinary power to be exercised only sparingly and in a clear case and usually to maintain the authority and integrity of the court process.

[7] The concept of "inherent jurisdiction" within CCAA proceedings is discussed in the recent decision of the British Columbia Court of Appeal in *Re Skeena Cellulose Inc.* (2003), 43 CBR (4th) 187 at 211-212 (BCCA). The court concludes that when one analyzes cases such as *Re Royal Oak Mines*, as well as others referred to by Farley J such as *Re Westar Mining Ltd.*, [1992] 6 WWR 331 (BCSC), the court's use of the term "inherent jurisdiction," is a misnomer. In these cases, the courts are exercising a statutory discretion given by the CCAA rather than their inherent jurisdiction. This is an important distinction, which Farley J recognizes in *Re Royal Oak Mines* in the passage quoted and in his reference to the decision of the Supreme Court of Canada in *Baxter*.

[8] I agree with the analysis in *Skeena Cellulose* that when a court grants a stay of proceedings under section 11 or approves a plan of arrangement under section 6, the court is not exercising a power that arises from its nature as a Superior Court, but rather is exercising the discretion granted to it under the broad statutory regime of the CCAA. The relief that Richtree requests whether under the CCAA or the *Securities Act* is discretionary. The question that arises then is whether the statutory discretion granted to a court under the CCAA can be exercised in the face of section 80 of the *Securities Act*, which provides that it is the Commission that may grant or refuse the exemptions sought.

[9] The answer is no. There is no provision of the CCAA that either addresses or contemplates an application to the court for exemption from the filing requirements of the *Securities Act*. The doctrine of paramountcy has been acknowledged to apply where the exercise of a court's discretion under the CCAA conflicts with the mandatory provisions of provincial legislation; see, for example, *Re Smoky River Coal Ltd.* (1999), 12 CBR (4th) 94 at 115 (Alta. CA); *Re Loewen Group Inc.* (2001), 32 CBR (4th) 54 at 58 (Ont. SCJ) However, it is worth noting that in neither case was it necessary to invoke the paramountcy doctrine. Here, as in the cases referred to, there is no inconsistency between federal and provincial law. The doctrine of paramountcy does not apply.

[10] Further, where a provincial statute is given exclusive jurisdiction to determine a matter, the court's discretionary power under the CCAA cannot be used to override it. Hence, a broad receivership power under federal bankruptcy legislation confers no authority on a bankruptcy court to determine whether a receiver that carries on the business of a debtor is a successor employer. This is within the exclusive jurisdiction of the Ontario Labour Relations Board: *GMAC Commercial Credit Corp. v. TCT Logistics Inc.* (2004), 238 DLR (4th) 677 (Ont. CA). On this point, the court was unanimous.

[11] Richtree relies on Orders made in CCAA proceedings in *Slater Steel* and *Air Canada* where the court granted extensions of time for calling an annual general meeting of shareholders. This is commonly done in CCAA proceedings. It is quite a different thing to relieve a reporting issuer from providing timely and accurate financial information to members of the public where, as here, the company's shares continue to trade. At the time of its application for exemption from filing requirements, Slater's shares had been delisted from the Toronto Stock Exchange and were no longer trading. Further, the OSC, as lead regulator, had granted Slater a filing exemption, which is recited in the Order of May 5, 2004.

[12] Richtree submits that the court should defer to the opinion of the directors of the company who are attempting to achieve the best results they can for the company and all of its stakeholders. I agree that the task of the directors is to focus their attention on assisting Richtree with its restructuring. However, the proper forum for debating the effect of the filing requirements on Richtree is not on this motion, but at the OSC. The legislature has decided that it is the proper forum for balancing the interests of the company and its stakeholders on the one hand and the interests of members of the public on the other. I conclude that the court has no jurisdiction under the CCAA to grant the exemptions sought.

[13] Having said this, I wish to make some comments about the reasons that the Richtree directors have come to court. The company does not plan to comply with its filing requirements and the directors have two concerns. The only evidence before the court is a solicitor's affidavit, which deposes in paragraph 2:

> … I understand that Richtree's directors are concerned that they could be required under applicable securities laws to notify the boards of any other public companies on which they serve or may in the future serve, of such filing requirement defaults. Moreover, I understand that Richtree's directors are concerned that they might be viewed as having acquiesced in a deliberate breach by Richtree of securities law and corporate legislation and thereafter suffer damage to their respective reputations.

[14] As to the first concern, the Richtree directors are already required to disclose that they have been directors of a company that has made a plan of arrangement under the CCAA. Specifically, the rules of the Toronto Stock Exchange require directors to disclose this on a Personal Information Form for all companies seeking to list, or that currently list their shares for trading on the TSX.

[15] The sole consequence of Richtree's failure to meet the filing requirements is that the company will be placed on the OSC's Default List. There is no requirement under Ontario securities law to disclose that an individual has been a director of a company that has been placed on the Default List. Although the OSC does place companies that are under CCAA protection on the Default List, there is no evidence that this has caused any harm to Richtree or indeed to other companies currently on the list, or to their directors.

[16] As to the second concern, I was informed that the Richtree directors, or at least some of them, are on several boards, and that this raises concerns for them about their reputations as directors of these boards or other boards they may be invited to join. I find this to be a disquieting submission. As directors of Richtree and as directors of any other boards on which they may now or in the future serve, they have fiduciary duties that

require them to act honestly and in good faith with a view to the best interests of the corporation. These duties are paramount. Reputational concerns of a personal nature play no role in assessing the alleged harm that may flow to a director from being a member of a board whose company is a defaulting issuer.

[17] The purpose of section 11 of the CCAA is to provide the court with a discretionary power to restrain conduct against a debtor company so as to permit it to continue in business during the arrangement period: see, *Quintette Coal Ltd. v. Nippon Steel Corp.* (1990), 2 CBR (3d) 303 at 312 (BCCA). As observed there, the power is discretionary and therefore is to be exercised judicially.

[18] Companies under CCAA protection are not immunized from complying with regulatory regimes. During a CCAA proceeding, directors are not immunized from carrying out their responsibilities or relieved of their obligations to serve the company and its stakeholders diligently. The order that is sought has nothing to do with Richtree's restructuring process. It is intended to grant the directors personal protection to their reputations. This is neither contemplated by section 11, nor are the directors entitled to this protection. Even if the court had the jurisdiction to grant the relief sought, I would not do so as this is an improper and injudicious exercise of the court's discretion under the CCAA.

NOTES

1. See new CCAA s. 11.1, inserted by the 2007 amendments. How does this provision affect the position as stated in *Richtree*?

2. Can the court stay a creditor's right of set-off? See CCAA s. 18.1 and *Re Air Canada* (2003), 45 CBR (4th) 13 (Ont. SCJ), extracted in Chapter 14, Section IV.

CHAPTER THIRTEEN

Carrying On Business During CCAA Proceedings

I. INTRODUCTION

This chapter deals with various aspects of carrying on business while subject to CCAA proceedings. The CCAA establishes a debtor-in-possession regime, on the rationale that, as a general rule, the debtor's existing management is likely to do a better job of running the debtor's business during the restructuring than an administrator or the like appointed from outside, who may not know the ins and outs of the business as well. On the other hand, leaving the current management in charge carries with it certain obvious concerns, not the least of which is that the debtor became insolvent on the current management's watch and this may reflect on its competence. To meet these concerns, the CCAA provides for the appointment of a monitor to perform a watchdog function: see Section II. Section III deals with directors' duties, the implications of the Supreme Court's decision in the *People's* case for the responsibilities of directors in the course of a restructuring, and the court's power to remove directors on the application of disaffected stakeholders. Section IV deals with the debtor's right to disclaim, affirm, and assign executory contracts in CCAA proceedings. Section V discusses the special provisions in the CCAA relating to derivatives or "eligible financial contracts." Section VI addresses the question of debtor-in-possession financing. If the debtor is to carry on business during the restructuring process, it will typically need a fresh injection of funds. On the other hand, potential new lenders may not be ready to come to the table unless the debtor can assure them of priority over existing creditors. This creates a conflict between the interest of the stakeholders at large in the debtor being able to continue in business and the interest of the subset of creditors whose priority position will be affected if the debtor accedes to the new lender's demands. Finally, Section VII deals with the debtor's right to sell assets outside the ordinary course of business, including the right to sell the business itself on a going-concern basis as an alternative to restructuring.

II. THE MONITOR

Andrew J.F. Kent, Wael Rostom, Adam Maerov, and Tushara Weerasooriya,
"Canadian Business Restructuring Law: When Should a Court Say 'No'?"
(2008), 24 *BFLR* 1, at 13-18 (footnotes omitted)

One possible counterweight to the powers given to the debtor under the Canadian system is provided by the requirement in CCAA proceedings to have a "monitor," and in BIA proceedings to have a trustee.

The requirement for an appointment by the Court of a monitor in CCAA proceedings is a relatively new development. Prior to 1997, the CCAA did not require the appointment of a monitor. However, in the years prior to that time a practice developed of having the Court appoint an accounting firm to perform an officially sanctioned role in the CCAA proceedings. At a time when there was relatively more suspicion about the restructuring process, their role was often analogized to that of an interim receiver appointed under s. 46 of the BIA to monitor the debtor's conduct while a disputed bankruptcy petition is outstanding. Indeed, in CCAA cases in the 1980s the monitors were often called "Interim Receivers" (see, for example, *Re United Co-Operatives of Ontario* and *Re Northland Properties Ltd.*). They could be selected and appointed directly or indirectly at the instigation of key creditors as a watchdog to observe the conduct of management and the operation of the business while a plan was being formulated. Over time, wise debtors co-opted the process by asking the Court to appoint "their" accounting firm to forestall the appointment of a different firm selected by the creditors.

One practical issue that led to the Court appointment of accounting firms was the protection of fees. When creditors instigated the appointment, they wanted the fees paid for by the debtor, and when the debtor instigated the appointment, the accountants wanted security of payment. After some judicial doubt, it was concluded that the Court had the jurisdiction to protect the fees on the basis that once appointed, the accounting firm was either an officer or an agent of the Court.

During the development of the 1997 round of insolvency law reform, the BIAC [Bankruptcy and Insolvency Advisory Committee] task force studying the CCAA recommended that the appointment of a monitor be made mandatory so as to "give creditors in CCAA applications the same protection of a professional and impartial "watchdog," as is provided to creditors in BIA reorganizations." When the CCAA was amended in 1997 to require the appointment of a monitor, the statutory language used to describe the monitor's role was consistent with the watchdog concept. The basic purpose of the appointment was described as being "to monitor the business and financial affairs of the company while the [initial order] remains in effect." The monitor was given express access to the debtor's books, records and property for the purpose, and was required to report "on the state of the company's business and financial affairs" if there was a material adverse change in the debtor's projected cash-flow or financial circumstances and also prior to creditor meetings. There were no other express powers or duties.

The Court was given the power to order the monitor "to carry out such other functions in relation to the company as the Court may direct." This catch-all provision has been used to adjust the role of the monitor on a case by case basis. It is now typical for an initial order under the CCAA to have numerous provisions dealing with the powers and duties of the monitor.

In most CCAA cases, the monitor plays a broader role than watchdog. In practice, the monitor plays an expanded role that depends firstly on management and secondly, where there are key creditors or groups of creditors, on the relationship between management and those key creditors. In practice, monitors are hired by the debtor and in substance often act as an advisor to the debtor, albeit with special responsibilities.

The role of the monitor is further confused by the role the monitor plays in court during proceedings under the CCAA. Because the monitor is appointed by the Court, early on the Courts concluded that the monitor was either an agent of the Court or an officer of the Court. The Courts have also concluded that the monitor has an "obligation to act independently and to consider the interest of the petitioners and its creditors." In one pre-1997 case, the Court commented:

> It is essential for the court to ensure that neither the shareholders nor the creditors have any influence over the monitor. As an agent of the court, the monitor must not be in a "conflict of interest" situation. The monitor's sole responsibility is to the court.

The fact that the monitor has been adviser to the debtor before the filing has not been considered problematic. However, disclosure at the time of the appointment is the correct practice and may be required under applicable professional rules.

Justice Farley commented in one case that the monitor "recognizes its role is to be neutral and to act in the best interests of all concerned." In another, he noted that there was no jurisprudence to support an argument that a monitor represents the interest of the creditors in the same way as a trustee in bankruptcy, receiver or liquidator. Some courts have viewed the monitor as a competent and independent expert providing advice to the Court on the merits of the reorganization plan, and another stated that "[t]he monitor must be an agent of the court, it must assist the court and it must be independent of any of the parties."

This view of the monitor has a number of consequences. First, the monitor can provide evidence by way of report rather than affidavit, and is generally not subject to cross-examination. The Courts understandably place great trust and confidence in the information provided by the monitor, and are unreceptive to criticisms or conflicting evidence. As a result, where the debtor and the monitor are in agreement, debtor's counsel put in little or no evidence and instead may rely on the monitor's reports. In practical terms, this makes it very difficult for stakeholders to challenge the debtor's position.

Second, in their reports monitors now routinely go beyond simply providing information. They will express views and make recommendations to the Court concerning matters before the Court. Once again, it is difficult for stakeholders to challenge the monitor's views as an independent expert and officer of the Court.

These factors have become increasingly significant as the shape of CCAA proceedings has changed. It used to be that the Courts provided a standstill while the principals negotiated. The major commercial transactions were implemented through the plan of arrangement and were therefore subject to prior creditor class approval. In effect, the

CCAA operated as a mandatory ADR process that encouraged resolution of business issues through negotiations between the parties whose interests were at stake.

But now major commercial transactions are implemented on an interim basis during the course of CCAA proceedings before a plan is filed, with Court approval being substituted for creditor approval. This can now extend to a sale of all or substantially all of the business or assets of the debtor. On application for approval of these transactions, invariably the monitor will file a report and make a recommendation as to whether the proposed transaction should be approved by the Court. Almost as invariably, the Courts will defer to the monitor's views. Accordingly, in substance these transactions are really subject to monitor approval. As a result the monitor's judgment has replaced the judgment of the Court or the creditors.

Monitors can use the threat of withholding their approval to negotiate with the debtor. The debtor knows that, as a practical matter, it will be difficult to obtain Court approval for a major transaction without having the monitor's prior approval. So the monitors can and do constructively influence the debtor's conduct. It can therefore be the reality that the real negotiations in the proceedings take place in secret between the monitor and management for the debtor. This has the odd result that one of the key negotiating parties has no direct economic stake in the outcome of the case.

It was the view of the the Insolvency Institute of Canada and the Canadian Association of Insolvency and Restructuring Professionals Joint Task Force on Business Insolvency Law Reform (the "JTF") on Independence issues and the role of the monitor, that the monitor must be the "ears and eyes" of the Court and that it was critical that the CCAA Monitor should not be put in a position where it acts as an advocate for the applicants. In the Report, the JTF stated that:

> While it is understood and accepted that in reporting on factual matters, a Monitor will necessarily put forward views—sometimes strong views—on business related matters affecting the applicants, a Monitor should not file a factum or take positions on the legal aspects of any contested issues in the CCAA proceeding. Instead, advocacy of those legal matters should be left to the applicants and any stakeholders who are challenging a position being taken by the applicants.

Based on that principle, the JTF recommended to Industry Canada that the legislation should:

(a) Provide that the party with the primary obligation to advance a position and adduce evidence before the Court should be the applicant and not the Monitor.

(b) Provide that the Monitor, unless otherwise required by the Court, should avoid taking any legal positions or filing a factum regarding contested legal disputes among the parties.

(c) Provide for an amendment to the CCAA section 11.7 to stipulate that the primary roles of the monitor are (a) to monitor the activities of the debtor for the benefit of all interested parties and the court, and (b) to work impartially with the debtor and all interested parties to facilitate the restructuring process.

None of these recommendations were adopted in the *Reform Act*.

NOTES

1. The 2007 amendments incorporate additional provisions relating to monitors. New CCAA s. 11.7 provides that the monitor must be a licensed trustee, and, as a general rule, a trustee may not be appointed as monitor if the trustee has served as a director or is connected with the debtor in various other specified ways. New CCAA s. 23 codifies the monitor's functions and duties. New CCAA, ss. 27-32 provide for supervision of monitors by the Office of the Superintendent of Bankruptcy.

2. Prior to the 2007 amendments, it had become quite common in some jurisdictions for the monitor also to be appointed as interim receiver pursuant to BIA s. 244, with power to take possession of the debtor's assets, operate its business, and, in some cases, sell the assets and distribute the proceeds: see Chapter 18, Section IV. This procedure was seen as useful in cases where creditors had lost faith in the debtor's management and were not prepared to allow the debtor to continue in business with the current managers still in place. The 2007 amendments preclude the appointment of an interim receiver for this purpose, but they have instead introduced a new form of receivership: see Chapter 18, Section VI. Removal or replacement of directors may be another option in cases where creditors have lost faith in the debtor's current management. Does the court have power to order the removal of directors on the application of one or more stakeholders? This question is addressed in Section III.

III. GOVERNANCE

Andrew J.F. Kent, Wael Rostom, Adam Maerov, and Tushara Weerasooriya,
"Canadian Business Restructuring Law: When Should a Court Say 'No'?"
(2008), 24 *BFLR* 1, at 6-13 (footnotes omitted)

Since most Canadian businesses involve corporations, a logical place to start the analysis of the rules that should govern the debtor is to consider the principles that apply to the governance of corporations.

In Canada, corporate governance laws are based on the *Canada Business Corporations Act* (the "CBCA") and that Act's provincial counterparts, as well as on common law principles derived from case law and rules that are imposed by stock exchanges and provincial securities laws. The management of corporations is overseen by the directors, who under s. 102(1) of the CBCA are granted authority, subject to any unanimous shareholder agreement, to manage or supervise the management of, the business and affairs of a corporation. In managing the corporation, the directors must govern in accordance with s. 122(1) of the CBCA, which states that:

> Every director and officer of a corporation in exercising their powers and discharging their duties shall
>> (a) act honestly and in good faith with a view to the best interests of the corporation; and
>> (b) exercise the care, diligence and skill that a reasonably prudent person would exercise in comparable circumstances.

These two directions outline what is at the core of corporate governance law in Canada. The decisions of directors must (a) be in the best interests of the corporation, commonly referred to as the fiduciary duty, and (b), those decisions must be made using the skill and judgment of the director to a standard of a reasonably prudent person in the circumstance that the director is in, commonly referred to as the duty of care.

The goals and standards of the two duties described above have been given more concrete meaning by the Courts. The CBCA uses the phrase "in the best interest of the corporation," but does not define which of the various stakeholders' interests should be considered, and how those interests should be balanced. Ever since Berle and Dodd debated this question over 75 years ago, the question of to whom directors owe their loyalty has been considered, with no satisfactory conclusion. In Canada, the Supreme Court considered this question in *Peoples Department Stores Inc. (Trustee of) v. Wise*. The Supreme Court was considering whether the fiduciary duties of the directors should shift to looking out for the interests of creditors where a corporation is nearing insolvency and it appears that a bankruptcy proceeding is likely. The Supreme Court answered this question by stating that the duty is not owed to one particular stakeholder, but to the corporation itself. The Supreme Court interpreted the best interests of the corporation to mean the maximization of value of the corporation, and to that end, the interests of various stakeholders may be considered:

> We accept as an accurate statement of law that in determining whether they are acting with
> a view to the best interests of the corporation it may be legitimate, given all the circum-
> stances of a given case, for the board of directors to consider, *inter alia*, the interests of
> shareholders, employees, suppliers, creditors, consumers, governments and the
> environment.

The decision by the Supreme Court to interpret the duty of directors as one towards "the corporation" does not, however, answer the question of how to balance stakeholder interests when those interests might be at odds. The Supreme Court noted that "where the corporation is profitable and well capitalized and has strong prospects" the interests of shareholders and creditors may be consistent with each other. However, in *Peoples* the corporation had entered bankruptcy proceedings, and the trustee in bankruptcy was unsatisfied with some of the business decisions that the directors made before bankruptcy which it felt were unfair and eroded the estate's value, sacrificing the interests of a group of creditors. The questions that the Supreme Court had to answer in *Peoples* had to do with how to consider the interests of creditors when "the corporation approaches what has been called 'the vicinity of insolvency,' [when] the residual claims of shareholders will be nearly exhausted. The Supreme Court dismissed any conflict by not recognizing any direct duty to the shareholders or creditors, but in maintaining that the director's fiduciary duty was only to the corporation.

The Supreme Court's consideration of whether directors' duties shift as a corporation reaches the vicinity of insolvency denies that there should be a shift in interest depending on the state of the corporation:

> The various shifts in interests that naturally occur as a corporation's fortunes rise and fall do
> not, however, affect the content of the fiduciary duty under s. 122(1)(a) of the CBCA. At all

times, directors and officers owe their fiduciary obligation to the corporation. The interests of the corporation are not to be confused with the interests of the creditors or those of any other stakeholders.

The Supreme Court maintains that there is one clear interest, that of the corporation, that can be maintained during financial difficulties. This allows the directors to avoid considering conflicting interests, as one observer has interpreted the Supreme Court decision:

> If a fiduciary duty were owed directly to creditors, directors could, among other things, face potentially conflicting duties between two manifestly opposing parties. Even if a company is insolvent or in the vicinity of insolvency, the duties of directors to it continue unabated. If, at the same time, directors owed duties to creditors of the company, an irreconcilable conflict would arise when, for example, directors seek additional credit for the company. Do they vigorously pursue the additional credit, thereby deepening the insolvency at the expense of creditors? Or do the directors disclose the company's financial plight, killing the company's chances of survival but minimizing the exposure of creditors. The Court's decision avoids hoisting directors on the horns of this potential conflict by clearly stating that the duty of directors never shifts and that, at least before bankruptcy, the interests of shareholders and creditors are always aligned.

However, arguing that the interests of the corporation, including those of the shareholders and creditors are always aligned before bankruptcy may ignore some conflicts in the interests of these stakeholders. For example, consider a situation where a corporation is near insolvent with little residual value remaining for shareholders. However, there is an opportunity to "bet the farm" in a strategy that might result in value for shareholders if successful, but leave little value for creditors in the likely event of failure. In such a situation, clearly the interests of the shareholders and creditors are not aligned.

If the duty of the directors is to the corporation, as decided by the Supreme Court, it should be asked whether that can include the value of the corporation in a liquidation or restructuring, options not mentioned by the Court in *Peoples*. Whether the interests of the corporation can be held separate from those of its stakeholders is a matter for debate and interpretation, and given that, as the example above shows, there can be opposing interests amongst stakeholders, it is unclear what guidance can be derived by directors considering the interests of the corporation as opposed to the interest of its stakeholders.

In *Re Stelco Inc.* the Ontario Court of Appeal considered the issue of corporate governance in the context of a company that had already entered a restructuring process under the CCAA. The appeal arose from a decision at the Superior Court to remove two directors representing shareholders appointed to the board during the restructuring process that had been made by Justice Farley who was supervising that process. Some of the unsecured creditors of Stelco feared that the represented shareholders' involvement as directors would lead to a restructuring process focused mainly on maximizing shareholder value at the expense of their interests. Justice Farley held that a supervising court can interfere with the composition of a board where there is sufficient reason to do so under the authority of s. 11 of the CCAA. Section 11 gives the supervising judge in a CCAA proceeding broad powers to, where considered appropriate and on an application made under the CCAA, make an order. In this case, Justice Farley was not prepared to adopt a "wait and see" approach in determining whether the directors would act in the best interests of the corporation, and used what he argued was the supervisory Court's inherent jurisdiction to order that the two directors [not be appointed to] the board.

In the unanimous appeal decision written by Justice Blair, the Ontario Court of Appeal overturned the Superior Court's ruling and reinstated the two new directors to the board. The Court of Appeal rejected Justice Farley's conclusion that a supervising court has the power to remove directors based on its inherent jurisdiction and its discretion under section 11 of the CCAA. The Court of Appeal found that a court should not step into the shoes of the directors, and that the governance of the company remains with the directors and the board during the restructuring process. Justice Blair wrote that:

> Although a judge supervising a CCAA proceeding develops a certain "feel" for the corporate dynamics and a certain sense of direction for the restructuring, this caution is worth keeping in mind. The court is not catapulted into the shoes of the board of directors, or into the seat of the chair of the board, when acting in its supervisory role in the restructuring.

The Court of Appeal found that section 11 only gives the supervising court a role in the process in so much as it can prevent the directors from taking certain actions as outlined in the CCAA. Justice Blair found that:

> What the court does under s. 11 is to establish the boundaries of the playing field and act as a referee in the process. The company's role in the restructuring, and that of its stakeholders, is to work out a plan or compromise that a sufficient percentage of creditors will accept and the court will approve and sanction. The corporate activities that take place in the course of the workout are governed by the legislation and legal principles that normally apply to such activities. In the course of acting as referee, the court has great leeway, as Farley J observed in *Lehndorff* [(1993), 17 CBR (3d) 24 (Ont. Gen. Div.)], at para. 5, "to make order[s] so as to effectively maintain the status quo in respect of an insolvent company while it attempts to gain the approval of its creditors for the proposed compromise or arrangement which will be to the benefit of both the company and its creditors." But the s. 11 discretion is not open-ended and unfettered. Its exercise must be guided by the scheme and object of the Act and by the legal principles that govern corporate law issues. Moreover, the court is not entitled to usurp the role of the directors and management in conducting what are in substance *the company's* restructuring efforts.

Although the Court of Appeal decided that there was no role in section 11 of the CCAA for a court to restrict the appointment of directors, the Court of Appeal did observe that under section 20 of the CCAA there was a way to bring in the oppression remedy and other provisions of the CBCA.

The combined effect of the *Peoples* and *Stelco* decisions is arguably to leave a vacuum. One way of interpreting *Peoples* is to say that the fiduciary duty concept is principally directed at self-dealing, and that absent self-dealing the directors will not be liable for breach of fiduciary duty. If so, fiduciary duty does not inform the directors about how and why the extraordinary powers of a debtor in a reorganization are to be exercised.

Of course, the directors are also subject to the standard of care under applicable corporate law. A key task of debtor's counsel in a restructuring proceeding is to advise the board about the processes to follow and what management and expert reports should be received in order to be able to document that the standard of care has been met. But this is ultimately a defensive exercise engaged in for the purpose of building protections against personal claims against the directors. It does not inform the board or the debtor about what should actually be done with the debtor's restructuring powers.

The Court of Appeal decision in *Stelco* refers to corporate law without recognizing that it was not developed with insolvency proceedings in mind. The decision then amplifies the corporate law vacuum by defining the role of the Courts in a restructuring proceeding as in effect being "hands off the debtor." Its primary justification for that role is a fiction that the role of the Court is to preserve the "status quo" pending a vote by the creditors on a restructuring plan.

In practice, a common tactic of a debtor in a restructuring proceeding is actually to try to alter the status quo before a vote is taken to such a degree that the creditors have no choice but to accept the ultimate restructuring plan as a *fait accompli*. Canadian courts have repeatedly used their powers to assist debtors in this endeavour.

It is inherent in the restructuring process that there be material changes in the status quo. It may be necessary for the debtor to borrow new funds secured in priority to pre-filing secured loans, to sell assets in breach of pre-filing covenants, and to terminate pre-filing contracts without paying damages for breach. These steps and many others are generally taken by the debtor before a plan is approved, often without any form of creditor approval and relying solely on the approval of the Court.

However, one can argue that, even if the status quo rationale for it is wrong, the "hands off the debtor" approach is still correct. A restructuring can involve many practical business decisions that are beyond the expertise of the Court. It can be cogently argued as a result that it would not be appropriate for a court to second guess management. A consequence of that view is that it renders the Court approval process largely meaningless. And what then are the checks and balances on the debtor?

As is apparent in the discussion above, the CBCA does not give specific direction on governance during an insolvency proceeding or restructuring. The CBCA is designed with the governance of solvent companies in mind, and primarily addresses the agency problems associated with the separation of ownership and control. The CBCA, for the most part, does not govern the relationship of companies and creditors, with the understanding that creditors are able to make contracts to protect themselves. However, where a court orders a stay under the CCAA, the creditors lose their contractual protection, and thus the assumptions made by the CBCA are not reflected in the resulting situation.

Finally, the uncertainties in the law have been compounded by the fact that the result in *Stelco* has in substance been overturned by the *Reform Act*. It gives the Courts the express power to remove directors during reorganization proceedings [new CCAA s. 11.5]. What does that do to the rationale of the *Stelco* decision?

NOTES

1. For a critical analysis of new CCAA s. 11.5, see Marie Bruchet, "Director Removal Under the CCAA" (2008), 24 *BFLR* 269.

2. The foregoing materials address the case of where creditors have lost faith in one or more directors, but the directors are reluctant to resign. The reverse scenario is also a concern—namely, where directors are reluctant to stay, even though creditors want the current management to remain in place. Directors may want to resign in order to avoid personal liability, both for the company's existing debts and for any further debts the company may incur going forward (provincial legislation makes directors personally responsible for the company's debts in certain circumstances). On the other hand, creditors may want the directors to stay—for example, because the directors have a close knowledge of the debtor's business that would be hard to replicate. The statute contains a number of provisions addressing this problem. CCAA s. 11.03 (formerly s. 11.5), authorizes the inclusion in the stay order of provisions staying proceedings against directors. Section 5.1 provides for the inclusion of directors in the debtor's plan. New s. 11.51 authorizes the court to impose a charge on the debtor's assets for the purpose of indemnifying a director against liabilities incurred after the commencement of the CCAA proceedings.

IV. EXECUTORY CONTRACTS

A. Introduction

Chapter 6 deals with the disclaimer, affirmation, and assignment of executory contracts in straight bankruptcy proceedings. The following commentary and materials relate to the disclaimer, affirmation, and assignment of contracts in CCAA proceedings. They should be read in conjunction with Chapter 6.

B. Disclaimer

The common law position is as follows. In the case of CCAA proceedings, where the debtor remains in possession, the right of disclaimer derives from the general law of contract. Outside CCAA proceedings, the debtor can disclaim a contract if it wants to, but in the absence of a lawful excuse, it would be liable in damages to the counterparty. The debtor in CCAA proceedings is the same legal entity as it was before (see *Re Air Canada* (2003), 45 CBR (4th) 13 (Ont. SCJ)) and, therefore, at least as far as the common law is concerned, it has the same right of disclaimer. In summary, as a general rule at common law, a debtor in CCAA proceedings is bound by its pre-filing contracts, unless it elects to disclaim them.

Disclaimer gives the counterparty a claim for damages. This claim is a provable one and the counterparty will end up recovering only so much of its claim as the plan allows. (As a general rule only pre-filing claims are provable claims, but the courts make an exception for post-filing damages claims arising from the disclaimer of contracts: see *Re Doman*, extracted below.)

Prior to the 2007 amendments, the CCAA said nothing about the disclaimer of contracts, but the courts interpreted CCAA s. 11 as empowering them to make provision for disclaimer in the initial order: see, for example, *Re Dylex Ltd.* (1995), 31 CBR (3d) 196 (Ont. SCJ) (commercial tenancy agreements); and *Re Doman Industries Ltd.* (2004), 45 BLR (3d) 78 (BCSC) (other contracts). To this extent, the CCAA cases simply track the common law. However, the courts went further by reserving to themselves a discretion to disallow disclaimer on application by the counterparty (there is no such discretion at common law, but the innovation could be justified on the ground of either inherent jurisdiction or the broad statutory discretion that CCAA s. 11 confers). *Re Doman*, below, deals with the factors the courts took into account when ruling on a disputed disclaimer.

Re Doman Industries Ltd.
(2004), 45 BLR (3d) 78 (BCSC)

TYSOE J: [1] One of the Petitioners, Western Forest Products Ltd. ("Western"), applies, in these proceedings under the *Companies' Creditors Arrangement Act* (the "CCAA") involving the Doman group of companies, for authorization or approval of the termination of contracts it has with Hayes Forest Services Ltd. ("Hayes") and Strathcona Contracting Ltd. ("Strathcona").

[2] The Doman group of companies ("Doman") carry on business in the BC forestry industry. Doman encountered financial difficulties and has been in the process of attempting to restructure under the CCAA for approximately one and a half years. The liabilities of *Doman* consist of secured term debt in the principal amount of US$160 million, unsecured term notes in the principal amount of US$513 million, unsecured trade debt in excess of $20 million, a secured operating line of credit and other miscellaneous obligations.

[3] The restructuring process is nearing completion. A plan of compromise and arrangement (the "Restructuring Plan") has been filed and the meeting of creditors to consider it has been scheduled to be held in approximately two weeks. The deadline for creditors to file proofs of claim is today.

[4] In very simple terms, the Restructuring Plan contemplates that the lumber and pulp assets of Doman will be transferred into new corporations and that the unsecured noteholders, trade creditors and other unsecured creditors will have their debt converted into shares in one of the new corporations, which will own the lumber assets and the shares of the other corporation holding the pulp assets. The secured term debt is to be refinanced and the secured operating line of credit will be unaffected. The existing shareholders of Doman are to receive warrants entitling them to purchase a limited number of shares in the new parent corporation.

[5] The implementation of the Restructuring Plan is subject to the fulfilment of numerous conditions precedent. One of the conditions is the termination of the contracts with Hayes and Strathcona which are the subject matter of this application.

[6] Western holds certain forest tenure, including licenses relating to an area known as the Nootka Region on Vancouver Island and at least one island off the coast of Vancouver Island called Nootka Island. In 1991, the BC government decided that logging contractors should have a form of security similar to the tenure enjoyed by license holders and created the concept of replaceable contracts under the *Forest Act*.

[7] The attributes of replaceable contracts were discussed at length by the BC Court of Appeal in *Clear Creek Contracting Ltd. v. Skeena Cellulose Inc.*, 2003 BCCA 344 and I will not repeat all of them here. In short, a replaceable contract is a form of evergreen contract which contains statutorily mandated provisions, the most important of which is that the license holder must offer a new or replacement contract to the contractor upon each expiry of the term of the contract as long as the contractor is not in default under the contract. If the parties are not able to agree on the new rates under the replacement contract, an arbitrator will determine the rates, which are mandated to be competitive within the industry and to permit the contractor to earn a reasonable profit on top of its costs. The contractors with such contracts are known in the industry as Bill 13 contractors. A license holder must have at least 50% of its annual allowable cut harvested by Bill 13 contractors.

[8] Western has 7 full-phase Bill 13 logging contracts with 6 contractors for the Nootka Region. Hayes is one of those contractors and it has the full-phase contract for the Plumper Harbour area of the Nootka Region. A full-phase contract includes all aspects of logging ranging from road construction, falling, hauling, sorting and delivery to transportation points. Hayes sold the road construction aspect of its contract, and the replaceable contract for road construction was assigned to Strathcona.

[9] When Doman first commenced these CCAA proceedings, it was anticipated that the restructuring process would be completed in a relatively short period of time. It was contemplated that all unsecured debt other than the unsecured bondholders would be paid in full and that the unsecured bondholders would take most, but not all, of the equity in Doman in exchange for some of the indebtedness owed to them and would take security for the remainder of their indebtedness. The confirmation or come-back Order of December 6, 2002 authorized a downsizing process for Doman, but it was not instituted in view of the anticipated restructuring.

[10] The restructuring initially contemplated by Doman did not take place, in part because I made a ruling that the covenants in the trust deed for the secured term debt could not be overridden into the future. By the beginning of April 2004, the unsecured bondholders were pressing for their own restructuring plan and had made it clear that there should be some downsizing in Doman's operations, particularly the closure of Doman's pulp mill in Port Alice. On April 6, 2004, I declined Doman's application for an extension of the stay for the sole purpose of pursuing refinancing of its debt and the sale of the Port Alice pulp mill, but I also declined an application of the unsecured bondholders to call a meeting of creditors to consider its plan of arrangement. I extended the stay for the purpose of allowing Doman to file its own restructuring plan while still pursuing refinancing and sale alternatives, but I imposed a fairly concrete deadline by directing that the creditors meeting be held on June 7. In my April 6 Order, I authorized Doman to reinstitute its downsizing process with special emphasis on the closure of the Port Alice pulp mill if a purchaser was not located. I also placed a restriction on any downsizing by providing that any termination of a replaceable contract under the *Forest Act* was not to be effective unless authorized by the court.

[11] By letters dated April 27, 2004, Western terminated its contracts with Hayes and Strathcona effective upon court approval of the terminations. An affidavit of Mr. Zimmer-

man, a Western employee, provided the following rationale for the decision to terminate these replaceable contracts:

> As part of the reorganization and "downsizing" processes of [Western], we have looked at methods to rationalize harvesting operations in the Nootka Region so as to reduce costs and improve profitability of [Western]. [Western] has worked in conjunction with representatives of the Bondholder committee who have asked for recommendations so as to increase profitability. [Western] has determined that within the Nootka Region, operational efficiencies can be achieved and significant cost savings can be achieved if the number of contractors is reduced and if that contractor's allocated volume is re-allocated to the remaining contractors. [Western] has recommended this reduction to the Bondholders Committee and the representatives of the Committee have asked that [Western] institute a rationalization and termination of contract, which is subject to Court approval as provided in this Court's Order of April 6, 2004.

The affidavit goes on to state that the rationalization can best be carried out by the termination of the Plumper Harbour contracts, principally because the contractor costs associated with this location are the highest in the Nootka Region. The volume under the contracts would then be re-allocated to other Bill 13 contractors in the Nootka Region. The average contract rate for logging a cubic metre of timber under the Hayes contract for the period from 1998 to 2001, as determined by arbitration, was approximately $4 higher than the average rate under the other contracts for the Nootka Region.

[12] Mr. Zimmerman's affidavit indicated that Western did not intend to harvest at Plumper Harbour for the next three years and set out the savings that Western would be able to achieve by terminating the Hayes and Strathcona contracts. These savings were estimated at $5 million over the next three years and $800,000 for each year thereafter. These included annual savings of approximately $165,000 in road building costs, but the main reason Western wants to terminate its contract with Strathcona is that the full-phase contractor replacing Hayes may have its own road building capabilities. Mr. Zimmerman also exhibited to his affidavit a proposal which Hayes had made to Western in 1999 whereby Hayes offered to exchange its rights under its Bill 13 contract for the exclusive right to do helicopter logging in the Nootka Region with an annual minimum guarantee. In the proposal, Hayes stated that the average cut for many of the Bill 13 contractors had been reduced below an efficient economic operating level and that higher costs were being passed on to Western. The proposal was not accepted by Western because it did not want to give exclusive rights for helicopter logging with a guaranteed entitlement.

[13] Representatives of Hayes and Strathcona swore affidavits disputing that the savings would be of the magnitude estimated by Mr. Zimmerman. They also set out the prejudice which their companies would suffer if the contracts were terminated, including the loss of employment and the inability to utilize fixed assets. Mr. Hayes deposed that there is no reasonable or rational economic reason for Western to forego harvesting in Plumper Harbour this year because most of the engineering and road construction costs have already been incurred. Mr. Hayes estimated that if Western harvested the timber on its logging plan for this year in Plumper Harbour, it would receive revenue, net of additional harvesting costs, of approximately $2 million.

[14] The affidavit of Mr. Hayes also stated that Hayes recognized that the operations of the Bill 13 contractors in the Nootka Region are inefficient, unwieldy and costly. Despite this acknowledgment, Mr. Hayes expressed a view that the termination of its contract will not have a material impact on cost reduction in the Nootka Region when one takes into account that the Province will be taking back approximately 20% of Western's annual allowable cut in the Nootka Region pursuant to the recently enacted *Forestry Revitalization Act* and will thereby cause a reduction in the volumes harvested by all of the Bill 13 contractors. No affidavit was sworn by a Western representative to dispute this statement.

[15] Mr. Zimmerman, Mr. Hayes and the deponent on behalf of Strathcona were cross-examined on their affidavits. In his cross-examination, Mr. Zimmerman stated that Western did intend to liquidate the developed timber at Plumper Harbour of approximately 130,000 cubic metres over the next two years before putting the area in abeyance for a three year period. Western has not introduced any evidence with respect to the anticipated costs if this developed timber is harvested or is harvested by other Bill 13 contractors rather than Hayes.

[16] In addition to the *Skeena Cellulose* decision which dealt with the termination of replaceable contracts in CCAA proceedings, counsel referred me to several other cases involving the termination of contracts, leases or licenses in CCAA proceedings.

[17] In *Re Dylex Ltd.*, [1995] OJ No. 595 (QL) (Ont. Ct. of Jus.), Farley J authorized the insolvent company to repudiate the leases of three of its stores as part of a program to close 200 of its stores across Canada. The three stores had been a financial drain on Dylex. Although the closures were going to have a detrimental effect on the shopping centres in which the stores were located, Farley J held that in weighing the balancing of interests in a CCAA context, the court's discretion should be exercised in favour of Dylex over the landlord, which was in sound financial condition. Farley J declined to import into the CCAA the requirement applicable to proposals under the *Bankruptcy and Insolvency Act* that the insolvent company has to show that it would not be able to make a viable proposal unless it terminated the leases in question.

[18] In *Re Blue Range Resource Corp.*, 1999 ABQB 1038, the insolvent company had been authorized by the court under the initial stay order to terminate such of its contracts as it deemed appropriate to permit it to proceed with an orderly restructuring of its business. Blue Range terminated some of its natural gas supply contracts and three of the parties to such contracts sought to challenge the termination of their contracts. One of the issues they raised was that the stay order should be varied to provide that Blue Range would only be permitted to terminate the contracts if it was incapable of performing them or if the termination was essential to the success of their restructuring. Lo Vecchio J dismissed the application to vary the stay order in this fashion. He made the following comments at paras. 36 through 38, which have been quoted in subsequent cases:

> The purpose of the CCAA proceedings generally and the stay in particular is to permit a company time to reorganize its affairs. This reorganization may take many forms and they need not be listed in this decision. A common denominator in all of them is frequently the variation of existing contractual relationships. Blue Range might, as any person might,

breach a contract to which they are a party. They must however bear the consequences. This is essentially what has happened here.

A unilateral termination, as in any case of breach, may or may not give rise to a legitimate claim in damages. Although the Order contemplates and to a certain extent permits unilateral termination, nothing in Section 16.e or in any other part of the Order would suggest that Blue Range is to be relieved of this consequence; indeed Blue Range's liability for damages seems to have been assumed by Duke and Engage in their set-off argument. The application amounts to a request for an order of specific performance or an injunction which ought not to be available indirectly. In my view, an order authorizing the termination of contracts is appropriate in a restructuring, particularly given that it does not affect the creditors' rights to claim for damages.

The Applicants are needless to say not happy about having to look to a frail and struggling company for a potentially significant damages claim. They will be relegated to the ranks of unsecured judgment creditors and may not, indeed likely will not, have their judgments satisfied in full. While I sympathize with the Applicants' positions, they ought not to, in the name of equity, the guide in CCAA proceedings, be able to elevate their claim for damages above the claims of all the other unsecured creditors through this route.

[19] Lo Vecchio J held that the court has the necessary jurisdiction to permit termination of contracts and that the termination of the contracts in question was necessary to the company's survival program.

[20] In *Re T. Eaton Co.*, [1999] OJ No. 4216 (QL) (Ont. Sup. Ct. of Jus.), Farley J refused to order specific performance of an exclusive license to provide credit card services that had been repudiated by the insolvent company as part of a sale of its assets which was the foundation of its restructuring plan. He held that the licensee could be adequately compensated in damages and should not have a higher claim than any other unsecured creditor. In the course of his reasons, he quoted the above portions of the *Blue Range* decision, and said the following at para. 7:

> It is clear that under CCAA proceedings debtor companies are permitted to unilaterally terminate in the sense of repudiate leases, and contracts without regard to the terms of those leases and contracts including any restrictions conferred therein that might ordinarily (i.e. outside CCAA proceedings) prevent the debtor company from so repudiating the agreement. To generally restrict debtor companies would constitute an insurmountable obstacle for most debtor companies attempting to effect compromises and reorganizations under the CCAA. Such a restriction would be contrary to the purposive approach to CCAA proceedings followed by the courts to this date.

Farley J also spoke about being cognizant of the function of a balancing of prejudices within the general approach to the CCAA.

[21] The issue of the court's jurisdiction to authorize the termination of replaceable contracts under the *BC Forest Act* was first addressed in the predecessor to the CCAA proceedings of Skeena Cellulose, *Re Repap British Columbia Inc.*, June 11, 1997, Docket No. A970588 (BCSC). Thackray J held that the court had the jurisdiction under the CCAA to authorize the insolvent company to terminate replaceable contracts. None of

the replaceable contracts in question were actually terminated until the subsequent Skeena Cellulose proceedings.

[22] In the Skeena Cellulose proceedings, the come-back order authorized the company to terminate replaceable contracts in order to facilitate the downsizing and consolidation of its business and operations. As part of Skeena Cellulose's plan of compromise and arrangement, a third party agreed to purchase the shares in the company for $8 million, which was to be used for distribution to the creditors having claims in excess of $400 million. It was a condition precedent to the purchase that two of Skeena Cellulose's five replaceable contracts be terminated, and letters of termination were sent. The two contractors applied to the court for a declaration that the terminations were invalid.

[23] Brenner CJSC dismissed the application. In his decision (cited at 2002 BCSC 1280), he said the following at para. 25:

> SCI has no authority to decline to replace the applicants' replaceable contracts under the terms of those contracts, or in accordance with the provisions of the Regulation that deal with when and how a replaceable contract can be terminated. The only authority for SCI to terminate, or indeed, jurisdiction for this court to approve such terminations, must be found in the terms of the Come-back Order, and in the provisions of the CCAA. To be effective, the terminations must:
>
> (a) comply with the procedures and conditions stipulated in the Come-back Order; and,
>
> (b) conform to the broader principles of economic necessity and fairness which underlie the court's discretionary jurisdiction under the CCAA.

Brenner CJSC expressed the view that the statutory privileges given to the Bill 13 contractors are not sufficient to justify the creation or recognition of a preference in favour of the contractors over other creditors.

[24] The appeal from Brenner CJSC's decision was dismissed. In its decision, the BC Court of Appeal held that the court had an equitable jurisdiction to supplement the CCAA by approving a plan of arrangement which contemplates the termination of contracts by the debtor corporation. Newbury JA held that in approving such a plan involving the termination of replaceable contracts, the court was not overriding provincial legislation because nothing in the legislation purported to invalidate a termination of a replaceable contract but that, in any event, the doctrine of paramountcy would result in preference being given to the CCAA over the *BC Forest Act* in the case of a conflict.

[25] The Court of Appeal found no error in the exercise of discretion by Brenner CJSC. Newbury JA said the following about the concept of fairness at para. 60:

> I have no difficulty in accepting the appellants' argument that fairness as between them and the other three evergreen contractors and as between the appellants and Skeena was a legitimate consideration in the analysis of this case. (Indeed, I believe the Chief Justice considered this aspect of fairness, even though he did not mention it specifically in this part of his Reasons.) The appellants are obviously part of the "broad constituency" served by the CCAA. But the key to the fairness analysis, in my view, lies in the very breadth of that constituency and wide range of interests that may be properly asserted by individuals, corporations, government entities and communities. Here, it seems to me, is where the flaw in the

appellants' case lies: essentially, they wish to limit the scope of the inquiry to fairness as between five evergreen contractors or as between themselves and Skeena, whereas the caselaw decided under the CCAA, and its general purposes discussed above, require that the views and interests of the "broad constituency" be considered. In the case at bar, the Court was concerned with the deferral and settlement of more than $400 million in debt, failing which hundreds of Skeena's employees and hundreds of employees of logging and other contractors stood to lose their livelihoods. The only plan suggested at the end of the extended negotiation period to save Skeena from bankruptcy was NWBC's acquisition of its common shares for no consideration and the acceptance by its creditors of very little on the dollar for their claims.

The Court of Appeal concluded that there was a business case for the terminations. Newbury JA stated that the situation in *Dylex* was no different in principle because, like the leases in *Dylex*, the replaceable contracts were too costly for Skeena Cellulose to continue operating under them.

[26] Although the Court of Appeal's decision in *Skeena Cellulose* settles that the court has the necessary jurisdiction to deal with the termination of contracts, none of the above decisions includes any detailed discussion with respect to the basis upon which the court becomes involved in decisions to terminate contracts. Newbury JA discussed the jurisdiction in terms of the court approving a plan of arrangement which involves the termination of contracts, but the court will often authorize the termination of contracts prior to the formulation of a plan of arrangement.

[27] If a debtor company repudiated a contract prior to commencing CCAA proceedings, the court would not have any direct involvement in the termination of the contract unless, possibly, the other party to the contract sought specific performance of the contract (which, as Brenner CJSC pointed out in *Skeena Cellulose*, is particularly inappropriate in an insolvency). The other party to the contract would have a claim for damages in respect of the repudiation and would be treated like any other unsecured creditor for the purposes of the plan of arrangement.

[28] Once an insolvent company seeks the assistance of the court by commencing CCAA proceedings, the company comes under the supervision of the court. The supervision also involves a consideration of the interests of the broad constituency served by the CCAA mentioned in *Skeena Cellulose* by Newbury JA. These interests, when coupled with the exercise by the court of its equitable jurisdiction, bring into play the requirements for fairness and reasonableness in weighing the interests of affected parties.

[29] Generally speaking, the indebtedness compromised in CCAA proceedings is the debt which is in existence at the time of the CCAA filing, and the debtor company is expected to honour all of its obligations which become owing after the CCAA filing. It is common for the initial stay order or the come-back order to provide that the debtor company is to continue carrying on its business and to honour its ongoing obligations unless the court authorizes exceptions.

[30] In many reorganizations under the CCAA, it is necessary for the insolvent company to restructure its business affairs as well as its financial affairs. Even if the financial affairs are restructured, the company may not be able to survive because portions of the business will continue to incur ongoing losses. In such cases, it is appropriate for the

court to authorize the company to restructure its business operations, either during the currency of the CCAA proceedings or as part of a plan of arrangement. The process is commonly referred to as a downsizing if it involves certain aspects of the business coming to an end. The liabilities which are incurred as a result of the restructuring of the business operations, for such things as termination of leases and other contracts, are included in the obligations compromised by the plan of arrangement even though the debtor company will have been honouring its ongoing commitments under the leases and other contracts after the commencement of the CCAA proceedings. The inclusion of these liabilities in the plan of arrangement is an exception to the general practice of debtor companies paying the full extent of post-filing liabilities and compromising only the pre-filing liabilities.

[31] It is within this context that the court is called upon to authorize the termination of contracts which the debtor company could have repudiated without any authorization prior to the commencement of CCAA proceedings. The liabilities to be compromised have, in general terms, been crystallized by the filing of the CCAA petition, and the affairs of the debtor company are under the supervision of the court, which is required to exercise its equitable jurisdiction fairly and reasonably.

[32] I do not approach the matter in the same fashion as Lo Vecchio J did in *Blue Range*. I do not see the resistance of a party to the termination of a contract with the debtor company to be an attempt to elevate their claim for damages above the claims of all the other unsecured creditors. Apart from any monies which may have been outstanding under the contract at the time of the CCAA filing, the party to the contract was not an unsecured creditor who was going to be subjected to a compromise under a plan of arrangement. The party only becomes a creditor in respect of its damage claim if the contract is terminated. Although Lo Vecchio J could be interpreted as suggesting in the quoted paragraphs 36 to 38 that a debtor company may terminate contractual relations as long as the resulting damage claim is included in its plan of arrangement, I do note that he subsequently commented that the termination of the contracts in that case was necessary to the company's survival program.

[33] I prefer the approach of Farley J in *Dylex*, which involves the court weighing the competing interests and prejudices in deciding what is fair and reasonable. I would anticipate that in the majority of cases a debtor company will be able to persuade the court to exercise its discretion in favour of the termination of contracts and other steps required to downsize or rationalize its business affairs. A debtor company must be insolvent to qualify under the CCAA and the insolvency may have been caused by overexpansion or continual losses by a part of the business. If the company is to have a reasonable prospect of surviving into the indefinite future, it will be appropriate to downsize its operations or bring an end to the losing aspects of the business. The interests of the broad constituency of stakeholders in taking reasonable steps to ensure the ongoing viability of the business will often outweigh the prejudice caused to parties having their contracts or other arrangements with the debtor company terminated and their consequential damage claim being included in the plan of arrangement. There is no single test for the debtor company to satisfy apart from demonstrating that the termination is fair and reasonable in all of the circumstances. As held in *Dylex*, it is not necessary

for the debtor company to demonstrate that the termination of the contract is essential to the making of a viable plan of arrangement.

[34] An example of this type of situation has already occurred in these proceedings. Doman's pulp mill at Port Alice has been losing money for a significant period of time and causing a financial drain on Doman's resources. At the suggestion of the bondholders, it was decided that the mill should be closed and should not be part of the restructured company. Although the closure of the mill would have had a devastating effect on the employees of the pulp mill and the Village of Port Alice as a whole, I authorized the closure because it would not have been reasonable to require the restructured company to operate a division of its business which was anticipated to continue to lose money. Fortunately, Doman was able to find another party who was willing to take over the pulp mill prior to its closure.

[35] On the other hand, there will be circumstances where it will not be appropriate to authorize the debtor company to terminate contracts. For example, suppose that a debtor company became insolvent because its business had been operating at a loss but market conditions had changed and, with a financial restructuring of its existing debt, it was expected to be profitable in the future. Suppose further that the debtor company was party to a contract which did not cause the company to operate the relevant aspect of its business at a loss but the contract was not as favourable as the market would permit the company to obtain if it could divest itself of the existing contract. If the company could terminate the contract and enter into a new one with different rates, it could become substantially more profitable into the future. In these circumstances, it may well be inappropriate for the court to authorize the termination of the contract. The risk of the failure of the debtor company after its restructuring would be relatively low and, depending on the terms of the plan of arrangement, the future benefit of the contract termination may accrue to the shareholders of the company or to the creditors of the company who took risks in exchange for high rates of return.

[36] On the present application, all that the evidence establishes is that Doman will likely be able to reduce its costs to some extent at some point in the future if it can terminate the two contracts in question. Mr. Zimmerman's affidavit states that the reason Western made the recommendation to terminate the two contracts was to improve or increase its profitability. There is no evidence on this application with respect to the following points:

(a) whether the logging at Plumper Harbour under the existing contracts has produced a loss in the past or is expected to produce a loss in the future;

(b) whether other logging operations of Doman produce a greater loss;

(c) whether other aspects of Doman's business produce a loss and, if so, what consideration has been given to rationalizing that loss in comparison to the termination of the contracts in question;

(d) whether it is expected that the restructured company will operate at a profit;

(e) what parts of the constituency of stakeholders will benefit from the termination of the contracts in question;

(f) whether the developed timber at Plumper Harbour can be harvested in the next two years by other contractors at a cost less than the cost under the contracts in question; and

(g) what is the fallacy, if any, in the assertion of Mr. Hayes that the termination of the contracts will have no material impact on cost reduction after taking into account the 20% government take-back.

[37] Some reliance was placed by counsel on the fact that the termination of these contracts is a condition precedent of the Restructuring Plan. In my view, this condition precedent is materially different than the condition precedent in *Skeena Cellulose*. In that case, it was an independent purchaser of the shares in *Skeena* that negotiated the condition on the basis that it was not prepared to purchase the shares unless two of the five replaceable contracts were terminated. The condition resulted from an arm's length negotiation which required the purchaser to put up funds to purchase the shares. In the present case, the bondholder committee produced the initial draft of the Restructuring Plan, which was finalized after a limited negotiation that served to advance the interests of the existing directors and shareholders of Doman. The condition precedent in question was not contained in the initial draft of the Restructuring Plan put forward by the bondholders and there is no evidence as to why the condition was inserted in the Restructuring Plan. I am unable to conclude that the condition precedent was the result of a truly adversarial negotiation and that, unlike the situation in *Skeena Cellulose*, the restructuring is unlikely to proceed if the condition is not satisfied.

[38] In my opinion, therefore, there is insufficient evidence for me to conclude that the proposed contract terminations are fair and reasonable in all of the circumstances. All that the evidence available to me supports is a conclusion that the restructured company will have an opportunity of being more profitable if the contracts are terminated. It has not been demonstrated that the loss of this opportunity will outweigh the prejudice which will be suffered by Hayes and Strathcona if the contracts are terminated. In weighing the competing interests on the evidence before me, it is my conclusion that I should exercise my discretion against approving the contract terminations. I dismiss the application with costs.

NOTES AND QUESTIONS

1. In *Re Doman*, Tysoe J favoured the *Re Dylex* "balancing-the-prejudices" approach over LoVecchio J's alternative approach in the *Blue Range* case. Section 365 of the US *Bankruptcy Code* requires court approval of rejection (disclaimer) and most courts apply a business judgment test. Under the business judgment test, the court defers to the trustee's business judgment as to whether rejection of the contract would be beneficial to the estate. In other words, the trustee may reject a contract more or less as of right, and this is comparable to LoVecchio J's approach. The balancing-the-prejudices test gives the court substantial discretion, whereas LoVecchio J's approach gives it very little. Does the balancing-the-prejudices test yield predictable outcomes? Lack of predictability is a concern in commercial litigation at large, but it is a particular concern in bankruptcy and insolvency proceedings. Can you see why?

2. The 2007 amendments enact a new CCAA s. 32 providing for the disclaimer of agreements. The main features of the provision are as follows:

- the monitor must first approve the proposed disclaimer;

- following this, the debtor must notify the counterparty, and the counterparty has 15 days to apply to the court for disallowance of the disclaimer;

- if the monitor does not approve the proposed disclaimer, the debtor may apply to the court for an order allowing the disclaimer;

- in hearing an application by either the counterparty or the debtor, the court must consider whether the disclaimer "would enhance the prospects of a viable compromise or arrangement being made in respect of the company" and whether the disclaimer "would likely cause significant financial hardship [to the counterparty]";

- if a contract is disclaimed, the counterparty has a provable claim in the CCAA proceedings for any loss;

- there are certain contracts to which the section does not apply, including eligible financial contracts, collective agreements, a lease of real property where the debtor is the landlord and an intellectual property licence where the debtor is the licensor.

There is no exception for (1) a contractual licence, other than an intellectual property licence where the debtor is the licensor; or (2) a lease of personal property where the debtor is the lessor. However, the court may disallow the disclaimer on application by the licensee (lessee) if, among other things, it would be likely to cause the licensee (lessee) significant financial hardship. Why should the law permit a debtor-licensee (or tenant) to disclaim, but not a debtor-licensor (or landlord)? See Anthony Duggan, "Partly Performed Contracts," in Stephanie Ben-Ishai and Anthony Duggan, eds., *Canadian Bankruptcy and Insolvency Law: Bill C-55, Statute c. 47 and Beyond* (Toronto: LexisNexis, 2007), at 26-27.

In terms of the factors relevant to the court's discretion, how, if at all, does the section change the law as stated in *Re Doman*? How does Canadian law compare with US law in relation to disclaimers?

3. New CCAA s. 32 provides that, in the event of disclaimer, the counterparty has a provable claim in the proceedings for its loss, but the section says nothing about valuation of the counterparty's claim. In particular, and in contrast to the position in straight bankruptcy and BIA proposal proceedings, there is no statutory limit on the amount a landlord may claim when the debtor disclaims a commercial tenancy agreement. In *Alternative Fuel Systems v. Remington Development Corp.* (2004), 47 CBR (4th) 1 (Alta. CA), the court held that the relevant provisions of the provincial commercial tenancy statutes were limited to straight bankruptcies and did not apply in CCAA proceedings. Further, it held that there was no justification for incorporating BIA s. 65.2 by reference into the CCAA. Consequently, there is one set of rules for valuing landlords' claims in straight bankruptcy proceedings, a different set of rules for BIA commercial proposal proceedings, and no hard-and-fast rules at all for CCAA proceedings. In *Alternative Fuel Systems*, the court justified these discrepancies by contrasting the BIA's essentially rule-driven approach with the high degree of flexibility

the CCAA offers debtors to propose a plan offering broad creditor support. Do you agree, or is this an aspect that the amendments should have addressed?

Syndicat national de l'amiante d'Asbestos inc. v. Jeffrey Mine Inc.
(2003), 40 CBR (4th) 95 (Que. CA)

DALPHOND JA (for the court): ... [6] Under the *Companies' Creditors Arrangement Act* (RSC 1985, c. C-36) (hereinafter referred to as the "CCAA"), could the Superior Court authorize the monitor, appointed by it and empowered to continue the operations of the debtor's enterprise not to comply with the provisions of the collective agreements concluded between the debtor and the appellant unions?

[7] Could the Superior Court authorize the monitor to cease making the payments required to offset the actuarial liability of the pension plan?

The Facts

[8] Jeffrey Mine Inc. is a company specialized in asbestos mining and processing. It operates, in Asbestos, the largest open-pit mine in the world. In early October 2002, faced with an untenable financial situation, the company's board of directors decided to avail themselves of the CCAA. All of the directors then resigned.

[9] On October 7, 2002, further to a motion that was not served on the appellants, the company obtained from the Superior Court an initial order designating the respondent company, Raymond Chabot inc., monitor. Under the draft arrangement contemplated by Jeffrey Mine Inc., the site would be salvaged and agreements would be concluded with secured creditors and governments with a view to possibly resuming operations or to selling the complex. The following passages from the initial order are relevant to the appeal:

[TRANSLATION]

[6] Orders the monitor to mail a copy of this order, within the next 10 days, to all ordinary creditors of Jeffrey Mine Inc., and, for the employees of Jeffrey Mine Inc., to their union; ...

[8] Authorizes Jeffrey Mine Inc. to file an arrangement with its creditors, the whole in accordance with the CCAA; ...

[16] Authorizes the monitor to take possession of all of the tangible and intangible assets, movable and immovable, belonging to Jeffrey Mine Inc. or used in its business operations; ...

[18] Authorizes the monitor to take all necessary action to preserve and maintain the property and premises of Jeffrey Mine Inc. according to commercial standards in the field; ...

[20] Authorizes the monitor to exercise the following powers: ...

(h) hire and retain the services of certain former directors of Jeffrey Mine Inc., and of any other person, whether a former employee or not of Jeffrey Mine Inc., according to the terms and conditions it deems appropriate, with a view to completing the collection of accounts receivable, the sale of finished products, the implementation of capital asset protection measures, the formulation of a plan to salvage assets and shut down the mining complex for a time, and the conclusion of an arrangement with Jeffrey Mine Inc.'s creditors;

(i) proceed with shutting down Jeffrey Mine Inc.'s production operations and with implementing measures to protect the company's capital assets; ...

(l) lay off Jeffrey Mine Inc.'s employees, and terminate their employment contracts, as it deems appropriate;

(m) retain, in the service of Jeffrey Mine Inc., all employees it deems appropriate for the purpose of implementing the arrangement;

(n) incur and pay, out of Jeffrey Mine Inc.'s receipts, the fees and expenditures relating to the arrangement, including, in particular, the salaries of the employees kept on and of the consultants hired, as well as the expenditures relating to the salvaging of Jeffrey Mine Inc.'s property;

[22] Authorizes the monitor to suspend, as it deems appropriate, any agreement obliging Jeffrey Mine Inc. to pay amounts on behalf of current or former Jeffrey Mine Inc. employees, with regard to the fringe benefits granted by Jeffrey Mine Inc. to its current and former employees, such as drug and dental insurance, life and disability insurance, and contributions to pension plans made by employees other than those kept on by the monitor, the whole reserving any right of such creditors to file a proof of claim; ...

[26] Declares that the monitor is not and cannot be considered an employer or the successor of Jeffrey Mine Inc., in any regard whatsoever concerning Jeffrey Mine Inc. or its current or former employees;

[27] Declares that the monitor and any persons whose services it retains under the present order and, subsequently, under the arrangement cannot incur statutory or civil liability for any action, decision or omission arising out of the exercise of the powers authorized under the terms of this order, or its renewal or amendment, and that no actions, suits or other proceedings may be brought against the monitor or any persons whose services it retains, without prior authorization from this Court;

. . .

[10] That very day, the monitor effected a mass layoff of Jeffrey Mine Inc.'s employees. At the time, there were 258 active, unionized employees, all members of one of the three appellant unions. As of the next day, the monitor gradually retained the services of some 90 people, 60 of whom belonged to the appellant unions. The monitor had each of them, irrespective of their status (manager, unionized employee or non-unionized employee), sign an individual employment contract in which the monitor described itself as acting in that position with respect to the arrangement and the affairs of Jeffrey Mine Inc. The following were among the provisions contained in the contract:

[TRANSLATION]

2. REMUNERATION
The Employee shall be remunerated weekly, on the basis of the customary hourly wage for the job held at Jeffrey Mine Inc.

3. HOLIDAYS AND FRINGE BENEFITS

Holidays and all fringe benefits, in whatever form, shall be paid to the Employee, as a taxable lump sum equivalent to twenty-two percent (22%) of gross remuneration, at the end of each week.

4. PENSION PLAN

A lump sum equivalent to eight percent (8%) of gross remuneration earned between October 7 and November 30, 2002 shall be paid to the pension plan of the Employee.

5. UNION DUES

The Employee specifically asks that the customary union dues be withheld from his/her remuneration by the Monitor, for remittance to the union of which the Employee is a member.

The Employee acknowledges that the Monitor is not and cannot be considered the Successor Employer of Jeffrey Mine Inc., and that the Monitor shall in no way assume any past or present debts or obligations Jeffrey Mine Inc. may have with respect to the Employee.

[11] In a letter dated October 23, 2002 addressed to the chair of the retirees committee of the pension plan of Jeffrey Mine Inc's hourly-paid employees, the monitor wrote the following, in accordance with the authorization in paragraph 22 of the initial order:

[TRANSLATION]

Jeffrey Mine Inc., as employer, is a party to the aforementioned pension plan and makes employer contributions to the pension fund on behalf of contributors and beneficiaries.

On October 7, the monitor effected a mass layoff of Jeffrey Mine Inc's employees, and kept on at Jeffrey Mine Inc. only a limited number of employees contributing to the pension plan.

With regard to contributions subsequent to October 1, 2002, the monitor will pay, on behalf of contributing employees whose services it retains, a lump sum equivalent to eight percent (8%) of the gross remuneration earned by each employee between October 7 and November 30, 2002. The contributions will be paid into the pension fund at the end of each month.

Lastly, given Jeffrey Mine Inc's precarious financial situation, the monitor notifies you that, beginning on October 1, 2002 and ending on a date to be determined, employer contributions will no Ionizer [read "longer"—eds.] be made to the pension fund for the purpose of offsetting the plan's actuarial liability.

. . .

[12] The evidence shows that the actuarial liability was between $30 million and $35 million at that time, and that there were 1200 retired employees. The actuarial liability had been evaluated at approximately $12 million in December 1999, and the debtor made monthly payments of $170,500 until September 1999 to absorb it. As indicated in the letter of October 23, the monitor suspended those payments in October 2002.

[13] The monitor also terminated the dental care, disability, medical and travel insurance plans provided for in the collective agreements, replacing them with a 22% increase in the salaries of the workers still actively employed.

[14] On November 7, 2002, further to a motion filed by the monitor, the Superior Court rendered a second order renewing the initial order to January 10, 2003, ordering

the calling of the creditors' meeting to be postponed indefinitely and authorizing the monitor to borrow and give guarantees in order to finance the expenditures and outlays necessary to salvage assets.

[15] At that time, the monitor mentioned a possible contract for 600 tonnes of asbestos with a US company, ATK Thiokol Propulsion Corp., a NASA supplier. The contract required operations to be resumed temporarily, for about four months. Upon leaving the hearing room, the monitor informed the president of the principal union that the contract was worthwhile only if the collective agreements were disregarded, and asked the president his opinion. The latter did not answer.

[16] In the following weeks, the monitor negotiated with bankers, secured creditors holding rights in regard to the facilities and certain suppliers, such as Hydro-Québec, with a view to executing the Thiokol contract. However, no attempt was made to negotiate with the appellants for the purpose of amending the collective agreements or temporarily suspending their application. On November 22, the monitor accepted Thiokol's order, then turned to the Superior Court to obtain various orders—including a declaration that it was not bound by the collective agreements—considered necessary to carrying out the contract. In its motion, the monitor alleged that [TRANSLATION] "the representatives of the Banner [*sic*—eds.] unionized employees of the Debtor informed the Monitor that they would demand that the latter apply all working conditions provided for in the Collective Agreements."

[17] On November 27, 2002, at around 7:20 p.m., the appellants' attorneys received the monitor's motion by fax, along with a notice of presentation for the next morning in Sherbrooke. ...

[19] On November 29, 2002, the trial judge allowed the motion and rendered a third order, without rising, authorizing the monitor to resume certain operations of Jeffrey Mine Inc. and hire all necessary personnel for the purpose of the Thiokol project, without having to comply with the collective agreements.

[20] Since then, the monitor has retained the services of some 220 employees belonging to one of the three appellant unions. Although the employees were hired in accordance with the rules of seniority set forth in the collective agreements, the appellant unions were not involved in any way. The monitor required each employee to sign an individual employment contract similar to the one described above.

[21] The salaries paid are consistent with those stipulated in the collective agreements, and the amounts granted for fringe benefits and the pension plan (30%) correspond to the costs assumed by the debtor in that regard before October 7, with the exception of the amount to offset the actuarial liability.

The Trial Judgment

[22] The order rendered on November 29, 2002 contained the provisions below:

[TRANSLATION]

[6] RENEWS to May 31, 2003 the second order, rendered by the Honourable Pierre C. Fournier JSC on November 7, 2002, as amended by this order;

[7] AUTHORIZES the monitor, in that position, to resume certain operations of Jeffrey Mine Inc., for and in the name of the latter, and, to that end, AUTHORIZES the monitor to exercise the following powers:

(a) hire and retain the services of any person, regardless of whether or not that person is a former employee of Jeffrey Mine Inc., according to the terms and conditions it deems appropriate;

(b) mine raw asbestos ore and convert it into a finished product; ...

(c) incur and pay, out of Jeffrey Mine Inc.'s receipts, the cost and expenditures relating to the resumption of operations for the purpose of the Thiokol project; ...

(f) exercise any other power necessary or helpful in managing the operations of Jeffrey Mine Inc.; ...

[12] DECLARES that the Monitor and any persons whose services it retains under the present order and, subsequently, under the arrangement, cannot incur statutory or civil liability for any action, decision, omission or damage arising out of the exercise of the powers authorized under the terms of this order, including, but without being limited to, any damage relating to the quality, and to the effects and consequences stemming from the sale, of asbestos fibre products further to the resumption of the operations of Jeffrey Mine Inc., or any environmental damage resulting from the resumption of the Debtor's operations, unless such a fact or damage is caused by gross negligence or wilful misconduct on their part; ...

[16] DECLARES that the Monitor is not bound by the collective agreements between Jeffrey Mine Inc. and its former unionized employees, and that, consequently, it is not required to comply with the provisions therein for the purpose of the Thiokol project; ...

[20] DECLARES this order executory notwithstanding all appeals; ...

The Arguments of the Parties

[23] The appellants argued that the impugned order allowed the monitor to operate the mine, manage its activities and lay off, hire and dismiss employees, and determine their working conditions, without respecting their rights relating to certification or meeting the obligations stemming from the collective agreements, the whole while enjoying civil and statutory immunity. In their opinion, under section 18.1 CCAA, the Monitor is the successor of Jeffrey Mine Inc., making it a new employer contemplated by section 45 of the *Québec Labour Code*. Accordingly, it is bound by the certifications and collective agreements. In their view, it follows that the impugned provisions of the orders (i.e. paras. 20(h), 20(1), 20(m), 22, 26 and 27 of the initial order; paras. 7(a), 12 and 16 of the third order) are contrary to the provisions pertaining to public order and the alienation of undertakings (ss. 39, 45 and 46 of the *Québec Labour Code*), and must be declared invalid. They further contended that the matters raised did not come under the jurisdiction of the Superior Court, but under that of specialized administrative tribunals.

[24] The respondent countered by stating that, pursuant to paragraph 26 of the initial order, it was not and could not be considered an employer or the successor of Jeffrey Mine Inc., and that it was too late for the appellants to request that this Court amend that

part of the initial order. In the respondent's opinion, it follows that it is not bound by the collective agreements.

[25] As for the parts of the third order pertaining to collective agreements, they would simply suspend them during the Thiokol project, which would in no way violate the employees' freedom of association and would be valid given the very broad powers—including the power to change the rights of the parties other than the debtor without their consent, where justified under the circumstances—conferred on the court under the CCAA.

The Relevant Legislative Provisions

[See CCAA ss. 11.3, 11.7, and 11.8—eds.]

Analysis

. . .

III. The Monitor's Role

[Dalphond JA found that the monitor of Jeffrey Mine was not a successor employer and that there was nothing in CCAA s. 11.8 to contradict this conclusion.]

IV. The CCAA and the Appellants' Exclusive Representation

[44] There is nothing in the orders rendered about the abolishment or modification of the certifications. Thus, the appellants' certifications are still valid and in effect. Furthermore, it is doubtful that the Superior Court would have jurisdiction to rule on such matters, as determined by the majority in conjunction with the winding-up of the *Coopérants (Syndicat des employés de coopératives d'assurance-vie v. Raymond, Chabot, Fafard, Gagnon inc.*, [1997] RJQ 776 (CA)), unless that were allowed under a constitutionally valid provision in the CCAA. It follows that the appellants' exclusive representation continues, which, incidentally, is recognized in paragraph 6 of the initial order, where it is stated that a notice to their union constitutes a notice to their employees.

[45] Since the certifications are still valid, their effects must be recognized, described as follows in *Noël v. Société d'énergie de la Baie-James*, [2001] 2 SCR 207, at paras. 41 and 42: ...

[46] Consequently, the monitor cannot disregard the appellants' exclusive representation with regard to the positions covered by certification units. Signing an individual contract with a person occupying any certified position violates the appellants' exclusive representation and is therefore illegal.

V. The Working Conditions of Employees Kept On or Recalled

[47] Under section 11.3 CCAA, a court cannot order suppliers of goods or services, including employees, to make their supply without receiving immediate payment from the monitor. As for the consideration payable, it cannot, in my opinion, be imposed unilaterally by the monitor or the court.

[48] Take the case of a fuel oil supplier. By virtue of the extended powers conferred on it under the CCAA with regard to protection of the status quo and stays of proceedings, the court can order the supplier to continue supplying the debtor even if the supplier's contract contains a clause allowing the contract to be disclaimed in the event of customer insolvency. In such a case, subsequent fuel oil deliveries are made at the price determined in the contract. If the monitor is not satisfied with that price, it must negotiate a reduction with the supplier or disclaim the contract. That said, I do not see by virtue of what power the court could order the price reduction deemed appropriate by the monitor given the debtor's financial situation.

[49] Similarly, I do not see any judicial basis that could be invoked by a court to order a lessor to agree to a reduction in the rent payable by a debtor placed under the CCAA. If the monitor cannot negotiate a rent reduction, its only option is to vacate the premises and cancel the lease.

[50] In short, nothing in the CCAA authorizes the monitor or the court to unilaterally determine the consideration payable to the supplier of goods or services to the debtor. Moreover, the consideration must be agreed upon with the supplier before the supply is made or before the initial order is rendered, as in the case of a contract of successive performance for example, or the consideration must be applicable by law, or under a regulation, a rate scale or market rules. Once again, the situation is comparable to that of a debtor governed by the BIA.

[51] In the case at bar, since the certifications are not contemplated in the orders rendered, and since the layoff of all unionized employees did not terminate the certifications and people were recalled the next day or later on to fill certified positions, it follows that the consideration to be paid to these people must be that provided for in the collective agreements or in any amendment of the agreements negotiated with the appropriate union. That consideration includes the salaries and other benefits associated with the services provided since the initial order. Moreover, like other suppliers, they cannot demand to be paid, over and above that consideration, the amounts owing at the time of the initial order (s. 11.3, para. (a) *in fine*). In the case of those amounts, they will be, within the meaning of the CCAA, creditors to whom the debtor will eventually propose an arrangement. ...

Appeal allowed in part.

NOTES AND QUESTIONS

1. In the same year the *Jeffrey Mines* case was decided, the Standing Senate Committee on Banking, Trade and Commerce recommended that the disclaimer of collective agreements should be allowed if the debtor (1) established inability or serious hardship in restructuring the enterprise without the disclaimer; (2) demonstrated that post-filing negotiations had been carried on, in good faith, for the relief of too onerous aspects of the collective agreement; and (3) satisfied the court that the disclaimer was necessary for a viable restructuring: *Debtors and Creditors Sharing the Burden: A Review of the Bankruptcy and Insolvency Act and Companies Creditors' Arrangement Act* (Ottawa, November 2003), Recommendation 30. This recommendation was based on s. 1113 of the US *Bankruptcy Code*. The 2007

amendments have added a new CCAA s. 33, dealing with collective agreements. How does this provision differ from the Senate Committee's recommendation? Should there be special rules for the disclaimer of collective agreements or should they be treated on the same footing as other contracts? What are the potentially adverse consequences of a debtor not being able to disclaim a collective agreement? For discussion, see David E. Baird and Ronald B. Davis, "Labour Issues," in Chapter 4 of Ben-Ishai and Duggan, above.

C. Affirmation and Assignment

The CCAA says nothing explicitly about the right to affirm contracts in CCAA proceedings. However, a right of affirmation derives by implication from the new statutory right of disclaimer in s. 32: the effect of this provision seems to be that if the debtor does not take the prescribed steps to disclaim a contract then, subject to what is said below, the contract remains on foot.

The matter becomes more complicated if the contract contains an *ipso facto* clause and the counterparty elects to terminate the contract upon commencement of the CCAA proceedings. Prior to the 2007 amendments, the courts relied on their s. 11 discretion to include in the initial order provisions aimed at preventing the counterparty from terminating. The 2007 amendments, in effect, codify this practice. The governing provision is new CCAA s. 34. Note that the new provision gives the court power, on application by the counterparty, to waive the application of the section on the ground of "significant financial hardship."

New CCAA s. 11.4 (critical suppliers) is also relevant. There is some overlap between ss. 11.4 and 34. For discussion, see Anthony Duggan, "Partly Performed Contracts," in Ben-Ishai and Duggan, above, at 39-40.

Prior to the 2007 amendments, a court could, in the exercise of its discretion under CCAA s. 11, authorize the assignment of a contract even if the contract contained an anti-assignment clause and the counterparty did not consent to the assignment. In *Re Playdium Entertainment Corp.* (2001), 31 CBR (4th) 302 (Ont. SCJ), Spence J, citing *Re Canadian Red Cross Society* (1998), 5 CBR (4th) 299 (Ont. Gen. Div.), held that the court must consider four main factors in the exercise of its discretion: (1) whether the debtor has made a sufficient effort to obtain the best price for the contract and has not acted improvidently; (2) the competing interests of the counterparty and the debtor's other stakeholders; (3) the efficacy and integrity of the process by which the offers were obtained; and (4) whether there has been any unfairness in the working out of the process. The 2007 amendments enact a new CCAA s. 11.3, which codifies the rules governing assignments. The new provision requires court approval and it directs the court to take account of whether (1) the monitor approved the proposed assignment; (2) the proposed assignee "would be able to perform the obligations [under the contract]"; and (3) it would be "appropriate" to assign the contract to the proposed assignee. How, if at all, are these considerations different from the ones Spence J identified in *Playdium*?

V. DERIVATIVES

Stephanie Ben-Ishai and Peter Kolla, "Derivatives and the CCAA"
in Stephanie Ben-Ishai and Anthony Duggan, eds., *Canadian Bankruptcy and Insolvency Law: Bill C-55, Statute c. 47 and Beyond* (Toronto: LexisNexis, 2007) 46, at 49-51 and 55-57 (footnotes omitted)

Overview of Derivatives

Derivatives are financial instruments whose price is derived from the underlying value of an asset such as a currency, a commodity, a stock, or an index. The respective rights of the parties to these derivatives are embodied in a derivatives contract, which has obligations that extend into the future concerning performance of the contract. As such, derivatives contracts are a category of executory contract. Businesses use derivatives contracts to manage the risks of changes in the price of an asset, because derivatives can act like a form of insurance to protect against unknown variables that can affect this future price. There are many types of derivatives, including forward contracts, options, and swaps.

The example of forward contracts in the commodities industry illustrates well the risk-managing purpose of derivatives. A forward contract is a contract where at a specified time in the future, the buyer agrees to purchase and the seller agrees to deliver a specified amount of a commodity at a specified price. For those using commodities as inputs, these contracts ensure a fixed supply of a commodity without the risk that its cost will increase. The forward contract also guarantees to those supplying the commodity a fixed market without the risk that the price will decrease. Of course, both parties eliminate the possibility of beneficial movements of prices. However, given the volatility of commodity prices, the large capital investments of extracting commodities or building facilities to utilize the commodities, and the length of time before such investments become profitable, it can be optimal to sacrifice the potential for a large windfall in exchange for increased certainty.

There are two principal types of derivatives. Over-the-counter (OTC) derivatives consist of customizable and privately negotiated contracts, while futures are derivatives that are standardized and traded on exchanges. Futures, traded on exchanges and guaranteed by a clearing organization, raise few concerns about the possibility of future contracts not being honoured. In contrast, since OTC derivatives are negotiated between two parties, the ongoing creditworthiness of the parties to the contract is an important issue. This is especially true when the purpose of entering a derivatives contract is to reduce risk, and since derivatives contracts involve the performance of future obligations.

The importance of risk management in OTC derivatives contracts is illustrated by the fact that most OTC contracts provide that security be demanded when one party is "out of the money" on its contractual obligations. This term refers to the situation where the price at which one party has agreed to buy, sell, or provide some other sort of protection has become negative when compared with the prevailing market price. Comparisons between the price of a derivative and the prevailing market price are known as "marking to market." After marking to market, the "in the money" counterparty to the derivatives contract faces the risk that the "out of the money" counterparty will not be able to fulfill the contractual obligation when it becomes due. The provision of security by the "out of the money" counterparty reduces that risk. In the event that the security cannot be provided, the "in the money" counterparty can terminate the derivatives contract, usually according to explicit provisions in the contract itself, and enter into another contract with a different counterparty.

Thus far, the discussion has centred upon single derivatives transactions. However, the standard form of derivatives transactions, developed by the International Swaps and Derivatives Association, Inc. (ISDA) and called the ISDA "master agreement," provides for derivatives contracts that are more complex than a single transaction. Master agreements can govern a series of discrete transactions, allowing for a net payment to be made on all the transactions occurring during a specified period between the counterparties instead of numerous payments back and forth. This represents the basis for another important characteristic of derivatives contracts that reduces risk, which is known as "close-out netting." Close-out netting is a process that, according to the contractual terms of the derivatives contract, occurs in the event of a default on the derivatives contract before the contractual maturity date. It allows the netting of all the "in the money" transactions against all "out of the money" transactions that are governed by a single master derivatives agreement. The close-out netting process provides that the outstanding financial value of the entire master agreement can be determined and paid out. Berl Nadler observes the following risk-reducing properties of the close-out netting process:

> Close-out netting is a critical risk reduction tool and has been estimated to reduce the value of exposures under derivatives transactions by as much as 70 percent. It does so by enabling parties to offset amounts owing under different transactions under a master agreement against each other upon termination of the master agreement, thereby reducing the financial exposure and credit risk of each of the parties to the master agreement.

What follows from this analysis of derivatives is that the primary objective of OTC derivatives contracts is to reduce risks that are inherent to business and finance. Whether by the very structure of the derivatives contract itself, a swap or a forward contract for example, or by the specific provisions within the contract, such as close-out netting, risk reduction is fundamental to derivatives contracts. Accordingly, Canadian bankruptcy and insolvency legislation affords special treatment for derivatives contracts. The mechanics of and reasons for this special treatment are the topics of the following sections.

Legislative History and Justifications for EFC Treatment

In 1992, the BIA was amended to exempt [derivatives] from the stay in bankruptcy proceedings, but a similar provision was not introduced into the CCAA. During its ultimately successful lobbying efforts to have EFCs exempted in CCAA restructurings, the Canadian Bankers Association provided the following justifications for its position:

> A recent amendment to Chapter 11 of the US *Bankruptcy Code* does permit counter-parties to terminate or close out hedging contracts during a stay period if one of these becomes insolvent. Similar legislation we feel is needed in Canada to ensure the continued competitiveness

of Canadian financial markets and their ability to be part of these contracts when the other party is in fact a US entity or a US citizen. The contracts being discussed, which we have called eligible financial contracts ["EFCs"], are, however, important in their limited sphere. They help Canadian and other corporations world wide to manage risks such as changes in interest rates and in currency exchange rates.

This passage highlights two main arguments in support of exempting EFCs in CCAA restructurings. The first is that EFCs help manage risks, and therefore the bankruptcy system should further this goal to promote stability. As Biery *et al.* have summarized,

> Given that the objective of most eligible financial contracts is to manage risk, there is logic to the view that a party who is essentially seeking insurance against risk should not be held in a contract with a debtor who may choose to terminate the contract if it becomes a money-losing proposition. Instead, the counter-party ought to be able to terminate its contract with the debtor and be entitled to move quickly to obtain the sort of protection it wants elsewhere, from a party who has the ability to provide it.

The second justification outlined by the Canadian Bankers Association is solely concerned with regulatory competition between the United States and Canada: in order for Canadian financial companies to remain competitive with their American counterparts, the argument goes, Canadian bankruptcy legislation must imitate American law. This, the second justification suggests, will level the playing field between the two countries. Additionally, even though this line of argument will not be pursued in this chapter, a public choice theory analysis reveals another motivation of the Canadian Bankers Association. Exemptions for EFCs in Canadian restructuring legislation can be assumed to benefit Canadian banks during restructurings, at the expense of debtors who are their counterparties in derivatives contracts.

The restructuring of affiliates of the Confederation Life Insurance Company in 1994 brought to light the consequences of the absence of EFC exemptions in the CCAA. Nadler has commented that Justice Houlden's order to stay proceedings, which prevented the termination of derivatives contracts, "effectively allowed the Applicants to 'cherry pick' Derivatives Contracts by choosing to terminate certain agreements in which the Applicants were in the money while continuing others." The pre-1997 CCAA structure clearly favoured the policy goal of restructuring companies, over that of reducing the risk of counterparties to derivatives contracts.

The Government of Canada released a white paper in 1995, entitled *Enhancing the Safety and Soundness of the Canadian Financial System*, which argued for excluding EFCs from the CCAA stay. The justification for this position was to reduce the exposure of financial institutions and their counterparties in derivatives contracts to unnecessary risk, due to an inability to terminate derivatives contracts in the event of insolvency. The claim followed from the fact that restructurings under the CCAA generally take between six and 12 months to complete, and that such a period of time without the risk reduction provided by EFCs was unacceptable. Justice Farley has emphasized the importance of derivatives contracts generally:

> It would seem as a matter of public policy that such a valuable tool which has become a key fundamental for the interlocking financial activities of virtually every major financial and

many major non-financial corporations in Canada (and having international links) should not be dealt with in such a manner as to seriously affect its efficiency.

As an expression of precisely this public policy, and after "intense lobbying by the financial industry," the CCAA was amended in September 1997 to include the section 11.1 exemptions for EFCs from a stay of proceedings.

NOTES

1. New CCAA s. 11.05, enacted as part of the 2007 amendments, replaces former CCAA s. 11.1. It provides that "no order may be made under this Act that has the effect of staying or restraining the exercise of a right to terminate or amend an eligible financial contract or claim an accelerated payment or a forfeiture of the term under it." The purpose of the new provision is to make it clear that the EFC exemption applies not just to the stay provision in s. 11.02, but also to the court's general power to make orders in s. 11.

2. "Eligible financial contract" was previously defined in CCAA s. 11.1(1) by reference to a long but incomplete shopping list of specific transactions. The courts had considerable difficulty with the definition: *Re Blue Range Resource Corp.* (2000), 20 CBR (4th) 187 (Alta. CA); *Re Androscoggin Energy LLC* (2005), 75 OR (3d) 552 (CA); *Re Calpine Canada Energy Ltd.* (2006), 19 CBR (5th) 187 (Alta. QB). In response to concerns voiced both by commentators and the courts themselves, the 2007 amendments repeal the old definition and provide instead for the definition to be prescribed by regulation: new CCAA s. 11.05(2). The aims are to facilitate changes to the definition in response to rapidly occurring developments in the marketplace and to achieve greater consistency with the United States and the European Union. The operative part of the new definition, as prescribed by the *Eligible Financial Contract General Rules* (*Companies' Creditor Arrangement Act*), reads as follows:

1. The following definitions apply in these Rules.

"derivatives agreement" means a financial agreement whose obligations are derived from, referenced to, or based on, one or more underlying reference items such as interest rates, indices, currencies, commodities, securities or other ownership interests, credit or guarantee obligations, debt securities, climatic variables, bandwidth, freight rates, emission rights, real property indices and inflation or other macroeconomic data and includes

(a) a contract for differences or a swap, including a total return swap, price return swap, default swap or basis swap;

(b) a futures agreement;

(c) a cap, collar, floor or spread;

(d) an option; and

(e) a spot or forward.

"financial intermediary" means

(a) a clearing agency; or

(b) a person, including a broker, bank or trust company, that in the ordinary course of business maintains securities accounts or futures accounts for others.

2. The following kinds of financial agreements are prescribed for the purpose of the definition "eligible financial contract" in section 2 of the *Bankruptcy and Insolvency Act*:

(a) a derivatives agreement, whether settled by payment or delivery, that

(i) trades on a futures or options exchange or board, or other regulated market, or

(ii) is the subject of recurrent dealings in the derivatives markets or in the over-the-counter securities or commodities markets;

(b) an agreement to

(i) borrow or lend securities or commodities, including an agreement to transfer securities or commodities under which the borrower may repay the loan with other securities or commodities, cash or cash equivalents,

(ii) clear or settle securities, futures, options or derivatives transactions, or

(iii) act as a depository for securities;

(c) a repurchase, reverse repurchase or buy-sellback agreement with respect to securities or commodities;

(d) a margin loan in so far as it is in respect of a securities account or futures account maintained by a financial intermediary;

(e) any combination of agreements referred to in any of paragraphs (a) to (d);

(f) a master agreement in so far as it is in respect of an agreement referred to in any of paragraphs (a) to (e);

(g) a master agreement in so far as it is in respect of a master agreement referred to in paragraph (f);

(h) a guarantee of, or an indemnity or reimbursement obligation with respect to, the liabilities under an agreement referred to in any of paragraphs (a) to (g); and

(i) an agreement relating to financial collateral, including any form of security or security interest in collateral and a title transfer credit support agreement, with respect to an agreement referred to in any of paragraphs (a) to (h).

3. As noted in Section IV, new CCAA s. 32 (disclaimer of contracts) and s. 34 (non-termination of contracts by counterparty) do not apply to eligible financial contracts. The rationale for these exemptions is explained in Ben-Ishai and Kolla, above.

VI. DEBTOR-IN-POSSESSION FINANCING

Michael B. Rotsztain and Alexandra Dostal, "Debtor-in-Possession Financing"
in Stephanie Ben-Ishai and Anthony Duggan, eds., *Canadian Bankruptcy and Insolvency Law: Bill C-55, Statute c. 47 and Beyond* (Toronto: LexisNexis, 2007),
at 227-29, 231, 233-34, 236-40

Although debtor-in-possession (DIP) or interim financing is a relatively new concept in Canadian insolvency proceedings, it has become an essential element of many Canadian corporate restructurings. The term "debtor-in-possession" is borrowed from American legislation, in which DIP financing is codified. ...

As a result of their precarious financial position, insolvent companies are often unable to access existing credit facilities or obtain new conventional credit facilities after they have commenced BIA or CCAA restructuring proceedings. A restructuring company needs a source of credit to finance continuing operations while it attempts to formulate and negotiate a plan of arrangement or considers other options. The funds borrowed in DIP financings can be used for a number of restructuring-related purposes, such as paying operating costs of the business during the restructuring proceedings and paying advisors. DIP financing may be sourced from either existing creditors or from parties with no interest in the restructuring; however, such financing is most often obtained from existing secured creditors who already have a large stake in the proceedings.

DIP financing is usually accompanied by charges over the debtor's assets, granted by the court to secure the repayment of the funds advanced by the DIP lender and related obligations of the debtor. These charges may rank subordinate to, equal to, or in priority to existing charges. The ranking of court-ordered DIP financing charges has been the most controversial aspect of DIP financing. Secured creditors' rights in collateral have historically been well protected in Canada. The security position of secured creditors whose charges are subordinated to DIP financing charges may, however, be eroded without their consent. As a result, some have argued that granting a priority DIP financing charge (or "priming" existing secured creditors) is tantamount to expropriation of the property of secured creditors, and that this should not be permitted without specific legislative authority. ...

When Canadian courts were first requested to approve secured interim financing under the CCAA, they searched for the jurisdictional basis for their authority to do so ... . Courts often fail to clarify the basis on which they grant insolvency relief that is not specifically authorized in the legislation: whether on the basis of inherent jurisdiction, statutory discretion, or both. Inherent jurisdiction is one of the common bases relied upon by courts to grant interim financing in insolvency proceedings. Canadian courts often refer to the following passage from Halsbury's Laws of England definition of "inherent jurisdiction":

> In sum, it may be said that the inherent jurisdiction of the court is a virile and viable doctrine, and has been defined as being the reserve or fund of powers, a residual source of powers, which the court may draw upon as necessary whenever it is just and equitable to do so, in particular to ensure the observance of due process of law, to prevent vexation or oppression, to do justice between the parties and to secure a fair trial between them.

In contrast, the court's exercise of statutory discretion arises not from its nature as a court of law, but rather from statute. Statutory discretion allows a court to supplement a statute by making orders that are consistent with the purposes and objects of the statute. ...

In *Re Royal Oak Mines* (1999), 6 CBR (4th) 414 (Ont. Gen. Div.) Justice Blair found the court's authority in a CCAA proceeding to subordinate existing secured charges to charges for interim financing in section 11 of the CCAA:

> Section 11 of the CCAA is the provision of the Act embodying the broad and flexible statutory power invested in the court to "grant its protection" to an applicant by imposing a stay of proceedings against the applicant company, subject to terms, while the company attempts to negotiate a restructuring of its debt with its creditors. It is well established that the provi-

sions of the Act are remedial in nature, and that they should be given a broad and liberal interpretation in order to facilitate compromises and arrangements between companies and their creditors, and to keep companies in business where that end can reasonably be achieved.

However, Justice Blair was careful to stress that DIP financing represents extraordinary relief:

> It follows from what I have said that, in my opinion, extraordinary relief such as DIP financing with super priority status should be kept, in Initial Orders, to what is reasonably necessary to meet the debtor company's urgent needs over the sorting-out period. Such measures involve what may be a significant re-ordering of priorities from those in place before the application is made, not in the sense of altering the existing priorities as between the various secured creditors but in the sense of placing encumbrances ahead of those presently in existence. Such changes should not be imported lightly, if at all, into the creditors mix; and affected parties are entitled to a reasonable opportunity to think about their potential impact, and to consider such things as whether or not the CCAA approach to the insolvency is the appropriate one in the circumstances—as opposed, for instance, to a receivership or bankruptcy—and whether or not, or to what extent, they are prepared to have their positions affected by DIP or super priority financing.

. . .

The case law discussed above makes it clear that the courts have characterized the granting of priority security for DIP financing as an extraordinary remedy and have issued caveats that inherent jurisdiction or statutory discretion should be exercised sparingly. Nevertheless, a body of jurisprudence has developed which permits charges in favour of existing secured creditors to be subordinated to CCAA DIP financing charges, where required, in order to facilitate restructurings. In recognition of the broad remedial purposes of the CCAA, the courts have been prepared to exercise their powers in this way to fill a gaping hole in the legislation currently in force. While this has been a positive development, there is a serious question as to whether judicial law-making ought to be the principal source of DIP financing law. ...

Commentators have attempted to rationalize the cases on DIP financing (primarily decided under the CCAA) in an effort to extract general principles that will provide guidance on courts' treatment of interim financing requests, regardless of whether the jurisdictional basis is inherent jurisdiction or statutory discretion. A previous article by one of the authors provides a summary of the principles as of 2000.

(1) A company with a viable basis for restructuring will be permitted to borrow funds for working capital and to grant security for such borrowings ranking ahead of the claims of unsecured creditors: *Re Westar Mining Ltd.*; *Re T. Eaton Co.*

(2) Super-priority DIP financing will be approved where all or substantially all the existing secured creditors acquiesce or consent: *Willann Investments Ltd. v. Bank of America Canada.*

(3) Super-priority for DIP financing will be granted where existing secured creditors will not be adversely affected thereby because the financing results in the creation

of new collateral assisting in repaying the DIP financing, specifically new receivables: *Re Dylex Ltd.*

(4) Super-priority DIP financing will be approved where the funds are used to pay essential expenditures which have priority in any event over existing secured lenders, who will therefore suffer little overall prejudice as a result, particularly where the new financing is "not very significant … relevant to the overall numbers involved": *Re SkyDome Corp.*

(5) In initial CCAA orders, which are usually granted on very short notice, extraordinary relief such as super-priority financing should be restricted to what is necessary to meet urgent short-term needs. Requests for additional DIP financing should be made on adequate notice to the affected parties so that they are provided with a reasonable opportunity to consider the impact of such financing and make their submissions to the court: *Re Royal Oak Mines Inc.*

(6) The court's inherent jurisdiction to grant super-priority financing does not extend so as to permit it to grant DIP financing super-priority over security (in this case, builders' liens under British Columbia legislation) which by statute is afforded priority over all other interests: *Re Royal Oak Mines Inc.*

(7) Deciding whether to grant super-priority DIP financing is an exercise of balancing the interests of the debtor and its stakeholders. The court should not permit super-priority DIP financing unless there is "cogent evidence that the benefit of DIP financing clearly outweighs the potential prejudice to the lenders whose security is being subordinated": *Re United Used Auto & Truck Parts Ltd.*, applied in *Re Sharp-Rite Technologies Ltd.* (In the latter case, despite its application of the *United Used Auto* decision, the court granted super-priority financing against the debtor's current assets where the first-ranking secured creditor raised no objection but other secured creditors did.)

(8) The interests of existing secured creditors can be prejudiced by the granting of super-priority financing only if the court is satisfied that this is justified in the circumstances of the case. The court will not be satisfied that there is such justification where the secured creditors have "a high level of distrust" and "wide ranging lack of confidence" in the debtor's managers and directors, and the appointment of an interim receiver under the BIA is found to be the more appropriate course of action. An order authorizing super-priority DIP financing "is only rarely made unless the security for such financing can be provided by hitherto unsecured assets": *General Electric Capital Canada Inc. v. Euro United Corp.*

There have not been significant departures from these judicial principles since 2000, with the exception of a contrary ruling in Alberta on principle 6 above.

The fact that the courts' inherent jurisdiction and statutory discretion have been the jurisdictional bases for as critical a matter as DIP financing has warranted reconsideration. Courts have thus far exercised their discretion on whether to approve DIP financing on a case-by-case basis. This flexibility has meant that although the principles articulated above have emerged, uncertainty continues to exist with regard to the appropriate limits of the courts' jurisdiction and discretion, thus making it difficult for secured creditors and other parties to predict how their interests may be affected if DIP financing is granted in a restructuring. There has also been a lack of uniformity on procedural issues, such as the appropriate notice, if any, to be provided to affected parties. Though rare, *ex parte* orders approving DIP financing are sometimes made. These uncertainties as to the appropriate limits to courts' jurisdiction and discretion and the lack of procedural uniformity have prompted calls to incorporate into the legislation express authority for the courts to grant DIP financing.

NOTES AND QUESTIONS

1. The 2007 amendments enact a new CCAA s. 11.2, which provides a new statutory scheme governing interim financing. These provisions are discussed below in note 3. These amendments seek to end the debate over the scope of the court's jurisdiction and discretion to issue DIP financing orders. The Alberta Court of Appeal in *Canada (Deputy Attorney General) v. Temple City Housing Inc.* (2009), 43 CBR (5th) 35 (Alta. CA), at para. 13, referred to the 2007 statutory changes noting that "[t]he amendments to the CCAA include specific authority to grant super-priority to DIP financing such as the loan in this case … . However, once it has been proclaimed in force, the issue of the CCAA judge's inherent jurisdiction to order such priorities will not be an issue in future CCAA proceedings."

2. In the lead-up to the 2007 amendments, there was some debate over the desirability of enacting legislative guidelines. Janis Sarra raised the question of whether statutory amendment was required:

> While this codification might create greater certainty, it reflects precisely what the courts are doing now, using the flexibility of the process to ensure a proper balancing of creditor and other stakeholder interests. It is worth noting that in the current debate about whether DIP financing should be the subject of statutory amendment, there are no cases cited in which the courts have failed to exercise their discretion reasonably and in a restrained manner. Thus, it is unclear why statutory amendment is required.

(Janis Sarra, "Debtor in Possession (DIP) Financing: The Jurisdiction of Canadian Courts to Grant Super-Priority Financing in CCAA Applications" (2000), 23 *Dal. LJ* 337, at 381.)

What are the advantages or disadvantages of allowing the courts to decide DIP issues on a case-by-case basis under their inherent or general statutory discretion? Are there any problems in providing a more detailed statutory scheme?

3. Section 11.2 of the CCAA makes two significant changes. First, the legislation gives the court the express power to grant security for interim financing in priority to existing charges or secured claims. Thus, secured creditor X, who may have been first in time and in priority, may well find itself second in priority to secured creditor Y, who has provided DIP financing. Second, s. 11.2 provides guidelines that the courts are to consider on an interim financing application. Although the Saskatchewan Court of Appeal in *National Bank of Canada v. Stomp Pork Farm Ltd.* (2008), 43 CBR (5th) 42 (Sask. CA) concluded that the 2007 amendments "confirm an authority that the courts have been exercising for some time," the legislation now provides detailed guidelines for the court to consider in assessing applications for DIP financing.

The main features of s. 11.2 follow:

- On application by a debtor company, a court may make an order declaring that all or part of the company's property is subject to a charge in favour of a person who agrees to lend to the company an amount approved by the court as required by the company.

- The application by the debtor company must be on notice to secured creditors who are likely to be affected by the security or charge.

- The security or charge may not secure an obligation that exists before the order is made.

- The new provisions enable the court to deal with the priority of existing secured creditors in relation to the new charge. The court may order that the security or charge rank in priority over the claim of any secured creditor of the company.

- The legislation also contemplates the possibility of more than one order for interim financing being made. Assume that the court made an order for interim financing in favour of A on July 15. If a subsequent application is made and an order is granted in favour of B, the court may only order that B has priority over A with A's consent.

- In deciding whether to make an order, the court is to consider among other things:

  — the period during which the company is expected to be subject to proceedings under the CCAA;

  — how the company's business and financial affairs are to be managed during the proceedings;

  — whether the company's management has the confidence of its major creditors;

  — whether the loan would enhance the proposal of a viable compromise or arrangement being made in respect of the company;

  — the nature and value of the company's property;

  — whether any creditor would be materially prejudiced as a result of the security or charge; and

  — the monitor's report if any.

4. Compare the statutory scheme with the case law principles extracted in Rotsztain and Dostal, above. Which regime, statutory or judicial, creates more certainty and fairness for the parties? How would the court balance material prejudice to an existing secured creditor with the claim that DIP financing will facilitate a viable compromise?

5. Before the 2007 amendments, courts sought to balance the interests of the debtor and stakeholders in assessing whether a DIP financing order was appropriate: see factor (7) in Rotsztain and Dostal, above. Janis Sarra has argued that "the court, in balancing prejudices, will weigh the possibility of a going-concern solution that potentially creates long-term upside value for numerous stakeholders, with the risk of further depletion of value that may be able to satisfy claims on a short term basis": *Rescue! Companies' Creditors Arrangement*

Act (Toronto: Carswell, 2007), at 96-97. For example, in *Re MEI Computer Technology Group Inc.*, (2005), 19 CBR 5th 257 (Que. SC), at para. 25, the court identified the following as a relevant factor: "Before allowing a DIP financing or creating a priority charge, a court should be satisfied with proper evidence that the benefits to all creditors, shareholders and employees clearly outweigh the potential prejudice to some creditors." In *Re Simpson's Island Salmon Ltd.*, (2005), 18 CBR (5th) 182 (NBQB), at para. 19, the court concluded that "a Court should not authorize DIP financing pursuant to the CCAA unless there is a reasonable prospect that the debtor will be able to make an arrangement with its creditors and rehabilitate itself." In what ways does s. 11.2 alter these judicial tests? Alternatively, are the judicial approaches and the new s. 11.2 in substance the same?

6. What is the policy rationale for requiring that secured creditors be given notice of the application? If an interim financing order could be made without notice, what implications would that have for secured lending?

7. Why are applications restricted to debtor companies? Should creditors have standing to make an application?

8. In addition to DIP financing, courts sometimes authorized the creation of a post-filing trade creditors' charge. Instead of paying cash for supplies acquired after the commencement of CCAA proceedings, the debtor sought to induce suppliers to continue to supply goods and services through a court-ordered charge on the assets that secured payment of these obligations. See *Re Westar Mining Ltd.* (1992), 14 CBR (3d) 88 (BCSC); *Re Smoky River Coal Ltd.* (2001), 28 CBR (4th) 127 (Alta. QB). The charge was usually afforded priority over existing secured creditors, but ranked below the other court-ordered charges. The 2007 amendments to the CCAA make no mention of this type of order. Can a court make this type of order following the amendment?

VII. ASSET SALES

The Senate Standing Committee on Banking, Trade and Commerce in its 2003 report, *Debtors and Creditors: Sharing the Burden*, recognized (at 146) that asset sales in the course of a CCAA proceeding provide an opportunity for the insolvent debtor to "sell part of its business in order to generate capital, avoid further diminution in value and/or focus better on the financially solvent aspects of its operations." Asset sales increase the chance of survival for the debtor company because the debtor obtains necessary capital while creditors, in turn, avoid further reductions in the value of their claims. However, asset sales are typically outside the debtor company's course of business and in some situations the sale "might involve the sale of the business in its entirety" (at 146).

In the absence of any express provisions in the CCAA that deal with asset sales, traditionally courts relied on two sources of jurisdiction to approve asset sales: (1) the power of the court to impose terms and conditions under a stay order under s. 11; and (2) inherent jurisdiction: see *Re Canadian Red Cross Society* (1998), 5 CBR (4th) 299, at para. 44 (Ont. Gen. Div.). In approving the sale of assets the courts to date have considered a number of factors on a case-by-case basis. For example, in *Re Canadian Red Cross Society*, above, at para. 47, the court concluded that the following were relevant factors to consider when approving a sale of assets:

1. whether the debtor company has made a sufficient effort to get the best price and has not acted improvidently;
2. the interests of the parties;
3. the efficacy and integrity of the process by which offers are obtained; and
4. whether there has been unfairness in the working out of the process.

As discussed below, in the notes following *Fracmaster*, new CCAA s. 36 now provides statutory guidelines for the courts to consider in the exercise of their discretion to approve asset sales. In reviewing the materials below, consider whether the issues raised in the case law have been adequately resolved by s. 36.

Re Consumers Packaging Inc.
(2001) 150 OAC 384

THE COURT: [1] Ardagh PLC ("Ardagh"), seeks leave to appeal and if leave is granted appeals the Order of The Honourable Mr. Justice Farley dated August 31, 2001 which approved a sale of certain assets of Consumers Packaging Inc. and Consumers International Inc. and 164489 Canada Inc. (hereinafter collectively "Consumers") to Owens-Illinois, Inc. ("Owens-Illinois").

[2] Consumers had filed for protection under the *Companies' Creditors Arrangement Act* (the "CCAA") on May 23, 2001 and Farley J made an initial order on that date approving an amendment and forbearance agreement between Consumers and its institutional lenders and arranging interim credit. KPMG Inc. was appointed Monitor under s. 11.7 of the CCAA. On June 18, 2001 Farley J authorized Consumers through an Independent Restructuring Committee and its Chief Restructuring Officer to fix a date upon which interested third parties were to submit firm, fully financed offers to purchase all or any part of Consumers' business. Both Ardagh and Owens-Illinois participated in the bid process. The Independent Restructuring Committee, the Chief Restructuring Officer and the Monitor agreed on behalf of Consumers that Owens-Illinois was the preferred bid. On the sale approval motion heard August 31, 2001, Farley J found as a fact that Consumers was "quite sick" and "financially fragile" and that there "exists a material risk that [Consumers] will be destabilized by a withdrawal of funding by the [consortium of lenders] which have been continuously adamant about a September 2001 deadline for pay out."

[3] On the evidence before us, the Owens-Illinois bid approved by Farley J on August 31, 2001 was the result of a fair and open process developed by Consumers and its professional advisors and carried out, after May 23, 2001, under the supervision of the court and with the participation of Ardagh. The Owens-Illinois bid provides more cash to Consumers' creditors than a proposal from Ardagh, has the least completion risk, is not conditional on financing, is likely to close in a reasonable period of time, is made by a credible purchaser (the largest glass bottle manufacturing company in the world) and will result in the continuation of Consumers' Canadian business, the retention of a vast majority of Consumers' 2,400 Canadian employees and the assumption by the purchaser

of significant obligations under Consumers' employee pension plan. It is supported by all parties before this court with the exception of Ardagh.

[4] The respondents on this motion submit that the restructuring proposals put forward by Ardagh were not backed by financing commitments, required further due diligence by Ardagh and its lenders, could not be completed in a timely way, offered less by way of recovery to Consumers' creditors and were no more than proposals to negotiate. It appears to have been the unanimous view of the Monitor, Consumers' Independent Restructuring Committee and Consumers' Chief Restructuring Officer that Ardagh's proposals were not viable and would, if pursued, result in the liquidation of Consumers, resulting in lower return to creditors, loss of jobs and cessation of business operations. This view was accepted by Farley J who stated in his endorsement approving the Owens-Illinois bid that it was the "only presently viable option better than a liquidation with substantially reduced realization of value."

[5] In our opinion, leave to appeal should not be granted. The authorities are clear that, due to the nature of CCAA proceedings, leave to appeal from orders made in the course of such proceedings should be granted sparingly: see *Algoma Steel Inc. (Re)*, a judgment of the Ontario Court of Appeal, delivered May 25, 2001, [2001] OJ No. 1943 at p. 3. Leave to appeal should not be granted where, as in the present case, granting leave would be prejudicial to the prospects of restructuring the business for the benefit of the stakeholders as a whole, and hence would be contrary to the spirit and objectives of the CCAA. The sale of Consumers' Canadian glass operations as a going concern pursuant to the Owens-Illinois bid allows the preservation of Consumers' business (albeit under new ownership), and is therefore consistent with the purposes of the CCAA. There is a real and substantial risk that granting leave to appeal in the present case will result in significant prejudice to Consumers and its stakeholders, in light of the significant time and financial constraints currently faced by Consumers. Both Farley J and KPMG Inc., the court-appointed Monitor in the CCAA proceedings, have concluded that the Owens-Illinois bid represents the only presently viable option available to Consumers, which would be better than a liquidation.

[6] The transactions contemplated by the Owens-Illinois bid are expected to close on September 28, 2001. If the Owens-Illinois bid does not close before the end of September, 2001, it is uncertain if, and for how long, Consumers would be able to continue its operations. The financial institutions that are prepared to finance these transactions have appeared before this court and have advised, both before and throughout the CCAA proceedings, that they will not fund the operations of Consumers beyond the end of September, the time at which Consumers' credit requirements seasonally increase on an annual basis. There is no evidence on the record, and certainly none from Ardagh, as to the manner in which the operations of Consumers would be funded until the Ardagh proposal contained in its bid, if successful, could be implemented.

[7] Further, despite its protestations to the contrary, it is evident that Ardagh is a disappointed bidder that obtained its security interest in the assets of Consumers in order to participate in their restructuring and obtain a controlling equity position in the restructured entity. There is authority from this court that an unsuccessful bidder has no standing to appeal or to seek leave to appeal. As a general rule, unsuccessful bidders do not have standing to challenge a motion to approve a sale to another bidder (or to appeal

from an order approving the sale) because the unsuccessful bidders "have no legal or proprietary right as technically they are not affected by the order": see the statement of Farley J, dealing with a receiver's motion to approve a sale, that is quoted with approval by O'Connor JA of this court in *Skyepharma plc v. Hyal Pharmaceutical Corp.* (2000), 47 OR (3d) 234 at 238 (CA). O'Connor JA went on to say at p. 242:

> There is a sound policy reason for restricting, to the extent possible, the involvement of prospective purchasers in sale approval motions. There is often a measure of urgency to complete court approved sales. This case is a good example. When unsuccessful purchasers become involved, there is a potential for greater delay and additional uncertainty. This potential may, in some situations, create commercial leverage in the hands [of] a disappointed would be purchaser which could be counterproductive to the best interests of those for whose benefit the sale is intended.

[8] The position of Ardagh is not advanced by the fact that it did not challenge the order of Farley J of June 18, 2001 which set out the parameters for the bidding. Instead it participated in the bidding process which it now attacks as being *ultra vires* the CCAA.

[9] Finally, while we do not propose to become involved in the merits of the appeal, we cannot refrain from commenting that Farley J's decision to approve the Owens-Illinois bid is consistent with previous decisions in Ontario and elsewhere that have emphasized the broad remedial purpose and flexibility of the CCAA and have approved the sale and disposition of assets during CCAA proceedings prior to a formal plan being tendered.

[10] Accordingly, leave to appeal is refused with costs.

QUESTIONS

Why is the sale of the debtor's assets consistent with the purposes of the CCAA? Are there any circumstances in which the interests of unsuccessful bidders should be taken into account by the court?

Re 1078385 Ontario Ltd.
(2004), 16 CBR (5th) 152 (Ont. CA)

J.M. SIMMONS JA: Randy Oram requests leave to appeal an order of Quinn J dated November 22, 2004, [2004] OJ No. 6101, sanctioning a plan of arrangement under the … CCAA … , and a related vesting order dated November 25, 2004, implementing the plan of arrangement. Pursuant to the terms of those orders, the assets of the applicants (the "debtor companies") were vested in a new company owned by an affiliate of Amico Contracting & Engineering (1992) Inc., the secured creditor that proposed the plan of arrangement.

The debtor companies are the developers of Bob-Lo Island, which is a relatively small island located in the Detroit River. Randy Oram is a shareholder of at least one of the debtor companies as well as an unsecured creditor. Under the agreement of purchase and sale forming part of the plan of arrangement, the assets of the debtor companies were sold for approximately $11,500,000 in satisfaction of secured creditors' claims totalling $19,219,744.

Randy Oram raises a number of proposed grounds of appeal. However, the focus of his objections is that the plan of arrangement is a secured-creditor-led plan that excludes the unsecured creditors from any realistic prospect of recovery, without requiring the secured creditors to go through the formal process of enforcing their security and without exposing the secured assets to the market.

Randy Oram submits that the significant issue raised for consideration on appeal is a review of the factors that should guide a court's exercise of discretion when considering secured-creditor-led plans of arrangement. He contends that, in this case, the motion judge erred by allowing the secured creditors to use the CCAA procedure as a shortcut for liquidating secured assets and by failing to require the secured creditors to proceed with enforcing their security in the ordinary course. ...

I reject Randy Oram's submission that the proposed appeal raises serious and arguable grounds that satisfy the test for granting leave to appeal for nine reasons.

First, although the question of whether a plan of arrangement under which the assets of the debtor company will be disposed of and the debtor company will not continue as a going concern is contrary to the purposes of the CCAA may not have been resolved by this court, contrary to Randy Oram's written submissions, this is not the first time a secured-creditor-led plan, which operates exclusively for the benefit of secured creditors and under which the assets of the debtor company will be disposed of and the debtor company will not continue as a going concern, has received court approval: see *Re Anvil Range Mining Corp.* (2001), 25 CBR (4th) 1 (Ont. SCJ), aff'd. on other grounds [2002] OJ No. 2606 (CA). (See also the discussion of the purposes of the CCAA in the cases referred to in *Re Anvil Range Mining Corp., supra*, at para. 11 (SCJ).)

Moreover, the fact that unsecured creditors may receive no recovery under a proposed plan of arrangement does not, of itself, negate the fairness and reasonableness of a plan of arrangement: *Re Anvil Range Mining Corp., supra*, at para. 31 (CA).

Based on the foregoing reasons, I conclude that Randy Oram failed to demonstrate arguable grounds for appealing the motion judge's finding that "the debt of the secured creditors exceeds the equity [in the debtor companies' property]." Randy Oram has not therefore established any reasonable possibility that he has an economic interest in the assets forming the subject matter of the proposed appeal. In addition, I conclude that to the extent there may be any arguable merit in the issue of whether the proposed plan of arrangement was contrary to the purposes of the CCAA, Randy Oram failed to demonstrate that there is sufficient merit in that issue to justify granting leave to appeal in the circumstances of this case.

Royal Bank of Canada v. Fracmaster Ltd.
(1999), 244 AR 93 (CA)

FRUMAN JA (orally): Fracmaster Ltd., an oil and gas services company with world-wide operations, encountered serious financial difficulties. With liabilities that greatly exceeded its assets, its inevitable insolvency gave rise to hurried attempts to restructure the company. A series of court proceedings and a court-authorized tender process, all conducted at break neck speed, resulted in a court order approving the sale of Fracmaster's assets to BJ Services Company for $80 million. That order, and the events which led up to it, are the subject of four appeals by prospective purchasers whose bids for Fracmaster were unsuccessful. ...

Fracmaster is an Alberta company. Beginning in the fall of 1998, when its financial condition was precarious, it unsuccessfully attempted to restructure its financial affairs. With the indulgence of a lending syndicate to whom Fracmaster owed $96 million, and whose debt was registered as a first charge on its assets, it subsequently filed a petition under the CCAA. On March 18, 1999, Fracmaster was granted an order imposing a stay of proceedings and appointing Arthur Andersen Inc. as the monitor. Fracmaster then conducted another sale process, in order to restructure the company, inject equity or sell its assets. The sale process was neither supervised nor controlled by the monitor. Several companies submitted offers or proposals, including UTI Energy Corp., Calfrac Limited and The Janus Corporation together with its principal, Alfred H. Balm.

When the matter returned to court in May of 1999 four applications were heard:

First, Fracmaster applied for approval of the sale of its assets to UTI. The members of the lending syndicate supported that application, in accordance with a contractual commitment they had made to UTI.

Second, that same lending syndicate, as an alternative to Fracmaster's application, applied to lift the stay, appoint Arthur Andersen as receiver, direct the receiver to approve the UTI sale and permit the lending syndicate to begin to realize on its security. ...

In reasons dated May 17, 1999, the chambers judge dismissed the Fracmaster, Balm/Janus and Calfrac applications. She appointed Arthur Andersen as the receiver/manager on certain terms and conditions, including the power to sell the assets of Fracmaster subject to court approval. She denied the lending syndicate's application to direct the receiver to sell the assets to UTI. Alive to concerns about delay, she asked the receiver to quickly report its recommendations about a sale of assets or other immediate action that the receiver considered appropriate for the benefit of all claimants, including the secured creditors (CCAA AB 333). The May 17 order in the CCAA proceedings is the subject of appeals by Balm/Janus and UTI.

The next day, May 18, the receiver returned to court with a notice of motion seeking directions for approval of a sale process by way of sealed bids. The process was designed to respond to the principles and objectives established by the chambers judge for a sale of assets. As there had been no independent valuations, the proposed tender process would test the market to determine whether offers were available in excess of the amount of the lending syndicate's secured debt. The process was also designed to maximize the value to the creditors; respond to concerns about delay and the need for finality; provide a process for the benefit of all creditors; and be fundamentally fair by establishing a level playing field for all participants. ...

Offers were submitted by UTI, Calfrac and BJ Services, a company which had previously shown interest in acquiring Fracmaster, but had not participated in the CCAA company-conducted sale process. Balm/Janus did not submit an offer. The lending syndicate continued to support the UTI offer, in accordance with a contractual commitment its members had made to UTI. The receiver recommended acceptance of the BJ Services offer, for a number of reasons, including the fact that it provided the highest cash purchase price, exceeding the Calfrac offer by $13 million and the UTI offer by $19.3 million. The chambers judge, in reasons dated May 21, 1999, approved the BJ Services offer recommended by the receiver. UTI and Calfrac appeal that decision. ...

UTI also appeals the May 17, 1999 order denying Fracmaster's application to approve the sale of its assets to UTI under the CCAA. The chambers judge noted that the proposed sale of assets to UTI did not create any monetary return for the unsecured creditors or shareholders of Fracmaster, nor did it contemplate that they would receive any benefit. The transaction was effectively a sale of assets for the benefit of the lending syndicate, a transaction which she concluded could be accomplished in a manner that did not require the use of the CCAA (CCAA AB 331-332). Without deciding whether the UTI offer was commercially provident, she concluded that the sale should not be approved under the CCAA, and dismissed Fracmaster's application.

Although there are infrequent situations in which a liquidation of a company's assets has been concluded under the CCAA, the proposed transaction must be in the best interest of the creditors generally: *Re Lehndorff General Partner Ltd.* (1993), 17 CBR (3d) 24 at 31 (Ont. Gen. Div.). There must be an ongoing business entity that will survive the asset sale. See, for example, *Re Canadian Red Cross Society*, [1998] OJ No. 3306 (Ont. Gen. Div.), online: QL (OJ); *Re Solv-Ex Corporation and Solv-Ex Canada Limited* (19 November, 1997), (Calgary), 9701-10022 (Alta. QB). A sale of all or substantially all the assets of a company to an entirely different entity, with no continued involvement by former creditors and shareholders, does not meet this requirement. While we do not intend to limit the flexibility of the CCAA, we are concerned about its use to liquidate assets of insolvent companies which are not part of a plan or compromise among creditors and shareholders, resulting in some continuation of a company as a going concern. Generally, such liquidations are inconsistent with the intent of the CCAA and should not be carried out under its protective umbrella. The chambers judge did not err in concluding ' that the sale of assets to UTI would be an inappropriate use of the CCAA. We grant leave to appeal to UTI, but dismiss its appeal.

Appeal dismissed

NOTES AND QUESTIONS

1. Which case, *1078385* or *Fracmaster*, is more consistent with the objectives of the CCAA? Should all liquidation proceedings take place under the BIA? Does the BIA offer any procedural safeguards that may not be found under a CCAA sale of assets? Are there any significant disadvantages in converting the CCAA proceeding to a proceeding under the BIA to enable a trustee in bankruptcy to take charge of the sale process? See *Caterpillar Financial Services Ltd. v. Hard-Rock Paving Co.* (2008), 45 CBR (5th) 87 (Ont. SCJ).

2. In *Re 843504 Alberta Ltd.* (2003), 4 CBR (5th) 306 (Alta. QB), the court contrasted the Alberta and Ontario positions on the liquidation issue:

[T]he courts in Alberta generally expect the corporate entity to continue in some form or another and do not allow for a liquidation proposal unless exceptional circumstances exist to justify it, notwithstanding that the CCAA seems to allow it (*Royal Bank of Canada v. Fracmaster Ltd.* …) Simply put, in this province the corporate entity is expected to continue in some form or another unless there are exceptional circumstances. Liquidation proceedings are typically reserved for receiverships, windings up or bankruptcy. This is quite different than in Ontario where apparently debtors can use the benefits of the legislation when there is no prospect of corporate survival or no plan of arrangement is proposed.

Several Ontario cases accept liquidation as a possible outcome in CCAA proceedings. See, for example, *Re Lehndorff General Partner Ltd.* (1993), 17 CBR (3d) 24, at 32 (Ont. Gen. Div.); *Re Anvil Range Mining Corp.* (2001), 25 CBR (4th) 1, at para. 11 (Ont. SCJ), aff'd. (2002), 34 CBR (4th) 157, at para. 32; *Re Olympia & York Developments* (1995), 34 CBR (3d) 93 (Ont. Gen. Div.), at 104; *TRG Service Inc.* (2006), 26 CBR (5th) 203, at para. 68 (Ont. SCJ).

3. In an annotation to the *1078385* case, two authors reached the following conclusion:

> The CCAA has traditionally been used as a vehicle through which insolvent companies could compromise the claims of creditors and enter into a restructuring arrangement that would allow them to continue in business as a going concern. Over the years, the concept of a liquidating plan developed when it became obvious that no restructuring was possible and efforts were generally made to accommodate unsecured and secured creditors. This recent recognition of the CCAA as an enforcement tool for secured creditors is a significant departure from its traditional purpose.

(Carole J. Hunter and Antonio Di Domenico, "The Evolving Role of the Companies' Creditors Arrangement Act: A Shortcut for Secured Creditors" (2004), 16 CBR 5th 152.)

4. What implications does *1078385* have for the role of secured creditors in a CCAA proceeding? The BC Court of Appeal, in *Caterpillar Financial Services Ltd. v. 360networks corp.* (2007), 279 DLR (4th) 701 stated (at para. 46):

> The Ontario Court of Appeal's decision in *Re 1078385 Ontario Ltd.* (2004), 206 OAC 17, 16 CBR (5th) 152 [*Bob-Lo Island*] suggests that secured creditors may assume a leadership role in a restructuring process that has traditionally been directed by debtor companies to the company's general benefit. Further, the decision appears to create an opportunity for secured creditors to use the CCAA as an efficacious shortcut to enforce their security. Ultimately, *Bob-Lo Island* represents the evolution of the role of secured creditors under the CCAA, and the use of the statute as a flexible and advantageous restructuring tool for secured creditors.

5. In *Cliffs Over Maple Bay Investments Ltd. v. Fisgard Capital Corp.* (2008), 296 DLR (4th) 577, the British Columbia Court of Appeal held that CCAA liquidation proceedings are inappropriate if there is no actual or proposed plan of arrangement to be voted on by the creditors: see Chapter 12, Section II, note following the *Lehndorff* extract. How does this position differ from the one articulated by the Alberta Court of Appeal in *Fracmaster*? Is it inconsistent with the position the Ontario courts have taken? See also *Humber Valley Resort Corp.—Re Companies Creditors' Arrangement Act* (2008), 48 CBR (5th) 128 (NLSC), where the court granted an extension application despite the absence of any plan, on the ground that otherwise the debtor's development project was likely to fail. Is this decision reconcilable with *Cliffs Over*?

6. The 2007 amendments enact a new CCAA s. 36 providing for a regime governing the disposition of business assets. The main features of the provision follow:

- a debtor company may not sell or otherwise dispose of assets outside the ordinary course of business unless authorized to do so by a court;

- despite any requirement for shareholder approval, the court may authorize the sale or disposition, even if shareholder approval was not obtained;

- a company applying for authorization to sell or otherwise dispose of assets must give notice of the application to secured creditors who are likely to be affected by the sale or disposition;

- when deciding whether to grant authorization to the debtor company to sell or dispose of assets, the court must consider, among other things, six listed factors in s. 36(3);

- if the proposed sale or disposition is to a person who is related to the company (defined in s. 36(5)), the court may, after considering the factors in s. 36(3), grant the authorization only if it is satisfied that

  — good-faith efforts were made to sell or otherwise dispose of the assets to persons who are not related to the company, and

  — the consideration to be received is superior to the consideration that would be received under any other offer made in accordance with the process leading to the proposed sale or disposition; and

- the court may grant an authorization only if it is satisfied that the company can and will make payments to employees that it would be required to make if the court had sanctioned a plan or arrangement.

7. Does the new s. 36 resolve the questions raised by *1078385* and *Fracmaster*? May a court approve a sale of all the debtor company's assets under s. 36?

8. What policy rationale underlies Parliament's decision to enable the court to authorize the sale or disposition even where shareholder approval was not obtained? What economic interest does a shareholder have in a CCAA asset sale process? See, for example, *Re Loewen Group Inc.* (2001), 32 CBR (4th) 54 (Ont. SCJ), discussed in Chapter 15.

CHAPTER FOURTEEN

Claims

I. INTRODUCTION

Section 2(1) of the CCAA defines a "claim" as any indebtedness, liability, or obligation that would be a debt provable in a bankruptcy under the BIA. Section 19(1) of the CCAA provides that the only claims that may be dealt with by a compromise or arrangement are (1) claims that relate to debts or liabilities, present or future, to which the company is subject on the day that restructuring proceedings are commenced; and (2) claims that relate to debts or liabilities, present or future, to which the company may become subject before the compromise or arrangement is sanctioned by reason of any obligation incurred by the company before restructuring proceedings are commenced. This language confirms that liabilities arising from the disclaimer of executory contracts that had been entered into before the commencement of restructuring proceedings are properly dealt with in a plan of compromise or arrangement

Section 19(1) of the CCAA thus differentiates between pre-filing obligations and post-filing obligations. Pre-filing obligations (those that relate to debts or liabilities that were incurred before the commencement of the insolvency proceedings or that arise out of the disclaimer of contracts that had been entered into before the commencement of restructuring proceedings) may be compromised or otherwise affected by a plan of compromise or arrangement. Claims that arise after this date are not affected by the plan. This does not mean that post-filing creditors are free of risk of loss. If the restructuring does not succeed and the debtor goes into bankruptcy, post-filing creditors will be adversely affected. For this reason, a company that is in restructuring proceedings often must take steps to ensure that the post-filing creditors either are paid in cash or that a post-filing trade creditors charge is created in order to induce them to extend credit to a financially distressed firm.

Unlike the BIA, the CCAA does not provide a statutory procedure for the proof and valuation of claims held by creditors. Instead, the claims process is established by a claims procedure order. The claims procedure order sets out the manner by which creditors are notified of the process and establishes the procedure that the creditors must employ to prove their claims. In some CCAA proceedings, a reverse claims procedure is used. The notice discloses the amounts owing to the various creditors based on the debtor's records, and the creditors are required to act only if they disagree with the amount disclosed in the notice.

The claims procedure order may provide that the monitor will determine the validity and amount of the claims. Alternatively, the order may provide for the appointment of a claims officer who is responsible for the validation and assessment of claims. The claims procedure order will also provide a claims bar date. Section 12 of the CCAA provides that the court may fix deadlines for the purposes of voting and for the purposes of distributions under a plan. Proofs of claims must be filed before the expiration of the claims bar date.

II. DISPUTED AND LATE CLAIMS

Pine Valley Mining Corp.
(2008), 41 CBR (5th) 43 (BCSC)

GARSON J: This is an application for directions respecting the process for the determination of the amount of Pine Valley Mining Corporation's ("PVM") claim against Falls Mountain Coal Inc. ("FMC") within a proceeding under the *Companies' Creditors Arrangement Act*, RSC 1985 c. C-36, as amended, (the "CCAA Proceeding"), in which both PVM and FMC are related parties and petitioners.

FMC is a wholly-owned subsidiary of PVM. PVM claims that FMC owes PVM $37,692,218. The other major creditors of FMC dispute that amount largely on the basis that the advances made to FMC are properly characterized as capital investment in FMC, not debt, and therefore PVM should rank behind the other unsecured creditors in the distribution of FMC assets. The Monitor appointed by this Court in the CCAA Proceeding has reviewed the accounts of PVM and FMC and determined that $27,070,166 is properly owed to PVM by FMC as debt. ...

A ten-day trial has been reserved for May of this year. The parties have reached an impasse on the two issues mentioned above. Mr. Sandrelli, counsel for PVM, says that "deference is owed to the Monitor's ... conclusions ... in [his] Fourth Report, such that the onus to challenge the Monitor's findings lies on the party appealing the Monitor's findings; and if deference is owed to the Monitor's findings, what standard of review applies to those findings."

I understood Mr. Sandrelli to use the term "appeal" in a loose sense. He acknowledged that this is not an appeal because Tercon did not participate in the original decision making process of the Monitor. He said in submissions that the process is more akin to a review on a correctness standard of review. He concluded his submissions by contending that Tercon should bear the onus of displacing the finding of the Monitor that PVM is owed $27 Million by FMC, and that PVM bears the onus of displacing the Monitor's finding that PVM is not entitled to the additional approximate $11 million it claims.

Mr. McLean, counsel for Tercon, contends that "the burden of proof lies upon the party who substantially asserts the affirmative of the issue": *Phipson on Evidence*, 14th ed. He says that PVM seeks to prove that it is a creditor of FMC and it must carry the burden of proof of that whole claim.

Mr. Sandrelli argues that in the special context of a CCAA proceeding the Monitor, who is appointed by the court, should be accorded deference and that the review of his decision is akin to a review of a CCAA claims officer's decision in a CCAA proceeding. He relies for this proposition on dicta in *Olympia & York Developments Ltd. v. Royal Trust Co.* (1993), 17 CBR (3d) 1 (Ont. Gen. Div.); *Air Canada, Re* (2004), 2 CBR (5th) 23 (Ont. SCJ [Commercial List]); *Canadian Airlines Corp., Re*, 2001 ABQB 146 (Alta. QB); *Matte v. Roux*, 2007 BCSC 902 (BCSC); *Triton Tubular Components Corp., Re*, [2005] OJ

No. 3926 (Ont. SCJ); and *Muscletech Research & Development Inc., Re* (2006), 25 CBR (5th) 231 (Ont. SCJ).

In *Olympia & York*, the decision under review was that made by a claims officer. The claims officer is akin to a judicial officer. The proceeding before him is an adversarial one and naturally he should be granted some deference. That decision is distinguishable on the grounds that the court appointed Monitor in this proceeding, while undoubtedly an impartial agent of the court, reviews the claim but is in no way engaged to conduct a hearing or any type of adversarial or quasi-judicial type proceeding. Similarly, *Air Canada* involved an appeal from a decision of a claims officer appointed in the CCAA proceeding in which the claims officer had dismissed a contingent claim. The appeal was dismissed. The *Air Canada* case is distinguishable for the same reasons as the *Olympia & York* case. In *Canadian Airlines*, the decision under review was also that of a claims officer appointed to determine disputed claims within a CCAA proceeding. Paperny J, as she then was, held that the review was a trial *de novo*, but that was because the law in Alberta differed from Ontario. The *Matte* case involved the standard of review of a master's decision and, for the same reasons, I find it unhelpful and distinguishable. *Triton* also involved the review of a claims officer's decision. The court determined that the standard of review was correctness but, for the same reasons as above, the case is distinguishable. The *Muscletech* case is similarly distinguishable.

In none of the cases cited above was the decision under review one of a monitor, not engaged in an adversarial process.

Paragraph 17 of the Claims Procedure Order pronounced December 8, 2006, provides:

> Where a Creditor delivers a Dispute Notice in accordance with the terms of this Order, such dispute shall be resolved as directed by this Court or as the Creditor in question, the Petitioners and Monitor may agree.

Section 12(2) of the CCAA provides in part as follows:

> For the purposes of this Act, the amount represented by a claim of any secured or unsecured creditor shall be determined as follows:
>
> > (a) the amount of the unsecured claim shall be the amount
> >
> > > (iii) in the case of any other company, proof of which might be made under the *Bankruptcy and Insolvency Act*, but if the amount so provable is not admitted by the company, the amount shall be determined by the court on summary application by the company or by the creditor;

I conclude from the CCAA and the Claims Procedure Order that the function of the Monitor, that is relevant to this application, is to determine the validity and amount of a claim on the basis of the evidence submitted. The Monitor's process in doing so is in no way akin to an adversarial process. Although his findings and opinion should be respectfully considered, he is not entitled to deference in the sense that would alter the burden of proof ordinarily imposed on the claimant. Counsel have not called my attention to any authority for either of the following propositions, either that the CCAA claim process alters substantive law that would otherwise apply to the determination of such a claim, or that a monitor appointed on the terms here is entitled to the deference accorded a quasi-judicial officer like a court appointed claims officer. It follows that PVM has the burden of proving its claim. PVM shall file a statement of claim. Tercon, with standing to defend on behalf of FMC, shall file a statement of defence. ...

Order accordingly.

Re Blue Range Resource Corp.
(2000), 193 DLR (4th) 314 (Alta. CA)

WITTMANN JA:

Introduction

The *Companies' Creditors Arrangement Act*, RSA 1985, c. C-36, as amended ("CCAA"), permits the compromise and resolution of claims of creditors against an insolvent corporation. In this appeal, as part of the ongoing resolution of the insolvency of Blue Range Resources Corporation ("Blue Range"), this Court has been asked to state the applicable criteria in considering whether to allow late claimants to file claims after a stipulated date in an order ("claims bar order").

In his decision below, the chambers judge determined that in the circumstances of this case it was appropriate to allow the respondents ("late claimants") to file their claims thus entitling them to participate in the CCAA distribution.

Facts

Blue Range sought and received court protection from its creditors under the CCAA on March 2, 1999. The claims procedure established by PriceWaterhouse Coopers Inc. ("the Monitor"), and approved by the court in a claims bar order, fixed a date of May 7, 1999 at 5:00 p.m. by which all claims were to be filed. Due to difficulties in obtaining the appropriate records, the date was extended in a second order to June 15, 1999 at 5:00 p.m., for the joint venture partners. The relevant orders stated that claims not proven in accordance with the set procedures "shall be deemed forever barred" (ABP01, ABP06). Under this procedure $270,000,000 in claims were filed.

The respondent creditors in this appeal fall into two categories: first, those who did not file their Notices of Claim before the relevant dates in the claims bar orders, and second, those who filed their initial claims in time but sought to amend their claims after the relevant dates. All of these creditors applied to the chambers judge for relief from the restriction of the date in the claims bar orders and to have their late or amended claims accepted for consideration by the Monitor.

The chambers judge allowed the late and amended claims to be filed. The appellants, Enron Capital Corp. ("Enron") and the Creditor's Committee, seek to have that decision overturned. I granted leave to appeal on January 14, 2000 on the following question:

> What criteria in the circumstances of these cases should the Court use to exercise its discretion in deciding whether to allow late claimants to file claims which, if proven, may be rec-

ognized, notwithstanding a previous claims bar order containing a claims bar date which would otherwise bar the claim of the late claimants, and applying the criteria to each case, what is the result? (AB928). ...

The Appropriate Criteria

The appellants advocated the adoption of the criteria under the US *Bankruptcy Rules*, Chapter 11, while the respondents favoured either the application of the tests under the BIA or some blending of the two standards.

Rule 9006 of the US *Bankruptcy Rules* deals with the extension of time in these circumstances. The relevant portion of the Rule states:

> 9006(b)(1) ... [W]hen an act is required or allowed to be done at or within a specified period by these rules or by a notice given thereunder or by order of court, the court for cause shown may at any time in its discretion (1) with or without motion or notice order the period enlarged if the request is made before the expiration of the period originally prescribed or as extended by a previous order or (2) on motion made after the expiration of the specified period permit the act to be done where the failure to act was the result of excusable neglect.

The key phrase in this section is "excusable neglect." In *Pioneer Investment Services Co. v. Brunswick Associates Ltd. Partnership*, 507 US 380, 113 S. Ct. 1489 (US Tenn. 1993) the US Supreme Court dealt with the interpretation of this phrase. In *Pioneer*, the creditor's attorney, due to disruptions in his legal practice and confusion over the form of notice, failed to file a Notice of Claim in time. The US Supreme Court noted that excusable neglect may extend to "inadvertent delays" (at pg 391) and went on to identify the relevant considerations when determining whether or not a delay is excusable. The Court said at 395:

> Because Congress has provided no other guideposts for determining what sorts of neglect will be considered "excusable," we conclude that the determination is at bottom an equitable one, taking account of all relevant circumstances surrounding the party's omission. These include, as the Court of Appeals found, the danger of prejudice to the debtor, the length of the delay and its potential impact on judicial proceedings, the reason for the delay, including whether it was within the reasonable control of the movant, and whether the movant acted in good faith.

The American authorities also seem to reflect that the burden of meeting all of these elements, including showing the absence of prejudice, lies with the party seeking to file the late claim: e.g. *Specialty Equipment Cos. Inc., Re*, 159 BR 236 (US Bankr. ND Ill. 1993).

The Canadian approach under the BIA has been somewhat different. Canadian courts have been willing to allow the filing of late or amended claims under the BIA when the claims are delayed due to inadvertence, (which would include negligence or neglect), or incomplete information being available to the creditors, see: *Mount James Mines (Que.) Ltd., Re* (1980), 110 DLR (3d) 80 (Ont. Bktcy.). The Canadian standard under the BIA is, therefore, less arduous than that applied under the US *Bankruptcy Rules*.

I accept that some guidance can be gained from the BIA approach to these types of cases but I find that some concerns remain. An inadvertence standard by itself might imply that there need be almost no explanation whatever for the failure to file a claim in time. In my view inadvertence could be an appropriate element of the standard if parties are able to show, in addition, that they acted in good faith and were not simply trying to delay or avoid participation in CCAA proceedings. But I also take some guidance from the US *Bankruptcy Rules* standard because I agree that the length of delay and the potential prejudice to other parties must be considered. To this extent, I accept a blended approach, taking into consideration both the BIA and US *Bankruptcy Rules* approaches, bolstered by the application of some of the concepts included in other areas, such as late reporting in insurance claims, and delay in the prosecution of a civil action. ...

Therefore, the appropriate criteria to apply to the late claimants is as follows:

1. Was the delay caused by inadvertence and if so, did the claimant act in good faith?

2. What is the effect of permitting the claim in terms of the existence and impact of any relevant prejudice caused by the delay?

3. If relevant prejudice is found can it be alleviated by attaching appropriate conditions to an order permitting late filing?

4. If relevant prejudice is found which cannot be alleviated, are there any other considerations which may nonetheless warrant an order permitting late filing?

In the context of the criteria, "inadvertent" includes carelessness, negligence, accident, and is unintentional. I will deal with the conduct of each of the respondents in turn below and then turn to a discussion of potential prejudice suffered by the appellants. ...

Prejudice

The timing of these proceedings is a key element in determining whether any prejudice will be suffered by either the debtor corporation or other creditors if the late and late amended claims are allowed. The total of all late and amended claims of the late claimants, secured and unsecured, is approximately $1,175,000. As set out above, in the initial claims bar order, the relevant date was 5:00 p.m. May 7, 1999. This date was extended for joint venture partners to 5:00 p.m. on June 15, 1999. The Plan of Arrangement, sponsored by Canadian Natural Resources Ltd. ("CNRL"), was voted on and passed on July 23, 1999. Status as a creditor, the classification as secured or unsecured, and the amount of a creditor's claim, are relevant to voting: s. 6 CCAA.

Enron and the Creditor's Committee claim that they would be prejudiced if the late claims were allowed because, had they known late claims might be permitted without rigorous criteria for allowance, they might have voted differently on the Plan of Arrangement. Enron in particular submits that it would have voted against the CNRL Plan of Arrangement, thus effectively vetoing the plan, if it had known that late claims would be allowed. This bald assertion after the fact was not sufficient to compel the chambers judge to find this would in fact have been Enron's response. Nowhere else in the evidence is there any indication that late claimants being allowed would have impacted the voting on the different proposed Plans of Arrangement. In addition, materiality is relevant to the issue of prejudice. The relationship of $1,175,000 (which is the total of late claims) to $270,000,000 (which is the total of claims filed within time) is .435 per cent.

Also, the contrary is indicated in the Third Interim Report of the Monitor where it is shown in Schedule D-1 (AB269) that $2 million was held as an estimate of unsecured disputed claims. Therefore, when considering which Plan of Arrangement to vote for, Enron, and all of the creditors, would have been aware that $2 million could still be legitimately allowed as unsecured claims, and would have been able to assess that potential effect on the amount available for distribution.

Further, the late claimants were well known to the Monitor and all of the other creditors. The evidence discloses that officials at Enron received an e-mail from the Monitor on May 18, 1999 indicating that there were several creditors who had filed late, after the first deadline of May 7, and the Monitor thought that even though they were late the court would likely allow them (AB1040). Finally, all of the late claimants were on the distribution list as having potential claims. (AB9-148). It cannot be said that these late claimants were lying in the weeds waiting to pounce. On the contrary, all parties were fully aware of who had potential claims, especially Enron and the Creditors Committee.

In a CCAA context, as in a BIA context, the fact that Enron and the other Creditors will receive less money if late and late amended claims are allowed is not prejudice relevant to this criterion. Re-organization under the CCAA involves compromise. Allowing all legitimate creditors to share in the available proceeds is an integral part of the process. A reduction in that share can not be characterized as prejudice: *Cohen, Re* (1956), 36 CBR 21 (Alta. CA) at 30-31. Further, I am in agreement with the test for prejudice used by the British Columbia Court of Appeal in *312630 British Columbia Ltd*. It is: did the creditor(s) by reason of the late filings lose a realistic opportunity to do anything that they otherwise might have done? Enron and the other creditors were fully informed about the potential for late claims being permitted, and were specifically aware of the existence of the late claimants as creditors. I find, therefore, that Enron and the Creditors will not suffer any relevant prejudice should the late claims be permitted. …

Conclusion

Applying the criteria established, I find that the conclusion reached by the chambers judge ought not to be disturbed, and the late claims filed by the respondents should be permitted under the CCAA proceedings. The appeal is dismissed.

Appeal dismissed.

NOTES

1. The claims procedure order in *Re Blue Range Resource Corp.* provided that claims that were not proven in accordance with the claims procedure "shall be deemed forever barred and may not thereafter be advanced as against Blue Range in Canada or elsewhere." The Alberta Court of Appeal also indicated that a claims bar order should not purport to "forever

bar" a claim without including a saving provision that makes it clear that a claimant may bring a claim after the claims bar date with leave of the court.

2. The failure to notify a known creditor of the CCAA proceedings as required by the claims procedure order will generally mean that the creditor is not bound by the plan of arrangement. See *Ivorylane Corp. v. Country Style Realty Ltd.*, 2004 CarswellOnt 2567 (SCJ). Even if a creditor has not been properly notified, the creditor may nevertheless be bound if the creditor knows of the CCAA proceedings but chooses not to participate in the hopes of obtaining the full value of its claim following the restructuring. See *Lindsay v. Transtec Canada Ltd.* (1994), 28 CBR (3d) 110 (BCSC).

3. Can a supervising court permit a plaintiff to file a proof of claim as a representative claim in an uncertified class proceeding? The court in *Re Muscletech Research & Development Inc.* (2006), 25 CBR (5th) 218 (Ont. SCJ), at para. 36, stated that "Canadian courts have not yet permitted a filing of a proof of claim by a plaintiff in an uncertified class proceeding on behalf of itself and other members of the class." Although it was of the opinion that it was not an appropriate case for a representative claim, it left open the possibility of representative claims in future CCAA cases.

III. PRIORITIES

The BIA establishes a statutory scheme of distribution for bankruptcy proceedings (see Chapter 9), but there are no corresponding provisions in the CCAA. Instead, the plan of compromise or arrangement determines the amounts that will be recovered by the various classes of claimants. This does not mean that priorities are irrelevant in a restructuring. The bargaining over the terms of the agreement occurs in the shadow of the law. A claim that is entitled to priority will usually be afforded more favourable treatment in the plan. A plan of arrangement will typically divide the creditor into a number of different classes—for example, the plan may create a class of unsecured creditors and a class of secured creditors. The class of secured creditors will not be inclined to vote in favour of the plan if their priority status is not recognized. Furthermore, a court will usually be unwilling to approve the plan if it gives a creditor less than what it would receive on a bankruptcy liquidation.

When determining priorities, one begins with the priority status of the claim under non-insolvency law principles. For example, the priority status of a consensual security interest in personal property is determined by provincial personal property security legislation. The priority of other kinds of proprietary claims may be governed by legislation. In the absence of any legislative priority rule, the priority status of the claim will be determined by the priority principles of property law. The CCAA contains a number of priority provisions that provide for an express priority rule for certain types of claims. In these instances, the non-insolvency priority rules are displaced and the express priority rule set out in the CCAA will govern.

A. Secured Creditors

Section 2(1) of the CCAA defines a "secured creditor." Like the definition of a secured creditor in the BIA, it covers security interests in real and personal property that arise consensually or by operation of law. Personal property security legislation does not subordinate an unperfected security interest on the commencement of restructuring proceedings. See *Re TRG Services Inc.* (2006), 26 CBR (5th) 203 (Ont. SCJ); *Re PSINet* (2002), 30 CBR (4th) 226 (Ont. SCJ). And see Anthony Duggan, "The Status of Unperfected Security Interests in Insolvency Proceedings" (2008), 24 *BFLR* 103. However, secured parties encounter difficulties when attempting to register a financing statement after restructuring proceedings are commenced, because the stay of proceedings may prevent creditors from taking such action. Although registration is not needed in order to give the security interest priority over the unsecured creditors who have not taken the appropriate steps to enforce their judgments, a secured creditor may wish to ensure that it is properly perfected if the restructuring is unsuccessful and the debtor goes into bankruptcy and also to preserve its priority against other parties who acquire an interest in the debtor's assets. If the stay of proceedings prevents registration, a secured creditor can apply to court to have the stay lifted in order to permit registration. In many instances, the drafting of the stay provision permits post-filing registration of security interests. If this is the case, a court application is not needed.

B. Unsecured Creditors

Unsecured creditors have no proprietary right in the debtor's assets, and therefore have no basis to claim priority over other claimants. The situation becomes more complicated if the unsecured creditor has obtained judgment and has registered or filed a writ or judgment against land. Many provinces also provide for registration of writs or judgments in the personal property security registry. If registration or filing has been effected, the unsecured creditor obtains priority over subsequently created interests in the asset. Registration under the PPSA also gives the writ or judgment priority over prior unperfected security interests. Unlike the case in bankruptcy proceedings, the commencement of restructuring proceedings does not extinguish the writ or judgment. Therefore, the priority of such interests over other subordinated claims to the same asset must be recognized in the restructuring proceedings.

C. Subordinated Claims

A creditor may subordinate or postpone its claim to others. The courts will generally give effect to a contractual subordination. However, this does not necessarily mean that all creditors will be able to take advantage of the subordination. See the discussion in Chapter 9, Section VII. As is the case in bankruptcy proceedings, the subordination provision is given effect by requiring the subordinated creditor to turn over any dividends or other amounts received in the insolvency proceedings to the benefiting creditors.

D. Crown Claims

Sections 38 and 39 of the CCAA are similar in operation to ss. 86 and 87 of the BIA. A Crown claim is only afforded the status of an unsecured claim unless (1) it is of a kind that is ordinarily available to other creditors; (2) the Crown claim is registered before the commencement of CCAA proceedings; or (3) the Crown claim is covered by the statutory garnishment device that is used to recover source deductions of income tax, Canada Pension Plan, and employment insurance. See the discussion of Crown claims in Chapter 8, Section III.

E. Deemed Trusts

Section 37 of the CCAA is similar to ss. 67(2) and (3) of the BIA. A statutory deemed trust in favour of the Crown is not effective unless it would have been effective in creating a trust in the absence of the statutory provision. An exception is made for the statutory deemed trust that secures unpaid source deductions of income tax, employment insurance, and Canada Pension Plan contributions. See the discussion of Deemed Trusts in Chapter 8, Section III.

Section 37 only covers deemed trusts in favour of the Crown. Legislation that creates statutory deemed trusts in favour of persons other than the Crown are not affected by this provision. However, if the restructuring is in the form of a liquidation plan in which the business is sold as a going concern to a third party, a supervising court may make an order that permits the company to be placed into bankruptcy. When this occurs, the bankruptcy scheme of distribution will determine the priorities of the various claims. Although a statutory deemed trust in favour of a person other than the Crown is fully effective under the CCAA, in bankruptcy it is rendered ineffective unless it would have been recognized as creating a trust in the absence of the statutory provision. See *British Columbia v. Henfrey Samson Belair Ltd.*, [1989] 2 SCR 24. The bankruptcy therefore has the effect of destroying the statutory deemed trust. The Ontario Court of Appeal in *Re Ivaco Inc.*, below, discusses the circumstances in which a court should make an order that permits bankruptcy proceedings to ensue following a liquidating plan.

Section 222 of the *Excise Tax Act*, RSC 1985, c. E-15, creates a statutory deemed trust in respect of GST that has been collected. The provision indicates that the deemed trust is effective despite any other legislation, other than the BIA. Section 67(2) of the BIA and s. 37 of the CCAA provide that a statutory deemed trust in favour of the Crown is ineffective in restructuring proceedings. Courts have given pre-eminence to the provision of the *Excise Tax Act*. See *Re Ottawa Senators Hockey Club Corp.* (2005), 6 CBR (5th) 293 (Ont. CA); *Re Gauntlet Energy Corp.* (2003), 49 CBR (4th) 213 (Alta. QB). As a result, the statutory deemed trust is effective in a restructuring under the CCAA, but it is not effective in a restructuring under the commercial proposal provisions of the BIA.

F. Thirty-Day Goods

Unlike the case in either bankruptcy or receivership proceedings, in CCAA proceedings, a supplier of goods is not given a special right to repossess 30-day goods—that is, goods delivered within 30 days before the bankruptcy or receivership. See BIA s. 81.1 and the discussion of unpaid suppliers in Chapter 9, Section II. It was thought that the right would interfere with attempts to rescue financially distressed debtors, and should be limited to insolvency proceedings that result in the liquidation of a commercial debtor. One may question whether this rationale holds true given the subsequent widespread use of the CCAA to liquidate companies. In the case of failed restructuring proceedings, courts have ordered that the restructuring period—that is, the time between the application for the initial order and the subsequent bankruptcy or receivership—should not be counted for the purposes of calculating the 30-day period. In many cases, this is a hollow right, as the goods will have been sold or transformed during this period. The statutory security in favour of agricultural suppliers created by s. 81.2 of the BIA is also limited to bankruptcy and receivership proceedings and does not arise in respect of restructuring proceedings.

G. Environmental Claims

The CCAA adopts the same approach as the BIA to environmental claims. See the discussion of environmental claims in Chapter 9, Section V. Section 11.8(8) of the CCAA creates a charge against the land affected by the environmental condition as well as on any contiguous real property. The charge has priority over any other claim, right, charge, or security against the property. Section 11.8(3) protects the monitor from liability for pre-appointment damage, and the monitor is liable for post-appointment damages only if they occur as a result of gross negligence or wilful misconduct. Section 11.8(5) provides that a monitor may choose to comply with the remediation order or may abandon the interest in the property.

H. Wage and Pension Claims

The *Wage Earner Protection Program Act* does not cover employees who have claims for unpaid wages in CCAA proceedings. See the discussion of these claims in Chapter 9, Sections III and IV. Nor does the statutory security for unpaid wages created by ss. 81.3 and 81.4 of the BIA apply in respect of restructuring proceedings. Instead, a limitation is imposed on a court's ability to sanction a plan under the CCAA. Section 6(5) of the CCAA permits a court to sanction a plan only if the employees and former employees receive no less than the amount secured by their statutory security for unpaid wages together with all wages and salary earned after the commencement of restructuring proceedings.

A similar approach is taken in respect of unpaid pension contributions. The statutory security created by ss. 81.5 and 81.6 of the BIA do not come into operation in restructuring proceedings. Section 6(6) of the CCAA permits a court to sanction a plan only if the employee pension contributions have been paid in full, or if the parties have entered into an agreement approved by the relevant pension regulator.

I. Equity Claims

As with bankruptcy proceedings, equity claims are effectively subordinated in restructuring proceedings. See Chapter 9, Section VIII. Section 22.1 of the CCAA provides that equity claimants must be placed in their own separate class and cannot vote on the plan unless a court orders otherwise. Section 6(8) of the CCAA prevents a court from sanctioning any plan that provides any distribution to equity claimants unless all non-equity claims are paid in full. See Chapter 15, Section V.

Re Ivaco Inc.
(2006), 275 DLR (4th) 132 (Ont. CA)

J. LASKIN JA:

. . .

[1] This appeal arises out of a priorities dispute between two groups of creditors of an insolvent company, Ivaco Inc., and its related group of companies. The dispute is over the sale proceeds of the assets of Ivaco. On one side of the dispute are the employees and retirees in Ivaco's underfunded non-union pension plans. They claim under the deemed trust and lien provisions of Ontario's *Pension Benefits Act*, RSO 1990, c. P.8, ss. 57(3), (4) ("PBA"), and seek to recover unpaid contributions to the plans outside of bankruptcy. On the other side of the dispute are Ivaco's financial and trade creditors. They wish to put Ivaco into bankruptcy in order to take advantage of the scheme of distribution under the federal *Bankruptcy and Insolvency Act*, RSC 1985, c. B-3 ("BIA"). The dispute arises because provincial deemed trusts do not, by virtue of that legislative designation, enjoy priority under the federal bankruptcy statute.

[2] Ivaco and its related group of companies (collectively "the Companies") became insolvent in 2003. In September 2003, the Companies sought and obtained court-ordered protection under the *Companies' Creditors Arrangement Act*, RSC 1985, c. C-36 ("CCAA"). All claims of creditors were stayed. A later order stayed the Companies' obligation to pay the outstanding past service contributions and special payments to the non-union pension plans. (Past service contributions are monies due to fund benefits or benefit enhancements for pension members' past service; special payments are extraordinary payments made because a pension plan is underfunded).

[3] The main purpose of CCAA proceedings is to facilitate the restructuring of an insolvent company so that it may stay in business. The Companies, however, were unable to restructure. In late 2004, virtually all of their assets were sold. All that remains is a pool of money: the proceeds of sale. All that remains to be done is to distribute this pool of money among the creditors.

[4] The Superintendent of Financial Services, representing the employees and retirees, brought a motion for an order that part of the sale proceeds be used to satisfy the unpaid past service and special contributions, which the Companies are deemed to hold in trust for the beneficiaries of the pension plans under the PBA. Alternatively, the Superintendent sought an order segregating this amount in a separate account. The Quebec Pension Committee ("QPC"), the administrator of the largest non-union plan, supported the Superintendent's motion. Two of the Companies' lenders, the Bank of Nova Scotia and the National Bank, brought motions for an order lifting the stay under the CCAA and petitioning the Companies into bankruptcy.

[5] Farley J, who had supervised these CCAA proceedings for over two and a half years, heard all three motions. By order dated July 18, 2005 he dismissed the Superintendent's motion and partly granted the banks' motions. He lifted the stay and permitted the bankruptcy petitions to proceed, but he did not put the Companies into bankruptcy.

. . .

[72] The Superintendent argues that the motions judge's order was unfair to the pension beneficiaries in three related ways. First, she points out that the pension benefici-

aries agreed to a stay of the past service contributions to keep the Companies afloat, which in turn permitted the going concern sale to Heico. That sale greatly enhanced the return to the creditors. The Superintendent contends that now permitting the bankruptcy petitions to proceed, which would potentially deprive the pension beneficiaries of their rights, produces an unfair outcome.

[73] Undoubtedly, and regrettably, the pension beneficiaries stand to suffer from the insolvency of the Companies. However, the Superintendent's argument implicitly assumes that the pension beneficiaries alone made sacrifices to maximize the recovery for all creditors. The motions judge rejected this assumption, which he said at para. 2 of his reasons, "somewhat overstates the situation." The motions judge accurately concluded:

> [O]ther stakeholders (such as the financial and trade creditors) as a result of the stay also contributed to the financial stability of the Ivaco Companies, fragile as their financial situation was, by not being paid interest as such became due nor for pre-filing indebtedness which was due.

In short, all creditors gave up something to permit the Companies to stay in business so that they could either reorganize or sell their assets in a going concern sale.

[74] Second, the Superintendent contends that the motions judge's order undermined his earlier pension stay order, which had expressly preserved the pension beneficiaries' deemed trust rights. I do not accept this contention. Although the pension stay order did not take away these deemed trust rights, it did not provide that the deemed trusts would be paid out of any sale proceeds. Instead, para. 4 of the pension stay order provided that the Companies would not incur any obligation because of their failure to pay past service contributions during the stay period. Moreover, even though the Superintendent and the QPC knew that a petition for bankruptcy (by the Bank of Nova Scotia) was pending when they agreed to the pension stay order, they did not ask that the order be conditional on payment of the amount of the deemed trusts when the stay was lifted.

[75] The third aspect of unfairness on which the Superintendent relies is that the motions judge's order fails to take account of the law's "special solicitude" for pensioners. Certainly provincial pension legislation has shown this solicitude. It has recognized the importance of ensuring that retirees have income security. Thus, it has legislated statutory trusts and liens to protect their pension claims. But federal insolvency law has not shown the same solicitude. It does not accord the claims of "sympathetic" creditors more weight than the claims of "unsympathetic" ones. Subject to specified exceptions, the BIA aims to distribute a bankrupt debtor's estate equitably among all of the estate's creditors. There are undoubtedly compelling policy reasons to protect pension rights in an insolvency. But, as I have said, it is for Parliament, not the courts, to do so.

[76] Therefore, I do not accept the Superintendent's unfairness argument. Also, in my view, numerous considerations supported the motions judge's decision to lift the stay and permit the bankruptcy petitions to proceed. These considerations include the following:

- The CCAA proceedings are spent. There are no entities to reorganize and no further compromises can be negotiated between the Companies and their creditors. There remains only a pool of money to distribute. The BIA is the regime Parliament has chosen to effect this distribution.

- The petitioning creditors have met the technical requirements for bankruptcy. And their desire to use the BIA to alter priorities is a legitimate reason to seek a bankruptcy order. See for example *Bank of Montreal v. Scott Road Enterprises Ltd.* (1989), 57 DLR (4th) 623 (BCCA), at 627, 630-631; *Harrop of Milton Inc., Re* (1979), 22 OR (2d) 239 (Ont. Bktcy.), at 244-245.

- The Superintendent and the QPC agreed to the CCAA process. They recognized that it benefitted the pension claimants. Thus, they did not oppose either the pension stay order or the sale to Heico. They did not ask to have the deemed trusts satisfied or an amount to satisfy them set aside, though they knew that bankruptcy was pending. They likely recognized that if they had insisted on a segregation order, the other creditors may not have agreed to the sale. It is now too late for the Superintendent and the QPC to ask for relief that they never sought during the entire CCAA process.

- The motions judge would have gone beyond his role as a referee in the CCAA proceedings if he had given effect to the Superintendent's claim. The Superintendent wants to jump ahead of all the other creditors by obtaining an extraordinary payment at the end of a long CCAA process. If the motions judge had ordered this payment, he would have upset the ground rules that all stakeholders agreed to and that he supervised for over two years.

[77] The motions judge took into account the likely result of the Superintendent's claims if the Companies are put into bankruptcy. He recognized that bankruptcy would potentially reverse the priority accorded to the pension claims outside bankruptcy. Nonetheless, having weighed all the competing considerations, he exercised his discretion to lift the stay and permit the bankruptcy petitions to proceed. In my view, he exercised his discretion properly. I would not give effect to this ground of appeal.

NOTES AND QUESTIONS

1. *Re Ivaco* was decided before the coming into force of section 6(6) of the CCAA. Would the outcome in this case be any different if that section had been in force at the time the case was decided?

2. Some of the priority rules provided in the CCAA are substantially similar to those that apply in a bankruptcy—for example, the rules concerning both Crown and environmental claims are the same; however, in other instances, the rules are different. A landlord's right of distress is ineffective in bankruptcy, but fully effective in a restructuring. A supplier may repossess 30-day goods in bankruptcy, but not in restructuring proceedings. A deemed trust in respect of GST is ineffective in bankruptcy, but effective in restructuring proceedings under the CCAA. This produces the possibility of regime-shopping. Parties will attempt to invoke the insolvency regime that gives them the most favourable priority status. The problem is compounded because CCAA restructuring proceedings are now frequently used to liquidate the business through a going-concern sale to a third party. See T. Buckwold and R. Wood, "Priorities," in *Canadian Bankruptcy and Insolvency Law: Bill C-55, Statute c. 47 and Beyond*, S. Ben-Ishai and A. Duggan, eds. (Toronto: LexisNexis Canada, 2007),

Chapter 5. For further treatment of asset sales in CCAA proceedings, see this text, Chapter 13, Section VII.

3. The employment standards legislation in some provinces creates a statutory charge or deemed trust in favour of unpaid employees. For example, s. 109 of the Alberta *Employment Standards Code*, RSA 2000, c. E-9 provides that unpaid wages to a maximum of $7,500 per employee are secured by a statutory security interest. It is given priority over any other claim other than a purchase-money security interest. This statutory security is ineffective in bankruptcy proceedings, because it conflicts with the bankruptcy scheme of distribution that gives employees a preferred claim in respect of unpaid wages to the extent of $2,000. Because there is no similar scheme of distribution set out in the CCAA, the statutory security interest in favour of employees will be effective in restructuring proceedings. However, the statutory security interest is lost if the restructuring involves a liquidating plan and the court permits the commencement of bankruptcy proceedings following the sale.

IV. AVOIDABLE TRANSACTIONS

The BIA contains provisions that give a trustee in bankruptcy the power to impugn certain types of pre-bankruptcy transactions as preferences or transfers at undervalue. See the discussion in Chapter 5. Earlier versions of the CCAA did not provide for the integration of these provisions. Although transactions could be impugned under provincial fraudulent conveyance and fraudulent preference law, the creditors were unable to use the avoidance powers in the BIA. A transaction could be impugned under the BIA only if it occurred within a fixed period prior to the date of the initial bankruptcy event. Although the filing of a notice of intention under the commercial proposal provisions qualified as such an initial bankruptcy event, the commencement of CCAA proceedings did not. As a consequence, persons who wished to challenge a transfer made by the debtor would seek leave to lift the stay of proceedings in order to make an application for a bankruptcy order. This was done simply to preserve the right to impeach the transaction using the avoidance powers set out in the BIA.

Once the 2005-2007 reforms come into force, it will no longer be necessary to take this step to preserve a right to impeach a preference or transfer at undervalue. The definition of "date of the initial bankruptcy event" has been amended so that it now includes commencement of CCAA proceedings. Section 36.1(1) of the CCAA gives the monitor the power to avoid or otherwise impeach transfers that occur before the commencement of restructuring proceedings. Section 36.1(2) provides that a reference to the "date of bankruptcy" is to be read as the day on which proceedings commence under the CCAA. Thus, the monitor may seek to avoid a preferential transfer or payment made by the insolvent debtor company to an arm's-length party in the three-month period prior to the commencement of CCAA proceedings or to a non-arm's-length party in the one-year period prior to the commencement of CCAA proceedings. Section 36.1(1) also incorporates s. 38 of the BIA. This gives creditors the option of instituting proceedings to impugn a transfer if the monitor decides not to do so.

The plan of compromise or arrangement may contain a provision by which the creditors agree not to invoke the avoidance powers. Section 23(1)(d.1) of the CCAA places a duty on the monitor to provide an opinion of the reasonableness of the term in its report on the state of the debtor's business.

QUESTION

Can a monitor use the BIA avoidance provisions to impugn transactions entered into by the debtor after the commencement of restructuring proceedings? Unlike in a bankruptcy, in which the debtor's assets vest in the trustee, in restructuring proceedings, title to the assets remains in the debtor and the debtor retains the capacity to deal with its assets.

V. SET-OFF

The issue of set-off was examined earlier in connection with bankruptcy proceedings. See Chapter 4, Section VIII. Issues of set-off arise in restructuring proceedings as well. As the next case illustrates, it may be easier for a party to assert a right of set-off in restructuring proceedings because the commencement of the proceedings does not result in a loss of mutuality of dealings between the parties.

Re Air Canada
(2003), 45 CBR (4th) 13 (Ont. SCJ)

FARLEY J: Bell Canada, Certain Airport Authorities (the Calgary Airport Authority et al) and the Bank of Nova Scotia in its capacity as Agent for the R/T Syndicate (collectively "Moving Creditors") brought motions to vary the Initial Order obtained by Air Canada ("AC") on April 1, 2003 by striking out the last seven words of the first sentence of paragraph 9 and the whole of the second sentence of paragraph 9.

At the present time the wording of paragraph 9 is as follows:

> [9] THIS COURT ORDERS that persons may exercise only such rights of set-off as are permitted under Section 18.1 of the CCAA as of the date of this order. For greater certainty, no person may set off any obligations of an Applicant to such person which arose prior to such date.

If the relief requested by the Moving Creditors were granted, then paragraph 9 would be revised to:

> [9] THIS COURT ORDERS that persons may exercise only such rights of set-off as are permitted under Section 18.1 of the CCAA.

> • • •

AC at paragraphs 19 and 20 of its factum stated:

> [19] The right of set-off is available as a defence to a proceeding and may arise in contract, in law, or in equity; however, in the context of the CCAA, it is the Applicants' position that post-filing claims can be set off against pre-filing claims only where there is a valid claim for equitable set-off such that the relationship between the two amounts are so closely related that it would be inequitable to sever the debts from one another by a CCAA Order.

[20] The Applicants submit that paragraph 9 of the Initial Order is consistent with existing law. It is respectfully submitted that contractual and legal set-off are not available to a creditor in relation to post-filing as against pre-filing claims as the required mutuality is severed by the CCAA filing. Pre-filing claims may be set off against each other and post-filing claims may be set off against each other but post-filing and pre-filing claims may only be set off against each other pursuant to the principles of equitable set-off in the appropriate case.

AC went on at paragraphs 53-55 of its factum to conclude:

[53] The law of set-off applies to obligations owed by, and claims owed to, a debtor company operating under the protection of a CCAA proceeding. However, pursuant to the law of set-off neither the requirements for legal set-off nor the requirements for contractual set-off are satisfied when dealing with pre-filing obligations owed by, and post-filing claims owed to, a debtor company operating under the protection of the CCAA. These types of set-off require, among other things, mutuality of parties in the same right. The fundamentally changed character of the debtor company and its obligations, which accrue post-CCAA filing, severs the requisite mutuality.

[54] Pursuant to the law of set-off, equitable set-off does not require the mutuality of obligations. Equitable set-off is therefore available in appropriate cases between pre- and post-filing obligations. Other requirements, such as the existence of a close connection between the obligations, limit the application of equitable set-off. Paragraph 9 of the Initial Order is consistent with section 18.1 of the CCAA as it necessitates a court-supervised application process to deal with creditors' claims for equitable set-off which may arise during the CCAA proceeding.

[55] For all the reasons stated above, the Applicants respectfully submit that the only amounts which are potentially susceptible to set-off are as follows:

1. Pre-filing liabilities that exist between a creditor and the Applicants can be set off against each other;

2. Post-filing liabilities between a creditor and the Applicants can be set off against each other; and

3. Set-off across the April 1, 2003 date in favour of a creditor will only be permitted where the Court determines pursuant to the principles of equitable set-off that pre- and post-filing debts are so closely connected that it would be inequitable to sever the two debts.

. . .

The requirements for legal set-off were stated in *Citibank Canada v. Confederation Life Insurance Co.* (1996), 42 CBR (3d) 288 (Ont. Gen. Div.) at p. 298, affirmed (1998), 37 OR (3d) 226 (Ont. CA).

For set-off at law to occur, the following circumstances must arise:

1. The obligations existing between the two parties must be debts, and they must be debts which are for liquidated sums or money demands which can be ascertained with certainty; and,

2. Both debts must be mutual cross-obligations, i.e. cross-claims between the *same parties* and in the same right.

(emphasis added).

In a bankruptcy, the trustee is inserted into the proceedings. Post-bankruptcy dealings of a creditor with the trustee in bankruptcy do not involve the same party, namely the debtor before the condition of bankruptcy. When a bankruptcy occurs, there is a new estate created: there is the estate of the debtor under the direction and control of the debtor before the bankruptcy which is a different estate than the one post-bankruptcy where there is an estate of the bankrupt under the direction and control of the trustee in bankruptcy. Thus, creditors who incur post-bankruptcy obligations to trustees in bankruptcy cannot claim legal set-off to avoid paying such obligations by setting-off such obligations against their proven (pre-bankruptcy) claims against the bankrupt. The same parties are not involved so there cannot be mutual cross-obligations. See *S. Piscione & Sons Ltd., Re*, [1965] 1 OR 515 (Ont. SC); *Reid, Re* (1964), 7 CBR (NS) 54 (Ont. Bktcy.); *First Canadian Land Corp. (Trustee of) v. First Canadian Plaza Ltd.* (1991), 6 CBR (3d) 308 (BCSC).

In *Husky Oil Operations Ltd. v. Minister of National Revenue* (1995), 128 DLR (4th) 1 (SCC), at pp. 24-5, Gonthier J for the majority observed:

> … for a particularly thorough and helpful discussion of the issues relating to set-off in bankruptcy and insolvency, see Kelly Ross Palmer, *The Law of Set-off in Canada* (Aurora, ON: Canada Law Book, 1993), at pp. 157-223.

AC relies on what it asserts is the similarity of s. 73(1) of the *Winding-up and Restructuring Act*, RSC 1985, c. W-11 ("WURA") to s. 18.1 of the CCAA. It provides:

> 73.(1) The law of set-off, as administered by the courts, whether of law or equity, applies to all claims on the estate of a company, and to all proceedings for the recovery of debts due or accruing due to a company *at the commencement of the winding-up of the company*, in the same manner and to the same extent *as if the business of the company was not being wound up* under this Act.

(emphasis added).

. . .

Palmer explored the aspect of mutuality regarding the appointment of a liquidator under Old WUA at pp. 209-210 as follows:

(ii) Mutuality

(a) Appointment of liquidator changes mutuality
One difference between bankruptcy and winding-up proceedings which, at first, would seem to be quite important is the lack of any vesting provisions in the *Winding-up Act*. Under the *Bankruptcy and Insolvency Act*, s. 71(2), the property of the bankrupt is assigned to the trustee upon an assignment into bankruptcy. A change in mutuality will therefore result. However, an equivalent section providing for an assignment of the assets of the insolvent corporation to the liquidator is not found in the *Winding-up Act*, with the initial result that

mutuality would appear not to change upon the appointment of a liquidator. This is not the case, however, as the Canadian courts have devised several descriptions of this event which effectively result in a change of mutuality.

Different Interests. The courts have noted that the liquidator is required to serve different interests than those served by the company and, accordingly, the appointment of the liquidator results in a change in the climate which debtors and creditors of the company faced prior to winding-up. "Prior to liquidation, the directors act in the interests of the shareholders but upon liquidation the liquidator represents the interests of the creditors and the shareholders." These different interests are sufficient to allow a court to effectively deal with mutuality as though it had changed, to the point of characterizing this change as being equivalent to an assignment. ...

Quasi-trust. A second view imports the notion of the establishment of a trust. While the *Winding-up Act* does not create a trust of the company's assets, the courts have seen the liquidator as holding the assets on a "quasi-trust" for the benefit of the shareholders and creditors of the company. The imposition of the trust therefore brings about a change of mutuality. ...

Change Assumed. Some courts do not define the basis for the change in mutuality upon the liquidator's appointment, but assume that it has occurred. The mere appointment of the liquidator does not destroy mutuality, however, as s. 73 of the *Winding-up Act* will preserve set-off rights that the appointment of a liquidator would otherwise remove.

· · ·

Again, I would emphasize that these three approaches analyzed by Palmer are all within a liquidation scenario. However while a liquidation scenario under the CCAA is possible, the CCAA proceedings in this AC case are not aimed at a liquidation, but at a restructuring. While it is quite conceivable that any restructuring that may be possible in these proceedings will either eliminate the present shares held by existing shareholders or vastly dilute the existing share capital in number and value by the issuance of a large number of new shares to compromised creditors or to new equity investors, it does not seem to me that given the difference in the wording between s. 18.1 of the CCAA and s. 73(1) of the WURA, especially as to the words which I have emphasized in the WURA, that I should apply the different interests approach to these present ... proceedings. That is particularly so when one appreciates that in the normal order under WURA, a liquidator as a Court officer is appointed to take charge of the liquidation (even though there is not a vesting of assets as in BIA with a trustee in bankruptcy). Here however the Court appointed Monitor does not have any similar powers to a liquidator. AC is in a restructuring mode, not a liquidation mode under the CCAA. It seems to me that it would take more explicit language in s. 18.1 of the CCAA where one is dealing with a restructuring situation to import the concepts of a section in the WURA which by the very wording of s. 73(1) requires that the company be in a liquidation mode. The draftsperson and Parliament had the advantage of reviewing the three insolvency statues and the set-off provisions (and specific wording thereof) in the first two statutes), the *Bankruptcy and Insolvency Act*, the Old WUA and the CCAA when s. 18.1 of the CCAA was drafted and enacted. Identical wording for set-off provisions was not adopted.

I have therefore reached the conclusion that paragraph 9 of the Initial Order should be modified by striking out the complained of wording so that paragraph 9 should be read as:

> [9] THIS COURT ORDERS that persons may exercise only such rights of set-off as are permitted under Section 18.1 of the CCAA.

· · ·

Motions granted.

QUESTIONS

A debtor company owes $25,000 to creditor A. The debtor company commences restructuring proceedings under the CCAA. During the restructuring proceedings, the debtor company supplies goods to A for $15,000 on unsecured credit terms. Instead of paying for the goods, A exercises its right of set-off. A's claim is thereby reduced to $10,000. Is it fair to the other creditors that A should receive such a benefit? Are there any means by which the other creditors can prevent A from benefiting in this way? What can the debtor company do to ensure that it will be paid?

CHAPTER FIFTEEN

Approval of CCAA Plans

I. INTRODUCTION

Unlike a private workout (a compromise or arrangement between debtor and creditors concluded outside a formal insolvency restructuring regime and governed by ordinary principles of contract law), creditors may be bound by a plan developed pursuant to the CCAA even if they did not consent to it. In order for a CCAA plan to become binding on creditors, the creditors must approve it. However, it is not necessary that this consent be unanimous. Under the CCAA, a plan may be forced on a dissenting creditor if a majority of creditors in the same class approve it. If so approved, the court must also sanction the plan. This permits the court to consider the plan's fairness—an important check on the actions and conduct of the debtor company and the other creditors.

II. VOTING AND CLASSIFICATION OF CLAIMS

Sections 4 and 5 of the CCAA permit a court to order a meeting of creditors. The court will issue a meeting and approval order that sets out the rules and procedure for the meeting. Section 6 of the CCAA provides that the plan must be approved by a majority in number representing two-thirds of the value of the creditors (where there is only one class of creditors) or two-thirds of the value of each class of creditors (where there is more than one class of creditors). The percentage requirements are calculated on the basis of the creditors who actually vote on the plan, rather than on the basis of all the creditors who are affected by it. For example, where there are 70 creditors, and 50 of them vote on the plan—whether for or against—the vote must be carried by at least 26 of the creditors (a majority in number) who hold two-thirds of the value of the claims.

A creditor may be related to the debtor company—for example, a wholly or partially owned subsidiary corporation may have made an intercorporate loan to the parent corporation. Section 22(3) of the CCAA provides that a creditor who is related to the debtor company may vote against but not for the plan.

Sometimes a class of creditor is not brought within the plan. These creditors are typically referred to as unaffected creditors, because they are not being asked to agree to a compromise or other alteration of their rights against the debtor company. Unaffected creditors do not vote on the plan, because their rights are not compromised or impaired. Once the stay of proceedings is lifted, they are entitled to exercise and enjoy their full legal rights against the debtor company.

The ability to bind dissenting creditors applies only within a class of creditors. A court cannot impose a plan on a class of creditors that does not approve the plan by a dual majority. Consider the following example. A plan of compromise and arrangement creates three classes of creditors: (1) secured creditors, (2) unsecured creditors, and (3) landlords. The secured creditors and unsecured creditors approve the plan by a dual majority, but the landlords do not. The class of landlords did not vote in favour of the plan and are not bound by it. An unresolved issue is whether the plan will nevertheless be binding on the two classes who voted in favour of it, or if the underlying assumption is that all classes must vote in favour of the plan for it to bind any class of creditor. A plan may contain a "drop-out" clause that provides that a class that does not approve a plan is to be treated as unaffected creditors. Courts have given effect to such provisions. See *Olympia & York Developments Ltd. v. Royal Trust Co.* (1993), 17 CBR (3rd) 1 (Ont. Gen. Div.). If the plan is silent, a court must decide the question. If the plan is not viable without the inclusion of the non-approving class of creditors, a court will be unlikely to sanction it so as to bind the classes of creditors who approved it.

The classification of claims is of fundamental importance under the CCAA. Not surprisingly, the debtor company and the various creditors will attempt to attain a classification scheme that gives them a superior bargaining position. A creditor would ideally wish to be placed in its own separate class, because this would give it the power to veto any plan. Failing this, a creditor would wish to be placed in a class in which it could block approval of the plan by the other creditors. For example, a creditor who holds 35 percent of the value of the claims of a class of creditors can prevent approval of the plan by the class. The debtor, in developing the plan, will attempt to structure the plan in such a way as to swamp any dissenting creditors within a class of creditors who are inclined to approve it. If, in the above example, the debtor company suspects that a majority of the landlords are not supportive of the restructuring and will vote against it, the debtor company may develop a plan that includes the landlords within the class of unsecured creditors in the hope that the other unsecured creditors will be able to carry the day. See, for example, *Re San Francisco Gifts Ltd.* (2004), 5 CBR (5th) 92 (Alta. QB).

Section 22(1) of the CCAA provides that the debtor must apply to court for approval of a classification scheme for voting at a meeting. The next case examines the principles that will be applied by a court in determining whether a classification scheme is fair and reasonable.

Norcen Energy Resources Limited v. Oakwood Petroleums
(1988), 72 CBR (NS) 20 (Alta. QB)

FORSYTH J: On 12th December 1988 Oakwood Petroleums Limited ("Oakwood") filed with the court a plan of arrangement ("the plan") made pursuant to the *Companies' Creditors Arrangement Act* (Canada), RSC 1970, c. C-25 [now RSC 1985, c. C-36] ("CCAA"), as amended, ss. 185 and 185.1 [now ss. 191 and 192] of the Canada *Business Corporations Act*, SC 1974-75-76 [now RSC 1985, c. C-44] as amended, and s. 186 of the *Business Corporations Act* (Alberta), SA 1981, c. B-15, as amended.

On 16th December 1988 Oakwood brought an application before me for an order which would, *inter alia*, approve the classification of creditors and shareholders proposed in the plan. I would note that the classifications requested are made pursuant to ss. 4, 5 and 6 of the CCAA for the purpose of holding a vote within each class to approve the plan.

Since my concern primarily is with the secured creditors of Oakwood, I shall set out, in part, the sections of the CCAA relevant to the court's authority with respect to compromises with secured creditors:

> 5. Where a compromise or arrangement is proposed between a debtor company and its secured creditors or any class of them, the court may ... order a meeting of such creditors or class of creditors. ...
>
> 6. Where a majority in numbers representing three-fourths in value of the creditors, or class of creditors, as the case may be, present and voting either in person or by proxy at the meeting or meetings ... held pursuant to sections 4 and 5 ... agree to any compromise or arrangement ... [it] may be sanctioned by the court, and if so sanctioned is binding on all the creditors. ...

The plan filed with the court envisions five separate classes of creditors and shareholders. They are as follows:

(i)   The secured creditors;

(ii) The unsecured creditors;

(iii) The preferred shareholders of Oakwood;

(iv) The common shareholders and holders of class A non-voting shares of Oakwood;

(v)   The shareholders of New York Oils Ltd.

With the exception of the proposed class comprising the secured creditors of Oakwood, there has been for the moment no objection to the proposed groupings. I add here that shareholders of course have not yet had notice of the proposal with respect to voting percentages and classes with respect to their particular interests. With that caveat, and leaving aside the proposed single class of secured creditors, I am satisfied that the other classes suggested are appropriate and they are approved.

I turn now to the proposed one class of secured creditors. The membership of and proposed scheme of voting within the secured creditors class is dependent upon the value of each creditor's security as determined by Sceptre Resources Ltd. ("Sceptre"), the purchaser under the plan.

As a result of those valuations, the membership of that class was determined to include: the Bank of Montreal, the ABC noteholders, the Royal Bank of Canada, the National Bank of Canada and the HongKong Bank of Canada and the Bank of America Canada. Within the class, each secured creditor will receive one vote for each dollar of "security value." The valuations made by Sceptre represent what it considers to be a fair value for the securities.

Any dispute over the amount of money each creditor is to receive for its security will be determined at a subsequent fairness hearing where approval of the plan will be sought. Further, it should be noted that all counsel have agreed that, on the facts of this case, any errors made in the valuations would not result in any significant shift of voting power within the proposed class so as to alter the outcome of any vote. Therefore, the valuations made by Sceptre do not appear to be a major issue before me at this time insofar as voting is concerned.

The issue with which I am concerned arises from the objection raised by two of Oakwood's secured creditors, namely, HongKong Bank and Bank of America Canada, that they are grouped together with the other secured creditors. They have brought applications before me seeking leave to realize upon their security or, in the alternative, to be constituted a separate and exclusive class of creditors and to be entitled to vote as such at any meeting convened pursuant to the plan.

The very narrow issue which I must address concerns the propriety of classifying all the secured creditors of the company into one group. Counsel for Oakwood and Sceptre have attempted to justify their classifications by reference to the "commonality of interests test" described in *Sovereign Life Assur. Co. v. Dodd*, [1892] 2 QB 573 (CA). That test received the approval of the Alberta Court of Appeal in *Savage v. Amoco Acquisition Co.* (1988), 59 Alta. LR (2d) 260, 68 CBR (NS) 154, 87 AR 321, where Kerans JA, on behalf of the court, stated [pp. 264-65]:

> We agree that the basic rule for the creation of groups for the consideration of fundamental corporate changes was expressed by Lord Esher in *Sovereign Life Assur. Co. v. Dodd*, [*supra*] when he said, speaking about creditors:
>
>> ... if we find a different state of facts existing among different creditors which may differently affect their minds and their judgments, they must be divided into different classes.
>
> In the case of *Sovereign Life Assur. Co.*, Bowen LJ went on to state at p. 583 that the class:
>
>> ... must be confined to those persons whose rights are not so dissimilar as to make it impossible for them to consult together with a view to their common interest.

Counsel also made reference to two other "tests" which they argued must be complied with—the "minority veto test" and the "bona fide lack of oppression test." The former, it is argued, holds that the classes must not be so numerous as to give a veto power to an otherwise insignificant minority. In support of this test, they cite my judgment in *Amoco Can. Petroleum Co. v. Dome Petroleum Ltd.*, Calgary No. 8701-20108, 28th January 1988 (not yet reported).

I would restrict my comments on the applicability of this test to the fact that, in the *Amoco* case, I was dealing with "a very small minority group of [shareholders] near the bottom of the chain of priorities." Such is not the case here.

In support of the "bona fide lack of oppression test," counsel cite *Re Alabama, New Orleans, Texas & Pac. Junction Ry. Co.*, [1891] 1 Ch. 213 (CA), where Lindley LJ stated at p. 239:

> The Court must look at the scheme, and see whether the Act has been complied with, whether the majority are acting *bona fide*, and whether they are coercing the minority in order to promote interests adverse to those of the class whom they purport to represent. ...

Whether this test is properly considered at this stage, that is, whether the issue is the constitution of a membership of a class, is not necessary for me to decide as there have been no allegations by the HongKong Bank or Bank of America as to a lack of bona fides.

What I am left with, then, is the application to the facts of this case of the "commonality of interests test" while keeping in mind that the proposed plan of arrangement arises under the CCAA.

Sceptre and Oakwood have argued that the secured creditors' interests are sufficiently common that they can be grouped together as one class. That class is comprised of six institutional lenders (I would note that the ABC noteholders are actually a group of ten lenders) who have each taken first charges as security on assets upon which they have the right to realize in order to recover their claims. The same method of valuation was applied to each secured claim in order to determine the security value under the plan.

On the other hand, HongKong Bank and Bank of America have argued that their interests are distinguishable from the secured creditors class as a whole and from other secured creditors on an individual basis. While they have identified a number of individually distinguishing features of their interests vis-à-vis those of other secured parties (which I will address later), they have put forth the proposition that since each creditor has taken separate security on different assets, the necessary commonality of interests is not present. The rationale offered is that the different assets may give rise to a different state of facts which could alter the creditors' view as to the propriety of participating in the plan. For example, it was suggested that the relative ease of marketability of a distinct asset as opposed to the other assets granted as security could lead that secured creditor to choose to disapprove of the proposed plan. Similarly, the realization potential of assets may also lead to distinctions in the interests of the secured creditors and consequently bear upon their desire to participate in the plan.

In support of this proposition, the HongKong Bank and Bank of America draw from comments made by Ronald N. Robertson, QC, in a publication entitled "Legal Problems on Reorganization of Major Financial and Commercial Debtors," Canadian Bar Association—Ontario Continuing Legal Education, 5th April 1983, at p. 15, and by Stanley E. Edwards in an earlier article, "Reorganizations Under the *Companies' Creditors Arrangement Act*" (1947), 25 *Can. Bar Rev.* 587, at p. 603. Both authors gave credence to this "identity of interest" proposition that secured creditors should not be members of the same class "unless their security is on the same or substantially the same property and in equal priority." They also made reference to a case decided under c. 11 of the *Bankruptcy Code* of the United States of America which, while not applying that proposition in that given set of facts, accepted it as a "general rule." That authority is *Re Palisades-on-the-Desplaines; Seidel v. Palisades-on-the-Desplaines*, 89 F 2d 214 at 217-18 (1937, Ill.).

Basically, in putting forth that proposition, the HongKong Bank and Bank of America are asserting that they have made advances to Oakwood on the strength of certain security which they identified as sufficient and desirable security and which they alone have the right to realize upon. Of course, the logical extension of that argument is that in the facts of this case each secured creditor must itself comprise a class of creditors. While counsel for the HongKong Bank and Bank of America suggested it was not necessary to do so in this case, as they are the only secured creditors opposed to the classification put forth, in principle such would have to be the case if I were to accept their proposition.

To put the issue in another light, what I must decide is whether the holding of distinct security by each creditor necessitates a separate class of creditor for each, or whether notwithstanding this factor that they each share, nevertheless this factor does not override the grouping into one class of creditors. In my opinion, this decision cannot be made without considering the underlying purpose of the CCAA.

· · ·

In this regard, I would make extensive reference to the article by Mr. Robertson, QC, where, in discussing the classification of creditors under the CCAA and after stating the proposition referred to by counsel for the HongKong Bank and Bank of America, he states at p. 16 in his article:

> An initial, almost instinctive, response that differences in claims and property subject to security automatically means segregation into different classes does not necessarily make economic or legal sense in the context of an act such as the CCAA.

And later at pp. 19 and 20, in commenting on the article by Mr. Edwards, he states:

> However, if the trend of Edwards' suggestions that secured creditors can only be classed together when they held [sic] security of the same priority, that perhaps classes should be subdivided into further groups according to whether or not a member of the class also holds some other security or form of interest in the debtor company, *the multiplicity of discrete classes or sub-classes might be so compounded as to defeat the object of the act*. As Edwards himself says, the subdivision of voting groups and the counting of angels on the heads of pins must stop somewhere and some forms of differences must surely be disregarded.

In summarizing his discussion, he states on pp. 20-21:

> From the foregoing one can perceive at least two potentially conflicting approaches to the issue of classification. On the one hand there is the concept that members of a class ought to have the same "interest" in the company, ought to be only creditors entitled to look to the same "source" or "fund" for payment, and ought to encompass all of the creditors who do have such an identity of legal rights. *On the other hand, there is recognition that the legislative intent is to facilitate reorganization, that excessive fragmentation of classes may be counterproductive and that some degree of difference between claims should not preclude creditors being put in the same class.*
>
> *It is fundamental to any imposed plan or reorganization that strict legal rights are going to be altered and that such alteration may be imposed against the will of at least some creditors.* When one considers the complexity and magnitude of contemporary large business organizations, and the potential consequences of their failure it may be that the courts will be compelled to focus less on whether there is any identity of legal rights and rather focus on whether or not those constituting the class are persons, to use Lord Esher's phrase, "whose rights are not so dissimilar as to make it impossible for them to consult together with a view to their common interest. ..."
>
> If the plan of reorganization is such that the creditors' particular priorities and securities are preserved, especially in the event of ultimate failure, *it may be that the courts will, for example in an apt case decide that creditors who have basically made the same kinds of loans against the same kind of security, even though on different terms and against different particu-*

*lar secured assets, do have a sufficient similarity of interest to warrant being put into one class
and being made subject to the will of the required majority of that class.* [emphasis added]

These comments may be reduced to two cogent points. First, it is clear that the CCAA
grants a court the authority to alter the legal rights of parties other than the debtor company without their consent. Second, the primary purpose of the Act is to facilitate reorganizations and this factor must be given due consideration at every stage of the process, including the classification of creditors made under a proposed plan. To accept the
"identity of interest" proposition as a starting point in the classification of creditors necessarily results in a "multiplicity of discrete classes" which would make any reorganization difficult, if not impossible, to achieve.

In the result, given that this planned reorganization arises under the CCAA, I must
reject the arguments put forth by the HongKong Bank and the Bank of America, that
since they hold separate security over different assets, they must therefore be classified as
a separate class of creditors.

I turn now to the other factors which the HongKong Bank and Bank of America submit distinguishes them on individual bases from other creditors of Oakwood. The HongKong Bank and Bank of America argue that the values used by Sceptre are significantly
understated. With respect to the Bank of Montreal, it is alleged that that bank actually
holds security valued close to, if not in excess of, the outstanding amount of its loans
when compared to the HongKong Bank and Bank of America whose security, those
banks allege, is approximately equal to the amount of its loans. It is submitted that a plan
which understates the value of assets results in the oversecured party being more inclined to support a plan under which they will receive, without the difficulties of realization, close to full payments of their loans.

The problem with this argument is that it is a throwback to the "identity of interest"
proposition. Differing security positions and changing security values are a fact of life in
the world of secured financing. To accept this argument would again result in a different
class of creditor for each secured lender, with the possible exception of the ABC noteholders who could be lumped with the HongKong Bank or Bank of America, as their
percentage realization under the proposed plan is approximately equal to that of the
HongKong Bank and Bank of America.

Further, the HongKong Bank and Bank of America also submit that since the Royal
Bank and National Bank of Canada are so much more undersecured on their loans, they
too have a distinct interest in participating in the plan which is not shared by themselves.
The sum total of their submissions would seem to be that, since oversecured and undersecured lenders have a greater incentive to participate, it is only those lenders, such as
themselves with just the right amount of security, that do not share that common interest. Frankly, it appears to me that these arguments are drawn from the fact that they are
the only secured creditors of Oakwood who would prefer to retain their right to realize
upon their security, as opposed to participating in the plan. I do not wish to suggest that
they should be chided for taking such a position, but surely expressed approval or disap-
proval of the plan is not a valid reason to create different classes of creditors. Further, as
I have already clearly stated, the CCAA can validly be used to alter or remove the rights
of creditors.

Finally, I wish to address the argument that, since Sceptre has made arrangements with the Royal Bank of Canada relating to the purchase of Oakwood, it has an interest not shared by the other secured creditors. The Royal Bank's position as a principal lender in the reorganization is separate from its status as a secured creditor of Oakwood and arises from a separate business decision. In the absence of any allegation that the Royal Bank will not act bona fide in considering the benefit of the plan of the secured creditors as a class, the HongKong Bank and Bank of America cannot be heard to criticize the Royal Bank's presence in the same class.

In light of my conclusions, the result is that I approve the proposed classification of secured creditors into one class. ...

Application granted.

NOTES

Paperny J, in *Re Canadian Airlines Corp.* (2000), 19 CBR (4th) 12 (Alta. QB), sets out the following principles for assessing commonality of interest (at para. 31):

1. Commonality of interest should be viewed based on the non-fragmentation test, not on an identity-of-interest test;

2. The interests to be considered are the legal interests that a creditor holds qua creditor in relationship to the debtor company prior to and under the plan as well as on liquidation;

3. The commonality of interests are to be viewed purposively, bearing in mind the object of the CCCA—namely to facilitate reorganizations if at all possible;

4. In placing a broad and purposive interpretation on the CCCA, the court should be careful to resist classification approaches that would potentially jeopardize viable plans;

5. Absent bad faith, the motivations of creditors to approve or disapprove are irrelevant;

6. The requirement of creditors being able to consult together means being able to assess their legal entitlement *as creditors* before or after the plan in a similar manner.

For an important judgment by Tysoe J applying a non-fragmentation test in determining which of the holders of different types of unsecured claims (terminated employees, a debenture holder, equipment financiers, creditors holding a guarantee from one debtor's parent company, and landlords whose lease had been repudiated) could be joined in a single class for voting on a plan of arrangement, see *Re Woodward's Ltd.* (1993), 20 CBR (3d) 74 (BCSC). The employees wished to be placed in their own separate class for the purposes of voting on the plan. Tysoe J refused this request on the ground that the employees and the other unsecured creditors had identical legal interests. He stated:

The legal rights of the terminated employees are the same as the legal rights of the trade suppliers. They are both creditors with unsecured claims against the Operating Company (the secured and preferred amounts payable to employees under provincial legislation and the *Bankruptcy and Insolvency Act* have already been paid to the terminated employees). In a bankruptcy or other liquidation they would both receive the same pro rata amount of their claims. They are to receive the same pro rata amount of their claims under the Reorganization Plan.

The fact that there is a recognized difference between contracts of employment and ordinary commercial contracts is not relevant because the contracts of employment of the terminated employees have come to an end. The terminated employees have claims for damages against Woodward's for wrongful dismissal. Once the amount of damages for an employee has been agreed upon or determined by the Court, the difference between the two types of contracts becomes historical and the employee has the same rights as any other unsecured creditor. The differences between the two types of contracts may result in the employees receiving higher amounts of damages but the differences do not warrant the terminated employees being entitled to a higher distribution than the other unsecured creditors.

Even if the legal rights of the creditors differ, they may be placed in the same class of creditors if the difference in legal rights does not prevent the creditors from sharing a sufficient commonality of interest. Tysoe J held that this commonality of interest is lacking when the plan denies some of the creditors a valuable right to which they would otherwise be entitled. The plan proposed that the same payment (37 percent of the value of their claim) would be made to creditors who held claims solely against the debtor company as well as to creditors who in addition had been given an unsecured guarantee by an affiliated company. Tysoe J held that the classification scheme was unfair to the extent that both kinds of creditors were placed in the same class. He stated:

> The Reorganization Plan ignores the fact that the holders of guarantees are unsecured creditors of both companies. It proposes that they receive the same 37% proportion of their indebtedness as the other General Creditors and their status as creditors of the Holding Company is not reflected.
>
> In view of the fact that the holders of guarantees do have different legal rights from the other members of the class of General Creditors, it is necessary to decide whether the rights are so dissimilar that they cannot vote on the Reorganization Plan with a common interest. It was submitted by counsel for Woodward's that there is a common interest because the holders of guarantees will still receive more under the Reorganization Plan than they will be paid upon a liquidation of the two companies. I do not think that this is sufficient to create a commonality of interest with the other members in the class of General Creditors who have lesser legal rights. To the contrary, I believe that this is an example of what Bowen LJ had in mind in the *Sovereign Life* case [[1892] 2 QB 573 (CA)], when he used the term "confiscation." By being a minority in the class of General Creditors, the holders of guarantees can have their guarantees confiscated by a vote of the requisite majority of the class who do not have the same rights. The holders of guarantees could be forced to accept the same proportionate amount as the other members of the class and to receive no value in respect of legal rights that they uniquely enjoy and that would have value in a liquidation of the two companies.

The US *Bankruptcy Code* gives a court the power to "cram down" a Chapter 11 plan on a dissenting class of creditors. However, a court may only exercise the power if it is fair and equitable to do so. This has been interpreted to mean that the plan must provide for a distribution strictly in accordance with the priority entitlements of the claimants (this is referred to as the "absolute priority rule"). In other words, the class that is subject to the cram-down must be paid in full before any class of claimants that are lower in priority ranking receive anything. Although US restructuring law adopts an identity of interest test that leads to a greater number of classes of creditors, this is mitigated by the power of the court to cram down the plan on a dissenting class. In contrast, the non-fragmentation approach leads to fewer classes of creditors, and, therefore, results in a lesser need for a cram-down power.

III. ACQUISITION OF CLAIMS

In re Allegheny International, Inc.
118 BR 282 (Bktcy. WD Pa. 1990)

JOSEPH L. COSETTI CJ:

. . .

Unless it is necessary to repeat certain facts in the interest of clarity, the court will not burden readers with the history of the first 22 months of this case. The parties to these matters are painfully aware of those facts. For the uninitiated, those facts are available in numerous memorandum opinions by this court, both published and unpublished. For the motions to designate, we take up the saga, beginning on December 29, 1989, when the debtor filed the instant plan of reorganization. The court conducted several days of hearings on the disclosure statement in January 1990. The court approved the debtor's disclosure statement on February 5, 1990, setting the last day to ballot on the debtor's plan as March 30, 1990, at 5:00 P.M.

However, on January 24, 1990, near the conclusion of the hearings on the debtor's disclosure statement, Japonica filed its plan of reorganization (the "Japonica plan") and disclosure statement which mirrored and utilized in large part the debtor's material and organization. The court was urged by Japonica not to approve the debtor's disclosure statement until Japonica's disclosure statement could be approved and a joint ballot distributed. Japonica requested an extraordinary reduction in the time the rules provided for confirmation. The court feared additional delay and denied the request. The court set separate schedules for confirmation of the plans and promised Japonica an opportunity for creditors to vote on the Japonica plan before any order of confirmation would be issued.

The Japonica plan offered cash equivalent to $6.42 per share with holdbacks, as compared to the debtor's proposed stock plan which offered $7.00 per share. Under the Japonica plan, Japonica would acquire control of the debtor ... . Although Japonica had indicated its interest in acquiring control of the debtor as early as July 1989, Japonica held no interest as a creditor or equity holder of the debtor until immediately prior to the filing of its proposed plan and disclosure statement. To qualify as a party in interest authorized to file a plan, Japonica purchased public subordinated debentures of the debtor with a face value of $10,000 for $2,712. At that time, the court was unaware that the purchase of claims would be the tactic used by Japonica to gain control. ...

On February 23, 1990, Japonica began purchasing claims of the secured bank lenders, Class 2.AI.2. This occurred after the debtor's disclosure statement was approved and the debtor's plan balloting had commenced. This was also after Japonica had proposed a plan and disclosure statement and had become a proponent of a plan. The purchase of the following claims gave Japonica control of approximately 27% of the claims in Class 2.AI.2. ...

On or about March 26, 1990, Japonica purchased the claim of Continental Bank, NA ("Continental"), with a face amount of $12,614,800, for $11,984,060, or 95% of the face amount. Following the purchase of the claim of Continental, Japonica held 33.87% of the claims in Class 2.AI.2, enabling Japonica to block an affirmative vote by that class on the debtor's plan of reorganization. 11 USC § 1126(c). After achieving its blocking position, Japonica purchased the claim of Bank of Hawaii, with a face amount of $2,242,630, for $1,838,956.60, or 82% of the face amount. Under the terms of the assignments by the aforementioned banks, Japonica caused the votes of the claims it purchased to be voted against the debtor's plan.

. . .

Japonica's actions with respect to the purchase of claims were in bad faith. Notwithstanding Japonica's allegedly longstanding interest in the debtor, Japonica filed its plan of reorganization at the eleventh hour. Notwithstanding Japonica's allegedly longstanding interest in the debtor, Japonica did not purchase significant claims until the voting period on the debtor's plan. Japonica was also at this time a proponent of a plan. The particular claims that Japonica purchased, and the manner in which they were purchased, can be used to determine their intent. Japonica purchased a clear blocking position in Class 2.AI.2, the secured bank lenders. Because that class was the most senior class, a negative vote in that class made confirmation extremely difficult, if not impossible. Japonica paid approximately 80% of the face amount for the first five claims in Class 2.AI.2. As Japonica approached ownership of 33% in amount of this class, it paid 85% of the face amount for the next claim, that of First National Bank of Boston. It then purchased the claim of Continental Bank for *95% of the face amount.* This gave Japonica 33.87% of the amount of Class 2.AI.2 claims. Thereafter, Japonica purchased one more bank claim, but only for 82% of the face amount. If Japonica purchased bank claims solely for economic purposes, it would not have paid 95% of the face amount and then returned to an 82% purchase. Instead, it purchased almost exactly the amount required to block the plan of reorganization.

. . .

A noted commentator suggests that the ultimate intent of bankruptcy is to maximize results for all creditors:

> The basic problem that bankruptcy law is designed to handle, both as a normative matter and as a positive matter, is that the system of individual creditor remedies may be bad for the creditors as a group when there are not enough assets to go around. Because creditors have conflicting rights, there is a tendency in their debt-collection efforts to make a bad situation worse. Bankruptcy law responds to this problem. …
>
> Bankruptcy provides a way to make these diverse individuals act as one, by imposing a *collective* and *compulsory* proceeding on them. …
>
> This is the historically recognized purpose of bankruptcy law and perhaps is none too controversial in itself.

T. Jackson, *The Logic and Limits of Bankruptcy Law*, 10-13 (1986).

The purpose of reorganization is to offer an opportunity to maximize results for all creditors and interest holders. Japonica's actions and statements make abundantly clear that it is "control" and "control profit" that they seek. This control profit will not be shared through a reorganization plan with all creditors and all interest holders. A control profit will be shared by only Japonica and their affiliates. Japonica intends to use its newly acquired control to extract economic profit for itself, not to maximize the results for all creditors.

Trading in claims to achieve profits on a specific claim may not be destructive of the reorganization process (a) when both buyer and seller are informed; (b) when the purchaser is willing to hold the claim until distribution; and (c) when the original claimant does not wish to hold the claim or needs immediate cash. However, the technical provisions of the Code, such as the automatic stay, are designed to achieve the purposes of the reorganization process and to maximize results for all creditors. These provisions are not designed to create delay and pressure claimants to sell. Delay reduces the value of claims. Japonica has deliberately created delay which has improved their ability to buy claims.

The confirmation process enables creditors to modify themselves. The purpose is to increase the pool of value for all creditors and shareholders. Here, Japonica clearly attempts to deprive creditors of the control premium by a manipulation of the reorganization process through the strategic purchase of claims. Acquiring claims with the clear purpose of achieving control of the debtor, thereby earning a control profit, does not maximize the result for all creditors. Such action manipulates the process.

NOTES

1. Under the US *Bankruptcy Code*, the bankruptcy court is permitted to disqualify votes where the creditor was not acting in good faith. Although the CCAA does not contain an express rule that permits a court to disqualify votes on the basis of bad faith, it is likely that this power would be derived from the broad remedial purpose of the legislation. Subsequent cases have held that the acquisition of claims by a creditor that is undertaken to improve the bargaining position of the creditor in the restructuring proceedings is not objectionable. A distinction is drawn between efforts to obtain a veto or blocking position in order to enhance its position as a creditor and actions and efforts to do so for an ulterior motive, such as eliminating a competitor, seeking preferential treatment by threatening to block a fair plan, or promoting a competing plan in which it is the chief beneficiary. See *In re Marin Town Center*, 142 BR 374 (ND Cal. Feb. 18, 1992).

2. A person who acquires a claim of another creditor is counted as a single creditor for the purposes of voting on the plan. In other words, the acquisition of the claim only affects the money value of the claim that can be voted by the creditor who acquired the claim—it does not give the creditor the right to be counted as two creditors for the purposes of the vote. See *Re Canadian Airlines Corp.* (2000), 19 CBR (4th) 12 (Alta. QB).

QUESTIONS

Can the trading of claims improve the position of creditors in a restructuring? In what respect does a creditor who sells its claim benefit? How might the concentration of claims by an investor benefit other creditors whose claims have not been acquired?

IV. TREATMENT OF SHAREHOLDERS

The CCAA does not itself indicate how existing shareholders of the debtor company are to be dealt with in the plan of arrangement. Instead, s. 42 of the CCAA provides that the Act may be applied together with the provisions of any other federal or provincial Act that authorizes or makes provision for the sanction of compromises or arrangements between a company and its shareholders. This implies that shareholders have some rights, even though their equity is worthless. Many of the Canadian incorporation statutes provide that a court may make an order amending the corporation's constating documents without the need for shareholder approval. See, for example, *Canada Business Corporations Act*, RSC 1985, c. C-44, s. 191. However, some incorporations statutes may not contain this type of provision, and this might imply that shareholders have the ability to demand some value in the restructuring in order to obtain their consent.

Farley J's judgment in *Re Loewen Group Inc.*, below, is important because he makes it clear that, for insolvency purposes, the assumption is not correct and the court can authorize the vesting of property under a plan free of shareholder claims even if the law governing the debtor's incorporation requires shareholder approval of any change in the company's structure. In practice, it is not uncommon for the plan to throw the existing shareholders a small bone (for example, 1 to 2 percent of the equity in the company's restructured capitalization) so as to enlist their support for approval of the new share structure before the court hearing the application under the relevant *Business Corporations Act*. In the light of Farley J's judgment, consider whether the CCAA court's approval is sufficient, or will this be deemed incompatible with the direction given in s. 42 of the CCAA?

Re Loewen Group Inc.
[2001] OJ no. 5640 (QL) (SC)

FARLEY J: [1] On Dec. 7, 2001, I heard the motion of The Loewen Group Inc. ("Loewen") and the other Companies listed in Schedule "A" requesting an order pursuant to s. 18.6(2) of the *Companies' Creditors Arrangement Act* ("CCAA") and s. 182 of the Ontario *Business Corporations Act* ("OBCA"). That relief, *inter alia* of recognizing the US plan of arrangement and granting a vesting order pursuant thereto, was granted that day. I noted that I was in agreement with the general thrust of the factum of the moving parties. It was observed that there did not seem to be any reported case to date dealing with the non-applicability of s. 126 of the British Columbia *Company Act*, RSBC 1996, c. 62 ("BC Company Act") or its equivalence under the corporations legislation in the other jurisdictions in Canada, given that this subject case dealt with a reorganization pursuant to the insolvency law. Perhaps this analysis will be of some assistance in filling that vacuum.

[2] I agreed with the assertion of the moving parties that s. 126 of the BC *Company Act* was not applicable in these circumstances so as to require a special resolution of the shareholders (members). Loewen was incorporated under the BC *Company Act*. S. 126 provides as follows:

126(1) The directors must not sell, lease or otherwise dispose of the whole or substantially the whole of the undertaking of the company unless they have the approval of the members given by a special resolution.

(2) If the approval required by subsection (1) has not been obtained, the court, subject to subsection (3), on application by any member, director or creditor of a company, may do one or more of the following:

(a) enjoin a proposed sale, lease or other disposition of the whole, or substantially the whole, of the undertaking of the company;

(b) set aside a sale, lease or other disposition;

(c) make any further order the court considers appropriate.

· · ·

[3] In my view s. 126 contemplates a voluntary disposal of the assets and undertaking of a corporation by the directors and not a transfer of property pursuant to a vesting order issued pursuant to the CCAA (or other federal bankruptcy and insolvency legislation), in this case pursuant to s. 18.6(2) of the CCAA. An arrangement between a bankrupt or insolvent corporation and its directors, including the disposal of the corporation's property to implement the arrangement, falls within the exclusive jurisdiction of the federal Parliament. Provincial legislation which would otherwise apply to the sale of the corporation's property has no application in such circumstances. See *Montreal Trust Company v. Abitibi Power & Paper Co. Ltd. et al.*, [1938] OR 589 (CA) at pp. 601-2.

[4] I note that s. 126 is directed against conduct by the directors of the corporation, not the fundamental capacity of the provincial corporate entity. In this regard, see s. 126(3) which provides that despite the failure of the directors to comply with s. 126(1), the disposition is valid if effected for valuable consideration and in good faith. Given the nature of these insolvency proceedings, the conditions of s. 126(3) would be met, even if s. 126 were applicable.

[5] I further note that if concurrent bankruptcy or insolvency proceedings are not pending, then pursuant to s. 252 of the BC *Company Act*, a transfer of the corporation's property could be ordered by a court pursuant to that provincial creditor arrangement without resort to s. 126. See also s. 254 regarding a provincial shareholder arrangement.

[6] In receiverships the directors' powers of management are curtailed or eliminated. See *Nova Metal Products Inc. v. Comiskey (Trustee of)* (1990), 1 CBR (3d) 101; 1 OR (3d) 289 (CA); *AIDC v. Co-operative Farmers and Graziers Direct Meat Supply Ltd.* 1978 VIC LEXIS 91 (Supreme Court of Victoria) at p. 32, citing *Moss Steam Ship Co. v. Whinney*, [1912] AC 254 at p. 263. See also s. 98 of the BC *Company Act* which provides:

98. If a receiver manager is appointed, the powers of the directors and officers of the corporation cease with respect to that part of the undertaking of the company unless they have the approval of the members given by a special resolution.

It seems to me that the Court's power and authority to grant a vesting order under the CCAA is analogous to the inherent process of a court in a receivership. The court's inherent powers to make orders in a CCAA proceeding have been analogized to those in receiverships for the purpose of recognizing the court's jurisdiction to grant super priorities for certain debtor expenses and debtor in possession (DIP) financing. These quasi-receivership powers permit the court to override the usual ordering of priorities accorded to secured creditors under provincial legislation. See *Re United Used Auto & Truck Parts Ltd.*, [2000] BCJ no. 409 (CA) at para. 22 where the British Columbia Court of Appeal held that the court's inherent jurisdiction in a CCAA proceeding is even broader than its inherent jurisdiction in a receivership.

[7] If a conflict arises between the CCAA and a provincial statute, then under the doctrine of paramountcy, the CCAA provision prevails and the conflicting provisions of the provincial statute are rendered inoperative. See *Pacific National Lease Holding Corp. v. Sun Life Trust Co.* (1995), 34 CBR (3d) 4 (BCCA) at pp. 11-2. Thus even if s. 126 of the BC *Company Act* were to be interpreted as applying (which I have found it does not), then in this case the Loewen shareholders would have an opportunity to veto a key component of the US Plan which is being recognized by this Court pursuant to s. 18.6(2) of the CCAA. Thus there would be an irreconcilable conflict between those provisions of the provincial statute and the CCAA.

[8] Under US bankruptcy law, shareholders having no economic interest to protect have no right to vote on a plan of reorganization. Consistent with that appropriate economic and legal principle, courts in Ontario and Alberta have held that where shareholders similarly have no economic interest to protect, it would defeat the policy objectives of the CCAA to give those shareholders a right to veto a plan of arrangement. In the subject case the shareholders of Loewen have no economic interest. Loewen has in fact to its credit consistently advised in press releases that it considered its shares to be valueless, notwithstanding that these shares continued to trade for somewhat more than nominal value during a considerable portion of the CCAA and US Chapter 11 *Bankruptcy Code* proceedings.

· · ·

[11] The conflict between, on the one hand, the recognition of the US Confirmation Order and the US Plan pursuant to s. 18.6(2) of the CCAA and, on the other hand, the shareholders voting rights mandated by s. 126 of the BC *Company Act* may be resolved by applying the constitutional doctrines of dual aspect and paramountcy. The disposition of all of Loewen's property in an insolvency restructuring has a dual aspect. Both s. 18.6 of the CCAA and s. 126 of the BC *Company Act* are constitutionally valid enactments: s. 18.6 of the CCAA falls within the scope of the federal legislative power over bankruptcy and insolvency and s. 126 of the BC *Company Act* falls under the scope of provincial legislative powers over the incorporation of provincial companies and property and civil rights. See *Re Olympia & York Developments Ltd.* (1993), 102 DLR (4th) 149 (Ont. Gen. Div.); *Multiple Access Limited v. McCutcheon*, [1982] 2 SCR 161.

[12] In *Olympia & York*, Blair J confirmed the dual aspect doctrine in the case of provincial shareholder arrangements in approving a shareholder arrangement with a solvent corporation (incorporated pursuant to the OBCA) which was part of a larger CCAA arrangement involving insolvent affiliates. The shareholder arrangement involved share transfers, reorganizations, corporate amalgamations, share cancellations and an exchange of shares; it was held that the shareholders would derive intrinsic benefit from such an arrangement. Blair J held that while the CCAA authorizes creditor arrangements, there is no federal legislation authorizing arrangements between provincially incorporated corporations and their shareholders and the provincial shareholder arrangement provisions fill this gap while operating harmoniously under CCAA creditor arrangements.

Olympia & York was an example of the practice which has developed of combining a plan of arrangement under the CCAA with a shareholder arrangement or other procedure under provincial corporate legislation. ...

[13] The doctrine of paramountcy has been applied where the exercise of a court's discretion under the CCAA conflicted with the mandatory provisions of provincial legislation. In *Luscar Ltd. v. Smoky River Coal Ltd.*, [1999] AJ no. 676 (CA), the Alberta Court of Appeal held as follows:

(a) The CCAA gave the Court discretion to establish a dispute resolution procedure, even though the parties had agreed to arbitrate their disputes.

(b) The Court acknowledged that in other cases, courts had sent specific issues to a provincial forum for resolution. However, in each of those cases the courts had determined that resolution in the other forum would promote the objectives of the CCAA. In this case, the CCAA judge had found that the objectives of the CCAA would be frustrated by a transfer of the dispute to provincial arbitration. The Court held that while a judge has the discretion under the CCAA to permit issues to be determined in another forum, he is under no obligation to do so.

(c) The Court confirmed that the CCAA authorized it to affect permanently the rights of third parties if their actions would potentially prejudice the success of the plan.

(d) Even if the provincial arbitration act required arbitration of the dispute in the circumstances, there would then be a conflict between the CCAA and the provincial act and the CCAA must prevail.

[14] It seems to me that the reasoning in Luscar is applicable in the subject case before me since:

(a) The US Plan is a US bankruptcy reorganization which can be recognized and implemented in Canada pursuant to s. 18.6(2) of the CCAA. It contains no proposal to restructure Loewen's share capital. Confirming the US Plan falls squarely within the jurisdiction of the US Court, and recognizing and effecting the US Court proceedings in Canada falls squarely within the jurisdiction of this Court pursuant to s. 18.6(2) of the CCAA.

(b) In confirming the US Plan under which shareholders received no value and on which they did not vote, the US Court confirmed that Loewen's shareholders have no economic interest to protect. This determination is consistent with recent developments in Canadian law, discussed above, and so there are strong policy reasons for the Ontario Court to recognize and give effect to it.

(c) In such circumstances, a requirement for shareholder approval would defeat the purpose of Loewen's bankruptcy reorganization because it would give shareholders, who have no economic interest to protect, a right to veto and potentially extract an economic benefit. This would give rise to irreconcilable conflict between s. 18.6(2) of the CCAA and s. 126 of the BC *Company Act*. Under the constitutional doctrine of paramountcy, s. 18.6(2) of the CCAA prevails.

Vesting order approved without necessity for shareholder approval.

V. TREATMENT OF EQUITY CLAIMS

Shareholders will usually receive little or nothing in a restructuring. Not surprisingly, they have sometimes attempted to improve their status by asserting a cause of action against the debtor company. The shareholders may assert a claim to be a creditor, on the ground that the company is obliged to pay them a dividend or some other form of corporate distribution. They may also attempt to sue the debtor company for damages for misrepresentation or seek to rescind the contract and recover the consideration that they paid in respect of the issuance of the shares. The courts generally disallowed such claims, and used a variety of legal techniques to reach this result. See *Re Central Capital Corp.* (1996), 38 CBR (3d) 1 (Ont. CA); *Re Blue Range Resource Corp.* (2000), 15 CBR (4th) 169 (Alta. QB). And see the discussion in Chapter 9 and Chapter 14, Section II.

The 2007 amendments to the CCAA have introduced statutory provisions ensuring that these types of claims will be subordinate to the claims of ordinary unsecured creditors. Section 2(1) of the CCAA defines an "equity claim." It includes a claim for a dividend, return of capital, a redemption or retraction obligation, and a monetary loss resulting from the ownership sale or purchase of an equity interest or rescission of a purchase or sale of an equity interest. Section 22.1 of the CCAA provides that holders of equity interests must be placed in their own separate class and do not have a right to vote on a plan unless a court orders otherwise. Section 6(8) of the CCAA provides that a court may not sanction a plan that provides any distribution to equity claimants unless all non-equity claims are paid in full.

One commentator has argued that this approach goes too far and that claims that arise pursuant to provincial securities regulation statutes that seek to protect investors from fraud or misrepresentation should not be postponed to the claims of other creditors. See J. Sarra, "From Subordination to Parity: An International Comparison of Equity Securities Claims in Insolvency Proceedings" (2007), 16 *Int'l Ins. Rev.* 181.

VI. COURT APPROVAL

The CCAA provides for certain mandatory features in a plan of compromise or arrangement. If the plan does not contain these features, a court cannot approve it and it therefore will not bind the creditors. There are three mandatory requirements. Section 6(3) of the CCAA provides that unremitted source deductions of income tax, Canada Pension Plan, and employment insurance that have been deducted from the pay of employees must be paid within six months after court approval of the plan unless the Crown agrees otherwise. Section 6(5) provides that the plan must give employees at least as much as the preferred amount that they would have been qualified to receive in a bankruptcy and all amounts earned after the commencement of the restructuring. Section 6(6) provides that the plan must provide for the payment of unremitted pension contributions, but this requirement can be omitted from the plan if the parties have reached an agreement concerning those amounts that has been approved by the relevant pension regulator.

The following two cases discuss the test that is used by courts in determining whether to sanction a plan and the criteria that it will use to determine if a plan is fair and reasonable.

Re Sammi Atlas Inc.
(1998), 3 CBR (4th) 171 (Ont. Gen. Div.)

FARLEY J: [1] This endorsement deals with two of the motions before me today:

1) Applicant's motion for an order approving and sanctioning the Applicant's Plan of Compromise and Arrangement, as amended and approved by the Applicant's unsecured creditors on February 25, 1998; and
2) A motion by Argo Partners, Inc. ("Argo"), a creditor by way of assignment, for an order directing that the Plan be amended to provide that a person who, on the record date, held unsecured claims shall be entitled to elect treatment with respect to each unsecured claim held by it on a claim by claim basis (and not on an aggregate basis as provided for in the Plan).

[2] As to the Applicant's sanction motion, the general principles to be applied in the exercise of the court's discretion are:

1) there must be strict compliance with all statutory requirements and adherence to the previous orders of the court;
2) all materials filed and procedures carried out must be examined to determine if anything has been done or purported to be done which is not authorized by the *Companies' Creditors Arrangement Act* ("CCAA"); and
3) the Plan must be fair and reasonable.

See *Northland Properties Ltd., Re* (1988), 73 CBR (NS) 175 (BCSC); affirmed (1989), 73 CBR (NS) 195 (BCCA) at p. 201; *Olympia & York Developments Ltd. v. Royal Trust Co.* (1993), 12 OR (3d) 500 (Ont. Gen. Div.) at p. 506.

[3] I am satisfied on the material before me that the Applicant was held to be a corporation as to which the CCAA applies, that the Plan was filed with the court in accordance with the previous orders, that notices were appropriately given and published as to claims and meetings, that the meetings were held in accordance with the directions of the court and that the Plan was approved by the requisite majority (in fact it was approved 98.74% in number of the proven claims of creditors voting and by 96.79% dollar value, with Argo abstaining). Thus it would appear that items one and two are met.

[4] What of item 3—is the Plan fair and reasonable? A Plan under the CCAA is a compromise; it cannot be expected to be perfect. It should be approved if it is fair, reasonable and equitable. Equitable treatment is not necessarily equal treatment. Equal treatment may be contrary to equitable treatment. One must look at the creditors as a whole (i.e. generally) and to the objecting creditors (specifically) and see if rights are compromised in an attempt to balance interests (and have the pain of the compromise equitably shared) as opposed to a confiscation of rights: see *Campeau Corp., Re* (1992), 10 CBR (3d) 104 (Ont. Gen. Div.) at p. 109. It is recognized that the CCAA contemplates that a minority of creditors is bound by the Plan which a majority have approved—subject only to the court determining that the Plan is fair and reasonable: see *Northland Properties Ltd.* at p. 201; *Olympia & York Developments Ltd.* at p. 509. In the present case no one appeared today to oppose the Plan being sanctioned: Argo merely wished that the Plan be amended to accommodate its particular concerns. Of course, to the extent that

Argo would be benefited by such an amendment, the other creditors would in effect be disadvantaged since the pot in this case is based on a zero sum game.

[5] Those voting on the Plan (and I note there was a very significant "quorum" present at the meeting) do so on a business basis. As Blair J said at p. 510 of *Olympia & York Developments Ltd.*:

> As the other courts have done, I observe that it is not my function to second guess the business people with respect to the "business" aspects of the Plan, descending into the negotiating arena and substituting my own view of what is a fair and reasonable compromise or arrangement for that of the business judgment of the participants. The parties themselves know best what is in their interests in those areas.

The court should be appropriately reluctant to interfere with the business decisions of creditors reached as a body. There was no suggestion that these creditors were unsophisticated or unable to look out for their own best interests. The vote in the present case is even higher than in *Central Guaranty Trustco Ltd., Re* (1993), 21 CBR (3d) 139 (Ont. Gen. Div. [Commercial List]) where I observed at p. 141:

> … This on either basis is well beyond the specific majority requirement of CCAA. Clearly there is a very heavy burden on parties seeking to upset a plan that the required majority have found that they could vote for; given the overwhelming majority this burden is no lighter. This vote by sophisticated lenders speaks volumes as to fairness and reasonableness.
>
> The Courts should not second guess business people who have gone along with the Plan. …

[6] Argo's motion is to amend the Plan—after it has been voted on. However I do not see any exceptional circumstances which would support such a motion being brought now. In *Algoma Steel Corp. v. Royal Bank* (1992), 11 CBR (3d) 11 (Ont. CA) the Court of Appeal observed at p. 15 that the court's jurisdiction to amend a plan should "be exercised sparingly and in exceptional circumstances only" even if the amendment were merely technical and did not prejudice the interests of the corporation or its creditors and then only where there is jurisdiction under the CCAA to make the amendment requested, I was advised that Argo had considered bringing the motion on earlier but had not done so in the face of "veto" opposition from the major creditors. I am puzzled by this since the creditor or any other appropriate party can always move in court before the Plan is voted on to amend the Plan; voting does not have anything to do with the court granting or dismissing the motion. The court can always determine a matter which may impinge directly and materially upon the fairness and reasonableness of a plan. I note in passing that it would be inappropriate to attempt to obtain a preview of the court's views as to sanctioning by bringing on such a motion. See my views in *Central Guaranty Trustco Ltd., Re* at p. 143:

> … In *Algoma Steel Corp. v. Royal Bank* (1992), 8 OR (3d) 449, the Court of Appeal determined that there were exceptional circumstances (unrelated to the Plan) which allowed it to adjust *where no interest was adversely affected*. The same cannot be said here. FSTQ aside from s. 11(c) of the CCAA also raised s. 7. I am of the view that s. 7 allows an amendment after an adjournment—*but not after a vote has been taken.* (emphasis in original)

What Argo wants is a substantive change; I do not see the jurisdiction to grant same under the CCAA.

[7] In the subject Plan creditors are to be dealt with on a sliding scale for distribution purposes only: with this scale being on an aggregate basis of all claims held by one claimant:

   i) $7,500 or less to receive cash of 95% of the proven claim;

   ii) $7,501-$100,000 to receive cash of 90% of the first $7,500 and 55% of balance; and;

   iii) in excess of $100,000 to receive shares on a formula basis (subject to creditor agreeing to limit claims to $100,000 so as to obtain cash as per the previous formula).

Such a sliding scale arrangement has been present in many proposals over the years. Argo has not been singled out for special treatment; others who acquired claims by assignment have also been affected. Argo has acquired 40 claims; all under $100,000 but in the aggregate well over $100,000. Argo submitted that it could have achieved the result that it wished if it had kept the individual claims it acquired separate by having them held by a different "person"; this is true under the Plan as worded. Conceivably if this type of separation in the face of an aggregation provision were perceived to be inappropriate by a CCAA applicant, then I suppose the language of such a plan could be "tightened" to eliminate what the applicant perceived as a loophole. I appreciate Argo's position that by buying up the small claims it was providing the original creditors with liquidity but this should not be a determinative factor. I would note that the sliding scale provided here does recognize (albeit imperfectly) that small claims may be equated with small creditors who would more likely wish cash as opposed to non-board lots of shares which would not be as liquidate as cash; the high percentage cash for those proven claims of $7,500 or under illustrates the desire not to have the "little person" hurt—at least any more than is necessary. The question will come down to balance—the plan must be efficient and attractive enough for it to be brought forward by an applicant with the realistic chance of its succeeding (and perhaps in that regard be "sponsored" by significant creditors) and while not being too generous so that the future of the applicant on an ongoing basis would be in jeopardy: at the same time it must gain enough support amongst the creditor body for it to gain the requisite majority. New creditors by assignment may provide not only liquidity but also a benefit in providing a block of support for a plan which may not have been forthcoming as a small creditor may not think it important to do so. Argo of course has not claimed it is a "little person" in the context of this CCAA proceeding.

[8] In my view Argo is being treated fairly and reasonably as a creditor as are all the unsecured creditors. An aggregation clause is not inherently unfair and the sliding scale provisions would appear to me to be aimed at "protecting (or helping out) the little guy" which would appear to be a reasonable policy.

[9] The Plan is sanctioned and approved; Argo's aggregation motion is dismissed.

. . .

Motion for approval granted; motion for amendment dismissed.

QUESTIONS

Is the inclusion of the sliding-scale formula truly intended to "help out the little guy," or is it included to ensure that the plan will obtain the support of a majority in number of the creditors? Or is it included in order to dissuade creditors from acquiring the rights of other creditors for the purpose of voting on the plan? Is it fair and reasonable that creditors who have identical legal rights are treated differently—that is, unsecured creditors with smaller claims obtain a higher recovery than those with larger claims?

ATB Financial v. Metcalfe & Mansfield Alternative Investments II Corp.
(2008), 296 DLR (4th) 135 (Ont. CA)

BLAIR JA:

A. Introduction

[1] In August 2007 a liquidity crisis suddenly threatened the Canadian market in Asset Backed Commercial Paper ("ABCP"). The crisis was triggered by a loss of confidence amongst investors stemming from the news of widespread defaults on US sub-prime mortgages. The loss of confidence placed the Canadian financial market at risk generally and was reflective of an economic volatility worldwide.

[2] By agreement amongst the major Canadian participants, the $32 billion Canadian market in third-party ABCP was frozen on August 13, 2007 pending an attempt to resolve the crisis through a restructuring of that market. The Pan-Canadian Investors Committee, chaired by Purdy Crawford, CC, QC, was formed and ultimately put forward the creditor-initiated Plan of Compromise and Arrangement that forms the subject-matter of these proceedings. The Plan was sanctioned by Colin L. Campbell J on June 5, 2008.

[3] Certain creditors who opposed the Plan seek leave to appeal and, if leave is granted, appeal from that decision. They raise an important point regarding the permissible scope of a restructuring under the *Companies' Creditors Arrangement Act*, RSC 1985, c. C-36 as amended ("CCAA"): can the court sanction a Plan that calls for creditors to provide releases to third parties who are themselves solvent and not creditors of the debtor company? They also argue that, if the answer to this question is yes, the application judge erred in holding that this Plan, with its particular releases (which bar some claims even in fraud), was fair and reasonable and therefore [erred] in sanctioning it under the CCAA.

. . .

B. Facts

(1) The Parties

[7] The appellants are holders of ABCP Notes who oppose the Plan. They do so principally on the basis that it requires them to grant releases to third party financial institutions

against whom they say they have claims for relief arising out of their purchase of ABCP Notes. Amongst them are an airline, a tour operator, a mining company, a wireless provider, a pharmaceuticals retailer, and several holding companies and energy companies.

[8] Each of the appellants has large sums invested in ABCP—in some cases, hundreds of millions of dollars. Nonetheless, the collective holdings of the appellants—slightly over $1 billion—represent only a small fraction of the more than $32 billion of ABCP involved in the restructuring.

[9] The lead respondent is the Pan-Canadian Investors Committee which was responsible for the creation and negotiation of the Plan on behalf of the creditors. Other respondents include various major international financial institutions, the five largest Canadian banks, several trust companies, and some smaller holders of ABCP product. They participated in the market in a number of different ways.

(2) The ABCP Market

[10] Asset Backed Commercial Paper is a sophisticated and hitherto well-accepted financial instrument. It is primarily a form of short-term investment—usually 30 to 90 days—typically with a low interest yield only slightly better than that available through other short-term paper from a government or bank. It is said to be "asset backed" because the cash that is used to purchase an ABCP Note is converted into a portfolio of financial assets or other asset interests that in turn provide security for the repayment of the notes.

[11] ABCP was often presented by those selling it as a safe investment, somewhat like a guaranteed investment certificate.

[12] The Canadian market for ABCP is significant and administratively complex. As of August 2007, investors had placed over $116 billion in Canadian ABCP. Investors range from individual pensioners to large institutional bodies. On the selling and distribution end, numerous players are involved, including chartered banks, investment houses and other financial institutions. Some of these players participated in multiple ways. The Plan in this proceeding relates to approximately $32 billion of non-bank sponsored ABCP the restructuring of which is considered essential to the preservation of the Canadian ABCP market.

· · ·

(3) The Liquidity Crisis

[17] The types of assets and asset interests acquired to "back" the ABCP Notes are varied and complex. They were generally long-term assets such as residential mortgages, credit card receivables, auto loans, cash collateralized debt obligations and derivative investments such as credit default swaps. Their particular characteristics do not matter for the purpose of this appeal, but they shared a common feature that proved to be the Achilles heel of the ABCP market: because of their long-term nature there was an inherent timing mismatch between the cash they generated and the cash needed to repay maturing ABCP Notes.

[18] When uncertainty began to spread through the ABCP marketplace in the summer of 2007, investors stopped buying the ABCP product and existing Noteholders ceased to roll over their maturing notes. There was no cash to redeem those notes. Al-

though calls were made on the Liquidity Providers for payment, most of the Liquidity Providers declined to fund the redemption of the notes, arguing that the conditions for liquidity funding had not been met in the circumstances. Hence the "liquidity crisis" in the ABCP market.

[19] The crisis was fuelled largely by a lack of transparency in the ABCP scheme. Investors could not tell what assets were backing their notes—partly because the ABCP Notes were often sold before or at the same time as the assets backing them were acquired; partly because of the sheer complexity of certain of the underlying assets; and partly because of assertions of confidentiality by those involved with the assets. As fears arising from the spreading US sub-prime mortgage crisis mushroomed, investors became increasingly concerned that their ABCP Notes may be supported by those crumbling assets. For the reasons outlined above, however, they were unable to redeem their maturing ABCP Notes.

. . .

(4) The Plan

a) Plan Overview

[24] Although the ABCP market involves many different players and kinds of assets, each with their own challenges, the committee opted for a single plan. In Mr. Crawford's words, "all of the ABCP suffers from common problems that are best addressed by a common solution." The Plan the Committee developed is highly complex and involves many parties. In its essence, the Plan would convert the Noteholders' paper—which has been frozen and therefore effectively worthless for many months—into new, long-term notes that would trade freely, but with a discounted face value. The hope is that a strong secondary market for the notes will emerge in the long run.

[25] The Plan aims to improve transparency by providing investors with detailed information about the assets supporting their ABCP Notes. It also addresses the timing mismatch between the notes and the assets by adjusting the maturity provisions and interest rates on the new notes. Further, the Plan adjusts some of the underlying credit default swap contracts by increasing the thresholds for default triggering events; in this way, the likelihood of a forced liquidation flowing from the credit default swap holder's prior security is reduced and, in turn, the risk for ABCP investors is decreased.

[26] Under the Plan, the vast majority of the assets underlying ABCP would be pooled into two master asset vehicles (MAV1 and MAV2). The pooling is designed to increase the collateral available and thus make the notes more secure.

[27] The Plan does not apply to investors holding less than $1 million of notes. However, certain Dealers have agreed to buy the ABCP of those of their customers holding less than the $1-million threshold, and to extend financial assistance to these customers. Principal among these Dealers are National Bank and Canaccord, two of the respondent financial institutions the appellants most object to releasing. The application judge found that these developments appeared to be designed to secure votes in favour of the Plan by various Noteholders, and were apparently successful in doing so. If the Plan is approved, they also provide considerable relief to the many small investors who find themselves unwittingly caught in the ABDP collapse.

b) The Releases

[28] This appeal focuses on one specific aspect of the Plan: the comprehensive series of releases of third parties provided for in Article 10.

[29] The Plan calls for the release of Canadian banks, Dealers, Noteholders, Asset Providers, Issuer Trustees, Liquidity Providers, and other market participants—in Mr. Crawford's words, "virtually all participants in the Canadian ABCP market"—from any liability associated with ABCP, with the exception of certain narrow claims relating to fraud. For instance, under the Plan as approved, creditors will have to give up their claims against the Dealers who sold them their ABCP Notes, including challenges to the way the Dealers characterized the ABCP and provided (or did not provide) information about the ABCP. The claims against the proposed defendants are mainly in tort: negligence, misrepresentation, negligent misrepresentation, failure to act prudently as a dealer/advisor, acting in conflict of interest, and in a few cases fraud or potential fraud. There are also allegations of breach of fiduciary duty and claims for other equitable relief.

[30] The application judge found that, in general, the claims for damages include the face value of the Notes, plus interest and additional penalties and damages.

[31] The releases, in effect, are part of a *quid pro quo*. Generally speaking, they are designed to compensate various participants in the market for the contributions they would make to the restructuring. Those contributions under the Plan include the requirements that:

a)   Asset Providers assume an increased risk in their credit default swap contracts, disclose certain proprietary information in relation to the assets, and provide below-cost financing for margin funding facilities that are designed to make the notes more secure;

b)   Sponsors—who in addition have cooperated with the Investors' Committee throughout the process, including by sharing certain proprietary information— give up their existing contracts;

c)   The Canadian banks provide below-cost financing for the margin funding facility and,

d)   Other parties make other contributions under the Plan.

[32] According to Mr. Crawford's affidavit, the releases are part of the Plan "because certain key participants, whose participation is vital to the restructuring, have made comprehensive releases a condition for their participation."

(5) The CCAA Proceedings to Date

[33] On March 17, 2008 the applicants sought and obtained an Initial Order under the CCAA staying any proceedings relating to the ABCP crisis and providing for a meeting of the Noteholders to vote on the proposed Plan. The meeting was held on April 25th. The vote was overwhelmingly in support of the Plan—96% of the Noteholders voted in favour. At the instance of certain Noteholders, and as requested by the application judge (who has supervised the proceedings from the outset), the Monitor broke down the voting results according to those Noteholders who had worked on or with the Investors' Committee to develop the Plan and those Noteholders who had not. Re-calculated on

this basis the results remained firmly in favour of the proposed Plan—99% of those connected with the development of the Plan voted positively, as did 80% of those Noteholders who had not been involved in its formulation.

[34] The vote thus provided the Plan with the "double majority" approval—a majority of creditors representing two-thirds in value of the claims—required under s. 6 of the CCAA.

[35] Following the successful vote, the applicants sought court approval of the Plan under s. 6. Hearings were held on May 12 and 13. On May 16, the application judge issued a brief endorsement in which he concluded that he did not have sufficient facts to decide whether all the releases proposed in the Plan were authorized by the CCAA. While the application judge was prepared to approve the releases of negligence claims, he was not prepared at that point to sanction the release of fraud claims. Noting the urgency of the situation and the serious consequences that would result from the Plan's failure, the application judge nevertheless directed the parties back to the bargaining table to try to work out a claims process for addressing legitimate claims of fraud.

[36] The result of this renegotiation was a "fraud carve-out"—an amendment to the Plan excluding certain fraud claims from the Plan's releases. The carve-out did not encompass all possible claims of fraud, however. It was limited in three key respects. First, it applied only to claims against ABCP Dealers. Secondly, it applied only to cases involving an express fraudulent misrepresentation made with the intention to induce purchase and in circumstances where the person making the representation knew it to be false. Thirdly, the carve-out limited available damages to the value of the notes, minus any funds distributed as part of the Plan. The appellants argue vigorously that such a limited release respecting fraud claims is unacceptable and should not have been sanctioned by the application judge.

[37] A second sanction hearing—this time involving the amended Plan (with the fraud carve-out)—was held on June 3, 2008. Two days later, Campbell J released his reasons for decision, approving and sanctioning the Plan on the basis both that he had jurisdiction to sanction a Plan calling for third-party releases and that the Plan including the third-party releases in question here was fair and reasonable.

[38] The appellants attack both of these determinations.

C. Law and Analysis

[39] There are two principal questions for determination on this appeal:

1) As a matter of law, may a CCAA plan contain a release of claims against anyone other than the debtor company or its directors?

2) If the answer to that question is yes, did the application judge err in the exercise of his discretion to sanction the Plan as fair and reasonable given the nature of the releases called for under it?

(1) Legal Authority for the Releases

[40] The standard of review on this first issue—whether, as a matter of law, a CCAA plan may contain third-party releases—is correctness.

[41] The appellants submit that a court has no jurisdiction or legal authority under the CCAA to sanction a plan that imposes an obligation on creditors to give releases to third parties other than the directors of the debtor company. The requirement that objecting creditors release claims against third parties is illegal, they contend, because:

a) on a proper interpretation, the CCAA does not permit such releases;

b) the court is not entitled to "fill in the gaps" in the CCAA or rely upon its inherent jurisdiction to create such authority because to do so would be contrary to the principle that Parliament did not intend to interfere with private property rights or rights of action in the absence of clear statutory language to that effect;

c) the releases constitute an unconstitutional confiscation of private property that is within the exclusive domain of the provinces under s. 92 of the *Constitution Act, 1867*;

d) the releases are invalid under Quebec rules of public order; and because

e) the prevailing jurisprudence supports these conclusions.

[42] I would not give effect to any of these submissions.

· · ·

[43] On a proper interpretation, in my view, the CCAA permits the inclusion of third party releases in a plan of compromise or arrangement to be sanctioned by the court where those releases are reasonably connected to the proposed restructuring. I am led to this conclusion by a combination of (a) the open-ended, flexible character of the CCAA itself, (b) the broad nature of the term "compromise or arrangement" as used in the Act, and (c) the express statutory effect of the "double-majority" vote and court sanction which render the plan binding on *all* creditors, including those unwilling to accept certain portions of it. The first of these signals a flexible approach to the application of the Act in new and evolving situations, an active judicial role in its application and interpretation, and a liberal approach to that interpretation. The second provides the entrée to negotiations between the parties affected in the restructuring and furnishes them with the ability to apply the broad scope of their ingenuity in fashioning the proposal. The latter afford necessary protection to unwilling creditors who may be deprived of certain of their civil and property rights as a result of the process.

[44] The CCAA is skeletal in nature. It does not contain a comprehensive code that lays out all that is permitted or barred. Judges must therefore play a role in fleshing out the details of the statutory scheme. The scope of the Act and the powers of the court under it are not limitless. It is beyond controversy, however, that the CCAA is remedial legislation to be liberally construed in accordance with the modern purposive approach to statutory interpretation. It is designed to be a flexible instrument and it is that very flexibility which gives the Act its efficacy: *Canadian Red Cross Society (Re)*, 1998 CanLII 14907 (ONSC), (1998), 5 CBR (4th) 299 (Ont. Gen. Div.). As Farley J noted in *Re Dylex Ltd.*, 1995 CanLII 7370 (ONSC), (1995), 31 CBR (3d) 106 at 111 (Ont. Gen. Div.), "[t]he history of CCAA law has been an evolution of judicial interpretation."

· · ·

[53] An interpretation of the CCAA that recognizes its broader socio-economic purposes and objects is apt in this case. As the application judge pointed out, the restructuring underpins the financial viability of the Canadian ABCP market itself.

[54] The appellants argue that the application judge erred in taking this approach and in treating the Plan and the proceedings as an attempt to restructure a financial market (the ABCP market) rather than simply the affairs between the debtor corporations who caused the ABCP Notes to be issued and their creditors. The Act is designed, they say, only to effect reorganizations between a corporate debtor and its creditors and not to attempt to restructure entire marketplaces.

[55] This perspective is flawed in at least two respects, however, in my opinion. First, it reflects a view of the purpose and objects of the CCAA that is too narrow. Secondly, it overlooks the reality of the ABCP marketplace and the context of the restructuring in question here. It may be true that, in their capacity as ABCP *Dealers*, the releasee financial institutions are "third-parties" to the restructuring in the sense that they are not creditors of the debtor corporations. However, in their capacities as *Asset Providers* and *Liquidity Providers*, they are not only creditors but they are prior secured creditors to the Noteholders. Furthermore—as the application judge found—in these latter capacities they are making significant contributions to the restructuring by "foregoing immediate rights to assets and ... providing real and tangible input for the preservation and enhancement of the Notes" (para. 76). In this context, therefore, the application judge's remark at para. 50 that the restructuring "involves the commitment and participation of all parties" in the ABCP market makes sense, as do his earlier comments at paras. 48-49:

> [48] Given the nature of the ABCP market and all of its participants, it is more appropriate to consider all Noteholders as claimants and the object of the Plan to restore liquidity to the assets being the Notes themselves. The restoration of the liquidity of the market necessitates the participation (including more tangible contribution by many) of all Noteholders.
>
> [49] In these circumstances, *it is unduly technical to classify the Issuer Trustees as debtors and the claims of the Noteholders as between themselves and others as being those of third party creditors,* although I recognize that the restructuring structure of the CCAA requires the corporations as the vehicles for restructuring. [Emphasis added.]

· · ·

[60] While there may be little practical distinction between "compromise" and "arrangement" in many respects, the two are not necessarily the same. "Arrangement" is broader than "compromise" and would appear to include any scheme for reorganizing the affairs of the debtor: Houlden & Morawetz, *Bankruptcy and Insolvency Law of Canada*, loose-leaf, 3rd ed., vol. 4 (Toronto: Thomson Carswell) at 10A-12.2, N§10. It has been said to be "a very wide and indefinite [word]": *Re Refund of Dues under Timber Regulations*, [1935] AC 184 at 197 (PC), affirming SCC [1933] SCR 616. See also, *Re Guardian Assur. Co.*, [1917] 1 Ch. 431 at 448, 450; *Re T&N Ltd. and Others (No. 3)*, [2007] 1 All ER 851 (Ch.).

[61] The CCAA is a sketch, an outline, a supporting framework for the resolution of corporate insolvencies in the public interest. Parliament wisely avoided attempting to anticipate the myriad of business deals that could evolve from the fertile and creative

minds of negotiators restructuring their financial affairs. It left the shape and details of those deals to be worked out within the framework of the comprehensive and flexible concepts of a "compromise" and "arrangement." I see no reason why a release in favour of a third party, negotiated as part of a package between a debtor and creditor and reasonably relating to the proposed restructuring cannot fall within that framework.

[62] A proposal under the *Bankruptcy and Insolvency Act*, RS, 1985, c. B-3 (the "BIA") is a contract: *Employers' Liability Assurance Corp. Ltd. v. Ideal Petroleum (1959) Ltd.*, 1976 CanLII 142 (SCC), [1978] 1 SCR 230 at 239; *Society of Composers, Authors & Music Publishers of Canada v. Armitage* 2000 CanLII 16921 (ONCA), (2000), 50 OR (3d) 688 at para. 11 (CA). In my view, a compromise or arrangement under the CCAA is directly analogous to a proposal for these purposes, and therefore is to be treated as a contract between the debtor and its creditors. Consequently, parties are entitled to put anything into such a plan that could lawfully be incorporated into any contract. See *Re Air Canada*, 2004 CanLII 34416 (ONSC), (2004), 2 CBR (5th) 4 at para. 6 (Ont. SCJ); *Olympia & York Developments Ltd. v. Royal Trust Co.* (1993), 12 OR (3d) 500 at 518 (Gen. Div.).

[63] There is nothing to prevent a debtor and a creditor from including in a contract between them a term providing that the creditor release a third party. The term is binding as between the debtor and creditor. In the CCAA context, therefore, a plan of compromise or arrangement may propose that creditors agree to compromise claims against the debtor and to release third parties, just as any debtor and creditor might agree to such a term in a contract between them. Once the statutory mechanism regarding voter approval and court sanctioning has been complied with, the plan—including the provision for releases—becomes binding on all creditors (including the dissenting minority).

· · ·

[68] Parliament's reliance on the expansive terms "compromise" or "arrangement" does not stand alone, however. Effective insolvency restructurings would not be possible without a statutory mechanism to bind an unwilling minority of creditors. Unanimity is frequently impossible in such situations. But the minority must be protected too. Parliament's solution to this quandary was to permit a wide range of proposals to be negotiated and put forward (the compromise or arrangement) and to bind *all* creditors by class to the terms of the plan, but to do so only where the proposal can gain the support of the requisite "double majority" of votes *and* obtain the sanction of the court on the basis that it is fair and reasonable. In this way, the scheme of the CCAA supports the intention of Parliament to encourage a wide variety of solutions to corporate insolvencies without unjustifiably overriding the rights of dissenting creditors.

· · ·

[69] In keeping with this scheme and purpose, I do not suggest that any and all releases between creditors of the debtor company seeking to restructure and third parties may be made the subject of a compromise or arrangement between the debtor and its creditors. Nor do I think the fact that the releases may be "necessary" in the sense that the third parties or the debtor may refuse to proceed without them, of itself, advances the argument in favour of finding jurisdiction (although it may well be relevant in terms of the fairness and reasonableness analysis).

[70] The release of the claim in question must be justified as part of the compromise or arrangement between the debtor and its creditors. In short, there must be a reasonable

connection between the third party claim being compromised in the plan and the restructuring achieved by the plan to warrant inclusion of the third party release in the plan. This nexus exists here, in my view.

[71] In the course of his reasons, the application judge made the following findings, all of which are amply supported on the record:

a) The parties to be released are necessary and essential to the restructuring of the debtor;

b) The claims to be released are rationally related to the purpose of the Plan and necessary for it;

c) The Plan cannot succeed without the releases;

d) The parties who are to have claims against them released are contributing in a tangible and realistic way to the Plan; and

e) The Plan will benefit not only the debtor companies but creditor Noteholders generally.

[72] Here, then ... there is a close connection between the claims being released and the restructuring proposal. The tort claims arise out of the sale and distribution of the ABCP Notes and their collapse in value, just as do the contractual claims of the creditors against the debtor companies. The purpose of the restructuring is to stabilize and shore up the value of those notes in the long run. The third parties being released are making separate contributions to enable those results to materialize. Those contributions are identified earlier, at para. 31 of these reasons. The application judge found that the claims being released are not independent of or unrelated to the claims that the Noteholders have against the debtor companies; they are closely connected to the value of the ABCP Notes and are required for the Plan to succeed. At paras. 76-77 he said:

> [76] I do not consider that the Plan in this case involves a change in relationship among creditors "that does not directly involve the Company." Those who support the Plan and are to be released are "directly involved in the Company" in the sense that many are foregoing immediate rights to assets and are providing real and tangible input for the preservation and enhancement of the Notes. It would be unduly restrictive to suggest that the moving parties' claims against released parties do not involve the Company, since the claims are directly related to the value of the Notes. The value of the Notes is in this case the value of the Company.
>
> [77] This Plan, as it deals with releases, doesn't change the relationship of the creditors apart from involving the Company and its Notes.

[73] I am satisfied that the wording of the CCAA—construed in light of the purpose, objects and scheme of the Act and in accordance with the modern principles of statutory interpretation—supports the court's jurisdiction and authority to sanction the Plan

· · ·

(2) The Plan Is "Fair and Reasonable"

[106] The second major attack on the application judge's decision is that he erred in finding that the Plan is "fair and reasonable" and in sanctioning it on that basis. This attack is centred on the nature of the third-party releases contemplated and, in particular, on the fact that they will permit the release of some claims based in fraud.

[107] Whether a plan of compromise or arrangement is fair and reasonable is a matter of mixed fact and law, and one on which the application judge exercises a large measure of discretion. The standard of review on this issue is therefore one of deference. In the absence of a demonstrable error an appellate court will not interfere: see *Re Ravelston Corp. Ltd.*, 2007 ONCA 268 (CanLII), (2007), 31 CBR (5th) 233 (Ont. CA).

[108] I would not interfere with the application judge's decision in this regard. While the notion of releases in favour of third parties—including leading Canadian financial institutions—that extend to claims of fraud is distasteful, there is no legal impediment to the inclusion of a release for claims based in fraud in a plan of compromise or arrangement. The application judge had been living with and supervising the ABCP restructuring from its outset. He was intimately attuned to its dynamics. In the end he concluded that the benefits of the Plan to the creditors as a whole, and to the debtor companies, outweighed the negative aspects of compelling the unwilling appellants to execute the releases as finally put forward.

[109] The application judge was concerned about the inclusion of fraud in the contemplated releases and at the May hearing adjourned the final disposition of the sanctioning hearing in an effort to encourage the parties to negotiate a resolution. The result was the "fraud carve-out" referred to earlier in these reasons.

[110] The appellants argue that the fraud carve-out is inadequate because of its narrow scope. It (i) applies only to ABCP Dealers, (ii) limits the type of damages that may be claimed (no punitive damages, for example), (iii) defines "fraud" narrowly, excluding many rights that would be protected by common law, equity and the Quebec concept of public order, and (iv) limits claims to representations made directly to Noteholders. The appellants submit it is contrary to public policy to sanction a plan containing such a limited restriction on the type of fraud claims that may be pursued against the third parties.

[111] The law does not condone fraud. It is the most serious kind of civil claim. There is therefore some force to the appellants' submission. On the other hand, as noted, there is no legal impediment to granting the release of an antecedent claim in fraud, provided the claim is in the contemplation of the parties to the release at the time it is given: *Fotinis Restaurant Corp. v. White Spot Ltd.*, 1998 CanLII 3836 (BCSC), (1998), 38 BLR (2d) 251 at paras. 9 and 18 (BCSC). There may be disputes about the scope or extent of what is released, but parties are entitled to settle allegations of fraud in civil proceedings—the claims here all being untested allegations of fraud—and to include releases of such claims as part of that settlement.

[112] The application judge was alive to the merits of the appellants' submissions. He was satisfied in the end, however, that the need "to avoid the potential cascade of litigation that ... would result if a broader 'carve out' were to be allowed" (para. 113) outweighed the negative aspects of approving releases with the narrower carve-out provision. Implementation of the Plan, in his view, would work to the overall greater benefit

of the Noteholders as a whole. I can find no error in principle in the exercise of his discretion in arriving at this decision. It was his call to make.

· · ·

[115] The appellants all contend that the obligation to release the third parties from claims in fraud, tort, breach of fiduciary duty, etc. is confiscatory and amounts to a requirement that they—as individual creditors—make the equivalent of a greater financial contribution to the Plan. In his usual lively fashion, Mr. Sternberg asked us the same rhetorical question he posed to the application judge. As he put it, how could the court countenance the compromise of what in the future might turn out to be fraud perpetrated at the highest levels of Canadian and foreign banks? Several appellants complain that the proposed Plan is unfair to them because they will make very little additional recovery if the Plan goes forward, but will be required to forfeit a cause of action against third-party financial institutions that may yield them significant recovery. Others protest that they are being treated unequally because they are ineligible for relief programs that Liquidity Providers such as Canaccord have made available to other smaller investors.

[116] All of these arguments are persuasive to varying degrees when considered in isolation. The application judge did not have that luxury, however. He was required to consider the circumstances of the restructuring as a whole, including the reality that many of the financial institutions were not only acting as Dealers or brokers of the ABCP Notes (with the impugned releases relating to the financial institutions in these capacities, for the most part) but also as Asset and Liquidity Providers (with the financial institutions making significant contributions to the restructuring in these capacities).

[117] In insolvency restructuring proceedings almost everyone loses something. To the extent that creditors are required to compromise their claims, it can always be proclaimed that their rights are being unfairly confiscated and that they are being called upon to make the equivalent of a further financial contribution to the compromise or arrangement. Judges have observed on a number of occasions that CCAA proceedings involve "a balancing of prejudices," inasmuch as everyone is adversely affected in some fashion.

[118] Here, the debtor corporations being restructured represent the issuers of the more than $32 billion in non-bank sponsored ABCP Notes. The proposed compromise and arrangement affects that entire segment of the ABCP market and the financial markets as a whole. In that respect, the application judge was correct in adverting to the importance of the restructuring to the resolution of the ABCP liquidity crisis and to the need to restore confidence in the financial system in Canada. He was required to consider and balance the interests of *all* Noteholders, not just the interests of the appellants, whose notes represent only about 3% of that total. That is what he did.

[119] The application judge noted at para. 126 that the Plan represented "a reasonable balance between benefit to all Noteholders and enhanced recovery for those who can make out specific claims in fraud" within the fraud carve-out provisions of the releases. He also recognized at para. 134 that:

> [134] No Plan of this size and complexity could be expected to satisfy all affected by it. The size of the majority who have approved it is testament to its overall fairness. No plan to address a crisis of this magnitude can work perfect equity among all stakeholders.

[120] In my view we ought not to interfere with his decision that the Plan is fair and reasonable in all the circumstances.

Appeal dismissed.

NOTE

1. In *Re Canadian Airlines Corp.* (2000), 20 CBR (4th) 1 (Alta. QB), Paperny J considered the following matters in deciding whether a plan was fair and reasonable:

   a. the composition of the unsecured vote;
   b. what creditors would receive on liquidation or bankruptcy as compared to the Plan;
   c. alternatives available to the Plan and bankruptcy;
   d. oppression;
   e. unfairness to shareholders; and
   f. the public interest.

2. If a plan is not approved by the creditors or is not sanctioned by the court, this does not result in an automatic bankruptcy, as is the case under the commercial proposal provisions of the BIA. Instead, the creditors are able to assert their enforcement rights and remedies as soon as the stay of proceedings granted by the court comes to an end. The usual result is that the debtor or the creditors will institute bankruptcy or receivership proceedings.

PART IV

BIA Proposals

CHAPTER SIXTEEN

BIA Commercial Proposals

I. GENESIS AND EVOLUTION OF COMMERCIAL PROPOSALS

The *Bankruptcy Act, 1919* contained skeletal provisions, copied from the British *Bankruptcy Act*, enabling insolvent debtors, not restricted to particular types of debtors, to make a proposal to their creditors for the payment of their debts and thereby avoid the fatal bankruptcy solution. However, the 1919 Act's commitment to a rescue philosophy was weak for the following reasons: (1) a proposal could only be made to unsecured creditors; (2) no interim period was allowed between initiating the proceedings and filing the proposal; and (3) filing the proposal did not entitle the debtor to repudiate executory contracts or preclude creditors from terminating their contracts with the debtor. Not surprisingly, therefore, proposals did not play an important role in Canada's bankruptcy regime in the interwar period, although factors other than the restricted scope of the device also accounted for its limited use.

In the post-World War II period, there was a strong revival of interest in strengthening the reorganizational options open to insolvent debtors. The Tassé Report (Chapters 1 and 2) [contained ambitious recommendations for recasting the proposal provisions and replacing the CCAA. These were incorporated in varying forms in successive bills introduced in Parliament between 1975 and 1984. However, none of the bills was enacted—for reasons that had less to do with the merits of the bills than with lack of political will by successive governments to secure the bills' adoption. To resolve the deadlock, the Colter Committee was established by the Mulroney government in 1984 (again, see Chapter 1) with the mandate to recommend changes to the bankruptcy regime that they deemed to be most urgent.

The Colter Committee's 1986 Report (Advisory Committee on Bankruptcy and Insolvency, *Proposed Bankruptcy Act Amendments; Report of the Advisory Committee on Bankruptcy and Insolvency* (Hull, QC: Supply and Services Canada, 1986)) singled out commercial and consumer proposals as two of the areas deserving prompt remedial action. As far as commercial proposals were concerned, the Report recommended the following changes: (1) the debtor should be allowed an interim period to give notice of intention to file a proposal before having to file the proposal itself; (2) proposals should be allowed to target secured as well as unsecured creditors (thereby also giving the debtor the benefit of a stay of proceedings by secured as well as unsecured creditors); and (3) the debtor should be allowed to disclaim executory contracts and realty leases, and third parties should be restrained from terminating contracts that were important for the debtor's economic survival.

The Committee's Report was critical of important aspects of Chapter 11 of the US *Bankruptcy Code* and thought that, overall, its provisions were too favourable to debtors and too harsh on secured creditors. The Committee favoured a "made-in-Canada" proposal regime that included strong checks and balances to prevent debtor abuse of its provisions. The

Committee made no recommendations with respect to the future of the CCAA, but apparently assumed the Act would fade away from disuse because of its restrictive provisions, which made it unsuitable for all but a tiny number of struggling enterprises.[1]

All of the Colter Committee recommendations involving commercial proposals were adopted in the BIA 1992 amendments. The key features of the regime are described below.[2] Commercial proposals (CPs) have proved popular with debtors from the beginning of the new regime. Their number increased steadily between 1993 and 2002 (from 1,005 in 1993 to 1,911 in 2002, and from 7.90 percent of the number of business filings in 1993 to 18.30 percent in 2002), then decreased over the next few years as the Canadian economy boomed. In 2004, the number of CPs declined by 5.4 percent to 1,728.[3] In the 12-month period ending August 31, 2008, there were 1,308 commercial proposals and 6,151 business bankruptcies. Impressive as these statistics are, it is important to bear in mind that the rate of successful completion of proposals has been much more modest than the number of proposal filings.[4]

The 1997 amendments to the BIA made some modest changes to commercial proposals. The really significant changes appear in the 2005-7 amendments to the BIA and, for the most part, are a mirror image of the changes made to the CCAA. The BIA commercial proposal changes cover the following main areas:

- Authorization of interim financing arrangements by court: s. 50.6. Compare new CCAA s. 11.2, discussed in Chapter 13, Section VI.

- No court approval of employer proposals unless employer has made good arrears in payments to employer–employee pensions funds and to defined pension benefit plans: s. 60(1.5). Compare new CCAA s. 6(5), discussed in Chapter 14, Section III.

- No release to debtor from s. 178(1) BIA debts unless prescribed conditions are met: s. 62(2.1)

- On application, court may remove director of debtor company and fill vacancy created by director's removal: s. 64. Compare new CCAA s. 11.5, discussed in Chapter 13, Section III.

- Court may authorize security to directors and officers of the debtor company against obligations incurred by them after the initiation of proposal proceedings: s. 64.1. Compare new CCAA s. 11.51, discussed in Chapter 13, Section III.

---

1. As described in Chapter 1, the Committee's assumption was mistaken because, between 1984 and 1992, the courts engaged in a radical reinterpretation of the CCAA provisions to make them much more user friendly.

2. The term "commercial proposal" in Part III, Division 1, of the BIA is misleading because its provisions apply to all insolvent debtors, whether engaged in business or not, and to individual as well as business debtors. In fact, from the introduction of the new proposal regime in 1992, the number of proposals made by individual debtors has greatly exceeded the number of proposals made by incorporated businesses.

3. OSB, *An Overview of Canadian Insolvency Statistics Up to 2004*, pp. 40 et seq. The OSB statistics refer to commercial proposals as "Business Proposals." For reasons of consistency, this chapter uses the statutory term of commercial proposals.

4. See below, Section IV.

- Court may also authorize security for costs, including legal expenses incurred by interim receivers, receivers, receiver-managers, and trustees of debtors involved in proposal proceedings: s. 64.2. Compare new CCAA s. 11.52.

- Existing invalidation of *ipso facto*, acceleration and forfeiture clauses extended to such clauses in security agreements with debtor: s. 65.1. Compare new CCAA s. 34, discussed in Chapter 13, Section IV, above.

- Debtor permitted, on application by trustee, to resiliate or disclaim agreements but subject to judicial veto if the other party objects: s. 65.11. Compare new CCAA s. 32, discussed in Chapter 13, Section IV.

- Provision for a new definition of "eligible financial contract" to be prescribed by regulation: s. 65.1(8) and Eligible Financial Contract General Rules (*Bankruptcy and Insolvency Act*). Compare new CCAA s. 11.05(2) and Eligible Financial Contract General Rules (*Companies Creditors' Arrangement Act*), discussed in Chapter 13, Section V.

- On application by trustee, court may authorize assignment of contracts: s. 84.1. Compare new CCAA s. 11.3, discussed in Chapter 13, Section IV.

- Court authorization for debtor to serve notice to bargain on other parties to employer-employee bargaining agreement: s. 65.12. Compare new CCAA s. 33, discussed in Chapter 13, Section IV.

- Restriction on disposition of assets, other than in ordinary course, without court approval: s. 65.13. Compare new CCAA s. 36, discussed in Chapter 13, Section VII.

- Subordination of equity claims: s. 54.1. Compare new CCAA s. 22.1, discussed in Chapter 15, Section V.

Given the fact that by far the largest number of commercial proposals to date have involved business and individual debtors with assets below $1 million, it is difficult to predict what impact the 2005-7 amendments will have on future proposals under the BIA. The likelihood is that most of them will have little, if any, impact.

The fact that the drafters of the 2005-7 CCAA amendments deemed it appropriate to duplicate the amendments in the BIA, nevertheless, raises anew the question, previously adverted to in earlier chapters of this casebook (see Chapters 1 and 12), whether it would not have been more efficient for the federal government to merge commercial proposals and the CCAA in a single reorganizational regime, but with differences to allow for the special needs of small reorganizations. An alternative approach would have been to integrate the CCAA with the BIA, but as a separate part of the BIA, to ensure that a common set of principles applied to all insolvency proceedings.[5] Regrettably, these options were never seriously considered because of strong opposition from the commercial insolvency bar and other professional organizations. They felt it best not to allow the CCAA to be tarred with the BIA

---

5. On these alternatives, see Jacob Ziegel, "The BIA and CCAA Interface," in Stephanie Ben-Ishai and Anthon Duggan, eds., *Canadian Bankruptcy and Insolvency Law: Bill C-55, Statute c. 47 and Beyond* (Toronto: LexisNexis, 2007), Chapter 12.

brush and were committed to retaining the autonomous character of the CCAA. A frequent argument heard before the 2005-7 amendments to the CCAA was that the rule-oriented character of the BIA commercial proposal regime was incompatible with the flexibility and judicial discretion that was the hallmark of the CCAA. This distinction between the two regimes is much more difficult to sustain in light of the many rule-oriented provisions added to the CCAA as a result of the 2005-7 amendments and, conversely, because of the many discretionary provisions added to Part III, Division 1, of the BIA. It is safe to predict that the last word has not been heard about this particular insolvency debate.

II. KEY FEATURES OF THE COMMERCIAL PROPOSAL REGIME

J.S. Ziegel and R.S. Sahni, "An Empirical Investigation of Corporate Division 1 Proposals in the Toronto Bankruptcy Region"
(2003), 41 *Osgoode Hall LJ* 665, at 673-81 (updated to incorporate references to the 2005-7 amendments; footnotes omitted)

A. Main Features of Part III.1

A reorganization can be initiated under the BIA either by the filing of a proposal [s. 50(1)] or the filing of a notice of intention (NOI) to file a proposal. [s. 50.4(1)]. Only an insolvent debtor can file a NOI, while a proposal can also be filed by a liquidator, a bankrupt person, the trustee of a bankrupt estate, or a receiver on behalf of secured creditors. In both cases, a stay of proceedings takes effect immediately on the filing of the document and is binding on all secured and unsecured creditors, including [with some exceptions] the Crown. [ss. 69, 69.1]. [The stay does not operate against a secured creditor who: (1) takes possession of the collateral before the filing of the NOI or proposal; or (2) serves a s. 244 enforcement notice more than 10 days before the NOI is filed]. There are no court proceedings at this stage and no creditor's consent is required. Equally important, the debtor company remains in possession and, so far as its resources permit, continues to carry on business as before.

In practice, most corporate debtors prefer to follow the NOI route. However, the Colter Committee was alert to the abuses to which a similar procedure has led under Chapter 11 of the US *Bankruptcy Code*. As a result, the Canadian regime contains the following safeguards to keep debtors on a short leash.

First, the debtor must appoint a trustee who is willing to act as monitor for the creditors' benefit and with whom the debtor must file a projected cash flow statement relating to the business within ten days of the NOI. The trustee in turn must sign a report on the reasonableness of the cash flow statement, which must be filed by the debtor with the official receiver together with the other documents. [s. 50.4(2)(b)]. The debtor must also give the trustee full access to its books for the purpose of monitoring the debtor's business and financial affairs. The trustee in turn is obliged to notify creditors of any adverse change in the debtor's financial condition subsequent to the initial filing [s. 50.4(7)].

Second, the debtor must file its proposal within thirty days of the NOI [s. 50.4(8)]; failure to do so results in an automatic deemed assignment in bankruptcy. The debtor can apply for an extension of time to file the proposal but no extension can run for more than forty-five days at a time. There is no restriction on the number of extensions for which the debtor can apply but they cannot exceed five months in duration from the end of the thirty days following the NOI [s. 50.4(9)]. The debtor must also meet some demanding tests before the court can grant an extension. The court must be satisfied that (a) the debtor is acting in good faith and with due diligence; (b) if given an extension, the debtor "would likely be able to make a viable proposal"; and, (c) "no creditor would be materially prejudiced if the extension being applied for were granted" [ibid.].

Third, any creditor is free at any time to apply for termination of the proceedings on the ground that the debtor "will not likely be able to make a proposal … that will be accepted by the creditors" [ibid., s. 50 (11)]. In practice, hostile creditors do not avail themselves of this ground as often as might be expected but seemingly prefer to wait until the creditors' meeting to cast their vote against the proposal.

B. Debtor in Possession Financing and Status of Executory Contracts

Given the fact that a proposal may not be presented to the creditors until six months have elapsed (although in practice most proposals are filed much sooner) and that an even longer period may elapse before the creditors meet to vote on the proposal, it is important to know whether the debtor will be in a position to stay in business this long. [Until the 2005-6 amendments, the BIA contained] no provisions authorizing debtor in possession (DIP) financing that can prime the claims of preferred or secured creditors. [See, however, *Re Bearcat* (2004), reproduced below, Section III]. However, so far as we have been able to ascertain, this does not appear to [have been] a significant problem in most BIA cases since the debtor's financial institution [was usually] willing to continue its secured line of operating credit if a line of credit [was] already in place and the financial institution [believed] itself to be adequately secured. Alternatively, the debtor's post-NOI cash flow may [have been] sufficient to keep the business afloat given the fact that the debtor is under no obligation to pay frozen claims during the stay period. The BIA does not state this explicitly but clearly implies the debtor's authority to pay post-filing claims incurred to enable the debtor to carry on business. [New BIA s. 50.6, enacted by the 2005-6 amendments, makes express provision for debtor-in-possession financing along the same lines as new CCAA s. 11.2].

· · ·

Contractual clauses purporting to terminate existing contracts, or that give the other contracting party the power to do so because of the initiation of insolvency proceedings, are declared unenforceable [s. 65.1(1)]. Similarly, leasing or licensing agreements cannot be terminated by the lessor or licensor in respect of the period preceding the NOI, if an NOI was filed, or in respect of the period preceding the proposal if no NOI was filed [s. 65.1(2)]. Likewise, suppliers of utility services cannot refuse to deal with the debtor so long as they are being paid promptly for post-NOI and post-proposal services and materials [ss. 65.1(3) and (4)]. [The 2005-6 amendments extend the application of s. 65.1 to *ipso facto* clauses in security agreements, and they create an exception preserving the repossession rights of a lessor of aircraft objects against a debtor-lessee].

C. Disclaimer of Executory Contracts

. . .

Sections 65.2 to 65.22 of the BIA contain specific provisions dealing with the repudiation of commercial realty leases which, in their earlier incarnation, provoked considerable litigation.

The pre-1997 version of section 65.2(2) provided that, within fifteen days of being given notice of the repudiation of a lease, the landlord could apply to the court for a declaration that the right of repudiation under subsection (1) was not to apply. Where such an application was made, the onus shifted to the debtor to show that it would not be able to make a viable proposal, or that the proposal the debtor had made would not be viable without repudiation of that lease and all other leases that the debtor had repudiated under subsection (1). Subsection (3) provided that if the repudiation was upheld, any proposal filed by the debtor also had to provide for payment to the landlord, immediately after court approval of the proposal, of compensation "equal to the lesser of an amount equal to six months rent under the lease, and the rent for the remainder of the lease, from the date on which the repudiation takes effect."

Debtor tenants objected that the obligation to pay the required compensation immediately on approval of the proposal was too onerous, especially in the case of debtors with many repudiated leases. Landlords, on the other hand, complained that the compensation provisions were inadequate in the case of long-term leases and given the poor market conditions for vacated premises. In response, the 1997 amendments eliminated the requirement for cash payment on approval of the proposal, denied the landlord any claim for accelerated rent, and required the proposal to offer the landlord a provable claim for the actual losses arising from the disclaimer of the lease, or for an amount equal to the lesser of:

(i)   the aggregate of

   (A) the rent provided for in the lease for the first year of the lease following the date on which the disclaimer becomes effective, and

   (B) fifteen per cent of the rent for the remainder of the term of the lease after that year, and

(ii) three years' rent [s. 65.2(4)].

The 1997 amendments also [contained] provisions for the classification of landlords' compensation claims that, subject to the availability of court review at the landlord's request, give the debtor the right either to put the landlord's claim in "a separate class of similar claims of landlords; or a class of unsecured claims that includes claims of creditors who are not landlords" [s. 65.2(5)]. The court is precluded from upholding a landlord's objection to disclaimer of the lease "if the court is satisfied that the insolvent person would not be able to make a viable proposal without the disclaimer of the lease and all other leases that the tenant has disclaimed under [the section]" [s. 65.2(3)].

So far there is very little jurisprudence interpreting [these] provisions [but see *Re Superstar Group of Companies* (2001), reproduced below, Section III]. If the issue were to arise, 1990s jurisprudence under the CCAA strongly suggests that Canadian courts will apply a balance of hardship test and uphold the lease repudiation if the consequences of not doing so will be more serious to the debtor than they would be for the landlord.

[Until the 2005-7 amendments, there were no provisions in the BIA relating to the disclaimer of other types of contract. However, it was generally assumed that the debtor remained free to exercise whatever rights existed at common law for this purpose in exchange for the creditor's entitlement to file a claim for damages: see Chapter 6, Section II. New BIA s. 65.11 fills this gap, giving the debtor in BIA commercial proposal proceedings a statutory right of disclaimer. The new provision does not apply to commercial tenancy agreements, which will continue to be governed by s. 65.2. There are various other exceptions, including eligible financial contracts, collective agreements, a financing agreement if the debtor is the borrower, and a lease of real property if the debtor is the lessor. Compare new CCAA s. 32: see Chapter 13, Section IV.]

D. Classification of Creditors and Voting on Proposal

The adroit classification of creditors—secured and unsecured—is of key importance to the debtor and its advisors in securing creditors' approval of a proposal, and has provoked much litigation in Canada, most of it under the CCAA. Section 50(1.2) of the BIA requires a proposal to be made to unsecured creditors generally as a mass or separated into classes but otherwise leaves it up to the debtor to decide which of its creditors it wishes to include in the proposal and how they are to be classified. There is almost no guidance with respect to the classification of unsecured claims although it is clear that there may be more than one class of unsecured creditors [s. 50.1(2)]. In the case of secured claims, section 50(1.4) provides that creditors may be included in the same class if the creditors holding those claims are sufficiently similar to give them a commonality of interest, taking into account:

(a) the nature of the debts giving rise to the claims;

(b) the nature and priority of the security in respect of the claims;

(c) the remedies available to the creditors in the absence of the proposal, and the extent to which the creditors would recover their claims by exercising those remedies;

(d) the treatment of the claims under the proposal, and the extent to which the claims would be paid under the proposal; and

(e) such further criteria, consistent with those set out in paragraphs (a) to (d), as are prescribed [s. 50(1.4)].

. . .

The test embodied in section 50(1.4) is generally assumed to follow the commonality of interest test adopted in Lord Justice Bowen's well-known judgment in *Sovereign Life Assurance Co. v. Dodd* [[1892] 2 QB 573]. That test has also been followed in Canada. However, starting in the late 1980s, Canadian courts veered away from the commonality test in favour of an "anti-fragmentation" test to prevent secured creditors from being able to torpedo an otherwise desirable proposal. The anti-fragmentation test is basically an economic test and asks whether, ignoring the legal distinctions between the secured parties' claims, the proposal treats them alike having regard to the market value of their securities and the terms of the proposal. Still more recently, a particularly reflective bankruptcy judge in British Columbia, while paying lip service to the commonality test, has embraced a "contextual" approach. This requires the court to look at all the circumstances surrounding the treatment of creditors' claims in a class of claims to determine how much they have in common having regard to the terms of the proposal. At bottom, this test seems to us not very different from the anti-fragmentation test. What is significant about the contextual approach is that it is as relevant in determining the classification of unsecured creditors' claims (and was so treated by Judge Tysoe in *Re Woodward's Limited* [(1993), 20 CBR (3d) 74 (BCSC)] as it is in dealing with secured creditors' claims. In our view, it also means that section 50(1.4) of the BIA will not give secured creditors as strong a veto power over the approval of BIA proposals as was previously thought. Instead, it seems much more likely that the courts will adopt a common approach to classification problems under the BIA and the CCAA even though the CCAA contains no counterpart to section 50(1.4).

. . .

E. *Voting of Creditors and Court's Approval*

The BIA requirements for creditor approval of the proposal are fairly straightforward. Creditor approval requires an absolute majority of the creditors in each class present and voting at the meeting and representing at least two-thirds in value of the claims in each class [s. 54(2)(d)]. Failure to obtain the required degree of approval results in a deemed assignment in bankruptcy by the debtor [s. 61(2)(b)]. Our study shows that in the Toronto bankruptcy region, the failure rate may be around 25 per cent. If the creditors have given their approval, the trustee must apply within five days for an appointment for a hearing to obtain the court's approval [s. 58(a)]. The court may refuse its approval if the court is of the opinion that the proposal is "not reasonable or ... not calculated to benefit the general body of creditors" [s. 59(2)]. Unless there are special circumstances, the court will almost invariably defer to the creditors' vote. For example, in the Toronto study we found that the court only withheld its approval in 6 out of 144 cases. Even in those cases, the court's refusal may have been based on the non-conformity of the proposal with the statutory requirements rather than on a finding of unreasonableness in the terms of the proposal. Failure by the debtor to secure the court's approval results in a deemed assignment into bankruptcy [s. 51(2)(a)].

If the debtor is in default of the terms of the proposal following the court's approval, the trustee must so inform the creditors unless the default has been waived by the inspectors (where inspectors have been appointed) or the default has been cured within the prescribed time [s. 52.1]. However, there is no automatic annulment of the proposal. Instead, an application must be made to the court for this purpose, although no one is obliged to bring such an application. If the annulment order is granted, a receiving order is deemed to be made simultaneously against the debtor and the usual consequences of a bankruptcy order will ensue. Judging by the results in the Toronto study, annulment of a proposal following the court's approval is a single-digit phenomenon and does not appear to be of greater significance at the national level.

[The 2005-6 amendments have enacted a new s. 54.1, stipulating that creditors holding equity claims are to be in the same class and may not vote on the proposal unless the court orders otherwise. Compare new CCAA s. 22.1, discussed in Chapter 15, Section V.]

NOTE ON STRIKING THE RIGHT BALANCE: SCREENS, GATEKEEPERS, AND GUILLOTINES

In a thoughtful article, "The Interplay Between Liquidation and Reorganization in Bankruptcy: The Role of Screens, Gatekeepers and Guillotines (1996), 16 *Int'l Rev. L & Econ.* 101, George Triantis discusses the role of checks and balances in the Canadian as well as the US Chapter 11 reorganizational legislative schemes. In the light of his discussion and the above extract from the article by Ziegel and Sahni, what screening, gatekeeper, and guillotining roles are played by courts, trustees, and creditors in the commercial proposal scheme and how effective are they in practice? (The practical aspects are considered further, below, Section IV.) Should the safeguards against debtor abuses be strengthened, or are they already too stringent? Consider too the many roles played by trustees. Note, however, that trustees are not required to advise creditors or the court whether they believe the debtor will be able to file a viable plan or, if a plan is put forward, whether the debtor is likely to be able to implement it successfully. Since trustees are retained and are paid by the debtor, is it realistic to expect them to blow the whistle on the debtor? (Recall that trustees are in a similar position of conflict when dealing with individual bankrupts, who look to them for guidance and advice and are responsible to them for their fees and expenses, yet trustees must report to creditors on the causes of the debtor's financial difficulties, must ensure that the debtor's non-exempt property is made available for distribution to creditors, and may (and sometimes do) oppose the bankrupt's discharge on a variety of grounds.)

III. CASE LAW

Compared with the abundant and generally fully reasoned CCAA judgments, the case law on Part III is relatively sparse and many of the judgments are quite brief. The difference between the two positions is explained in part by the relatively short period during which revamped Part III.1 has been in force. A still more important reason is that, generally speaking, much smaller amounts of money are involved in Part III.1 proposals and those debtors cannot afford to litigate as freely or as heavily as can the large corporations usually involved in CCAA proceedings. The cases reproduced in this section are designed to show students how the courts have responded to key features of the commercial proposal regime and how some of the problems have been resolved.

A. Dismissal of Proceedings

Re Cumberland Trading Inc.
(1994), 23 CBR (3d) 225 (Ont. Gen. Div.)

[Motions by the secured creditor for a declaration that stay provisions of the *Bankruptcy and Insolvency Act* no longer operated to prevent it from enforcing its security, for a declaration that the 30-day period to file a proposal had terminated, and for an order allowing substitution of trustee.]

FARLEY J: Skyview International Finance Corporation ("Skyview") brought this motion for a declaration that the stay provisions (ss. 69 and 69.1) of the *Bankruptcy and Insolvency Act*, RSC 1985, c. B-3 as amended ("BIA") no longer operate in respect of Skyview taking steps to enforce its security (including accounts receivable and inventory) given by Cumberland Trading Inc. ("Cumberland") which it has been financing for the last 9 years. In addition Skyview moved for a declaration that the 30 day period to file a proposal mentioned in s. 50.4(8) BIA was terminated. Thirdly, Skyview was asking for an order removing Doane Raymond Limited ("Doane") which was Cumberland's choice as trustee and substituting A. Farber Associates ("Farber") as trustee under the Notice of Intention to File a Proposal of Cumberland. In the alternative to the relief awarded in the last two aspects, Skyview wished to have an order appointing Farber as interim receiver.

On January 5, 1994 Skyview demand payment in full of its operating financing loan to Cumberland and gave a s. 244 BIA notice of its intention to enforce its security in ten days. The affidavit filed on behalf of Skyview indicated that Cumberland was not cooperating with it in providing appropriate financial information for the last half year. This was disputed in the affidavit filed by Cumberland. Suffice it to say that there has been a falling out between the two. Skyview asserted that it was owed $966,478 and that there was an exposure to it under a guarantee given on Cumberland's behalf to a potential of approximately $200,000 US. Skyview's deadline for repayment was January 16th. On January 14th Cumberland filed with the Official Receiver a Notice of Intention to make a Proposal (s. 50.4(1) BIA) and pursuant to s. 69 BIA there would a stay of proceedings upon this filing.

Skyview's president swore that:

> 21. In light of the unpleasant and frustrating experience Skyview has had to endure over the preceding 3 to 4 months with Cumberland, including specifically the persistent refusal by Cumberland to account for its sales from the Retail Business, the misrepresentation of Cumberland's pre-sold orders referred to above and particularly its secretive purported "Termination" of its direction to accord to pay sums to Skyview in reduction of Cumberland's indebtedness, Skyview's faith and confidence in the management of Cumberland has been irreparably damaged such that Skyview would not be prepared to vote in terms of any proposal which Cumberland may make.

and further that

24. The continued operation of a stay of proceedings preventing Skyview from enforcing its security will be materially prejudicial to the rights of Skyview. The assets of Skyview consist primarily of inventory and receivables (both from the Distribution Business and the Retail Business). With each day that passes Cumberland is converting its inventory (financed by Skyview) into cash (primarily in the Retail Business) and receivables (primarily in the Distribution Business) and it is Skyview's fear that those sums will be used by Cumberland to pay its other creditors and to fund the professional costs which it inevitably must incur in formulating and implementing a proposal. This fear is especially heightened insofar as the receivables generated from the Retail Business are concerned as they are under the direct and immediate control of Cumberland and are not collected by Accord.

Cumberland's Notice of Intention to File a Proposal acknowledges that Skyview is owed $750,000. On that basis Skyview has 95% in value of Cumberland's admitted secured creditors' claims and 67% of all creditors' claims of whatever nature. No matter what, Skyview's claim is so large that Skyview cannot be swamped in any class in which it could be put. Clearly Skyview would have a veto on any vote as to a proposal, at least so far as the secured class, assuming that secureds are treated as a separate class. This leaves the interesting aspect that under the BIA regime one could have a proposal turned down by the secured creditor class but approved by the unsecured creditor class and effective vis-à-vis this latter class, but with the secured class being able to enforce their security. One may question the practicality [*sic*] proposal affecting only unsecured creditors becoming effective in similar circumstances to this situation.

Cumberland's essential position is that it must have some time under BIA to see about reorganizing itself. While I am mindful that both BIA and the *Companies' Creditors Arrangement Act*, RSC 1985, c. C-36 ("CCAA") should be classified as debtor friendly legislation since they both provide for the possibility of reorganization (as contrasted with the absence of creditor friendly legislation which would allow, say, creditors to move for an increase in interest rates if inflation became rampant), these acts do not allow debtors absolute immunity and impunity from their creditors. I would also observe that all too frequently debtors wait until virtually the last moment, the last moment, or in some cases, beyond the last moment before even beginning to think about reorganization (and the attendant support that any successful reorganization requires from the creditors). I noted the lamentable tendency of debtors to deal with these situations as "last gasp" desperation moves in *Re Inducon Development Corp.* (1992), 8 CBR (3d) 308 (Ont. Gen. Div.). To deal with matters on this basis minimizes the chances of success, even if "success" may have been available with earlier spadework. It is true that under BIA an insolvent person can get an automatic stay by merely filing a Notice of Intention to File a Proposal—as opposed to the necessity under the CCAA of convincing the court of the appropriateness of granting a stay (and the nature of the stay). However BIA does not guarantee the insolvent person a stay without review for any set period of time. To keep the playing field level and dry so that it remains in play, a creditor or creditors can apply to the court to cut short the otherwise automatic (or extended) stay; in this case Skyview is utilizing s. 50.4(11) to do so.

Cumberland relies upon *Re N.T.W. Management Group Ltd.* (1993), 19 CBR (3d) 162 (Ont. Bktcy.), a decision of Chadwick J. Skyview asserts that *N.T.W.* is distinguishable or incorrectly decided and secondly that the philosophy of my decision in *Re Triangle Drugs Inc.* (1993), 16 CBR (3d) 1 (Ont. Bktcy.) should prevail. In *Triangle Drugs* I allowed the veto holding group of unsecured creditors to in effect vote at an advance poll in a situation where there appeared to be a gap in the legislation. The key section of BIA is s. 50.4(11) which provides:

. . .

It does not seem to me that there is any gap in this sector of the legislation.

As the headnote in *N.T.W.* stated, Chadwick J viewed a situation similar to this one as requiring that the debtor must have an opportunity to put forth its proposal when he stated at p. 163:

> The bank had stated that it would not accept any proposal. However, since the companies had not yet had the opportunity to put forth their proposal, it was impossible to make a final determination under s. 50.4(11)(c). The companies should have the opportunity to formulate and make their proposal.

However, I note that in this instance Cumberland has filed its Notice of Intention to File a Proposal the day before Skyview's s. 244 notice would have allowed it to take control of the security. Cumberland's president swore that:

> 2. The efforts which Cumberland is currently undertaking represent a bona fide effort, made in good faith, to restructure its finances in order to preserve the business of the company for the benefit of all of the creditors of the company, including Skyview. It is my belief that the proposal process will represent a significantly better treatment of all such creditors then would be available through either an enforcement by Skyview of its security against the assets of Cumberland, a bankruptcy of Cumberland or other processes available in the circumstances.

and further that:

> I intend to submit a proposal, pursuant to the provisions of the *Bankruptcy and Insolvency Act*, which represent the most advantageous treatment available, in my view, to all of the creditors of Cumberland and which allows for the continued viability of the business of Cumberland. This proposal is being prepared, and will be presented, in complete good faith. In the course of reviewing and preparing this proposal material with Mr. Godbold, I have determined that the legitimate claim of Skyview does not, in fact, represent in excess of 66⅔ of all the claims against Cumberland. At this time, Doane Raymond Limited is already in the position of Trustee under the proposal, in accordance with the provisions of the *Bankruptcy and Insolvency Act*. In addition, as noted above, I am prepared to consent to the appointment of Doane Raymond Limited as interim receiver of Cumberland. In the circumstances, I respectfully submit that the stay in favour of Cumberland pursuant to the *Bankruptcy and Insolvency Act* should not be lifted.

No explanation was given as to the lower share indicated for Skyview but in any event there was no assertion that Skyview lost its veto.

However we do not have any indication of what this proposal proposes to be—notwithstanding that 10 days have now passed since Cumberland filed its Notice of Intention to File a Proposal and five days since Skyview served Cumberland with this motion.

In a practical sense one would expect, given Skyview's veto power and its announced position, that Cumberland would have to present "something" to get Skyview to change its mind—e.g. an injection of fresh equity or a take out of Skyview's loan position. However there was not even a germ of a plan revealed—but merely a bald assertion that the proposal being worked on would be a better result for everyone including Skyview. This is akin to trying to box with a ghost. While I agree with the logic of Chadwick J when he said at p. 168 of *N.T.W.* that:

> CIBC the major secured creditor has indicated they will not accept any proposal put forth, other than complete discharge of the CIBC indebtedness. Other substantial creditors have taken the same position. There is no doubt that the insolvent companies have a substantial obstacle to overcome. *As the insolvent companies have not had the opportunity to put forth this proposal, it is impossible to make the final determination.* In *Triangle Drugs Inc.* Farley J had the proposal. Well over one-half of the secured [*sic*; in reality unsecured] creditors indicated they would not vote for the proposal. As such, he then terminated the proposal. We have not reached that stage in this case. The insolvent companies should have the opportunity of putting forth the proposal.

[Emphasis added.]

However this analysis does not seem to address the test involved. With respect I do not see this logical aspect as coming into play in s. 50.4(11)(c) which reads:

> The court may, on application by … a creditor, declare terminated, before its actual expiration, the thirty day period mentioned in subsection (8) … if the court is satisfied that
>
> • • •
>
>   (c) the insolvent person will not likely be able to make a proposal, before the expiration of the period in question, that will be accepted by the creditors, or
>
> • • •
>
> and where the court declares the period in question terminated, paragraphs (8)(a) to (c) thereupon apply as if that period had expired.

It seems to me that clause (c) above deals specifically with the situation where there has been no proposal tabled. It provides that there is no absolute requirement that the creditors have to wait to see what the proposal is before they can indicate they will vote it down. I do no see anything in BIA which would affect a creditor (or group of creditors) with a veto position from reaching the conclusion that nothing the insolvent debtor does will persuade the creditor to vote in favour of whatever proposal may be forthcoming. I think that this view is strengthened when one considers that the court need only be satisfied that "the insolvent person will not *likely* be able to make a proposal, before the expiration of the period in question, that will be accepted by the creditors …" (emphasis added). This implies that there need not be a certainty of turndown. The act of making the proposal is one that is still yet to come. I am of the view that Skyview's position as indicated above is satisfactory proof that Cumberland will not likely be able to make a proposal that will be accepted by the creditors of Cumberland.

Skyview of course also has the option of proceeding under s. 69.4 BIA. …

• • •

Is Skyview entitled to the benefit of s. 69.4(1) BIA? I am of the view that the material prejudice referred to therein is an objective prejudice as opposed to a subjective one—i. e., it refers to the degree of the prejudice suffered vis-à-vis the indebtedness and the attendant security and not to the extent that such prejudice may affect the creditor *qua* person, organization or entity. If it were otherwise then a "big creditor" may be so financially strong that it could never have the benefit of this clause. In this situation Skyview's prejudice appears to be that the only continuing financing available to Cumberland is that generated by turning Chamberland's [*sic*] accounts receivable and inventory (pledged to Skyview) into cash to pay operating expenses during the period leading up to a vote on a potential proposal, which process will erode the security of Skyview, without any replenishment. However, Skyview does not go the additional step and make any quantitative (or possibly qualitative) analysis as to the extent of such prejudice so that the court has an idea of the magnitude of materiality. In other words, Skyview presently estimates that it would be fortunate to realize $450,000 on Cumberland's accounts receivables and inventory, but it does not go on to give any foundation for a conclusion that in the course of the next month $x of this security would be eaten up or alternatively that the erosion would likely be in the neighbourhood of $y per day of future operations. The comparison would be between the "foundation" of a maximum of $450,000 and what would happen as to deterioration therefrom if the stay is not lifted. I note there was no suggestion from Cumberland that there would be no erosion of Skyview's position by, say, getting a cash injection or by improving margins by increasing revenues or decreasing expenses. Skyview's request for its first relief request is dismissed since in my view Skyview did not engage in the correct comparison of material prejudice.

I note that Cumberland does not oppose Skyview's request for an interim receiver. But for my conclusion that Skyview succeeds in its second relief request (to have the 30 day period in which to file a proposal terminated) and the ancillary third relief request of substitution of Farber for Doane as trustee, I would have granted the fourth relief request of appointing Farber as interim receiver. I would also award Skyview costs of $600 payable out of the estate of Cumberland from the proceeds first realized.

Order accordingly.

B. Interim Financing Applications

Re Bearcat Explorations Ltd.
(2004), 3 CBR (5th) 167 (Alta. QB)

ROMAINE J (orally): [1] Through the efforts of Mr. Czechowskyj, I have received a letter from the office of the Superintendent of Bankruptcy, Ms. Maj, the Division Assistant Superintendent, that advises me that the Senate Committee on Banking Trade and Commerce issued a report in the fall of 2003 recommending that amendments be made to both the *Bankruptcy and Insolvency Act* and the *Company's Creditors Arrangement Act* to specifically provide for DIP financing in corporate reorganizations. However, she also advises that the Superintendent of Bankruptcy wishes to remain neutral on this issue at this time.

[2] Further to my refusal last week to allow DIP financing that would rank in priority to Knox LLC, Locke, Stock & Barrel Company Ltd. now applies for an order granting approval for it to advance debtor-in-possession financing of up to $450,000 to Bearcat Exploration Ltd. and Stampede Oils Inc. to be a second charge on the assets of Bearcat and Stampede, ranking after the security of Knox but prior to all other secured and unsecured creditors.

[3] This application is supported by the secured creditors other than Knox, and, albeit reluctantly, by the unsecured creditors who were represented at the hearing. It is opposed by Knox and Anadarko, for many of the same reasons they opposed the previous application.

[4] The Proposal Trustee supports the application on the basis that, without this funding, the issues between Knox and Bearcat and Stampede will not be resolved through a trial process, and that finality on these issues is important to the creditors generally.

[5] The first issue, which I did not decide at the time of the last application, is whether DIP financing is available or appropriate under proposal proceedings pursuant to the *Bankruptcy and Insolvency Act*, or whether it should only be available pursuant to the *Companies' Creditors Arrangement Act*. Counsel have been unable to refer a case to me where DIP financing was considered by a court overseeing a bankruptcy proposal process, other than *AgriBio Tech Canada Inc.*, which I have previously indicated is not helpful due to its unusual facts.

[6] The courts have found authority for the use of DIP financing in CCAA scenarios both under the legislation and through the exercise of their inherent jurisdiction. The brevity of the CCAA and its remedial nature has allowed the courts to be creative in ensuring the objects of the legislation are met.

[7] In contrast, the BIA proposal provisions are specific and detailed. They are designed to provide a quick and inexpensive process for an insolvent debtor to resolve issues with its unsecured creditors and emerge from the proposal process. However, there is nothing in these provisions that precludes the concept of super-priority financing, nor would DIP financing be in conflict with the proposal provisions under the BIA.

[8] Inherent jurisdiction is a "residual source of powers, which the court may draw upon as necessary whenever it is just and equitable to do so, in particular, to ensure the observance of the due process of law ... to do justice between the parties and to secure a fair trial between them.": in *Royal Oak Mines Inc., Re* (14 March 1999) Ontario Court File No. 98-CL-3278 (OSCJ) (Com. List) [1999 CarswellOnt 988 (Ont. Gen. Div. [Commercial List])], Farley J at paragraph 22, citing Halsbury, Volume 37, 4th edition, at paragraph 14. Because it is an extraordinary power, it should be exercised only sparingly and in a clear case: *Baxter Student Housing Ltd. v. College Housing Co-operative Ltd.* (1975), [1976] 2 SCR 475 (SCC), at 480.

. . .

Application allowed.

NOTES

Re Bearcat Exploration Ltd. appears to be the first reported case in which the court exercised its inherent jurisdiction to fill a gap in the BIA commercial proposal provisions of the BIA. The Colter Committee must certainly have been aware of the interim financing provisions in Chapter 11 of the US *Bankruptcy Code*, yet did not recommend their inclusion in the Canadian regime. Presumably, the drafters of the 1992 BIA amendments also decided against the inclusion of the provisions. Given this history, was it still appropriate for Justice Romaine to invoke the inherent jurisdiction doctrine to bridge what she perceived to be a gap? Was she entitled to anticipate that the 2005-7 BIA amendments would confer an explicit interim financing power on the courts (see new BIA s. 50.6, but unproclaimed as of the end of 2008)? Should she have told the debtor applicants to proceed under the CCAA where the courts' interim financing jurisdiction was already well established? Compare *Re Farmpure Seeds Inc.*, 2008 SKQB 381, where the court, in granting a debtor-in-possession (DIP) financing application, took account of the pending BIA amendments and also considered and followed *Bearcat*. Given the lacunae in the BIA proposal provisions, why did the debtors in *Bearcat* opt to proceed under the BIA at all?

C. Disclaimer of Leases

Re Carr-Harris & Co.
(1993), 23 CBR (3d) 74 (BCSC)

[An application by a landlord that s. 65.2(1) of the *Bankruptcy and Insolvency Act* did not apply and that notice of repudiation was not effective.]

Master PATTERSON [In Chambers] (orally): Carr-Harris & Company is a professional law corporation which carries on business in Vancouver primarily in the area of personal injury litigation. The law firm has encountered financial problems and on September 16, 1993, filed a notice of intention to make a proposal pursuant to the provisions of the *Bankruptcy and Insolvency Act*, RSC 1985, c. B-3. Subsequently, on October 15, 1993, a proposal was filed.

The essence of the proposal is that by 1996 all creditors will be paid 100% of their claims but there will be no entitlement to interest. The proposal is contingent upon Carr-Harris & Company working out an arrangement with the Royal Bank of Canada, a secured creditor owed approximately $100,000 by the terms of which the bank is to be paid $10,000 per month commencing December 20th, 1993. The proposal requires the law firm to pay $8,500 per month to the trustee for the benefit of creditors commencing in March 1994. A number of creditors with claims less than $500 will be paid in full and forthwith. It follows that during the term of the proposal, the law firm will be required to pay for all expenses including rent in cash and not on credit.

The law firm has prepared a projected cash flow statement for the months October, 1993, to March, 1994. That cash flow projection shows total revenue for the six-month period as $1,266,166. The revenue projection is based on the receipt of contingency fees consequent upon the settlement of various personal injury actions. Most, if not all, of the clients retaining the law firm do so on a contingency basis. Usually the contingency agreements will provide that a fee based on a percentage of recovery is payable when the matter is settled or judgment is obtained. The agreements generally provide that the clients will pay necessary disbursements as and when they are incurred.

On October 15, 1993, Carr-Harris & Company delivered to its landlord, Standard Life Assurance Company, a notice of repudiation of lease pursuant to Section 65.2(1) of the *Bankruptcy and Insolvency Act*. The landlord has now applied pursuant to Section 65.2(2) for a declaration that subsection 1 does not apply. If the landlord is successful, the notice of repudiation would be ineffective. Section 65.2 of the *Bankruptcy and Insolvency Act* is as follows:

. . .

Section 65.2(2) [see now s. 65.2(3)—eds.] clearly places the onus on the insolvent person to satisfy the court that the proposal would not be viable without the repudiation of the lease. This Section only came into force in late 1992, and counsel were able to find only one reported decision, that of *Re Janpar Produits de Bureau Inc.* (1993), 20 CBR (3d) 8, a decision of the Quebec Superior Court, Bankruptcy Division. The headnote for that case indicates the court found Section 65.2 not to be unconstitutional and that the Federal Bankruptcy Legislation prevailed over Provincial laws governing landlords and tenants. Otherwise, the decision does not appear to assist in the determination of the viability of the proposal, without the repudiated lease.

On September 1, 1987, the law firm first occupied premises on the second floor at 900 Howe Street, Vancouver. In August, 1992, the law firm renewed its existing lease with Standard Life and at the same time, leased an additional 2,463 square feet. This extra space is not contiguous and effectively doubled the size of the office. Combined rent for both parts of the office is $11,971.03 per month effective November 1, 1993, and approximately half of that relates to the extra space. It is for the extra space that notice of repudiation was given not for the original office space. Carr-Harris & Company did not pay any rent for June, July, August, and September 1993, but has paid all rent due for October of 1993, even thought the notice of repudiation was delivered on October the 15th.

The principal of Carr-Harris & Company has sworn an affidavit in which he states that the decision to expand into extra offices was ill-advised. The extra offices (described as the south wing) are now empty and will not be required during the term of the proposal because various lawyers formerly associated with the practice will no longer be there. Mr. Carr-Harris, after reviewing actual fees received by the law firm, swears this in his affidavit sworn November 1, 1993:

> 21. For the reasons given, I verily believe that the proposal the Corporation has made will not be viable in the sense that it will not be one which the corporation is capable of performing, if it is required to continue leasing empty space in the south wing.

David Gray, a partner with Campbell Saunders Ltd., the trustee under the proposal in his affidavit sworn November 1, 1993, swears:

> 6. In the context of preparing the Proposal as well as the supporting cash flow statements, it became apparent that the lease, which is the subject matter of this application (the "Lease") may well inhibit the performance of the Proposal by the firm. Accordingly, and

based upon my recommendation after discussion with counsel, Mr. Carr-Harris was advised to repudiate the Lease. A copy of the repudiation is attached as Exhibit "A" to the Affidavit of Richard J. Olson filed in these proceedings on October 18th, 1993. That notice of repudiation was prepared by the Trustee.

7. Based upon my knowledge of the affairs of the Firm, it is my opinion that the Firm's financial position has been enhanced by repudiation of the Lease. As well, the repudiation of the Lease has enhanced the likelihood of the success of the Proposal.

In the trustee's preliminary report to creditors, Mr. Gray reviews the assets of the law firm and writes this about the biggest asset which is work in progress.

The law corporation shows a value of $2,500,000.00 for its work in progress. This amount is calculated on the total potential volume of work that the firm has contracted for based on assumptions regarding the projected amount of the claim. It does not include the time incurred at standard hourly rates that has been incurred to date on the client file. We have arbitrarily reduced the law corporation's value to $1,000,000.00 to reflect the fact that not all of the time has been incurred and also to reflect the fact that not all of the files will result in a successful claim.

The trustee then continues and points out that on a liquidation basis, the value of work in progress could be nothing.

In attempting to assess the viability of the proposal, it is clearly necessary to try and define "viable" as there is no definition in the *Bankruptcy and Insolvency Act*. "Viable" is defined variously as capable of functioning or capable of existing or maintaining an existence. In *Re Janpar*, a distinction is drawn between a viable proposal and the wording of Section 65.2(2) [now s. 65.2(3)—eds.] which speaks of a "proposal (which) would not be viable, without the repudiation of that lease." It follows, in my view, that the first determination is whether the insolvent person has shown that the proposal is viable or workable if the lease were not a factor at all and would not work if there were a requirement to pay the additional rent. In other words, in this case, would the payment of an extra $6,000 per month rent render the proposal of [*sic*] unworkable?

Contingency fees received by the law firm for the past five months are as follows:

June, 1993	$ 44,715.11
July, 1993	$ 22,422.44
August, 1993	$ 33,304.74
September, 1993	$ 43,975.19
October, 1993	$ 71,310.64
	$215,728.12

The average receipts are $43,145 per month. This is a far cry from the cash flow projections of the law firm which project average monthly receipts of $204,000 per month. For the one month where there is a prediction and actual receipts, the difference is dramatic. In October of 1993, the law firm predicted receipts of $153,000, actually received $71,310.64, leaving a shortfall of $81,689.36.

Under the proposal, the law firm will have to make the following fixed payments:

Revenue Canada	$ 2,500.00
Royal Bank	$10,000.00
Trustee.	$ 8,500.00
Rent (remaining office only).	$ 6,000.00
	$27,000.00

If one assumes that average receipts will continue at approximately $43,000 per month then approximately $16,000 remains after paying the fixed costs to cover all other expenses, including salaries, benefits, source deductions, telephones and supplies, with no allowance being made for income tax, PST or GST. The cash flow projection made by the law firm for January, 1994, shows projected expenses of $70,234. If that figure is reduced by $11,000 to reflect the payment of one-half the rent and no shareholder's draw, the expenses are still $59,000. This is amply covered by the projected income of $153,000 but not covered by the current average receipts. I note that the trustee in his report of the projected cash flow statement writes this:

> Since the projection is based on assumptions regarding future events, actual results will vary from the information presented even if the hypothetical assumptions occur and the variations may be material. Accordingly, we express no assurance as to whether the projections will be achieved.

After reviewing the projections as carefully as time permits, reviewing actual receipts, and taking into account the fact that rent was unpaid for four months in 1993, that BC Telephone Company is owed in excess of $37,000, it is my view that this proposal made by the law firm has only a slim chance of working whether the extra lease payment is a factor or not. The revenue projections appear to be optimistic and there are no assurances from the trustee. Mr. Carr-Harris believes that this proposal will not be viable if he has to continue to lease empty space. The trustee will only say that repudiation of the lease enhances the company's financial position and the likelihood of the success of the proposal. The trustee does not say that the proposal is workable but for the payment of rent for the extra space.

Simply put, the lease payment must be the factor that makes the proposal unworkable, it must be the straw that breaks the camel's back. While I have the greatest sympathy for the law firm and the efforts made to try and resolve its problems, I do not think that this proposal is going to work with the present debtload, with or without the lease payment for the extra space.

Carr-Harris & Company has not satisfied the onus upon it to show that "the proposal ... would not be viable, without the repudiation of that lease" for the extra space. The landlord, Standard Life, is entitled to a declaration, that Section 65.2(1) does not apply to the lease of the extra space, and, consequently, the notice of repudiation is ineffective.

Application allowed.

Re Superstar Group of Companies
(2001), 25 CBR (4th) 119 (BCSC)

SIGURDSON J:

Introduction

This application concerns an insolvent person's attempt to disclaim a number of leases prior to filing a proposal. Certain affected landlords served with notices of disclaimer of their leases applied for declarations that the insolvent person could not disclaim their leases. Their opposition is on the grounds that the insolvent person's disclaimer is premature and the disclaimer of their particular leases is unnecessary.

Background

. . .

These reasons deal with an application by two landlords, the Manufacturer's Life Insurance Company and Richmond Developments Ltd., for declarations that section 65.2(1) of the Act, the section that allows for disclaimers of leases, does not apply to the leases held by them. I advised the parties by memorandum that I had decided in favour of the insolvent person, the Superstar Group. These are my reasons.

Facts

The Superstar Group was a collection of 17 corporations operating 49 retail outlets. Its principal trading banners are Shoestrings and Superstar. In late December 2000, its 49 stores in British Columbia and Alberta had sales in excess of $60 million and employed 650 employees. The group began to take steps to downsize, but by the end of 2000 it continued to face financial difficulty. By early January 2001, it was facing imminent action by creditors, including landlords threatening termination of some leases. Its inventory financier and secured creditor, Congress Financial Corporation (Canada) Ltd., was out of margin by $560,000. It also faced potential action from its other secured creditor, Montreal Trust.

On January 17, 2001, the Superstar Group, on a consolidated basis, filed a Notice of Intention to make a proposal. PricewaterhouseCoopers was appointed trustee and has monitored the affairs of the Superstar Group since that time.

Part of the plan was to downsize its operation to its more profitable or promising stores. The Superstar Group's plan was to conduct liquidation sales, reduce debt to its inventory financier on the understanding further inventory would be supplied, transfer inventory from closed stores and eliminate the lease payments, salary and head office overhead on its closed stores. The group anticipated that operations would be normalized and that a short time after the end of February 2001 the Group would be in a position to assess its viability and as well to assess the future support of the necessary stakeholders, creditors, suppliers, landlords and other unsecured creditors.

On January 17, 2001, the group forwarded disclaimers to landlords with respect to 23 leases (one was later withdrawn). Most landlords have not contested the disclaimers, with the exception of four who brought this application. Three of the leases are held by

ManuLife and one is held by Richmond Developments. The three ManuLife stores, numbers 8, 135 and 402, are now closed and are located in Metrotown Burnaby. The store leased by Richmond Developments Ltd. is number 114. It was expected to be closed February 12, 2001.

These two landlords seek a declaration under section 65.2(2) that the insolvent person's disclaimer does not apply in respect of their leases.

The relevant [provisions are] sections 65.2(1), (2) and (3). ...

Discussion

It is conceded that the burden is on the insolvent person, the Superstar Group, to demonstrate that it would not be able to make a viable proposal without "the disclaimer of the lease and all other leases that the tenant has disclaimed ... ." The insolvent person opposes the declaration sought by the two landlords that section 65.2(1) does not apply in respect of each of their leases.

The landlords make two main points.

First they say that the disclaimers and this application are premature because the insolvent person has not yet filed a proposal, and it is therefore too early to tell if there is viable proposal without the disclaimer of the leases or any of them.

Second, the landlords say that the insolvent person has not discharged the burden on it to demonstrate that each particular lease of the four leases in question must be disclaimed for there to be a viable proposal.

As to the first point, I do not think that this application or the disclaimer of these leases is premature.

The language of section 65.2 as a whole clearly contemplates the possible disclaimer of a lease prior to the actual making of a proposal. The introductory words of section 65.2 indicate that the insolvent person may disclaim the lease on notice "at any time between the filing of a notice of intention and the filing of a proposal, or on the filing of a proposal ... ." That language indicates that the proposal does not have to be filed prior to the insolvent person disclaiming a lease. Given that a proposal need not be filed until 30 days after a notice of intention is filed, a declaration under section 65.2(2) can conceivably be made prior to filing a proposal. Subsection (3) does not prevent the court from making the declaration in the event that the proposal is not viable, but instead prevents that declaration if the court is satisfied the insolvent person "would not be able to make a viable proposal ... ." That language also contemplates an actual proposal being made after the question of the disclaimed lease is considered.

Moreover the Act not only allows for the disclaimer of leases before a proposal is filed, but also provides for an insolvent person to apply to court to extend the time to file a proposal. This also suggests that the present application is not premature. Section 50.4(9)(b) provides that an extension may be granted if "the insolvent person would likely be able to make a viable proposal if the extension ... were granted ... ." The scheme of the Act appears to contemplate that the issue of whether a challenged disclaimer is valid might be resolved prior to the filing of a proposal.

The landlords find some support for their position in *Re Carr-Harris & Co.* (1993), 23 CBR (3d) 74 (BC Master). That case concerned one lease and a filed proposal. Master Patterson held that the insolvent person had not satisfied the onus to show that "the proposal ... would not be viable without the repudiation of that lease." He said, "the first determination is whether the insolvent person has shown that the proposal is viable or workable if the lease were not a factor at all and would not work if there were a requirement to pay the additional rent." I think that *Re Carr-Harris & Co.* is distinguishable because there was an existing proposal and the court concluded it was unworkable with or without the lease payment for the extra space.

Accordingly I conclude that the disclaimers and this application are not premature.

I turn to the second point. The landlords say that the insolvent group has not demonstrated that it would not be able to make a viable proposal without the disclaimer of any of the individual leases.

The language of section 65.2(3) does not assist the landlords on this argument. The section does not provide that the disclaimer should not be permitted in the event that the insolvent person would not be able to make a viable proposal without the disclaimer of the particular lease. Rather it reads that there should be no disclaimer where the insolvent person would not be able to make a viable proposal "without the disclaimer of the lease *and all other leases that the tenant has disclaimed* ... ." The language of the section suggests that at least initially the court must address this question by considering whether the insolvent person has demonstrated that it would not be able to make a viable proposal without the disclaimer of all of the leases that the tenant has disclaimed under section 65.2(1), including any where the disclaimer is challenged.

I think the evidence demonstrates that the group would not be able to make a viable proposal without the disclaimer of the leases it has disclaimed. Darryl Eddy, a Senior Vice-President of PricewaterhouseCoopers Inc., deposed that he reviewed the projected cash flows and balance sheets of the Superstar Group. They indicated that the group did not have sufficient cash flow and financing ability to properly stock inventory in all 49 stores and that the closure of the 22 stores and consolidation of the inventory into the remaining stores, after a liquidation of as much inventory as possible, was immediately required. Paul Dusanj, the Chief Executive Officer of the group, deposed that the Superstar Group did not have the cash flow sufficient to fund the operations of the entire 49 stores and had to take immediate steps to stop ongoing losses. He opined that the disclaimers would result in an immediate savings of $230,000 per month. The projections for each of the stores show a cash loss before taking into consideration the contribution of each store for depreciation, interest expense and administrative overhead cost.

I do not interpret the section to require an insolvent person to demonstrate that it still could not make a viable proposal if it continued to be bound by one of the leases in question.

I have concluded that the landlords are not entitled to the declaration they seek. The Superstar Group has demonstrated that it would not be able to make a viable proposal without a disclaimer of these four leases and all the other leases that it has disclaimed under sub-section (1). The evidence as a whole also suggests that the disclaimer of the particular leases in question was reasonable, and is a reasonable part of a plan to make a viable proposal. ...

Applications dismissed.

NOTES AND QUESTIONS

The lease provisions in s. 65.2, referred to in *Carr-Harris & Co.*, were amended in 1997, but the amendments do not affect the debtor's right of repudiation and the lessor's right to challenge the repudiation. Given the debtors' poor financial position in this case, what did the landlord hope to gain by opposing repudiation of the lease? Was the landlord hoping to extract more concessions from the law firm? Should the law firm have opted for bankruptcy? (Yes, lawyers and law firms have declared bankruptcy.) Were the lawyers concerned about the impact of bankruptcy on their image and their ability to attract future clients, or were they concerned that, if they declared bankruptcy, the landlord would have a claim against their personal assets? Could the lawyers have avoided these troubles by incorporating a company to hold the lease (a common practice among large law firms) or would the landlord have insisted on a personal guarantee from the partners? Is a personal guarantee always as onerous as primary liability under an obligation?

D. Classification of Creditors

Re Points West Fashion Outlets Inc.
(1996), 39 CBR (3d) 249 (BCSC)

BOYD J: The Court has before it applications for the approval of the Amended Proposals of Points West Fashion Outlets Inc., Points West Fashion Outlets Langley Ltd. and Points West Fashion Outlets Westgate Ltd., which I will collectively refer to as the "Amended Proposals." The Amended Proposals were approved by a majority of the creditors of the subject companies, which majority comprised two-thirds of the dollar value percentage of the vote. It is not contested that the creditors in attendance voted in favour of the Amended Proposals by a very narrow margin of approximately 69% of the dollar value.

These three applications for approval of the Amended Proposals are opposed by the National Apparel Bureau, Inc., which is an association representing a number of fashion retailers across Canada including 41 of the 49 creditors who opposed the approval of the Amended Proposals at the meeting held March 15, 1996. At the risk of being over-simplistic, I understand that the National Apparel Bureau opposes this Court's approval of the Proposals on three grounds:

(1) That two particular groups of creditors ought not to have been included in a single class of unsecured creditors but rather ought to have voted separately in one or two classes of preferred creditors;

(2) That the Amended Proposals themselves are sufficiently lacking in particularity and detail as to not constitute formal offers which are capable of being accepted by virtue of the operation of the vote held at the meeting of March 15, 1996; and finally

(3) That following the meeting of March 15, 1996, the Trustee discounted the votes cast by certain creditors, as a result of which the results of the vote are not reliable.

Dealing with the first issue, it is the National Apparel Bureau's position that two particular groupings of creditors ought not to have been included in the single class of unsecured creditors. Firstly, Mr. Hobbs points out that 12 of the creditors who voted in favour of the proposals are suppliers who have assigned their accounts receivable to Accord Business Credit Ltd., a factoring company. He further notes that both of the debtors' landlords, Skeena Holdings and Colonial Developments, were categorized as unsecured creditors by the Trustee notwithstanding the fact that there is some evidence Colonial was originally identified by the Trustee to be a secured creditor.

As I understand Mr. Hobbs' submission, it is that some separate class or classes of preferred creditors ought to have been created by the Trustee to include the 12 creditors who assigned their accounts receivable to Accord, as well as the two landlords, and that this class or classes of creditors ought to have voted separately from the balance of the unsecured creditors. In the end result, Mr. Hobbs submits that their votes would not have had the effect of creating an affirmative vote in favour of the Amended Proposals.

In support of his submission, Mr. Hobbs relies upon a series of cases decided in CCAA proceedings in which the court applied what is described as a "contextual approach" in the determination of whether one or more classes of unsecured creditors ought to be created. (*Re Grafton-Fraser Inc. and Canadian Imperial Bank of Commerce et al.* (1992) 90 DLR (4th) 285 [Ont. Gen. Div.)] and *Re Woodward's Ltd.* (1993) 20 CBR (3d) 74 (BCSC).)

I agree with the Trustee's and the various debtors' counsel's submissions that the *Bankruptcy and Insolvency Act* (the "Act") makes no provision for the creation of a class of preferred creditors separate from the class or classes of unsecured creditors allowed for under the Act. Reading together s. 50 and s. 54 of the Act, it is clear that for the purposes of voting at a meeting of creditors, there are two classes of claimants secured and unsecured creditors. If the creditors are unsecured creditors, then they all fall into a single mass class unless the proposal provides otherwise. I agree with both Mr. Grieve and Mr. Reardon that if it were otherwise, and preferred creditors always constituted a separate class or classes of claimants, such creditors would be accorded the potential to exercise an unwarranted degree of power, totally out of keeping with the dollar value of their claims relative to the value of the claims of the unsecured creditors as a whole.

There may well be cases in which the debtor decides, for good tactical reasons, to include certain unsecured creditors in a class of their own, holding the power to prevent acceptance of the proposal unless two-thirds of their dollar value in votes supports the proposal. This usually occurs in situations where the smallest claimants are offered close to one hundred cents on the dollar, thus assuring a yes vote from that class. While the debtor has the option to create such separate classes of unsecured creditors, there is nothing contained anywhere in the legislation or the case law which forces a debtor (in a situation akin to that faced by the Point West companies) to create some separate class for preferred creditors. Thus, the National Apparel's opposition on this ground cannot be supported.

A second major ground for opposing the proposal is the contention that the proposal itself is replete with a number of gaps and a lack of detail, such that it cannot constitute an offer capable of being accepted by the result of a vote and thus does not amount to a contract in law.

Mr. Hobbs points out that the Amended Proposals contain no definition of what constitutes a "secured creditor," which creditors are "ordinary creditors," and precisely when and in what amounts the creditors shall be paid out.

While I agree that the Proposals are inelegantly drafted, and contain a number of gaps, I am satisfied that given the underlying legislative framework of the Act, there was no doubt in the minds of the various creditors who attended the creditors' meeting as to the precise terms of the Amended Proposals put forward upon which votes were cast in the form of Voting Letters. I accept that for good practical reasons such Proposals are often amended in the course of a creditors' meeting and then put to the assembled creditors for a vote to be taken at the meeting. Not surprisingly, many such documents are inelegantly phrased and likely contain many gaps. Relying upon the underlying legislation and the appointment of inspectors to ensure the carrying out of the Proposal in the terms voted upon, I cannot accede to the National Apparel Bureau's suggestion that I should reject the Proposals because of the various gaps identified.

· · ·

In the end result, having reviewed the three Amended Proposals and the Trustee's report, I am satisfied that a majority of the creditors voted in favour of the Amended Proposals and that the Proposals are reasonable, are calculated to benefit the general body of creditors, and ought to be approved.

Proposals Approved

NOTES AND QUESTIONS

Boyd J does not draw attention to the fact that s. 60(1) of the BIA provides that a proposal shall not be approved by the court if it fails to provide for payment in priority of claims so entitled in the distribution of the debtor's property (as to which see BIA s. 136(1)). Would it have made a difference if his attention had been drawn to the section? Why should the debtor alone, and not creditors as well, have a say in determining whether there should be one or more classes of unsecured creditors? If the concern is that fragmentation of creditors for voting purposes will jeopardize the prospect of a successful proposal, could the same concerns not be addressed by giving Canadian courts a Chapter 11-type "cram-down" power with respect to recalcitrant creditors who have opposed the proposal to extract unjustified better treatment of their claims?

E. Approval/Refusal of Proposals

Re Wandler
(2007), 32 CBR (5th) 292 (Alta. QB) (footnotes omitted)

TOPOLNISKI J:

. . .

I. The Application

Donald Wandler ("Debtor") applies for court approval of his Division I, *Bankruptcy and Insolvency Act* ("BIA") proposal to his unsecured creditors, made November 18, 2006 ("Proposal"). The application is opposed by the Debtor's largest unsecured creditor, Canada Revenue Agency ("CRA"), on the ground of non-compliance with s. 59(3) of the BIA, which requires that security be provided for the performance of the Proposal ("performance security").

II. Background

The facts are straightforward. The Proposal affects eight unsecured creditors ("creditors"), whose claims total $148,001.00. CRA's claim is for $90,000.00, or about 60 percent of the total unsecured debt. The Proposal provides that the Debtor will pay $18,000.00 from his future earnings in satisfaction of the Trustee's fees and expenses (about $5,400.00) and the creditors' claims ("Payment"). The Payment is due in thirty-six installments of $500.00 each, the first due on filing of the Proposal ("Initial Payment") and continuing monthly thereafter. The Proposal also provides that the Debtor will file a provisional income tax return.

A representative of CRA told the Trustee before the meeting of creditors to vote on the Proposal that she had sent CRA's negative vote and proxy via the mail, and did not plan to attend the meeting. As matters unfolded, the vote and proxy did not arrive in time for the meeting. The Proposal was approved by two creditors with a combined claim value of $13,645.56.

The Trustee reports that the Debtor's insolvency is attributable to relationship breakdown, overuse of credit, tax liability, and his son's drug problems. The Debtor's 2006 net income to November was $60,000.00. The realizable value of his assets is $9,202.00, of which he claims that all but $2,002 is exempt [under the provisions of the *Civil Enforcement Act*, RSA 2000, c. C-15] or encumbered.

The Trustee recommends that the Court approve the Proposal as it is advantageous to the creditors and they voted in favour of it, urging a generous interpretation of s. 59(3) to ensure that consumer debtors are not deprived of the right to make Division I proposals to their creditors. The Trustee says there is authority for the proposition that s. 59(3) may not require performance security per se, but rather a reasonable chance that the Proposal will succeed.

The Debtor did not attend the application or proffer any evidence to support his application.

CRA contends that s. 59(3) mandates performance security in the Debtor's circumstance.

A. General Principles Governing Applications for Court Approval of Proposals

A debtor bears the onus of establishing that a proposal should be approved. Where a proposal calls for payment over an extended time, the debtor must show a reasonable prospect of being able to generate the money to make the payments.

As a proposal substantially interferes with creditors' rights, the provisions of the BIA must be complied with strictly.

Proposals are clearly preferable to bankruptcies. Nonetheless, the court must consider all of the stakeholders' interests on an application to approve a proposal: the debtor's interest in restructuring debt; the creditors' interests in resolving claims in a reasonable fashion; and the public interest in maintaining the integrity of the bankruptcy process and commercial morality.

Because proposals are arrangements submitted for the approval of creditors, at least some of whom may not have had the benefit of legal advice and may be unfamiliar with legal nuance, the words used in proposals should be given their plain and ordinary meaning.

B. The Statutory Framework

Natural persons whose debts do not exceed $75,000.00 have recourse to the "consumer proposal" provisions in Part III, Division II of the BIA. For corporations and natural persons whose debts exceed $75,000.00, recourse is under Part III, Division I of the BIA. In either case, the law recognizes that proposals have significant impact on the stakeholders. The Act addresses those impacts through express provisions to safeguard stakeholder interests, just one of which is the requirement for court scrutiny of all proposals accepted by the creditors.

Section 59 provides the framework for and considerations governing the court's scrutiny of Division I proposals. Section 59 reads as follows:

> (1) The court shall, before approving the proposal, hear a report of the trustee in the prescribed form respecting the terms thereof and the conduct of the debtor, and, in addition, shall hear the trustee, the debtor, the person making the proposal, any opposing, objecting or dissenting creditor and such further evidence as the court may require.
>
> (2) Where the court is of the opinion that the terms of the proposal are not reasonable or are not calculated to benefit the general body of creditors, *the court shall refuse* to approve the proposal, *and the court may refuse* to approve the proposal whenever it is established that the debtor has committed any one of the offences mentioned in sections 198 to 200.
>
> (3) Where any of the facts mentioned in section 173 are proved against the debtor, *the court shall refuse* to approve the proposal *unless* it provides reasonable security for the payment of not less than fifty cents on the dollar on all unsecured claims provable against the debtor's estate or such percentage thereof as the court may direct. [Emphasis added.]

Section 173 of the BIA enumerates certain circumstances and behaviour relating to a debtor. It reads in relevant part as follows:

The facts … are:

> [T]he assets of the bankrupt are not of a value equal to fifty cents on the dollar on the
> amount of the bankrupt's unsecured liabilities, unless the bankrupt satisfies the court
> that the fact that the assets are not of a value equal to fifty cents on the dollar on the
> amount of the bankrupt's unsecured liabilities has arisen from circumstances for
> which the bankrupt cannot justly be held responsible.

The requirement of performance security for court approval of proposals has been a
feature of the BIA dating to *The Bankruptcy Act*, SC 1919, c. 36, s. 13(9). In 1949, the Act
was amended (*Bankruptcy Act*, SC 1949, c. 7, s. 34(3)) to allow the court the discretion
to lower the percentage of the security. The requirement of performance security and the
court's discretion in terms of the percentage has remained unchanged ever since.

C. The Jurisprudence

A review of the jurisprudence concerning the mandate for performance security under
s. 59(3) of the BIA, its predecessor provisions, and parallel legislation in the United Kingdom is helpful.

Re P.F. Murray, A Debtor, Ex parte The Debtor v. Official Receiver concerned the performance security required for a scheme of arrangement under s. 16(10) of the English
Bankruptcy Act, 1914. Like s. 59(3) of our BIA, that provision required a threshold level
of performance security, but unlike s. 59(3) it did not allow the court the discretion to
lower the threshold amount. The scheme of arrangement in that case provided for
monthly cash payments and allowed the debtor six months to obtain planning approval
to redevelop and sell his matrimonial home, failing which the trustee could sell the property. On appeal, the court reversed the initial ruling that the security was unacceptable
as not providing the creditors with the required amount in the six month time allotted,
finding that there was a reasonable probability that the performance security could be
paid in a reasonably short period. At p. 445, Cross J commented that a broad view of the
words "reasonable security" should be taken when a proposal is highly favourable to the
creditors and has been accepted by them.

The proposal in *Re Dolson* did not provide for performance security and the payment
under the proposal was by installments, the first payment being due thirty days after approval of the proposal. Anderson J refused to approve the proposal, stating that where a
debtor, as in that case, had previously taken advantage of the BIA (a bankruptcy and another proposal), only extraordinary circumstances would justify the court in exercising
its discretion to reduce the percentage of the performance security. No such circumstances were found.

In *Re McNamara*, the performance security offered consisted of assets minimally worth
20 cents on the dollar which had vested in the trustee. Saunders J refused to exercise his
discretion to reduce the amount of security from the statutory minimum, noting that there
was inadequate evidence as to the proposal's viability, and commenting that the debtors'
inability to provide security up to the statutory requirement was a factor in assessing the
reasonableness of the proposal under the equivalent of s. 59(2) of the present Act.

In *Re Mernick*, the proposal in effect was a bankruptcy without investigative assistance. Farley J found the proposal unreasonable on its face, noting that it was for a frac-

tion of a cent on the dollar and fell below the minimum statutory threshold required by s. 59(3). The case took an unusual turn when the creditor opposing the application in the first instance settled with the debtor and entered into a consent order allowing an appeal of Farley J's decision, which had the effect of remitting the matter for a rehearing. In granting the consent order, the Ontario Court of Appeal noted that it did not reflect on the court's view of the merits of the appeal from the initial decision. The eventual outcome of the case is not reported.

Re Orchid Fashions Inc. is another case in which the court refused to approve a proposal for a variety of reasons. The court suggested that great care and caution must be exercised before approving a proposal that does not provide for reasonable security where there is a "fact" or bankruptcy offence in the relevant predecessor provisions to s. 173 and ss. 198 to 200.

Re Sumner Co. is yet another case where approval of a proposal was objected to on the basis of performance security. The court refused to approve the proposal, in part as the performance security failed to comply with the predecessor of s. 59(3).

Performance security is sometimes plainly set out as such in the proposal or it may be implicit. However, it must be meaningful, the onus of proof of which rests with the debtor. *Re National Fruit Exchange Inc.* is an example of a proposal which was not approved for want of meaningful security. The court in that case rejected the debtors' principals' personal guarantees as performance security because there was no evidence to show that the principals had assets to support the guarantees.

III. Analysis

McNamara, Mernick, and implicitly *Orchid,* consider the adequacy of performance security simply to be one factor, albeit an important one, in the overall assessment of the reasonableness of a proposal. This approach requires reading in language or reading ss. 59(2) and (3) conjunctively, an exercise which, in my view, is unwarranted given the purpose of the BIA proposal provisions generally, the specific purpose of s. 59, and the express language of ss. 59(2) and (3). Another approach, which I find more appealing given the express language of s. 59(3) which directs that the court do certain things if s. 173 "facts" are made out, is to read these subsections disjunctively.

The s. 59(3) requirement for performance security is designed to further the interests of creditors and the public. It is a requirement that, in my view, is additional to the requirements enunciated in s. 59(2). As compared to the s. 59(2) requirements, which apply to all proposals, the requirement under s. 59(3) for performance security applies only in a specified circumstance; where the debtor's situation or past conduct is blameworthy, falling within s. 173.

While s. 173 facts might well lead to a measure of skepticism that the debtor will satisfy his or her obligations under the proposal, they serve primarily as a reflection of public policy. Section 59(3) and s. 172(2) both refer to the facts set out in s. 173.

Section 172(2) stipulates that, on proof of any of those facts, the court shall refuse to discharge the bankrupt, shall suspend the discharge for a period that the court thinks proper, or shall grant the discharge on condition that the bankrupt perform such acts, pay such moneys, consent to such judgments or comply with such other terms as the court may direct.

In *Ex parte Reed; In Re Reed, Bowen & Co.*, Lord Esher MR commented on the reason why the English *Bankruptcy Act* of 1883 had been passed, stating:

> It was because of the known and proved behaviour of creditors with regard to their insolvent debtors that this Act was passed, taking away from the majority of creditors that power which they had so recklessly and carelessly used, and putting a controlling power into the hands of the Court for the purpose of protecting the creditors against their own recklessness; for the purpose of preventing a majority of creditors from dealing thus recklessly, not only with their own property, but with that of the minority, *and of enforcing, so far as the legislature could, a more careful and moral conduct on the part of debtors.* [Emphasis added.]

In moving in Canada for leave to introduce Bill No. 25 in respect of bankruptcy on March 27, 1918, Mr. S.W. Jacobs stated:

> At present no distinction whatever is made as between the honest and the dishonest debtor in the matter of obtaining a discharge; they are all thrown into the discard. By this measure it is proposed that the courts shall carefully scrutinize the business dealings and the business relations of traders, and shall make a distinction—shall separate the sheep from the goats. When the court is of the opinion that a debtor has been obliged to assign through misfortune, he shall be given the necessary relief. *If, on the other hand, it should be found, in scrutinizing his affairs, that he wrecked his own business wilfully, then, of course, he should receive no relief whatever.* That is the crux of every bankruptcy law ... [Emphasis added.]

That Bill was not passed, but the one which was during the next session of Parliament, and which was the forerunner of the current BIA, reflected the same public policy of fostering moral conduct on the part of debtors.

Like the s. 172(2) requirement, the prohibition against approving a proposal where any of the s. 173 facts have been proved against the debtor unless the debtor provides reasonable security for the payment serves to protect not only the interests of creditors but also the public's interest in commercial morality.

As stated in Houlden and Morawetz's *Bankruptcy and Insolvency Law of Canada*:

> In deciding whether the proposal should be approved, the court must take the following interests into account: (a) the interests of the debtor in making a settlement with creditors; (b) the interests of creditors in procuring a settlement which is reasonable and which does not prejudice their rights; and (c) the interests of the public in the fashioning of a settlement which preserves the integrity of the bankruptcy process and complies with the requirements of commercial morality.

The Debtor's assets in the present case clearly are less than fifty cents on the dollar of his unsecured liabilities. Accordingly, the onus shifts to him to show that this situation has arisen from circumstances for which he cannot justly be held responsible. He offered no evidence in support of his application and chose not to appear at it. The Trustee says that he could not muster such evidence. Consequently, s. 59(3) is triggered.

Viewed in its best light, the Initial Payment might be considered performance security implicit in the Proposal. The Initial Payment equates to .027 percent of the total amount due under the Proposal. That is not reasonable performance security.

In *Dolson*, Anderson J stated that the lack of any performance security is fatal to a proposal, but suggested that the court might exercise its discretion to reduce the percentage of security required, at least in extraordinary circumstances. Presumably he meant that the court could reduce the security to zero. I disagree. I prefer the view taken in Houlden and Morawetz that if no performance security is offered under a proposal, the court cannot approve it since s. 59(3) requires that there be a percentage of fifty cents on the dollar and zero is not a percentage of fifty cents. In any event, there must be some evidence presented to justify the court exercising its discretion to lower the percentage of performance security, and here there was none other than the creditors' approval of the Proposal, which alone is insufficient.

The desirability of promoting proposals over bankruptcies is obvious. However, even such a laudable objective cannot override Parliament's directive that there be reasonable creditor protection by way of performance security for Division I proposals if, as here, a s. 173 "fact" is established.

. . .

Application dismissed.

NOTES AND QUESTIONS

1. Why did the two creditors who appeared at the hearing support the proposal despite the fact they would have derived a negligible benefit from the proposed payout? Why did the trustee support the proposal? Was it because the trustee felt it owed a greater loyalty to the debtor than to Revenue Canada? Would the debtor have fared better if he had appeared at the hearing and pleaded his cause in person?

2. BIA s. 173, much discussed in Topolniski J's judgment, applies to discharge applications only if the discharge is opposed. In that case, the court must refuse the application, attach conditions to the discharge, or suspend the discharge. Where the court attaches conditions, a common one is that the bankrupt must pay a given percentage of the debts owing to creditors or pay a fixed amount to the trustee for distribution to the creditors. In other words, the court has a broad discretion, but cannot give the bankrupt an unconditional discharge. Presumably, it is for this reason that s. 59(3) provides, in the case of an application for approval of the proposal, that the debtor must provide performance security of not less than 50 cents on the dollar or such percentage thereof as the court may direct.

F. Secured Claims

Bruncor Leasing Inc. v. Zutphen Bros. Construction Ltd. (Trustee of)
(1994), 26 CBR (3d) 258 (NSCA)

HALLETT JA: The main issue in this appeal is whether the appellant, the trustee named in a Proposal made by Zutphen Bros. Construction Limited under the *Bankruptcy and Insolvency Act*, RSC 1985, c. B-3, as amended, erred in disallowing the respondent's claim that it had security against an asset of Zutphen. The respondent was the assignee of a conditional sales contract entered into between a seller of motor vehicles and Zutphen with respect to a sale to Zutphen of a Volvo dump truck. The trustee disallowed the claim to security on the ground that there was a failure to register the conditional sales contract in the registration district for the City of Halifax as required by the *Conditional Sales Act*, RSNS 1989, c. 84.

To determine if the trustee erred it is essential to review the terms of Zutphen's proposal. Clause 4 in the Proposal states:

> Whereas the Company is of the view that to provide for the orderly realization of its principal assets through a Trustee under the Proposal will recover significantly more for the benefit of its creditors generally than would be recovered through a Receivership or other forced liquidation initiated by a single creditor, to the point that the Company is of the view that its assets will likely exceed its liabilities, thus ensuring that all creditors will ultimately be paid in full.

Clause 5 of the Proposal sets out the background of the Company; it states in part:

> … The Company is of the view that its insolvency is a result of the drain upon cash flow made by certain investments in subsidiary companies and projects in the United States of America, which have failed to yield any return. This, and the reluctance of the Company's banker to advance further credit, has caused the Company to be unable to make payments to its creditors on the due dates which has, in turn, led to delay in resolving matters on the two major contracts. The Company is of the view it is best able to resolve the outstanding matters in respect to these contracts and that these contracts alone will ultimately yield sufficient funds to pay substantially all, if not all, of the claims of all preferred and ordinary creditors.

Clause 6 describes the "purpose" of the Proposal as including the objectives set out in the latter part of Clause 5 and further to enable the company to continue with the available cash after meeting the claims of its creditors to settle deficiencies and to provide ongoing warranty where required on existing contracts and to bid and finance new work. Clauses 7 … and 10 of the Proposal provide as follows:

> 7. There shall be one class of Secured Creditors, being all the creditors with a charge or security over assets of the company. …
>
> (2) Creditors with a priority under Section 136.1 of the *Bankruptcy and Insolvency Act* shall be a class of "Preferred" creditors.
>
> (3) All other creditors, being the ordinary creditors of the Company without any security, shall be one class of creditor. …
>
> VESTING OF CERTAIN ASSETS AND CONTINUED OPERATIONS
>
> 10. Upon acceptance of this Proposal, the Company shall vest in the Trustee under the Proposal its interest in its equipment and the Trustee shall enter into an Auction Contract with Ritchie Bros.
>
> Auctioneers which will provide for a net guarantee of $2.759 million, which guarantee shall be secured by a Letter of Credit, pursuant to an offer from Ritchie Bros. Auctioneers dated March 11, 1993, attached as Schedule A to this Proposal.

Clause 11 provides for the vesting of Zutphen's interest in certain real property in the trustee for the purpose of sale. Clause 12 vests in the trustee Zutphen's interest in the net proceeds of certain contracts. Clause 13 provides that the assets aforementioned are being vested in the trustee so that the current value would not become co-mingled with new work generated and undertaken by the Company. Clause 14 provides that the company would continue to operate in the ordinary course of business and to use cash flow generated by assets other than those vested in the trustee to maintain its corporate presence and meet its overhead and operating expenses with two exceptions.

Clause 15 provides for a scheme of distribution. I will not set it out in its entirety; the part that is relevant to this decision is Clause 15(1)(i):

• • •

15. The proceeds of realization shall be distributed in the following manner:

Secured Creditors

(1) To the extent secured creditors hold a specific charge (which shall include a crystallized floating charge) over a single asset or group of assets, they shall be paid from the net proceeds of realization, an amount sufficient to discharge their claim, limited to the actual net realization, which is defined as follows:

(i) In the case of a charge over equipment, the net proceeds of sale as guaranteed by Ritchie Brothers on the attached schedule, plus their pro-rata share of the net proceeds in excess of the total guarantee of Ritchie Brothers, to the limit of their indebtedness.

Clauses 7 and 15(1)(i) are particularly relevant to the issues before the Court. Other clauses show the intention of Zutphen to carry on its business despite the fact that significant assets are vested in the trustee for disposition. This type of proposal is often referred to as a "vesting proposal" in contrast to the more usual proposal in which assets remain in the hands of the debtor.

The Proposal was accepted by the creditors and approved by the court pursuant to the provisions of the *Bankruptcy and Insolvency Act*. The Volvo dump truck and other equipment was sold by Ritchie Bros. Auctioneers. The appellant then disallowed the respondent's claim that it held security against the Volvo.

The respondent appealed the disallowance to the Registrar in Bankruptcy who dismissed the appeal. ... The respondent then appealed the Registrar's decision to the Supreme Court of Nova Scotia. Anderson J allowed the appeal ... ; that decision ... has given rise to this appeal by the trustee.

The appellant's counsel states the issue as being whether the respondent is a secured creditor for the purpose of the distribution of the proceeds realized under the proposal. As set out in paragraph 12 of its factum:

The Appellant's position can be simply stated. The Respondent is not a secured creditor. The Conditional Sales Contract held by the Respondent was not properly registered. The title retention provisions are, in the circumstances of this case, void and of no effect as against the Appellant by virtue of s. 3(1) of the *Conditional Sales Act*.

• • •

The appellant's counsel argues that the trustee is either or both an assignee for the general benefit of the creditors and/or a trustee under the *Bankruptcy Act*; that the trustee in disallowing the claim was enforcing the rights of unsecured creditors who did not have notice of the retention, in the respondent, of title to the Volvo because of the failure to register the conditional sales contract in Halifax and, therefore, pursuant to s. 3(1) of the Act the conditional sales contract is void as against the trustee. Counsel considers it of great significance that the Proposal vests substantially all of Zutphen's assets in the trustee for disposition. There is evidence that certain of Zutphen's creditors, at the time they extended credit to Zutphen, did not have notice that title to the Volvo was in the respondent. Counsel for the appellant takes the position:

> that the purpose (or at least one of the primary purposes) of the Proposal is to enforce the rights of creditors of Zutphen Bros. (including those who had no notice of the Respondent's Conditional Sales Contract at the time of becoming creditors) by vesting the property of Zutphen Bros. in the Trustee for the purpose of liquidating the property in order to satisfy the claims of those creditors. The Proposal is a mechanism for enforcing the respective rights of creditors to payment of their claims.

. . .

With respect, I do not see the issue quite the same way as counsel for the appellant. I am of the opinion the appeal ought to be dismissed on the ground that the Trustee's decision to disallow the respondent's claim to security was founded on his misinterpretation of the terms of the Proposal.

A proposal to creditors, once accepted and approved by the court, becomes a binding contract between the parties with respect to the payment of the creditors' claims (*Employers Liability Insurance Corp. Ltd. v. Ideal Petroleum (1959) Ltd.* (1976), 75 DLR (3d) 63 (SCC)). The Proposal in this case provided that there would be one class of secured creditors "being all creditors with a charge or security over assets of the company." The critical point is that the respondent vis-à-vis Zutphen had security over the Volvo pursuant to the conditional sales contract as it had retained title and had the right to take possession of the Volvo if Zutphen defaulted. Section 3(1) of the *Conditional Sales Act* does not make the security void as between Zutphen and the respondent. The respondent, like other creditors with security, gave up their rights in exchange for Zutphen's undertaking in Clause 15 of the Proposal that those creditors with a specific charge on equipment would be paid from the net proceeds of realization from the sale by Ritchie Bros. In my opinion the respondent, as holder of the conditional sales contract on the Volvo, was a secured creditor within the meaning of that term as defined in Clause 7 of the Proposal.

A proposal is very different from an assignment in bankruptcy, even in a case such as this, where the debtor proposes that most of its assets will be sold by the trustee. The essence of a proposal is that it is an offer of terms by an insolvent person to its creditors to settle its debts and, if accepted by the required statutory majority of the various classes of creditors and approved by the court, becomes a binding contract between the parties. In this case that contract should have been interpreted by the Trustee in a manner that would give effect to its terms and purpose. The clear intention of the parties was that creditors with security against equipment would be paid from the proceeds of the Ritchie Bros sale. In disallowing the respondent's claim to security the trustee failed to give effect to this intention and therefore misinterpreted the Proposal.

Apart from the contractual intention of Zutphen in making the offer as set out in the Proposal and the creditors in accepting it, there are a number of factors, when taken together with the terms of the Proposal, have led me to the foregoing conclusion.

There is no express authority in the *Bankruptcy and Insolvency Act* to authorize a trustee named in a proposal to disallow a claim to security. While the trustee has this right when acting as a trustee in bankruptcy (s. 135), a trustee could only invoke the power when acting in a proposal by application of s. 66(1) of the Act.

As so often stated, the proposal, once accepted and approved, is a contract between the insolvent person and his creditors. Had Zutphen and the creditors wished the trustee to be empowered to challenge securities held by various creditors they would likely have provided in the Proposal a mechanism for doing so similar to that found in the proposal that was reviewed by this Court in *Neiff Joseph Land Surveyors Limited v. Bruce* (1976), 23 CBR (NS) 172 affirmed, 23 CBR (NS) 258. That proposal contained a term that the trustee could attack any preference to the same extent as if there had been an assignment in bankruptcy. This Court was of the opinion that the trustee could exercise this authority conferred on him by the terms of the proposal.

In an annotation to the report of the decision of Anderson J in *Re Mercantile Steel Products Limited* (1978), 27 CBR (NS) 161 (Ont. SC) C.H Morawetz, QC contrasted the *Mercantile* decision, which held that a trustee named in a proposal could not challenge the validity of a creditor's security, with that of this Court in the *Neiff Joseph* case. Morawetz expressed a view that he doubted if the parties to a proposal could confer such authority on a trustee. He was of the view that the wording of the Act reserves this power to a trustee when acting in a bankruptcy. In the *Neiff Joseph* case there was a vesting of assets in the trustee as in this case. I would infer that Mr. Morawetz was of the opinion at the time he penned the annotation that if there is a vesting of assets in the trustee this might be sufficient to enable the creditors to clothe the trustee with the power to review and disallow claims to security but he had "doubts." These two decisions were rendered prior to the 1992 amendments to the Act which, for the first time, provided statutory authority to allow an insolvent person to make a proposal to classes of secured creditors and, if accepted, would be binding on all within the class.

In *Re Henfrey Samson Belair Ltd. and Wedgewood Village Estates Ltd. et al.* (1984), 7 DLR (4th) 79 the British Columbia Court of Appeal held that Section 46(1) of the *Bankruptcy Act*, RSC 1970, c. B-3, which provided that "all the provisions of the Act, insofar as they are applicable, apply *mutatis mutandis* to proposals," has the effect of making ss. 69, 73, 74 and 78 (dealing with fraudulent settlements and preferences) applicable to a proposal in which the debtor's property vests in the trustee. In that case the proposal had been made by a Mr. Scalbania and his company.

In that proposal the trustee was expressly authorized to use the fraudulent preference sections of the Act to set aside any transaction to the same extent as if Scalbania had made an assignment in bankruptcy. Nemetz CJ, writing for the court, made reference to the decision of this court in the *Neiff Joseph* case but made a point of stating that the trustee's power to invoke the fraudulent preference provisions of the Act depended not so much on the spirit and intent of the proposal but on the provisions of s. 46(1) of the Act, the predecessor section to s. 66(1) of the present Act. Applying this reasoning then a trustee named in a proposal would appear to have the power to disallow a claim for security by the application of s. 66(1) of the Act.

The 1992 amendments to the *Bankruptcy Act* included the addition of s. 101.1 which empowers a trustee named in a proposal to challenge preferences and settlements. ...

Sections 91 to 101 authorize a trustee in bankruptcy to challenge certain settlements and preferences. Therefore, pursuant to s. 101.1, unless the proposal otherwise provided, a trustee can challenge settlements and preferences. There is nothing in the Act that expressly authorizes a trustee named in a proposal to disallow a claim to security. Section 135 is in Part V of the Act which parts deals with the administration of the estates of bankrupt.

The case law with respect to the right of a trustee named in the proposal to challenge security for non perfection is in conflict. In the *Mercantile* case Anderson J stated that a trustee under a proposal could not challenge a creditor's security. While the decision turned on other issues Anderson J stated at p. 164:

> My conclusions have been arrived at on the wording of the Act [the *Ontario Personal Property Security Act*] and on the relevant provisions of the *Bankruptcy Act*. I am fortified in my conclusions, however, by consideration of the ultimate purpose and effect of a proposal, and the bearing which that has on the attack made on the position of a secured creditor. The purpose sought by a proposal is continuation of the business carried on by the debtor. While the proposal must present benefits for creditors, it is fundamentally a mechanism for the advantage of the debtor making it. That being the case, it would be anomalous if the debtor could improve its position through objections put forward by the trustee concerning security, of a nature such that they could not have been successfully asserted by the debtor directly. If the proposal succeeds, the ordinary creditors will have received what they contracted to accept and there is no reason why it should be augmented by an amount realized at the expense of a secured creditor. If this proposal does not succeed, bankruptcy will ensue and the trustee in bankruptcy can assert all the rights created by the Act.

This statement was made with reference to a proposal which did not contain a provision for vesting assets in a trustee for disposition and was decided before the 1992 amendments to s. 135 that gave trustees in bankruptcy a new power to disallow claims to security. Prior to this a trustee in bankruptcy could challenge security that was void under provincial legislation but he could not disallow a security claim. The effect of the amendment is to give the trustee this power and then the onus is on the creditor claiming security to appeal the trustee's disallowance to the courts. There is nothing in s. 135 that would indicate an intention of Parliament that trustees named in proposals had a duty to disallow claims to security.

In *Re Toronto Permanent Furniture Showrooms Co. Ltd.* (1960) 1 CBR (NS) 16 (Ont. SC) it was held that a trustee on a proposal has the same powers to disallow claims as a trustee in bankruptcy. That case did not deal with setting aside a security. But as argued by counsel for the appellant it is relevant since the 1992 amendments which allow proposals to be made to secured creditors and in particular the amendment to s. 135 which authorizes a trustee in bankruptcy to disallow claims to security. It would be a logical extension of this decision that the trustee under a proposal could disallow security claims.

In *Bankruptcy Law of Canada*, 3rd edition, Houlden and Morawetz seemed to come down on each side of the issue. At p. 3-75 the authors state:

> A trustee under a proposal cannot challenge a security interest for failure to comply with the PPSA, even though the proposal purports to confer such powers on the trustee. A trustee under a proposal does not represent the creditors of the debtor; he represents the creditors only to the extent necessary to assure performance of the proposal: *Re Mercantile Steel Products Ltd.* (1978), 20 OR (2d) 237, 27 CBR (NS) 161 (SC).

At p. 5-89/90, in reviewing s. 135 of the Act, the authors state:

> In the case of a proposal the trustee is also under a responsibility to see that only provable claims are paid in accordance with their priorities. The appropriate provisions of s. 135 are, by virtue of s. 66, applicable to proposals. Therefore, it would appear that the trustee is entitled to disallow the claim of a creditor for priority also in the case of a proposal and not only in the case of a bankruptcy and this would even be so if the proposal provides for payment in full of all claims: *Re Toronto Permanent Furniture Showrooms Co. (Ont.)* (1960), 1 CBR (NS) 16 (Ont. SC). Apparently the right of a trustee under a proposal to disallow a claim has always been assumed in Ontario: See *Re McKay* (1922), 2 CBR 462 (Ont. SC); *Re Jacobs* (1922), 3 CBR 419 (Ont. SC); or in New Brunswick: *Re McIntyre* (1922), 2 CBR 396 at 408 (NBSC), and has now been settled by the *Toronto Permanent Furniture* case, *supra*. On the other side is the Quebec decision of *Re Marcotte Inc.* (1959), 38 CBR 129 (Que. SC). However, this decision appears rather isolated and seems based on rather exceptional circumstances and, although considered by the court in Ontario in the *Toronto Permanent Furniture* case, was not followed.
>
> The powers of a trustee with regard to the allowing or disallowing of claims in a proposal is the same as the powers of the trustee acting in a bankruptcy."

Under a heading "Disallowance of Secured Claims" (1994—Release 2) the authors state at p. 5-90:

> By reason of the changes made in s. 135 in 1992, the trustee can now disallow a secured claim by the summary procedure in s. 135: s. 135(2)(c).
>
> It was held in *Bruncor Leasing Inc. v. Zutphen Bros. Construction Ltd. (Trustee of)* (1993), 21 CBR (3d) 1 (NS SC) that, by reason of the changes in s. 135(2), the trustee under a proposal may disallow the claim of a secured creditor. In the Bruncor case, the interests of the debtor in its equipment was vested in the trustee under proposal for realization and distribution of the proceeds to creditors; the result can therefore be justified. However, if the debtor is continuing in business and using the equipment of a secured creditor, it is difficult to see why a trustee under a proposal should be able to disallow a secured claim, and, if the trustee is successful in the disallowance, only pay the secured creditor the same settlement that unsecured creditors are receiving under the proposal.

With the exception of the above reference to the Registrar's decision in this proceeding the quoted authorities for the foregoing statements from Houlden and Morawetz's text were made before the 1992 amendments to the Act.

In face of the uncertainty of the law respecting whether a trustee acting under a proposal had power to disallow claims to security for non perfection of registration requirements of provincial statutes it would seem to me that in 1992, when considering the substantial amendments to the proposal sections of the Act, that had Parliament intended that trustees acting under proposals be empowered to disallow such claims, as a trustee can now clearly do when administering a bankrupt estate, Parliament would have expressly stated that a trustee acting in a proposal have this power, just as Parliament did with respect to extending the power to attack preferences and settlements to trustees when administering a proposal. Other than the Registrar's decision in this proceeding we have not been referred to any authority which has expressly held that a trustee acting under a proposal has power to disallow or challenge a security claim unless it was a fraudulent preference or settlement as in the Scalbania proposal. In the annotation to the decision of *Mercantile Steel* previously referred to, Morawetz obviously approved the approach taken by Anderson J in the statement I have quoted from his decision in that case; that is that a trustee under a proposal represents the creditors only to the extent necessary to assure performance of the proposal and not any broad general sense.

· · ·

Given the nature of a proposal, the most recent statement in Houlden and Morawetz accords with my view as to the proper role of the trustee in administering this proposal and accords with the similar views of this Court in the *Neiff Joseph* decision and with the Quebec Court of Appeal in the *Toronto-Dominion Bank v. Seward* (1991), AQ No. 1250.

Section 66(1) of the Act states that all the provisions of the Act insofar as they are applicable apply with such modifications as the circumstances require to proposals. Therefore, it might be reasonable to interpret s. 135(2) as authorizing a trustee named in a proposal to disallow claims to security for non-compliance with the registration requirements of provincial legislation. However, in every case one must look to the terms of the proposal to ascertain the intention of the insolvent person and the creditors as to the role and duties of the trustee named therein.

· · ·

Appeal dismissed.

NOTES AND QUESTIONS

1. The proposition, which is the foundation of the court's judgment in *Bruncor Leasing*, that an approved proposal constitutes an agreement between the creditors and the debtor, was articulated in *Re Lipson* as early as 1925 and is now established law. However, is the contract analogy apt? If the debtor fails to honour the terms of the proposal, does it mean every creditor has a right of action against the debtor for breach of contract? Presumably the answer is "no," because BIA s. 63(1) provides that only the court can annul the proposal. Is s. 60(1) incompatible with the right of creditors to sue the debtor individually, where the debtor has promised to make direct payment to the creditors? Conceptually, is it also correct to speak of creditors "agreeing" to a proposal where only a majority voted in its favour?

2. As far as the main issue in *Bruncor Leasing* is concerned, the right of the trustee of a proposal to challenge the validity of a security interest held by a creditor has much broader implications than just for the BIA. It arises frequently, for example, in CCAA proceedings

where a creditor alleges a security interest is unenforceable because the secured party has failed to file a financing statement in time or because the statement was defective in a material respect. It seems well established that a CCAA monitor is not a representative of creditors and is therefore not an eligible person to challenge the security interest. Should the BIA and the CCAA be amended to provide that the trustee in a proposal has the status to do so, whether before or after acceptance of a proposal, and that the monitor is deemed to have the same powers as a trustee? See Anthony Duggan, "The Status of Unperfected Security Interests in Insolvency Proceedings" (2008), 24 *BFLR* 103.

3. BIA s. 50.1 governs the valuation of a secured creditor's claim for voting purposes. In *Re Workgroup Designs Inc.* (2008), 292 DLR (4th) 185 (OCA), the Royal Bank of Canada held a general security interest in the debtor's assets. Relying on BIA s. 135, the bank filed a proof of claim as a secured creditor, which the proposal trustee disallowed. The trustee's position was that all the debtor's assets were encumbered by the Canada Revenue Agency in priority to the bank so that, on a liquidation, there would be nothing left for the bank. The consequence was to deny the bank its right to vote on the proposal as a secured creditor. The court held that s. 50.1, not s. 135, was the governing provision. Applied to the facts of the present case, s. 50.1 meant that the bank was entitled to vote the full amount of its claim as a secured creditor, and taking this vote into account resulted in rejection of the proposal by the secured creditor's class.

G. Claims of Post-Proposal Creditors

Re Model Craft Hobbies Ltd.
(1981), 39 CBR (NS) 97 (Ont. SC)

ANDERSON J: This is a motion for directions brought by the trustee pursuant to s. 16 of the *Bankruptcy Act*, RSC 1970, c. B-3. The motion relates to the disposition of funds in the hands of a receiver appointed pursuant to a debenture. The funds are the proceeds of sale of the assets covered by that debenture, a sale which was effected with the co-operation of the trustee in bankruptcy.

The principal issue to be resolved relates to the status of the creditors who were creditors of the debtor before a proposal was made, a group that I will refer to for the purpose of these reasons as the pre-proposal creditors, and the creditors who became such during the currency of the proposal, a group which I shall refer to for the purposes of these reasons as the post-proposal creditors.

… The facts which give rise to the matter are not in dispute and are conveniently taken from the affidavit of Alan G. Driver, a senior vice-president of Coopers & Lybrand Limited, the trustee in bankruptcy. Model Craft Hobbies Limited filed a proposal on January 25, 1980, which was amended on February 19, 1980. On February 19th, the amended proposal was accepted by the creditors and on April 2, 1980, was approved by the Court.

The amended proposal provided for payment by Model Craft to the trustee of an amount equal to 20% of the sum of the claims of ordinary creditors on June 30, 1980. Model Craft was unable to comply with this on the date provided but was able to do so with an extension of time. The balance to implement the first payment was distributed to creditors on February 10, 1981. The result is that the first payment of 20% has been paid. During the month of January, 1981, Mr. Driver was informed by Wayne Lucas, the president of Model Craft, that it would be unable to pay an amount equal to 25% of the sum of the claims of ordinary creditors on January 31, 1981, as required by the proposal. No extension was granted. Failure to make the payments required by the amended proposal was a default under the proposal. On the application of the trustee an order was made on February 25th annulling the proposal.

Pursuant to the terms of the proposal, Model Craft had granted a debenture to the trustee containing a floating charge on the assets of Model Craft. The debenture was duly filed pursuant to the requirements of the *Corporation Securities Registration Act*, RSO 1970, c. 88 [now RSO 1980, c. 94], and registered under the provisions of the *Personal Property Security Act*, RSO 1970, c. 344 [now RSO 1980, c. 375]. By appointment in writing pursuant to the terms of the debenture, on February 6, 1981, the trustee under the proposal appointed Robert E. Lowe, the president of Coopers & Lybrand, as receiver and manager of the property, undertaking and assets of Model Craft pursuant to the debenture. As a result of the enforcement of the debenture and with the co-operation of the trustee the fund in question, amounting to some $282,000, has been realized from the assets covered by the debenture.

During the currency of the proposal Model Craft carried on business pursuant to its terms, but has not paid all the claims of all creditors in respect of goods supplied, services rendered or other consideration given subsequent to the date of filing of the proposal. If the money realized by the receiver is distributed to the creditors claiming under the proposal, there will be no assets left for distribution to creditors whose claims arose subsequent to the filing of the proposal or whose claims were deferred pursuant to the proposal with the exception of any assets which may be recovered by action instituted by the trustee and which would not be subject to the secured claims under the debenture. ...

Paragraph 3 of the proposal is in these terms:

> THAT provision for payment for all proper fees, expenses, liabilities and obligations of the trustee and interim receiver and legal fees on and incidental to the proceedings arising out of this proposal, including advice to the debtor in connection therewith, shall be made in priority to all claims of preferred and ordinary creditors.
>
> THAT provision for the payment of all claims of ordinary creditors, being those claims not referred to in paragraphs 1, 2 and 3 of this proposal, including claims of every nature and kind, whether due or not due for payment, as of the date of this proposal including contingent or unliquidated claims arising out of any transactions entered into by the debtor prior to the date of this proposal, shall be made as follows.

Then follow provisions as to the scheme of payments which I do not intend to set out at length. Paragraph 6 of the proposal is as follows:

> THAT claims arising in the respect of goods supplied, services rendered or other consideration given to the debtor subsequent to the date of the filing of this proposal shall be paid in the ordinary course of business by the debtor.

THAT if this proposal is accepted by the creditors and approved by the court, the share-holders of Model Craft Hobbies Limited, Mrs. E.M. Lucas and Mrs. Jo-Anne Lucas shall waive their rights to dividends as ordinary creditors under the terms of this proposal, but shall be otherwise unaffected by the terms of this proposal.

THAT the debtor will not declare or pay any dividends or make any payments of principal, interest or otherwise in respect of its capital stock, shareholder loans or loans payable to Mrs. E.M. Lucas or Mrs. Jo-Anne Lucas until the terms of this proposal have been satisfied in full.

As security for the payments in paragraphs 2, 3 and 4 above the debtor shall issue to the trustee a debenture in the amount of $2,000,000 charging all of the assets of the debtor. The trustee, at the request of the debtor, shall postpone this debenture to the security interest of the debtor's bankers up to but not exceeding an amount equal to the sum of $600,000 plus any amounts paid by the debtor to the trustee under paragraph 4 above.

THAT if this proposal is accepted by the creditors and approved by the court, the debtor will forthwith make application for amendment of its letters patent to permit the issue of redeemable preferred shares, which shares shall be issued to Mrs. Jo-Anne Lucas at par, in satisfaction of monies advanced to the company.

The debenture is in a form commonly in use in commercial practice and accords in its terms with the provision for it in the proposal. I propose to refer briefly to only two sections of the debenture. First, the opening words of para. 2:

The company, as security for the due payment of those certain sums set out in paragraphs 2, 3 and 4 of the proposal referred to in section 1 hereof, and all other monies from time to time owing hereunder, but subject to the reservation as to leaseholds contained in sections 5 hereof, hereby charges with such payments as and by way of a first floating charge, its undertaking and all its property and assets. ...

And the opening portion of s. 6 of the debenture in these terms:

The monies hereby secured shall become immediately payable and the security hereby constituted shall become enforceable in each and every [one] of the events following:

(a) If the company makes default in any payments referred to in either this debenture or the proposal mentioned in section 1 hereof. ...

The questions as raised by the notice of motion are put in these terms:

1. Should the proceeds be paid to creditors who filed claims in the proposal on the grounds that they are secured creditors, or

2. Should the funds be paid to all creditors rateably including creditors whose claims arose subsequent to the date of filing of the proposal.

It was suggested in the course of argument that some slight variation of these questions might be appropriate and I shall return to that in due course.

• • •

The argument on behalf of the pre-proposal creditors is basically very simple. It is that they take all of the fund because all of the proceeds from the sale of assets charged and seized under the debenture will be required to satisfy the pre-proposal creditors for whose benefit the debenture was taken. It is pointed out that by the terms of the proposal and the debentures, the latter was taken for the benefit of those entitled to payment under paras. 2, 3 and 4 of the debenture and that the post-proposal creditors do not fall within any of those groups. I propose to deal first with that general issue and then to return to a disposition of the question or questions relating to the shareholders, the two Mrs. Lucas.

The arguments of counsel for the post-proposal creditors rests principally upon para. 6 of the debenture which, for convenience of reference, I set out again:

> THAT claims arising in the respect of goods supplied, services rendered or other consideration given to the debtor subsequent to the date of the filing of this proposal shall be paid in the ordinary course of business by the debtor.

Counsel for the post-proposal creditors first points out that as matters developed under the proposal, the great majority of those providing goods, services or other consideration subsequent to the filing of the proposal have been paid in full and that it would be inequitable that others, having such dealings with the debtor, should not have equal treatment. Further, he argues that s. 6 properly interpreted implies a priority in favour of the persons there described over the pre-proposal creditors.

Both counsel make reference to two cases, a brief discussion of which will point up the relatively narrow focal point of difference between the two arguments. The first of these cases is *Re M. Thoun Estate* (1925), 29 OWN 68, [1925] 4 DLR 242, 7 CBR 251. The [CBR] headnote with respect to that case reads in part as follows:

> Under sec. 51(4) of *The Bankruptcy Act* all debts proved in the bankruptcy or under an assignment shall be paid *pari passu* and consequently persons, becoming creditors after a composition which has been approved by the Court, are not entitled to priority in payment of their claims over the persons who became creditors prior thereto. ...
>
> But where the persons who became creditors prior to the composition agree "that all new goods accounts are to constitute a preferred claim against the assets" as one of the terms of the composition, they have contracted themselves out of the above section and are estopped from contesting the priority of the subequent creditors.

One of the terms of the proposal in that case was "that all new goods accounts are to constitute a preferred claim against the assets." On my reading of the case the disposition indicated in the concluding portion of the headnote depended upon that provision in the proposal.

The second of the two cases referred to by counsel is *Re Ogden Enterprises Ltd.*, the report of which is found in (1978), 22 NBR (2d) 344 ... . In that case also the rights of pre-proposal and post-proposal creditors fell to be determined and the case also involved debentures as does the present case.

The critical paragraph of the proposal, which is found at p. 346 of the report, is in these terms:

> That all claims arising and amounts payable (including principal and interest) in respect of goods supplied, services rendered, lease agreements, current business and property taxes and consideration given (including loans or advances arranged, and specifically, but without limiting the foregoing, the financing provided for in paragraph 6) after the date of the within

proposal, shall be paid in full in the ordinary course of business and in priority to the claims of the unsecured creditors of the Company (whether preferred or ordinary) as existing at the effective date of the within proposal.

The disposition in the case was a holding that in the circumstances the debentures were subject to the specific priority created by the proposal in favour of the post-proposal creditors.

Dealing with these cases, counsel for the pre-proposal creditors in the matter before me submits that the post-proposal creditors in *Thoun* and *Ogden* prevailed because of the express terms of the proposal which gave them a priority. He submits that such express terms are lacking in the proposal before me and that therefore the post-proposal creditors fail. Counsel for the post-proposal creditors says that, properly interpreted in the context of a proposal, s. 6 of the proposal should be held to give a priority and the result should be as in *Thoun* and *Ogden*.

… I am not prepared to accept that submission. In my view, so long as the proposal was in existence and operative, para. 6 was in existence and operative, and it was open to the debtor to pay the claims described in s. 6 of the proposal pursuant to the terms of that section. In my view that section had force and governed only while the proposal was *in esse* and not otherwise or afterwards. This conclusion substantially disposes of the issue between the pre-proposal and post-proposal creditors. The first group takes the fund.

· · ·

Judgment accordingly.

NOTES

1. The position, as expounded by Anderson J in the above case, is still good law and the warning it conveys to post-NOI/proposal creditors is *caveat creditor*. Is this a fair allocation of risks between the pre-NOI and proposal creditors and subsequent creditors? Does it make a difference whether or not post-NOI/proposal creditors were aware of the proposal proceedings? If they were not aware (and, remember, there is no statutory obligation on a proposal debtor to advertise or otherwise alert post-NOI/proposal creditors of insolvency), presumably the creditors must have assumed the normal risk of not being paid and of having to share the bankrupt's estate with other unsecured creditors. Should it make a difference that the post-proposal creditors knew of the proposal proceedings? Can they rely on an implicit understanding, in the absence of an explicit BIA provision, that if the proposal fails their claims will have priority over the claims of pre-NOI/proposal creditors because otherwise post-proposal creditors will always insist on being paid before or at the time of rendering services or supplying goods? It might also be argued that insolvency law should accept the priority of post-proposal creditors' claims in the interests of efficiency and minimizing contracting costs.

2. The last argument is supported by the well-established legal position that, in straight bankruptcies, trustees of the estate are personally liable for post-bankruptcy debts unless they have expressly disclaimed personal liability. It is true most Canadian courts have rationalized this result on the basis that the trustee contracts as principal, and not as agent for

the estate, which, recall, has no legal personality under the BIA. Nevertheless, the result makes good sense because it puts the burden on the trustee to limit or exclude his liability and the trustee is in a much better position to assess the estate's post-bankruptcy ability to meet its new debts than are outsiders.

3. The results in *Model Craft Hobbies Ltd.* were particularly striking. This is because Anderson J not only upheld the validity of the general security interest given by the proposal-debtor in favour of the pre-proposal creditors, but also because he held that the post-proposal creditors were not entitled to share in the assets subject to the security interest. Intuitively one feels there is something wrong about this result. Anderson J said the post-proposal creditors should have appreciated this risk as well. Do you agree? How would you frame your argument in legal terms?

H. Annulment of Proposals

Re No. 289 Taurus Ventures Ltd.
(2000), 16 CBR (4th) 112 (BCSC)

LOWRY J: [1] Application is made under s. 63 of the *Bankruptcy and Insolvency Act*, RSC 1985, c. B-3 for the annulment of amended bankruptcy proposals which are in default. It is opposed in the main on the ground that the petitioning creditors will derive no gain from the bankruptcy that will result, and the court is asked to exercise the discretion the Act affords in favour of allowing the respondent companies more time to meet their obligations.

[2] Application is also made by the companies for an order that the trustee pay their solicitors' fees incurred in connection with the amended proposals out of funds it received to support the proposals when they were made. The application is opposed on the basis that the companies are not entitled to the payment of their solicitors' fees out of those funds.

[3] The petitioners are 22 of a large number of the unsecured creditors of No. 289 Taurus Ventures Ltd., 544553 BC Ltd., and Prema Systems Ltd. The three are related companies that own 125 acres of commercial property on River Road in Richmond, BC The Royal Bank is the holder of the first mortgage security. Foreclosure proceedings were initiated some time ago, and an order has been made giving the bank conduct of sale at the end of May in ten weeks time. In May 1999, faced with bankruptcy proceedings commenced by unsecured creditors, the respondents filed notice under the Act of their intention to make proposals for the orderly discharge of their unsecured debt. The proposals were made in November and, as amended, were approved by the court in December. They required payments of $500,000 in January and $2,000,000 in February. Nothing has been paid to the creditors. The trustee continues to hold the funds ($100,000) received at the time the proposals were made.

[4] The proposals were made only after all of the time for extensions the Act affords was exhausted. They were to have been funded by a Byron Seaman. The affidavit material filed to obtain the extensions that were granted is replete with assurances of a transaction being negotiated with Mr. Seaman that would provide all of the funding required. The

principles [*sic*] of the companies now say they were overly optimistic at the time the proposals were made that they would reach agreement with Mr. Seaman, but they continue to insist that a "deal" is imminent. There is, however, nothing from Mr. Seaman in this regard as would be expected if he was interested in making a substantial investment, and it is acknowledged that the companies have been unable to obtain anything from him in writing to assist them in resisting the application with which they are now confronted.

[5] Nonetheless, the companies maintain that the proposals should not be annulled. While throughout these proceedings they have been contending the appraised value of the land was sufficiently high to cover all of the debt, they now say that if the appraisals of the land upon which the bank relied in the foreclosure proceedings are sound, the unsecured creditors will gain nothing in a bankruptcy because those appraisals show the bank will suffer a substantial shortfall. The companies say the proposals should be varied to defer the payments to the end of May on the premise that, if they are unable to reorganize their affairs by the time the bank is entitled to take conduct of the sale of the land, they will then have to accept the consequences of the proposals being annulled.

[6] They contend further that under the Act they are entitled to a period of grace running to 60 days from the date of default in any event. They say this is so because s. 63 must be read with s. 62.1 of the Act and s. 93 of the Bankruptcy Rules, CRC 1978, c. 368. But the point taken has already been addressed by this court on this application: *In the Matter of the Bankruptcy of 544553 BC Ltd.*, [2000] BCJ no. 323, 2000 BCSC 277. The application was adjourned then so the point was not decided, but the companies' contention was fully considered and rejected. I respectfully adopt what has already been said in this regard. Section 63 is a discreet provision unencumbered by any prescriptions of time.

[7] The petitioners point out that the companies are insolvent and there have been two defaults in proposals they made that it is now clear were based on misplaced optimism with respect to obtaining the funding required. There can be no confidence in the companies' continuing assurances that any funding is forthcoming. Almost 11 months have now elapsed since the companies gave notice of their intention to make proposals and the proceedings that have followed have brought the parties to court no less than 18 times largely with respect to the extensions the companies repeatedly sought and the various adjournments that were necessitated along the way. This application alone has been adjourned twice. The petitioners say with good reason "enough is enough." They have decided that their interests will be better served in a bankruptcy than if the proposals are varied as the companies propose and the proceedings further protracted.

[8] Section 63(1) of the Act provides:

> Where default is made in the performance of any provision in a proposal, or where it appears to the court that the proposal cannot continue without injustice or undue delay or that the approval of the court was obtained by fraud, the court may, on application thereto, with such notice as the court may direct to the debtor, and, if applicable to the trustee and to the creditors, annul the proposal.

[9] The authorities that bear on the exercise of the court's discretion under s. 63 are not many. They reflect a divergence of views as to whether a proposal should be annulled if there will be no gain to the creditors involved. In Alberta it has been held that it should: *Re Continental Express Lines Ltd. (M. & P. Transport Ltd.)* (1973), 18 CBR (NS) 143

(Alta. TD) at 146, and that the requirement of a benefit is not to be found in the wording of the section: *Northlands Café Inc., Re* (1996), [1997] 2 WWR 52 (Alta. QB) paras. 10-12. The decision of the New Brunswick Court of Queens Bench in *Barclays Bank of Canada v. Coopers & Lybrand Ltd.* (1995), 35 CBR (3d) 217 would appear to be consistent with that view. However, in *T.E. Quinn Truck Lines, Re* (1987), 64 CBR (NS) 255 at 259, the Ontario Supreme Court distinguished *Continental Express* factually and, relying on Halsbury, 4th ed., Vol. 3, p. 250, para. 437, held that discretion will not be exercised in favour of annulment if it can be seen plainly that the creditors will gain nothing.

[10] In *Gavex, A Resource Corp., Re* (1989), 77 CBR (NS) 102, this court applied what was described as the narrower view expressed in *T.E. Quinn* in annulling a proposal, but held [that] creditors would benefit from the annulment in any event. In *Skalbania, Re* (1990), 2 CBR (3d) 205, this court found that the annulment sought would probably not benefit the creditors, but the application was nonetheless allowed in part. Quoting O'Halloran JA in *Re City Construction Co.* (1961), 29 DLR (2d) 568 (BCCA) at 570, it was held that s. 63 could be interpreted widely enough to permit the court to amend, alter, or vary the proposal and it was amended to best accommodate the somewhat unusual circumstances that had arisen.

[11] *Gavex* and *Skalbania* do not in my respectful view lead to a clear determination of which view is to be preferred by this court. *Gavex* would have been decided as it was regardless, and *Skalbania* did not squarely address the point.

[12] However, even assuming that it is the narrower view that should prevail, it appears to me the companies bear the burden of establishing plainly that the unsecured creditors will gain nothing from the resulting bankruptcy. This they have not done. Whatever gain they may enjoy appears for all practical purposes to turn on the value of the land and, as indicated, the companies have maintained until now that it was sufficiently high to cover their debt. They cannot be heard to contend for a lower value now to resist the application with which they are confronted. In any event, it is far from clear on the evidence adduced that the unsecured creditors will gain nothing from the deemed assignment that will follow the proposals being annulled. It is at best a matter of speculation.

[13] The 22 unsecured creditors speculate that they will benefit from the annulment they seek. The companies have not established that they are wrong. I am told that the remainder of the unsecured creditors have been notified of this application (counsel is to file proof) and only one lends support to the position the companies take.

Proposals annulled.

IV. OPERATIONAL EXPERIENCE UNDER PART III.1

**Jacob S. Ziegel, "New and Old Challenges in Approaching Phase Three
Amendments to Canada's Commercial Insolvency Laws"**
(2002), 37 *CBLJ* 75, at 81-83 (footnotes omitted)

On balance, I believe the impact of the 1992 and 1997 BIA amendments has been very
positive and that, with two exceptions, the amendments have achieved their proponents'
objectives. The exceptions involve the unpaid suppliers' rights and the international insolvency provisions, both of which will be discussed hereafter.

The impact of the new BIA Division III.1 is particularly significant. I discuss below the
ongoing controversy whether Canada should retain the two quite separate reorganizational
vehicles. Let me at this juncture report briefly on operational experience with the BIA-
driven commercial proposals. The overriding goal of Division III.1 is to encourage commercial reorganizations or going concern sales as an alternative to straight liquidation, to
make the new procedure easily accessible to debtors while leaving the debtor in possession
of the enterprise, to allow secured creditors to be included in a proposal (and meanwhile
to be bound by the stay of proceedings), and to offer unsecured creditors the prospect of
a substantially higher rate of return than is normally available in a straight liquidation.

The available statistics show that these objectives have been met, but there are also
some negative features. The number of individual Division III.1 proposals grew from 217
in 1993 to 966 by 1999, an increase of 345%. However, the failure rate was also significant
and fluctuated between 46.3% in 1993 and 24% in 1998. Corporate Division 1 proposals
grew from 534 in 1993 to 797 in 1999, an increase of 49%. The failure rate was also very
high and fluctuated between 54.6% in 1994 and 65.9% in 1996.

Table 1, which is derived from an empirical study of all corporate BIA III.1 filings in
the Toronto regional office between November 1992 (the implementation date of the new
provisions) and the end of 1997, provides a closer insight into the actual operation of
Division III.1 corporate proposals. The study yielded 148 files for which complete or
nearly complete data were available. The performance profile was as follows:

Table 1

Final Outcome	Count	%
A. Proposal Fully Implemented	48	33
B. Failure to File Cashflow Statement	6	3
C. Failure to File Proposal	26	17
D. Proposal Rejected by Creditors	26	18
E. Proposal Rejected by Court	6	4
F. Default by Debtor after Court Approval	17	12
G. Approved by Creditors, Current Status Unknown	1	1
H. Approved by Creditors & Court, Still in Progress	9	6
I. Proposal Failed for Other Reason	7	5
J. File Missing from OSB	2	1
Total:	148	100

The estimated median realization rate for unsecured creditors under the proposals was 31.5%, compared with an average realization rate of 6.89% in straight liquidations. The median assets, medium encumbered assets, and medium deficit in our sample were respectively $505,215, $415,502, and $712,004. These modest figures reflect the fact that since the late 1980s most large reorganizations have been conducted under the CCAA. However, Table 2 shows that the *average* assets and liabilities were much larger than the median figures.

Table 2

	Average	Median	Minimum	Maximum
Total Assets	$2,197,028	$ 505,215	0	$53,029,000
Encumbered				
Assets	$2,008,220	$ 415,502	0	$53,029,000
Unencumbered				
Assets	$ 188,808	0	0	$ 3,590,000
Liabilities	$4,398,527	$1,794,677	$ 98,472	$74,477,176
Deficit	$2,201,498	$ 712,004	+$17,755,472	$ 4,477,176
			(surplus)	

It seems reasonable to conclude, based on the rapid increase in the number of commercial proposals, that the ease of initiating proceedings, the debtor's right to remain in possession, and the automatic stay of proceedings by secured as well as unsecured creditors are proving very attractive to small and medium sized insolvent businesses. However, the easy access comes at a steep price in the form of a high failure rate, although most of the failures occur within the first six months of the initiation of proceedings.

NOTE ON PAPILLON/GOSSELIN QUEBEC STUDY (2005)

In 2005, Professors Benoit Mario Papillon and Jocelyn Gosselin of the Université du Quebec at Trois Rivières reported on a study of BIA proposal procedures used by 2,704 incorporated businesses in Montreal and Quebec City between 1998-2003. See "Empirical Analysis of the Effectiveness of the Reorganization Procedures Under the BIA and the CCAA" found at http://www.ic.gc.ca/epic/site/bsf-osb.nsf/vwapj/Papillon-Gosselin-2005-ENG.pdf/$FILE/Papillon-Gosselin-2005-ENG.pdf. The authors presented an updated analysis of their results at the 4th Academic Conference, *Office of the Superintendent of Bankruptcy*, May 12-13, 2008, Ottawa.

The study yielded the following results on geographical differences in BIA commercial proposal procedures, among many others. The number of proposals accepted by creditors in Montreal was 44 percent compared with 53 percent in Quebec City. In Montreal, the number of proposals performed without notice of default was 34 percent of the number of proposals accepted and 15 percent of the total number of files. In Quebec City, the corresponding figures were 54 percent and 29 percent. The average value of assets was $700,000 and the authors observed a downward trend in the average value of assets-to-liabilities ratio from 0.51 in 1995 to 0.39 in 2005.

CHAPTER SEVENTEEN

Consumer Proposals

I. ALTERNATIVES TO CONSUMER BANKRUPTCIES

There are various reasons why an insolvent consumer may prefer to seek debt relief by other means than a bankruptcy:

1. to avoid the stigma of bankruptcy (perhaps now of diminishing concern, but still relevant, especially among professionals);

2. to protect non-exempt assets that would become part of the estate in a bankruptcy;

3. to avoid having to pay unaffordable trustee fees and disbursements (a relevant consideration in Canada before trustees were willing to accept payment by installments); and

4. in response to the stricter rules governing discharge from bankruptcy where the debtor has surplus income. (Prior to the 2007 amendments, the trustee had discretion to oppose the 9-month automatic discharge on the ground of the "debtor's ability to make payments": BIA ss. 168.1, 170, and 170.1. The 2007 amendments have substituted a hard-and-fast rule that debtors with surplus income must wait 21 months (first-time bankrupts) or 26 months (second-time bankrupts) before being eligible for discharge: new s. 168.1. Moreover, a debtor with more than $200,000 personal income tax debt representing 75 percent or more of the debtor's total unsecured debts is not eligible for automatic discharge, and an application for discharge is required: new s. 172.1.)

Creditors also have their own reasons for supporting alternatives to bankruptcy. To them, bankruptcy sends the wrong message—that is, it's easy to slough off debts and walk away from one's obligations—whereas the various alternatives to straight bankruptcy involve the debtor making at least partial payments on the debts for a substantially longer period. In practice, however, the difference between straight bankruptcy and the most common alternative in use in Canada today, a consumer proposal under BIA Part III.2, is more a question of degree and perception than of substance. The reason for this is that, generally, only debtors with surplus income are able to opt for a consumer proposal, and these are the same debtors that would be required to make income contributions throughout the bankruptcy period in a straight bankruptcy.

A. Evolution of Alternatives

In Canada, viable alternatives to straight bankruptcy were slow to develop. The 1919 *Bankruptcy Act* contained provisions enabling any debtor, not just consumer debtors, to make a proposal to the debtor's creditors instead of filing for bankruptcy. However, the provisions were not consumer-friendly and, in any event, a 1923 amendment permitted the presentation of a proposal only after bankruptcy. In 1932, Manitoba enacted an *Orderly Payment of Debts Act*, which introduced a simple procedure that enabled a debtor to apply to the clerk of the county court for an order staying creditors' collection efforts while the debtor made installment payments that the clerk determined to be reasonable, based on the debtor's aggregate debts. However, the debtor was still obliged to pay off all the debts. Alberta adopted similar legislation in 1959, but it was struck down by the Supreme Court of Canada as unconstitutional. See *Reference re Orderly Payment of Debts Act 1959 (Alberta)*, [1960] SCR 571, excerpted in Chapter 2.

To fill the gap created by the decision, in 1965, the federal government added new Part X to the BIA, essentially replicating the Manitoba and Alberta provisions. Part X applies only in Alberta, Saskatchewan, Nova Scotia, and Prince Edward Island. Before 1992, Part X enjoyed considerable popularity among low-income consumers. Since then, support has dropped off significantly. In 1998, the total number of Part X orders amounted to only 1,539. The reasons for this decline were: (1) Part X does not provide for remission of any part of the debts and, therefore, does not help those consumers with heavy debt burdens and negligible surplus income; (2) consumer bankruptcies have become much more accessible and affordable even for low-income consumers; and (3) BIA Part III.2, added in 1992, provides more effective relief than does Part X.

B. Consumer Proposals Under BIA Part III.2

The addition of a new part to the BIA to deal with consumer proposals, as a counterpart to the new provisions on commercial proposals in BIA Part III.1, was first recommended in the Colter report of 1986. Nevertheless, consumer debtors' initial response to Part III.2 was modest. The number of consumer proposals in 1995—2,491—was only 341 more than the number of Part X orders for that year. The number of consumer proposals grew to 4,737 in 1997 and to 19,486 in 2007. In 2006, 19.5 percent of all consumer insolvency files were proposals, compared with only 3.8 percent in 1983. The increase is probably due to the 1997 amendments to the BIA, requiring individual bankrupts to make mandatory surplus income payments. Another plausible reason is that in 1998 the fee structure in the bankruptcy rules was substantially changed to give trustees a stronger incentive than they had before to recommend consumer proposals to their clients. Other factors include:

- protection of equity in home;

- on filing a consumer proposal, stay of proceedings comes into effect (see BIA s. 69.2(1)); the stay is similar to the bankruptcy stay, and remains effective until the consumer proposal has been withdrawn, refused, annulled or deemed annulled, or the administrator has been discharged;

- protection of RRSPs;

- existence of tax debt; and

- stigma.

C. Structure of BIA Part III.2

The following are the key features of the consumer proposal provisions:

- Part III.2 is available only to a natural person who is bankrupt or insolvent, and whose aggregate debts, excluding any debts secured by the person's principal residence, do not exceed $250,000 or such other maximum as may be prescribed. (Before the 2007 amendments, the maximum was $75,000) (s. 66.11).)

- A consumer proposal must be made to creditors, generally, but is not binding on secured creditors who have not filed a proof of claim under BIA ss. 124-134 (s. 66.28(2)).

- The debtor must use the services of an administrator (defined in s. 66.13) who, after investigating the debtor's financial circumstances, will file a consumer proposal on the debtor's behalf with the official receiver. Within 10 days of the filing of the consumer proposal, the administrator is required to file a report with the official receiver (s. 66.14) setting out (1) the results of the administrator's inquiries into the debtor's assets and liabilities; (2) the administrator's opinion about whether the consumer proposal is reasonable and fair to the consumer debtor and the creditors, and whether the consumer debtor will be able to perform it; and (3) a list of the creditors whose claims exceed $250. The administrator is also required to forward the creditors a copy of the consumer proposal and statement of affairs referred to in s. 66.13(2)(d) together with a proof of claim form.

- Ordinarily, no meeting of creditors is necessary to vote on a consumer proposal. Instead, when returning their proofs of claim, creditors will indicate their assent to or dissent from the consumer proposal (s. 66.17(1)).

- A meeting of creditors to consider a consumer proposal is only necessary (1) if required by the official receiver, or (2) if, within 45 days following the filing of the consumer proposal, creditors holding claims equal to at least 25 percent of the value of proven claims request such a meeting (s. 66.15(2)). (In practice, creditors rarely require a meeting to consider the consumer proposal.)

- If there is no obligation to call a meeting, the consumer proposal is deemed to be approved (s. 66.18(1)).

- Ordinarily, the court's approval is not necessary before the consumer proposal becomes effective. There is an exception where the official receiver or "any other interested party" requests a review by the court (s. 66.22(1).)

D. Division II Consumer Proposals Versus Business Division I Proposals

The distinction between a consumer proposal and a business proposal (discussed in Chapter 16) is not always clear. The distinction under the BIA is based on the amount of debt the debtor has accumulated. Any natural person who is insolvent, including a bankrupt, whose debts are less than $75,000, excluding a home mortgage, can make a consumer proposal. Recently there have been an increasing number of individuals filing business Division I proposals. This pattern may shift following the increase in the cap for filing a consumer proposal from $75,000 to $250,000, introduced as part of the 2007 amendments. It is interesting that, for the purpose of data collection and reporting, the OSB does not rely on the amount of debt, but rather defines a consumer proposal as one where 50 percent of the debt is consumer related. A consumer proposal is more favorable to a debtor than a business Division I proposal for the following reasons:

- It provides for a simplified and less costly process—for example, if no objections are received after the requisite notice periods, the proposal is deemed to have been accepted by the creditors and the court without the necessity of holding creditors' meetings or going to court for approval; this is not the case for a Division 1 proposal.

- The debtor is not automatically bankrupt if a consumer proposal is not accepted, as is the case for a Division 1 proposal.

- On the other hand, a business Division 1 proposal may be attractive to a debtor for the following reasons:

  — there is no debt restriction; and

  — if the proposal is accepted, counselling is not required; in contrast, under Division II, the debtor is required to participate in two mandatory counselling sessions.

E. Scope of Consumer Proposals

The BIA is flexible with respect to the permissible scope of a consumer proposal—see the definition of "proposal" in s. 2(1), which permits a proposal in the form of a composition, extension of time, or scheme of arrangement. (The first and third terms are not defined and are derived from 19th century English usage in commercial reorganizations.) In practice, most consumer proposals will be in the form of a composition—that is, payment of a percentage of the debts over a prescribed period or as a lump sum. However, a consumer proposal cannot run for more than five years and must provide for payment in priority of all preferential claims under s. 136(1) of the BIA: s. 66.12(6). All payments to creditors under the consumer proposal must be channeled through the administrator.

Amendments to a consumer proposal after it has been approved are permitted, in which case all Division II provisions apply to the consumer proposal and amended consumer proposal, with any modification that the circumstances require (s. 66.37).

F. Annulment of Consumer Proposals (Section 66.3)

The BIA recognizes two types of annulment of a consumer proposal: (1) automatic annulment, which occurs where payments under the consumer proposal are to be made monthly or more frequently and the debtor is in default for an amount that is equal to or more than the amount of three payments; similarly, where payments are due less frequently than monthly and the debtor is in default for more than three months on any payment: s. 66.31; and (2) court-approved annulment, which is necessary or available in other cases where, *inter alia*, the debtor is in default of performance of any other provision of the consumer proposal or where the court is satisfied that the consumer proposal cannot continue without injustice or undue delay: s. 66.3.

The failure rate for consumer proposals is high. In 2002, of 13,803 completed files, 37 percent of Division II consumer proposals failed. In 2003, the failure rate was 40.2 percent of the 12,966 completed proposals. (This was the most recent data available at the time of writing. The OSB does not track the number of failures and completion rate of consumer proposals.) This is probably due to excessive optimism by debtors when anticipating their future income stream and their inability to maintain a rigorous financial self-discipline during the life of the consumer proposal, which is normally three years. Canadian studies also show that some trustees are more aggressive than others in promoting the virtues of consumer proposals to debtors. Whatever the reasons, the high failure rate gives cause for concern because it means that debtors who are forced into bankruptcy, after having started with a consumer proposal, are worse off than they would have been had they gone into bankruptcy to begin with.

A recent empirical study (Janis Sarra, *Economic Rehabilitation: Understanding the Growth in Consumer Proposals*, commissioned by the Office of the Superintendent in Bankruptcy, 2008) found that the points of failure for consumer proposals were significant for an understanding of which aspects of the process need to be improved to increase success rates. The points of failure from 2002-4 were:

- 4-6 percent withdrew before approval;

- 8-12 percent failed because creditors rejected the proposal;

- Less than 0.08 percent failed due to lack of court approval; and

- 87 percent (2002), 84 percent (2003), and 81 percent (2004) failed due to automatic (or deemed) annulment.

Under the 2007 amendments, the administrator, in the case of a deemed annulment of a consumer proposal made by a person other than a bankrupt, may revive the proposal if he or she considers it appropriate. To do so, the administrator must send a notice in the prescribed form to both the official receiver and the creditors within 10 days of the proposal's deemed annulment, stating that the proposal will be automatically revived within 45 days of its deemed annulment unless a notice of objection is filed with the administrator. If an objection to the revival is filed, the administrator must notify both the official receiver and creditors that the proposal will not be revived. The administrator may also apply to the court at any time, on notice to the official receiver and creditors, to have the consumer debtor's proposal revived, if the consumer debtor is not a bankrupt. The court may revive the consumer proposal on any terms it considers appropriate. When a consumer proposal is revived, the administrator must file a report with the official receiver in relation to the revival and must send notice of the revival to the creditors informing them of the revival.

G. Comparison to the United States

Prior to the 2005 amendments, the discharge rate of Chapter 13 filings was less than one-third of cases filed. (Jean Braucher, "A Fresh Start for Personal Bankruptcy Reform: The Need for Simplification and a Single Portal" (2006), 55 *Am. UL Rev.* 1295, at 1298 and 1318.)

Two-thirds of debtors who file Chapter 13 do not complete their plans. Excluding cases "never confirmed by a bankruptcy court (22.8 percent of Chapter 13 cases filed), the completion rate in Chapter 13 increases to 42.7 percent" (Jean Braucher, "Comparative Study of Repayment Forms of Consumer Bankruptcy: Identifying Common Empirical Criteria and Analysing Available Data" (2008), Arizona Legal Studies Discussion Paper no. 08-09, available at SSRN online, http://ssrn.com/abstract=1116011, citing Scott F. Norberg and Andrew J. Velkey, "Debtor Discharge and Creditor Repayment in Chapter 13" (2006), 39 *Creighton L Rev.* 473, at 477-78, 533-35, and note 164 (using this measure)).

The ratio of Chapter 13 to Chapter 7 filings in the United States is approximately 2:3, based on annual non-business filings data for 2007 (US Courts, Bankruptcy Statistics, "2007 Calendar Year by Chapter," available online, at http://www.uscourts.gov/bnkrpctystats/statistics.htm#calendar).

Some of the reasons for the greater popularity of Chapter 13 filings in the United States as compared with consumer proposals in Canada are the following:

1. Prior to the 2007 BIA amendments, Chapter 13 had a substantially higher ceiling for the admissible amount of debt. (The BIA amendments raise the debt ceiling to $250,000 excluding a mortgage; in the United States, the unsecured debt ceiling is $250,000 and the secured debt ceiling is $750,000.)

2. Chapter 13 permits the debtor to modify the rights of holders of secured claims, other than a claim secured only by a security interest in the debtor's principal residence, and provides for the curing or waiving of any default, including default in payments on a residential mortgage.

3. The list of non-dischargeable debts is significantly smaller in Chapter 13 cases than it is for Chapter 7 filings, whereas BIA Part III.2 draws no distinction for this purpose between consumer proposals and bankruptcies.

4. In cases of hardship and subject to other conditions, the US bankruptcy court may discharge the balance of the consumer's debts even though the debtor has not met the terms of the plan. A Canadian court has no such power under BIA Part III.2. (It seems, however, that, in practice, US courts are reluctant to grant hardship relief.)

5. The addition of a means test as a result of the 2005 US bankruptcy amendments is also aimed at making it more difficult for debtors to file for Chapter 7, thus supposedly increasing the number of Chapter 13 filings.

The US failure rate under Chapter 13 has been between 60 and 70 percent for a substantial number of years and is therefore about twice as high as the Canadian rate based on the most recent available data. The higher US figure is probably due to a number of reasons. First, the number of proposals to bankruptcies is about 40 percent higher in the United States than in Canada. Second, US consumers have stronger incentives to opt for Chapter 13. Third, US observers have found that local bankruptcy judges and bankruptcy attorneys play an important role in persuading consumers to opt for a Chapter 13 over a Chapter 7 bankruptcy and may do so, even when the prospects for successful plan completion are not good.

H. Non-Profit Debt Repayment and Credit Counselling Service Agencies

Apart from the statutory facilities under BIA Parts III.2 and X, overindebted Canadian consumers also have access to non-profit and non-statutory debt repayment and credit counselling service agencies (more commonly referred to as CCS agencies), of which there are now one or more outlets in most provinces. The largest and oldest of the credit counselling agencies in Ontario is Credit Counselling Service of Toronto, which was established in 1965. In the province of Quebec, credit counselling services are provided by ACEF, *Association coopérative d'économie familiale*. ACEF differs from the agencies in the English-speaking provinces because it accepts no funds from creditors and creditors are not represented on its board of directors. There are 24 non-profit credit counselling agencies in Ontario, all members of an umbrella organization, the Ontario Association of Credit Counselling Services (OACCS). "Credit counselling" is a misnomer because, from the beginning, the agencies have been equally active in running debt management programs for the benefit of debtors and their creditors. For example, in fiscal year 1998, the OACCS opened 13,944 new counselling cases and 4,275 new debt management files. Under debt management plans, $22.5 million was distributed to creditors: *OACCS Statistical Highlights 1998*. The debt repayment program of the OACCS members has assumed much greater importance since the withdrawal of provincial financial support in March 1992 and the enhanced reliance of the agencies on financial contributions from creditor members of individual agencies.

Canadian creditors strongly support the voluntary CCS agencies because they see them as a foil to burgeoning consumer bankruptcies. Creditors are often strongly represented on the board of directors of the CCS agencies and senior members of the operating staff of the agencies have quite often previously worked for consumer loan companies or other financial intermediaries. As far as their debt repayment functions are concerned, the CCS agencies differ from BIA consumer proposals because they do not normally seek remission of payment of any part of the debts nor do they have the power to impose a compromise of debts on the creditors. In effect, this means that, to ensure their ability to meet a repayment plan, CCS debtors must have either higher average incomes than bankrupt consumers or lower debt-to-income ratios.

In the United States, CCS agencies have been criticized because of their close ties with the credit industry, their failure to protect debtors against contract abuses or statutory violations by creditors, and their unwillingness to recommend bankruptcy relief when it would be in the best interests of the debtor. See D.A. Lander, "Recent Developments in Consumer Debt Counselling Agencies" (2002), 21 *Am. Bankr. Inst. J* 14; D.A. Lander, "Snapshot of an Industry in Turmoil: The Plight of Consumer Debt Counseling" (2000), 54 *Cons. Fin. LQ Rep.* 330;

and H.B. Hoffman, "Consumer Bankruptcy Filers and Pre-Petition Consumer Credit Counseling: Is Congress Trying To Place the Fox in Charge of the Henhouse?" (1999), 54 *Bus. Law.* 1629; Karen Gross and Susan Block-Lieb, "Empty Mandate or Opportunity for Innovation? Pre-Petition Credit Counseling and Post-Petition Financial Management Education" (2005), 13 *Am. Bankr. Inst. L Rev.* 549; Lea Krivinskas, " 'Don't File!': Rehabilitating Unauthorized Practice of Law-Based Policies in the Credit Counseling Industry" (2005), 79 *Am. Bankr. LJ* 51; Leslie E. Linfield, "Lightening Strikes Thrice: Emerging Issues in Bankruptcy Credit Counseling" (2006), 25 (1) *Am. Bankr. Inst. J* 16; Robert M. Hunt, "Whither Consumer Credit Counseling" (2005), SSRN online, at http://ssrn.com/abstract=905263; US Congress, Senate Committee on Governmental Affairs, Permanent Subcommittee on Investigations, "Profiteering in a Non-Profit Industry: Abusive Practices in Credit Counseling" (2004), online, at http://purl.access.gpo.gov/GPO/LPS54863. There are no comparable Canadian studies.

II. CASE LAW ON CONSUMER PROPOSALS

There is a substantial body of case law on consumer proposals. Most of the decisions are by registrars. Space does not permit reproduction of many of the cases. The following cases have been selected because of their general importance for the administration of consumer proposals.

Automotive Finance Corp. v. Davies
2002 BCSC 509

BOYD J: [1] This is an application by Automotive Finance Corporation ("AFC") for an order that the Consumer Proposal of the respondents, John Geraint (Gary) Davies ("GD") and April Violet Davies ("AD"), be annulled pursuant to s. 66.3 of the *Bankruptcy and Insolvency Act*, RSC 1985, c. B-3 as am. SC 1992, c. 27 ("the Act").

[2] Since the date of the application I have been advised that AFC has withdrawn its application in respect of AD, with no costs payable by either party. Further AFC has discontinued its claim in the related civil action, Vancouver Registry No. S015819, in respect of AD.

[3] GD and AD were officers and directors of Alda Wholesale Ltd., doing business as Alda Auto Sales ("Alda"). On March 11, 1997, GD, on behalf of Alda, entered into a written Floorplan Loan Agreement and a written Security Agreement with AFC. Under the terms of those agreements, Alda was eligible to be loaned up to $100,000 by AFC in credit for the financing of automobile purchases by Alda. On March 11, 1997, GD and AD executed and granted a written guarantee whereby they jointly and severally guaranteed repayment to AFC of any and all obligations of Alda to AFC under the Floorplan Loan Agreement and Security Agreement.

[4] On August 28, 1998, a further Floorplan Loan Agreement and written Security Agreement with AFC were executed by GD, on behalf of Alda. Pursuant to the terms of these agreements, the amount of credit extended by AFC to Alda was increased to $300,000 for the financing of automobile purchases by Alda. On that same date, GD and

AD again executed and granted a written guarantee whereby they jointly and severally guaranteed repayment to AFC of any and all obligations of Alda to AFC under the security agreements.

[5] As at June 25, 1999 AFC had advanced $277,004.40 in purchase money pursuant to the earlier security agreements.

[6] On June 25, 1999 Alda filed an assignment under the Act with the Official Receiver.

[7] On July 6, 1999, AFC filed a Proof of Claim with the Trustee in the sum of $277,004.40, plus interest. This amount was the principal sum of the debt owed by Alda to AFC as at the date of bankruptcy.

[8] There is no dispute that pursuant to the terms of the Unconditional Guarantees referred to earlier, both GD and AD had jointly and severally guaranteed full and prompt payment to AFC of all debts owed by Alda to AFC, including interest and solicitors' fees.

[9] On August 30, 1999, GD and AD made a Consumer Proposal which was filed with the Official Receiver by Deloitte & Touche Inc. on September 1, 1999, pursuant to s. 66.13 of the Act.

[10] For the purposes of this application AFC accepts that GD and AD approached Mr. John Todd ("Todd") of Todd McMahon Inc., Trustees in Bankruptcy, in order to obtain advice concerning their rights under the Act. By virtue of Alda's bankruptcy, both GD and AD anticipated their guarantees could indeed be enforced by AFC and they were aware that neither had sufficient assets to satisfy the face amount of the debt owing by Alda to AFC.

[11] Again, for the purposes of this application, it is accepted that, in the course of receiving advice from Todd, both GD and AD disclosed to him all possible liabilities they faced including the potential claim by AFC under their personal guarantees.

[12] Mr. Todd advised GD and AD that it would be in their interest to file a Consumer Proposal under the Act, rather than to declare bankruptcy. In order to be eligible to file a Consumer Proposal, an individual's aggregate debts, excluding any debts secured by his/her principal residence, must not exceed $75,000 (s. 66.11).

[13] AFC's position is that by virtue of GD and AD providing unconditional guarantees to AFC, AFC had a claim provable against them, in the full amount. Specifically, AFC relies upon s. 121(1) which defines "claims provable" as "all debts and liabilities, present or future, to which the bankrupt is subject on the day on which the bankrupt becomes bankrupt or to which the bankrupt may become subject before the bankrupt's discharge. ..." While Ms. Ferris, on behalf of GD, did not concede that the guaranteed debt amounted to a "claims provable" within bankruptcy, she nevertheless conceded that contrary to Mr. Todd's views and practice, that amount ought to have been included in the Consumer Proposal prepared on GD's and AD's behalf and distributed to the creditors.

[14] As a result of the advice received by Todd, the amount of the AFC guarantee was not disclosed in the Consumer Proposal and Todd determined the debtors were indeed eligible to file a Consumer Proposal since their joint debt was less than an aggregate of $150,000.

[15] The Consumer Proposal was filed, distributed to all creditors other than AFC and ultimately approved. GD and AD complied with the terms imposed by the creditors and successfully completed the requirements of their Consumer Proposal by July 24, 2001.

[16] In the interim, AFC had no notice of GD's and AD's Consumer Proposal. In his most recent affidavit sworn March 8, 2002, GD has sworn that he had two specific conversations with Mr. Roach of AFC during the period July 1999-November 2001, at one or two of several car auctions held during that period. He states:

> During my attendance at the Auctions, I recall specifically two conversations I had with Mr. Roach regarding my personal situation and the bankruptcy protection I had sought. I recall one conversation with Mr. Roach at the Auction in September or October of 1999. The second conversation was held with Mr. Roach at the same location in the spring of 2000.

[17] Ms. Ferris notes that this evidence remains uncontroverted and accordingly, she suggests the Court should infer that Mr. Roach of AFC indeed had notice of the Consumer Proposal which was underway.

[18] In my view, the evidence from GD goes no further than to state that he had at least generally advised Mr. Roach he was seeking "bankruptcy protection." The evidence does not support the conclusion that:

(a) he specifically advised Mr. Roach he had elected to proceed by way of Consumer Proposal; nor that

(b) AFC or Mr. Roach or any representative at AFC had any specific notice of such proposal.

Ms. Ferris conceded that the Consumer Proposal was never provided to AFC during this period. Indeed, the evidence is clear that AFC's first receipt of the Consumer Proposal was on October 29, 2001.

[19] At no point since the filing of the Consumer Proposal, has Todd, as Administrator, taken any steps to inform either the creditors or the Official Receiver that the Consumer Proposal was wrongly filed. (See s. 66.13(4)).

Issue

[20] Ought the Court to exercise its discretion to grant an annulment of the Consumer Proposal in issue?

Discussion

[21] It is agreed the Court retains the discretion to determine whether an annulment of a Consumer Proposal ought to be allowed. Section 66.3(1) provides:

> Where default is made in the performance of any provision in the Consumer Proposal, or where it appears to the court:
>
> (a) that the debtor was not eligible to make a Consumer Proposal when the Consumer Proposal was filed,
>
> (b) that the Consumer Proposal cannot continue without injustice or undue delay, or
>
> (c) that the approval of a court was obtained by fraud,
>
> the court may, on application with such notice as the court may direct to the consumer debtor, and, if applicable, to the administrator and to the creditors, annul the Consumer Proposal.

[22] The real issues are the factors to be considered by the court in exercising the discretionary power provided in s. 66.13. Ms. Ferris submits that considering the terms of s. 66.13(4), it is clear that a consumer debtor's simple ineligibility to file a Consumer Proposal will not automatically result in annulment. Section 66.13(4) provides:

> Where the administrator determines, after filing a Consumer Proposal under paragraph 2(d), that it should not have been filed because the debtor was not eligible to make a Consumer Proposal, the administrator shall forthwith so inform the creditors and Official Receiver, but the Consumer Proposal is not invalid by reason only that the debtor was not eligible to make the consumer proposal.

[23] Both counsel point to the decision of the court in *Minister of National Revenue v. Engdahl* (1994), 27 CBR (3d) 114 (Sask. QB in Bankruptcy); affirmed on appeal 29 CBR (3d) 111 (Sask. CA) as setting out the factors to be taken into account in the exercise of the court's discretion.

[24] In *Engdahl*, the debtor filed a Consumer Proposal disclosing his debts and liabilities, including a liability to Revenue Canada. At that point, the outstanding liability was $13,200 for the 1990 and 1991 tax years and an estimated liability of $12,600 for the 1992 tax year. The proposal was approved. The debtor's 1992 tax return was later reassessed disclosing an indebtedness to Revenue Canada of $39,756.03. Then, upon the 1990 and 1991 returns being reassessed, a further indebtedness of $92,819.89 was disclosed.

[25] After the Certificate of Full Performance of the Consumer Proposal was issued by the debtor's administrator, Revenue Canada applied for an order under s. 66.3(1) of the Act to annul the proposal. As in the case at bar, the application was based on the proposition that the debtor had not been eligible to make a Consumer Proposal since his unsecured debts exceeded $75,000 at the time he filed the proposal.

[26] At page 124 of the trial judgment, Gunn J noted as follows:

> The function of a court sitting in bankruptcy and insolvency matters is to take into account the interests of a debtor and his creditors and balance their interests while maintaining the integrity and confidence of the public.

[27] Considering that statement of principle, he concluded at page 125:

> … In the circumstances of this case I do not feel it is an appropriate case in which to annul the Consumer Proposal given the actions of Revenue Canada Taxation. I accept that the debtor did not know he was ineligible at the time of making the proposal. He has completed all his requirements pursuant to the proposal and has received the Certificate of Compliance from the administrator. I am not satisfied any benefit will accrue to the unsecured creditors if the proposal were to be annulled, based on the debtor's belief he will be forced to make an assignment in bankruptcy if the proposal were to be annulled.

[28] Likewise in this case, Ms. Ferris submits that at the time they filed their Consumer Proposal, neither GD nor AD had any idea they were ineligible to make such a proposal, and that they relied innocently on Todd's advice that their guarantees of Alda's debt were not matters which required disclosure in the Consumer Proposal forms. GD and AD have completed all requirements pursuant to their proposals and they have likewise received Certificates of Compliance from their Administrator. It is unclear that any

benefit will necessarily accrue to the unsecured creditors if their proposals were to be annulled.

[29] Finally, Ms. Ferris submits that the Court must balance the interest of the debtors and the creditors while maintaining the integrity and confidence of the public, as Gunn J noted in *Engdahl*. She submits that the public's confidence in the Act and the process of consumer proposals would be lost, were innocent debtors like GD and AD to find their Consumer Proposals annulled in circumstances such as those in the case at bar.

[30] I am not persuaded that the decision in *Engdahl* is of any particular assistance to the respondent. In *Engdahl*, there was no evidence of anything more than a small debt owed to Revenue Canada as at the time the Consumer Proposals were filed. The much larger debt to Revenue Canada, as revealed by the assessments, did not accrue until after the proposals were filed. In the case at bar, GD's exposure under the guarantees was well understood by him, and indeed it was that exposure which led him to seek out the advice of Todd. As I understand the evidence, excluding AFC, GD's and AD's total debt was in the sum of approximately $192,280. Neither Mr. Schwartz nor Ms. Ferris were able to say what portion of that debt constituted the mortgage on the personal residence which was to be excluded from the calculation.

[31] In any case, by any measure, the largest single creditor which loomed on the debtors' horizon was AFC, which held a guarantee worth in excess of $277,000. This debt was not included in the Statement of Affairs completed by GD and AD. Nor was AFC provided with any notice of the Consumer Proposal.

[32] Ms. Ferris has submitted that Gunn J's reasons in Engdahl, were aimed at ensuring the exercise of judicial discretion such as to maintain the public's confidence in the "integrity" of the bankruptcy process. She submitted that the granting of the annulment of the Consumer Proposal in the case at bar would undermine the debtor's, as well as the other creditors' reliance upon the process, and the certificates granted.

[33] It strikes me that if the Consumer Proposal process is to have any "integrity," it must rest firmly on the foundation that all proper debts and liabilities will be disclosed by debtors seeking the protection of the Act; that the administrators will properly investigate the debtor's financial affairs; and that all creditors will be provided with proper notice of a Consumer Proposal so as to be able to elect to participate in the process if they choose. Assuming the Act is complied with, the debtors, creditors and the public generally, can expect that the purpose of the Act will be fulfilled _ that is there will be an orderly and equitable distribution of the debtors' assets.

[34] If a clear error, such as that which was committed in the case at bar, is allowed to stand without ramification, leaving the creditor (who received no notice of the Consumer Proposal) to absorb the loss, then the integrity of the process has surely been undermined. The creditor would be left with no remedy either against the debtor or for that matter the Administrator, whose error caused the loss.

· · ·

Consumer proposal annulled.

Re Jalal
(2003), 42 CBR (4th) 260 (Ont. SCJ)

DEPUTY REGISTRAR NETTIE: [1] This is the application by the Administrator under the Consumer Proposal of Mohammed Ferhang Jalal (the "Proponent") for Court approval of the Proposal.

Facts

[2] The Proposal was lodged with the Administrator on October 28, 2002, and filed that day with the Official Receiver. According to the Administrator's report to the Court, the aggregate of the unsecured indebtedness of the Proponent did not exceed $75,000.00, based upon the Proponent's Statement of Affairs. The Proposal was deemed, under s. 66.18 of the *Bankruptcy and Insolvency Act*, RSC 1985, c. B-3 (the "Act"), to have been accepted by the creditors on December 12, 2002. As no one requested that the Administrator seek Court approval of the Proposal, within the 15 day period after acceptance by the creditors, the Court was deemed, under s. 66.22(2) of the Act, to have approved the Proposal. The effective date of Court approval was December 27, 2002.

[3] Sometime after December 27, 2002, and neither the materials nor counsel were clear as to the exact date, the Administrator became aware that the unsecured indebtedness of the Proponent totalled $81,693.60. I assume that the date was shortly before the date of the Report of the Administrator made January 28, 2003. There is no evidence to suggest otherwise, and I find that to be an appropriate inference to make, as I have no reason to suspect that the Administrator delayed in carrying out its duties under s. 66.13(4) of the Act. The source of this knowledge was, presumably, the sum of the proofs of claim filed with the Administrator by the creditors. This fact rendered the Proponent ineligible to make a consumer proposal, as he did not come within the definition of a "consumer debtor" as set out in s. 66.11 of the Act.

[4] Having discovered that the Proposal was wrongly filed, as the Proponent was not a consumer debtor, the Administrator quite properly prepared and served a Report under s. 66.13(4) of the Act. In that Report, the Administrator advised that it was going to seek Court approval of the Proposal. Towards that end, on February 19, 2003, the Administrator prepared a Report to the Court and served a copy of that latter Report on the creditors and the Official Receiver.

Analysis

[5] The facts raise, in my view, two questions. Firstly, must Court approval of a consumer proposal be sought when it has already been deemed to have been given, and it is subsequently discovered that the proponent is ineligible to make such a proposal? Secondly, if the answer to the first question is in the affirmative, can the Court approve a consumer proposal filed by someone who is not a consumer debtor?

[6] The answer to the first question is no. The Act sets out a comprehensive regime for the making of consumer proposals by those defined therein to be consumer debtors. That regime differs materially from the regime prescribed for proposals under Division I, in that a meeting of the creditors for the purposes of approving the consumer proposal

and an application to the Court for its approval are clearly anticipated to be done on an exception basis. Proposals under Division II are intended to be less labour intensive and less costly for smaller debtors, and the regime recognizes that creditors in those smaller estates are less likely to be inclined to commit their resources to meeting and the like, as are required for Division I proposals. It is clear from the Act that Parliament anticipated, given less formal review, that some persons might make a consumer proposal where all concerned believed that the proponent was a consumer debtor, only to discover at some point in the process that the proponent was ineligible to make a consumer proposal. Section 66.13(4) of the Act speaks directly to that point it provides:

> Where the administrator determines, after filing a consumer proposal under paragraph (2)(d), that it should not have been filed because the debtor was not eligible to make a consumer proposal, the administrator shall forthwith so inform the creditors and the official receiver, but the consumer proposal is not invalid by reason only that the debtor was not eligible to make the consumer proposal.

[7] In the present matter, the ineligibility of the Proponent to make a consumer proposal was discovered after it was deemed accepted by the creditors, and approved by the Court. Nothing in the Act changes these facts or renders the consumer proposal invalid. Accordingly, it is completely unnecessary and redundant to ask the Court to approve that which it has already approved, by operation of law. If Parliament had intended to require the matter of the debtor's subsequently discovered ineligibility to be put before the Court, it could have mandated that. Instead, it only mandated advising the creditors and the Official Receiver, who could, if so inclined, apply to the Court to annul the Proposal under s. 66.3 of the Act. No such application has been made.

[8] Given my finding regarding the first question, it is not necessary to answer the second question. However, given the apparent lack of case law on the point, and in the event that I am wrong in my answer to the first question, I will do so. The answer to the second question is yes. If an application to the Court was mandated by s. 66.22 of the Act, then s. 66.24 makes it clear that refusal of the consumer proposal on the ground of ineligibility to make the proposal is permissive, not mandatory. Refusal is only mandatory if the terms of the consumer proposal are not reasonable; if they are not fair to the consumer debtor or the creditors; or if the consumer proposal does not comply with ss. 66.12(5) and (6). Clearly, then, approval of the consumer proposal in all other cases is in the discretion of the Court. In coming to this conclusion, I have considered the matter of *Re Bouillion*, [2001] OJ No. 1758 [now reported at (2001), 25 CBR (4th) 15 (Ont. SCJ)], a decision of Deputy Registrar Sproat of this Court, as she then was. In *Bouillion*, Registrar Sproat appears to have been considering whether or not the ineligibility of the proponent may be waived by the Court, prospectively. That is to say, before the consumer proposal is filed. In that instance, I agree with the Registrar. Section 66.13(3) of the Act makes it quite clear that an administrator is not to file a consumer proposal if the proponent is not eligible to make same. As well, the Court has no ability to arrogate to itself jurisdiction to change the definition of an eligible person from that set out by Parliament. I would, however, clearly distinguish *Bouillion* from those cases where the ineligibility is discovered after filing of the consumer proposal, and an application is made to the Court for approval of the consumer proposal under s. 66.22(1) of the Act. In the latter case,

Parliament has clearly given the Court the jurisdiction to approve the consumer proposal notwithstanding the proponent's ineligibility to make such a proposal. If it were necessary to grant Court approval to this consumer proposal, I would exercise my discretion to do so. In my view, the consumer proposal is reasonable and fair to the debtor and his creditors, and exceeds the realization available in a bankruptcy. I am also persuaded that approval of the Court is appropriate given that no interested party has come forward to object to the Administrator's advice that it would be seeking such Court approval.

[9] As set out in the facts recited, above, I have inferred from the evidence that the discovery of ineligibility was made after the Court was deemed to have approved the Proposal. If that were not the case, and the ineligibility was discovered after filing, and prior to deemed approval of the Court, then it would be appropriate for the Administrator to apply, of its own volition, to the Court for approval under s. 66.22(1) of the Act. The Administrator is clearly an interested party, and as such has standing to make such an application under that section of the Act. As an officer of the Court, the Administrator would have a positive obligation to bring the ineligibility to the Court's attention in those circumstances, and apply for Court approval. It would, of course, be obliged to adhere to the provisions of both ss. 66.13(4) and 66.23 of the Act. If that had been the basis for this application, I would have exercised my discretion to approve the Proposal, for the reasons set out in the preceding paragraph.

. . .

Order that consumer proposal was properly filed.

Re H. and K. Ter Mors
(1998), 5 CBR (4th) 109 (QB)

REGISTRAR LEE: [1] Deloitte & Touche Inc., as administrators of the consumer proposal of Henry John Ter Mors and Karen Ter Mors, made application to the court for a review of the consumer proposal of the consumer debtors which had been accepted by the creditors at a meeting held on March 26, 1998. The administrator filed a report as required by s. 66.14(a), expressing the opinion that the proposal is reasonable and fair to the consumer debtors and the creditors and that the proposal offers on a voluntary basis more to creditors than would be available in bankruptcy.

[2] The proposal and the report together with a notice of creditors' meeting and proofs of claim were sent to all creditors and the consumer proposal was accepted by the creditors at a meeting held March 26, 1998. However, the Official Receiver requested that the administrator apply to the court for review of the proposal due to the provisions of s. 66.11 of The *Bankruptcy and Insolvency Act*.

[3] [Section] 66.11(d) provides that ... [a] person whose aggregate debts exceed $75,000.00 is ineligible to make a consumer proposal. However, the administrator submits that a consumer proposal is in the interests of the debtors and the creditors, that the proposal has been approved by the creditors and that the cost structure is such that the consumer proposal under Division II is advantageous, whereas a Division I proposal would not be advantageous.

· · ·

[5] According to the statement of affairs, the debtors have unsecured liabilities in the amount of $39,899.06. There is no evidence as to the amount of proven unsecured debt. Also, it should be noted that this is a joint proposal of a husband and wife. There is no indication as to whether all of the unsecured indebtedness is joint or whether some of the debt is in the name of one or other of the parties. There is secured debt on the principal residence of the debtors which is disclosed in the statement of affairs to be an amount of $140,240.16. Also, there is a secured debt with respect to two vehicles, secured debt with respect to a 1995 Acclaim in the amount of $14,500.00 and secured debt with respect to a 1994 Sunbird in the amount of $6,000.00. Finally, there is secured debt with respect to a second residential property in the amount of $52,357.53.

[6] The proposal provides that payments to secured creditors will be made directly to the secured creditors by the debtors in accordance with the terms of the security agreements and sets out payments to be made for the benefit of the unsecured creditors.

[7] [Section] 66.12 (1) (1.1) of the Act provides that:

> Two or more consumer proposals may, in such circumstances as are specified in directives of the Superintendent, be dealt with as one consumer proposal where they could reasonably be dealt with together because of the financial relationship of the consumer debtors involved.

[8] Directive 2R issued December 19, 1997 provides that:

> 6. Consumer proposals may be dealt with as one consumer proposal where the debts of the individuals making the joint consumer proposal are substantially the same and the administrator of consumer proposals is of the opinion that it is in the best interest of the debtors and the creditors."

[9] In the subject proposal, the administrator has expressed the opinion that the proposal is in the interest of the debtors and creditors. As stated earlier, there is no identification as to whether the liabilities set out in the statement of affairs are all joint and several or whether certain of the liabilities are owing by one or the other debtor. I will assume, however, that the administrator has considered the nature of the liabilities and determined that the debts of the debtors are substantially the same. Assuming all of the debt is joint debt, each of the debtors has liabilities in excess of $75,000.00. However, collectively, the two debtors have liabilities, excluding the liabilities associated with the principal residence, in the amount of $112,756.59.

[10] If each of the debtors was responsible for only one-half of the debts the amount of indebtedness other than the indebtedness relating to the principal residence would be $56,378.30 each which is under the $75,000.00 limit stipulated in s. 66.11. Unfortunately, given the necessary assumption that the liabilities are, for the most part, joint, each party has liabilities in excess of the prescribed limit and each of the debtors is ineligible to make a consumer proposal under the provisions of Division II.

[11] This, however, does not end the matter. S. 66.24(2) provides in part that:

> ... and the court may refuse to approve the consumer proposal whenever it is established that the consumer debtor

(b) was not eligible to make a consumer proposal when the consumer proposal was filed with the official receiver.

[12] Accordingly, the court is provided with a discretion which it may exercise in the case where the consumer debtor was not eligible to make a consumer proposal. Failure to comply with the provision of s. 66.11 as to the limit of the liabilities is a matter of eligibility. This matter was previously determined in *Minister of National Revenue v. Engdahl* (1994), 27 CBR (3d) 114. In that case Gunn J concluded that although the consumer debtor was ineligible because the liabilities of the debtor ultimately exceeded the $75,000.00 limit due to a reassessment of tax liability, it was an appropriate situation to refuse to annul the proposal. He stated at p. 124:

> The function of a court sitting in bankruptcy and insolvency matters is to take into account the interests of a debtor and his creditors and balance their interests while maintaining the integrity and confidence of the public.

[13] In the subject case, the debtors have advanced a proposal which has been accepted by the creditors. The administrator has rendered a favourable opinion with respect to the proposal. The maximum indebtedness of the two debtors, based on the statement of affairs and disregarding the indebtedness with respect to the principal residence, is $112,756.59. Two separate debtors could make separate proposals with liabilities totalling $150,000.00, excluding the liability associated with a principal residence. The total unsecured indebtedness of the joint debtors is $39,899.06. The balance of the debts are secured and the proposal contemplates payment to all of the secured creditors in accordance with the terms of the security agreements. The debt which causes the debtors to be ineligible under the provisions of s. 66.11 is the secured debt associated with a rental property which is an income generating property owned by the debtors.

[14] Considering all of the above factors, I am satisfied that it is in the interest of the creditors and the debtors to exercise the discretion provided to the court pursuant to s. 66.24(2) and approve the consumer proposal as submitted. It should be noted that all of the proven creditors were given notice of the hearing of the application for court review of the consumer proposal in accordance with the provisions of s. 66.23(a) and the Official Receiver was sent a copy of the required report in accordance with the provisions of s. 66.23(b) and no-one appeared to take any position one way or the other with respect to the matter.

[15] Although I have determined that the proposal should be approved, I would like to comment on one final issue. S. 66.13(3)(a) provides that:

> The administrator shall not file a consumer proposal under paragraph (2)(d) if he has reason to believe that the debtor is not eligible to make a consumer proposal;

[16] This would appear to be an absolute sanction against an administrator filing a consumer proposal under circumstances where it is clear that the debtor is ineligible, such as in the present circumstances. The administrator has not provided any evidence as to why it may have believed the debtor was eligible to make a proposal. Nevertheless, the consumer proposal was filed on January 20, 1998 and the Official Receiver accepted the filing.

[17] Once the filing has been accepted, I am not certain that the court should refuse to exercise its discretion to make a determination on the merits. However, it seems that if the legislation is to have any meaning, the Office of the Superintendent should not accept a consumer proposal which is ineligible on its face or should otherwise impose sanctions on an administrator who is in breach of the provisions of s. 66.13(3). Otherwise, an administrator may feel that the eligibility requirements for a Division II proposal can simply be ignored.

Standing Senate Committee on Banking, Trade and Commerce, *Debtors and Creditors Sharing the Burden: A Review of the Bankruptcy and Insolvency Act and the Companies' Creditors Arrangement Act*
(Ottawa: November 2003), at 15 and 190-92

To be eligible to make a consumer proposal, an individual's debts cannot exceed $75,000, excluding the mortgage on a principal residence, and he or she must have adequate resources to enable the development of a fair and realistic proposal. Consumer proposals are not binding on secured creditors; these creditors retain their right to realize on their security if timely payments are not made. Commercial proposals can be filed regardless of the amount of indebtedness, and secured creditors are similarly able to realize on their security if timely payments are not made. ...

When the consumer proposal provisions were included in the BIA in 1992, it was expected that the administration of consumer proposals would be relatively straightforward and would not warrant the more complex and costlier option provided for commercial reorganizations. The $75,000 liability threshold, however, may be prompting many self-employed individuals and higher-income debtors to use the more complex and costlier option.

In the view of the Personal Insolvency Task Force, the current definition of "consumer debtor" is too restrictive, and the more complex process is not justified or needed for many of the debtors now using it. Higher costs reduce recovery for creditors, and failure of a commercial proposal results in automatic bankruptcy for the insolvent debtor; there is no "deemed bankruptcy" when a consumer proposal fails. It recommended that the BIA be amended to include a revised definition of "consumer debtor" for those filing a consumer proposal; it should include "an individual whose indebtedness, consequent of commercial or self-employed activity, does not exceed $100,000 or such other amount as is prescribed" and should include no ceiling on the amount of non-business indebtedness or on the debtor's assets. ...

The Committee believes that consumers should pursue a consumer proposal rather than a commercial reorganization, if possible. We hold this view because failure in the former situation does not result in a "deemed bankruptcy," while in the latter case it does. Moreover, the consumer proposal option should be pursued because it is simpler and less costly. We recognize, however, that the current indebtedness threshold may be limiting the extent to which consumers are eligible to pursue a consumer proposal. One of the fundamental principles articulated ... is accessibility. Clearly, accessibility is hampered if the indebtedness threshold needed to access the simpler, less costly process is a barrier. It is from this perspective that the Committee recommends that:

The Bankruptcy and Insolvency Act be amended to raise the indebtedness threshold contained in the definition of "consumer debtor" to $100,000, with annual increases thereafter to reflect increases in the cost of living as measured by the Consumer Price Index. Moreover, two years after the new indebtedness threshold comes into force, the federal government should initiate a review of the degree to which insolvent debtors are using the consumer proposal option rather than pursuing a commercial reorganization. [Emphasis in original.]

NOTE

The 2007 BIA amendments have adopted the Senate Committee's recommendation. However, the indebtedness threshold contained in the definition of "consumer debtor" has been set at $250,000, rather than the committee's recommended $100,000. The aim may have been to achieve parity with the American ceiling.

III. CREDIT COUNSELLING AND CONSUMER EDUCATION AS PART OF THE BANKRUPTCY PROCESS

The concept of credit counselling—teaching consumers how to use credit wisely and how to manage household budgets—has strong roots in Canada, as it has in many Western countries with growing debt problems. In 2005, the United States followed the Canadian model and made credit counselling a *mandatory* part of the consumer bankruptcy process. The following extracts describe the Canadian requirements and provide a preliminary assessment of the effectiveness of the requirement.

J.S. Ziegel, *Comparative Consumer Insolvency Regimes*
(Oxford: Hart Publishing, 2003), at c. 2.14 (footnotes omitted)

Canada was the first common law jurisdiction to introduce mandatory credit counselling as part of the consumer bankruptcy process. The requirement was first introduced as part of the 1992 amendments to the BIA and was extended in the 1997 amendments to consumer proposals. Failure to comply with the requirement deprives the debtor of the right to an automatic discharge. In addition to the counselling, which only takes place after the assignment or filing of a proposal, the trustee or administrator of a proposal must also complete an assessment of the debtor *before* the assignment or proposal. The assessment requirement arises from an OSB directive and not from the Act. Nevertheless, it is an essential component of the counselling process since the trustee or administrator is obliged to review the debtor's income, assets and liabilities and to advise the debtor of the various options open to him to address his financial problems. The debtor must also be told about the surplus income payment requirements under s. 68 if a straight bankruptcy is his choice and, if a proposal is under consideration, the trustee/administrator must satisfy herself that the debtor is in a position to make a viable proposal. A difficulty about the assessment requirement is that the trustee/administrator may not be perceived to be wholly disinterested since the size of their fees will depend on the nature of the debtor's choice.

So far as the statutory counselling is concerned, it has two stages. The first stage must be conducted 10-60 days after the assignment or filing of the proposal; the second stage cannot occur before 30 days following the end of the first session and cannot be later than 120 days after the effective date of the bankruptcy or filing of the consumer proposal. The first counselling session is quite benign and is designed to instruct the debtor in proper money management, spending and shopping habits, and obtaining and using credit. The second counselling session is much more controversial and apparently envisages the counsellor playing the combined role of social worker and psychologist to determine whether there are non-budgetary reasons for the debtor's financial problems. Not surprisingly, many trustees feel uncomfortable filling this role.

Credit counselling has very much become the flavour of the month in all jurisdictions grappling with the problems of overcommitted debtors. Nevertheless, the lasting value of counselling provided after the damage has been done still has to be proven. There is broad consensus that ideally budgetary management courses should be included in high school curricula but the prospects of this happening on a widespread basis appear slim. Educational authorities in Canada complain that the high school calendar is already too crowded.

Saul Schwartz, "Counselling the Overindebted: A Comparative Perspective"
(2005), OSB online,
at http://strategis.ic.gc.ca/epic/site/bsf-osb.nsf/en/br01672e.html

. . .

Based on the observation of a number of first and second counselling sessions and on interviews with several experienced counsellors, it is clear that the sessions are often used primarily to maintain contact with the debtors, to provide rudimentary budget advice and to address questions and issues related to the bankruptcy process that the debtor is experiencing. For example, in one interview, the bankrupt had suffered a nervous breakdown, an event that led, at least indirectly, to his insolvency. In the interview I observed, the bankrupt was clearly having trouble understanding any questions beyond the most simple and straightforward. He knew that his wife was dealing with all the financial affairs of the family and was clearly focused on making sure that he remembered to give the trustee the cheques representing the trustee's fee. The trustee asked several questions about "how things were going" and could draw out only perfunctory answers. Since it was evident that any efforts at financial education would be futile, the trustee quickly ended the session.

Another session with another trustee involved a woman who, while working full-time, had established a small gift shop with financial support of her family. For a time, business was good and the woman and her family prospered. Then two simultaneous events destroyed that prosperity. First, the woman lost her voice, for reasons that have eluded her doctors. She could not work any longer, either on her full-time job or in the gift shop. Second, the SARS crisis hit Toronto and the gift shop failed. When I observed her second counselling session, she could speak only with evident discomfort and in a voice that was barely audible. And even that level of function was an improvement, the result of non-traditional treatment in her native Lebanon. The woman was accompanied by her brother, a Toronto-area financial planner who had been supporting her since her misfortunes had begun some years earlier. In this case, the counsellor first went through the events of the past months to make sure that there had been no material change in the woman's circumstances. The woman had run up substantial credit card debts, before the loss of her voice and the collapse of her business, and the counsellor thought it necessary to remind the bankrupt that it would have been more prudent to have limited the size of her credit card balances, even when times were good, in anticipation of the possibility that times would turn bad. That advice, plus some suggestions that the woman should explore job possibilities that did not require speech, comprised the financial education component of the session.

At the suggestion of the OSB, I interviewed two counsellors—one a trustee and one a counselling specialist—who strongly believe in the efficacy of Canadian bankruptcy counselling.

The trustee supports mandatory counselling despite believing, as do most trustees, that bankruptcy is not often an avoidable consequence of personal irresponsibility or ignorance. Counselling is therefore not necessarily about teaching all bankrupts about prudent financial management. Instead, he believes that counselling provides the opportunity to provide advice that is tailored to individual situations and that can help the debtors with the rehabilitation process, understood as "getting back on their feet" after the bankruptcy. He gave the example of a bankrupt who had been a vice-president in a major bank before losing his job. The trustee said that it was clear that the sort of financial counselling envisioned under the BIA would not be of benefit to this particular bankrupt. Instead, the trustee focused on assuring the bankrupt that even though he had lost his job, he was still a competent individual and would be able to find new work that would be both remunerative and satisfying. In other words, the counselling was not about financial matters but about building the confidence of the bankrupt and helping him rehabilitate himself.

This trustee thought that every bankrupt could benefit from the counselling, as long as the counsellor was sensitive to the needs of the bankrupt. Nonetheless, this trustee was clear that beneficial counselling was the exception rather than the norm under the current system. Nonetheless, he felt that even if only 1 in 10 bankrupts benefited from counselling, the counselling was worthwhile and should be continued. He gave the example of an immigrant who was bankrupt because he really did not understand how the Canadian financial system worked. In that case, the trustee provided the sort of fast-paced course in financial management mentioned above. As a result, the bankrupt was able to re-establish his life and, when the trustee later met him in other contexts, always credited the trustee's advice for his later success. Even if this kind of success is unusual, the trustee believed that it is "worth it."

I asked if trustees should try to identify those who could benefit from counselling and counsel only those who needed it. He was reluctant to move toward such a system, however, because he saw such choices as "too much responsibility" for the trustees.

The second person to whom I was referred by the OSB has been involved in mandatory bankruptcy counselling in Canada since its inception in 1992. In the early days of the system, she toured Canada with Dave Stewart talking to trustees about how the new system would work. She believes passionately in the efficacy of counselling as an educational process and believes that its apparent ineffectiveness could be overcome through a more intense commitment on the part of the insolvency community and by providing better training for counsellors.

Many trustees believe that their clients' bankruptcies are unavoidable because they are caused by events such as unemployment, illness or family disruption. This counsellor believes, however, that prudent financial management would prevent most bankruptcies even when unemployment, illness or family disruption are involved. Her rationale is that prudent financial management demands that individuals and families protect themselves from insolvency either by saving enough to carry them through unemployment, illness or family disruption or by not borrowing when those events are possible. She therefore believes that 90 per cent of bankruptcies would not be necessary if the bankrupts had been financially prudent. Driven by that belief, she provides all bankrupts with extensive information on prudent financial behaviour and believes that many are able to use that information to better manage their personal finances. The information she provides differs in both volume and depth from the information provided by most other trustees.

She also differs from most trustees in how hard she works to discover the cause of bankruptcy. While some trustees might simply scribble "bad management" or "unemployment" in the relevant part of Form xxx, this counsellor tries to confront bankrupts with what she believes to be the true cause. Given her view that most bankruptcies are the responsibility of the bankrupt, she tries to force the debtor to accept that responsibility. She does not shy away from asking whether the debtor has drug problems or a gambling addiction or a predilection toward compulsive shopping. Because she believes so strongly in the therapeutic effects of accepting responsibility, she is ready for the debtor to be upset by these investigations and prepared to support [the debtor] in the aftermath with referrals to appropriate sources of help.

In summary, I believe that Canadian bankruptcy counselling does not fulfill the promise of financial education. Even if the system helps the rare bankrupt, it seems wasteful to have a system in which the vast majority of counselling is either unnecessary or ineffective. And, since I do not believe that most bankruptcies are the result of financial imprudence, I do not think it advisable to train all counsellors to follow the example the counsellor discussed in the last paragraph.

Nonetheless, the counselling still plays a valuable role in the bankruptcy process by facilitating and informing that process. Whether this role implies mandatory sessions or face-to-face contact, however, is arguable.

PART V

Receiverships

CHAPTER 18

Receiverships

I. INTRODUCTION

Secured creditors who have been granted an all-encompassing security interest in the debtor's assets will usually also be given the power to appoint a receiver-manager in the event of a default under the security agreement. If this power is exercised, the receiver-manager will take possession and control of the business from the debtor. The receiver-manager will operate the business in the hope of selling it to a buyer as a going concern.

The law relating to receiverships is complicated by the fact that there are two different sources of receivership law. A receiver-manager may be appointed pursuant to the contractual power contained in the security agreement. Alternatively, a court exercising its equitable jurisdiction may appoint a receiver-manager. The rules and principles governing these two types of receiverships differ in many important respects, although these differences have been reduced somewhat by legislation. The law relating to receiverships is also complicated by the fact that there are several different federal and provincial statutes that regulate receiverships, and there is considerable overlap in their provisions.

II. THE POSITION AT COMMON LAW

For several centuries, equity has employed the remedial device of a court-appointed receiver and manager to administer assets while a dispute is being resolved or to assist in the enforcement of a judgment where the legal enforcement mechanisms were inadequate. The privately appointed receivership has a much shorter history and traces its genesis to, approximately, the middle of the 19th century. Historically, in the case of realty mortgages, mortgagees were reluctant to take possession of the land because the courts held the mortgagees strictly to account for maladministration. Mortgagees were reluctant to apply for court-appointed receivers because the device is expensive and can require many court hearings. Ingenious counsel thereupon hit on the device of a contractual clause allowing the secured creditor, on the debtor's default, to appoint a private receiver-manager to take possession of the collateral and manage the business until it is disposed of. To make sure that the secured creditor could not be held responsible for the receiver's actions, and that the receiver would have plenary powers to manage the business, the clause also provided (and continues to provide) that the receiver shall be deemed to be the debtor's agent.

Strictly speaking, a distinction is drawn between a person who is appointed to collect income and rent from a property and a person who also has the power to manage the business of the debtor. The former is referred to as a receiver, while the latter is referred to as a receiver and manager (or receiver-manager). The appointee is virtually always given a power of management over the business, and it has therefore become usual to refer to the latter simply as a receiver. This usage will be adopted here, but it should be kept in mind that the receiver must be given a power of management either by the security agreement (in the case of a privately appointed receiver) or by the court order (in the case of a court-appointed receiver).

The powers of a court-appointed receiver were derived from the order appointing the receiver. The powers of a privately appointed receiver were derived from the terms of the security agreement. A secured creditor who had the power to appoint a privately appointed receiver pursuant to its security agreement was not compelled to do so and could instead seek to have a receiver appointed by a court. A secured creditor could also seek to have a privately appointment receiver converted into a court-appointed receiver. The next case discusses the difference between these two kinds of receiverships.

Ostrander v. Niagara Helicopters Ltd.
(1973), 19 CBR (NS) 5 (Ont. HCJ)

STARK J: In spite of the lengthy evidence that was taken in these proceedings continuing over many days, I am satisfied that the real questions involved have become quite narrowed and confined. This result was mainly achieved by the very careful and thorough arguments of all counsel and by their careful review of the evidence. Summarily stated the facts are briefly these. The company known as Niagara Helicopters Limited (hereinafter referred to for convenience as "Niagara"), was founded by the plaintiff Paul S. Ostrander who was the owner of 90% of the stock of the company. This company operated out of the City of Niagara Falls providing charter commercial air services, a flight school, tourist operations and various other services using helicopters. While Ostrander was an experienced helicopter pilot he proved to be an inept financial manager and when the company experienced serious financial difficulties the defendant Roynat was approached for a substantial loan by way of bond mortgage. A debenture dated October 1, 1969, (ex. 1) was entered into between Niagara Helicopters Limited and the Canada Trust Company as trustee, as a result of which Roynat became the single debenture holder. An initial advance of $125,000 was made on November 4, 1969. Two or three months later Niagara defaulted on the loan and the insurance on its aircraft was cancelled. On January 16, 1970, the defendant, C.R. Bawden, was appointed as receiver-manager by virtue of the default provisions contained in the deed of trust. It was admitted by counsel for the plaintiff and was placed on the record that all powers of the trustee were properly delegated to Roynat pursuant to s. 9.2 of the debenture and, in effect, Bawden was appointed receiver and manager as the agent of Roynat for the purpose of protecting and enforcing its security. The defendant Bawden was considered by Roynat to be an experienced receiver-manager, having acted in that capacity on many previous occasions. Bawden took immediate steps to reinstate the insurance, came to the conclusion that the company was a viable operation, although it lacked working capital, and a further $15,000 was advanced under the debenture. Bawden's duties as receiver-manager were then terminated but Roynat insisted that the company retain a financial adviser; and with the consent of Ostrander, indeed it appears with the urging of Ostrander, Bawden acted in this capacity.

However, during this period the financial position of Niagara deteriorated mainly because of Ostrander's inability to operate the company efficiently and due also to his frequent absences from the company for various reasons and Roynat became increasingly concerned as to the safety of its security. Thus, ex. 50 indicated that during the year ending December 31, 1970, a loss of $84,000 had been incurred as opposed to a net loss the previous year of $65,000. By February 24, 1971, it was necessary to again call in the loan and once again Bawden was appointed receiver-manager in accordance with the terms of the debenture and was instructed by Roynat to find a buyer for the shares as being the best possibility for all concerned. Bawden had had some previous satisfactory dealings with principals in the defendant company New Unisphere and this company displayed interest in Niagara. Negotiations were opened between New Unisphere and Ostrander, both parties being represented by independent counsel, and an agreement was formalized. The agreement was finally negotiated and signed and appears herein as ex. 20. No evidence was presented to indicate undue influence by Bawden or anyone else with respect to the negotiations and execution of this agreement. Indeed, from Ostrander's standpoint it was a highly desirable agreement in which Ostrander would have received a substantial payment for his shares. It appears from the evidence that Bawden did all he could reasonably do to assist in the completion of this deal and in postponing public sale of the assets as long as this could be done. However, delays occurred, probably caused by both parties in meeting the terms of the agreement, and as the fall of 1971 approached Roynat became increasingly concerned about the position of its security and urged and instructed Bawden to proceed with preparations for the sale of the assets by public tender. Conditions for sale were prepared, advertisements were duly inserted in the newspapers and a closing date fixed for the receipt of bids. The final date for the receipt of bids was September 24, 1971. ...

Only two tenders for the working assets of the company as listed in the conditions of sale were received. One of these tenders was a hastily written offer which turned out to be ambiguous in meaning, made by White and prepared in the few moments that preceded the opening. The other tender was the Toprow tender, the benefits of which were later assigned to Baltraco. It was admitted by all parties that since the defendant New Unisphere is the sole owner of its subsidiaries Baltraco Limited and Toprow Investments Limited, that the Toprow bid may fairly be regarded as in fact the bid of New Unisphere Limited. After two or three days' consideration, the Toprow tender was accepted, the decision being made by Roynat's representatives acting on its own views and acting as well on the advice of Bawden. ...

Commencing in June, 1971, and continuing until November of the same year, Bawden began purchasing for his own personal account through his broker shares in New Unisphere. The total of his purchases amounted to 42,000 shares for a total purchase price of approximately $20,000. These shares represented a 2% interest in the total issued shares of New Unisphere. The shares of that company are listed on the public exchanges. Bawden admitted quite frankly in his evidence that under the circumstances this was a "stupid" thing to do. His own counsel admitted to the Court that, "of all the matters brought before this Court by the plaintiff, this was the only one which has any appearance of substance. There is no question, whatever, that Mr. Bawden should not in the circumstances have been purchasing shares in New Unisphere." Bawden in his evidence

contended that his decision to purchase New Unisphere shares had no connection whatever with Niagara, that he does speculate in the market to a considerable extent and that
he was interested in this company because of its holdings in certain well known oil producing companies. In placing great stress upon these dealings, the plaintiff submits that
Bawden, acting as receiver-manager was in a fiduciary position, that even if there was no
actual fraud involved there was constructive fraud, that Bawden had created a conflict
between his interests and his duty and that these dealings must vitiate the ultimate deal
with Toprow. He argues also that Roynat must be responsible for the misdeeds of its
agents. I should hasten to point out that there is not one shred of evidence to indicate
that Roynat, Canada Trust or New Unisphere or its subsidiaries had any knowledge of
these purchases by Bawden. However, because of the suspicious nature of these circumstances it appeared to me that there was an onus thrown upon the defendants to uphold
the validity of the Toprow sale and to satisfy the Court that the decision to make that sale
was not in any way affected or influenced by Bawden's foolish purchase of these shares.

My decision might well be otherwise if I had come to the conclusion that Bawden as
receiver-manager was acting in a fiduciary capacity. I am satisfied that he was not. His
role was that of agent for a mortgagee in possession. The purpose of his employment was
to protect the security of the bondholder. Subsequently his duty was to sell the assets and
realize the proceeds for the benefit of the mortgagee. Of course he owed a duty to account in due course to the mortgagor for any surplus; and in order to be sure there would
be a surplus he was duty bound to comply with the full terms of the conditions of sale set
out in the debenture, to advertise the property and to take reasonable steps to obtain the
best offer possible. Certainly he owed a duty to everybody to act in good faith and without fraud. But this is not to say that his relations to Ostrander or to Niagara or to both
were fiduciary in nature. A very clear distinction must be drawn between the duties and
obligations of a receiver-manager, such as Bawden, appointed by virtue of the contractual
clauses of a mortgage deed and the duties and obligations of a receiver-manager who is
appointed by the Court and whose sole authority is derived from that Court appointment and from the directions given him by the Court. In the latter case he is an officer of
the Court; is very definitely in a fiduciary capacity to all parties involved in the contest.
The borrower, in consideration of the receipt by him of the proceeds of the loan agrees
in advance to the terms of the trust deed and to the provisions by which the security may
be enforced. In this document he accepts in advance the conditions upon which a sale is
to be made, the nature of the advertising that is to be done, the fixing of the amount of
the reserve bid and all the other provisions contained therein relating to the conduct of
the sale. In carrying on the business of the company pending the sale, he acts as agent for
the lender and he makes the decisions formerly made by the proprietors of the company.
Indeed, in the case at hand, Mr. Bawden found it necessary to require that Ostrander absent himself completely from the operations of the business and this Ostrander consented to do. As long as the receiver-manager acts reasonably in the conduct of the business
and of course without any ulterior interest, and as long as he ensures that a fair sale is
conducted and that he ultimately makes a proper accounting to the mortgagor, he has
fulfilled his role which is chiefly of course to protect the security for the benefit of the
bondholder. I can see no evidence of any fiduciary relationship existing between
Ostrander and Bawden. Mr. Papazian in his able argument put it very forcibly to the

Court that the duties and obligations of a receiver-manager appointed by the Court and a receiver-manager appointed under the terms of a bond mortgage without a Court order, were in precisely the same position, each being under fiduciary obligations to the mortgagor. I do not accept that view and I am satisfied that the cases clearly distinguish between them. A good example of the obligation placed upon the Court-appointed receiver-manager is provided by *Re Newdigate Colliery, Ltd.*, [1912] 1 Ch. 468. That case was authority for the proposition that it is the duty of the receiver and manager of the property and undertaking of a company to preserve the goodwill as well as the assets of the business, and it would be inconsistent with that duty for him to disregard contracts entered into by the company before his appointment. At p. 477 Buckley LJ, described the duties of the Court-appointed receiver and manager in this way:

> The receiver and manager is a person who under an order of the Court has been put in a position of duty and responsibility as regards the management and carrying on of this business, and has standing behind him—I do not know what word to use that will not create a misapprehension, but I will call them "constituents"—the persons to whom he is responsible in the matter, namely, the mortgagees and the mortgagor, being the persons entitled respectively to the mortgage and the equity of redemption. If we were to accede to the application which is made to us, and to allow the receiver and manager to sell the coal at an enhanced price, the result would be that the enhanced price would fall within the security of the mortgagees and they would have the benefit of it; but, on the other hand, there would be created in favour of the persons who had originally contracted to purchase the coal a right to damages against the mortgagor, the company, with the result that there would be large sums of damages owing.

Lord Justice Buckley then continued with language which further accentuates the difference between the two classes of receiver-managers:

> It has been truly said that in the case of a legal mortgage the legal mortgagee can take possession if he choose of the mortgaged property, and being in possession can say "I have nothing to do with the mortgagor's contracts. I shall deal with this property as seems to me most to my advantage." No doubt that would be so, but he would be a legal mortgagee in possession, with both the advantages and the disadvantages of that position. This appellant is not in that position. He is an equitable mortgagee who has obtained an order of the Court under which its officer takes possession of assets in which the mortgagee and mortgagor are both interested, with the duty and responsibility of dealing with them fairly in the interest of both parties.

It appears to me unfortunate that the same terms "receiver-manager" are customarily applied to both types of offices, when in fact they are quite different. The difference is well pointed out in the case of *Re B. Johnson & Co. (Builders) Ltd.*, [1955] 1 Ch. 634, where it was held that a receiver and manager of a company's property appointed by a debenture holder was not an officer of the company within the meaning of the *Companies Act*. The language of Evershed MR, at p. 644 is in point:

> The situation of someone appointed by a mortgagee or a debenture holder to be a receiver and manager—as it is said, "out of court"—is familiar. It has long been recognized and established that receivers and managers so appointed are, by the effect of the statute law, or of the

terms of the debenture, or both, treated, while in possession of the company's assets and exercising the various powers conferred upon them, as agents of the company, in order that
they may be able to deal effectively with third parties. But, in such a case as the present at
any rate, it is quite plain that a person appointed as receiver and manager is concerned, not
for the benefit of the company but for the benefit of the mortgagee bank, to realize the security; that is the whole purpose of his appointment. …

Again, at p. 662, Lord Justice Jenkins stated:

The company is entitled to any surplus of assets remaining after the debenture debt has been
discharged, and is entitled to proper accounts. But the whole purpose of the receiver and
manager's appointment would obviously be stultified if the company could claim that a receiver and manager owes it any duty comparable to the duty owed to a company by its own
directors or managers.

* * *

The duties of a receiver and manager for debenture holders are widely different from
those of a manager of the company. He is under no obligation to carry on the company's
business at the expense of the debenture holders. Therefore he commits no breach of duty
to the company by refusing to do so, even though his discontinuance of the business may be
detrimental from the company's point of view. Again, his power of sale is, in effect, that of a
mortgagee, and he therefore commits no breach of duty to the company by a bona fide sale,
even though he might have obtained a higher price and even though, from the point of view
of the company, as distinct from the debenture holders, the terms might be regarded as
disadvantageous.

In a word, in the absence of fraud or mala fides (of which there is not the faintest suggestion here), the company cannot complain of any act or omission of the receiver and manager, provided that he does nothing that he is not empowered to do, and omits nothing that he
is enjoined to do by the terms of his appointment. If the company conceives that it has any
claim against the receiver and manager for breach of some duty owed by him to the company, the issue is not whether the receiver and manager has done or omitted to do anything
which it would be wrongful in a manager of a company to do or omit, but whether he has
exceeded or abused or wrongfully omitted to use the special powers and discretions vested
in him pursuant to the contract of loan constituted by the debenture for the special purpose
of enabling the assets comprised in the debenture holders' security to be preserved and
realized.

* * *

While I find that the purchase by Mr. Bawden of the shares in New Unisphere, in the
amounts and at the times when he did, were purchases which he should better not have
made, I cannot find anything in these transactions to impugn the validity of the final sale
by tender. I am satisfied that Mr. Bawden and his principal Roynat did the very best they
could to protect their own security but at the same time went out of their way to assist Ostrander in so far as his private negotiations had any hopes of success. Other than the tact-
less purchase of these shares and the minor misjudgment with respect to certain payments
with which I have already dealt, I can find nothing censurable in Mr. Bawden's conduct. I
am satisfied that the power of sale was exercised in a fair and proper manner and that in

the opinion of Roynat and its advisers the better offer was obtained. I do not consider it necessary to analyse in detail the nature of the offers that were being considered because no evidence has been placed before the Court to show that the Toprow offer was a disadvantageous one or that the White offer was a better one. Certainly as far as New Unisphere and its subsidiaries are concerned there is no evidence to indicate that they had the slightest knowledge of the purchases by Bawden and they are in the position of purchasers in good faith without notice of any such wrongdoing, if such it were, and accordingly the sale must stand. No legal or moral stigma of any kind should be attached to any defendant in this action and the most that can be said against Mr. Bawden is that he was guilty of misjudgment in certain respects. There was an aura of suspicion which had to be dispelled by the defendants and which they have succeeded in doing. I do not think the plaintiff should be further penalized than by dismissing his action against the defendants with costs, except that in the case of the proceedings against Bawden who was separately represented, the action should be dismissed without costs. As already indicated, there should be a reference to pass accounts and to fix the receiver-manager's costs. If any questions arise as to the drawing up of the judgment, I may of course be spoken to.

Order accordingly.

NOTE

A security agreement that provides for the appointment of a receiver will virtually always also contain a deemed agency clause that provides that the receiver is deemed to act as agent of the debtor. The unusual feature of a deemed agency clause is that although the receiver's power to manage the business is derived from the debtor (the debtor is the principal and the receiver is the agent), the principal is not permitted to revoke the agency, and the agent's primary obligation is owed to the secured creditor rather than to the principal. This gives the receiver the power to carry on the debtor's business. It also has the effect of insulating the secured creditor from liability arising out of wrongful acts of the receiver. However, a privately appointed receiver will not be considered an agent of the debtor for all purposes.

Peat Marwick Ltd. v. Consumers' Gas Co.
(1980), 35 CBR (NS) 1 (Ont. CA)

HOULDEN JA: Peat Marwick Limited, the receiver and manager of the undertaking and assets of Rigidflex Canada Limited, brought this action for (a) recovery of the sum of $2,823.33 paid to the Consumers' Gas Company under protest, (b) a declaration that it was entitled to a supply of gas pursuant to s. 55 of the *Public Utilities Act*, RSO 1970, c. 390, to the premises at 55 Denison Rd. E., in the Boroughs of North York and York, and (c) a declaration that Consumers' Gas was not entitled to discontinue gas services to the said premises. Galligan J dismissed the action with costs: see 23 OR (2d) 659. In this appeal, Peat Marwick asks that it be awarded judgment against Consumers' Gas for the amount paid under protest together with interest from the date of payment to the date of judgment.

Canadian Imperial Bank of Commerce was the banker of Rigidflex Canada Limited, a manufacturer of garden hose and plastic pipe. As security for advances made to Rigidflex, the bank held the following security:

(1) Security by way of assignment under s. 88 of the *Bank Act*, RSC 1970, c. B-1, on all the inventory of Rigidflex;

(2) A floating charge debenture dated 6th December 1976, in the amount of $2,300,000. The debenture was properly registered in accordance with the *Corporation Securities Registration Act*, RSO 1970, c. 88.

(3) A general security agreement dated 20th December 1976. The agreement was properly registered in accordance with the *Personal Property Security Act*, RSO 1970, c. 344.

. . .

The floating charge debenture, like the general security agreement, charged all the property of Rigidflex in favour of the bank as security for a loan of $2,300,000. If default occurred in payment of principal or interest, the bank had the power by instrument in writing to appoint a receiver (which term included a receiver and manager). The debenture conferred wide powers on the receiver, including the right to take possession of the premises of Rigidflex and to carry on the business. The clause listing the powers of the receiver contained the following provision:

> The receiver shall for all purposes be deemed to be the agent of the Company and not of the Bank, and the Company shall be solely responsible for his acts or defaults and for his remuneration.

Default having occurred in the payments to the bank, the bank, by letter dated 31st August 1977, appointed Peat Marwick as receiver and manager pursuant to the floating charge debenture and to the general security agreement, and as agent pursuant to the bank's s. 88 security. The bank instructed the receiver and manager to enter into possession of the property of Rigidflex and to carry on the business. Rigidflex was the tenant of the premises at 55 Denison Rd. E., in the Boroughs of North York and York. Acting on the bank's instructions, Peat Marwick took possession of the said premises and proceeded to liquidate the assets covered by the bank's security. It took its instructions regarding the realization of the assets from the bank, not from Rigidflex.

By letter of 2nd September 1977 Peat Marwick advised Consumers' Gas of its appointment as receiver and manager. The letter read in part as follows:

> You are hereby advised that our firm has been appointed Receiver and Manager for the above Three Companies [one of which was Rigidflex] pursuant to debenture security held by the Canadian Imperial Bank of Commerce as of August 31, 1977.
>
> In this connection we request that you contact a Representative of Peat Marwick Limited at 248-5544 and arrange forthwith to have particular Meter Readings taken in order to determine the status of your account with the above Three Companies as of the above date.
>
> In our capacity as Receiver and Manager of the above Three companies, we hereby undertake to be responsible for consumption subsequent to the meter reading as referred to above.

At this time, there was $2,823.33 owing to Consumers' Gas for gas supplied to 55 Denison Rd. E. prior to the appointment of the receiver.

The arrangements suggested by Peat Marwick in its letter of 2nd September 1977 were not satisfactory to Consumers' Gas, and on 12th September 1977 it terminated the supply of gas to 55 Denison Rd. E. An application was then made by Peat Marwick to Osler J for a mandatory injunction requiring Consumers' Gas to open a new account in the name of Peat Marwick and to provide an adequate supply of gas to the said premises. On 4th October 1977 Osler J delivered written reasons dismissing the application: see 18 OR (2d) 631, 26 CBR (NS) 195, 83 DLR (3d) 450. Peat Marwick then arranged with Consumers' Gas to pay the arrears of $2,823.33 under protest without prejudice to its rights to seek recovery of the said sum in this action.

Sections 55 and 59 of the *Public Utilities Act* are relevant for this appeal. They provide:

> 55. Where there is a sufficient supply of the public utility the corporation shall supply all buildings within the municipality situate upon land lying along the line of any supply pipe, wire or rod, upon the request in writing of the owner, occupant or other person in charge of any such building. ...
>
> 59. If any person supplied with any public utility neglects to pay the rent, rate or charge due to the company at any of the times fixed for the payment thereof, the company, or any person acting under its authority, on giving forty-eight hours previous notice, may stop the supply from entering the premises of the person by cutting off the service pipes or by such other means as the company or its officers consider proper, and the company may recover the rent or charge due up to that time, together with the expenses of cutting off the supply, notwithstanding any contract to furnish it for a longer time.

Consumers' Gas is a supplier of a public utility. Section 55 requires it to supply gas to the owner, occupant or other person in charge of a building. Section 59, however, is designed to protect Consumers' Gas and other suppliers of public utilities from being required to continue the supply of a utility if their accounts are not being paid. Mr. Thomson conceded that, if Peat Marwick when it took possession of the premises of Rigidflex was, in fact, acting as the agent of Rigidflex, then Consumers' Gas was entitled under s. 59 to terminate the supply of gas; however, he contended that, notwithstanding the wording of the floating charge debenture, Peat Marwick was acting not as the agent of Rigidflex but as the agent of the bank.

. . .

It seems to me that the receiver and manager in a situation like the present is wearing two hats. When wearing one hat, he is the agent of the debtor company; when wearing the other, the agent of the debenture holder. In occupying the premises of the debtor and in carrying on the business, the receiver and manager acts as the agent of the debtor company. In realizing the security of the debenture holder, notwithstanding the language of the debenture, he acts as the agent of the debenture holder and thus is able to confer title on a purchaser free of encumbrances.

There are substantial benefits which accrue to a debenture holder from providing in a debenture that a receiver and manager, when appointed, shall be deemed to be the agent of the debtor company. Gower, *Modern Company Law*, 3rd ed. (1969), at p. 436 summarizes the effect of such a provision in these words:

> A receiver appointed out of court, on the other hand, might be expected to be an agent of the party appointing him, namely, the debentureholder or trustee, but in practice, the debenture will invariably provide, expressly or impliedly, that the receiver shall be deemed to be the agent of the company. Prior to the 1948 Act [s. 369(2) of the *Companies Act, 1948* (11 & 12 Geo. 6), c. 38], this distinction had important consequences, for the former type of receiver would be personally liable on contracts into which he entered, whereas the latter would not, unless he pledged his personal credit.

There is no legislation in Ontario equivalent to s. 369(2) of the English *Companies Act* of 1948 so that the distinction mentioned by Gower still has important consequences in this province: see also *Kerr on Receivers*, 15th ed. (1978), pp. 325-26.

The Canadian law as to the effect of appointing a receiver as agent for the debtor company is well summed up in Fraser & Stewart, *Company Law of Canada*, 5th ed., p. 448:

> Unless the trust deed states, as it ought, that the receiver is to be deemed the agent of the company, he will be deemed to be the agent of the bondholders or the trustee, who will be liable for any default on his part: *Re Vimbos Ltd.*, [1900] 1 Ch. 470; *Robinson Printing Co. Ltd. v. Chic Ltd.*, [1905] 2 Ch. 123 (debenture holders held to be personally liable for debts incurred by the receiver). If the receiver is the agent of the bondholders he can claim remuneration from them: *Deyes v. Wood*, [1911] 1 KB 806 (CA). It is now the practice to use apt words making the receiver the agent of the company and expressly excluding any liability of the bondholders not only to the receiver for his remuneration and expenses, but also to anyone having any dealings with the receiver: *Cully v. Parsons*, [1923] 2 Ch. 512, 93 LJ Ch. 42. See *Central London Electricity Ltd. v. Berners*, [1945] 1 All ER 160, [1945] WN 51 (undertaking given by receiver on behalf of bondholders without authority).

The decision of *Re Smith; Ex parte Mason*, [1893] 1 QB 323, while it did not involve a receiver and manager, is, I believe, of assistance. In that case, a receiving order in bankruptcy was made against the debtor, and the official receiver took possession of the debtor's premises. The gas company cut off the supply of gas to the premises and refused to reconnect it until its account was paid. The official receiver paid the amount of the arrears under protest. Subsequently the debtor was adjudged bankrupt, and the trustee in bankruptcy applied for an order that the amount paid to the gas company should be refunded to the bankrupt estate. Vaughan Williams J dismissed the application on the ground that, when the official receiver took possession of the debtor's premises, the debtor's occupation of the premises had not come to an end and, therefore, the gas company was entitled under statutory powers similar to s. 59 of the *Public Utilities Act* to refuse to supply gas to the official receiver. Similarly, in this case, it seems to me that, by virtue of the wording of the debenture, Rigidflex's possession did not come to an end when Peat Marwick, as receiver and manager, took possession of its premises. Consequently, the gas company was entitled to exercise the powers conferred by s. 59 of the *Public Utilities Act* and to refuse to supply gas unless the arrears were paid.

If the court were to hold, as Mr. Thomson has submitted, that the receiver and manager was the agent of the bank and hence not liable for the amount owing for gas supplied prior to the appointment of the receiver and manager, then it would, as I see it, give the bank the best of both worlds. If the receiver and manager became involved in some difficulty, the bank, to avoid liability, could claim that the receiver and manager was the agent of the debtor company: see Fraser & Stewart, p. 448. If, however, there were amounts owing for public utilities supplied prior to the appointment of the receiver and manager, the bank, to avoid liability, could claim that the receiver and manager was its agent.

If the bank chooses to provide in its debenture that the receiver and manager shall be deemed to be the agent of the debtor company, then it must not only take the benefits, but it must also accept the detriments which flow from such a provision. The gas was supplied to Rigidflex. The bank took possession of the premises as the agent of Rigidflex and did not pay the arrears owing for gas supplied to Rigidflex. Consumers' Gas was, therefore, entitled to exercise the powers given to it by s. 59 of the *Public Utilities Act* and to terminate the supply of gas.

For the foregoing reasons, I would dismiss the appeal with costs.

Appeal dismissed.

NOTES

1. A deemed agency provision is a contractual provision between the debtor and the secured creditor. Upon a bankruptcy of the debtor, the deemed agency clause ceases to operate because the debtor's title to the assets and the debtor's power to deal with the assets is automatically transfereed to the debtor's trustee in bankruptcy. See *Gosling v. Gaskell*, [1897] AC 575 (HL).

2. A court-appointed receiver has independent status and acts as neither agent of the secured creditor nor the debtor. As a consequence, a court-appointed receiver is personally liable for any post-receivership contracts that are entered into, but has a right of indemnity from the assets under receivership. A privately appointed receiver is not personally liable on such contracts, because the receiver acts as agent of the debtor in incurring the obligation. However, a receiver may expressly or impliedly consent to personal liability on such obligations.

III. THE STATUTORY REGULATION OF RECEIVERSHIPS

During the 1970s and 1980s, secured creditors typically chose to appoint a privately appointed receiver, rather than apply for the appointment of a court-appointed receiver. There were two reasons for this preference. First, a private appointment was usually less expensive than a court-appointed one. Second, the privately appointed receiver owed his or her primary obligation to the secured creditor and was not required to consider the interests of other parties. At common law, a privately appointed receiver is under no obligation to tell the debtor's unsecured creditors what is happening and owes no general duty of care to them or the debtor with respect to the assets under the receiver's control.

The widespread use of receiverships by secured creditors gave rise to a number of concerns. Secured creditors would often appoint a private receiver immediately upon a default by the debtor. Within hours, the receiver would take over control of the business. The privately appointed receiver owed its primary obligation to the secured creditor, leaving the other interested parties in the dark concerning the conduct of the receivership, because they had no right to information or an accounting. As long as the sale of the assets was fairly conducted, the receiver was under no obligation to consider the interests of any other party.

Legislation was subsequently introduced to address these problems. Unfortunately, these provisions are scattered across a number of different federal and provincial statutes, and there is a considerable degree of overlap. The *Canada Business Corporations Act* (CBCA) contains receivership provisions as do some, but not all, provincial business corporations statutes. The provincial *Personal Property Security Acts* also contain provisions respecting receiverships.

In 1992, Part XI (ss. 243-252) was added to the BIA. Its provisions impose a number of different accounting and reporting obligations on receivers, which ensures that interested third parties will have access to relevant information. The statutes significantly modify the obligation owed by a privately appointed receiver, who is required to act in good faith and in a commercially reasonable manner: see BIA s. 247. Many of the statutes also give the court broad supervisory powers over privately appointed receivers. For example, s. 100 of the CBCA gives the court the power to make the following orders:

> (a) an order appointing, replacing or discharging a receiver or receiver-manager and approving their accounts;
>
> (b) an order determining the notice to be given to any person or dispensing with notice to any person;
>
> (c) an order fixing the remuneration of the receiver or receiver-manager;
>
> (d) an order requiring the receiver or receiver-manager, or a person by or on behalf of whom the receiver or receiver-manager is appointed, to make good any default in connection with the receiver's or receiver-manager's custody or management of the property and business of the corporation, or to relieve any such person from any default on such terms as the court thinks fit, and to confirm any act of the receiver or receiver-manager; and
>
> (e) an order giving directions on any matter relating to the duties of the receiver or receiver-manager.

Note that s. 100(d) permits a court to make a secured creditor liable for the wrongful conduct of a receiver. This gives the court the power to override a deemed agency clause, which would otherwise be effective in insulating a secured creditor from liability. Under what circumstances would a court be justified in invoking this provision?

The BIA also imposes a number of restrictions on the persons who may act as receiver. Section 13.4 provides that a trustee may not act for a secured creditor or realize collateral unless the trustee has a written opinion from independent legal counsel that the security is valid and enforceable against the estate. The trustee must also notify the superintendent and the estate's creditors and inspectors that he is also acting for the secured creditor. The 2007 amendments to the BIA added a new qualification requirement. Only a licensed trustee may act as receiver. See s. 243(4).

Section 244 of the BIA requires that a secured creditor give notice of its intention to appoint a receiver or otherwise enforce a security interest in substantially all the assets of the debtor. The courts had developed the common law reasonable notice doctrine. A secured creditor was not permitted to immediately enforce a security interest upon default, but was required to give the debtor a reasonable time to satisfy the obligation. One of the difficulties with this doctrine was that the amount of time required to be given depended on all the facts and circumstances of the case, and this uncertainty gave rise to much litigation.

John Deere Credit Inc. v. Doyle Salewski Lemieux Inc.
(1997), 36 OR (3d) 259 (CA)

GOUDGE JA (for the court): The appellant is a secured creditor of Ready Rental and Supply Limited ("RRSL"). The respondent is the trustee of RRSL pursuant to a notice of intention to make a proposal under the *Bankruptcy and Insolvency Act*, RSC 1985, c. B-3, as am. by SC 1992, c. 27.

The order under appeal allowed the respondent's motion. It restrained the appellant from realizing on its security and further required the appellant to return any security interest of which it had already taken possession. The order also dismissed the appellant's cross-motion for an order that it be permitted to realize on its security unimpeded by the stay provided by s. 69(1) of the *Bankruptcy and Insolvency Act* or, alternatively, that it be released from the operation of that stay on equitable grounds.

The facts relevant to this appeal are straightforward. On May 29, 1997 the appellant delivered by hand to RRSL, pursuant to s. 244(1) of the *Bankruptcy and Insolvency Act*, a notice of intention to enforce security for each conditional sales agreement it had with RRSL. On Sunday, June 8, 1997, RRSL transmitted a notice of intention to make a proposal to the office of the Official Receiver in Toronto. The next day, June 9, when the office reopened, this notice was filed with the Official Receiver. Thereafter, when the appellant attended at RRSL to repossess the equipment, the debtor company asserted the protection of the stay provided in the legislation and the motions referred to above were brought.

The central issue on this appeal is whether the appellant's rights as a secured creditor are stayed by the filing by RRSL of the notice of intention to make a proposal. The germane sections of the *Bankruptcy and Insolvency Act* are as follows: ... [See BIA ss. 50.4(1), 69(1), and 244—eds.]

Also of relevance is Rule 112 of the Bankruptcy and Insolvency Rules, CRC 1978, c. 368:

> 112. Where the time for doing any act or taking any proceeding expires on a Sunday or other day on which the offices of the court are closed, and by reason thereof the act or proceeding cannot be done or taken on that day, the act or proceeding shall, for the purpose of determining the time when the act was done or the proceeding taken, be deemed to be done or taken on the next day on which such offices are open.

Finally, regard must be had to s. 26 of the *Interpretation Act*, RSC 1985, c. I-21:

> 26. Where the time limited for the doing of a thing expires or falls on a holiday, the thing may be done on the day next following that is not a holiday.

Section 244 requires a secured creditor to send the prescribed notice and then wait ten days before enforcing the security.

Section 69 entitles the insolvent person to file a proposal and thereby prevent a secured creditor from enforcing the security unless that creditor had sent the prescribed notice more than ten days earlier.

While these are separate legislative provisions, in my view they cover the same time period. Until a secured creditor, having sent the prescribed notice, has waited the time necessary before being able to enforce the security, the insolvent person can file a proposal staying that creditor's right to proceed to enforce the security.

Hence, for the purposes of the issue on appeal, the effect of ss. 244 and 69 taken together is that a secured creditor must send a notice of intention to enforce his security and then wait for the expiry of ten days. Only thereafter can the security interest be enforced without the consent of the insolvent person. The latter has the same ten days following the day on which the notice was sent to file a notice of intention to make a proposal and gain the protection of the stay provisions. In effect, the two sections are designed so that the insolvent person has these ten days to determine whether to give up the security provided or to continue with the proposal proceedings.

Where the ten-day period available to the insolvent person to file and thereby gain the protection of a stay expires on a Sunday, it is my view that the insolvent person may file a notice of intention to make a proposal on Monday, the next day, so as to trigger the stay provided by s. 69. While Rule 112 is not felicitously worded, when s. 26 of the *Interpretation Act* is used to inform its meaning, this result is clearly prescribed. In *Ohayon Jewelry Inc. v. Libarian Jewels & Settings Ltd. (Trustee of)* (1987), 63 OR (2d) 157, 66 CBR (NS) 302 (SC), the court adopted this interpretation of the statutory scheme. Indeed, without this interpretation the insolvent person would have to file his notice on the preceding Friday (since filing is impossible on either Saturday or Sunday) and would therefore have only eight days to decide which way to proceed rather than the ten days prescribed by s. 69(2)(b).

I therefore conclude that on the central issue the appellant fails. Its notice of intention to enforce security was sent on May 29, 1997. The ten-day period that followed ended on Sunday, June 8. This permitted RRSL to file its notice of intention to make a proposal on Monday, June 9, so as to raise the stay provided for in s. 69(2)(b).

The appellant also argued that it ought to be relieved from the effect of the stay for equitable reasons, as is permitted by s. 69.4 of the *Bankruptcy and Insolvency Act*. Given that the material filed by the appellant on this issue was no more than a bare assertion of the possibility of the value of its security declining over time if it could not repossess that security, I am unprepared to allow the appeal on this basis. ...

Appeal dismissed.

Beresford Building Supplies (1984) Ltd. v. Caisse Populaire de Petit-Rocher Ltée
(1996), 38 CBR (3d) 274 (NBQB)

McINTYRE J: [1] On February 21, 1994 the defendant Caisse Populaire de Petit-Rocher (La Caisse) crystallized a debenture dated March 2, 1990. It appointed the second defendant Belliveau, Pellerin as receiver and closed down the plaintiffs' business. The plaintiffs take action claiming that no notice was given, as required, both at common law and under subsection 244(1) of the *Bankruptcy and Insolvency Act*, RSC 1985, ch. B-3 as amended. The plaintiffs' action is also founded on trespass, conversion and breach of fiduciary duty.

. . .

[3] Clifford and Martin Comeau purchased Beresford Building Supplies (B.B.S.) in 1984. They incorporated the business under the corporate name Beresford Building Supplies (1984) Ltd. and became owners at 50% each. From 1984 until 1990 B.B.S. conducted its banking business with the National Bank in Petit-Rocher with an operating line of credit of $650,000.

[4] In 1990 B.B.S. approached La Caisse with a view of obtaining a loan for a new business venture. The then manager, after reviewing the financial statements, offered to become B.B.S.'s banker. B.B.S. accepted. La Caisse gave B.B.S. a line of credit of $875,000 plus an additional $260,000 loan secured by a demand note. La Caisse further secured its loans by a debenture, an assignment of accounts receivable, promissory notes and the personal guarantees of Clifford and Martin Comeau. The land and building as well as the chattels of B.B.S. had previously been mortgaged in favour of the Federal Business Development Bank.

[5] Between 1987 and 1992 the financial statements of B.B.S. showed a reasonable profit. In 1988 the net income was $75,007, in 1989 it was $118,984 and $57,475 in 1990. The financial picture changed in 1991 with a net loss of $7,334 followed by net losses of $95,961 in 1992 and $533,740 in 1993.

[6] In June 1992 Gilles Poirier, former manager at the National Bank in Petit-Rocher, became the new manager at La Caisse. It took him little time to become aware of B.B.S.'s financial difficulties. Indeed, by October 30, 1992, B.B.S. had exceeded its allowable credit by almost $400,000.

. . .

[8] With the financial situation of B.B.S. deteriorating from day to day La Caisse, on July 19, 1993, served on B.B.S. and Clifford and Martin Comeau a notice of intention to enforce security pursuant to subsection 244(1) of the *Bankruptcy and Insolvency Act*, as well as a letter of demand for payment of $1,070,905.59. B.B.S. was given 30 days or until August 19th to pay. Clifford and Martin Comeau were also served with a demand under their personal guarantees.

[9] Following service of the demand the parties met in an attempt to prevent the closure of the business. La Caisse manager, Mr. Poirier, had heard that Clifford and Martin had a brother who may have been able to provide financial assistance and he discussed that possibility with Clifford Comeau. He was told that Henry Comeau would not be interested unless there was something in it for him. Poirier says he had given the lengthy 30 days' notice precisely because he wanted to give B.B.S. every opportunity to find a

solution to its financial problems. At the last hour, on August 19, 1993, a conditional agreement was reached between B.B.S. and La Caisse. Basically the agreement provided for the payment of $300,000 by November 30, 1993 and subsequent payments of $100,000 and $200,000 on the 30th of November in each subsequent year until 1998. The agreement, which was confirmed and approved by the Board of Directors of La Caisse on August 20th, contains the proviso, however, that the demand of July 19, 1993 is to remain effective until the payment is made of $300,000 due by November 30, 1993. The July 19th demand notice was to become null and void upon receipt of $300,000 by the stipulated date. On the same date, August 19th, B.B.S. made a deposit of $88,000. $18,000 of the amount was to remain in the account as working capital and $70,000 was assessed against the debt. It was the last amount which La Caisse was to receive. La Caisse did not receive the additional $230,000 by November 30, 1993. No additional payments were made on the debt after August 19, 1993. Any amount deposited after that date was to cover cheques in circulation.

[McIntyre J refers to evidence that Comeau had told Poirier in December 1993 or early January 1994 that Comeau would soon receive $50,000 from Mario Jean and that Poirier had said that if the $50,000 was paid in reduction of the debt he would recommend to the Caisse Populaire's board of directors that Beresford should be given more time to pay the balance of the debt. Comeau never paid the $50,000. The judgment continued:]

[13] … When Poirier found out that La Caisse was not going to receive any money from the Mario Jean receivable, he did not present the draft letter of February 1st to his Board. When the Board met in mid-February the decision was made to call in the receiver. A declaration of crystallization and a notice of appointment of a receiver were served on B.B.S. and on Clifford and Martin Comeau. The inventory was sold "en bloc" on May 5th and, as earlier indicated, there is no dispute as to the amount recovered. B. B.S. filed for bankruptcy shortly thereafter. It is agreed that the trustee has consented to the continuance of the present action.

· · ·

[14] Considering the events that transpired following the agreement of August 20, 1993, B.B.S. contends that La Caisse had, in effect, nullified its notice of July 19, 1993, thereby requiring new notice. To put it in the words of counsel for the plaintiffs in his pre-trial brief, "La Caisse had in effect misrepresented its position throughout to B.B.S. and its principals, obtaining as much security as they possibly could, and then without notice, precipitously closed down the family business. This completely prevented the Comeau's from obtaining other funds (which could have been hundreds of thousands of dollars) from their brother Henry, which would have alleviated entirely the situation with La Caisse and even allowed B.B.S. to seek alternative financing with other bankers with whom the Comeau's had a relationship."

[15] That a debtor is entitled to reasonable notice from a creditor making a demand for payment is now settled law. See *Lister v. Dunlop Canada Ltd.*, [1982] 1 SCR 726, *Royal Bank of Canada v. Estabrooks Pontiac Buick Ltd.* (1985), 60 NBR (2d) 160 (NBCA), *Canadian Imperial Bank of Commerce v. Prosser* (1982), 41 NBR (2d) 656. Although the length of the notice will vary depending on the particular circumstances in each case, the authorities

agree that it will generally be of short duration. To put it in the words of McLachlin J (as she then was) in *C.I.B.C. v. Quesnel Machinery Ltd.*, 62 CBR (NS) 91 at 93:

> What constitutes reasonable notice depends on the facts of the particular case; thus depending on the circumstances, reasonable notice may range from a few days, as in Lister, to no time at all.

See also *Jeannette B.B.Q. Ltée and Haché v. Caisse Populaire de Tracadie Ltée* (1991), 117 NBR (2d) 129 (NBCA) and *Kavcar Investments Ltd. et al. v. Aetna Financial Services Ltd. and Coopers and Lybrand* (1989), 35 OAC 305; 62 DLR (4th) 277 (Ont. CA).

[16] The common law requirement of notice to the debtor before calling in the receiver became statutory in certain cases by the enactment of the *Bankruptcy and Insolvency Act*, RSC 1985, ch. B-3. Subsection 244(1) and (2) provides as follows:

...

[17] It is argued by counsel for the plaintiffs that the common law requirement of reasonable notice continues to exist despite the statutory notice in section 244 of the *Bankruptcy and Insolvency Act*. I agree that there may indeed be circumstances calling for notice to be given outside the context of the *Bankruptcy and Insolvency Act*. The plaintiffs argue that before calling in the receiver on February 21, 1994 the defendant should have served another section 244 notice and at the very least it had an obligation to give the plaintiffs reasonable notice (the common law notice) of its decision to bring in the receiver.

[18] The situation in this case is not much different than that in *Delron Computers Inc. v. Peat Marwick Thorne Inc.* (1995), 31 CBR (3d) 75 (Sask. QB). *Delron* was cited by both parties to these proceedings but to advance two different positions. Delron had given security interest in its personal property to ITT in exchange for two lines of credit. As a result of a breach of the covenants in the agreement, ITT delivered a notice of intention to enforce security, a letter demanding repayment, and a letter of proposal suggesting a plan to maintain the credit for two months which Delron accepted but then failed to respect the terms thereof. ITT appointed a receiver who took possession of the premises and of the assets. Delron brought an application for a stay pursuant to paragraph 248(1)(b) of the *Bankruptcy and Insolvency Act* on grounds that ITT had failed to give notice under subsection 244(1) of its intention to enforce the security. In dismissing the application, Gerein J concluded that a second statutory notice was not required as the parties had not entered into a "new" or "replacement" security agreement. The purpose of the proposal being strictly to "better safeguard the position of ITT in return for it (Delron) maintaining their existing lines of credit." The proposal pertained to the operation of Delron's business and not to the original agreements. In the circumstances, the provisions contained in the proposal did not constitute a new agreement.

[19] In the present case I conclude that the acceptance by La Caisse on August 20, 1993 (Exhibit No. 2, Tab 127) of B.B.S.'s refinancing proposal was intended as a means of securing La Caisse's position whilst allowing B.B.S. to continue operating. It was not, in any manner, meant to replace the existing security agreements. In fact, it is so stated clearly at the last line on page one, "Toutes les garanties déjà existantes demeurent en vigueur." That being so, it was not necessary to give a second section 244 notice.

[20] The plaintiffs submit, however, that the Court must be satisfied not only that the statutory requirements of notice have been complied with but also the common law requirements as well. Like Gerein J in *Delron*, I adopt the position taken by Farley J in *Prudential Assurance Co. v. 90 Eglinton Ltd. Partnership* (1994), 25 CBR (3d) 139 (Ont. Gen. Div.) at pp 152-3, that it is unnecessary to give both a statutory notice and a common law notice. One notice is sufficient. Whenever the provisions of the *Bankruptcy and Insolvency Act* apply a minimum 10-day notice is required in order to enforce a demand loan. Where no minimum notice is required whether by statute or otherwise the common law principle of reasonable notice applies.

[21] In the present case I am satisfied on a balance that La Caisse never revoked the notice of July 19th to call in its loan. An arrangement was worked out on August 20, 1993 to keep B.B.S. in operation but B.B.S.'s failure to pay $300,000 by November 30, 1993 amounted to a breach of the repayment arrangement. It was explicit in the offer of August 20th that the notice to call in the loan remained in effect until the amount of $300,000 was paid. The November 30th deadline passed and no amount was paid. In my view La Caisse was then in a position to call in the receiver at anytime without further notice. The fact that it waited until February 21st, 1994 indicates only that it gave B.B.S. every opportunity to find a solution to its financial problem. The argument that they expected to receive a second or final notice before making a final effort at looking for financing from another source is not realistic and is unacceptable. As for the draft letter of February 1st, 1994, I am satisfied, on a balance, that Clifford Comeau knew that Poirier could not make such a commitment on his own. Mr. Comeau is an experienced businessman who knew that Poirier required the approval of his Board before the draft of February 1st could become a formal proposal. In any event, the $50,000 promised from the Mario Jean receivable was never paid. I conclude that on February 21st La Caisse had every right to call in the receiver without further notice to B.B.S. I agree with the statement of Gerein J in *Delron* at pp. 84-85:

> To my way of thinking, it is not inconsistent for a creditor to intend to realize on its security; give notice to that effect; and still be willing to resolve or attempt to resolve the difficulty. The creditor is simply communicating the fact that its intended course is capable of change. If one were to adopt the applicant's position, a creditor would always be at risk if an arrangement was entered into; for it may be construed as establishing a lack of the intent required by the section. This certainly would be contrary to business efficacy.

> · · ·

Appeal dismissed.

NOTE

Why should the 10-day notice requirement under s. 244(1) apply only where the collateral covers all or substantially all of the debtor's inventory, accounts receivable, or other property? Does this notice serve a different function than the pre-sale notification requirement in the PPSA? See, for example, OPPSA s. 63(4); APPSA s. 60(4).

Consider also the circumstances in *Re Great Alberta Barbecue Inc.*, [1996] AJ no. 947 (QL) (QB). The secured creditor seized equipment essential for the operation of the debtor's business without giving a s. 244(1) notice. The debtor argued that a notice was required and obtained an interim order for the return of the equipment. In addressing the issue whether s. 244 applied, Fraser J observed as follows:

> [19] Section 244(1) applies to a secured creditor who intends to enforce a security on "all or substantially all" of the "other property" of an insolvent person that was used in relation to a business carried on by such person. The evidence is that the "other property" of the debtor corporation consists of food inventory which was spoiled, a lease of the land and buildings, office equipment and fixtures. The security held by the creditor corporation does not apply to the food inventory, the lease, office equipment or fixtures other than those covered by its contract. It may be argued therefore that the security does not cover substantially all of the other property. On the other hand, there is evidence that the equipment removed is essential and critical to the operation of the Barbecue and it would be reasonable to infer that it constitutes substantially all of the kitchen equipment of the Barbecue without which it cannot operate. Further, so far as value is concerned, it is reasonable to assume that the value of the kitchen equipment which has been seized constitutes a substantial proportion of the realizable value of all of the assets of the debtor corporation. That view is based on the evidence that food left on the premises at the time of the seizure to the value of $5,000.00 was spoiled; the view that the office furniture and fixtures required for a catering operation would not be extensive and would therefore likely be of little realizable value; and the view that the lessee's interest in a lease presumably negotiated in the summer of 1996 (when the kitchen equipment was purchased) would also probably be of little realizable value. If, based on the value of the kitchen equipment seized it constituted a substantial proportion of the realizable value of all of the debtor corporation's assets, it may be strongly argued that the statutory condition imposed by s. 244(1), that enforcement of the security be on substantially all of the other property would be satisfied. Taking this argument into account, a serious issue with respect to this point can also be said to exist.

IV. PRIORITIES

As a general rule, the invocation of a receivership does not affect the priority ranking of the persons who hold interests in the debtor's assets. The priority will therefore be governed by the ordinary rules regulating such interests. This means that a landlord who has exercised a right of distress will be entitled to priority over a secured creditor. Similarly, a statutory deemed trust will generally be entitled to priority over a secured creditor if the deemed trust was the first to attach or if the statute creating it contains a priority provision that subordinates a prior secured creditor. However, there are a number of provisions in the BIA that alter the ranking of certain types of claims in respect of receiverships. These are summarized below:

Thirty-day goods: The right of a supplier to repossess 30-day goods under s. 81.1 also applies to a receivership.

Agricultural supplier charge: The statutory charge on inventory in favour of a farmer, fisherman, or aquaculturalist created by s. 81.2 applies to a receivership.

Employee charge: A statutory charge that secures the unpaid wages of employees up to a maximum of $2,000 per employee is created by s. 81.4 and is applicable to receiverships.

Pensions charge: A statutory charge that secures unpaid pension contributions is created by s. 81.6 and is applicable to receiverships.

Environmental charge: The statutory charge that secures environmental remediation costs created by s. 14.06(7) also applies to a receivership.

However, BIA ss. 86 and 87 or ss. 67(2) and (3) do not apply to receiverships. As a consequence, statutory deemed trusts and statutory liens or charges in favour of the Crown are fully effective in a receivership. Although a landlord's right to distress is extinguished by the commencement of bankruptcy proceedings, the same does not hold true in a receivership. The statutory scheme of distribution that classifies certain types of claims as preferred claims applies only in bankruptcy proceedings. There is therefore no conflict between the federal and provincial statutes. By way of contrast, the conflict between the federal bankruptcy scheme of distribution and provincial statutes that purported to give the claim a higher priority led the Supreme Court of Canada to conclude that provincial statutes were inoperative in bankruptcy proceedings. See *Husky Oil Operations Ltd. v. Canada (Minister of National Revenue—MNR)*, excerpted in Chapter 8, Section III.

Secured creditors who have caused a receiver to be appointed often attempt to invoke bankruptcy proceedings in order to improve their priority ranking. The courts have not interceded to prevent them from doing so. See *Bank of Montreal v. Scott Road Enterprises Ltd.*, excerpted in Chapter 3, Section II. In "Priorities," in S. Ben-Ishai and A Duggan, eds., *Canadian Bankruptcy and Insolvency Law: Bill C-55, Statute c. 47 and Beyond* (Toronto: LexisNexis, 2007), 101, Buckwold and Wood have observed that the existence of different priority rankings in bankruptcy, restructuring, and receivership proceedings results in regime shopping by creditors. They argue that this creates greater uncertainty for creditors in assessing insolvency risk, and that, insofar as possible, the same priority ranking should govern. They conclude (at 143):

> Fierce debates inevitably arise in insolvency law reform over the relative merits of certain claimants, and whether a particular class of claimants, such as unpaid employees, should be ranked higher than others. These are matters of central importance in insolvency law reform. However, these debates tend to overshadow an equally important matter. The priority rules differ within the major insolvency regimes, and these differences provide a strong incentive for parties to engage in strategic behaviour that seeks to procure the insolvency regime under which their claim is afforded the highest ranking. The recent legislative trend has been to create priority rules that operate with substantially similar effect within each of the insolvency regimes. This is an encouraging development. However, comprehensive insolvency law reform must go further than this. It must not be content with ensuring this only in respect of new priority rules that are enacted. It must attempt, as far as possible, to create a consistent set of priority rules that operate across all insolvency regimes.

V. THE RISE AND FALL OF THE INTERIM RECEIVER

The 1992 amendments to the BIA provided for the appointment of an interim receiver by a court. This was introduced at the same time that the 10-day notice of intention to enforce a security was enacted in s. 244. In order to alleviate the risk that the debtor might dispose of or dissipate the assets during this period, the secured creditor was given the ability to apply to court for the appointment of an interim receiver. However, in appointing an interim receiver under the BIA, courts did not limit the receiver's powers to those necessary to preserve the asset. Section 47(2)(c) provided that the court could order an interim receiver to "take such other action as the court considers advisable." In *Canada (Minister of Indian Affairs & Northern Development) v. Curragh Inc.* (1994), 27 CBR (3d) 148 (Ont. Gen. Div.), Justice Farley decided that this allowed a court to give an interim receiver the power to manage the business and to sell it as a going concern. In other words, the interim receiver was permitted to operate in much the same manner as a court-appointed receiver appointed under provincial jurisdiction.

The appointment of an interim receiver under the BIA had the advantage of being a national appointment. This meant that the order had full force and effect throughout Canada and it was not necessary to seek the aid, recognition, and assistance of superior courts in other provinces to give effect to the order. However, the provisions of the BIA that governed receivers did not apply to interim receivers. This meant that special priority rules in the BIA that would normally apply in a receivership did not apply where an interim receiver was appointed. Similarly, the provisions in the BIA that imposed obligations on receivers did not apply to an interim receiver.

The appointment of interim receivers to liquidate a business grew in popularity. In addition to the power to both carry on business and sell the assets, the order often contained provisions that purported to exempt the receiver from liability pursuant to both employment and environmental legislation. The orders were often obtained on an *ex parte* basis without notice to parties whose rights were affected by the order. See P. Farkas, "Why Are There So Many Court-Appointed Receiverships?" (2003), 20 *Nat. Insol. Rev.* 37. However, some courts were concerned about the appropriateness of such broad orders as well as their jurisdiction to grant them.

Re Big Sky Living Inc.
(2002), 37 CBR (4th) 42 (Alta. QB)

SLATTER J: The issue on this application is the proper scope of an *ex parte* order appointing an interim receiver under the *Bankruptcy and Insolvency Act*, RSC 1985, c. B-3.

Facts

The debtor Big Sky Living Inc. owns and is developing a piece of land in Parkland County, just west of Edmonton. HSBC Bank of Canada provided financing for the project, and took as security a general security agreement and a mortgage on the lands. HSBC has advanced approximately $1.5 million to Big Sky.

There are other creditors and interested parties. Country Squire 2000 Inc., the previous owner of the lands, has a second mortgage on the title. 416099 Alberta Ltd. claims an interest in the lands and has filed a caveat to protect it. Atco Gas and Pipelines Inc. has a right-of-way across the lands, and proposes to install a high pressure gas pipeline which may require an increased setback between the right-of-way and the development, and which may therefore affect the value of the property. Eng-Con Holdings Ltd. has been installing utility infrastructure on the lands. On May 23, 2002 Eng-Con filed a builder's lien on the property for $587,887.

The filing of the builder's lien caused concerns for HSBC. On May 30, 2002 HSBC gave Big Sky ten days' notice of its intention to enforce its security, as required by s. 244 of the *Bankruptcy and Insolvency Act*. On May 31, 2002 HSBC commenced these proceedings, and on June 3, 2002 it applied to Smith J for an interim receiver under s. 47 of the *Bankruptcy and Insolvency Act*. Smith J was apparently concerned by the short notice that had been received by some of the other interested parties, a problem that was compounded by the breadth and complexity of the proposed order, which is 15 pages long. For ease of reference a copy of the order that Smith J granted is attached to these reasons, with those portions that she added in handwriting shown in italics. As can be seen, Smith J granted the order effective until Friday, June 7, 2002 only, and directed that the order be renewed in Chambers on that date. On June 7th the matter came before me in Chambers for review. Upon reviewing the Order I became concerned about the breadth of some of the clauses, and I indicated to counsel that I was not prepared to grant the Order in the form tendered. I invited counsel to provide me with argument and authorities as to the proper scope of the Order, and to permit counsel to do so I extended the Order twice. Counsel appeared before me on June 21, 2002 and presented argument, at which point I extended the Order again, pending delivery of these Reasons for Decision.

Counsel advises that Big Sky, 416099, and Eng-Con are now consenting to the Order. Country Squire and Atco are not opposing it. This eliminates any concerns that the Court might have had about the impact of the Order on those parties. There remain, however, concerns about the scope and breadth of the Order.

The Statutory Framework

The jurisdiction to appoint an interim receiver is found in s. 47 of the *Bankruptcy and Insolvency Act*. ...

It is precondition to the appointment of an interim receiver under this section that notice of intention to enforce security has or is about to be sent. That condition has been complied with in this case. The test is then whether it is "necessary for the protection of the estate or the creditors" to appoint an interim receiver. Smith J obviously felt that this condition had been satisfied, and I respectfully agree. The question is then what powers and directions should be given to the interim receiver. The wording of s. 47(2) is very wide, but in granting powers to the interim receiver the Court should have regard to what is truly "necessary for the protection" of the estate or the creditor.

Section 47 appears to contemplate that an interim receiver will be appointed for a brief period only, to protect the interest of the creditors while the 10-day notice period under s. 244 is running. The section does not appear to contemplate that the interim receiver will actually carry on the business of the debtor, although that is the intention of HSBC in this case. However, given the consent or lack of opposition by the key players described above, this issue need not be explored further. HSBC had the power to appoint a receiver under its general security agreement, and it could also have applied for a receiver under the *Judicature Act*, or it could have petitioned Big Sky into bankruptcy. HSBC obviously found the interim receivership route to be more convenient, and the other parties concur.

Statutory Protection for an Interim Receiver

There are a number of provisions in the *Bankruptcy and Insolvency Act* that provide some protection to an interim receiver. These provisions are primarily designed to allow the interim receiver to deal with the debtor's assets in an orderly way, without being bombarded by litigation or burdened by frequent court appearances. They protect the interim receiver from some risks and claims which Parliament has obviously felt should not, for reasons of fairness or convenience, be visited upon the receiver. By limiting the exposure of receivers, these provisions undoubtedly helped reduce the overall costs of receiverships.

The key provisions that provide protection for an interim receiver are [ss. 14.06 and 215]. ...

In addition to s. 14.06(2), other sections of the Act deal with environmental risks in some detail. Section 14.06(4) limits the obligation of the interim receiver to comply with orders made to remedy any environmental condition. To obtain the protection of this section, the interim receiver must either comply with the order, abandon the property in question, contest the order, or apply for a stay of the order. The Act also provides a super priority for the costs of remedying certain environmental damage.

The Order applied for by HSBC is in many respects prospective, and it goes far beyond the provisions of the Act. It gives the interim receiver the power to deal with matters that have not yet arisen, and in all likelihood will never arise. The Order might be described as a "standard form order," and it attempts to anticipate problems or issues that might arise in a receivership. It obviously makes sense for the Order to be wide enough that the Interim Receiver does not have to be back in Court continuously seeking advice and direction on small points. There is nothing particularly objectionable in using precedents and standard form orders. However, an applicant tendering an order for signature by the court has a duty to edit it in each case to make sure that it is appropriate for the particular circumstances.

Of greater concern is the fact that the Order purports to affect the rights of parties that have not been served with the proceedings to date, and have probably not even been served with the Order. Those parties include employees, unsecured creditors, government agencies, landlords, and many others. While it is appropriate to anticipate *powers* that the Interim Receiver might require in the future, it is less appropriate to try and anticipate and cut off *rights* of third parties that might exist. When an order purports to affect the rights of persons who have not been given notice of the proceedings, then it is an *ex parte* order as against those persons and the usual principles apply. The Applicant has a duty to make full disclosure to the Court. The relief sought is extraordinary, and should only be granted in a clear case. Generally speaking, the order should be no wider than the circumstances require. Relief which is not urgent should not be granted *ex parte*, but should await proper notice. Further, it is generally contemplated that *ex parte* orders will be served forthwith on all affected parties; it is clear that the Applicant does not propose to serve all affected parties (for example landlords, employees and contractors) until some particular need arises.

A further problem with the Order in question is that it is in some respects "legislative" in nature. Not only does it purport to give the Interim Receiver certain powers, and to cut off the rights of others, it then goes on to provide sweeping definitions and descriptions of what those rights and immunities encompass. In many cases the provisions of the Order go far beyond the statutes that are in place. It is generally inappropriate for the Court to define what Parliament has chosen not to define, and to expand at large on what particular statutory provisions mean. These parts of the Order are declaratory in nature. The Court has always been careful about issuing declaratory judgments, and will not issue them when the issues are moot, where the issues are overly abstract or academic, or where there is no necessity on the facts of the particular case to issue a declaration. There are good reasons for these rules, relating to the constitutional division of powers and relating to the role of a common law court in developing the law. Some clauses in the tendered Order are objectionable on this basis.

Counsel for the Applicant was unable to provide any authority supporting an order of the scope asked for. He was able to provide copies of two interim receivership orders granted by the Ontario Superior Court of Justice—Commercial List, but these were simply copies of the orders as granted and there were not written reasons provided to explain the orders.

With those general comments in mind, some of the specific clauses in the order require examination.

· · ·

Bankruptcy

Paragraph 5(u) of the Order authorizes the Interim Receiver to assign the debtor into bankruptcy, and "to act as Trustee in Bankruptcy of the estate." Section 13.3(2) of the Act recognizes that it is not always appropriate for a receiver to act as a trustee in bankruptcy. There is no urgency involved, and nothing on the record to justify this relief. The provision anticipates a future state of affairs that is unknown, and this provision is not justified.

· · ·

Contracting Parties

Paragraph 7 of the Order is directed at those who have contracts with the debtor, including "all persons, firms, corporations, governments, governmental agencies, municipalities, counties and other entities of any kind or nature," including all of the officers, directors and agents of Big Sky. Each of these persons are restrained from "varying, amending, terminating, cancelling or breaching any contracts or agreements with the debtor." In case someone should discover any way of circumventing the staggering breadth of this provision in the Order, the topic is picked up again in paragraphs 9(c), (d), (e) and (f). By paragraph 9(c) all persons are restrained from "accelerating, terminating, suspending, modifying or cancelling any agreements." Paragraph 9(c) ends up with a form of mandatory *ex parte* injunction requiring all persons to "continue to perform and observe" all agreements. It would appear to be wide enough to prevent any employee from resigning. Paragraph 9(f) of the Order restrains the exercise of certain options, remedies or rights, most of which would arise by contract. Paragraph 9(e) restrains even the "asserting or perfecting" of any right.

There are innumerable contracting parties who might be affected by these provisions, most of whom have no notice of the proceedings. Assuming that the contracting parties would have the right to act as contemplated under their contracts but for the provisions of this Order, then their rights are being interfered with without notice to them. If it is being suggested that this interference with contractual rights is the legal consequence of an interim receivership, then the provisions of the Order are merely declaratory and probably redundant. As such they would fall afoul of the rule against abstract and potentially moot declarations. These provisions of the order are also legislative in nature. There is nothing in the *Bankruptcy and Insolvency Act* which restrains contracting parties in the manner set out in this Order. Parliament not having seen fit to enact such a provision, it is inappropriate for the Court to attempt to do so under the guise of granting a receivership order.

In any event the rights of contracting parties should not be swept away or crystalized in a court order on an *ex parte* basis unless urgency can be shown. There is nothing on the record that would establish why such relief is necessary for the protection of the debtor's estate. There is also no evidence of any urgency justifying this relief being granted *ex parte*.

The only portion of these clauses which is justified is the provision in the middle of paragraph 9(c) which restrains the interference with any utilities or telecommunications being provided to the debtor. Because of the duty of public utilities to provide service on payment, and the severe effect that disruption to these services would have, those provisions may remain in the Order. The Applicant has leave to make further submissions justifying any other provision of clauses 7 and 9.

• • •

Environmental Risks

The increased societal sensitivity to environmental damage and contamination created new issues for receivers and trustees in bankruptcy. Particularly problematic were provisions in environmental legislation that imposed liability not only on those who contaminated property, but on those who thereafter came to own or control that property. In 1992 Parliament addressed those problems by the new provisions found in s. 14.06 of the *Bankruptcy and Insolvency Act*, which provisions were modified and extended to interim receivers in 1997: see Marin and Ilchenko, "Environmental Liabilities of Trustees and Receivers" (1997), 14 *Nat. Ins. Rev.* 19. In addition to limiting the liability of trustees and interim receivers for environmental damage, the Act now provides a super priority for the costs of environmental clean-ups.

• • •

In Alberta, it is clear that receivers are bound by environmental legislation. They are expressly included among the "persons responsible" mentioned in sections 1(tt)(iii) and 134 (b)(vi) of the *Environmental Protection and Enhancement Act*, RSA 2000, ch. E-12 ("*EPE Act*"). The scope of the liability of a receiver was discussed by the Court of Appeal in *Panamericana de Bienes y Servicios SA v. Northern Badger Oil & Gas Ltd.* (1991), 81 DLR (4th) 280, 80 CBR (NS) 84 (Alta. CA). There is no basis for holding that a receiver in Alberta has any immunity for environmental damage beyond what is found in s. 14.06, or the *EPE Act* itself. As was held in *Lindsay*, the Court has no general jurisdiction to grant exemptions from statutes.

The provisions of s. 14.06(2) are fairly short and ... [are found in] paragraph 10. Essentially they provide that a receiver is only liable for environmental damage arising after the receiver's appointment and because of its gross negligence or wilful misconduct. The Court is given no power to extend or limit the protection given. The Applicant has turned those brief provisions into over one page of text in the Order, encompassing clauses 22 through 28.

The initial problem with the proposed environmental provisions in the Order is that they contradict other provisions of the Order. Paragraph 2 of the Order places all of the assets of the debtor under the power of the Interim Receiver. Paragraph 28 then provides that the Order does not vest in the Interim Receiver care or control of any property which "may be" environmentally polluted. This latter clause is unacceptable, because at best it creates great uncertainty as to which properties are under the control of the Interim Receiver, and at worst it gives the Interim Receiver some sort of *ex post facto* right to elect whether it has been in control of property or not. Sections 14.06(4)(c) and 14.06(6) contemplate the abandonment of contaminated property by the receiver, which is the process that should be followed if this later becomes necessary.

There would be nothing objectionable to a provision in the Order which essentially parallels s. 14.06(2) of the *Bankruptcy and Insolvency Act*. While such a provision might be redundant in legal terms, it is helpful to note those provisions in the Order. However, the Order as drafted goes considerably beyond this. First of all, it deems the Interim Receiver not to be an occupier for the purposes of "environmental legislation." The *Bankruptcy and Insolvency Act* does no such thing. There is no indication what environmental legislation is being referred to, or whether the Court has any jurisdiction to make this type of declaration. No notice has been given to any Department of Environment or other regulator who might have an interest in the matter. These provisions are legislative in nature, in the sense that the Court is being asked to extend general and unlimited immunity to the Interim Receiver.

Paragraph 23 of the Order does roughly parallel section 14.06(2) of the *Bankruptcy and Insolvency Act*. However, it goes further in that it states that the Interim Receiver's immunity comes into effect on the later of the appointment of the Interim Receiver, or the date the Interim Receiver goes into possession. Section 14.06(2) contains no such provision. Presumably if Parliament had intended to extend that type of immunity, it would have done so.

Paragraphs 26 and 27 of the Order purport to define "Environmental Legislation" and "Adverse Environmental Condition." Parliament did not see fit to define either of these terms, and did not see fit to exempt trustees from all of the requirements of environmental legislation as implied by paragraph 23 of the Order. For example, I note that clause 14.06(3) of the Act requires the Interim Receiver to make any reports or disclosures called for by such legislation. Counsel for the Applicant indicated that these definitions were to "provide comfort" to the Interim Receiver, and to clarify what the Act "really means." He indicated that receivers have more faith in court orders than in the *ex post facto* interpretation of statutory provisions. Whether that be so, Parliament did not see fit to define these terms, and I cannot see why the Court should do so prospectively and in a factual vacuum.

Paragraph 25 of the Order limits the Interim Receiver's liability for environmental damage to the "Net Realizable Value of the Property" in the estate. Again, the *Bankruptcy and Insolvency Act* contains no such provision. If Parliament had intended a cap on the liability of receivers, it presumably would have provided for one. Furthermore, I note that the Net Realized Value of the property is defined in paragraph 29 as being net of the remuneration of the Interim Receiver and a number of other items including "distributions of proceeds." Accordingly, if the estate was only large enough to pay the secured creditors and the Interim Receiver's compensation, there would be nothing left and the Interim Receiver would be absolved of any liability whatsoever. After distribution of the assets, the Interim Receiver's liability is limited under the Order to the amount of its fees. I am unable to see on what basis the Court could grant this sort of relief *ex parte* and before the Interim Receiver has even gone into possession.

In summary, the environmental clauses provided in this order are inappropriate. The Applicant is at liberty to insert a clause which essentially parallels the provisions of s. 14.06(2) of the Act.

General Protection of the Receiver

Paragraph 29 purports to limit the liability of the Interim Receiver to the Net Realizable Value of the estate. I have already commented on the breadth and effect of the definition of Net Realizable Value of the assets.

Paragraph 29 purports to protect the Interim Receiver from all kinds of liability "whatsoever," including negligence and wilful misconduct. Paragraph 29 is so broad it even appears to protect the Interim Receiver if one of its employees negligently injured someone in a motor vehicle accident while acting in the scope of the employee's duties. It contradicts s. 247 of the Act which requires the receiver to act honestly and in a commercially reasonable manner. It purports to cap the liability of the Interim Receiver in connection with any environmental legislation, or labour or employment laws, something that s. 14.06(1.2) does not do. There is no obvious jurisdiction in the Court to exempt anybody from the general operation of statutes, or excuse liability for their own negligence, or to limit their liability. Apart from the environmental damage cases mentioned, there does not appear to be a decision where it has been attempted. Even the *Lundrigans* case is based on the premise that it was merely declaratory of the law. There is no provision in the *Bankruptcy and Insolvency Act* which provides any limit on the liability of receivers, whether tied to the net value of the estate or otherwise. There may be situations, such as the one that arose in *Lundrigans*, where the public interest requires a receiver to wind up a high risk enterprise but no one will accept the assignment without some protection. Whether the Court can grant that protection will have to be decided when the point arises. But these protective clauses should not be included in all receivership orders as a matter of routine, and they should only be granted on notice to all governments and interested parties. In my view, the provisions of Clause 29 are unjustified on this record. The Applicant may include in the Order a provision that paraphrases s. 215. A provision paraphrasing s. 247 should also be included.

The indemnity in paragraph 16 is acceptable, but the reference to "gross negligence" should be a reference to "commercial reasonableness," the standard found in s. 247.

Conclusion

In conclusion, the Applicant has established that it is entitled to an interim receivership order in accordance with s. 47 of the *Bankruptcy and Insolvency Act*. However, the order tendered for signature is overly broad, and overly declaratory and legislative in nature. It purports to affect in general terms the rights of broad and undefined classes of parties who have not received notice of this application. It goes far beyond what is necessary for the protection of the estate of the debtor. It attempts to provide the Interim Receiver with immunities and protections that are not authorized by statute. The Order as presently granted will be extended for a further five days from the date of these Reasons, during which time the Applicant can draft and submit a further order for signature.

Order accordingly.

NOTES

Labour relations legislation provides that a subsequent employer is bound by the employment obligations found in the collective agreements of its predecessor. The statutes give exclusive jurisdiction to labour relation boards to decide successor employer issues. Receivers were concerned that they might be exposed to liability under these statutes. Two devices were employed by courts to immunize a receiver from potential liability under these statutes. Some courts purported to make a declaratory order pursuant to s. 47 of the BIA that the receiver was not subject to liability as a successor employer. Other courts used s. 215 of the BIA to limit liability. This section provided that no action could be brought against a trustee or an interim receiver without leave of the court. By refusing leave to bring the provincial labour relations proceedings, the court could prevent the provincial labour relations board hearing the matter.

The Supreme Court of Canada, in *GMAC Commercial Credit Corp.—Canada v. TCT Logistics Inc.*, [2006] 2 SCR 123, rejected both these devices. The court held that although s. 47 of the BIA was sufficiently open-ended to authorize a wide range of conduct, including the management and sale of the business, it did not authorize the court to make unilateral declarations about the rights of third parties affected by other statutory schemes. The provincial labour relations board was given exclusive jurisdiction to decide questions of successor employer liability, and the bankruptcy court had no jurisdiction to make a declaration about or immunize the receiver from successor employer liability, nor could s. 215 of the BIA be used to achieve this objective. The provision was intended to provide protection only against frivolous or vexatious litigation and could not be used to permit the court to immunize an interim receiver against a legitimate claim under successor employer legislation. Although the BIA immunized a trustee or receiver from certain types of liabilities, it did not do so with respect to successor employer liability.

The 2007 amendments to the BIA have specifically addressed the question of successor liability. Section 14.06(1.2) provides that a trustee or receiver is not by reason of that fact personally liable in respect of a liability, including one as a successor employer, that exists before the trustee or receiver is appointed or that is calculated by reference to a period before the appointment. Would the result in *TCT Logistics* have been any different if this new provision were in force?

VI. TEMPLATE RECEIVERSHIP ORDERS

Uncertainty over the appropriateness of terms in a receivership order led to the development of template receivership orders. In Ontario, a subcommittee of the Commercial List Users' Committee developed a standard form receivership order together with an explanatory note. Similar template receivership orders have been developed in British Columbia, Alberta, and Saskatchewan. The template receivership order provided for the concurrent appointment of a receiver pursuant to both s. 47 of the BIA as well as provincial legislation. The dual appointment ensured that the federal and provincial statutes that regulated receiverships were brought into play. The template receivership orders were drafted to avoid the excesses of earlier orders in that they did not attempt to immunize the receiver from liability beyond that provided by statute. Variation in a template order was possible, but the changes had to be blacklined or struck out so as to specifically bring them to the attention of the court.

The template receivership orders include the following features:

1. Concurrent appointment of the receiver as an interim receiver under the BIA and as a receiver-manager pursuant to provincial legislation.

2. Conferral of a wide range of powers on the receiver, including the power to:

   - take possession and control of the property and protect and preserve it;

   - manage, operate, and carry on the business;

   - cease carrying on all or part of the business and performing any contract;

   - engage consultants and experts;

   - commence, continue, or defend a legal action and settle or compromise legal proceedings;

   - market the property for sale; and

   - report to, meet, and discuss matters concerning the property with interested stakeholders.

3. Provisions that prevent commencement or continuation of any proceedings against the debtor or the debtor's property and that stay all rights and remedies against the debtor or the receiver or those affecting the property except with the consent of the receiver or the leave of the court.

4. Provisions that prevent any person from terminating, repudiating, or failing to perform any right, renewal right, contract, or licence or from discontinuing the supply of goods or services pursuant to an agreement or a statutory or regulatory mandate without the consent of the receiver or the leave of the court.

5. Provision for the creation of a superpriority charge on the assets under receivership that secure the receiver's fee and a charge that secures any borrowings by the receiver that has priority over any prior secured creditor.

6. A comeback clause under which any interested party can apply to the court to vary or amend the order.

The template receivership orders in Ontario and British Columbia provide that a receiver incurs no liability or obligation as a result of its appointment or carrying out the provisions of the order except for any gross negligence or wilful misconduct on its part. The template receivership orders in Alberta and Saskatchewan do not attempt to limit a receiver's liability in this way.

VII. THE NEW APPROACH TO RECEIVERSHIPS

The 2007 amendments to the BIA have introduced major changes. The most significant change is that the powers of an interim receiver have been curtailed and the duration of the appointment has been limited. Section 47(1) provides that the appointment of an interim receiver is effective for 30 days unless the court orders a longer period. It also comes to an end if a receiver or trustee takes possession of the property. The powers of an interim receiver have been limited to those of a conservatory nature. Section 47(2) provides that a court may direct that an interim receiver take possession of the property, exercise control over the debtor's business, take conservatory measures, and summarily dispose of assets that are perishable or likely to depreciate rapidly in value. The court is not given the power to direct a sale of the assets or the business, and the court no longer has the power to direct the interim receiver to "take such other action as the court considers advisable." As a result, interim receivers can no longer be used to liquidate the debtor's business. Instead, interim receivership is to be used where a secured creditor has a legitimate concern that the assets will be dissipated or disposed of before the secured creditor is able to enforce its security.

Although an interim receiver can no longer be used to liquidate the debtor's business, new provisions have been added that give the bankruptcy court the power to appoint a receiver, including a national receiver. Section 243(1) allows the bankruptcy court to appoint a receiver with power to take possession of the debtor's assets, exercise control over the debtor's business, and take any other action that the court considers advisable. This allows the court to create the same kinds of powers that were formerly afforded to interim receivers. Section 243(1.1) provides that a court may not appoint a receiver before the expiration of the 10-day notice period under s. 244 unless the debtor consents to earlier enforcement or if the court considers it appropriate to do so. Section 243(5) provides that the application is to be made to the bankruptcy court having jurisdiction in the judicial district of the locality of the debtor.

The provisions of the BIA that impose obligations on receivers or create special priority rules in respect of receivers apply to a receiver appointed by a bankruptcy court pursuant to s. 243(1). These provisions continue to apply to receivers appointed by a provincial superior court under business corporations legislation, personal property security legislation, or pursuant to the court's equitable jurisdiction to appoint receivers (recognized in the provincial judicature statutes, such as s. 101(1) of the Ontario *Courts of Justice Act*, RSO 1990, c. C.43), as well as to privately appointed receivers.

QUESTIONS

To what extent will the cases appointing an interim receiver under former s. 47 be relevant in respect of the court appointment of a nationally appointed receiver under s. 243(1)? How might these new provisions affect the practice of obtaining a concurrent appointment under the BIA and under provincial statute? Has the development of template receivership orders resolved all the concerns expressed by Justice Slatter in *Big Sky Living*? Will these changes result in secured creditors choosing to appoint privately appointed receivers instead of court-appointed receivers?

PART VI

International Insolvencies

CHAPTER 19

International Insolvencies

I. INTRODUCTION

This chapter deals with a branch of the conflict of laws commonly referred to as "cross-border insolvency law" or "international insolvency (or bankruptcy) law." The following example illustrates some of the issues that may arise.

X, a corporation incorporated under Delaware law and having its head office in Los Angeles, has branch offices across Canada. X also has a subsidiary operating in Canada which was incorporated under provincial law. X is hammered by the financial crisis of 2008 and files for protection for itself and its Canadian subsidiary under Chapter 11 of the US *Bankruptcy Code*.

1. Will the Canadian courts recognize the Chapter 11 proceedings with respect to (a) the Canadian incorporated subsidiary, and (b) the Canadian branches?

2. Can Canadian creditors initiate bankruptcy proceedings in Canada against the Canadian subsidiary despite the US proceedings?

3. Can Canadian creditors enforce security interests given them by X against assets held by the branches and assets owned by the subsidiary despite a stay of proceedings, applicable to creditors worldwide, under s. 306 of the US *Bankruptcy Code*?

4. Whose bankruptcy rules, Canadian or US, will apply to determine the priority rights of Canadian employees of the subsidiaries and the Canadian branches of X?

The conflict-of-law rules concerning cross-border insolvencies fall under two main headings: (1) the rules governing the assumption of jurisdiction by Canadian courts over insolvent companies and individuals ("jurisdictional rules") (see questions 1 to 3, above), and (2) the rules governing the recognition of foreign insolvency proceedings, the status of corporate groups, and the treatment of Canadian-based assets and liabilities of such entities ("recognitional and enforcement rules") (see question 4, above). Both types of problem are of great practical importance and arise on a daily basis. However, it is the second heading— the recognition and enforcement of foreign insolvency orders—that has triggered most of the Canadian litigation since the early 1990s.

815

II. JURISDICTION OF CANADIAN COURTS

From the beginning, the jurisdiction of Canadian courts over insolvent individuals and companies has been determined by Canadian bankruptcy legislation. In the case of involuntary proceedings, the BIA provides that the bankruptcy petition may be brought in Canada against a "debtor." "Debtor," as defined in s. 2(1), "includes an insolvent person and any person who, at the time an act of bankruptcy was committed by him, resided or carried on business in Canada and, where the context requires, includes a bankrupt." "Insolvent person" is defined (s. 2(1)) as "a person who is not bankrupt and who resides, carries on business or has property in Canada, whose liabilities to creditors provable as claims under this Act amount to one thousand dollars, and (a) who is for any reason unable to meet his obligations as they generally become due, (b) who has ceased paying his current obligations in the ordinary course of business as they generally become due, or (c) the aggregate of whose property is not, at a fair valuation, sufficient, or, if disposed of at a fairly conducted sale under legal process, would not be sufficient to enable payment of all his obligations, due and accruing due." Section 43(5) is also relevant. It provides that the petition must be filed in the court having jurisdiction in the judicial district of the locality of the debtor. "Locality of the debtor" is defined in s. 2(1) and its function is to pinpoint the domestic place in Canada where the petition must be brought once it is established that the debtor meets the requirements of a "debtor" in the statutory definition.

As far as an assignment in bankruptcy is concerned, an assignment can be made by an "insolvent person." Put more succinctly, a debtor can make an assignment if the debtor resides or carries on business or has property in Canada.[1] Despite the broad definition of debtor, it is not clear whether the location of property is alone sufficient to give the court jurisdiction in involuntary proceedings. The point can be argued both ways. For recent cases applying these provisions, see *Re Dalsto* (2002), 38 CBR (4th) 181 (Ont. SC) and *Re Chauvco Resources International* (1999), 9 CBR (4th) 235 (Alta. QB).

The BIA does not address the question of what is to happen if the debtor has already been made bankrupt in another jurisdiction at the time of the Canadian proceedings.[2] However, it is well established in Anglo-Canadian jurisprudence that this fact will not bar the Canadian court's jurisdiction and that, in such cases, the Canadian court will do its best to cooperate with the foreign court to administer the two estates in the best interests of the creditors in both countries and without sacrificing the interests of Canadian creditors. See, for example, *Allen v. Hansen* (1890), 18 SCR 667.

The trustee is entitled to claim the debtor's property wherever it is located—in Canada or elsewhere. See BIA s. 67(1) and the definition of "property." Likewise, the debtor's foreign as

---

1. The "property" jurisdictional base was added to the BIA in 1997 and greatly increases the jurisdiction of Canadian courts, particularly because there is no requirement that the bulk of the debtor's property must be located in Canada.

2. The parties may have various reasons for initiating Canadian proceedings. An important reason is to prevent Canadian assets being removed to the foreign jurisdiction without the creditors' consent. Another reason may be to ensure that the Canadian-based assets are distributed in accordance with the BIA distributional rules. Similar considerations come into play where the parties must decide whether to initiate reorganizational proceedings in Canada where reorganizational proceedings have also been started in a foreign jurisdiction.

well as Canadian creditors will be subject to the Canadian court's jurisdiction and will be entitled to file proofs of claim. See BIA s. 2(1), definition of "creditor." Absent special BIA rules, the question whether the estate has a valid claim to particular property and whether a creditor has a valid secured or unsecured claim will be governed by general conflict of laws principles. See, further, American Law Institute (ALI), Transnational Insolvency Project, *International Statement of Canadian Bankruptcy Law*, Part II.D (2002). Difficulties also arise in determining the ranking of foreign creditors under BIA s. 136(1). It seems clear that non-preferred creditors, Canadian and foreign, will be treated alike. It is unsettled, however, whether foreign employees of a debtor company are to be treated as preferred creditors and whether, contrary to the normal conflict of laws rule, foreign revenue claims are entitled to recognition in the administration of the estate. See *Re Sefel Geophysical Ltd.* (1988), 54 DLR (4th) 117 (Alta. QB), where on the particular facts Justice Forsyth recognized the US tax claim.

An unresolved issue in Canada is whether, if the insolvency proceedings are in Canada, the Canadian laws dealing with preferences, transfers at undervalue, fraudulent conveyances, and the like apply to transactions that took place in a foreign country. The following leading US decision addresses the question in a British–US context.

In re Maxwell Communication Corporation plc
93 F3d 1036 (2d Cir. 1996)

CARDAMONE Circuit Judge: The demise of the late British media magnate Robert Maxwell and that of the corporation bearing his name, the Maxwell Communication Corporation plc, followed a similar and scandalous path, spawning civil and criminal litigation in England and around the world. This case illustrates that some positive consequences have resulted from these parallel demises. From Maxwell's mysterious death, which forced his international corporation into bankruptcy, was born a unique judicial administration of the debtor corporation by parallel and cooperative proceedings in the courts of the United States and England aimed at harmonizing the laws of both countries and also aimed at maximizing the benefits to creditors and the prospects of rehabilitation.

We have before us a small but significant piece of the swirling legal controversy that followed the collapse of Robert Maxwell's media empire. The question to be addressed is whether Maxwell Communication, as a debtor estate in Chapter 11, may recover under American law millions of dollars it transferred to three foreign banks shortly before declaring bankruptcy. It has sought such relief in adversary proceedings in the bankruptcy court under those sections of the United States *Bankruptcy Code*, 11 USC §§101-1330 (1994) (*Bankruptcy Code* or Code), providing for what is known as "avoidance" of prepetition transactions. Because, in our view, the doctrine of international comity supports deferring to the courts and laws of England, we affirm the dismissal of the Chapter 11 debtor's complaints.

Background

. . .

A. Events Preceding the Dual Filings

The debtor was originally incorporated in England over 60 years ago as a limited company. Robert Maxwell acquired control of this limited company 15 years ago. The following year, the company was re-registered under English law as a public limited company and, in 1987, it became Maxwell Communication Corporation plc (hereafter Maxwell or the debtor). Before filing for bankruptcy protection, Maxwell functioned as a holding company for Robert Maxwell's "public side" holdings—as distinguished from Maxwell's private holdings, which at one time included the *New York Daily News*—and controlled a variety of media-related companies. Although Maxwell was headquartered and managed in England and incurred most of its debt there, approximately 80 percent of its assets were located in the United States, most notably its subsidiaries Macmillan, Inc. and Official Airlines Guide, Inc.

Maxwell alleges that in the fall of 1991, less than 90 days before its Chapter 11 filing, it made several transfers—transfers it now seeks to avoid—to three European banks (collectively, the banks) with whom it had credit arrangements. Two of these banks are Barclays Bank plc (Barclays) and National Westminster Bank plc (National Westminster), both of which have their headquarters in London and maintain an international presence, with branches in New York and elsewhere. The other bank is Société Générale, a French Bank headquartered in Paris with offices, among other places, in London and New York.

. . .

B. The Dual Insolvency Proceedings

On December 16, 1991 Maxwell filed a petition for reorganization under Chapter 11 of the United States *Bankruptcy Code* in the Bankruptcy Court for the Southern District of New York. The next day, it petitioned the High Court of Justice in London for an administration order. Administration, introduced by the *Insolvency Act 1986*, is the closest equivalent in British law to Chapter 11 relief. Acting under the terms of the *Insolvency Act*, Justice Hoffman, then of the High Court (now a member of the House of Lords), appointed members of the London office of the accounting firm of Price Waterhouse as administrators to manage the affairs and property of the corporation.

Simultaneous proceedings in different countries, especially in multi-party cases like bankruptcies, can naturally lead to inconsistencies and conflicts. To minimize such problems, Judge Brozman appointed Richard A. Gitlin, Esq. as examiner, pursuant to 11 USC §1104(c), in the Chapter 11 proceedings. The order of appointment required the examiner, *inter alia*, to investigate the debtor's financial condition, to function as a mediator among the various parties, and to "act to harmonize, for the benefit of all of [Maxwell's] creditors and stockholders and other parties in interest, [Maxwell's] United States chapter 11 case and [Maxwell's] United Kingdom administration case so as to maximize [the] prospects for rehabilitation and reorganization."

Judge Brozman and Justice Hoffman subsequently authorized the examiner and the administrators to coordinate their efforts pursuant to a so-called Protocol, an agreement between the examiner and the administrators. In approving the Protocol, Judge Brozman recognized the English administrators as the corporate governance of the debtor-in-possession. As the bankruptcy judge later explained, this recognition was motivated not only by the need for coordination but also because Maxwell was "incorporated in England and run ... by [Maxwell] executives out of Maxwell House in London subject to the direction of an English board of directors." *Maxwell I*, 170 BR at 817. Justice Hoffman reciprocated, granting the examiner leave to appear before the High Court in England.

These joint efforts resulted in what has been described as a "remarkable sequence of events leading to perhaps the first world-wide plan of orderly liquidation ever achieved." Jay Lawrence Westbrook, "The Lessons of Maxwell Communication," 64 *Fordham L Rev.* 2531, 2535 (1996). The administrators, the examiner, and other interested parties worked together to produce a common system for reorganizing Maxwell by disposing of assets as going concerns and distributing the proceeds to creditors. *Maxwell I*, 170 BR at 802. The mechanism for accomplishing this is embodied in a plan of reorganization and a scheme of arrangement, which are interdependent documents and were filed by the administrators in the United States and English courts respectively.

· · ·

Despite the unusual degree of cooperation and reconciliation of the laws of the two forums, the plan and scheme predictably did not resolve all the problems that might arise from the concurrent proceedings. For example, these documents did not specify which substantive law would govern the resolution of disputed claims by creditors. More importantly, they did not address the instant dispute regarding the debtor's ability to set aside pre-petition transfers to certain creditors.

· · ·

Maxwell and the examiner appealed. We consolidated the three cases on January 15, 1996 and now address the merits.

Discussion

· · ·

II. *International Comity*

A. *The Doctrine*

Analysis of comity often begins with the definition proffered by Justice Gray in *Hilton v. Guyot*, 159 US 113, 163-64, 16 S Ct. 139, 143, 40 L Ed. 95 (1895): "'Comity,' in the legal sense, is neither a matter of absolute obligation, on the one hand, nor of mere courtesy and good will, upon the other. But it is the recognition which one nation allows within its territory to the legislative, executive or judicial acts of another nation, having due regard both to international duty and convenience, and to the rights of its own citizens or of other persons who are under the protection of its laws." Although *Hilton* addressed the degree to which a foreign judgment is conclusive in a court of the United States, the principle expressed is one of broad application.

· · ·

Comity is exercised with reference to "prevalent doctrines of international law." *Lauritzen*, 345 US at 577, 73 S Ct. at 926. The management of transnational insolvencies is concededly underdeveloped. However, certain norms shared among nations are relevant to the present case and have guided the choice-of-law analysis in such cases as *Lauritzen* and *Romero*. See also *Alcoa*, 148 F2d at 443 (referring to similar norms). The same principles are set forth in §403(1) of the *Restatement (Third) of Foreign Relations* (1986), which provides that states normally refrain from prescribing laws that govern activities connected with another state "when the exercise of such jurisdiction is unreasonable."

Whether so legislating would be "unreasonable" is determined "by evaluating all relevant factors, including, where appropriate," such factors as the link between the regulating state and the relevant activity, the connection between that state and the person responsible for the activity (or protected by the regulation), the nature of the regulated activity and its importance to the regulating state, the effect of the regulation on justified expectations, the significance of the regulation to the international system, the extent of other states' interests, and the likelihood of conflict with other states' regulations. *Restatement* §403(2).

· · ·

B. Primacy of English Law

England has a much closer connection to these disputes than does the United States. The debtor and most of its creditors—not only the beneficiaries of the pre-petition transfers—are British. Maxwell was incorporated under the laws of England, largely controlled by British nationals, governed by a British board of directors, and managed in London by British executives. These connecting factors indicated what the bankruptcy judge called the "Englishness" of the debtor, which was one reason for recognizing the administrators—who are officers of the High Court—as Maxwell's corporate governance. *Maxwell I*, 170 BR at 817 n. 23. These same factors, particularly the fact that most of Maxwell's debt was incurred in England, show that England has the strongest connection to the present litigation.

Although an avoidance action concededly affects creditors other than the transferee, because scrutiny of the transfer is at the heart of such a suit it is assuredly most relevant that the transfers in this case related primarily to England. The $30 million received by Barclays came from an account at National Westminster in London and, while it was routed through Barclays' New York branch like all payments received in US dollars, it was immediately credited to an overdraft account maintained in England. Plaintiffs claim no particular United States connection to the other alleged transfers to Barclays, all of which were denominated in the amended complaint in pounds sterling. Similarly, the transfers to National Westminster and Société Générale were made to and from accounts maintained in Great Britain.

Further, the overdraft facilities and other credit transactions between the transferee banks and the debtor resulted from negotiations that took place in England and were administered primarily there. English law applied to the resolution of disputes arising under such agreements. We recognize that some of the money transferred to the banks came from the proceeds of the sale of Maxwell subsidiaries in the United States, which is a subject we discuss in a moment. In almost all other respects, however, the credit transactions were centered in London and the fund transfers occurred there.

C. *Relative Interests of Forum and Foreign States*

Given the considerably lesser American connection to the dispute, the bankruptcy court believed its forum's interests were "not very compelling." *Maxwell I*, 170 BR at 818. Virtually the only factor linking the transfers to the United States—that the sale of certain Maxwell subsidiaries in the United States provided the source of some of the funds—is not particularly weighty because those companies were sold as going concerns. Hence, the potential effect that such sales might have had on local economies is not here implicated.

The examiner warns that dire consequences would result from a failure to enforce the Code's avoidance provision. The first one he mentions is that such a course ignores §103(a) of the Code. This contention is one we have already addressed and rejected. The examiner next urges that the purposes underlying §547 and §502(d) would be thwarted unless both of these provisions were applied in all Chapter 11 proceedings. Although the non-application of these or other *Bankruptcy Code* provisions certainly might detract from the Code's policies in other cases, here the negative effects are insubstantial. The principal policies underlying the Code's avoidance provisions are equal distribution to creditors and preserving the value of the estate through the discouragement of aggressive pre-petition tactics causing dismemberment of the debtor. *Wolas*, 502 US at 161, 112 S Ct. at 533. These policies are effectuated, although in a somewhat different way, by the provisions' British counterpart. *See Maxwell I*, 170 BR at 818.

In the present case, in which there is a parallel insolvency proceeding taking place in another country, failure to apply §547 and §502(d) does not free creditors from the constraints of avoidance law, nor does it severely undercut the policy of equal distribution. All avoidance laws are necessarily limited in scope because time limits and other conditions are imposed on the voidability of transactions. Although a different result might be warranted were there no parallel proceeding in England—and, hence, no alternative mechanism for voiding preferences—we cannot say the United States has a significant interest in applying its avoidance law. Moreover, as noted, international comity is a policy that Congress expressly made part of the *Bankruptcy Code*, and a decision consistent with comity therefore furthers the Code's policy.

Because of the strong British connection to the present dispute, it follows that England has a stronger interest than the United States in applying its own avoidance law to these actions. Its law implicates that country's interest in promoting what Parliament apparently viewed as the appropriate compromise between equality of distribution and other important commercial interests, for instance, ensuring potentially insolvent debtors' ability to secure essential ongoing financing. In addition, although complexity in the conduct of transnational insolvencies makes choice-of-law prognostication imprecise, we agree with the lower courts that English law could have been expected to apply.

. . .

Appeal dismissed.

NOTE

Jay Westbrook, a leading American international insolvency scholar, who was retained as *amicus curiae* by the District Court, favoured adoption of the "home jurisdiction" rule (that is, in the case of a corporate debtor, the law of incorporation of the debtor corporation) on the grounds of its simplicity and predictability of outcome and the advantage it confers in enabling contracting parties to plan their affairs with greater certainty. See Ian F. Fletcher, *Private International Law* (1999), at 77, n. 169. As the above judgment shows, the US Circuit Court rejected this approach and, probably, rightly so. The place of incorporation may be quite arbitrary and, if used as a touchstone, would enable the parties to incorporate in an offshore haven, or to reincorporate there, in order to take advantage of lax avoidance rules. The suggestion that parties, engaged in what may appear to them to be quite normal and legitimate pre-bankruptcy transactions, consider at the time what the law of the debtor's incorporation may have to say about the transaction will often be quite fanciful. Consider the following example. X, a Canadian bank located in Toronto, makes a loan to Y, a US company incorporated under Delaware law. Y is delinquent in repaying the loan and X threatens to sue if Y does not make prompt payment. Y makes the payment. It is unlikely that the parties will consult Delaware law, or even the US *Bankruptcy Code*, to determine whether the repayment can be impeached as a preferential payment. An effectiveness or interest test, such as the test adopted in *Maxwell*, strikes a better balance between a home jurisdiction test (as favoured by Westbrook) and a territorial test, turning on the law of the jurisdiction in which the bankruptcy proceedings are initiated. Canadian bankruptcy lawyers seem to favour the territorial test, but only if the bankruptcy proceedings take place in Canada.

III. RECOGNITION AND ENFORCEMENT OF FOREIGN INSOLVENCIES

A. Evolution of Canadian Law

Until recently, the common law rule applied by Canadian courts was that recognition would be given to a foreign bankruptcy order if made by a court or agency of competent jurisdiction in the jurisdiction of the debtor's domicile. "Domicile" here meant (as elsewhere in the conflict of laws) the jurisdiction with which the debtor was deemed to have the closest connection. In the case of a corporation, this meant the corporation's place of incorporation. See, for example, *Williams v. Rice*, [1926] 3 DLR 225 (Man. KB) and *Re IIT* (1975), 58 DLR (3d) 55 (Ont. HC), both cited in Registrar Funduk's lively judgment in *Re Singer Sewing Machine Co. of Canada Ltd.*, [2000] 5 WWR 598 (Alta. QB), below.

Commonwealth authors argued for more expanded grounds of recognition of foreign insolvency proceedings because it was felt that the debtor's domiciliary jurisdiction often only has a tenuous connection with the location of the debtor's main business operations. Another reason advanced for a broader basis of recognition was that because Commonwealth courts themselves assume jurisdiction over an insolvent debtor, where the debtor resides or has a place of business in the forum, they should be willing to concede the same jurisdiction to foreign courts. Recent Canadian cases, particularly Ontario cases, have used the language of comity in hearing applications for recognition of US insolvency proceedings in Canada or requests to stay proceedings against the debtor or the debtor's affiliate. See, for example, Farley J's important (and controversial) judgment in *Re Babcock & Wilcox Canada Ltd.* (2000), 18 CBR (4th) 157 (Ont. SC), also extracted below.

In using the comity test, these courts relied on the Supreme Court of Canada's seminal decision in *Morguard Investments Ltd. v. De Savoye*, [1990] 3 SCR 1077. *Morguard* involved the recognition of an Alberta judgment in British Columbia, and not the recognition of foreign insolvency proceedings. Nevertheless, many subsequent lower courts interpreted the Supreme Court's judgment as meaning that, absent special circumstances, a foreign judgment will be enforced in Canada if there is a "substantial connection" between the foreign jurisdiction and the defendant. The Supreme Court confirmed the correctness of this interpretation in *Beals v. Saldanha*, [2003] 3 SCR 416. If the comity test is retained, presumably the domiciliary test will fade into the background and Canadian courts will basically look to see whether there is sufficient connection between the debtor and the foreign insolvency proceedings to justify recognizing the proceedings in Canada.

As further discussed below, the 1997 BIA and CCAA amendments (BIA Part XIII; CCAA s. 18.6)[3] included several substantially identical sections dealing with international insolvencies, but they threw no light on which recognitional test should be applied by Canadian courts. The thrust of these provisions was to emphasize coordination of the Canadian proceedings with the foreign proceedings. However, BIA s. 268(5) (CCAA s. 18.6) also provided that "[n]othing in this Part prevents the court, on the application of a foreign representative or any other interested person, from applying such legal or equitable rules governing the recognition of foreign insolvency orders and assistance to foreign representatives as are not inconsistent with the provisions of this Act," which returns us to our starting point.

B. Treatment of Corporate Groups

Another and still more difficult issue is whether, and to what extent, Canadian courts will recognize a foreign insolvency order (typically, in the North American context, a US Chapter 11 case) involving several or all members of a corporate group, some of which are located in Canada and may not even be insolvent. In *Singer Canada*, above, Registrar Funduk gave two reasons for refusing to recognize the Chapter 11 proceedings as far as they purported to apply to the Canadian affiliate. The first was that the Canadian company was not insolvent, and the other was that the US bankruptcy court lacked jurisdiction over the Alberta incorporated company. His decision stands in contrast to Farley J's decision in *Babcock & Wilcox* (B & W), below, where the latter extended recognition in Canada to a stay-of-proceedings order issued by Judge Brown in Louisiana against asbestos tort claimants seeking to sue B & W's Canadian subsidiary in Canada. Farley J granted Brown J's request for assistance even though B & W Canada was not a party to the US proceedings and was not itself insolvent. The two decisions are difficult to reconcile and clearly took a different view of what comity involves in the corporate group area.

---

3. These provisions will be replaced by the modified UNCITRAL Model Law on Cross-border Insolvency, adopted in the 2005-2007 amendments to the BIA and the CCAA when these provisions are proclaimed to come into effect. The new provisions are discussed below.

C. Effects of Recognition of Foreign Insolvency Proceedings

Legal systems differ most in their treatment of foreign insolvency orders. Countries sub-scribing to a "territorialist" theory of recognition (until recently, many civil law jurisdic-tions, as well as many US courts before adoption of the 1978 US *Bankruptcy Code*) refuse to give effect to a foreign order as far as it affects property and rights in the forum state or, at any rate, will subordinate foreign creditor claims to the claims of local creditors.[4] Other the-orists subscribe to a "universalist" conception of insolvency pursuant to which an insolvency order made by a court or official organ of the country in which the debtor has its main in-terests is entitled to recognition and assistance in all other jurisdictions.[5] In the past, Can-adian courts have generally followed the British model of "modified universalism," which involves recognizing and giving effect to foreign insolvency orders, but with a substantial number of exceptions and qualifications. In particular, Anglo-Canadian courts have consis-tently held that the existence of insolvency proceedings in a foreign jurisdiction does not preclude initiation of proceedings in Canada or the United Kingdom, although, as a matter of practice, the bankruptcy order is usually confined to assets of the debtor located within the jurisdiction.

As far as the US approach is concerned, before 1978, US state courts often embraced a territorialist philosophy and gave priority to the satisfaction of local creditor claims before allowing the foreign representative to take control of locally situated assets. However, this was changed in 1978 with the enactment of the *Bankruptcy Code* and its important s. 304. Section 304 adopted a modified universalist approach but with stricter rules for giving effect to the foreign order than those applied at common law in England or Canada. Section 304 was replaced in 2005 by a new Part XV of the US *Bankruptcy Code* as part of the *Bankruptcy Abuse Prevention and Consumer Protection Act of 2005* (BAPCPO) adopted by Congress. Part XV adopts almost verbatim the UNCITRAL Model Law on Cross-border Insolvency.

The modified universalism practised by Canadian courts before the (still unproclaimed) 2005-2007 BIA and CCAA amendments adopting a modified version of the UNCITRAL Model Law led to the following results:

1. The status of the foreign representative was recognized for the purpose of enabling the representative to bring or defend proceedings in Canada as long as insolvency proceedings had not been initiated in Canada with respect to the Canadian based assets (see above).[6]

---

4. British lawyers refer to this approach as "ring fencing" of locally based assets. Still more colourfully, Jay Westbrook describes it as the "grab rule."

5. Westbrook is a strong advocate of the universalist theory. He has argued in many articles that the universalist approach makes most sense, is more efficient than the other theories, and provides greater predictability of results in a world dominated by large multinational corporations, where the most important assets of a debt-or are often held in intangible form and their location can be switched to another jurisdiction with the click of a computer button.

6. Difficulties arise in Chapter 11-type cases where the debtor remains in possession and has no trustee or other independent representative. US courts have overcome this difficulty by designating a special examiner or other person to represent the debtor for foreign recognitional purposes. In Canada, Canadian courts would probably authorize a CCAA case monitor to serve the same function for external purposes.

2. Canadian courts would enjoin proceedings in Canada against the foreign debtor. See, for example, *Roberts v. Picture Butte Municipal Hospital*, [1999] 4 WWR 443 (Alta. QB) and pre-2005 BIA s. 269 and CCAA s. 18.6.

3. The foreign representative was allowed to take control of the debtor's assets in Canada where there was no creditor opposition. See, for example, *Re IIT* (1975), 58 DLR (3d) 55 (Ont. HC), cited in Registrar Funduk's judgment in *Singer Canada*.

If Canadian creditors objected, the Canadian court could impose restrictions on the foreign representative's power to liquidate, transfer, or distribute the proceeds of the Canadian assets.[7] There was also another qualification. Canadian courts have said in the past that a foreign insolvency order cannot affect title to immovables in Canada. See *Macdonald v. Georgian Bay Lumber Co.* (1878), 2 SCR 364. In practice, courts have overcome this anomalous rule[8] by recognizing the status of a local receiver of the property appointed by the foreign representative.

D. Chattel Security Problems

It is a well-established rule in the conflict of laws that the validity, effect, and priority of security interests in personal property is governed by the *lex situs* of the property at the time of creation of the security interest.[9] The rule applies equally in Canadian bankruptcies (1) because BIA s. 71(1) provides that title to the debtor's property vests in the trustee, subject to the right of secured creditors; and (2) because BIA s. 72(1) preserves the substantive provisions of any other law or statute relating to property and civil rights that is not in conflict with the BIA.[10] Prior to the Supreme Court's decision in *Holt Cargo Systems Inc. v. ABC Containerline N.V. (Trustees of)*, [2001] 3 SCR 907, extracted below, it was generally assumed that a Canadian court would not allow a trustee to remove Canadian-situated assets out of Canada without the secured party's consent or without the court being satisfied that the security interest would be recognized and given the same priority in the foreign jurisdiction as it enjoyed under Canadian law. One of the clearly stated objectives of the BIA Part XIII amendments was to ensure that Canadian secured parties would continue to enjoy this protection in the future. However, it was unclear whether Canadian courts would show the

---

7. In practice, Canadian creditors concerned about not being treated fairly or expeditiously in the foreign jurisdiction initiate their own insolvency proceedings in Canada, thereby triggering concurrent proceedings in Canada and the foreign jurisdiction and giving Canadian creditors a direct input into the disposition of the Canadian assets.

8. "Anomalous" because, presumably, Canadian courts would not object to the foreign representative assuming control of shares in a Canadian-based realty company owned by the foreign debtor where the company's assets include real property in Canada.

9. These rules are now enshrined in ss. 5 to 8 of the Ontario *Personal Property Security Act* (PPSA) and the near identical provisions in the PPSAs of the other provinces. The same rules apply even more strongly to security interests in real property.

10. For the BIA rules governing proofs of claim, realization of the secured party's collateral, and other aspects, see Chapter 8.

same solicitude for security interests against property situated *outside Canada* in favour of foreign secured parties where the property was subsequently brought into Canada. In *Holt Cargo*, in an unusual factual setting, the Supreme Court answered "yes" to the question and Justice Binnie's comprehensive judgment for the court reaffirmed Canada's support for a modified form of universalism.

E. Discharge of Debts Under Foreign Insolvency Law

This is another issue that has given difficulties in the past. The general Anglo-Canadian conflict of laws rule is that the discharge of a debt is governed by the proper law of the debt, which may be that of Canada or any other country deemed to have a close connection with the debt. However, the rule does not apply to the discharge of debts under the BIA because the discharge provisions (ss. 168.1 *et seq.*) have always been understood to apply to *all* debts, whatever the governing law of the debt, unless otherwise provided in the BIA. Section 178 enumerates non-dischargeable debts, but these provisions also do not turn on the proper law of the debt.

Nevertheless, in an 1890 decision, the English Court of Appeal decided in *Gibbs & Sons v. Société Industrielle et Commerciale* (1890), 25 QBD 399[11] that a foreign insolvency law or order discharging or modifying a debt or other contractual obligation, or a claim for damages for breach of such an obligation, will not be recognized unless the discharge or variation is also recognized under the proper law of the debt or obligation. *Gibbs & Sons* was approved, with surprisingly little hesitation, by the Privy Council in an 1898 decision: *New Zealand Loan and Mercantile Agency Co. v. Morrison*, [1898] AC 349.[12] The rule has not been much discussed in Canadian cases, but has been recognized or enforced in the context of personal insolvencies: *International Harvester Co. v. Zarbok*, [1918] 3 WWR 38 (Sask. QB); *Re Taylor* (1988), 68 CBR (NS) 93 (PEISC); *Re Bialek* (1994), 18 OR (3d) 462 (Gen. Div.), extracted below. The rule has been much criticized by commentators[13] as seriously at odds with the principles underlying the recognition of foreign insolvencies, and also because the English and Canadian bankruptcy acts themselves provide for discharges from personal insolvencies regardless of the proper law of the debts being discharged. It seems reasonable to conclude, therefore, that the *Gibbs* rule is ripe for reconsideration by the Supreme Court of Canada and will probably not be followed.

---

11. A case involving the liquidation of a French incorporated company. French law did not permit proof of claim for damages for breach of an executory contract. The plaintiffs sued the company in England for damages for breach of contract governed by English law. It was held that they were entitled to do so despite the French liquidation rules.

12. For a powerful criticism of this aspect of the decision, as well as other aspects, see John Honsberger, "Canadian Recognition of Foreign Judicially Supervised Arrangements" (1990), 76 CBR (NS) 204.

13. In addition to the criticisms by Honsberger, see I.F. Fletcher, *The Law of Insolvency*, 4th ed. (London: Sweet & Maxwell, 2009) (criticizing Lord Esher's judgment as "insular and xenophobic in the extreme") and Philip Smart, *Cross-Border Insolvency* (London: Butterworths, 1991), Chapter 8.

F. Recognition and Effects of Foreign Reorganizational Proceedings

Until the early 1990s, there was much uncertainty about how much recognition would be given in Canada to foreign reorganizational proceedings, particularly those involving Chapter 11 of the US Code. For the details, see ALI, *International Statement of Canadian Bankruptcy Law*, above, part II.E.2. The doubts were inspired by a number of factors, such as the rule in *Gibbs & Sons*, previously discussed; the Privy Council decision in *New Zealand Loan & Mercantile Agency Co. v. Morrison*, [1898] AC 349; and unease about recognizing Chapter 11 proceedings in which the old management was allowed to continue to run the company's affairs.

Since then, there has been a near-total sea change in the attitude of Canadian courts. It is now safe to state that our courts no longer draw a distinction between straight bankruptcy and reorganizational proceedings for such purposes as recognizing the foreign proceedings; restraining actions in Canada against the foreign debtor (at least in those cases where the domiciliary jurisdictional test is satisfied with respect to the foreign court's competence); and cooperating with US courts where there are concurrent proceedings in Canada and the United States. See, further, J. Ziegel, "Cross-Border Insolvencies," in Stephanie Ben-Ishai and Anthony Duggan, eds., *Canadian Bankrupcy and Insolvency Law. Bill C-55, Statute c. 47 and Beyond* (Toronto: LexisNexis, 2007), Chapter 11.

G. Cross-Border Insolvency Provisions

Over the past 25 years or so, many efforts have been made, domestically and internationally, to bring about greater harmonization of rules for the recognition of cross-border insolvency proceedings. Here we can sketch only a few of the many initiatives. For fuller details, see I.F. Fletcher, *Insolvency in Private International Law*, 2nd ed. (Oxford: Oxford University Press, 2005) and J.S. Ziegel, ed., *Current Developments in International and Comparative Corporate Insolvency Law* (Oxford: Oxford University Press, 1994).

At the country and regional levels, the European Union opened for signature in 1995 an ambitious Convention on Insolvency Proceedings, applicable only to EU members, covering jurisdictional, recognitional, and choice-of-law issues. The Convention never took effect because the United Kingdom withheld its approval. (The United Kingdom was upset about some EU members' reactions to the "mad cow" disease in the United Kingdom.) However, the EU managed to sidetrack the diplomatic contretemps by adopting the Convention in 2000 in the form of an EU regulation: Council regulation (EC) no. 1346/2000 of May 29, 2000 on insolvency proceedings.

The EU regulation covers both jurisdictional and choice-of-law issues. For jurisdictional purposes, the regulation distinguishes between insolvency proceedings initiated in a member country that is a debtor's centre of main interest (COMI) and proceedings brought in a non-COMI member country. An order made in a COMI jurisdiction is binding on all EU members and entitles the insolvency administrator to take control of the debtor's assets wherever situated, to realize the assets, and to distribute the net proceeds in accordance with the COMI jurisdiction's distributional rules unless otherwise provided in the regulation. Note that a judgment rendered by a national tribunal that a debtor's COMI is situated in its territory must be recognized by all other member states (art. 16(1)), and can only be refused recognition on the ground of public policy, narrowly defined (art. 26(1)). Two leading cases that illustrate the powerful impact of these rules are *Re Daisytek-ISA Ltd.*, [2003] BCC 562 (England) and the ECJ's judgment in *Eurofood IFSC Ltd.*, case C-341/04 (2 May 2006). See, further, J. Ziegel, "Cross-Border Insolvencies," in Ben-Ishai and Duggan, above, Chapter 11, at 288-89.

Much less ambitious in scope than the EU regulation, but probably more important for international harmonization goals is the UNCITRAL Model Law on Cross-Border Insolvency. This was approved by the UN in 1997 and, as of 2008, had been adopted in 15 countries including the United States, the United Kingdom, Japan, Mexico, South Africa, and other smaller countries. (Canada also incorporated a much modified version of the Model Law in the 2005-2008 BIA and CCAA amendments, but they are not yet in effect.) The Model Law does not deal with choice-of-law and equally contentious substantive issues, but focuses its attention on questions related to the recognition of foreign insolvency proceedings and the protection of the assets of foreign estates. For this purpose, the Model Law addresses the four sequential steps generally deemed necessary for an optimally successful international insolvency regime: *access* by the foreign representative to the local insolvency courts; *recognition* of the status of the foreign representatives when the prescribed prerequisites are met; *assistance* to the foreign representatives by granting orders for the stay of proceedings against locally based assets of the foreign estate; and, finally, *cooperation* between the courts of the recognizing state and the foreign state.

These features must be read in conjunction with the following definitions in art. 2 of the Model Law:

(a) "Foreign proceeding" means a collective judicial or administrative proceeding in a foreign State, including an interim proceeding, pursuant to a law relating to insolvency in which proceeding the assets and affairs of the debtor are subject to control or supervision by a foreign court, for the purpose of reorganization or liquidation;

(b) "Foreign main proceeding" means a foreign proceeding taking place in the State where the debtor has the centre of its main interests;

(c) "Foreign non-main proceeding" means a foreign proceeding, other than a foreign main proceeding, taking place in a State where the debtor has an establishment within the meaning of subparagraph (f) of this article;

(d) "Foreign representative" means a person or body, including one appointed on an interim basis, authorized in a foreign proceeding to administer the reorganization or the liquidation of the debtor's assets or affairs or to act as a representative of the foreign proceeding;

(e) "Foreign court" means a judicial or other authority competent to control or supervise a foreign proceeding;

(f) "Establishment" means any place of operations where the debtor carries out a non-transitory economic activity with human means and goods or services.

As will be seen from these definitions, like the EU regulation, the Model Law also distinguishes between a "foreign main proceeding" (FMP) and a "foreign non-main proceeding" (FNMP) and adopts the COMI test to determine whether a foreign insolvency proceeding falls under the first or the second heading. There is, however, this vital difference: under the Model Law, courts are not bound by the COMI/non-COMI determination made in another Model Law jurisdiction and are free to make their own determination.[14] The Model Law also

---

14. As has indeed happened in the United States under Chapter 15 of the *Bankruptcy Code*. For a leading case, see *In re Bear Stearns High-Grade Structured Credit Strategies Master Fund Ltd.*, 389 BR 325 (SDNY 2008).

distinguishes between the effects of recognition of an FMP (art. 20) and the relief that *may* be granted on recognition of a foreign proceeding (art. 21). The assistance to which an FMP is entitled under art. 20 is mandatory; the relief that may be accorded an FMP and FNMP under art. 21 is discretionary.

However, even in the case of an FMP, the required assistance is restricted to three types—stay of action against the debtor and the debtor's property; stay of execution against the debtor's property; and suspension of the debtor's right to transfer, encumber, or otherwise dispose of the debtor's assets. The foreign representative's power to administer the assets in the enacting state and to distribute the assets do not fall into this category.[15] All other forms of relief in the case of an FMP are in the discretion of the court and fall under art. 21. Article 21 also applies to *all* forms of relief in the case of an FNMP. This very much reduces the significance of the recognition of FNMP in the enacting states because even a stay of proceedings against the foreign debtor and its property requires the court's approval. Article 21(3) narrows the scope of relief still further in the case of an FNMP because it provides, which is somewhat puzzling, that the court must be satisfied that the relief relates to assets which, under the law of the enacting state, "should be administered in the foreign non-main proceeding or concerns information required in that proceeding."

Other features of art. 21 also emphasize the cautiousness with which the Model Law approaches the exercise of the court's discretionary powers. Before entrusting the foreign representative with the administration or distribution of assets located in the enacting state, the court must be satisfied that the interests of (local) creditors are adequately protected.[16] In fact, concern over adequate protection for creditors and other interested parties preyed heavily on the national representatives gathered in Vienna to draft the Model Law, for it surfaces again in art. 22(1). This time it is more broadly based and applies to all relief granted under arts. 19 and 21, and the court is told that it "must be satisfied" that the interests of creditors and other interested persons, including the debtor, are adequately protected.

H. Impact of Model Law on the BIA and CCAA

1. *Pre-Model Law Developments in Canada*

Canada's concern in the post-World War II period with respect to the impact of foreign insolvencies in Canada and the recognition of Canadian proceedings in other countries (principally the United States) has a long history. The 1970 Tassé Report recommended legislation to facilitate the recognition of foreign bankruptcy orders in Canada. Bill C-17, introduced in Parliament in 1984, gave effect to this recommendation and contained four substantial sections (ss. 313-317) devoted to this topic. Of particular interest was s. 316, which was a Canadian version of s. 304 of the US Code, but less restrictive in its preconditions.

Work was resumed in the 1990s on a new set of cross-border insolvency provisions as part of Phase III of the BIA amendment process. Influential Canadian practitioners felt that the 1984 proposals were too liberal. There was particular concern by banking representatives that the proposals would permit foreign representatives to move Canadian assets, or

---

15. They fall into the area of discretionary powers governed by art. 21(2).

16. Article 21(2).

the proceeds from their disposition, out of Canada. There was also a strong bias in favour of concurrent proceedings for the administration of Canadian-situated assets and for close cooperation between Canadian and foreign (especially US) judges in the administration of the debtor's Canadian and foreign assets. These perspectives are reflected in Part XIII of the BIA, adopted in the 1997 amendments, and the substantially identical provisions in s. 18.6 of the CCAA. The key features were the following:

1. A stay of proceedings existing against creditors of a debtor in foreign proceedings would not apply to creditors residing or carrying on business in Canada with respect to assets in Canada except where such a stay was imposed as a result of proceedings taken in Canada (BIA s. 269).

2. A foreign representative would have liberal access to the assistance of Canadian courts and, where such an application was made, the court could stay or dismiss any action or proceedings in Canada against the debtor or its property (BIA s. 271(2)).[17.]

3. Where concurrent proceedings were in progress in both Canada and a foreign jurisdiction, the Canadian court could limit the property to which the authority of a Canadian representative extended to that situated in Canada (BIA s. 268(2)).

4. The foreign representative would also have status to commence or continue insolvency proceedings in Canada as if the foreign representative were a creditor, trustee, liquidator, or receiver of the debtor (BIA s. 272).

5. Section 268(5) was an important saving provision and stated that nothing in BIA Part XIII prevented the court, on the application of a foreign representative or other interested person, from applying any legal or equitable rules governing the recognition of foreign insolvency orders and assistance to foreign representatives that are not inconsistent with the provisions of the BIA. Farley J relied on s. 268(5) in *Babcock & Wilcox*, extracted below, to justify imposing a stay against future tort claims brought against the non-debtor affiliate company in Canada.

Boiled down to their essentials, the 1997 amendments supported cooperation with, and assistance to, foreign insolvency representatives as long as the cooperation did not prejudice the interests of Canadian creditors.

2. Canadian Version of the Model Law

On the whole, senior Canadian insolvency lawyers were unenthusiastic about Canada adopting the Model Law. This was not because they were opposed to greater harmonization between insolvency law systems and improved cooperation in the treatment of cross-border insolvencies, but because they felt the Model Law provisions were unnecessary and would

---

17. See also BIA s. 271(3) (appointment of interim receiver) and BIA s. 271(4) (examination of debtor or other person in Canada at foreign representative's request) for other forms of assistance made available to the foreign representative.

only add a new layer of complexity. The opponents felt that Canadian and US counsel, and Canadian and US courts, had developed a good working relationship in the handling of Canadian–US cross-border insolvencies (by far the largest number of cross-border insolvencies coming before Canadian courts) and that, as far as Canada was concerned, BIA Part XIII and CCAA s. 18 provided an adequate statutory structure. Other Canadian counsel felt that, if Canada were to adopt the Model Law, its recognitional provisions should be restricted to those foreign jurisdictions that had also enacted it.

Despite the lack of enthusiasm by the insolvency bar, the Senate Committee's report recommended that Canada adopt the Model Law and did not favour the inclusion of a reciprocity provision: Standing Senate Committee on Banking, Trade and Commerce, *Debtors and Creditors Sharing the Burden: A Review of the Bankruptcy and Insolvency Act and Companies' Creditors Arrangements Act* (Ottawa, 2003), at 112-17. The federal government followed the Senate Committee's recommendation in the 2005-2007 amendments to the BIA and CCCA, and a version of the Model Law appears in new Part XIII of the BIA and new Part IV of the CCAA. Unfortunately, the Canadian version of the Model Law is not the same as the UNCITRAL version. In particular, the Canadian version contains provisions that are not replicated in the UNCITRAL version and contains an even larger number of provisions that deviate from the Model Law or have no Model Law counterparts. The following extract gives the flavour of the Canadian deviations.

Jacob Ziegel, "Cross-Border Insolvencies"
in Stephanie Ben-Ishai and Anthony Duggan, *Canadian Bankruptcy and Insolvency Law: Bill C-55, Statute c. 47 and Beyond* (Toronto: LexisNexis, 2007), Chapter 11, at 297-301 (footnotes omitted)

Part XIII Provisions That Deviate From or Have No Model Law Counterparts

There are 11 such provisions, several of them of considerable significance. The deviating provisions are the following:

(a) *Section 268(1).* The definition of FNMP ... differs substantially from the definition in the Model Law. Article 2(c) of the Model Law requires the debtor to have an "establishment" in the place of the foreign proceedings. "Establishment" is defined in art. 2(f) as any place of operations where the debtor carries out a non-transitory economic activity with human means and involving goods or services. S[ection] 268(1) does not require the debtor to have an "establishment" in the foreign jurisdiction. Instead, it defines FNMP as "a foreign proceeding *other than* a foreign main proceeding" (italics added). This suggests that a Canadian court will or may be obliged to cooperate with or recognize a foreign proceeding even if the debtor has no place of business in the foreign jurisdiction. This open-ended provision is at odds with the standard *Morguard* test adopted by Canadian courts in many recent cross-border proceedings that there must be a substantial connection between the debtor and the foreign jurisdiction before the Canadian court will extend its assistance to the foreign order.

(b) Section 270 deals with an order recognizing a foreign proceeding. Section 270 is more concise than Model Law article 17 but appears to impose the same essential requirements.

(c) Section 271 deals with the effect of recognition of an FMP. Section 271(2) has no counterpart in art. 20 of the Model Law. It excludes subsection (1) entirely if BIA proceedings are in progress in Canada at the time of the foreign representative's application. Subsection (3) also has no Model Law counterpart. It makes the recognition of an FMP subject to exceptions that would apply if the foreign proceedings had taken place in Canada under the BIA. It is not clear what types of exclusions the Bill C-55 drafters had in mind. Section 271(4) also has no Model Law counterpart and may conflict with art. 28 of the Model Law, which deals with proceedings in the enacting state after recognition of an FMP. Section 271(4) retains the right of parties to commence or continue proceedings under the BIA, the CCAA or the WURA. Section 271(4) conflicts with the Model Law philosophy that the locus of the debtor's main interests should govern all proceedings against the debtor and that proceedings against the foreign debtor in the enacting state should be confined to proceedings involving locally situated assets. Section 271(4) may need to be amended to reflect the same policy.

(d) Section 272 deals with the orders a Canadian court can make on recognition of the foreign proceedings. Section 272 has no counterpart to article 21(2) of the Model Law authorizing the forum court to approve "distribution"[18] of all or part of local assets to the foreign representative if the court is satisfied that the assets of local creditors are adequately protected. Presumably the Canadian drafters were concerned that the Model Law power might be abused, but this could be said of all discretionary powers under the Model Law or the BIA. There appears to be no good reason to exclude article 21(2) of the Model Law.

(e) Section 274 has no Model Law counterpart and provides that if a recognitional order is made respecting the foreign representative, the foreign representative may commence or continue proceedings under BIA ss. 43, 46-47.1, 49, 50(1) and 50.4(1) as if the foreign representative were a creditor of the debtor. These provisions seem unobjectionable and reflect the partiality shown in existing Part XIII for Canadian initiated proceedings over recognition of foreign proceedings and foreign insolvency orders. Section 274 *would* be objectionable if the courts used these provisions as an excuse not to recognize the foreign proceedings or for refusing the court's assistance to the foreign representative.

(f) Section 275 deals with forms of cooperation between Canadian and foreign courts. Section 275 is not as explicit as are articles 25-27 of the Model Law in spelling out the forms of cooperation between the Canadian and foreign courts. It is not obvious what objections the Canadian drafters found in the more detailed Model Law provisions and it is arguable that, in the interests of uniformity of the Model Law provisions among enacting countries the fuller Model Law provisions should have been retained.

(g) Section 281 has no counterpart in the Model Law provisions. Section 281 provides that the foreign representative may make an application to the Canadian court under Part XIII even though an appeal is pending in a foreign court. S[ection] 281 does not state what type of appeal the drafters had in mind. Presumably it must implicate the foreign representative's standing in the Canadian proceedings since otherwise there would be no reason why the Canadian court should be concerned about the foreign representative's entitlement to bring the proceedings.

---

18. Question whether "distribution" should read "release" of the debtor's assets in the enacting state? [eds.]

(h) Section 284(1) is another troubling provision in Bill C-55 which has no counter-part in the Model Law. Subs[ection] 1 provides that nothing in Part XIII prevents the court on the application of a foreign representative or other interested person from ap-plying any legal or equitable rules governing the recognition of foreign insolvency orders and assistance to foreign representatives "that are not inconsistent with the provisions of this Act." S[ection] 284(1) is a reincarnation of existing BIA s. 268(5), which was invoked by Farley J in *Babcock & Wilcox Canada*[19] to recognize the ch 11 order in Canada with-out requiring the US debtor to initiate new insolvency proceedings under the BIA. The author has explained elsewhere the origin of s. 268(5) and its weakening effect on ss. 268(2) and (3) of the BIA. Will s. 284(1) have a similar diluting effect in new Part XIII? Can it be used to undermine the careful structure of the Model Law provisions? We cannot be sure because everything will depend on whether the court will perceive the requested order to be inconsistent with the other provisions in new Part XIII.

(i) Section 284(2) is also a carry-over from existing Part XIII, in this case, s. 268(6). S[ection] 284(2) provides that nothing in new Part XIII requires the court to make any or-der that is not in compliance with the laws of Canada or to enforce any order made by a foreign court. Section 268(6) was designed to prevent giving *per se* effect to foreign insol-vency orders in Canada and to require the Canadian court's imprimatur before a foreign insolvency order could be implemented in Canada. Is there a conflict between s. 284(2) and the other new Part XIII provisions? One hopes not, though one cannot be sure. The drafters of Bill C-55 would surely have done better to leave this relic of an earlier age be-hind and to have sufficient confidence in the capacity of the new Part XIII provisions to stand on their own feet and to strike a fair balance between the interests of Canadian based creditors and the interests of the foreign based debtor and its foreign creditors.

Overall Conclusion. Given the many differences between Canada's version of the Model Law and the UNCITRAL version it is difficult to predict how important the dif-ferences will turn out to be in practice. However, one prediction can be made with some certainty. The Canadian version will do little to promote the greater certainty and pre-dictability in outcomes the Model Law was designed to achieve and it may also encour-age other states to adopt their idiosyncratic version of the Model Law.

I. Case Law

1. Recognition of Foreign Insolvency Proceedings

Re Singer Sewing Machine Co. of Canada Ltd.
[2000] 5 WWR 598 (Alta. QB)

REGISTRAR FUNDUK: [1] The issue is whether I should recognize and enforce an American chapter 11 bankruptcy court order which includes in its scope a Canadian company carrying on business only in Canada and whose assets are all in Canada.

[2] The answer is no.

---

19. See below for an extract from Farley J's judgment. [eds.]

[3] The facts are not in dispute.

[4] The Singer Company, N.V. ("Singer") is incorporated under the laws of the Netherland Antilles. Its principal executive office is in New York. Singer is the "parent company" of numerous foreign companies, including Singer Sewing Machine Company of Canada Limited ("Singer Canada").

[5] Singer is the direct or indirect beneficial owner of all the shares in Singer Canada.

[6] Singer got a chapter 11 order from the American bankruptcy court for itself. It also managed to convince the American bankruptcy court to include all the foreign companies under the protective umbrellas of the order, including Singer Canada. The fact that Singer Canada is a Canadian company carrying on business solely in Canada and whose assets are solely in Canada does not appear to have been cause for pause by the American bankruptcy court.

[7] The American bankruptcy court's attitude is this:

B. The Debtors are part of a global group of companies (the "Singer Group") engaged in business under the trademarks of "Singer" and "Pfaff." Certain of the Debtors are incorporated, domiciled or have a principal place of business outside the United States.

C. Given the international identities and operations of the Debtors and the other members of the Singer Group, maximizing the value of the Debtors' businesses and assets for the benefit of all stakeholders wherever located in the world will be facilitated by coordinating the Singer Group's activities on a global basis such that (1) the core businesses within the Singer Group can be reorganized on a consistent global basis, and (2) the non-continuing businesses within the Singer Group can be liquidated on an organized basis, rather than piecemeal.

D. In situations where the Debtors and other members of the Singer Group are subject to insolvency proceedings outside the United States ("Relevant Foreign Proceedings"), such value maximization will be best achieved through cooperation and coordination with the within chapter 11 proceedings with the Relevant Foreign Proceedings. ...

G. Pursuant to United States law and jurisprudence, prepetition management of a debtor remains in place as postpetition management of the debtor in possession, except under rare circumstances not present here. Consistent with the foregoing, it is this Court's preference and desire that foreign courts and office holders accord recognition to debtors in possession in United States chapter 11 proceedings as the duly-authorized representatives of the debtors' estates.

H. Notwithstanding the foregoing, it is the collective experience and leaning of this Court and the other bankruptcy judges in the District and elsewhere that some foreign jurisdictions and foreign courts are not necessarily accustomed to the concept of prepetition management remaining in place as management of the postpetition debtor in possession. As a result, some foreign jurisdictions and courts, and some foreign office holders, by law or by custom, may be reluctant to recognize a debtor in possession as the representative of a US debtor's estate.

I. In light of the foregoing, and without derogating the importance of the debtor in possession concept in the United States or the role of Skadden, Arps, Slate, Meagher &

Flom LLP and law practice affiliates as the Debtors' Lead counsel, both domestically and internationally, this Court is appointing the Foreign Representatives with the desire that, in foreign situations where there may be some reluctance to recognize a debtor in possession, the Foreign Representatives be recognized as the official representatives of the Debtors' estates.

[8] That appears to be a "we can do it best" attitude untrammelled by the fact that Canadian private international law does not recognize an American bankruptcy court's jurisdiction over a Canadian not resident in the United States, not carrying on business in the United States, and not having any assets in the United States.

[9] The American bankruptcy court goes on to order: ...

[10] The Murrays got a substantial money judgment against Singer Canada. The Murrays are Canadians, domiciled and resident in Alberta. They would now have to prove their claim in the United States bankruptcy proceeding and be subject to United States law.

[11] Canadian law says that a corporation is a person in law. Canadian law says that a corporation has an existence separate from its shareholders. Canadian law says that a shareholder is not liable for the corporation's debts. Canadian law says that a shareholder does not own the corporation's assets. Canadian law says that a corporation's business activities are not the shareholder's business activities.

. . .

[14] Counsel refer to *Re Graham*, [1929] 3 DLR 353 (Sask. KB); *Re IIT*, 58 DLR (3d) 55 (Ont. HC); *Microbiz Corp. v. Classic Software Systems Inc.*, [1996] OJ No. 5094 (Ont. CJ); *Re Cumberland Trading Inc.*, [1994] OJ No. 132 (Ont. CJ); *Pitts v. Hill & Hill Truck Line Inc.*, 53 Alta. LR (2d) 219 (M); and *Best Electric & Heating v. MacKillop*, [1993] BCJ No. 1156 (BSSC).

[15] The headnote in *Re Graham* says all that is necessary. It says:

Property, situated in a Province, of a person domiciled in England at the time when he was adjudicated a bankrupt under the English *Bankruptcy Act* will be vested in his English trustee by order of a provincial Court having bankruptcy jurisdiction whose aid is requested under s. 122 of that Act.

That is not helpful to Singer Canada's representative. He does not seek assistance in Alberta in realizing on assets in Alberta owned by Singer i.e., the shares. That is not what this application is about.

[16] *Re IIT* is also not helpful. That is also a case of a foreign "bankrupt" with assets in Canada. The bankruptcy judge said, p. 58:

On the material before me I have no hesitation in finding that the Luxembourg Court had the authority to make the order appointing the liquidators. Indeed, I do not think that any other jurisdiction would have had authority to appoint liquidators for IIT: *National Trust Co. Ltd. v. Ebro Irrigation & Power Co. Ltd. et al; National Trust Co. Ltd. v. Catalonian Land Co. Ltd. et al.*, [1954] OR 463 at p. 477, [1954] 3 DLR 326 at p. 340. The liquidators were given status by the law of Luxembourg and in my opinion that status should be recognized by the Courts of this Province.

The question then arises—what form of recognition should be given by this Court? Since the assets have been vested in the liquidators by the Luxembourg Court, I believe the proper form of recognition in these circumstances is an order vesting the Ontario assets in the liquidators. The alternative would be to appoint a receiver to administer the Ontario assets, but in my opinion, in view of the substantial amount of assets involved and the ramifications of administering those assets this would not be a convenient procedure to adopt.

[17] That has no application to the case before me.

[18] Microbiz Corp. is also not helpful to the representative of Singer Canada. There the bankrupt was a United States corporation which had no assets in Ontario and carried on business in Ontario only through a distributor. The bankruptcy judge says:

> … There is no doubt that under the principles laid down in the Morguard Investments case, that judgment of the US Court should be recognized in Canada as there is a real and substantial connection between the US Court's judgment and the subject matter of the proceeding. More importantly, both Classic Software and Haggerty have recognized the judgment and in fact have filed Proofs of Claim in the US proceeding to take advantage of the mechanism provided therein for adjudication of their claims and recovery to the extent of 17.5% of their proven claims. To participate in the US proceedings is beneficial in that it allows Classic and Haggerty to prove their claims and obtain collection in one proceeding rather than obtain judgment on their claims in Ontario and in a separate proceeding in New Jersey seek to effect recovery against the estate of MicroBiz. By filing their Proofs of Claim, Classic and Haggerty have thereby attorned to the jurisdiction of the US Court in New Jersey.

[19] What is the "real and substantial connection" between the American bankruptcy court's order and Singer Canada?

[20] The Murray's have not attorned to the jurisdiction of the American bankruptcy court.

[21] The relevance of *Re Cumberland Trading Inc.* entirely escapes me.

[22] Pitts is also a case of an American bankrupt with assets in Alberta, an American judgment in favour of a creditor and the creditor then attorning to the American bankruptcy court's jurisdiction. It also does not help the representative of Singer Canada.

[23] *Best Electric & Heating Ltd.* helps the Murrays. It points out the drastic difference between a chapter 11 bankruptcy and a Canadian bankruptcy. The order sought to be recognized in Alberta lets Singer Canada keep possession of its assets and stay in business without paying its current creditors.

[24] The Murrays are creditors only of Singer Canada. They are not creditors of Singer or of any of the foreign companies. If they are to be prohibited from pursuing their claim against Singer Canada it must be by Canadian law, not American Law.

· · ·

[26] Comity does not require me to recognize a chapter 11 order over a Canadian company carrying on business only in Canada and whose assets are all in Canada. Who the shareholders are is irrelevant and who the creditors are is irrelevant. Under Alberta law neither gives an American bankruptcy court jurisdiction over Singer Canada.

[27] As Mr. McKenzie rightly points out, if Singer Canada is insolvent it can resort to Canadian legislation.

Application dismissed.

NOTES AND QUESTIONS

Registrar Funduk's judgment in *Singer Sewing Machine Co.* has been reproduced here because the precedents he cites faithfully reflected the Anglo-Canadian conflict-of-law rules as generally understood and applied prior to Farley J's judgment in *Re Babcock & Wilcox Canada*, extracted below. This was true with respect to (1) the basis for the recognition of foreign insolvency orders, and (2) recognition of the separate legal personalities of parent and subsidiary companies for conflict-of-law as well as domestic purposes. Would Registrar Funduk's reaction to the US court order have been more benign if the order had been less aggressive and imperative in tone? Registrar Funduk's application of the traditional rules also reflects the difficulties facing a multinational corporation, like Singer Sewing Machine, that seeks to reorganize parent and subsidiary companies, located in different countries, where some members of the group are solvent and others are not and where the applicable legal systems hold different views about the nature of legal personality.

Re Babcock & Wilcox Canada Ltd.
(2000), 18 CBR (4th) 157 (Ont. SC)

FARLEY J: [1] I have had the opportunity to reflect on this matter which involves an aspect of the recent amendments to the insolvency legislation of Canada, which amendments have not yet been otherwise dealt with as to their substance. The applicant, Babcock & Wilcox Canada Ltd. ("BW Canada"), a solvent company, has applied for an interim order under s. 18.6 of the *Companies' Creditors Arrangement Act* ("CCAA"):

> (a) that the proceedings commenced by BW Canada's parent US corporation and certain other US related corporations (collectively "BWUS") for protection under Chapter 11 of the US *Bankruptcy Code* in connection with mass asbestos claims before the US Bankruptcy Court be recognized as a "foreign proceeding" for the purposes of s. 18.6;
> (b) that BW Canada be declared a company which is entitled to avail itself of the provisions of s. 18.6;
> (c) that there be a stay against suits and enforcements until May 1, 2000 (or such later date as the Court may order) as to asbestos related proceedings against BW Canada, its property and its directors;
> (d) that BW Canada be authorized to guarantee the obligations of its parent to the DIP Lender (debtor in possession lender) and grant security therefor in favour of the DIP Lender; and
> (e) and for other ancillary relief.

[2] In Chapter 11 proceedings under the US *Bankruptcy Code*, the US Bankruptcy Court in New Orleans issued a temporary restraining order on February 22, 2000 wherein it was noted that BW Canada may be subject to actions in Canada similar to the US asbestos claims. US Bankruptcy Court Judge Brown's temporary restraining order was directed against certain named US resident plaintiffs in the asbestos litigation:

> ... and towards all plaintiffs and potential plaintiffs in Other Derivative Actions, that they are hereby restrained further prosecuting Pending Actions or further prosecuting or com-

mencing Other Derivative Actions against Non-Debtor Affiliates, until the Court decides whether to grant the Debtors' request for a preliminary injunction.

Judge Brown further requested the aid and assistance of the Canadian courts in carrying out the US Bankruptcy Court's orders. The "Non-Debtor Affiliates" would include BW Canada.

[3] Under the 1994 amendments to the US *Bankruptcy Code*, the concept of the establishment of a trust sufficient to meet the court determined liability for a mass torts situations was introduced. I am advised that after many years of successfully resolving the overwhelming majority of claims against it on an individual basis by settlement on terms BWUS considered reasonable, BWUS has determined, as a result of a spike in claims with escalating demands when it was expecting a decrease in claims, that it is appropriate to resort to the mass tort trust concept. Hence its application earlier this week to Judge Brown with a view to eventually working out a global process, including incorporating any Canadian claims. This would be done in conjunction with its joint pool of insurance which covers both BWUS and BW Canada. Chapter 11 proceedings do not require an applicant thereunder to be insolvent; thus BWUS was able to make an application with a view towards the 1994 amendments (including s. 524(g)). This subsection would permit the US Bankruptcy Court on confirmation of a plan of reorganization under Chapter 11 with a view towards rehabilitation in the sense of avoiding insolvency in a mass torts situation to:

> enjoin entities from taking legal action for the purpose of directly or indirectly collecting, recovering, or receiving payment or recovery with respect to any claims or demand that, under a plan of reorganization, is to be paid in whole or in part by a trust.

[4] In 1997, ss. 267-275 of the *Bankruptcy and Insolvency Act*, RSC 1985, c. B-3 as amended ("BIA") and s. 18.6 of the CCAA were enacted to address the rising number of international insolvencies ("1997 Amendments"). The 1997 Amendments were introduced after a lengthy consultation process with the insolvency profession and others. Previous to the 1997 Amendments, Canadian courts essentially would rely on the evolving common law principles of comity which permitted the Canadian court to recognize and enforce in Canada the judicial acts of other jurisdictions.

· · ·

[6] In *ATL Industries Inc. v. Han Eol Inc. Co.* (1995), 36 CPC (3d) 288 (Ont. Gen. Div.) at pp. 302-3 I noted the following:

> Allow me to start off by stating that I agree with the analysis of MacPherson J in *Arrowmaster Inc. v. Unique Forming Ltd.* (1993), 17 OR (3d) 407 (Gen. Div.) when in discussing *Morguard Investments Ltd. v. De Savoye*, [1990] 3 SCR 1077, … he states at p. 411:
>
>> The leading case dealing with the enforcement of "foreign" judgments is the decision of the Supreme Court of Canada in *Morguard Investments, supra.* The question in that case was whether, and the circumstances in which, the judgment of an Alberta court could be enforced in British Columbia. A unanimous court, speaking through La Forest J, held in favour of enforceability and, in so doing, discussed in some detail the doctrinal principles governing inter-jurisdictional enforcement of orders. I think

it fair to say that the overarching theme of La Forest J's reasons is the necessity and desirability, in a mobile global society, for governments and courts to respect the orders made by courts in foreign jurisdictions with comparable legal systems, including substantive laws and rules of procedure. He expressed this theme in these words, at p. 1095:

> Modern states, however, cannot live in splendid isolation and do give effect to judgments given in other countries in certain circumstances. Thus a judgment *in rem*, such as a decree of divorce granted by the courts of one state to persons domiciled there, will be recognized by the courts of other states. In certain circumstances, as well, our courts will enforce personal judgments given in other states. Thus, we saw, our courts will enforce an action for breach of contract given by the courts of another country if the defendant was present there at the time of the action or has agreed to the foreign court's exercise of jurisdiction. *This, it was thought, was in conformity with the requirements of comity, the informing principle of private international law, which has been stated to be the deference and respect due by other states to the actions of a state legitimately taken within its territory. Since the state where the judgment was given has power over the litigants, the judgments of its courts should be respected.* (emphasis added in original)

Morguard Investments was, as stated earlier, a case dealing with the enforcement of a court order across provincial boundaries. *However, the historical analysis in La Forest J's judgment, of both the United Kingdom and Canadian jurisprudence, and the doctrinal principles enunciated by the court are equally applicable, in my view, in a situation where the judgment has been rendered by a court in a foreign jurisdiction. This should not be an absolute rule—there will be some foreign court orders that should not be enforced in Ontario, perhaps because the substantive law in the foreign country is so different from Ontario's or perhaps because the legal process that generates the foreign order diverges radically from Ontario's process.* (my emphasis added)

Certainly the substantive and procedural aspects of the US *Bankruptcy Code* including its 1994 amendments are not so different and do not radically diverge from our system.

· · ·

[9] In the context of cross-border insolvencies, Canadian and US Courts have made efforts to complement, coordinate and where appropriate accommodate the proceedings of the other. Examples of this would include Olympia & York Developments Ltd., Everfresh Beverages Inc. and The Loewen Group Inc. Other examples involve the situation where a multi-jurisdictional proceeding is specifically connected to one jurisdiction with that jurisdiction's court being allowed to exercise principal control over the insolvency process: see *Roberts v. Picture Butte Municipal Hospital*, [1998] AJ No. 817 (QB) at pp. 5-7; ...

[10] In *Roberts*, Forsythe J at pp. 5-7 noted that steps within the proceedings themselves are also subject to the dictates of comity in recognizing and enforcing a US Bankruptcy Court stay in the Dow Corning litigation as to a debtor in Canada so as to promote greater efficiency, certainty and consistency in connection with the debtor's

restructuring efforts. Foreign claimants were provided for in the US corporation's plan. Forsyth J stated:

> Comity and cooperation are increasingly important in the bankruptcy context. *As internationalization increases, more parties have assets and carry on activities in several jurisdictions. Without some coordination there would be multiple proceedings, inconsistent judgments and general uncertainty.*
>
> ... *I find that common sense dictates that these matters would be best dealt with by one court, and in the interest of promoting international comity it seems the forum for this case is in the US Bankruptcy Court.* Thus, in either case, whether there has been an attornment or not, I conclude it is appropriate for me to exercise my discretion and apply the principles of comity and grant the Defendant's stay application. I reach this conclusion based on all the circumstances, including the clear wording of the US *Bankruptcy Code* provision, the similar philosophies and procedures in Canada and the US, the Plaintiff's attornment to the jurisdiction of the US Bankruptcy Court, and the incredible number of claims outstanding .... (emphasis added)

[11] The CCAA as remedial legislation should be given a liberal interpretation to facilitate its objectives. See *Re Chef Ready Foods Ltd.* (1990), 4 CBR (3d) 311 (BCCA) at p. 320; *Re Lehndorff General Partners Ltd.* (1993), 17 CBR (3d) 24 (Ont. Gen. Div.).

[12] ... The philosophy of the practice in international matters relating to the CCAA is set forth in *Olympia & York Developments Limited v. Royal Trust Co.* (1993), 20 CBR (3d) 165 (Ont. Gen. Div.) at p. 167 where Blair J stated:

> The Olympia & York re-organization involves proceedings in three different jurisdictions: Canada, the United States and the United Kingdom. Insolvency disputes with international overtones and involving property and assets in a multiplicity of jurisdictions are becoming increasingly frequent. Often there are differences in legal concepts—sometimes substantive, sometimes procedural—between the jurisdictions. The Courts of the various jurisdictions should seek to co-operate amongst themselves, in my view, in facilitating the trans-border resolution of such disputes as a whole, where that can be done in a fashion consistent with their own fundamental principles of jurisprudence. The interests of international co-operation and comity, and the interests of developing at least some degree of certitude in international business and commerce, call for nothing less.

Blair J then proceeded to invoke inherent jurisdiction to implement the Protocol between the US Bankruptcy Court and the Ontario Court. See also my endorsement of December 20, 1995 in *Re Everfresh Beverages Inc.* where I observed: "I would think that this Protocol demonstrates the 'essence of comity' between the Courts of Canada and the United States of America." *Everfresh* was an example of the effective and efficient use of the Cross-Border Insolvency Concordat, adopted by the Council of the International Bar Association on May 31, 1996 (after being adopted by its Section on Business Law Council on September 17, 1995), which Concordat deals with, *inter alia*, principal administration of a debtor's reorganization and ancillary jurisdiction. See also the UNCITRAL Model Law on Cross-Border Insolvency.

. . .

Interim order granted.

NOTES

Farley J's decision in *Babcock & Wilcox* is critically examined by Ziegel in "Corporate Groups and Canada–US Cross-Border Insolvencies: Contrasting Judicial Visions" (2001), 35 *CBLJ* 459, in which the author makes the following points:

1. The history of Part XIII of the BIA and s. 18.6 of the CCAA did not support Justice Farley's conclusion that "debtor" in s. 18.6(1) was not meant to be restricted to insolvent debtors. Ziegel argues that, even if Farley J were correct on the constructional issue, there was still the constitutional issue—whether the federal government's insolvency power in the *Constitution Act* also extends to solvent debtors. (Recall that B & W Canada was not insolvent and was not included in the US Chapter 11 proceedings.)

2. In Ziegel's view, reliance on such an open-ended concept as "comity" is not helpful in addressing the complex and nuanced issues that arise in international insolvencies.

3. He also finds that the precedents cited by Justice Farley were distinguishable because they all involved cases where the Canadian creditor had submitted to the US court's jurisdiction by filing a claim or had otherwise accepted the US court's jurisdiction.

4. Justice Farley failed to discuss the important Australian decision in *Taylor v. Dow Corning Australia Pty Ltd.* (December 19, 1997), no. 8438/95 (Vict. SC), not officially reported, where the court refused to stay the plaintiff's action, seeking damages because of an alleged defective breast implant, against the Australian subsidiary Dow Corning US and was not willing to give extraterritorial effect to the US stay of proceedings order against the Australian subsidiary.

5. As far as the merits of the US court's request in *Babcock & Wilcox* were concerned, Ziegel suggests that, before staying actions by Canadian plaintiffs against a solvent Canadian subsidiary at the request of a US or other foreign court, the Canadian court should conduct an inquiry to satisfy itself that a stay order will not unfairly prejudice the plaintiffs. In his view, such an inquiry is necessary because once a stay order is made (as happened in *Babcock*), it is difficult to reverse without causing international embarrassment.

Holt Cargo Systems v. ABC Containerline N.V. (Trustees of)
[2001] 3 SCR 907

BINNIE J (For the Court): [1] The problems of international bankruptcies have excited much recent judicial and academic commentary. In this appeal, we are required to determine whether a maritime law proceeding by a US creditor against a Belgian ship in a Canadian court ought to have been stayed in deference to a Belgian court dealing with the subsequent bankruptcy of its Belgian shipowner. Deference to the Belgian bankruptcy court, it is argued, was required by the principles of international comity. Despite the obvious benefits of international coordination of bankruptcies that spread their financial wreckage across multiple jurisdictions, the Federal Court of Canada declined to stay its proceedings under Canadian maritime law. The present appeal is from its decision. The companion case, *Antwerp Bulkcarriers, N.V. (Re)*, [2001] 3 SCR 951, 2001 SCC 91, released at the same time, deals with the appeal from the Quebec Court of Appeal on the bankruptcy side of the concurrent and interconnected proceedings.

[2] The history of this litigation, in brief summary, is as follows. On March 30, 1996, the M/V "Brussel" (the "Ship") was arrested in Canadian waters near the entrance to Halifax harbour by order of the Federal Court of Canada. A week later, its Belgian owner made an assignment in bankruptcy at Antwerp with debts vastly exceeding its assets. The US creditor, Holt Cargo Systems Inc. ("Holt"), persisted with its *in rem* action. Four months later, after a storm of motions and applications in the Federal Court and the Superior Court of Quebec sitting in Bankruptcy, with periodic interventions by the Eleventh Chamber of the Commercial Court of the Judicial District of Antwerp (the "Belgian bankruptcy court") and a related order by a US bankruptcy court, the Ship was sold over the objection of the trustees in bankruptcy. The Federal Court ruled that the proceeds of the sale are eventually to be distributed to secured creditors, including the respondent, depending on the outcome of this appeal.

[3] The Superior Court of Quebec sitting in Bankruptcy (the "Canadian bankruptcy court") played a potentially important role in responding to the request for assistance from the Belgian Commercial Court exercising Belgian bankruptcy jurisdiction. However, I believe the trustees asked for more assistance from the Canadian bankruptcy court than could lawfully be given, and that the Federal Court did not err in principle in refusing a stay of the maritime law proceedings.

[4] I would therefore dismiss the appeal.

I. Facts

[5] The Ship was arrested at Halifax under a warrant of arrest issued at the instance of Holt, a US company incorporated under the laws of New Jersey. The warrant for arrest was issued in connection with an *in rem* action commenced by Holt the same day in the Federal Court of Canada against the "owners, charterers and all others interested in the ship," and the Ship itself. The M/V "Brussel" was owned by Antwerp Bulkcarriers N.V. which, with other interrelated companies, carried on the business of international carriage of goods by sea.

[6] Holt's action was for unpaid fees and charges for stevedoring and other related services provided to the Ship at Gloucester City, New Jersey, in the United States between 1994 and 1996 inclusive. No part of the debt was incurred in Canada and neither the Ship nor its creditors were ordinarily resident here.

[7] Following the arrest of the Ship, cargo and container owners, shippers, suppliers, insurers and others also filed claims in the Federal Court. In total, statements of claim were filed in 27 separate actions. Moreover, notices of claim were filed in Holt's *in rem* action against the Ship by more than 20 claimants in response to the Federal Court's order, discussed below, that the Ship be appraised and sold.

[8] On April 5, 1996, a week after the Ship's arrest, the shipowner was adjudged bankrupt by the Belgian bankruptcy court, which appointed the appellants, T. Van Doosselaere

and F. De Roy, as trustees in bankruptcy (the "Trustees"). Under Belgian law, the Trustees were required to take possession of all assets of the bankrupt holding company and its bankrupt affiliated companies, wherever situated. The major assets of the group of bankrupt companies were six cargo vessels, and at the time of the bankruptcy order at least five of these were under arrest in ports in Israel, Singapore, New Zealand, the Bahamas and, as stated, Canada. Other assets owned or leased by the debtors, including unpaid freight and shipping containers, had also been arrested, detained or threatened with seizure at various locations throughout the world. The Trustees filed applications in jurisdictions where proceedings had been commenced against the debtors seeking the release of the bankrupts' assets from arrest, preventing further seizure and arrest of their assets, and directing the submission of all claims against them to the bankruptcy proceedings in Belgium.

[9] Faced with these difficult circumstances, the appellant Trustees urged on the Federal Court on several occasions the need for international cooperation in the resolution of bankruptcies and insolvencies that cross national boundaries. The effect of these arguments was to advocate deference to the Belgian courts, being the courts of the bankrupts' domicile. Adherence to what is sometimes called the "Grab Rule," in which each national court takes charge of assets in its own jurisdiction for the benefit of creditors who win the race to its courthouse, was said to be destructive of international order and fairness. (As will be seen, there is much merit in these submissions.)

[10] The "universalist" position advocated by the appellant Trustees was put forward in a series of motions and applications before the courts of Quebec and the Federal Court of Canada. A detailed summary of the complicated procedural history of this dispute is set out in an Appendix to the judgment in the companion case, *Antwerp Bulkcarriers, N.V., supra*.

· · ·

[11] It is clear from the order of June 28, 1996 that the Canadian bankruptcy court is now asserting control over the Ship and the related proceedings. It "permits" the sale ordered by MacKay J to proceed, but only if it is completed by July 12. The proceeds of sale are to go to the appellant Trustees, not to the secured claimants who are litigating in the Federal Court. If the sale is not completed by July 12, the Ship is to be turned over to the Trustees irrespective of the orders of the Federal Court. The Supreme Court of Nova Scotia is requested to "aid" in giving effect to these directions.

[12] As of July 1996, it will be noted, default judgment had been signed in the *in rem* action, the Ship had been appraised, and bids were being invited from potential purchasers. MacKay J eventually ruled that the Trustees could obtain the proceeds of sale only if they posted security to answer the claims of the secured creditors. This was never forthcoming. His reasons were compendiously explained in a subsequent judgment of April 9, 1997, as will now be described.

· · ·

IV. Analysis

[20] In this appeal we are urged to adopt a "universalist approach" to bankruptcies and insolvencies that affect more than one jurisdiction. I accept at the outset that bankruptcies that engage multiple jurisdictions may not be administered effectively if each

national court goes its own way with the assets that happen physically to be within its control. The chaotic fact situation faced by the Trustees in this case, from Singapore to the Bahamas and Israel to New Zealand, is eloquent testimony to the need for judicial cooperation and international comity.

[21] Moreover, it must also be freely acknowledged that the connection between this litigation and Canada is relatively weak. None of the parties (including the Ship) resides here. The debt was incurred in the United States. The shipowner resides in Belgium. There are no bankruptcy proceedings in Canada other than those initiated by the appellant Trustees for recognition of various orders of the Belgian bankruptcy court.

[22] Canadian courts have become seized with the dispute only because the vagaries of maritime commerce carried the M/V "Brussel" into Canadian waters on March 30, 1996. It was certainly open to the Federal Court to defer in these matters to the bankruptcy court of the bankrupt's domicile. The question is whether, as contended by the appellant Trustees, the Federal Court was obliged to do so. If not, did the Federal Court nevertheless commit an error in the exercise of its discretion not to stay the *in rem* action in deference to the Belgian bankruptcy court?

[23] For present purposes, I accept the following convenient definitions of the "universalist approach" and the "territorialist approach" (sometimes referred to as the "Grab Rule"):

> ... [C]ourts and commentators have identified two general approaches to distributing assets in such proceedings. Under the "territoriality" approach, or the "Grab Rule," the court in each jurisdiction where the debtor has assets distributes the assets located in that jurisdiction pursuant to local rules. Under the "universality" approach, a primary insolvency proceeding is instituted in the debtor's domiciliary country, and ancillary courts in other jurisdictions—typically in jurisdictions where the debtor has assets—defer to the foreign proceeding and in effect collaborate to facilitate the centralized liquidation of the debtor's estate according to the rules of the debtor's home country. (*In re Treco*, 240 F3d 148 (2d Cir. 2001), at p. 153)

[24] The Federal Court was clearly of the view that it was not in this case choosing between the "universalist" approach and the "Grab Rule." It was making a choice between the conflicting demands of two international systems of commercial dispute resolution, namely the rules of maritime law, with long historical roots in the practicalities of ocean shipping, and more recent legal initiatives to establish coherent rules for the administration of international bankruptcies and insolvencies. In its view, I think correctly, the choice was dictated not by some abstract rule of "universalism" but by what the Federal Court understood to be the specific circumstances and justice of this particular case.

· · ·

B. Foreign Bankruptcy Orders

[28] The appellant Trustees take the position that once the Canadian bankruptcy court was activated on this file, its power and authority occupied the field in relation to matters pertaining to the bankrupt, so to speak, to the exclusion of courts not possessing bankruptcy jurisdiction. This proposition is, in my view, too broad.

[29] I propose to make a few preliminary observations about the appellant Trustees' position. More detailed consideration follows.

[30] The first preliminary observation is that Antwerp Bulkcarriers, N.V. was not placed in bankruptcy under the laws of Canada. The only proceedings before a Canadian bankruptcy court were for the recognition and implementation of the orders of the Belgian bankruptcy court. Part XIII of the *Bankruptcy and Insolvency Act* (the "Act"), entitled "International Insolvencies," was not yet in force at the time of these events. Nevertheless, Canadian bankruptcy courts have long exercised a jurisdiction to come to the aid of foreign bankruptcy courts where it has been in their power to do so. Part XIII put the stamp of parliamentary approval on an initiative supported by judges and scholarly practitioners, both before and after enactment of Part XIII. ...

[31] My second preliminary observation is that the bankruptcy courts in Belgium and Canada had (and have) a legitimate interest in the *in rem* action in the Federal Court. On May 9, 1996, when the Trustees obtained the order of recognition of the Belgian judgment, title to the M/V "Brussel," however heavily encumbered, was still registered in the name of the bankrupt. It is true that the market value of the Ship (ultimately sold for US$4.6 million) was a mere fraction of the first mortgage (about $68 million) held by the Belgian state bank, Société Nationale de Crédit à l'Industrie S.A. ("SNCI"). It is also true that there were maritime liens and statutory charges that ranked ahead of the first mortgage. The bankrupt company nevertheless retained legal title, and to that extent the Ship constituted part of the property of the bankrupt, at least as that term is understood in Canadian law: *Federal Business Development Bank v. Quebec (Commission de la santé et de la sécurité du travail)*, [1988] 1 SCR 1061.

[32] Counsel for the respondent appeared to consider it dispositive of the appeal to characterize the issue before us as concerning "maritime law" as opposed to "bankruptcy law." The facts here present both aspects, and in my view, with respect, the issue before the Federal Court was one of finding the proper balance of relevant factors on the stay application as opposed to trying to preempt further debate with a "pith and substance" characterization of the nature of the proceeding.

[33] Thirdly, a Canadian bankruptcy court has a responsibility to consider the interests of the litigants before it and other affected parties in this country as well as the desirability of international cooperation and other relevant circumstances. Its function is not simply to rubber stamp commands issuing from the foreign court of the primary bankruptcy. Thus the exigencies of international cooperation were significant to both the Federal Court and the Canadian bankruptcy court, but they were not a factor that necessarily trumped all other factors.

[34] Fourthly, the Canadian bankruptcy court derives its authority from Canadian law. When called upon to lend assistance to foreign bankruptcy courts, Canadian law requires our courts to consider as one of the relevant circumstances the juridical advantage which those disadvantaged by deferral to the foreign court would enjoy in a Canadian court. I appreciate that over-emphasis on juridical advantage as a factor would lead to enthronement of the "Grab Rule" because claimants in the Canadian court will inevitably have a good reason why they do not wish to take their chances in the general bankruptcy in the court of the bankrupt's domicile. Nevertheless, all of the relevant factors must be

weighed in a stay application and the nature and extent of juridical advantage for the various parties was clearly an important factor to throw into the balance.

[35] Fifthly, the public policy expressed in our own bankruptcy laws is a relevant consideration. Bankruptcy usually signals at least a temporary "cease fire" against the bankrupt's estate. However, if this had been a Canadian bankruptcy, the statutory stay of a creditor's action would have been of little practical relevance because s. 69.3 of the Act exempts from the statutory stay (with exceptions not relevant here) proceedings by secured creditors to realize on their security. Section 69.3(2)(a) would have authorized the Canadian bankruptcy court to order a postponement of no more than six months. The effect of the Canadian bankruptcy court's order in this case was a permanent stay of proceedings for realization of the security of the Ship in Canada.

[36] I now turn to the more detailed submissions of the parties.

C. Issues Raised by the Present Appeal

[37] It is common ground that ordinarily the Federal Court, Trial Division, would have jurisdiction to arrest the Ship, to entertain Holt's claim for debts incurred on the Ship's behalf, to assess the validity of Holt's claim to a maritime lien, to order the appraisal and sale of the Ship and to see the successful secured claimants paid out of the proceeds of sale.

[38] The Trustees advance three broad submissions in support of their position that once the shipowner was declared bankrupt on April 5, 1996, the Federal Court was "bound to act in comity with the direction" given by the Belgian bankruptcy court, whose edicts were recognized and accepted by the Canadian bankruptcy court. Firstly, as already mentioned, they say that Canadian courts should follow a "universalist" rather than a "territorialist" approach to bankruptcy. Secondly, they say that a Canadian court exercising admiralty jurisdiction (the Federal Court) must defer to or at least cooperate with (which in their eyes seems to amount to the same thing) the Canadian court exercising bankruptcy jurisdiction (the Quebec Superior Court). Thirdly, the Trustees say that the response of Canadian courts should be "uniform" by which they appear to mean the Federal Court should have acceded to the request of the Belgian court because the Quebec Superior Court sitting in Bankruptcy had already done so.

[39] In light of these preliminary observations, I think the Trustees' arguments may be conveniently addressed under the following headings:

1. Did the respondent Holt possess a valid claim to a maritime lien under Canadian law against the M/V "Brussel" prior to the Belgian bankruptcy of the owners on April 5, 1996?

2. Did Holt thereby enjoy a juridical advantage in Canada that would be in jeopardy if the Federal Court proceedings were stayed in deference to the Belgian bankruptcy court?

3. Did the Federal Court err in treating Holt as a "secured creditor" as that term is understood in Canadian bankruptcy law?

4. Did the Belgian bankruptcy of April 5, 1996 give the Belgian Trustees a valid claim to the Ship?

5. Did the Federal Court of Canada lose jurisdiction to proceed as a result of the various orders of the Quebec Superior Court sitting in Bankruptcy?

6. Even if the Federal Court retained jurisdiction, ought it nevertheless to have deferred to the Belgian bankruptcy court on the basis of "international comity" and the need for an integrated "universalist" approach to the bankruptcy?

7. In light of the foregoing, did the Federal Court err in the exercise of its discretion to deny the Trustees' application for a stay of proceedings?

[40] I will address each of these issues in turn.

[Binnie J answered the first three questions in Holt's favour, then continued:]

4. Did the Belgian Bankruptcy of April 5, 1996 Give the Belgian Trustees a Valid Claim to the Ship?

[54] Under the Belgian bankruptcy court's order of April 5, 1996, the Trustees were given the duty and power to take possession of the assets of the bankrupt wherever located. At that stage, the Ship was no longer in the possession of the bankrupt shipowner. It was in the possession of the Marshal of the Federal Court at Halifax and subject to further orders of that court.

[55] In Canada, the bankruptcy order pronounced by the court of the domicile operated as an assignment by operation of law of the moveable assets of the bankrupt shipowner located in Canada, including its interest in the M/V "Brussel," but this assignment is subject to any prior charges upon it recognized by Canadian law (J.-G. Castel, *Canadian Conflict of Laws* (4th ed. 1997), at pp. 564-65).

[56] In this respect, our conflict of laws rule is the same as the English rule set out by the editors of *Dicey and Morris on the Conflict of Laws* (13th ed. 2000), vol. 2, at p. 1184:

> The general principle of English law is that bankruptcy, or any proceeding in the nature of bankruptcy, in a foreign country whose courts have jurisdiction over a debtor operates as an assignment to the trustee, assignees, curators, syndics or others, who under the law of that country are entitled to administer his property, of all his movables in England, if that is its effect under the foreign law.

See also I.F. Fletcher, *Insolvency in Private International Law* (1999), at pp. 61-62. As in Canada, the assignment by operation of law of the debtor's property is subject to a number of limitations, one of which as noted is that the property passes subject to existing charges recognized under English law:

> The property in England passes subject to any existing charges upon it recognised by the law of England, even if these charges would be postponed under the law of the place of bankruptcy to the claim of the creditors, and even if under the English bankruptcy the charges would be defeated by the title of the trustee in bankruptcy. (*Dicey and Morris on the Conflict of Laws, supra,* at pp. 1184-85)

. . .

6. *Even If the Federal Court Retained Jurisdiction, Ought It Nevertheless to Have Deferred to the Belgian Bankruptcy Court on the Basis of "International Comity" and the Need for an Integrated "Universalist" Approach to the Bankruptcy?*

[67] I should first of all address the issue of "international comity" as it pertains to the present appeal and then move on to consider some of the more specific approaches that have been devised to solve problems arising from international bankruptcies. I will then outline what I believe is the preferred approach in cases of this kind.

(a) The Role of International Comity

[68] In *Zingre v. The Queen*, [1981] 2 SCR 392, Dickson J (as he then was) commented at p. 401 that "the courts of one jurisdiction will give effect to the laws and judicial decisions of another jurisdiction, not as a matter of obligation but out of mutual deference and respect."

[69] Subsequently, in *Spencer v. The Queen*, [1985] 2 SCR 278, at p. 283, Estey J accepted as accurate the following definition of international comity:

> "Comity" in the legal sense, is neither a matter of absolute obligation, on the one hand, nor of mere courtesy and good will, upon the other. But it is the recognition which one nation allows within its territory to the legislative, executive or judicial acts of another nation, having due regard both to international duty and convenience, and to the rights of its own citizens or of other persons who are under the protection of its laws: *Hilton v. Guyot*, 159 US 113 (1895), at pp. 163-64.

[70] The Canadian bankruptcy court in this case did not have a monopoly in the determination of what level of "deference and respect" was owed to the Belgian bankruptcy court. Within its own bankruptcy jurisdiction, of course, it could and did make that determination. Insofar as Holt's claim was "integrally connected to maritime matters," it lay within the jurisdiction of the Federal Court (*Ordon Estate v. Grail*, [1998] 3 SCR 437, at para. 73) and it was for that court to decide whether to defer to the Belgian bankruptcy court "having due regard both to international duty and convenience, and to the rights of its own citizens or of other persons who are under the protection of its laws."

[71] In *Morguard Investments Ltd. v. De Savoye*, [1990] 3 SCR 1077, the Court expanded on the definition of international comity by noting that the twin objectives sought by private international law in general and the doctrine of international comity in particular were order and fairness. This was reiterated in *Hunt v. T&N PLC*, [1993] 4 SCR 289, at p. 325, and again in *Tolofson v. Jensen*, [1994] 3 SCR 1022, at p. 1058, where the Court gave pre-eminence to the objective of order:

> While, no doubt, as was observed in Morguard, the underlying principles of private international law are order and fairness, order comes first. Order is a precondition to justice.

[72] It has been, of course, the objective of international maritime law for centuries to create conditions of order and fairness for those engaged in maritime commerce.

(b) The "Universalist" Approach

[73] The Trustees argue that to achieve the twin objectives of order and fairness in an international insolvency, it is necessary to adopt the "universalist" approach because in fairness "the claims of creditors can be finally determined only by the court of the debtor's domicile in accordance with the law of that place" (Castel, *supra*, at p. 553). They advocate a "close networking between courts on an international level" (factum, at para. 36).

[74] In the case at bar the debtor's domicile was Belgium, and the Trustees contend that the Federal Court erred in not requiring Holt and the other secured creditors to pursue their claims in that country. The Trustees also argue that as the Quebec Superior Court decided to come to the aid of the Belgian bankruptcy court, the Federal Court ought, as a matter of "domestic" comity, to have deferred to that decision.

[75] There is much to be said for the proposition that primary insolvency proceedings having been instituted in Belgium, other jurisdictions where the bankrupt possessed assets should cooperate to the extent permitted by their respective laws with the Belgian courts. The need for such international cooperation in bankruptcy and insolvency has been evident for a very long time, though the ever-continuing ascendancy of multi-national enterprises and acceleration towards a global economy have made the underlying problems more acute. As long ago as 1883, in the case of *Canada Southern Railway Co. v. Gebhard*, 109 US 527 (1883), the United States Supreme Court said, at p. 539:

> Unless all parties in interest, wherever they reside, can be bound by the arrangement which it is sought to have legalized the scheme may fail. All home creditors can be bound. What is needed is to bind those who are abroad. Under these circumstances the true spirit of international comity requires that schemes of this character, legalized at home, should be recognized in other countries.

[76] The essence of the universalist approach advocated by the Trustees is that there ought to be a primary bankruptcy proceeding, title to assets locally situated should be vested in the foreign representative of the bankrupt estate, creditors should not be permitted to realize on a foreign debtor's assets in the local courts outside the framework of the primary bankruptcy, and orders made in foreign bankruptcy proceedings should be recognized and enforced elsewhere.

[77] Professor J.S. Ziegel contrasts the "universalist" approach to the "territorialist" approach, earlier referred to as the "Grab Rule," and concludes that most jurisdictions exhibit elements of both approaches:

> International insolvency jurists have long classified countries and their conflict of laws rules according to their willingness to recognize and give effect to foreign insolvency orders and judgments. Those regimes that are hospitable to extending such recognition are labelled universalist; those that deny such recognition are classified as territorialist. Common law countries are often described as belonging among the universalist families, while civil law systems are believed to be territorialist.
>
> However, the pigeonholing is misleading. Common law countries differ as widely in their international insolvency rules as do civil law jurisdictions. On closer examination it will be found that some of the jurisdictions that claim to be universalist only practise a very diluted form of universalism while countries labelled as territorialist in fact extend varying

measures of recognition to foreign insolvency orders and foreign insolvency representatives.

("Ships at Sea, International Insolvencies, and Divided Courts" (1998), 50 CBR (3d) 310. See also *In re Treco, supra*, and Castel, *supra*, at pp. 553-54.)

[78] Traditionally, only some of the key components of the universalist approach have been reflected in Canadian law. While our courts generally favour a process of universal distribution and recognize a foreign trustee's title to property, they also permit concurrent bankruptcies and protect the vested rights of what we regard as secured creditors under Canadian law. With respect to the latter, the usual Canadian position has been that a foreign trustee in bankruptcy should have no higher claim on the secured assets of a bankrupt than if the bankruptcy had occurred here. In a true universalist system the question of encumbrances would be settled by the law of the place of the bankruptcy (which may, as in this case, produce a result contrary to Canadian maritime law).

[79] Further, Canadian law has always recognized that initiation of foreign bankruptcy proceedings does not prevent concurrent insolvency proceedings in Canada: see Castel, supra, at p. 565; *Allen v. Hanson* (1890), 18 SCR 667; *Re Breakwater Co.* (1914), 33 OLR 65 (HC), and *Re E.H. Clarke & Co.*, [1923] 1 DLR 716 (Ont. SC). The existence of two sets of proceedings obviously raises the spectre of conflicting decisions or approaches, although as noted in 1890 by Ritchie CJ of this Court in *Allen, supra*, at p. 674, it is "the duty of the courts of both countries to see no conflict should arise." Conflict avoidance can take many forms, including dismissing or staying Canadian proceedings. Section 43(7) of the *Bankruptcy and Insolvency Act* permits the court to dismiss a petition if it has "sufficient cause." This requirement may be satisfied if the debtor has been declared bankrupt elsewhere. In fact, the courts have stayed liquidation proceedings where bankruptcy proceedings are on foot in a foreign jurisdiction: *Re Stewart & Matthews, Ltd. and The Winding-Up Act* (1916), 10 WWR 154 (Man. KB). Similarly, in an appropriate case, the Federal Court can avoid conflict by staying its proceedings pursuant to s. 50 of the *Federal Court Act*.

[80] In short, Canada has adhered to a middle position (dignified by the name "plurality approach") which recognizes that different jurisdictions may have a legitimate and concurrent interest in the conduct of an international bankruptcy, and that the interests asserted in Canadian courts may, but not necessarily must, be subordinated in a particular case to a foreign bankruptcy regime. The general approach reflects a desire for coordination rather than subordination, with deference being accorded only after due consideration of all the relevant circumstances rather than automatically accorded because of an abstract "universalist" principle. As pointed out by Professor Castel, supra, at pp. 554-55:

> Under the doctrine of plurality which prevails in Canada, each country has the right, if it deems it advisable, to allow bankruptcy proceedings to begin in its territory by virtue of its bankruptcy law. The court applies its own substantive law. Thus, bankruptcies may be initiated in a number of countries with respect to the same debtor. In Canada, this rigid doctrine is partially tempered by close cooperation with foreign courts.

[81] The question is whether, as argued by the appellant Trustees, this orientation in Canada ought now to be changed to a more "universalist" approach.

(c) The 1997 Amendments to the Act

[82] In April 1997 Parliament enacted Part XIII of the *Bankruptcy and Insolvency Act*, entitled "International Insolvencies." It applies only to bankruptcy proceedings initiated after September 30, 1997, and thus has no direct application here. Nevertheless, it is worth noting that Parliament has continued the diluted universalism (or "plurality approach") adopted by Canadian courts under the common law. There is now, under Part XIII, specific authority to come to the aid of foreign courts and "foreign representatives" in the administration and adjudication of insolvencies that have international dimensions. There is also authority for Canadian courts, under s. 271(1), to request "the aid and assistance of a court, tribunal or other authority in a foreign proceeding." The objective of these provisions is to facilitate the coordination of foreign and domestic insolvency proceedings. Nevertheless, there is no rule requiring Canadian courts to refrain from entertaining concurrent proceedings. On the contrary, concurrent proceedings are anticipated as Canadian courts are given authority under s. 268(3) to make orders that will result in a coordination of domestic and foreign proceedings, not the elimination of one in preference to the other. By authorizing a Canadian court under subs. (2) to limit the domestic trustee's authority to property situated in Canada, Parliament obviously anticipated that in certain cases a territorialist approach would be acceptable. The amendments provide specifically that a court is not compelled to enforce any order made by a foreign court: s. 268(6).

[83] Moreover, s. 269 explicitly denies extraterritorial reach to foreign stay orders. It says that a foreign stay of proceedings "does not apply in respect of creditors who reside or carry on business in Canada with respect to property in Canada unless the stay of proceedings is the result of proceedings taken in Canada."

[84] It thus appears that Canadian public policy, expressed as recently as 1997 by Parliament, endorses the plurality approach developed over the years by the courts.

(d) The Preferred Approach

[85] Given the almost infinite variations in circumstances that can occur in an "international bankruptcy," the pragmatism of the "plurality" approach continues to recommend itself. International coordination is an important factor, but it is not necessarily a controlling factor.

[86] Where a stay is sought of Canadian proceedings in deference to a foreign bankruptcy court, the Canadian court before which the stay application is made (in this case the Federal Court) ought to be mindful of the difficulties confronting the bankruptcy trustees in the fulfilment of their public mandate to bring order out of financial disorder and the desirability of maximizing the size of the bankrupt estate. These objectives are furthered by minimizing the multiplicity of proceedings, and the attendant costs, and the possibility of inconsistent decisions in relation to the same claims or assets.

[87] Nevertheless, courts must have regard to the need to do justice to the particular litigants who come before them as well as to the public interest in the efficient administration of bankrupt estates. It would be inappropriate to elevate any one consideration to a controlling position in the exercise of a bankruptcy court's discretion to dismiss a petition under s. 43(7) or to stay proceedings under Part XIII of the Act or in the Federal Court's decision to stay proceedings under s. 50 of the *Federal Court Act*. Discretion

should not be thus predetermined. The desirability of international coordination is an important consideration. In some cases, it may be the controlling consideration. The courts nevertheless have to exercise their discretion to stay or not to stay domestic proceedings according to all of the relevant facts of a particular case.

· · ·

Appeal dismissed.

NOTES

1. Justice Binnie does not refer to Farley J's judgment in *Babcock & Wilcox*, above, but it is clear that he takes a more nuanced view of the rule of comity with respect to the recognition and enforcement of foreign insolvency orders than does Farley J, even assuming that the comity test is appropriate to resolve insolvency issues. Given the conflict between the two approaches, which approach should lower Canadian courts follow in the future?

2. Ziegel examines the lower court decisions in *Holt Cargo* in "Ships at Sea, International Insolvencies, and Divided Courts" (1998), 29 *CBLJ* 417 and Comment (2000), 33 *CBLJ* 476. Among the points he makes are the following.

   1. In his view, the Quebec bankruptcy court judges lacked jurisdiction in purporting to recognize the Belgian insolvency proceedings and declaring the Belgian curators entitled to take possession of the "Brussels" in Canada. This was because the jurisdiction of Canadian bankruptcy courts is only derived from the BIA and at the time of the Quebec hearings, Part XIII of the BIA had not yet been enacted.

   2. Ziegel accepts the proposition that a Canadian court should not release assets in Canada to a foreign representative unless the foreign bankruptcy court recognizes the validity of a security interest validly created under the relevant *lex situs*. However, he disagrees with the argument, accepted by MacKay J in the Federal Court and endorsed by Justice Binnie in the Supreme Court of Canada's judgment, that the Canadian assets should not be released unless the foreign court will give the security interest the same ranking as it would enjoy under Canadian bankruptcy law. In Ziegel's words (at 432), "If we require the law of the home jurisdiction to mirror the Canadian characterization and ranking rules faithfully then it is unlikely that a Canadian court will ever agree to release assets subject to a security interest or where the claimants have preferred status under Canadian law. If we agree, on the other hand, on the need for elasticity in applying our concept of fairness in the international context then we must also accept the consequence that Canadian creditors may not fare as well abroad as they would at home if the assets were retained and administered in Canada."

   3. Ziegel expresses the view that the Supreme Court of Canada, in *Todd Shipyards Corp. v. Altema Compania Maritima S.A.*, [1974] SCR 1248, erred in holding that where there are multiple maritime liens against a vessel created under different laws, Canadian law will govern their ranking because the ranking of liens is a question of procedure. In his opinion, the better view is that the ranking of secured claims is a question of substantive law and should be determined by the law governing the cre-

ation of the liens, at least where the liens are created in the same jurisdiction. (This is the position adopted in Canada with respect to chattel security interests in the provincial *Personal Property Security Acts*.)

4. Ziegel argues that it is still a mistake to treat Canadian secured creditors' immunity from the bankruptcy process as a fundamental feature of Canadian law, as Justice Binnie did in *Holt Cargo*. "Case law developments, the dramatic transformation of the *Companies' Creditors Arrangement Act* ... and the 1992 amendments to the BIA have substantially reduced secured creditors' rights of seizure, both by requiring prior notice of the secured creditor's intention to seize where s. 244 applies and by greatly expanding the debtor's opportunity to restructure its affairs. This being the case, the Belgian trustees' quest for an orderly liquidation of Bulkcarriers' fleet of ships and, for all we know, an opportunity to consider the feasibility of restructuring the company's affairs, would have been consistent with Canadian insolvency policy" (29 *CBLJ*, at 434, footnotes omitted).

2. *Cooperation with and Release of Assets to Foreign Jurisdiction*

In re HIC Casualty and General Insurance Ltd.
[2008] 1 WLR 852 (HL)

[In this important decision of the House of Lords, the law lords were called on to decide the following two questions: (1) whether English courts had jurisdiction under the English *Insolvency Act* to authorize release to Australian liquidators of English-based assets being administered by English provisional liquidators, even though some of the English creditors would not fare as well under the Australian distributional scheme as they would under the English Act; and (2) whether s. 426(4) of the English *Insolvency Act* authorized the release of the assets under such circumstances, whether or not it was also possible under the general provisions of the Act. Four of the law lords (Hoffmann, Philipps, Scott, and Walker) were evenly divided on the first question (Lord Neuberger took no position on the question), but they all agreed that s. 426(4) gave the English court this discretionary power. The full facts are stated in Lord Hoffmann's judgment, below, together with his exposition of the conflicting views on the first question.]

LORD HOFFMAN: ... This appeal arises out of the insolvent liquidation of the HIH group of Australian insurance companies. On 15 March 2001 four of them presented winding up petitions to the Supreme Court of New South Wales. Some of their assets— mostly reinsurance claims on policies taken out in London—were situated in England. To realise and protect these assets, provisional liquidators were appointed in England. In Australia, the court has made winding up orders and appointed liquidators. The Australian judge has sent a letter of request to the High Court in London, asking that the provisional liquidators be directed, after payment of their expenses, to remit the assets to the Australian liquidators for distribution. The question in this appeal is whether the English court can and should accede to that request. The alternative is a separate liquidation and distribution of the English assets in accordance with the *Insolvency Act 1986*.

The English and Australian laws of corporate insolvency have a common origin and their basic principles are much the same. The general rule is that after payment of the costs of liquidation and the statutory preferred creditors, the assets are distributed *pari passu* among the ordinary creditors: see section 107 of the 1986 Act and section 555 of the *Corporations Act 2001* (Cth). But Australia has a different regime for insurance companies. I need not trouble your Lordships with the details. It is sufficient to say that, in broad outline, it requires assets in Australia to be applied first to the discharge of debts payable in Australia … and the proceeds of reinsurance policies to be applied in discharge of the liabilities which were reinsured … . It is agreed that if the English assets are sent to Australia, the outcome for creditors will be different from what it would have been if they had been distributed under the 1986 Act. Some creditors will do better and others worse. … Generally speaking, insurance creditors will be winners and other creditors will be losers.

The Australian court made its request pursuant to section 426(4) of the *Insolvency Act 1986*: "The courts having jurisdiction in relation to insolvency law in any part of the United Kingdom shall assist the courts having the corresponding jurisdiction in … any relevant country. …"

The Secretary of State has power under subsection (11) to designate a country as "relevant" and has so designated Australia. Subsection (5) describes the assistance which a UK court may give. A request from the court of a relevant country is

> authority for the court to which the request is made to apply, in relation to any matters specified in the request, the insolvency law which is applicable by either court in relation to comparable matters falling within its jurisdiction. In exercising its discretion under this subsection, a court shall have regard in particular to the rules of private international law.

This provision was introduced into insolvency law in consequence of a recommendation in fairly general terms by the Cork Committee in 1982: see *Report of the Review Committee on Insolvency Law and Practice* (Cmnd 8558), ch 49. The committee drew attention to the inadequacy of the statutory provisions for international co-operation in personal bankruptcy and their complete absence in the law of corporate insolvency.

Despite the absence of statutory provision, some degree of international co-operation in corporate insolvency had been achieved by judicial practice. This was based upon what English judges have for many years regarded as a general principle of private international law, namely that bankruptcy (whether personal or corporate) should be unitary and universal. There should be a unitary bankruptcy proceeding in the court of the bankrupt's domicile which receives worldwide recognition and it should apply universally to all the bankrupt's assets.

This was very much a principle rather than a rule. It is heavily qualified by exceptions on pragmatic grounds; elsewhere I have described it as an aspiration: see *Cambridge Gas Transportation Corpn v. Official Committee of Unsecured Creditors of Navigator Holdings plc* [2007] 1 AC 508, 517, para. 17. Professor Jay Westbrook, a distinguished American writer on international insolvency has called it a principle of "modified universalism": see also Fletcher, *Insolvency in Private International Law*, 2nd ed (2005), pp 15-17. Full universalism can be attained only by international treaty. Nevertheless, even in its modified and pragmatic form, the principle is a potent one.

In the late 19th century there developed a judicial practice, based upon the principle of universalism, by which the English winding up of a foreign company was treated as ancillary to a winding up by the court of its domicile. There is no doubt that an English court has jurisdiction to wind up such a company if it has assets here or some other sufficient connection with this country .... And in theory, such an order operates universally, applies to all the foreign company's assets and brings into play the full panoply of powers and duties under the *Insolvency Act 1986* like any other winding up order: see Millett J in *In re International Tin Council* [1987] Ch 419, 447: "The statutory trusts extend to [foreign] assets, and so does the statutory obligation to collect and realise them and to deal with their proceeds in accordance with the statutory scheme."

But the judicial practice which developed in such a case was to limit the powers and duties of the liquidator to collecting the English assets and settling a list of the creditors who sent in proofs. The court, so to speak, "disapplied" the statutory trusts and duties in relation to the foreign assets of foreign companies. This practice was based partly upon the pragmatic consideration that any foreign country which applied our own rules of private international law would not recognise the title of an English ancillary liquidator to the company's assets. But it was also based upon the principle of universalism. In *In re Matheson Brothers Ltd* (1884) 27 Ch D 225 Kay J appointed a provisional liquidator, as in this case, to protect the English assets of a New Zealand company which was being wound up in New Zealand. He said, at pp 230 and 231:

> [W]hat is the effect of the winding up order which it is said has been made in New Zealand? This court upon principles of international comity, would no doubt have great regard to that winding up order and would be influenced thereby"—but there was nevertheless jurisdiction to make a winding up order, and therefore to appoint a provisional liquidator, to protect the English assets.
>
> I consider that I am justified in taking steps to secure the English assets until I see that proceedings are taken in the New Zealand liquidation to make the English assets available for the English creditors *pari passu* with the creditors in New Zealand.

It seems clear from the last sentence that Kay J envisaged the English assets being distributed in the New Zealand liquidation, provided that English creditors shared *pari passu* with New Zealand creditors. It was on the authority of this and similar statements in other cases that Sir Richard Scott V-C held in *In re Bank of Credit and Commerce International SA (No 10)* [1997] Ch 213, 247 that an English court had power in an ancillary liquidation (provisional or final) to authorise the English liquidators to transmit the English assets to the principal liquidators. The basis for the practice could only be what Kay J called principles of international comity, the desirability of a single bankruptcy administration which dealt with all the company's assets.

It is this jurisdiction, reinforced by the provisions of section 426, which the Australian liquidators (supported by two Australian insurance creditors who stand to gain from the application of Australian law) invite the court to exercise. But David Richards J [2006] 2 All ER 671, in a judgment which carefully examined all the arguments and authorities, held that the jurisdiction did not extend to authorising the assets to be remitted to principal liquidators for distribution which was not *pari passu* but gave preference to some creditors to the prejudice of others. The Court of Appeal ... held that there was such a jurisdiction, which might be exercised if distribution in the country of the principal liquidation produced advantages for the non-preferred creditors which counteracted the prejudice they suffered. But the present case offered no such advantages. The appeal was therefore dismissed.

My Lords, I would entirely accept that there are no administrative savings to be gained from remitting the assets to Australia. In order to avoid delay in distributing the available assets, the English provisional liquidators and the Australian liquidators have co-operated in securing the approval of two alternative schemes of arrangement, one based on the outcome which would occur if all the assets were distributed according to Australian law and the other on the outcome of separate liquidations in England and Australia. Depending upon your Lordships' decision, one or the other will be carried into effect. All that remains is to press button A or button B. So the question is whether an order for remittal should be made, not to achieve any economies in the winding up, but simply because it is the right thing to do. Is it what principle and justice require?

The judge denied the existence of a power to order remittal to Australia on two grounds. The first was the absence of a power in the English court to disapply any part of the statutory scheme for the collection and distribution of the assets of an insolvent company. That included the provision in section 107 for *pari passu* distribution. The second was the weight of authority, in the specific context of an ancillary winding up, which laid emphasis upon the fact that the co-operation of the English court was given on the assumption that there would be a *pari passu* distribution in the principal liquidation.

In my opinion there is force in both of these reasons but the judge carried them too far. There is no doubt that, at least until the passing of section 426, an English court and an English liquidator had no option but to apply English law to whatever they actually did in the course of an ancillary winding up. As Wynn-Parry J said of an ancillary winding up in *In re Suidair International Airways Ltd* [1951] Ch 165, 173: "this court sits to administer the assets of the South African company which are within its jurisdiction, and for that purpose administers, and administers only, the relevant English law. ..."

Similarly Sir Richard Scott V-C decided in *In re Bank of Credit and Commerce International SA (No 10)* [1997] Ch 213 that in settling a list of creditors, the English court was bound to apply English law. It could not disregard rule 4.90 of the *Insolvency Rules 1986* (SI 1986/1925), which requires that the amount owing by the company to the creditor or vice versa shall be determined after setting off mutual debts against each other.

However, Sir Richard Scott V-C went further and directed the English ancillary liquidators not to remit the assets in their hands to the principal liquidators in Luxembourg (which did not recognise rights of set off) without making provision to ensure that the overall distributions to English creditors were in accordance with English law.

On the facts of the case I think, if I may respectfully say so, that the decision was correct. ...

Where I respectfully part company with my noble and learned friend, Lord Scott, is in relation to the reason which he gave, and maintains in his speech in this appeal (which I have had the privilege of reading in draft) for deciding that he should not remit the assets to Luxembourg without protecting the position of creditors who had proved in England. In my opinion he was right to do so as a matter of discretion. But he says that he had no jurisdiction to do otherwise because creditors in an English liquidation (principal or ancillary) cannot be deprived of their statutory rights under English law.

In my opinion, however, the judicial practice to which I have referred and which [Lord Scott] approved in *In re Bank of Credit and Commerce International SA (No 10)* [1997] Ch 213 is inconsistent with the broad proposition that creditors cannot be deprived of their statutory rights under the English scheme of liquidation. The whole doctrine of ancillary winding up is based upon the premise that in such cases the English court may "disapply" parts of the statutory scheme by authorising the English liquidator to allow actions which he is obliged by statute to perform according to English law to be performed instead by the foreign liquidator according to the foreign law (including its rules of the conflict of laws.) These may or may not be the same as English law. Thus the ancillary liquidator is invariably authorised to leave the collection and distribution of foreign assets to the principal liquidator, notwithstanding that the statute requires him to perform these functions. Furthermore, the process of collection of assets will include, for example, the use of powers to set aside voidable dispositions, which may differ very considerably from those in the English statutory scheme.

Once one accepts, as my noble and learned friend rightly accepted in *In re Bank of Credit and Commerce International SA (No 10)*, that the logic of the ancillary liquidation doctrine requires that the court should have power to relieve an English ancillary liquidator from the duty of distributing the assets himself but can direct him to remit them for distribution by the principal liquidator, I think it must follow that those assets need not be distributed according to English law. The principal liquidator would have no power to distribute them according to English law any more than the English liquidator, if he were doing the distribution, would have power to distribute them according to the foreign law.

It would in my opinion make no sense to confine the power to direct remittal to cases in which the foreign law of distribution coincided with English law. In such cases remittal would serve no purpose, except some occasional administrative convenience. And in practice such a condition would never be satisfied. Almost all countries have their own lists of preferential creditors. These lists reflect legislative decisions for the protection of local interests, which is why the usual English practice is, when remittal to a foreign liquidator is ordered, to make provision for the retention of funds to pay English preferential creditors. But the existence of foreign preferential creditors who would have no preference in an English distribution has never inhibited the courts from ordering remittal. I think that the judge was inclined to regard these differences as *de minimis* variations which did not prevent the foreign rules from being in substantial compliance with the *pari passu* principle. But they are nevertheless foreign rules. The fact that the differences were minor might be relevant to the question of whether a court should exercise its discretion to order remittal. But any differences in the English and foreign systems of distribution must destroy the argument that an English court has absolutely no jurisdiction to order remittal because it cannot give effect to anything other than the English statutory scheme.

· · ·

It follows that in my opinion the court had jurisdiction at common law, under its established practice of giving directions to ancillary liquidators, to direct remittal of the

English assets, notwithstanding any differences between the English and foreign systems of distribution. These differences are relevant only to discretion.

Even on the question of whether the court should make the kind of provision for protecting rights of set off which Sir Richard Scott V-C made in *In re Bank of Credit and Commerce International SA (No 10)* [1997] Ch 213, much will depend upon the degree of connection which the mutual debts have with England. If the country of principal liquidation does not recognise bankruptcy set off and the mutual debts arise out of transactions in that country, it is hard to see why an English court should insist on rights of set off being preserved in respect of claims by the foreign creditors against assets which happen to be in England. The English court would be entitled to exercise its discretion by remitting the assets to the principal jurisdiction and leaving it to apply its own law. (Compare *In re Paramount Airways Ltd* [1993] Ch 223, discussing the discretion not to apply the English law on voidable dispositions.)

It was submitted by the appellants that the argument for the existence of such a jurisdiction under section 426 was even stronger, because it expressly gives the court power to apply the foreign insolvency law to the matter specified in the request. As Sir Andrew Morritt C said [2007] Bus LR 250, para. 49, section 426 is "itself part of the statutory scheme," no less than section 107. The court therefore has power to apply the Australian law of distribution. It may be that it does, but in my opinion that is not what a court directing remittal of the assets is doing. It is exercising its power under English law to direct the liquidator to remit the assets and leave their distribution to the courts and liquidators in Australia. It is they who apply Australian law, not the English ancillary liquidator. As Morritt LJ said in *Hughes v. Hannover Rückversicherungs-AG* [1997] 1 BCLC 497, 517, a court asked for assistance under section 426 may exercise "its own general jurisdiction and powers" as well as the insolvency laws of England and the corresponding laws of the requesting state. The power to direct the remittal of assets collected in an ancillary liquidation falls within the former category.

This point highlights, I think, the difference between my noble and learned friend Lord Scott and myself. In relying upon section 426, Lord Scott holds that a court which directs remittal of the English assets to the Australian principal liquidator is applying the insolvency law of Australia. My own view is that the order cannot be characterised in this way and that the court is exercising a power, established well before the 1986 Act, under the insolvency law of England.

The power to remit assets to the principal liquidation is exercised when the English court decides that there is a foreign jurisdiction more appropriate than England for the purpose of dealing with all outstanding questions in the winding up. It is not a decision on the choice of the law to be applied to those questions. That will be a matter for the court of the principal jurisdiction to decide. Ordinarily one would expect it to apply its own insolvency laws but in some cases its rules of the conflict of laws may point in a different direction. Section 426, on the other hand, extends the jurisdiction of the English court and the choice of law which it can make in the exercise of its own jurisdiction, whether original or extended. For example, section 426 can confer jurisdiction to make an administration order in respect of a foreign company when that jurisdiction is ordinarily confined to UK companies: *In re Dallhold Estates (UK) Pty Ltd* [1992] BCLC 621. Or it may enable the court to apply a foreign law when, as in *In re Suidair International Airways Ltd*

[1951] Ch 165, it would otherwise be obliged to apply only English law, as in *England v. Smith* [2001] Ch 419 (Australian law applied to examination of accountant connected with insolvent Australian company). But the present case involves neither an extension of the English jurisdiction or an application by the English court of a foreign law.

I therefore agree with the Court of Appeal that the court has jurisdiction, even if not for precisely the same reasons. But the Court of Appeal nevertheless decided that the jurisdiction should not be exercised because the outcome for some creditors would be worse than if the English assets were distributed according to English law. There was, said Carnwath LJ [2007] Bus LR 250, para. 72, no "rule of private international law, or any other countervailing benefit" which would require the court to disregard the principles applicable under English insolvency law.

I must respectfully disagree. The primary rule of private international law which seems to me applicable to this case is the principle of (modified) universalism, which has been the golden thread running through English cross-border insolvency law since the 18th century. That principle requires that English courts should, so far as is consistent with justice and UK public policy, co-operate with the courts in the country of the principal liquidation to ensure that all the company's assets are distributed to its creditors under a single system of distribution. That is the purpose of the power to direct remittal.

In the present case I do not see that it would offend against any principle of justice for the assets to be remitted to Australia. In some cases there may be some doubt about how to determine the appropriate jurisdiction which should be regarded as the seat of the principal liquidation. I have spoken in a rather old-fashioned way of the company's domicile because that is the term used in the old cases, but I do not claim it is necessarily the best one. Usually it means the place where the company is incorporated but that may be some offshore island with which the company's business has no real connection. The Council Regulation on insolvency proceedings (Council Regulation (EC) No 1346/2000 of 29 May 2000) uses the concept of the "centre of a debtor's main interests" as a test, with a presumption that it is the place where the registered office is situated: see article 3(1). That may be more appropriate. But in this case it does not matter because on any view, these are Australian companies. They are incorporated in Australia, their central management has been in Australia and the overwhelming majority of their assets and liabilities are situated in Australia.

It is true that Australian law would treat insurance creditors better and non-insurance creditors worse than English law did at the relevant time. But that seems to me no reason for saying that the Australian law offends against English principles of justice. As it happens, since the appointment of the provisional liquidators, English law has itself adopted a regime for the winding up of insurance companies which gives preference to insurance creditors: see regulation 21(2) of the *Insurers (Reorganisation and Winding Up) Regulations 2004* (SI 2004/353), giving effect to the European Parliament and Council Directive 2001/17/EC on the reorganisation and winding up of insurance companies. So English courts are hardly in a position to say that an exception to the *pari passu* rule for insurance creditors offends against basic principles of justice.

Furthermore, it seems to me that the application of Australian law to the distribution of all the assets is more likely to give effect to the expectations of creditors as a whole than the distribution of some of the assets according to English law. Policy holders and other creditors dealing with an Australian insurance company are likely, so far as they think about the matter at all to expect that in the event of insolvency their rights will be determined by Australian law. Indeed, the preference given to insurance creditors may have been seen as an advantage of a policy with an Australian company.

As for UK public policy, I cannot see how it would be prejudiced by the application of Australian law to the distribution of the English assets. There is no question of prejudice to English creditors as such, since it is accepted that although section 116(3) of the *Insurance Act 1973* (Cth) gives creditors whose debts are payable in Australia a first call upon Australian assets, this provision will not in practice prejudice the interests of creditors in the English assets. Furthermore, if there were to be a separate liquidation of the English assets in England, all creditors would be entitled to prove. Those Australian (or other foreign) creditors who see an advantage in proving in England after bringing into hotchpot their dividends in Australia would no doubt do so. But UK public policy does not require them to be afforded this facility.

The fact that there are assets in England is principally the result of the companies having placed their reinsurance business in the London market. For the purposes of deciding how the assets should be distributed, that seems to me an entirely adventitious circumstance. Indeed, it may not be to the advantage of London as a reinsurance market if the distribution of the assets of insolvent foreign reinsurance companies is affected by whether they have placed their reinsurance business in London rather than somewhere else.

In my opinion, therefore, this is a case in which it is appropriate to give the principle of universalism full rein. There are no grounds of justice or policy which require this country to insist upon distributing an Australian company's assets according to its own system of priorities only because they happen to have been situated in this country at the time of the appointment of the provisional liquidators. I would therefore allow the appeal and make the order requested by the Australian court.

NOTES

1. The BIA has never had a provision comparable to s. 426(4) of the English *Insolvency Act* and no such provision was included in the 1997 BIA and CCAA amendments dealing with cross-border insolvencies. However, for the reasons given in Lord Hoffmann's judgment, Canadian courts would have approved the release of Canadian assets to a foreign administrator after the claims of Canadian creditors had been satisfied and, presumably, would have authorized the release of assets if satisfied that Canadian creditors would be treated equitably under the foreign law and no less well than under Canadian law.

2. With the rapid proliferation of cross-border insolvencies from the early 1990s onward, the issue of cooperation between Canadian and foreign (principally US) administrators assumed great importance in the case of corporate debtors with substantial assets and business activities in both jurisdictions. The *Maxwell Communications* case (see above) was the first reported case where the English and US judges appointed joint US and English administrators and also approved a protocol prepared by the administrators setting forth their respective functions and the terms of their cooperation. The *Maxwell* precedent was taken up enthusiastically by INSOL and other groups of international insolvency lawyers and quickly found a place in Canada–US cross-border insolvency proceedings. (Farley J was an

early and strong supporter of such protocols and of close cooperation between the Canadian and US courts.) As seen earlier, the UNCITRAL Model Law also places great emphasis on cooperation among courts in cross-border insolvencies, though without converting them into binding norms.

3. There is no reported Canadian case raising the same or similar issues as in *HIC*—that is, the court being asked to approve the release of assets to the foreign administrator for distribution in the foreign jurisdiction on terms less favourable to Canadian creditors than under the Canadian distributional rules. The closest case is Blair J's judgment in *Menegon v. Philip Services Corp.* (1999), 11 CBR (4th) 262 (Ont. Sup. Ct.). Philip Services was the subject of Chapter 11 proceedings in the United States and CCAA proceedings in Canada and was also a defendant in class action proceedings in Canada and the United States for misrepresentations in the sale of its securities. Additionally, the Royal Bank of Canada had a large claim against Philips arising out of equipment leases it had helped to finance for Philip. Philip's US lawyers had secured the US bankruptcy court's approval for settlement of the class actions and the claims of the Royal Bank under US law and also sought Blair J's approval of the proposed settlement terms. Blair J rejected the request on the ground that Philip's Canadian creditors were entitled to have their claims adjudicated in accordance with Canadian law, which was significantly more favourable to them than US law. See his judgment at paras. 38-40.

3. Recognition of Discharge of Debts Under Foreign Bankruptcy Law

Re Bialek
(1994), 18 OR (3d) 462 (Gen. Div.)

D. LANE J: Barry Benjamin Bialek applies for discharge from bankruptcy. Dr. Bialek was born and educated in the United States as a doctor of medicine, graduating in 1985. In gaining that education he relied extensively upon financial aid from various United States government-funded student loan programs. These loans totalled some US$104,000 over the four years of his studies. With interest, they have resulted in a claim proved in the estate at over $200,000. This was his second degree, the first being a degree in mathematics and science and a teaching certificate earned in 1974. He spent two-and-a-half years in Nepal as a teacher after his math degree and then worked in the US until entering the medical course. His experience in Nepal has had a strong influence upon him. For several years he has returned more or less annually to work as a volunteer in that country. Dr. Bialek interned in Canada and also did a six-month residency in Toronto. He has practised since then in Ontario, primarily as an emergency room physician on a part-time basis in hospitals in Toronto during the week and in Woodstock and Campbellford on the weekends. His wife is expecting a child in June.

Dr. Bialek's agreement with the US lending agencies required him to begin repayment upon graduation. In 1987 he paid $6,400 but he obtained a deferral of the balance of his obligation in 1988 upon the basis that he was going to Nepal to work for five years. He testified that he did intend to do so, but political unrest in Nepal forced him to leave after a few months and he came to Canada. He did not advise the US lending authorities of this change in plans. In 1989 or 1990 they contacted his mother and he told her to give them his address in Canada. They were soon in contact with him. It appears that he had the impression that so long as he was in Canada, the US authorities either could not, or would not, seek to enforce repayment of his obligations, but this proved not to be the case. Collection agencies began to call him. In March 1992, he went to Nepal for a month. In June 1992, he made an assignment in bankruptcy. It was apparent to me from the evidence that the bankruptcy was largely as a result of his discovery that the US loans were enforceable in this country.

> ...

The opposition to discharge comes from two sources. The US authorities oppose on the basis that their loans got him the education that enables him to earn an exceptional income and that the principles applied in this court to Canadian student loans should apply equally to them. The Royal Bank opposes on the basis that he obtained credit from them knowing that he was insolvent and that he committed fraud upon them by concealing his US indebtedness when applying for credit.

I can see no reason why the student loans should not receive the same consideration as similar loans by Canadian student lenders. In such cases the court takes into account whether the earning capacity of the bankrupt has been enhanced for the future by the education paid for by the loans. If so, and assuming that there is a present capacity to pay, it is surely necessary, for fairness and for the protection of the integrity of the bankruptcy system, that some of that enhanced earning capacity be harnessed for the benefit of the creditors as a whole, including the student-loan lender ... .

> ...

Counsel for the bankrupt asks for an absolute discharge. He says that it was the bankrupt's devotion to Nepal that caused these troubles, the cause is praiseworthy and is an extenuating circumstance. I do not agree. In the first place, the evidence does not show that the loan proceeds were devoted to Nepal. Even if they had been, that was not their disclosed purpose. It is not open to an insolvent debtor to divert the funds available to pay his creditors in favour of a charitable enterprise, however worthy, and then come for an absolute discharge. The creditors have the right to pick their own uses for the money owed to them.

Counsel for the US student lenders took the position that those loans would not be discharged by any order of this court. They would no longer be enforceable in this country, but would be in the US Counsel for the bankrupt argued that I should not hear counsel for the US opponent because the opponent was refusing to submit to the jurisdiction of the court. He relied on the decision of McQuaid J in *Re Taylor* (1988), 68 CBR (NS) 93, 215 APR 177 (PEISC), where US student lender agencies took the same position as is taken before me. He also relied on *Paul Magder Furs Ltd. v. Ontario (Attorney General)* (1991), 6 OR (3d) 188, 85 DLR (4th) 694 (CA), where the court refused an audience to an appellant who had repeatedly disobeyed an order of the court and would not undertake to obey it pending his appeal. In *Magder*, the appellant was in contempt already and was refusing to obey in Ontario an order of an Ontario court. These opponents are admitting that the order of discharge from bankruptcy would be effective and would be obeyed by them in this country. They assert that the court's jurisdiction does not extend to discharging a debt incurred under a contract governed by the law of the United States. I do not think that the Magder principle applies to the case before me.

...

Counsel for the opponent submits that a discharge under the bankruptcy laws of this country of a contractual debt governed by the law of the US, while fully effective here, cannot, under recognized rules of private international law, prevent enforcement of the debt in the US. If this position is correct according to our concepts of private international law, then there can be no objection to his stating that position before me. It would not be a question of refusing to submit to the jurisdiction of the Ontario court, but rather one of drawing to this court's attention a recognized limit on its jurisdiction.

In the 12th edition of *Dicey and Morris on the Conflict of Laws* (1993), at p. 1181:

> ... a discharge of a contractual debt under the bankruptcy law of the country whose law governs the contract is a valid discharge in England. Conversely, a discharge of a contractual debt under the bankruptcy law of any other foreign country ... is not a valid discharge in England.

In support of this statement, the authors cite, *inter alia*, *International Harvester Co. v. Zarbok*, [1918] 3 WWR 38, 11 Sask. LR 354 (KB), where the court cited a statement from *Halsbury's Laws of England*, vol. 6, p. 247, to the same effect. The modern *Halsbury*, the 4th edition, vol. 8 in the article "Conflict of Laws," para. 702, is to the same effect: a foreign discharge is not recognized in England

> ... unless it is a discharge under the proper law of the contract giving rise to the debt.

Zarbok, supra, is also cited as authority for a statement to the same effect in Houlden and Morawetz, *The Bankruptcy and Insolvency Act* (1993), p. 350, para. H§24.1; see also *Gibbs & Sons v. Société Industrielle et Commerciale des Métaux* (1890), 25 QBD 399, [1886-90] All ER Rep. 804 (CA), and *Marine Trust Co. v. Weinig*, [1935] 3 DLR 282, [1935] OWN 150 (SC).

The contracts under which the debt in question arose were a series of promissory notes in favour of US banks, guaranteed by the US government under the US Health Education Assistance Loan Program authorized by legislation. Each note was accompanied by an application form filled out by Barry Bialek, giving his US citizenship, a US address and stating an intent to enrol in a US educational institution. Each note specifies that it is to be construed according to the US legislation authorizing the program. The proper law of these contracts can only be US law, being that law with which the contracts have their closest and most real connection.

Thus, according to our own notions of private international law, a bankruptcy discharge would not affect the debt arising from these contracts unless it is a discharge of the courts of the US as the proper law of the contracts. The position of the United States' government before me is thus not a refusal to accept the jurisdiction of the court, but merely a statement of the limits of that jurisdiction according to our own law.

For these reasons, and with great respect, I cannot follow *Re Taylor*. My normal reluctance to differ from a judge in a sister province is reduced by the fact that, as is noted by the learned judge, the point was one on which no jurisprudence had been brought to his attention.

Order for conditional discharge.

NOTES

1. In your opinion, did Lane J correctly interpret and apply the *Gibbs & Son* rule with respect to the non-dischargeability of the US student loan in Canadian bankruptcy proceedings? Is there anything in the BIA, and s. 178 in particular, that suggests that foreign law has any input in determining what debts are *not* dischargeable in BIA proceedings? Could one nevertheless rationalize Lane J's decision on the ground that he was entitled to consider the US student loan in determining whether to grant Dr. Bialek an absolute or conditional discharge from his debts?

2. As far as the rule in *Gibbs & Son* is concerned, is it compatible with the *Morguard* doctrine in Canada (see the introductory notes to this chapter) and the doctrine's application in recent Canadian judgments recognizing foreign insolvency proceedings? The *Personal Insolvency Task Force Report*, c. 2.VI was concerned that the *Gibbs & Son* rule might still be good law in Canada. It therefore proposed a complex set of amendments giving Canadian bankruptcy courts jurisdiction over former Canadian residents who had obtained a US (or other foreign) discharge from their debts and enabling the Canadian court to grant a discharge from the Canadian debts. Are such amendments necessary or desirable given the paucity of Canadian cases on the *Gibbs* rule? Would the Canadian creditors not be inclined to raise objections to recognizing the foreign discharge in the Canadian discharge proceedings? Happily, the Task Force's recommendations never found their way into the 2005-2007 BIA amendments.